THE ANALYSIS AND USE OF FINANCIAL STATEMENTS

Second Edition

GERALD I. WHITE, CFA
Grace & White, Inc.

ASHWINPAUL C. SONDHI, Ph.D.
A. C. Sondhi & Associates, LLC

DOV FRIED, Ph.D.
Stern School of Business
New York University

JOHN WILEY & SONS, INC

New York • Chichester • Weinheim • Brisbane • Toronto • Singapore

To Penny, Rachel, and Our Families and Friends

ACQUISITIONS EDITOR   Rebecca Hope
MARKETING MANAGER   Wendy Goldner
PRODUCTION EDITOR   Deborah Herbert
COVER DESIGN   Harry Nolan
INTERIOR DESIGN   Lee Goldstein
ILLUSTRATION   Eugene Aiello

This book was set in 10/12 Times Roman by BI-COMP, INC. and
printed and bound by Hamilton Printing Company. The cover was printed by Phoenix Color Corp.

Recognizing the importance of preserving what has been written, it is a
policy of John Wiley & Sons, Inc. to have books of enduring value published
in the United States printed on acid-free paper, and we exert our best
efforts to that end.

Library of Congress Cataloging in Publication DATA:
White, Gerald I.
    The analysis and use of financial statements/Gerald I. White,
Ashwinpaul C. Sondhi, Dov Fried.—2nd ed.
        p.   cm.
    Includes bibliographical references and index.
    ISBN 0-471-11186-4 (cloth: alk. paper)
    1. Financial statements.   I. Sondhi, Ashwinpaul C.   II. Fried,
Dov.   III. Title.
HF5681.B2W4678   1997
657'.3—dc21   97-12618
                                      CIP

ISBN 0-471-11186-4

Printed in the United States of America

20   19   18   17   16   15   14   13   12

PREFACE

The objective of this book is the presentation of financial statement analysis from the point of view of the primary users of financial statements: equity and credit analysts. The analysis and use of financial statements is not restricted to analysts, however. Managers, auditors, educators, and regulators can also benefit from the insights and analytic techniques presented in this text.

Corporate managers, and those training to be managers, require an understanding of how financial statements provide information regarding an enterprise. This book is intended for use as a university level textbook for MBA and advanced undergraduate financial statement analysis courses. In addition, it should help equip businesspeople to prepare, audit, or interpret financial information. Finally, the text is designed to be a useful reference for both neophytes and informed readers.

WHO SHOULD READ THIS BOOK?

We believe that our work will be valuable to numerous audiences. First, it will benefit the working financial analyst. Some of the areas covered (off balance sheet financing and hedging techniques, for example) are rarely covered either in the professional literature or in accounting textbooks. While many analysts are familiar with some of the techniques in this book, we believe that even the most experienced analyst will find fresh insights on financial reporting issues.

Financial analysis, in some cases, is nothing more than journalism. Analysts accept the financial statements and what management tells them at face value. Good analysis is hampered by the inadequacies of published financial data. Many analysts examine the trend of reporting earnings but are unable to go "behind the numbers" or beyond them. The analysis taught in most textbooks starts and ends with reported financial statements or computerized databases.

Our view is that good financial analysis requires the analyst to understand how financial statements are generated in order to *separate the economic process that generates the numbers from the accounting process that (sometimes) obscures it.* Such analysis requires the use of assumptions and approximations, as reported financial data are often inadequate. We may dislike the need to make assumptions, but most financial analysis depends on them. Good analysis also requires the recasting of reported data into other formats when the latter yield superior insights.

However, we do not believe that there are always simple solutions to analytic problems. There is, for example, no precisely correct or "optimal" leverage ratio;

there are many possible ratios, depending on the goals of the analysis and the judgement of the analyst. Our view is that asking the right questions is more than half the battle. This text asks many questions, and suggests some answers.

Previous financial analysis books have been written from an academic point of view, stressing either an accounting or an empirical (data analysis) approach. While both financial accounting and empirical analysis are present in this text, they are integrated with, and subordinated to, user oriented analysis. They are subjected to the test of relevance: how do they aid in the interpretation of financial statement data?

Most of the analysis presented is based on the financial statements of actual companies. While such analysis can be frustrating (due to inadequate data), we believe that financial analysis can be presented best in a real world setting. While "models" are sometimes required for exposition purposes (such as for the analysis of foreign operations), the principles learned are always applied to real company statements.

The end-of-chapter materials (all problems and solutions were written by the authors) are also largely based on real corporate data. Some problems are adapted from the Chartered Financial Analyst examination program. Readers and students need to apply the text material to actual financial statements and the problems are designed to test their ability to do so.

ORGANIZATION AND CONTENT

A few comments on the organization and content of the book may be helpful to both reader and instructor. As already stated, we have integrated accounting, economic theory, and empirical research into a financial analysis framework. In doing so, we realize that some topics may be more important to some readers than to others. For that reason some advanced material (e.g., the Analysis of Oil and Gas Disclosures in Chapter 7) appears in appendices. Within chapters, we have organized some material into boxes that are available to interested readers without distracting those who are not.

As the globalization of financial markets continues apace, we include discussions and comparisons of relevant foreign and international (IASC) accounting standards throughout the text. Some of this material is in separate "international" sections but much of it is integrated. As the comparative analysis of companies using different accounting standards is an increasingly common concern, our goal is to help the user who must make an investment decision despite the lack of comparability. In some chapters, non-U.S. companies are used to illustrate international accounting differences. An example is Chapter 14 (Business Combinations), where the crossborder merger of SmithKline (U.S.) and Beecham (U.K.) is used to analyze different merger accounting methods. Non-U.S. companies are also used extensively in the cases and problem sections.

The first five chapters introduce the essential elements of financial statement analysis. Chapter 1 provides the framework, including discussions of data sources and the roles of preparers, auditors, and standard setters in the financial reporting process.

Chapter 2 describes the accrual method of accounting and its implications for financial reporting, leading to a discussion of the income statement and balance sheet. Chapter 3 describes the cash flow statement and cash flow analysis. Chapter 4 presents ratio analysis, suggesting both its advantages and its limits. Chapter 5 reviews empirical research, emphasizing its implications for financial analysis.

Chapters 6 to 15 focus on specific areas of analysis, ranging from inventories to multinational corporations. Throughout these chapters our goal is to show how differences in accounting methods and estimates affect reported financial condition, results of operations (including cash flows), and ratios. In many cases, analytic techniques are used to restore comparability, enhancing the decision usefulness of financial data. Each chapter includes a discussion of international accounting differences and relevant empirical research findings.

Chapter 6 considers the analysis of inventories, where differing methods have far-reaching effects on financial data. Chapter 7 (Long-Lived Assets) addresses the capitalization versus expensing decision, which has pervasive effects on reported financial statements. Chapter 8 considers differing methods of allocating capitalized costs to operations and the thorny topics of impairment and restructuring. Chapter 9 concerns income tax accounting, and focuses on the information content of income tax disclosures.

Chapter 10, the first of a series of long-term liabilities, provides an analysis of varying forms of debt. Chapter 11 turns to off-balance-sheet financing techniques, with particular emphasis on leases. Chapter 12 considers pension and other postemployment benefits (including stock options).

The next three chapters focus on problems resulting from the combination of more than one enterprise. Chapter 13 considers the cost, mark-to-market, equity method, and consolidation issues resulting from intercorporate investments, including joint ventures. Chapter 14 presents the alternative methods of accounting for business combinations, as well as the analysis of leveraged buyout firms (LBOs) and spinoffs. Chapter 15 describes the impact of changing exchange rates on multinational firms and suggests how available data can be used to separate exchange rate and accounting effects from operating results.

Chapter 16 examines risk management activities (including hedging), an area of inconsistent accounting standards and incomplete disclosures.

Chapters 17 through 19 pull together all previous text material. Chapter 17 shows how to use financial statement disclosures to prepare current cost balance sheets and to normalize reported income and cash flows. Such recast data, we believe, provide superior input for investment decisions. Chapter 18 demonstrates how financial data can be used to assess different forms of risk. Chapter 19 presents a variety of valuation models, and relates their use to the material covered earlier in the text. The final section of Chapter 19 considers forecasting models, for which financial data constitute the input.

Changes in Second Edition

This edition is substantially rewritten:

1. Chapter length is reduced by reorganizing the material into 19 chapters.
2. Some introductory material is removed and advanced material is placed in appendixes to reduce chapter length.
3. Except for Chapters 1 and 5, each chapter has one or more cases that apply the chapter material to the analysis of real firms. Many of these cases require comparisons of U.S. firms with foreign competitors.
4. The international content is increased by including more non-U.S. firms and by addressing all significant IASC standards.
5. The text is updated to include all major FASB and IASC standards (and many exposure drafts) issued as of February, 1997.

ACKNOWLEDGEMENTS

We acknowledge the help of our many teachers, mentors, colleagues, and friends throughout our respective careers. In particular, we thank the late Oliver R. Grace and Professors Michael Schiff, George Sorter, Joshua Livnat, and Sanford C. Gunn.

Many colleagues and friends read parts of the manuscript during its preparation, offering us encouragement and constructive criticism. In particular we would like to thank Terry Arndt, CFA (Ball State University), Phil Malone, CFA (University of Mississippi), James B. Rosenwald III, CFA (Rosenwald Capital Management), Rolf Rundfelt (Bohlins), and Stephen Ryan (New York University).

Lawrence D. Brown (State University of New York), Carl Crego (Pace University), Gerald Lobo (Syracuse University), David Mielke (Marquette University), Haim Mozes (Fordham University), R.D. Nair (University of Wisconsin), David Smith (University of Dayton), and Walter Teets (University of Illinois), the reviewers of the first edition, deserve special thanks for their valuable insights and suggestions. Many students at New York University and Columbia University field tested the manuscript and problems.

The main reviewer for the second edition was Eric Press (Temple University), whose comments and suggestions were enormously valuable to the authors. Other second edition reviewers, whose contributions are hereby acknowledged, include John Brozovsky (Virginia Polytechnic Institute), Charles Caliendo (University of Minnesota), Ray Carroll (Dalhousie University), James Deitrick (University of Texas at Austin), Patricia Fairfield (Georgetown University), Peter Knutson (University of Pennsylvania), Belinda Mucklow (University of Wisconsin–Madison), Stephen Penman (University of California, Berkeley), and Joseph Weintrop (CUNY–Baruch).

Research assistance was provided by Aryeh Glatter and Patricia D. McQueen, to whom we express our appreciation. Invaluable help in preparing the manuscript was provided by Kimberly Phillips and Shevon Nurse Estwick. Our Wiley editors, Karen Hawkins (1st edition) and Rebecca Hope (2nd edition), encouraged us throughout the writing process. Micheline Frederick (1st edition) and Deborah Herbert (2nd edition) ably steered us through the rigors of editing and production.

Despite the help provided by the many people mentioned, errors may remain, for which we accept full responsibility. Comments are welcome and should be directed to us in care of John Wiley & Sons.

GERALD I. WHITE
ASHWINPAUL C. SONDHI
DOV FRIED

May 1997

CONTENTS

1. FRAMEWORK FOR FINANCIAL STATEMENT ANALYSIS 1

Introduction 2

Need for Financial Statement Analysis 2

Focus on Investment Decisions 4

Classes of Users, 4

Financial Information and Capital Markets, 5

The Financial Reporting System 6

General Principles and Measurement Rules, 6

The U.S. Financial Reporting System 7

The Securities and Exchange Commission, 7

The Financial Accounting Standards Board, 8

International Accounting Standards 12

International Organization of Securities Commissions, 12

International Accounting Standards Committee, 12

European Financial Reporting Standards, 13

SEC Reporting Requirements for Foreign Registrants 14

Multijurisdictional Disclosure System, 15

Principal Financial Statements 15

The Balance Sheet, 16

The Income Statement, 17

The Statement of Cash Flows, 19

The Statement of Stockholders' Equity, 19

Footnotes, 20

Contingencies, 21

Supplementary Schedules, 22

Other Sources of Financial Information 23

Management Discussion and Analysis, 23

Other Data Sources, 24

Role of the Auditor 24

Reporting on Uncertainties, 26

Summary 28

Problems 28

2. ACCOUNTING INCOME AND ASSETS: THE ACCRUAL CONCEPT 35

Introduction 36

Income, Cash Flows, and Assets: Definitions and Relationships 36

The Accrual Concept of Income 40

Income Statement, 43

Accounting Income: Revenue and Expense Recognition, 48

Summary of Revenue Recognition Methods, 57

Nonrecurring Items 58

Types of Nonrecurring Items, 58

Analysis of Nonrecurring Items, 63

The Balance Sheet 69

Format and Classification, 69

Measurement of Assets and Liabilities, 72

Uses of the Balance Sheet, 73

The Statement of Stockholders' Equity 74

Format, Classification, and Use, 74

Summary 76

Case 2-1: Thousand Trails, Inc. I, 76

Problems 79

3. ANALYSIS OF CASH FLOWS 87

Statement of Cash Flows 88

Direct and Indirect Method Cash Flow Statements, 88

The Preparation of a Statement of Cash Flows, 91

Transactional Analysis, 91

Preparation of a Direct Method Statement of Cash Flows, 93

The Indirect Method, 97

Reported Versus Operating Changes in Assets and Liabilities, 97

Effect of Exchange Rate Changes on Cash, 102

Example: DuPont   102

Analysis of Cash Flow Information   104

Free Cash Flows and Valuation, 104

Relationship of Income and Cash Flows, 105

Analysis of Cash Flow Trends, 110

Cash Flow Classification Issues, 112

Cash Flow Statements: An International
    Perspective   117

Summary   119

Case 3-1: Thousand Trails, Inc. II, 119

Problems   122

4. FOUNDATIONS OF RATIO AND
    FINANCIAL ANALYSIS   139

Introduction   140

Purpose and Use of Ratio Analysis, 141

Ratio Analysis: Cautionary Notes, 141

Common-Size Statements   144

Discussion of Ratios by Category   150

Activity Analysis, 151

Liquidity Analysis, 155

Long-Term Debt and Solvency Analysis, 160

Profitability Analysis, 165

Operating and Financial Leverage, 168

Earnings per Share and Other Ratios Used in
    Valuation   172

Earnings per Share, 172

Cash Flow per Share, 179

EBITDA per Share, 179

Book Value per Share, 179

Price-to-Earnings and Price-to-Book Value
    Ratios, 180

Dividend Payout Ratio, 180

Ratios: An Integrated Analysis   182

Analysis of Firm Performance, 183

Economic Characteristics and Strategies, 186

Classification and Selection of Ratios, 192

Patterns of Ratio Disclosure, Definitions,
    and Use, 194

Summary   198

Case 4-1: Integrated Analysis of DuPont, Dow
    Chemical, and ICI   198

Problems   199

Appendix 4-A: Estimating Operating
    Leverage   211

Step 1: Examine Individual Components, 212

Step 2: Use Regression Analysis to Estimate
    V, 213

Step 3: Estimate Fixed Costs, 213

5. EMPIRICAL RESEARCH: IMPLICATIONS FOR
    FINANCIAL STATEMENT ANALYSIS   215

Introduction   216

The Classical Approach   218

Market-Based Research   219

Efficient Market Theory, 220

Modern Portfolio Theory, 221

Tests of the EMH Versus the Mechanistic
    Hypothesis, 223

The Ball and Brown Study, 225

Information Content Studies, 226

The Relationship Between Earnings and Stock
    Returns, 227

Market-Based Research: Current Status, 230

Market Anomalies, 233

Positive Accounting Research   237

Disclosure and Regulatory Requirements, 238

Agency Theory, 238

The Bonus Plan Hypothesis, 239

The Debt Covenant Hypothesis, 240

The Political Cost Hypothesis, 240

Summary of the Research, 241

Direction of Current Research   244

Back to the Future?, 245

Implications of Empirical Research for Financial
    Statement Analysis   250

Problems   251

6. ANALYSIS OF INVENTORIES   257

Introduction   258

Inventory and Cost of Goods Sold: Basic
    Relationships   259

Scenario 1: Stable Prices, 259

Scenario 2: Rising Prices, 259

Comparison of Information Provided by
  Alternative Methods 261
Balance Sheet Information: Inventory
  Account, 261
Income Statement Information: Cost of Goods
  Sold, 261
LIFO Versus FIFO: Income, Cash Flow, and
  Working Capital Effects 264
Adjustment from LIFO to FIFO 267
Adjustment of Inventory Balances, 267
Adjustment of Cost of Goods Sold, 268
Adjustment of Income to Current
  Cost Income 270
Financial Ratios: LIFO Versus FIFO 273
Profitability: Gross Profit Margin, 274
Liquidity: Working Capital, 275
Activity: Inventory Turnover, 276
Solvency: Debt to Equity Ratio, 279
Declines in LIFO Reserve 280
LIFO Liquidations, 280
Declining Prices, 281
Initial Adoption of LIFO and Changes to and
  from LIFO 283
Initial Adoption of LIFO, 284
Change from LIFO Method, 285
LIFO: A Historical and Empirical
  Perspective 289
Overview of FIFO/LIFO Choice, 289
Summary of FIFO/LIFO Choice, 291
Concluding Comments on Accounting for
  Inventories 293
International Accounting and Reporting
  Practices 294
IASC Standard 2, 294
Using Inventory Balances to Aid in
  Forecasting 295
Summary 296
Case 6-1: Inventory Analysis of Nucor 297
Problems 299
Appendix 6-A: LIFO Measurement Issues 311
LIFO Inventory Methods, 311
Interim Reporting Under LIFO, 313
Appendix 6-B: The FIFO/LIFO Choice:
  Empirical Studies 315

7. ANALYSIS OF LONG-LIVED ASSETS, PART I:
  The Capitalization Decision 321
Introduction 322
Acquiring the Asset: The Capitalization
  Decision 322
Capitalization Versus Expensing: Conceptual
  Issues 323
Financial Statement Effects of Capitalization, 323
Capitalization Versus Expensing: General
  Issues 328
Capitalization of Interest Costs, 328
Intangible Assets, 331
Asset Revaluation, 334
Capitalization Versus Expensing: Industry
  Issues 336
Regulated Utilities, 336
Computer Software Development Costs, 338
Accounting for Oil and Gas Exploration, 340
Analytic Adjustments for Capitalization and
  Expensing 342
Need for Analytic Adjustments, 342
Valuation Implications, 345
Other Economic Consequences, 345
Additional Analysis of Fixed Asset Data, 345
Summary 350
Case 7-1: Adjustments for Capitalization and
  Expensing: Digital Equipment 351
Problems 352
Appendix 7-A: Research and Development
  Affiliates 365
Research and Development Partnerships, 365
Appendix 7-B: Analysis of Oil and Gas
  Disclosures 367
Introduction, 367
SFAS 69: Disclosures Regarding Oil and Gas
  Reserves, 370

8. ANALYSIS OF LONG-LIVED ASSETS, PART II:
  Analysis of Depreciation and Impairment 377
Introduction 378
The Depreciation Concept 378
Depreciation Methods, 379
Depletion, 385
Amortization, 385

Depreciation Method Disclosures, 386

Impact of Depreciation Methods on Financial
  Statements, 387

Accelerated Depreciation and Taxes, 388

The Impact of Inflation on Depreciation, 388

Changes in Depreciation Method, 391

Analysis of Fixed Asset Disclosures   **393**

Estimating Relative Age and Useful Lives, 395

Estimating the Age of Assets, 395

Example: Forest Products Industry
  Comparison, 397

Impairment of Long-Lived Assets   **398**

Financial Reporting of Impaired Assets, 398

Financial Statement Impact of Impairments, 402

Effect of SFAS 121 on Analysis of
  Impairment, 403

Empirical Findings, 403

**Liabilities for Closure and Environmental
  Costs**   **406**

Summary   **408**

**Case 8-1: Analysis of Fixed Assets in the
  Swedish Forest Products Industry**   **409**

Problems   **410**

**Appendix 8-A: Analysis of Changing Prices
  Information**   **414**

Introduction, 414

Analysis of General Inflation, 415

Analysis of Firm-Specific Inflation, 417

9. ANALYSIS OF INCOME TAXES   **425**

Introduction   **426**

Accounting for Income Taxes: Basic Issues   **428**

Deferred Tax Assets and Liabilities, 430

SFAS 109: The Liability Method   **433**

Effect of Tax Rate and Tax Law Changes, 434

Treatment of Operating Losses, 437

Deferred Tax Assets and the Valuation
  Allowance, 437

Financial Statement Presentation and Disclosure
  Requirements, 438

Deferred Taxes: Analytical Issues   **439**

Factors Influencing the Level and Trend of
  Deferred Taxes, 439

Liability or Equity?, 442

Analysis of Deferred Tax Assets, 444

Effective Tax Rates, 445

Accounting for Taxes: Specialized Issues   **447**

Temporary Versus Permanent Differences, 447

Indefinite Reversals, 447

Accounting for Acquisitions, 449

Analysis of Income Tax Disclosures: DuPont   **449**

Analysis of the Effective Tax Rate, 450

Analysis of Deferred Income Tax Expense, 452

Using Deferred Taxes to Estimate Taxable
  Income, 453

Analysis of Deferred Tax Assets and
  Liabilities, 453

Other Issues in Income Tax Analysis, 455

**Financial Reporting Outside the
  United States**   **555**

IASC Standards, 455

Non-U.S. Standards, 456

Summary   **459**

**Case 9-1: Comprehensive Analysis of Income
  Tax Disclosures**   **459**

Problems   **463**

**Appendix 9-A: The Deferral Method of Income
  Tax Accounting**   **470**

10. ANALYSIS OF FINANCING LIABILITIES   **473**

Introduction   **474**

Balance Sheet Debt   **475**

Current Liabilities, 475

Long-Term Debt, 476

Debt with Equity Features, 490

Effects of Changes in Interest Rates, 496

Debt of Firms in Distress, 502

Retirement of Debt Prior to Maturity, 503

Bond Covenants   **506**

Nature of Covenants, 506

Calculation of Accounting-Based Constraints, 508

**International Accounting and Reporting
  Practices**   **513**

Summary   **515**

**Case 10-1: Comparative Analysis of the Financing
  Liabilities of DuPont, Dow Chemical, and
  Imperial Chemical Industries PLC (ICI)**   **515**

Problems   **517**

11. LEASES AND OFF-BALANCE-SHEET DEBT   531

Introduction   532

Leases   533

Incentives for Leasing, 533

Lease Classification: Lessees, 534

Financial Reporting by Lessees: Capital Versus Operating Leases, 537

Analysis of Lease Disclosures, 540

Off-Balance-Sheet Financing Activities   547

Take-or-Pay and Throughput Arrangements, 548

Sale of Receivables, 548

Finance Subsidiaries, 554

Joint Ventures and Investment in Affiliates, 555

Other Off-Balance-Sheet Activities, 556

Analysis of OBS Activities: Ashland Oil   557

International Accounting and Reporting Practices   561

Lease Accounting Outside the United States, 561

Summary   562

Case 11-1: Off-Balance-Sheet Financing Techniques for Texaco and Caltex   562

Problems   571

Appendix 11-A: Financial Reporting by Lessors and for Sale Leasebacks   582

12. PENSIONS AND OTHER EMPLOYEE BENEFITS   591

Introduction   593

Pension Plans   594

Defined Contribution Plans, 596

Defined Benefit Plans, 596

Defined Benefit Pension Plans   597

Estimating Benefit Obligations, 597

Factors Affecting Benefit Obligations, 599

Factors Affecting Plan Assets, 601

Funded Status of Pension Plan, 602

Accounting for Pensions: SFAS 87   603

Pension Cost: Components and Measurement, 603

Disclosure of Plan Status, 605

Analysis of Pension Costs and Liability   608

Importance of Assumptions, 608

Analysis of Plan Status, Costs, and Cash Flows, 611

Analysis of DuPont Pension Plan Disclosures, 616

Impact of Discontinuities   623

Acquisitions and Divestitures, 623

Curtailments and Settlements, 623

Non-U.S. Reporting Requirements   624

Other Postemployment Benefits   628

Estimating Health Care Benefits, 631

Computing Postretirement Benefit Cost, 632

Disclosure of Plan Status, 632

Importance of Assumptions, 633

Effects of Transition Methods, 635

Analysis of DuPont's Postretirement Health Care Costs, 637

Using SFAS 106 Disclosures, 639

Postretirement Benefits Outside the United States, 639

Preretirement Benefits   640

Stock Compensation Plans   640

Using SFAS 123 Disclosures, 643

Summary   644

Case 12-1: Analysis of Pension Plan Disclosures: GM   644

Introduction and Case Objectives, 644

The GM Pension Plan, 645

Analysis of GM's Pension Status, 647

Analysis of GM Pension Trends, 652

GM's Pension Plans: Concluding Comments, 654

Case 12-2: DBP Corp.   656

Defined Benefit Plan Example, 656

Problems   658

13. ANALYSIS OF INTERCORPORATE INVESTMENTS   671

Introduction   672

Investments in Securities   673

Cost Method, 674

Market Method, 674

Lower of Cost or Market Method, 675

U.S. Accounting Requirements, 675

Analysis of Marketable Securities   678

Separation of Operating from Investment Results, 678

Effects of Classification of Marketable Securities
    Under SFAS 115, 679
Analysis of Investment Performance, 683
Summary of Analytical Procedures, 685
Financial Reporting for Marketable Securities
    Outside the United States, 686
Equity Method of Accounting   **686**
Conditions for Use, 686
Illustration of the Equity Method, 687
Comparison of the Equity Method and
    SFAS 115, 688
Equity Accounting and Analysis, 689
Consolidation   **692**
Conditions for Use, 693
Illustration of Consolidation, 693
**Comparison of Consolidation with the Equity
    Method**   **696**
Consolidation Versus the Equity Method:
    Analytic Considerations, 697
Proportionate Consolidation, 701
Significance of Consolidation: Summary, 708
Analysis of Minority Interest   **709**
**Consolidation Practices Outside the United
    States**   **711**
Analysis of Segment Data   **711**
Illustration of Industry Segments: DuPont, 713
Illustration of Geographic Segments: DuPont, 715
Management Discussion and Analysis, 715
Uses and Limitations of Segment Data, 716
Proposed Changes in Segment Reporting, 717
Using Segment Data to Estimate Consolidated
    Earnings and Risk, 719
Segment Reporting Outside the United
    States, 721
Summary   **721**
Case 13-1: Coca-Cola   **722**
Consolidation Versus Equity Method, 722
Problems   **726**

**14. ANALYSIS OF BUSINESS
    COMBINATIONS**   **743**
Introduction   **744**
Accounting for Acquisitions   **745**

Conditions Necessary for Use of the Pooling of
    Interests Method, 746
**Illustration of the Purchase and Pooling
    Methods**   **747**
The Purchase Method, 747
The Pooling of Interests Method, 750
Effects of Accounting Methods   **751**
Comparison of Balance Sheets, 751
Comparison of Income Statements, 753
Cash Flow Statement Effects, 759
Impact on Ratios, 762
**Complicating Factors in Purchase Method
    Acquisitions**   **763**
Contingent Payments, 763
In-Process Research and Development, 764
**Income Tax Effects of Business
    Combinations**   **764**
**International Differences in Accounting for
    Business Combinations**   **765**
Differences in Treatment of Goodwill, 766
**Illustration of International Differences:
    The Acquisition Activities of SmithKline
    Beecham**   **767**
Differences in Accounting Methods, 767
The Merged Balance Sheet, 768
Balance Sheet Restatement, 771
Income Statement Effects, 773
Income Statement Restatement, 776
Financial Ratio Effects, 777
Summary, 778
Analysis of Goodwill   **778**
Goodwill Amortization, 779
Choosing the Acquisition Method   **780**
Income Maximization as Motivation for the
    Pooling/Purchase Choice, 782
Market Reaction and the Pooling/Purchase
    Choice, 782
Interpreting the Research Results, 783
Other Factors Influencing Mergers, Bid Premia,
    and the Pooling/Purchase Choice, 784
Summary, 787
Push-Down Accounting   **787**
Push-Down in Practice: The GM–Hughes
    Transaction, 788

Impact on the Balance Sheet, 788

Impact on the Income Statement, 789

Effect on Cash Flows, 790

Effect on Financial Ratios, 790

Push-Down Summed Up, 791

Spinoffs   **791**

Analysis of Spinoffs, 792

Reasons for Investment in Spinoffs, 793

Example: Emerson Electric's Spinoff of ESCO
   Electronics, 794

Summary   **794**

**Case 14-1: Analysis of a Purchase Method
   Acquisition: Georgia Pacific's Purchase of
   Great Northern Nekoosa**   **795**

**Case 14-2: Analysis of a Pooling Method
   Acquisition: The ConAgra–Golden
   Valley Merger**   **798**

Problems   **801**

**15. ANALYSIS OF MULTINATIONAL
   OPERATIONS**   **819**

Introduction   **821**

Effects of Exchange Rate Changes   **821**

Basic Accounting Issues   **823**

**Foreign Currency Translation Under
   SFAS 52**   **824**

Role of the Functional Currency, 825

The Temporal Method or Remeasurement, 825

The All-Current Method or Translation, 827

Treatment of Exchange Rate Gains and
   Losses, 827

Remeasurement Versus Translation, 828

**Illustration of Translation and
   Remeasurement**   **830**

Translation: The All-Current Method, 830

Cumulative Translation Adjustment, 833

Remeasurement: The Temporal Method, 835

**Comparison of Translation and
   Remeasurement**   **837**

Income Statement Effects, 837

Balance Sheet Effects, 840

Impact on Financial Ratios, 841

Impact on Reported Cash Flows, 844

Analysis of Foreign Currency Disclosures   **846**

Exchange Rate Changes: Exposure and
   Effects, 847

Hyperinflationary Economies   **852**

Alternative Accounting Methods for
   Hyperinflationary Subsidiaries, 853

Effects of Debt Denominated in
   Hyperinflationary Currencies, 853

Changes in Functional Currency   **854**

Example: Alcoa of Australia, 854

**Analytic Difficulties Related to Foreign
   Operations**   **857**

Relationships Among Interest Rates, Inflation,
   and Exchange Rates, 858

Consistency in Reporting, 859

Economic Interpretation of Results, 860

Impact of SFAS 8 and SFAS 52 on Management
   and Investor Behavior, 862

**Financial Reporting Outside of the United
   States**   **864**

Foreign Currency Translation, 864

Foreign Currency Transactions, 864

International Accounting Standards, 865

Summary   **866**

Case 15-1: AFLAC   **866**

Analysis of Exchange Rate Effects: Single
   Currency, 866

Case 15-2: IBM   **871**

Analysis of Exchange Rate Effects: Multiple
   Currencies, 871

Problems   **881**

**16. DERIVATIVES AND HEDGING
   ACTIVITIES**   **893**

Introduction   **894**

Defining Risk   **895**

Foreign Currency Risk, 895

Interest Rate Risk, 897

Commodity Risk, 898

Risk of Changes in Market Value, 898

Hedging Techniques   **898**

Forward Contracts, 899

Options, 901

Economic Hedges, 903

Accounting for Hedging Activities   **905**

Recognition Issues, 907

Measurement Issues, 907

Forecasted Transactions, 907

Hedging Portfolios, 909

Rolling Hedges, 909

Imperfect Hedges, 910

Current Accounting Standards for Hedging
Activities, 910

Analysis of Hedging Disclosures   **914**

Analysis of DuPont Risk Management
Disclosures, 914

**Non-U.S. Financial Reporting of Hedging
Activities**   **916**

Summary   **917**

**Case 16-1: Enron Corp.: Analysis of Risk
Management Activities**   **918**

Problems   **925**

**17. ANALYSIS OF FINANCIAL STATEMENTS:
A SYNTHESIS**   **931**

Introduction   **932**

**Analysis of and Adjustments to the Balance
Sheet**   **933**

Analysis of Book Value, 933

Adjustments to Assets, 934

Adjustments to Liabilities, 934

Balance Sheet Adjustments for DuPont, 935

Adjustments to Stockholders' Equity, 944

Adjusted Book Value per Common Share, 945

Analysis of Capital Structure, 946

Balance Sheet Adjustments for Non-U.S.
Companies, 948

Adjustments to Reported Income   **948**

Normalization of Reported Income, 948

Analytic Treatment of Nonrecurring Items, 951

Income Normalization for Non-U.S. Firms, 953

Normalization Over the Economic Cycle, 954

Acquisition Effects, 954

Exchange Rate Effects, 955

Effect of Accounting Changes, 955

Quality of Earnings, 956

Comprehensive Income, 958

Analysis of Cash Flow   **959**

Analysis of Cash Flow Components, 960

Free Cash Flow, 963

International Cash Flow Comparisons, 964

Adjusted Financial Ratios   **965**

International Ratio Comparisons, 966

Summary   **966**

**Case 17-1: Comparison of Dow and ICI with
DuPont**   **967**

**Case 17-2: Alcoa: Analysis of Current Cost
Balance Sheet and Normalized Income**   **968**

**Case 17-3: A. M. Castle: Analysis of a Cyclical
Company**   **974**

Case 17-4: Deere: Cash Flow Analysis   **979**

**18. ACCOUNTING- AND FINANCE-BASED
MEASURES OF RISK**   **983**

Introduction   **984**

Earnings Variability and Its Components, 987

The Prediction of Bankruptcy   **992**

Usefulness of Bankruptcy Prediction, 992

Research Results, 993

Bankruptcy Prediction and Cash Flows, 1000

Bankruptcy and Financial Distress: Concluding
Comments, 1000

The Prediction of Debt Risk   **1001**

The Prediction of Bond Ratings, 1001

Usefulness of Bond Ratings Predictions, 1005

The Significance of Ratings: Another Look, 1009

Equity Risk: Measurement and Prediction   **1012**

Risk and Return: Theoretical Models, 1012

Importance and Usefulness of Beta (β), 1014

Review of Theoretical and Empirical
Findings, 1015

The Attack on the CAPM and β, 1021

Summary   **1025**

**Case 18-1: Analysis of the Debt Ratings and
Default Risk of DuPont, Dow Chemical, and
Imperial Chemical Industries**   **1026**

Problems   **1026**

19. VALUATION AND FORECASTING   **1035**

Introduction   **1037**

VALUATION MODELS   **1037**

Overview of Models   **1037**

Asset-Based Valuation Models   **1038**

Market Price and Book Value: Theoretical
  Considerations, 1039

Book Value: Measurement Issues, 1040

Tobin's Q Ratio, 1041

Stability and Growth of Book Value, 1041

Discounted Cash Flow Valuation Models   **1043**

Dividend-Based Models, 1044

Earnings-Based Models, 1045

Free Cash Flow Approach to Valuation, 1059

The Abnormal Earnings or EBO Model   **1062**

EBO Versus DCF Models, 1065

The EBO Model: Concluding Comments, 1072

**FORECASTING MODELS AND TIME-SERIES
  PROPERTIES OF EARNINGS**   **1072**

Forecasting Models   **1073**

Extrapolative Models, 1073

Index Models, 1076

Forecasting with Disaggregated Data, 1076

**Comparison with Financial Analyst
  Forecasts**   **1080**

Analyst Forecasts: Some Caveats, 1083

Summary   **1084**

Case 19-1: Valuation of DuPont   **1085**

Problems   **1087**

Appendix 19-A: Multistage Growth Models   **1100**

Valuing a Nondividend-Paying Firm, 1100

Shifting Growth Rate Patterns, 1101

**Appendix 19-B: The EBO and Terminal Value
  Assumptions**   **1102**

**APPENDIX A: DUPONT FINANCIAL
  STATEMENTS**   **1105**

**APPENDIX B: DOW CHEMICAL
  COMPANY**   **1147**

**APPENDIX C: ICI FINANCIAL
  STATEMENTS**   **1167**

PRESENT VALUE TABLES   **1192**

BIBLIOGRAPHY   **1197**

INDEX   **1211**

1

FRAMEWORK FOR FINANCIAL STATEMENT ANALYSIS

CHAPTER OUTLINE

CHAPTER OBJECTIVES

INTRODUCTION

NEED FOR FINANCIAL STATEMENT ANALYSIS

FOCUS ON INVESTMENT DECISIONS
Classes of Users
Financial Information and Capital Markets

THE FINANCIAL REPORTING SYSTEM
General Principles and Measurement Rules

THE U.S. FINANCIAL REPORTING SYSTEM
The Securities and Exchange Commission
The Financial Accounting Standards Board
  FASB Conceptual Framework

INTERNATIONAL ACCOUNTING STANDARDS
International Organization of Securities
Commissions
International Accounting Standards Committee
European Financial Reporting Standards

SEC REPORTING REQUIREMENTS FOR FOREIGN REGISTRANTS
Multijurisdictional Disclosure System

PRINCIPAL FINANCIAL STATEMENTS
The Balance Sheet
  Elements of the Balance Sheet
The Income Statement
  Elements of the Income Statement
  Comprehensive Income
The Statement of Cash Flows
The Statement of Stockholders' Equity
Footnotes
Contingencies
  Risks and Uncertainties
Supplementary Schedules

OTHER SOURCES OF FINANCIAL INFORMATION
Management Discussion and Analysis
Other Data Sources

ROLE OF THE AUDITOR
Reporting on Uncertainties

CONCLUSION

CHAPTER OBJECTIVES

The goals of this chapter are to:

1. Introduce the reader to the financial reporting system.
2. Discuss the general principles of that system.
3. Identify the organizations that set accounting standards worldwide.

4. Briefly describe the financial statements and other elements of financial reporting.
5. Describe other sources of financial data.
6. Discuss the role of the independent auditor.

INTRODUCTION

Why are financial statements useful? Because they help investors and creditors make better economic decisions. The goal of this book is to enhance financial statement users' understanding of financial reporting in order to facilitate improved decision making. We will examine the impact of the differential application of accounting methods and estimates on financial statements, with particular emphasis on the effect of accounting choices on reported earnings, stockholders' equity, cash flow, and various measures of corporate performance (including, but not limited to, financial ratios). We will also stress the use of cash flow analysis to evaluate the financial health of an enterprise.

Financial statements are, at best, only an approximation of economic reality because of the selective reporting of economic events by the accounting system, compounded by alternative accounting methods and estimates. The tendency to delay accounting recognition of some transactions and valuation changes means that financial statements tend to lag behind reality as well.

This chapter provides a framework for the study of financial statement analysis. This framework consists of the users being served, the information system available to them, and the institutional structure within which they interact.

NEED FOR FINANCIAL STATEMENT ANALYSIS

The United States has the most complex financial reporting system in the world. Detailed accounting principles are augmented by extensive disclosure requirements. The financial statements of large multinationals add up to dozens of pages, and many of these firms voluntarily publish additional "fact books" for dissemination to financial analysts and other interested users.

Financial reporting in other major developed countries and many emerging markets has also evolved substantially during the last five years, with an increasing emphasis on providing information useful to both domestic and foreign creditors and equity investors.

In an ideal world, the user of financial statements could focus only on the bottom lines of financial reporting: net income and stockholders' equity. If financial statements were comparable among companies (regardless of country), consistent over time, and always fully reflected the economic position of the firm, financial statement analysis would be simple, and this text a very short one.

The financial reporting system is not perfect. Economic events and accounting entries do not correspond precisely; they diverge across the dimensions of timing, recognition, and measurement. Financial analysis and investment decisions are further complicated by variations in accounting treatment among countries in each of these dimensions.

Economic events and accounting recognition of those events frequently take place at different times. One example of this phenomenon is the recognition of capital gains and losses only upon sale in most cases. Appreciation of a real estate investment, which took place over a period of many years, for example, receives income statement recognition only in the period management chooses for its disposal.[1]

Similarly, long-lived assets are written down, most of the time, in the fiscal period of management's choice. The period of recognition may be neither the period in which the impairment took place nor the period of sale or disposal. Accounting for discontinued operations, in the same manner, results in recognition of any loss in a period different from when the loss occurred or the disposal is consummated.[2]

In addition, many economic events do not receive accounting recognition at all. Most contracts, for example, are not reflected in financial statements when entered into, despite significant effects on financial condition and operating and financial risk. Some contracts, such as leases and hedging activities, are recognized in the financial statements by some companies but disclosed only in footnotes by others. Disclosure requirements for derivatives and hedging activities are in place, but comprehensive financial reporting (recognition and measurement) is still in its infancy.

Further, generally accepted accounting principles (GAAP) in the United States and elsewhere permit economic events that do receive accounting recognition to be recognized in different ways by different financial statement preparers. Inventory and depreciation of fixed assets are only two of the significant areas where comparability may be lacking.

Financial reports often contain supplementary data that, although not included in the statements themselves, help the financial statement user to interpret the statements or adjust measures of corporate performance (such as financial ratios) to make them more comparable, consistent over time, and more representative of economic reality. When making adjustments to financial statements, we will seek to discern substance from form and exploit the information contained in footnotes and supplementary schedules of data in the annual report and SEC filings. The analytic treatment of "off-balance-sheet" financing activities is a good example of this process. We also illustrate the use of reconciliations to U.S. GAAP in foreign registrants' Form 20-F filings.

Finally, information from outside the financial reporting process can be used to make financial data more useful. Estimating the effects of changing prices on corporate performance, for example, may require the use of price data from outside sources.

---

[1] However, in countries (such as the United Kingdom) where periodic asset revaluation is permitted, balance sheet recognition of market value changes may occur much sooner.

[2] In the United States, Statement of Financial Accounting Standards (SFAS) No. 121, Accounting for the Impairment of Long-Lived Assets and for Long-Lived Assets to Be Disposed of, constrains but does not eliminate management control over the timing and measurement of impairment recognition. In most foreign countries, there are few, if any, guidelines governing the accounting for such impaired assets (in April 1996, the U.K. Accounting Standards Board issued a discussion paper, "Impairment of Tangible Fixed Assets"). The treatment of discontinued operations is similarly varied across countries.

FOCUS ON INVESTMENT DECISIONS

This book is concerned with the concepts and techniques of financial analysis employed by users of financial statements who are external to the company. Principal emphasis is on the financial statements of companies whose securities are publicly traded. The techniques described are generally applicable to the analysis of financial statements prepared according to U.S. GAAP. However, we will also discuss the pronouncements of the International Accounting Standards Committee (IASC) and standard setters in other countries, compare them to U.S. GAAP, and analyze financial statements prepared in accordance with these other reporting standards.

The common characteristic of external users is their general lack of authority to prescribe the information they want from an enterprise. They depend on general-purpose external financial reports provided by management. The objectives of these external users are aptly described by the Financial Accounting Standards Board (FASB) in its Statement of Financial Accounting Concepts (SFAC) 1, Objectives of Financial Reporting by Business Enterprises:

Information Useful in Investment and Credit Decisions
Financial reporting should provide information that is useful to present and potential investors and creditors and other users in making rational investment, credit, and similar decisions. The information should be comprehensible to those who have a reasonable understanding of business and economic activities and are willing to study the information with reasonable diligence.[3]

Classes of Users

External users of financial information encompass a wide range of interests but can be classified into three general groups:

1. Credit and equity investors
2. Government (the executive and legislative branches), regulatory bodies, tax authorities
3. The general public and special interest groups, labor unions, and consumer groups

Each of these user groups has a particular objective in financial statement analysis, but, as the FASB stated, the *primary users are equity investors and creditors.* However, the information supplied to investors and creditors is likely to be generally useful to other user groups as well. Hence, financial accounting standards are geared to the purposes and perceptions of investors and creditors. That is the group for whom the analytical techniques in this book are intended.

The underlying objective of financial analysis is the comparative measurement of risk and return to make investment or credit decisions. These decisions require estimates of the future, be it a month, a year, or a decade. General-purpose financial statements, which describe the past, provide one basis for projecting future earnings and cash flows. Many of the techniques used in this analytical process are broadly applicable to all types of decisions, but there are also specialized techniques concerned

---

[3]SFAC 1, para. 34.

with specific investment interests or, in other words, risks and returns specific to one class of investors or securities.

The equity investor is primarily interested in the long-term earning power of the company, its ability to grow, and, ultimately, its ability to pay dividends and increase in value. Since the equity investor bears the residual risk in an enterprise, the largest and most volatile risk, the required analysis is the most comprehensive of any user and encompasses techniques employed by all other external users.

Creditors need somewhat different analytical approaches. Short-term creditors, such as banks and trade creditors, place more emphasis on the immediate liquidity of the business because they seek an early payback of their investment. Long-term investors in bonds, such as insurance companies and pension funds, are primarily concerned with the long-term asset position and earning power of the company. They seek assurance of the payment of interest and the capability of retiring or refunding the obligation at maturity. Creditor risks are usually smaller than equity risks and may be more easily quantifiable.

More subordinated or junior creditors, especially owners of "high-yield" debt, however, bear risks similar to those of equity investors and may find analytic techniques normally applied to equity investments more relevant than those employed by creditors.

Financial Information and Capital Markets

The usefulness of accounting information in the decision-making processes of investors and creditors has been the subject of much academic research during the last 30 years. That research has examined the interrelationship of accounting information and reporting standards on financial markets in great detail. At times, the research conclusions are highly critical of the accounting standard-setting process and of the utility of financial analysis. This criticism, it should be noted, is based on research performed in a capital market setting. These findings do not negate the usefulness of financial analysis of individual securities that may be mispriced or for decisions made outside a capital market setting.[4]

Some researchers argue that financial data are useful to investors only for prediction of a firm's risk characteristics. To a great extent, this line of reasoning is influenced by the finance literature and the prevalent acceptance of the efficient market hypothesis. Others argue that the impact of accounting is not so much in its information content per se, but rather in the "economic consequences" to the firm resulting from contracts (implicit or explicit) that are based on or driven by accounting-determined variables.[5]

By and large, the early conclusions of the academic literature have proven to be somewhat premature. More recent research demonstrates that the interplay between markets and information is richer and more sophisticated than originally thought. In fact, the trend in research is now to incorporate techniques of fundamental analysis in model development and research design.

Various research trends and relevant economic considerations are discussed throughout the book, with varying emphasis from topic to topic. Chapter 5 is devoted entirely to a review of the major strands of empirical research in order to set the stage

---

[4]Examples include acquisitions and credit decisions made by banks or other institutional lenders.

[5]Management compensation contracts and covenants contained in debt agreements are two examples of such contracts.

for discussions of other topics, where appropriate, in subsequent chapters. Throughout the text we focus on what the analyst can learn from the research and how its implications are relevant to analysis.

THE FINANCIAL REPORTING SYSTEM

An understanding of the conceptual bases of the financial reporting system and the preparation of financial statements is an essential prerequisite to financial analysis. Financial statements are issued by corporate management, which is responsible for their form and content. It is management that selects accounting methods, compiles accounting data, and prepares the financial statements. For smaller companies, portions of the preparation work may be carried out by auditors.

The accounting process or financial reporting system, which generates financial information for external users, encompasses four principal financial statements:

- Balance sheet (statement of financial position)
- Income statement (statement of earnings)
- Statement of cash flows
- Statement of stockholders' equity

These four financial statements, augmented by footnotes and supplementary data, are interrelated. Collectively, they are intended to provide relevant, reliable, and timely information essential to making investment, credit, and similar decisions, thus meeting the objectives of financial reporting. An example is the 1994 financial statements of duPont, contained in Appendix A at the end of this book, which will be used to illustrate financial analysis throughout the text.

General Principles and Measurement Rules

Financial statements provide information about the assets (resources), liabilities (obligations), income and cash flows, and stockholders' equity of the firm. The effects of transactions and other events are recorded in the appropriate financial statement(s). The balance sheet shows assets, liabilities, and stockholders' equity; the statement of stockholders' equity reports capital transactions with owners. The income statement reflects revenues, expenses, and gains and losses; the statement of cash flows includes operating, investing, and financing inflows and outflows; many transactions are reflected in more than one statement so that the entire set is required to evaluate the firm.

The financial reporting system is based on data generated from *accounting events and selected economic events*. The financial statements recognize events and transactions meeting certain criteria, primarily exchange transactions (the exchange of cash or another asset for a different asset or to create or settle a liability). Other events recognized in the financial reporting system include the passage of time (e.g., accrual of interest), the use of services (e.g., insurance) or assets (e.g., depreciation), estimates such as bad debts or accruals for warranties, and the impact of some contracts (e.g., capital leases). Selected external or economic events, including some market value changes, are also recognized. However, many contractual arrangements and market value changes are disclosed only in the footnotes or in supplementary schedules.

The emphasis on reporting exchange transactions does not mean that the exchange of cash is necessary for the recognition of revenue and expense events. Under *accrual accounting*, revenues are recognized when goods are delivered or services are performed and expenses are recorded as services are used, rather than when cash is collected or expenditures incurred for these transactions. Accrual accounting rests on the *matching principle*, which says that performance can be measured only if the related revenues and costs are accounted for in the same period.

Financial statements are prepared using a monetary unit to quantify (measure) the operations of the firm. Transactions are generally measured at their *historical cost*, the amount of cash or other resources exchanged for the asset or liability; changes in value subsequent to acquisition are usually ignored. The advantage of historical cost is that it is objective and verifiable. Its utility declines as specific prices or the general price level changes; as a result, the SEC, FASB, and non-U.S. standard setters have added disclosure and accounting standards for financial instruments.[6]

Financial reporting also relies on the *going concern assumption*, that the firm will continue in operation indefinitely. The alternative assumes liquidation or sale of the firm, which requires different measures of assets and liabilities. Only by assuming normal future operations is it possible, for example, to depreciate fixed assets over their useful life rather than valuing them at their estimated disposal value.

THE U.S. FINANCIAL REPORTING SYSTEM

In the United States, the form and content of the financial statements of companies whose securities are publicly traded are governed by the Securities and Exchange Commission through its regulation S-X. Although the SEC has delegated much of this responsibility to the FASB, it frequently adds its own requirements. The SEC functions as a highly effective enforcement mechanism for standards promulgated in the private sector.

The Securities and Exchange Commission

As stated above, while financial reporting standards are developed primarily in the private sector, the SEC often augments the FASB's work. For example, the SEC-mandated Management Discussion and Analysis (MD&A) provides helpful information regarding past operating results and current financial position. In such areas as segment data, leases, the effects of changing prices, and disclosure of oil and gas reserves, SEC-required disclosures preceded FASB action.

Audited financial statements, related footnotes, and supplementary data are presented in both annual reports sent to stockholders and those filed with the SEC. These filings often contain other valuable information not presented in stockholder reports. Exhibit 1-1 contains a listing of SEC-required filings. Quarterly financial reports and SEC 10-Q filings, both of which contain abbreviated financial statements, may be reviewed by auditors but are rarely audited.[7]

---

[6]In 1991, the FASB issued SFAS 107 requiring disclosure of the market values of certain financial instruments, and in 1994, the FASB added SFAS 119 calling for expanded disclosures about derivatives and other similar financial instruments. In June 1995, the IASC issued IAS 32 concerning disclosure and presentation of financial instruments.

[7]In 1989, the SEC issued a concepts release seeking comments on a proposal to require timely reviews by independent auditors of interim period registration statements and quarterly filings. No action has been taken to date.

EXHIBIT 1-1
Corporate Filings: Securities and Exchange Commission

10-K Annual Report

Contents   (partial listing):
            Business of Company
            Properties
            Legal Proceedings
            Management Discussion and Analysis
            Changes or Disagreements with Auditors
            Financial Statements and Footnotes
            Investee Financial Statements (where applicable)
            Parent Company Financial Statements (where applicable)

            Schedules:
              I. Condensed Financial Information
             II. Bad Debt and Other Valuation Accounts
            III. Real Estate and Accumulated Depreciation
             IV. Mortgage Loans on Real Estate
              V. Supplementary Information Concerning Property-Casualty Insurance Oper-
                 ations

Due Date: 3 months following end of fiscal year.

10-Q Quarterly Report

Contents   Financial Statements
            Management Discussion and Analysis

Due Date: 45 days following end of fiscal quarter. Not required for fourth quarter of fiscal
year.

8-K Current Reports

Contents   (used to report important events):
            Change in Control
            Acquisitions and Divestitures
            Bankruptcy
            Change in Auditors
            Resignation of Directors

Due Date: 15 days following event.

Source: Adapted from SEC Regulation S-X.

The Financial Accounting Standards Board

The FASB is a nongovernmental body with seven full-time members. The board sets
accounting standards for all companies issuing audited financial statements. Because
of Rule 203 of the American Institute of Certified Public Accountants (AICPA), all
FASB pronouncements are considered authoritative; new FASB statements immediately become part of GAAP. Prior to creation of the FASB in 1973, accounting

standards were set by an AICPA committee known as the Accounting Principles Board (APB). Unless superseded, APB opinions remain part of GAAP.[8]

Because the SEC recognizes FASB statements as authoritative (as it recognized APB opinions prior to 1973), there is only one body of GAAP applicable to the United States. There are a few instances (earnings per share, e.g.) in which nonpublic companies are exempted from certain GAAP requirements. Generally speaking, however, all audited statements are prepared using the same financial reporting framework.

The FASB is an independent body whose members are required to sever all ties with previous employers. Although historically most board members have been former auditors, others have come from the corporate world, government service, and academia. The analyst community is currently represented on the board by Anthony Cope, CFA; Frank Block, CFA, served from 1979 to 1985.

Before issuing a new Statement of Financial Accounting Standards (SFAS), the FASB staff often works with a task force—composed of public accountants, representatives from industry, academics, regulators, and financial statement users—to develop a discussion memorandum. After public comments are received and hearings held, the staff prepares an exposure draft (a proposed standard) for public comment.[9] The FASB also collaborates with other standard-setting authorities. For example, recent proposals on earnings per share and segment reporting have been developed in conjunction with the IASC and the Canadian Accounting Standards Board.

The board's due process rules necessitate extensive dissemination of its agenda. SEC rulemaking is also normally preceded by a request for comments on a proposed set of rules. Thus, it is possible to anticipate new accounting and disclosure standards well in advance of their issuance and implementation.

FASB Conceptual Framework

The conceptual basis for U.S. GAAP stems from FASB concepts statements that create a "constitution" or conceptual framework used by the board to set standards. Many critics of the FASB view the conceptual framework as a failure.[10] They state that the definitions are unduly vague and that the board has repeatedly deferred difficult decisions (such as how to measure income). Others believe that the conceptual framework has helped the board set better standards.

For the analyst, the conceptual framework is an important building block in understanding the information provided by financial statements. The conceptual framework delineates the characteristics accounting information must possess to be useful in investment and other economic decisions.

---

[8]FASB statements and interpretations, Accounting Principles Board (APB) opinions, and AICPA accounting research bulletins constitute the highest level of authority in the hierarchy of accounting principles. These are followed in descending order of authority by FASB technical bulletins, cleared AICPA industry audit guides, and AICPA statements of position at level B. ("Cleared" means that the FASB has not objected to the issuance of the guide or the statement of position.) Positions of the FASB Emerging Issues Task Force and cleared AcSEC practice bulletins constitute level C, followed by AICPA accounting interpretations, question-and-answer guides published by the FASB staff, uncleared AICPA statements of position, and uncleared AICPA industry audit and accounting guides. The lowest authoritative level includes FASB concepts statements, APB statements, AICPA issues papers, IASC statements, and so on.

[9]The FASB sometimes issues an intermediate document, labeled preliminary views or tentative conclusions, to obtain comment on difficult issues.

[10]For example, see David Solomons, "The FASB's Conceptual Framework: An Evaluation," *Journal of Accountancy*, June 1986, pp. 114–124.

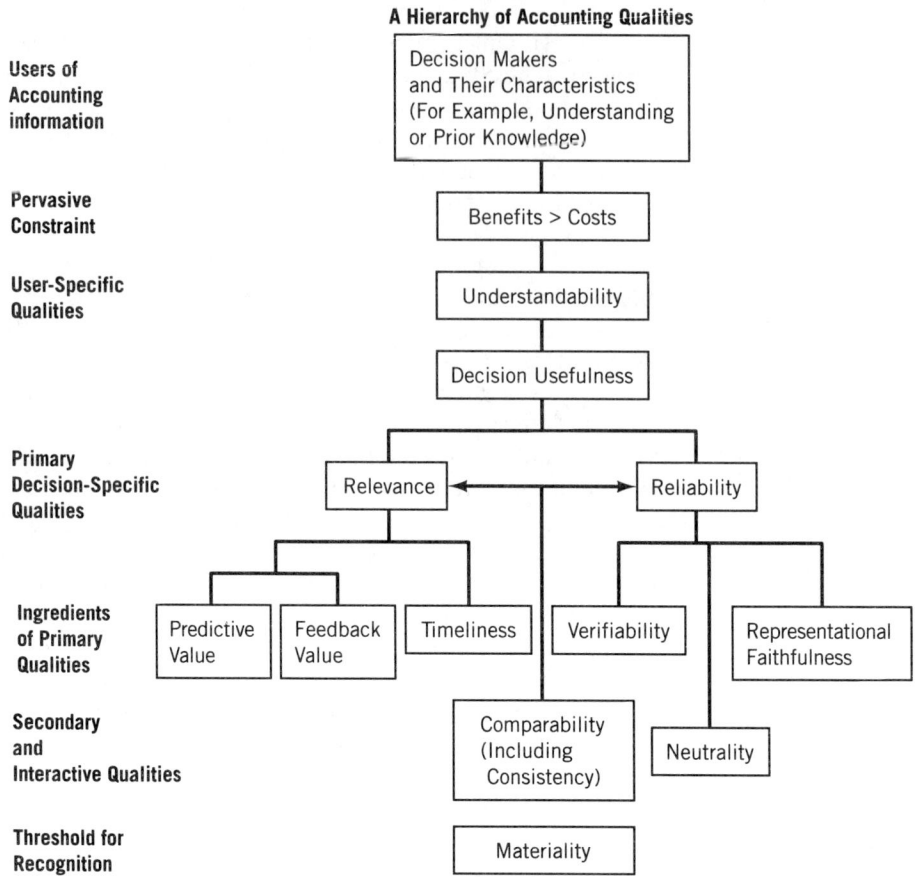

FIGURE 1-1 A hierarchy of accounting qualities. *Source*: Figure 1 of FASB Concepts Statement No. 2, *Qualitative Characteristics of Accounting Information*, copyright by Financial Accounting Standards Board, Norwalk, CT.

We have already addressed Statement of Financial Accounting Concepts (SFAC) 1, which sets forth the objectives of financial reporting. SFAC 2 is concerned with the Qualitative Characteristics of Accounting Information. These characteristics are shown in Figure 1-1, which is reproduced from the statement. A brief discussion follows.[11]

Qualitative Characteristics of Accounting Information. Analysts' concern with the qualitative characteristics of accounting information derives from the need for information that facilitates comparison of firms using alternative reporting methods and is useful for decision making. Although some of these characteristics are self-evident, others require some explanation. We start with relevance and reliability, key characteristics from the analyst point of view.

---

[11]SFAC 3, Elements of Financial Statements of Business Enterprises, has been superseded by SFAC 6, Elements of Financial Statements, which is discussed in detail in subsequent sections of this chapter. The topics covered by SFAC 4, Objectives of Financial Reporting by Nonbusiness Organizations, are beyond the scope of this text. The remaining concepts statement, SFAC 5, Recognition and Measurement in Financial Statements of Business Enterprises, is addressed elsewhere in this chapter.

Relevance is defined as "the capacity of information to make a difference in a decision. . . ."[12] In practice, of course, the relevance of information depends on the decision maker. To a technical analyst (chartist), all financial data are irrelevant. For fundamental analysts, the relevance of information varies with the method of analysis (emphasis on income statement, cash flow, balance sheet, etc.).

Timeliness is an important aspect of relevance. Information loses value rapidly in the financial world. Market prices are predicated on estimates of the future; data on the past are helpful in making projections. But as time passes and the future becomes the present, past data become increasingly irrelevant.

Reliability encompasses *verifiability*, *representational faithfulness*, and *neutrality*. The first two elements (verifiability and representational faithfulness) are concerned with whether financial data have been measured accurately and whether they are what they purport to be. Data without these characteristics cannot be relied on in making investment decisions.

Neutrality is concerned with whether financial statement data are biased. FASB proposals are frequently the object of complaints that companies will be adversely affected by the new standard. The principle of neutrality states that the board should consider only the relevance and reliability of the data, not any possible economic impact.

Unfortunately, relevance and reliability tend to be opposing qualities. For example, the audit process improves the reliability of data, but at the cost of timeliness. For that reason, financial statement users have generally not supported the auditing of quarterly data, believing that the time delay does not compensate for any improved data quality.

Relevance and reliability also clash strongly in a number of accounting areas. Market value data are probably the best example. Information on the current market value of investments may be highly relevant (see Chapter 13) but may be accurate (reliable) only to a limited extent. Yet historical cost, although highly reliable, may have little relevance. It is the old argument as to whether it is better to be "precisely wrong" or "approximately right."

Analysts have generally opted for approximately right. They have supported the disclosure of supplementary data in such areas as natural resources (SFAS 69, Chapter 7), off-balance-sheet financing (Chapter 11), and segment data (SFAS 14, Chapter 13). Auditors and preparers, more concerned with reliability (and legal liability), have often opposed the inclusion of less reliable data in the financial statements.

Consistency and *comparability* are also key characteristics of accounting information from the analyst perspective. Consistency refers to use of the same accounting principles over time. A broader term, comparability, refers to comparisons among companies.

Consistency is affected by new accounting standards and voluntary changes in accounting principles and estimates. Accounting changes hinder the comparison of operating results between periods when the accounting principles used to measure those results differ. As the transition provisions of new accounting standards vary, it is frequently difficult to obtain a consistent time series of earnings properly adjusted for such changes. For voluntary changes (such as depreciation methods and lives), the effect of the change is generally disclosed only for the year of the change.

Comparability is a pervasive problem in financial analysis. Companies are free to choose among different accounting methods and estimates in a variety of areas, making

[12]SFAC 2, Glossary.

comparisons of different enterprises difficult or impossible. Although the FASB (and to a lesser extent, foreign standard setters and the IASC) has narrowed these differences somewhat in recent years, new types of transactions (such as securitization of assets) create new sources of noncomparability. Even when accounting differences do not exist, however, comparability may be missing because of real differences between the firms (e.g., one has foreign operations and the other does not).

INTERNATIONAL ACCOUNTING STANDARDS

Growing international trade, multinational industrial and financial enterprises, and increasingly global capital markets have significantly expanded investment opportunities. Creditors and equity investors need to analyze both domestic and foreign companies. Yet differences in accounting and reporting standards make it difficult to compare domestic companies with those in other countries. Furthermore, as accounting standards are established separately in each country, it is difficult to generalize about those differences.

Financial reporting requirements are a function of tax regulations, corporate law, the comparative significance of capital markets and financial institutions in industrial development, and cultural differences. However, as capital markets and international investments expand, the need for global accounting standards is obvious.

Two questions arise: Who should develop such standards and who would enforce them?

This section provides a brief discussion of the International Organization of Securities Commissions (IOSCO), the International Accounting Standards Committee (IASC), and European financial reporting standards; a review of SEC reporting requirements for foreign registrants follows. These discussions indicate limited progress toward harmonization of international reporting requirements.

International Organization of Securities Commissions

IOSCO is an organization of securities regulators from more than 65 countries, including the SEC from the United States. IOSCO's Technical Committee investigates regulatory issues related to international securities transactions and is charged with developing solutions to problems in these areas.

IOSCO is also involved in standard setting through the Technical Committee's Working Party 1 on Multinational Disclosure and Accounting that is charged with advocating financial reporting regulation, which facilitates cross-border securities offerings and promotes effective and efficient international capital markets.

The Technical Committee's Working Party has established a comprehensive core set of international accounting standards that could be recognized by IOSCO members for use in cross-border offerings and global multiple listings. However, each country's regulatory agency would have to approve these standards. It appears that enforcement would also remain a country-by-country matter.

International Accounting Standards Committee

The IASC, established in 1973, attempts to harmonize (conform) the accounting standards of different nations. The IASC is a nongovernmental body with representatives from national accounting federations, stock exchanges, financial institutions, and other groups (including the International Coordinating Committee of Financial

Analysts Associations). Members of these diverse groups give IASC standards a comprehensive due process similar to that used by the FASB.

Lacking an enforcement mechanism, the IASC historically strove for consensus, resulting in broad standards allowing alternative methods. Starting in 1989, with increasing support from IOSCO, the IASC became more aggressive in limiting accounting alternatives.

In 1989, the IASC issued Exposure Draft 32 (E32), Comparability of Financial Statements, which dealt with 29 accounting issues. E32 was designed to eliminate all but one accounting treatment where the alternatives represented a free choice for similar transactions and events and to ensure that alternative treatments are used only under different circumstances. In some cases, E32 identified benchmark (preferred) and allowed alternative standards. When the allowed alternative was used, firms were to be required to reconcile reported net income and stockholders' equity to amounts determined using the preferred treatment. In 1990, the IASC revised E32, and 21 proposals contained in the original E32 were subsequently incorporated in the IAS without substantive changes.

As of December 31, 1995, the IASC has issued 32 international accounting standards (IAS) and is expected to issue an additional 16 standards by the end of 1999.[13] It has also issued its Framework for the Preparation and Presentation of Financial Statements, similar to the FASB conceptual framework, used to review existing standards and develop future IAS. This framework is also used to promote harmonization of regulations and standard setting by providing a basis for reducing the number of alternative accounting treatments permitted by the IASC.

The IASC has largely "caught up" with the FASB. In the early 1990s, the IASC developed standards dealing with issues such as joint ventures that the FASB has yet to resolve. Despite the handicaps of part-time members, a limited budget, and the need to achieve consensus among a large (and diverse) membership, the IASC has emerged as a rival source of accounting standards. Individual IASC standards are discussed in each chapter of this text as appropriate.

In October 1993, IOSCO and the IASC reached two milestones in their quest for globally acceptable accounting standards for cross-border securities offerings and multiple listings. IOSCO endorsed IAS 7, Cash Flow Statements, and published a list of core standards that would form the basis for a reasonably complete set of global standards. As of December 1995, IOSCO has also approved 14 of the existing IASC standards. The IASC intends to complete work on the remaining core standards by 1999 to obtain full approval from IOSCO. The IASC clearly aspires to be the body that sets global GAAP.

As capital markets become more international in scope, the need for global accounting standards and the demand for multiple listings grow. Discussion of financial reporting in Europe will be followed by an examination of the SEC's efforts to facilitate foreign listings.

European Financial Reporting Standards

Financial reporting requirements in Europe differ from those in the United States and other countries because of differences in their economies, relevance of local commercial law to the development of reporting standards, comparative importance

---

[13]The additional 16 standards include 13 IOSCO core standards, two revised standards, and one noncore standard on agriculture issues.

of capital markets and banks as a source of financing, and the degree to which tax laws influence financial reporting.

Within the European Economic Community (EEC), attempts have been made to reduce reporting differences. The Fourth Directive (1978) attempted to provide a framework for a common level of disclosure, with an emphasis on accounting rules and measurement (valuation) methods. This directive permitted some choice as to format and required content of the balance sheet and income statement and did not mandate a cash flow statement. The directive was a preliminary attempt at harmonization, and its adoption followed the passage of the directive into law in each member country.

In 1983, the EEC issued the Seventh Directive with an effective date of January 1, 1990. This directive is similar to international practice, particularly in the requirement for consolidated financial statements. The level of compliance and the impact on financial statement analysis were observable from 1991 onward when the first statements prepared under it were published.

Harmonization in Europe may prove to be difficult if only because of critical differences between U.K. and German GAAP. It is quite likely that the European union will foster greater cooperation between standard setting organizations across Europe and thereby contribute to international harmonization. Such harmonization is likely, however, to take the form of adoption of IASC standards rather than "European GAAP."

SEC REPORTING REQUIREMENTS FOR FOREIGN REGISTRANTS

Foreign issuers may sell their securities in the United States by registering with the SEC and are subject to substantially the same reporting requirements as their domestic counterparts. Some foreign issuers may elect to file the registration and reporting forms used by domestic issuers (see Exhibit 1-1). Alternatively, foreign filers may elect to file the generally less stringent Forms 20-F (similar to 10-K) and 6-K (similar to 8-K). Issuers of American Depositary Receipts (ADRs)[14] may register either Form F-6 or 20-F and are exempt from Form 8-K requirements.

Form 20-F filings are commonly used by foreign issuers, thereby making them exempt from requirements to file proxies and insider trading reports. Form 20-F annual reports are due six months after the fiscal year end, quarterly reports are optional, and relatively little business and segment data disclosure is required.

Form 20-F filers must identify both the reporting principles used and the material variations from U.S. GAAP and reconcile reported income and stockholders' equity to U.S. GAAP. These reconciliations provide insights into the differences in reporting requirements across countries and the tasks involved in developing universal financial reporting standards. (See Chapter 14 for an example of the analysis of and the utility of data provided in Form 20-F reconciliations.)

The SEC issued Staff Accounting Bulletin (SAB) 88 in August 1990 clarifying disclosures and quantitative reconciliations required by Item 17 of Form 20-F. The new guidance requires some additional disclosures regarding pension obligations (SFAS 87) and financial instruments (SFAS 105) in the MD&A. However, SAB 88 does not

---

[14]ADRs are depositary shares representing a specified number of shares and are issued against the deposit of a foreign issuer's securities. ADRs must be registered on Form F-6 unless another registration form is more appropriate.

mandate disclosures required by U.S. GAAP or the SEC but not by the foreign issuer's local GAAP.[15]

If a foreign registrant uses IAS 7, Cash Flow Statements, no further reconciliation is required. In 1994, the SEC eliminated the requirement for foreign issuers to reconcile to U.S. GAAP for differences stemming from the use of IAS 21, The Effects of Changes in Foreign Exchange Rates [Financial Reporting Release (FRR) 43, December 13, 1994]. Similarly, no reconciliation to U.S. GAAP is required when the registrant uses IAS 22, Business Combinations (FRR 45, December 13, 1994).

These amendments reflect two parallel developments. First, some IAS standards have achieved acceptance for filing requirements in the United States. Second, U.S. filing requirements for foreign registrants have affected requirements for U.S. entities. FRR 44 (December 13, 1994) eliminated the requirement for domestic issuers to file schedules with data on marketable securities, property, plant, and equipment, accumulated depreciation, and short-term borrowings. Although these amendments "leveled the field" for domestic and foreign filers, they also eliminated a significant amount of information useful in financial analysis.

Multijurisdictional Disclosure System

In 1991, to facilitate efficient international capital formation and growth, and to harmonize disclosure standards, the SEC entered into an agreement, the multijurisdictional disclosure system (MJDS), with Canadian regulators. Under this agreement, large Canadian companies can issue certain classes of securities in the United States using financial statements prepared according to Canadian GAAP (and vice versa). Reconciliation to U.S. GAAP is not required for the offering of highly rated bonds and preferred shares. Although the original intent of the MJDS was to end the reconciliation requirement for filings subsequent to July 1, 1993, the SEC decided to maintain that requirement.

The United States and Canada have similar financial reporting standards, but Canada requires substantially less disclosure. Discussions with several European countries along the same lines have taken place. However, European GAAP is quite different, and the development of similar agreements with the European community would appear to be more difficult than the current MJDS with Canada.

Thus, it seems likely that the further internationalization of the securities markets requires a common set of accounting standards. As the IASC continues to establish a credible set of standards, those standards become the only candidate for "world GAAP." Major IASC and foreign standards are discussed in the appropriate chapters of this book.

PRINCIPAL FINANCIAL STATEMENTS

The preceding sections described the general principles and measurement rules of the basic accounting process applicable to financial reporting in the United States. They also examined the role of international and domestic standard-setting bodies (the SEC and FASB) and the latter's conceptual framework that guides this process, along

---

[15]See R. Dieter and J. A. Heyman, "Implications of SEC Staff Accounting Bulletin 88 for Foreign Registrants," *Journal of Accountancy*, Aug. 1991, pp. 121–125.

with the qualitative characteristics of accounting information. This section provides a detailed discussion of the output of this system: the different financial statements, footnotes, and supplementary data.

The Balance Sheet

The balance sheet (statement of financial position) reports major classes and amounts of assets (resources owned or controlled by the firm), liabilities (external claims on those assets), and stockholders' equity (owners' capital contributions and other internally generated sources of capital) and their interrelationships at specific points in time.

Assets reported on the balance sheet are either purchased by the firm or generated through operations; they are financed, directly or indirectly, by the creditors and stockholders of the firm. This fundamental accounting relationship provides the basis for recording all transactions in financial reporting and is expressed as the balance sheet equation:

$$\text{Assets (A)} = \text{Liabilities (L)} + \text{Stockholders' Equity (E)}$$

In the United States, firms issue balance sheets at the end of each quarter and the end of the year. Annual or semiannual reporting is the norm in most other countries.

Elements of the Balance Sheet

SFAC 6 discusses the elements of financial statements. Although this statement also deals with nonprofit organizations, we restrict our comments to business enterprises.
Assets are defined in SFAC 6 as

> probable future economic benefits obtained or controlled by a particular entity as a result of past transactions or events. (para. 25)

This definition seems to be noncontroversial. Its weakness is its lack of reference to risk. It seems to us that an enterprise that retains the risks of ownership still "owns" the asset. This issue is important, for example, as it relates to the sale of assets (such as accounts receivable, loans, and mortgages; see Chapter 11) when the seller retains some risk of loss.
Liabilities are defined, similarly, as

> probable future sacrifices of economic benefits arising from present obligations of a particular entity to transfer assets or provide services to other entities in the future as a result of past transactions or events. (para. 35)

Again, the definition reads well. Yet it permits the nonrecognition of contractual obligations such as operating leases (see Chapter 11). The interpretation of "present obligation" and "result of past transactions or events" is key to accounting for all such contracts; some believe that only payments immediately due as a consequence of completed transactions create liabilities. Others believe that all long-term contracts should be recognized as long-term liabilities.[16] Another important problem area is the

---

[16]The capitalization of all executory contracts is advocated in the AIMR position paper "Financial Reporting in the 1990s and Beyond" (1993).

derecognition of liabilities that have been prerefunded but remain outstanding (see the discussion of defeasance in Chapter 10).[17]

As required by the fundamental accounting equation, *stockholders' equity* is therefore

the residual interest in the net assets of an entity that remains after deducting its liabilities. (para. 49)

In practice, some financial instruments have characteristics of both liabilities and equities, making them difficult to categorize. Convertible debt and redeemable preferreds are two common examples examined in Chapter 10.

The Income Statement

The income statement (statement of earnings) reports on the performance of the firm, the result of its operating activities. It explains some but not all of the changes in the assets, liabilities, and equity of the firm between two consecutive balance sheet dates. Use of the accrual concept means that income and the balance sheet are interrelated.

The preparation of the income statement is governed by the matching principle, which states that performance can be measured only if revenues and related costs are accounted for during the same time period. This requires the recognition of expenses incurred to generate revenues in the same period as the related revenues. For example, the cost of a machine is recognized as an expense (it is depreciated) over its useful life (as it is used in production) rather than as an expense in the period it is purchased.[18]

Elements of the Income Statement

Revenues are defined in SFAC 6 as

inflows. . . of an entity. . . from delivering or producing goods, rendering services, or other activities that constitute the entity's ongoing major or central operations. (para. 78)

Expenses are defined as

outflows. . . from delivering or producing goods, rendering services, or carrying out other activities that constitute the entity's ongoing major or central operations. (para. 80)

These definitions explicitly exclude *gains and losses*, defined as

increases (decreases) in equity (net assets) from peripheral or incidental transactions. . . . (para. 82)

Gains or losses are, therefore, nonoperating events. Examples would include gains and losses from asset sales, lawsuits, and changes in market values (including currency rates).

---

[17]SFAS 125 (1996), Accounting for Transfers and Servicing of Financial Assets and Extinguishments of Liabilities, prohibits derecognition of liabilities using in-substance defeasance.

[18]Note that no depreciation would be recorded if the products manufactured were not sold in the period the machine was used; the cost of using the machine would be added to work-in-process or finished goods inventories and carried on the balance sheet as an asset until the goods were sold.

These definitions are, like the others in SFAC 6, easy to accept as stated. The difficulties come in practice. For example, investment activities may be "central" to a financial institution but "peripheral" to a manufacturing company. Similarly, sales of assets such as automobiles may be "incidental" to a retailer but "central" to a car rental firm. The write-down of inventories due to obsolescence is more problematic: Is this an expense or a loss? To some extent, the distinction between revenue and expense on the one hand and gains and losses on the other is a precursor of the controversy over "extraordinary items." From the analyst point of view, disclosure is more important than classification; analysts prefer to make their own distinctions between operating and nonoperating events in many instances. From the point of view of database users, however, the outcome of the debate is important.

Comprehensive Income

The notion of *comprehensive income* is perhaps the most innovative (and potentially most useful) concept in SFAC 6. It is defined as

> the change in equity (net assets). . . from transactions and other events and circumstances from nonowner sources. It includes all changes in equity during a period except those resulting from investments by owners and distributions to owners. (para. 70)

On October 11, 1996, the FASB issued an exposure draft: Reporting Comprehensive Income. The proposed standard, which would become effective in 1997, would require:

- Either a separate Statement of Comprehensive Income or expansion of the income statement to a Statement of Income and Comprehensive Income
- Classification of items of comprehensive income by their nature
- Reclassification adjustments to avoid double counting when, for example, unrecognized capital gains are later recognized and included in reported income
- Reporting comprehensive income per share

The comprehensive income concept has several applications. Financial statements contain increasing numbers of valuation adjustments—foreign currency translation, market values of investments, and minimum pension liability are but three that are commonly found. Such adjustments, and the plethora of "restructuring" and other "nonrecurring" items, make it difficult to discern the operating results of an enterprise. Also, the FASB may eventually require financial statement recognition and measurement of many financial instruments (particularly, the consequences of hedging and derivative transactions) at fair value. However, the treatment of resulting unrealized gains and losses on these instruments is unsettled. The concept of comprehensive income holds a solution to these problems.[19]

Changes in carrying amounts of assets and liabilities could be accounted for as part of comprehensive income, yet kept outside of "income from continuing operations," which most analysts use as the best guide to future earnings of an enterprise.

---

[19]Financial reporting in the United Kingdom complements the traditional income statement with a Statement of Total Recognized Gains and Losses in which firms report comprehensive income. (See U.K. Financial Reporting Standard 3, Reporting Financial Performance.)

The Statement of Cash Flows

The statement of cash flows reports cash receipts and payments in the period of their occurrence, classified as to operating, investing, and financing activities. It also provides supplementary disclosures about noncash investing and financing activities. Cash flow data also help explain changes in consecutive balance sheets and supplement the information provided by the income statement.

SFAS 95, Statement of Cash Flows (1987), defines investing cash flows as those resulting from:

- Acquisition or sale of property, plant, and equipment
- Acquisition or sale of a subsidiary or segment
- Purchase or sale of investments in other firms

Similarly, financing cash flows are those resulting from:

- Issuance or retirement of debt and equity securities
- Dividends paid to stockholders

The standard requires gross rather than net reporting of significant investing and financing activities, thereby providing improved disclosure. For example, cash flows for property acquisitions must be shown separately from those related to property sales.

Significant noncash investing and financing activities (such as capitalized leases) must be disclosed separately within the cash flow statement or in a footnote elsewhere in the financial statements. Complex investment and financing transactions sometimes involve combinations of cash, debt, and other resources—these separate but related components must be reported separately.

Cash from Operations. This key performance measure includes the cash effects of all transactions that do not meet the definition of investing or financing. In effect, they are the cash flow consequences of the revenue-producing activities of the firm. They may be reported either directly, using major categories of gross cash receipts and payments, or indirectly by providing a reconciliation of net income to net cash flow from operating activities. Both methods require separate disclosure of the cash outflows for income taxes and interest within the statement or elsewhere in the financial statements.

The Statement of Stockholders' Equity

This statement reports the amounts and sources of changes in equity from capital transactions with owners and may include the following components:

1. Preferred shares
2. Common shares (at par or stated value)
3. Additional paid-in capital
4. Retained earnings
5. Treasury shares (repurchased equity)
6. Employee Stock Ownership Plan (ESOP) adjustments

7. Minimum pension liability
8. Valuation allowance (marketable equity securities)
9. Cumulative translation allowance (foreign operations)

Equity events and transactions are generally recognized as they occur, but capital market developments have created significant measurement and classification problems in transactions with owners.

The firm usually records the issuance of preferred and common stock at par (or stated) value and the amounts received in excess of par as additional paid-in capital. Repurchases or retirements of common stock may be reported as treasury shares, a contra account, which reflects a reduction in common stock outstanding. Retained (reinvested) earnings, which increase with income and decline with dividend declarations, are also reported. Finally, this statement also includes adjustments made in a quasireorganization (see Chapter 14).

The minimum pension liability results from reconciliation of the accounting liability for pensions with the economic liability (see Chapter 12). The valuation allowance for noncurrent investments and the cumulative foreign currency translation adjustment result from selective recognition of market value changes (see Chapter 13) and exchange rate changes (see Chapter 15), respectively.

Footnotes

Information provided in the financial statements is augmented by footnotes and other supplementary disclosures. Footnotes are an integral part of the financial statements and provide data on such subjects as business segments, the financial position of retirement plans, and off-balance-sheet obligations. These data are required by either GAAP (FASB standards) or regulatory authorities (the SEC). The financial statements and footnotes in the annual report and the SEC 10-K filings are audited.

Supplementary schedules, some required by the SEC in 10-K filings (see Exhibit 1-1), provide additional useful information. Some of these supplementary data are unaudited.

Footnotes provide information about the accounting methods, assumptions, and estimates used by management to develop the data reported in the financial statements. They are designed to allow users to improve assessments of the amounts, timing, and uncertainty of the estimates reported in the financial statements. Footnotes provide additional disclosure related to such areas as:

1. Fixed assets
2. Inventories
3. Income taxes
4. Pension and other postemployment benefit plans
5. Debt (interest rates, maturity schedules, and contractual terms)
6. Lawsuits and other loss contingencies
7. Marketable securities and other investments
8. Significant customers, sales to related parties, and export sales

Contingencies

Footnotes often contain disclosures relating to contingent[20] losses. Firms are required to accrue a loss (recognize a balance sheet liability) when *both* of the following conditions are met:

1. It is probable that assets have been impaired or a liability has been incurred.

2. The amount of the loss can be reasonably estimated.

If the loss amount lies within a range, the most likely amount should be accrued. When no amount in the range is a better estimate, the firm may report the minimum amount in the range.[21]

SFAS 5 defines *probable* events as those "more likely than not" to occur, suggesting that a probability of more than 50% requires recognition of a loss. However, in practice, firms generally report contingencies as losses only when the probability of loss is significantly higher.

Footnote disclosure of (unrecognized) loss contingencies is required when it is *reasonably possible* (more than remote but less than probable) that a loss has been incurred or when it is probable that a loss has occurred but the amount cannot be reasonably estimated. The standard provides an extensive discussion of loss contingencies.

The recognition and measurement of loss contingencies are problematic because they involve judgment and are subjective at best. External analysis is hampered by the paucity of data, as disclosures are often vague. Footnote disclosures and the SEC-mandated MD&A are the best sources of information.

Significant problem areas include environmental remediation liabilities, litigation, expropriation, self-insurance, debt guarantees, repurchase agreements, take-or-pay contracts, and throughput arrangements. In later chapters we provide discussion of analytical techniques applicable to many of these contingencies and examples of losses recognized in the financial statements as well as others disclosed only in footnotes.

DuPont's Note 28, Commitments and Contingent Liabilities, typifies disclosures of contingencies (Appendix A). Although the note contains considerable uninformative "boilerplate," it does tell us that:

- DuPont has accrued $616 million for environmental obligations, and its ultimate liability may be higher. Additional discussion of the company's environmental problems takes up more than two pages of the MD&A.

- Debt guarantees total $845 million, almost all for direct guarantees of the obligations of affiliates and other firms.

Note 3, concerning a fungicide recall, indicates that it is difficult for firms to estimate contingent liabilities. DuPont accrued $212 million for this problem in 1992, an additional $200 million in 1993, and $175 million more in 1994.

---

[20]The FASB defines a contingency as an "existing condition, situation, or set of circumstances involving uncertainty as to possible gain or loss" (SFAS 5, para. 1).

[21]See FASB Interpretation No. 14, Reasonable Estimation of the Amount of a Loss.

Footnote and MD&A disclosures of contingencies should be read carefully, as they provide clues about possible future expense provisions and cash outflows.[22] In extreme cases (asbestos, for example), environmental claims have driven firms into bankruptcy. Lawsuits and claims are, in addition, sometimes indicators of illegal acts or poor management practices.

Risks and Uncertainties

In 1994, the AICPA issued Statement of Position (SOP) 94-6, Disclosure of Certain Significant Risks and Uncertainties.[23] Although most AICPA SOPs are narrow in scope, applying to only one industry or narrow category of transactions, SOP 94-6 has broad application. It requires that audited financial statements report the following information:

1. *Nature of operations.* A description of the firm's major business activities and markets.

2. *Use of estimates.* A statement that financial statements use estimates.

3. *Certain significant estimates.* When it is reasonably possible that an estimate used to prepare financial statements will change in the near term, and such change would have a material impact on those statements, then disclosures must be made regarding the nature of the uncertainty involved. Examples include the effect of technological obsolescence on operating assets, capitalized costs that might not be recoverable from operations, and contingent liabilities for environmental remediation or litigation.

4. *Current vulnerability due to certain concentrations.* Firms must disclose concentrations when it is reasonably possible that there could be a severe impact in the near term. Examples include concentrations in customers, suppliers, or markets.

For companies subject to SEC reporting requirements, the SOP has limited effect,[24] although it was intended to help firms (and their auditors) understand the application of SFAS 5 (Contingencies). The major effect of the SOP is on nonpublic companies, whose disclosures are not governed by the SEC; their disclosures were inadequate to analysts accustomed to reviewing the financial statements of public companies.

Supplementary Schedules

In some cases, additional information about the assets and liabilities of a firm is provided within the financial statement footnotes, or as supplementary data outside the financial statements. Examples include:

• Oil and gas companies provide additional data on their exploration activities, quantities and types of reserves, and the present value of cash flows expected from those reserves (see Chapter 7).

---

[22]See M. E. Barth and M. F. McNichols, "Estimation and Valuation of Environmental Liabilities," *Journal of Accounting Research*, Supplement 1994, pp. 177–209.

[23]One of the authors of this text was a member of the task force that prepared the SOP.

[24]SFAS 14 (see Chapter 13) requires more detailed segment data. The SOP permits the use of imprecise language such as "approximately."

- Supplemental disclosures of the impact of changing prices (see Appendix 8-A).
- Disclosure of sales revenue, operating income, and other data for major business segments (see Chapter 13) and by geographic areas (see Chapter 15). Firms also provide additional information about export sales.
- Increased disclosures related to financial instruments and hedging activities (see Chapter 16).

OTHER SOURCES OF FINANCIAL INFORMATION

Stockholder reports often contain useful supplementary financial and statistical data as well as management comments. In some cases, the stockholder report is included ("incorporated by reference") in the SEC filing, or vice versa. The MD&A required by the SEC may appear in either reports to stockholders or SEC filings. A brief discussion of the contents of the MD&A is followed by a discussion of other sources of financial data.

Management Discussion and Analysis

Companies with publicly traded securities have been required since 1968 to provide a discussion of earnings in the MD&A section.[25] The MD&A included in the financial statements of duPont (Appendix A at the end of the book) is one example. In 1980,[26] the SEC expanded the requirements to a comprehensive, broad-based discussion and analysis of the financial statements to encourage more meaningful disclosure.

The MD&A is required to discuss:

- Results of operations, including discussion of trends in sales and categories of expense
- Capital resources and liquidity, including discussion of cash flow trends
- Outlook based on known trends

In 1989, the SEC issued an interpretive release providing additional guidance on compliance in the following areas:

1. Prospective information and required discussion of significant effects of currently known trends, events, and uncertainties, for example, decline in market share or impact of inventory obsolescence. Firms may voluntarily disclose forward-looking data that anticipate trends or events.
2. Liquidity and capital resources: Firms are expected to use cash flow statements to analyze liquidity; provide a balanced discussion of operating, financing, and investing cash flows; and discuss transactions or events with material current or expected long-term liquidity implications.
3. Discussion of discontinued operations, extraordinary items, and other "unusual or infrequent" events with current or expected material effects on financial condition or results of operations.

---

[25]Securities Act Release No. 4936, Dec. 9, 1968 (33 FR 18617) and Securities Act Release No. 5520, Aug. 14, 1974 (39 FR 31894).

[26]Securities Act Release No. 6231, Sept. 2, 1980 (45 FR 63630).

4. Extensive disclosures in interim financial statements in keeping with the obligation to periodically update MD&A disclosures.

5. Disclosure of a segment's disproportionate need for cash flows or contribution to revenues or profits. Also, disclosure of any restrictions on a free flow of funds between segments.

Other Data Sources

Many companies prepare periodic "fact books" containing additional financial and operational data. Corporate press releases also provide new information on a timely basis. Computerized services (e.g., the Dow Jones News Retrieval System) and various on-line services provide databases of corporate releases and other business news. In addition, many companies hold periodic meetings or conference telephone calls to keep the financial community apprised of recent developments regarding the company. In between such meetings, or in lieu of, a company officer may be designated to answer questions and provide additional data to analysts following the company.

Industry data and other information about a company also may be obtained from sources outside the company. Trade publications, the general business press, computerized databases, investment research reports, and the publications of competitors are among the sources that may supplement company-originated financial data.

The growth of the Internet has greatly improved access to data relevant to investment decisions. Given the rapid change in Internet offerings, we have not attempted to compile a specific list. Examples include:

1. Company home pages that contain financial, product, and other data
2. EDGAR, which contains corporate filings with the SEC
3. Market data from exchanges and private data providers
4. Tax regulations
5. Economic data

A comprehensive analysis of a company requires the use of all these sources of information.

When reviewing corporate reports to stockholders and other publications, it is important to remember that they are written by management. Management often views annual reports as public relations or sales materials, intended to impress customers, suppliers, and employees, as well as stockholders. As a result, these reports must be read with at least some degree of skepticism. Only the financial statements (including footnotes and other disclosures labeled "audited") are independently reviewed and attested to by outside auditors.

ROLE OF THE AUDITOR

The auditor (independent certified public accountant) is responsible for seeing that the financial statements issued conform with generally accepted accounting principles. Thus, the auditor must agree that management's choice of accounting principles is appropriate and any estimates are reasonable. The auditor also examines the company's accounting and internal control systems, confirms assets and liabilities, and generally tries to be sure that there are no material errors in the financial statements.

EXHIBIT 1-2. PRICE WATERHOUSE
Report of Independent Accountants

To the Stockholders and the Board of Directors of
E. I. Du Pont de Nemours and Company

In our opinion, the consolidated financial statements appearing on pages 39–63 of this Annual Report present fairly, in all material respects, the financial position of E. I. du Pont de Nemours and Company and its subsidiaries at December 31, 1994 and 1993, and the results of their operations and their cash flows for each of the three years in the period ended December 31, 1994 in conformity with generally accepted accounting principles.

These financial statements are the responsibility of the company's management; our responsibility is to express an opinion on these financial statements based on our audits. We conducted our audits in accordance with generally accepted auditing standards which require that we plan and perform the audit to obtain reasonable assurance about whether the financial statements are free of material misstatement. An audit includes examining, on a test basis, evidence supporting the amounts and disclosures in the financial statements, assessing the accounting principles used and significant estimates made by management, and evaluating the overall financial statement presentation. We believe that our audits provide a reasonable basis for our opinion.

As discussed in Note 1 to the consolidated financial statements, the company changed its method of accounting for postretirement benefits other than pensions and for income taxes in 1992.

Price Waterhouse LLP, Philadelphia, Pennsylvania 19103, February 16, 1995

Source: E. I. Du Pont de Nemours and Company, *1994 Annual Report.*

The auditor will often review interim reports and "unaudited" portions of the annual report. Although hired by the company (often through the audit committee of the board of directors), the auditor is supposed to be independent of management and to serve the stockholders and other users of the financial statements.

Audited financial statements are always accompanied by the auditor's report, often referred to as an "opinion." Because of the "boilerplate" nature of these reports, there is a tendency to skip over them when reviewing financial statements. Failure to read this report, however, may cause the financial analyst to miss significant information.

Exhibit 1-2 is the independent auditor's report issued by Price Waterhouse after its audit of duPont for fiscal 1994. The first two paragraphs of the report are standard and are required by Statement of Auditing Standards (SAS) 58, Reports on Audited Financial Statements,[27] that addresses the audit report in which auditors express their opinion on the financial statements developed by management. It clarifies the scope of the assurance provided by the auditors and briefly describes the audit work. The report tells us the following:

1. Although the financial statements are prepared by duPont management and are the responsibility of management, the auditor has performed an independent review of the statements.

---

[27]Auditing Standards Board of the American Institute of Certified Public Accountants, 1989.

2. The audit has been conducted using generally accepted auditing standards (GAAS) that require the auditor to provide "reasonable assurance" that there are no material errors in the financial statements. The auditor does not guarantee that the statements are free from error or no fraud is present. The auditor has performed tests of the company's accounting system designed to ensure that the statements are accurate.

3. DuPont's financial statements are prepared in accordance with GAAP. The auditor is satisfied that the accounting principles chosen and the estimates employed are reasonable.

An auditor's report on GAAP-based financial statements will always include these three claims.

SAS 58 also requires the addition of an explanatory paragraph to the auditor's report when accounting methods have not been used consistently among periods. For duPont, the final paragraph tells us that the company changed its method of accounting for income taxes (SFAS 109) and for postretirement benefits other than pensions (SFAS 106) in 1992.

Reporting on Uncertainties

In some cases, the SAS requires the addition of an explanatory paragraph (following the "opinion" paragraph) that reports and describes material uncertainties affecting the financial statements, and it references the footnote(s) to the financial statements that further detail those uncertainties. The auditor's report on material uncertainties depends on the probability of material loss due to uncertainty. If the probability of a loss is remote, the auditor issues a standard, unqualified opinion.

An explanatory paragraph is required when a material loss is probable and the amount of the loss cannot be reasonably estimated. Exhibit 1-3 contains examples of three types of report paragraphs:

1. For the Morrison Knudsen Corporation, doubt regarding the "going concern" assumption that underlies the preparation of financial statements

2. For the Columbia Gas System, Inc., uncertainty regarding the valuation or realization of assets and payment of liabilities

3. For both the Morrison Knudsen Corporation and Columbia Gas System, Inc., uncertainty due to litigation

Whenever the auditor's report contains any of the three types of disclosures just listed, or the consistency exception, the financial statements should be examined closely. Note that "subject to" and "except for" disclosures no longer appear in auditors' reports; they were replaced in 1989 by the language (SAS 58) discussed above.

The first category is the most serious. A "going concern" qualification conveys doubt that the firm can continue in business. It may be that the firm requires financing due to losses or a lack of liquidity. This paragraph should be viewed as the equivalent of a flashing red light.[28]

---

[28]Recent empirical studies [e.g., Carcello et al. (1995) and Rama et al. (1995)] have indicated that approximately 60% of bankrupt firms received a prior going-concern modified audit report and approximately 10% of firms receiving a first-time going concern qualification entered into bankruptcy within one year of the date of the financial statements.

EXHIBIT 1-3
Uncertainty Paragraphs

Independent Auditor's Reports

Morrison Knudsen Corporation

The accompanying consolidated financial statements have been prepared assuming that the Corporation will continue as a going concern. As discussed in "Notes to Consolidated Financial Statements—Basis of Presentation and Management's Plans," the Corporation had substantial losses and negative cash flow from operations in 1994, which significantly reduced stockholders' equity and resulted in a substantial retained deficit and working capital deficit at December 31, 1994; was not in compliance with certain financial covenants of certain of its credit agreements at December 31, 1994 and subsequently failed to meet scheduled repayment terms; and will require additional funding to cover substantial expected negative cash flows in 1995. In addition, substantially all of the Corporation's short-term debt agreements expire on July 31, 1995. If the Corporation is unable to obtain adequate financing, it may be required to seek protection under the United States Bankruptcy Code in order to continue operating. These conditions raise substantial doubt about the Corporation's ability to continue as a going concern. Management's plans in this regard are also described in the "Notes to Consolidated Financial Statements—Basis of Presentation and Management's Plans." The consolidated financial statements do not include any adjustments that might result from the outcome of this uncertainty.

As emphasized in "Notes to Consolidated Financial Statements—Estimated Losses on Uncompleted Contracts," the Corporation recorded significant provisions for losses during 1994 related to revised estimates of costs to be incurred to complete certain transit car contracts. These management estimates are based on numerous assumptions which, if not ultimately achieved, could result in additional revisions of the estimates of costs to complete the transit car contracts and such revisions could be material.

The Columbia Gas System, Inc.

On July 31, 1991, the Corporation and Columbia Gas Transmission Corporation ("Columbia Transmission"), a wholly owned subsidiary, filed separate petitions seeking protection under Chapter 11 of the Federal Bankruptcy Code. Note 2 discusses, among other matters, uncertainties associated with Chapter 11 proceedings, including the status of the Corporation's loans to Columbia Transmission, certain prepetition intercompany asset transfers and the measurement of certain liabilities. This note also discusses purported class action and other complaints which have been filed against the Corporation generally alleging violations of certain securities laws. The accompanying financial statements do not reflect any liability associated with these complaints as the Corporation believes that it has meritorious defenses to these actions; however, the ultimate outcome is uncertain. As a result of these matters, the Corporation may take, or be required to take, actions which may cause assets to be realized or liabilities to be liquidated for amounts other than those reflected in the financial statements. These factors create substantial doubt about the Corporation's ability to continue as a going concern. The accompanying financial statements have been prepared assuming that the Corporation and Columbia Transmission will continue as going concerns which contemplate the realization of assets and payment of liabilities in the ordinary course of business. The appropriateness of the Corporation continuing to present financial statements on a going concern basis is dependent upon, among other things, the terms of the ultimate plan of reorganization and the ability to generate sufficient cash from operations and financing sources to meet obligations.

Source: Annual reports of Morrison Knudsen Corporation and the Columbia Gas System, Inc.

The other two categories suggest problems that are significant, but may not threaten the firm's existence. In these cases, an explanatory paragraph is included at the auditor's discretion when a material loss is reasonably possible. The paragraph's appearance depends on whether the probability of loss is closer to remote (unlikely) or probable (likely) and on the magnitude of the possible loss.

The auditor also performs other services less visible to readers of financial statements. The auditor examines the internal control system of the company and reports any weaknesses to management or the audit committee of the board of directors. The report to the audit committee sometimes also contains information regarding significant audit adjustments, unusual transactions, disagreements with management, or serious audit difficulties. This report is generally not available to outside financial statement users. In 1989, the Auditing Standards Board (ASB) of the American Institute of Certified Public Accountants issued two standards dealing with these reports.

Changes in auditors have become more frequent in recent years. In many cases, changes are due to an effort to reduce audit costs or to personality issues. Some changes, however, result from disagreements regarding the application of accounting principles. When an auditor is willing to lose a client because of such a disagreement, the financial analyst should exercise extreme caution with respect to the financial statements of the company in question.

SUMMARY

Chapter 1 provided an informational background for the study of financial statement analysis. It examined the sources of financial data and the institutional framework in which accounting and disclosure standards are set. In addition, it provided a general guide to the contents of the financial statements and the roles played by statement preparers and auditors. In Chapters 2 and 3, we build on this informational framework by addressing the financial statements—the raw material of analysis.

Chapter **1**

Problems

1. [Conceptual basis for accounting standards] In February 1993, the Chinese Ministry of Finance awarded a contract to develop accounting standards for China. Assume that you are employed on that project. Discuss how the standards to be developed would be affected by:

- **(i)** Decisions regarding the relative importance of different classes of financial statement users
- **(ii)** The choice between relevance and reliability
- **(iii)** The importance placed on comparability
- **(iv)** Political, legal, and cultural factors

2. [Conceptual basis for accounting standards] Explain why accounting standards might be different if they were established by:

   (i) Short-term lenders such as banks

   (ii) Long-term equity investors

   (iii) Tax authorities

   (iv) Corporate managers

3. [Basic accounting concepts] Describe the relationship between the matching principle and the accrual method of accounting in the preparation of financial statements.

4. [Basic accounting concepts] Describe why the going concern assumption is important in the preparation of financial statements.

5. [Sources of information] Contrast investors in public companies with those in private companies with respect to access to financial and other information useful for investment decisions.

6. [Sources of information] Contrast investors in public companies in the United States with those in foreign countries with respect to access to financial and other information useful for investment decisions.

7. [Sources of accounting standards] Contrast the roles of the Financial Accounting Standards Board and the Securities and Exchange Commission in the setting of accounting standards for American companies.

8. [Basic accounting concepts] Explain why the definitions of assets and liabilities affect accounting standards and, therefore, the preparation of financial statements.

9. [Basic accounting concepts] Explain why the distinction between liabilities and equity is important to investors and creditors.

10. [Basic accounting concepts] Explain why the difference between historical cost and market value affects the relevance and reliability of financial statement data.

11. [Basic accounting concepts] Contrast the role of contra accounts and adjunct accounts in financial statements.

12. [Basic accounting concepts]

   A. Contrast gains and losses with revenues and expenses. Explain why the distinction is important for financial analysis.

   B. Define *comprehensive income* and explain how that concept might make financial statements more useful for financial analysis.

13. [Basic concepts] Explain why the distinction between recurring and nonrecurring income is important for financial analysis.

14. [Basic concepts] Explain why cash flows are classified into three categories. Discuss the usefulness of each category.

15. [Basic concepts] Differentiate between financial statement footnotes and supplementary schedules as sources of financial data.

16. [Basic concepts] Discuss the SEC requirement for MD&A and explain how MD&A disclosures can assist financial analysis.

17. [Role of auditor] You are reviewing a company's financial statements. Its auditor has issued an unqualified opinion regarding the financial statements. Discuss what that opinion tells you about:

    (i) Possible changes in accounting principles

    (ii) Possible changes in accounting estimates

    (iii) The existence of significant risks regarding the future operations of the company

    (iv) The possibility that the financial statements are fraudulent

18. [Role of auditor, accounting changes] Exhibit 1P-1 contains an extract from the auditor's report and footnotes of Deere's fiscal *1992 Annual Report.*

A. Discuss whether the auditor's report should have referred to the change in accounting principle. Your answer should include *both* reasons why and reasons why not.

EXHIBIT 1P-1. DEERE & COMPANY
Extracts from Financial Statements

Independent Auditors' Report

Deloitte & Touche

Deere & Company:

We have audited the accompanying consolidated balance sheets of Deere & Company and subsidiaries as of October 31, 1992 and 1991 and the related statements of consolidated income and of consolidated cash flows for each of the three years in the period ended October 31, 1992. These financial statements are the responsibility of the company's management. Our responsibility is to express an opinion on these financial statements based on our audits.

    We conducted our audits in accordance with generally accepted auditing standards. Those standards require that we plan and perform the audit to obtain reasonable assurance about whether the financial statements are free of material misstatement. An audit includes examining, on a test basis, evidence supporting the amounts and disclosures in the financial statements. An audit also includes assessing the accounting principles used and significant estimates made by management, as well as evaluating the overall financial statement presentation. We believe that our audits provide a reasonable basis for our opinion.

    In our opinion, such consolidated financial statements present fairly, in all material respects, the financial position of Deere & Company and subsidiaries at October 31, 1992 and 1991 and the results of their operations and their cash flows for each of the three years in the period ended October 31, 1992 in conformity with generally accepted accounting principles.

Chicago, Illinois
December 9, 1992

Excerpt from Footnote on Income Tax

In the second quarter of 1992, the company adopted FASB Statement No. 109, "Accounting for Income Taxes." There was no cumulative effect of adoption or current effect on continuing operations mainly because the company had previously adopted FASB Statement No. 96, "Accounting for Income Taxes," in 1988.

Source: Deere & Company, *1992 Annual Report.*

B. Discuss why knowledge of the change in accounting principle is important for analysis purposes despite its immaterial effect on 1992 results.

19. [Role of auditor] Compare the role of the auditor with that of the financial statement preparer (firm being audited) in preparation of the firm's financial statements.

20. [Sources of information] Discuss the importance to investors of the controversy over the conditions under which companies may issue securities in foreign jurisdictions.

21. [Contingencies; 1988 CFA adapted] Bonnywill Auto produced 10,000 Fiery models. On December 31, 19X2, company engineers discovered a possible fire hazard for this model. The probability of fire is estimated at 0.00009. If a fire occurs, the company's liability is estimated at $100,000 per occurrence, plus or minus $30,000. When answering the following questions, show any calculations.

A. Describe the most likely treatment of this contingency in Bonnywill's 19X2 financial statements.

B. Suggest an alternative treatment that would portray the liability more accurately.

22. [Contingencies] Consider two firms that self-insure for workers' compensation losses. Assume that the annual probability of a claim is 1 in 1,000 for each firm and that each claim has an expected value of $10,000.

A. Firm A has 3 employees.

B. Firm B has 10,000 employees.

Discuss how each firm should account for its liability for workers' compensation benefits. If there is any difference in your answers, explain why.

23. [Contingencies] Exhibit 1P-2 contains excerpts from the *1995 Annual Report* of Bristol-Myers Squibb Company. The exhibit includes the 1995 Note 2 on Special Charges and Notes on Contingencies (for four years from 1992 to 1995), which provide a review of the firm's disclosures on breast implant litigation.

A. The firm did not record a liability for the breast implant litigation for the year ended December 31, 1992. Comment on the footnote disclosure in 1992.

B. The firm recorded a special charge and related liability in the fourth quarter of 1993, 1994, and 1995. This liability has been offset by $1.0 billion of expected insurance proceeds. The firm is engaged in coverage litigation with some of its insurers. Comment on the impact of this offset on the income statement and the balance sheet.

C. Compute the actual cash outflow related to this litigation during the years 1994 and 1995.

EXHIBIT 1P-2. BRISTOL-MYERS SQUIBB COMPANY
Selected Financial Statement Data

1995 Note 2: Special Charges

Years Ended December 31 ($ in millions)

Income Statement	1995	1994	1993
Special charge	$ 950	$ 750	$ 500
Net earnings	$1,812	$1,842	$1,959
Balance Sheet			
Noncurrent Assets			
Insurance recoverable	959	968	1,000
Product Liability			
Current portion	700	635	100
Noncurrent portion	$1,645	$1,201	$1,370

1995 Note 17: Contingencies

As of December 31, 1995, approximately 20,000 plaintiffs had filed suit against the company, its subsidiary, Medical Engineering Corporation (MEC), and certain other subsidiaries, in federal and state courts and in certain Canadian provincial courts, alleging damages for personal injuries of various types resulting from polyurethane covered breast implants and smooth walled breast implants. Most of these plaintiffs are participants in a 1994 class action settlement approved by the Federal District Court in Birmingham, Alabama; that settlement is now subject to appeals. A revision of that settlement, known as the revised settlement, which includes the company, MEC and certain other defendants, was approved on December 22, 1995. The order approving the settlement has been appealed. The revised settlement, applicable only to domestic claimants, currently does not include approximately 2,600 claimants who may assert claims based upon MEC implants and who opted out of the original settlement. Separate class action settlements for eligible claimants have been approved in the provincial courts of Quebec and Ontario. In January 1996, a notice of the revised settlement was mailed to approximately 450,000 persons. Class members who wish to do so may now opt out of the revised settlement although the Court has cautioned class members against doing so until they receive additional information as to the status of their claims. It is not possible on any reliable basis to estimate how many class members will participate in or opt out of the settlement. The cost of the settlement is dependent upon complex and varying factors, including the number of class members that participate in the settlement, the kinds of claims approved and their dollar value. The cost to the company of resolving opt out claims is also subject to a number of complex uncertainties in addition to the unknown quantity and quality of such claims. In light of the uncertainties attendant to these and other factors, it is difficult at this time to estimate with any precision the cost of the breast implant product liability claims to the company. Note 2 sets forth the special charges recorded in connection with this litigation. An additional charge to earnings may be required as additional information relating to the revised settlement and the litigation becomes known.

1994 Note 18: Contingencies

As of December 31, 1994, approximately 20,000 plaintiffs have filed suit against the company, its subsidiary, Medical Engineering Corporation (MEC), and certain other subsidiaries, in federal and state courts and in certain Canadian provincial courts, alleging damages for personal injuries of various types resulting from polyurethane covered breast implants and smooth walled breast implants. Most of these plaintiffs are participants in a class action settlement approved by the

EXHIBIT 1P-2. (*continued*)

federal District Court in Birmingham, Alabama, and that settlement is now subject to appeals. Of those who have chosen to opt out of the settlement, the company estimates that approximately 3,000 United States claimants may assert claims based upon MEC implants. Under the settlement, the company would make payments totaling $1.154 billion over a period of 30 years. Note 2 sets forth the special charges recorded in connection with this litigation. If the value of approved current disease claims under the settlement exceeds certain limits, payments to claimants would be reduced and claimants would have another opportunity to opt out of the settlement. If this were to occur, the company and other defendants could renegotiate the terms of the settlement or withdraw. The company is unable to predict when these events may occur but, based on information available at this time, it does not seem likely before late 1995. Dependent on these and other future developments, the company would record such additional charge as may be required. The amount of such a charge, if any, cannot be estimated.

1993 Note 18: Contingencies

As of December 31, 1993, approximately 10,000 plaintiffs have filed suit against the company, its subsidiary, Medical Engineering Corporation, and certain other subsidiaries, in federal and state courts and in certain Canadian provincial courts, alleging damages for personal injuries of various types resulting from polyurethane covered breast implants and smooth walled breast implants. Certain of these cases are class actions which seek to allege claims on behalf of all breast implant recipients. All federal court actions have been consolidated for pre-trial proceedings in federal District Court in Birmingham, Alabama. See Note 2 relating to the special charge recorded in connection with this litigation.

1992 Note 17: Contingencies

The company is a defendant in a number of actions brought against it and other pharmaceutical companies in federal and state courts by the children or grandchildren of women who ingested diethylstilbestrol (DES), a product which had been, but is no longer, manufactured or sold by an affiliate of the company.

The company is a defendant in a substantial number of actions filed in various U.S. federal and state courts and in certain Canadian provincial courts by recipients of two types of breast implants, formerly manufactured and sold by a subsidiary of the company, alleging damages for personal injuries of various types. Certain of these cases are class actions, some of which seek to allege claims on behalf of all breast implant recipients. All federal court actions have been consolidated for pre-trial proceedings in federal District Court in Birmingham, Alabama. In the case of *Pamela Jean Johnson* v. *Medical Engineering Corporation*, tried in state Court in Harris County, Texas, a jury on December 23, 1992 awarded plaintiff compensatory and punitive damages totaling $25 million. Absent settlement, the company's subsidiary will appeal this verdict.

Source: Bristol-Myers Squibb Company, 1992–1995 Annual Reports.

2

ACCOUNTING INCOME AND ASSETS: THE ACCRUAL CONCEPT

CHAPTER OUTLINE

CHAPTER OBJECTIVES

INTRODUCTION

INCOME, CASH FLOWS, AND ASSETS: DEFINITIONS AND RELATIONSHIPS

THE ACCRUAL CONCEPT OF INCOME
Income Statement
   Format and Classification
   Components of Net Income
Accounting Income: Revenue and Expense Recognition
   Departures from the Sales Basis of Revenue Recognition
   Percentage-of-Completion and Completed Contract Methods
   Comparison of Percentage-of-Completion and Completed Contract Methods
   Installment Method of Revenue Recognition
   Cost Recovery Method
   Revenue Recognition: Special Situations
Summary of Revenue Recognition Methods

NONRECURRING ITEMS
Types of Nonrecurring Items
   Unusual or Infrequent Items
   Extraordinary Items
   Discontinued Operations
   Accounting Changes
   Prior Period Adjustments
Analysis of Nonrecurring Items
   Income Statement Impact of Nonrecurring Items
   Cash Flow and Valuation Impact
   Implications for Continuing Operations
   Management Discretion and Earnings Manipulation

THE BALANCE SHEET
Format and Classification
Measurement of Assets and Liabilities
Uses of the Balance Sheet

THE STATEMENT OF STOCKHOLDERS' EQUITY
Format, Classification, and Use

SUMMARY

CASE 2-1 THOUSAND TRAILS, INC. I

CHAPTER OBJECTIVES

From this chapter, readers should obtain an under-standing of the:

1. Accrual principle of accounting
2. Format and classification of the income statement
3. Components of the income statement
4. Criteria for revenue and expense recognition
5. Percentage-of-completion and completed contract methods of contract accounting

6. Analysis of nonrecurring items, including extraordinary items, discontinued operations, the cumulative effect of accounting changes, and prior period adjustments
7. Significance of nonrecurring items to firm valuation
8. The format and components of the balance sheet
9. Information contained in the statement of stockholders' equity

INTRODUCTION

The primary objective of this book is to help users of financial statements develop the skills needed to analyze financial statement data and use these data when making rational investment, credit, and similar decisions. Such decisions require comparison of the risk and return characteristics of alternative investments. Risk and return projections depend on income and cash flow forecasts and assessments of firm assets and liabilities.

Financial statements are the starting point for analysis as they report data about income, cash flows, and assets and liabilities that users can tailor to their specific needs. To do so, they need to understand the information provided by financial statements and the shortcomings of those data. In addition, financial statement users must be able to rearrange the information provided in a manner consistent with their objectives.

The first question is how should income and cash flow be defined and measured? Are they simply the amounts provided by financial statements or should reported amounts be adjusted? Reporting methods, measurement techniques, and the presentation of financial information can all be criticized in many cases; good analysis requires skepticism.

Comprehensive financial analysis, therefore, requires a thorough understanding of the financial reporting system and its output. Chapter 1 provided a general overview of the accounting process, the reporting system, and their product: the financial statements.

The next two chapters take us to the next step. Chapter 2 deals with the income statement and balance sheet—products of the accrual system of accounting. Chapter 3 considers the statement of cash flows. For exposition purposes, we use duPont's financial statements provided in Appendix A.

INCOME, CASH FLOWS, AND ASSETS: DEFINITIONS AND RELATIONSHIPS

As background for the discussion of net income and cash flows in this and the following chapter, we first examine conceptual definitions of "income." We will then explore the relationship between these concepts of income and "accounting income" reported by the current financial reporting system. We use insights from this discussion to delve into the relationship among income, cash flows, and assets as the first stage of the development of our understanding of "return" in our study of comparative risk-return analyses. Later chapters will broaden our understanding of the analysis and use of financial statement information in the evaluation of different elements of risk and return.

This section introduces several conceptual definitions of income, measured in terms of cash flows and changes in the market values of assets.

In a world of certainty,[1] the interrelationship among income, cash flow, and assets is captured by the concept of *economic earnings*, defined as net cash flow plus the change in market value of the firm's net assets. The market value of the firm's assets in this certain world is equal to the present value of their future cash flows discounted at the (risk-free) rate r.

We illustrate this concept using a two-period model with the following assumptions:

- The entity has a single asset, an investment with zero liquidation value.
- The entity has no debt; the asset is 100% equity-financed.
- The investment generates a return of $100 at the end of each of two years.
- The $100 received at the end of year 1 is distributed to the owners and not reinvested in the firm.

Because the cash received at the end of each period equals $100 and $r = 5\%$, the value of the firm's assets is

$$\text{Beginning of period 1} = \$100/(1.05) + \$100/(1.05)^2 = \$185.94$$
$$\text{Beginning of period 2} = \$100/(1.05) = \$95.24$$

and economic earnings equals cash flow plus the change in net asset value[2]:

$$\text{Period 1:} \quad \$100 + (\$95.24 - \$185.94) = \$9.30$$
$$\text{Period 2:} \quad \$100 + (\$0 - \$95.24) = \$4.76$$

Note that economic income in each year is equal to the rate of return times the opening value of the assets.

$$\text{Period 1:} \quad 0.05 \times \$185.94 = \$9.30$$
$$\text{Period 2:} \quad 0.05 \times \$95.24 = \$4.76$$

Equivalently, the market value at the beginning of the period is equal to a (constant) multiple of earnings equal to $1/r$. In this example, the price/earnings multiple is 20 (1/0.05).

However, future cash flows and interest rates are uncertain in the real world, and the interrelationships are not as neat. Therefore, market prices of assets are also uncertain;[3] available prices may be difficult to relate to the present value of generally

---

[1]This would include perfect financial markets.

[2]The change in net asset value in this example is often referred to as economic depreciation (see Chapter 8).

[3]Some assets are heavily traded on regulated markets (common stock of companies like IBM and General Electric), others may be thinly traded (stocks of small companies), and still others have limited secondary markets from which verifiable prices can be obtained (most manufacturing equipment).

unknown, estimated future cash flows discounted at estimated interest rates. These estimates of future cash flows and interest rates and their interrelationships depend on the expectations of different decision makers.

Moreover, the market value of an asset may be measured in various (often inconsistent) ways, for example, as its replacement cost or liquidating value. *In this world of uncertainty, income (however measured) is, at best, only a proxy for economic income.* Thus, economists, analysts, and others have developed a number of analytic and practical definitions of earnings to serve as proxies of economic earnings.

BOX 2-1
Elaboration of Conceptual Income, Cash Flow, and Asset Relationships

The following discussion assumes that all income is paid out as dividends, allowing us to avoid considering reinvestment of income in the firm.

Case A

Assume that a firm purchases an asset at the beginning of each period for $10 and sells it for $12 at the end of each period. Further, assume that this markup of 20% is equivalent to the interest (discount) rate.* Under these conditions, the market value of the firm at the beginning of the period equals the $10 paid for the asset.

The market value of $10 can be derived in a single- or multiperiod context. For a single period, the present value of the end-of-period cash flow is $12/1.20 = $10. If we use a multiperiod model, the firm will earn $2 ($12 sale price less $10 cost of asset). The present value of $2 per period earned for an infinite period equals $2/0.20 = $10.

The economic earnings of the firm equal the cash flow of $2 ($12 − $10), the expected level of earnings in the future; the market value of the firm is a constant $10. Based on this same calculation, the distributable income is also $2, since paying out $2 will not change the value of the firm. Similarly, sustainable income is also $2, as that amount can be distributed without altering the firm's level of operations (buying and selling one asset per period). Finally, since the value of the firm is $10, permanent earnings equal $2 (0.2 × $10). Thus, economic, distributable, sustainable, and permanent earnings are all identical in this simplified case.

However, introducing uncertainty and changing one assumption make the problem much more complex.

Case B

Now assume that the sale price of the asset suddenly increases to $13.20. Accordingly, the purchase price of the asset should also increase as its one-period present value is now $13.20/1.20 = $11.00. Thus, if the firm replaces the asset at the end of that period, economic earnings are the sum of the cash flow of $2.20 ($13.20 − $11.00) and an increase in the market value of the firm of $1.00 (from $10.00 to $11.00), for a total of $3.20.

What are the expected earnings of the firm, given the change in the value of the asset? The answer is clearly not $3.20. It depends on the assumption one makes as to the level of operations the firm maintains.

Maintenance of Physical Level of Assets

If the firm retains the original level of *physical* assets, now valued at $11.00, the expected earnings are $2.20 (20% of $11.00). Note that economic earnings now have two components: operating earnings of $2.20 and a *holding gain* of $1.00. The holding gain results from owning an asset while its market value increases. This "one-time" occurrence cannot be expected to recur. Expected earnings would be the operating earnings as this amount can be expected to continue into the future given the level of physical assets.†

Maintenance of Monetary Level of Assets

If we assume that the asset is divisible and the firm does not replace the entire asset but only maintains its *monetary* level of assets by purchasing $10.00 of the now more expensive asset, economic earnings for the current period will still be $3.20.

Net cash flow will be $3.20 ($13.20 sales proceeds − $10.00 reinvestment). Since the market value of assets remains $10.00, economic earnings are $3.20 as above. Expected earnings, however, differ. If the firm retains the original level of monetary assets of $10.00, expected earnings are $2.00 (20% of $10.00).

What happens to the other definitions of income under this scenario? Distributable income is $3.20, which maintains the initial wealth level of $10.00, equivalent to economic earnings. However, sustainable income, the achievable earnings level of the firm in the future, is only $2.00 (if we assume that $3.20 is distributed).

However, if the firm maintains the same physical level of assets and we consider the Hicksian definition of income in terms of the physical measure of assets, both distributable and sustainable income equal $2.20. Similarly, permanent earnings depend on whether the firm retains its original physical asset base (whose value is now $11.00), or whether it retains its original monetary asset base of $10.00. In the former case, permanent earnings are $2.20; in the latter, they will be $2.00.

Under real-world conditions, income measures become judgmental. The neat mappings from one definition to another no longer hold as they become situation-specific.

---

*Under conditions of certainty, the rate of return earned on the asset (the 20% markup) equals the prevailing interest rate.

†See Box 19-1 for an elaboration of the differing market valuation of permanent and transitory earnings components.

Distributable earnings are defined as the amount of earnings that can be paid out as dividends without changing the value of the firm. This concept is derived from the Hicksian definition of income:

> The amount that a person can consume during a period of time and be as well off at the end of that time as at the beginning.[4]

A related measure, *sustainable income,* refers to the level of income that can be maintained in the future given the firm's stock of capital investment (e.g., fixed assets and inventory).

Permanent earnings[5] is used by analysts for valuation purposes. It is the amount that can be normally earned given the firm's assets and equals the market value of those assets times the firm's required rate of return. Similar to economic earnings, it is the base to which a multiple is applied to arrive at a "fair price."[6]

All these definitions are attempts to capture the concept of economic earnings. Box 2-1 provides a discussion of the difficulties associated with applying these concepts in practice due to measurement and asset valuation problems.

[4]J. R. Hicks, *Value and Capital,* 2nd ed. (Oxford: Chaundon Press, 1946), p. 176.

[5]Normalized earnings and earnings power are similar concepts.

[6]The price/earnings ratio used by analysts represents this conceptual relationship.

As a result of these difficulties, the financial reporting concept of income—*accounting income*—is often quite different. The analyst, therefore, needs to relate accounting income to the income concepts just discussed.

Accounting income is measured using the accrual concept and provides information about the ability of the enterprise to generate future cash flows.[7] It is not, *a priori*, equivalent to any of the definitions discussed earlier.

THE ACCRUAL CONCEPT OF INCOME

Accounting and economic income both define income as the sum of cash flows and changes in net assets. However, in financial reporting, the determination of:

- Which cash flows are included in income and when
- Which changes in asset values are included in income
- How and when the selected changes in asset values are measured

is based on accounting rules and principles that make up generally accepted accounting principles (GAAP). With a few exceptions, the accounting process only recognizes value changes arising from actual transactions.

Accounting income represents a *selective* recognition of both current period actual cash flows and changes in asset values. Reported income under the accrual concept provides a measure of current operating performance[8] not solely based on actual current period cash flows. Cash inflows and outflows (past, present, and future) are recognized in income in the "appropriate" accounting periods, that is, as goods and services are provided and used rather than as cash is collected and expenditures incurred. *The selected period "best" indicates the firm's present and continuing ability to generate future cash flows.*

The accrual concept of accounting income assumes that forecasts of future cash flows require more than historical cash flow data:

> Information about enterprise earnings based on accrual accounting generally provides a better indication of an enterprise's present and continuing ability to generate cash flows than information limited to the financial effects of cash receipts and payments.[9]

The accrual basis of accounting thus allocates (recognizes as revenue and expense) many transactions and events producing cash flows to time periods other than those in which the cash flows occur. Accrual accounting principles are, fundamentally, the decision rules that tell preparers of financial statements when to recognize the revenue and expense consequences of cash flows and other events.

The recognition of revenues and expenses in periods other than when cash is actually received or spent has a corollary effect on the balance sheet. *Under accrual accounting, asset and liability recognition and measurement are not determined exoge-*

---

[7]Beaver (1989) refers to this as the "informational perspective" of accounting earnings.

[8]However, see the discussion of nonrecurring items later in this chapter.

[9]SFAC 1, Objectives of Financial Reporting by Business Enterprises, Nov. 1978, p. ix.

nously but rather flow from the accrual concept of income itself. The differences between the income recognized and actual cash flows for the period are *accrued* as assets or liabilities.

Consider case A in Box 2-1. In that example, an item purchased for $10 at the beginning of period 1 is sold for $12 at the end of that period and replaced at the start of the next period at a cost of $10. If we assume that the sale is made on credit and cash will be collected in the following period, the actual cash outflow in period 1 is $10, the cost of acquiring the asset at the beginning of period 1. Under accrual accounting, the revenue (expected future cash flow) is recognized at the time of sale, and income is $2.

The expected cash flow, revenue, is shown as an increase of $12 in the asset accounts receivable. Income is thus equal to the change in assets plus actual cash flows:

Income = $12 Increase in Accounts Receivable − $10 Cash Outflow = $2

Which is a better indicator of the earning power of the firm and its ability to generate future cash flows: the cash outflow of $10 or the income of $2? Income computed using the accrual concept, which reports an income of $2, generally provides better forward-looking information than pure cash flow accounting.

The Matching Principle. Revenue and expense recognition are also governed by the *matching principle*, which states that operating performance can be measured only if related revenues and expenses are accounted for during the same time period. It is the matching principle that requires the expense (cost of goods sold) of inventory to be recognized in the same period in which the sale of that inventory is recorded. This facilitates measurement of the periodic income, that is, operating performance generated by selling inventories during the period regardless of when collections or expenditures occur.

Over the life of the firm, income and cash flows converge. They differ only as to timing of recognition. The recognition of revenues and expenses in particular accounting periods is both the strength and the weakness of the accrual method. It is a strength in that it results in more meaningful measurement of current operating performance (income statement) and a better indicator of future operating performance and earnings power. If accrual accounting did not exist, financial analysts would have to invent it.[10] The weakness is that the amount and timing of accruals are subject to management discretion and are based on estimates that can and do change over time. Analysts need to differentiate between real events and accruals stemming from management choice.

Overall, as the empirical evidence in Box 2-2 indicates, the accrual process does provide information and enhances the predictive ability of cash flows. However, as the evidence also indicates (and as we elaborate on in Chapter 3), it does not mean that cash flows are not relevant. They provide information as to the "quality" of accounting earnings and can be used to "shore up" the weaknesses of the accrual process.

---

[10]This occasionally happens. Because of the deficiencies of (cash-based) regulatory accounting in the insurance industry, analysts developed methods of analysis in the 1960s that eventually were adopted as GAAP by the industry. More recently, German analysts developed their own method of adjusting tax-based income statements.

The determination of accounting earnings is also governed by:

1. General principles and measurement rules underlying all accounting transactions and events
2. Specific rules to determine revenue, expense, gain, and loss recognition

For example, the *historical cost-based* approach underlying GAAP results in rules that exclude from income *many* unrealized holding gains or losses (increases/decreases in the market value of assets and liabilities held by the firm). Recognition of these gains/losses must await the disposal of the assets and the retirement or settlement of the liabilities.

However, some nontransaction-related declines in asset values *can* affect reported income. Current assets must be evaluated at each financial statement date and any estimated declines in asset values recognized as losses. SFAS 121, Accounting for the Impairment of Long-Lived Assets and for Long-Lived Assets to Be Disposed of, extended this requirement to most classes of fixed assets. The amount and timing

---

BOX 2-2
Accrual Income Versus Cash Flow: Some Empirical Evidence

A number of empirical studies have compared the benefits of accrual income versus those of cash flows. A comparison of Cash from Operations (CFO) with accrual income by Dechow (1994) showed that accrual income more closely measured firm performance (as reflected in stock returns) than CFO. Moreover, she found that the "superiority" of accrual income as a predictor of stock returns was more likely to occur in those situations where it is hypothesized that cash flows would have greater timing and matching problems. That is, accrual income performed better:

- The shorter the interval over which performance is measured
- The more volatile the working capital requirements and investment and financing activities
- The longer the operating cycle of the firm

The above study compared accrual income directly with CFO. Other studies examined whether given one of the measures, the other provided *incremental* information. The studies* offer consistent evidence that, given cash flows from operations, accruals give incremental information.† Bernard (1989) notes that such results demonstrate that "increases in accruals, including receivables and inventory, translate on average into increases in expected future cash flows."

These results do not necessarily mean that the information contained in the CFO and accruals components of income are identical. Sloan (1996) found that the CFO component of income was more "persistent" than the accrual component; that is, CFO levels achieved were more likely to carry into the future, whereas accruals were (relative to CFO) more transitory and likely to be reversed. Sloan noted that this finding was consistent with the approach advocated by those financial analysts who related CFO to reported net income to test the "quality" of earnings. Interestingly, Sloan also found that the market seemed to ignore this distinction, lending credence to investing strategies that attempted to find mispriced securities by exploiting the differences between CFO and net income.

Bowen et al. (1987) compared market reaction to cash flows and net income. They found that cash flow and net income data are useful to investors. Specifically, they determined that, after controlling for earnings, cash flow data had incremental information, and separately, after controlling for the information provided by CFO, they found that earnings also contained incremental information.

Livnat and Zarowin (1990) found that, although aggregate CFO did not provide additional informational content, individual components from both CFO and financing cash flows did add incremental information. This, however, does not mean that cash flow information is superior to accrual information as the relevant comparison would have to be individual components of accrual income.

Bernard and Stober (1989) noted that the variation in cash flow results found by some studies may be caused by using models that do not capture the specific implications of any particular company or situation. That is, in many cases the relative benefits of accruals versus cash flows may be firm-, industry-, and/or situation-specific.‡ They suggest that "further progress in this line of research will require a better understanding of the economic context in which the implications of detailed earnings components are interpreted."§

---

*See, for example, Judy Rayburn, "The Association of Operating Cash Flow and Accruals With Security Returns," *Journal of Accounting Research,* Supplement 1986 and G. Peter Wilson, "The Relative Information Content of Accruals and Cash Flows: Combined Evidence at the Earnings Announcement and Annual Report Release Date," *Journal of Accounting Research,* Supplement 1986, in addition to Robert M. Bowen, David Burgstahler, and Lane A. Daley, The Incremental Information Content of Accrual Versus Cash Flows," *The Accounting Review,* Oct. 1987, discussed shortly.

†In Chapter 5, we provide a more detailed look at and critique of the nature of the "information content" line of empirical research.

‡To some extent, the Dechow study, noted earlier, examined some of these factors.

§Victor Bernard and Thomas Stober, "The Nature and Amount of Information in Cash Flows and Accruals," *The Accounting Review,* Oct. 1989, p. 648.

---

of loss recognition remain substantively discretionary because these assets must be evaluated for declines only when certain impairment criteria are present.[11]

Changes in market values of assets and liabilities may occur over a number of periods. However, they are either recognized in income in the period of disposal or when certain impairment criteria are met. The result is current period income that may be distorted and may not be indicative of normal earning power. As an initial step, one needs to understand the components that make up the income statement.

Income Statement

Format and Classification

U.S. GAAP do not specify the format of the income statement. Actual formats vary across companies, especially in the reporting of equity in earnings of affiliates, and nonoperating income and expense. In some cases, income statement detail appears in financial statement footnotes. Consequently, the sample "format" presented below should be viewed in a generic sense rather than as a strict rendition of how an income

---

[11]See Chapter 8 for a discussion of this standard.

statement is laid out:

Sample Income Statement Format

	Revenues from the sales of goods and services:
+	Other income and revenues
−	Operating expenses
−	Financing costs
+/−	Unusual or infrequent items
=	Pretax earnings from continuing operations
−	Income tax expense
=	Net income from continuing operations*
+/−	Income from discontinued operations (net of tax)*
+/−	Extraordinary items (net of tax)*
+/−	Cumulative effect of accounting changes (net of tax)*
=	Net income*

*Per share amounts are reported for each of these items.

Components of Net Income

The format typically found in actual statements may not be the most useful for analytical purposes. It is important for the analyst to be cognizant of the various categories or groupings into which the income statement components *can* be combined. These groupings do not necessarily coincide with the classifications presented in actual financial statements (or our sample income statement above). In our discussion of the income statement components, we shall follow the suggested groupings presented below. These groupings provide information about different aspects of a firm's operations:

Suggested Format

	Revenues from the sales of goods and services:
−	Operating expenses
=	Operating income from continuing operations
+	Other income and revenues
=	Recurring income before interest and taxes from continuing operations
−	Financing costs
=	Recurring (pretax) income from continuing operations
+/−	Unusual or infrequent items
=	Pretax earnings from continuing operations
−	Income tax expense
=	Net income from continuing operations
+/−	Income from discontinued operations (net of tax)
+/−	Extraordinary items (net of tax)
+/−	Cumulative effect of accounting changes (net of tax)
=	Net income

The income statement reports revenues generated by the sales of goods and services from a firm's continuing operations. The costs and expenses incurred to generate these revenues follow. The costs of manufacturing or purchasing the goods sold are normally listed first since they are directly related to the period's revenues. Indirect costs of selling and administrative activities, and expense categories such as research and development are reported next. The excess of revenues over expenses (before interest expense) measures the firm's *operating income from continuing operations*, which is independent of its capital structure.

In addition to its core business, a firm may have income (loss) from other activities, such as interest or dividends from investments, equity in (share of) the income of its unconsolidated affiliates, and gains or losses on sales or disposal of assets. *Recurring earnings before interest and taxes from continuing operations* usually include these items and are also independent of the firm's capital structure. Deducting financing costs (interest expense) results in *recurring (pretax) income from continuing operations*.

Unusual or infrequent items, such as pretax gains and losses from the sale or impairment of assets or investments,[12] are often shown as separate line items yielding *pretax income from continuing operations*. Income tax expense is usually the final deduction before arriving at *net income from continuing operations*.

The income statement effects of discontinued operations are segregated and reported net of income tax to emphasize the fact that these operations will not contribute to future revenues and income. The net of tax effect of "extraordinary items" is also reported separately because they are incidental to the firm's operating activities, unusual in nature, and not expected to be a normal, recurring component of income and cash flows.

Finally, the income statement separately reports the cumulative effect of accounting changes adopted during the period since they are unrelated to the period's income or operating activities and rarely have any impact on cash flows.[13] Footnotes provide detailed information on both mandatory and voluntary changes in accounting methods, which must be analyzed to evaluate the impact on present and future reported earnings.

A more detailed description and discussion of an income statement and related footnotes using duPont as an example are provided in Box 2-3.

Recurring Versus Nonrecurring Items. Reported net income is only loosely related to the concept of *comprehensive income* discussed in Chapter 1. It contains income from operations as well as all realized (but only some unrealized) changes in the market value of assets and liabilities.

From an analyst's perspective, however, it may not be the most informative number. Generally, income from a firm's recurring operating activities is considered the best indicator of future income. The predictive ability of reported income is enhanced if it excludes the impact of transitory or random components, which are not directly related to operating activities and are generally more volatile. If we use the definitions of income discussed earlier (and elaborated on in Box 2-1), transitory gains or losses should not be regarded as components of permanent, or sustainable income. The concept of recurring income is similar to permanent or sustainable income in the sense

---

[12]The appropriate income statement classification of such items and their analytic significance are discussed later in this chapter.

[13]Actual cash flows are not affected by accounting changes unless the firm also changes the method used for income tax reporting (e.g., LIFO, discussed in Chapter 6). However, changes in accounting methods may affect the classification of cash flows, as discussed in Chapter 3.

BOX 2-3. DUPONT
Income Statement Components

DuPont's income statement, included in Appendix A, illustrates the income statement format of a manufacturing company. Comments on the individual line items follow. In addition, we provide below an "index" showing in which book chapters the various income statement components are discussed in greater detail:

	Chapter Index
Sales—revenue recognition	2
Other income	
Income from affiliates	13
Cost of goods sold	6
Depreciation expense	8
Exploration expenses	7, Appendix 7-B
Research and development	7
Interest (capitalized interest)	10 (7)
Restructuring costs	2, 8
Write-downs (acquisitions)	8 (14)
Income taxes	9
Extraordinary items (debt retirement)	2 (10)
Accounting changes (income taxes, post-retirement benefits)	2 (9, 12)
Earnings per share	4

(In the discussion that follows, all "Note" references are to the financial statement footnotes of duPont.)

Sales include revenues from duPont's operating activities. The note reveals that reported sales include excise taxes paid to governments by the company's petroleum division. As some firms report sales *net* of such taxes, comparisons will suffer unless an adjustment is made. Since excise taxes are beyond management control and have no impact on profitability, such payments should be excluded from reported sales for analytic purposes. Reported sales are also affected by management's choice of *revenue recognition* methods. To the extent that different firms choose different methods, sales are not comparable.

Other income is broken down in note 2. The largest component is duPont's share of the earnings of affiliates accounted for using the equity method. Most of the increase in other income, however, was due to "miscellaneous income and expenses—net" for which no further explanation is provided.

Cost of goods sold and other operating expenses constitute more than half of total expenses. Note 3 reveals that this item includes accruals for the estimated costs of the recall of the fungicide "Benlate" DF50. Note 12 reports that Du Pont uses the LIFO method to account for 88% of inventories and there was a LIFO liquidation in 1993.

Selling, general, and administrative expenses (SG&A) include operating expenses not reported as components of *costs of goods and other operating expenses*. The division between cost of goods sold and SG&A expenses depends on the company's accounting system, and the breakdown may not be comparable among firms. SG&A expenses are not always directly related to sales levels as they contain fixed components.

Depreciation, depletion, and amortization expenses represent the allocation of past expenditures for property, plant, and equipment and intangible assets. The allocation depends on the company's choice of accounting method, asset lives, and residual values.

Exploration expenses reflect both current expenditures for exploration and the amortization of past expenditures.

Under U.S. GAAP, all *research and development expenditures* must be recorded as expenses in the year they are incurred.

Interest and debt expenses include interest and amortization of financing costs less capitalized interest (Note 4).

Note 9 shows that *taxes other than on income* include the petroleum excise tax included in sales, payroll, property, and other taxes not based on earnings.

DuPont recorded *restructuring charges* (discussed later in this chapter) in each year shown. *Write-down of intangible assets* reflects the 1993 write-down of intangible assets connected with 1989 acquisitions.

Sales and other income, net of all expenses, produce earnings before income tax expenses. Subtracting the provision for income taxes results in net income before extraordinary items and the effect of accounting changes.

Extraordinary items include the 1992 and 1993 recognition of losses from the early retirement of debt (see the discussion in Chapters 2 and 10).

Transition effect of changes in accounting principles reports on the 1992 adoption of two new standards. SFAS 106 (Other Postretirement Benefits) and SFAS 109 (Income Taxes). The cumulative effect of adopting these standards reduced reported income.

Earnings per share are reported for income before extraordinary items and effects of accounting changes, and separately for both extraordinary items and the cumulative effect of accounting changes. Note 9 discloses the number of shares used to compute the earnings per share.

that it is persistent; that is, its level or rate of growth is relatively predictable, and cash flows will eventually follow at the predicted levels and growth rates.

If we use the terminology above:

- Recurring (pretax) income from continuing operations

or on a posttax basis:

- Net income from continuing operations after adjustment[14] for unusual or infrequent items (after tax)

should be the primary focus of analysis.

Segregation of the results of normal, recurring operations from the effects of nonrecurring items facilitates the forecasting of future earnings and cash flows. Financial reporting defines nonrecurring by the *type of transaction or event.* However, depending on the firm, the nature of the event, and to some extent management

---

[14]The adjustment would be effected by either (1) adding back to net income from continuing operations the after-tax consequences of unusual or infrequent items, that is,

Net Income from Recurring Operations =
Net Income from Continuing Operations $+/-$ [Unusual or Infrequent Items $\times$ (1 − Tax Rate)]

or (2) adjusting recurring income from continuing operations directly for taxes:

Net Income from Recurring Operations =
Recurring Income from Continuing Operations $\times$ (1 − Tax Rate)

discretion, similar transactions may be included in operating income or reported below the line. Operational definitions of "operating," "nonrecurring," and "extraordinary" are elusive and accounting standards setters have struggled with this issue for decades.

For purposes of analysis, however, the important issue is whether the amount of nonrecurring income or loss in a given year is a good predictor of future income or loss. For example, for some firms, a material gain or loss from the sale of fixed assets will be rare; the amount reported has no predictive value. Other firms retire fixed assets each year and regularly report gains or losses (e.g., consider a car rental company that retires part of its fleet of cars annually). In the latter case, the analytic issue is whether this year's income or loss from the sale of retired property is higher or lower than the "normal" amount.

Ultimately, the analyst must evaluate the role of nonrecurring items, whether they are called extraordinary, unusual, or something else, in the prediction of earnings power. The goal of analysis of the income statement is to derive an effective measure of future earnings and cash flows. Therefore, analysts often exclude components of reported income (regardless of their accounting label) that may reduce its predictive ability.

Fairfield et al. (1996) examined whether the classification scheme used in financial statements can improve predictive ability. Their results (discussed in more detail in Chapter 19) indicated that the forecasting of one-year ahead profitability, that is, return on equity (ROE), was improved by disaggregating previous year's ROE into the separate components discussed earlier. They found that extraordinary items and discontinued operations were not useful in predicting bottom-line ROE or ROE from continuing operations *although unusual and infrequent items were.* This latter result implies that, on average, unusual or infrequent items contain a recurring element.

The predictive ability objective does not mean that financial analysis of the income (or other financial) statements is simply the extrapolation of previous trends. Rather, all financial statement information should be viewed as part of a database that provides limited information about future prospects and opportunities facing the firm. For example, an increase in the sale of cameras provides useful information not only for forecasts of future camera sales but also for related products, such as film and film development services.

Nonrecurring items can also provide such information, but in a different fashion. The implication of the sale of an operating asset, for example, depends on the utilization of the cash generated by the sale, and how its productive capacity will be replaced.

We return to nonrecurring items later in the chapter. First, however, we look at the revenue and expense recognition rules used to report a firm's recurring operations.

Accounting Income: Revenue and Expense Recognition

When accrual accounting is used to prepare financial statements, two revenue and expense recognition issues must be addressed:

1. *Timing.* When should revenue and expense be recognized?

2. *Measurement.* How much revenue and expense should be recognized?

The responses to these questions determine the amount and timing of periodic revenue and expense. In practice, there is considerable scope for management discretion with respect to both revenue and expense recognition. At this point, however, the focus of our discussion is revenue recognition and how the application of the *matching principle* relates expense recognition to revenue recognition.[15] Other issues of expense recognition are discussed, on an issue-by-issue basis, in the chapters that follow.

Statement of Financial Accounting Concepts (SFAC) 5, Recognition and Measurement in Financial Statements of Business Enterprises, specifies *two conditions that must be met for revenue recognition to take place.* These conditions are:

1. Completion of the earnings process
2. Assurance of payment

To satisfy the first condition, the firm must have provided all or virtually all the goods or services for which it is to be paid, and it must be possible to measure the total expected cost of providing the goods or services; that is, the seller must have no remaining significant contingent obligation. If the seller is obligated to provide future services, for example, warranty protection, but cannot estimate the cost of doing so, this condition is not satisfied.

Revenue recognition also requires a second condition: the quantification of cash or assets expected to be received for the goods or services provided. Reliable measurement encompasses the realizability (collectibility) of the proceeds of sale. If the seller cannot reasonably estimate the probability of nonpayment, realization is not reasonably assured, and the second condition is not satisfied.

The general rule for revenue recognition includes this concept of realizability: Revenue, measured as the amount expected to be collected, can be recognized when goods or services have been provided and their cost can be reliably determined.

The amount of revenue recognized at any given point in time is measured as

$$\frac{\text{Goods and Services Provided to Date}}{\text{Total Goods and Services to Be Provided}} \times \text{Total Expected Revenue}$$

This equation measures the amount of revenue recognized *cumulatively* to date. Revenue reported for the current period is the *cumulative total less revenue recognized in prior periods.*

The most common case is revenue recognition at the time of sale. Goods or services have been provided, and the sale is for cash or to customers whose ability to pay is reasonably assured.[16]

In some cases, payment is received prior to the delivery of goods or services. Examples include:

1. Magazine publishers receive subscription payments in advance; the receipts represent an obligation to provide periodic delivery of the publication. Revenues are recognized in proportion to issues delivered.

---

[15]Direct costs, such as cost of goods sold, are recognized as related revenue is recognized under accrual accounting. Note that the cost of goods sold often includes depreciation expense or capitalized overhead. However, other expenses cannot be directly related to revenues and must be recognized using different principles. Some, called period costs (e.g., advertising costs), are expensed as incurred. Other costs are recognized as time passes, for example, interest costs. Finally, some costs may be based on other criteria, for example, taxes on income.

[16]In some cases, the buyer has a right to return unsold goods. If the risks or benefits (or both) of ownership are retained by the "seller," the transaction is, in economic substance, a consignment rather than a completed sale. SFAS 48, Revenue Recognition When Right of Return Exists, governs such sales. See also SFAS 49, Accounting for Product Financing Arrangements.

2. Credit card fees are recognized as advances from customers; revenue is recorded as the right to use the cards expires over time.

3. Revenue from leased equipment is recognized as time passes or based on usage (copier rental is sometimes based on a per copy charge).

These examples show that revenue recognition can be measured by cash expenditures, the passage of time, or the provision of service (measured in physical units) to the customer.

Departures from the Sales Basis of Revenue Recognition

Revenue may be recognized *prior* to sale or delivery when the earnings process is substantially complete and the proceeds of sale can be reasonably measured. For example, revenue is recognized at the completion of production in the case of commodities (such as oil or agricultural products) with highly organized and liquid markets or, in the case of long-term construction contracts, as production takes place.

Alternatively, revenues may not be recognized even at the time of sale if there is significant uncertainty regarding the seller's ability to collect the sales price (the resulting accounts receivable) or to estimate remaining costs. Either the installment method or the more extreme cost recovery method, both discussed shortly, must be used in such cases.

Percentage-of-Completion and Completed Contract Methods

The *percentage-of-completion method* recognizes revenues and costs in proportion to the work completed; production activity is considered the critical event signaling completion of the earnings process rather than delivery or cash collections. The percentage-of-completion method is used for long-term projects when there is a contract, and reliable estimates of production completed, revenues, and costs are possible.

The *completed contract method* recognizes revenues and expenses only at the end of the contract. It must be used when any one of the conditions required for use of the percentage-of-completion method is not met, generally when no contract exists or estimates of selling prices or collectibility are not reliable. It must be used for short-term contracts.[17]

The percentage-of-completion method measures progress using *either:*

- Engineering estimates (or physical milestones such as distance of road completed), or
- Ratios of costs incurred to expected total costs

The latter method may overstate revenues and gross profit if expenditures made are recognized before they contribute to completed work, for example, when the costs of raw materials and advance payments to subcontractors are included in the determination of work completed.

---

[17]SFAS 56 (1982) emphasizes that the percentage-of-completion and completed contract methods are not "intended to be free-choice alternatives under either Accounting Research Bulletin 45 (ARB 45) or AICPA Statement of Position 81-1 (SOP 81-1)." ARB 45 states that the percentage-of-completion method is preferable when estimates of costs to complete and degree of completion are reliable. SOP 81-1 reiterates this position.

When estimates of revenue or costs change, there is a "catch-up" effect included in the earnings of the period in which the change in estimate is made. That effect is recognized currently as a change in accounting estimate, and *the earnings of prior periods are not restated.* Whenever there is an estimated loss on a contract, that loss must be recognized when the amount can be estimated.

Comparison of Percentage-of-Completion and Completed Contract Methods

Exhibit 2-1 compares the percentage-of-completion and completed contract revenue recognition methods.

EXHIBIT 2-1. JUSTIN CORP.
Comparison of Percentage-of-Completion and Completed Contract Revenue Recognition Methods

In 1992, Justin Corp. entered into a construction project with the following terms:

Total contract price	$6,000,000
Total expected cost	$4,800,000

Actual production costs over the duration of the contract and cash inflow information are provided as follows ($ in thousands):

	1992	1993	1994	1995
Costs incurred				
Current year	$ 600	$1,200	$1,800	$1,200
Cumulative	600	1,800	3,600	4,800
Estimated *remaining* costs to complete (as of December 31)	4,200	3,000	1,200	0
Cash received during the year	$1,500	$1,500	$1,500	$1,500

A. Income Statement ($ in thousands)

	Percentage-of-Completion Method			Completed Contract Method		
	Revenue	Expense	Income	Revenue	Expense	Income
1992	$ 750*	$ 600	$ 150	$ 0	$ 0	$ 0
1993	1,500†	1,200	300	0	0	0
1994	2,250‡	1,800	450	0	0	0
1995	1,500§	1,200	300	6,000	4,800	1,200
Total	$6,000	$4,800	$1,200	$6,000	$4,800	$1,200

* $\dfrac{\$600}{\$4,800} \times \$6,000 = \$750.$

† $\dfrac{(\$600 + \$1,200)}{\$4,800} \times \$6,000 = \$2,250 - \$750 = \$1,500.$

‡ $\dfrac{(\$600 + \$1,200 + \$1,800)}{\$4,800} \times \$6,000 = \$4,500 - \$2,250 = \$2,250.$

§ $\dfrac{(\$600 + \$1,200 + \$1,800 + \$1,200)}{\$4,800} \times \$6,000 = \$6,000 - \$4,500 = \$1,500.$

EXHIBIT 2-1. (*continued*)

B. Balance Sheet and Cash Flow ($ in thousands)

Percentage-of-Completion Method

	Assets	=	Liabilities	+	Equity
	Cash	=	Advances	+	Retained Earnings
1992					
Cash received	$ 1,500		$ 1,500		
Revenue			(750)		$ 750
Costs incurred	(600)				(600)
Year-end balances	$ 900	=	$ 750	+	$ 150
1993					
Cash received	1,500		1,500		
Revenue			(1,500)		1,500
Costs incurred	(1,200)				(1,200)
Year-end balances	$ 1,200	=	$ 750	+	$ 450
1994					
Cash received	1,500		1,500		
Revenue			(2,250)		2,250
Costs incurred	(1,800)				(1,800)
Year-end balances	$ 900	=	$ 0	+	$ 900
1995					
Cash received	1,500		1,500		
Revenue			(1,500)		1,500
Costs incurred	(1,200)				(1,200)
Year-end balances	$ 1,200	=	$ 0	+	$ 1,200

Completed Contract Method

	Assets			=	Liabilities	+	Equity
	Cash	+	Inventory	=	Advances	+	Retained Earnings
1992							
Cash received	$ 1,500				$ 1,500		
Costs incurred	(600)		$ 600				
Year-end balances	$ 900	+	$ 600	=	$ 1,500	+	$ 0
1993							
Cash received	1,500				1,500		
Costs incurred	(1,200)		1,200				
Year-end balances	$ 1,200	+	$ 1,800	=	$ 3,000	+	0
1994							
Cash received	1,500				1,500		
Costs incurred	(1,800)		1,800				
Year-end balances	$ 900	+	$ 3,600	=	$ 4,500	+	0
1995							
Cash received	1,500				1,500		
Costs incurred	(1,200)		1,200				
Revenue					(6,000)		6,000
Expense			(4,800)				(4,800)
Year-end balances	$ 1,200	+	$ 0	=	$ 0	+	$ 1,200

EXHIBIT 2-1. (continued)

C. Change in Estimated Cost to Complete

On December 31, 1994, Justin Corp. determines that the total cost of the project will be $5,400, making remaining costs to complete $1,800, an increase of $600 from the original estimate. This changes *both* revenue and expense for 1994 under the percentage-of-completion method. The adjustment is made on a cumulative basis; revenue and expense reported for previous years are *not* restated.

Cumulative revenue recognized is

$$\frac{\$3,600 \text{ (cumulative costs incurred)}}{\$5,400 \text{ (revised total cost)}} \times \$6,000 \text{ (estimated revenue)}$$
$$= \$4,000, \text{ of which } \$2,250 \text{ was recognized as revenue in 1992 and 1993}$$

Therefore, $1,750 ($4,000 − $2,250) is recognized as revenue for 1994.

Cumulative expense recognized is $3,600, the total incurred. Expense recognized for 1994 remains unchanged at $1,800. As a result, income recognized in 1994 is

$$\$1,750 - \$1,800 = (\$50) \text{ Loss}$$

This loss reflects *both* the income on the portion of the contract completed during 1994 ($200) *and* the loss resulting from the overestimation of project in 1992 and 1993 ($250 loss).*

Revised Income Statements ($ in thousands)

	Percentage-of-Completion Method			Completed Contract Method		
	Revenue	Expense	Income	Revenue	Expense	Income
1992	$ 750	$ 600	$ 150	$ 0	$ 0	$ 0
1993	1,500	1,200	300	0	0	0
1994	1,750	1,800	(50)	0	0	0
Subtotal	$4,000	$3,600	$ 400			
1995	2,000	1,800	200	6,000	5,400	600
Total	$6,000	$5,400	$ 600	$6,000	$5,400	$600

*Using the revised estimate of cost to complete, year-by-year revenue, expense, and income would have been ($ in thousands):

Year	Revenue	Expense	Income
1992	$ 667	$ 600	$ 67
1993	1,333	1,200	133
1994	2,000	1,800	200
Total	$4,000	$3,600	$400

Part A compares the revenues, expenses, and income reported under each method for each year. Computations for the percentage-of-completion method use the ratio of costs (assumed to provide a reliable measure of actual work performed) incurred each period to expected total costs. In 1992, 12.5% of estimated costs are incurred, so that revenue recognized for that year equals 12.5% of the contract price. As a result, if we use the matching principle, the same percentage (12.5%) of expected total expenses and total income is recognized for 1992. This pattern is repeated as long as actual results closely mirror expectations.

Under the completed contract method, revenues, expenses, and income are recognized only at the end of the contract period; no revenue, expense, or income is reported during the first three years.

As a result, the two different revenue recognition methods produce different patterns of reported revenue, expense, and income, although total revenue, expense, and income over the life of the contract are identical under both methods.

The percentage-of-completion method provides both a better measure of operating activity and a more informative disclosure of the status of incomplete contracts. For a firm with constant revenues the two methods produce identical results.[18] However, since the business world is rarely in a steady state of equilibrium, *the percentage-of-completion method reports income earlier and is a better indicator of trends in earning power.* Although better disclosure of contracts in progress under the completed contract method would help analysts forecast future operating results and cash flows, the percentage-of-completion method is more informative.

The choice of method also affects the reported assets and liabilities on the balance sheet. Under the completed contract method, expenditures prior to completion are reported as inventory and cash receipts as advances from customers. Under the percentage-of-completion method, any difference between cash received and revenue recognized is treated as accounts receivable. Part B shows the balance sheet and cash flow statement effects of the two methods. The most important difference is that, during the first three years, the completed contract method reports higher assets since construction in process is reported as inventory. Because the percentage-of-completion method recognizes revenues during the life of the contract, inventory is replaced by receivables that are then collected.

Reported cash flows, however, are identical under both approaches. As a result, the completed contract method reports:

1. *Larger total assets* because it accumulates inventory and
2. *Lower net assets (equity),* since no income is recognized until the end of the contract.

These differences are critical when comparing the size, return on assets, and return on equity ratios of U.S. construction firms with their European and Japanese competitors, who generally use the completed contract method.[19]

Part C shows the impact of a change in estimate: The estimated cost to complete is increased at the end of the third year (1994). This increase is recognized in 1994, and that year's loss reflects the income on work completed during the period offset by the impact of the change in estimate. Note that the cumulative income correctly reflects the degree of completion using the revised cost estimate.[20]

---

[18]This statement assumes that, with a large number of contracts, income recognized from contracts completed in each period would be equal to the income recognized from the partial completion of contracts in process.

[19]However, German and Japanese regulators now recommend use of the percentage-of-completion method.

[20]The firm has completed two-thirds ($3,600 of costs incurred to date out of total expected costs of $5,400) of the work on the project and at the end of the year will have recognized $400 or two-thirds of expected income of $600 ($150 in 1992, $300 in 1993, and a loss of $50 in 1994).

Similarly, if the firm estimated the remaining cost to complete the project at $2,750,000 at the end of 1994 (rather than the original $1,200,000), the expected loss of $350,000 (on the entire contract) would be recognized in that year. The previously recognized earnings would be offset and the full contract loss would be recognized in 1994, the year in which it can be estimated, even though some of that loss will be incurred in 1995.

Newcor Company changed its accounting method from the completed contract method to the percentage-of-completion method in 1991. The company restated its income statements for the previous three years, as shown in Exhibit 2-2.

Part A includes excerpts from Newcor's 1991 income statement and its MD&A, which contains a brief description of its revenue and expense recognition methods. Part B reproduces excerpts from a news release issued by the firm in February 1992 and contains a restatement of its 1989 to 1991 income statements from the completed contract to the percentage-of-completion method.

The following points should be noted when comparing the revised statements with the original ones. Revenue (and income) under the completed contract method is volatile. No trend is apparent. A decline in 1990 is followed by an increase in 1991. The results are driven by the timing of completed projects and do not inform us about the firm's activity level or profitability. The revised percentage-of-completion income statement not only reports more stable revenue but also that firm's volume of business seems to be declining. Paradoxically, its income is increasing, indicating that whereas the firm has taken on fewer projects, the profit margin on those projects is greater.[21]

Installment Method of Revenue Recognition

Revenues should not be recognized at the time of sale or delivery when there is no reasonable basis to estimate collectibility of the sales proceeds. The installment method recognizes gross profit in proportion to cash collections, resulting in delayed recognition of revenues and expenses as compared with full recognition at the time of sale. This method is sometimes used to report income from sales of noncurrent assets and real estate transactions.

Cost Recovery Method

Revenue recognition on sale or delivery is also precluded when the costs to provide goods or services cannot be reasonably determined, for example, in the development of raw land. This occurs when completion of the sale is dependent on expenditures to be made in the future (e.g., road construction) and it is impossible to estimate the amount of those expenditures (which may depend on zoning or environmental factors).

In many cases, there is also substantial uncertainty about revenue realization since only small downpayments may be required with nonrecourse financing provided by the seller. With both future costs and collection uncertain, the cost recovery method requires that all cash receipts be first accounted for as a recovery of costs. Only after all costs are recovered can profit be recognized under this method.

The installment and cost recovery methods may be used to recognize franchise revenues[22] when revenue is collectible over an extended period and there is no reasonable basis to estimate that collectibility. These methods may also be used, under specific circumstances, in real estate sales and retail land sales.[23]

Revenue Recognition: Special Situations

The foregoing discussion of recognition methods should be viewed in terms of laying a conceptual understanding of the factors that must be considered when deciding

---

[21]See Problem 12 for additional analysis of Newcor's (original and revised) income.

[22]See SFAS 45, Accounting for Franchise Fee Revenue, para. 6 (FASB, 1981).

[23]See SFAS 66, Accounting for Sales of Real Estate (FASB, 1982).

EXHIBIT 2-2. NEWCOR, INC.
Comparison of Completed Contract and Percentage-of-Completion Methods

A. Completed Contract Method

Original Income Statement

	1989	1990	1991
Sales	$100,436	$79,865	$98,747
Cost of sales	83,884	64,211	76,872
SGA	10,418	11,123	12,536
	$ 6,134	$ 4,531	$ 9,339

Newcor, Inc. is organized into two business segments: special machines and precision machined parts. Special machines are custom-designed and sold individually on a made-to-order basis or incorporated into complete systems. Revenue and costs for special machines are determined under the completed contract method of accounting, which can result in significant fluctuations in sales and net income between accounting periods. In addition, the cyclical nature of this segment can result in sharp changes in the order backlog, working capital, and bank borrowings.

B. Percentage-of-Completion Method

Restated Income Statement

	1989	1990	1991
Sales	$ 95,974	$92,160	$89,309
Cost of sales	79,473	74,203	69,225
SGA	10,517	11,307	12,491
	$ 5,984	$ 6,650	$ 7,593

News Release

Newcor, Inc., Troy, Michigan, February 18, 1992. Richard A. Smith, President and Chief Executive Officer, Newcor, Inc., announced today that the company has adopted the percentage-of-completion method of accounting for revenue and costs associated with long-term contracts within the company's special machinery segment. In the opinion of management, with concurrence from the company's outside auditors, the percentage-of-completion method of accounting is the preferable method for reporting the financial results of the special machinery segment. The percentage-of-completion method of accounting will be implemented in the first quarter of fiscal 1992. In all prior years, the completed contract method of accounting was utilized to determine revenue and costs.

Source: Newcor, Inc., *1991 Annual Report* and Feb. 1992 press release.

whether revenue recognition criteria have been met. Generally, application of the criteria is straightforward. In certain industries, however, the nature of the revenue-generating process leads to reasonable and legitimate doubt as to when revenue should be recognized. In other cases, the particular way a firm does business can lead to similar questions. Four examples follow:

1. In the broadcast industry, television stations buy the rights to show a film for a given period of time. Should the revenue be recognized by the film's owner:

- When the agreement is signed?
- When the film is physically transferred to the television station?
- Over time as the film is shown?

2. Mortgage issuers charge a fee, *origination points*, that is, in effect, interest paid in advance. Points are not refundable even if the mortgage is repaid before its due date. Should the fee be recognized as income:

- Over time?
- At the time of origination?

3. Insurance policies cover life or property over specified time periods. Should revenue be recognized:

- When the policy is sold?
- Over its life?
- When premiums are paid?

4. A company offers price incentives or preferential access to goods to induce customers to purchase future period requirements in advance.[24] The result is an increase in current period revenues. Should all sales be recognized in the current period?

These are but a few examples of complex revenue recognition issues. Case 2-1 deals with the well-known revenue recognition example of Thousand Trails. Other examples are provided in the problems at the end of this chapter. It should be clear, however, that the analyst must have a thorough understanding of the nature of the business and its relationship to revenue recognition.

Summary of Revenue Recognition Methods

The preceding sections discuss the conceptual bases and financial statement effects of different revenue recognition methods. The analyst must be aware of the assumptions underlying these methods both for interfirm comparisons and because questionable revenue is a poor predictor of future cash flows.

Generally, revenues and related receivables are recognized at the time of sale. The percentage-of-completion method for long-term contracts, however, accrues revenues in proportion to services performed and the firm's assessment of the realizability of those revenues. This method highlights the relationship among the income statement (reported revenues), balance sheet (resulting receivables), and the cash flow statement (current collections). It is designed to measure current operating performance and facilitate forecasts of future performance and cash flows.

The completed contract method lies at the other extreme since it recognizes revenues and expenses only when the contract has been completed. Under this method, the analyst may need to rely on the statement of cash flows to assess the contribution of long-term contracts to the firm's profitability.

The installment and cost recovery methods are used when there is uncertainty regarding the amount or collectibility of future cash flows. The installment method is similar to the percentage-of-completion method for contracts in that it reports earnings in stages (in this case, as funds are received). The cost recovery method is similar to

---

[24]See, for example, M. Maremont, "Blind Ambition," *Business Week*, Oct. 23, 1995, pp. 78–92, where it is alleged that Bausch and Lomb carried out similar practices.

the completed contract method in that it postpones income recognition (but not recognition of revenue and expense) until all uncertainties have been eliminated. Whichever method is used, the analyst needs to monitor the cash flow statement and its relationship to the income statement. As discussed in the next chapter, the statement of cash flows can warn the financial statement user that overly aggressive revenue recognition methods are being used.

NONRECURRING ITEMS

Analysis of the income statement for most firms is affected by nonrecurring items. As companies have increased their effort to explain earnings variations, they have made greater use of the "unusual" and "nonrecurring" labels, especially for items that reduce reported income. We have previously noted that, when estimating a firm's earning power, analysts should exclude items that are unusual or nonrecurring in nature. However, this does not mean that everything management labels nonrecurring should be ignored. In this section, we discuss the extent to which such items provide useful information and how they should be treated in financial analysis.

Types of Nonrecurring Items

The income statement format previously described contains four categories of nonrecurring income:

1. Unusual or infrequent items
2. Extraordinary items
3. Discontinued operations
4. Accounting changes

The first of these appear "above the line" as part of "income from continuing operations" and are presented on a pretax basis. The other three categories are "below the line," excluded from "income from continuing operations," and presented net of tax.[25] We first describe these classifications and then discuss their analytic implications.

Unusual or Infrequent Items

Transactions or events that are *either unusual in nature or infrequent in occurrence but not both* may be disclosed separately (as a single-line item) as a component of income from continuing operations. These items must be reported pretax in the income statement; the tax impact (or the net-of-tax amount) may be disclosed separately. Common examples are:

1. Gains or losses from disposal of a portion of a business segment
2. Gains or losses from sales of assets or investments in affiliates or subsidiaries

---

[25]The fact that some nonrecurring items are presented pretax (and included in income from continuing operations) but others are reported after tax (excluded from income from continuing operations) hampers analysis. Attention to detail and a little thought, however, can conquer the inconsistent presentation of nonrecurring items.

3. Provisions for environmental remediation

4. Impairments, write-offs, write-downs, and restructuring costs

DuPont's income statement contains several examples. "Restructuring" provisions are present in each year, 1992 through 1994. The details of the 1992 and 1993 provisions are contained in Note 6, which states that they include:

- Employee separation costs
- Plant shutdown costs
- Write-downs of assets to be sold

The 1992 provision of $475 million was primarily for termination incentives and payments and it included some restructuring costs. The 1993 charges perfunctorily reported in the *1993 Annual Report* are disclosed in substantial detail in the 1994 statements. (The 1994 disclosure reflects stricter enforcement by the SEC.)

The total charge in 1993 was $1,621 million, including $665 million for employee separation and the remaining $956 million for asset write-downs and facility shutdowns. Note the detailed discussion of the number of employees involved, the initial restructuring liability recorded, the amounts settled, and the remaining balance of the restructuring liability on the balance sheet.

Restructuring provisions are estimates and subject to change. In 1994, the restructuring provision originally established in 1993 was reduced by $167 million and the 1992 charge was increased by $25 million, increasing 1994 pretax income by $142 million.

In 1993, duPont also wrote down goodwill and other intangible assets obtained in its 1989 acquisitions.

However, nonrecurring items are not always disclosed as separate line items in the income statement. They are often included in the catch-all "other income" classification or may be buried in COGS or SG&A. Both footnote disclosures and the MD&A should be scrutinized for events and transactions that may have had a material impact on earnings, but that management has chosen to treat as normal, recurring items.

Extraordinary Items

APB 30 (1973) created the U.S. GAAP income statement format discussed earlier. It defines *extraordinary items* as transactions and events that are *unusual in nature and infrequent in occurrence and are material in amount.* Extraordinary items must be reported separately, net of income tax. Firms are also required to report per share amounts for these items and encouraged to provide additional footnote disclosures. Extraordinary items are intended to be rare; based on APB 30, such events as losses due to a foreign government's expropriation of assets qualify as an extraordinary item, whereas gains or losses on the sale of noncurrent assets do not.

In the early 1970s, high interest rates and an economic recession led firms with depressed profits to refinance low coupon debt, whose market value was below the face amount, with high coupon debt, reporting an accounting gain.[26] SFAS 4 (1975)

---

[26]See Chapter 10 for a comparison of the accounting and economic consequences of refinancing.

broadened the classification of extraordinary items by requiring that *gains or losses on qualifying early retirement of debt*[27] be classified as extraordinary.

In recent years, firms have refinanced high coupon debt, whose market value exceeded face amount after sharp declines in interest rates, These debt retirements have resulted in reported extraordinary losses. Of the sample of 600 companies in the 1994 *Accounting Trends and Techniques*, 59 reported extraordinary items and all of these were gains or losses on the early retirement of debt.

Referring to duPont's income statement, we see extraordinary charges in 1992 and 1993. Both result from the early extinguishment of debt, which resulted in call premiums as duPont paid more than the carrying amount of the liability to retire this debt.

Discontinued Operations

The discontinuation or sale of a business segment may indicate that it:

- Has inadequate or uncertain markets or prospects.
- Has an unsatisfactory contribution to earnings and cash flows.
- Is no longer considered by management to be a strategic fit.
- Can be sold at a significant profit.

Operating income from discontinued operations, and any gains or losses (net of taxes) from their sale are segregated in the income statement, since these activities will not contribute to future income and cash flows. As in the case of extraordinary items, this segregation makes the reported information more useful for analysis.

A business segment is defined as a "component of an entity whose activities represent a separate major line of business or class of customer" (APB 30, para. 13). Subsidiaries and investees also qualify as separate segments.

To qualify for treatment as discontinued operations, the assets, results of operations, and investing and financing activities of a business segment must be separable from those of the firm. APB 30 states that the separation must be possible physically and operationally, and for financial reporting purposes.

Once management develops or adopts a formal plan for the sale or disposal of a segment (the *measurement date*), the operating results of the segment are segregated within the income statement. The income statement will report the income or loss from operations of the discontinued segment only on a net-of-tax basis. A condensed income statement for the segment is usually shown in a footnote. Prior period income statements are restated as well.

At the measurement date, the firm will accrue any estimated loss from operations during the "phase-out" period, that is, from the measurement date to the disposal date,[28] and any estimated loss on sale or disposal. However, any gain on disposal (net

---

[27]Gains and losses on early retirement of debt are considered extraordinary, except for those related to sinking fund requirements (SFAS 4, 1975).

[28]The disposal date is the date the sale is completed or the operations are shut down if the segment is abandoned or discontinued.

of expected operating losses during the phase-out period) can be reported only after disposal, that is, when realized.[29]

An example of the income statement reporting of discontinued operations appears in Exhibit 2-3, which reproduces the income statement and partial footnotes of the Heico Corporation. The income statement shows the two components of the required disclosure of discontinued operations. Note that the sales and operating losses of the laboratory products segment have been excluded from reported sales and income from continuing operations. Previously reported sales and earnings have been restated to exclude the discontinued segment.

Note 2 of the financial statements shows that Heico entered into an agreement to sell the segment in December 1989, recorded a provision for the loss that year, and then recognized an additional loss when the sale was completed during the first quarter of 1990. This note also provides summary disclosure of the net assets and operating results of the discontinued segment.

In addition, Heico's Note 3 discloses information regarding several "nonrecurring" costs related to a proxy contest and restructuring costs. The note shows that the 1989 posttax loss was $1,316,000 or $0.41 per share. Note that these nonrecurring items are reported pretax as part of the income from continuing operations.

Accounting Changes

Accounting changes fall into two general categories: those undertaken voluntarily by the firm and those mandated by new accounting standards. Generally, accounting changes do not have direct cash flow consequences.

The change from one acceptable accounting method to another acceptable method is reported in the period of change. Any cumulative impact on *prior period* earnings is reported net of tax after extraordinary items and discontinued operations on the income statement.[30] Firms are required to provide footnote disclosure of the impact of the change on current period operations (and on each prior period, if restated) and their justification for the change. However, accounting changes also affect future operating results. That impact is rarely disclosed but can sometimes be estimated. Accounting changes are dealt with frequently in the remaining chapters of the text.

---

[29]These rules also apply [see Accounting Interpretations of APB 30 (AICPA, Nov. 1973)] when only a portion of a business segment, for example, a factory, plant, or group of machines, is to be sold, disposed of, or abandoned. However, any gain or loss from the sale of a portion of a segment must be reported pretax as a separate component of income from continuing operations rather than as a discontinued operation. Firms are encouraged to disclose separately the affected assets and liabilities on the balance sheet. However, the income or loss from operations from the beginning of the year to the measurement date is not always segregated on the income statement. Some firms provide footnote disclosure of this datum for all years presented. The income or loss during the phase-out period and the gain or loss on sale or disposal are included in income from continuing operations.

[30]In most cases, prior period results are not restated. The cumulative impact is computed under the assumption that the new method had been used in all past periods and is therefore the difference between reported income and what income would have been if the new method had been applied.

In some cases, prior period results are restated; the portion of the cumulative impact applicable to periods preceding those for which an income statement is presented is shown as an adjustment to retained earnings.

EXHIBIT 2-3. HEICO CORPORATION
Disclosure of Discontinued Operations

HEICO CORPORATION AND SUBSIDIARIES
Notes to Consolidated Financial Statements
for the years ended October 31, 1990, 1989 and 1988

NOTE 2 – DISCONTINUED OPERATIONS – SALE OF LABORATORY PRODUCTS SEGMENT

In March 1990, the Company completed the sale of the stock of its various laboratory products segment subsidiaries to Varlen Corporation for $11.5 million cash consideration and the assumption of related liabilities of $4.7 million. In fiscal 1989, the Company recorded a $5.6 million provision representing an estimated loss pursuant to the terms of a letter of intent entered into with Varlen in December 1989. The sale, as consummated, resulted in an additional charge of $2,480,000, or $.78 per share, in the first quarter of fiscal 1990. The sale resulted in capital losses aggregating approximately $7 million which can be used to offset any capital gains realized over the next five years.

The results of operations of the laboratory products segment have been reported as discontinued operations for the three-year period ended October 31, 1990 and reported separately from the results of continuing operations. The 1990 and 1989 provisions for loss on disposal of the laboratory products segment include a provision for fiscal 1990 operating losses prior to disposition of $159,000 and $400,000, respectively.

The Company's net investment in the laboratory products segment at October 31, 1989, after reduction for the $5.6 million estimated loss on disposal, is included in current assets. A summary of the net assets as of October 31, 1989 follows:

Trade accounts receivable, net	$ 3,832,000
Inventories	9,496,000
Other current assets	91,000
Property, plant and equipment, net	5,140,000
Intangible assets, net	3,955,000
Other assets	131,000
Current liabilities	(1,774,000)
Long-term debt	(2,897,000)
Deferred income taxes	(214,000)
Provision for loss on disposal	(5,600,000)
	$ 12,160,000

Summary operating results for the laboratory products segment are as follows:

	Period from November 1, 1989 through disposal (March 5, 1990)	Fiscal Year Ended October 31	
		1989	1988
Net sales	$ 6,013,000	$ 20,599,000	$ 20,236,000
Operating loss	$ (770,000)	$ (951,000)	$ (856,000)
Loss, net of income taxes	$ (559,000)	$ (769,000)	$ (746,000)

With the discontinuance of the laboratory products segment, the Company's operations are within a single business segment, the aviation and defense products industry.

NOTE 3 – NON-RECURRING CHARGES

During fiscal 1989, the Company incurred the costs of a proxy contest relating to the election of directors and the subsequent litigation contesting that election aggregating $717,000. In December 1989, a settlement was reached whereby, among other things, the Company and its insurers agreed to reimburse the plaintiff shareholder group for certain expenses in connection with the proxy contest and litigation. A provision of $855,000 for the costs associated with the settlement was recorded in the fiscal 1989 financial statements.

In October 1989, the Company announced restructuring plans to further integrate the operations of its aviation and defense products subsidiaries. A $500,000 provision was charged against income in the fourth quarter of 1989 to cover the expenses associated with this plan. These expenses together with the charges discussed in the preceding paragraph have been set forth separately in the Consolidated Statements of Income for fiscal 1989 as non-recurring charges. These non-recurring charges adversely affected income from continuing operations and the net loss by $1,316,000, or $.41 per share, in fiscal 1989.

HEICO CORPORATION AND SUBSIDIARIES
CONSOLIDATED STATEMENTS OF INCOME
For the years ended October 31, 1990, 1989 and 1988

	1990	1989	1988
Net sales	$26,239,000	$26,473,000	$22,925,000
Operating costs and expenses:			
Cost of products and services sold	19,165,000	17,239,000	13,600,000
Selling, general and administrative expenses	5,205,000	5,291,000	5,100,000
Non-recurring charges	–	2,072,000	–
Total operating costs and expenses	24,370,000	24,602,000	18,700,000
Income from operations	1,869,000	1,871,000	4,225,000
Interest expense	(181,000)	(131,000)	(173,000)
Interest and other income	970,000	751,000	788,000
Income from continuing operations before income taxes	2,658,000	2,491,000	4,840,000
Income taxes	697,000	770,000	1,608,000
Income from continuing operations	1,961,000	1,721,000	3,232,000
Discontinued operations (Note 2):			
(Loss) from operations of discontinued laboratory products segment (less applicable tax benefits of $442,000 in 1989 and $407,000 in 1988)	–	(769,000)	(746,000)
(Loss) on disposal of laboratory products segment (includes a provision for operating losses prior to disposition of $159,000 in fiscal 1990 and $400,000 in fiscal 1989)	(2,480,000)	(5,600,000)	–
Net income (loss)	$ (519,000)	$ (4,648,000)	$ 2,486,000
Income per share from continuing operations	$ .66	$ .54	$1.00
Net income (loss) per share	$(.17)	$(1.45)	$ .77
Weighted average number of common and common equivalent shares outstanding	2,992,947	3,213,355	3,237,488

See notes to consolidated financial statements.

Source: Heico Corp. 1990 Annual Report.

APB 20 (1971) identifies several exceptions to the general treatment of accounting changes. These are:

1. Change from LIFO to another inventory method (see Chapter 6)
2. Change to or from the full cost method (see Chapter 7)
3. Change to or from the percentage-of-completion method
4. Change in accounting methods prior to an initial public offering

These exceptions require retroactive restatement of all years presented.

In 1992, duPont adopted two new accounting standards: SFAS 106, Postretirement Benefits Other than Pensions (see Chapter 12), and SFAS 109, Income Taxes (see Chapter 9). The combined cumulative (net-of-tax) effect of these accounting changes, a $4,833 million reduction in earnings, is shown as a separate line item in the income statement, following the extraordinary items previously discussed.

A change from an incorrect to an acceptable accounting method is treated as an error, and its impact is reported as a *prior period adjustment.*

Prior Period Adjustments

On occasion, newly available information clarifies transactions that were accounted for in prior periods. In some cases, the appropriate adjustment is not reported as a component of current period income, but recorded directly to retained earnings. SFAS 16, Prior Period Adjustments, restricts this treatment to accounting errors. In most cases, however, these adjustments are included in reported income of the period in which the new information becomes available.

Outside of the United States, the rules on prior period adjustments are sometimes more lenient. For example, Suncor, a Canadian company, included the following note in its *1993 Annual Report:*

Legal Claim Settlement
During 1993, a settlement was reached on all actions initiated by the company in 1989 against defendants for damages caused by the October 1987 fire at its Oil Sands operations. Accordingly, the financial impact was reflected retroactively in 1987 earnings and 1992 opening retained earnings was increased by $16 million.[31]

Under U.S. GAAP, since the settlement was reached in 1993, the settlement gain of $16 million would be recorded in the 1993 income statement. Either way, an analyst would treat it as a nonrecurring item and exclude it from earnings used for valuation.

Analysis of Nonrecurring Items

The preceding discussion of unusual items, extraordinary items, and discontinued operations illustrates the difficulty presented by nonrecurring items. Accounting standard setters cannot draw "bright lines" that are adequate to separate clearly "unusual" items. In practice, gains tend to be buried in continuing operations, whereas losses are often shown separately; disclosure is not always sufficient. In some cases, the

---

[31]Suncor's *1993 Annual Report,* Notes to Financial Statements.

MD&A provides more information about unusual items than the financial statements themselves.

When estimating a firm's "earning power," analysts normally exclude items that are unusual or nonrecurring in nature. Yet such events seem to recur, more so in some companies than others. Some companies seem to be "accident prone," although each "accident" is different. Nonrecurring items are not all alike. Although the sale of assets, divisions, or segments may not be part of continuing operations, such sales may recur, albeit sporadically. Recurring and nonrecurring are not two distinct categories but rather a continuum. The objective, therefore, is to place each item in its appropriate place on the spectrum.

Income Statement Impact of Nonrecurring Items

The current period income statement effect of nonrecurring items is generally clearly stated. However, such items also have implications for previously reported income and future earnings.

Some nonrecurring items are, in effect, a "correction" of prior period income. The Suncor case discussed above is one example. A more common example is asset write-downs, frequently included in "restructuring" provisions. Such write-downs suggest that prior period depreciation or amortization changes were insufficient and reported income for these periods was overstated.

The effect on future income is frequently the reverse. To the extent that assets are written down, future depreciation and amortization expense will be lower than would otherwise have been the case. The accrual of future lease rental expense and employee severance costs also affects future earnings, which will no longer be saddled with these costs. The restructuring charges recorded by duPont in 1993 and 1994 both contain asset write-downs that reflect on both past and future reported earnings.

These implications for previous and future earnings must be carefully considered. *If nonrecurring charges are really prior year expenses taken too late or future expenses charged off early, then the practice of ignoring nonrecurring charges and focusing on recurring operating income results in an overestimation of the firm's earnings trend.*

The ever-increasing spate of restructurings and special charges (e.g., duPont had at least one in each of the years 1992 to 1994) has been criticized by some as being motivated by the desire to paint a better earnings picture:

> . . . How can repeated write-offs be nonrecurring or extraordinary? *How can investors believe that reported earnings are real and won't be canceled by subsequent write-offs?* . . .
>
> Here's how this kind of charge can boost earnings. Say Company XYZ reports rising profits of $1 million in year 1 and $1.2 million in year 2; in year 3, XYZ takes a restructuring charge of $5 million for the cost of closing a few businesses. The charge turned year 3's net into a loss of $3.5 million—but XYZ says profit would have been $1.5 million before the charge. The next year, year 4, the upward trend resumes as XYZ reports profits of $1.8 million. But the results are helped because $2 million of the company's year 4 expenses—say, for severance payments and plant closings—can be counted against the charge already taken in year 3. . . .
>
> . . . *The most obvious way restructuring charges make companies' earnings look better is if the companies can convince investors that operating earnings—before the charges—provide a more meaningful indication of trends.* . . .
>
> Wall Street analysts often use some version of operating earnings—not counting charges—to track a company's earnings trend. Thus, many analysts and research services that follow AT&T show a tidy growth track for the company: $3.13 a share for 1994,

$3.45 for 1995, and $3.95 for 1996. But that doesn't include AT&T's 1995 charges of $5.4 billion, or $3.35 a share. . . .[32]

Cash Flow and Valuation Impact

Nonrecurring items with cash flow consequences do affect the wealth of the firm. However, they should still be segregated because their valuation implications differ from recurring income. As outlined in Box 2-1 and discussed in greater detail in Chapter 19, (true) nonrecurring components of income have only a one-time dollar-for-dollar effect on valuation, whereas the multiple for changes in recurring income (the price-earnings multiple) is greater.

The analyst must distinguish among items that:

- Have no cash flow implications (e.g., asset write-downs)
- Affect current period cash flow only (e.g., employee severance costs)
- Have future cash flow effects (e.g., lease payments for closed facilities)

Careful attention must be paid to footnote disclosures to ascertain the cash flow effects of "restructuring" provisions in particular. In some cases, the cash drain from such provisions extends years into the future.

The 1993 restructuring charges and write-down of intangible assets of $1,621 million reported by duPont provide a good example of these issues. Note 6 states that the termination of approximately 10,900 employees accounted for $665 million. The firm had paid $420 million as of December 31, 1994, reduced its estimate by $45 million, and anticipated completing this program during the following year. The remaining $200 million was, therefore, expected to be paid in 1995.

Various write-downs and the discontinuance of certain facilities accounted for $956 million. The write-downs and write-offs have no current cash flow implications. The subsequent sale of a polymers plant and continued operation of certain operations generated higher proceeds and led to a revision of the 1993 charges and the benefit of $122 million is reflected in 1994 earnings. The firm discloses a reserve balance of $100 million at year-end, but it is not possible to determine cash consequences, if any, of this amount.

Implications for Continuing Operations

Nonrecurring events, even those without cash flow effects, may also provide useful information about the firm. A plant closing and the write-off of its book value are one example. The actual cash outflows occurred in the past and are only now being expensed. The value implication of the gain or loss reported on the income statement may be nonexistent. The plant closing itself may, however, help forecast the firm's future sales, earnings, and cash flows. Similarly, duPont's 1994 restructuring charge included employee severance costs. Future reported earnings should be higher than previously expected because its employment costs are reduced. Benefit accruals (see Chapter 12) will also be affected by the reduced number of employees.

[32]Quotations are excerpted from "Are Companies Using Restructuring Costs to Fudge The Figures?: A Repeated Strategic Move Makes Future Earnings Seem Unrealistically Rosy," *Wall Street Journal,* Jan. 30, 1996 (emphasis added).

Management Discretion and Earnings Manipulation

When estimating earnings trends, the analyst must also be wary of the discretionary nature of the income statement. Items requiring separate disclosure on the income statement may be discretionary with respect to the:

1. Timing of the occurrence (e.g., the disposal of an asset or the discontinuation of a segment)
2. Classification of the item (ordinary, unusual, or extraordinary)

In addition, changes in accounting methods can alter reported income statement trends. In many cases, there is no disclosure (except in the aggregate) of the effects of the accounting change on income reported in individual prior periods, making adjustment difficult.

The discretionary nature of income permits an examination of the degree of management manipulation of earnings under one or more of the following guises:

1. Classification of good news/bad news
2. Income smoothing
3. Big bath behavior
4. Accounting changes

Classification of Good News/Bad News. Management prefers to report good news "above the line" as part of continuing operations and bad news "below the line" as extraordinary or discontinued operations. For example, management determines whether the component of the firm sold meets the definition of a segment and hence given below-the-line treatment as income from discontinued operations. As SFAS 14 notes, the

> determination of enterprise industry segments must depend to a considerable extent on the judgment of the management of the enterprise.[33]

This ambiguity permits management to report unusual items most favorably. Exhibit 2-4 shows the findings of Rapaccioli and Schiff (1991) that are consistent with such behavior. In their sample of 504 disposals carried out in 1985 and 1986, approximately 60% of the cases were accorded the more favorable treatment, with 61% of gains reported above the line and 57% of losses reported below the line.

Income Smoothing. Some firms reduce earnings in good years (defer gains or recognize losses) and inflate earnings in bad years (recognize gains or defer losses) in order to report stable earnings. Ronen and Sadan (1981) demonstrated that managements can and do engage in such behavior by engaging in two types of smoothing. *Intertemporal smoothing* refers to either:

- Timing expenditures such as research and development, repairs and maintenance, and asset disposals, or
- Choosing accounting methods (e.g., capitalization or expensing) that allocate the expenditure over time

---

[33]SFAS 14, para. 12

EXHIBIT 2-4
Percentages of Gains and Losses from the Sale of Business Components Reported Above-the-Line and Below-the-Line for 1985 to 1986

	% of Sales Reported Above-the-Line	% of Sales Reported Below-the-Line
Gain	61%	43%
Loss	39%	57%

Source: Donna Rapaccioli and Allen Schiff, "Reporting Segment Sales Under APB Opinion No. 30," *Accounting Horizons,* Dec. 1991, pp. 53–59, Table 1 on p. 55.

Classificatory smoothing is smoothing by choosing to classify an item as either income from continuing operations, or extraordinary income.[34] The implicit assumption is that analysts focus on ordinary income and ignore nonrecurring/extraordinary items. Thus, by shifting items above or below the "line," management can report a desired trend.

Asset sales are an example of a nonrecurring item that has been used as both an intertemporal and classificatory smoothing instrument. Bartov (1993) showed that such sales have been *timed* to smooth income. Furthermore, as there is discretion in how a segment is defined, the sale of a portion of a business can be classified as part of continuing operations or as a discontinued operation. Fried et al. (1996) showed that the *classification* choices made by their sample of firms were consistent with smoothing.

Ronen and Sadan have argued that smoothing is not necessarily "bad." Rather, by engaging in smoothing, management may be aiding the predictive ability of reported earnings by conveying information about the future prospects of the firm.[35] Moses (1987) made similar arguments. Possible incentives for earnings manipulation are varied [see the discussion in Bartov (1993)] and not necessarily limited to the desire to show stable earnings and/or aid predictive ability. A number of authors [e.g., Healy (1985), Holthausen et al. (1995), and Gaver et al. (1995)] examined executive bonus plans and showed that depending on the structure of such plans, management may be motivated to engage in discretionary accruals, manipulating earnings in an upward or downward direction. Jones (1991) showed that firms that would benefit from import relief (e.g., tariff increases and quota reductions) decrease income through earnings manipulation in order to influence the U.S. International Trade Commission. Bartov, on the other hand, demonstrated that firms attempt to manipulate earnings in an upward direction in order to escape possible restrictions imposed by their bond covenant agreements.

[34]Because of the looser classification standards in the United Kingdom, the distinction between ("above-the-line") exceptional items and ("below-the-line") extraordinary items became a major reporting issue in that country. Financial Reporting Standard (FRS) 3, which became effective for fiscal years ending after June 22, 1993, virtually eliminated extraordinary items under U.K. GAAP.

[35]Gonedes (1978), testing for such signaling behavior, however, found that extraordinary items *did not* convey any incremental information above that of contemporaneously reported income numbers. In an earlier study, Gonedes (1975) found that special items *did* convey information to investors. In reconciling the two studies, Gonedes (1978, p. 74) noted that the latter study included only those items reported "below the line" as extraordinary items, whereas the earlier study also included items for which separate disclosure was recommended or required whenever material—even though these additional items were not considered "extraordinary" according to GAAP.

EXHIBIT 2-5
Income Effects of Changes in Accounting Method by Type of Change (1976 to 1984)

	Number of Firms	Average EPS* Effect of the Change		Number (%) of Cases in Which Change Increases Income	
		Mean	Median		
Voluntary changes					
FIFO to LIFO	116	−0.0977	−0.0666	5	4.3%
Other to LIFO	16	−0.0795	−0.0832	2	12.5%
Def. to FT-ITC	20	0.1275	0.0596	18	90.0%
ACC. to SL deprec.	9	0.0509	0.0260	9	100.0%
Other depreciation	21	0.2216	0.0609	15	71.4%
Pension	11	0.1244	0.0761	8	72.7%
Capitalize to expense	7	−0.0793	−0.0448	2	28.5%
Expense to capitalize	17	0.1207	0.0442	12	70.6%
Revenue recognition	18	0.0165	0.0238	11	61.1%
Miscellaneous voluntary	52	0.0992	0.0479	35	67.3%
Total voluntary	285	0.0098	−0.0234	118	41.0%
Mandatory changes					
SFAS 13—Leases	21	−0.0018	0.0000	2	9.5%
SFAS 34—Interest capitalization	83	0.1667	0.0579	79	95.2%
SFAS 43—Vacation accruals	50	−0.0016	0.0000	4	8.0%
SFAS 52—Foreign currency	143	0.4133†	0.0900	118	82.5%
Miscellaneous mandatory	30	0.1795	0.0093	17	56.7%
Total mandatory	327	0.2392	0.0404	220	67.3%
Total all changes	612	0.1324	0.0155	337	55.0%

*Impact of change in accounting method on change year EPS divided by annual report EPS before the accounting change. A positive value indicates an increase in earnings.
†Three cases larger than three standard deviations from the mean account for the high mean value. With these omitted, the mean is 0.1493.

Source: John A. Elliott and Donna R. Philbrick, "Accounting Changes and Earnings Predictability," *The Accounting Review,* Jan. 1990, pp. 157–174, Table 3 on p. 162.

"Big Bath" Accounting. In contrast to income smoothing, the big bath hypothesis suggests that management will report additional losses in bad years in the hope that, by taking all available losses at one time, they will "clear the decks" once and for all. The implicit assumption is that future reported profits will increase.

This hypothesis is more widely accepted in the financial press than in the academic literature. Elliott and Shaw (1988) found that analyst forecasts following large write-offs are not consistent with the big bath theory. Rather than increasing following a write-off, indicating a clearing of the deck, forecast earnings tended to decrease. Fried et al. (1989) reported that a firm taking an asset write-down in one year is likely to take another one soon after. This is inconsistent with big bath behavior, which argues that firms would overestimate rather than underestimate the size and amounts of write-offs.[36]

---

[36]See the discussion of impairment in Chapter 8 for more details of these results.

Accounting Changes. Regardless of whether accounting changes are voluntary or mandatory, they typically have no direct cash flow consequences for a U.S. company.[37] Thus, such changes can be viewed as a form of earnings manipulation. Empirical research has studied accounting changes extensively, focusing on both managerial motivations and stock market reaction. We shall refer to many of these studies in later chapters.

Elliott and Philbrick (1990) examined the effects of accounting changes on earnings predictability. They examined both voluntary and mandated changes and partitioned their sample on the basis of whether analysts, prior to making their forecasts, had information about the change. In the period studied, 1976 to 1984, 1,273 firms had accounting changes large enough to generate a consistency exception in the audit opinion. From this set of firms, they were able to obtain usable data for 612 accounting changes.

Exhibit 2-5 shows income effects by the type of change. Not surprisingly, they found that analysts had difficulty forecasting earnings for the year of the change. That difficulty was more pronounced for mandatory changes, for which there was no prior information regarding the change. Moreover, they found that when analysts had no prior information about the change, the effect of the accounting change tended to be in the *opposite* direction of forecast revisions made by analysts in the latter part of the fiscal year (fourth quarter). For example, accounting changes that *increased* income were associated with *downward* forecast revisions; that is, when income was lower than originally expected (causing downward forecast revisions), accounting changes were adopted that raised reported income. This behavior, the authors concluded, was consistent with management's use of accounting changes to manipulate or smooth earnings.

THE BALANCE SHEET

The balance sheet (statement of financial position) reports the categories and amounts of assets (firm resources), liabilities (claims on those resources), and stockholders' equity at specific points in time. In the United States, balance sheets are generally issued at the end of each quarter and the end of the fiscal year; outside of the United States, annual or semiannual reporting is the general rule.

Format and Classification

The definitions of assets, liabilities, and stockholders' equity are discussed in Chapter 1. We now discuss the format and classification prevalent in most companies in the United States. Box 2-4 lists and discusses duPont's balance sheet components.

Assets and liabilities are classified according to liquidity, that is, their expected use in operations or conversion to cash in the case of assets and time to maturity for liabilities. Assets expected to be converted to cash or used within one year (or one operating cycle, if longer than one year) are classified as current assets. Current liabilities include obligations the firm expects to settle within one year (or one operating cycle, if longer).

Assets expected to provide benefits and services over periods exceeding one year and liabilities to be repaid after one year are classified as long-term assets and liabilities.

---

[37]The FIFO to LIFO change is the major exception in the United States (see Chapter 6).

BOX 2-4. DUPONT
Balance Sheet Components

Although every firm's financial statements are unique, we can use duPont's balance sheet to briefly define and discuss the components of the balance sheet. As in Box 2-3, we provide an "index" showing in which book chapters the balance sheet components are discussed in greater detail:

Assets	Chapter Index	Liabilities	Chapter Index
Cash and cash equivalents	3	Accounts payable	4
Marketable securities	13	Current liabilities	4
Accounts receivable	2, 4	Debt—short- and long-term	10
Inventory	4, 6	Capital leases	11
Prepaid expenses		Deferred taxes	9
Deferred taxes	9	Pensions and postretirement benefits	12
Current assets	4	Minority interest	13
Fixed assets	7		
(Accumulated depreciation)	8	Stockholders' Equity	2
		Cumulative translation adjustment	15
Capital leases	11		
Investment in affiliates	13, 15	Minimum pension liability	12
Prepaid pension costs	12	Unrealized gains/losses	13
Intangible assets	7, 14		

(In the discussion that follows, all "Note" references are to the financial statement footnotes of duPont.)

Assets

SFAS 95 defines *cash and cash equivalents* as risk-free assets with original maturities of 90 days or less. Thus, bank accounts, U.S. Treasury Bills, and similar assets qualify. Note that the "bottom line" of the statement of cash flows is the change in these assets for the period.

Marketable securities include equity and trading securities, which must be carried at market value under SFAS 115. Fixed-income securities may be carried at either market value or amortized cost. In some cases, marketable securities are similar to cash equivalents; in other cases, there is substantial risk. Footnote data often provide more detail.

Accounts and notes receivable contain both trade receivables and notes receivable (e.g., from asset sales). The distinction is important. Trade receivables reflect credit sales of products and services and their analysis over time is an important indicator of liquidity and the soundness of revenue recognition methods. The maturity and collectibility of notes receivable may have important implications for the future cash flow and liquidity of the firm. Note 11 separates the two components.

The accounting method used for *inventories* (Note 12) can significantly affect the measurement of this important operating asset as well as the level and trend of reported income.

Prepaid expenses include tax and insurance prepayments, items that will appear as expenses in future income statements.

Deferred income taxes represent deferred tax assets. Note 7 provides detail regarding the firm's income tax position.

Total current assets include all of duPont's assets that are expected to generate cash within one year or one operating cycle. However, most of these assets revolve; new receivables and inventories arise as old ones are realized. Thus, current assets alone are not a forecast of future cash flow.

For duPont, as for most industrial and manufacturing firms, *Property, plant, and equipment* is the largest asset category. The stated amount is a function of accounting policies regarding capitalization, depreciation, and impairment. Note 13 contains a breakdown of duPont's fixed assets and states that a small amount of capital leases are included. Assets under operating leases are not included in the PPE total; Note 20 contains data on duPont's operating leases.

Investments in affiliates reflect the investment in and advances to affiliates accounted for using the equity method. Note 14 contains summarized financial data for these affiliates and states that duPont has guaranteed the debt of some affiliates.

The components of *other assets* are shown in Note 15. The largest single item is prepaid pension cost (see Note 20). DuPont also includes intangible assets here, a common practice.

Liabilities

Note 16 reports the components of *accounts payable*. Trade payables are the largest item and are useful in assessing a firm's cash cycle. Payables to banks should be treated as debt.

Short-term borrowings and capital lease obligations are detailed in Note 17.

As mentioned earlier, Note 7 provides details of *income taxes.*

Other accrued liabilities are shown in Note 18. Details on pensions and other postretirement benefits are contained in Notes 25 and 26.

Total current liabilities represent the required payments over the next year *if nothing else takes place.* In reality, of course, duPont will repay some of these obligations but incur new ones.

Long-term borrowings and capital lease obligations are detailed in Note 19. Note 20 shows both the capitalized leases that are reported in duPont's balance sheet and the operating leases that are not reflected there.

Note 21 states that the largest component of *other liabilities* is accrued postretirement benefit costs (see Note 25). Note 7 contains details on *deferred income taxes.*

Minority interests in consolidated subsidiaries represent the equity held by investors other than duPont in those subsidiaries.

Stockholders' Equity

Stockholders' equity for duPont contains four components. Preferred stock represents a prior claim on the firm's net assets. As shown in the Consolidated Statement of Shareholders' Equity, duPont has two classes of preferred. Although these issues are callable at duPont's option, they are not redeemable. Preferred shares that are redeemable at the stockholders' option must be shown outside (normally just above) the stockholders' equity section. Preferred shares are reported as the amount of cash received when they were issued; the redemption or liquidation value may be higher. When computing book value per share, the redemption or liquidation value should be used (see Chapter 17 for the duPont computation).

The next two components, *common stock* and *additional paid-in capital,* represent the amount received from the sale or other issuance of common stock. *Reinvested* (retained) *earnings* represent the accumulation of duPont earnings over its corporate life, reduced by dividends paid. For most companies, the distinction among these three components is unimportant. In rare cases, however, a low level (or absence) of retained earnings may affect the firm's ability to declare dividends or the tax treatment of those dividends.

Although not present in duPont's case, stockholders' equity may contain the following additional components:

- Treasury stock: expenditures to repurchase shares
- Employee Stock Option Plan (ESOP) accruals
- Unrealized gains and losses on securities
- Deferred translation gains and losses
- Minimum pension liability

Tangible assets and liabilities are generally reported before intangibles and other assets and liabilities whose measurement is less certain.

This classification scheme can be used to develop ratios employed in financial analysis. The current–noncurrent distinction can be used to measure liquidity, for example. In recent years, however, that distinction has become somewhat arbitrary as differences between short-term and long-term investments and debt are sometimes difficult to discern.

The most liquid assets, cash and cash equivalents, precede marketable equity securities, receivables, inventories, and prepaid expenses in the current asset section of the balance sheet. Long-lived assets, including property, plant, and equipment, investments in affiliated companies, and intangible assets such as brand names, patents, copyrights, and goodwill, are reported as noncurrent assets.

Short-term bank and other debt, the current portion of long-term debt and capitalized leases, accounts payable to suppliers, accrued liabilities (amounts owed to employees and others), interest, and taxes payable are classified as current liabilities. Long-term debt, capitalized lease obligations, pension obligations, and other "liabilities" (such as deferred income taxes and minority interest in the net assets of consolidated affiliates) are commonly observed noncurrent liabilities.

Stockholders' equity (the residual interest in the firm) lists components in order of their priority in liquidation with any preference (preferred) stock listed before common stock, treasury stock, and reinvested earnings. This section may also include the additional components shown in Box 2-4.

Measurement of Assets and Liabilities

Most components of the balance sheet are reported at historical cost, that is, the exchange price at their acquisition date. As noted earlier in this chapter, in the discussion of the accrual concept of income, the nature (and amount) of a recognized asset is a function of the firm's revenue recognition method.

In some cases (e.g., accounts receivable), valuation allowances (reserve for uncollectible receivables) adjust the originally recorded amount to an approximation of net realizable value. The reserve for uncollectibles is an estimate of bad debts, reported as a deduction from the gross receivables balance; this is called a "contra" account. (Accumulated depreciation is also a contra account since it reduces the carrying value of long-lived assets to reflect their use.)

Changes in some other assets or liabilities are accumulated in "adjunct" accounts, such as the premium on bonds payable that records the excess of the bond's issue price over its face value. These contra and adjunct accounts allow firms to report both the original, historical cost (e.g., gross plant assets) and the net carrying amount (plant assets net of accumulated depreciation). They also reflect management's estimate of realizable values of the underlying assets, for example, receivables net of the allowance for uncollectibles. However, these are accounting estimates of net realizable values and not market values.[38]

Lower of cost or market and impairment rules may, however, require write-downs to fair or market values when they are below cost. In most cases, however, market values are not reflected in the balance sheet prior to realization, and recoveries (reversal of previous write-downs) to the original acquisition cost are not allowed under U.S.

---

[38]The level and trend of the allowance for uncollectible receivables may, however, help assess the market value of receivables, as well as the firm's credit policies and revenue recognition method.

GAAP. The exception to this rule is the accounting for investments in securities (see Chapter 13).[39]

Finally, the assets and liabilities of foreign affiliates or those denominated in other currencies are reported at amounts translated from other currencies at the exchange rate prevailing on the financial statement date or a combination of this current rate and specific historical rates for certain components.[40]

The balance sheet does not report all assets and liabilities of the firm, but reflects only those meeting specific recognition criteria.[41] Some assets and liabilities meet these criteria, but are not reported because they cannot be reliably measured (see the discussion of contingencies in Chapter 1).

Some intangible assets have extremely uncertain or hard-to-measure benefits, for example, customer lists or brand names, and they are recognized only when acquired in a purchase method acquisition. Similarly, liabilities may exist as a result of legal action, but because they are not reliably measurable, only footnote disclosure may be required (see, e.g., Note 28 on commitments and contingencies in duPont's financial statements).

Thus, a balance sheet does not report the market value of a firm's assets, liabilities, or equity, although the information provided can be useful when estimating the market value of the firm or its securities.

Uses of the Balance Sheet

The reported balance sheet is one starting point for the analysis of a firm. It provides information about a firm's resources (assets) and obligations (liabilities), including liquidity and solvency. For creditors, the balance sheet provides information about the nature of assets that the firm uses as debt collateral.

The balance sheet also reports on a firm's earnings-generating ability in two ways. Assets are defined as economic resources that are expected to provide future benefits. Consistent with the long-run "going concern" perspective of the firm, these future benefits are not only cash flows but also the ability to generate earnings.

Receivables are forecasts of cash collections. Fixed assets and inventory, on the other hand, are assets that generate future sales. Increases and decreases in such assets assist forecasts of the firm's sales and profitability.

Second, proper evaluation of a firm's profitability must consider the amount of resources, that is, the level of investment, required for a specified level of sales or profitability. The balance sheet provides such data and (together with the income

---

[39]Companies also record acquired assets and liabilities at fair market value when the purchase method is used. See Chapter 14 for a comparison of purchase and pooling methods.

[40]See Chapter 15 for a detailed discussion.

[41]SFAC 5, Recognition and Measurement in Financial Statements of Business Enterprises (FASB 1984), requires financial statement recognition when four basic criteria are met:

Definition. The item qualifies as an element (e.g., asset or liability) of financial statements.

Measurability. It can be reliably measured.

Relevance. The information provided by the item can make a difference in user decisions.

Reliability. The information is representationally faithful, verifiable, and neutral.

Recognition is subject to cost/benefit and materiality constraints.

statement) can be used to measure the efficiency of a firm's operations and its return on investment.

The balance sheet can also generate forecasts about a firm's future cash flow needs. The asset levels needed to generate certain operating levels as well as the age of the firm's assets are useful inputs in assessing when a firm may have to replace its assets.

Finally, the reported balance sheet is the starting point for the preparation of an adjusted balance sheet and book value using current cost data.[42] In Chapter 17, we prepare such a balance sheet for duPont, using adjustments discussed in many chapters along the way.

Limitations of the Balance Sheet. The usefulness of the balance sheet is limited by the following factors:

1. *Selective reporting.* Important assets and liabilities may be omitted from the balance sheet because GAAP does not require their inclusion. One example is operating leases and other off-balance-sheet financing techniques (see Chapter 11). Some included assets may have no real value (see the discussion of goodwill in Chapter 14).

2. *Measurement.* Some assets and liabilities are carried at historical cost, others at market value. Historical costs may bear little relationship to their real market value. Inventories (Chapter 6) and long-lived assets (Chapter 7) are good examples.

3. *Delayed recognition.* GAAP permits companies to delay recognition of value changes. An important example is employee benefit plans, discussed in Chapter 12.

Fortunately, footnote and supplementary data are often used by analysts to adjust reported balance sheets and thereby improve their usefulness. Starting with Chapter 6, we discuss the adjustments that can be made to prepare a current cost balance sheet that provides a better measure of a firm's resources and obligations. In Chapter 17, as already stated, we prepare a current cost balance sheet for duPont.

THE STATEMENT OF STOCKHOLDERS' EQUITY

This statement reports components of stockholders' equity or the investment of the owners in the firm, the earnings reinvested in the business, and various accounting adjustments that reflect selected market value changes in noncurrent assets, any minimum pension liability, and the effect of exchange rate changes on certain foreign subsidiaries.

Format, Classification, and Use

U.S. firms generally report components of stockholders' equity in order of preference upon liquidation. For each class of shares, firms report the number of shares authorized, issued, and outstanding at each balance sheet date.

---

[42]See Chapter 17 for additional discussion.

Preferred (preference) stock has priority for liquidation and dividends. Common characteristics and related disclosure requirements include but are not limited to:

- Cumulative rights to dividends that may be:
  1. Fixed.
  2. Floating rate.
  3. Tied to amounts declared for common stock.
- Callable by issuer; call price must be disclosed.
- Convertible into common stock; specified prices must be disclosed.

These features must be evaluated to determine the treatment of different classes of preferred stock in the analysis of leverage, capital structure, and earnings per share.

Redeemable preferred stock is redeemable by the holder or according to a fixed time schedule. Such issues must be excluded from stockholders' equity, and reported after liabilities but before the equity section of the balance sheet.[43] The liquidation preference or redemption price should be used in the computation of book value per share, leverage, and capital ratios.

Common stock represents the owners' residual interest in the firm after all other claims have been met. Firms may issue one or more classes of common stock. The balance sheet or related footnotes generally disclose the various rights (such as voting rights and dividends) of the different classes of common stock. The par (or stated) value of common stock is normally reported separately from any additional paid in capital. The latter represents the cumulative difference between the par value of common and the amount received when issued.[44]

Firms often purchase their own common stock on the open market when management thinks it is undervalued, for reissue, or to prevent hostile takeovers. Treasury stock is reported as a contra account within stockholders' equity. Although such repurchases are largely a U.S. phenomenon, this practice has started to spread to other countries.

The Statement of Stockholders' Equity also reconciles the beginning and ending balance of retained earnings reinvested in the firm. This reconciliation reports the net income for the period, preferred and common dividends declared during the year, and any adjustments for stock splits, stock dividends, and acquisitions or quasireorganizations.

The statement may also report:

- A minimum liability recognized for underfunded pension plans (see Chapter 12)
- Market value changes in noncurrent investments (see Chapter 13)
- Cumulative effect of exchange rate changes (Chapter 15)
- Unearned shares issued to employee stock ownership plans (ESOPs)

---

[43]Rule 5-02(28) of Regulation S-X requires the exclusion of mandatorily redeemable preferred stock from the equity section of the financial statements. Preferred stocks that are not redeemable or are redeemable only at the option of the holder and common stock should be included in the equity section. Staff Accounting Bulletin 64 details the accounting treatment of redeemable preferred.

[44]Some companies report the difference between the purchase price of treasury stock and the price at subsequent reissuance of that treasury stock as a component of additional paid-in capital. Other firms reflect this difference as an adjustment to retained earnings.

The valuation allowance for changes in the carrying amount of investment securities and the cumulative translation adjustment are examples of reserves permitted by U.S. GAAP. For many foreign companies, the statement of stockholders' equity includes reserve accounts that are required or discretionary under financial reporting standards or tax rules. Some foreign firms appropriate some percentage of earnings to preserve liquidity by limiting earnings available for dividends. The use of conservative accounting rules can achieve the same goal.

Some foreign countries permit firms to account for selected transactions as direct charges to the additional paid in capital account. These include debt and equity issue and repurchase costs (including premiums and discounts on debt) and organization costs. Finally, some countries allow the revaluation of assets with the resulting gain or loss reported in a revaluation reserve. U.K. GAAP (SSAP 6) requires a statement or a separate footnote on changes in reserves.

The growth of international capital markets has increased the transparency of reserves reported by foreign multinationals. Examples are provided and analyzed in various chapters in the text.

Example: DuPont. The Consolidated Statement of Stockholders' Equity for duPont is included in Appendix A. The statement reports the:

1. Number of shares authorized and issued for two series of no par, cumulative, callable preferred shares, as well as dividends and call prices.

2. Par value and number of common shares authorized and outstanding as of year-end.

3. Related additional paid-in capital and common shares issued in connection with compensation plans. Notes 22 and 23 provide additional data on common and additional paid-in capital.

4. Change in reinvested earnings, including net income, and preferred and common dividends declared.

SUMMARY

This chapter introduces the balance sheet, income statement, and the accrual concept that links them together. Financial statements are interrelated and good financial analysis requires the use of all available information. Our introduction, therefore, is incomplete.

The next chapter discusses the use of the cash flow statement and cash flow data in the assessment of the firm. It begins with the cash flow statement and the information it contains, and then develops the relationship between cash flow and income. The next chapter concludes our introduction to a firm's financial statements, the "raw materials of analysis."

CASE 2-1

Thousand Trails, Inc. I

REVENUE AND EXPENSE RECOGNITION

Thousand Trails owned and operated private membership resort campgrounds (preserves) in the United States and Canada. Membership allowed a member's family an unlimited number of visits to any of the company's campgrounds for an initial membership fee and annual dues. Memberships could be used over the lifetime of the member and passed on to heirs (transfer limited to one generation). The company was not contractually obligated to provide additional campgrounds or additional facilities at existing sites. The company, however, did promise (and planned) to develop and operate additional sites.

In addition to membership sales, the company earned income from (1) interest on installment receivables generated by membership sales and (2) annual dues paid by existing members. Membership sales, however, were by far the primary source (approximately two-thirds) of Thousand Trails' income.

Thousand Trails' net income (see income statement, Exhibit 2C-1) increased almost fourfold

EXHIBIT 2C-1. THOUSAND TRAILS, INC. AND SUBSIDIARIES
Consolidated Statements of Earnings

Year ended December 31	1983	1982	1981
Membership sales	$79,971,000	$56,454,000	$40,006,000
Costs attributable to membership sales			
Marketing expenses	35,209,000	24,892,000	19,831,000
Preserve land and improvement costs	13,047,000	8,389,000	5,753,000
General and administrative expenses	11,827,000	8,612,000	7,141,000
Provision for doubtful accounts	3,977,000	2,241,000	1,866,000
	64,060,000	44,134,000	34,591,000
Income from membership sales	15,911,000	12,320,000	5,415,000
Preserve operations			
Membership dues	7,355,000	4,982,000	3,304,000
Trading post and other sales	2,749,000	2,015,000	1,482,000
	10,104,000	6,997,000	4,786,000
Less			
Cost of trading post sales	2,400,000	1,839,000	1,346,000
Maintenance and operations expense	5,709,000	3,860,000	2,560,000
General and administrative expenses	1,506,000	973,000	711,000
	9,615,000	6,672,000	4,617,000
Income from preserve operations	489,000	325,000	169,000
Other income (expense)			
Interest income	10,147,000	6,622,000	4,153,000
Interest expense	(3,957,000)	(4,203,000)	(3,213,000)
Other	42,000	35,000	(147,000)
	6,232,000	2,454,000	793,000
Earnings before deferred income taxes	22,632,000	15,099,000	6,377,000
Deferred income taxes	10,628,000	7,338,000	3,050,000
Net earnings	$12,004,000	$ 7,761,000	$ 3,327,000
Net earnings per share			
Primary	$1.85	$1.45	$0.71
Fully diluted	$1.81	$1.34	$0.68

Source: Thousand Trails, Inc., *1983 Annual Report.*

(from $3.3 million to $12 million) in the period 1981 to 1983. Most of the increase was attributable to the high growth rate of membership sales, which increased by 40% in each of the years 1982 and 1983. Income from membership sales increased almost three times over the same period.

REVENUE RECOGNITION BY THOUSAND TRAILS

Thousand Trails' revenue recognition footnote stated:

> The Company sells memberships for cash or on installment contracts. Revenues are recorded in full upon execution of membership agreements. Installment sales require a down payment of at least 10% of the sales price. All marketing costs and an allowance for estimated contract collection losses (based on historical loss occurrence rates) are recorded currently.

The footnote indicated that revenue was recognized in full for both cash and installment sales as long as a down payment of 10% was received. Other footnotes indicated that installment sales had terms of 24 to 84 months, with an average term of 61 months.

EXPENSE RECOGNITION BY THOUSAND TRAILS

Thousand Trails incurred two types of expenditures in generating sales of memberships: (1) marketing costs and (2) preserve development costs. Marketing costs were charged to expense as incurred. Preserve development costs were treated as stated in the revenue recognition footnote:

> Operating preserve land and improvement costs, including the estimated costs to complete preserves in accordance with the Company's development plans, are aggregated by geographical region and recorded as a cost of membership sales based upon the ratio of actual memberships sold within each region to the total memberships planned by the Company to be available for sale within the region.

For expense recognition, Thousand Trails used a percentage-of-completion method and allocated (actual and planned) costs to expenses based on the ratio of actual to planned sales. The company stated that

> as of December 31, 1983, the Company had 51,000 members which represented approximately one-third of the total planned memberships for sale on its 36 operating preserves.

Required:

Discuss the impact of Thousand Trails' revenue and expense recognition methods on current and future income. Your answer should address the following issues:

1. Did Thousand Trails' method of revenue recognition meet the required criteria; that is,
   - Had Thousand Trails provided all or substantially all the required services to its customers?
   - Was cash collectibility reasonably assured?
2. Were the reported amounts of expense (and income) reliable and/or consistent with the revenue recognition criteria used by the company?
3. How well did Thousand Trails' revenue and expense recognition methods "forecast" future cash flows? Were reported growth rates sustainable? What problems might the company face in the future?
4. Thousand Trails had three sources of revenues: membership sales, preserve operations, and interest income. At present, the most prominent was membership sales. Looking to the future, which source(s) may be most relevant? What does that tell you about the company's future prospects? How can the present information be used in assessing future prospects?
5. What impact do Thousand Trails' revenue and expense recognition methods have on the amounts reported on the balance sheet?

Chapter 2

Problems

1. [Revenue recognition criteria] Describe the conditions under which revenue would be recognized:

(i) At the time of production, but prior to sale

(ii) At the time of sale, but prior to cash collection

(iii) Only when cash collection has occurred

2. [Revenue recognition criteria; 1989 CFA adapted] In October 1997, the Terry Company ships a new product to retailers.

A. Discuss how each of the following conditions would affect the timing of revenue recognition as reflected in its financial statements for the year ended December 31, 1997.

(i) Retailers are not required to pay for the product until January 31, 1998.

(ii) Retailers have an unlimited right to return an unsold product. As the product is new, the company cannot reliably estimate the return rate.

B. Discuss which balance sheet accounts would be misstated if the Terry Company accelerates revenue recognition contrary to the economic substance of the transaction implied by conditions A(i) and A(ii).

3. [Earning volatility—percentage-of-completion versus completed contract; 1992 CFA adapted]

A. Compare the volatility of reported earnings over the life of a contract between the completed contract and percentage-of-completion accounting methods.

B. Discuss the difference in volatility when a firm has many contracts.

C. Discuss how the volatility discussed in parts A and B impacts the usefulness of the information provided by the statement of cash flows.

4. [Percentage-of-completion versus completed contract method] Compare the effect during the contract period of the completed contract and percentage-of-completion methods of accounting on the level and trend of reported:

(i) Revenues and cost of goods sold

(ii) Earnings

(iii) Operating cash flows

(iv) Accounts receivable, total current assets, and total long-term assets

5. [Balance sheet effects of revenue recognition methods] Exhibit 2P-1 presents the current assets and liabilities accounts of the Morrison Knudsen Corporation, a construction company.

A. What is the nature of the two accounts listed below?

• Costs and earnings in excess of billings on uncompleted contracts: current asset

• Billings in excess of costs and earnings on uncompleted contracts: current liability

EXHIBIT 2P-1. MORRISON KNUDSEN CORPORATION
Balance Sheet

	1993	1992
Current Assets		
Cash and cash equivalents	$ 91,879	$134,011
Short-term investments, at cost that approximates market	—	43,681
Accounts receivable including retentions of $62,800 and $44,871	231,021	160,196
Refundable federal income taxes	21,096	18,365
Inventories	133,350	78,856
Costs and earnings in excess of billings on uncompleted contracts	185,221	127,254
Investments in construction joint ventures	83,116	68,904
Deferred income taxes	23,019	36,135
Other	22,519	14,010
Total current assets	$793,221	$681,412
Current Liabilities		
Short-term and current portion of long-term debt	$ 37,238	$ 5,757
Accounts payable including retentions of $45,951 and $44,806	293,746	209,418
Accrued salaries, wages and benefit plan liabilities	46,507	49,649
Other accrued expenses	53,372	55,483
Billings in excess of costs and earnings on uncompleted contracts	104,460	58,966
Advances from customers	147,788	223,501
Dividends payable	6,423	5,956
Total current liabilities	$689,534	$608,730

Source: Morrison Knudsen, *1993 Annual Report.*

B. To what other accounts on the company's balance sheet are these accounts similar?

C. What method does the company use to account for its long-term construction projects?

6. [Percentage-of-completion] On April 1, 19X6, Pine Construction enters into a fixed price contract to construct an apartment building for $6 million. Pine uses the percentage-of-completion method. Information related to the contract follows:

	December 31, 19X6	December 31, 19X7
Percentage-of-completion	20%	60%
Estimated total construction cost	$4,500,000	$4,800,000
Income recognized to date	$ 300,000	$ 720,000

A. Calculate the following for both 19X6 and 19X7:

(i) Revenue recognized

(ii) Costs incurred

B. Assume that during 19X7, Pine purchases and pays for $0.3 million of products and services that will be used in construction during 19X8. What is the impact of these expenditures on Pine's revenue recognition for 19X7?

7. [Percentage-of-completion; 1996 CFA adapted] Sousa Corporation uses the percentage-of-completion method to recognize revenue. In 1994, Sousa agreed to construct a facility at a total contract price of $27 million and a total expected cost of $24 million. Actual costs and cash inflow information are presented below (in $ millions):

	1994	1995	1996
Costs incurred			
Current year	$ 4.7	$ 9.4	$ 9.9
Cumulative	4.7	14.1	24.0
Estimated remaining costs to complete (as of December 31)	19.3	9.9	0.0
Cash received during the year	6.8	10.0	10.2

A. Determine Sousa's income from the contract for each year 1994 to 1996.

B. Assume that in 1995 actual costs incurred are $10.0 million and expected costs for 1996 are revised upward to $10.3 million. If the contract price of $27 million is not adjusted, what will Sousa report as income in 1995 and 1996?

8. [Percentage-of-completion and completed contract; 1988 CFA adapted] James Construction enters into a contract in 19X5 to build a tunnel at a cost of $11 million. The company estimates that the total cost of the project will be $10 million and it will take three years to complete. Actual costs incurred and billings are as follows:

Year	Costs Incurred	Billings
19X5	$ 2.5 million	$ 2.0 million
19X6	4.0	3.5
19X7	3.5	5.5
Totals	$10.0 million	$11.0 million

A. Calculate James Construction's reported sales, operating profit, and operating cash flows for each year using the percentage-of-completion method of accounting.

B. Calculate James' reported sales, operating profit, and operating cash flows for each year using the completed contract method of accounting.

C. Assume that, just prior to the end of 19X6, the estimated cost to complete the tunnel increases to $11 million, with that additional $1 million of cost to be incurred in 19X7. Under that assumption, calculate 19X6 sales and operating profit for the project assuming use of the percentage-of-completion method.

D. Using your answers to parts A through C, discuss the advantages and disadvantages of the two accounting methods from the point of view of a financial analyst.

9. [Revenue recognition methods, income and cash flow effects] The Able, Baker, Charlie, and David companies are identical in every respect except for their revenue recognition methods:

(i) Able recognizes sales when an order is received.

(ii) Baker recognizes sales at the time of production.

(iii) Charlie recognizes sales at the time of shipment.

(iv) David recognizes sales when cash is collected.

After the first year of operations, Charlie's closing inventory was $30,000 and accounts receivable was $50,000. Backorders, for which production had not yet started, were $10,000. Charlie recognized sales of $100,000 for the year.

A. Assuming that each company charges a markup of 100% over cost, complete the following table:

	Able	Baker	Charlie	David
Sales	————	————	$100,000	————
Cost of goods sold	————	————	————	————
Net income	————	————	————	————

B. Ignoring income taxes, which company will have the largest cash balance at year-end?

C. Which company will report the largest cash from operations?

10. [Effect of revenue recognition methods on bonus] The Kwai Co. has obtained a contract to build a bridge over the Celluloid River. The bridge will take three years to construct and will require of Kwai cash outflows of $1.0 million, $0.5 million, and $0.5 million in years 1, 2, and 3, respectively. Kwai will receive the $3 million contract price in three equal installments of $1 million. As manager of this project, you have three revenue recognition choices:

    (i) Completed contract

    (ii) Percentage-of-completion

    (iii) Installment basis

A. Assume that your objective is to maximize the present value (the discount rate is 12%) of your bonus. Bonus payments are made at the end of each year. Which accounting method would you choose if the bonus were based on:

    (i) 10% of annual income

    (ii) 10% of annual revenue

    (iii) 10% of cash flows from operations

For each case, explain your reasoning.

B. Assume that bonuses are calculated on an annual basis but paid only when the bridge is completed. Explain how your answers to part A would change.

Note: This problem (parts A and B) can be solved without calculations. The answer can be deduced with some thought and by inspection of the data.

11. [Revenue and expense recognition: Pricing season tickets—The Toronto Raptors, courtesy of Professor I. Krinsky] The Toronto Raptors, a 1995 NBA expansion team, announced an elaborate season-ticket plan with a ticket price and vantage point to satisfy almost every need. Ticket prices range from $85 per game for 45 games—*plus a one-time license fee of $8,750*—for the best seats, to $10 per game—*plus a one-time license fee of $750*—for the cheapest seats; the team has eight ticket prices.

    The license fee, used for the first time by a sports team in Canada, entitles the holder to a de facto lease on the seat. The license holder retains the right to buy the accompanying ticket and may sell that right to anyone at a mutually agreed on price.

A. Discuss how the Toronto Raptors should recognize revenue from ticket sales and the license fee under this system.

B. Discuss how a corporation that purchases Toronto Raptors tickets and gives them to its customers should recognize the license fee.

C. As an analyst, how would you incorporate

- The licensing fee
- Season-ticket sales

in your estimation of the Toronto Raptors' expected earnings?

12. [Change from completed contracted to percentage-of-completion] Exhibit 2-2 in the text presents three years of income statements for Newcor, Inc., as originally reported (completed contract basis) and restated (percentage-of-completion basis).

A. On the completed contract basis, Newcor shows an increase in revenues of 24% from 1990 to 1991. On the percentage-of-completion basis, it shows a decrease of 3%. Explain this difference.

B. Newcor's total revenues recognized over the period 1989 to 1991 are greater under the completed contract basis, although the percentage-of-completion method generally recognizes revenues sooner. Explain why.

C. Discuss the trend in Newcor's gross profit margin (sales less cost of sales) over the period 1989 to 1991. Explain why the change in accounting method affected that trend. Which accounting method provides an earlier indication of changes in firm profitability?

D. Discuss the effects of the change in accounting method on Newcor's balance sheet. Your answer should focus on the inventory, accounts receivable, and advances from customer accounts.

13. [Effects of nonrecurring events, courtesy of Professor M. Schiff] Monsanto's *1994 Annual Report* stated that the Chairman and CEO, Richard J. Mahoney, would retire on March 31, 1995. Mahoney's cash compensation for 1994 consisted of:

Salary	$ 950,000
Annual incentive award (based primarily on achieving or exceeding a net income goal)	1,680,000
Total cash compensation	$2,630,000

In addition, Mahoney participated in a long-term compensation plan that granted annual stock option awards if the return on stockholders' equity (ROE) exceeded 20%. Monsanto's reported ROE was

$$\text{Net Income} = \$\ 622 \text{ million}$$
$$\text{Opening Stockholders' Equity} = 2,855 \text{ million}$$
$$\text{Closing Stockholders' Equity} = 2,948 \text{ million}$$

$$\text{ROE} = \frac{\text{Net Income}}{\text{Average Stockholders' Equity}} = \frac{622}{2,902} = 21.4\%$$

EXHIBIT 2P-2. MONSANTO
Excerpts from *1994 Annual Report* ($ in millions)

	1994	1993	1992
Net income (loss)	$622	$494	($88)
ROE	21.4%	16.9%	(2.6%)

Note: Restructurings and Other Actions

In December 1994, the board of directors approved a plan to eliminate redundant staff activities across the company and consolidate certain staff and administrative business functions. The plan will result in reductions in worldwide employment levels of approximately 500 people. In addition, the company will close or exit certain facilities and programs. These workforce reductions and closures will be substantially completed by the end of 1995. The pretax expense related to these actions was $89 million ($55 million after tax).

In September 1994, Monsanto received $67 million from the U.S. Internal Revenue Service in settlement of certain tax matters related to the 1985 acquisition of Searle. This settlement included interest of $33 million ($21 million after tax), recorded as a one-time gain. Most of the remainder of the proceeds reduced the balance of unamortized goodwill related to the Searle acquisition. . . .

. . . Restructuring expenses are recorded based on estimates prepared at the time the restructuring actions are approved by the board of directors. In the fourth quarter of 1994, the board approved the reversal of $49 million of pretax excess restructuring reserves from prior years. The excess was primarily due to higher than expected proceeds and lower exit costs from the sale and shutdown of nonstrategic businesses and facilities included in the 1993 and 1992 restructuring actions. The balance in restructuring reserves as of Dec. 31, 1994, was $254 million, and consisted primarily of workforce reduction costs under the 1994 actions and planned facility dismantling and site closure costs remaining under previous restructurings. Management believes that the balance of these reserves as of Dec. 31, 1994, is adequate for completion of those activities. . . .

Source: Monsanto, *1994 Annual Report.*

Given the reported ROE of 21.4%, Mahoney was granted options for 275,000 shares at $77.75 per share, the market price on the grant date. At the end of November 1995, the market price of Monsanto shares was $120 per share. If exercised and sold, the options would have gained about $11,600,000 ($42.25 × 275,000).

A. Using the information presented and Exhibit 2P-2, discuss whether Mahoney's stock options were deserved. Provide at least one argument for and one argument against the option award.

B. Discuss whether the nonrecurring events disclosed in Exhibit 2P-2 should be included in management performance measures such as ROE.

C. Using the information presented and Exhibit 2P-2, discuss the expected level of Monsanto's future income and ROE.

14. [Recurring and nonrecurring income, courtesy of Professor M. Schiff] Many analysts focus on recurring income and ignore nonrecurring charges. Exhibit 2P-3, adapted from AT&T's *1995 Annual Report*, reports sales and operating income (earnings before interest and taxes) for the 11-year period 1985 to 1995. The exhibit also provides information about the company's restructuring charges and other write-downs.

EXHIBIT 2P-3. AT&T
Revenues and Operating Income, 1985 to 1995, ($ in millions)

	1995*	1994	1993†	1992	1991‡	1990	1989	1988§	1987	1986**	1985
					Results of Operations						
Total revenues	**$79,609**	$75,094	$69,351	$66,647	$64,455	$63,228	$61,604	$62,067	$60,726	$61,975	$63,159
Operating income (loss)	**1,215**	7,949	6,498	6,529	1,428	5,358	4,751	(2,500)	4,071	974	3,561

*1995 Data reflect $7.8 billion of pretax business restructuring and other charges.
†1993 Data reflect $0.5 billion of pretax business restructuring and other charges.
‡1991 Data reflect $4.5 billion of pretax business restructuring and other charges.
§1988 Data reflect a $6.7 billion pretax charge due to accelerated digitization of the long-distance network.
**1986 Data reflect $3.2 billion of pretax charges for business restructuring, and accounting change and other items.
   Source: Adapted from AT&T's *1995 Annual Report.*

A. Compute AT&T's operating income before nonrecurring charges.

B. Compare the trend in AT&T's reported operating income with the trends of sales and adjusted income computed in part A. (Graphical analysis may be useful.)

C. Discuss which set of operating income data is most relevant in analyzing AT&T. State any other adjustments or data needed.

D. In 1995, AT&T adopted SFAS 121, Accounting for Impairment of Long-Lived Assets and for Long-Lived Assets to Be Disposed of. In its footnotes, AT&T states:

> Effective October 1, 1995, we adopted Statement of Financial Accounting Standards (SFAS) No. 121, "Accounting for Impairment of Long-Lived Assets and for Long-Lived Assets to Be Disposed of." This standard requires that long-lived assets and certain identifiable intangibles held and used by an entity be reviewed for impairment whenever events or changes in circumstances indicate that the carrying amount of an asset may not be recoverable. *The adoption of this standard did not materially affect our reported earnings, financial condition or cash flows because this was essentially the same method we used in the past to measure and record asset impairments.* Our 1995 restructuring and other charges included recognition of asset impairments. (emphasis added)

Do you agree with the italicized statement? What does the statement mean?

3

ANALYSIS OF CASH FLOWS

CHAPTER OUTLINE

CHAPTER OBJECTIVES

STATEMENT OF CASH FLOWS
Direct and Indirect Method Cash Flow
Statements
The Preparation of a Statement of Cash Flows
Transactional Analysis
Preparation of a Direct Method Statement of
Cash Flows
Cash Flows from Operations
Investing Cash Flow
Financing Cash Flow
The Indirect Method
Reported Versus Operating Changes in Assets
and Liabilities
Acquisitions and Divestitures
Translation of Foreign Subsidiaries
Effect of Exchange Rate Changes on Cash

EXAMPLE: DUPONT

ANALYSIS OF CASH FLOW INFORMATION
Free Cash Flows and Valuation
Relationship of Income and Cash Flows
Income, Cash Flow, and the Going Concern
Assumption
Income, Cash Flow, and the Choice of
Accounting Policies
Income, Cash Flow, and Liquidity
Analysis of Cash Flow Trends
Cash Flow Classification Issues
Classification of Cash Flows for Property,
Plant, and Equipment
Effect of Differences in Accounting Methods
Interest and Dividends Received
Interest Paid
Noncash Transactions

CASH FLOW STATEMENTS: AN
INTERNATIONAL PERSPECTIVE

SUMMARY

CASE 3-1: THOUSAND TRAILS, INC. II

CHAPTER OBJECTIVES

Chapter 1 introduced the reader to the financial reporting process and Chapter 2 presented a detailed review of the accrual process, its role, and its impact on a firm's income statement and balance sheet. This chapter focuses on the statement of cash flows (SoCF) that recasts the financial statement data provided by the accrual process. It discusses the use and analysis of the information provided by the SoCF on its own and in conjunction with other financial statement data.

This chapter will enable readers to:

1. Understand the process by which cash flow statements are generated.

2. Recast an indirect statement of cash flows to a direct basis or to any format desired.

3. Understand how classification rules and accounting policies can affect the components of the cash flow statement.

4. Use the cash flow statement to examine a firm's liquidity position and the basic assumptions inherent in the accrual process.

5. Understand how cash flow statements can be used to derive information about a firm's acquisitions and how such activities can distort reported operating cash flows.

6. Analyze trends in cash flow components.

Continuing with the approach utilized in the previous chapter, we use duPont's financial statements to illustrate many of the points raised in the chapter.

STATEMENT OF CASH FLOWS

Cash flow data supplement the information provided by the income statement as both link consecutive balance sheets. The statement of cash flows is intended to report all the cash inflows and outflows (classified among operating, investing, and financing activities) of the firm for a specified period. It also provides disclosures about that period's noncash investing and financing activities.

The classification of cash flows among operating, financing, and investing activities is essential to the analysis of cash flow data. Net cash flow (the change in cash and equivalents during the period) has little informational content by itself; it is the classification and individual components that are informative.

Cash flow from operating activities (cash from operations or CFO) measures the amount of cash generated or used by the firm as a result of its production and sales of goods and services. Although deficits or negative cash flows from operations are expected in some circumstances (e.g., rapid growth), for most firms positive operating cash flows are essential for long-run survival. Internally generated funds can be used to pay dividends or repurchase equity, repay loans, replace existing capacity, or invest in acquisitions and growth.

Investing cash flow (CFI) reports the amount of cash used to acquire assets such as plant and equipment as well as investments and entire businesses. These outlays are necessary to maintain a firm's current operating capacity and to provide capacity for future growth. CFI also includes cash received from the sale or disposal of assets or segments of the business.

Financing cash flow (CFF) includes cash flows related to the firm's capital structure (debt and equity), including proceeds from the issuance of equity, returns to shareholders in the form of dividends and repurchase of equity, and the incurrence and repayment of debt.

Direct and Indirect Method Cash Flow Statements

SFAS 95, Statement of Cash Flows (1987), permits firms to report cash from operations either *directly,* using major categories of gross cash receipts and payments, or *indirectly* by providing a reconciliation from accrual-based net income to CFO.

Exhibit 3-1 contrasts the direct and indirect cash flow statements of the WSF Company. These statements are generated from the company's balance sheet (Exhibit 3-2) and income statement (Exhibit 3-3).

EXHIBIT 3-1. THE WSF COMPANY
Statement of Cash Flows for Year Ended December 31, 1997

A. Direct Method

Cash collections		$ 2,675,000
Less: Cash inputs	$(1,750,000)	
Cash expenses (rent, operating)	(430,000)	
Cash interest	(125,000)	(2,305,000)
Cash flow from operations		**$370,000**
Capital expenditures	(500,000)	
Investment in affiliate	(710,000)	
Cash flow from investments		**(1,210,000)**
Short-term borrowing	500,000	
Dividends paid	(35,000)	
Cash flow from financing		**465,000**
Net cash flow		**$ (375,000)**
Cash balance, as of December 31		
1997	$ 3,625,000	
1996	4,000,000	
Net change		**$ (375,000)**

B. Indirect Method

Net income		78,870
Add: Noncash expenses		
Depreciation expense		175,000
		$ 253,870
Changes in operating accounts		
(Increase) in receivables	(224,500)	
Decrease in inventories	425,000	
(Decrease) in accounts payable	(475,000)	
Increase in accrued liabilities	50,000	
Increase in interest payable	125,000	
Increase in taxes payable	40,630	
Increase in advances from customers	175,000	116,130
Cash flows from operations		**$ 370,000**

Note: Cash flow from investing and financing identical to that shown on direct method. The firm would also provide a separate footnote on cash payments for interest and taxes. The WSF Company paid $125,000 in interest, but it made no tax payments during the year ended December 31, 1997.

Under the indirect method, CFO is computed by adjusting net income for all:

1. Noncash revenues and expenses

2. Nonoperating items included in net income

3. Noncash changes in operating assets and liabilities

Enterprises using the direct method must also provide such a reconciliation. Firms using both methods must disclose the cash outflows for income taxes and interest within the statement or elsewhere in the financial statements (e.g., in the footnotes).[1]

[1] Required by para. 29 of SFAS 95.

EXHIBIT 3-2. THE WSF COMPANY
Balance Sheets at December 31, 1996 and 1997

	1996	1997
Assets		
Cash	$4,000,000	$3,625,000
Accounts receivable	0	224,500
Inventory	850,000	425,000
Current assets	$4,850,000	$4,274,500
Investment in affiliates	0	710,000
Buildings	3,500,000	4,000,000
Less: Accumulated depreciation	0	(175,000)
Long-term assets	$3,500,000	$4,535,000
Total assets	$8,350,000	$8,809,500
Liabilities		
Short-term debt	$0	$500,000
Advances from customers	0	175,000
Accounts payable	850,000	375,000
Accrued liabilities	0	50,000
Interest payable	0	125,000
Taxes payable	0	40,630
Dividends payable	0	35,000
Current liabilities	$ 850,000	$1,300,630
Bonds payable	2,500,000	2,500,000
Total liabilities	$3,350,000	$3,800,630
Common stock	1,000,000	1,000,000
Additional paid-in capital	4,000,000	4,000,000
Retained earnings	0	8,870
Stockholders' equity	$5,000,000	$5,008,870
Total liabilities and equities	$8,350,000	$8,809,500

Cash flow statements prepared using the indirect method have a significant drawback. Because of the *indirect format, it is not possible to compare operating cash inflows and outflows by function with the revenue and expense activities that generated them, as is possible from cash flow statements prepared using the direct method.* In the absence of acquisitions, divestitures, and significant foreign operations, the indirect method simply recasts the income statement and the balance sheet, providing little new information on or insight into a firm's cash-generating ability. As a majority of firms prepare the SoCF using the indirect method,[2] it is often necessary to convert an indirect statement into a direct one.

[2]Of the 600 firms surveyed by the AICPA in the 1994 *Accounting Trends and Techniques,* only 14 report using the direct method.

EXHIBIT 3-3. THE WSF COMPANY
Income Statement for Year Ended December 31, 1997

Net sales		$ 2,724,500
Less: Cost of goods sold		(1,700,000)
Gross margin		$ 1,024,500
Less: Operating expense	$360,000	
Depreciation expense	175,000	
Rent expense	120,000	
Interest expense	250,000	(905,000)
Income before taxes		119,500
Tax expense		(40,630)
Net income		$ 78,870

Statement of Retained Earnings

Beginning balance, January 1, 1997	$	0
Net income		78,870
Dividends declared		(70,000)
Ending balance, December 31, 1997	$	8,870

The Preparation of a Statement of Cash Flows

The cash flow statement combines cash flows for events that are reported on the balance sheet (e.g., purchases of assets) and the income statement (e.g., the sale of goods). The process is complicated by differences between the time cash flows occur and when they are recognized as revenues, expenses, assets, or liabilities. The next section discusses methods used to prepare direct and indirect method cash flow statements.

Transactional Analysis

Transactional analysis[3] is a technique that can be used to create a cash flow statement for firms that do not prepare such statements in accordance with SFAS 95 and IAS 7.[4] It can also be used to convert indirect method cash flow from operations to the direct method.

One objective of transactional analysis is to understand the relationship between the accrual of revenues, expenses, assets, and liabilities and their cash flow consequences. Another goal is to classify cash flows among operating, financing, and investing activities as required by SFAS 95.

[3] See Ashwinpaul C. Sondhi, George H. Sorter, and Gerald I. White, "Transactional Analysis," *Financial Analysts Journal,* Sept./Oct. 1987, pp. 57–64. "Cash Flow Redefined: FAS 95 and Security Analysis," *Financial Analysts Journal,* Nov./Dec. 1988, pp. 19–20 by the same authors links the transactional analysis method of preparing cash flow statements to those required by SFAS 95.

[4] The number of non-U.S. companies preparing statements of cash flows is on the increase. IAS 7, Cash Flow Statements, was issued a few years after SFAS 95; foreign firms using IAS 7 are not required to reconcile their cash flow statements to U.S. GAAP. Despite these trends, many foreign firms do not report any cash flow statement or report changes in funds (see "Cash Flow Statements: An International Perspective," near the end of this chapter).

The method reconciles line-item changes in the balance sheet with their related income statement components to derive the cash flow consequences of the reported transactions and events. These changes are grouped according to whether they are operating, investing, or financing in nature. The classification and cash flow description for a typical firm follow:

Changes Included in Cash Flow from *Operating* Activities (CFO)

Balance Sheet Account	Cash Flow Description
Accounts receivable	Cash received from customers
Inventories	Cash paid for inputs (materials)
Prepaid expenses	Cash expenses
Accounts payable	Cash paid for inputs/expenses
Advances from customers	Cash received from customers
Rent payable	Cash expenses
Interest payable	Interest paid
Income tax payable	Income taxes paid
Deferred income taxes	Income taxes paid

Changes Included in Cash Flow from *Investing* Activities (CFI)

Balance Sheet Account	Cash Flow Description
Property, plant, and equipment	Capital expenditures
	Proceeds from property sales
Investment in affiliates	Cash paid for acquisitions and investments

Changes Included in Cash Flow from *Financing* Activities (CFF)

Balance Sheet Account	Cash Flow Description
Notes payable	Increase or decrease in debt
Short-term debt	Increase or decrease in debt
Long-term debt	Increase or decrease in debt
Bonds payable	Increase or decrease in debt
Common stock	Equity financing or repurchase
Retained earnings	Dividends paid

The relationship between balance sheet changes and cash flows can be summarized as follows:

- Increases (decreases) in assets represent net cash outflows (inflows). If an asset increases, the firm must have paid cash in exchange.
- Increases (decreases) in liabilities represent net cash inflows (outflows). When a liability increases, the firm must have received cash in exchange.

While these points are simplistic (they ignore payments or receipts other than cash), they are useful in practice.

Two examples clarify the application of these points to transactional analysis:

1. When accounts receivable increase, the period's sales revenues must have exceeded cash collections. Thus, the increase in receivables must be deducted from the accrued sales revenue to derive the cash collected from customers during the period.
2. When interest payable increases, that means the firm did not pay all the interest expense accrued during the period. Hence, the increase in interest payable must be deducted from the interest expense to compute the amount of interest paid during the period.

Preparation of a Direct Method Statement of Cash Flows

Exhibit 3-4 illustrates the use of transactional analysis to prepare a direct method statement of cash flows for the WSF Company. This simplified example allows us to explain the method without the complications present in most actual financial statements.

We use the data from Exhibits 3-2 and 3-3. A brief discussion of the most critical problems in the preparation of cash flow statements is provided later.

Cash Flows from Operations

Cash Collections. The principal component of CFO is the cash collections for the period. To derive this amount, we start with WSF net sales of $2,724,500 in 1997. The increase of $224,500 in the balance of accounts receivable means that cash has not yet been collected for all the sales recognized. In addition, the firm received cash advances ($175,000) for which revenue has not yet been recognized.

We modify net sales by deducting the increase in accounts receivable and adding the increase in advances, to arrive at cash collections. This is the amount of cash actually received during the period as a result of sales activities, regardless of when the related revenues were recognized.

Cash Outflows. The next stage involves the computation of operating cash outflows incurred to generate the cash collections. The first component is the cash outflow for inputs into the manufacturing or retailing process. The decrease in inventory balances[5] (cash outflow occurred in the prior period) is subtracted from, and the decrease in accounts payable (cash outflow in the current period for goods received in a prior period) is added to the cost of goods sold to determine the cash inputs or outflow for the manufacturing process.

The remaining income statement accounts and their related balance sheet accounts are similarly modified to their cash analogs to determine the cash outflows for operating expenses, interest, and taxes. In each case, the goal is to link the income statement account with related balance sheet accounts. By related, we mean that the balance sheet account contains cash flows that either have been recognized in that income statement category (accruals and payables) or will be recognized in the future (prepayments).

---

[5]The cash outflow for inputs is not affected by the inventory valuation method used by the firm, facilitating comparison across firms.

EXHIBIT 3-4. THE WSF COMPANY
Transactional Analysis ($ 000)

	Income Statement	Balance Sheet 12/31/96	12/31/97	Change	Cash Effect	Cash	
Cash Collections							
Net sales	2,724.5				Increase	2,724.5	
Accounts receivable		—	224.5	224.5	(Decrease)	(224.5)	
Advances		—	175.0	175.0	Increase	175.0	**2,675.0**
Cash Inputs							
COGS	(1,700.0)				(Decrease)	(1,700.0)	
Inventory		850.0	425.0	(425.0)	Increase	425.0	
Accounts payable		850.0	375.0	(475.0)	(Decrease)	(475.0)	**(1,750.0)**
Cash Expenses							
Operating expense	(360.0)				(Decrease)	(360.0)	
Rent expense	(120.0)				(Decrease)	(120.0)	
Accrued liabilities		—	50.0	50.0	Increase	50.0	**(430.0)**
Cash Taxes Paid							
Tax expense	(40.63)				(Decrease)	(40.63)	
Taxes payable		0	40.63	40.63	Increase	40.63	—
Cash Interest Paid							
Interest expense	(250.0)				(Decrease)	(250.0)	
Interest payable		0	125	125	Increase	125.0	**(125.0)**
							370.0
Operating Cash Flow							
Capital Expenditures							
Depreciation	(175.0)				(Decrease)	(175.0)	
Buildings—Net		3,500	3,825	325.0	(Decrease)	(325.0)	**(500.0)**
Cash Invested in Affiliates							
Investment in affiliates		—	710.0	710.0	(Decrease)		**(710.0)**
							(1,210.0)
Investing Cash Flow							
Cash from Borrowing							
Short-term debt		—	500.0	500.0	Increase	500.0	
Bonds payable		2,500	2,500	—		—	**500.0**

EXHIBIT 3-4. (*continued*)

	Income Statement	Balance Sheet			Cash Effect	Cash	
		12/31/96	12/31/97	Change			
Equity Financing							
Common stock		1,000	1,000	—			
Additional paid-in capital		4,000	4,000	—			—
Dividends							
Net income	78.87						
Dividends declared					(Decrease)	(70.0)	
Dividends payable		—	35.0		Increase	35.0	**(35.0)**
							465.0
Financing Cash Flow							
Change in cash							**(375.0)**

In many cases, disclosures are inadequate to do this precisely. Educated guesses and approximations may be necessary. For example, we assume that accounts payable reported by WSF relate only to the purchase of inventory for operating purposes although they may also be related to other operating expenses.

A careful reading of footnote data is necessary to obtain additional information on aggregated balance sheet accounts, permitting finer breakdowns of assets and liabilities. For example, in addition to trade accounts receivable, the amounts reported on the balance sheet may include notes and loans receivable, which either belong to the miscellaneous category of operating cash flows or represent investment cash flows.

Additionally, balance sheet and income statement accounts may require reallocation of some components. For example, when depreciation expense is not reported separately in the income statement, we must reduce COGS by the amount of depreciation expense to accurately reflect cash inputs and create a "depreciation expense" account to correctly estimate cash invested in property. The depreciation expense may be disclosed separately in footnotes, or in the indirect cash flow statement.

Cash flows that are considered nonrecurring[6] or peripheral to the basic activities of the firm are combined in the miscellaneous category, which also includes the cash impact of transactions for which the financial statements and the footnotes do not provide information enabling more precise classification.

Investing Cash Flow

Capital expenditures for long-term assets such as plant and machinery are usually the primary component of investing cash flow. As depreciation changes (net) property, plant, and equipment, the calculation of capital expenditures requires the amount of

---

[6]However, the transaction should be analyzed to determine whether it is best classified as operating, investing, or financing.

depreciation, depletion, and amortization expense in addition to the changes in all related long-term asset accounts.[7]

Capital expenditures may be calculated net or gross of proceeds on the sales of these assets. The cash flows from such sales are considered investment cash flows, regardless of whether they are netted in capital expenditures. Trends in gross capital expenditures contain useful insights into management plans. Segment disclosures should be monitored for differential investment patterns.

Other components of cash flows from investing activities include cash flows from investments in joint ventures and affiliates and long-term investments in securities.[8] The cash flow consequences of acquisitions and divestitures must also be reported in this category. Footnote disclosures (when available) should be used to segregate operating assets and liabilities obtained (relinquished) in acquisitions (divestitures). This analysis, as discussed below, may be necessary to calculate CFO.

Financing Cash Flow

Components of financing cash flow include inflows from additional borrowing and equity financing, and outflows for repayment of debt, dividend payments, and equity repurchases. Debt financing for the period is the sum of the changes in short- and long-term debt accounts.

The calculation of equity financing cash flows requires analysis of the change in stockholders' equity, separating:

- Net income
- Dividends declared
- Shares issued or repurchased
- Changes in valuation accounts included in equity (each of these may require reallocation to appropriate operating or investing cash flow categories[9])

Once this is done, every change in the balance sheet has been included (net income is included by incorporating each of its components) except cash. The net cash flow must, by definition, be equal to the change in cash. This identity provides a check on computations.[10]

The last step is to summarize the cash flows from operations, financing, and investing activities. The result is a direct method statement of cash flows, as shown in Exhibit 3-1A.

---

[7]Thus, the deduction for depreciation expense is not taken because depreciation represents a cash flow; rather, because it is needed to calculate the cash capital expenditures.

[8]The nature of the relationship between parent and subsidiary or joint venture affiliate should be reviewed periodically to ensure proper classification; in some cases, affiliates may be more accurately considered part of operations. However, contractual arrangements may constrain the parent's control over or access to cash flows from affiliates. (See Chapter 13 for a detailed discussion of these issues.)

[9]For example, the change in the unrealized gains (losses) on investments account must be reflected as a component of investment cash flows (see Chapter 13).

[10]As an additional check, make sure that the income statement components used in the transactional analysis add up to net income.

The Indirect Method

Exhibit 3-1B presents the indirect method statement of cash flows for the WSF Company. The reporting of investing and financing activities is identical to the direct method. *The reporting of cash flow from operations, however, is quite different.* Under the indirect method, the starting point is the period's net income. Two types of adjustment are then made to net income to arrive at the CFO:

1. All "non-cash" expense (revenue) components of the income statement are added (subtracted).
2. Changes in operating accounts are added/subtracted as follows:

- Increases (decreases) in the balances of operating asset accounts are subtracted (added).
- Increases (decreases) in the balances of operating liability accounts are added (subtracted).

The second type of adjustment represents the same balance sheet changes that were used to arrive at cash from operations under the direct method. As these adjustments are provided by the reconciliation in the indirect cash flow method, it is possible to use them to derive a direct method cash flow statement from an indirect one.

In Box 3-1, we demonstrate this process using duPont's indirect method Statement of Cash Flows reproduced in Exhibit 3-5. As the discussion in the box indicates, careful analysis of footnote information is required to make the necessary adjustments.

Two important requirements of SFAS 95 must, however, be explained before proceeding to Box 3-1:

1. *Changes in operating accounts shown on duPont's Statement of Cash Flows do not equal the balance sheet changes.* For example, in the 1994 cash flow statement, accounts receivable *decreases by $30;* on the balance sheet (Appendix A), it *increases by $319.* What accounts for this and similar discrepancies in other operating assets and liabilities?
2. DuPont's Statement of Cash Flows contains the *effect of exchange rate changes on cash* (in addition to the three cash flow categories: operating, investing, and financing). The 1994 amount is $94 million. What does it represent?

We address both issues below.

Reported Versus Operating Changes in Assets and Liabilities

The discrepancies between the changes in accounts reported on the balance sheet and those reported in the cash flow statement are due to two factors:

- Acquisitions and divestitures
- Foreign subsidiaries

BOX 3-1
DuPont—1994
Derivation of CFO Using Direct Method ($ in millions)

EXHIBIT 3-5. E. I. DUPONT DE NEMOURS AND COMPANY AND
CONSOLIDATED SUBSIDIARIES
Consolidated Statement of Cash Flows ($ in millions)

	1994	1993	1992
Cash and cash equivalents at beginning of year	$ 1,109	$ 1,640	$ 468
Cash provided by operations			
Net income (loss)	2,727	555	(3,927)
Adjustments to reconcile net income to cash provided by operations			
Extraordinary charge from early extinguishment of debt (Note 8)	—	11	69
Transition effect of accounting changes (Notes 1, 7, and 25)	—	—	4,833
Depreciation, depletion, and amortization	2,976	2,833	2,655
Dry hole costs and impairment of unproved properties	152	201	185
Other noncash charges and credits—net	(140)	843	(174)
Decrease in operating assets			
Accounts and notes receivable	30	103	104
Inventories and other operating assets	19	664	219
Increase (decrease) in operating liabilities			
Accounts payable and other operating liabilities	(432)	686	907
Accrued interest and income taxes (Notes 4 and 7)	332	(516)	(483)
Cash provided by operations	5,664	5,380	4,388
Investment activities (Note 24)			
Purchases of property, plant, and equipment	(3,050)	(3,621)	(4,448)
Investments in affiliates	(90)	(70)	(127)
Payments for businesses acquired	(5)	(409)	—
Proceeds from sales of assets	432	1,160	179
Investments in short-term financial instruments—net	(379)	(85)	(70)
Miscellaneous—net	(41)	(53)	(87)
Cash used for investment activities	(3,133)	(3,078)	(4,553)
Financing activities			
Dividends paid to stockholders	(1,247)	(1,201)	(1,182)
Net increase (decrease) in short-term borrowings	(517)	(2,024)	2,310
Long-term and other borrowings			
Receipts	824	1,806	2,976
Payments	(2,032)	(1,392)	(2,711)
Common stock issued in connection with compensation plans	94	67	86
Cash provided by (used for) financing activities	(2,878)	(2,744)	1,479
Effect of exchange rate changes on cash	94	(89)	(142)
Cash and cash equivalents at year-end	$ 856	$ 1,109	$ 1,640
Increase (decrease) in cash and cash equivalents	$ (253)	$ (531)	$ 1,172

	1994	
Cash collections from customers		
Sales (not including excise taxes)	$ 34,042	
Change in accounts and notes receivable	30	**34,072**
Cash payments for inputs		
COGS	(21,977)	
Change in inventories and other operating assets	19	
Change in payables and operating liabilities (see discussion)	172	**(21,786)**
Cash payments for SG&A		
Selling, general and administrative	(2,888)	
Change in payables and operating liabilities (see discussion)	149	**(2,739)**
Cash for research and development		**(1,047)**
Exploration expenses including dry hole and impairment	(357)	
Less adjustment for noncash expense	152	**(205)**
Taxes other than income		
Excise taxes received	5,291	
Taxes other than income	(6,215)	
Change in taxes other than income (see discussion)	42	**(882)**
Miscellaneous		
Other income	926	
Change in payables and liabilities (see discussion)	(204)	
Other noncash charges and credits	(140)	**582**
Restructuring	142	
Change in payables and liabilities (see discussion)	(591)	**(449)**
Interest and debt expense		**(559)**
Income taxes		
Tax expense	(1,655)	
Change in accrued interest and income taxes	332	**(1,323)**
Cash from operations		**$ 5,664**

Discussion

The category "changes in accounts payable and other operating liabilities" appearing in duPont's (indirect) cash flow statement in Exhibit 3-5 is an aggregation of many categories. Details can be found in Notes 16 and 18 reproduced below. The sum of the changes in these accounts is 290 + (748) = (458). DuPont's cash flow statement shows a change of (432).

In order to obtain the direct cash flow statement, a number of assumptions and simplifications were made. First, as the difference between (458) and (432) (due to acquisitions and/or the effect of exchange rate changes) is not significant, (26), it can be safely ignored* without affecting the thrust of the analysis. Then, where possible, each of the individual categories in Notes 16 and 18 was identified with its "associated activity" (see last column).

Note 16: Accounts Payable

	1994	1993	Change	Associated Activity
Trade	$1,847	$1,675	$172	Inputs
Payables to banks	321	264	57	
Compensation awards	222	94	128	SG&A
Other	344	411	(67)	
	$2,734	$2,444	$290	

Note 18: Other Accrued Liabilities

	1994	1993	Change	Associated Activity
Payroll and other employee benefits	$ 725	$ 694	$ 31	SG&A
Taxes other than on income	422	380	42	Taxes other than income
Postretirement benefits other than pensions	333	343	(10)	SG&A
Restructuring charges	219	810	(591)	Restructuring
Miscellaneous	1,431	1,651	(220)	
	$3,130	$3,878	$(748)	

The identified items from Notes 16 and 18 are aggregated and listed below. These were used to modify their respective associated activity from the income statement to calculate the cash disbursement for that activity.

Changes in Payables and Operating Liabilities

Inputs	$ 172
SG&A	149
Taxes other than income	42
Restructuring	(591)
	$(228)

This leaves a remaining balance of (432) − (228) = (204) in the miscellaneous activity, comprised of:

Payables to banks	$ 57
Other	(67)
Miscellaneous	(220)
	(230)
Acquisition or exchange rate adjustment*	26
	$(204)

---

*Alternative approaches may be to assume that the 26 is associated with inputs or with inputs and SG&A and aggregate cash disbursement for inputs and expenses as one item.

Acquisitions and Divestitures

Changes in reported balances of operating asset and liability accounts may include the effects of both operating activities and acquisitions or divestitures. Thus, for example, the inventory account may be increased as a result of:

1. Purchase of inventory from a supplier (an operating activity)
2. Acquisition of (merger with) another firm that has inventory as a component of its balance sheet (an investing activity)

SFAS 95 requires that CFO include only operating transactions and events. Thus, for firms that acquire operating assets and liabilities, the changes reported in the statement of cash flows as adjustments to income to arrive at CFO will not match the increase or decrease reported on the balance sheet.

The difference between the changes reported in the two statements provides useful information to the analyst. If the difference for any balance sheet account represents the amount of that component acquired through a merger, *the analyst can reconstruct the assets and liabilities obtained by the firm through an acquisition.*[11] This information is generally not provided anywhere else.

It should be noted that although the reporting requirements accomplish the necessary segregation in the period of the acquisition (or divestiture), cash flows for subsequent periods may be distorted. For example, cash paid for the accounts receivable of an acquired firm is reported as an investment cash (out)flow. However, the subsequent cash collection of that receivable will be a component of operating cash flows. The result is overstated cash flows from operations as the cost of acquiring the accounts receivables was never reflected in cash outflows for operations.[12] *Acquisitions, divestitures, and continuing corporate reorganizations can therefore distort trends in both cash flows from operations and investing cash flows.* These issues are examined in greater detail in Chapter 14.

Translation of Foreign Subsidiaries

The second difference between the changes reported on the cash flow statement and those reported on the balance sheet relates to foreign operations. The assets and liabilities of foreign subsidiaries must be translated into the reporting currency (i.e., U.S. dollars) upon preparation of consolidated financial statements. This process generates a U.S. dollar balance for each asset and liability account that includes both operating changes (representing real cash flow effects) and exchange rate effects that have no current cash flow consequences.

For example, assume a firm has a foreign subsidiary that has an opening and closing accounts receivables balance of 10,000 lira. Assume further that at the beginning of the year 1 lira is worth $1.00, but at the end of the year a lira is worth $1.10. Upon consolidation, the parent's balance sheet will include

---

[11]This can be done if we assume that the confounding effect of exchange rate changes (discussed next) is not significant. Thus, ignoring that issue for the moment, one would estimate that duPont's accounts receivable increased by $349 million ($319 + $30) due to an acquisition.

[12]Similarly, cash received for accounts receivable of a divested business is reflected as an investment cash inflow, whereas the cash outflow required to generate the receivable (purchase of inventory, selling costs) was previously reported as a component of CFO.

Opening accounts receivable from foreign subsidiary (10,000 lira × opening exchange rate of 1)	$10,000
Closing accounts receivable from foreign subsidiary (10,000 lira × closing exchange rate of 1.1)	$11,000
Change	$ 1,000

This increase of $1,000 appears as part of the balance of accounts receivable on the balance sheet. However, it will not appear as a component of cash collections for the period because it is not a change resulting from operations. Thus, CFO does not include the effects of the translation process.

Effect of Exchange Rate Changes on Cash

An explanation of the item *effect of exchange rate changes on cash* follows directly from our previous discussion. Suppose the foreign subsidiary in our previous example had a cash balance of 4,000 lira at the beginning and end of the year. Upon consolidation, the parent's reported cash balance includes $4,000 at the beginning of the year and $4,400 (4,000 lira × 1.10) at the end of the year. This change of $400 needs to be reported as it does not appear as an operating, investing, or financing activity.

Translation gains and losses resulting from exchange rate changes are excluded from cash flows from operating, investing, and financing activities. The sum of these excluded gains and losses is reported as the effect of exchange rate changes on cash (further discussion of these issues occurs in Chapter 15).

EXAMPLE: DUPONT

DuPont's Statement of Cash Flows is reproduced in Exhibit 3-5. We examine each component of duPont's cash flow statement, in turn, to demonstrate the use and analysis of cash flow statements.

Cash from Operations. DuPont reports cash flows using the *indirect method.* As a result, the company provides a reconciliation of the difference between net income and CFO. The reconciling adjustments fall into three categories:

1. Noncash expenses
2. Nonoperating cash flows
3. Changes in operating assets and liabilities

Noncash expenses consist mostly of the amortization of past investment outflows. Although the matching principle requires amortization when computing net income, it is not a current period cash flow.

For 1992, the transition effects of adopting new accounting standards for income tax and other postemployment benefits must be removed. The adoption of these standards had no cash flow impact.[13]

---

[13]See Chapters 9 and 12.

Nonoperating cash flows relate to investment and financing activities. For example, gains and losses from the sales of investments result from investment activities (discussed below) and must be excluded from the CFO. Similarly, the 1992 and 1993 extraordinary losses relate to the early extinguishment of debt, a financing activity, and must also be excluded from the computation of the cash flows from operations.

Finally, cash from operations reports changes in balance sheet accounts that are operating in nature. Such accounts include inventories, accounts receivable and payable (excluding amounts relating to investing and financing activities), and accruals for such operating items as interest,[14] income taxes, and employee benefits.

The reconciliation only uses the changes due to operating activities and excludes two other sources of changes in operating assets and liabilities: acquisitions and the impact of changes in exchange rates. We will see shortly how these are treated in the cash flow statement.

Investing Cash Flow. DuPont's major investment activity from 1992 to 1994 has been the purchase of property, plant, and equipment (PP&E). There are additional outflows for acquisitions, investments in affiliates, and net investment in short-term financial instruments. DuPont has received cash inflows from the sale of assets.

Gains or losses from the sale of long-term assets are excluded from CFO. Although duPont's cash flow statement does not explicitly report such gains or losses, Note 2 (Appendix A) reveals that gains are included in other income. Thus, we assume that they have been removed from CFO (probably in the "other noncash charges and credits—net" entry).

Note 2 also reports duPont's equity in the earnings of affiliates. Note 14 states that, in 1994, affiliates paid $326 million in dividends to duPont, roughly the same as duPont's equity in the earnings of those affiliates. The difference[15] is another adjustment to CFO (again, probably included in the "other—net" item). Many companies report the deduction for "undistributed earnings" or "equity earnings in excess of dividends received" as a separate reconciling item in the CFO section of their cash flow statement.

The separate disclosure of cash outflows for acquisitions is an important feature of the cash flow statement. These amounts reflect the assets purchased less liabilities assumed in acquisitions accounted for using the purchase method (see Chapter 14 for a full discussion). *The cash outflows for the acquisitions of operating assets and liabilities of the acquired firm are excluded from CFO but included in CFI.*

The change in duPont's investment in short-term financing instruments requires some discussion. These investments are not considered "cash equivalents" because they do not meet the SFAS 95 definition (risk-free with maturities of less than three months). Nonetheless, from a practical point of view, they may be little different. If their risk is low and liquidity high, they should be treated analytically as cash equivalents as they represent additional short-term liquidity. Note that changes in the level of these investments are reported net, one of the exceptions to the "gross" reporting requirements of SFAS 95. Under that standard, changes in balance sheet assets and liabilities that turn over frequently (another example is credit card receivables) may be reported

---

[14]In a subsequent section of this chapter, we make the argument that cash flows for interest represent financing rather than operating activities.

[15]Generally, the cash dividends received from investees are more appropriately analyzed as components of investment cash flows.

net. Investments that are long-term, less liquid, and riskier (e.g., stocks or long-term bonds) should be treated differently (such investments are discussed in Chapter 13).

Financing Cash Flow. This category contains cash flows between the firm and suppliers of its debt and equity capital. For duPont, debt origination and repayment are the principal items. Note that whereas changes in long-term debt are gross, the change in short-term debt is shown net (another exception to the gross reporting requirement). Dividends paid to shareholders and cash received from the sale of common stock are also included in CFF.

Effect of Exchange Rate Changes on Cash. DuPont has foreign subsidiaries and cash balances denominated in foreign currencies. Changes in exchange rates create translation gains and losses that are not cash flows, but must be reported for the cash flow statement to balance. The $94 million reported by duPont captures, in a single number, the effect of exchange rate changes on the firm's foreign cash holdings.

Change in Cash and Cash Equivalents. The net reconciling number is the period's change in the balance of cash and equivalents, equal to the sum of the three major cash flow components (CFO, CFI, and CFF) and any exchange rate effects. This number is necessarily equal to the difference between cash at the beginning of the year and the amount at the end of the year. However, although this number is easy to measure, it has no analytic value. Firms can influence the net change by accelerating or delaying payments, or by making use of short-term financing facilities.

ANALYSIS OF CASH FLOW INFORMATION

The cash flow statement is intended to help predict the firm's ability to sustain (and increase) cash from current operations. In doing so, the statement provides more objective information about:

- A firm's ability to generate cash flows from operations
- Trends in cash flow components and cash consequences of investing and financing decisions
- Management decisions regarding such critical areas as financial policy (leverage), dividend policy, and investment for growth

Neither the statement of cash flows nor the income statement alone contain sufficient information for decision making. (See Box 2-2 for some empirical evidence in this respect.) Income statement and balance sheet data must be combined with cash flows for insights into the firm's ability to realize assets based on reported revenues and settle liabilities resulting from accrued expenses and thereby assist the analyst in the development of other valuation-relevant measures.

Free Cash Flows and Valuation

An important but elusive concept often used in cash flow analysis is *free cash flow* (FCF). It is intended to measure the cash available to the firm for discretionary uses after making all required cash outlays. The concept is widely used by analysts and in the finance literature as the basis for many valuation models (see Chapter 19). The basic elements required to calculate FCF are available from the cash flow statement. In practice, however, the definition of FCF varies widely, depending on how one defines required and discretionary uses.

The basic definition used by many analysts is cash from operations less the amount of capital expenditures required to maintain the firm's *present* productive capacity.[16] Discretionary uses include growth-oriented capital expenditures and acquisitions, debt reduction, and stockholder payments (dividends and stock repurchase). The larger the firm's FCF, the healthier it is because it has more cash available for growth, debt payment, and dividends.

The argument for this definition is similar to Hicks' argument regarding the computation of net income discussed in the previous chapter. If historical cost depreciation provided a good measure of the use of productive capacity, then FCF would equal CFO less depreciation expense. However (as discussed in Chapter 8), historical cost depreciation is arbitrary and measures the cost to replace operating capacity only by coincidence.

The obvious alternative to depreciation is the amount of capital expenditures made to maintain current capacity, excluding the expansion portion of capital expenditures. In practice, however, it is difficult to separate capital expenditures into expansion and replacement components. Lacking better information, all capital expenditures are subtracted from CFO to obtain FCF.

Subtracting all capital expenditures from CFO to arrive at FCF brings the definition of FCF closer to the one used in finance valuation models. In these models, required outflows are defined as operating cash flows less capital expenditures to replace current operating capacity *as well as capital expenditures necessary to finance the firm's growth opportunities.* Growth opportunities are defined as those in which the firm can make "above normal" returns. It is difficult to determine *a priori* the amount of capital expenditures required to maintain growth and the discretionary portion of these expenditures; pragmatically, FCF is generally measured as CFO less capital expenditures.

Valuation models do, however, differ as to whether FCF is measured by *FCF available to the firm [i.e., all providers of capital (debt and equity)]* or *FCF available to equity shareholders.* In the former case, required payments *do not* include outlays for interest and debt. In the latter case, they do. Thus, for FCF to the firm, one cannot use reported CFO because it includes outlays for interest expense. We return to this point later in this chapter. In Chapter 19, we elaborate on the differing definitions of FCF and their implications for valuation models.

Relationship of Income and Cash Flows

When periodic financial statements are prepared, estimates of the revenues earned and expenses incurred during the reporting interval are required. As discussed in the previous chapter, these estimates require management judgment and are subject to modification as more information about the operating cycle becomes available. Accrual accounting can therefore be affected by management's choice of accounting policies and estimates. Furthermore, accrual accounting *by itself* fails to provide adequate information about the liquidity of the firm and long-term solvency. Some of these problems can be alleviated by the use of the cash flow statement in conjunction with the income statement.

---

[16]IAS 7 on cash flow statements recommends this disclosure.

Cash flow is relatively (but not completely) free of the drawbacks of the accrual concept. It is less likely to be affected by variations in accounting principles and estimates, making it more useful than reported income in assessing liquidity and solvency.

As a result, the level and trend of cash flow and reported income vary, as illustrated in Figure 3-1. Three different types of company are presented: Kmart, Union Camp, and Intel. Reported income and CFO were taken directly from the firms' financial statements. Two measures of free cash flow are used:

FCF1 equals CFO minus (net) capital expenditures.
FCF2 equals CFO minus CFI and thus includes expenditures (receipts) for acquisitions (divestitures) and other investments.

Note that CFO (generally) exceeds income for all three companies because CFO is not reduced by the cost of productive capacity.[17] Depreciation is usually the largest component of the adjustment from income to CFO. When the cost of productive capacity is included, as in FCF1, the relationship is company-specific and varies from year to year.

Intel is a "growth" company; its income and CFO show steady growth from 1991 to 1994. FCF1 is below income in each period, reflecting capital expenditures for expansion as well as for replacement. FCF1 is positive in each year, a healthy sign given rapid growth. FCF2, on the other hand, is near or below zero each year. FCF patterns have to be monitored carefully for growth companies to ensure that they are not growing too fast, which can cause liquidity problems.

Kmart was experiencing operating difficulties during this time period as reflected in its income and cash flow patterns. CFO exceeded income in 1994; in 1993 and 1995, CFO was lower. In 1994, Kmart reported the highest CFO, but the lowest profitability! Finally, unlike Intel, its FCF2 exceeded CFO in 1995.

The explanation for Kmart's pattern of CFO and income is its (current) operating assets. Increases in receivables and inventories reduced CFO below reported income in some years. Revenues were recognized without receipt of cash, increasing receivables; cash outflows for (increased) inventories were not expensed.

Although Intel also reported higher receivables and inventory, the nature of the growth was not the same. *Intel's operating assets grew in proportion to the firm's sales.* As Intel grew, more working capital was required to maintain that growth. *In Kmart's case, the lack of sales growth, coupled with increases in working capital growth, reduced CFO, reflecting slow receivable collections and inventory buildup.* In 1994, on the other hand, Kmart cut back and decreased its operating assets, increasing CFO.

The FCF patterns for Kmart also differ considerably from those for Intel. Note the increase in FCF1 reported by Kmart in 1994 and FCF2 in 1994 and 1995. The increases in 1994 were partially due to the increases in CFO discussed earlier. Additionally, in 1994, Kmart cut capital expenditures. The sharp increase in FCF2 in 1995 is a result of Kmart's sale of some investments (in its noncore operations) to raise needed cash.

Union Camp is an example of a cyclical company. In 1992 and 1993, it was in the trough of the cycle. In 1991, it had just entered the trough and, in 1994, it was coming out of it. The differences between income and cash flows are largely due to timing

---

[17]This point is elaborated on further in the section entitled, "Cash Flow Classification Issues."

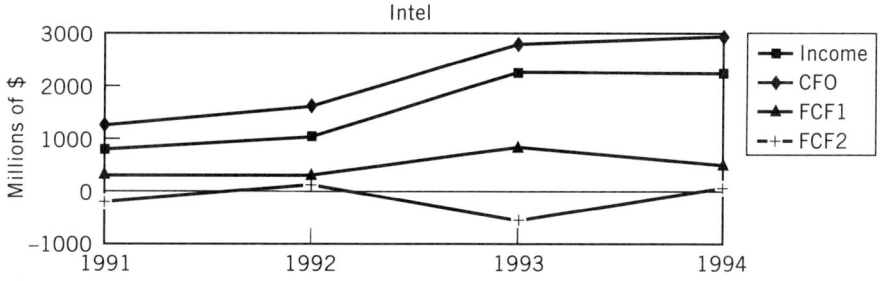

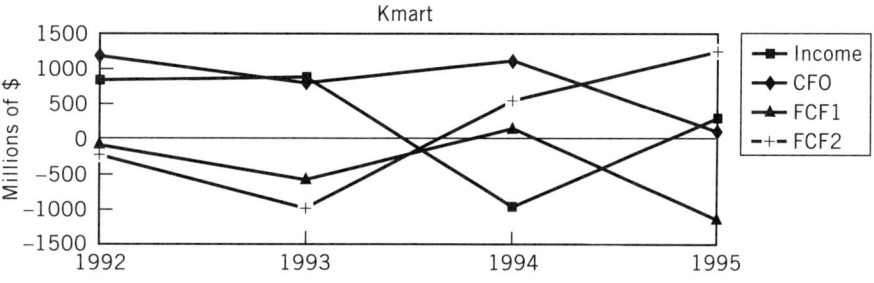

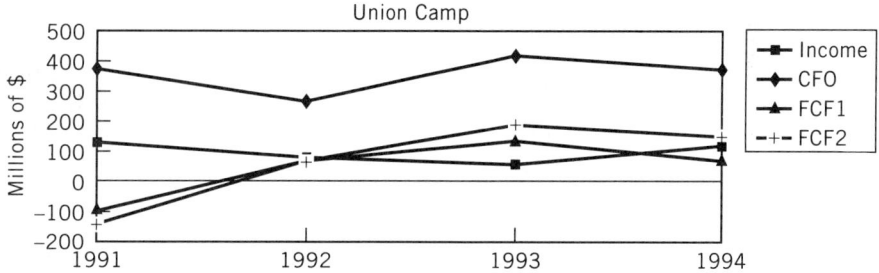

Legend: Income and CFO as per firm's financial statements.
FCF1 = CFO - (net) Capital Expenditures
FCF2 = CFO - CFI

FIGURE 3-1 Comparison of patterns of income, CFO, and free cash flows.

differences. The company cut production and capital expenditures during the downturn. However, depreciation on existing capacity had to be recognized. The result was high (relative to income) CFO, FCF1, and FCF2 in those years. Capital expenditures may not have been enough to replace existing capacity as all three cash flow measures were above income. In 1991 and 1994, however, the company increased capital expenditures, reducing FCF below income.

The above discussion indicates that cash flow statements should be used together with information from the income statement, the balance sheet, and footnotes to assess the cash-generating ability of a firm. This assessment should consider the firm's liquidity, the viability of income as a predictor of future cash flows, and the effect of timing and recognition differences. We elaborate on these points in the next sections.

Income, Cash Flow, and the Going Concern Assumption

As noted earlier, income statement amounts based on accrual accounting are generally presumed to be good predictors of future cash flows. That predictive ability is subject to a number of implicit assumptions, including the going concern assumption. For example, the classification of inventories as assets rather than expenses implicitly assumes that they will be sold in the normal course of business. Similarly, the accrual of revenue from credit sales and the valuation of receivables assume that the firm will continue to operate normally; failing firms may find that customers are unwilling to pay.

When the going concern assumption is subject to doubt, revenue recognition and asset valuation can no longer be taken for granted. To some extent, this was the situation in which Kmart found itself in 1994. The value of inventory and receivables declines sharply when they must be quickly liquidated. Long-term assets (especially intangibles and other assets with little or no value in a nonoperating framework) also must be reexamined when the going concern assumption is questioned. In this respect, *the statement of cash flows serves as a "check" on the assumptions inherent in the income statement.*

To find out why income can fail as a predictor of cash-generating ability (uncollected receivables or unsold inventories) requires a comparison of amounts recorded as sales and cost of goods sold on the income statement with the pattern of cash collections from customers and cash paid for inventories on the cash flow statement. A direct method cash flow statement is helpful in this regard.

Income, Cash Flow, and the Choice of Accounting Policies

Consider the income statements for the three hypothetical companies presented in Exhibit 3-6. They are based on the example illustrated in Exhibit 2-1.

Their income patterns differ only because of the choice of accounting policy. The policies selected convey information about management expectations. In case A, income is positive each year as management expects to complete the project within budget. In case B, a more conservative management recognizes income only when the project is completed. The annual income statement reports no activities during the first three years. Finally, in case C, management assumes that the eventual collectibility of the revenues is uncertain and thus does not recognize profit until collections are sufficient to recover all costs.

The periodic net income differs because accounting methods and assumptions of managers differ, not because their economic activities differ. *The cash flow statement allows the analyst to distinguish between the actual events that have occurred and the accounting assumptions that have been used to report these events.* This is not to say that the assumptions made by management are wrong. The assumptions may provide useful information. The user of financial statements needs to understand the interrelationship between these events and financial reporting choices.

The cash flow statement shows that the cash collected, cash disbursed, and the cash flow from operations is identical for all three companies because the economic activities of these companies are identical. The three companies differ only with respect to reported income, which is a function of different accounting assumptions and policies.

Case 3-1, an extension of Case 2-1 on Thousand Trails, shows how cash flow data can be used to examine the effect of revenue and expense recognition methods on a

EXHIBIT 3-6
Derivation of Cash from Operations Under Alternative Accounting Methods

	Year			
	1	2	3	4
Indirect Method				
Company A: Percentage of Completion				
Revenue	$ 750	$ 1,500	$ 2,250	$ 1,500
Expense	(600)	(1,200)	(1,800)	(1,200)
Net income	$ 150	$ 300	$ 450	$ 300
Add: Increase in advances	750	0	(750)	0
Cash from operations	$ 900	$ 300	$ (300)	$ 300
Company B: Completed Contract				
Revenue	$ 0	$ 0	$ 0	$ 6,000
Expense	0	0	0	(4,800)
Net income	$0	$0	$0	$1,200
Add: Increase in advances	1,500	1,500	1,500	(4,500)
Subtract: Increase in inventory	(600)	(1,200)	(1,800)	3,600
Cash from operations	$ 900	$ 300	$ (300)	$ 300
Company C: Cost Recovery				
Revenue	$ 600	$ 1,200	$ 1,800	$ 2,400
Expense	(600)	(1,200)	(1,800)	(1,200)
Net income	$ 0	$ 0	$ 0	$ 1,200
Add: Increase in advances	900	300	(300)	(900)
Cash from operations	$ 900	$ 300	$ (300)	$ 300
Direct Method: Identical for All Three Companies				
Cash collections*	$1,500	$ 1,500	$ 1,500	$ 1,500
Cash disbursements†	(600)	(1,200)	(1,800)	(1,200)
Cash from operations	$ 900	$ 300	$ (300)	$ 300

*Cash collections = revenue + increase in advances (e.g., for year 1, Company A = $750 + $750; Company B = 0 + $1,500; and Company C = $600 + $900).

†Cash disbursements = expense + increase in inventory (e.g., for year 1, Company A and Company C = $600 + $0; Company B = $0 + $600).

firm's reported financial statements. Analysis that considers this effect properly can improve forecasts of future cash flows and earnings.

Income, Cash Flow, and Liquidity

Companies can grow too fast, resulting in liquidity problems. Although Intel, discussed above, does not suffer from liquidity problems, its cash flow pattern can be a prelude to such problems. Another fast-growing company, The Discovery Zone, an operator of children's indoor entertainment facilities, provides such an example. The company filed for bankruptcy reorganization under Chapter 11 in 1995. At that time, its CEO stated:

> A successful Chapter 11 reorganization will address the problems caused by the company's *rapid expansion* and put Discovery Zone on stronger financial footing.

Rapid growth is often accompanied by increases in capital expenditures and negative free cash flows. Moreover, growth companies may also report weak operating cash flows because they must finance growth in current operating assets. As firms usually pay for inventories before they are sold and collect sales proceeds subsequent to sale, there may be a long time lag between payments to suppliers and receipts from customers.

The cash flow statement provides information about the firm's liquidity and its ability to finance its growth from internally generated funds. It can highlight potential liquidity problems, such as an increasing need for operating capital or lagging cash collections.

However, reliance on the cash flow statement is insufficient for a complete assessment of the underlying strength of the company. Trends in sales and earnings must be evaluated from income statement data to determine whether there is a strong growth pattern that indicates a sustainable ability to generate cash flows in the future.

Analysis of Cash Flow Trends

The data contained in the statement of cash flows can be used to:

1. Review individual cash flow items for analytic significance.

2. Examine the trend of different cash flow components over time and their relationship to related income statement items.

3. Consider the interrelationship between cash flow components over time.

We examine each of these uses continuing with duPont as an example. A summary of duPont's cash flow statements for 1992 to 1994 is presented below:

DuPont Statement of Cash Flows

1992 to 1994 ($ in millions)

	1992	1993	1994
Cash from operations (CFO)	$ 4,388	$ 5,380	$ 5,664
Investing cash flow (CFI)	(4,553)	(3,078)	(3,133)
Financing cash flow (CFF)	1,479	(2,744)	(2,878)
Effect of exchange rate changes	(142)	(89)	94
Change in cash and equivalents	$ 1,172	$ (531)	$ (253)

The CFI portion of duPont's cash flow statement is especially revealing. Investment in property, plant, and equipment declined by nearly one-third from 1992 to 1994. DuPont's segment data (Note 30) reveal sharp declines in capital spending in the fibers, polymers, and diversified businesses segments. All three segments have shown large increases in profitability over the same time span. CFI also shows substantial asset sales in 1993 and 1994. These data suggest a useful line of questioning for management regarding the company's future growth.

For an example of the second type of analysis, we look at cash from operations. Because CFO is subject to random and cyclical influences, it should be analyzed over long periods (three to five years) of time. In general, CFO should be positive and increase over time because it provides the resources to service debt, invest in growth, and reward shareholders.

DuPont's CFO grew by $1,266 million or 29% from 1992 to 1994. Given the company's sales growth and improved profitability, increased CFO is a healthy sign. Significant growth often results in negative CFO for brief periods, as the required increase in working capital more than offsets growth in income. This is not the case for duPont, which reduced its operating assets (see Exhibit 3-5 for changes in operating assets and liabilities), especially in 1993, contributing to the improved CFO.[18]

In other cases, however, weak CFO may reflect operating problems such as unrealistic revenue recognition accounting policies or the inability to collect receivables. A comparison of revenue and expense trends with the pattern of cash collections from customers and cash payments should reveal the causes of lower CFO and suggest whether the trend is likely to reverse.

Direct method statements allow analysts to make such comparisons because they provide information better suited to trend analysis. Direct method statements reveal, for example, whether CFO is increasing because cash collections are increasing or payments to suppliers are decreasing. The discussion of duPont that follows uses the method outlined in Box 3-1.

First, we compute a "cash gross margin" percentage and compare it to one based on income:

DuPont: Cash and Income-Based Gross Margins

1992 to 1994 ($ in millions)			
	1992	1993	1994
Cash Flow Statement			
Cash collections	$ 33,249	$ 32,724	$ 34,072
Cash inputs	(21,752)	(21,177)	(21,786)
Cash gross margin	$ 11,497	$ 11,547	$ 12,286
Percent	34.6%	35.3%	36.1%
Income Statement			
Sales	$ 33,291	$ 32,621	$ 34,042
COGS	(22,046)	(21,624)	(21,977)
Gross margin	$ 11,245	$ 10,997	$ 12,065
Percent	33.8%	33.7%	35.4%
Other Ratios			
Cash collections/sales	99.9%	100.3%	100.1%
Cash for inputs/COGS	98.7%	97.9%	99.1%

[18]The ratio analysis of DuPont in Chapter 4 provides further insight into this issue.

DuPont's cash gross margin increased by $789 million over the 1992 to 1994 period, accounting for 62% of the improvement in CFO. This is a good sign as it indicates that the improvement is primarily because duPont has been able to control costs and keep cash outflows steady while sales and cash collections increased. Both the income statement and cash gross margin ratios are stable and improving over time. The cash margins are slightly higher than the income margins. The relative stability in the ratios suggests that duPont has successfully controlled its working capital requirements.

The cash collections/sales ratio is stable and hovers at the 100% level, indicating good credit management. The cash for inputs/COGS ratio fluctuates, declining in 1992 to 1993 and increasing in 1994. This pattern may be due to declining inventory levels in 1992 and 1993 (see Exhibit 3-5). The increase in the cash for inputs/COGS ratio in 1994 may indicate that duPont has reached the point at which further reductions are not likely and, although the increased levels of CFO may be maintainable, the *rate of increase* in CFO may not be sustainable. Additionally, firms that decrease inventories relative to sales increase their cash gross margin, regardless of the income statement gross margin. This explains why duPont's cash gross margin "leads" the income statement gross margin.

The third type of analysis of cash flow components looks at the relationship among those components over time. An example is provided by duPont's free cash flows.

DuPont Free Cash Flows

1992 to 1994 ($ in millions)			
	1992	1993	1994
Cash from operations	$4,388	$5,380	$5,664
Capital expenditures	4,448	3,621	3,050
Free cash flow	$ (60)	$1,759	$2,614

DuPont's FCF increased significantly over the 1992 to 1994 period. This increase reflects increases in CFO coupled with sharp declines in capital expenditures. The sharpness of that decline makes projections regarding CFO and FCF premature. Unless duPont increases capital expenditures or makes acquisitions, further increases in CFO are unlikely. The trend in FCF will also depend on management's future growth plans.

Trend analysis of cyclical companies requires more than the evaluation of data for individual years; aggregated data should be evaluated as well. In Box 3-2, we provide an analysis of A. M. Castle (a cyclical company) over the five-year period 1987 through 1991.

Cash Flow Classification Issues

Although the classification of cash flows into the three main categories is important, we must recognize that classification guidelines can be arbitrary. The resulting data may require selective adjustment before they are used to make investment decisions.

The classification guidelines of SFAS 95 often create problems for users of the cash flow statement in the following areas:

1. Cash flows involving property, plant, and equipment
2. Differences due to some accounting methods
3. Interest and dividends received
4. Interest paid
5. Noncash transactions

Some of these issues have been touched on earlier in the chapter. We discuss each in greater detail now.

BOX 3-2
A. M. CASTLE
Analysis of Cash Flow, 1987 to 1991 ($ in thousands)

	1987	1988	1989	1990	1991
Cash collections	$ 364,224	$ 487,448	$ 509,046	$ 483,464	$ 441,442
Cash material cost	(268,890)	(408,664)	(371,943)	(388,878)	(313,033)
Cash operating expense	(71,947)	(85,066)	(102,062)	(99,857)	(95,711)
Interest paid	(3,433)	(5,135)	(4,886)	(6,324)	(7,340)
Income tax paid	(5,018)	(7,870)	(5,422)	(3,116)	(283)
Cash from operations	$ 14,936	$ (19,287)	$ 24,733	$ (14,711)	$ 25,075
Capital expenditures	(2,605)	(7,816)	(10,381)	(13,390)	(3,305)
Proceeds from property sales	1,888	503	196	34	5,490
Acquisitions	—	—	—	(2,529)	—
Cash from investment	$ (717)	$ (7,313)	$ (10,185)	$ (15,885)	$ 2,185
Net change in debt	(10,816)	28,184	(9,687)	33,967	(23,329)
Net issue of equity	204	21	32	50	25
Dividends paid	(3,040)	(3,442)	(4,640)	(4,931)	(3,927)
Cash from financing	$ (13,652)	$ 24,763	$ (14,295)	$ 29,086	$ (27,231)
Net change in cash	$ 567	$ (1,837)	$ 253	$ (1,510)	$ 29
Ratios					
Cash material/cash collections	0.738	0.839	0.730	0.804	0.709
Cash operations/cash collections	0.198	0.174	0.200	0.207	0.217
Cost of materials/net sales*	0.750	0.751	0.760	0.759	0.759
Operating expense/net sales*	0.199	0.185	0.193	0.204	0.213

*Latter two ratios based on income statement data not shown.

Discussion

A direct method cash flow statement for A. M. Castle for the five years from 1987 to 1991 is presented. The direct method statements were derived from the indirect statements presented by the company using the methodology shown in Box 3-1.

Castle is a metals wholesaler. Its revenues and earnings are heavily influenced by the business cycle. Because of this cyclicality, we start by looking at cash flows over the entire five-year period:

Cash from operations		$ 30,746
Capital expenditures	$(37,497)	
Property sales	8,111	
Acquisitions	(2,529)	
Cash from investment (reported)		$(31,915)
Less: reclassification of sale-leaseback		(5,317)
Cash from investment (adjusted)		(37,232)
Net change in debt	$ 18,319	
Net issue of equity	332	
Dividends paid	(19,980)	
Cash from financing (reported)		(1,329)
Less: reclassification of sale-leaseback		5,317
Cash from financing (adjusted)		3,988
Net change in cash		$ (2,498)

Aggregate cash from operations was approximately $31 million, although CFO was negative for two of the five years. Total capital expenditures were $37 million, suggesting that free cash flow was negative. Before adopting this conclusion, however, we would question management to see how much of capital spending over the five-year period represented expansion rather than replacement of capacity. Given the lack of sales growth, for the purposes of this discussion, we assume that none of the capital expenditure was for expansion. The 1990 acquisition, however, would be considered a cash outflow for expansion.

Turning to financing cash flow, Castle paid dividends of $20 million over the five-year period while increasing debt by $18 million. Reclassification of the sale/leaseback transaction† changes the debt increase to more than $23 million.

In rough terms, therefore, it appears that Castle's operating cash flow was insufficient to cover capital expenditures necessary to maintain its operating capacity. The shortfall and cash dividend payments were financed by an increase in debt. Long- and short-term debt increased from less than $45 million at the end of 1986 (87% of stockholders' equity) to more than $63 million (98% of equity) five years later.

Looking at the components of CFO, cash material cost has been highly variable relative to cash collections. Although the accrual-based cost of materials has been quite stable (75 to 76% of sales), the cash basis ratio has ranged from 71 to 84% over the five-year period. Swings in inventory levels and prices (which do affect cash flows, even when LIFO is used for accrual purposes) create that volatility. It may explain why Castle has substantial lines of credit.

---

†Proceeds from the sales of property were $8 million over the five-year period, but most of that resulted from a 1991 sale and leaseback transaction. The proceeds of that sale are really a financing transaction and should not be considered a reduction of cash for investment. This is another case where good analysis requires the reclassification of reported cash flows.

Classification of Cash Flows for Property, Plant, and Equipment

Consider the components of cash flow from operations in the following simple example:

Net income	$30,000
Noncash expense: depreciation	5,000
	$35,000
Change in operating accounts: decrease in inventory	15,000
= Cash from operations	$50,000

The cash flow statement adds both depreciation expense (a noncash expense) and the decrease in inventory (change in operating accounts) to net income to arrive at cash from operations for the current period. Their differing classifications suggest that the reason for these addbacks is not identical. On the one hand, both adjustments reflect cash outflows that occurred in prior periods but are recognized in income in the current period. Depreciation allocates the cost of fixed assets to the current period, the period in which they are used. Similarly, the cost of goods sold allocates the cost of inventory to the current period, when the inventory is actually sold.

The difference between the two adjustments is the classification of the initial cash outlays. In one sense, both initial outlays were for investments. In one case, the firm invested in fixed assets; in the other, it invested in inventories. The latter, however, is classified as an operating cash outflow,[19] deducted from CFO in the period of the initial outlay and added back to income when expensed to avoid double counting.

The original investment in fixed assets was reported as an investment cash outflow, and its allocation (depreciation expense) is added back to income because it is never classified as an operating flow, but always as an investment flow.[20]

The implications of this classification issue follow:

1. Cash from operations does not include a charge for use of the firm's operating capacity. Cash required to replace the productive capacity or physical plant used during operations is not included in CFO.

2. Firms reporting positive CFO may not thrive unless the CFO (generated and retained) is sufficient to replace the productive capacity used to generate the operating cash flow.

3. Identical firms with equal capital intensity will report different CFOs when one firm leases plant assets and the other owns its assets. The firm that leases reports lower CFO because lease rentals are operating expenditures (operating cash flows), whereas the other firm's expenditures are reported as investment cash flows.[21]

---

[19]An exception occurs, as discussed, when inventory is acquired as part of an acquisition (see Chapter 14).

[20]The distinction between adding back to avoid double counting or because of nonclassification as an operating item can perhaps best be seen if we consider what happens to the current period cash outflows for inventory and plant assets acquired and used during the period. For inventory, no adjustment is required. The current period allocation of the investment in plant assets (depreciation expense) must be added back as the outflow has been recorded as an investing cash outflow.

[21]See Chapter 11 for a detailed discussion of the financial statement impacts of the lease versus buy decision.

4. Cash payments for inventory may also be excluded from CFO. When an acquired firm has inventories, the cash paid for those inventories is included in investing cash flow. However, the proceeds from the subsequent sale of such "purchased" inventory are included in CFO, distorting reported CFO because its purchase cost is never reported in CFO.

5. An additional problem is that "investment" is not precisely defined. Two examples follow:

   • Hertz classifies its investment in rental cars as inventory, and purchases are included in CFO. In this case, CFO is understated relative to a firm that classifies its operating assets as property (see problem 10).

   • Media companies consider programming purchases as long-term fixed assets. Although amortization impacts reported earnings, purchase costs are never reported in CFO. Yet financial markets seem to value such firms based on multiples of CFO per share rather than earnings per share!

Free cash flow, which deducts capital expenditures (however defined) from CFO, is generally free from this problem. However, the classification decision can have a significant impact on reported CFO.

Effect of Differences in Accounting Methods

We previously demonstrated that CFO is not affected by the timing differences generated by revenue and expense recognition methods. In that sense, CFO is less affected by differing accounting policies. However, *CFO is affected by reporting methods that alter the classification of cash flows among operating, investing, and financing categories.* If one accounting method results in the classification of a cash flow as investing and an alternative results in its classification as operating, then the reported CFOs will differ. Moreover, unlike revenue and expense differences in accounting policies that reverse over time, *the differences in CFO classification caused by reporting methods are permanent and do not reverse.*[22]

The capitalization of expenditures such as computer software leads to the classification of cash outflows as investing cash flows. However, they are reported as operating cash flows when expensed immediately.[23] Chapter 7 contains an extensive discussion of this issue. Lease classification (discussed in Chapter 11) also affects cash flow components for both lessors and lessees. We shall demonstrate various other examples throughout the book.

Interest and Dividends Received

Interest income and dividends received from investments in other firms are classified under SFAS 95 as operating cash flows. *As a result, the return on capital is separated*

---

[22]The effects on the calculation of free cash flows must also be considered. If the classification difference is just between CFO and CFI, then Free Cash Flow = CFO − CFI will not be affected. However, if the classification difference results in a shift between CFO and CFF (as in the case of leasing), FCF can be affected as well.

[23]This effect depends on the cash flow classification of the capitalized amount. Overhead capitalized in inventory, for example, will not change reported CFO because changes in inventory are also included in CFO. Overhead capitalized in fixed assets, however, will result in reclassification of the outflow from operating to investing cash flow.

from the return of capital.[24] Combining these two returns to report cash flow to and from investees facilitates analysis. More important, the reclassification of after-tax dividend and interest from operating to investing cash flows has the advantage of reporting operating cash flows that reflect only the operating activities of the firm's core business.[25]

Interest Paid

Interest payments are classified as operating cash outflows under SFAS 95. Such payments are the result of capital structure and leverage decisions and they reflect financing rather than operating risk. The reported CFOs of two firms with different capital structures are not comparable because returns to creditors (interest) are included in CFO, whereas returns to stockholders (dividends) are reported as financing cash flows. For analytic purposes, therefore, interest payments (after tax to reflect the cash flow benefits of tax deductibility) should be reclassified as financing cash flows. The resulting operating cash flow is independent of the firm's capitalization, facilitating the comparison of firms with different capital structures.

Noncash Transactions

Some investing and financing activities do not require direct outlays of cash. For example, a building may be acquired by assuming a mortgage. Under current disclosure rules, such transactions do not appear as cash from financing or investing activities but are given separate footnote disclosure as "Significant Noncash Financing and Investment Activities."

For analytic purposes, however, this transaction is identical to the issuance of a bond to a third party, using the proceeds to acquire the building. *The "noncash" transaction reflects both a financing and investing activity and should be included in each category.* Knowledge of the firm's cash requirements for investing activities is as important as the method of financing. The latter provides information about future cash flow needs for interest and the repayment of principal.

The classification issues discussed in this section should provide the reader with an awareness that the cash flow statement is based on assumptions, definitions, and (somewhat arbitrary) accounting rules. Knowledge of these assumptions and rules allows the analyst to make informed adjustments that may be better suited for analytical purposes.

CASH FLOW STATEMENTS: AN INTERNATIONAL PERSPECTIVE

Although income statements and balance sheets are required as part of the periodic financial statements virtually around the world, there is no cash flow statement required in many countries. For example, Germany and The Netherlands have no requirement;

---

[24]Only the nominal (cash) return (dividend or interest received) is reported as an operating cash flow; the real (total) return (which includes capital gain or loss) is split between operating and investing cash flow.

[25]However, some investments and joint ventures are operating in nature. Such investments may assist in current and future operations, require significant financing commitments, and provide some control over the cash flows generated by the investee. See Chapter 13 for more discussion of these issues.

in Japan, it is only required of listed companies as part of an unaudited schedule. When none is provided, the analyst should use the transactional analysis method (Exhibit 3-4) to generate a direct method cash flow statement.

When cash flow statements are required, their format varies greatly across countries. In the United Kingdom, interest and dividends paid (returns to providers of capital) are grouped in a separate category, not included as part of either CFO or CFF. Although we believe this format is superior to the SFAS 95 format, reported cash flows are not comparable without adjustment.

Some countries, notably in South America, still present a *statement of changes in funds. Funds are defined as net working capital* (current assets less current liabilities) and the focus of the statement is the *change in working capital.* Under this definition, funds are regarded as an appropriate measure of liquidity because near-cash current accounts are considered to be cash surrogates; that is, it is irrelevant whether funds are held as cash, receivables, or inventories. Prior to SFAS 95, the funds flow approach was used in the United States. However, its limitations were recognized in the late 1970s and early 1980s.[26]

The primary difference between the funds flow statement and the cash flow statement is the treatment of changes in operating accounts. The indirect method CFO requires the addition to or subtraction from net income of changes in current operating accounts as well as non-cash or non-operating income statement items. In contrast, funds from operations (FFO) equals net income adjusted *only* for the non-cash income statement items. *No adjustment is made for the changes in the current operating accounts.*

A second major difference between the funds flow and cash flow approaches is the treatment of short-term debt. Under the funds flow approach, short-term debt remains a component of working capital and is not removed to CFF.

Because of these two differences, FFO is not a true measure of the cash generated from operating activities. Empirical evidence shows that FFO does not add informational value to net income, but CFO does.

Cash flow analysis is an important tool for international comparisons because of significant accounting differences across countries. As noted, cash flows (CFO and FCF) are generally less susceptible than income to variations resulting from differences in accounting methods. However, differences in accounting methods do affect cash flow classifications. Thus, international comparisons may require the adjustment of reported cash flows.[27]

---

[26]The credit crunch and high-interest-rate environment of the 1970s made liquidity and cash itself more critical: Greater emphasis was placed on shortening the cash-generating cycle of the firm's operations, leading to the decline of working capital and funds as indicators of liquidity. As noted earlier, two major components of working capital—receivables and inventories—need careful evaluation as both FFO and income can increase with little or no cash generated if the receivables increase without a corresponding increase in collections or inventories increase because they are not being sold. The W. T. Grant bankruptcy [see Largay and Stickney (1980)] is a classic example of increasing working capital and income but declining cash. Furthermore, CFO is favored because reported FFO varies more readily with accounting methods used but actual cash flows are less prone to manipulation.

[27]See, for example, Kenneth S. Hackel and Joshua Livnat, "International Investments Based on Free Cash Flow: A Practical Approach," *The Journal of Financial Statement Analysis,* Fall 1995, pp. 5–14 where such an approach is applied to a sample of firms. See also Chapter 10 of *Cash Flow and Security Analysis,* 2nd ed., (Irwin, 1995) by the same authors.

SUMMARY

This chapter completes our discussion of the basic framework for financial statement analysis. We have discussed financial statements that are the raw data of financial analysis and introduced users of financial statements to the interrelationship among them.

In the next chapter, we examine financial statement ratios, which are used as shorthand indicators of firm performance. Although some ratios use data from only one financial statement (debt/equity ratio), others use data from several statements (return on equity). Sound investment decisions, based on the comparative assessment of alternative investments, require the use and analysis of all three financial statements as well as footnote and supplementary disclosures.

In the following chapter, we review trends in empirical research to gain insight into the information content of financial data. Starting in Chapter 6, we examine areas of financial reporting more specifically, seeking to apply the general principles articulated in these first three chapters.

CASE 3-1

Thousand Trails, Inc. II

INCOME AND CASH FLOW ANALYSIS

The statement of changes in financial position (see Exhibit 3C-1) provided by Thousand Trails was required prior to the adoption of SFAS 95. The layout of that statement and cash flow classifications in that statement differ from those specified by SFAS 95. However, as it is the information contained in financial statements, not their format, that determines their usefulness, we can make use of this statement (together with those provided in Exhibit 2C-1) to shed further light on Thousand Trails' operations.

Thousand Trails reported that CFO (before and after preserve improvements) lagged reported income (see Exhibit 2C-1). Given the growth in Thousand Trails' income and revenue, this lag may have been purely a function of Thousand Trails' growth. As Thousand Trails used the direct method, a separate comparison of its pattern of revenue growth with its cash inflows and of its expenses with cash outflows is possible.

Required
Discuss how the information provided by the statement of cash flows sheds light on Thousand Trails'

1. Future cash flows and long-term growth prospects
2. Liquidity position
3. Revenue and expense recognition methods
4. Balance sheet

In particular, the following points should be considered in your analysis:

- How does the amount of revenue recognized with respect to membership sales compare with the cash inflows from those activities?
- How does the amount of expense recognized with respect to preserve improvements compare with the cash outlows from those activities?
- What are Thousand Trails' cash requirements and free cash flows?

Note: To answer the above questions regarding cash flows, you may want to make reference to Thousand Trails' balance sheet (Exhibit 3C-2).

EXHIBIT 3C-1. THOUSAND TRAILS, INC. AND SUBSIDIARIES
Consolidated Statements of Changes in Financial Position, 1981 to 1983

Year ended December 31	1983	1982	1981
Operations			
Cash received			
Membership sales	$ 27,738,000	$ 22,582,000	$18,003,000
Collections on contracts receivable, including interest	28,619,000	19,278,000	13,258,000
Dues and preserve revenues	10,507,000	7,336,000	5,133,000
Other	211,000	133,000	(69,000)
	67,075,000	49,329,000	36,325,000
Cash expended			
Marketing expenses	34,211,000	23,211,000	19,983,000
General and administrative expenses	11,788,000	7,739,000	7,130,000
Preserve maintenance and operations	9,001,000	6,127,000	4,571,000
Principal payments on debt related to preserve properties	4,337,000	3,744,000	2,032,000
Interest expense	3,957,000	4,203,000	3,213,000
	63,294,000	45,024,000	36,929,000
Cash provided by (used in) operations before preserve improvements	3,781,000	4,305,000	(604,000)
Cash expended for preserve improvements	(18,391,000)	(11,275,000)	(6,837,000)
Cash used in operations	(14,610,000)	(6,970,000)	(7,441,000)
Other sources (uses) of cash			
Issuance of common stock	17,756,000	4,161,000	10,000
Proceeds of borrowings collateralized by contracts receivable	851,000	8,646,000	9,069,000
Principal payments on notes payable and credit line arrangements	(1,109,000)	(735,000)	(743,000)
Acquisition of preferred stock		(3,000,000)	
Purchase of construction and operating equipment, net of related borrowings of $1,388,000, $1,072,000, and $1,588,000	(2,943,000)	(1,490,000)	(789,000)
Other, net	122,000	(81,000)	(566,000)
	14,677,000	7,501,000	6,981,000
Increase (decrease) in cash	67,000	531,000	(460,000)
Cash			
Beginning of year	703,000	172,000	632,000
End of year	$ 770,000	$ 703,000	$ 172,000

Source: Thousand Trails, Inc., *1983 Annual Report.*

EXHIBIT 3C-2. THOUSAND TRAILS, INC. AND SUBSIDIARIES
Consolidated Balance Sheets

Assets December 31,	1983	1982
Current assets		
Cash	$ 770,000	$ 703,000
Current portion of notes, contracts, and accounts receivable		
Membership contracts	20,382,000	13,568,000
Other	1,558,000	1,025,000
	21,940,000	14,593,000
Allowance for doubtful accounts	(1,111,000)	(646,000)
	20,829,000	13,947,000
Inventory and prepaid expenses	2,067,000	1,331,000
Total current assets	23,666,000	15,981,000
Notes, contracts, and accounts receivable, less current portion		
Membership contracts	66,740,000	42,546,000
Real estate contracts	732,000	788,000
Other	218,000	179,000
	67,690,000	43,513,000
Allowance for doubtful accounts	(3,638,000)	(2,025,000)
	64,052,000	41,488,000
Operating preserves		
Land	17,702,000	12,347,000
Improvements	64,580,000	43,820,000
	82,282,000	56,167,000
Costs applicable to membership sales	(38,466,000)	(25,427,000)
	43,816,000	30,740,000
Preserves under development, at cost	6,592,000	2,244,000
Investment in real estate, at cost	2,773,000	2,793,000
Construction and operating equipment, net of accumulated		3,480,000
depreciation of $3,174,000 and $2,085,000	5,293,000	
Other assets, at cost	5,575,000	5,573,000
	$151,767,000	$102,299,000

Liabilities and shareholders' equity December 31,	1983	1982
Current liabilities		
Accounts payable	$ 2,415,000	$ 1,836,000
Accrued salaries	3,714,000	1,949,000
Prepaid membership dues	1,887,000	1,064,000
Other liabilities	1,180,000	1,289,000
Current portion of long-term debt	5,896,000	4,350,000
Deferred income taxes	7,026,000	4,513,000
Total current liabilities	22,118,000	15,001,000
Long-term debt, less current portion	47,343,000	43,112,000
Deferred income taxes	22,007,000	13,992,000
Commitments and contingencies (Note G)		
Shareholders' equity		
Common stock, no par value	29,358,000	11,252,000
Retained earnings	30,941,000	18,942,000
	60,299,000	30,194,000
	$151,767,000	$102,299,000

Source: Thousand Trails, Inc., *1983 Annual Report.*

Chapter 3

Problems

1. [Cash flows; 1992 CFA adapted] The cash flow data of Palomba Pizza Stores for the year ended December 31, 1991 follow:

Cash payment of dividends	$ (35,000)
Purchase of land	(14,000)
Cash payments for interest	(10,000)
Cash payments for salaries	(45,000)
Sale of equipment	38,000
Retirement of common stock	(25,000)
Purchase of equipment	(30,000)
Cash payments to suppliers	(85,000)
Cash collections from customers	250,000
Cash at December 31, 1990	50,000

A. Prepare a statement of cash flows for Palomba for 1991. Classify cash flows as required by SFAS 95.

B. Discuss, from an analyst's viewpoint, the purpose of classifying cash flows into the three categories used in part A.

C. Discuss whether any of the cash flows should be classified differently.

D. Discuss the significance of the change in cash during 1991 as an indicator of Palomba's performance.

2. [Cash flows; 1994 CFA adapted] The following information was obtained for the CF Company:

Cash payments for interest	$ (12)
Retirement of common stock	(32)
Cash payments to merchandise suppliers	(85)
Purchase of land	(8)
Sale of equipment	30
Payments of dividends	(37)
Cash payments for salaries	(35)
Cash collections from customers	260
Purchase of equipment	(40)

A. Calculate, *using the provisions of SFAS 95,* the firm's:
  (i) Cash flows from operating activities
  (ii) Cash flows from investing activities
  (iii) Cash flows from financing activities

B. Redo (A), suggesting other amounts that may be more appropriate to use for analytic purposes.

C. Calculate the firm's *free cash flow*.

3. [Cash flows; 1996 CFA adapted] The following information applies to a firm during a recent fiscal year:

Paid cash for land	$ 20,000
Paid cash for salaries	60,000
Paid cash to suppliers	40,000
Collected cash from customers	150,000
Collected cash from sale of equipment	75,000
Depreciation expense	10,000

A. If the firm is not subject to income taxes, calculate its net cash flow from operating activities.

B. Assume that in addition to the above items, the firm also paid $20,000 in cash for interest to bondholders. How would that affect your answer in part A?

4. [Revenue and expense recognition, cash flow analysis] The accrual concept results in the recognition of revenue at the time a sale is made. However, as some customers will surely default, an allowance must be made for bad debts. The Stengel Company showed the following pattern of sales, bad-debt expense, and net receivables for 19X1 through 19X5 ($ in millions):

	19X1	19X2	19X3	19X4	19X5
Sales	$140	$150	$165	$175	$195
Bad-debt expense	7	7	8	10	10
Net receivables*	40	50	60	75	95
Net receivables* at 19X0 = 30					

*At year-end.

A. Calculate the cash collected from customers each year from 19X1 to 19X5.

B. Based on the pattern of sales, net receivables, and cash collections in part A, discuss the adequacy of the provision for bad debts.

5. [Cash flow, transactional analysis; 1990 CFA adapted] The following financial statements are from the *19X2 Annual Report* of the Niagara Company:

Income Statement for Year Ended December 31, 19X2

Sales	$1,000
Cost of goods sold	(650)
Depreciation expense	(100)
Sales and general expense	(100)
Interest expense	(50)
Income tax expense	(40)
Net income	$ 60

Balance Sheets at December 31, 19X1 and 19X2

	19X1	19X2
Assets		
Cash	$ 50	$ 60
Accounts receivable	500	520
Inventory	750	770
Current assets	$1,300	$1,350
Fixed assets (net)	500	550
Total assets	$1,800	$1,900
Liabilities and equity		
Notes payable to banks	$ 100	$ 75
Accounts payable	590	615
Interest payable	10	20
Current liabilities	$ 700	$ 710
Long-term debt	300	350
Deferred income tax	300	310
Capital stock	400	400
Retained earnings	100	130
Total liabilities and equity	$1,800	$1,900

Prepare a statement of cash flows for the year ended December 31, 19X2. Use the direct method.

6. [Cash flow and income analysis] The financial statements of the M company and G Company are contained in Exhibit 3P-1.

A. Derive the 19X4 income statement for the G Company.

B. Derive the 19X4 cash receipts and disbursements for the M Company.

C. Convert the schedules of cash receipts and disbursements for the years 19X0 through 19X4 for both the G Company and M Company to statements of cash flows segregating the cash from operations, financing, and investment. Use the direct method.

D. As a bank loan officer, would you prefer to lend to the G Company or M Company? Justify your answer.

7. [Preparation of cash flow statement—indirect method; 1996 CFA adapted] The balance sheet and income statement for the Green Company are presented in Exhibit 3P-2.

A. Based on the financial statements provided, prepare the company's Statement of Cash Flows using the indirect method.

B. Calculate the company's free cash flow.

8. [Statement of cash flows—direct method] Redo the previous problem using the *direct* method.

EXHIBIT 3P-1. M COMPANY
Comparative Balance Sheets at December 31, 19X0 to 19X4 ($ in thousands)

	19X0	19X1	19X2	19X3	19X4
Cash	$ 34	$ 35	$ 50	$ 30	$ 46
Accounts receivable	365	420	477	545	599
Inventory	227	265	304	405	458
Current assets	$626	$720	$831	$ 980	$1,103
Property, plant, and equipment	120	137	174	204	237
Less: Accumulated depreciation	(40)	(50)	(61)	(73)	(87)
Total assets	$706	$807	$944	$1,111	$1,253
Accounts payable	$104	$118	$125	$ 113	$ 104
Taxes payable	81	95	113	130	133
Short-term debt	181	246	238	391	453
Current liabilities	$366	$459	$476	$ 634	$ 690
Long-term debt	48	46	143	143	239
Total liabilities	$414	$505	$619	$ 777	$ 929
Common stock	81	72	80	73	76
Retained earnings	211	230	245	261	248
Total equity	$292	$302	$325	$ 334	$ 324
Total liabilities and equity	$706	$807	$944	$1,111	$1,253

M COMPANY
Income Statements for Years Ended December 31, 19X0 to 19X4 ($ in thousands)

	19X0	19X1	19X2	19X3	19X4
Sales	$1,220	$1,265	$1,384	$1,655	$1,861
Cost of goods sold	818	843	931	1,125	1,277
Operating expenses	298	320	363	434	504
Depreciation	9	10	11	12	14
Interest	15	19	16	21	51
Taxes	38	33	27	26	6
Total expenses	$1,178	$1,225	$1,348	$1,618	$1,852
Net income	$ 42	$ 40	$ 36	$ 37	$ 9

M COMPANY
Cash Receipts and Disbursements, 19X0 to 19X4 ($ in thousands)

	19X0	19X1	19X2	19X3	19X4
Cash Receipts from					
Customers	$1,165	$1,210	$1,327	$1,587	$?
Issue of stock	5	5	8	3	?
Short-term debt	64	65	—	153	?
Long-term debt	—	—	100	—	?
Total receipts	$1,234	$1,280	$1,435	$1,743	$?

EXHIBIT 3P-1. (*continued*)

	19X0	19X1	19X2	19X3	19X4
Cash Disbursements for					
Cost of goods sold and operating expenses	1,130	1,187	1,326	1,672	?
Dividends	20	21	21	21	?
Taxes	23	19	9	9	?
Interest	15	19	16	21	?
Property, plant, and equipment purchase	14	17	37	30	?
Repurchase of stock	22	14	—	10	?
Repayment of long-term debt	2	2	3	—	?
Repayment of short-term debt	—	—	8	—	?
Total disbursements	$1,226	$1,279	$1,420	$1,763	$?
Change in cash	$ 8	$ 1	$ 15	$ (20)	$?

G COMPANY
Comparative Balance Sheets at December 31, 19X0 to 19X4 ($ in thousands)

	19X0	19X1	19X2	19X3	19X4
Cash	$ 28	$ 32	$ 35	$ 54	$ 19
Accounts receivable	249	321	419	549	711
Inventory	303	391	510	672	873
Current assets	$580	$744	$ 964	$1,275	$1,603
Property, plant, and equipment	200	200	220	230	230
Less: Accumulated depreciation	(10)	(20)	(32)	(46)	(61)
Total assets	$770	$924	$1,152	$1,459	$1,772
Accounts payable	$102	$134	$ 177	$ 235	$ 309
Income tax payable	20	25	36	38	45
Short-term debt	138	190	281	284	344
Current liabilities	$260	$349	$ 494	$ 557	$ 698
Long-term debt	40	63	83	208	258
Total liabilities	$300	$412	$ 577	$ 765	$ 956
Common stock	440	440	445	490	520
Retained earnings	30	72	130	204	296
Total equity	$470	$512	$ 575	$ 694	$ 816
Total liabilities and equity	$770	$924	$1,152	$1,459	$1,772

EXHIBIT 3P-1. (*continued*)

G COMPANY
Income Statements for Years Ended December 31, 19X0 to 19X4 ($ in thousands)

	19X0	19X1	19X2	19X3	19X4
Sales	$1,339	$1,731	$2,261	$2,939	$?
Cost of goods sold	1,039	1,334	1,743	2,267	?
Operating expenses	243	312	398	524	?
Depreciation	10	10	12	14	?
Interest	11	13	23	29	?
Taxes	13	20	27	31	?
Total expenses	$1,316	$1,689	$2,203	$2,865	$?
Net income	$ 23	$ 42	$ 58	$ 74	$?

G COMPANY
Cash Receipts and Disbursements, 19X0 to 19X4 ($ in thousands)

	19X0	19X1	19X2	19X3	19X4
Cash Receipts from					
Customers	$1,110	$1,659	$2,163	$2,809	$3,679
Issue of stock	10	—	5	45	30
Short-term debt	80	52	91	3	60
Long-term debt	40	23	20	125	50
Total receipts	$1,240	$1,734	$2,279	$2,982	$3,819
Cash Disbursements for					
Cost of goods sold and operating expenses	1,214	1,702	2,217	2,895	3,778
Dividends	—	—	—	—	—
Taxes	13	15	16	29	35
Interest	11	13	23	29	41
Property, plant, and equipment purchase	—	—	20	10	—
Repurchase of common stock	—	—	—	—	—
Repayment of long-term debt	—	—	—	—	—
Repayment of short-term debt	—	—	—	—	—
Total disbursements	$1,238	$1,730	$2,276	$2,963	$3,854
Change in cash	$ 2	$ 4	$ 3	$ 19	$ (35)

9. [Cash flow, conversion of indirect to direct method] Exhibit 3P-3 contains balance sheets, income statements, and cash flow statements for Mercantile Stores, a department store company, for the two years ended January 31, 1992. The statement of cash flows is prepared using the indirect method as permitted by SFAS 95.

A. Using the data in Exhibit 3P-3, prepare a statement of cash flow from operations, using the direct method, for the year ended January 31, 1992.

EXHIBIT 3P-2. THE GREEN COMPANY
Balance Sheet and Income Statement

Balance Sheet

As of December 31	1995	1996
Assets		
Cash	$ 1,000	$ 1,100
Accounts receivable	1,500	1,650
Inventory	2,000	2,200
Total current assets	4,500	4,950
Fixed assets—at cost*	11,000	12,150
Accumulated depreciation	4,500	5,100
Net fixed assets	6,500	7,050
Total assets	$11,000	$12,000
Liabilities and Equity		
Accruals	$ 800	$ 880
Accounts payable	1,200	1,320
Notes payable	5,500	6,050
Total current liabilities	7,500	8,250
Long-term debt	2,000	1,602
Common stock	1,000	1,000
Retained earnings	500	1,148
Total liabilities and equity	$11,000	$12,000

*No fixed assets were sold during 1996.

Income Statement for the Year

Ending December 31, 1996

Sales	$10,000
Cost of goods sold	6,000
Depreciation	600
Selling, general and administrative expenses	1,000
Interest expense	600
Taxable income	1,800
Taxes	720
Net income	$ 1,080

EXHIBIT 3P-3. MERCANTILE STORES
Consolidated Balance Sheets

$ in thousands January 31,	1992	1991
Assets		
Current assets		
Cash and cash equivalents	$ 122,458	$ 44,655
Receivables		
Customer	606,189	626,656
Other	50,239	40,944
Inventories	381,406	393,304
Deferred income taxes	6,470	6,668
Other current assets	3,846	4,515
Total current assets	1,170,608	1,116,742
Investments and other noncurrent assets	40,928	35,192
Property and equipment		
Land	17,640	17,640
Building and improvements	396,473	377,832
Fixtures	243,307	223,114
Leased property	65,525	61,001
	722,945	679,587
Less accumulated depreciation	261,382	234,891
Property and equipment—net	461,563	444,696
Total	$1,673,099	$1,596,630

$ in thousands January 31,	1992	1991
Liabilities and Stockholders' Equity		
Current liabilities		
Current maturities of long-term debt	$ 7,030	$ 7,985
Note payable	6,401	—
Accounts payable	86,414	88,112
Other current liabilities	44,628	46,379
Accrued income taxes	18,192	18,465
Accrued payroll	19,160	21,307
Total current liabilities	181,825	182,248
Long-term debt	207,150	207,906
Due to affiliated companies	17,792	17,372
Deferred income taxes	7,217	6,520
Other long-term liabilities	8,067	8,453
Stockholders' equity		
Common stock: $.14 2/3 par value, issued 36,887,475 shares, outstanding 36,844,050 (after deducting 43,425 treasury shares)	5,403	5,403
Additional paid-in capital	6,018	6,018
Retained earnings	1,239,627	1,162,710
Total stockholders' equity	1,251,048	1,174,131
Total	$1,673,099	$1,596,630

Statements of Consolidated Income and Retained Earnings

$ in thousands January 31,	1992	1991	1990
Net sales	$2,442,425	$2,367,210	$2,312,802
Cost, expenses, and other income			
Cost of goods sold (including occupancy and central buying expenses)	1,720,947	1,670,555	1,594,849
Selling, general and administrative expenses	546,682	527,467	502,537
Provision for relocation	—	—	10,000
Interest expense	23,390	23,422	22,818
Interest income	(4,511)	(4,160)	(4,289)
Other income	(30,485)	(29,186)	(26,156)
	2,256,023	2,188,098	2,099,759
Income before income taxes	186,402	179,112	213,043
Income taxes			
Currently payable	71,468	85,327	99,845
Deferred	895	(29,829)	(17,145)
	72,363	55,498	82,700
Net income	$ 114,039	$ 123,614	$ 130,343
Retained earnings at beginning of year	1,162,710	1,065,900	969,454
	1,276,749	1,189,514	1,099,797
Dividends declared (1)	37,122	26,804	33,897
Retained earnings at year-end	$1,239,627	$1,162,710	$1,065,900
Net income per share	$ 3.10	$ 3.36	$ 3.54
(1) Dividends Paid	$ 37,122	$ 35,278	$ 32,792

Statements of Consolidated Cash Flows

$ in thousands January 31,	1992	1991	1990
Cash flows from operating activities			
Net income	$114,039	$123,614	$130,343
Adjustments to reconcile net income to net cash provided by operating activities			
Depreciation and amortization	70,607	63,158	54,478
Deferred taxes	895	(29,829)	(17,145)
Provision for relocation	—	—	10,000
Equity in unremitted earnings of affiliated companies	(931)	(1,840)	(1,873)
Net pension benefit	(4,256)	(6,248)	(4,468)
Change in inventories	11,898	15	(31,282)
Change in accounts receivable	11,172	(22,967)	(19,434)
Change in accounts payable	(1,698)	(4,634)	8,206
Net change in other working capital items	(2,854)	(17,921)	(6,276)
Net cash provided by operating activities	198,872	103,348	122,549
Cash flows from investing activities			
Cash payments for property and equipment	(79,931)	(82,944)	(97,196)
Net change in other noncurrent assets and liabilities	(1,163)	(3,719)	(190)
Net change in notes receivable	—	(165)	249
Net cash used in investing activities	(81,094)	(86,828)	(97,137)

EXHIBIT 3P-3. (*continued*)

$ in thousands January 31,	1992	1991	1990
Cash flows from financing activities			
Payments of long-term debt	(9,254)	(7,860)	(8,194)
Increase in note payable	6,401	—	—
Dividends paid	(37,122)	(35,278)	(32,792)
Net cash used in financing activities	(39,975)	(43,138)	(40,986)
Net increase (decrease) in cash and cash equivalents	77,803	(26,618)	(15,574)
Cash and cash equivalents at beginning of year	44,655	71,273	86,847
Cash and cash equivalents at year-end	$122,458	$ 44,655	$ 71,273
Supplemental cash flow information			
Interest paid	$ 23,397	$ 23,453	$ 22,865
Income taxes paid	$ 71,741	$100,440	$103,019
Noncash investing and financing activities			
Leases capitalized	$ 7,543	$ 16,681	$ 10,073

Source: Mercantile Stores, *1991 Annual Report.*

B. Discuss the usefulness of the direct method statement, with particular emphasis on insights not provided by the income statement and indirect method cash flow statement.

10. [Cash flow from operations, free cash flows] Hertz is the world's largest provider of rental cars and trucks. Extracts from its statement of cash flows follow:

Cash Flows of Hertz Corp.

	1989	1990	1991
Net income	$ 108	$ 89	$ 48
Depreciation of revenue equipment	475	530	497
Depreciation of property	57	69	75
Self-insurance and other accruals	100	85	122
Purchases of revenue equipment	(3,003)	(4,024)	(4,016)
Sales of revenue equipment	2,354	3,434	3,784
Changes in operating assets and liabilities (net)	(141)	13	(118)
Payment of self-insurance claims	(67)	(104)	(106)
Cash flow from operations	$ (117)	$ 92	$ 286
Cash flow for investing	(133)	(79)	(72)
Net change in debt	241	(4)	(84)
Dividends paid	(90)	(64)	(62)
Cash flow from financing	$ 151	$ (68)	$ (146)
Effect of foreign exchange rates	1	11	0
Net increase (decrease) in cash	$ (98)	$ (44)	$ 68

Source: Hertz Corp., *1991 Annual Report.*

Note that Hertz includes the purchases and sales of revenue equipment (cars and trucks to be rented) in cash flow from operations.

A. Recompute cash flow from operations, classifying the purchases and sales of revenue equipment as investing cash flows.

B. Compare the trend of cash flow from operations as reported with the trend after reclassification.

C. Recompute cash flow for investing, classifying the purchases and sales of revenue equipment as investing cash flows.

D. Compare the trend of cash flow for investing as reported with the trend after reclassification.

E. Which classification provides the better measure of cash flow from operations for Hertz? Define and compute a useful measure of free cash flow for Hertz. State your assumptions.

F. Assume that Hertz leases (rather than purchases) some of its rental cars and trucks. Discuss the impact of leasing (rather than buying) on cash flow from operations as reported by Hertz.

G. Discuss the impact of leasing on cash flow from operations, assuming that the purchases of revenue equipment are reported as cash flows from investing. (Hint for parts F and G: Think of leasing and buying as expensing and capitalizing, respectively.)

11. [Income statement and cash flow analysis, courtesy of Professor I. Krinsky] The income statement and statement of cash flows of the Radloc Company are presented in Exhibit 3P-4. The company is a merchandising company that has been expanding rapidly.

EXHIBIT 3P-4. THE RADLOC COMPANY
Income and Cash Flow Statements

Income Statement			
	1994	1993	1992
Net sales	**$2,748,634**	$2,414,124	$2,127,684
Cost of merchandise sold	**1,975,332**	1,742,276	1,527,731
Gross margin	**772,302**	671,648	599,953
Selling, general and administrative	**605,538**	520,685	458,804
Depreciation and amortization	**48,478**	40,501	34,954
Preopening expense	**7,574**	8,228	3,492
Facilities relocation expense	**3,786**		
Interest expense	**34,948**	34,904	39,934
Earnings before provision for income taxes, extraordinary items, and cumulative effects of accounting changes	**71,928**	67,530	62,769
Income tax provision	**27,569**	26,152	25,507
Earnings before extraordinary loss and cumulative effect of accounting changes	**44,359**	41,378	37,262
Extraordinary loss		(5,378)	
Cumulative effect of accounting changes		(2,768)	(2,812)
Net earnings	**$ 44,359**	$ 33,232	$ 34,450

EXHIBIT 3P-4. (*continued*)

| | *Statement of Cash Flows* | | |
	1994	1993	1992
Cash flows from operating activities			
Net earnings	**$ 44,539**	$ 33,232	$ 34,450
Expenses not requiring the outlay of cash			
Amortization of debt issuance costs	**1,000**	1,537	2,051
Depreciation and other amortization	**48,478**	40,501	34,954
Cumulative effect of accounting changes		4,500	2,812
Deferred income taxes	**1,594**	501	4,090
Extraordinary loss on early retirement of debt		5,430	
Loss on disposal of property and equipment	**1,359**	650	
Changes in working capital and other accounts			
Accounts receivable	**(4,475)**	6,837	8,121
Merchandise inventories	**(82,863)**	(60,893)	(28,401)
Prepaid expenses and other	**(3,358)**	(2,137)	1,317
Accounts payable	**(6,620)**	61,020	53,718
Accrued wages and benefits	**7,321**	(652)	4,038
Other accrued liabilities	**5,990**	5,293	(10,017)
Federal and state income tax payable	**17,567**	2,662	9,003
Other assets and long-term liabilities	**342**	254	246
Net cash provided by operating activities	**$ 30,794**	$ 98,735	$100,140
Cash flows from investing activities			
Capital expenditures	**(90,009)**	(110,534)	(48,878)
Acquisition of leasehold interests	**(8,025)**	(21,894)	(36,602)
Net cash used in investing activities	**$(98,034)**	$(132,428)	$ (85,480)
Cash flows from financing activities			
Retirement of senior notes		(200,000)	
Proceeds from borrowings under term loan		180,000	
Proceeds from borrowings under revolving credit	**70,243**		
Proceeds from long-term debt	**(19,432)**	(3,831)	(3,276)
Proceeds from of common stock	**34**	53,334	
Proceeds from exercise of warrants and options	**1,016**	1,126	1,995
Net cash provided by (used in) financing activities	**$ 51,361**	$ 30,629	$ (1,281)
(Decrease) increase in cash	**$(15,379)**	$ 3,064	$ 13,379

Assume that you are the credit manager of a bank and the company approaches you for a loan in the first quarter of 1995. Would you grant the company a loan? As *part* of your analysis, you should:

(i) Compute (to the extent possible) a direct cash flow statement.

(ii) Compare the trends in

- Cash collections from customers
- Cash payments to suppliers
- Cash payments for expenses

with their "counterparts" in the income statement.

(iii) Examine trends in income, CFO, and free cash flow.

12. [Cash flow statement—effects of acquisitions and relationship to other statements] Excerpts from A. M. Castle's balance sheet and cash flow statements are presented below:

Consolidated Statement of Cash Flows

	1990	1991
Cash from operations		
Net income	$ 3,128	$ 201
Add/subtract		
Depreciation	5,215	5,273
Provision for bad debts	790	522
Gain on sale of equipment	(17)	(635)
Increase in deferred taxes	71	728
Other	876	(1,109)
Changes in		
Accounts receivable	3,818	4,479
Inventories	(13,592)	25,601
Accounts payable	(11,709)	(7,541)
Accrued payroll	(3,034)	(1,701)
Accrued liabilities	267	91
Current deferred taxes	(524)	(834)
	$(14,711)	**$ 25,075**
Cash from investing		
Acquisition of Norton Steel	$ (2,529)	
Proceeds from sales of facilities/equipment	34	5,490
Capital expenditures	(13,390)	(3,305)
	(15,885)	**2,185**
Cash from financing	29,086	(27,231)
Change in cash	$ (1,510)	$ 29

Consolidated Balance Sheets

	1989	1990	1991
Current Assets			
Cash	$ 1,812	$ 302	$ 331
Accounts receivable	51,068	49,043	44,564
Inventories	96,299	113,893	88,292
Total current assets	149,179	163,238	133,187
Prepaid expenses and other assets	7,798	8,640	9,813

	1989	1990	1991
Property, plant, and equipment, at cost			
Land	3,687	4,115	4,115
Buildings	26,896	33,893	34,688
Machinery and equipment	52,531	59,340	54,653
	83,114	97,348	93,456
Less accumulated depreciation	37,839	42,583	46,041
	45,275	54,765	47,415
Total assets	**$202,252**	**$226,643**	**$190,415**
Liabilities and Stockholders' Equity			
Current liabilities			
Accounts payable	$ 53,520	$ 44,915	$ 37,374
Accrued payroll and employee benefits	8,477	5,443	3,742
Accrued liabilities	3,101	3,624	3,715
Short-term debt	500	11,900	200
Current deferred income taxes	3,907	3,335	2,501
Current portion of long-term debt	3,846	4,107	5,925
Total current liabilities	73,351	73,324	53,457
Long-term debt, less current portion	51,019	76,725	63,278
Deferred income taxes	8,138	8,282	9,010
Stockholders' equity	69,744	68,312	64,670
Total liabilities and stockholders' equity	**$202,252**	**$226,643**	**$190,415**

A. In 1990, as indicated by the cash flow statement, Castle acquired Norton Steel. Estimate the impact of the acquisition on the following components of operating working capital:

   (i) Accounts receivable

   (ii) Inventory

   (iii) Accounts payable

B. Estimate the amount of property, plant, and equipment purchased in the acquisition.

C. In 1991, Castle's income declined. Its CFO, however, increased dramatically.

   (i) Explain how this difference occurred.

   (ii) Explain how the acquisition of Norton may have affected the trend in CFO.

13. [Cash flows, free cash flows; effect of acquisitions 1989 CFA adapted] In October 1988, Philip Morris announced an unsolicited cash tender offer for all the 124 million outstanding shares of Kraft at $90 per share. Kraft subsequently accepted a $106-per-share all-cash offer from Philip Morris. Following the completion of the acquisition of Kraft, Philip Morris released its 1988 year-end financial statements.

A. Prepare a statement of cash flows for Philip Morris Companies, Inc. based on the format utilized in SFAS 95 using only the actual 1988 financial data contained in Exhibit 3P-5.

EXHIBIT 3P-5. PHILIP MORRIS COMPANIES, INC.
Balance Sheets at December 31, 1987–1988 ($ in millions)

	1987	1988
Assets		
Cash and cash equivalents	$ 90	$ 168
Accounts receivable	2,065	2,222
Inventories	4,154	5,384
Current assets	$ 6,309	$ 7,774
Property, plant, and equipment (net)	6,582	8,648
Goodwill (net)	4,052	15,071
Investments	3,665	3,260
Total assets	$20,608	$34,753
Liabilities and Stockholders' Equity		
Short-term debt	$ 1,440	$ 1,259
Accounts payable	791	1,777
Accrued liabilities	2,277	3,848
Income taxes payable	727	1,089
Dividends payable	213	260
Current liabilities	$ 5,448	$ 8,233
Long-term debt	6,293	17,122
Deferred income taxes	2,044	1,719
Stockholders' equity	6,823	7,679
Total liabilities and stockholders' equity	$20,608	$34,753

PHILIP MORRIS COMPANIES, INC.
Income Statement for Year Ended December 31, 1988 ($ in millions)

Sales	$ 31,742
Cost of goods sold	(12,156)
Selling and administrative expenses	(14,410)
Depreciation expense	(654)
Goodwill amortization	(125)
Interest expense	(670)
Pretax income	$ 3,727
Income tax expense	(1,390)
Net income	$ 2,337

Dividends declared $941 million

PHILIP MORRIS PURCHASE OF KRAFT
Allocation of Purchase Price ($ in millions)

Accounts receivable	$ 758
Inventories	1,232
Property, plant, and equipment	1,740
Goodwill	10,361
Short-term debt	(700)
Accounts payable	(578)
Accrued liabilities	(530)
Long-term debt	(900)
Purchase price (net of cash acquired)	$11,383

(*Important Note:* The acquisition of Kraft requires that you remove the assets acquired and liabilities incurred as a result of that acquisition from the balance sheet changes used to prepare the statement of cash flows. Philip Morris paid $11.383 billion for Kraft, net of cash required. A breakdown of the purchase is contained in Exhibit 3P-5.)

B. Based on your answer to part A, compute Philip Morris' free cash flow for 1988 and discuss how free cash flow may impact the company's future earnings and financial condition.

C. In the Philip Morris cash flow statement prepared in part A, the cost of Kraft's inventories and receivables acquired by Philip Morris was classified as cash from investment rather than cash from operations. Discuss how this classification may distort the trend in CFO, and state under what conditions this distortion will occur.

4

FOUNDATIONS OF RATIO AND FINANCIAL ANALYSIS

CHAPTER OUTLINE

CHAPTER OBJECTIVES

INTRODUCTION
Purpose and Use of Ratio Analysis
Ratio Analysis: Cautionary Notes
 Economic Assumptions
 Benchmarks
 Timing and Window Dressing
 Negative Numbers
 Accounting Methods

COMMON-SIZE STATEMENTS

DISCUSSION OF RATIOS BY CATEGORY
Activity Analysis
 Short-Term (Operating) Activity Ratios
 Long-Term (Investment) Activity Ratios
Liquidity Analysis
 Length of Cash Cycle
 Working Capital Ratios and Defensive Intervals
Long-Term Debt and Solvency Analysis
 Debt Covenants
 Capitalization Table and Debt Ratios
 Interest Coverage Ratios
 Capital Expenditure and CFO-to-Debt Ratios

Profitability Analysis
 Return on Sales
 Return on Investment
 Profitability and Cash Flows
Operating and Financial Leverage
 Operating Leverage
 Financial Leverage

EARNINGS PER SHARE AND OTHER RATIOS USED IN VALUATION
Earnings per Share
 Simple Capital Structure
 Complex Capital Structure
 Adjustments for Options and Warrants
 Adjustments for Convertible Securities
 Limitations of EPS Calculations
Cash Flow per Share
EBITDA per Share
Book Value per Share
Price-to-Earnings and Price-to-Book Value Ratios
Dividend Payout Ratio
 Effect of Dividend Policy on per Share Growth

RATIOS: AN INTEGRATED ANALYSIS
Analysis of Firm Performance
 Disaggregation of ROA

Disaggregation of ROE and Its Relationship to ROA
Economic Characteristics and Strategies
  Competing Strategies
  Product Life Cycle
  Interindustry Economic Factors
  Trends in ROE
Classification and Selection of Ratios
Patterns of Ratio Disclosure, Definitions, and Use
  Perceived Importance and Classification

Disclosure of Ratios
Industry Norms as Benchmarks

SUMMARY

CASE 4-1: INTEGRATED ANALYSIS OF DUPONT, DOW CHEMICAL, AND ICI

APPENDIX 4–A: ESTIMATING OPERATING LEVERAGE

CHAPTER OBJECTIVES

This chapter introduces ratios, the basic tools of financial analysis. Our goals are to:

1. Examine the purpose and use of ratios and provide some cautionary notes.
2. Explain the use of common-size statements.
3. Discuss the construction and use of:
   - Activity (turnover) ratios that measure the efficiency with which the firm uses its resources.
   - Liquidity ratios that assess the firm's ability to meet its near-term obligations.
   - Solvency ratios that examine capital structure and the firm's ability to meet long-term obligations and capital needs.
   - Profitability ratios that measure income relative to revenues and invested capital.
4. Define and compute measures of operating and financial leverage.
5. Examine the computation and usefulness of earnings per share and other ratios used for valuation purposes.
6. Show how the integrated analysis of ratios can be used to evaluate corporate performance.

INTRODUCTION

Financial ratios are used to compare the risk and return of different firms in order to help equity investors and creditors make intelligent investment and credit decisions. Such decisions range from an evaluation of changes in performance over time for a particular investment to a comparison among all firms within a single industry at a specific point in time.

    The informational needs and appropriate analytical techniques used for these investment and credit decisions depend on the decision maker's time horizon. Short-term bank and trade creditors are primarily interested in the immediate liquidity of the firm. Longer-term creditors (e.g., bondholders) are interested in long-term solvency. Creditors seek to minimize risk and ensure that resources are available for the payment of interest and principal obligations.

Equity investors are primarily interested in the long-term earning power of the firm. As the equity investor bears the residual risk (which can be defined as the return from operations after all claims from suppliers and creditors have been satisfied), it requires a return commensurate to that risk. The residual risk is highly volatile and difficult to quantify, as is the equity investor's time horizon. Thus, analysis by the equity investor needs to be the most comprehensive, and it subsumes the analysis carried out by other users.

Purpose and Use of Ratio Analysis

A primary advantage of ratios is that they can be used to compare the risk and return relationships of firms of different sizes. *Ratios can provide a profile of a firm, its economic characteristics and competitive strategies, and its unique operating, financial, and investment characteristics.*

This process of standardization may, however, be deceptive as it ignores differences between industries, the effect of varying capital structures, and differences in accounting and reporting methods (especially when comparisons are international in scope). Given these differences, changes (trends) in a ratio and variability over time may be more informative than the level of the ratio at any point in time.

Four broad ratio categories measure the different aspects of risk and return relationships:

1. Activity analysis. Evaluates revenue and output generated by the firm's assets.
2. Liquidity analysis. Measures the adequacy of a firm's cash resources to meet its near-term cash obligations.
3. Long-term debt and solvency analysis. Examines the firm's capital structure in terms of the mix of its financing sources and the ability of the firm to satisfy its longer-term debt and investment obligations.
4. Profitability analysis. Measures the income of the firm relative to its revenues and invested capital.

These categories are interrelated rather than independent. For example, profitability affects liquidity and solvency, and the efficiency with which assets are used (as measured by activity analysis) impacts profitability. Thus, financial analysis relies on an integrated use of many ratios, rather than a selected few.

Ratio Analysis: Cautionary Notes

Ratio analysis is essential to comprehensive financial analysis. However, ratios are based on implicit assumptions that do not always apply. Ratio computations and comparisons are further confounded by the lack or inappropriate use of benchmarks, the timing of transactions, negative numbers, and differences in reporting methods. This section presents some important caveats that must be considered when interpreting ratios.[1]

---

[1] For explanatory purposes, this discussion uses specific ratios as examples; these ratios are defined later in the chapter.

Economic Assumptions

Ratio analysis is designed to facilitate comparisons by eliminating size differences across firms and over time. Implicit in this process is the *proportionality assumption* that the economic relationship between numerator and denominator does not depend on size. This assumption ignores the existence of fixed costs. When there are fixed costs, changes in total costs (and thus profits) are not proportional to changes in sales.

Moreover, the implicit assumption of a linear relationship between numerator and denominator may be incorrect even in the absence of a fixed component. For example, the inventory turnover ratio, COGS/inventory, implies a constant relationship between the volume of sales and inventory levels. Management science theory, however, indicates that the optimum relationship is nonlinear and inventory levels may be proportional to the square root of demand.[2] Thus, a doubling in demand should increase inventory by only 40% (approximately) with a consequent 40% increase in the turnover ratio. *The inventory turnover ratio is clearly not size-independent.*

Benchmarks

Ratio analysis often lacks appropriate benchmarks to indicate optimal levels. The evaluation of a ratio often depends on the question posed by the analyst. For example, from the point of view of a short-term lender, a high liquidity ratio may be a positive indicator. However, from the perspective of an equity investor, it may indicate poor cash or working capital management.

Using an industry average as the benchmark[3] may be useful for comparisons within an industry, but not for comparisons between companies in different industries. Even for intraindustry analysis, the benchmark may have limited usefulness if the whole industry or major firms in that industry are doing poorly.

Timing and Window Dressing

Data used to compute ratios are available only at specific points in time when financial statements are issued. For annual reports, the fiscal year-end may correspond to the low point of a firm's operating cycle, when reported levels of assets and liabilities may not reflect the levels typical of normal operations. As a result, especially in the case of seasonal businesses, ratios may not reflect normal operating relationships. For example, inventories and accounts payable may be understated. Reference to interim statements is one way of alleviating this problem. However, most foreign countries either do not require interim statements or require them less frequently.[4] Moreover, foreign filings are generally less timely than U.S. reports.

The timing issue leads to another problem. Transactions at year-end can lead to manipulation of the ratios to show the firm in a more favorable light, often called *window dressing*. For example, a firm with a current ratio (current assets/current liabilities) of 1.5 ($300/$200) can increase it to 2.0 ($200/$100) by simply using cash of $100 to reduce accounts payable immediately prior to the period's end.

---

[2]See Chapter 6 for a more detailed discussion of this issue.

[3]See the last section of the chapter, where we discuss databases that provide industry averages.

[4]Foreign firms using Form 20-F filings to sell securities in the United States are not required to provide interim statements if there is no home-country filing requirement.

Generally, any ratio where a transaction affects the numerator and denominator can be manipulated as follows. If the ratio is greater than 1, it can be increased by a transaction that subtracts the same amount from both the numerator and denominator. If it is less than 1, it can be increased by a transaction that adds the same amount to both the numerator and denominator.[5]

Negative Numbers

Two examples illustrate the care that must be taken in ratio analysis when negative numbers occur.

■ **Example 1: Return on Equity** $= \dfrac{\text{Income}}{\text{Equity}}$

	Income	Equity	ROE
Company A	$ 10,000	$ 100,000	10%
Company B	(10,000)	(100,000)	10%

Ratio analysis without reference to the underlying data can lead to wrong conclusions as it appears that both companies earn identical returns on their (equity) investment. Because much financial and ratio analysis today is computer-generated, the existence of negative numbers will be overlooked unless the program is well written.

■ **Example 2: Dividend Payout Ratio** $= \dfrac{\text{Dividend}}{\text{Income}}$

	Dividend	Income	Payout Ratio
Company A	$10,000	$ 50,000	20%
Company B	10,000	30,000	33%
Company C	10,000	(50,000)	(20%)

Ranking these firms by payout ratio (highest to lowest) would list them as B, A, and C. However, in reality, Company C has the highest payout ratio. That ratio is intended to measure the extent to which income is paid to shareholders rather than retained in the business. For the same income, a higher dividend increases the proportion paid out (higher payout ratio). As income approaches zero, the payout ratio approaches infinity. The payment of dividends despite negative income indicates a high payout ratio.

Accounting Methods

The choice of accounting methods and estimates can greatly affect reported financial statement amounts. In addition, as described in Chapter 3, even "pure" numbers such as cash flows from operations may be affected by accounting choices. Thus, ratios are

---

[5]To decrease the ratio, for ratios greater (less) than 1, the same amount is added to (subtracted from) the numerator and denominator.

not comparable between firms (with differing accounting methods) or for the same firm over time (when it changes accounting methods). To interpret such ratios, it may be necessary to convert from one accounting method to another. A strong understanding of accounting rules and a judicious eye for information contained in the notes to financial statements are musts for this type of analysis. Subsequent chapters will detail the impact of specific accounting methods on affected ratios.

The balance of this chapter describes specific ratios, primarily in narrative form. We illustrate the calculation and interpretation of these ratios in Exhibits 4-4, 4-6, 4-7, 4-8, and 4-12 through 4-14, using the financial statements of duPont, a leading firm in the chemical industry. DuPont's financial statements are presented in Appendix A at the end of the book. Case 4-1 asks you to compare the financial data and ratios of duPont with those of two competitors, Dow Chemical and ICI.

The calculations in these exhibits are intended for illustrative purposes; in most cases, they are based on data taken directly from financial statements without any adjustments. The required adjustments will become clearer as we progress through the book. Ratios should not be viewed as an end unto themselves, but rather as a starting point for further analysis. Ratios highlight where further investigation and adjustment may be needed. In that sense, even ratios calculated with unadjusted data can serve a useful purpose.

COMMON-SIZE STATEMENTS

A pervasive problem when comparing a firm's performance over time is that the firm's size is always changing. Firms of different sizes are also difficult to compare. Common-size statements are used to standardize financial statement components by expressing them as a percentage of a relevant base. For example, balance sheet components can be shown as a percentage of total assets; revenues and expenses can be computed as a percentage of total sales, and in the direct method cash flow statement, the components of cash flow from operations can be related to cash collections.

Common-size statements should not, however, be viewed solely as a scaling factor for standardization. They provide the analyst with useful information as a first step *in developing insights into the economic characteristics of different industries and of different firms in the same industry*. For example, significant changes in net income over time may be traced to variations in cost of goods sold (COGS) as a percentage of sales. Changes in this ratio may indicate the efficacy of the firm's efforts to streamline its operations and/or a change in pricing strategies. Additionally, differences over time in a single firm or between firms due to operating, financing, and investing decisions made by management and external economic factors are often highlighted by common-size statements.

Exhibit 4-1 compares the 1994 balance sheets and income statements of duPont, Dow Chemical, and ICI, including both the actual data and common-size statements. Exhibit 4-2 presents common-size balance sheets and income statements for the chemical industry and selected other industries. The scaling factors are total assets for the balance sheets and sales for the income statements.

Cross-Sectional Comparisons. Comparison of the three companies based on actual reported data is fraught with problems because of the disparity in size. Both duPont and Dow are considerably larger than ICI; comparisons of assets, working capital, and income cannot provide much insight unless the numbers are scaled.

EXHIBIT 4-1
Comparative Balance Sheets and Income Statements, 1994 Data

A. *Comparative Balance Sheets*

	As Reported			Common-Size (%)		
	DuPont ($ millions)	ICI (£ millions)	Dow ($ millions)	DuPont	ICI	Dow
Cash and marketable securities	$ 1,109	1,759	$ 1,134	3	20	4
Accounts receivable	5,213	1,629	4,458	14	18	17
Inventories	3,969	1,233	2,712	11	14	10
Prepaid expenses	259	112	—	1	1	0
Deferred taxes	558	—	389	2	0	1
Current assets	$ 11,108	4,733	$ 8,693	30%	53%	33%
Net property, plant, and equipment	21,120	3,861	8,726	57	43	33
Investment in affiliates	1,662	171	931	5	2	4
Other assets	3,002	239	8,195	8	3	31
Total assets	$ 36,892	9,004	$ 26,545	100%	100%	100%
Short-term debt	1,292	369	1,275	4	4	5
Accounts and notes payable	2,734	1,077	2,562	7	12	10
Income taxes payable	409	233	720	1	3	3
Other current liabilities	3,130	929	2,061	8	10	8
Current liabilities	$ 7,565	2,608	$ 6,618	21%	29%	25%
Long-term debt	6,376	1,529	5,303	17	17	20
Other liabilities	8,438	772	3,240	23	9	12
Deferred income taxes	1,494	21	644	4	0	2
Total liabilities	$ 23,873	4,930	$ 15,805	65%	55%	60%
Minority interests	197	338	2,506	1	4	9
Preferred stock	237	—	22	1	0	0
Common stock and APIC	5,179	1,293	1,144	14	14	4
Retained earnings	7,406	2,443	7,068	20	27	27
Total equity	$ 13,019	4,074	$ 10,740	35%	45%	40%
Total liabilities and equity	$ 36,892	9,004	$ 26,545	100%	100%	100%

Note: Common-size columns may not add due to rounding.

Common-size balance sheets and income statements provide such insight. Looking at the common-size balance sheets, we immediately see that:

- ICI is the strongest financially, as total debt (short- and long-term) of 21% of assets exceeds cash and marketable securities of 20%. Dow and duPont have total debt (short- and long-term) of 25% and 21% of assets respectively. As their cash and marketable securities are considerably lower than for ICI, their net debt burden is much higher. ICI also has the highest ratio of equity to total assets.

EXHIBIT 4-1 (*continued*)

B. *Comparative Income Statements*

	As Reported			Common-Size (%)		
	duPont ($ millions)	ICI (£ millions)	Dow ($ millions)	duPont	ICI	Dow
Sales	$ 39,333	9,189	$ 20,015	100	100	100
Cost of goods sold*	(24,953)	(6,502)	(13,219)	(63)	(71)	(66)
Selling, general, and administrative expenses	(2,888)	(2,005)	(3,061)	(7)	(22)	(15)
Research and development expenses	(1,047)	(184)	(1,261)	(3)	(2)	(6)
Interest expense	(559)	(186)	(537)	(1)	(2)	(3)
Restructuring and write-downs	142	(137)	—	0	(1)	—
Other operating expenses	(6,572)	(39)	(229)	(17)	(0)	(1)
Income from operations	$ 3,456	136	$ 1,708	9%	1%	9%
Other income	926	272	344	2	3	2
Income before taxes	4,382	408	2,052	11%	4%	10%
Provision for taxes	(1,655)	(164)	(779)	(4)	(2)	(4)
Income before minority interests, extraordinary items, and accounting changes	$ 2,727	244	$ 1,273	7%	3%	6%
Less minority interests, extraordinary items, and accounting changes	—	(56)	(335)	—	(1)	(2)
Net income	$ 2,727	188	$ 938	7%	2%	5%

*Includes depreciation.
Note: Common-size columns may not add due to rounding.

- DuPont has the largest relative property investment, at 57% of total assets, followed by ICI (43%) and Dow (33%).
- DuPont has a disproportionate amount of "other liabilities." We will find (in Chapter 12) that this liability reflects its unfunded postretirement benefit obligation.

Turning to the income statement, we find that:

- DuPont reports the highest net income as a percentage of sales. Dow reports much lower net income ($938 million versus $2,727 million for duPont), but the difference is much smaller as a percentage of sales (5% compared to 7%).[6] ICI reports the lowest net income relative to sales.
- DuPont has the lowest ratio of cost of goods sold to sales and the lowest relative selling expense. ICI has the highest ratios.
- Dow reports the highest R&D expense as a percentage of sales.

[6]This difference is affected by the inclusion of excise taxes in the sales figures reported by duPont. That firm's income as a percentage of sales increases to 8% if excise taxes are excluded.

EXHIBIT 4-2
Industry Comparisons, 1994: Common-size Balance Sheets and Income Statements

	Retailers		Manufacturers					
	Groceries	Depart-ment Stores	Rubber and Plastic Footwear	Pulp and Paper	Drugs and Medi-cines	Industrial Chemicals	Iron and Steel	Petroleum Refining
A. Comparative Balance Sheets (%)								
Cash and equivalents	11	6	6	7	14	7	6	7
Receivables	5	12	29	22	23	27	26	27
Inventories	32	49	23	18	24	22	25	22
Other	2	2	1	1	2	2	1	2
Current assets	50%	68%	59%	49%	63%	58%	57%	58%
Fixed assets (net)	37	24	33	42	27	32	34	32
Intangibles (net)	3	2	2	2	5	4	1	1
Other	10	7	5	8	6	7	8	9
Total assets	100%	100%	100%	100%	100%	100%	100%	100%
Notes payable	5	6	10	8	5	8	9	6
Current portion of long-term debt	5	3	4	3	3	3	4	3
Trade payables	20	16	15	15	14	17	14	20
Inc. taxes payable	1	1	2	1	1	1	2	1
Other	10	8	8	6	9	9	8	8
Current liabilities	41%	35%	39%	33%	32%	37%	36%	39%
Long-term debt	24	19	17	19	14	15	18	17
Deferred taxes	0	0	1	2	1	1	2	2
Other	3	3	4	3	3	4	5	2
Total liabilities	69%	57%	60%	57%	50%	56%	61%	60%
Equity	31%	43%	40%	43%	51%	44%	39%	41%
Total liabilities + equity	100%	100%	100%	100%	100%	100%	100%	100%
B. Comparative Income Statements (%)								
Sales	100	100	100	100	100	100	100	100
Cost of sales	−77	−67	−72	−75	−57	−68	−79	−78
Gross profit	23%	33%	28%	25%	43%	32%	21%	22%
Operating expenses	−22	−32	−23	−20	−35	−26	−17	−19
Operating profit	1%	2%	5%	5%	8%	6%	4%	3%
Other expenses	0	0	−2	−1	−1	−1	−2	−1
Profit before tax	1%	2%	4%	4%	7%	5%	3%	2%

Source: Reprinted with permission, copyright Robert Morris Associates 1994. Data adapted from the ALL SIZES column appearing in 1994 *Annual Statement Studies.* RMA cautions that the studies be regarded only as a general guideline and not as an absolute industry norm. This is due to limited samples within categories, the categorization of companies by their primary Standard Industrial Classification (SIC) number only, and different methods of operations by companies within the same industry. For these reasons, RMA recommends that the figures be used only as general guidelines in addition to other methods of financial analysis.

Differences in operating characteristics may explain some of these differences. Different accounting methods may also play some part. Common-size analysis has provided a starting point for analysis, however.

Industry Comparisons. Some of the differences among the three firms may reflect differences in the industry segments in which they operate. Industry comparisons in Exhibit 4-2 show that balance sheet compositions differ widely. For example:

- The two retailer categories (groceries and department stores) show (as would be expected) the lowest levels of receivables and highest inventory balances. Customers generally pay for purchases with cash (or with credit cards), keeping receivables low. Inventories are relatively high as customers demand a variety of goods.
- Pulp and paper manufacturers report the highest fixed assets, reflecting large required investments in plants and natural resources.
- The drugs and chemicals sectors report the highest intangibles, probably due to patents and acquisition intangibles.

Common-size income statements also delineate some critical income statement differences. Groceries show low gross margins and drugs the highest, reflecting the economic characteristics and cost structures of these industries. Groceries have the lowest operating profit margin, typical of a low-margin, high-turnover business. Drugs and medicines have the highest operating margins, reflecting their high-research, patent-protected position.

Comparisons over Time. Common-size statements can also be used to compare the performance of a single company over time. Exhibit 4-3A shows actual and common-size income statements for duPont over the period 1990 to 1994. Sales declined slightly from $40,047 million to $39,333 million, whereas profits increased 18% from $2,310 million to $2,727 million. The common-size statements indicate considerable stability in the components of operating expense, perhaps surprising for a company in a cyclical industry. Other income, restructuring charges, and write-downs were highly variable. Both interest expense and the provision for income taxes declined. Significant charges for restructuring (1991 to 1993) and the adoption of two new accounting methods in 1992 explain most of the variations in duPont's performance during the 1991 to 1993 period.

Exhibit 4-3A also illustrates the use of common-size statements for trend analysis. A base year is selected, 1990 in this case, and data for all subsequent years (1991 to 1994 for duPont) are shown as percentages of base year data. This statement reveals an 81% increase in other income and declines of 28% in interest expense and 10% for the provision for income taxes. The analyst must review the financial statements to determine the sources of other income, evaluate the cause of the decline in reported interest expense, and assess the reason for the lower income tax rate.

Changes in balance sheet and cash flow statement components can also be analyzed over time. Exhibit 4-3B applies common-size analysis to duPont's direct method statement of cash flows, derived in Chapter 3; cash collections is the appropriate scaling factor. The insights obtained from the analysis of common-size statements facilitate detailed analysis of the firm and comparative analysis of firms—issues discussed in the following sections.

EXHIBIT 4-3. E.I. DUPONT DENEMOURS
Common-Size Income Statements and Statement of Cash Flows, 1990 to 1994

A. Common-Size Income Statements

	1990	1991	1992	1993	1994
As Reported ($ in millions)					
Sales	$ 40,047	$ 38,695	$ 37,799	$ 37,098	$ 39,333
Cost of goods sold	(22,945)	(22,528)	(22,046)	(21,624)	(21,977)
Gross profit	17,102	16,167	15,753	15,474	17,356
Other operating expenses	(12,687)	(12,988)	(13,377)	(12,830)	(13,483)
Restructuring and write-downs	0	(828)	(475)	(1,835)	142
Income from operations	4,415	2,351	1,901	809	4,015
Other income	512	828	553	743	926
Income before interest and taxes	4,927	3,179	2,454	1,552	4,941
Interest expense	(773)	(752)	(643)	(594)	(559)
Income before taxes	4,154	2,427	1,811	958	4,382
Provision for taxes	(1,844)	(1,415)	(836)	(392)	(1,655)
Income before extraordinary items and accounting changes	2,310	1,012	975	566	2,727
Extraordinary items and accounting changes	—	—	(4,902)	(11)	—
Net income	$ 2,310	$ 1,012	$ (3,927)	$ 555	$ 2,727
As % of Total Sales					
Sales	100%	100%	100%	100%	100%
Cost of goods sold	−57	−58	−58	−58	−56
Gross profit	43	42	42	42	44
Other operating expenses	−32	−34	−35	−35	−34
Restructuring and write-downs	0	−2	−1	−5	0
Income from operations	11	6	5	2	10
Other income	1	2	1	2	2
Income before interest and taxes	12	8	6	4	13
Interest expense	−2	−2	−2	−2	−1
Income before taxes	10	6	5	3	11
Provision for taxes	−5	−4	−2	−1	−4
Income before extraordinary items and accounting changes	6	3	3	2	7
Extraordinary items and accounting changes	0	0	−13	0	0
Net income	6%	3%	−10%	1%	7%
As % of 1990 Level					
Sales	100%	97%	94%	93%	98%
Cost of goods sold	100	98	96	94	96
Gross profit	100	95	92	90	101
Other operating expenses	100	102	105	101	106
Restructuring and write-downs*	—	100	57	222	−17
Income from operations	100	53	43	18	91
Other income	100	162	108	145	181
Income before interest and taxes	100	65	50	31	100
Interest expense	100	97	83	77	72
Income before taxes	100	58	44	23	105

149

EXHIBIT 4-3 (*continued*)

A. Common-Size Income Statements

	1990	1991	1992	1993	1994
Provision for taxes	100	77	45	21	90
Income before extraordinary items and accounting changes	100	44	42	25	118
Extraordinary items and accounting changes					
Net income	100%	44%	−170%	24%	118%

*1991 used as base year as none in 1990.

B. Common-Size Statement of Cash Flows

Years ended December 31	1990	1991	1992	1993	1994
As % of Cash Collections					
Cash collections	100.0%	100.0%	100.0%	100.0%	100.0%
Cash inputs	−63.5	−64.0	−65.0	−65.0	−63.9
Cash expenses	−19.0	−19.0	−13.0	−17.0	−14.3
Cash taxes paid	−5.0	−5.5	−9.6	−3.0	−3.9
Cash interest paid	−3.0	−3.0	−2.8	−2.0	−1.6
Misc. cash flow	2.5	1.0	0.0	2.0	0.4
Cash flow from operations	12.0%	9.5%	9.6%	15.0%	16.6%
As % of 1990 Level					
Cash collections	100.0%	98.0%	93.0%	92.0%	95.0%
Cash inputs	100.0	98.0	96.0	93.0	96.0
Cash expenses	100.0	98.0	59.0	78.0	83.0
Cash taxes paid	100.0	116.0	205.0	58.0	72.0
Cash interest paid	100.0	102.0	90.0	84.0	75.0
Misc. cash flow	100.0	45.0	15.0	82.0	52.0
Cash flow from operations	100.0	80.0	76.0	118.0	108.0

Note: Common-size columns may not add due to rounding.

DISCUSSION OF RATIOS BY CATEGORY

The ratios presented here and their mode of calculation are neither exhaustive nor uniquely "correct." The definition of many ratios is not standardized[7] and may vary from analyst to analyst, textbook to textbook, and annual report to annual report.[8] Not all such variations are logical or useful; we believe that the ratios presented in this book meet both these criteria.

[7]In this chapter, when one of the components of the ratio comes from the balance sheet and the other from the income or cash flow statement, the balance sheet number is an average of the beginning and ending balances. An exception is the cash flow from operations to debt ratio. In practice, some analysts use beginning or ending balances for such "mixed" ratios.

[8]For example, see Gibson (1982, 1987), discussed in the section in this chapter entitled "Patterns of Ratio Disclosure, Definitions, and Use."

The analyst's primary focus should be the relationships indicated by the ratios, not the details of their calculation. As we proceed through this book, we will suggest many adjustments to and modifications of these basic ratios.

Activity Analysis

A firm's operating activities require investments in both short-term (inventory and accounts receivable) and long-term (property, plant, and equipment) assets. Activity ratios describe the relationship between the firm's level of operations (usually defined as sales) and the assets needed to sustain operating activities.

The higher the ratio, the more efficient the firm's operations, as relatively fewer assets are required to maintain a given level of operations (sales). Trends in these ratios over time and in comparison to other firms in the same industry can indicate potential trouble spots or opportunities. Furthermore, although these ratios do not measure profitability or liquidity directly, they are important factors affecting those performance indicators.

Activity ratios can also be used to forecast a firm's capital requirements (both operating and long-term). Increases in sales will require investments in additional assets. Activity ratios enable the analyst to forecast these requirements and to assess the firm's ability to acquire the assets needed to sustain the forecasted growth.

Short-Term (Operating) Activity Ratios

The *inventory turnover ratio*, defined as

$$\text{Inventory Turnover} = \frac{\text{Cost of Goods Sold}}{\text{Average Inventory}}$$

measures the efficiency of the firm's inventory management. A higher ratio indicates that inventory does not remain in warehouses or on the shelves but rather "turns over" rapidly from the time of acquisition to sale. This ratio is affected by the choice of accounting method; an explanation and an adjusted ratio are discussed in Chapter 6.

The inverse of this ratio can be used to calculate the average number of days inventory is held until it is sold:[9]

$$\frac{\text{Average No. Days}}{\text{Inventory in Stock}} = \frac{365}{\text{Inventory Turnover}}$$

The *receivables turnover ratio* and the *average number of days of receivables outstanding* can be calculated similarly as

$$\text{Receivables Turnover} = \frac{\text{Sales}}{\text{Average Trade Receivables}}$$

---

[9]For manufacturing firms, the computation is less straightforward. See the discussion in Box 4-1.

and

$$\frac{\text{Average No. Days}}{\text{Receivables Outstanding}} = \frac{365}{\text{Receivables Turnover}}$$

The receivables turnover ratios:

1. Measure the effectiveness of the firm's credit policies.
2. Indicate the level of investment in receivables needed to maintain the firm's sales level.

Receivables turnover should be computed using only trade receivables in the numerator in order to evaluate operating performance. Receivables generated from financing (unless customer financing is provided as a normal component of sales activities) and investment activities (e.g., receivables from the sale of an investment) should be excluded as they do not represent normal recurring operating transactions. Adjustments may also be necessary if the firm has sold receivables during the period.[10]

The *accounts payable turnover ratio* and *number of days payables are outstanding* can be computed in a similar fashion as

$$\text{Payables Turnover} = \frac{\text{Purchases}}{\text{Average Accounts Payable}}$$

and

$$\frac{\text{Average No. Days}}{\text{Payables Outstanding}} = \frac{365}{\text{Payables Turnover}}$$

Although accounts payable are liabilities rather than assets, their trend is significant as they represent an important source of financing for operating activities. The time spread between when suppliers must be paid and when payment is received from customers is critical for wholesale and retail firms with their large inventory balances. The relationship among accounts payable, accounts receivable, and inventories will be seen shortly when we examine the operating and cash cycles.

The *working capital turnover ratio*, defined as

$$\text{Working Capital Turnover} = \frac{\text{Sales}}{\text{Average Working Capital}}$$

is a summary ratio that reflects the amount of working (operating) capital needed to maintain a given level of sales. Only operating items should be used to compute this measure. Short-term debt, marketable securities, and excess cash should be excluded as they are not required for operating activities.

In Chapter 1, we discussed the going concern assumption, a basic tenet of accrual accounting. The deferral of inventory cost until the item is sold and recognition of revenues prior to cash collection assume that the inventories will be sold and the receivables collected.

---

[10]See Chapter 11 for a discussion of this issue.

Similarly, the use of working capital as a proxy for cash flow (and liquidity—see the next section) is contingent on this assumption. The level and trends of turnover ratios provide information as to the validity of this assumption. Declining turnover ratios, indicating longer shelf time for inventory and/or slower collection of receivables, could be indicators of reduced demand for a firm's products or of sales to customers whose ability to pay is less certain. This might signal one or more of the following:

1. The firm's income may be overstated because reserves are required for obsolete inventory or uncollectable receivables.
2. Future production cutbacks may be required.
3. Potential liquidity problems may exist.

When activity ratios decline, the statement of cash flows helps assess whether income is overstated relative to cash collections. As will be discussed shortly, profitability and liquidity ratios can also improve our understanding of the cause(s) of lower turnover ratios.

Long-Term (Investment) Activity Ratios

The *fixed asset turnover ratio* measures the efficiency of (long-term) capital investment. The ratio, defined as

$$\textbf{Fixed Assets Turnover} = \frac{\textbf{Sales}}{\textbf{Average Fixed Assets}}$$

reflects the level of sales generated by investments in productive capacity.

The level and trend of this ratio are affected by characteristics of its components. First, sales growth is continuous, albeit at varying rates. Increases in capacity to meet that sales growth, however, are discrete, depending on the addition of new factories, warehouses, stores, and so forth. Compounding this issue is the fact that management often has discretion over the timing, form, and financial reporting of the acquisition of incremental capacity.

The combination of some of these factors, as Figure 4-1 shows, results in an erratic turnover ratio. The life cycle of a company or product includes a number of stages: startup, growth, maturity (steady state), and decline. Startup companies' initial turnover may be low, as their level of operations is below their productive capacity. As sales grow, however, turnover will improve continually until the limits of the firm's initial capacity are reached. Subsequent increases in capital investment decrease the turnover ratio until the firm's sales growth catches up to the increased capacity. This process continues until maturity when sales and capacity level off, only to reverse when the firm enters its decline stage.

Additional problems can result from the timing of a firm's asset purchases. Two firms with similar operating efficiencies, having the same productive capacity and the same level of sales, may show differing ratios depending on when their assets were acquired. The firm with older assets has the higher turnover ratio, as accumulated depreciation has reduced the carrying value of its assets. Over time, for any firm, the accumulation of depreciation expense improves the turnover ratio (faster for firms that use accelerated depreciation methods or short depreciable lives) without a corresponding improvement in actual efficiency. The use of gross (before depreciation)

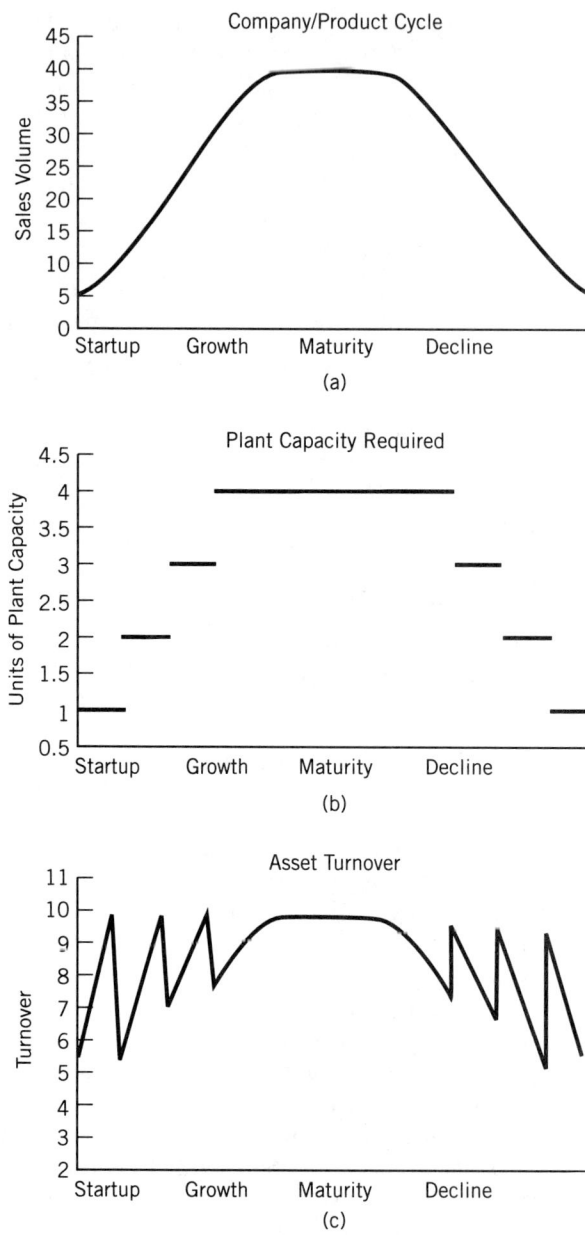

FIGURE 4-1 Asset turnover and capacity requirements.

rather than net fixed assets alleviates this shortcoming. However, this is rarely done in practice.

An offsetting and complicating factor is that newer assets generally operate more efficiently due to improved technology. However, due to inflation newer assets may be more expensive and thus decrease the turnover ratio. Using current or replacement cost rather than historical cost to compute the turnover ratio is one solution to this

EXHIBIT 4-4. E.I. DUPONT DENEMOURS AND COMPANY AND CONSOLIDATED SUBSIDIARIES
Activity Analysis

Years Ended December 31,	1990	1991	1992	1993	1994	Average
Inventory turnover[a]	**4.68**	**4.83**	**4.95**	**5.21**	**5.64**	**5.06**
No. of days[b]	78	76	74	70	65	72
Accounts receivable turnover[c]	**8.39**	**8.13**	**8.80**	**8.99**	**9.52**	**8.77**
No. of days[d]	44	45	41	41	38	42
Fixed assets turnover[e]	**2.00**	**1.86**	**1.78**	**1.71**	**1.85**	**1.84**
Total assets turnover[f]	**1.10**	**1.04**	**1.01**	**0.98**	**1.06**	**1.04**

1994 Calculations:

[a]**Inventory Turnover = COGS/Avg. inventory** = $\{21,977/[(3,969 + 3,818)/2]\}$ = **5.64**

[b]Avg. No. Days Inventory Stock = 365/Inventory Turnover = 365/5.64 = 65

[c]**Accounts Receivable Turnover = Net Sales/Avg. AR(Trade)** = $\{39,333/[(4,244 + 4,020)/2]\}$ = **9.52**

[d]Avg. No. Days Receivables Outstanding = 365/AR Turnover = 365/9.52 = 38

[e]**Fixed Assets Turnover = Sales/Avg. Fixed Assets** = $\{39,333/[(21,120 + 21,423)/2]\}$ = **1.85**

[f]**Total Assets Turnover = Sales/Avg. Total Assets** = $\{39,333/[(36,892 + 37,053)/2]\}$ = **1.06**

Comments: DuPont does not provide a breakdown of the raw materials, work-in-process, and finished goods inventory balances. It is, therefore, not possible to compute turnover ratios for the components. The gross inventory turnover ratio has improved significantly from 4.68 (78 days) in 1990 to 5.64 (65 days) in 1994. The receivables turnover ratio shows similar improvement over the 1990 to 1994 period. These ratios reflect better operating performance.

problem. Finally, it should be noted that methods of acquisition (lease versus purchase) and subsequent financial reporting choices (capitalization versus operating lease reporting) also affect turnover ratios for otherwise similar firms. See Chapter 11 for a discussion of these issues.

Total asset turnover is an overall activity measure relating sales to total assets:

$$\text{Total Asset Turnover} = \frac{\text{Sales}}{\text{Average Total Assets}}$$

This relationship provides a measure of overall investment efficiency by aggregating the joint impact of both short- and long-term assets. This comprehensive measure is a key component of the disaggregation of return on assets, presented in a later section of this chapter. The computation and analysis of turnover measures are illustrated, using duPont as an example, in Exhibit 4-4.

Liquidity Analysis

Short-term lenders and creditors (such as suppliers) must assess the ability of a firm to meet its current obligations. That ability depends on the cash resources available as of the balance sheet date and the cash to be generated through the operating cycle of the firm.

Figure 4-2 is a schematic representation of the operating cycle of a firm. The firm purchases or manufactures inventory, requiring an outlay of cash and/or the creation of trade payables debt. The sale of inventory generates receivables that, when collected, are used to satisfy the payables, and the cycle is begun again. The ability to repeat

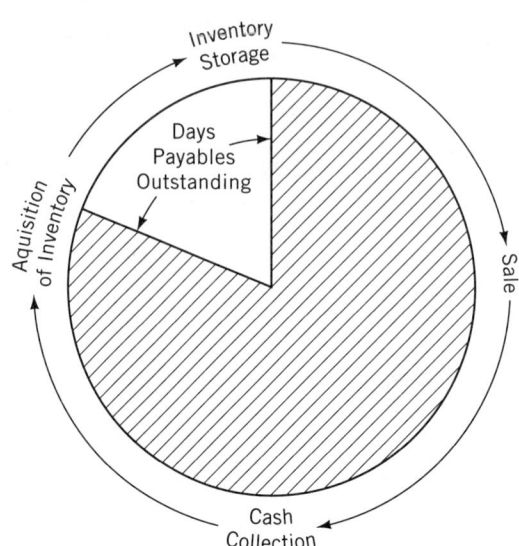

Shaded Area Circumference = Cash Cycle

FIGURE 4-2 Operating and cash cycles.

this cycle on a continuous basis depends on the firm's short-term liquidity and cash-generating ability.

Length of Cash Cycle

One indicator of short-term liquidity uses the activity ratios as a liquidity measure. The *operating cycle* of a merchandising firm is the sum of the number of days it takes to sell inventory and the number of days until the resultant receivables are converted to cash. The circumference of the circle in Figure 4-2 represents the length of this cycle. If a firm operates without credit, it also represents the total number of days cash is tied up in operating assets.

To the extent a firm uses credit, the length of the cash (operating) cycle is reduced. Subtracting the number of days of payables outstanding from the operating cycle results in the firm's *cash cycle*, the number of days a company's cash is tied up by its current operating cycle (the circumference of the shaded portion of the circle in Figure 4-2). The cash cycle[11] captures the interrelationship of sales, collections, and trade credit in a manner that the individual numbers may not. The shorter the cycle, the more efficient the firm's operations and cash management.

For a manufacturing firm, further refinements and approximations may be necessary to calculate the length of the operating and cash cycle. They are discussed in Box 4-1.

---

[11]The inverse of the working capital turnover ratio (times 365) is sometimes used as a crude approximation of the cash cycle. [See Richards and Laughlin (1980) for an extended discussion.]

BOX 4-1
Estimating the Operating and Cash Cycle for a Manufacturing Firm

---

A merchandising firm holds only one type of inventory: finished goods inventory. Consequently, the inventory turnover ratio measures only one time stage: the time from inventory purchase until its sale. For a manufacturing firm, on the other hand, inventory is held through three stages:

1. As raw material, from purchase to beginning of production
2. As work in process, over the length of the production cycle
3. As finished goods, from completion of production until sale

Only the last stage (as finished goods) is comparable to a merchandising firm. The inventory turnover ratio, COGS/average finished goods inventory, computes the length of time from completion until sale.

The length of time inventory is in the production cycle (stage 2) can be calculated as

$$365 \times \frac{\text{Average Work-in-Process Inventory}}{\text{Cost of Goods Manufactured}}$$

The length of time it takes for raw material to enter production is

$$365 \times \frac{\text{Average Raw Material Inventory}}{\text{Raw Materials Used}}$$

The breakdown among finished goods, work in process, and raw materials inventory is often available in the notes to financial statements. Cost of goods manufactured can be calculated from financial statements as cost of goods sold + ending (finished goods) inventory − beginning (finished goods) inventory. However, the amount of material used in production is rarely available making the calculation of the length of stage 1 infeasible. Some approximations are possible. The first involves calculating the combined length of stage 1 and 2 as

$$365 \times \frac{\text{Average (Work in Process and Raw Material) Inventory}}{\text{Cost of Goods Manufactured}}$$

The accuracy of this approximation depends on the proportion of the various inventories and the degree to which the individual ratios differ. Another (less accurate but perhaps simpler) approximation ignores this whole discussion and uses the composite turnover ratio, thereby mirroring the merchandising firm:

$$365 \times \frac{\text{Average (Total) Inventory}}{\text{Cost of Goods Sold}}$$

Exhibit 4-5 presents the operating and cash cycles for Kmart, a major discount retailer, over the 10-year period 1985 to 1994. Inventory turnover declined gradually over this period; receivables turnover declined sharply. Suppliers appear to have tightened credit terms in 1990, perhaps reflecting Kmart's poor operating performance. As a result, both the operating cycle and cash cycle lengthened considerably over the period. This analysis illustrates the importance of examining the relationship among cash cycle components.

EXHIBIT 4-5. KMART CORPORATION
Analysis of Operating and Cash Cycle

	1985	1986	1987	1988	1989	1990	1991	1992	1993	1994
				A. Turnover Ratios						
Inventory	3.7	3.5	3.6	3.5	3.5	3.5	3.5	3.6	3.5	3.2
Receivables	134.5	82.7	63.2	69.0	62.0	48.2	45.0	43.1	37.3	28.7
Payables	9.0	8.4	8.7	8.4	8.6	9.9	10.3	10.6	10.5	8.4
				B. Average No. of Days						
Inventory in stock	98	103	102	105	103	106	106	102	104	114
Receivables outstanding	3	4	6	5	6	8	8	8	10	13
Operating cycle	100	107	108	111	109	113	114	110	114	127
Less payables outstanding	41	43	42	43	42	37	35	35	35	43
Cash cycle	60	64	66	67	67	76	78	76	79	83

Comments: The decline in inventory and receivables turnover occurs steadily over the 10-year period shown. However, supplier concern is evident in the decline in number of days payables were outstanding beginning in 1989. These factors contributed to the significant deterioration in both the operating and cash cycles.

Working Capital Ratios and Defensive Intervals

The concept of working capital relies on the classification of assets and liabilities into "current" and "noncurrent" categories. *The traditional distinction between current assets and liabilities is based on a maturity of less than one year or (if longer) the operating cycle of the company.*

The typical balance sheet has five categories of current assets:

1. Cash and cash equivalents
2. Marketable securities
3. Accounts receivable
4. Inventories
5. Prepaid expenses

and three categories of current liabilities:

1. Short-term debt
2. Accounts payable
3. Accrued liabilities

By definition, each current asset and liability has a maturity (the expected date of conversion to cash for an asset; the expected date of liquidation for cash for a liability) of less than one year. However, in practice the line between current and noncurrent has blurred in recent years. Marketable securities and debt are particularly susceptible to arbitrary classification. For this reason, working capital ratios should be used with caution.

Short-term liquidity analysis compares the firm's cash resources with its cash obligations. Cash resources can be measured by either:

1. The sum of the firm's current cash balance and its potential sources of cash, or
2. Its (net) cash flows from operations

Cash obligations can be measured by either:

1. Current obligations requiring cash, or
2. Cash outflows arising from operations

The following table summarizes the ratios commonly used to measure the relationship between resources and obligations:

	Numerator Cash Resources	Denominator Cash Obligations
Level	Current assets	Current liabilities
Flow	Cash flow from operations	Cash outflows for operations

Conceptually, the ratios differ in whether *levels* (amounts shown on the balance sheet) or *flows* (cash inflows and outflows) are used to gauge the relationship.

Three ratios compare levels of cash resources with current liabilities as the measure of cash obligations. The *current ratio* defines cash resources as all current assets:

$$\text{Current Ratio} = \frac{\text{Current Assets}}{\text{Current Liabilities}}$$

A more conservative measure of liquidity is the *quick ratio:*

$$\text{Quick Ratio} = \frac{\text{Cash + Marketable Securities + Accounts Receivable}}{\text{Current Liabilities}}$$

which excludes inventory from cash resources, recognizing that the conversion of inventory to cash is less certain both in terms of timing and amount.[12] The included assets are "quick assets" because they can be quickly converted to cash.

Finally, the *cash ratio*, defined as

$$\text{Cash Ratio} = \frac{\text{Cash + Marketable Securities}}{\text{Current Liabilities}}$$

is the most conservative of these measures of cash resources as only actual cash and securities easily convertible to cash are used to measure cash resources.

The use of either the current or quick ratio implicitly assumes that the current assets will be converted to cash. In reality, however, firms do not actually liquidate their current assets to pay their current liabilities. Minimum levels of inventories and

---

[12]Inventory balances of actively traded commodities such as oil, metals, or wheat can be considered very liquid and should be included in the quick ratio.

receivables are always needed to maintain operations. If all current assets are liquidated, the firm has effectively ceased operations. As suggested earlier by Figure 4-2,
the process of generating inventories, collecting receivables, and paying suppliers is
ongoing. These ratios therefore measure the "margin of safety" provided by the cash
resources relative to obligations rather than expected cash flows.

Liquidity analysis, moreover, is not independent of activity analysis. Poor receivable or inventory turnover limits the usefulness of the current and quick ratios. Obsolete inventory or uncollectible receivables are unlikely to be sources of cash. Thus,
levels and changes in short-term liquidity ratios over time should be examined in
conjunction with turnover ratios.

The *cash flow from operations ratio*:

$$\text{Cash Flow from Operations Ratio} = \frac{\text{Cash Flow from Operations}}{\text{Current Liabilities}}$$

measures liquidity by comparing actual cash flows (instead of current and potential cash
resources) with current liabilities. This ratio avoids the issues of actual convertibility
to cash, turnover, and the need for minimum levels of working capital (cash) to
maintain operations.

An important limitation of liquidity ratios is the absence of an economic or "real-
world" interpretation of those measures. Unlike the cash cycle liquidity measure,
which reflects the number of days cash is tied up in the firm's operating cycle, there
is no intuitive meaning to a current ratio of 1.5. For some companies that ratio would
be high, for others dangerously low.

The *defensive interval*, in contrast, does provide an intuitive "feel" for a firm's
liquidity, albeit a most conservative one. It compares the currently available "quick"
sources of cash (cash, marketable securities, and accounts receivable) with the estimated outflows needed to operate the firm: projected expenditures. There are different
definitions of both cash resources and projected expenditures.[13] We present here only
the basic form:

$$\text{Defensive Interval} = 365 \times \frac{\text{Cash + Marketable Securities + Accounts Receivable}}{\text{Projected Expenditures}}$$

The calculation of the defensive interval for duPont (Exhibit 4-6) uses current
year income statement data to estimate projected expenditures. The defensive interval
represents a "worst case" scenario indicating the number of days a firm could maintain
the current level of operations with its present cash resources but without considering
any additional revenues.

Long-Term Debt and Solvency Analysis

The analysis of a firm's capital structure is essential to evaluate its long-term risk and
return prospects. Leveraged firms accrue excess returns to their shareholders as long

---

[13]See Sorter and Benston (1960). The most conservative variation, the "no credit" interval, measures
the number of days the firm could survive if it loses all access to trade credit. In this version, accounts
payable are subtracted from the numerator.

EXHIBIT 4-6. E. I. DUPONT DENEMOURS AND COMPANY AND CONSOLIDATED SUBSIDIARIES
Liquidity Analysis

Years Ended December 31,	1990	1991	1992	1993	1994	Average
Average no. of days inventory in stock[a]	78	76	74	70	65	72
+ Days of receivables outstanding[a]	44	45	41	41	38	42
Length of operating cycle	**122**	**121**	**115**	**111**	**103**	**114**
− Payables outstanding[b]	32	32	31	31	29	31
Length of cash cycle	**90**	**89**	**84**	**80**	**74**	**83**
Current ratio[c]	**1.22**	**1.45**	**1.20**	**1.15**	**1.47**	**1.30**
Quick ratio[d]	0.68	0.80	0.68	0.64	0.84	0.73
Cash ratio[e]	**0.06**	**0.06**	**0.16**	**0.13**	**0.15**	**0.11**
Cash from operations ratio[f]	0.51	0.73	0.43	0.57	0.75	0.60
Defensive interval no. of days[g]	**75**	**67**	**77**	**70**	**71**	**72**

1994 Calculations:

[a]Average no. of days inventory stock and receivables outstanding computed in Exhibit 4-4.

[b]Purchases = COGS + Change in Inventory = [21,977 + (3,969 − 3,818)] = 22,128

Average No. Days Payables Outstanding = 365*[Avg. AP(Trade)/Purchases] = {365*[((1,847 + 1,675)/2)/22,128]} = 29

[c]**Current Ratio = Current Assets/Current Liabilities = 11,108/7,565 = 1.47**

[d]Quick Ratio = (Cash + Marketable Securities + AR)/Current Liabilities = (856 + 253 + 5,213)/7,565 = 0.84

[e]**Cash Ratio = (Cash + Marketable Securities)/Current Liabilities = (856 + 253)/7,565 = 0.15**

[f]CFO = Operating Cash Flow (computed in the consolidated statement of cash flows)

Cash from Operations Ratio = CFO/Current Liabilities = 5,664/7,565 = 0.75

[g]**Projected Expenditures = Cost of Goods Sold + Other Operating Expenses except Depreciation Expense =**
21,977 + 2,888 + 357 + 1,047 + 6,215 = 32,484

Defensive Interval No. Days = 365*[(Cash + Marketable Securities + AR)/Projected Expenditures] =
365*(856 + 253 + 5,213)/32,484 = 71

Comments: Both the operating and cash cycle have improved over the last 5 years. Similarly, improved operating performance is seen in all the liquidity ratios. The defensive interval suggests that the firm has 71 days of expenditures on hand, compared to 75 days in 1990 and 72 days on average. This decline may be the result of improved operations and resource management.

as the rate of return on the investments financed by debt is greater than the cost of debt. The benefits of financial leverage bring additional risks, however, in the form of fixed costs that adversely affect profitability (see the next section) if demand or profit margins decline. Moreover, the priority of interest and debt claims can have a severe negative impact on a firm when adversity strikes. The inability to meet these obligations can lead to default and possible bankruptcy.

Debt Covenants

To protect themselves, creditors often impose restrictions on the borrowing company's ability to incur additional debt and make dividend payments. These *debt covenants* are often based on working capital, cumulative profitability, and net worth. It is, therefore, important to monitor the firm to ensure that ratios comply with levels specified in the debt agreements. Violations of debt covenants are frequently an "event of default" under loan agreements, making the debt due immediately. When covenants are violated, therefore, borrowers must either repay the debt (not usually possible) or obtain waivers from lenders. Such waivers often require additional collateral, restrictions on firm operations, or higher interest rates.[14]

Capitalization Table and Debt Ratios

Long-term debt and solvency analysis evaluate the level of risk borne by a firm, changes over time, and risk relative to comparable investments. A higher proportion of debt relative to equity increases the riskiness of the firm. Exhibit 4-7 presents capitalization tables for duPont. Two important factors should be noted:

1. The relative debt levels themselves, and
2. The trend over time in the proportion of debt to equity

Debt ratios are expressed either as

$$\textbf{Debt to Total Capital} = \frac{\textbf{Total Debt (Current + Long-Term)}}{\textbf{Total Capital (Debt + Equity)}}$$

or

$$\textbf{Debt to Equity} = \frac{\textbf{Total Debt}}{\textbf{Total Equity}}$$

The definition of short-term debt used in practice may include operating debt (accounts payable and accrued liabilities). The short-term debt shown in Exhibit 4-7 excludes operating debt because it is a function of the firm's operations and its essential business and contractual relationship to its suppliers rather than external lenders. However, many lenders define debt as equal to total liabilities.

As with other ratios, industry and economy-wide factors affect both the level of debt and the nature of the debt (maturities and variable or fixed rate). Capital-intensive industries tend to incur high levels of debt to finance their property, plant, and equipment. Such debt should be long-term to match the long time horizon of the assets acquired.

An important measurement issue is whether to use book or market values to compute debt ratios. Valuation models in the finance literature that use leverage ratios as inputs are generally based on the market value of debt and equity. Market values of both debt and equity are available or can readily be estimated, and their use can make the ratio a more useful analytical tool.

The use of market values, however, may produce contradictory results. The debt of a firm whose credit rating declines may have a market value well below face amount. A debt ratio based on market values may show an "acceptable" level of leverage. A ratio that would "control" for this phenomenon and can be used in conjunction with book- or market-based debt ratios is one that compares debt measured at book value to equity measured at market:

$$\frac{\textbf{Total Debt at Book Value}}{\textbf{Equity at Market}}$$

---

[14]The relationship between debt covenants and ratios is explored in greater detail in Chapter 10.

If the market value of equity is higher than its book value, the above ratio will be lower than the debt-to-equity ratio using book value.[15] This indicates that market perceptions of the firm's earning power would permit the firm to raise additional capital at an attractive price. If this ratio, however, exceeds the book value debt-to-equity measure, it signals that the market is willing to supply additional capital only at a discount to book value.

The measurement of debt and equity used to compute leverage ratios may require adjustments to reported data. Leases (whether capitalized or operating), other off-balance-sheet transactions such as contractual obligations not accorded accounting recognition, deferred taxes, financial instruments with debt and equity characteristics, and other innovative financing techniques must all be considered when making these calculations. These issues are discussed in later chapters. Exhibit 4-7 shows the computation and interpretation of long-term debt and solvency measurements for duPont.

Interest Coverage Ratios

Debt-to-equity ratios examine the firm's capital structure and, indirectly, its ability to meet current debt obligations. A more direct measure of the firm's ability to meet interest payments is

$$\text{Times Interest Earned} = \frac{\text{Earnings Before Interest and Taxes (EBIT)}}{\text{Interest Expense}}$$

This ratio, often referred to as the *interest coverage ratio*, measures the protection available to creditors as the extent to which earnings available for interest "cover" interest expense.[16] A more comprehensive measure, the *fixed charge coverage ratio*, includes all fixed charges:

$$\text{Fixed Charge Coverage} = \frac{\text{Earnings Before Fixed Charges and Taxes}}{\text{Fixed Charges}}$$

where fixed charges include contractually committed interest and principal payments on leases as well as funded debt.

This coverage ratio may also be computed using adjusted operating cash flows (cash from operations + fixed charges + tax payments) as the numerator:

$$\text{Times Interest Earned (Cash Basis)} = \frac{\text{Adjusted Operating Cash Flow}}{\text{Interest Expense}}$$

$$\text{Fixed Charge Coverage Ratio (Cash Basis)} = \frac{\text{Adjusted Operating Cash Flow}}{\text{Fixed Charges}}$$

Capital Expenditure and CFO-to-Debt Ratios

Internally generated cash flows are needed for investment as well as debt service. The coverage ratios discussed do not take this into consideration. Cash flow from opera-

---

[15]The analysis assumes that all debt has been included. See Chapter 11 for a discussion of off-balance sheet financing techniques.

[16]Because firms may capitalize some interest expense, using reported interest expense may overstate the coverage ratio. See Chapter 10 for a discussion of capitalized interest and adjustments to coverage ratios.

EXHIBIT 4-7. E. I. DUPONT DENEMOURS AND COMPANY AND CONSOLIDATED SUBSIDIARIES
Long-Term Debt and Solvency Analysis

Years Ended December 31,	1990	1991	1992	1993	1994	Average
Capitalization Table ($ in millions)						
Short-term debt	2,932	693	3,223	1,499	714	1,812
Current long-term debt	996	1,148	576	1,297	578	919
Long-term debt	5,663	6,456	7,193	6,531	6,376	6,444
Total debt	**9,591**	**8,297**	**10,992**	**9,327**	**7,668**	**9,175**
Trade payables[a]	3,437	3,174	3,372	3,145	3,565	3,339
Total debt (including trade)	**13,028**	**11,471**	**14,364**	**12,472**	**11,233**	**12,514**
Capital stock	4,981	5,058	5,193	5,304	5,416	5,190
Retained earnings	11,437	11,681	6,572	5,926	7,406	8,604
Total equity	**16,418**	**16,739**	**11,765**	**11,230**	**12,822**	**13,795**
Total capital	**26,009**	**25,036**	**22,757**	**20,557**	**20,490**	**22,970**
Total capital (including trade)	**29,446**	**28,210**	**26,129**	**23,702**	**24,055**	**26,308**
Debt						
To equity[b]	**0.58**	**0.50**	**0.93**	**0.83**	**0.60**	**0.67**
To capital[c]	0.37	0.33	0.48	0.45	0.37	0.40
Debt (including trade)						
To equity[d]	**0.79**	**0.69**	**1.22**	**1.11**	**0.88**	**0.91**
To capital[e]	0.44	0.41	0.55	0.53	0.47	0.48
Times interest earned[f]	**6.37**	**4.75**	**3.82**	**2.61**	**8.84**	**5.28**
Capital expenditure ratio[g]	0.95	2.26	0.88	1.58	2.16	1.56
CFO to debt[h]	**0.54**	**0.66**	**0.40**	**0.58**	**0.74**	**0.58**

1994 Calculations:

   [a]Trade Payables = Accounts Payable + Nonincome Taxes + Income Taxes = 2,734 + 422 + 409 − 3,565
   [b]**Debt to Equity = Total Debt/Total Equity = 7,668/12,822 = 0.60**
   [c]Debt to Capital = Total Debt/Total Capital = 7,668/20,490 = 0.37
   [d]**Debt (including trade) to Equity = Total Debt (including trade)/Total Equity = 11,233/12,822 = 0.88**
   [e]Debt (including trade) to Capital = Total Debt (including trade)/Total Capital (including trade) =
      11,233/24,055 = 0.47
   [f]**Times Interest Earned = EBIT/Interest Expense = 4,941/559 = 8.84**
   [g]CFO/Capital Expenditures
    Capital Expenditure Ratio = 5,664/2,618 = 2.16
   [h]**CFO to Debt = CFO/Total Debt = 5,664/7,668 = 0.74**

Comments: Leverage ratios show substantial improvement since the lows of 1992. However, lower reported equity in 1992 is due to significant charges taken for accounting changes. Restructuring charges reduced earnings in 1993.

tions, as noted in Chapter 3, ignores the cost of additions to operating capacity. Net income, with its provision for depreciation, amortizes the original cost of existing fixed assets. However, given their relatively long service life, the replacement costs of these assets (even with minimal inflation) may be significantly higher, and historical cost depreciation cannot adequately provide for their replacement.[17] Neither net income

---

[17]See Chapter 8 for a discussion of these issues.

nor cash from operations, of course, makes any provision for the capital required for growth.

A firm's long-term solvency is a function of:

1. Its ability to finance the replacement and expansion of its investment in productive capacity, as well as
2. Its generation of cash for debt repayment

The *capital expenditure ratio*

$$\text{Capital Expenditure Ratio} = \frac{\text{Cash from Operations (CFO)}}{\text{Capital Expenditures}}$$

measures the relationship between the firm's cash-generating ability and its investment expenditures. To the extent the ratio exceeds 1, it indicates the firm has cash left for debt repayment or dividends after payment of capital expenditures.

The *CFO-to-debt ratio*[18]

$$\text{CFO to Debt} = \frac{\text{CFO}}{\text{Total Debt}}$$

measures the coverage of principal repayment requirements by the current CFO. A low CFO-to-debt ratio could signal a long-term solvency problem as the firm does not generate enough cash internally to repay its debt.

Profitability Analysis

Equity investors are concerned with the firm's ability to generate, sustain, and increase profits. Profitability can be measured in several differing but interrelated dimensions. First, there is the relationship of a firm's profits to sales, that is, the residual return to the firm per sales dollar. Another measure, return on investment (ROI), relates profits to the investment required to generate them. We briefly define these ratios and then elaborate on their use in financial statement analysis.

Return on Sales

One measure of profitability is the relationship between the firm's costs and its sales. The ability to control costs in relation to revenues enhances earnings power. A common-size income statement shows the ratio of each cost component to sales. In addition, six summary ratios measure the relationship between different measures of profitability and sales:

1. The *gross (profit) margin* captures the relationship between sales and manufacturing or merchandising costs:

$$\text{Gross Margin} = \frac{\text{Gross Profit}}{\text{Sales}}$$

---

[18]The definition of debt may depend on the objective of the analysis. It should include all short- and long-term debt and may include trade debt.

2. The *operating margin*, calculated as

$$\text{Operating Margin} = \frac{\text{Operating Income}}{\text{Sales}}$$

provides information about a firm's profitability from the operations of its "core" business, excluding the effects of:
- Investments (income from affiliates or asset sales)
- Financing (interest expense)
- Tax position

3. A profit margin measure that is independent of both the firm's financing and tax position is the

$$\text{Margin Before Interest and Tax} = \frac{\text{EBIT}}{\text{Sales}}$$

4. The pretax margin is calculated after financing costs (interest) but prior to income taxes:

$$\text{Pretax Margin} = \frac{\text{Earnings Before Tax (EBT)}}{\text{Sales}}$$

5. Finally, the overall profit margin is net of all expenses:

$$\text{Profit Margin} = \frac{\text{Net Income}}{\text{Sales}}$$

The five ratios listed above can be computed directly from a firm's financial statements.

6. Another useful profitability measure is the contribution margin ratio, defined as

$$\text{Contribution Margin} = \frac{\text{Contribution}}{\text{Sales}}$$

where contribution = sales − variable costs.

The contribution margin ratio, however, cannot be computed directly from a firm's financial statements as the breakdown between fixed and variable costs is rarely provided. Appendix 4-A, however, discusses how to estimate this breakdown.

Return on Investment

Return on investment (ROI) measures the relationship between profits and the investment required to generate them. Diverse measures of that investment result in different forms of ROI.

Return on Assets. The return on assets (ROA) compares income with total assets (equivalently, total liabilities and equity capital). It can be interpreted in two ways.

First, it measures management's ability and efficiency in using the firm's assets to generate (operating) profits. Second, it reports the total return accruing to all providers of capital (debt and equity), independent of the source of capital.

The return is measured by net income prior to the cost of financing and is computed by adding back (after-tax) interest expense to net income:[19]

$$\text{ROA} = \frac{\textbf{Net Income + After-Tax Interest Cost}}{\textbf{Average Total Assets}}$$

ROA can also be computed on a pretax basis using EBIT as the return measure. This results in a ROI measure that is unaffected by differences in a firm's tax position as well as financial policy:

$$\text{ROA} = \frac{\textbf{EBIT}}{\textbf{Average total assets}}$$

In practice, however, the ROA measure is sometimes computed using either net income or EBT as the numerator. Such postinterest ROI ratios make leveraged firms appear less profitable by charging earnings for payments (interest) to some capital providers (lenders) but not others (stockholders). Preinterest ROI ratios, in contrast, facilitate the comparison of firms with different degrees of leverage. Therefore, ROI ratios that use total assets in the denominator should *always* include total earnings (before interest) in the numerator. As interest is tax-deductible, posttax profit measures should add back net-of-tax interest payments.

Return on Total Capital. One particularly useful ROI measure is the *return on total capital* (ROTC). This ratio uses the sum of *external* debt and equity instead of total assets as the base against which the firm's return is measured. ROTC measures profitability relative to all (nontrade) capital providers.

Return can be measured either (pretax) by EBIT or (after tax) by net income plus after-tax interest:[20]

$$\text{ROTC} = \frac{\textbf{EBIT}}{\textbf{Average (Total Debt + Stockholders' Equity)}}$$

or

$$\text{ROTC} = \frac{\textbf{Net Income + After-Tax Interest Expense}}{\textbf{Average (Total Debt + Stockholders' Equity)}}$$

Return on Equity. The return on total stockholders' equity (ROE) excludes debt in the denominator and uses either pretax income (*after* interest costs) or net income:

$$\text{ROE} = \frac{\textbf{Pretax Income}}{\textbf{Average Stockholders' Equity}}$$

[19]The after-tax interest cost is calculated by multiplying the interest cost by $(1 - t)$, where t is the firm's marginal tax rate.

[20]As in the case of ROA, preinterest measures of profitability should be used to compute ROTC, as total capital includes debt obligations.

Relationship of ROA and ROE to Providers of Investment Base

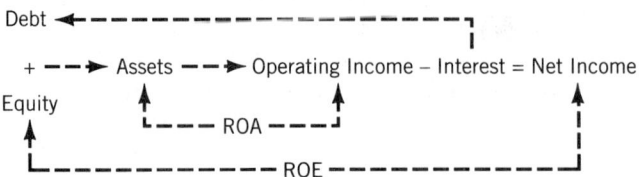

FIGURE 4-3 Relationship of ROA and ROE to providers of investment base.

or

$$ROE = \frac{\text{Net Income}}{\text{Average Stockholder's Equity}}$$

For companies with preferred equity, another ROI measure focuses on the returns accruing to the residual owners of the firm—common shareholders:

$$\text{Return on Common Equity (ROCE)} = \frac{\text{Net Income} - \text{Preferred Dividends}}{\text{Average Common Equity}}$$

The relationship between ROA and ROE reflects the firm's capital structure. As shown in Figure 4-3, creditors and shareholders provide the capital needed by the firm to acquire the assets used in the business. In return, they receive their share of the firm's profits.

ROA and ROTC measure returns to all providers of capital. ROCE measures returns to the firm's common shareholders and is calculated after deducting the returns paid to the creditors (interest) and other providers of equity capital (preferred shareholders).

Profitability and Cash Flows

Profitability ratios traditionally use accrual-based income measures, as shown for duPont in Exhibit 4-8. Cash flow analogues for these ratios should also be calculated. Examples include cash gross margin (cash collections less cash paid for inputs) and ROI measures using CFO in the numerator (either before or after interest, depending on the denominator). A direct method cash flow statement is required for ratios such as cash gross margin and operating margin. There is empirical evidence (see the discussion of Gombola and Ketz, 1983 that follows) that such cash-flow-based ratios have different properties from traditional profitability measures.

Operating and Financial Leverage

Profitability ratios imply that profits are proportional to sales, which may belie the true relationship among sales, costs, and profits. Generally, a doubling of sales would be expected to double income only if all expenses were variable. Conceptually, expenses can be classified into variable (V) and fixed (F) components. Variable expenses

EXHIBIT 4-8. E. I. DUPONT DENEMOURS AND COMPANY AND CONSOLIDATED SUBSIDIARIES
Profitability Analysis

Years Ended Dedember 31,	1990	1991	1992	1993	1994	Average
Gross margin (%)[a]	42.70	41.78	42.18	42.33	44.13	42.62
Operating margin (%)[a]	**11.02**	**8.22**	**6.29**	**7.13**	**9.85**	**8.50**
Preinterest and tax margin (%)[a]	12.30	9.23	6.49	4.18	12.56	8.95
Pretax margin (%)[a]	**10.37**	**7.28**	**4.79**	**2.58**	**11.14**	**7.23**
Profit margin (%)[a]	**5.77**	**3.63**	**(10.39)**	**1.50**	**6.93**	**1.49**
ROA (preinterest)						
After tax (%)[b]	**7.52**	**4.79**	**(9.55)**	**2.39**	**8.32**	**2.69**
Pretax (%)[c]	13.53	9.62	6.55	4.09	13.36	9.43
ROE						
After tax (%)[d]	**14.34**	**8.46**	**(27.55)**	**4.83**	**22.68**	**4.55**
Pretax (%)[e]	25.79	17.00	12.71	8.33	36.44	20.05
ROTC (preinterest)						
After tax (%)[f]	**11.00**	**6.96**	**(14.99)**	**4.18**	**14.98**	**4.43**
Pretax (%)[g]	19.79	13.99	10.27	7.17	24.07	15.06

1994 Calculations:

[a]Return on sales and margins from Exhibit 4-3.

[b]After Tax (%) = {[Net Income + (Interest Expense*(1 − Effective Tax Rate))]/Avg. Assets}*100 =
{2,727 + [559*(1 − 0.378)/(36,892 + 37,053)/2)]}*100 = 8.32%

[c]Pretax (%) = (EBIT/Avg. Assets)*100 = {4,941/[(36,892 + 37,053)/2)]}*100 = 13.36

[d]After Tax (%) = (Net Income/Avg. Equity)*100 = (2,727/[12,822 + 11,230)/2]*100 = 22.68%

[e]Pretax (%) = (EBT/Avg. Equity)*100 = {4,382/[(12,822 + 11,230)/2]}*100 = 36.44%

[f]After Tax (%) = {[Net Income + (Interest Expense*(1 − Effective Tax Rate))]/Avg. Total Capital [Debt + Equity]}*100
= {[2,727 + (559*(1 − 0.378))]/(20,490 + 20,557)/2}*100 = 14.98%

[g]Pretax (%) = [EBIT/Avg. Total Capital (Debt + Equity)]*100 = {4,941/[(20,490 + 20,557)/2]}*100 = 24.07%

Comments: See the section on "common-size statements" for a discussion of trends in margins. Trends in ROA/ROE are discussed later with reference to Exhibits 4-12 and 4-14.

tend to be operating in nature, whereas fixed costs are the result of operating, investing, and financing decisions.[21]

The mix of variable and fixed operating cost components in a firm's cost structure often reflects the industry in which the firm operates. Fixed investing and financing costs depend on the asset intensity of the firm's operations and (somewhat related) on the amount of debt financing used by the firm.

Leverage, which is the proportion of fixed costs in the firm's overall cost structure, can be subdivided into fixed operating costs that reflect *operating leverage* (the proportion of fixed operating costs to variable costs), and fixed financing costs or *financial leverage*.

Leverage trades risk for return. Increases in fixed costs are risky because they must still be paid as demand declines, depressing the firm's income. At high levels of demand, fixed costs are spread over a larger base, enhancing profitability. These concepts are illustrated in Exhibit 4-9.

[21]Financial markets sometimes create investing and financing transactions with variable payment streams such as lease payments tied to revenues (e.g., retailers) and adjustable rate loans. These payments may have both variable and fixed components.

EXHIBIT 4-9
Illustration of Operating, Financial, and Total Leverage Effects

General Assumptions	Company V	Company F
Fixed costs	$ 0	$ 40
Variable costs/sales	80%	40%
Assets	$200	$200

A. Assume 0% Financing, Debt $0, Equity $200

	No Leverage Company V			Operating Leverage Company F		
Scenario	A	B	C	A	B	C
Sales	$50	$100	$150	$50	$100	$150
Variable cost	40	80	120	20	40	60
Contribution	$10	$ 20	$ 30	$30	$ 60	$ 90
Fixed cost	0	0	0	40	40	40
Operating income	$10	$ 20	$ 30	($10)	$ 20	$ 50
Return						
On sales	20%	20%	20%	(20%)	20%	33%
On assets	5%	10%	15%	(5%)	10%	25%
On equity	5%	10%	15%	(5%)	10%	25%

B. Assume 50% Financing, Debt 100, Equity 100, Interest rate = 5%

	Financial Leverage Company V			Total Leverage Company F		
Scenario	A	B	C	A	B	C
Operating income	$10	$ 20	$ 30	($10)	$ 20	$ 50
Interest	5	5	5	5	5	5
Net income	$ 5	$ 15	$ 25	($15)	$ 15	$ 45
Return						
On assets	5%	10%	15%	(5%)	10%	25%
On equity	5%	15%	25%	(15%)	15%	45%

Operating Leverage

Part A of Exhibit 4-9 illustrates operating leverage. With sales of $100 (scenario B), Company V and Company F have the identical return on sales of 20% and ROA (= ROE) of 10%. The return on sales is constant for Company V, since its operating costs are completely variable. Changes in net income are directly proportional to changes in demand—a 50% increase in sales to $150 results in a 50% increase in income to $30. Company F's profitability, on the other hand, varies by more than changes in demand. A 50% change in demand changes net income by 150%. Because of fixed costs, the return on sales does not remain constant with volume.

The *contribution margin ratio* is a useful measure of the effects of operating leverage on the firm's profitability:

$$\text{Contribution Margin Ratio} = \frac{\text{Contribution}}{\text{Sales}} = 1 - \frac{\text{Variable Costs}}{\text{Sales}}$$

This ratio indicates the incremental profit resulting from a given dollar change in sales. For Company V this ratio is 20% (1 − 80%), and for Company F it is 60% (1 − 40%). Thus, a change of $50 in sales results in a change in operating income of

$$\text{Company V: 20\% } \times \text{ \$50} = \text{\$10}$$

$$\text{Company F: 60\% } \times \text{ \$50} = \text{\$30}$$

The *operating leverage effect (OLE)* is defined as

$$\text{OLE} = \frac{\text{Contribution Margin Ratio}}{\text{Return on Sales}} = \frac{\text{Contribution}}{\text{Operating Income}}$$

and is the ratio of the contribution margin to operating income. The OLE can be used to estimate the percentage change in income (and ROA) resulting from a given percentage change in sales volume:

$$\text{\% Change in Income} = \text{OLE} \times \text{\% Change in Sales}$$

When OLE is greater than 1, operating leverage exists. However, this measure of operating leverage is not constant across all levels of activity.[22] *The OLE is a relative measure and varies with the level of sales.*

For Company V, the OLE is equal to 1, at all sales levels, because its costs are completely variable. Thus, for Company V, a given percentage change in sales results in equivalent percentage changes in income and ROA.

For Company F, however, the OLE varies: It is equal to 3 (60%/20%) for scenario B. A 50% change in sales (to scenario A or scenario C) will result in a threefold percentage change (3 × 50% = 150%) in income and ROA. Using scenario C as the base starting point, however, results in an OLE measure of 1.8 (60%/33%). A 33% drop in sales from scenario C to scenario B ($150 to $100) results in a 60% (1.8 × 33%) drop in income ($50 to $20) and ROA.[23]

Financial Leverage

The effects of financial leverage can also be measured. From the point of view of common shareholders, financial leverage is, like operating leverage, a risk and return trade-off. The firm takes on the risk of fixed financing costs, anticipating that higher returns will accrue to the common shareholders at higher levels of demand.

In part B of Exhibit 4-9, we assume that each company is 50% financed by debt and interest costs = $5 (5% interest rate). For Company V (which has no operating leverage), changes in net income are now proportionally higher than changes in de-

---

[22]Similarly, the financial leverage measure discussed shortly is also a function of the chosen starting point.

[23]In all cases, the ROE is identical to ROA, as we have assumed no financing in Panel A.

mand; changes of 50% in volume are accompanied by changes of 67% in profit and ROE. (Note that ROA, because it is computed before interest expense, is unaffected by the existence of financial leverage.)

The *financial leverage effect* (FLE) relates operating income to net income:

$$FLE = \frac{\textbf{Operating Income}}{\textbf{Net Income}}$$

The FLE for Company V is (at scenario B) $20/$15 = 1.33. Thus, a 50% change in sales (and operating income) results in a 67% (1.333 × 50%) shift in income (from $15 to $25) and ROE (from 15% to 25%).

For Company F, the changes in income relative to changes in demand are even higher. Here, the effects of *both* operating and financial leverage work together, giving a *total leverage effect* (TLE) equal to the product of the individual leverage effects:

$$TLE = OLE \times FLE = \frac{\textbf{Contribution}}{\textbf{Net Income}}$$

$$TLE = 3 \times 1.333 = 4.00$$

A 50% decline in Company F's sales (from $100 to $50) results in a 200% (4 × 50%) decline in income (from $15 to $-15). This suggests that firms with high operating leverage take on high financial leverage only at their peril. Traditionally, high debt ratios have been considered acceptable only for firms with low operating leverage or with stable operations (such as public utilities), where the risk of combining operating and financial leverage was low. In recent years, however, financial leverage has been applied to companies with high operating leverage as well (airlines, for example), resulting in financial distress or even bankruptcy during periods of economic adversity.[24]

EARNINGS PER SHARE AND OTHER RATIOS USED FOR VALUATION

Ratios are often used explicitly or implicitly for securities valuation. Equity valuation models use ratios such as earnings per share and book value per share. Fixed income ratings and valuation techniques also lean heavily on ratios. This section introduces the ratios used in these models; their use in ratings and valuation models is discussed in Chapters 18 and 19.

Earnings per Share

Earnings per share (EPS) is probably the most widely available and commonly used corporate performance statistic for publicly traded firms. It is used to compare operating performance and for valuation purposes either directly or together with market prices in the familiar form of price/earnings (P/E) ratios. The EPS and P/E ratios are reported in the business section of many newspapers. Unlike other ratios discussed in this chapter, however, the calculation of EPS is governed and mandated by GAAP.

In the United States, EPS reporting requirements are governed by Accounting

---

[24]The growth in off-balance sheet financing can be partly explained by the desire of firms to report lower levels of operating and financial leverage. The use of operating leases allows firms to avoid the recognition of debt and related financing costs. All leverage ratios should be adjusted for operating leases and other forms of off-balance sheet financing. (See Chapters 10 and 11.)

Principles Board (APB) Opinion 15, Earnings per Share, as subsequently amended by the FASB.[25] Box 4-2 provides details on these reporting requirements and a comparison with worldwide standards. The following discussion summarizes the important issues.

Simple Capital Structure

For firms that have only common shares, the computation of EPS is relatively straightforward. In such cases, the computation is

$$\textbf{Basic EPS} = \frac{\textbf{Earnings Available to Common Shareholders}}{\textbf{Weighted-Average Number of Shares of Common Stock Outstanding}}$$

or

$$\frac{\textbf{Net Income} - \textbf{Preferred Dividends}}{\textbf{Weighted-Average Number of Shares of Common Stock Outstanding}}$$

where the shares are usually weighted by the number of months those shares were outstanding.[26] The numerator used to calculate EPS must equal earnings available for distribution to common shareholders. Therefore, preferred stock dividends, whether declared or cumulative, must be deducted from net income.

Complex Capital Structure

Companies whose capital structures include options or convertible securities (preferred shares and debt) are said to have complex capital structures. *These firms must recognize the potential effect on EPS upon conversion of those securities if such a conversion will result in dilution (lowering) of EPS.*[27] These firms must report two EPS numbers:

1. Primary earnings per share (PEPS) to report the effects of securities that derive a significant portion of their value from their conversion right. Such securities are called common stock equivalents (CSEs).[28] Options and warrants are always considered to be CSEs. Convertible debt and preferred shares are considered to be CSEs only when their effective yield is less than two-thirds of the average Aa bond yield at the date of issuance:[29]

$$\textbf{PEPS} = \frac{\textbf{Net Income Available for Common} + \textbf{Adjustment for CSEs}}{\textbf{Weighted-Averaged Common Shares} + \textbf{Weighted-Average CSEs}}$$

[25] AICPA interpretations cover some issues left unclear by APB 15. As these interpretations are "unofficial," they are not always followed. See footnote 8 in Chapter 1, which details the five authoritative levels in the hierarchy of accounting principles; "unofficial" AICPA interpretations are classified as level 4.

[26] EPS calculations may also be based on daily or weekly weighting.

[27] Firms are required to report only basic EPS if the FDEPS results in a dilution of less than 3% from basic EPS. Note that this materiality test is applied in the aggregate to all dilutive securities, whereas the antidilutive exception is based on an analysis of each security.

[28] Nonconvertible participating securities and two-class common stock are CSEs if their claim on earnings is substantially equivalent to that of common shareholders.

[29] This classification is permanent; subsequent changes in interest rates or market prices do not affect the classification. When a newly issued convertible security is classified as a CSE, all previously or subsequently issued securities with similar terms must also be classified as CSEs.

BOX 4-2
Earnings per Share: Additional Issues

Earnings per share is probably the most widely used indicator of corporate performance. Yet, most who use it do not understand how it is computed. Fewer still understand how it is affected by the issuance of convertibles, options, or other potentially dilutive securities. In the text, we outlined some of the procedures used in its calculation. In this box, we discuss computational issues, disclosure requirements, proposed changes in current U.S. practice, and a comparison with international standards.

Computational Issues Under U.S. GAAP

Weighted-Average Number of Common Shares Outstanding

The denominator must reflect all stock dividends and stock splits effective during the period and those announced after the end of the reporting period (but before the financial statements are issued) as if effective at the beginning of the reporting period. All prior periods presented are restated for comparability.

Acquisitions

Shares issued in purchase method acquisitions (see Chapter 14) are included in the denominator only for the period following the acquisition date. Similarly, only the postacquisition results of operations of the acquired firms are included in the numerator of the EPS computation. Note that no restatement of prior periods is permitted for purchase method acquisitions.

The impact of the pooling method is quite different. Merged firms are considered combined entities for all years presented. The shares issued in the combination are assumed to have been outstanding for all periods presented, and the results of operations for the two firms are also combined for those periods in the EPS calculation.

Contingent Shares

Acquisitions and incentive compensation plans may require the issuance of common shares if specific conditions, such as the passage of time, achievement of income levels, or specified market prices of the common stock, are met. Securities whose issuance depends solely on the passage of time are always included in the weighted-average shares outstanding. Other contingent shares are included in the computation of primary and fully diluted EPS if the required income levels or market prices have been reached at the end of the reporting period.

When the issuance of contingent shares depends on the achievement of earnings targets and it is likely that those targets will be achieved, the computation of fully diluted earnings per share includes both the incremental shares and the level of income assumed to have been achieved. These adjustments to the EPS measures are required even if the incremental shares are to be issued at a later date.

Convertible Securities

All dilutive CSEs that are convertible within 5 years of the financial statement date are included in PEPS and FDEPS. CSEs exercisable after 5 years but within 10 years of the statement date enter FDEPS calculations *only*. However, conversion is not assumed for either PEPS or FDEPS if the conversion privilege is not effective within 10 years of the reporting period.

For options and warrants, the treasury stock method is used only when the market price exceeds the exercise price for "substantially all"* of three consecutive months ending on the last month of the reporting period. *PEPS calculations are based on the average market price and FDEPS on the higher of the end-of-period market price or average market price for the period.*

EPS Computations for Two-Class Securities

Some firms issue more than one class of common stock or have "participating" securities that are entitled to share in the dividends paid on common stock. EPS computations for each class of nonconvertible† two-class securities are based on an allocation of earnings according to dividends paid and participation rights in undistributed earnings.

Additional Disclosure Requirements Under U.S. GAAP

Firms with convertible securities or options must also disclose:

1. Dividend and liquidation preferences
2. Participation and voting rights
3. Call dates and prices
4. Conversion (or exercise) dates and prices

The actual conversion of CSEs (bonds or preferred stock) into common shares may not change the total capital of the firm. However, such conversions or the issuance of shares (exercise of options) change the number of shares outstanding and the trend of reported EPS. Firms must disclose the impact of these changes on primary EPS even if the event occurs after the close of the reporting period (but before the financial statements are issued). Such supplementary disclosure assumes that the events occurred at the beginning of the reporting period. The SEC requires separate disclosure of EPS calculations if they cannot be determined directly from the financial statements or other disclosures.‡

International Differences

Earnings per share computations and disclosure requirements under U.S. GAAP are more comprehensive than those of other countries. U.K. and Canadian standards are closest in that they require firms to calculate basic and fully diluted EPS. Potential dilution is reflected only in fully diluted EPS, but neither country employs the treasury stock method; proceeds of exercise are assumed to be invested to generate a notional return, which is included in earnings when computing fully diluted earnings per share.

The most important international differences are that:

1. The computation of fully diluted earnings per share is not required in most countries.
2. The concept of common stock equivalents is not used in other countries.
3. Rights issues are common in other countries; they are included in basic EPS. A denominator adjustment is required for the bonus element when rights are issued below the current market price.

Proposed Changes in EPS Computation

The FASB and the IASC have undertaken a joint EPS project with the goal of international harmonization. Both approaches will simplify the computation of EPS by requiring firms to report basic and diluted EPS number, eliminating the (U.S.) primary earnings per share. The two approaches are similar and the important differences are mitigated by disclosure requirements.

However, some conceptual and practical differences remain. An important difference lies in the objectives: The FASB proposes to incorporate the potential dilutive effect of all securities that may have a claim on earnings, whereas the IASC objective is to provide a warning signal of the risk or variability of EPS. However, significant disclosures will be available to facilitate comparability.

Another significant difference stems from the choice of the "control number" used to compute dilution: The FASB uses income from continuing operations, whereas the IASC has proposed net income attributable to ordinary shareholders. EPS computations based on FASB proposals should be more informative (more comparable over time and across firms) as they will not be affected by management discretion over the amount and timing of voluntary accounting changes, different methods used to adopt mandatory accounting changes, discontinuance of operations, and extraordinary items.

The FASB also would require the disclosure of EPS for all the components of income. The IASC, in contrast, only calls for the disclosure of EPS based on net income attributable to ordinary shareholders. Again, the FASB requirement is more informative.

Two other differences deserve mention. First, the FASB would require computation of basic and diluted EPS using the new number of shares outstanding following stock dividends, stock splits, or reverse stock splits that occur after the end of the period but before the issuance of financial statements. The IASC proposal mandates the use of actual shares outstanding at period-end, but calls for the disclosure of such transactions and pro-forma EPS amounts.

The second distinction involves the use of different methods in the case of rights offers containing bonus elements. The IASC proposal adjusts for the fair value of the theoretical ex-rights, whereas the FASB uses the treasury stock method. This difference is unlikely to be material unless the rights offer is for a substantial number of shares. Rights offers with a large bonus element are rare in the United States.

The two proposals constitute significant progress toward harmonization and will promote cross-border investment by ensuring that the denominator of the EPS measures will be comparable across countries. However, comparability of the numerator (the earnings number) continues to require a lot more work.

---

*"Substantially all" means 11 of 13 weeks over the last 3 months. Similar rules apply to interim EPS. See AICPA Interpretation 63.

†If shares of one class are convertible into shares of the other class, as is normally the case, the problem is simplified. EPS is computed based on the number of shares outstanding if we assume conversion. Although the AICPA interpretations suggest that the "two-class method" should be used when it results in greater dilution, in practice this advice is not followed.

‡Item 601, Exhibit 11 of Regulation S-K. This exhibit is required even when the dilution is less than 3% and APB 15 would not require the dual presentation.

2. Fully diluted earnings per share (FDEPS) to reflect the maximum potential dilution due to CSEs and all other convertible securities not considered CSEs [such securities are called *other potentially dilutive securities* (OPDS)]:

$$\text{FDEPS} = \frac{\textbf{Net Income Available for Common} + \textbf{Adjustments for CSEs and OPDS}}{\textbf{Weighted-Average Common Shares} + \textbf{Weighted-Average CSEs and OPDS}}$$

To account for the potential dilution, assumptions must be made with respect to:

• Whether the conversion or exercise will actually take place, and
• How the proceeds of exercise will be used

Unfortunately, these assumptions are in many ways arbitrary and not necessarily tied to economic reality. Thus, for companies with complex or changing capital structures, both the level and trend of reported EPS are affected by the assumptions made.

Adjustments for Options and Warrants

APB 15 uses the *treasury stock method* to calculate the dilutive impact of options and warrants on EPS. This method assumes that the proceeds from exercise are used by the firm to (re)purchase common shares on the open market. As long as the market price (MP) is greater than the exercise price (EP), the effect will be dilutive and the options and warrants will affect (both primary and fully diluted) EPS calculations. *The denominator*[30] *of the EPS ratio is adjusted by adding the incremental (I) shares* equal to

$$I = \frac{MP - EP}{MP} \times N$$

where *N* equals the number of shares issuable on exercise. No adjustment is made to the numerator.

Adjustments for Convertible Securities

The dilutive effect of convertible bonds and preferred stock is computed using the "if converted" method, which assumes that securities were converted[31] into common shares at the beginning of the period or on the date of issuance, whichever is later. *The denominator is adjusted by including the new shares issued and the numerator is adjusted by eliminating the (after-tax) interest and/or preferred dividend payments made on the convertible security.*

Example of EPS Computation. Exhibit 4-10 shows an actual earnings per share computation. Two points require emphasis. First, since the convertible bond was not classified as a CSE at issuance, conversion is not assumed when computing primary EPS; conversion is assumed for fully diluted EPS as the security is dilutive. Second, options are always CSEs, and since in this case they are dilutive, they enter into the computation of both primary and fully diluted EPS. The difference is that, for the fully diluted calculation, the period-end stock price is used if higher (hence, more dilutive) than the period-average price.

Limitations of EPS Calculations

The following limitations of EPS as a measure of profitability should be considered before using that ratio for valuation or comparison purposes:

- CSE classification for convertibles is permanently decided on the basis of the Aa bond yield at the time of issuance. However, subsequent changes in market prices affect the value of the conversion feature and change the probability that conversion (dilution) will actually occur.

---

[30] A modified treasury stock method is used when the proceeds would result in the assumed repurchase of more than 20% of the outstanding common stock. Proceeds in excess of amounts needed to purchase 20% of the common are assumed to be used first to retire short-term debt and then long-term debt. Any balance is assumed invested in government securities. If debt is assumed to be retired or government securities are assumed to be purchased, there will be a numerator effect in that income will be increased (or loss decreased) by the assumed decrease in interest expense or increased interest income (both posttax).

[31] For PEPS, the earliest conversion rate should be used for securities with changing conversion rates over time. FDEPS is based on the conversion rate (applicable over the next 10 years) most favorable to the holder to reflect maximum potential dilution.

EXHIBIT 4-10
Computation of Earnings per Share

Assumptions

1996	Net income	$500,000
	Average common shares	100,000
	Tax rate	40%

Convertible bond, issued July 1, 1996:

Face amount	$1,000,000
Rate	8% (semiannual)
Convertible	25 shares per $1,000 bond
Aa bond rate	9%

Options on common stock, issued December 31, 1995:

Number of shares	25,000
Exercise price	$25.00 per share
Average price during 1996	$27.50 per share
Year-end price at December 31, 1996	$30.00 per share

Primary Earnings per Share

The convertible bond would not be considered a CSE for PEPS as the rate on the bonds of 8% exceeds two-thirds of the Aa rate ($2/3 \times 9\% = 6\%$). The option is considered a CSE, and since the (average) market price is greater than the exercise price, the effect will be dilutive.

$$\text{PEPS} = \frac{\text{Net Income} + \text{Interest Adjustment (Net of Taxes)}^*}{\text{Average Common Shares} + \text{Additional Shares}\dagger}$$

$$\frac{\$500,000}{100,000 + 2,273} = \frac{\$500,000}{102,273} = \$4.89$$

Fully Diluted Earnings per Share

$$\text{FDEPS} = \frac{\text{Net Income} + \text{Interest Adjustment (Net of Taxes)}\ddagger}{\text{Average Common Shares} + \text{Additional Shares}\S}$$

$$\frac{\$500,000 + \$24,000}{100,000 + 12,500 + 4,167} = \frac{\$524,000}{116,667} = \$4.49$$

---

*No adjustment is required since the bonds are not CSEs.

†Incremental shares from the assumed exercise of options using the average market price:

$$I = \frac{\text{MP} - \text{EP}}{\text{MP}} N = \frac{27.50 - 25}{27.5} \times 25,000 = 2,273$$

‡Interest Expense = $ 40,000   (8% × $1,000,000 × 1/2 year)
     Tax Effect = <u>(16,000)</u>   (40% × $40,000)
     Adjustment = <u>$ 24,000</u>

§12,500 shares from the assumed conversion of bonds. 4,167 incremental shares from the assumed exercise of options. Incremental shares from the assumed exercise of options using the higher year-end price:

$$I = \frac{\text{MP} - \text{EP}}{\text{MP}} N = \frac{30 - 25}{30} \times 25,000 = 4,167$$

- The Aa bond yield is the wrong benchmark for most firms. Its use results in a lower probability of CSE classification for lower-rated firms, as it is less likely that they could sell securities with an effective yield below two-thirds of the Aa bond yield.
- The assumptions behind the treasury stock method are unrealistic; they mirror the actual impact of exercise only in rare cases.
- EPS growth rates can be distorted by a firm's dividend and financing policies. Firms with lower dividend payout ratios will show higher EPS growth rates than firms with higher payout ratios (see below).

Cash Flow per Share

Cash flow per share is calculated using CFO as the numerator. Computed in this manner, it reports on the cash-generating ability of the firm. Like all summary measures, cash flow per share should be used with caution. CFO/share suffers from the following problems:

- Variability from year to year
- Dependent on accounting methods
- Does not reflect cash needed for required debt payments
- Does not reflect cash required for maintenance of productive capacity

EBITDA per Share

Earnings before interest, taxes, depreciation, and amortization (EBITDA) is computed by adding depreciation and amortization expense to earnings before interest and taxes (EBIT). It is often used as a measure of cash flow, but suffers from many limitations in that it ignores:

1. Variations in accounting methods
2. Cash required for working capital
3. Debt service and other fixed charge requirements
4. The need to maintain productive capacity

For these reasons, it should not be used blindly for valuation purposes.

Book Value per Share

This ratio represents the equity of the firm (common equity less preferred shares at liquidation value) on a per share basis (number of shares outstanding at balance sheet date) and is sometimes used as a benchmark for comparisons with the market price per share. As will be discussed in Chapter 19, recent work by Ohlson (1995) has renewed interest in book value (and the price-to-book ratio) as an input in accounting-based valuation models.

Book value per share, however, has limitations as a valuation tool as it is subject to valuation measures based on GAAP:

- Which are bound by historical cost rather than current market value conditions, and

• Whose definition of what constitutes an asset or liability may not coincide with economic reality.

Thus, the balance sheet may contain goodwill or other intangible assets of uncertain value; the market value of investments and fixed assets may differ markedly from the balance sheet valuation and there may be significant adjustments for off-balance sheet activities.

Price-to-Earnings and Price-to-Book Value Ratios

The P/E ratio measures the degree to which the market "capitalizes" a firm's earnings. The P/E ratio has been the subject of much scrutiny in the academic as well as the professional world. Its theoretical underpinnings, empirical behavior, and its relationship to the price-to-book value ratio are discussed in greater detail in Chapter 19.

Book value per share and its relationship to price in the form of the price-to-book (P/B) ratio has received recent attention in the finance and accounting literature. The Ohlson (1995) valuation model noted above is one reason. Additionally, Fama and French (1992) found that the P/B ratio (along with size) was the best predictor of future stock returns. Firms with low P/B ratios subsequently had consistently higher returns than firms with high P/B ratios. We discuss this research further in Chapters 5 and 18.

Dividend Payout Ratio

The dividend payout ratio equals the percentage of earnings paid out as dividends, that is,

$$\text{Dividend Payout} = \frac{\text{Dividends}}{\text{Net Income}}$$

Generally, "growth" firms have low dividend payout ratios as they retain most of their income to finance future expansion. More established "mature" firms tend to have higher payout ratios.

Effect of Dividend Policy on per Share Growth

The (ir)relevance of a firm's dividend policy has been the subject of much debate in the finance literature. It is important to note, however, that a firm's payout ratio (combined with its financing policy) can lead to differing growth rates in EPS and book value per share. Firms with low dividend payout ratios will show higher growth than those with high payout ratios. As a result, misleading conclusions can arise when firms with different dividend policies are compared.

Firm A, shown in Exhibit 4-11, has a low dividend payout ratio of 10%. The reinvestment of earnings produces steady growth in EPS given a constant ROE of 10% and no issuance of new stock. Firm B pays out all net income as dividends. To obtain capital for growth, it sells new shares at the price indicated (for simplicity, we assume a constant price-earnings ratio of 10). Although both firms show the same (9%) growth rate for net income, Firm B shows no growth in per share earnings and book value. The growth in shares outstanding is as rapid as the growth in earnings

EXHIBIT 4-11
Effect of Dividend Policy on Growth of Earnings and Book Value per Share

	19X1	19X2	19X3	19X4	19X5
Firm A: Low Dividend Payout					
Net income ($000)	1,000	1,090	1,188	1,295	1,411
Average shares (000)	1,000	1,000	1,000	1,000	1,000
Earnings per share ($)	1.00	1.09	1.19	1.30	1.41
Dividends paid ($000)	100	109	119	130	141
Book value ($000)*	10,900	11,881	12,950	14,115	15,385
Book value/share ($)*	10.90	11.88	12.95	14.11	15.38
Firm B: High Dividend Payout					
Net income ($000)	1,000	1,090	1,188	1,295	1,411
Average shares (000)	1,000	1,090	1,188	1,295	1,411
Earnings per share ($)	1.00	1.00	1.00	1.00	1.00
Dividends paid ($000)	1,000	1,090	1,188	1,295	1,411
Stock issued ($000)	900	981	1,069	1,165	1,270
Assumed price per share ($)	10.00	10.00	10.00	10.00	10.00
No. of shares issued (000)	90	98	107	116	127
Book value ($000)*	10,900	11,881	12,950	14,115	15,385
Book value/share ($)*	10.00	10.00	10.00	10.00	10.00
Firm A Compared to Firm B					
Ratio of earnings per share	1.00	1.09	1.19	1.30	1.41
Ratio of book value per share	1.09	1.19	1.30	1.41	1.54

*At year-end.
Note: Opening Book Value January 1, 19X1, assumed to be $10,000,000.

and book value. The last part of the exhibit shows the widening differential between the two firms.

Although this example may appear unrealistic, it is a reasonable description of the plight of public utility companies (gas, electric, water) in the United States. To attract investors, these firms historically paid out most of their earnings as dividends. To finance growth, they periodically sold additional common shares. As a result, EPS growth rates were low. These firms were trapped in a vicious cycle. If they reduced their dividend rates, their EPS growth rates would rise, and they might be considered growth companies rather than bond substitutes.[32]

---

[32] In recent years, some utilities have reduced their dividends or restricted dividend growth to increase retained earnings available for new investment. Other utilities have long been successful in promoting themselves as growth companies by paying low dividends and/or stock dividends and retaining their earnings for growth.

RATIOS: AN INTEGRATED ANALYSIS

The ratios surveyed in this chapter measure such diverse aspects of an enterprise's performance as its efficiency of operations (activity ratios), liquidity, solvency, and profitability. The discussion thus far has focused on the characteristics of individual ratios. Comprehensive financial analysis requires a review of three interrelationships among ratios:

1. *Economic relationships.* Interdependent changes in various components of the financial statements stem from underlying economic relationships. For example, higher sales are generally associated with higher investment in working capital components such as receivables and inventory. Ratios comprising these elements should be correlated.

2. *Overlap of components.* The components of many ratios overlap due to the inclusion of an identical term in the numerator or denominator, or because a term in one ratio is a subset or component of another ratio.[33] Change in one of these identical terms will change a number of ratios in the same direction. Similarly, ratios that aggregate other ratios can be expected to follow patterns over time consistent with those of their components. For example, the total assets turnover ratio is essentially a (weighted) aggregation of the individual turnover ratios. Trends in this ratio will mirror those observed in the inventory, accounts receivable, and fixed asset turnover ratios.

3. *Ratios as composites of other ratios.* Some ratios are related to other ratios across categories. For example, the ROA ratio is a combination of profitability and turnover ratios:

$$\frac{\textbf{Income}}{\textbf{Assets}} = \frac{\textbf{Income}}{\textbf{Sales}} \times \frac{\textbf{Sales}}{\textbf{Assets}}$$

A change in either of the ratios on the right-hand side will change the return on assets as well.

The interrelationships among ratios have important implications for financial analysis. Disaggregation of a ratio into its component elements allows us to gain insight into factors affecting a firm's performance; for example, significant changes in ROA may be best understood through an analysis of its components. Further, ratio differences can highlight the economic characteristics and strategies of:

- The same firm over time
- Firms in the same industry
- Firms in different industries
- Firms in different countries

These relationships among ratios imply that one might be able to "ignore" some component ratios and use a composite or representative ratio to capture the information contained in other ratios. For example, in the ROA relationship described earlier,

[33]An example of the first type is the use of sales in various activity and profitability ratios. Examples of the second category include cash as a component of quick assets, which in turn are a part of current assets.

the effect of the two ratios on the right side of the equation may be captured by the ROA ratio. For certain analytic purposes, this composite ROA ratio may suffice.

Analysis of Firm Performance

This section will exploit some of these interrelationships to analyze a firm's performance by focusing on disaggregations of the overall profitability measures ROA and ROE.

Disaggregation of ROA

The ROA ratio can be disaggregated as follows:

$$\text{ROA} = \text{Total Asset Turnover} \times \text{Return on Sales}$$

$$= \frac{\text{Sales}}{\text{Assets}} \times \frac{\text{EBIT}}{\text{Sales}}$$

The firm's overall profitability is the product of an activity ratio and a profitability ratio. A low ROA can result from low turnover, indicating poor asset management, low profit margins, or a combination of both factors.

Exhibit 4-12 (part A) presents an analysis of duPont's ROA for the period 1990 to 1994. Note that profitability is measured by EBIT. The use of EBIT (rather than net income) shows trends independent of the capital structure and tax position of the firm.

EXHIBIT 4-12. E. I. DUPONT DENEMOURS AND COMPANY AND CONSOLIDATED SUBSIDIARIES
Disaggregation of Pretax ROA and ROE

	A. Return on Assets				B. Return on Equity		
	Preinterest and Tax Margin[a] $\times$	Asset Turnover[b] =	Preinterest ROA[c]	Interest on Assets[d] $-$	Postinterest ROA[e] =	Leverage[f] $\times$	Pretax ROE[g] =
	$\dfrac{\text{EBIT}}{\text{Sales}}$ $\times$ (%)	$\dfrac{\text{Sales}}{\text{Average Total Assets}}$ =	$\dfrac{\text{EBIT}}{\text{Average Total Assets}}$ (%)	$\dfrac{\text{Interest Expense}}{\text{Average Total Assets}}$ (%) $-$	$\dfrac{\text{EBT}}{\text{Average Total Assets}}$ (%) =	$\dfrac{\text{Average Total Assets}}{\text{Average Common Equity}}$ $\times$	$\dfrac{\text{EBT}}{\text{Average Common Equity}}$ (%) =
Average	8.95 $\times$	1.04 =	9.30	1.79 $-$	7.51 =	2.70 $\times$	20.28 =
1990	**12.30** $\times$	**1.10** =	**13.53**	2.12 $-$	**11.41** =	**2.26** $\times$	**25.79** =
1991	**9.23** $\times$	**1.04** =	**9.62**	2.03 $-$	**7.59** =	**2.24** $\times$	**17.00** =
1992	**6.49** $\times$	**1.01** =	**6.55**	1.71 $-$	**4.84** =	**2.63** $\times$	**12.71** =
1993	**4.18** $\times$	**0.98** =	**4.09**	1.56 $-$	**2.51** =	**3.30** $\times$	**8.33** =
1994	**12.56** $\times$	**1.06** =	**13.36**	1.51 $-$	**11.85** =	**3.07** $\times$	**36.44** =

1994 Calculations (numbers have been rounded):

[a]Preinterest and Tax Margin (%) = (EBIT/Sales)*100 = (4,941/39,333)*100 = 12.56%

[b]Asset Turnover = Sales/Avg. Total Assets {39,333/[(36,892 + 37,053)/12]} = 1.06

[c]Preinterest ROA = Preinterest and Tax Margin * Asset Turnover = 12.56*1.06 = 13.36

[d]Interest on Assets = (Interest Expense/Avg. Total Assets)*100 = {559/[(36,892 + 37,053)/2]}*100 = 1.51

[e]Postinterest ROA = Preinterest ROA − Interest on Assets = 13.36 − 1.51 = 11.85

[f]Leverage = Avg. Total Assets/Avg. Common Equity = {(36,892 + 37,053)/2]/[(12,822 + 11,230)/2]} = 3.07

[g]Pretax ROE = Postinterest ROA Leverage = 11.85*3.07 = 36.44

EXHIBIT 4-13
Disaggregation of ROA into Basic Components

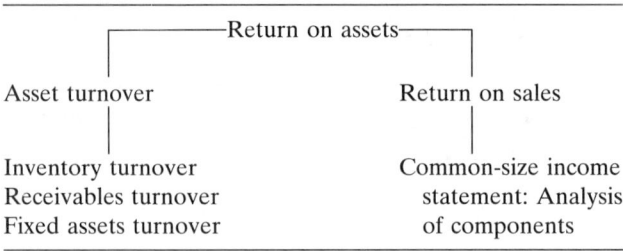

Comparing 1994 with 1990, we find that duPont's ROA showed little change. The individual components of ROA, profit margins and asset turnover, also showed little change. If we turn our attention to the changes in duPont's ROA on a year-to-year basis, our findings are somewhat different. Changes in profitability (EBIT/sales) were largely responsible for the variability of ROA.

The analysis of changes in ROA can be refined further by examining individual turnover ratios (Exhibit 4-4) and the elements of profitability (Exhibit 4-8). Exhibit 4-13 provides an overall summary of this hierarchical analysis.

Disaggregation of ROE and Its Relationship to ROA

The next logical step is a detailed examination of ROE. Exhibit 4-9 illustrates the relationship between ROA and ROE. At low levels of volume when the ROA is equal to the 5% cost of debt, there are no benefits to Company V from financial leverage. As volume increases and the ROA is greater than the cost of debt, the excess return accrues to the common shareholders.

The relationship between ROE and ROA is a function of the proportion of debt used for financing and the relationship of the cost of that debt to ROA. This can be formally expressed as

$$\textbf{ROE} = \textbf{ROA} + \left[(\textbf{ROA} - \textbf{Cost of Debt}) \times \frac{\textbf{Debt}}{\textbf{Equity}} \right]$$

In effect, the benefit of financial leverage is the product of the excess returns earned on the firm's assets over the cost of debt[34] and the proportion of debt financing to equity financing. If there are no excess returns (i.e., ROA < cost of debt), then ROE will be lower than ROA.

The relationship between ROA and ROE may also be expressed as

$$\textbf{ROE} = \left(\textbf{ROA} - \frac{\textbf{Interest Cost}}{\textbf{Assets}} \right) \times \frac{\textbf{Assets}}{\textbf{Equity}}$$

Exhibit 4-12 illustrates the ROA and ROE relationship on a pretax basis using duPont. Part B extends the ROA calculation, deducting the interest component and multiplying by the assets/equity ratio.

---

[34]This relationship is, of course, just another manifestation of the financial leverage effect defined earlier as operating income/net income, where net income = operating income − interest costs.

The assets/equity ratio is a capital structure/financial leverage ratio indicating the degree to which assets are internally financed. A higher ratio indicates more outside financing. The ratio equals 1 plus the debt/equity ratio, where debt is defined as total liabilities.[35] Thus, if we recall the components of ROA, ROE is a function of three of the four categories discussed.[36] That is,

$$\textbf{ROE = Profitability} \times \textbf{Activity} \times \textbf{Solvency}$$

$$= \frac{\textbf{Income}}{\textbf{Sales}} \times \frac{\textbf{Sales}}{\textbf{Assets}} \times \frac{\textbf{Assets}}{\textbf{Equity}}$$

Exhibit 4-14 (part A) disaggregates duPont's ROE into these three components for the years 1990 to 1994. The analysis can be expanded by examining the individual components (from Exhibits 4-4, 4-7, and 4-8) making up these categories.

The analysis of the components of ROE, which is frequently known as the *duPont model*,[37] enables the analyst to discern the contribution of each factor to the change in ROE.

From Exhibit 4-12 we learn that, from 1990 to 1994, duPont's ROE increased from 25.8% to 36.4% (we ignore, for the moment, the lower returns in 1991 through 1993). The increased ROE resulted primarily from a significant increase in leverage; the ratio of average total assets to average common equity increased from 2.26 (1990) to 3.07 (1994). Profit margins (EBIT/sales) and asset turnover (sales/average assets) showed little change over the 1990 to 1994 period (note that their product, ROA, showed a minimal decline.)

Exhibit 4-14, using posttax data, shows similar results. ROE increased considerably from 1990 to 1994 because of an increased after-tax profit margin and much higher leverage. On a short-term (year-to-year) basis, variations in ROE were due primarily to changes in profit margins.

Although the three-component model shown is the standard duPont analysis, that model can be developed further. In many cases, it is worthwhile to look at the effect of interest payments or tax payments. To do so, we must disaggregate the profitability ratio further as follows:

$$\frac{\textbf{Net Income}}{\textbf{EBT}} \times \frac{\textbf{EBT}}{\textbf{EBIT}} \times \frac{\textbf{EBIT}}{\textbf{Sales}} = \frac{\textbf{Net Income}}{\textbf{Sales}}$$

[35]Recall that assets = liabilities (debt) + equity.

[36]Selling and Stickney (1990) disaggregate ROE as follows:

$$ROE = ROA \times \frac{Assets}{Equity} \times \frac{Net\ Income}{Operating\ Income}$$

The terms to the right of ROA are clearly measures of financial leverage. Because the assets/equity ratio (capital structure leverage) discussed earlier will always be greater than 1, its effect is to increase ROE relative to ROA. The ratio of net income to operating income (the common earnings leverage) is the inverse of the financial leverage and will always be less than 1, tending to drive ROE below ROA. Whether ROE is greater or less than ROA depends on whether the positive effects of capital structure leverage outweigh the negative effect of earnings leverage; do the returns on all assets that accrue to common shareholders (capital structure leverage effects) exceed the cost of external financing (common earnings leverage)?

[37]This model was originated by duPont. See C. A. Kline, Jr. and H. L. Hissler, "The duPont Chart System for Appraising Operating Performance," *NACA Bulletin*, Aug. 1953.

EXHIBIT 4-14. E. I. DUPONT DENEMOURS AND CONSOLIDATED SUBSIDIARIES
Disaggregation of Return on Equity (After Tax)

A. Three-Component Disaggregation of ROE

	(Profitability × Turnover)				× Solvency = ROE	
	Net Income / Sales	× Sales / Average Total Assets	= Net Income / Average Total Assets	× Average Total Assets / Average Common Equity	= Net Income / Average Common Equity	
1990	5.77%	× 1.10	= 6.35%	× 2.26	= 14.34%	
1991	3.63%	× 1.04	= 3.78%	× 2.24	= 8.46%	
1992	−10.39%	× 1.01	= −10.49%	× 2.63	= −27.55%	
1993	1.50%	× 0.98	= 1.47%	× 3.30	= 4.83%	
1994	6.93%	× 1.06	= 7.37%	× 3.07	= 22.68%	
Average	1.49%	× 1.04	= 1.55%	× 2.94	= 4.55%	

B. Five-Component Disaggregation of ROE

Effects of:	(Profitability) Taxes Net Income / EBT	Financing × EBT / EBIT	Operations × EBIT / Sales	= Net Income / Sales	× Turnover) × Sales / Average Total Assets	= Net Income / Average Total Assets	× Solvency = ROE × Average Total Assets / Average Common Equity	= Net Income / Average Common Equity
1990	0.56	× 0.84	× 12.30%	= 5.77%	× 1.10	= 6.35%	× 2.26	= 14.34%
1991	0.50	× 0.79	× 9.23%	= 3.63%	× 1.04	= 3.77%	× 2.24	= 8.46%
1992	−2.17	× 0.74	× 6.49%	= −10.39%	× 1.01	= −10.49%	× 2.63	= −27.55%
1993	0.58	× 0.62	× 4.18%	= 1.50%	× 0.98	= 1.47%	× 3.30	= 4.83%
1994	0.62	× 0.89	× 12.56%	= 6.93%	× 1.06	= 7.37%	× 3.07	= 22.68%
Average	0.21	× 0.78	× 8.95%	= 1.49%	× 1.04	= 1.55%	× 2.94	= 4.55%

yielding a five-way breakdown of ROE. This decomposition is presented in Exhibit 4-14 (part B); it allows the analyst to view the income tax burden (element one is 1 minus the tax rate) separately from the interest burden (element 2, which shows the percentage of EBIT that is not paid to debtholders) and each separately from operating profitability (EBIT/sales).

DuPont's tax and interest burdens declined from 1990 to 1994. These factors explain why duPont's posttax profitability rose, increasing ROE, although (as noted earlier) EBIT/sales and (consequently) pretax ROA showed little change.

Economic Characteristics and Strategies

Ratios are not randomly distributed among companies; management strategy, industry characteristics, and product life cycle all are reflected in a firm's ratios. In this section, we examine these influences.

Competing Strategies[38]

Firms (and industries) can often be differentiated by whether they employ a high-turnover/low-margin strategy or a low-turnover/high-margin strategy to generate profits. The high-turnover/low-margin firm sells large volumes at low prices and profit margins; to be successful, the firm must carefully control costs. The firm must also control investment to achieve an acceptable ROI. The supermarket industry generally follows this strategy.

The low-turnover/high-margin firm, in contrast, competes on the basis of attributes other than price (quality or product differentiation). If successful, the firm is able to charge a high price, generating higher profit margins. Cost control is less important when costs can be passed on to the customer through higher prices. Specialty (gourmet) food shops would follow this strategy by offering goods and service not generally available from supermarkets.

Product Life Cycle

The *product life cycle* concept affects the firm's financial performance as it passes through the four stages in the cycle. Figure 4-1 and our discussion of asset turnover ratios is one example of such an analysis.

Savich and Thompson (1978) discuss the impact of product cycle stages on balance sheet, income statement, and cash flow components. Based on their discussion, we expect to see the following pattern of ratios:

1. Startup

    a. High short-term activity ratios but low liquidity ratios. Although seemingly contradictory, these reflect low inventory and receivable levels; the company is cash "hungry" and cannot build these elements of working capital.

    b. Profits and cash from operations are very low (or even negative). Thus, all ratios—profitability, solvency, and liquidity—with these components in the numerator will tend to be poor.

    c. Debt (both short- and long-term) will be high.

2. Growth

    a. Profits grow, but cash from operations lags; cash receipts are based on past sales levels, whereas disbursements are geared toward higher expected sales levels. Thus, ratios based on income tend to improve prior to those based on cash flows.

    b. Investment in capacity also rises, decreasing long-term activity (turnover) ratios. At the same time, expansion in productive capacity delays the full benefit of operating leverage; fixed costs remain high relative to sales. Profits and ROA, as a result, remain low. Debt ratios remain high. At later stages, these ratios will approach the pattern typical of the maturity stage.

---

[38]Much of the discussion of economic characteristics and strategies is based on Thomas Selling and Clyde P. Stickney, "The Effects of Business Environment and Strategy on a Firm's Rate of Return on Assets," *Financial Analysts Journal*, Jan.–Feb. 1989, pp. 43–52.

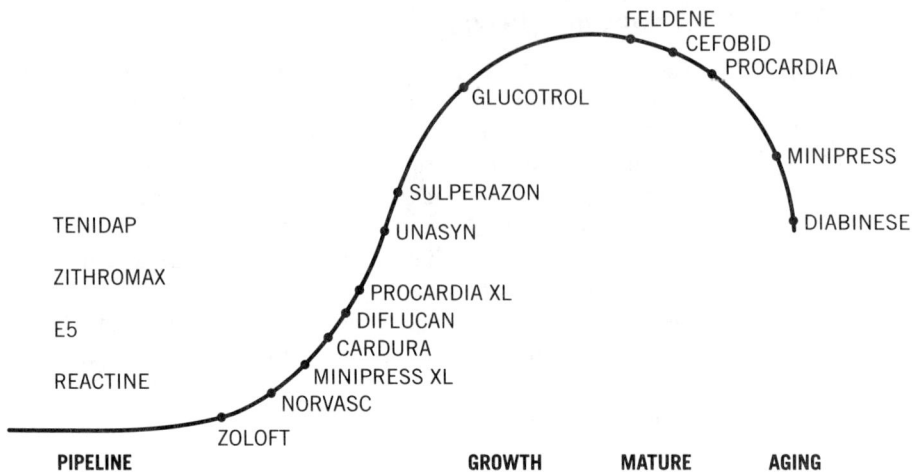

FIGURE 4-4 Illustration of product life cycle.

3. Maturity and

4. Decline (Harvest)

   a. The firm reaches its optimal operating levels, and ratios approach industry norms. Profit margins and turnover ratios are high. Debt declines relative to equity as retained earnings grow; funds are not needed for expansion. Liquidity is high as CFO has "caught up" with profits.

   b. As the firm begins the decline (harvest) stage, cash flows resulting from past investments remain positive even when current profits decline. Moreover, with a reduced asset base, ROA peaks as the firm enters this last stage.

The product life cycle concept, although providing some useful insights, can be overrated. The concept is primarily product-based. Successful firms build a portfolio of products, continually introducing new ones; at any one time, a firm will most likely have products at each stage of the cycle. The stage of the firm depends on the stage of the preponderance of its products. Figure 4-4, from the cover of Pfizer's *1990 Annual Report*, provides a good illustration of this concept.

Interindustry Economic Factors

Our earlier discussion of common-size statements and Exhibit 4-2 demonstrate that "industry norm" ratios reflect industry characteristics. Gombola and Ketz (1983) compared the means of 58 ratios for two broad-based industry classifications: manufacturing and retail firms. Finding differences in ROA, activity ratios, and profit margins, they stated that

> All of the income measures expressed as a percentage of sales are much smaller for retail firms than manufacturing firms. All of the turnover ratios show much higher values for retail firms than for manufacturing firms. Retail firms also tend to show less cash and fewer receivables than manufacturing firms as well as somewhat more debt than manufacturing firms.[39]

[39]Michael J. Gombola and J. Edward Ketz, "Financial Ratio Patterns in Retail and Manufacturing Organizations," *Financial Management*, Summer 1983, pp. 45–56.

EXHIBIT 4-15
Distributions of ROA, Profit Margin, and Asset Turnover, Selected Industries

	ROA	Profit Margin	Asset Turnover
Publishing	11.5	8.7	1.41
Chemicals	9.0	7.0	1.40
Food processors	8.5	4.3	2.28
Paper	8.3	6.9	1.29
Metal products	7.8	5.3	1.53
Department stores	7.7	3.6	2.27
Telecommunications	7.0	16.1	0.49
Petroleum	6.9	5.3	1.47
Glass	6.8	6.3	1.07
Rubber	6.6	4.0	1.66
Grocery stores	6.6	1.5	5.00
Transportation equipment	6.4	4.0	1.69
Wholesale equipment	6.4	2.8	1.93
Engineering/architecture	6.4	4.1	1.89
Real estate	6.3	12.1	0.75
Apparel	6.3	3.4	1.80
Industrial equipment	5.6	3.8	1.38
Trucking	5.6	3.5	1.80
Textiles	5.3	3.1	1.64
Oil exploration	5.1	8.1	0.47
Lumber	5.1	3.1	2.10
Steel	4.0	3.3	1.25

Source: Thomas Selling and Clyde Stickney, "The Effects of Business Environment and Strategy on a Firm's Rate of Return on Assets," *Financial Analysts Journal,* Jan.–Feb. 1989, pp. 43–52, Table IV, p. 51 (adapted).

Selling and Stickney examined ROAs for 22 industries over the period 1977 to 1986 as well as the components that make up ROA. Their results are reproduced in Exhibit 4-15 and plotted in Figure 4-5. They noted that the same overall ROA (represented by the solid lines in Figure 4-5) can result from an infinite number of different combinations of turnover and return on sales. For example, both rubber manufacturers and grocery stores have ROAs of 6.6%. Their turnover ratios and profit margins, however, differ significantly as indicated by their different locations along the turnover and profit margin axes.

They explained these differences by distinguishing between capital-intensive and noncapital-intensive industries. Capital-intensive industries tend to have low asset turnover and higher fixed costs. As a result, profit margins can fluctuate greatly due to the effects of operating leverage.

Competitive Factors. The microeconomics literature classifies firms' operating environments as ranging from monopolistic at one extreme to pure competition at the other. Monopolistic industries are characterized by high barriers to entry, high capital intensity, and high profit margins. High capital intensity results in low turnover ratios and "monopoly" profits. In addition, barriers to entry, whether a result of regulation, technology, or capital requirements, also give rise to "monopoly" profits. Pure competition, on the other hand, is characterized by low barriers to entry, low levels of capital intensity, and correspondingly low profit margins. Products are commoditylike in

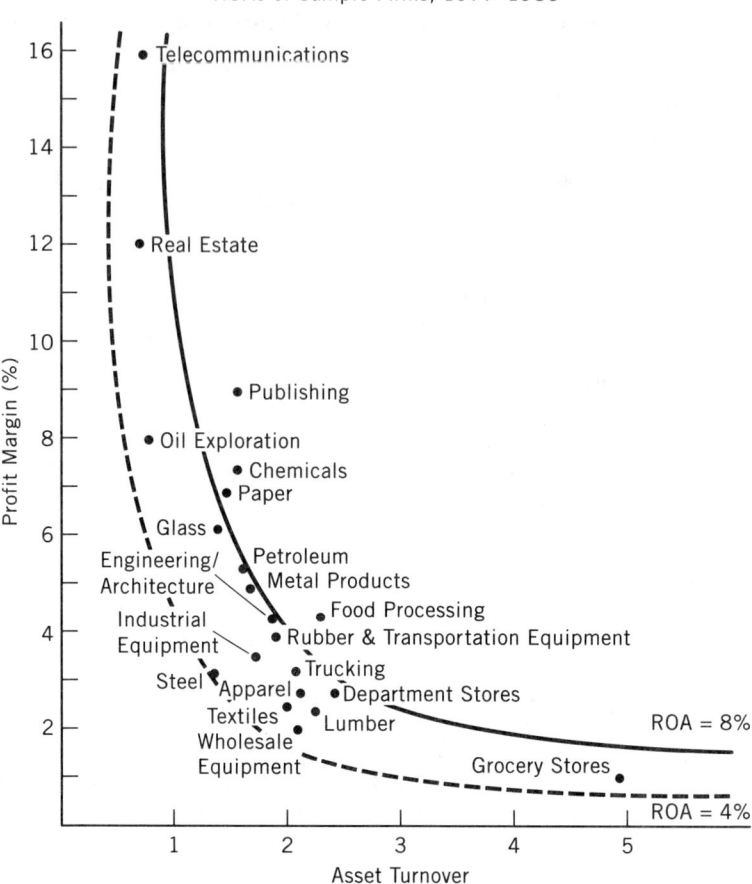

FIGURE 4-5 ROAs of sample firms, 1977–1986.
Source: Thomas Selling and Clyde Stickney, "The Effects of Business Environment and Strategy on a Firm's Rate of Return on Assets," *Financial Analysts Journal,* (Jan.–Feb. 1989), pp. 43–52, Fig. 1, p. 48.

nature and product differentiation is limited. Companies in highly competitive industries attempt to generate higher returns through increased efficiency and turnover.

Oligopolistic or multifirm industries, finally, have turnover ratios and profit margins at the midpoint of the continuum. Selling and Stickney summarize the argument with the following table:

Capital Intensity	Nature of Competition	Strategy
High	Monopoly	High profit margin
Medium	Oligopolistic	Combination of profit margin and turnover
Low	Pure competition	High turnover

Source: Thomas Selling and Clyde Stickney, "The Effects of Business Environment and Strategy on a Firm's Rate of Return on Assets," *Financial Analysts Journal,* Jan.–Feb. 1989, pp. 43–52, Table II on p. 47 (adapted).

ROE for portfolios formed on ROE for formation and subsequent years.

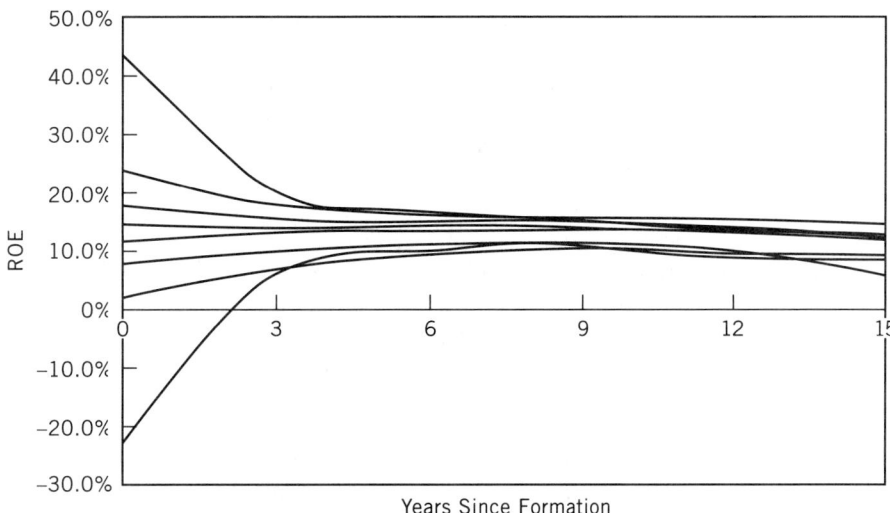

FIGURE 4-6 ROE for portfolios formed on ROE for formation and subsequent years.
Source: Based on (eight) selected portfolios from Stephen H. Penman, "An Evaluation of Accounting Rate-Of-Return," *Journal of Accounting, Auditing & Finance,* Spring 1991, pp. 233–256, Table 1, p. 238.

Trends in ROE

ROE is an important summary measure of a firm's profitability and return on investment. As the duPont model suggests, it captures many facets of a firm's operating, investing, and financing characteristics. In Chapter 19, ROE is used as a key input in an accounting-based valuation model.

Given its importance, it is worthwhile asking whether current ROE can be used to forecast future ROE levels. A related question is whether abnormally high levels of profitability can be expected to continue into the future. Some insight into these questions can be derived from Penman (1991).

Penman ranked firms (each year in the 1969 to 1985 period) by ROE and formed 20 equal-sized portfolios based on those rankings. He then remeasured the average ROE of those portfolios for the next 15 years. Figure 4-6 presents the trend in ROE for eight (the highest, lowest, and three others above and below the median ROE portfolio) of those portfolios.

The following points are apparent from the graph:

1. In the short term, approximating five years (except for the extreme portfolios), curent levels of ROE persist into the future.

2. Over the long-term, ROEs tend to revert toward an average "economy-wide" ROE.

3. Although there is a trend toward the mean, the portfolio rankings persist. That is, the portfolios with higher (lower) ROE tend to have higher (lower) ROEs in the future; however, the differences between the portfolios narrow.

Classification and Selection of Ratios

The ratios discussed in this chapter are by no means exhaustive, and a full list of the ratios available (and used) in our four categories would include nearly 100 different ratios. One possible reason for the proliferation of ratios is that ratio analysis is used not only in (external) financial analysis but also as a tool in internal management analysis and evaluation.

Ratios designed for managerial analysis may not add information to those already used for financial analysis as the needs of these two types of users are not the same. Management needs detailed information to pinpoint and remedy specific "problem" areas. The financial analyst's needs, however, are more general and thus may be satisfied with a ratio that captures the effects of other ratios or is highly correlated with other ratios. Unfortunately, once a ratio is developed for one purpose, it tends to be used in ways never intended. Ratio analysis is an area where more is not necessarily better.

Much empirical work on ratios has been descriptive: to examine the properties of and correlations among the ratios available in an attempt to find a manageable set of ratios suitable for analytic purposes. The benefit for financial analysis is a reduction in the number of ratios that must be computed and monitored. The reduced set can be used for decision making directly[40] or as a signal that more detailed analysis is required.

Horrigan (1965) examined the statistical properties of ratios and, as expected, found that many of the ratios were positively correlated with one another. In addition, some ratios, especially those with relatively stable components (e.g., long-term debt, fixed assets), were correlated over time. Industry classification was found to be the primary factor explaining ratio dispersion, although characteristics such as firm size, seasonality, and cyclical conditions also had an impact. As Horrigan stated:

> This presence of collinearity is both a blessing and a curse for financial ratio analysis. It means that only a small number of financial ratios are needed to capture most of the information ratios can provide, but it also means that this small number must be selected very carefully.[41]

Using a small subset of ratios to represent the whole set requires choosing ratios that are both:

1. Highly correlated with those ratios excluded, and

2. Not correlated with the other ratios in the subset

Condition 1 ensures that any information available from excluded ratios is captured, whereas condition 2 ensures no overlap and hence maximum information provided by the ratios included.

Several academic studies have attempted to identify ratio subsets that meet these conditions. Multivariate statistical analysis tools such as factor analysis and principal

---

[40]A second empirical approach (described in Chapter 18) uses these results to identify ratios as inputs in specific predictive models of risk in the analysis of bankruptcy, bond ratings, and beta (equity risk).

[41]James O. Horrigan, "Some Empirical Bases of Financial Ratio Analysis," *The Accounting Review*, July 1965, pp. 558–568.

EXHIBIT 4-16
Partitioning of Ratios

Return on Investment	Financial Leverage	Capital Turnover	Short-Term Liquidity	Cash Position	Inventory Turnover	Receivable Turnover
Total income/ Sales	Debt/Net plant	Cash flow/Sales	Current liabilities/ Net worth	*Cash/Total assets	Current assets/ Sales	*Receivables/ inventory
Cash flow/Total assets	*Debt/Total capital	Current assets/ Total assets	*Current assets/ Current liabilities	Cash/Current liabilities	*Inventory/ Sales	Inventory/ Current assets
Cash flow/Net worth	Total liabilities/ Net worth	Quick assets/ Total assets	Current liabilities	Cash/Sales	Sales/	*Receivables/ Sales
Total income/ Total assets	Total assets/Net worth	Net worth/Sales	Inventory/ Working capital	*Cash/Fund expenditures	Working capital	Quick assets/ Sales
Net income/ Total assets	*Debt/Total assets	*Sales/Total assets	*Quick assets/ Current liabilities		*Cost of goods sold/ Inventory	
*Net income/ Net worth	Total liabilities/ Total assets	*Sales/Net plant	Current liabilities/ Total assets			
Earnings before interest and taxes/Total assets		Sales/Total capital				
Earnings before interest and taxes/Sales						
Cash flow/Total capital						
*Total income/ Total capital						

*Indicates two most "representative" ratios for each factor.
  Source: Reprinted by permission of the publisher from George E. Pinches, A. A. Eubank, Kent A. Mingo, and J. Kent Caruthers, "The Hierarchical Classification of Financial Ratios," *Journal of Business Research,* pp. 295–310, copyright Oct. 1975 by Elsevier Science Publishing Co., Inc., Table 5, p. 303.

components have been used to partition ratios into groups that meet the two conditions listed above. Each of these partitions is assumed to be affected by an underlying factor, the nature of which is not specified by the statistical model. Rather, the researcher, after examining the ratios grouped in a given partition, attempts to find the unifying theme descriptive of the ratios in the group.

Pinches et al. (PEMC, 1975) examined 48 different ratios and found that they could be "explained" by only 7 empirical factors. These factors are consistent with the classifications used in our earlier discussions. Exhibit 4-16 lists, for each factor, the two ratios that best represent that classification. The utility of these results is that one ratio for each factor will fully provide the incremental information present in that partition. The study used data for 1966 through 1969. The results were found to be stable over the four-year period. Other studies using different sample firms, time periods, and sets of ratios reported alternative factor groupings. Chen and Shimerda (1981) reconciled these studies and showed that the apparent differences were due to nomenclature and were subsumed by the seven factors found by PEMC.

These studies confined themselves to manufacturing firms. Johnson (1979), using data from 1972 and 1974, extended the analysis to retail firms as well. Although median ratios between the two groups differ significantly (as discussed earlier), Johnson found that PEMC's seven "factors" for manufacturing companies were also descriptive of retail firms.

Gombola and Ketz (1983) also examined retail and manufacturing firms, using data from 1971 through 1980. They added improved analysis of the cash flow components of ratios. Previous studies estimated cash flows by simply adding depreciation to net income. The fact that these ratios were found to group together with profitability ratios

> could stem from the use of net income plus depreciation as a proxy for cash flow in all of these studies. Cash flow from operations, properly defined as cash receipts minus cash disbursements, is an accounting construct that differs markedly from profit. The empirical similarity between profitability measures using net income plus depreciation therefore suggests that net income plus depreciation might be measuring profitability instead of cash flow.[42]

Gombola and Ketz extended the PEMC study, adding eight cash ratios, four of which used cash flows in the numerator and four of which used working capital in the numerator. (The denominators were sales, equity, assets, and debt). In addition, for the two defensive interval ratios examined, they used actual cash expenditures in the denominator as well as the accrual-based expenses from the income statement. (Cash and quick assets were used in the numerator.)

Gombola and Ketz found that these new cash-based ratios did not group with the original seven factors. Rather, two additional factors appeared: a cash flow factor and a cash expenditures factor.

> Appearance of separate factors for cash flow and cash expenditures point to the empirical materiality of accrual and deferral items other than depreciation as well as the empirical materiality of the difference between expenses and expenditures. Such results should at least caution researchers or other users interested in cash flow performance using simple proxies for the cash flow construct or using expenses, an accrual concept, as a proxy for expenditures, a cash concept.[43]

The cash flow and cash expenditure factors were also found to be important for retail firms. These results are consistent with our view that ratios based on income/expense flows should also be examined on a cash flow basis.

Patterns of Ratio Disclosure, Definition, and Use

Before concluding this chapter, we remind the reader that the definitions and classifications of ratios we have presented are not set in stone. The proper definition of a ratio is not mandated, and there is wide diversity in practice regarding definition, relative importance, and even the categorization of particular ratios (do turnover ratios measure activity, liquidity, or profitability?). This section presents some evidence regarding:

1. How analysts classify and rank ratios
2. Which ratios are most commonly disclosed by firms
3. Publicly available industry norms

[42]Gombola and Ketz, p. 47.
[43]Ibid., pp. 54–55.

Perceived Importance and Classification

Gibson (1987) asked 52 CFA (Chartered Financial Analyst) charterholders to classify a set of 60 ratios in terms of whether they measure profitability, liquidity, or debt and to rank (on a scale of 0 to 9) their relative importance. The analysts agreed on the classification of very few ratios (net profit margin before and after tax and the current, cash and quick ratios). They gave profitability ratios the highest significance rating of any classification category, followed by debt and then liquidity ratios.

Disclosure of Ratios

Ratios are readily derived from financial statement information. There is rarely any explicit disclosure requirement. When firms do disclose ratios, the chosen ratios are consistent with those perceived to be most important by the analysts. That is, ROA, ROE, profit margins, and the debt-to-equity ratio are disclosed most often. A number of studies have examined the disclosure of ratios provided in financial statements along two dimensions:

1. The (lack of) uniformity in their calculation
2. The motivation for voluntarily disclosing the ratio

Gibson (1982) documented the wide disparity in ratio definitions across a sample of 100 annual reports. The following table lists five such ratios and statistics documenting the variability of definitions:

Ratio	Frequency of Appearance	Number of Variations	Frequency of Most Common Definition
Debt/capital	23	11	7
Debt/equity	19	6	7
Return on equity	62	5	53
Profit margin	58	8	40
Return on capital	21	12	6

Williamson (1984) examined the 1978 annual reports of 141 Fortune 500 firms for voluntary disclosure of ratios. His purpose was to test if firms engaged in selective disclosure; that is, were the ratio values of reporting companies significantly different from (better than) those of nonreporting companies? The ratio values for the reporting companies and nonreporting companies were compared on three dimensions:

1. The ratio itself
2. The ratio's percentage deviation from the industry median
3. The percentage change in the ratio from the previous year

The following results of the study show the relationship between disclosure and ratio levels:

Ratio	Percentage Reporting (%)
Significantly higher for reporting companies	
Return on equity	58
Current ratio	51
Return on sales	50
No significant difference between reporting and nonreporting	
Debt/assets	49
Dividend payout	18
Return on assets	16
Inventory turnover	8
Receivables turnover	7
Times interest earned	6
Asset turnover	6
Working capital turnover	2

These results provide evidence of selective disclosure for the three ratios that have the highest frequency of voluntary disclosure. Williamson's results also provide indirect evidence that the industry norm is a relevant benchmark. The strongest results are consistent with the hypothesis that firms tend to disclose a ratio voluntarily when that ratio exceeds the industry norm.

Industry Norms as Benchmarks

Lev (1969) and Frecka and Lee (1983) provide further evidence that industrywide norms are relevant benchmarks. They found that ratios of individual firms tend to converge toward the industrywide average.[44]

Two differing explanations are offered:

1. Managers view the industry norms as targets and "aim" their ratios accordingly. This is done by the choice of accounting method, allocation of resources, or both.

2. Industrywide economic characteristics operate on the firm to "correct" deviations from the industry norm.

More recently, Davis and Peles (1993) extended earlier work by Peles and Schneller (1989) and examined which of the above reasons were more prevalent and whether the speed of adjustment toward a "target" ratio varied by type of firm or ratio. They found that on average the management effect is faster than the industry

---

[44]These ratios were calculated by Lev (1969) and Frecka and Lee (1983) from the firms' annual reports. They were not necessarily disclosed by the firms.

EXHIBIT 4-17
Industry Norm Ratios Available

	Robert Morris Associates	Dun & Bradstreet
A. Activity		
A/R turnover Collection period	Yes	Yes
Inventory turnover	COGS/Inventory	Sales/Inventory
Payables turnover	Yes	N/A
Working capital turnover	Yes	Yes
Fixed asset turnover	Yes	N/A
Total asset turnover	Sales/Assets	Assets/Sales
B. Liquidity		
Quick ratio	Yes	Yes
Current ratio	Yes	Yes
C. Debt and Solvency		
Interest coverage	Yes	Yes
Current liabilities/ Net worth	N/A	Yes
Debt to equity	Yes	Yes
Fixed assets to equity	Fixed assets/Tangible net worth	Fixed assets/Net worth
Cash flow to debt	(Net income + depreciation)/ Current portion long-term debt	N/A
Current liabilities/ Inventory	N/A	Yes
D. Profitability		
Return on sales	N/A	Yes
Return on assets	EBT/Assets	Net income/Assets
Return on equity	EBT/Tangible net worth	EBT/Net worth
Depreciation/Sales	Yes	N/A
Officers', directors', owners' compensation/Sales	Yes	N/A

N/A = Not available.

one, although both contributed significantly to the total adjustment. In terms of individual ratios:

> The results show that when firms experience a liquidity shock, equilibrating forces counterbalance a little more than a third of the shock in the next period. This finding suggests that firms' liquidity ratios have a fast adjustment to equilibrium values. EPS ratios also have a high adjustment rate to equilibrium value; about one-third to one-half of the shock is adjusted within one period. For performance measures (net operating income over sales or assets), for the equity to debt and gross margin ratios, the findings imply a relatively long adjustment process to equilibrium values.[45]

[45]H. Z. Davis and Y. C. Peles, "Measuring Equilibrating Forces of Financial Ratios," *The Accounting Review*, Oct. 1993, pp. 725–747.

Finally, they found that smaller firms tend to adjust toward the optimal target more swiftly than larger firms.

Industry norms may be calculated directly through the use of computerized databases such as Standard & Poor's Compustat database. Alternatively, industry profiles are available from sources such as Robert Morris Associates (RMA) and Dun & Bradstreet's (D&B) Industrial Handbook. These sources provide common-size balance sheet, income statements, and selected ratios on an industry basis.

Exhibit 4-17 compares the ratios provided by each source. The ratios are presented within the categories used in this chapter. Where the sources differ in their calculation of the ratios with respect to one another or as compared to the presentation suggested in the chapter, the ratios are defined explicitly. For example, for the profitability ratios, RMA calculates ROA and ROE on a pretax basis,[46] whereas D&B does it on an after-tax basis.

SUMMARY

This chapter provides an overview of ratios most commonly used in the analysis of financial statements. These ratios, classified as activity, liquidity, solvency, and profitability indicators, are designed to measure different aspects of a firm's operating, investment, and financing activities. Ratios are used to standardize financial statements across firms and over time, facilitating comparative analysis. Ratios also provide insight into firm performance and economic relationships when evaluated in an integrated analysis.

Ratio analysis is not intended to provide all the answers about a firm, but rather to point to the relevant questions. Throughout the remainder of this book, we will address the questions raised by these ratios and show how an understanding of the accounting process facilitates their use.

CASE 4-1

Integrated Analysis of duPont, Dow Chemical, and ICI

Dow Chemical and ICI operate in some of the same markets as duPont. Their financial statements are contained in Appendices B and C, respectively, found at the end of this book. Note that the ICI statements are prepared in British pounds and in accordance with U.K. GAAP.

Required

1. For both Dow and ICI, compute ratios in the following categories, using the duPont exhibits cited as a guide:
   - Activity (Exhibit 4-4)
   - Liquidity (Exhibit 4-6)
   - Solvency (Exhibit 4-7)
   - Profitability (Exhibit 4-8)

---

[46]Somewhat surprisingly, but consistent with the CFA rankings in Gibson (1987), both calculate ROA on an "after-interest" basis.

2. Using your answers to Question 1 and the corresponding duPont data, compare the ratios of the three companies in these categories. Discuss factors that limit the usefulness of this comparison and additional data that would be needed to improve it.

3. Prepare an integrated ratio analysis of Dow and ICI, using Exhibits 4-12 and 4-14 as a guide.

4. Using your answers to Question 3, determine the key ratios that explain changes in ROE from 1993 to 1994.

5. Compare the 1994 ROE of duPont, Dow, and ICI, and determine the key ratios that explain differences in ROE. Discuss other factors that might explain the differences in ROE and any additional data needed to adjust for these factors.

6. Exhibit 4-2 contains common-size financial statement data for a group of industries. Compare these with the corresponding data for duPont, Dow, and ICI, and discuss the differences. Discuss the limitations inherent in this comparison.

Chapter 4

Problems

General Note: For ratios that are generally calculated on average data, use year-end data when prior year information is not available.

Problems 1 and 2 are based on the financial statements of Walt Disney in Exhibit 4P-1.

1. [1994 CFA adapted; ratio calculations] Calculate the ratios below for Disney at September 30, 1993 (use ending balance sheet amounts). Briefly explain the use of each of these ratios in the evaluation of a company's operations:

   (i) Accounts receivable turnover

  (ii) Total asset turnover

 (iii) Current ratio

  (iv) CFO to current liabilities

   (v) Debt to equity

  (vi) Times interest earned

 (vii) Operating income to sales

(viii) Return on sales

  (ix) Return on assets

2. [1994 CFA adapted; duPont model]

A. Using the duPont method, identify and calculate the five primary components of Disney's return on equity for each of the two fiscal years ended September 30, 1989 and September 30, 1993. Using these components, calculate Disney's return on equity for each year.

B. Identify the two components that contributed most to the observed change in Disney's return on equity from 1989 to 1993. State two reasons for the observed change in each of these components.

EXHIBIT 4P-1. THE WALT DISNEY COMPANY
Selected Financial Statement and Other Data, Years Ending September 30
($ in millions except per share data)

	1993	1989
Income Statement		
Revenue	$ 8,529	$ 4,594
Operating expenses	−6,805	−3,365
Operating income	$ 1,724	$ 1,229
General and administrative expenses	−163	−119
Interest expense	−158	−24
Investment and interest income	186	67
Income (loss) from Euro Disney	−515	0
Pretax income	$ 1,074	$ 1,153
Taxes	−403	−450
Net income	$ 671	$ 703
Earnings per share	$ 1.23	$ 1.27
Dividends per share	$ 0.23	$ 0.11
Balance Sheet		
Cash	$ 363	$ 381
Receivables	1,390	224
Inventories	609	909
Other	1,889	662
Current assets	$ 4,251	$ 2,176
Property, plant, and equipment	5,228	3,397
Other assets	2,272	1,084
Total assets	$ 11,751	$ 6,657
Current liabilities	$ 2,821	$ 1,262
Borrowings	2,386	861
Other liabilities	1,514	1,490
Stockholders' equity	5,030	3,044
Total liabilities and stockholders' equity	$ 11,751	$ 6,657
Cash Flow from Operations		
Net income	$ 671	$ 703
Depreciation	364	272
Other	1,110	300
Total	$ 2,145	$ 1,275
Other Data		
Common shares outstanding (millions)	544	552
Closing price—common stock per share	$ 37.75	$ 30.22

Problems 3 to 6 are based on the financial statements of Chicago Refrigerator, Inc.
[Exhibit 4P-2].

3. [1986 CFA adapted] Calculate the following ratios for 19X5:

    A. Activity ratios

      (i) Inventory turnover

     (ii) Accounts receivable turnover

    (iii) Fixed asset turnover

    (iv) Total asset turnover

EXHIBIT 4P-2. CHICAGO REFRIGERATOR, INC.
Balance Sheet, at December 31, 19X4 to 19X5 ($ in thousands)

	19X4	19X5
Assets		
Current assets		
Cash	$ 683	$ 325
Accounts receivable	1,490	3,599
Inventories	1,415	2,423
Prepaid expenses	15	13
Total current assets	$3,603	$ 6,360
Property, plant, equipment, gross	1,498	2,296
Less: Accumulated depreciation	(432)	(755)
Property, plant, equipment (net)	1,066	1,541
Other	123	157
Total assets	$4,792	$ 8,058
Liabilities		
Current liabilities		
Notes payable to bank	$ —	$ 875
Current portion of long-term debt	38	116
Accounts payable	485	933
Estimated income tax	588	472
Accrued expenses	576	586
Customer advance payments	34	963
Total current liabilities	$1,721	$ 3,945
Long-term debt	122	179
Other liabilities	81	131
Total liabilities	$1,924	$ 4,255
Shareholders' Equity		
Common stock	$ 550	$ 829
Preferred stock (10%)	500	450
Additional paid-in capital	450	575
Retained earnings	1,368	1,949
Total shareholders' equity	$2,868	$ 3,803
Total liabilities and shareholders' equity	$4,792	$ 8,058

EXHIBIT 4P-2 (*continued*)

CHICAGO REFRIGERATOR, INC.
Income Statement, for Years Ended December 31, 19X4 to 19X5
($ in thousands)

	19X4	19X5
Net sales	$7,570	$12,065
Other income (net)	261	345
Total revenues	$7,831	$12,410
Cost of goods sold	$4,850	$ 8,048
General administrative and marketing expense	1,531	2,025
Interest expense	22	78
Total costs and expenses	$6,403	$10,151
Net income before tax	$1,428	$ 2,259
Income tax expense	628	994
Net income	$ 800	$ 1,265

CHICAGO REFRIGERATOR, INC.
Cash Flow Statement, 19X5

Cash from operations		$ (256)
Cash for investments		(832)
Cash from financing		
Debt	$1,060	
Issue of shares	354	
Dividends paid	(684)	
		730
Change in cash		$ (358)

B. Liquidity ratios

   (i) Length of operating cycle

  (ii) Length of cash cycle

 (iii) Current ratio

  (iv) Quick ratio

   (v) Cash ratio

  (vi) CFO to current liabilities

 (vii) Defensive interval

C. Solvency ratios

   (i) Debt to equity

  (ii) Debt to capital

 (iii) Times interest earned

  (iv) Capital expenditures ratio

D. Profitability ratios

   (i) Gross margin

   (ii) Operating income to sales

   (iii) Return on sales

   (iv) Return on assets

   (v) Return on equity

4. [Disaggregation of ROE] Disaggregate the 19X5 return on equity of Chicago Refrigerator, Inc., using the three-component and five-component models.

5. [Effect of growth on ratios]

   A. Chicago Refrigerator grew considerably in 19X5, with total assets nearly doubling. Discuss how this rapid growth may have affected the ratios calculated in Problem 3 relative to those of the previous year.

   B. By calculating some ratios based on the average of opening and closing balances, we make the implicit assumption that changes in these accounts occurred uniformly throughout the year. Sometimes, however, the actual change occurs unevenly, perhaps due to an acquisition. In such cases, ratios based on averages will be distorted. Discuss how you would calculate the return on assets ratio if the growth in assets occurred:

   (i) At the beginning of the year

   (ii) At the end of the first quarter

   (iii) At the end of the second quarter

   (iv) At the end of the fourth quarter

6. [Operating and financial leverage, effects of growth]

   A. Estimate Chicago Refrigerator's fixed and variable costs for 19X5.

   B. Estimate Chicago Refrigerator's operating, financial, and total leverage effects for 19X4 and 19X5.

   C. Discuss how the company's rapid growth in 19X5 may have distorted the estimates calculated in parts A and B.

Problems 7 and 8 are based on the common-size statements presented in Exhibit 4P-3.

7. [Common-size statements—ratios] Using the common-size statements of Company 1 in Exhibit 4P-3, calculate the following ratios:

   (i) Inventory turnover

   (ii) Receivable turnover

   (iii) Length of operating cycle

   (iv) Length of cash cycle

   (v) Fixed asset turnover ratio

   (vi) Cash ratio

   (vii) Quick ratio

   (viii) Current ratio

EXHIBIT 4P-3
Common-Size Balance Sheets

Company	1	2	3	4	5	6	7	8	9
Cash and short-term investments	2%	13%	37%	1%	1%	3%	1%	22%	6%
Receivables	17	8	22	28	23	5	11	16	8
Inventory	15	52	15	23	14	2	2	0	5
Other current assets	6	0	5	1	4	2	2	1	0
Current assets	40%	73%	79%	53%	42%	12%	16%	39%	19%
Gross property	86	40	26	44	63	112	65	1	106
Less: Accumulated depreciation	(50)	(19)	(8)	(15)	(23)	(45)	(28)	0	(34)
Net property	36%	21%	18%	29%	40%	67%	37%	1%	72%
Investments	3	1	0	0	3	14	16	55	0
Intangibles and other	21	5	3	18	15	7	31	5	9
Total assets	100%	100%	100%	100%	100%	100%	100%	100%	100%
Trade payables	11	21	22	13	26	7	11	NA	20
Debt payable	4	0	3	6	4	6	2	46	4
Other current liabilities	9	43	0	0	1	4	1	16	8
Current liabilities	24%	64%	25%	19%	31%	17%	14%	62%	32%
Long-term debt	20	5	12	27	23	34	24	27	21
Other liabilities	16	0	1	21	16	12	13	5	12
Total liabilities	60%	69%	38%	67%	70%	63%	51%	94%	65%
Equity	40	31	62	33	30	37	49	6	35
Total liabilities and equity	100%	100%	100%	100%	100%	100%	100%	100%	100%

NA = Not available.

Common-Size Income Statements

Company	1	2	3	4	5	6	7	8	9
Revenues	100%	100%	100%	100%	100%	100%	100%	100%	100%
Cost of goods sold	58	81	58	63	52	0	59	0	0
Operating expenses	21	7	24	28	33	84	29	55	91
Research and development	7	5	9	0	1	NA	0	0	0
Advertising	3	0	3	2	5	NA	NA	0	2
Operating income	11%	7%	6%	7%	9%	16%	12%	45%	7%
Net interest expense	1	(1)	0	2	2	6	3	41	1
Income from continuing operations before tax	10%	8%	6%	5%	7%	10%	9%	4%	6%
Asset turnover ratio	0.96	1.12	0.94	1.38	1.82	0.45	0.96	0.15	0.96

NA = Not available.

(ix) Debt to equity 　　**(xiii)** EBIT/assets

(x) Interest coverage　　**(xiv)** EBT/assets

(xi) EBIT/sales　　　　**(xv)** Assets/equity

(xii) Sales/assets　　　**(xvi)** EBT/equity

Hint: Ratios for which one component is derived from the balance sheet and the other from the income statement can be calculated by making use of the asset turnover ratio, which is given in Exhibit 4P-3.

8. [Ratio analysis—industry characteristics] The nine companies in Exhibit 4P-3 are drawn from the following nine industries:

    (i) Aerospace

   (ii) Airline

  (iii) Chemicals and drugs

  (iv) Computer software

   (v) Consumer foods

  (vi) Department stores

 (vii) Consumer finance

(viii) Newspaper publishing

  (ix) Electric utility

    A. Based on the common-size statements, match each company to its industry.

    B. Briefly discuss the balance sheet and income statement characteristics that enabled you to identify the industry to which each company belonged.

9. [1995 CFA adapted] Discuss two uses of common-size financial statements for financial analysis.

10. [Liquidity analysis] The working capital accounts of Queen Chana, a retailer, are as follows:

Year	19X1	19X2	19X3
Cash	$1,000	$ 1,500	$ 2,000
Accounts receivable	2,000	4,000	6,000
Inventory	2,000	4,500	8,000
Current assets	$5,000	$10,000	$16,000
Accounts payable	2,000	3,500	4,500
Short-term debt	500	1,500	3,500
Current liabilities	$2,500	$ 5,000	$ 8,000

    A. For years 19X1 to 19X3, calculate Queen Chana's:

   (i) Current ratio

  (ii) Quick ratio

 (iii) Cash ratio

    B. What other useful indicators of the firm's liquidity can be calculated from the data given?

    C. Using the trend in the ratios calculated in part A and the indicators in part B, discuss the firm's liquidity.

D. What other information or ratios would help you confirm your analysis? What would you expect these ratios to show?

11. [Comprehensive review of ratios, operating and financial leverage, and financial statements] Company C and Company L operate in the same industry and have equal market shares. Their operating and financing characteristics differ as Company C has adopted newer manufacturing practices: It operates highly automated plants and maintains tight control of inventories consistent with just-in-time inventory techniques. To achieve these inventory levels, close coordination with suppliers and customers is needed; collections and payments are relatively prompt.

Financial data for 19X2 for Company C and Company L follow:

	Company C	Company L
Gross plant assets	$175,000	$65,000
Current ratio	9.475	3.592
Quick ratio	8.875	3.192
Return on equity	0.130	0.167
Cash from operations/ current liabilities	5.275	0.942
Decline in receivables	($3,000)	($4,500)
Decline in inventory	0	($6,000)
Decline in accounts payable	0	($5,000)
Cash from operations	$52,750	$28,250
Cash from financing: decline in short-term debt	($1,000)	($5,000)
Cash for investment	0	0

Common-size statements for Company C and Company L, prepared by your assistant, follow, but they are unidentified as to which company they belong to. Sales in 19X2 for both companies were one-sixth less than in 19X1.

Common-Size Statements

	Company?		Company?	
	19X1	19X2	19X1	19X2
Sales	100.00%	100.0%	100.00%	100.00%
COGS	63.89	66.67	58.33	66.67
Sales and administrative expenses	19.44	20.00	17.78	20.00
Interest	1.67	2.00	3.89	4.67
Taxes	3.75	2.83	5.00	2.17
Subtotal	88.75%	91.50%	85.00%	93.50%
Net income	11.25%	8.50%	15.00%	6.50%

Finally, your assistant also computed the ratios shown for 19X2 (again unidentified as to company). In addition, the ratios are mixed up: Some in column 1 belong to

Company C and some to Company L (similarly, the ratios in column 2 are a mixture of Company C and Company L):

	Column 1	Column 2
Inventory turnover	6.667	16.667
Receivable turnover	11.111	7.409
Payable turnover	25.000	4.444
Long-term debt to capital	0.195	0.429

When answering the following questions, round all numbers to the nearest $50.

A. Identify the common-size statements and each ratio with Company C or L. Briefly explain your reasoning.

B. Recreate the income statements for 19X1 and 19X2 for Company C and Company L.

C. Using the two years of data available, estimate for each company:

(i) Level of fixed costs

(ii) Variable costs (as a percentage of sales)

D. The recession is expected to continue with a 20% drop in sales in 19X3. Forecast the 19X3 income statements for each company.

E. Comment briefly on the impact of operating and financing leverage on the 19X1 to 19X3 financial performance of the two firms.

12. [Extension of Problem 11]

A. For Company C or L, recreate the balance sheet for 19X1 and 19X2. The balance sheet will have the following components:

Assets	Liabilities
Cash	Accounts payable
Accounts receivable	Short-term debt
Inventory	Long-term debt
Property, plant, and equipment	
Less Accumulated depreciation	Shareholders' equity

B. For the same company selected, forecast the balance sheet and cash from operations for 19X3. (*Hint:* Use the ratios to make the required assumptions regarding levels of inventories, payables, and receivables.)

C. Assess the strength of the cash position and cash flows of the company analyzed.

13. [Relationship of ROE, ROA, leverage, and cost of debt] The Vac Company has an ROA of 10%. The company has no debt (not even trade liabilities). Its total assets are $1 million and its tax rate is 20%. The company is considering borrowing some money and using the proceeds to buy back outstanding stock. The bank has stated that the interest rate charged will depend on the level of bank debt according to the following schedule:

Debt to Equity	Interest Rate
(1) 0.25	6%
(2) 0.50	8%
(3) 1.00	10%
(4) 1.50	12%
(5) 2.00	15%

A. Compute the company's current ROE.

B. Using the formula in the chapter that related ROE to ROA and interest costs, calculate the expected ROE for each level of debt.

C. Confirm your calculation of cases (1) and (5) by completing the following for each case:

   (i) Debt in dollars

   (ii) Equity in dollars

   (iii) Income before interest and taxes

   (iv) Interest expense

   (v) Tax expense

   (vi) Net income

   (vii) Return on equity

D. What does this table imply about "optimal" levels of debt and limits to the use of leverage?

14. [Relationship of ROE, ROA, leverage, and cost of debt] Redo Problem 13, assuming that the company has trade payables of $200,000 and intends to maintain that level. Note that the debt-to-equity ratio in the schedule is calculated by excluding the trade payables; that is, debt is defined as bank debt only. [*Hint:* The formula used in part B will require adjustment of the interest cost as the trade payables carry a zero interest rate.]

15. [Analysis of liquidity, profitability, and cash flow—extension of Problem 6 from Chapter 3] In Problem 6 in Chapter 3, you were asked to analyze the liquidity of the M and G companies based on income and cash flow trends.

A. What ratios could you use to support the conclusions reached in Problem 6, Chapter 3?

B. Calculate those ratios for the years 19X0 to 19X4, using the data in Exhibit 3P-1.

C. Discuss how the ratios computed in part B affect the conclusions reached in Problem 6, Chapter 3.

16. [Profitability analysis] The financial statements of Harley-Davidson, Inc., for the period 1985 to 1990 are presented in Exhibit 4P-4. Harley-Davidson is considered one of the success stories of the last decade, having introduced "world-class" management techniques to turn around the company. At the same time, however, an examination

EXHIBIT 4P-4. HARLEY-DAVIDSON INC.
Comparative Income Statements, for Years Ended 1985 to 1990 ($ in millions)

	1985	1986	1987	1988	1989	1990
Sales	$287.48	$295.32	$685.36	$757.38	$790.97	$864.60
Cost of goods sold	209.69	210.45	506.91	559.53	582.70	619.10
Selling, general, and administrative expense	57.34	60.06	104.14	111.91	127.61	144.27
Depreciation	7.53	8.72	14.86	15.73	14.23	16.45
Operating income after depreciation	$ 12.91	$ 16.10	$ 59.45	$ 70.20	$ 66.42	$ 84.78
Interest expense	(9.41)	(9.51)	(25.51)	(24.67)	(17.96)	(11.44)
Other income (expense)	(0.34)	0.75	0.52	4.38	4.54	(2.12)
Special items	0	0	(3.60)	(3.90)	0	(8.60)
Pretax income	$ 3.16	$ 7.33	$ 30.85	$ 46.01	$ 53.01	$ 62.62
Income tax expense	0.53	3.03	13.18	18.85	20.40	24.31
Income before extraordinary items	$ 2.64	$ 4.31	$ 17.67	$ 27.16	$ 32.61	$ 38.31
Extraordinary items and discontinued operations	7.32	0.56	3.54	(3.24)	0.33	(0.48)
Net income	$ 9.95	$ 4.87	$ 21.21	$ 23.91	$ 32.94	$ 37.83

HARLEY-DAVIDSON INC.
Condensed Comparative Balance Sheets, 1985 to 1990 ($ in millions)

	1985	1986	1987	1988	1989	1990
Assets						
Current assets	$ 72.89	$148.76	$197.90	$211.29	$187.67	$196.68
Net property	38.73	90.93	100.43	110.79	115.70	136.05
Intangibles	—	82.11	74.16	70.21	66.19	63.08
Other assets	2.47	5.39	8.38	8.82	9.36	11.65
Total assets	$114.09	$327.19	$380.87	$401.11	$378.92	$407.46
Liabilities and Equity						
Current debt	$ 2.88	$ 18.09	$ 28.33	$ 33.23	$ 26.93	$ 23.86
Other current liabilities	53.77	90.73	105.35	103.16	109.43	122.67
Long-term debt	51.50	191.59	178.76	135.18	74.79	48.34
Other liabilities	1.32	0.62	5.52	7.89	11.52	13.82
Total liabilities	$109.47	$301.03	$317.96	$279.46	$222.67	$208.69
Stockholder's equity	4.62	26.16	62.91	121.65	156.25	198.77
Total liabilities and equity	$114.09	$327.19	$380.87	$401.11	$378.92	$407.46

techniques to turn around the company. At the same time, however, an examination of the company's return on equity indicates that, after initial growth, the ratio stabilized and then declined.

Analyze the factors (sales growth, efficient use of assets, cost control) contributing to Harley-Davidson's increased profitability. How do these factors explain the changes in ROE over the period 1985 to 1990?

17. [CFA adapted; primary and fully diluted EPS calculations] The following information is provided regarding the capital structure of WFA, Inc., at December 31, 1992:

Common shares outstanding at December 31, 1992	2,700,000
Weighted-average common shares outstanding during 1992	2,500,000
Convertible bonds (issued December 31, 1989) (5% coupon, convertible into common shares at $30 per share)	$12,000,000
Convertible preferred shares (issued July 1, 1992) ($4.00 dividend per share, 5.5% effective yield, each share convertible into 5 common shares)	70,000
Options outstanding at December 31, 1992 (exercise price $15 per share)	200,000

WFA common shares on December 31, 1992, had a market price of $25. The weighted-average market price per share for 1992 was $20.

   (i) The Aa corporate bond yield was:

      (a) 8.5% at December 31, 1989

      (b) 7.5% at July 1, 1992

      (c) 7.0% at December 31, 1992

  (ii) Net income for 1992 was $6,500,000.

 (iii) WFA's tax rate for 1992 was 40%.

A. Compute *basic* earnings per share for 1992.

B. Which securities are considered to be common stock equivalents? Explain why. Compute the number of common and common equivalent shares used to compute primary earnings per share for 1992.

C. Compute *primary* earnings per share for 1992.

D. Compute the number of common shares used to compute fully diluted earnings per share. Explain any differences between your answer and the number of shares required to compute basic and primary EPS.

E. Compute *fully diluted* earnings per share for 1992. Explain any difference between the numerator (earnings) used to compute basic, primary, and fully diluted EPS.

F. Explain how your answers to parts A through D would change if:

  (i) WFA's common share price was $30 at December 31, 1992.

 (ii) The Aa bond rate was 9% at December 31, 1992.

G. WFA's 1992 results have been restated for a pooling acquisition made on March 31, 1992. WFA issued 240,000 shares and the acquired firm earned $600,000 in 1992 ($150,000 per quarter).

  (i) Compute WFA's basic and primary EPS for 1992, assuming that the acquisition had not been made.

    (ii) Compute WFA's basic and primary EPS for 1992, assuming that the acquisition was accounted for as a purchase (remember that the shares are considered outstanding and the earnings of the acquired firm are included only for the period following the acquistion).

18. [1989 CFA adapted] Champion Lion Tamers has 2 million shares outstanding on December 31, 1987. On March 31, 1988, Champion pays a 10% stock dividend. On June 30, 1988, Champion sells $10 million of 5% convertible debentures, convertible into common shares at $5 per share. The Aa bond rate on the issue date is 8%. On September 30, 1988, Champion issues 800,000 warrants, exercisable at $5 per share. The market price of Champion shares is $8 on December 31, 1988; the average price for the fourth quarter of 1988 is $4.

    A. Compute the number of shares used to compute *basic* earnings per share for 1988.

    B. Compute the number of common and common equivalent shares used to compute *primary* earnings per share for 1988.

    C. Compute the number of shares used to compute *fully diluted* earnings per share for 1988.

    D. Discuss how your answers to parts A, B, and C would change under the following conditions:

        (i) Champion's share price is $10 at December 31, 1988.

        (ii) Champion's average share price for the fourth quarter of 1988 is $8.

        (iii) The Aa bond rate at December 31, 1988 is 7%.

Appendix 4-A

Estimating Operating Leverage

Throughout this appendix, we use the following notation:

$$S = \text{Sales}$$

$$F = \text{Fixed costs}$$

$$V = \text{Variable costs}$$

$$v = \text{Variable costs as a percentage of sales, that is, } V = vS$$

$$TC = \text{Total costs} = F + V = F + vS$$

$$(1 - v)S = \text{Contribution}$$

$$N = \text{Net income} = S - TC = S - F - vS = (1 - v)S - F$$

In a simple world, where cost relationships are constant and not subject to random error, estimating a firm's variable and fixed cost components would be straightforward. A plot of total costs against sales would yield a straight line. The equation of the line would be the equation for total cost: $TC = F + vS$. The slope of the line v would be the variable cost percentage, and the point of intersection of the line with the TC axis (the y intercept) would be the fixed costs F.

The exact values of v and F would be calculated by using any two adjacent periods. For years 1 and 2,

$$v = \frac{TC\,(\text{year 2}) - TC\,(\text{year 1})}{S\,(\text{year 2}) - S\,(\text{year 1})} \tag{4-A.1}$$

and then, using either year, we obtain

$$F = TC - vS \tag{4-A.2}$$

Unfortunately, actual cost structures are not so simplistic. There are many problems when these equations are applied to real data:

- Fixed and variable costs are defined conceptually by whether they are affected by the level of output. Fixed costs do, however, change as a result of such factors as general inflation and changes in rents, property taxes, salary levels, and interest rates. Hence, TC changes from one year to the next independent of the level of v.

- The distinction between fixed and variable costs is valid only within a narrow range. For example, rent may be considered a fixed cost only when output falls within the firm's current capacity. When output exceeds capacity and new facilities are acquired, rent increases.[1]

- Variable costs, by definition, depend on the level of physical output. Unfortunately, unit data are rarely available, and estimates must be based on sales dollars. Thus, changes in prices affect total revenues, distorting the estimate of v. One solution is to deflate revenues to a base year before conducting further analysis. For public companies, the Management Discussion and Analysis (MD&A) sometimes provides information regarding price changes.

- The equations assume a linear relationship between costs and output. The real relationship may, however, be nonlinear,[2] and the linear relationship used is, at best, an approximation.

Fortunately, it is possible to estimate operating leverage in this more complex world. We suggest the following procedure.

Step 1: Examine Individual Components

An examination of the components of total cost often provide insight into which costs are fixed and which variable. For example, depreciation and rent expense may be assumed to be fixed, whereas the cost of goods sold in a merchandising operation can readily be assumed to be variable (for a manufacturer, COGS may include overhead and depreciation). For a manufacturer, the materials component and to some extent the labor cost component (if available) of the cost of goods sold can be assumed to be variable.

---

[1]In economics, this is often expressed as a short-run/long-run dichotomy. In the short run, there are some fixed costs; in the long run, all costs are viewed as variable.

[2]Introductory microeconomics textbooks generally depict the cost–output relationship as nonlinear.

Segregate identifiable items and estimate their status for each year separately.[3] This simplifies the estimation procedure for the other cost components.

Step 2: Use Regression Analysis to Estimate *v*

After disaggregating the "known" fixed costs, we can estimate the variable cost component *v* by regressing the remaining costs against sales, using an equation of the form:

$$\text{Costs} = a + b\ (\text{sales}) + e$$

where *a* and *b* represent estimates of the fixed and variable cost components and *e* represents the error term. Run the regression using changes in costs rather than changes in sales to alleviate the autocorrelation problem usually found in time series data. The intercept *a* would incorporate changes in (fixed) costs due to factors other than volume.

This procedure assumes that cost structures do not change over the time period examined. To check this assumption, estimate a sequence of *v*'s [using Eq. (4-A.1)] for the regression period. If the *v*'s do not exhibit a trend and are fairly consistent, use the regression results. Otherwise, the best estimate of *v* may be the estimate obtained from the last two years' data using Eq. (4-A.1).

Step 3: Estimate Fixed Costs

After estimating *v*, use Eq. (4-A.2) to estimate fixed costs using the most recent year's data.

---

[3]Each cost component should be classified as fixed or variable and reestimated each period. Levels and cost behavior can change over time. Depreciation, for example, will decline when an accelerated depreciation method is used. Similarly, depreciation will increase with capital spending, regardless of the level of output.

5

EMPIRICAL RESEARCH: IMPLICATIONS FOR FINANCIAL STATEMENT ANALYSIS

CHAPTER OUTLINE

CHAPTER OBJECTIVES

INTRODUCTION

THE CLASSICAL APPROACH

MARKET-BASED RESEARCH
Efficient Market Theory
Modern Portfolio Theory
Tests of the EMH versus the Mechanistic
Hypothesis
The Ball and Brown Study
Information Content Studies
The Relationship Between Earnings and Stock
Returns
  Accounting Variable
  Market-Based Variable
  *Test of the Relationship Between the Good
  News/Bad News Parameter and Abnormal
  Returns*

Market-Based Research: Current Status
  Critical Evaluation of Research Findings
Market Anomalies

POSITIVE ACCOUNTING RESEARCH
Disclosure and Regulatory Requirements
Agency Theory
  The Bonus Plan Hypothesis
  The Debt Covenant Hypothesis
  The Political Cost Hypothesis
Summary of the Research

DIRECTION OF CURRENT RESEARCH
Back to the Future?
  Ball and Brown Revisited
  Fundamental Analysis: Contextual Approaches
  *Coming Full Circle: From Edwards and Bell to
  Ohlson*

**IMPLICATIONS OF EMPIRICAL RESEARCH FOR
FINANCIAL STATEMENT ANALYSIS**

CHAPTER OBJECTIVES

The goals of this chapter are to:

1. Review the classical approach to accounting theory and the framework that still underlies most accounting standard-setting activities.
2. Survey market-based accounting research that examines the relationship between stock prices and financial reporting.
3. Explain "positive" accounting theory and its em-

phasis on the effect of financial reporting on management, creditor, and regulatory decision making.

4. Examine the current trend of accounting research.
5. Discuss the relevance of empirical research to financial statement analysis.

INTRODUCTION

The objectives, methodology, and underlying philosophies of accounting research have changed enormously over the past quarter-century. To a great extent, these changes mirrored (or, some would argue, merely followed) shifts in financial economic theory. This chapter presents an overview of the research. We will not try to review all this research here but rather:

- Characterize the nature of the research.
- Indicate the relevance of the research for financial analysts and where in the book it is discussed in further detail.
- Summarize important research findings without getting bogged down in detail.

The first three sections of the chapter examine three major approaches to accounting theory and research. Figure 5-1 presents these approaches schematically. In the first section, we briefly review the classical approach to accounting theory prior to the mid–1960s and the framework still underlying much of existing accounting regulation. This approach attempts, using a theoretical perspective, to develop an optimal or "most correct" accounting representation of some true (but unobservable) reality.

The second section deals with what is commonly referred to as market-based accounting research. Criticizing the classical approach for its lack of testability, market-based research takes a more empirical, as well as user-oriented, perspective. Its primary focus is the market reaction to (or association with) reported accounting data. Market-based research uses observable relationships between reported earnings[1] and market returns to draw conclusions about the role of accounting information.

The "positive" accounting theory approach, the subject of the third section, also focuses on observable reactions to accounting numbers, but this is not its primary focus. As Figure 5-1 indicates, it broadens the research perspective in two ways. First, in addition to financial markets, it includes other "environments" influenced by financial statements: management compensation plans, debt agreements with creditors,

---

[1]We use the term earnings here and throughout the chapter in a generic sense. It is not meant to preclude other measures of firm performance examined by researchers.

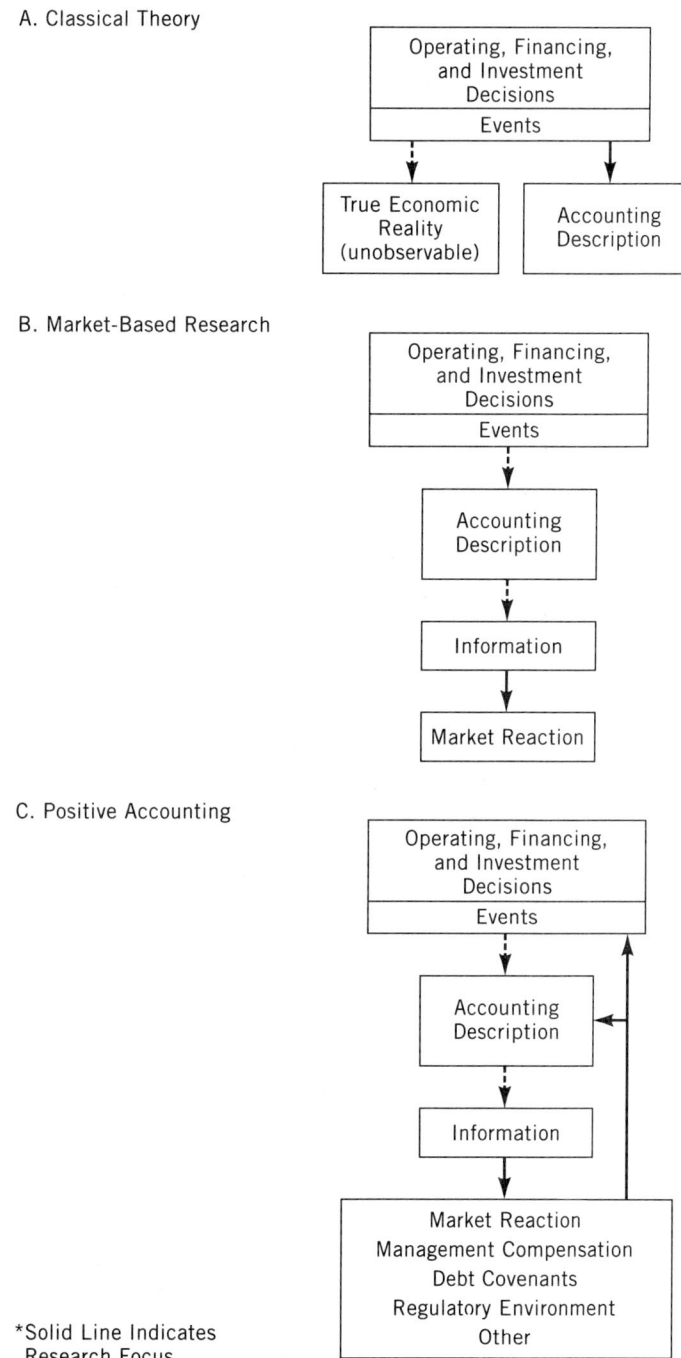

FIGURE 5-1 Schematic representation of three approaches to accounting theory and research.

and the host of regulatory bodies interacting with the firm. More important, it recognizes that, since financial statements impact these other environments, there are incentives for accounting systems to be used not only to measure the results of decisions but, in turn, to influence these decisions in the first place. This "feedback" interaction can influence both management's operating decisions and accounting choices.

These three approaches view the underlying economic reality of a firm in different ways. In the classical approach, an underlying reality exists, and it is the role of accounting to best describe it. Market-based research, on the other hand, views reality as determined by market value—"what you see is what you get"—and accounting alternatives, *a priori*, really do not make any difference. The positive approach adds a new twist: Accounting alternatives (help) define and determine reality.

These competing approaches evolved over time in response to both research results and new developments in information economics and finance theory. Empirical research began in the 1960s with much fanfare and promise, only to be tempered over time both by the economic (in)significance of the results and by perplexing elements of reality, or what academics euphemistically call anomalies.

The concluding section of the chapter examines the present direction of accounting research. This trend is characterized by a return to the examination of *a priori* linkages between financial statements, the analysis thereof, and security valuation. It grew out of extensions of market-based research on an empirical level and, on a theoretical level, a rediscovery of a valuation paradigm built on fundamental accounting variables and relationships. This underlying structural or fundamental analysis,[2] in some respects, combines the direction of the classical approach with the empiricism of market-based research. This "neoclassical" approach is still in the developmental stage. Given the experience of the last two decades, we hesitate to make any prediction as to its ultimate success.

Discussion of this research is intended to provide a context for the remainder of this book, in two respects. First, the financial reporting system has been shaped by accounting research (especially the classical approach), and users of that system must understand the factors that influence it. Second, accounting research provides valuable insights into the usefulness of financial statement data.

THE CLASSICAL APPROACH

Classical accounting theory approaches issues from a normative point of view. Writers such as Edwards and Bell (1961), Chambers (1966), and Sterling (1970) evaluate accounting methods and technologies in terms of how close reported information comes to some preconceived "true" picture of the firm. In this approach, the ideal picture is viewed as determinable within the accounting system itself. Concepts such as economic profit and its relationship to accounting income are a key focus of debate. Thus, much discussion (without consensus) ensues over topics such as current cost versus replacement cost versus historical cost accounting frameworks.

The classical approach is concerned with deducing correct accounting methods from a stated set of concepts, principles, and objectives. Implicit in this approach is the view that financial statement users accept (and react to) those statements at face

---

[2]Use of the term "structural" for modeling the *a priori* linkages can be traced to Ryan (1988). Using fundamental (or financial statement) analysis to classify the research can be attributed to empirical studies by Ou and Penman (1989), Ou (1990), and Penman (1991, 1992).

value; thus, great importance is attached to ensuring that statements reflect the firm's true financial status.[3] Moreover, as the nature of users' reactions to financial information is deemed predictable, no explicit effort is made to examine, empirically or otherwise, the interrelationship between financial statements and users' motivations and/or reaction to the information contained in those statements.

Concurrent with the early development of this approach to accounting theory, the teachings of Graham and Dodd reigned supreme in the academic and professional finance communities. In their world, stocks have "intrinsic" value and investors could use ratios and other financial analysis techniques based on financial statement data to develop filter rules that identify stocks as over- or undervalued.

Simultaneously (and, perhaps, paradoxically), it was argued that, although determining a company's true financial picture was a worthwhile objective, accounting rules did not actually mirror the underlying reality. Thus, financial statements were often seen as meaningless and of little use to investors. Canning (1929) was often quoted in support of this viewpoint:

> What is set out as a measure of net income can never be supposed to be a fact in any sense at all except that it is the figure that results when the accountant has finished applying the procedures which he adopts.[4]

The classical approach fell out of favor in academic circles due to its lack of testability. It was argued that the usefulness of accounting information could be evaluated only by observing its effects on financial statement users. The research emphasis turned to empirical investigations of the decision relevance of the information contained in accounting reports.

Accounting regulators never *fully* embraced this new (empirical) approach to accounting theory.[5] Whether this was because they did not agree with it philosophically or because they felt that its results had no practical implications is a matter of debate. It is important to note that existing accounting rules, which make up GAAP, are greatly influenced by and are still a product of the classical approach; in the concluding section of this chapter, we return to this point.

MARKET-BASED RESEARCH

Advances in finance theory in the mid- and late 1960s were the primary catalyst for the shift in accounting research described in this section. Academic accounting research moved from the classical deductive approach to a more empirical approach that focused primarily on three issues:

1. What are users' reactions to financial statements?
2. Do alternative accounting methods affect users' reactions?
3. Given users' needs, could accounting methods be set to maximize the utility of financial statements to various user-groups?

[3]This is equivalent to the concept of representational faithfulness discussed in Chapter 1.

[4]John B. Canning, *The Economics of Accountancy* (New York: Ronald Press Co., 1929), p. 98.

[5]There are some exceptions. For example, the change in the current cost disclosures from mandatory to voluntary required by Financial Accounting Standards Board No. 33 was partially a result of empirical evidence indicating that the market ignored the information.

The two major advances in finance literature that influenced accounting research in this period were the efficient market hypothesis and modern portfolio theory.

Efficient Market Theory

Underlying the new approach to accounting theory and research was the widespread interest in (and increasing acceptance of) the efficient market hypothesis (EMH) in the academic and professional finance community. The EMH, as defined by Fama (1970), states that a market is efficient if asset prices "fully reflect" the information available. "Fully reflecting" means that knowledge of that information does not allow anyone to profit from it, because prices already incorporate the information. Further, the information is impounded in the prices correctly and instantaneously as soon as it becomes known.

Information is classified into three sets, resulting in three forms of the EMH:

1. *The weak form.* The information set includes information about past securities prices only.
2. *The semistrong form.* The information set includes all publicly available information.
3. *The strong form.* The information set includes all information, including privately held (insider) information.

Empirical evidence in the accounting and finance literature during this period supported the weak and semistrong forms. The weak form implies that series of past security prices cannot be successfully used to predict future prices. Hence, charting techniques (head and shoulder patterns, double tops, etc.) and other types of technical analysis are deemed meaningless and unprofitable.

The information set assumed to be used by financial markets under the semistrong form includes all publicly available information, such as financial statements, government reports, industry reports and analysis. Two key implications for accounting research, policy, and analysis flow from the semistrong form of the EMH.

First, financial statements are not the only source of information for making investment decisions. Second, and more important, no trading advantages accrue to users of financial statements because the information contained in them is instantaneously impounded in prices as soon as the information becomes public. This latter point was a direct attack on fundamental analysis—the mainstay of financial analysts who searched for stocks that were over- or undervalued relative to their intrinsic value. Benjamin Graham himself said in 1976:

> I am no longer an advocate of elaborate techniques of security analysis in order to find superior value opportunities. This was a rewarding activity, say, forty years ago . . . but the situation has changed a good deal since then. In the old days any well-trained security analyst could do a good professional job of selecting undervalued issues through detailed studies; *but in light of the enormous amount of research being carried out, I doubt whether in most cases such extensive efforts will generate sufficiently superior selections to justify their cost. To that very limited extent I'm on the side of the "efficient market" school of thought.*[6]

[6]John Train, *Money Masters* (New York: Harper & Row, 1987), emphasis added.

The ironic part of the argument (as indicated by the preceding quotation) is that the very analysts engaging in fundamental analysis looking for the bargains ensure that there are no bargains to be found. Their research results in prices that fully reflect all available information:

> This error takes the form of asserting that accounting data have no value. . . . The efficient market in no way leads to such implications. It may very well be that the publishing of financial statements data is precisely what makes the market as efficient as it is.[7]

The EMH also had implications for the setting of accounting standards; no longer did such standards have to specifically protect the naive investor. Sophisticated analysts and investors, who ensure that prices correctly and instantaneously reflect available information, protect the naive investor. Any trades by such investors are made at "fair" prices.

Modern Portfolio Theory

The second trend in finance theory impacting accounting theory and research was modern portfolio theory (MPT), as embodied in the capital asset pricing model (CAPM). The CAPM characterizes the relationship between a common stock's expected return and risk as

$$E(R_i) = R_f + \beta_i [E(R_m) - R_f]$$

where

R_i = the rate of return on stock i

R_f = the risk-free rate of return

R_m = the rate of return on the market as a whole

β_i = the "beta" of firm i that measures the comovement of that firm's returns with those of the overall market

$E(*)$ = the symbol representing the expected value

The realized return on stock i is therefore [removing the expectation symbol $E(*)$]

$$R_i = R_f + \beta_i(R_m - R_f) + e_i$$

where *e is the unexpected or abnormal return.* In other words, e_i represents the portion of a stock's realized return that is different from its expected return (given existing market conditions).

Under MPT, higher risks are associated with higher (expected) returns, but the relationship holds only for that portion of risk that cannot be diversified away. Risk is classified as either systematic or unsystematic. Systematic risk is that portion of

---

[7]William Beaver, "What Should Be the FASB's Objectives?", *Journal of Accountancy*, August 1973, pp. 49–56.

uncertainty faced by a firm that is due to common factors facing all firms[8]: the business cycle, interest rates, inflation, and so on. Its measure under CAPM is the "beta" of the firm, β_i.

Unsystematic risk is the uncertainty specific to a given firm. The unsystematic return is the return e_i accruing to the firm after accounting for the systematic effects. The unsystematic risk can be diversified away by investors holding well-diversified portfolios. Thus, as this risk can be diversified away, there is no reward to investors (higher returns) for bearing this risk; the expected abnormal return is $E(e_i) = 0$. The systematic risk, on the other hand, which cannot be diversified away, must be rewarded by offering the investor a higher expected return.

MPT and the CAPM impacted accounting theory development in a number of ways. First, it provided a model to measure market returns and the reaction to earnings. Deviations from expected earnings could be shown to influence the realized rate of return or, more specifically, the unexpected portion (the abnormal return e_i).

Second, it implied that, since the expected return for a given firm does not depend on risks that can be diversified away, information regarding the outlook for a *specific* firm was largely irrelevant. The only thing that mattered was the systematic risk of the firm and its relationship to the total portfolio:

> In an efficient market, the usefulness of financial statement data to individual investors is not to find mispriced securities *since they are nonexistent. What then is the value, if any?* The value lies in the ability of financial statement data to aid in risk prediction.[9]

The ability of accounting data to predict and provide measures of risk thus became an avenue of accounting research, with the evidence indicating that such data could be used to enhance the prediction of risk measures such as beta. What is surprising is that this line of research, although promising, did not *originally* play a bigger role.

Recent empirical findings, however, have once again brought attention to the area of risk measurement. Contrary to the relationship predicted by the CAPM, Fama and French (1992) conclude that, during the period 1963 to 1990, beta was not related to average returns on stocks. On the other hand, measures such as company size, the market-to-book ratio, leverage, and the price-earnings ratio were found (by Fama and French as well as others) to be related to average returns.

These findings have triggered considerable debate among academics.[10] Explanations[11] of these "risk"/return relationships include the following:

1. Securities are mispriced, that is, the market is not as efficient as the (semi-strong form of) EMH assumes.

2. The CAPM model is flawed as a description of risk/return relationships.

3. There are other measures acting as proxies for risk.

---

[8]The single-index model just defined only has a provision for systematic risk on an economywide basis. Multiindex models, however, can capture industrywide effects.

[9]Beaver (1973), p. 55, emphasis added.

[10]See, for example, Fama and French (1993, 1995), Kothari, et al. (1995) and Lakonishok, et al. (1994). We return to the Lakonishok et al. paper later in this chapter in our discussion of market anomalies.

[11]Points 1 and 2 serve as a reminder that any market-based test of a valuation model is a joint test of both the model itself and the EMH. Unexpected findings may indicate either that the model is flawed or the EMH does not hold (or both).

4. The empirical tests are flawed due to measurement errors; either the market index is misspecified or the *ex post* measures of beta are not good predictors of the *ex ante* beta that should be used in portfolio formation.

We return to the issue of market inefficiency later in the chapter. A detailed review of the research that relates accounting variables to risk is presented in Chapter 18, where overall risk and credit analysis is discussed.

In addition to the prediction of risk measures, market-based research studies can be classified into the following categories:

1. Tests of the EMH versus the classical approach

2. Tests of the informational content of accounting alternatives

3. Tests of the earnings/return relationship

Tests of the EMH versus the Mechanistic Hypothesis

The mechanistic hypothesis, consistent with the classical approach to accounting theory, holds that users of financial statements accept the information provided at face value.[12] Implicit in this hypothesis is the assumption that users of financial statements do not access other sources of information nor do they adjust financial statements for the effects of alternative accounting methods. Clearly, the mechanistic hypothesis stands in opposition to the EMH, which holds that current prices reflect all information available.

The mechanistic hypothesis was tested by examining the stock market reaction to changes in accounting methods that increase reported income but have no cash flow effect. Specifically, firms that changed their depreciation method for financial reporting (but not for tax) purposes from accelerated to straight line (see Chapter 8 for a discussion of these methods) were examined by both Archibald (1972) and Kaplan and Roll (1972). Since this change increases reported income, the mechanistic hypothesis leads us to expect increases in stock prices. The EMH would argue that the market sees through the change and no stock price reaction should result.

The research methodology[13] consisted of measuring the abnormal return e_i around the time of the earnings announcement for a sample of firms that made the accounting change. Under the mechanistic approach, we expect $e_i > 0$; under the EMH, we expect $e_i = 0$. Figure 5-2 presents the results of Kaplan and Roll, who examined the price reaction in the 60-week period surrounding the earnings announcement. Around the time of the earnings announcement, which occurs at week 30, both the cumulative abnormal return (CAR) and the abnormal return itself are insignificantly different

---

[12]The mechanistic view is sometimes referred to as "functional fixation."

[13]The actual approach used in many studies is not strictly the CAPM but variations of it, such as the market model. The CAPM is a theoretically derived model based on a number of specific assumptions as to the nature and structure of capital markets. The "market" model does not have elaborate underpinnings, but rather is based on the intuitive argument that returns of a firm are a function of common and firm-specific factors. The linear equation that describes such a relationship is

$$R_i = a_i + \beta_i R_m + e_i$$

where a_i and e_i measure the firm-specific factor and $\beta_i R_m$ measures the common factors. Again, the $E(e_i) = 0$. The similarities between this model and the CAPM should be clear.

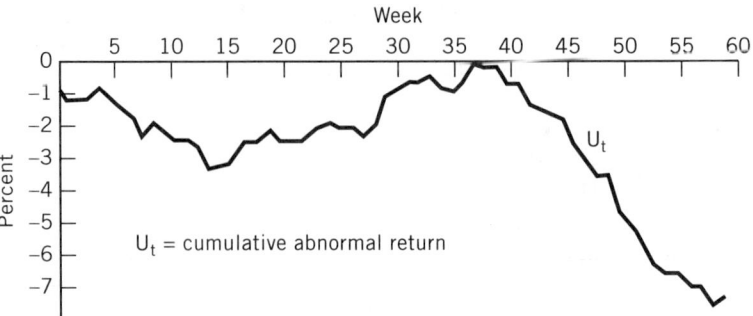

FIGURE 5-2 Kaplan and Roll results.

Source: Robert S. Kaplan and Richard Roll, "Investor Evaluation of Accounting Information: Some Empirical Evidence," *Journal of Business,* Vol. 45, April 1972, pp. 225–257, Figure 1, Panel C, p. 239 (adapted), ©University of Chicago.

from zero. About six weeks following the earnings announcement (week 36), there is a pronounced negative abnormal return for the sample firms. These results are inconsistent with the mechanistic hypothesis.[14]

Tests of the mechanistic hypothesis versus the EMH eventually became passé.[15] Although there was much disagreement as to the types of information markets reacted to, the general consensus[16] was that the market does not follow reported earnings blindly and adjusts the information accordingly:

> Many reporting issues are trivial. . . . The properties of such issues are twofold: (1) there is essentially no difference in cost to the firm of reporting either method. (2) There is essentially no cost to statement users in adjusting from one method to the other. In such cases there is a simple solution. Report one method, with sufficient footnote disclosure to permit adjustment to the other and let the market interpret implications of the data for security prices. . . . If there are no additional costs of disclosure to the firm, there is *prima facie* evidence that the item in question should be disclosed.[17]

On the other hand, studies of changes in accounting method continued with other objectives in mind. Switches from first-in, first-out (FIFO) to last-in, first-out (LIFO),

---

[14]These results, although offering some support for the EMH, also pose some problems for it. A possible explanation for the negative abnormal returns is that those firms that made the change were experiencing difficulty and management made the change in an attempt artificially to hide earnings declines. It should be remembered that market efficiency does not mean that everyone (in this case, management) believes it is efficient. The negative reaction is, therefore, nothing more than the market reacting to falling earnings. The problem for the EMH with these results is related to the fact that the negative reaction does not happen instantaneously at the time of the announcement and that it persists for a number of weeks (week 36 to week 60).

[15]Recently, however, in light of some of the anomalies associated with the EMH, the functional fixation hypothesis has returned in the form of the extended functional fixation hypothesis [see Hand (1990)]. Under this guise, it is argued that some unsophisticated investors on the margin can and do affect prices.

[16]The general consensus here refers to the academic accounting community and sizable portions of the professional community. This is not to say that some accountants and accounting policymakers as well as managers themselves did not believe that the investors needed to be protected from blindly following reported results.

[17]Beaver (1973), p. 51.

which have real cash flow effects due to their tax consequences, were studied extensively; these results are discussed in detail in our discussion of inventory accounting in Chapter 6. In addition, positive accounting theory suggested motivations for accounting changes beyond those provided by market-based accounting research. These motivations and related research are discussed shortly in the section on positive accounting theory.[18]

The belief that the market does not follow reported numbers blindly led researchers to question how (if at all) markets react to accounting information. The methodology and philosophy underlying this mode of research can be understood best with an in-depth analysis of the seminal Ball and Brown (1968) study.

The Ball and Brown Study

The goal of Ball and Brown was to document the association between the price (returns) of a firm's securities and the accounting earnings of the firm. To do so, they partitioned the firms in their sample into "good news"/"bad news" groupings. Based on a firm's reported earnings, a company was classified as reporting good (bad) news if the reported earnings were above (below) those predicted by a time-series forecasting model. Then, acting as if this knowledge was known as far back as March of the year in question, two portfolios were constructed on the basis of the good news/bad news partition.

Ball and Brown's main finding is reproduced in Figure 5-3, which compares the cumulative abnormal returns over the year for the good and bad news portfolios.[19] Good (bad) news firms enjoyed, on average, abnormally positive (negative) returns as measured by e_i. Ball and Brown demonstrated a clear (empirical) association between earnings and stockmarket reaction.

These results, although opening the door to future avenues of research, also raised many questions. As can be seen in Figure 5-3, the abnormal good/bad market reaction began one year prior to the announcement date. Further, there is little information content to the announcement itself. Ball and Brown estimated that 80 to 85% of the abnormal market performance occurred *prior* to the publication of the annual report. This suggests that although earnings are meaningful measures of a firm's financial performance, by the time they are published they are redundant and have little or no market impact:

> They demonstrate that the information contained in the annual income number is useful in that as actual income differs from expected income, the market typically has reacted in the same direction. . . .
>
> However, most of the information contained in reported income is anticipated by the market before the annual is released. In fact, anticipation is so accurate that the actual income number does not appear to cause any unusual jumps. . . in the announcement month.[20]

---

[18]Mandatory switches caused by changes in accounting standards, as opposed to voluntary switches instigated by management, are another avenue of research into the effects of accounting changes; we discuss such research in the next section.

[19]The graph depicts one (EPS, naive model) of the three variations of earnings examined by Ball and Brown.

[20]Ray Ball and Philip Brown, "An Empirical Evaluation of Accounting Income Numbers," *Journal of Accounting Research*, Autumn 1968, pp. 159–178.

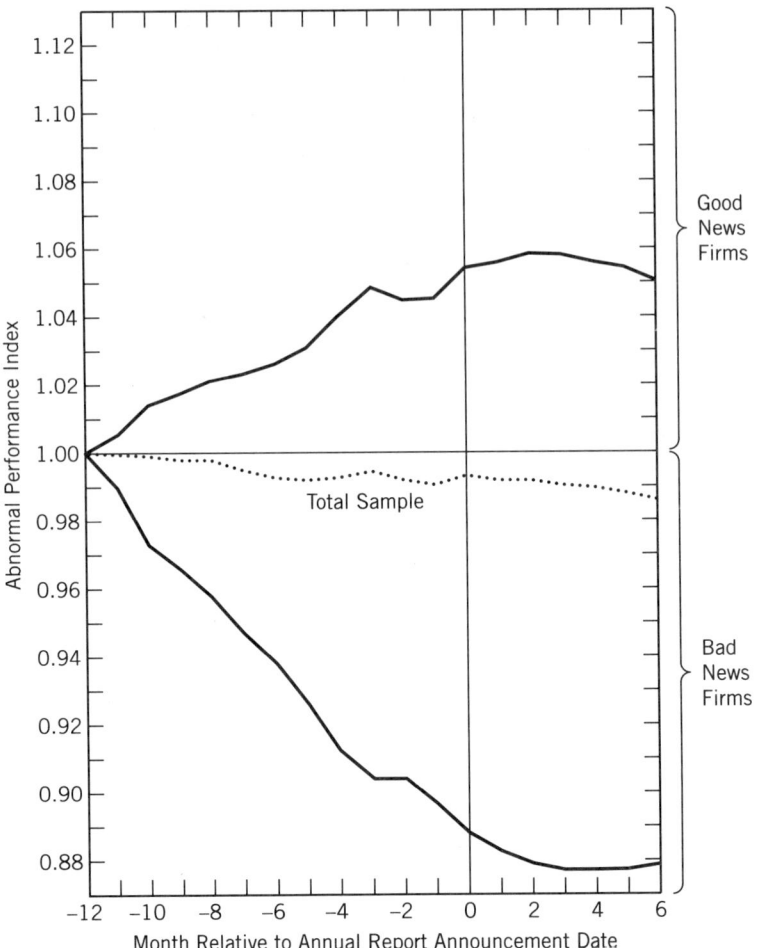

FIGURE 5-3 Ball and Brown results.

Source: Ray Ball and Philip Brown, "An Empirical Evaluation of Accounting Income Numbers," *Journal of Accounting Research*, Autumn 1968, pp. 159–178, Figure 1, p. 169 (adapted), reprinted with permission.

The market anticipation of reported earnings raises questions about the *timeliness of annual reports* and is a reminder that the annual report is not the sole source of information available to the marketplace. Competing sources of information about the economy as a whole, the industry the firm operates in, and the firm itself are available from the media, government reports, industry associations, financial analyst reports, and management announcements, as well as the firm's own interim reports.

    Ball and Brown triggered an explosion of empirical accounting research over the next two decades that can be roughly described as studies of either the information content of earnings or the overall relationship between stock returns and reported earnings.

Information Content Studies

Ball and Brown spurred a series of studies intended to examine the "information content" of accounting data, with information content measured by market reaction to the announced earnings and its deviation from expected earnings. The procedure generally involved calculating cumulative abnormal returns resulting from alternative measures of earnings.

For example, Beaver and Dukes (1972) compared the informational content of earnings with and without the deferral of income taxes. Others examined the information content of segment earnings, unusual items, capitalized leases, alternative accounting methods for oil and gas properties, and so on. These individual studies are discussed in the chapters where the related accounting principles are presented.

At first, researchers argued that, given a choice of accounting alternatives, the most desirable was the one that triggered the greatest market reaction, that is, had the most information content. This notion was soon abandoned, not because earnings and market reaction were unrelated, but rather because any transactions (purchase/sale of shares) or change in market prices made some people better off than others. Thus, deciding the best alternative necessarily involved judgments affecting social consequence and the general welfare, which were deemed to be "political" in nature and beyond the realm of academic research[21]:

> A second erroneous implication is, simply find out what method is most highly associated with security prices and report that method in the financial statements. As it stands, it is incorrect for several reasons. One major reason is that such a simplified decision rule fails to consider the costs of providing the information. . . . Moreover, the choice among different accounting methods involves choosing among differing consequences. . . .
>
> Hence, some individuals may be better off under one method, while others may be better off under an alternative method. . . . The issue is one of social choice, which in general is an unresolvable problem.[22]

The reluctance to prescribe normative solutions did not diminish the quantity of research carried out in this area; it just shifted the emphasis. Recognition was now being given to the implicit cost/benefit trade-offs resulting from any disclosure requirement. Some of the implications of viewing information as an economic commodity will be discussed in further detail later in this chapter.

The Relationship Between Earnings and Stock Returns

Studies of the earnings/return relationship were by far the most prevalent form of market-based research. Organizing and classifying the nature of this research are best done by reference to Ball and Brown. Their study included the following interrelated categories and subcategories, and we summarize the nature of the research along those lines:

1. Accounting variable:
   a. Choice of the appropriate accounting variable
   b. Expectations of accounting variables
   c. Measurement of good news and bad news

---

[21] In this way of thinking, intrinsic value, even if it existed, was not necessarily a standard by which to measure the choice of accounting alternatives since somebody may "suffer" if the "truth" be known. An extensive rationale for this argument can be found in Gonedes and Dopuch (1974).

[22] Beaver (1973), p. 55. This position was something of a reversal for Beaver. In an earlier paper (1972, p. 321), Beaver and Dukes (1972) took the position, consistent with the general approach of the time, that the accounting method most closely associated with security prices is the one that should be reported.

2. Market-based variable:
    a. Choice of market model
    b. Measurement of "abnormal" market performance
    c. Measurement period ("window") for market performance
3. Test of the relationship between the good news/bad news parameter and abnormal returns

A great deal of this research explored the foregoing elements as both variations of Ball and Brown's approach and legitimate areas of research in their own right. Some research was broad in scope; others merely replicated previous studies, with an emphasis on methodological refinements. All in all, the research results were somewhat disappointing, with no major breakthroughs in terms of understanding the role of accounting earnings in the stock return generating process. *In addition, some of the research began to turn up evidence that seemed to contradict the semistrong form of market efficiency.*

Accounting Variable

Choice of the Appropriate Accounting Variable. Ball and Brown used annual net income and earnings per share (EPS). Other researchers [e.g., Foster (1977), Bathe and Lorek (1984)] used quarterly earnings with similar results, indicating that quarterly reports also possess "information content." However, a number of studies [see Ball (1978) and Joy and Jones (1979) for surveys] began to document postannouncement drift, whereby positive (negative) abnormal return patterns continued for some time after the announcement of good (bad) news quarterly earnings. This phenomenon was contrary to the EMH assertion that information was *immediately* impounded by prices.

Gonedes (1975, 1978) and Ronen and Sadan (1981), among others, focused on the appropriate definition of income—operating income, income from continuing operations, or net income—by examining whether the inclusion of special, nonrecurring, or extraordinary items had any impact on security returns. The spate of restructuring and write-offs in the 1980s rekindled research in this area.

More recently, in line with the current focus on cash flows in accounting and finance, research has examined the informational content of cash flows relative to net income. As discussed[23] in Chapter 2, the results do not generally show additional information content in cash flow data over that found in accrual-based earnings data.

Finally, in response to criticisms [such as Lev (1989), discussed shortly] that using a single number such as earnings to explain return behavior was too simplistic, some studies examined the relationship between returns and various components of earnings (Lipe, 1986) and between returns and cash flow components (Livnat and Zarowin, 1990).

Expectations of Accounting Variables. Earnings forecasts play an important role in many finance valuation models and are thought to be of great interest to investors. An important by-product of the earnings/return relationship research, which soon became a major area of research in its own right, lay in the development and construction of earnings forecasting models. Simple and complex time-series models, using

---

[23]See Box 2-2.

annual and/or quarterly data, were compared against one another and with those generated by financial analysts and management to examine two independent but closely related questions:

1. Which forecasting model or forecast has the best predictive ability?
2. Which forecasting model or forecast most closely mirrors the market's expectations?

The first issue is discussed in detail in Chapter 19, where various forecasting models are described and compared.

Research into the second issue (also discussed in Chapter 19) suggests that financial analysts' forecasts are a better surrogate for market expectations than models based solely on the historical time series of reported income.[24] This superiority was attributed [Brown et al. 1987)] to the fact that analysts have both more timely information and a broader set of information on which to base forecasts.

The fact that market expectations coincide with those of financial analysts led researchers to examine whether financial analysts in some sense lead the market and the market derives its expectations from analyst forecasts. Such studies found that there is indeed market reaction to changes in analysts' forecasts. Givoly and Lakonishok (1979), however, also indicated that abnormal returns could be earned by trading on revisions of analyst forecasts, again raising questions as to the efficiency of capital markets.

Measurement of Good News/Bad News. Refinements in this respect were primarily methodological. Ball and Brown defined good news/bad news simply on the basis of the direction of the forecast error, that is, whether reported earnings were above or below expectation. Beaver et al. (1979) considered the magnitude of the error, weighting their portfolios by the size of the error. Others [Rendelman et al. (1982)] carried this a step further by weighting the forecast error by a measure of the earnings stream's overall variability. This latter study also documented evidence of post-announcement drift.

Market-Based Variable

Choice of Market Model and Measurement of Abnormal Market Performance. Generally, the market-based variable used was abnormal returns. However, the security pricing model used varied. The primary candidates were the CAPM and the "market" model.[25] Other research used control firms matched to the sample by size and industry classification and, instead of examining the abnormal return, compared the difference in actual returns between the control group and the study sample. In addition, other studies focused on trading volume or risk measures such as total variance of the return and/or "beta."

The choice of an appropriate model is grounded to a great extent in the finance literature and is not the focus of this book. However, it should be noted that any test carried out of the earnings/return relationship is as much a test of the underlying asset

---

[24]O'Brien (1988), however, presents contradictory findings.

[25]See footnote 13 for a description of the market model. In addition, some studies use models such as the Black–Scholes option pricing model and the arbitrage pricing model.

pricing model as it is of the relationship itself. To the extent that these models do not accurately describe the market process, conclusions drawn from them are suspect.

Measurement Period (Window) for Market Performance. Ball and Brown examined monthly returns over a full year. Other studies, depending on the issue examined, used weekly (or daily) returns in the periods immediately surrounding the announcement.[26] The trade-off between using narrow (short) versus wide (long) windows is that in the former case there is less risk that the market could be reacting to information other than that being tested. Wider windows have the advantage of allowing for the possibility of information "leakage," thus implying earlier market reaction. In addition, and perhaps more important, the significance of a piece of information may not be known until a later date. Using too narrow a window would miss this reaction. The emergence of postannouncement drift, alluded to earlier,[27] increased the relevance of this issue.

Test of the Relationship Between the Good News/Bad News Parameter and Abnormal Returns

Early studies, as we have discussed, grouped firms into good news/bad news portfolios by the sign and/or magnitude of the earnings forecast error. There was no explicit theoretical consideration or measurement of the relationship between earnings and returns. Later studies explicitly related the response of stock returns to earnings by the introduction of the earnings response coefficient (ERC).[28]

ERC studies tested for differential reactions across firms and for differential reactions to various components of earnings. Moreover, the ERC permitted testing of explicit relationships between prices and earnings as implied by finance valuation models. Collins and Kothari (1989) show that, as predicted by such models, risk and growth variables explain some of the cross-sectional differences in ERCs.

ERCs were typically found to be much lower than expected. This finding led to interest in the "persistence" issue, namely which components of earnings were permanent and hence had implications for future valuation and market reaction, and which were transitory and thus had limited implications. Kormendi and Lipe (1987), for example, found that the greater the persistence, the higher the ERC.

Chapter 19, which deals with earnings forecasts and valuation models, discusses the ERC, issues of persistence, and their relationship to the price/earnings (P/E) ratio in greater detail.

Market-Based Research: Current Status

The end of the 1980s triggered a number of "20-year" retrospectives of developments since Ball and Brown. The consensus was not complimentary. In addition, cracks in the efficient market hypothesis began to appear. This section reviews the conclusions of two of these retrospective papers. The next section summarizes EMH anomalies that have important implications for financial statement analysis.

---

[26]Patell and Wolfson (1982, 1984) focused on the intraday measure of market reaction.

[27]See the subsequent discussion of market anomalies.

[28]The ERC is the coefficient b in the regression equation $R = a + b\mathrm{E}$, where R and E measure returns and earnings, respectively.

Critical Evaluation of Research Findings

Lev[29] reviews and assesses this literature. His overall evaluation is critical:

> What is the incremental contribution of the recent methodological improvements in the returns/earnings research to our understanding of how and to what extent earnings are used by investors? What is the contribution. . . to the deliberations of accounting policymakers? The answer seems to be—very little.[30]

He argues that when all is said and done, the earnings/return research paradigm leaves much to be desired:

> If one considers the persistence research, for example, the idea that investors react differently to the earnings of different firms and that such differential reaction is related to the future implications of earnings (persistence) is not particularly revealing.[31]

Bernard[32] points out some research benefits:

> Some impacts of the research are more subtle, but nevertheless important. Imagine what our view of the role of accounting information might be if Ball and Brown had found, as many predicted they would, that accounting earnings were completely uncorrelated with the information used by investors![33]

Notwithstanding the foregoing, however, he notes that pessimism about the research had set in by the mid–1970s[34] and further that:

> The emphasis on methodology throughout the 1980s sharpened our tools in important ways but the "love affair" with sophisticated statistical techniques may have diverted our attention from more central problems of model specification. In the area of valuation, a substantial amount of work appears to be guided by the philosophy that the accounting system produces only one number—earnings—that tracks performance with error. As a result, we have probably overinvested in analyses of the details of the simple returns-earnings regression without considering a richer information set.[35]

Lev surveyed approximately 20 studies which, for the most part, were methodological refinements of Ball and Brown. These refinements mirrored those already described. Lev noted that the R^2 scores found by these studies were low. (The R^2 measures the percentage of variation in returns explained by variations in earnings. A high R^2

---

[29]Baruch Lev, "On the Usefulness of Earnings and Earnings Research: Lessons and Directions from Two Decades of Empirical Research," *Journal of Accounting Research*, Supplement 1989, pp. 153–192.

[30]Ibid., p. 172.

[31]Ibid., p. 172.

[32]Victor L. Bernard, "Capital Market Research During the 1980's: A Critical Review," in Thomas Frecka (ed.), *The State of Accounting Research as We Enter the 1990's* (Urbana-Champaign University of Illinois, 1989), pp. 72–120.

[33]Ibid., p. 5.

[34]See Figure 5-7, from Bernard's original working paper.

[35]Victor L. Bernard, "Capital Market Research During the 1980's: A Critical Review" (working paper), p. 53.

implies a strong earnings/return association). On average, no more than 5% of the variation in returns can be explained by earnings. The relationship, although it may have *statistical significance*, has little or *no economic significance*. It docs not provide a meaningful explanation of the relationship between earnings and returns.

Lev proceeds to list a number of reasons for this failure and suggests directions for future research:

1. Researchers used reported earnings and did not adjust for accounting manipulations by managers, year-to-year random occurrences, or the inherent arbitrariness of many accounting measurement and valuation techniques.

> No serious attempt is being made to question the quality of the reported earnings number. . . . While various deficiencies in earnings are obviously adjusted for by financial analysts and even in the media, most researchers. . . accept the reported numbers at face value.[36]

2. There is little or no knowledge as to how accounting information is disseminated in the marketplace; that is, what is it that financial analysts do with the information? Lev suggests that accounting research should study how analysts disseminate and use the information provided in financial statements:

> Research on the quality of earnings and other financial information items and on the way investors disseminate such information (namely, adjust for quality deficiencies) offers a promising extension. . . .
>
> Adjustments of reported data are an essential element of financial statement analysis or the information dissemination process in capital markets. However, surprisingly little is known about this important process.
>
> In general, the research line suggested here is aimed at understanding the use of financial data by investors. (a) What financial variables play a role in asset valuation? . . . (b) What are the specific adjustments made by analysts to reported data?[37]

Lev's criticisms suggest an interesting irony of accounting research. Although researchers have argued that financial analysis is meaningless since the market is not fooled by reported data, they tested their arguments using the same data that the market supposedly adjusts.[38]

3. Lev argues for a research emphasis on the quality of earnings that incorporates the effects of alternative GAAP measures on earnings and their relationship to valuation models. Elements of this paradigm include:

- Measuring earnings/returns relationships on a portfolio basis may not be meaningful since analysts usually view firms on an individual rather than portfolio basis.

---

[36]Lev (1989), pp. 175–176.

[37]Ibid., pp. 178–181.

[38]The rationale offered is that with large samples the noise resulting from nonadjustment would tend to be averaged away. This contention itself is subject to empirical verification as it would depend on whether the errors cancel, or they are in some fashion systematically related. Subject to the evidence on this issue, it would seem that many researchers suffer from a form of functional fixation.

- Looking at the immediate effect of a *single period's* earnings on stock prices may not be as meaningful as averaging the earnings numbers over time.[39]
- Time horizons studied should be extended; future year impacts should also be studied. This requires more careful analysis of valuation models as they relate to accounting and earnings.
- Earnings components used in the research should incorporate all possible adjustments, not just one at a time, to arrive at a more comprehensive and meaningful analysis.

Bernard echoes Lev's suggestions:

> 1) Progress will require that we end reliance on simple, naive models. . . . An injection of knowledge about the accounting system and fundamental analysis is necessary. . . .
> 2) It would frequently be useful to sacrifice large sample sizes and sophisticated statistics for the sake of achieving a deeper understanding of the relations among accounting variables, and between those variables and equity values. . . .
> 3) Further reliance on formal modeling would be fruitful.[40]

The relationship between these recommendations and the objectives laid out in the study of financial statement analysis can best be summed up in Lev's words:

> Capital market research should, therefore, shift its focus to the role of accounting measurement rules in asset valuation. Such research involves both positive and normative aspects. Regarding the former, the proposed research is aimed at understanding the use of financial information by investors, that is, a thorough investigation of the financial statement analysis process. . . . The normative aspect. . . is aimed at filling a current void in financial economic modeling. Economic models posit a relation between generic financial variables (e.g., "income") and market values, leaving unspecified the nature of the financial variables. The research conjectures proposed above are aimed at adding a fundamental element to this relation—the impact of GAAP and GAAP alternatives on market values, via the impact of accounting techniques on the predictive power of financial variables.[41]

Market Anomalies

A number of anomalies have been found that question the validity of the EMH and the conclusions drawn from the research described previously. Some of these anomalies are related to the relationship between earnings and returns, whereas others seem to be purely market-based. Additionally, some of the anomalies tend to overlap. For example, the Monday effect and postannouncement drift are most pronounced for small-size firms.

January Effect. Empirical evidence suggests that markets perform relatively well during the month of January. This would seem to be a violation of the weak form of

---

[39]To test for this, Lev examined the relationship of earnings and returns taken over a five-year period. He argued that over a longer period manipulations and smoothing tend to even out and earnings mirror cash flows. The R^2 over this longer period proved to be 35%—seven times the R^2 for the one-year data.

[40]Bernard, "Capital Markets Research in Accounting During the 1980's," pp. 99–100.

[41]Lev, pp. 185–186.

the EMH, as knowledge of this pattern could lead to abnormal gains by buying stock at the end of December.

Monday Effect. After the weekend, market prices tend to open at lower levels, suggesting an advantageous strategy of selling short at the Friday close and covering the short position Monday morning.

Size Effect. Smaller firms (measured by total assets or total capitalization) tend to outperform the market even when returns are adjusted for risk. This suggests that investing in a portfolio of smaller-sized firms is a sound investment strategy.

Price-Earnings Ratio. Firms with low P/E ratios tend to outperform the market even when returns are adjusted for risk. This suggests that investing in a portfolio of firms with low P/E ratios is a sound investment strategy.

Book-to-Market Ratios. Fama and French (1992) found that the book-to-market ratio was a strong predictor of average returns. Figure 5-4 (based on Fama and French) shows that firms with higher book-to-market ratios had higher monthly returns than firms with lower ratios. This suggests investing in firms with high book-to-market ratios.

Postannouncement Drift. The EMH holds that stock prices adjust instantaneously to new information. Empirical evidence, however, suggests that price changes persist for some time after the initial announcement.

The Briloff Effect. Professor Abraham Briloff, an outspoken critic of some accounting practices, analyzed the financial reports of some firms in *Barron's*; he was highly critical of their reporting practices. The common stocks of these firms typically suffered large price drops (see Figure 5-5) following publication. Since Briloff's analysis is

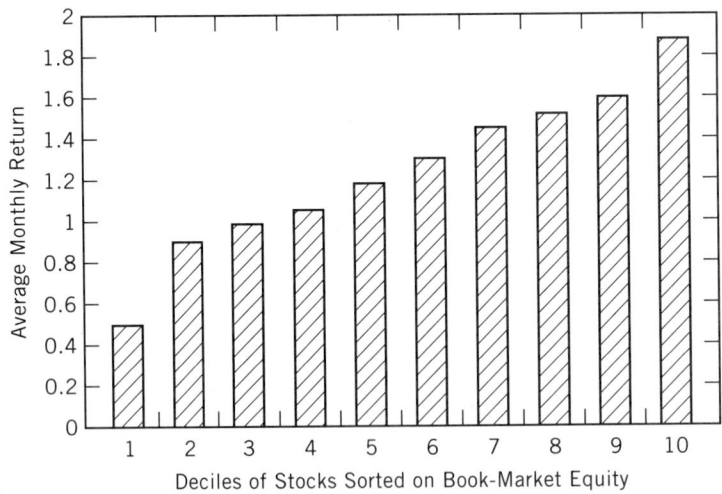

FIGURE 5-4 Evidence of book-market effect. Note that the ranking of book-market equity goes from the lowest (1) to the highest (10) decile.

Source: Data based on E. F. Fama and K. R. French, "The Cross-Section of Expected Stock Returns," *Journal of Finance*, June 1992, Table 2, p. 436.

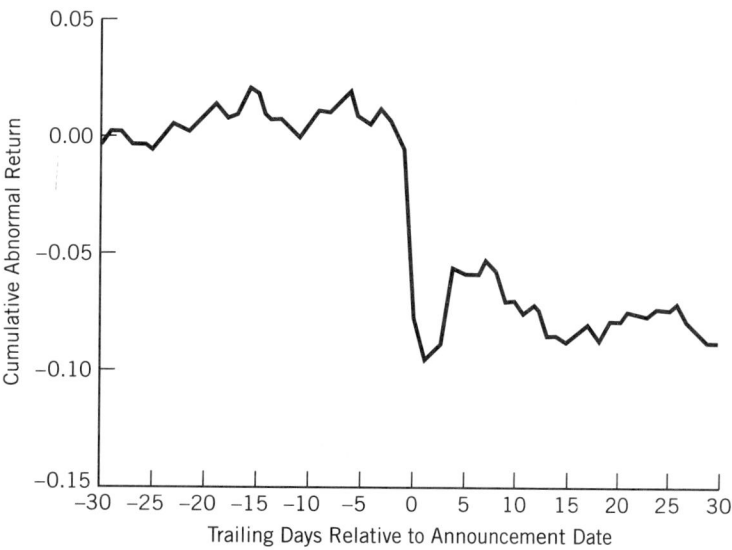

FIGURE 5-5 The Briloff effect: Market reaction for 28 stocks.

Source: George Foster, "Briloff and the Capital Market," *Journal of Accounting Research*, Spring 1979, pp. 262–274, Figure 1, p. 266, reprinted with permission.

based on publicly available information, it would seem that the market price prior to Briloff's analysis did not fully reflect all the available information.

Value Line. Figure 5-6 presents the performance of the stock groupings ranked by Value Line Investment Services. The continued and consistent performance of these groupings, relative to the market, implies that Value Line is able to "beat the market."

Overreactive Markets: Contrarian Strategy. DeBondt and Thaler (1985) found that if stocks were ranked by their performance over a previous five-year period (the base period), those firms with the worst base-period investment performance outperformed those firms with the best base-period performance over the next three years. This suggests that markets overreact and a contrarian investment strategy of buying recent losers and avoiding recent winners will be successful.

Lakonishok et al. (1994) extend this argument to explain the book-to-market phenomenon.[42] They argue that when a firm's earnings decline, the market overreacts, driving the price down (and the book-to-market ratio up) sharply. Similarly, when a firm reports good earnings, the market "chases" the stock price up (and the book-to-market ratio down). Over time, the extent of the overreaction becomes clear and prices reverse, yielding above (below) average returns for high (low) book-to-market firms.[43]

---

[42]See also Zarowin (1989, 1990) who argues that the overreaction effect may just be another manifestation of the size effect.

[43]The interested reader is referred to Robert A. Haugen, *The New Finance: The Case Against Efficient Markets* (Englewood Cliffs, N.J.: Prentice Hall, 1995).

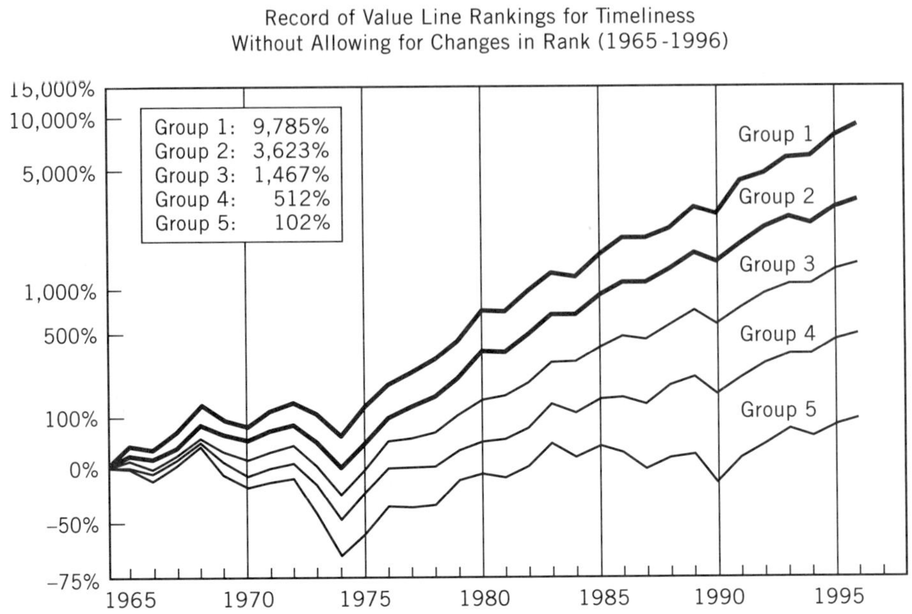

Record of Value Line Rankings for Timeliness
Without Allowing for Changes in Rank (1965-1996)

FIGURE 5-6 Performance of Value Line groups. Group 1 = highest predicted performance; group 5 = lowest predicted performance.

Source: Value Line Selection and Opinion, *New Line,* July 19, 1996, p. 7337.

Although all these anomalies have implications for analysts, explanations of the book-market effect, size effect, Briloff effect, and the Value Line results relate most directly to the role of financial analysts in the capital markets. The results of Lakonishok et al. with respect to the book-market effect justify a (contrarian and) "value" approach to investments *a la* Graham.[44] *Underpriced securities exist if the market overreacts.*

The size effect is often attributed to the fact that smaller firms are followed by fewer analysts than larger firms. Thus, not all information available about these firms is immediately incorporated in stock prices, leaving room for abnormal returns to be earned by those who trade on the information early enough. The excess returns on small-firm portfolios may also represent compensation for the cost and difficulty of analyzing underfollowed companies.

As a possible explanation of the Briloff effect, Foster noted that Briloff's superior accounting knowledge and analytical insights were in a sense nonpublic information, and hence capital market efficiency was not violated per se. This suggests that Briloff could earn a (competitive) return from using his superior skills. The so-called information market, rather than the capital market, is seen as the explanation for the research results.[45]

Value Line rankings are based on the performance of variables referred to as "earnings momentum" and "earnings surprise." The former relates to changes in

[44]David Dreman ("Value Will Out," *Forbes,* June 17, 1996, p. 146) makes the point that the academic community has finally come around to recognizing the teachings of Graham and Dodd. This is ironic given the earlier quotation (p. 220) from Graham.

[45]George Foster, "Briloff and the Capital Market," *Journal of Accounting Research,* (Spring 1979), pp. 262–274.

quarterly earnings over time, whereas the latter relates to the deviation between actual and forecasted earnings. Whether this qualifies as statistical or fundamental analysis is open for debate. The results, however, indicate that superior analysis can lead to results that outperform the market.

In summing up the evidence on efficient markets, we leave the reader with the following:

> The lesson is clear. An overly doctrinaire belief in efficient markets can paralyze the investor and make it appear that no research effort can be justified. This extreme view is probably unwarranted. There are enough anomalies in the empirical evidence to justify the search for underpriced securities that clearly goes on. The bulk of the evidence, however, suggests that any supposedly superior strategy should be taken with many grains of salt. The market is competitive enough that only differentially superior information or insight will earn money; the easy pickings have been picked.[46]

POSITIVE ACCOUNTING RESEARCH

Watts and Zimmerman (1990), the "fathers" of this line of research, note that the term positive accounting research

> was used to distinguish research aimed at explanation and prediction from research whose objective was prescription. . . . A positive theory differs from a normative theory, though a positive theory can have normative implications once an objective function is specified.[47]

The positive accounting approach is sometimes referred to as "contracting theory" or as "the economic consequences of accounting" literature. This approach assumes that accounting variables are not exogenous to the firm, but are an integral part of the firm and its organizational structure. The financial information interacts with the firm's investment, production, and financing decisions. This information is the basis on which resources are allocated, management is compensated, debt restrictions are measured, and so on. Management, therefore, would be expected to take into consideration financial information effects by changing their decisions and/or altering their choice of accounting methods. Operationally, the positive theory approach moved the focus away from tests of market reaction to accounting numbers to, as Figure 5-1C indicates, a study of the incentives underlying management's behavior in terms of:

- Their operating, investing, and financing decisions, and
- Their choice of alternative accounting numbers

Although both types of research fall into this paradigm, the "Rochester school," which popularized and applied to it the label of "positive accounting" [see Watts and Zimmerman (1986)], focused most of its attention on the second type.[48] Hence, studies

---

[46]Zvi Bodie, Alex Kane, and Alan J. Marcus, *Investments* (Homewood Ill.: Richard D. Irwin 1996), p. 377.

[47]Ross Watts and Jerold L. Zimmerman, "Positive Accounting Theory: A Ten Year Perspective," *The Accounting Review*, Jan. 1990, pp. 131–156.

[48]Research on the effects of accounting on management's operating decisions, in fact, preceded the research on the choice of an accounting method.

of the incentives underlying accounting choices are most closely identified with positive accounting research.

Market studies also play a role, but that emphasis is secondary. Accounting changes have an informational impact, but are more significantly a result of the interaction of the alternative choice with the production-financing-investment opportunities of the firm. As the opportunity set changes, so does the appropriate informational environment. It is for this reason that mandated rather than voluntary choices of accounting method are perceived to have more of a market impact. Voluntary changes are anticipated or predictable as the firm itself changes. For example, as it changes its primary industry classification, a firm is likely to change its accounting policies. Since the change in industry emphasis is somewhat predictable, so is the change in accounting policy.

Impetus for this broadened approach was once again led by changes in the finance and economics literature.

Disclosure and Regulatory Requirements

Economists examining regulation and its effects began to question the belief that all regulation was motivated by concern with the public good and regulation necessarily increased social welfare. Politicians and regulators were now viewed as motivated by their own self-interest and, hence, have private incentives to promulgate certain regulations.

Disclosure requirements were also viewed in this light. The benefits from increased disclosure requirements were not automatically assumed to outweigh the costs. Moreover, it was argued (further elaborated on shortly) that firms have private incentives to produce information so long as the cost of disseminating and producing the information does not outweigh its potential rewards. These cost/benefit trade-offs are believed to influence the choice of accounting alternatives. The motivations for accounting choices, however, still required explanation. Furthermore,

> Firms in the same industries tended to change procedures at the same time, just as at any given time firms in the same industry tend to use the same procedures. *This systematic behavior caused researchers to question the no-effects hypothesis.*[49]

Agency Theory

The agency theory literature also took as a starting point the argument that people are motivated by their own self-interest. Thus, managers take steps to maximize the value of the firm only if that is consistent with their own best interests. If managers could, moreover, *in the absence of a monitoring device,* enhance their well-being (1) by appropriating resources for themselves in addition to their agreed-on compensation or (2) by shirking their duties, equity or debt investors could be reluctant to provide financing to the firm.

Similarly, in the absence of a monitoring device, managers might engage in risk taking and other activities that would hurt the bondholder to the advantage of the equityholder. Thus, a monitoring device is needed to ensure that the agreements (contracts) among managers, shareholders, and creditors are adhered to. This discussion leads to viewing a firm not as an independent entity but rather as a "nexus of

---

[49]Ross Watts and Jerold L. Zimmerman, *Positive Accounting Theory* (Englewood Cliffs, N.J.: Prentice-Hall, 1986), p. 178, emphasis added.

contracts"[50] (explicit or implicit) between parties, each motivated by its own self-interest. The role of accounting in this scenario is to provide one of the monitoring devices enabling the contracting process to function.

This approach to the accounting process views financial statements as the means by which contracting parties measure, monitor, and enforce the objectives of the various contracts.[51] Thus, as mentioned in the introduction to this chapter, accounting data do not merely *describe* reality—they in effect *define* reality, as real economic consequences flow from the reported numbers. Positive accounting research, it should be noted, does not exclude market-based research. Rather, its approach subsumes the market-based research as a component of an overall research paradigm:

> The hypothesis that accounting and auditing arose as a monitoring device for the firm's contracts contrasts with the common hypothesis that investors demand accounting reports as a source of information for investment and valuation decisions. The information hypothesis . . . asserts that investors demand information on current and future cash flows and the market value of assets and liabilities. . . .
>
> The two hypotheses are not mutually exclusive. Both the contract and information roles could exist at the same time. Information that enables individuals to determine certain contractual requirements have been met is often useful in valuing the firm's securities.[52]

The specific hypotheses flowing from the positive theory approach to accounting that are most often tested are the:

- Bonus plan hypothesis
- Debt covenant or debt/equity hypothesis
- Political process hypothesis

The Bonus Plan Hypothesis

The "contract" between management and shareholders concerns the performance expected from the manager and his or her level of compensation. Under the *bonus plan* hypothesis, managers are compensated for how well they manage the firm. The financial statements are used (often explicitly identified by the firm's executive compensation plan) as the benchmark for the firm's performance. Thus, it is in the best interest of the firm's management to choose "liberal" accounting policies to improve their own compensation.

The motivation for choosing liberal accounting policies under this approach is not posited in terms of "fooling" the market, with all the implications vis-à-vis the efficient market hypothesis. Rather, motivation is simply the increased management compensation resulting from higher reported earnings.[53]

---

[50]This term can be traced to Jensen and Meckling (1976).

[51]Under this view, the choice of accounting policy by management may not necessarily have "sinister" implications. The various parties view the accounting process as an efficient way to operate the firm. Otherwise, if there were no proper monitoring device, equity shareholders would be reluctant to hire managers (or they would pay them less). Thus, management has an incentive to have a "proper" monitoring system in place.

[52]Watts and Zimmerman, *Positive Accounting Theory*, pp. 197–198.

[53]As footnote 51 points out, the management compensation hypothesis is also consistent with an efficiency point of view and not necessarily tied to "opportunistic" behavior on the part of managers.

At the same time, however, more complicated applications of the bonus plan hypothesis are also possible:

> A bonus plan does not always give managers incentives to increase earnings. If, in the absence of accounting changes, earnings are below the minimum level required for payment of a bonus, managers have incentives to reduce earnings this year because no bonuses are likely to be paid. Taking such an "earnings bath" increases expected bonuses and profits in future years.[54]

Similarly, when earnings exceed the maximum rewarded under the compensation plan, there is no incentive to increase earnings any further. On the contrary, it may become worthwhile to recognize losses (as long as earnings remain above the maximum threshold) currently as opposed to (saving them for) future years.

Healy (1985) provides some evidence on this effect. He found that managers tend to change their accounting policies based on bonus plan incentives and these changes are associated with the initial inception or modification of the plan. However, he also reports that managers do not seem to alter accounting policies if they are either below the minimum threshold or above the maximum ceiling for the current period. More recent studies by Holthausen et al. (1995) and Gaver et al. (1995) further refined the interrelationships between bonus plans and accounting choices.

The Debt Covenant Hypothesis

Bondholders and other creditors want to ensure repayment of their principal and interest. To protect themselves, they impose restrictions on the borrower as to payments of dividends, share repurchases, and issuance of additional debt. These restrictions are often expressed in terms of accounting amounts and ratios. Typical covenants also call for the maintenance of acceptable levels of working capital, interest coverage, net worth, and similar variables.

Accounting choices can greatly affect measures of these variables and consequently define whether a firm is in "technical default" of debt covenants. The debt covenant hypothesis states that managers are motivated to choose accounting methods that minimize the likelihood that covenants would be violated. Operationally, this is often expressed as the debt/equity hypothesis that asserts firms with higher debt/equity ratios tend to choose accounting policies that increase current income at the expense of future income. More recent papers have refined this measure by incorporating explicit debt covenants and estimates of the cost of violation. A more elaborate description of the nature of bond covenants and research in this area is provided in Chapter 10.

Political Cost Hypothesis

Our previous discussion of regulation implied that the political process imposes costs on the firm. When politicians and regulators can enhance their (or their constituents') interests at the expense of others, they will often do so. Financial data, and how it is perceived, play an important role in this process. If it is believed that a firm or an industry is taking advantage of the public and is making "obscene" profits, then reported earnings will be examined to see if profits are excessive. This may result in

---

[54]Watts and Zimmerman, "Positive Accounting Theory: A Ten Year Perspective," p. 139.

pressures for companies to reduce prices (drug industry) or for regulators to impose a "windfall profits" tax (oil industry).

Affected firms may be induced to choose accounting methods that reduce reported profits so as to lower their political risk. For example, some oil companies reduced reported earnings in 1991 (when oil prices were high because of the Kuwait crisis) by making provisions for environmental costs or asset impairment.

Similarly, accounting methods that reduce income reported to shareholders can be motivated by the desire to use those same methods on tax returns. Even though alternative methods are permissible,[55] it is less "embarrassing" to be paying little or no taxes if financial statement income is also low. Utilities, on the other hand, whose revenues are determined on the basis of accounting rules, can be motivated to lobby for rules that are most favorable from a rate-setting point of view.

The political cost hypothesis is often tested in the research literature as a size hypothesis. It is argued that large firms are most susceptible to political costs and pressures. The larger the firm, the more likely it would choose accounting methods that lower profits and hence lessen political pressures. One example is the oil industry. Large firms uniformly use the successful efforts method (see Chapter 7), which minimizes reported earnings; among smaller firms the full cost method is more common.

Summary of the Research

Positive accounting research takes on forms that we describe from a general perspective. Details of specific studies are provided in the chapters dealing with the related accounting issue.

Although our discussion of the three hypotheses focused on the choice of accounting method, the same hypotheses can be used to examine the effects of accounting data on management operating decisions. Thus, for example, the requirement that research and development costs be expensed rather than capitalized (SFAS 2) lowers reported earnings for many firms. This could induce a cutback in the amount of actual research and development work undertaken if managers felt that the lower earnings would hurt their compensation and/or imperil the status of the firm's bond covenants. A number of studies examining this issue are discussed in Chapter 7. Similarly, studies dealing with the interaction of accounting methods and the incentives for mergers and acquisitions, pension plan terminations, and oil exploration are discussed in the chapters dealing with these topics.

Market-based studies have examined mandated accounting changes in the oil and gas industry, purchase versus pooling accounting, and voluntary switches similar to the depreciation changes described earlier. The approach, however, differs because rather than just viewing returns as a function of earnings, it is now posited that return reaction may vary across firms as a function of a number of variables in addition to earnings, such as debt/equity, size, and management compensation. Changes that increase earnings, for example, could result in positive market reaction for firms with high debt/equity ratios because the increased income would permit wealth transfers from the firm's existing bondholders to equity shareholders as additional debt could be taken on without affecting the reported debt/equity ratio.

---

[55]In the United States, LIFO conformity (see Chapter 6) requires the use of the same accounting method for financial reporting as for tax reporting. However, in many industrial countries firms must use the same accounting methods for both purposes, strengthening the motivation to use "conservative" methods.

On the other hand, for large-sized firms, the increased income could increase the possibility of political costs, thus resulting in negative market reaction. Generally, research results are consistent, albeit weakly, with the predicted relationships for mandated accounting changes but not for voluntary ones. This finding is consistent with the theory described earlier.

The emphasis of positive accounting research was not market-based. Most of the research dealt with why firms chose among accounting alternatives. We briefly review one paper in the area to give the reader a "feel" for the nature of the research.

Zmijewski and Hagerman (ZH) (1981) focused on firms' choices with respect to four sets of accounting alternatives[56] that could increase or decrease reported net income:

Policy	Income Effect	
	Increase	Decrease
1. Inventory	FIFO	LIFO
2. Investment tax credit	Flowthrough	Deferral
3. Pensions: Amortization of past service costs	<30 years	>30 years
4. Depreciation	Straight line	Accelerated

Source: Mark Zmijewski and Robert Hagerman, "An Income Strategy Approach to the Positive Theory of Accounting Standard Setting/Choice," *Journal of Accounting and Economics,* Vol. 3, 1981, pp. 129–149, Table 1 on p. 135 (summary only).

For each choice, increasing (decreasing) income, a score of 1 (0) was assigned.[57] Thus, a firm's score for income strategy could vary from 0 (all decreasing) to 4 (all increasing). The distribution of the strategy scores for the 300 firms in their sample follows:

Number of Income Increasing Choices	Frequency	Percentage
Zero	10	3.33%
One	49	16.33
Two	107	35.67
Three	107	35.67
Four	27	9.00
	300	100.00%

Source: Zmijewski and Hagerman (1981).

[56] As the investment tax credit expired, it is no longer an accounting issue, except for firms that still have deferred credits that are being amortized against current earnings. The pension alternatives examined in Zmijewski and Hagerman (1981) were permitted by APB 8, which was replaced by SFAS 87 (see Chapter 12) in 1985.

[57] Other weighting schemes giving smaller weights to the pension and investment tax credit choices were also tested, with results similar to the equal-weighted scores reviewed here.

The following explanatory variables were used to explain the choices and thus test the underlying theory:

- *Bonus plan variable* (*B*). A score of 1 if the firm had a management compensation plan; 0 otherwise. The presence of a compensation plan was expected to increase the strategy score.
- *Debt variable* (*D*). The debt/assets ratio was used to measure the (relative) debt of the firm. Higher debt increased the likelihood that the strategy score would be higher.
- *Political cost variables* (P_1, P_2, P_3, and P_4). Four variables were used to measure different aspects related to political pressure: size, industry concentration (indicating the degree of monopoly power), capital intensiveness, and beta. Political cost variables were expected to decrease the frequency of choosing income-increasing alternatives.

The following equation was then tested[58] to determine the relationship between the strategy scores and explanatory variables:

$$Strategy = c_0 + c_1B + c_2D + c_3P_1 + c_4P_2 + c_5P_3 + c_6P_4$$

Based on the theory, we would expect the coefficients (c_1 and c_2) of the bonus and debt variables to be positive but the coefficients (c_3–c_6) for the political process variables to be negative. The results were consistent with the predicted relationships in terms of the signs of the coefficients, and the overall equation proved to be significant.

Other studies using similar techniques focused on single-choice alternatives as opposed to the Zmijewski and Hagerman study, which examined multiple choices. In reviewing the research, Watts and Zimmerman contend that the results are generally consistent with the bonus plan, debt/equity, and political cost hypotheses. With respect to the political cost hypothesis:

> However, the result only appears to hold for the largest firms and is driven by the oil and gas industry.[59]

Moreover, with echoes of Lev's analysis:

> While bonus, debt and political process variables tend to be statistically significant. . . in many studies the explanatory power (R^2) of the models is low.[60]

Christie (1990) addressed the issue of the low significance levels found in many of the studies by "aggregating" results across studies. The thrust of his findings (in nonstatistical terms) was that although (the results of) each study taken by itself was "circumstantial" and noncompelling, a multitude of such circumstantial evidence leads to a compelling case.

---

[58]The method of analysis used was probit analysis, which is similar to regression analysis but is more appropriate when the dependent variable is discrete (i.e., in our case, it can only be one of five values).

[59]Watts and Zimmerman, "Positive Accounting Theory: A Ten Year Perspective," p. 140.

[60]Ibid.

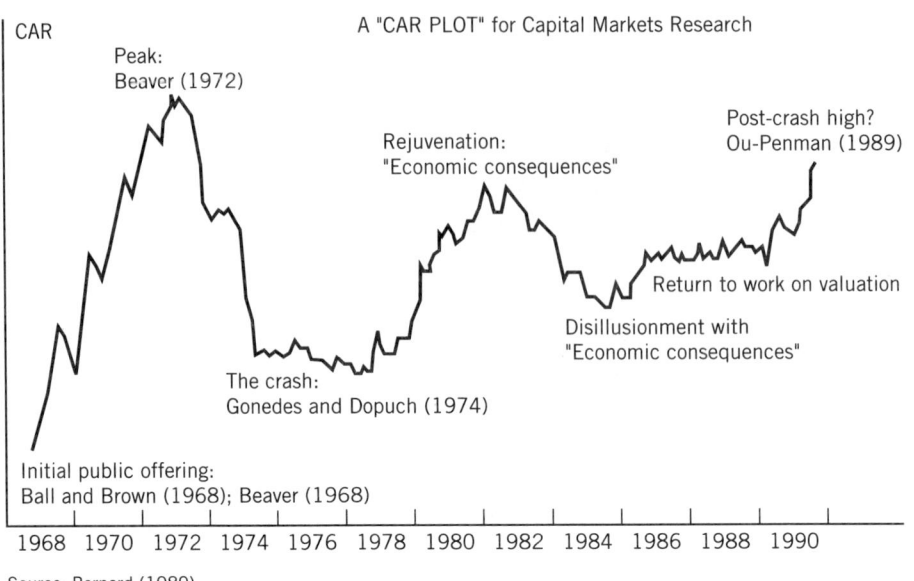

Source: Bernard (1989)

FIGURE 5-7 A "CAR plot" for capital markets research, 1968 to 1990.

Source: Victor L. Bernard, "Capital Market Research During the 1980's: A Critical Review," 1989, Figure 1 on p. 3 (working paper).

In their discussion of avenues for further research in the area, Watts and Zimmerman note that most of the studies have been concerned with incentives for management to behave opportunistically as these tend to be the most observable (and hence testable) phenomena. However, they argue that more work needs to be done in terms of strengthening the relationship between theory and empirical testing in determining whether management choices are made purely for opportunistic reasons, or the choices are motivated by efficiency considerations inherent in the firm's organizational structure and/or industrial dynamics.

DIRECTION OF CURRENT RESEARCH

Bernard (1989) summarized the accounting research of the last quarter-century by means of a "cumulative abnormal return" plot reproduced in Figure 5-7. The early promise of the market-based research (begun by Ball and Brown, and Beaver) was soon tempered by the realization that the desirability of accounting principles could not be determined solely on the basis of information content considerations. The economic consequences or positive theory approach provided the next "high." However, "disillusionment" with this line of research resulted as scant evidence of economic consequences was found.[61]

This brings us to the present state and direction of research. It is difficult to categorize what is still evolving. It is, however, possible to describe some of its attributes.

---

[61]Bernard, it should be noted, was specifically addressing evidence with respect to the area of capital market research and the positive (economic consequences) approach. As noted in the previous section, this is only one area of the overall positive accounting approach.

Current research involves a return to principles of valuation. No longer are prices or returns taken as given and accounting data just tested to justify their usefulness.[62] The emphasis is no longer on stock behavior, but rather on forecasting future *accounting* attributes such as ROE and book values. Emphasis has shifted to the information derived from accounting data and its relationship to value. Furthermore, that value may or may not be the same as that reflected in market prices. This shift signals a return to the thinking inherent in the classical approach (i.e., accounting data could yield information about value); however, with a major difference. The relationships posited had to be justified empirically.

The current approach, thus, in some sense, synthesizes elements of the classical and market-based approaches; it borrows elements from both. Initially, the trend evolved from market-based research. However, it has been sustained to a great degree by the application of theoretical valuation models originally developed close to a half-century ago in the works of the classical writers.

Much of the empirical research was, at first, cast as a refinement of earlier information content studies. However, eventually a difference set in. Research on the diversity of the earnings response coefficient across firms led to a rethinking of basic price/earnings relationships. Evidence that prices could be used to forecast future earnings led to the (re)awareness (in research design) that prices react to not only changes in current earnings but also changes in expected earnings. Consistent with these directions in the research were calls for a return to fundamental analysis. As Ou and Penman (1989) noted:

> There have been many claims of market efficiency with respect to "publicly available" information, but (astonishingly, when one considers the many tests of technical analysis) little research into the competing claim of fundamental analysis.[63]

Back to the Future?

Ball and Brown Revisited

Ou (1990) is indicative of the *initial* trend in this research. We describe this study in some detail because its research design contrasts with Ball and Brown, discussed at the beginning of the chapter.

Figure 5-8 captures Ou's salient results. Similar to Ball and Brown, Ou separates firms into good and bad news categories. The graphs marked E^+ and E^-, in fact, are replications of Ball and Brown's study and are based on whether a firm's reported earnings for the year were above (good news) or below (bad news) earnings predicted by a time-series forecasting model.

Acting as if this knowledge were known as far back as March of the year in question, two portfolios are constructed on the basis of the good news/bad news partitions. The positive (negative) abnormal returns for the good (bad) news portfolios result in the E^+ and E^- graphs. These graphs indicate that earnings have informational content and earnings are associated with prices. The assumption is that prices are "correct" insofar as impounding available information, and the question is whether

---

[62] As Penman (1992) notes when advocating the new direction for research: "Fundamental analysis, in contrast, involves the discovery of price without reference to price" (p. 466).

[63] Jane A. Ou and Stephen Penman, "Financial Statement Analysis and the Prediction of Stock Returns," *Journal of Accounting and Economics*, Nov. 1989, pp. 295–329.

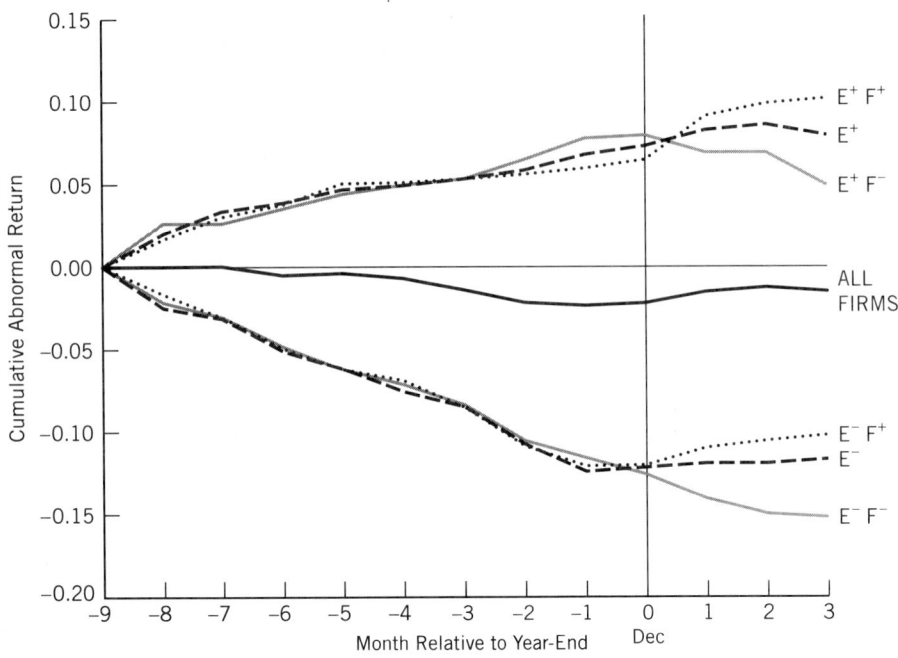

FIGURE 5-8 Ou's results.

Source: Jane A. Ou, "The Information Content of Nonearnings Accounting Numbers as Earnings Predictors," *Journal of Accounting Research*, Spring 1990, pp. 144–162, Figure 1 on p. 158, reprinted with permission.

earnings convey the same information. No more can be said as the portfolios were formed "as if" the knowledge with respect to the abnormal earnings was available in advance. Implications for valuation from this design are limited.[64]

Ou extended this analysis by partitioning the firms on the basis of both current year earnings and a forecast of the next year's earnings. A model was designed to predict whether the reported next year's earnings would be above (F^+ = good news) or below (F^- = bad news) the earnings forecast by a time-series model. This resulted in the formation of four portfolios:

Portfolio	Reported This Year	Predicted Next Year
E+F+	Good news	Good news
E+F−	Good news	Bad news
E−F+	Bad news	Good news
E−F−	Bad news	Bad news

The next year forecast was in the form of a probability assessment (Pr) as to whether next year's earnings would be above or below those predicted by a time-series model.

[64]As Penman (1991) notes, "Fundamental analysis concerns the measurement of investment worth and the 'information perspective' is limited in providing insights about this" (p. 5).

The following variables went into the model[65]:

1. Percentage growth in the ratio of inventory to total assets
2. Percentage growth in the total asset turnover (net sales/total assets)
3. Change in dividends per share relative to previous year
4. Percentage growth in depreciation expense
5. Percentage growth in the ratio of capital expenditures to total assets
6. Percentage growth in the previous year's ratio of capital expenditures to total assets
7. Return on equity
8. Change in return on equity relative to the previous year

These variables, culled from a list of 61 variables, are characteristic of those commonly used in financial statement analysis. As the graph indicates, all the E^+ portfolios and all the E^- portfolios moved together until year-end. Then, from January on, the F^+ portfolios (good news forecasts) moved upward, whereas the F^- (bad news forecasts) turned downward. The results indicate that the forecast model could be used successfully to predict (the direction of) future prices.

Ou's study is characterized by two attributes that differentiate it from previous market-based research. First, the analysis is not motivated to show whether accounting information is associated on an *ex post* basis with market prices, but rather whether the information can be used *ex ante* as a basis of valuation. Second and consistent with this *ex ante* approach, Ou broadens the set of accounting information by utilizing "tools of fundamental analysis" in her research design.

Subsequent papers by Ou and Penman (1989)[66] and Holthausen and Larcker (1992) using similar "tools of fundamental analysis" examined whether financial ratios could be used in a successful trading strategy. Ou and Penman (1989) was an extension of Ou (1990). Their purpose was to see whether a trading strategy[67] based on earnings forecasts (Pr) would prove to be fruitful. It was; the average market-adjusted return was 14.5% per annum over a 24-month holding period.

Holthausen and Larcker (1992) "replicated" Ou and Penman with some variation. They did not use ratios to forecast earnings first and then "trade" based on the expected earnings. Rather, they developed a model to forecast "abnormal" returns directly. Implementation of this model proved to be more successful in earning abnormal returns than Ou and Penman's strategy.

It is worth noting that we refer to these approaches *as utilizing tools of fundamental analysis rather than fundamental analysis itself.* All firms and variables were subjected to identical statistical analysis. The utilization of variables in these studies was done

---

[65]Jane A. Ou, "The Information Content of Nonearnings Accounting Numbers as Earnings Predictors," *Journal of Accounting Research*, Spring 1990, pp. 144–162.

[66]There is much debate [see Ball, 1992] as to whether Ou and Penman's results are an example of market inefficiency as the returns they garnered were "abnormal," or whether their model allowed them to predict better expected earnings relative to the CAPM. We do not intend to enter that debate. What is important is that under either premise, the variables proved to be valuation-relevant.

[67]Specifically, they tested the following trading strategy. If the Pr was greater than 60%, indicating at least a 60% probability that the earnings change would be positive, a long position in the firm's stock was taken. If the Pr was less than 40%, equivalent to a greater than 60% probability that the earnings change will be negative, a short position in the firm's stock was taken.

in a purely mechanical fashion.[68] *Fundamental analysis requires more in-depth analysis, the nature of which varies from firm to firm. Additionally, it needs theoretical underpinnings.* Both these attributes are missing from these studies. Ou and Penman (1995), in a subsequent paper, recognize this drawback and note (p. 5) that their

> approach was an empirical analysis, without a guiding conceptual foundation.[69]

Fundamental Analysis: Contextual Approaches

Lev and Thiagarajan (1993) took a step in this direction. Rather than just allowing statistical models to "select" their predictive variables, they attempted to, *a priori*, select predictive variables claimed to be useful by financial analysts. The variables they examined included:

1. Indications of future growth, for example,
   a. Levels of investment (capital expenditures and R&D)
   b. The percentage change in inventory and receivables relative to that of sales
2. Profitability measures, for example,
   a. Changes in the gross margin percentage
   b. The rate of change in SG&A expenses
3. "Quality" of earnings indicators, for example,
   a. LIFO versus FIFO earnings
   b. Audit qualification
4. Leading indicators, for example,
   a. Order backlog
   b. Change in labor force indicating changes in future costs

Additionally, the authors allowed for the possibility that the effects of these variables might vary (contextual approach), depending on the state of the economy or industry. For example, the impact of changes in inventory levels may depend on whether the firm itself increases inventory levels, or the economy as a whole is expanding.

They found that the variables were generally value-relevant and could be used to "forecast" abnormal returns. Moreover, varying economic and industry conditions had the desired effect. The interpretation of the financial variables, however, could be quite subtle and situation-specific:

> The above findings indicate that the valuation-relevance of earnings is assessed by investors within a broad context of financial information. Thus, for example, a positive

---

[68]If anything, this shortcoming may have biased the results downward; more promising results may be obtainable with more in-depth analyses.

[69]Holthausen and Larcker, similarly, viewed their results as somewhat of a puzzle for similar reasons:

> We find it surprising that a statistical model, derived without any consideration of any economic foundations, can earn excess returns of the magnitude determined here. Had our trading strategy been based on some new economic insight that others had never considered, or if it had been based upon hours of diligent investigation of annual reports of the firm, its suppliers, customers, the industry, and/or government documents, we would be more convinced that the trading strategy was earning "true" excess returns. As such, we view the results of our paper as something of a puzzle, similar in spirit to other evidence which is inconsistent with joint tests of market efficiency and asset pricing. (R. W. Holthausen and D. F. Larcker, "The Prediction of Stock Returns Using Financial Statement Information," *Journal of Accounting and Economics*, June/Sept. 1992, p. 410.)

earnings surprise combined with a disproportionate inventory increase, or an order backlog decrease, will have different valuation implications than an identical earnings surprise accompanied by an order backlog increase or a labor force decrease. . . .[70]

On an industry level, a number of studies have taken a contextual approach. Amir and Lev (1996) examined the wireless communication industry and showed that accounting information had relevance only once nonaccounting industry-specific variables were considered. A number of studies [e.g. Beatty et al. (1995), Collins, et al. (1995), and Bishop (1996)] have looked at the banking industry. Eccher (1996) examined the computer software industry.

Although many of these latter studies are an improvement insofar as they are based on *a priori* relationships, they still lack a formal model relating firm value to accounting variables.

Coming Full Circle: From Edwards and Bell to Ohlson

This gap is filled by Ohlson, whose research took time to be accepted by the rest of the academic community. With Ohlson (1995) and Feltham and Ohlson (1995), accounting research came full circle.[71] These papers rediscovered and expanded on valuation equations originally put forth by Edwards and Bell (1961) and Preinreich (1938). Ou and Penman, referring to the valuation relationships emanating from the EBO (Edwards and Bell, and Ohlson) paradigm, note (p. 8) that the equations

. . . are presumably what traditional fundamental analysts had in mind when they talked of "buying (future) earnings."

Unlike valuation models in vogue in the finance literature that "undo" the accounting (accrual) process, using (free) cash flows to arrive at value, these (i.e., Ohlson's) models express value using basic accounting variables such as earnings, ROE, and book values. These models:

1. Provide theoretical underpinnings for some of the results of market-based empirical research, and
2. More important, supply a framework for future research by directly connecting accounting variables and (intrinsic) value.

In doing so, these models have become "hot." Bernard (1995) refers to the work by Ohlson and Feltham as one of the most important developments in capital market research in the last several years. These studies have spawned a number of papers and research directions. For example, Easton et al. (1992) show that over long horizons, price changes can be explained by a prespecified earnings model. The results of Ohlson (1989) provide insight as to whether ERCs should be defined in terms of earnings levels or earnings changes (or both). Penman (1996) analyzes which variables are relevant in differentiating price/book and price/earnings ratios.

---

[70]Baruch Lev and S. Ramu Thiagarajan, "Fundamental Information Analysis," *Journal of Accounting Research*, Autumn 1993, pp. 190–215.

[71]These papers were originally completed in 1991 and 1992, respectively, and earlier versions were well known in the academic community. As noted, it took some time until the work was accepted.

More detailed discussion of the valuation models as well as research in this area is deferred to Chapter 19. As with any research effort in its development stages, judgment with respect to its ultimate efficacy must be suspended.

IMPLICATIONS OF EMPIRICAL RESEARCH FOR FINANCIAL STATEMENT ANALYSIS

The empirical studies reviewed in this chapter put to rest a number of beliefs, some of which, with hindsight, may have been overly naive in the first place. Financial markets are not simplistic and do not react in knee-jerk fashion to accounting information. On the contrary, the reactions seem to be complex enough that the vast methodological carpet bombing of the past quarter-century has not been able to uncover them.

The current state of academic research can be summarized as having one or more of the following characteristics:

- Further *theoretical development* and *empirical validation* of valuation models that relate accounting variables to value
- Development of (forecasting) models that predict *future values* of those *accounting variables deemed relevant by the theoretical models*
- Analysis of *firm-specific* and/or *industry-specific* valuation models

These characteristics indicate that future research should focus on understanding the work of the financial analyst as well as the relationships between accounting variables and market prices. Analysts seem to be the driving force keeping the market intelligent, and there is evidence that they lead the market.[72] Moreover, it is acknowledged that "better" analysts can carve out worthwhile areas of expertise.

Positive theory has contributed by pointing out that there are important contractual considerations that cannot be ignored when examining accounting data.

Classical theory, at the same time, cannot be discarded for two reasons. Even if one disagrees with the view that theory can dictate "correct" accounting standards, the fact remains that much of GAAP is based on the measurement of theoretical constructs. Thus, in analyzing financial statements, it is important to know the underlying principles that argue for a given treatment before interpreting or adjusting it to the analyst's own view. Second, empirical evidence shows that accounting data generated by the accrual process are value-relevant both *ex post* and *ex ante*.

At the same time, the analyst must be aware that the relationships governing accounting information involve complex interactions among investors, managers, and regulators and these interactions may have powerful implications for securities valuation.

In conclusion, accounting research has clearly not proven that financial analysis is a futile exercise. On the contrary, it is trying to get a better understanding of how financial analysis works. Although financial markets have become increasingly sophisticated in recent years, we believe that superior financial analysis is still rewarding. We advance three arguments for this belief:

1. The ability to understand the impact of alternative accounting methods places the investor at a competitive advantage in a world of increasingly complex transactions and sophisticated analytic techniques.

---

[72] A more detailed discussion of analyst forecasts and other forecasting models is presented in Chapter 19.

2. Market efficiency cannot be taken for granted, especially for smaller, less intensively researched companies.

3. Recent financial history provides many cases where financial markets ignored warning signals, at least in retrospect. Those left "holding the bag" suffered significant financial losses. Investors in banks and other financial intermediaries are but one example of this phenomenon.

At the same time, we would be foolish to ignore the lessons learned from the research and theory reviewed. Successful investing cannot simply focus on financial statements themselves. An awareness of the environment of the firm and its management is needed for proper analysis.

As Bernard stated:

There is much groundwork to be laid. . . moving to within-industry analyses, explicitly considering how the information conveyed by accounting numbers is conditioned on the accounting context, gaining a better understanding of the relations among accounting numbers before understanding price data, emphasizing economic interpretation more and statistics less—may be useful in laying that groundwork.[73]

We agree with that point of view and believe that this book can be useful in laying such a groundwork. It is with this belief that we continue with the remaining chapters of this book.

Chapter 5

Problems

1. [Approaches to accounting standard setting] In Chapter 1 (see p. 11) under the topic of "the hierarchy of accounting qualities," one of the elements discussed is the quality of neutrality:

Neutrality is concerned with whether financial statement data are biased. FASB proposals are frequently the object of complaints that companies will be adversely affected by the new standard. The principle of neutrality states that the Board should consider only the relevance and reliability of the data, not any possible economic impact.

Contrast this approach to accounting standard setting with that taken:

(i) By academics in drawing conclusions from "information content" studies

(ii) By proponents of the "positive" approach to accounting theory

2. [Predictability, "surprises," and information content] Suppose it were possible to evaluate the effects on stock prices of two information systems: Alpha and Gamma. Each produces two accounting reports. The second report of each system will be identical. Information system Alpha allows you to predict the second report more accurately than the Gamma system.

[73]Bernard, p. 106

A. Which of the two systems do you believe to be a better information system?

B. Under which system would the second report show more information content?

C. What is the implication of your replies to parts A and B on the factors that must be considered when evaluating the usefulness of financial reporting systems?

D. Ingberman and Sorter in their paper, "The Role of Financial Statements in an Efficient Market," *Journal of Accounting, Auditing and Finance*, Fall 1978, pp. 58–62, suggest that

> . . . financial statements are seldom the place in which significant firm-related events are initially reported. Instead, these statements help the investor to construct a forecasting model for future income and cash flows. During the period, firm-related events become known in various ways, and these are inserted into the forecasting model.

How does this view relate to your reply to parts A through C and the approach used by information content studies?

3. [Efficient market hypothesis, 1994 CFA adapted] The efficient market hypothesis (EMH) exists in three forms: *weak, semistrong*, and *strong*.

A. Briefly discuss the implications of each of these forms for investment policy as it applies to:

(i) Technical analysis (e.g., charting), and

(ii) Fundamental analysis

B. *Assuming the EMH holds*, discuss two major roles or responsibilities of portfolio managers in an efficient market hypothesis.

C. *Given the empirical evidence to date*, what are possible roles for investment managers?

4. [Implications of adjusting for general market conditions] Assume that new information arrived affecting all aspects of the economy. Under standard research procedures, using a model such as the capital asset pricing model to test for market reaction, what would the results show? What does this imply about the nature of conclusions that can be drawn from certain market studies? Can you think of any (mandated) accounting standards that may have had pervasive effects across many sectors of the economy?

5. [Accounting standard setting] It has been said by some that

> generally accepted accounting principles are anything but principled. How could they be? They are a product of a political process.

How would the proponents of the three approaches to accounting theory view this statement?

6. [Motivation for income manipulation] A *Business Week* (February 14, 1994, pp. 78–92) article entitled, "Did Pfizer Doctor Its Numbers," suggests that for the 1993 fiscal year, Pfizer, a pharmaceutical and chemical company, "managed down the numbers." Specifically, the article contends that:

> the company is spending heavily and delaying sales to deliberately dampen Pfizer's profit growth rates. . . . Pfizer pinched fourth-quarter sales while boosting expenses. . . . Pfizer also boosted R&D spending more than its rivals.

Can you suggest why Pfizer might have engaged in such actions?

7. [Implications for analysis] WSF Investment Services has a policy of completing a "company profile" for each new company whose financial statements it intends to analyze. You have been hired by WSF as an instructor in their training program. For each item on the checklist, explain to a trainee what the relevance might be for financial analysis:

(i) Terms of labor contract

(ii) Number of analysts following the company

(iii) Details of management compensation plans

(iv) Capitalization size

(v) The proportion of stock held by managers

(vi) Industry classification

8. [Mandated accounting changes, economic consequences, market reaction] *Newsweek* (January 11, 1993, p. 59) reports that a survey

> found that two-thirds of major corporations have curtailed retiree health plans or intend to in 1993.

The article attributes the curtailment of such benefits to

> a change in the national accounting rules that, beginning this year, require companies to carry the cost of such benefits as liabilities on their balance sheets. Technically, the new rule is a hit only on paper. But critics say many companies are using it as an excuse to cut costs and renege on past promises to workers.

Evaluate the argument made in the *Newsweek* article in the context of the accounting theories discussed in the chapter. Consideration should be given to the following points:

A. How consistent is the article with the efficient market and/or positive theory views of accounting?

B. The possibility that firms were not aware of the magnitude of the health costs until the new accounting rule came into effect.

C. What market reaction might you expect to the

(i) New accounting rule?

(ii) Subsequent balance sheet disclosures?

(iii) "Results" of the survey?

D. Do curtailments of health plans around the time of the implementation of the new accounting rule necessarily show the "economic consequences" of accounting rules?

EXHIBIT 5P-1
Selected Indices and News Reports, February 24–25, 1993

February 24, 1993

	Close	Change	Percent
Overall Averages			
Dow Jones Industrial Average	3356.50	+33.23	1.0%
S&P 500	440.87	+6.07	1.4%
NASDAQ Composite	662.46	+10.90	1.7%
Technology (Dow Jones)	331.14	+6.81	2.1%
Industry Group Performance			
Biotechnology	669.27	+34.50	5.4%
Computers	275.35	+3.00	1.1%
Heavy machinery	167.73	+4.73	2.9%
Closing Prices			
Amgen	46¼	+2¾	6.3%
Dell Computers	30⅛	−6⅛	−16.9%
Deere	50¾	+2½	5.2%

The following news items are from *The New York Times*, Feb. 25, 1993, p. D3.

Amgen Shares Plummet After Profit Forecast

Shares of Amgen, Inc., a biotechnology company, plunged in after-hours trading yesterday after the company said it expected its first-quarter earnings to come in well below Wall Street expectations. Amgen made the disclosure after regular trading hours, when its shares had closed on NASDAQ at $46.25, up $2.75. But in the half-hour of after-hour trading, shares plummeted $9, to $37.25.

Amgen's chief financial officer, Lowell Sears, said the company had anticipated that earnings per share for the first quarter would be 10 to 15 percent lower than Wall Street's average estimate of 60 cents a share. . . .

Dell's Stock Price Plunges After Forecast
by Thomas C. Hayes

Dallas, Feb. 24—The stock of the Dell Computer Corporation plummeted nearly 17 percent today after analysts said an earnings projection for the current fiscal year raised worries that the fast-growing maker of personal computers had quietly reduced its long-term profit goal to below 5 percent of sales.

The projection by Dell's chief financial officer was part of the announcement that it had withdrawn an offering of four million new common shares because its stock price fell sharply recently and because declining interest rates made borrowing more attractive.

The earnings and revenue projections were interpreted as a sign of Dell's determination to expand in the months ahead a price war [sic] that has crimped its profitability and pushed smaller rivals into financial distress.

Dell's stock fell $6.125 today, to $30.125, on volume of more than 9.5 million shares—the heaviest in NASDAQ trading. The stock hit an all-time high of $49.875 only last month.

Deere Plans to Expand Production This Year

Deere & Company, the world's largest producer of agricultural machinery, told shareholders yesterday at its annual meeting in Moline, Ill., that it would expand production this year for the first time since 1990. Hans W. Becherer, chairman and chief executive, said output would grow 5 percent this year, thanks to sharp reductions in inventories at dealers, renewed buying from American farmers and the appeal of new products. Growth would be even stronger, he said, but for declines in the European market, where debates about the level of farm price and production supports have made farmers cautious about investing in new machinery.

9. [News releases, market reaction, and abnormal returns] Exhibit 5P-1 contains information as to:

(i) Closing prices and news items/releases of three companies

(ii) The performance of various market indices on February 24, 1993

A. Ignoring the news items for the moment, which of the three stocks do you believe exhibited abnormal returns? How would you go about determining whether that was the case?

B. The Amgen news was disclosed after the market close. Thus, the closing price and price change do not reflect the news. Is the sharp market reaction to the news an indication of market efficiency, or does the lack of anticipation of the news indicate inefficiency? Can this same type of question be asked with respect to the price change in the last month of Dell's shares?

C. The news items for Amgen and Dell imply that the price change was in reaction to the news reported. In the case of Deere, although that argument can be made, the article does not do so. For which of these news releases can you argue that the market reaction is associated with the news release?

D. In the case of Dell, why is it particularly difficult to determine the "cause" of the market reaction?

E. Most research studies would test for the market reaction to an announcement coming after the close of the market on the basis of the market reaction of the following day. In the case of Amgen, its shares on February 25, 1993, the following day, closed at 37, down 9.25 or 20%. The biotechnology index closed at 591.07, down 11.68%.

(i) Under these circumstances why might a research study underestimate the effects of the earnings announcement?

(ii) *The Wall Street Journal* reported that the weakest stocks in the biotechnology group (on February 25, 1993) were Amgen, Chiron, and Centocor. Chiron stock fell by 1.02% and Centocor was unchanged. How does this information affect your response to (i)?

F. These news items are examples of the flow of information about a company during the year. Assuming the projections implied by these news items prove to be true, what should the market reaction be when the financial statements are released? Do these news items make financial statements irrelevant?

G. The Deere article does not deal with earnings, but rather with production. Do financial statements have any relevance in the context of news items of this sort?

10. [Disclosure, need for regulation] In describing the financial reporting environment, William H. Beaver (*Financial Reporting: An Accounting Revolution*, Englewood Cliffs, N.J. Prentice Hall, 1989) portrays an environment in which investors with (perhaps) limited access to or knowledge of financial information make use of financial intermediaries/analysts. These intermediaries provide information gathering as well as investment services and compete with each other in the information processing function. Managers and firms compete for investors' capital by producing and disseminating information to investors and their intermediaries. The information provided is often more timely than the annual report or SEC filings.

Given this environment, Beaver suggests that there exist incentives for firms to produce information on their own in the absence of any regulation. Given this argument, discuss the need for regulators such as the SEC and FASB to mandate the type and form of disclosure required.

[*Note*: The interested reader is referred to Chapter 7 of Beaver's book.]

11. [Regulatory accounting, market reaction, and economic consequences] Certain regulated industries such as utilities, banks, and insurance companies are subject to accounting rules, known as Regulatory Accounting Principles (RAP). These RAP rules, which can differ from GAAP, are the basis by which, for example, the permitted rate of profit is calculated. Additionally, for many of these industries, certain minimum net worth requirements must be met. RAP governs how these requirements are measured.

The following article, by Greg Steinmetz, appeared in *The Wall Street Journal* on January 8, 1993:

Certain Life Insurers Plan Reserves for Real Estate Losses due to New Rule

Giant, policyholder-owned life insurance companies plan to set aside billions of dollars in coming months to cover potential losses from real estate holdings.

The actions do not signify further deterioration in the companies' real estate holdings, nor will they seriously weaken the companies' financial strength. Rather, they stem from an accounting change that affects already identified problems. The change will bring the insurers' reserves up to the levels already established by publicly traded insurers. . . .

The new rules, established by the National Association of Insurance Commissioners, require companies to build reserves to a level determined by a complicated formula. Insurers have several years to build the reserve to their minimum requirement.

The new rules came in response to criticism that insurance accounting practices let insurers hide losses. The rules are also part of an effort to ward off federal regulation of insurance, which is now overseen by states.

In anticipation of the new rules, some insurers began to voluntarily put up real estate reserves in 1991.

A. Notwithstanding the manner in which the first paragraph was written, no actual cash is set aside in these reserves. They are merely accounting entries. Would proponents of the efficient market hypothesis view this accounting change as cosmetic? Should one expect the market to react when it first "heard" about the accounting change? Can you predict what the nature of the reaction might be?

B. Would one expect to see any market reaction around the time this article was published? In what direction?

C. Discuss the similarities between the implications of changes in RAP and the "positive accounting" approach to GAAP.

12. [Market "crashes" and efficient markets] On October 19, 1987, the Dow Jones Industrial Average dropped by over 500 points. Overall market value on the New York Stock Exchange stocks fell by close to 25% on that day. What are the implications of the crash for the efficient market theory?

6

ANALYSIS OF INVENTORIES

CHAPTER OUTLINE

CHAPTER OBJECTIVES

INTRODUCTION

INVENTORY AND COST OF GOODS SOLD: BASIC RELATIONSHIPS
Scenario 1: Stable Prices
Scenario 2: Rising Prices

COMPARISON OF INFORMATION PROVIDED BY ALTERNATIVE METHODS
Balance Sheet Information: Inventory Account
   Inventory Valuation: Lower of Cost or Market
Income Statement Information: Cost of Goods Sold

LIFO VERSUS FIFO: INCOME, CASH FLOW, AND WORKING CAPITAL EFFECTS

ADJUSTMENT FROM LIFO TO FIFO
Adjustment of Inventory Balances
   Example: Sun Company
Adjustment of Cost of Goods Sold
   Example: Sun Company

ADJUSTMENT OF INCOME TO CURRENT COST INCOME
   Example: Amerada-Hess

FINANCIAL RATIOS: LIFO VERSUS FIFO
Profitability: Gross Profit Margin
Liquidity: Working Capital
Activity: Inventory Turnover
   Inventory Theory and Turnover Ratios
   Economic Order Quantity
   Just in Time
   The FIFO/LIFO Choice and Inventory Holding Policy
Solvency: Debt to Equity Ratio

DECLINES IN LIFO RESERVE
LIFO Liquidations
Declining Prices
   Example: Wyman-Gordon

INITIAL ADOPTION OF LIFO AND CHANGES TO AND FROM LIFO
Initial Adoption of LIFO
Change from LIFO Method
   Example: Champion Enterprises

LIFO: A HISTORICAL AND EMPIRICAL PERSPECTIVE
Overview of FIFO/LIFO Choice
Summary of FIFO/LIFO Choice

CONCLUDING COMMENTS ON ACCOUNTING FOR INVENTORIES
   Example: British Petroleum

257

INTERNATIONAL ACCOUNTING AND REPORTING PRACTICES
IASC Standard 2

USING INVENTORY BALANCES TO AID IN FORECASTING

SUMMARY

CASE 6-1: INVENTORY ANALYSIS OF NUCOR

APPENDIX 6-A: LIFO MEASUREMENT ISSUES
LIFO Inventory Methods
Interim Reporting Under LIFO

APPENDIX 6-B: THE FIFO/LIFO CHOICE: EMPIRICAL STUDIES

CHAPTER OBJECTIVES

In this chapter, we discuss:

1. The alternative accounting methods used by companies to account for product inventory: LIFO, FIFO, and average cost.

2. The usefulness of inventory and cost of goods sold data provided by these different accounting methods

3. Cash flow and working capital effects of the choice of inventory method

4. How price increases and decreases affect reported income under different accounting methods

5. The effect of inventory method on financial ratios

6. How to adjust the financial statements of companies using different accounting methods to achieve comparability

7. How reported financial results can be adjusted to remove distortions caused by price changes

8. The two very different signals transmitted by a decline in the LIFO reserve

9. What research tells us about why firms choose to adopt (or not to adopt) the LIFO method

10. The inventory methods used outside the United States

INTRODUCTION

In early August 1990, after the invasion of Kuwait by Iraq, the spot price of oil rose from approximately $20 a barrel to almost $30 a barrel. Simultaneously, the price of gasoline sold at the pump increased by 15 to 20%. Consumers and politicians criticized oil companies for immediately raising the price of gasoline sold at the retail level. They argued that the gasoline being sold had been refined from oil purchased at a price of $20 a barrel and, hence, raising the price of this "old" gasoline resulted in windfall profits.

The oil companies countered that since the market price of oil had risen, replacing the old oil now cost more and thus raising the price of gasoline was justified and reflective of current market conditions.

The accounting choice of last-in, first-out (LIFO) versus first-in, first-out (FIFO) for inventory and cost of goods sold (COGS) mirrors this debate as to the more appropriate measure of income. The choice affects the firm's income statement, balance sheet, and related ratios. Perhaps more important, the decision has real cash flow effects as taxes paid by the firm are affected by its choice of accounting method.

INVENTORY AND COST OF GOODS SOLD: BASIC RELATIONSHIPS

The inventory account is affected by two events: the purchase (or manufacture) of goods (P) and their subsequent sale (COGS). The relationship between these events and the balance of beginning inventory (BI) and ending inventory (EI) can be expressed as

$$EI = BI + P - \text{COGS} \quad \text{or}$$
$$BI + P = \text{COGS} + EI$$

For any period, prior to the preparation of financial statements for the period, the left side of the equation is known: the beginning inventory plus purchases (cost of goods acquired for sale during the period). Preparation of the income statement and balance sheet for the period requires the allocation of these costs ($BI + P$) between COGS and ending inventory. This process is illustrated under two scenarios:

Beginning inventory: 200 units @ $10/unit = $2,000

Quarter	Purchases Units	Scenario 1: Stable Prices Unit Cost	Scenario 1: Stable Prices Purchases Dollars	Scenario 2: Rising Prices Unit Cost	Scenario 2: Rising Prices Purchases Dollars
1	100	$10	$1,000	$11	$1,100
2	150	10	1,500	12	1,800
3	150	10	1,500	13	1,950
4	100	10	1,000	14	1,400
Total	500		$5,000		$6,250
			$BI + P = \$7,000$		$BI + P = \$8,250$

Units sold: 100 units per quarter for a total of 400 units
Ending inventory: 300 units

Scenario 1: Stable Prices

Beginning inventory plus purchases equals $7,000. Since unit costs are constant at $10 per unit and 400 units were sold, the COGS equals $4,000 (400 × $10) and the cost of the 300 units in ending inventory equals $3,000 (300 × $10).

$$BI + P = \text{COGS} + EI$$
$$\$2,000 + \$5,000 = \$4,000 + \$3,000$$

However, perfectly stable prices are the exception rather than the norm. In addition to general inflationary pressures, costs and prices for specific goods are constantly changing. Accounting for inventory and COGS in such an environment, as a result, becomes more complex.

Scenario 2: Rising Prices

Beginning inventory plus purchases equals $8,250. Unlike the case of stable prices, the allocation between COGS and the cost of ending inventory requires an assumption as to the flow of costs. Essentially, three alternative assumptions are possible: *FIFO; LIFO; and weighted-average cost.*

EXHIBIT 6-1
Allocation of Costs Under Different Inventory Methods, Scenario 2

A. FIFO

The 400 units sold (COGS) are assumed to carry the earliest costs incurred and the 300 units left in inventory carry the latest costs:

COGS	Ending Inventory
200 @ $10 = $2,000	100 @ $14 = $1,400
100 @ $11 = $1,100	150 @ $13 = $1,950
100 @ $12 = $1,200	50 @ $12 = $ 600
400 $4,300	300 $3,950

B. LIFO

The 400 units sold (COGS) are assumed to carry the latest costs incurred and the 300 units left in inventory carry the earliest costs:

COGS	Ending Inventory
100 @ $14 = $1,400	200 @ $10 = $2,000
150 @ $13 = $1,950	100 @ $11 = $1,100
150 @ $12 = $1,800	
400 $5,150	300 $3,100

C. Weighted-Average

The total costs for the 700 units = $8,250. On a per unit basis, this results in a weighted-average unit cost of:

$$\frac{\$8,250}{700} = \$11.786$$

$$COGS = 400 \times \$11.786 = \$4,714$$
$$\text{Ending inventory} = 300 \times \$11.786 = \$3,536$$

FIFO accounting assumes that the costs of items *first purchased* are deemed to be the costs of items *first sold* and these costs enter COGS; ending inventory is made up of the cost of the most recent items purchased.

At the opposite extreme is LIFO accounting where items *last purchased* are assumed to be the ones *first sold* and the ending inventory is made up of the earliest costs incurred.

Finally, as its name implies, weighted-average cost accounting uses the (same) average cost for both the items sold and those remaining in closing inventory.

In our example, *the assumptions of rising prices and an increase in the inventory balance generate three alternative allocations of the cost of goods available for sale,* (*BI + P*), on the income statement and balance sheet (the calculations are shown in Exhibit 6-1):

	BI	+	P	=	COGS	+	EI
FIFO	$2,000	+	$6,250	=	$4,300	+	$3,950
Weighted-average	2,000	+	6,250	=	4,714	+	3,536
LIFO	2,000	+	6,250	=	5,150	+	3,100

COMPARISON OF INFORMATION PROVIDED BY ALTERNATIVE METHODS

This section compares the information provided by the three alternative accounting methods.

Balance Sheet Information: Inventory Account

The ending inventory consists of 300 units. At current replacement cost (i.e., the fourth-quarter unit cost of $14), the inventory would have a carrying value of $4,200. The FIFO inventory of $3,950 comes closest to this amount because FIFO allocates the earliest costs to COGS, leaving the most recent costs in ending inventory.

Conversely, the LIFO balance of $3,100 is furthest from the current cost as LIFO accounting allocates the earliest (outdated) costs to ending inventory. In fact, the cost of ending inventory for many companies using LIFO may be decades old[1] and virtually useless as an indicator of the current or replacement cost of inventories on hand.

From a balance sheet perspective, therefore, inventories based on FIFO are preferable to those presented under LIFO, as carrying values most closely reflect current cost. In other words, FIFO provides a measure of inventory that is closer to its current (economic) value.

The carrying amount of inventory can also be affected by changes in market value as discussed below.

Inventory Valuation: Lower of Cost or Market

GAAP requires the use of the lower-of-cost-or-market-valuation basis (LCM) for inventories, with market value defined as replacement cost.[2] The LCM valuation basis follows the principle of conservatism (on both the balance sheet and income statement) since it recognizes losses or declines in market value as they occur, whereas increases are reported only when inventory is sold. LCM can be used with LIFO for financial statement purposes. However, for tax purposes LIFO cannot be combined with LCM. Firms using LIFO cannot recognize (and obtain tax benefits from) write-downs and declines in market value for tax purposes.[3]

Income Statement Information: Cost of Goods Sold

Consider a situation where an item purchased for $6 is sold for $10 at a time when it costs $7 to replace it. Prior to replacement of the item, reported income is $4 ($10 − $6). However, if income is defined as the amount available for distribution to shareholders without impairing the firm's operations, then it can be argued that income is only $3, as $7 (not the original cost of $6) are needed to replace the item in inventory and continue operations. The $1 difference between the original cost of the item and

---

[1]For example, Caterpillar's *1995 Annual Report* states that the LIFO method "was first adopted for the major portion of inventories in 1950."

[2]However, replacement cost cannot exceed the net realizable value or be below the net realizable value less the normal profit margin.

[3]Otherwise, the firm could have the best of both worlds and obtain tax savings whether costs were rising or declining.

the cost of replacement is referred to as a holding gain or inventory profit,[4] and it is debatable whether this amount should be considered income.[5]

In our hypothetical case, *only if the item were not replaced* would there be $10 to distribute to shareholders, indicating income of $4. Under a going concern assumption, however, firms that sell their inventory need to replenish it constantly for sales in the future. Thus, income should be measured after providing for the replacement of inventory. In addition, the increase in inventory costs suggests that income of $3 is a better indicator of expected future income than $4.

In our example, the replacement cost of the items sold (using the unit cost for each quarter) is $5,000[6] [(100 × $11) + (100 × $12) + (100 × $13) + (100 × $14)]. As U.S. GAAP use a historical cost framework, however, replacement cost accounting is not permitted. LIFO allocates the most recent purchase prices to COGS. The reported LIFO COGS of $5,150 is, therefore, closest to the replacement cost, with the FIFO COGS of $4,300 furthest from this cost. During periods of rising prices and stable or growing inventories, LIFO is the most informative accounting method for income statement purposes, in that it provides a better measure of current income and future profitability. This leaves us in something of a quandary, since FIFO provides the best measure for the balance sheet.[7]

The preceding discussion implied the use of a single method for all inventories of the firm. In practice, firms often use more than one inventory method. They may use different methods for their foreign operations since LIFO is rarely used outside the United States, or they may use different methods for particular business segments. This factor serves to disguise further the impact of reported inventory on the income statement and balance sheet.

Additionally, the LIFO measurements are based on assumptions and estimates that are complex in a multiproduct environment, and are affected by management choice. These problems are detailed in Appendix 6-A.

Finally, the use of FIFO, LIFO, or weighted-average for the allocation of cost of goods available for sale is preceded by the determination of costs to be included in inventory. In a manufacturing environment, as Box 6-1 illustrates, that determination is also affected by management choice.

From an analyst's perspective the use of different methods is not so grim. Information is often available to permit restatement of financial statements from one method to the other. Such restatement is illustrated later in the chapter. Our discussion now, however, turns to pragmatic differences between LIFO and FIFO.

---

[4]If we use the terminology of Chapter 2, economic income equals 4. As the holding gain is 1, sustainable income is 3.

[5]The situation is analogous to having purchased a home before a rapid increase in real estate prices and not being able to benefit from your good fortune because any replacement home would cost as much as the home you live in now.

[6]If the computation is done on an annual basis, the replacement cost would be $5,600 (400 × $14) using the most recent purchase price to measure replacement cost.

[7]The weighted-average method falls someplace in between the FIFO and LIFO methods both in terms of the balance sheet and income statement. It is seen by some as a compromise method. Alternatively, we can argue that it is the worst of the three choices: Unlike LIFO and FIFO, which provide good information on one financial statement, the weighted-average method does not do so for either statement. Practically speaking, however, the weighted-average method tends to be closer to FIFO than LIFO, especially with respect to inventory costs on the balance sheet.

BOX 6-1
Inventory Costing in a Manufacturing Environment

Accounting for inventories in a manufacturing environment adds another dimension to the problem of inventory costing. A merchandising operation has only one type of inventory, finished goods, and the costs of obtaining that inventory can be determined directly. They are the amounts charged by the supplier of the finished goods.

Manufacturing operations, on the other hand, carry three types of inventory:

1. Raw material
2. Work in process
3. Finished goods

Costs included in the various stages of inventory are raw material costs and labor and overhead costs that are needed to transform the raw material into finished goods. Determining the amount of overhead costs, or indirect costs, poses the most problems. The magnitude of these problems can be appreciated if we consider the nature of some of the items included in (factory) overhead:

- Supervisors' salaries
- Rent of factory plant and equipment
- Depreciation of factory plant and equipment
- Utilities
- Employee benefits such as pensions, health insurance, etc.
- Repairs and maintenance
- Engineering costs
- Quality control

Let us consider the utility bill in a factory producing 50 different product lines. How much of the utility cost should be charged to each product line? Costs of this kind are *joint costs* and, in a multiproduct environment, it is impossible to determine, *a priori*, how much of the cost should be charged or allocated to any given product. An estimated allocation method is required. As the amount charged to any one product line depends on the chosen allocation procedure, results can be somewhat arbitrary and capable of manipulation. That is, manufacturers can increase income by choosing an allocation scheme that charges more of the overhead costs to slow-moving items. These costs then remain in inventory as an asset and their expense recognition is delayed until the products are sold.

A second aspect of this problem relates to the fixed nature of many of these costs. Items such as depreciation, rent, or supervisors' salaries will not increase (in the short run) with changes in production. Therefore, allocating their cost to products involves an averaging process that is subject to manipulation by changing levels of production. A simple example in a single product environment will illustrate this.

Assume a company has factory rent of $12,000 and it sells 10,000 units. If it only produces 10,000 units, the full $12,000 of factory rent will flow through COGS (at a rate of $1.20/unit) and be expensed. If the company increases production to 12,000 units, then factory rent is charged at $1.00/unit. But if it sells only 10,000 units, then $2,000 of rent cost will remain in inventory and only $10,000 will be expensed as part of COGS. The company has increased income by manipulating production rather than increasing sales.

It should be noted that although we speak of manipulation, it does not mean such manipulation must be willful. As the allocation method is by necessity based on estimation, any resultant income number is suspect because a different allocation method would have yielded a different income number. This inherent arbitrariness makes it imperative for the analyst to monitor:

- The accounting policies used by different firms in the same industry
- The effects of fluctuations in production on COGS and reported income.

Finally, it must be noted that there does not exist uniformity as to which costs are charged to inventory (and then expensed when sold) and which costs are expensed as incurred. Schiff (1987) notes that although it is commonly suggested in accounting textbooks that fixed overhead costs must be allocated to inventory, in practice, many companies* have (historically) charged certain overhead costs directly to expense. Examples of such costs are depreciation, pension costs, and property taxes. For companies that expense these costs, variations in production and inventory levels will not affect the amount expensed. It will always equal the amount incurred. However, in firms that allocate these costs to inventory, when inventory levels increase, the amount expensed will be less than the amount actually incurred with the difference remaining in inventory. On the balance sheet, those firms that capitalize more costs in inventory will have higher carrying values of inventory, working capital, and equity balances. Unfortunately, not all companies disclose their practices in this respect. This can make comparisons between companies difficult.

In recent years, a number of firms that had been expensing such items have changed their inventory costing method and begun to capitalize them.† The motivation may be to conform to their method of tax accounting since the Tax Reform Act of 1986 limited the number of items that could be expensed directly. Alternatively, with the beginning of the recession at the end of the 1980s, firms changed their method to improve reported income, keeping some of their fixed costs off the income statement by capitalizing them.

Additionally, with the increased emphasis in recent years on improving their manufacturing process, many firms have been adjusting their method of inventory costing. This does not relate to only the issue of which items to include as part of inventory cost, but also the allocation procedures used.

---

*The steel industry is one example noted by Schiff.

†Bartley and Chen (1992) report 27 companies that changed their inventory accounting method in this fashion in the two-year period 1986 to 1987. All the changes resulted in an increase in income.

LIFO VERSUS FIFO: INCOME, CASH FLOW, AND WORKING CAPITAL EFFECTS

The above example illustrates that, in periods of rising prices and stable or increasing inventory quantities, the use of LIFO results in higher COGS expense and lower reported income. In the absence of income taxes, there would be no difference in cash flow. Cash flow would equal payments made for inventory purchases and be independent of the accounting method used.

When LIFO is a permitted method for income taxes, however, lower income translates into lower taxes and thus higher cash flows. In the United States, unlike other accounting policy choices that allow differing methods of accounting for financial statements and tax purposes, *IRS regulations require that the same method of inventory accounting used for tax purposes also be used for financial reporting.* From an economic perspective, given rising prices, LIFO is the better choice, as taxes will be lower and cash flows will be higher despite the lower reported income.[8]

---

[8]The question of why, given the foregoing, all firms do not use LIFO will be considered later in the chapter.

In Chapter 4 (concerning ratios), it was noted that working capital is used as an expanded liquidity measure because it includes cash and near-cash assets. Inventory accounting can distort the working capital measure and lead to erroneous and contradictory conclusions. LIFO accounting results in higher cash flows, but it reports lower working capital because the inventory balances retain earlier (lower) costs and the cash saved is only a percentage (the marginal tax rate) of the difference in inventory values.

In periods of rising prices and stable or increasing inventory quantities, the impact of LIFO and FIFO on the financial statements can be summarized as

	LIFO	FIFO
COGS	Higher	Lower
Income before taxes	Lower	Higher
Income taxes	Lower	Higher
Net income	Lower	Higher
Cash flows	**Higher**	**Lower**
Inventory balance	Lower	Higher
Working capital	Lower	Higher

Cash flow has been highlighted because it is the only amount with direct economic impact. The others are accounting constructs and their economic significance is indirect and informational.

Continuing with the previous numeric example and assuming that 400 units are sold for $10,000 (average price of $25) with a tax rate of 40%, we can illustrate the above differences as follows. The resulting income statements are

	FIFO	LIFO	LIFO Higher/(Lower) by
Sales	$10,000	$10,000	$ 0
COGS	4,300	5,150	850
Income before tax	$ 5,700	$ 4,850	(850)
Income tax @ 40%	2,280	1,940	(340)
Net income	$ 3,420	$ 2,910	$(510)

If we assume that sales are for cash and payments for purchases and taxes are made immediately, then cash flows are

	FIFO	LIFO	LIFO Higher/(Lower) by
Sales inflows	$10,000	$10,000	$ 0
Purchases	6,250	6,250	0
Inflows before tax	$ 3,750	$ 3,750	0
Income tax paid	2,280	1,940	(340)
Net cash flows	$ 1,470	$ 1,810	$ 340

Therefore, changes in balance sheet accounts are

Assets

	FIFO	LIFO	LIFO Higher/(Lower) by
Cash*	$1,470	$1,810	$ 340
Inventory†	1,950	1,100	(850)
Working capital	$3,420	$2,910	$(510)

Liabilities and Stockholders' Equity

	FIFO	LIFO	LIFO Higher/(Lower) by
Retained earnings‡	$3,420	$2,910	$(510)

*Net cash flow for period.
†Purchases less COGS.
‡Net income for period.

The difference in net income of $510 and the difference in cash flows of $340 are related to the difference in COGS (equivalently the difference in inventory balances) of $850 as follows:

$$\begin{aligned}
\text{Difference in Income} &= (1 - \text{Tax Rate}) \times \text{Difference in COGS} \\
\$510 &= 0.6 \times \$850 \\
\text{Difference in Cash Flow} &= \text{Tax Rate} \times \text{Difference in COGS} \\
\$340 &= 0.4 \times \$850
\end{aligned}$$

However, these differences are in *opposite directions* with higher income for the FIFO firm and higher cash flows for the LIFO firm. The difference in working capital is the net of the difference in inventory balance and cash flow:

$$\$510 = \$850 - \$340$$

This results in misleading liquidity measures for the LIFO firm as its working capital is understated[9]: The increase in cash is more than offset by the understatement of inventory.

Our illustration has indicated that the choice of inventory method can greatly affect reported operating results. Moreover, depending on whether the focus is the balance sheet or income statement, differing methods may be preferred. Thus, the analyst needs to be able to adjust between LIFO and FIFO in order to:

- Eliminate differences between firms due to accounting methods so that any remaining differences reflect economic and operating variations.
- Obtain the measure(s) most relevant for their analytic purpose.

The next sections describe how such adjustments can be made.

[9]Johnson and Dhaliwal (1988) studied firms that abandoned LIFO in favor of FIFO. Their evidence suggests one possible motivation for the abandonment decision was to increase their reported working capital. Compared to firms that retained LIFO, the abandonment firms had tighter working capital constraints under their debt covenants.

ADJUSTMENT FROM LIFO TO FIFO

Adjustment of Inventory Balances

LIFO inventory balances generally contain older costs with little or no relationship to current costs. Because of this deficiency, firms are required to disclose the *LIFO reserve*. The LIFO reserve (usually shown in the financial statement footnotes, but sometimes on the face of the balance sheet) is the difference between the inventory balance shown on the balance sheet and the (approximately current or replacement cost) amount that would have been reported had the firm used FIFO.

To adjust inventory balances of firms using LIFO to current or FIFO cost, we must add the LIFO reserve to the LIFO inventory amount. We can express this as

$$\text{LIFO Reserve} = \text{Inventory}_F - \text{Inventory}_L$$

or

$$\text{Inventory}_F = \text{Inventory}_L + \text{LIFO Reserve}$$

(where the subscripts F and L represent the accounting methods FIFO and LIFO, respectively).

Example: Sun Company

Exhibit 6-2 contains details of inventory and portions of financial statement footnotes from the *1994 Annual Report* of Sun Company, a large oil refiner. Sun uses the LIFO method to account for virtually all crude oil and refined product inventories. Materials and supplies are excluded as LIFO accounting is not permitted for inventories not intended for sale to customers.

Exhibit 6-3A shows the adjustment of inventory from LIFO to FIFO, adding the LIFO reserve to the LIFO inventory. Sun's LIFO reserve is large, indicating that the balance sheet carrying amount significantly understates inventories. This understate-

---

EXHIBIT 6-2. SUN COMPANY
Inventory Disclosures

Inventories of crude oil and refined products are valued at the lower of cost or market. The cost of such inventories is determined principally using LIFO. Materials, supplies, and other inventories are valued principally at the lower of average cost or market.

Inventories at December 31 ($ in millions)	1991	1992	1993	1994
Crude oil	$147	$109	$140	$193
Refined products	229	261	244	335
Materials, supplies, and other	106	81	80	85
Total	$482	$451	$464	$613

The current replacement cost of all inventories valued at LIFO exceeded their carrying amount by $536, $530, $390, and $459 million at December 31, 1991 through 1994, respectively.

Source: Sun Company, *1992–1994 Annual Reports.*

EXHIBIT 6-3. SUN COMPANY
Adjustment from LIFO to FIFO, 1991 to 1994

Years Ended December 31 ($ in millions)

A. Adjusting LIFO Inventory to FIFO (Current) Cost

All Inventories	1991	1992	1993	1994
Total reported inventories*	$ 482	$ 451	$ 464	$ 613
LIFO reserve	536	530	390	459
Inventories at FIFO	$1,018	$ 981	$ 854	$1,072
Inventories Carried at LIFO				
Crude oil and refined products at LIFO	$ 376	$ 370	$ 384	$ 528
LIFO reserve	536	530	390	459
Crude oil and refined products at FIFO	$ 912	$ 900	$ 774	$ 987

B. Adjusting LIFO COGS to FIFO COGS

COGS at LIFO	$8,460	$7,192	$5,821	$6,276
Less: LIFO effect†	(299)	(6)	(140)	69
Equals: COGS at FIFO	$8,759	$7,198	$5,961	$6,207

*See Exhibit 6-2 for components and inventory methods used.
†Change in LIFO reserve.
Source: Sun Company, *1991–1994 Annual Reports.*

ment is typical of firms whose products have risen in price and that have used LIFO for many years. In the case of Sun, the LIFO cost (of inventories carried at LIFO) is only 54% of the FIFO cost in 1994.

Adjustment of Cost of Goods Sold

COGS can be derived using the opening and closing inventory balances and purchases for the period:

$$\textbf{COGS} = \textbf{\textit{BI}} + \textbf{\textit{P}} - \textbf{\textit{EI}}$$

Thus, to arrive at FIFO cost of goods sold ($COGS_F$), these figures need to be restated on a FIFO basis. The LIFO-to-FIFO adjustment in inventory balance was illustrated earlier. Purchases (which are not a function of the accounting method used) need not be adjusted and can be derived directly from the (opening and closing) inventory balances and COGS as stated in the financial statements:

$$\textbf{\textit{P}} = \textbf{COGS}_\text{L} + \textbf{\textit{EI}}_\text{L} - \textbf{\textit{BI}}_\text{L}$$

Example: Sun Company

For Sun Company, purchases for 1994 can be calculated ($ in millions) as

$$P = \$6,276 + \$613 - \$464$$
$$= \$6,425$$

To convert COGS from LIFO to FIFO, we need the restated inventories on a FIFO basis previously calculated in Exhibit 6-3A.

Using 1994 purchases, just calculated, and the FIFO inventory amounts derived in Exhibit 6-3 yields the 1994 COGS on a FIFO basis for Sun:

$$COGS_F = BI_F + P - EI_F$$
$$= \$854 \text{ million} + \$6,425 \text{ million} - \$1,072 \text{ million}$$
$$= \$6,207 \text{ million}$$

Thus COGS on a FIFO basis is lower than on a LIFO basis by \$69 million (\$6,276 million − \$6,207 million). The astute reader will note that this amount equals the increase in the LIFO reserve during the year (from \$390 to \$459 million). This is no coincidence and the adjustment from LIFO to FIFO COGS can be made directly from the LIFO reserve accounts without going through the intermediate steps of calculating purchases and adjusting inventories. The direct adjustment is[10]

$$\textbf{COGS}_F = \textbf{COGS}_L - \textbf{Change in LIFO Reserve}$$

or

$$\textbf{COGS}_F = \textbf{COGS}_L - (\textbf{LIFO Reserve}_E - \textbf{LIFO Reserve}_B)$$
$$\textbf{\$6,207 million} = \textbf{\$6,276 million} - (\textbf{\$459 million} - \textbf{\$390 million})$$

---

[10]For those with a more mathematical bent, this result can be proven as follows:

$$COGS_F = BI_F + P - EI_F \tag{1}$$

Similarly,

$$COGS_L = BI_L + P - EI_L \tag{2}$$

or

$$P = COGS_L + EI_L - BI_L \tag{3}$$

Substituting expression (3) for P in expression (1) (since the purchases P are identical for both accounting methods) and rearranging yield

$$COGS_F = COGS_L - [(EI_F - EI_L) - (BI_F - BI_L)] \tag{4}$$

Since the two terms in brackets—$(EI_F - EI_L)$ and $(BI_F - BI_L)$—on the right side of the equation are just the LIFO reserve at the end and beginning of the period, respectively, Eq. (4) can be expressed as

$$COGS_F = COGS_L - [(\text{LIFO Reserve}_E - \text{LIFO Reserve}_B)] \tag{5}$$

where the subscripts E and B refer to ending (inventory) and beginning (inventory), respectively. The change in LIFO reserve during the year, sometimes called the *LIFO effect* for the year, is thus the difference between the COGS computed under the two methods.

Before leaving this discussion, consider two questions. First, why does conversion to FIFO in 1991 to 1993 increase COGS (see Exhibit 6-3B) when we normally expect $COGS_F$ to be lower than $COGS_L$? Second, why did the LIFO reserve decrease in those years?

The answer to both questions is the same: Oil prices decreased. This decline reduced the difference between inventory cost on a LIFO basis and cost on a FIFO basis. The LIFO reserve, which represents this difference, is thus reduced. In 1993, for example, use of the LIFO method reduced COGS by $140 million, increasing pretax earnings by an equal amount. The lesson here should be clear: *When prices are declining, LIFO produces lower COGS and, therefore, higher earnings.*

In 1994, when prices (and the LIFO reserve) increased, the expected effect was obtained. $COGS_L$ was higher and pretax income was reduced by the amount of increase in the LIFO reserve.

ADJUSTMENT OF INCOME TO CURRENT COST INCOME

This section discusses the adjustment of FIFO COGS to reflect current costs. It is important to distinguish between the adjustment of FIFO COGS to current costs and the estimation of LIFO COGS. As long as the firm does not deplete any of its opening inventory, these two adjustment techniques produce equivalent results. When inventory quantities are reduced, however, further adjustment is required.

LIFO COGS and income are both distorted when the firm reduces its opening inventory (known as a LIFO liquidation), as old costs flow into the income statement and COGS no longer reflects the current cost of inventory sold. When a LIFO liquidation occurs, LIFO COGS does not equal current cost COGS; a further adjustment is required. LIFO liquidations are discussed in a subsequent section of the chapter and we illustrate there how to adjust for LIFO liquidations. For the moment, therefore, we ignore this problem and use the terms LIFO and current cost interchangeably. The reader should, however, keep this important caveat in mind.

For firms using FIFO, *only the adjustment of the FIFO COGS to LIFO COGS is relevant.* Adjustments of inventory balances to LIFO serve no purpose, as LIFO inventory costs are outdated and almost meaningless. However, information needed to adjust COGS to LIFO is not generally provided in the financial statements. An approximate adjustment, however, is often possible.[11]

This adjustment involves multiplying the opening inventory by the (specific) inflation rate and adding the product to $COGS_F$ to arrive at $COGS_L$. More formally,

$$COGS_L = COGS_F + (BI_F \times r)$$

---

[11] A more detailed adjustment taking into consideration the firm's inventory turnover is possible. Falkenstein and Weil (1977) discuss the use of turnover, but note (p. 51 of their article) that estimates from the more basic procedure (used in this text) have always approximated the estimates from the more complex methods.

BOX 6-2
Derivation of Current Cost Adjustment

The appropriateness of the approximation can be illustrated by the following "proof." Assume that a firm carries a *quantity* Q of inventory and this quantity is equal to three months of inventory. The inventory level Q is replenished every three months. Assume further that the inflation rate over the year is equal to r. Finally, let P be the unit cost at which the opening inventory Q_0 was purchased at the end of the previous year. Thus, the unit cost of the inventory at the end of the current year will equal $P(1 + r)$. The following illustrates the actual flow of goods purchased throughout the year:

$$\text{Beginning Inventory} = Q_0 = \text{Sales during 1st Quarter}$$
$$\text{End of 1st Quarter Purchase} = Q_1 = \text{Sales during 2nd Quarter}$$
$$\text{End of 2nd Quarter Purchase} = Q_2 = \text{Sales during 3rd Quarter}$$
$$\text{End of 3rd Quarter Purchase} = Q_3 = \text{Sales during 4th Quarter}$$
$$\text{End of 4th Quarter Purchase} = Q_4 = \text{Ending Inventory}$$

Under FIFO, the cost of Q_0, Q_1, Q_2, and Q_3 will appear in the COGS. Under LIFO, the cost of Q_1, Q_2, Q_3 and Q_4 will appear in the COGS. Thus, the difference between the two methods lies in the difference between the cost of the beginning (Q_0) and ending (Q_4) inventory. Hence, the difference between LIFO and FIFO equals

$$Q_4 P(1 + r) - Q_0 P = Q_0 Pr$$

since the inventory quantity purchased each period is the same.

---

where r is the *specific inflation rate appropriate for the products in which the firm deals*. A simple derivation of this adjustment is presented in Box 6-2.

To the extent a firm's inventory purchasing policies are uniform, the adjustment suggested here will approximate the actual FIFO-to-LIFO (current cost) adjustment. The inflation rate needed for the adjustment is not a general producer or consumer price index, but rather should be the specific price index appropriate to the firm in question. (For a multi-industry firm, the calculation would have to be done on a segmented basis.) Many industry indices are readily available, published by the U.S. Department of Commerce. For companies whose inputs are commodities (oil, coffee, steel scrap), the spot price for the commodity may be used.

The example that follows illustrates an alternative basis for obtaining the specific price level change, derived from a competing (LIFO) firm in the same industry as the firm under examination.

Example: Amerada Hess

Exhibit 6-4 contains inventory and COGS data for Amerada Hess, a major oil producer and refiner, along with related footnotes. The firm uses the FIFO method for 60% of its crude oil and refined product inventories and average cost for the balance.[12] Our objective is to adjust COGS for 1994 to a LIFO basis. There are two reasons for

---

[12]For simplicity, our analysis assumes that Amerada uses FIFO for all crude oil and refined product inventories.

EXHIBIT 6-4. AMERADA HESS
Inventories, December 31, 1993 to 1994

Years Ended December 31 ($ in millions)	1993	1994
Inventories at year-end		
Crude oil	$ 299	$ 250
Refined and other finished products	436	583
Subtotal	$ 735	$ 833
Materials and supplies	118	113
Total inventory	$ 853	$ 946
Cost of products sold and operating expenses	$4,287	$4,450

Inventories: Crude oil and refined product inventories are valued at the lower of cost or market value. Cost is determined on the FIFO method for approximately 60% of the inventories and the average cost method for the remainder. Inventories of materials and supplies are valued at or below cost.

Source: Amerada Hess, *1993–1994 Annual Reports.*

making this adjustment. One is to estimate the impact of changing oil prices on Amerada's sales and earnings; we wish to separate price effects from operating effects. The second reason is to compare Amerada with other firms in the oil industry using LIFO accounting. There are several ways to achieve our objective.

If the increase in specific price index (obtained, e.g., from government statistics) for oil products was 10% in 1994, then the addition to FIFO COGS would be $73.5 million (0.10 × $735 million), where the latter is the inventory (excluding materials and supplies) balance at the beginning of 1994. This $73.5 million, it should be noted, is the holding gain portion of the income reported under the FIFO method. Removing the holding gain from income (adding it to COGS) results in a better measure of reported income ($ in millions):

COGS (reported)	$4,450.0
Adjustment for holding gain	73.5
COGS (approximate LIFO)	$4,523.5

An alternative approach to arrive at the specific price index appropriate for the oil refining industry would be to examine the financial statements of a competing firm in that industry using LIFO. The LIFO reserve information presented earlier in Exhibit 6-3 for Sun Company can be used to approximate the effect of LIFO on Amerada Hess.

The 1994 increase in Sun's LIFO reserve of $69 million ($390 to $459 million) represents the increase in current costs during 1994. The specific inflation rate was, therefore,

$$\frac{\$69 \text{ million}}{\$774 \text{ million}} = 8.9\%$$

where $774 million is Sun's inventory balance (excluding materials and supplies), on a FIFO basis on December 31, 1993.

Since Amerada Hess is in the same industry, we can assume that it faced the same inflation rate, leaving us with an adjustment of

$$\$735 \text{ million} \times 0.089 = \$65.5 \text{ million}$$

to FIFO COGS, bringing Amerada Hess's COGS on a LIFO basis to

$$\text{COGS}_L = \$4,450 \text{ million} + \$65.5 \text{ million} = \$4,515.5 \text{ million}$$

Adjusting weighted-average COGS (with subscript W) to LIFO can be done in a similar fashion; the adjustment to opening inventory can be approximated[13] by one-half the (specific) inflation rate:

$$\text{COGS}_L = \text{COGS}_W + \left(BI_W \times \frac{r}{2} \right)$$

FINANCIAL RATIOS: LIFO VERSUS FIFO

Exhibit 6-5, based on Dopuch and Pincus (1988), compares selected financial characteristics of FIFO and LIFO firms. The comparison is done first on the basis of amounts reported in financial statements (part A) and again after adjusting to the alternative accounting method (part B).

Using reported financial data, part A of the table indicates that, based on median values, LIFO firms have higher turnover ratios, less inventory as a percentage of sales or total assets, and lower variation in inventory levels and pretax income.[14] However, for the most part, these differences are not real operating differences but rather are differences due to the accounting choice. In part B the FIFO firms are adjusted to LIFO and the LIFO firms are adjusted to FIFO. The appropriate comparison can now be made with all firms using the same accounting method; that is, the numbers in part B should be compared with those directly above them in part A.

Once the data are adjusted for accounting methods, the differences tend to disappear. For example, the inventory turnover ratio as reported is 4.97 for LIFO firms and 3.88 for FIFO firms—a difference of 28%. After we adjust to the same method, the turnover ratios are:

1. With all firms on FIFO, 4.03 for LIFO reporting firms and 3.88 for FIFO reporting firms—a difference of only 4%
2. With all firms on a LIFO basis, 4.97 versus 4.72, respectively—a difference of only 5%

Similar patterns exist for the other variables.

---

[13]When weighted-average cost is used, the inventory turnover rate affects the adjustment.

[14]The variation in inventory and pretax income is measured by the coefficient of variation—standard deviation divided by the mean.

EXHIBIT 6-5
Analysis of FIFO/LIFO Firms Based on Median Data, 1963 to 1981

A. Data as Reported

	LIFO	FIFO
COGS/average inventory	4.97	3.88
Inventory/sales	0.16	0.20
Inventory/assets	0.21	0.29
C.V. inventory*	0.42	0.63
C.V. pretax income	0.74	0.79

B. FIFO Firms Adjusted to LIFO and LIFO Firms to FIFO

	FIFO to LIFO	LIFO to FIFO
COGS/average inventory	4.72	4.03
Inventory/sales	0.17	0.22
Inventory/assets	0.25	0.24
C.V. inventory	0.52	0.67
C.V. pretax income	0.81	0.77

*C.V. is the coefficient of variation (standard deviation divided by the mean).
Source: Nicolas Dopuch and Morton Pincus, "Evidence of the Choice of Inventory Accounting Methods: LIFO Versus FIFO," *Journal of Accounting Research,* Spring 1988, pp. 28–59, Tables 4 and 5, p. 44 (adapted).

With Exhibit 6-5 as a prologue, we now focus on the distortions in measures of financial performance that result from the FIFO/LIFO choice.

The FIFO/LIFO choice impacts reported profitability, liquidity, activity, and leverage ratios. For some ratios, LIFO provides a better measure, whereas for others, FIFO does. The LIFO-to-FIFO and FIFO-to-LIFO adjustment procedures discussed earlier, however, allow one to make the appropriate adjustments to arrive at the "correct" ratio regardless of the firm's choice of accounting method. *The general guideline is to use LIFO numbers for ratio components that are income-related and FIFO-based data for components that are balance-sheet-related.*

Profitability: Gross Profit Margin

The argument that LIFO better measures current income can be made with reference to gross profit margins. When input prices increase, firms pass along the added costs to customers. Moreover, they try to mark up not only those items purchased at the higher price but also all goods previously purchased. (This policy, it should be noted, is economically defensible using the argument made earlier that the real cost of an item sold is its replacement cost.)

Thus, if the pricing policy of the firm in our opening example is to mark up cost by 100% (implying a gross profit margin of 50% of sales), the $10,000 of sales in our example would have been arrived at as follows:

Sales: 100 units per quarter for a total of 400 units
Sales Price: determined as 100% markup over current costs

Quarter	Unit Cost	Unit Price	Sales Units	Sales Dollars
1	$11	$22	100	$ 2,200
2	12	24	100	2,400
3	13	26	100	2,600
4	14	28	100	2,800
Total			400	$10,000

Gross profit margin under FIFO and LIFO would be

	Sales	− COGS	= Gross Profit	Percent Margin
FIFO	$10,000	$4,300	$5,700	$5,700/$10,000 = 57.0%
LIFO	$10,000	$5,150	$4,850	$4,850/$10,000 = 48.5%

The gross profit margin measured when LIFO inventory accounting is used is clearly closer to the profit margin implied by the firm's pricing policy. FIFO accounting, in times of rising (falling) prices, will tend to overstate (understate) reported profit margins.

The gross profit margin, by measuring the profitability of current sales, also provides an indication of the potential future profitability of a firm. Clearly, FIFO net income (which includes holding gains resulting from rising prices) inflates expectations regarding the future profitability of the firm as future holding gains may be smaller if future price increases are lower. LIFO gives a more accurate rendering of the firm's future prospects by removing the impact of price changes.

Liquidity: Working Capital

Working-capital-based ratios are misstated under LIFO because, as already discussed, the inventory component of working capital reports outdated costs. As the purpose of the current ratio is to compare a firm's cash or near-cash assets and liabilities, use of the current value of inventory (FIFO) results in the better measure.

For Sun, working capital and current ratios for 1991 to 1994 based on reported data are

Sun Company
Current Position Based on Reported LIFO Inventory

	($ in millions)			
	1991	1992	1993	1994
Current assets	$1,632	$1,331	$1,277	$1,508
Current liabilities	1,899	1,746	1,505	1,915
Working capital	**(267)**	**(415)**	**(228)**	**(407)**
Current ratio	**0.86**	**0.76**	**0.85**	**0.79**

Adjusting LIFO inventory (and hence current assets) to current cost (FIFO) by adding the LIFO reserves (see Exhibits 6-2 and 6-3) results in the following picture of Sun's current position:

Sun Company
Adjusted Current Position Based on Current Cost (FIFO) Inventory

	($ in millions)			
	1991	1992	1993	1994
Current assets	$1,632	$1,331	$1,277	$1,508
LIFO reserve	536	530	390	459
Adjusted current assets	$2,168	$1,861	$1,667	$1,967
Current liabilities	1,899	1,746	1,505	1,915
Adjusted working capital	**269**	**115**	**162**	**52**
Adjusted current ratio	**1.14**	**1.07**	**1.11**	**1.03**

The adjustments convert negative working capital to a positive measure. Similarly, adjusted current ratios are approximately 30% higher than the unadjusted measures.

Activity: Inventory Turnover

Inventory turnover, defined in Chapter 4 as COGS/average inventory, is often meaningless for LIFO firms due to the mismatching of costs. The numerator represents current costs, whereas the denominator reports outdated historical costs. Thus, the turnover ratio under LIFO will, when prices increase, trend higher irrespective of the trend of physical turnover.

This point is illustrated in Exhibit 6-6. We assume an actual physical turnover of four times per year; that is, the average inventory is sufficient for one quarter. Further, it is assumed that unit costs increase 10% per quarter.

The FIFO inventory ratio is unaffected by the change in price, and at 3.77 it is a rough approximation of the actual physical turnover of 4. The LIFO-based ratios of 5.11, 7.47, and 10.94 are, however, far from the actual measure of 4, and the discrepancy grows from quarter to quarter. Thus, to arrive at a reasonable approximation of the inventory turnover ratio for a LIFO firm, we must first convert stated inventory to FIFO.

The preferred measure of inventory turnover is the one labeled current cost. It combines the two methods, using LIFO COGS in the numerator and the FIFO inventory balance in the denominator. This approach provides the best matching of costs, as current costs are used in both the numerator and denominator.

Referring once again to the Sun Company (Exhibit 6-3), we see that the inventory turnover ratio (using total inventories) for 1994 is

$$\text{LIFO (reported)} = \frac{\$6,276}{(\$464 \text{ million} + \$613 \text{ million})/2} = 11.65$$

$$\text{FIFO (adjusted)} = \frac{\$6,207}{(\$854 \text{ million} + \$1,074 \text{ million})/2} = 6.44$$

$$\text{Current Cost} = \frac{\$6,276}{(\$854 \text{ million} + \$1,074 \text{ million})/2} = 6.51$$

EXHIBIT 6-6
Illustration of Turnover Ratio Under LIFO and FIFO

Year	Quarter	Purchases = Sales	Cost per Unit	Total	For Entire Year		
Opening inventory		100	$10.00	$1,000			
1	1	100	$11.00	$1,100	FIFO	COGS	$ 4,641
1	2	100	$12.10	$1,210		Avg. inv.	$ 1,232
1	3	100	$13.31	$1,331	LIFO	COGS	$ 5,105
1	4	100	$14.64	$1,464		Avg. inv.	$ 1,000
2	1	100	$16.11	$1,611	FIFO	COGS	$ 6,795
2	2	100	$17.72	$1,772		Avg. inv.	$ 1,804
2	3	100	$19.49	$1,949	LIFO	COGS	$ 7,474
2	4	100	$21.44	$2,144		Avg. inv.	$ 1,000
3	1	100	$23.58	$2,358	FIFO	COGS	$ 9,948
3	2	100	$25.94	$2,594		Avg. inv.	$ 2,641
3	3	100	$28.53	$2,853	LIFO	COGS	$10,943
3	4	100	$31.38	$3,138		Avg. inv.	$ 1,000

Turnover Ratios

	Year 1	Year 2	Year 3
FIFO	3.77	3.77	3.77
LIFO	5.11	7.47	10.94
Current cost	4.14	4.14	4.14

Note the decline in the ratio from that reported on a LIFO basis. The LIFO ratio is overstated, implying very fast turnover. The adjusted ratios imply a less than two-month supply of inventory on hand rather than a one-month supply.

Also note that there is little difference between the FIFO ratio and the more refined current cost ratio. This is empirically true in most situations, and for all practical purposes these two ratio calculations are equivalent as long as prices are not rising too rapidly.

We can compute inventory turnover for Amerada Hess for 1994, using the data in Exhibit 6-4:

$$\text{Inventory Turnover (FIFO)} = \frac{\$4,450 \text{ million}}{(\$853 \text{ million} + \$946 \text{ million})/2} = 4.95$$

Comparing the inventory turnover ratios for Amerada and Sun, we see the importance of making the calculations comparable. With only the reported data used (LIFO for Sun, FIFO for Amerada), it would appear that Sun turns its inventory more than two times faster (11.65 versus 4.95). If we put both on a FIFO basis, Sun still appears more efficient (6.44 versus 4.95), but the gap is smaller. *Having made the ratios comparable (by eliminating the effect of different accounting methods), we now have a reasonable basis to look for other explanations for the difference in the ratio.*

Inventory Theory and Turnover Ratios

Computing the inventory turnover ratio implies that there is some standard against which to measure or there is an optimal ratio. As for all turnover ratios, one's first instinct is to believe that higher is better, that more rapid inventory turnover indicates a more efficient use of capital. In practice, however, that assumption may be overly simplistic.

The management science literature has devoted much study to the design of optimal inventory ordering policies. The traditional literature in the United States has focused on the economic order quantity (EOQ). More recently, in line with developments in Japanese management practices, focus has turned to just-in-time inventory policies. It is worthwhile to note the implications of these theories for the interpretation of the turnover ratio.

Economic Order Quantity

The construction and use of ratios for cross-sectional and time-series comparisons implicitly assume (as discussed in Chapter 4) that the relationship between the numerator and denominator is linear. Applying this assumption to the inventory turnover ratio implies that, as demand increases, the quantity of inventory held should increase proportionately. The EOQ model, however, argues that the optimal level of inventory is proportionate to the *square root* of demand.

Thus, for example, if demand (COGS) increases by four times, one would expect average inventory to double (2 = the square root of 4). Exhibit 6-7 indicates that the turnover ratio should rise as sales increase. Smaller firms should have lower turnover ratios based on the EOQ. A high turnover ratio for a small firm would not be a sign of efficiency but, on the contrary, an indication that the firm was not managing its inventories in the most economic fashion.

Just in Time

Japanese management practices strive for the ideal that firms should not hold any inventory but rather should receive and ship orders "just in time" (JIT) as needed. Carried to its ultimate, this would argue for a turnover ratio approaching infinity with zero inventory held. Hence, we would expect the turnover ratios of Japanese firms to

EXHIBIT 6-7
Economic Order Quantity

Assume that for a firm whose demand is 120 units annually, the optimal inventory quantity based on the EOQ model is 10, implying an inventory turnover ratio of 12 (120/10). Using the equation $Q = (2DS/H)^{1/2}$, where D is demand, S setup cost, and H holding cost, we can solve to get $S/H = 5/12$. Using this value for S/H, we can compute the EOQ (Q) for any level of demand (D).

Demand	EOQ	Turnover (Demand/EOQ)
600	22.36	26.83
480	20.00	24.00
240	14.14	16.97
120	**10.00**	**12.00**
60	7.07	8.50
30	6.00	5.00

be considerably higher than those of American firms. To the extent that U.S. firms adopt these practices, they can be expected to have higher turnover ratios in the future.

One interesting by-product of the trend toward JIT inventory is that it renders the LIFO/FIFO choice less meaningful. If a firm has no inventories (or relatively small quantities), then there is no significant difference between FIFO and LIFO.[15]

The FIFO/LIFO Choice and Inventory Holding Policy

Another important consideration is that the LIFO/FIFO choice may be related to a firm's actual inventory holding policy. Biddle (1980) found that LIFO firms tended to carry higher inventory balances (in terms of quantity) than comparably sized FIFO firms. This finding is consistent with the following factors:

1. Firms with higher inventory balances have larger potential tax savings from the use of LIFO. Thus, the higher inventory balances that result from the firm's production and operating environment may explain why the firm chose LIFO in the first place.

2. These higher balances may result from the LIFO choice, as LIFO firms attempt to get the most advantage from it by increasing their inventory balances.

3. To avoid LIFO liquidations and consequent higher income taxes, LIFO firms must buy (produce) as many goods as they sell each year. For LIFO firms it is costly to lower inventory levels.

Barlev et al. (1984) examined Canadian and Israeli firms that were not permitted to use LIFO but used an alternative method of tax adjustment for inflation. They found that inventory balances were higher for firms with large tax benefits from the inflation adjustment.

Solvency: Debt-to-Equity Ratio

We have argued that, to compute liquidity ratios, understated LIFO inventory balances should be restated at current cost by adding the LIFO reserve. For the same reason, the firm's stockholders' equity should also be increased by the LIFO reserve.[16] The rationale for this adjustment is that the reported equity of the firm is understated because the firm owns inventory whose current value exceeds its carrying value.[17]

---

[15]However, inventory may be carried by suppliers; if a firm owns or controls its suppliers, it may bear the residual risk usually borne by the suppliers. To be most useful and relevant, turnover ratios and other inventory measures should be based on consolidated financial statements, where consolidation reflects economic rather than legal or regulatory control. Admittedly, such consolidation is not always feasible given the paucity of disclosure regarding such relationships. Further discussion of the issue of consolidation appears in Chapter 13.

[16]Lasman and Weil (1978) suggest that the LIFO reserve should not be adjusted for taxes unless a liquidation of LIFO layers is assumed. Further, as liquidations are reported in reverse LIFO order (latest layers are liquidated first), the largest gains reside in the earliest layers. Thus, there is a low probability that the tax effect of "minor" liquidations will be significant and (if we assume that the firm remains in business) extensive liquidations are unlikely, also arguing against tax adjustment. Note that firms have strong incentives to avoid liquidations that would result in significant tax payments.

[17]Using FIFO values for equity does not contradict our notion that the optimal choice for income presentation is LIFO. Recalling the house example in footnote 5, the fact that your house doubled in value from $100,000 to $200,000 at a time when all houses doubled in value, means that you do not benefit from selling the house as you will need the money to buy a replacement house. The value of (your equity) in your house is, nevertheless, $200,000.

For analytical purposes, the inventory choice should be treated like other accounting choices. The fact that the Internal Revenue Service does not permit any difference between financial reporting and tax accounting methods should not tie the hands of the analyst. The valuation of a LIFO firm should not be penalized because it takes advantage of the tax savings inherent in LIFO.

DECLINES IN LIFO RESERVE

LIFO reserves can decline for either of the following reasons:

1. Liquidation of inventories
2. Price declines

In either case, COGS will be smaller (and income larger) relative to what it would have been had the reserve not declined. *The response of the analyst should not be the same in both cases, however.* For LIFO liquidations, the analyst should "back out" the effects of the LIFO liquidation to arrive at a better measure of the firm's operating results. In the second case, no adjustment is required, as price decreases are a normal part of the firm's operating results (just as much as price increases).

LIFO Liquidations

The discussion of LIFO in this chapter thus far has generally assumed that inventory quantities are stable or increasing. When more goods are sold than are purchased (or manufactured), goods held in opening inventory are included in the COGS. For LIFO companies, this results in liquidating LIFO layers established in prior years, and such "LIFO liquidations" can materially distort reported operating results.

The carrying cost of the old inventories (which becomes the cost of goods sold associated with the inventory reduction) may be abnormally low and the gross profit margin abnormally high and unsustainable because the LIFO opening inventory carries old, *low* costs. Thus, LIFO cost no longer approximates current cost. For companies whose base inventory is very old, the distortion from these "paper profits" can be quite large; for analysis, that distortion needs to be removed.

The increased income from LIFO liquidations results in higher taxes and lower cash flows as the taxes that have been avoided to date through the use of LIFO must now be paid. To defer taxes indefinitely, purchases (production) must always be greater than or equal to sales. [See Biddle (1980) and the discussion of the impact of LIFO/FIFO on inventory purchases and holding policy.]

LIFO liquidations may result from inventory reductions because of strikes, recession, or declining demand for a particular product line. In recessionary periods companies that lay off workers and close down plants may appear, paradoxically, to report respectable profits, as production cuts result in the liquidation of LIFO inventories.

Exhibit 6-8 shows the significant LIFO liquidations of major industrial firms during the recessionary period of 1980 to 1981. In many cases, LIFO layers being liquidated dated back as far as World War II. Companies in Exhibit 6-8 experienced LIFO liquidations in more than one year. This result is consistent with that of Stober (1986), who examined 272 companies reporting LIFO liquidations in the period 1979 to 1983. He found that over 60% had liquidations in more than one year and 33% experienced

EXHIBIT 6-8
The Significance of LIFO Liquidation, 1980 to 1981

Company	Year	Net Income Before Taxes ($ in millions)	LIFO Liquidation as a Percentage of Income
Bethlehem Steel	1980	$ 95	77%
Bethlehem Steel	1981	293	16
National Steel	1980	31	31
LTV Corp.	1980	161	31
Firestone Tire	1980	164	65
Firestone Tire	1981	189	13
American Can	1981	107	18
General Motors	1980	(1,369)	16
General Motors	1981	(138)	39
U.S. Steel	1980	607	29

Source: Allen Schiff, "The Other Side of LIFO," *Journal of Accountancy,* May 1983, pp. 120–121, Exhibit 1, p. 120.

liquidations in three or more years. Furthermore, fully 85% of the latter occurrences were cases where a LIFO liquidation was disclosed one year earlier.

Thus, a LIFO liquidation may not be a one-time, random occurrence but a signal that a company is entering an extended period of decline. Further evidence to this end has been documented by Davis et al. (1984), who found that liquidations were industry-related, indicating a systematic effect, and by Fried et al. (1989), who found that write-downs and/or restructurings are often preceded by LIFO liquidations. (See Chapter 8 for a discussion of asset impairments and their relationship to LIFO liquidations.)

Given the trend toward lower inventory levels in recent years as companies move toward just-in-time or other means of reducing their investment in inventories, LIFO liquidations have become a common occurrence. Such liquidations are usually disclosed in the inventory footnote of the financial statements. As profits from LIFO liquidations are not operating in nature, they should be excluded from computations of recurring earnings for purposes of analysis (see the Wyman-Gordon example in Exhibit 6-9).

Declining Prices

Our discussion thus far has assumed rising price levels. In the case of Sun, we saw that the LIFO reserve declines when prices fall. In some industries (notably those that are technology-related), input prices decline steadily over time; in others (mainly commodity-based industries such as metals and petroleum), prices may fluctuate cyclically.

Declines in LIFO reserves occur whenever inventory costs fall as the lower-cost current purchases enter reported LIFO COGS, decreasing the cost differences between LIFO and FIFO ending inventories. Such declines are not considered LIFO liquidations, and disclosure of their impact is not required.

The theoretical arguments as to which accounting method provides better information still hold. LIFO provides more recent (or current) cost on the income statement and outdated costs on the balance sheet. The direction of the LIFO versus FIFO

EXHIBIT 6-9. WYMAN-GORDON
Inventories and Declines in LIFO Reserve

Inventory and Change in LIFO Reserve, 1992 to 1993

	($ in millions)		
	1991	1992	1993
Inventory		$ 53,688	$ 42,388
LIFO reserve	64,203	41,365	33,448
Change in LIFO reserve (LIFO effect)		$(22,838)	$ (7,917)

If all inventories valued at LIFO cost had been valued at FIFO cost or market, which approximates current replacement cost, inventories would have been $41,365,000 and $33,448,000 higher than reported at December 31, 1992 and 1993, respectively.

Inventory quantities were reduced in 1991, 1992, and 1993, resulting in the liquidation of LIFO inventories carried at lower costs prevailing in prior years as compared with the cost of current purchases. The effect of lower quantities decreased 1991 loss from operations by $1,529,000, increased 1992 income from operations by $18,388,000, and decreased 1993 loss from operations by $5,469,000, whereas the effect of deflation had no impact on 1991 loss from operations, increased 1992 income from operations by $4,450,000, and decreased 1993 loss from operations by $2,448,000.

Source: Wyman-Gordon, *1993 Annual Report.*

differences, however, is reversed when prices decline. LIFO closing inventories are overstated, and FIFO COGS tends to be higher. Thus, although the pragmatic incentives to use LIFO for tax purposes are lost in an environment of declining prices[18] (LIFO results in higher taxes and lower cash flow), the nature of the information provided does not change. The LIFO amounts on the balance sheet are not current and require adjustment, whereas the income statement amounts are current and do not need adjustment.

Example: Wyman-Gordon Exhibit 6-9 presents data from the inventory footnote for Wyman-Gordon, a producer of components for the aerospace industry. Wyman-Gordon has used the LIFO method for many years and has a large LIFO reserve on its balance sheet. Weak industry conditions led to inventory declines, resulting in significant LIFO liquidations; declining prices also reduced the LIFO reserve. The exhibit indicates that in 1992 and 1993 the LIFO reserve declined $22.838 and $7.917 million, respectively. Wyman-Gordon reported the effects of liquidations and price declines separately:

	($ in thousands)	
	1992	1993
Effect of LIFO liquidation	$(18,388)	$(5,469)
Effect of lower prices	(4,450)	(2,448)
Total LIFO effect	$(22,838)	$(7,917)

[18]In addition, companies whose inventories are subject to obsolescence often take advantage of the ability (not available, for tax purposes, under LIFO) to write down inventory to market value.

LIFO liquidations added to Wyman's reported earnings (or reduced reported losses) in each of the years 1991 to 1993. As the effect of LIFO liquidations is completely nonoperating in nature, operating results, (COGS) should be adjusted to exclude it. Adjustments to gross margin for each year follow:

Wyman-Gordon
Effects of LIFO Liquidations ($ in millions)

	Reported			Adjusted		
	1991	1992	1993	1991	1992	1993
Sales	$355.4	$298.9	$239.8	$355.4	$298.9	$239.8
COGS	310.5	234.6	210.1	310.5	234.6	210.1
LIFO liquidation effect	0	0	0	1.5	18.4	5.5
Adjusted COGS	$310.5	$234.6	$210.1	$312.0	$253.0	$215.6
Gross margin	**44.9**	**64.3**	**29.7**	**43.4**	**45.9**	**24.2**
GM percentage	**12.6%**	**21.5%**	**12.4%**	**12.2%**	**15.4%**	**10.1%**

Based on reported results, the 1992 gross margin increased by 43% (from $44.9 to $64.3 million), although sales declined by 15%, as the gross margin percentage increased 71% from 12.6 to 21.5%. When the LIFO liquidation is removed, there is a minimal increase in gross margin and the gross margin percentage increase is a much more modest 26% (at a lower level of 15.4%).

The adjusted results are a better measure of current (and future) operating performance and show lower gross margin percentages for all years. The adjusted margins better reflect the firm's ability to mark up the current cost of inputs.

Given our knowledge of the 1992 price declines, the increase in the gross margin percentage suggests that the company was able to capture that decline for itself without passing it on to customers. However, this advantage seems to have been short-lived; gross margins in 1993 were considerably below even their 1991 level.

Removing the LIFO liquidation effectively adjusts reported LIFO COGS to a current cost basis. The effects of declining prices on current purchases and sales, which are operating in nature, were not removed. However, *for purposes of comparison with firms using FIFO* (i.e., calculating COGS on a FIFO basis), adjustment should be made for the total LIFO effect (liquidations *and* declining prices).

INITIAL ADOPTION OF LIFO AND CHANGES TO AND FROM LIFO

Changes in inventory accounting method require examination for two reasons:

1. Reporting methods for these changes are not symmetric; changing from FIFO to LIFO is not accorded the same treatment as a LIFO-to-FIFO switch.
2. The implications and motivation behind the accounting change are equally important; the change itself may convey information about the company's operations.

Initial Adoption of LIFO

In the United States the change to LIFO is made only on a prospective basis: GAAP do not require either retroactive restatement or the disclosure of any cumulative effect of the adoption of LIFO. Records necessary for restatement or *pro forma* disclosures often do not exist. Opening inventory in the year of adoption is the base period inventory for subsequent LIFO computations.

Because LIFO is a cost method, switching from lower-of-cost-or-market (LCM) methods may require a write-up to the cost basis when a write-down to (lower) market value has been previously recorded. Generally, such write-ups are reported as other income and may offset decreases in income due to the adoption of LIFO. The adoption of LIFO also has an adverse cash effect since the LIFO book-tax conformity rule requires the restoration of previous write-downs to taxable income over a three-year period beginning with the adoption year. However, this requirement is not a significant economic disadvantage (in terms of cash flows), because inventory write-down rules under non-LIFO methods have become considerably more restrictive over the years.

When LIFO is adopted, required footnote disclosures include the impact of the adoption on the period's income before extraordinary items, net income, and related earning per share amounts. A brief explanation of the reasons for the change in method must be provided and the absence of any cumulative effect disclosures or retroactive adjustment must be noted.

Exhibit 6-10 provides an example of the required disclosures. Effective July 1, 1988, Quaker Oats extended its use of the LIFO method to some grocery products inventories that had been valued using average cost. As a result of the change, the percentage of the company's inventories accounted for using LIFO rose from 29 to 65%, with the remainder at average cost (21%) or FIFO (14%).

EXHIBIT 6-10. QUAKER OATS COMPANY
Notes to the Consolidated Financial Statements

Inventories

Inventories are valued at the lower of cost or market, using various cost methods, and include the cost of raw materials, labor, and overhead. The percentage of year-end inventories valued using each of the methods is as follows:

June 30	1989 (%)	1988 (%)	1987 (%)	1986 (%)
Average quarterly cost	21	54	52	51
LIFO	65	29	31	21
FIFO	14	17	17	28

Effective July 1, 1988, the Company adopted the LIFO cost flow assumption for valuing the majority of remaining U.S. Grocery Products inventories. The Company believes that the use of the LIFO method better matches current costs with current revenues. The cumulative effect of this change on retained earnings at the beginning of the year is not determinable, nor are the *pro forma* effects of retroactive application of LIFO to prior years. The effect of this change on fiscal 1989 was to decrease net income by $16.0 million, or $0.20 per share.

If the LIFO method of valuing certain inventories was not used, total inventories would have been $60.1 million, $24.0 million, and $14.6 million higher than reported at June 30, 1989, 1988, and 1987, respectively.

Source: Quaker Oats, *1987 and 1989 Annual Reports.*

Extension of the use of LIFO increased COGS by $25.6 million (disclosed elsewhere), reducing net income by $16 million or $0.20 per share for the fiscal year ended June 30, 1989. As Quaker reported earnings per share of $2.56 for that year, the extension of LIFO reduced reported earnings by 7.2% from the $2.76 that would have been reported without the accounting change.

Quaker also reported that its LIFO reserve rose from $24.0 million at June 30, 1988, to $60.1 million at June 30, 1989. Using the data on the effect of the accounting change, we see that the source of the increase in the LIFO reserve was:

Balance at June 30, 1988	$24.0 million
LIFO effect on inventory (29%) previously on LIFO	10.5
LIFO effect on extension (36%)	25.6
Balance at June 30, 1989	$60.1 million

The change to LIFO is often made to take advantage of the tax benefits inherent in the LIFO method and the propensity to switch is often a function of inflationary conditions. For example, in the early 1970s, over 400 firms switched to LIFO, reflecting double-digit inflation. Interestingly, the stock market did not always regard such switches favorably despite their (positive) cash flow implications. The empirical section of the chapter examines the reasons for this market reaction more closely.

Change from LIFO Method

Unlike changes to LIFO, changes from LIFO to other methods require retroactive restatement of reported earnings to the new method for prior years. The cumulative effect of adopting the new inventory accounting method is credited to retained earnings at the beginning of the earliest restated year to avoid a misstatement of current period income.

SEC regulations require a preferability letter from the firm's independent auditor stating its concurrence with and the rationale for the change. Additionally, a change from LIFO requires Internal Revenue Service approval.[19] The IRS considers changes from LIFO as a loss of tax deferral privileges, and the previous LIFO reserve becomes immediately taxable. Thus, a change from LIFO may bring significant adverse tax and cash flow consequences and requires evaluation of the impact on operations as well as management incentives for the switch. These motivations are also discussed in the empirical section to follow.

Example: Champion Enterprises

In fiscal 1992, Champion Enterprises, a producer of manufactured housing, buses, and recreation vehicles, changed from the LIFO to the FIFO method of inventory valuation. The analysis of this change allows us to integrate many of the concepts in this chapter. Specifically, we explore the following (interrelated) issues:

1. What were the financial statement consequences to Champion of making the change and were these consequences in the direction expected?

2. What were the tax effects of the change?

---

[19]Firms switching from LIFO to another method also agree not to switch back to LIFO for at least 10 years, except under "extraordinary circumstances."

EXHIBIT 6-11. CHAMPION ENTERPRISES
Analysis of Change from LIFO to FIFO

A. Inventory Footnote (1992 Annual Report)

During the fourth quarter of fiscal 1992, the Company changed its method of accounting for inventory from the LIFO method to the FIFO method. Management believes that the FIFO method provides a more meaningful presentation of the Company's financial position including significant financial statement amounts and ratios, as well as shareholders' equity. As required by generally accepted accounting principles, the Company has retroactively adjusted prior years' financial statements for this change. The effect of the restatement was to increase retained earnings at March 4, 1989 by $10,522,000. The restatement reduced net income in 1991 by $2,120,000 or $0.31 per share, and increased the net loss in 1990 by $517,000, or $0.07 per share.

Selected Balance Sheet Data Before and After Restatement for Accounting Change

	March 1, 1991	
Data ($ in thousands)	Originally Reported	After Restatement
Inventory	$19,027	$26,912
LIFO reserve		
Opening	10,258	N/A
Closing	8,138	N/A
Current assets	48,038	55,923
Total assets	76,993	84,878
Current liabilities	40,467	40,467
Total debt	10,548	10,548
Stockholders' equity	$24,079	$31,964

Note 3: Inventories (1991 Annual Report)

During fiscal 1991 and 1990, inventory quantities valued on the LIFO method were reduced. These reductions resulted in a liquidation of quantities carried at costs prevailing in prior years which were lower than current costs. The effect of these reductions was to reduce the cost of sales and other income by $2.2 million in fiscal 1991, and to reduce the cost of sales by $952,000 in fiscal 1990.

B. Letter to Shareholders (1992 Annual Report)

During the fourth quarter we elected to change our accounting method for inventory valuation from the LIFO to FIFO method in order to more appropriately represent our inventory and book value. The change does not create current tax liability, but reduces our operating loss carryforward. This accounting change actually reduces our reported earnings for the 1991 and 1992 fiscal years even though the Company's net worth increased by approximately $7.9 million. All historical data in this report have been restated to conform to the new FIFO method.

C. Long-Term Debt Footnote (1992 Annual Report)

Under an agreement with a bank, the Company can borrow up to $4 million and issue letters of credit up to $8 million through July 31, 1993. The credit facility is secured by certain accounts receivable, inventories, and equipment. The agreement, among other things, precludes the payment of cash dividends on common stock, requires the Company to maintain compliance with certain financial covenants. . . .

EXHIBIT 6-11 (*continued*)

D. *Revenues, Income, and Equity 1992 to 1994 (1992–1994 Annual Reports)*

	($ in thousands)		
	1992	1993	1994
Revenues	$270,554	$341,940	$615,668
Net income	2,869	11,183	27,098
Shareholders' equity	34,037	45,922	75,294

Source: Champion *1991–1994 Annual Reports.*

3. What was Champion's motivation for making the change?

4. What was the long-term impact of the change on Champion?

The answers to these questions may be obtained (in part) from the firm's financial statements. Some answers, however, are not apparent from the financial statements issued when the change was made; we must go back to prior year statements. In certain cases, future year statements provide further insight. Exhibit 6-11 contains required data from Champion annual reports.

Financial Statement Effects (Exhibit 6-11A). The accounting change increased Champion's stockholders' equity at March 1, 1991 by $7,885 thousand, as follows:

Increase in retained earnings at March 4, 1989	$10,522 thousand
Decrease in net income, year ended March 2, 1990	(517)
Decrease in net income, year ended March 1, 1991	(2,120)
Total effect of change	$ 7,885 thousand

The change in inventory method required the restatement of previously reported earnings for fiscal 1990 and 1991. The major effect of the change, however, was on periods prior to fiscal 1990, with that cumulative effect shown as an adjustment to retained earnings at March 4, 1989.

Note that this change in shareholders' equity equals the amount of the March 1991 inventory restatement. As originally reported (at LIFO), inventory was $19,027 thousand; restated to FIFO, it was $26,912 thousand, $7,885 higher.[20]

The increase in inventory and shareholders' equity from the change to FIFO is expected. However, adoption of FIFO *reduced* net income in fiscal 1990 and 1991, the opposite of our expectation. The explanation lies in our discussion of LIFO reserve declines due to deflation and/or LIFO liquidations.

The LIFO reserve declined by $2,220 thousand in 1991 and the 1991 inventory footnote shows that LIFO liquidations added $2.2 million to income in that year and nearly $1.0 million to income in fiscal 1990. The change to FIFO, applied retroactively,

[20]The reader may have noticed that the LIFO reserve was reported as $8,138 thousand on March 1, 1991; the difference between that amount and the $7,885 thousand effect of changing from LIFO to FIFO is not explained in Champion's financial statements. One possible explanation is that, when inventory was restated to its (higher) FIFO level, a lower of cost or market write-down was required.

eliminated that source of profit, far exceeding any increase in the LIFO reserve from current period price increases.

Note that the explanation for the surprising effect on restated earnings was derived from Champion's 1991 financial statements (when the company used LIFO), not the 1992 statements in which the change to FIFO was disclosed.

As the change was made in the fourth quarter, the company also reported the effects on the first three quarters of 1992 and on a quarter by quarter basis for fiscal 1991. The impact on the quarterly income for these periods was

Effect of Change from LIFO to FIFO on Net Income
($ in thousands)

	Fiscal 1991	Fiscal 1992
Quarter 1	$ 68	$90
II	(523)	90
III	(161)	(22)
IV	(1,504)	N/R
Totals	$(2,120)	N/R

N/R= Not reported.

Tax Effects (Exhibit 6-11B). The fact that the stockholders' equity restatement of $7,885 thousand equals the inventory statement indicates that there was no (immediate) *net* tax effect from the accounting change. As the change to FIFO was made for tax reporting as well, we would expect the change in shareholders' equity to be reduced by the incremental tax payable. Champion's *Letter to Shareholders*, however, disclosed the company's use of operating loss carryforwards to offset the income tax payments that would otherwise result from the accounting change.

Motivation for Change in Inventory Method (Exhibit 6-11C). The availability of operating loss carryforwards to neutralize the tax liability triggered by the change in inventory method eliminates the principal barrier to such changes for profitable firms. The expiration of tax loss carryforwards may provide an incentive to change inventory methods. In Champion's case, another effect of the accounting change was to *increase* the reported loss for both fiscal 1990 and 1991. Moreover, while Champion did not report the effect on all of 1992, the impact on the first three quarters was not significant. Thus, reporting higher current income was probably not the principal motivation for this accounting change.

Although Champion's financial statements are vague, it did report that

> under an agreement with a bank, the Company can borrow up to $4 million and issue letters of credit up to $8 million through July 31, 1993. The credit facility is secured by . . . *inventories and . . . requires the Company to maintain compliance with certain financial covenants. . . .* [emphasis added][21]

---

[21] *1992 Annual Report,* Note 4.

Champion had reported net losses for each year starting in fiscal 1986. Stockholders' equity had declined from nearly $60 million at the end of fiscal 1985 to approximately $24 million (prior to restatement) at the end of fiscal 1991. Although the company's debt was modest (approximately $10.5 million in fiscal 1991) and there was no indication that Champion was not in compliance with debt covenants, it is possible that the company was concerned about losing its access to credit.[22]

The major impact of the change to FIFO was on Champion's reported inventory and stockholders' equity. Fiscal 1991 equity was restated upward by nearly $8 million (from $24.1 million to nearly $32 million); the restated debt-to-equity ratio declined from 43.8% ($10,548/$24,079) to 33.0% ($10,548/$31,964). Similarly, the current ratio for fiscal 1991 was restated upward from 1.19 ($48,038/$40,467) to 1.38 ($55,923/$40,467).

The effect of the change to FIFO was to *both* increase inventories and improve Champion's reported financial condition (including working capital, current ratio, stockholders' equity, and debt-to-equity ratio). Thus, the major motivation for the accounting change may have been the need to comply with these covenants. Moreover, as the debt was secured by inventory, it is possible that by increasing the carrying value of the inventory, Champion increased its borrowing capacity.

Prospective Effects of Accounting Change (Exhibit 6-11D). Given the passage of time since Champion adopted FIFO, we can use the advantage of hindsight to evaluate the change on Champion in the years following the accounting change. The company's operating results have improved sharply since that time, with sales growing to $615 million in calendar 1994 and net income increasing to $27 million in that year. As a result, stockholders' equity exceeded $79 million at December 31, 1994. Champion's pretax earnings for the period March 1, 1992 through December 31, 1994 exceeded $52 million, virtually exhausting the company's tax loss carryforwards and resulting in significant current tax payments. We can assume that Champion's current tax liability would be lower if it had remained on LIFO. Although Champion's reported financial condition at the time of the accounting change improved, the adoption of FIFO has almost certainly had adverse cash flow consequences now that the firm has returned to profitability.

LIFO: A HISTORICAL AND EMPIRICAL PERSPECTIVE

Overview of FIFO/LIFO Choice

Exhibit 6-12 contains data from "Accounting Trends and Techniques"[23] regarding current LIFO use. Out of 600 (generally very large) firms in the sample, more than 350 consistently use LIFO for at least part of their inventories. Few firms use LIFO for all inventories. Use by industry classification (not shown here) varies widely; 97% of forest products companies use LIFO, whereas only 8% of firms in the "computers, office equipment" sector do so.

---

[22]See the discussion of debt covenants in Chapter 10.

[23]*Annual Survey of Accounting Practices Followed in 600 Stockholders' Reports,* American Institute of Certified Public Accountants, 1995 edition.

EXHIBIT 6-12
Survey of Inventory Methods Used in the United States

Inventory Cost Determination

| | Number of Companies | | | |
	1994	1993	1992	1991
Methods				
First-in first-out (FIFO)	417	417	415	421
Last-in first-out (LIFO)	351	350	358	361
Average cost	192	189	193	200
Other	42	42	45	50
Use of LIFO				
All inventories	17	17	23	23
50% or more of inventories	186	191	189	186
Less than 50% of inventories	98	92	91	95
Not determinable	50	50	55	57
Companies using LIFO	**351**	**350**	**358**	**361**

Source: American Institute of Certified Public Accountants, "1995 Accounting Trends and Techniques," Table 2-8.

Given the powerful incentives to use LIFO (tax savings and cash flow), two interrelated[24] questions arise:

1. Why do some firms continue to use FIFO?
2. Are firms that use LIFO perceived as being "better off" by the market despite lower reported earnings?

Many empirical studies have examined these issues; in this section we summarize their findings. The large number of studies devoted to the FIFO/LIFO choice is due to its richness as the choice has opposite effects on reported income and cash flow. Moreover, the ability to adjust from one method to the other permits "as if" comparisons in research design.

The choice enables researchers to test whether the market exhibits myopic behavior by being functionally fixated on reported income or the market is efficient and recognizes the beneficial cash flow effects of LIFO. Alternatively, the financial contracting approach can be used to examine the (potential) impact of reported income on management compensation and debt covenant restrictions.

The main empirical findings are relevant to the analyst as they provide evidence that the implications of the FIFO/LIFO choice (or any other accounting choice) are often complex and go beyond the simple tradeoff of lower taxes (higher cash flow) versus higher reported income articulated in research designs. Given the scope of this topic and the spectrum of research approaches covering it, a detailed discussion of

[24]These questions are interrelated because if the market reacts (for whatever reason) negatively to a switch to LIFO, it may explain why some firms choose to remain on FIFO.

the empirical studies is presented in Appendix 6-B. The objective of that appendix is to enable the reader to better appreciate the subtleties involved in the choice of, and the information provided by, alternative accounting reporting methods. We provide a synopsis of the findings in the next section, using the work of Cushing and LeClere (1992) to motivate the discussion.

Summary of FIFO/LIFO Choice

Cushing and LeClere (1992) asked 32 LIFO firms and 70 FIFO firms to rank their reasons for their choice of inventory method. For LIFO firms, the overwhelming primary reason was the favorable tax effect. This result is consistent with research findings that firms using LIFO are primarily motivated by its favorable tax effects and these firms stand to gain the most from using LIFO.

A switch to LIFO, however, is not always regarded favorably by the market. By switching to LIFO, the firm may be providing (unfavorable) information about its sensitivity to changing prices (or other firm characteristics). Thus, reaction to a change in accounting method may reflect this other information rather than the tax advantage alone. This leads to the possibility that the reaction to a switch may vary[25] with factors such as the:

- Time period estimated
- Market and analyst understanding of the effects of inflation
- Extent a change to LIFO can be anticipated

If the market (i.e., analysts) did not anticipate the change or were unable to accurately estimate the effects of inflation on the firm, the market may react negatively at the time of the switch. This, as noted in our earlier discussion of initial LIFO adoptions, may explain why firms that switched to LIFO in the early 1970s met with negative market reactions.

Reasons for choosing FIFO are complex. Based on the responses in Cushing and LeClere, no single reason emerges as most important for FIFO firms. Over half suggested economic reasons as their motivation. Twenty of the 70 firms (approximately 30%) indicated that LIFO did not provide them with any tax benefits (e.g., declining prices). Others claimed that the accounting and administrative costs to maintain LIFO records and/or ensure that there are no LIFO liquidations kept them from using LIFO. However, just as many firms stated that they chose FIFO because it was a "better accounting method" as it better reflected the physical flow of goods. Close to 40% indicated, as one of their two primary reasons, their concern about the lower earnings resulting from LIFO.[26]

Consistent with the tax effects argument, Dopuch and Pincus (1988) found that FIFO firms were less likely (relative to LIFO firms) to have significant tax savings from LIFO. With respect to the income enhancing arguments, Hunt (1985) did find some evidence that supported the bonus plan hypothesis.

Many of the inventory studies found the choice of inventory method closely related to industry and size factors, with larger firms opting for LIFO. The industry factor is a consequence of similar production, operating, and inflation conditions faced by firms

---

[25]See Figure 6B-1 on p. 317.

[26]These numbers, it should be noted, are considerably higher than those reported by Granof and Short (1984) in an earlier survey.

EXHIBIT 6-13
Variables Hypothesized to Affect FIFO-LIFO Choice

1. *Estimated tax savings* from use of LIFO expected to be larger for LIFO companies.
2. *Inventory materiality:* The larger a firm's inventory balance, the greater the incentive to use LIFO as the potential tax saving is larger.
3. *Tax loss carryforward:* The larger a firm's tax loss carryforward, the less incentive it has to use LIFO.
4. *Inventory variability:* The more variable a firm's inventory balance, the more likely it is to face inventory liquidations. This would tend to favor choosing FIFO over LIFO.
5. *Inventory obsolescence:* If a firm's inventory tends to become obsolete because of new product innovation, then the replacement of old products by new ones raises a difficult LIFO accounting question for which there is no authoritative answer. Such companies may prefer FIFO.
6. *Size as proxy for bookkeeping costs:* The larger the accounting costs required to use LIFO, the less likely a firm would choose LIFO. Larger firms would be able to absorb these costs more readily.
7. *Leverage:* Under the debt covenant hypothesis, firms with higher leverage would prefer FIFO as it would improve their debt/equity ratios.
8. *Current ratio:* Under the debt covenant hypothesis, firms with low current ratios would prefer FIFO, which improves their current ratio.

Source: Barry E. Cushing and Marc J. LeClere, "Evidence on the Determinants of Inventory Accounting Policy Choice," *The Accounting Review,* April 1992, pp. 355–366, Table 4, p. 363.

in the same industry. The size factor has been explained in two ways. As noted, adoption of LIFO increases inventory management and control costs, which mitigate the benefit received from tax savings. For large firms, these costs are more readily absorbed and small relative to the potential tax benefits. Alternatively, the size effect reflects the fact that, for political reasons, larger firms tend to choose accounting methods that lower reported earnings.

Exhibit 6-13, based on Cushing and LeClere (1992), is a useful summary of their findings; the variables and the rationale behind them are indicated in the table. Seven of the eight variables that explain the FIFO/LIFO choice are significant in the predicted direction. The estimated tax savings are significantly greater for LIFO firms. Consistent with this, FIFO firms have higher average loss carryforwards. Inventory variability is higher for FIFO firms, increasing the chances of LIFO liquidations. FIFO firms tend to be smaller, more highly leveraged, and less liquid. Similarly, the likelihood of inventory obsolescence is also a significant factor. Only the materiality measure is not statistically significant.

These variables indicate possible motivations to stay on FIFO. For a given firm, it is worthwhile knowing which of these motivations apply and thus, whether the firm is justified in staying on FIFO or management is inefficient (or self-serving) by giving up the LIFO tax advantage. Management that forgoes significant tax savings for motives that are either selfish or based on the belief that the market can be fooled should not inspire confidence.[27]

[27]See the discussion of "quality of earnings" in Chapter 17.

CONCLUDING COMMENTS ON ACCOUNTING FOR INVENTORIES

The choice of accounting method for inventories is one of the basic decisions made by nearly all companies engaged in the manufacturing and distribution of goods. Ideally, the method chosen should result in the best measure of income and financial condition. However, no single method accomplishes these objectives in most cases.

For companies operating in the United States, under conditions of rising prices, the cash flow advantage of LIFO usually dictates the choice of that method. When LIFO is not chosen, therefore, the first question should be: Why not? As the empirical work indicates, managers offer a number of reasons for not using LIFO, only some of which appear valid. Thus, companies that should use LIFO but do not may not be attractive to investors.

In many cases, the analytical techniques presented in this chapter enable the analyst to approximate the effect of LIFO on a company using FIFO or average cost. Such analysis can result in estimates of both the cash savings forgone (relevant to the discussion in the previous paragraph) and the inclusion of holding gains in reported income.

Example: British Petroleum

Occasionally, management makes the required adjustments available. Exhibit 6-14 contains data from the *1994 Annual Report* of British Petroleum (BP). Given the fluctuations in oil prices, holding gains and losses are a recurring feature of that company's income statement. As LIFO is generally not acceptable for income tax use outside of the United States, there is no incentive to use it for financial reporting.

The data in Exhibit 6-14 speak for themselves. Historical cost profit (before extraordinary items) was little changed in 1994, as compared with 1990. However, substantially lower profits were reported in 1991 to 1993. Historical cost-basis earnings per ordinary (common) share reflect these results. When holding gains and losses are excluded, however, a different picture emerges: replacement cost profit (before extraordinary items) rose 42% from 1990 to 1994. Reported operating earnings over

EXHIBIT 6-14. BRITISH PETROLEUM
Comparison of Historic and Replacement Profit, 1990 to 1994

	1990	1991	1992	1993	1994
	Pounds in millions				
Profit (historical)*	1,511	308	430	844	1,544
Holding (gains) losses	(472)	620	106	281	(62)
Profit (replacement)	1,039	928	536	1,125	1,482
	Pence per Ordinary Share				
Profit (historical)*	31.50 p	7.70 p	(8.50) p	11.30 p	28.80 p
Profit (replacement)	19.04	17.20	9.90	20.70	27.10
Dividend	16.05	16.80	10.50	8.40	10.50

*Before extraordinary items
Source: British Petroleum, *1994 Annual Report.*

this time period were significantly affected by inventory holding gains or losses virtually every year.

If we recall our discussion (Chapter 2) of the meaning of income, it seems clear that replacement cost profit is a better measure of BP's earnings. Holding gains and losses are not predictable. Moreover, holding gains must be reinvested in inventory for the firm to remain in business; they are not available for distribution.

British Petroleum lowered its per share dividend nearly 35% over the 1990 to 1994 period. Relative to both the reported (historical cost) and replacement cost profit, the dividend payout ratio declined. However, BP sustained its investments and reduced debt by cutting dividends during the lean period of 1991 to 1993.

Although BP, given wide swings in the price of oil, may be an extreme case, it illustrates the necessity of analyzing the inventory accounting of a firm to understand the impact of changing prices on its earnings and net worth.

INTERNATIONAL ACCOUNTING AND REPORTING PRACTICES

FIFO and the weighted-average method are the most commonly used methods worldwide. Historically, the use of LIFO was essentially limited to companies in the United States, and the significant tax benefits this method can provide suggest that the method will continue to enjoy widespread acceptance. These benefits have resulted in gradual adoption of LIFO as a permitted alternative in countries such as Germany, Italy, and Japan.[28] In some countries, LIFO is allowed for financial reporting but not income taxes, which may account for its lack of popularity in these countries. In practice, LIFO is rarely used in these countries, perhaps because of the low inflation rates of recent years. Non-U.S. reporting standards do not require disclosure of LIFO reserves, reducing the analyst's ability to make some of the balance sheet adjustments discussed in this chapter.

In the United Kingdom, Statement of Standard Accounting Practice (SSAP) 9 holds that LIFO may not result in a true and fair valuation and, in addition, the method is not allowed for tax purposes.

Average cost is the most widely used method in Germany, although LIFO has been allowed for tax purposes since 1990, and it may change reporting habits.

IASC Standard 2

In 1993, the IASC issued revised International Accounting Standard (IAS) 2, designating FIFO and weighted-average costs as the benchmark treatments and LIFO as the allowed alternative. Firms using LIFO are required to provide FIFO/weighted-average or current cost disclosures facilitating the adjustments discussed in this chapter.

Inventories (other than LIFO) are reported at the lower of cost or market value; cost depends on the method used. Market is generally defined as the net realizable value with specific limitations in the United States[29]; any write-down is determined on an item-by-item basis. Revised IAS 2 limits itself to net realizable value (NRV), and it does not specify whether the cost versus NRV comparison should be made on an item-by-item basis or by groups of similar items. This standard is similar to those of most other countries.

---

[28]As discussed in Chapter 1, financial reporting and tax reporting are identical in these countries.

[29]Generally, these limitations ensure that inventories are written down to approximately their current cost.

USING INVENTORY BALANCES TO AID IN FORECASTING[30]

Changes in inventory balances can provide signals about a firm's future sales and earnings prospects. Unfortunately, such signals are ambiguous. An unanticipated (from the analyst's perspective) increase in the inventory balance may signal either:

1. An unexpected decrease in recent demand, causing an unplanned increase in inventory that signals lower future demand, or[31]
2. A (planned) increase in inventory levels by management anticipating higher future demand

These two arguments are, of course, mutually exclusive. Which condition prevails cannot be determined from the changes in the inventory account itself. Rather, the change itself acts as a signal for the analyst to investigate (using other sources of information) which condition is most likely for the company in question.[32]

The above discussion relates only to changes in finished goods inventory. In a manufacturing environment, changes in work-in-process inventory (and to some degree changes in raw materials inventory) may indicate that management is increasing production to meet an increase in actual or anticipated orders.

The balances in the inventory account (Exhibit 6-15) of BMC Industries Inc. for 1989 to 1990 illustrate this phenomenon. Total inventory increased by 44% but the bulk of the increase was due to a 180% change in the work-in-process component. This increase implies there was increased production in anticipation of future sales, which materialized in the second quarter of 1991 (Exhibit 6-15B). After the second quarter, sales (and inventories) reverted to "normal" levels. Generally, when such increases occur, the analyst must determine if the sales increase is "one shot" or signals an ongoing trend. Although both cases enhance the company's value, there is a difference in degree. In BMC's case, management stated in the 1990 MD&A that the buildup in inventory was a result of a one-time order for delivery in the second quarter of 1991.

On a more general level, Bernard and Noel (1991) examined whether changes in inventory could be used to forecast future sales and earnings. They found that the implications of inventory changes are not homogeneous for all firms, but differ between retailers and manufacturers. Even among manufacturers, the implications depend on the component of inventory that changes.

For retailers, inventory increases signal higher sales but lower earnings and profit margins. This may seem paradoxical but the explanation is straightforward. Increases in inventory were usually a result of argument (1) above; a drop in demand resulted in increased inventory. To eliminate this "excess" inventory, retailers reduced prices to stimulate sales ("dumping" inventory). Therefore, sales increased but with lower earnings. These effects were generally short-lived as the effect on sales dissipated over time.

---

[30]See Bernard and Noel (1991) for a more elaborate discussion of the issues discussed in this section.

[31]Throughout this section, a distinction between demand and sales must be kept in mind. Lower current demand can be associated with higher future sales if a company, in response to lower demand, cuts prices, thus stimulating sales.

[32]The analyst must also be sure that the change is not a result of a change in accounting method or management acquiring more inventory in an attempt to "beat" an anticipated price increase.

EXHIBIT 6-15. BMC INDUSTRIES
Increase in Work in Process Inventory as Indicator of
Future Sales

A. Changes in Components of Inventory Account, 1989 to 1990

	($ in millions)		
	1989	1990	% Increase
Raw material	$ 9.7	$ 13.1	35%
Work in process	4.7	13.3	180
Finished goods	14.7	15.7	7
Total	$ 29.2	$ 42.1	44%

B. Comparison of Quarterly Sales 1990 and 1991

	Quarterly Sales		
	1990	1991	% Change
First	$ 43.6	$ 44.5	2%
Second	46.1	62.2	35
Third	39.2	42.5	8
Fourth	46.1	54.0	17
Total	$175.0	$203.2	16%

Source: BMC Industries, *1990–1991 Annual Report.*

For manufacturers, increases in finished goods inventory again indicate lower future demand; these increases are followed by higher sales and lower earnings in the short run as manufacturers dump unwanted inventory. However, unlike retailers, in the long run (once the initial increase is worked down) the drop in demand persists and future sales and earnings decrease. For raw materials and work in process, on the other hand, increases in inventory levels are consistent with higher future demand and higher future sales.

Unplanned inventory changes may also have a direct impact on future unit production costs. When excess inventory must be worked off, production levels decline and unit costs increase as fixed overhead is spread over fewer units. Conversely, production increases reduce unit costs by spreading overhead over increased production.

This concluding section of the chapter provides a different analytical application of information contained in financial reports. The lessons of the earlier sections, however, must not be forgotten. Any changes in inventory balances must take into consideration the inventory method used. Thus, for a LIFO company, analysis of changes should be based on current cost inventory amounts. In addition, an effort should be made to ensure that the change in inventory balances is driven by quantity changes, not increased prices for the same inventory quantity.

SUMMARY

In an environment of changing prices, assumptions as to the flow of costs affect reported income, balance sheet amounts, and associated ratios. More important, the FIFO/LIFO choice has real cash flow consequences because of LIFO's tax and financial reporting conformity requirement in the United States. The chapter compares the financial statement effects of the FIFO/LIFO choice and demonstrates how the analyst can adjust from one method to another. It also explores the effects of liquidations and inventory costing in a manufacturing environment. The incentives for firms to opt for one method over another as well as the stock market reaction to these choices are also analyzed. After a comparison of United States GAAP with those of other countries, the chapter concludes with a description of how changes in inventory balances can be used to improve forecasts of sales and earnings.

CASE 6-1

Inventory Analysis of Nucor

Nucor is one of the largest U.S. steel companies. Exhibit 6C-1 contains financial data for the five years ended December 31, 1995. Nucor has used the LIFO method for all inventories during the entire time period. There were no LIFO liquidations.

CASE OBJECTIVE

The objective of this case is to show the impact of Nucor's use of the LIFO inventory method on its:

1. Balance sheet
2. Income statement
3. Cash from operations
4. Financial ratios

Required:
The following questions should be answered using the data provided in Exhibit 6C-1:

1. Calculate gross margin (both level and as a percent of sales) under both the LIFO and FIFO methods for the years 1990 to 1995.

EXHIBIT 6C-1. NUCOR
Selected Financial Data, Years Ended December 31 ($ in millions)

	1989	1990	1991	1992	1993	1994	1995
Income Statement							
Sales		$1,481,630	$1,465,457	$1,619,235	$2,253,738	$2,975,596	$3,462,046
Cost of products sold		1,293,083	1,302,744	1,417,376	1,965,847	2,491,760	2,900,168
Pretax income		111,215	95,816	117,326	187,110	356,933	432,335
Net income		75,065	64,716	79,226	123,510	226,633	274,535
Earnings per share		$ 0.88	$ 0.75	$ 0.92	$ 1.42	$ 2.60	$ 3.14
Tax rate		34%	34%	34%	35%	35%	35%
Balance Sheet							
LIFO inventory	$139,450	$ 136,644	$ 186,075	$ 206,405	$ 214,015	$ 243,027	$ 306,773
LIFO reserve	43,723	50,903	37,208	29,631	67,128	81,662	93,932
Current assets		312,637	334,293	381,517	468,232	638,701	830,741
Current liabilities		202,789	229,166	271,972	350,491	382,465	447,136
Stockholders' equity	584,445	652,757	711,609	784,231	902,167	1,122,610	1,382,112
Per share	$ 6.83	$ 7.59	$ 8.23	$ 9.04	$ 10.36	$ 12.85	$ 15.78
Statement of Cash Flows							
Cash from operations		$ 214,330	$ 173,396	$ 205,409	$ 271,793	$ 424,946	$ 447,160

Source: Nucor, *1990–1995 Annual Reports.*

2. Discuss the differences in the level, trend, and variability of gross margins under the two methods.

3. Calculate net income, assuming Nucor had used the FIFO method of reporting for 1990 to 1995, and discuss differences in the level, growth rate, and variability of net income under the two methods.

4. Calculate Nucor's cash from operations, assuming Nucor had used the FIFO method of reporting for 1990 to 1995. Compare your results to reported cash from operations and discuss the difference in level and growth rate.

5. Calculate stockholders' equity per share, stating inventories at current cost. Compare your results to reported equity and discuss the difference in level and growth rate.

6. Calculate the following ratios for Nucor, using both reported data and current cost, for 1990 to 1995:

   • Current ratio

   • Return on (average) equity

   Discuss the effect of using LIFO on the level and variability of both ratios.

7. Calculate Nucor's inventory turnover ratios for 1990 to 1995, using:

   (a) LIFO data

   (b) FIFO data

   (c) Current cost data

   Discuss the differences among these three turnover ratios and select the method that provides the best measure of economic turnover. Discuss the trend in Nucor's inventory turnover over the 1990 to 1995 period and factors that might account for the variability of reported turnover.

8. Using the results of Questions 1 through 7 and the data in Exhibit 6C-1, discuss the advantages and disadvantages to Nucor of using the LIFO method over the 1990 to 1995 time period.

9. Birmingham Steel Corporation, a competitor of Nucor, uses the FIFO method of accounting for its inventories. Selected data ($ in thousands) from its *1995 Annual Report* are presented below:

Sales	885,553
COGS	723,558

	Opening Balance	Closing Balance
Inventory	132,459	173,053
Shareholders' equity	439,049	459,719

(a) Compare Nucor and Birmingham Steel's reported 1995:

   • Inventory turnover ratio
   • Gross profit margin
   • ROE

(b) Redo (a) using adjusted ratios for Nucor and Birmingham Steel. For each ratio, use the method(s) you deem to be most appropriate and justify your choice.

Chapter 6

Problems

1. [Allocation of purchase costs under different inventory methods; 1996 CFA adapted] Assume the following:

Quarter	Units Purchased	Per Unit Cost	Dollar Purchases	Unit Sales
I	200	$22	$ 4,400	200
II	300	24	7,200	200
III	300	26	7,800	200
IV	200	28	5,600	200
Year	1,000		$25,000	800

Inventory at beginning of Quarter I: 400 units at $20 per unit = $ 8,000.
Inventory at end of Quarter IV: 600 units.

A. Calculate reported inventory at the end of the year under *each* of the following inventory methods:

   (i) FIFO

   (ii) LIFO

   (iii) Average cost

B. Calculate the cost of goods sold for the year under *each* method listed in part A.

C. Discuss the effect of the differences among the three methods on:

   (i) Reported income for the year

   (ii) Stockholders' equity at the end of the year

2. [Effect of inventory methods on financial statements; 1996 CFA adapted] Compare the effect of the use of the LIFO inventory method with use of the FIFO method on each of the following, assuming rising prices and stable inventory quantities:

   (i) Net income

   (ii) Cash from operations

   (iii) Inventory balances

   (iv) Working capital

   (v) Inventory turnover ratio

3. [Ratio effects of choice of inventory method; 1995 CFA adapted] CMU Corporation uses FIFO instead of LIFO as its inventory valuation method. Explain the effect of using FIFO instead of LIFO during a period of rising prices on *each* of the following ratios:

   (i) Gross profit margin

   (ii) Inventory turnover

   (iii) Debt-to-equity

4. [FIFO and LIFO: basic relationships] The Mogul Company, expecting that decreases in oil prices are only temporary, increases its monthly purchases as the price of oil decreases. Mogul's 19X8 monthly oil purchases follow:

Period	Quantity (bbl)	Price/Barrel ($)
First quarter		
January	100,000	25
February	100,000	25
March	100,000	25
Second quarter		
April	125,000	20
May	125,000	20
June	125,000	20
Third quarter		
July	150,000	18
August	150,000	18
September	150,000	18
Fourth quarter		
October	200,000	15
November	200,000	15
December	200,000	15

Assumptions:

- The company has no opening inventory.
- Sales are 100,000 barrels per month for the period January through June and 150,000 per month for the period July through December.
- Mogul uses the LIFO inventory method.
- The company's tax rate is 40%.

A. Compute the difference in *each* of the following dollar amounts that Mogul would report under its present accounting method (LIFO), as compared with use of the FIFO method. (*Note:* The solution does not require long calculations; focus on the *differences* between FIFO and LIFO levels, not the actual amounts.)

  (i) Inventory purchases

  (ii) Closing inventory

 (iii) COGS

  (iv) Pretax income

  (v) Income tax expense

  (vi) Net income

 (vii) Cash flow from operations

(viii) Working capital (year-end)

B. Assume that Mogul liquidates its entire inventory at year-end. Discuss how the answers to part A would differ.

5. [Inventory costing; basic relationships] During its first year of operations, Metro Retailers made the following inventory purchases:

February 1	1,000 units @ $2 each
April 1	2,800 units @ $3 each
August 1	1,000 units

For the year, it reported COGS of $10,500 and ending inventory of $3,500 using the weighted-average method.

A. Compute the price at which the August 1 purchase was made.

B. Compute COGS and ending inventory under *both* the LIFO and FIFO methods.

6. [Inventory methods, basic relationships, impact on turnover ratio] The Renemax Co. begins operations on December 31, 19X0, with $500 of inventory, enough for one month's (January 19X1) sales. During 19X1, the company maintains its inventory at one month's sales. Monthly sales (in units) are constant, and the company replenishes inventory each month.

At the end of 19X1, Renemax must choose an inventory method. The following additional information is available:

· The cash flow difference between the FIFO and LIFO methods is $400. (*Note:* You do not know which is higher.)

· The COGS is $12,000 using the weighted-average method.

· The company's tax rate is 40%.

· Prices change only in one direction during the year.

A. Using the information provided, fill in the following blanks:

	FIFO	Weighted Average	LIFO
Opening inventory	_____	_____	_____
Purchases	_____	_____	_____
COGS	_____	$12,000	_____
Closing inventory	_____	_____	_____
Inventory turnover (reported)	_____	_____	_____
Inventory turnover (physical)	_____	_____	_____

(*Hint:* The firm's physical inventory turnover is 12. Use this insight to complete the blanks for the weighted-average method. Then consider the effect of price changes on the amounts computed under the LIFO and FIFO methods.)

B. Compare the inventory turnover ratio reported under each method. Discuss which method provides the ratio that most accurately portrays the actual *physical* turnover.

C. Discuss the impact of the choice of accounting method on cash flow from operations and total cash flows.

7. [Inventory methods, basic relationships] The M&J Co. begins operations on January 1, 19X0, with the following balance sheet:

Cash	$10,000	Common stock	$10,000

During the year, the company maintains its inventory accounts using the FIFO method. Before a provision for income tax, the balance sheet at December 31, 19X0, is:

Cash	$ 5,000	Common stock	$10,000
Inventory	10,000	Pretax income	5,000
	$15,000		$15,000

M&J has 19X0 sales of $25,000. The company sells half of the *units* purchased during the year. Operating expenses (excluding COGS) are $12,000.

Prior to issuing financial statements, the company considers its choice of inventory method. Assume a tax rate of 40% and a dividend payout ratio of 50%.

A. Using the information provided, complete the following table:

	FIFO	Weighted-Average	LIFO
Sales	$25,000	$25,000	$25,000
COGS			
Other expenses	12,000	12,000	12,000
Pretax income			
Income tax expense			
Net income			
Dividends paid			
Retained earnings			
Cash from operations			
Closing cash balance			
Closing inventory	10,000		
Inventory purchases			

B. Prepare a balance sheet for M&J at December 31, 19X0, assuming use of:
 (i) The LIFO inventory method
 (ii) The weighted-average method
 (iii) The FIFO inventory method

C. Discuss the advantages and disadvantages of *each* of the three possible choices of inventory method.

8. [LIFO, FIFO, holding gains and comprehensive income; 1988 CFA adapted] The Quickie Rice Company sells Rice-O-Matics, devices that reduce the time required to prepare rice.

- Inventory at the beginning of the accounting period was one unit at $35.
- Two more units were purchased during the period, the first at $39 and the second at $43.
- One unit was sold at $65.
- Replacement cost at the close of the accounting period was $46.

Calculate, on both the FIFO and LIFO basis, Quickie's

  (i) Ending inventory

  (ii) Gross profit

  (iii) Unrealized inventory holding gain

  (iv) Comprehensive income (reported income plus unrealized holding gain).

9. [Declining costs, LOCM] Prices for the ZB Company's products are falling due to lower production costs. On September 30, 1994, the company had the following inventory balance:

$$100 \text{ units @ } \$44 \qquad \$ 4,400$$

Fourth-quarter purchases were

$$
\begin{array}{lll}
200 \text{ units @ } & \$43 & \$ 8,600 \\
300 \text{ units @ } & \$40 & \$12,000
\end{array}
$$

Fourth-quarter sales were

$$125 \text{ units @ } \$50 \qquad \$62,500$$

A. Compute the balance in the inventory account on December 31, 1994 using the following accounting methods:

  (i) FIFO

  (ii) LIFO

B. Which method will result in lower income taxes? Compute the tax savings from the method producing the lower tax. Assume a 40% tax rate.

C. Now assume that, on December 31, 1994, a competitor announces a new model and selling prices drop to $40. Describe the accounting (journal) entry necessary and state the effect of that entry on income taxes assuming the company uses:

  (i) FIFO

  (ii) LIFO

Problems 10 and 11 are based on the following data, adapted from the actual financial statements of two firms in the automobile replacement parts industry.

Zenab Distributors, Balance Sheets, at December 31

	19X5	19X6
Cash	$ 500	$ 100
Accounts receivable (net)	8,100	8,300
Inventory	24,900	25,200
Current assets	$33,500	$33,600
Current liabilities	$11,600	$12,700

Zenab Distributors uses the LIFO method of accounting for 70% of its inventories; it uses FIFO for the remainder. If all inventories were carried at FIFO, inventory would be higher by $3,600 and $5,100 in 19X5 and 19X6, respectively.

Faybech Parts, Balance Sheets, at December 31

	19X5	19X6
Cash	$ 1,000	$ 600
Accounts receivable (net)	11,400	13,900
Inventory	22,300	30,300
Current assets	$34,700	$44,800
Current liabilities	$10,700	$12,200

Faybech Parts uses FIFO accounting for all inventories.

Income Statements, Year Ended December 31, 19X6

	Zenab	Faybech
Sales	$92,700	$77,000
COGS	61,300	52,000
Gross profit	$31,400	$25,000
Selling and general expense	26,400	21,500
Pretax income	$ 5,000	$ 3,500
Income tax expense	2,000	1,400
Net income	$ 3,000	$ 2,100

10. [Adjusting LIFO to FIFO and FIFO to LIFO/current cost] Using the financial data provided:

A. Calculate Zenab's COGS and pretax income on a FIFO basis.

B. Calculate Faybech's COGS and pretax income on a LIFO/current cost basis.

C. Discuss the circumstances under which income tax expense should be adjusted when computing net income in parts A and B.

11. [LIFO versus FIFO; effect on ratios; adjusting ratios]

A. Using *only reported* financial data, compute each of the following ratios for both Zenab and Faybech:

    (i) Current ratio (19X5 and 19X6)

    (ii) Inventory turnover (19X6)

    (iii) Gross profit margin (19X6)

    (iv) Pretax profit margin (EBT to sales) (19X6)

B. Briefly compare the performance of the two firms in 19X6 based on the ratios computed in part A.

C. Recalculate each of the ratios in part A with both companies:

    (i) On FIFO

    (ii) On LIFO

    (iii) Using the current cost method

D. Select the basis of comparison for *each* of the four ratios that you feel is most meaningful. Justify *each* choice.

12. [LIFO versus FIFO; effect on ratios; adjusting ratios; 1990 CFA adapted] The Zeta Corp. uses LIFO inventory accounting. The footnotes to the 19X4 financial statements contain the following data as of December 31:

	19X3	19X4
Raw materials	$392,675	$369,725
Finished products	401,325	377,075
Inventory on FIFO basis	$794,000	$746,800
LIFO reserve	(46,000)	(50,000)
Inventory on LIFO basis	$748,000	$696,800

You are also provided with the following data:

    • The company has a marginal tax rate of 35%.

    • COGS for 19X4 is $3,800,000.

    • Net income for 19X4 is $340,000.

    • Return on equity for 19X4 is 4.6%.

A. Calculate 19X4 net income for Zeta, assuming that it uses the FIFO inventory method.

B. Calculate the company's inventory turnover ratio on both a FIFO and LIFO basis.

C. Calculate Zeta's return on equity on a FIFO basis. (Remember to adjust both the numerator and denominator.)

D. Discuss the usefulness of the adjustments made in parts A, B, and C to a financial analyst.

E. Describe alternative measures of inventory turnover and return on equity that would be more useful to assess Zeta's operating performance.

13. [Adjusting for LIFO liquidations] The Jofen Company uses the LIFO inventory method. In 19X3, anticipating a downturn in demand, the company decides not to replenish inventory levels at year-end. The resulting LIFO liquidation increases pretax income by $300,000. Ending inventory on December 31, 19X3, is $2,000,000, a reduction of $700,000 from the level at January 1, 19X3.

A. Compute the LIFO cost of inventory at January 1, 19X3.

B. Compute the additional purchases that would have been required to fully replenish inventories, thus avoiding the LIFO liquidation during 19X3.

C. Describe the impact of the LIFO liquidation on cash flow from operations.

D. Describe how the foregoing data could be used to adjust reported income for 19X3.

E. Explain why net income as adjusted in part D is more useful for financial analysis.

14. [Inventory turnover ratio] General Electric reported that its inventory turnover ratio increased from 5.3 times in 1992 to 6.0 times in 1993 and 6.9 times in 1994. The following data appear in GE's 1994 annual report:

Years Ended December 31 ($ in millions)

	1991	1992	1993	1994
Revenues	$37,496	$37,906	$37,777	$39,543
Cost of goods and services sold	27,871	28,389	28,914	28,962
Year-end inventories at FIFO	7,333	6,382	5,453	5,312
Year-end inventories at LIFO	5,321	4,574	3,824	3,880

Note: All data exclude GE's financial services.
Source: General Electric, *1993-1994 Annual Reports.*

A. Compute GE's inventory turnover ratios for 1992 to 1994, using:
   (i) Cost of goods and services sold and LIFO inventory
   (ii) Cost of goods and services sold and FIFO inventory

B. Some firms calculate inventory turnover using sales rather than COGS in the numerator. Calculate GE's 1991 to 1994 turnover, using:
   (i) Sales and LIFO inventory
   (ii) Sales and FIFO inventory

C. Which method does it appear that GE uses?

D. Which method would you choose to evaluate GE's performance? Justify your choice.

15. [Effect of using LIFO; decline in reserve] The New York Times Company inventory footnote in 1991 follows:

Inventories as shown in the accompanying Consolidated Balance Sheets are composed of the following:

December 31, 1990 to 1991 ($ in thousands)

	1990	1991
Newsprint and magazine paper	$40,312	$33,393
Work in process	6,003	7,451
Total inventory	$46,315	$40,844

Utilization of the LIFO method reduced inventories as calculated on the FIFO method by approximately $7,882,000 and $3,619,000 at December 31, 1990 and 1991, respectively.
Source: New York Times Company, *1991 Annual Report.*

A. Calculate the effect of the use of LIFO by The New York Times Company on 1991 reported pretax income.

B. Calculate the change in total reported inventory balances if the firm had used the FIFO method for 1990 and 1991.

C. The 1991 decline in the LIFO reserve and inventory did not represent a LIFO liquidation. Explain what may have caused it.

16. [Inventory costing for pricing purposes] The following paragraph was taken from the "Message to Stockholders" section of the Driver-Harris *1980 Annual Report:*

We would like to call your attention to a major effect caused by inflation. Our results are significantly affected by the use of LIFO accounting. We believe that this method better reflects the results of operations in inflationary times, even though, had the FIFO method been used for inventory valuation, our 1980 results before income taxes would have been approximately $1,800,000 better. Unfortunately, some of our competitors throughout the world are still using the FIFO method, and thus tend to offer unrealistically low prices, based on outdated costs.

Discuss the validity of this paragraph.

17. [Declines in inventory; choice of method] Control Data Corporation was a manufacturer of computer equipment. It used FIFO or average cost for all inventories. Inventory levels were

December 31	1989	1990
Finished goods	$ 84.1 million	$ 46.7 million
Work in process	38.5	49.3
Raw materials	122.4	86.0
Total	$245.0 million	$182.0 million

A. Suggest three factors that would explain *all or part* of the 1990 inventory decline.

B. Explain which of the factors in your answer to part A justified Control Data's decision not to use the LIFO inventory method.

Control Data stated:

> Costs incurred in placing developed standard commercial products into production are capitalized and amortized based upon the quantity of units shipped during an 18- to 24-month period after commencement of production.

C. Discuss how this policy affects trends in the company's COGS.

18. [Measuring operating performance in service economy] The inventory turnover ratio measures one aspect of a firm's operating efficiency. For companies that do not have significant inventories (i.e., service industries), this measure cannot be used. In some cases, even for firms that maintain inventory, the measure is inappropriate. Examples include:

- Airlines
- Car rental firms
- Private hospitals

A. Explain why the inventory turnover ratio is not a useful measure for firms in these industries.

B. Suggest and justify possible alternative measures of operating efficiency for such companies.

19. [Effect of inventory methods on contracts] The Sechne Company has entered into a number of agreements in the past year. These agreements contain provisions that depend on the firm's reported financial statements:

    (i) *Management compensation plan.* Bonuses are based on a weighted-average of reported net income and cash from operations.

    (ii) *Bond indenture.* Specifies that the firm must maintain a minimum level of working capital and dividend payments to shareholders require a minimum level of retained earnings.

    (iii) *Labor contract.* Employees have a profit-sharing plan that pays them a share of reported net income in excess of a specified level.

Sechne's corporate controller, who is *both* a manager and shareholder, must select the accounting methods used for financial reporting. Discuss how these agreements may affect the controller's choice of an inventory accounting method for Sechne.

20. [Inventory obsolescence under LIFO] Monarch Machine Tool reported losses in each year for 1992 to 1994 as a result of highly competitive conditions. Its 1994 inventory footnote follows:

3. Inventories

Inventories, aggregating approximately $15,293,000 and $16,246,000 at December 31, 1994 and 1993, respectively, were valued at the lower of last-in, first-out (LIFO) cost or market. The remaining inventories of approximately $4,894,000 and $5,355,000 at December 31, 1994 and 1993, respectively, were valued at the lower of first-in, first-out (FIFO) cost or market.

At December 31, 1994 and 1993, inventories are summarized as follows ($ in thousands):

	1994	1993
Finished goods	$ 6,561	$ 6,904
Work in process	27,047	27,231
Raw materials, parts, and supplies	1,203	1,318
Total FIFO cost	$34,811	$35,453
Less allowance to adjust the carrying value of inventories to LIFO basis	14,624	13,851
Inventories at LIFO	$20,187	$21,602

The Company provides for potential losses from obsolete and slow-moving inventory in the period in which they are identified. The charge to earnings in 1994, 1993, and 1992 related to obsolete and slow-moving inventory was $748,000, $1,377,000 and $1,430,000, respectively.

Assume that the charges for inventory obsolescence relate to inventories carried on the LIFO method.

A. Discuss how these obsolescence charges affect:

  (i) Reported earnings

  (ii) Tax return earnings

  (iii) Cash from operations

B. Given your answers to part A, discuss the disadvantage to Monarch of using the LIFO method for nearly all inventories.

C. Discuss why Monarch has not changed its inventory method despite the disadvantage discussed in part B.

21. [Effect of LIFO liquidation on gross margins] The Deere Company reported the following operating results:

Years Ended October 31 ($ in millions)

	1991	1992	1993
Sales	$5,848	$5,723	$6,479
COGS	4,894	4,891	5,375
Gross margin	$ 954	$ 832	$1,104

Deere's inventory footnote reported LIFO liquidations that increased profits by $128, $65, and $51 million in 1991, 1992, and 1993 respectively.

A. Calculate the company's gross margin percentage for 1991 to 1993, using reported data.

B. Calculate Deere's COGS, gross margin, and gross margin percentage for 1991 to 1993 *excluding* the benefit of the LIFO liquidation.

22. [DuPont; adjusting for alternative accounting methods; effects of liquidation] DuPont reported a LIFO liquidation benefit of $50 million for 1993. Selected financial data ($ in millions) for 1992 to 1994 are presented below:

	1992	1993	1994
Sales	$37,799	$37,098	$39,333
COGS	22,046	21,624	21,977
Inventory (88% LIFO)	4,401	3,818	3,969
LIFO reserve	$ 1,187	$ 766	$ 819

A. Compute duPont's 1993 and 1994 COGS using the FIFO method.

B. Excluding the benefit of the LIFO liquidation, compute duPont's COGS for 1993 using:

(i) DuPont's current accounting method

(ii) The FIFO method for all inventories

C. Calculate duPont's inventory purchases in 1993 and 1994.

D. LIFO liquidations result from not buying (producing) enough inventory to replace units sold. Calculate the amount of duPont's purchases required to avoid the LIFO liquidation.

E. Using your answers to parts A through D, estimate the following:

(i) 1993 and 1994 gross profit margin

(ii) 1993 and 1994 inventory turnover ratio excluding the effect of all price changes

(iii) Rate of change in price level for 1993 and 1994

F. Describe how to use the inventory footnote data to adjust duPont's net worth (book value) to a current cost basis for 1993 and 1994.

23. [Estimating company–specific inflation rates] Pope & Talbot's inventory footnote for 1991 states that

> the portion of lumber and raw materials inventories determined using the last-in, first-out (LIFO) method aggregated $10,491,000 and $7,166,000 at December 31, 1991 and 1990, respectively. The cost of these LIFO inventories valued at the lower of average cost or market (which approximates current cost) at December 31, 1991 and 1990, was $16,141,000 and $11,480,000.

A. Using the foregoing footnote data and adjustment method described in the chapter, calculate the rate of price change experienced by Pope & Talbot during 1991.

Commodity Price Index—Lumber and Wood Products
(1982 = 100)

December 1990	126.8		
January 1991	127.6	July	136.9
February	127.2	August	133.3
March	127.8	September	133.4
April	129.2	October	133.3
May	132.3	November	133.3
June	136.2	December	134.3

Source: Survey of Current Business, Jan. 1992.

B. Based on the Commodity Price Index data, calculate the rate of price change for lumber and wood products for 1991.

The method used in the chapter to estimate price level changes assumes that inventory levels do not change during the year. Pope & Talbot, however, increased its inventory level considerably during the year.

C. Describe how the increase in Pope & Talbot's inventory levels during 1991 may have affected the estimate derived in part A.

D. Discuss other factors that may explain why the estimates derived in parts A and B differ.

Appendix 6-A

LIFO Measurement Issues

This appendix is concerned with two measurement issues that arise when the LIFO method is used:

- Different varieties of LIFO
- Difficulties when LIFO is applied to interim earnings

Although these issues arise frequently, they are segregated within this appendix to simplify the presentation in the chapter itself.

LIFO INVENTORY METHODS

The discussions in the chapter implicitly assume that:

- Firms account for each inventory item
- There is only one manner of applying the LIFO method of accounting

Neither assumption is correct. In practice, all but the smallest firms have far too many inventory items to use specific item-based costing methods efficiently. The potential for LIFO liquidations and the resulting loss of tax benefits are additional deterrents to the use of specific item methods. More efficient methods of applying LIFO to inventories involve the pooling of "substantially identical" inventory units to compute unit costs and physical quantities.

Reeve and Stanga (1987) found that a majority of LIFO method companies use a single pool, generally defined by the natural business unit, and they use the same pooling method for financial reporting and taxes although conformity is not required. The number of pools used was inversely related to the magnitude of tax benefits (companies with large tax savings from LIFO tended to use fewer pools).

They also reported substantial variation in the number of pools used within an industry and across all the firms in their sample. The impact on cash flows and financial statements suggests that analysts should carefully evaluate announcements of changes in LIFO pools to understand the impact of the change on reported earnings.

EXHIBIT 6A-1. MOBIL CORPORATION ($ in millions)
Effects of Changes in LIFO Measurement

	1992	1993	1994
Inventories	$ 4,354	$ 4,156	$ 3,302
Total current assets	10,956	11,217	11,181
Total current liabilities	12,629	12,351	13,418
Total assets	$40,561	$40,733	$41,542
Total liabilities	24,021	23,496	24,396
Stockholders' equity	16,540	17,237	17,146
Percent at LIFO	70%	70%	57%
LIFO reserve U.S.	N/A	N/A	$ 1,086
LIFO reserve foreign	N/A	N/A	88
LIFO reserve total	$ 372	—	1,174
Sales and services revenues	$63,564	$63,474	$66,757
Cost of products sold	36,639	35,622	36,665
Gross margin	26,925	27,852	30,092
Gross margin percent	42.4%	43.9%	45.1%
Pretax income	$ 2,875	$ 4,015	$ 3,678
Income tax	1,567	1,931	1,919
Net income	1,308	2,084	1,759
Cumulative effect (after tax)			$ 680
Earnings per share	$ 3.13	$ 5.07	$ 4.28
Cumulative effect per share			1.71

Example: Mobil

Mobil, a major international oil company, uses the LIFO method for 57% of its worldwide inventories. Prior to 1994, the company aggregated its worldwide inventories into a single pool for purposes of determining whether a lower of cost or market (LCM) adjustment is required. Effective January 1, 1994, Mobil changed to a country-by-country measurement basis.

Under the old method, low-cost U.S. inventories offset higher-cost foreign inventories. On a combined basis, Mobil took a LCM write-down of $250 million (after tax) in 1993; under the new method, that write-down would have been only $60 million (after tax). Mobil's accounting change resulted in a $680 million after-tax charge to earnings in the first quarter of 1994. This charge permanently reduced the carrying value of non-U.S. inventories, reducing the likelihood of future LCM write-downs. Mobil's intent was clearly to reduce the influence of future price changes on its reported earnings. (Mobil's future return on equity will also be higher as a result of the inventory write-down.)

Inventories may also be pooled on the basis of similarity of use, production method, or raw materials used. Liquidations are reduced because these "dollar value" LIFO methods compute inventories using dollars facilitating substitutions of items in the pools. Inventory layers may be priced using indices published by the Bureau of Labor Statistics or internally developed indices. The differences can be substantial.

For example, during 1990 Kmart switched to internally generated indices (from the U.S. Department of Labor's Department Store Price Index) for its U.S. merchandise inventories. The financial statement footnote states the firm's belief that the internal index "results in a more accurate measurement of the impact of inflation on the prices of merchandise sold in its stores." The change reduced its COGS by $105 million (net of tax), increasing income by $0.52 per share (32.3% of reported income for the year).

Retailers use more complex LIFO methods. Interested readers are referred to intermediate and advanced accounting texts for explanations of the LIFO Retail and Dollar Value LIFO Retail methods.

INTERIM REPORTING UNDER LIFO

As discussed in Chapter 1, interim reporting creates special problems for both financial reporting and financial analysis. Because LIFO is a tax-based inventory method, its use creates additional problems. The actual LIFO effect for the year cannot be known until the year is complete. *Thus, LIFO charges for interim periods require management assumptions regarding both inventory quantities and prices at the end of the year.*

Technological changes, fluctuations in demand, and strikes may also result in a reduction in LIFO layers during the year. The application of LIFO during interim periods may result in substantial distortions (income statement and balance sheet) if the factors causing the LIFO liquidations are temporary and the layers will be replenished prior to year-end.

Financial reporting for interim periods is governed by APB Opinion 28, which provides special inventory valuation procedures during interim periods when the firm experiences a LIFO liquidation during one or more of the first three quarters.

Permanent liquidations must be reported in the quarter of occurrence. However, when management believes that the liquidated layer(s) will be replenished before year-end, the cost of goods sold for the quarter must include the estimated cost of replacing the temporary liquidation rather than the LIFO cost of the goods sold. The application of this method is illustrated using the following example:

Assumptions: All transactions occur during the second quarter
Beginning inventory (LIFO): 10 units @ $10   = $100
    LIFO reserve (@ $20)   = $200
    Inventory @ FIFO   = $300
Purchases: 20 units @ $30   = $600
Goods available for sale   = $700
Sales: 21 units @ $40   = $840

Management determines that the liquidation is temporary and expects the next purchase price (cost to replace) to be $35. GAAP requires the use of $35 rather than the unit cost of the liquidated layer. COGS is reported at

$635 (20 units @ $30 plus 1 unit @ $35)

Inventory is reduced by

$610 (20 units @ $30 and 1 unit @ $10)

The firm recognizes a current liability (called the LIFO base liquidation) for the difference of $25, indicating that the firm has temporarily "borrowed" a unit from the base layer.[1] The next purchase of inventory is used to eliminate the current liability and replenish the LIFO base layer. This method eliminates any distortion in reported gross profit and income numbers due to temporary interim period liquidations.

Year-end LIFO liquidations are permanent reductions in LIFO layers, and the reported gross profit must include the impact of the reduction in LIFO reserves. If the foregoing scenario occurs during the fourth quarter, the firm would report a COGS of $610 [(20 × $30) + (1 × $10)] and separately disclose the impact of the LIFO liquidation on COGS and net income in the footnotes.

Example: Nucor

The following example illustrates the impact of volatile prices and the procedures required for interim reporting. It is based on Nucor Corp., a steel and steel products manufacturer that uses the LIFO method of inventory accounting. Steel scrap is a major component of inventory cost, and since scrap prices can be volatile, Nucor must estimate its year-end position at the end of each interim period. That is, it must estimate both physical inventory and the price of scrap at year-end to establish the appropriate LIFO reserve at the end of each interim period.

In 1981, scrap prices rose during the first part of the year, but declined in the second half. The LIFO reserve declined for 1981 as a whole, reflecting a decline in the price of steel scrap. (At the end of 1981, the difference between the LIFO and FIFO cost of its inventory was lower than it had been one year earlier.)

During the first two quarters, Nucor assumed that scrap prices would be higher at the end of 1981 than one year earlier and accrued additional LIFO reserves. Because of the decline in steel scrap prices late in the year, these earlier accruals were reversed in the fourth quarter. The impact of the interim changes in the LIFO reserve can be seen in the following table:

Reported Nucor Quarterly Results 1981 ($ in thousands)

Quarter	I	II	III	IV	Year
Pretax income	$13,087	$11,204	$ 4,637	$15,901	$44,829
LIFO effect	1,873	1,900	0	(5,134)	(1,361)
LIFO reserve (end of period) (12/31/80 = $23,727)	$25,600	$27,500	$27,500	$22,366	$22,366

Source: Nucor, 1981 annual and interim reports.

[1]An AICPA issues paper, "Identification and Discussion of Certain Financial Accounting and Reporting Issues Concerning LIFO Inventories" (AICPA, 1984), suggests that the interim liquidation may also be credited directly to inventories.

Although the interim LIFO accruals (LIFO effect = change in reserve) were made in good faith, in retrospect we can see that they were incorrect and distorted operating results. To correct that distortion, we can (with perfect hindsight) reallocate the decrease in the LIFO reserve for the year so that an equal amount is credited to each interim period. We can obtain the "true" interim results by restating the LIFO impact as follows:

Adjusted Nucor Quarterly Results 1981 ($ in thousands)

Quarter	I	II	III	IV	Year
Pretax income	$13,087	$11,204	$4,637	$15,901	$44,829
LIFO adjustment*	2,213	2,240	340	(4,793)	0
Adjusted pretax	$15,300	$13,444	$4,977	$11,108	$44,829
% Change from reported	16.9%	20.0%	7.3%	(30.1)%	0

*Difference between original LIFO effect and true LIFO effect (one-fourth of annual). For example, the first quarter adjustment is $1,873 - (-$1,361/4).

The Nucor case indicates that management assumptions can play a major role in reported interim earnings and the application of LIFO accounting to interim periods can result in large distortions in interim comparisons. It should also be noted that there are many ways of making interim LIFO calculations. This illustration also serves as an example of fourth-quarter adjustments that have a significant impact on reported earnings and trends reflected during the previous three quarters.

Appendix 6-B

The FIFO/LIFO Choice: Empirical Studies

As the chapter discussion indicates, there are sound reasons for firms to stay on FIFO. In addition to those related to LIFO liquidations and declining prices, these reasons include burdensome recordkeeping requirements, the inability to write down obsolete inventory, and the desire to maximize taxable income when using up a tax loss carryforward.

Other reasons relate to the desire to avoid the negative effect of LIFO on a firm's reported earnings. The motivations ascribed to this effect depend on whether (as discussed in Chapter 5) a market-based or financial contracting argument is used.

The market-based argument says that whether or not the market is efficient and can see through the FIFO/LIFO choice to the real economics of the firm, managers who believe that the market can be fooled by lower reported earnings are reluctant to use LIFO.

Alternatively, the financial contracting approach examines the impact of the FIFO/LIFO choice on management compensation and debt covenant restrictions. The bonus plan hypothesis argues that when top management compensation is based on income, the firm is less likely to use the LIFO method if the resultant lower earnings reduce their compensation.

The debt covenant hypothesis argues that the negative effect of LIFO on a firm's reported income and ratios increases the probability that a firm will violate such debt covenants as working capital maintenance, net worth maintenance, income maintenance, and dividend payout ratio. Highly leveraged firms may be especially reluctant to use LIFO for that reason, notwithstanding the tax benefits.

Studies of the FIFO/LIFO choice generally examine the impact of the choice on firms' financial performance in terms of both market reaction and management behavior, as well as the effect on firms' financial statements. These studies and the hypotheses tested are affected by both the progression in academic accounting theory and economic factors (such as higher inflation) that caused a resurgence in the adoption of LIFO in the mid-1970s.

LIFO has been permitted in the United States since before World War II, and its rate of adoption understandably follows the rate of inflation. In the 1970s, when the rate of inflation reached the double-digit range, LIFO adoptions soared. Approximately 400 companies switched from FIFO to LIFO in 1974 alone. This period coincided with heavy academic emphasis on market-based empirical research and the efficient market hypothesis, and the effect of the FIFO/LIFO switch was viewed as an ideal area for research.

Given these conditions, the functional fixation hypothesis was tested to see whether:

- The market accepts financial statements as presented and thus views the switch to LIFO unfavorably since income is depressed.
- The market is efficient in the sense that it sees through reported data and views the switch to LIFO positively since cash flow increases.

Proponents of the efficient market hypothesis predicted that the market would see through the switch and react favorably to the cash flow effects.

Surprisingly, the results were equivocal. Sunder (1973) examined a sample of firms that changed to LIFO in the period 1946 to 1966 and found that prior to the switch these firms experienced positive abnormal returns (Figure 6B-1a). At the time of the change itself, the reaction was slightly negative or nonexistent as investors seemed to ignore the positive cash flow effect. Moreover, the risk (beta) of firms that switched to LIFO increased in the months surrounding the switch.

This result was similar to that of Ball (1972), who examined the market reaction to several accounting changes, FIFO/LIFO included. The positive reaction in the year of the switch was interpreted by some as a sign that the market anticipated the switch and had reacted prior to the actual announcement. Others felt that firms that switched had been having "good" years and could thus "afford" the negative impact of the switch, and that these studies suffered from a self-selection bias.

Subsequent studies such as Eggleton et al. (1976), Abdel-khalik and McKeown (1978), Brown (1980), and Ricks (1982) extended this research by controlling for earnings-related variables and focusing on the large number of firms that switched in the 1974 to 1975 period. Generally, their results confirmed a negative market reaction in the year of the switch.

Ricks, for example, used a control sample of non-LIFO adopters (matched on the basis of industry and earnings calculated "as if" the control company was also on LIFO) and computed the cumulative average return differences between the two groups. His results, presented in Figure 6B-1b, clearly indicate better market perfor-

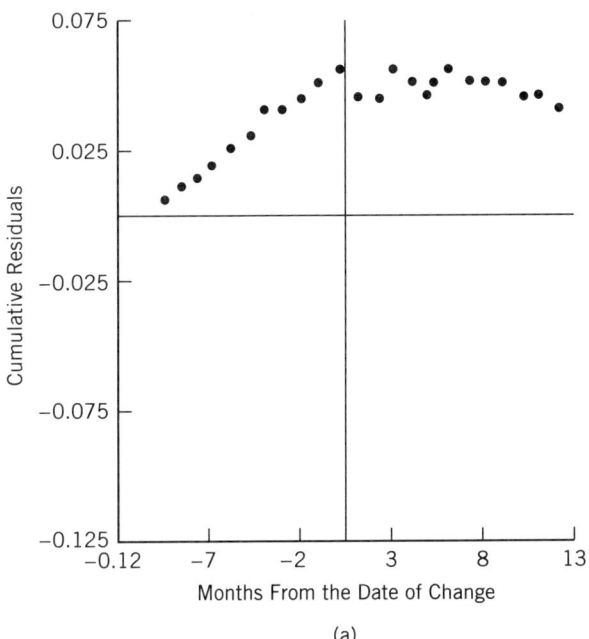

(a)

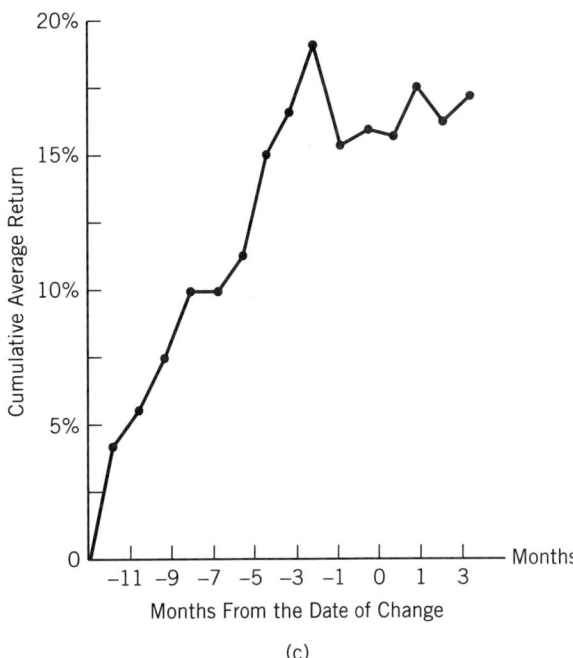

(c)

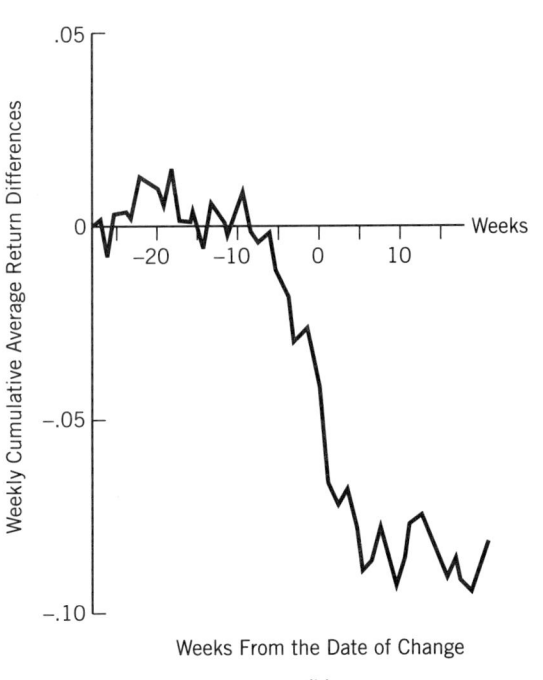

Weeks From the Date of Change

(b)

FIGURE 6B-1 Abnormal returns: Inventory method studies. *Sources:* (*a*) 1946–1966 Adopters: Shyam, Sunder, "Relationship Between Accounting Changes and Stock Prices: Problems of Measurement and Some Empirical Evidence," *Journal of Accounting Research*, Supplement 1973, pp. 1–45, Fig. 2, p. 18. (*b*) 1974–1975 Adopters: William E. Ricks, "The Market's Response to the 1974 LIFO Adoption," *Journal of Accounting Research*, Autumn 1982, pp. 367–387, Fig. 2, p. 378. (*c*) 1973–1982 Adopters: Gary C. Biddle and Fredrick W. Lindahl, "Stock Price Reactions to LIFO Adoptions: The Association Between Excess Returns and LIFO Tax Savings," *Journal of Accounting Research*, Autumn 1982, pp. 551–588, Fig. 1, p. 569.

mance for firms that did not adopt LIFO. Although these lower market returns were reversed within a year, the initial prolonged negative reaction is difficult to understand.

One explanation for this anomalous behavior is that firms that switched to LIFO were those most affected by inflation. Thus, the market may have reacted negatively to the added risk (higher inflation) of these firms, explaining the lower returns and higher risk measures.

The difficulty with this explanation is that the sample firms were matched by industry. Thus, we must assume that the sample firms were somehow more adversely affected by inflation than other firms in the same industry. Biddle and Ricks (1988), discussed shortly, also found evidence consistent with this explanation. Implicitly, these studies help explain why firms stayed on FIFO; they wanted to avoid the unfavorable market reaction resulting from the adoption of LIFO.

Biddle and Lindhal (1982) attempted to resolve some of these issues by arguing that previous studies did not consider the amount of tax savings from the LIFO adoption. They found a positive association (see Figure 6B-1c) between the market reaction and the estimated tax savings:

> The results in this study are consistent with a cash-flow hypothesis which suggests that investor reactions to LIFO adoptions depend on the present value of tax-related cash-flow savings. After controlling for abnormal earnings performance, larger LIFO tax savings were found to be (cross-sectionally) associated with larger cumulative excess returns over the year in which a LIFO adoption (extension) first applied.[1]

Biddle and Lindhal studied 311 LIFO adopters from the period 1973 to 1980. The pattern of abnormal returns reported is similar to Sunder's findings (Figure 6B-1a). Both studies did not use a control group,[2] making these results not directly comparable to those of Ricks. Thus, it is possible that there was some systematic as yet unexplained factor affecting the 1974 to 1975 adoptions, and that the research results were sensitive to the research design and the time horizon examined.

Biddle and Ricks (1988), using daily data, confirmed that there were

> negative excess market returns around the preliminary dates of firms adopting LIFO in 1974. There is little evidence of significant excess returns (negative or positive) near the preliminary dates of firms adopting LIFO in other years.[3]

To explain the negative returns, they examined analyst forecast errors for the 1974 LIFO adopters. They found that analysts significantly overestimated the earnings and did not fully appreciate the magnitude of the impact of inflation.[4] In other years,

---

[1] Gary C. Biddle and Frederick W. Lindahl, "Stock Price Reactions to LIFO Adoptions: The Association Between Excess Returns and LIFO Tax Savings," *Journal of Accounting Research*, Autumn 1982, Part II, pp. 551–588.

[2] Biddle and Lindahl instead used the size of the tax saving as a "within-group" control.

[3] Gary C. Biddle and William E. Ricks, "Analyst Forecast Errors and Stock Price Behavior Near the Earnings Announcement Dates of LIFO Adopters," *Journal of Accounting Research*, Autumn 1988, pp. 169–194.

[4] At that time, LIFO adoptions were unusual, and it took time for analysts to learn to estimate the impact. That they did learn is evidenced by the reduced earnings forecast errors for LIFO adopters in later years.

however, the error in analyst forecasts for LIFO adopters was not significant. Further, they found that the negative returns were positively correlated with the forecast error, indicating that the market (as well as analysts) was surprised by the actual reported earnings. Thus, the negative returns were due to the "surprise" when the market realized that it had underestimated the impact of inflation. As the firms that adopted LIFO were presumably those most affected by inflation, the negative surprise reaction hit them hardest. In later years, however, the market learned from experience and the impact of inflation was more readily factored into earnings estimates.

Although these studies shed some light on the market reaction to LIFO adoption, they still do not explain why some firms remain on FIFO. On the contrary, Biddle (1980) found

> surprising the finding that many firms voluntarily paid tens of millions of dollars in additional income taxes by continuing to use FIFO rather than switching to LIFO.[5]

The contracting theories of accounting choice focus on this issue. Abdel-khalik (1985) examined the bonus plan hypothesis and its implicit corollary that management-controlled firms, in which ownership is widely held, are more likely to use FIFO than owner-controlled firms. The rationale for this argument is that when management is more removed from ownership of the firm, then management compensation rather than the wealth of the firm becomes the primary motivator for manager actions. Thus, the LIFO-induced tax savings are less important in the management-controlled firm.

Abdel-khalik found that manager-controlled FIFO firms had relatively higher income-based bonuses. On the other hand, there was no evidence that differences in compensation plans were related to the FIFO/LIFO choice. In explaining this (non)finding, Abdel-khalik hypothesizes that either

> (1) firms switching to LIFO modify their compensation arrangements, or
> (2) as some executives have indicated to me, the FIFO-based income continues to be used in determining annual bonus.[6]

Hunt (1985) examined the bonus plan and debt covenant hypotheses. His results did not support the bonus plan hypothesis. Contrary to expectations, he found that LIFO firms tended to be less owner-controlled. Hunt, however, did find support for the debt covenant hypothesis, especially with respect to the leverage and interest coverage ratios. His evidence also indicates a threshold level of dividend payout ratios above which firms are reluctant to use LIFO.

Dopuch and Pincus (1988) examined the bonus plan, debt covenant, and taxation hypotheses in one study and found that the taxation effect provided the best explanation for the LIFO/FIFO decision. They compared the holding gain that would have accrued to LIFO firms had they stayed on FIFO with the holding gain for firms that remained on FIFO.

They found larger holding gains for LIFO firms, resulting in higher tax savings. In addition, the holding gain grew as they approached the switch date. Dopuch and

---

[5]Gary C. Biddle, "Accounting Methods and Management Decisions: The Case of Inventory Costing and Inventory Policy," *Journal of Accounting Research*, Supplement 1980, pp. 235–280.

[6]A. Rashad Abdel-Khalik, "The Effect of LIFO-Switching and Firm Ownership on Executive's Pay," *Journal of Accounting Research*, Autumn 1985, pp. 427–447.

Pincus argued that this indicated

> the long-term FIFO firms in our sample have not been forgoing significant tax savings, in which case remaining on that method is certainly consistent with FIFO being an optimal tax choice, given other considerations. In contrast, long-term LIFO firms would have forgone significant tax savings. . . . Finally, using the long-term FIFO sample's average holding gains as a base, our change-firms' average holding gains became significantly larger than the FIFO average as they approached the year in which they switched, and this difference continued to grow subsequently.[7]

Further, Dopuch and Pincus argued that financial analysts could have calculated the increased holding gains for the switch firms and thus anticipated the switch. Therefore, the inconclusive findings of the market reaction studies could be a result of ignoring the "advance warning" market agents had regarding the switch.

More recently, Jennings et al. (1992) found evidence supporting this advance warning contention. They constructed a model that predicted which firms in the 1974 to 1975 period were more likely to adopt LIFO. The model accurately forecast adopting/nonadopting firms approximately two-thirds of the time. Furthermore, the prior probability of adoption affected the market reaction. The less likely candidates for adoption (according to the model) had more positive market reactions when they adopted LIFO. Similarly, firms that were originally viewed as likely candidates for adoption, but did not adopt, suffered negative market reaction when they failed to adopt LIFO.

However, in summing up the research in this area, the editor of the *Accounting Review* stated

> We continue to be relatively uninformed about these issues and know little about the real reasons that many firms do not switch to LIFO when it appears that they would benefit by positive tax savings.[8]

---

[7]Nicholas Dopuch and Morton Pincus, "Evidence of the Choice of Inventory Accounting Methods: LIFO Versus FIFO," *Journal of Accounting Research*, Spring 1988, pp. 28–59.

[8]Editor's Comments, *The Accounting Review*, Vol. 67, No. 2, April 1992, p. 319.

7

ANALYSIS OF LONG-LIVED ASSETS, PART I
The Capitalization Decision

CHAPTER OUTLINE

CHAPTER OBJECTIVES

INTRODUCTION

ACQUIRING THE ASSET: THE CAPITALIZATION DECISION

CAPITALIZATION VERSUS EXPENSING: CONCEPTUAL ISSUES

Financial Statement Effects of Capitalization

Income Variability

Profitability

Cash Flow from Operations

Leverage Ratios

CAPITALIZATION VERSUS EXPENSING: GENERAL ISSUES

Capitalization of Interest Costs

Example: Amerada Hess

Interest Capitalization Outside the United States

Intangible Assets

Recognition and Measurement Issues

Research and Development

Patents and Copyrights

Franchises and Licenses

Brands and Trademarks

Advertising Costs

Goodwill

Asset Revaluation

CAPITALIZATION VERSUS EXPENSING: INDUSTRY ISSUES

Regulated Utilities

Computer Software Development Costs

Example: IBM

Accounting for Oil and Gas Exploration

ANALYTIC ADJUSTMENTS FOR CAPITALIZATION AND EXPENSING

Need for Analytic Adjustments

Valuation Implications

Other Economic Consequences

Additional Analysis of Fixed Asset Data

Capital Expenditures

Sale or Retirement of Assets

SUMMARY

CASE 7-1: ADJUSTMENTS FOR CAPITALIZATION AND EXPENSING: DIGITAL EQUIPMENT

APPENDIX 7-A: RESEARCH AND DEVELOPMENT AFFILIATES

Research and Development Partnerships

Analysis of Firms with R&D Affiliates

APPENDIX 7-B: ANALYSIS OF OIL AND GAS DISCLOSURES

Introduction

Motivations for Accounting Choice

Changing Accounting Methods

SFAS 69: Disclosures Regarding Oil and Gas Reserves

Disclosure of Physical Reserve Quantities

Disclosure of Capitalized Costs

CHAPTER OBJECTIVES

The objectives of Chapter 7 are to:

1. Discuss the effects of capitalization versus expensing on:
   - Income variability.
   - Profitability.
   - Cash from operations.
   - Financial ratios used to measure leverage.
2. Explain the rules governing the capitalization of interest and the effects of such capitalization on financial statements.

3. Review the circumstances under which intangible assets are capitalized.
4. Examine the effects of revaluation of long-term assets.
5. Consider the accounting for industries with unusual capitalization practices and the effects of accounting choices on reported financial data.
6. Adjust reported financial statements for differences in capitalization policy.
7. Discuss the valuation implications of expenditures that may be either capitalized or expensed.

INTRODUCTION

The long-lived operating assets of a firm, unlike inventory, are not held for resale, but are used in the firm's manufacturing, sales, and administrative operations. Such assets include tangible fixed assets (plant, machinery, and office facilities) as well as intangible assets such as computer software, patents, and trademarks.

This chapter examines financial reporting and analysis issues when the assets are originally acquired, with emphasis on:

- Which costs are included
- The capitalization of interest
- Financial statement effects of capitalization

Chapter 8 discusses the accounting for and analysis of the use, impairment, and disposal of these long-lived assets.

ACQUIRING THE ASSET: THE CAPITALIZATION DECISION

The costs of acquiring resources that provide services over more than one operating cycle are capitalized and carried as assets on the balance sheet. All costs incurred until the asset is ready for use must be capitalized, including the invoice price, applicable sales tax, freight and insurance costs incurred delivering the equipment, and any installation costs.

However, considerable debate surrounds the application of these principles and significant differences remain (across countries and firms) with respect to three major issues:

1. Should some components of acquisition cost be included in the capitalized cost (e.g., interest during construction)?

2. Do some types of costs merit capitalization (e.g., software development and research and development costs)?

3. What accounting method should be used to determine the amount of costs capitalized (e.g., oil and gas properties)?

These choices affect the balance sheet, income and cash flow statements, and ratios both in the year the choice is made and over the life of the asset. Management discretion can result in smoothing or manipulation of reported income, cash flows, and other measures of financial performance. Moreover, unlike some accounting choices whose effects reverse or "even out" over time, effects of the decision to capitalize or expense may never reverse.

This chapter is devoted to the controversial issue of capitalization versus expensing of expenditures for long-lived assets. We start with an overview of the conceptual issues and a review of the implications of capitalization for financial statement analysis. The remaining sections then examine the specific components and categories of cost where capitalization practices vary.

CAPITALIZATION VERSUS EXPENSING: CONCEPTUAL ISSUES

The Financial Accounting Standards Board (FASB), in its Statement of Financial Accounting Concepts (SFAC) 6,[1] defines accounting assets as probable future economic benefits. Analytically, the concept of long-lived assets can also serve as:

1. An index of initial investment outlays, used as a base for measuring profitability (return on assets)

2. A measure of the firm's wealth, used for solvency and valuation

3. Inputs in the firm's production function, used to measure capital intensity, leverage, and operating efficiency

Different analytical objectives require distinct definitions of what constitutes an asset. Although returns on research and development should be evaluated in the same way as returns on a purchased factory, measurement problems may preclude recognition of such expenditures as assets for assessment of shareholder wealth or collateral for bondholders.

For this reason, traditional, historical cost-based accounting rules cannot satisfy all contexts; analysts must evaluate asset definitions used for financial reporting and make necessary adjustments. The appropriate adjustment may require the capitalization of previously expensed costs,[2] or the reverse.[3] In some cases, particularly for intangible assets, there is no one "correct" choice that serves all analytical needs.

Financial Statement Effects of Capitalization

Box 7-1 uses a simple illustration to demonstrate the financial statement effects of the capitalize-versus-expense choice on two growing firms. That choice may have

---

[1] See Chapter 1 for a discussion of SFAC 6.
[2] See the Merck illustration in Exhibit 7-4.
[3] See the IBM example related to Exhibit 7-2.

BOX 7-1
Comparison of Financial Statement Effects: Capitalization Versus Expensing

For our illustration we consider two hypothetical firms, each with an asset base of $1,000 on which it earns $150, which begin to grow. Growth requires the acquisition of an "asset," which has a three-year life. Each asset costs $100 and generates cash flows of $50 per year. The pattern of growth* (the number of assets acquired each year and the replacement of old assets) is illustrated in Figure 7-1.

Growth is assumed to continue for 15 years after which maturity is reached, and all subsequent acquisitions are for replacement only. We further assume that the asset cost may be capitalized or expensed at the discretion of management under the provisions of generally accepted accounting principles (GAAP). One firm capitalizes the acquisition cost; the other expenses it. The firms are otherwise operationally identical. Their reported income, cash flow from operations, and related ratios, however, will differ markedly.

Figure 7-2 compares the pattern of reported income. The "expensing" firm exhibits a fluctuating pattern of income growth through maturity. The "capitalizing" firm, on the other hand, exhibits a smooth pattern of income growth. For firms that are initially larger,† the fluctuations are not as great throughout the growth and maturity cycle because of the larger base.

Figure 7-3 compares the return on assets (ROA) ratio for the two firms. The choice of accounting method affects both the numerator and denominator of the ROA. The expensing firm, having fewer recorded assets, will have a smaller denominator, increasing its reported ROA. The numerator (earnings) is volatile, so that sometimes ROA increases but at other times decreases. At the early stage of growth, the expensing firm's ROA gyrates about that of the capitalizing firm but will initially tend to be lower. As the expensing firm grows larger,

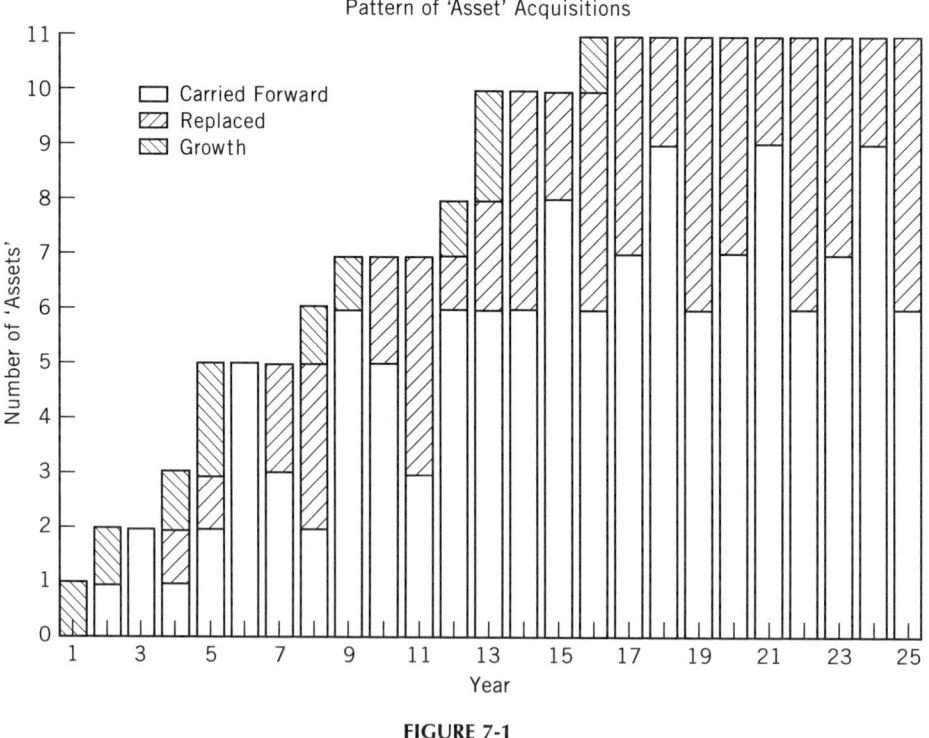

FIGURE 7-1

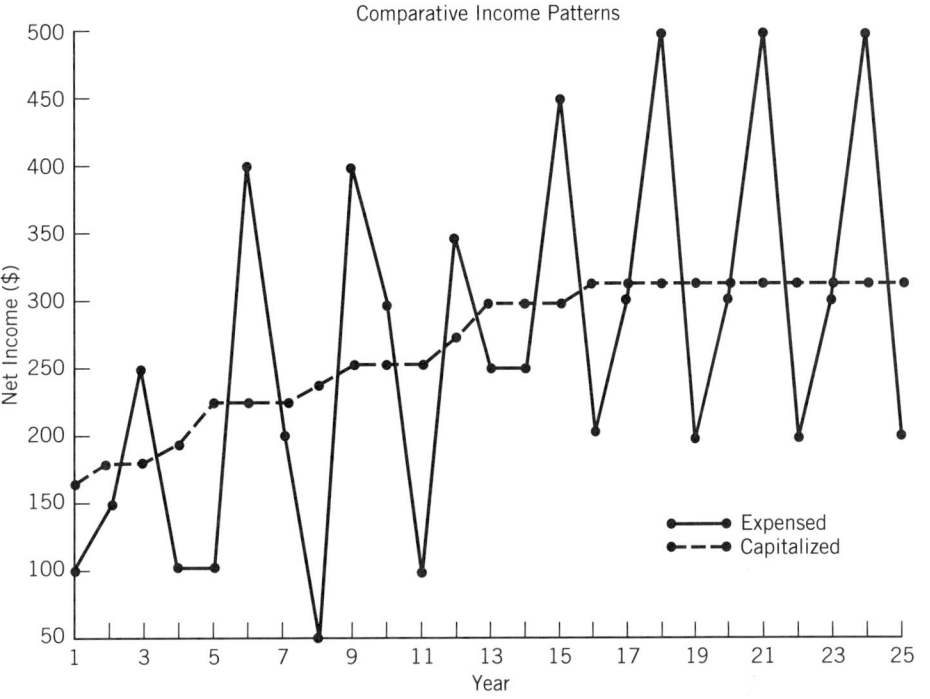

FIGURE 7-2

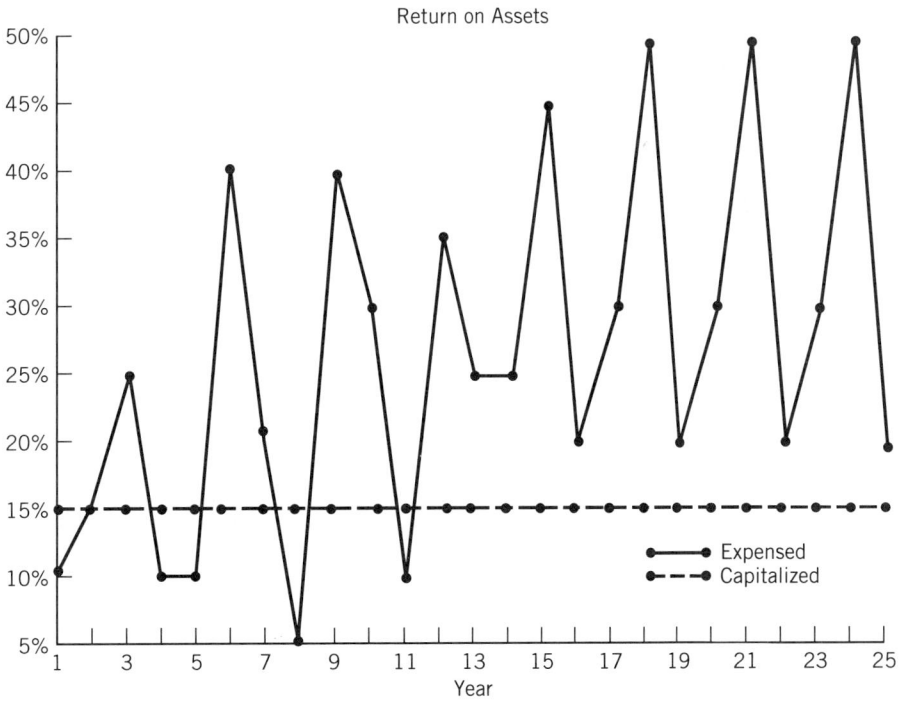

FIGURE 7-3

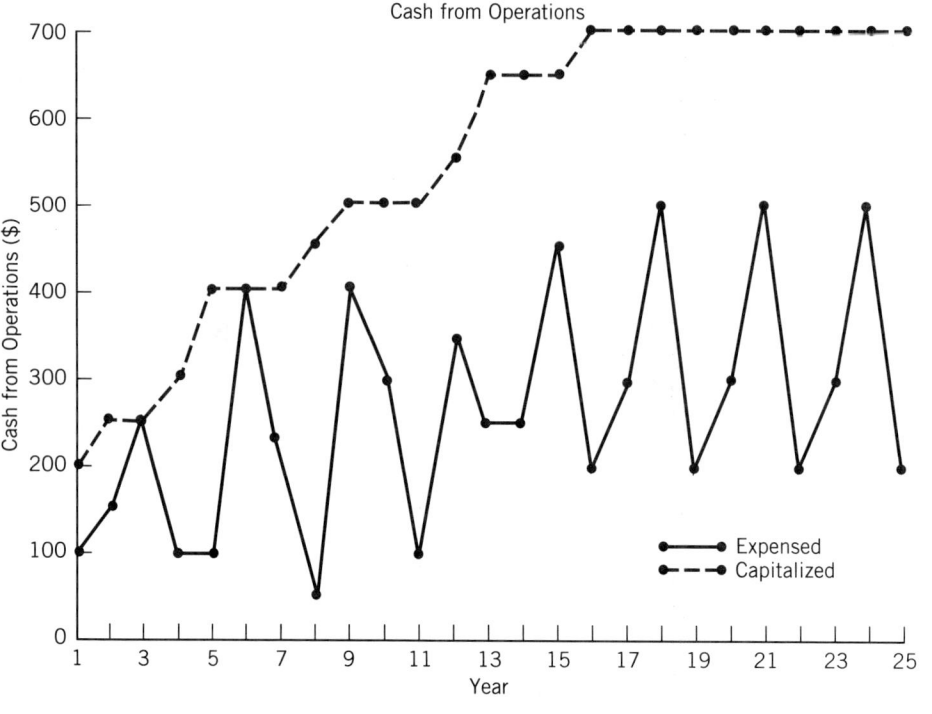

FIGURE 7-4

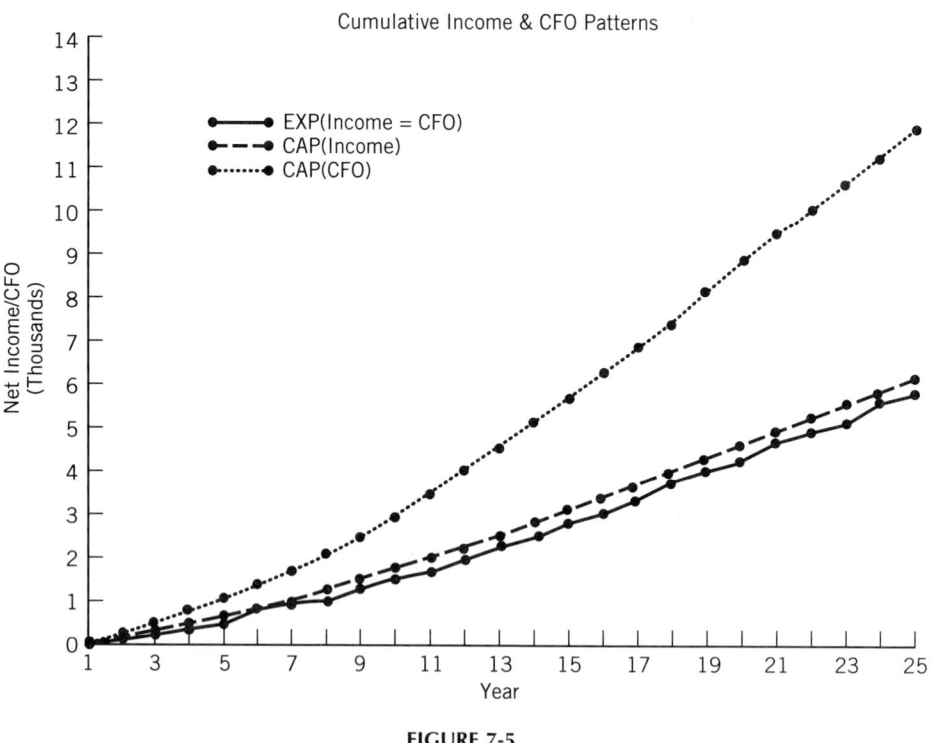

FIGURE 7-5

the fluctuations persist, but its ROA is higher because the effect of lower reported assets on the denominator dominates.

Figure 7-4 compares reported cash from operations for the capitalizing and expensing firms. The capitalizing firm always shows higher cash from operations; the difference increases and does not reverse over the life of the asset (see Figure 7-5).

---

*A variable growth rate is used in the illustration because it is more descriptive of reality (it has greater external validity). Any growth rate, other than a perfectly constant one, will create a similar pattern of differences between a capitalizing and expensing firm. At maturity or steady state, a constant growth rate generates identical (and constant) total expense for both firms. (ROA and cash flow from operations would still differ.)

†The term "larger" does not necessarily relate only to absolute size. It can also denote that the firm engages in other activities that offset the variability of the costs that are expensed.

significant effects on the cash flow statement, as well as the balance sheet and income statement.

Income Variability

Firms that capitalize costs and depreciate them (systematically allocate them to income) over time show "smoother" patterns of reported income (Figure 7-2). Firms that expense costs as incurred have greater variance in reported income. That variance declines as the firm matures and is lower for larger firms (or those with other sources of income).

Profitability

The effects on profitability depend on the actual pattern of expenditures. In the early years, expensing lowers profitability, both in absolute terms and relative to assets, sales, etc. In later years, as the firm reaches maturity and *growth subsides,* return on sales remains lower for expensing firms. However, because they report lower assets (and equity), their ROA/ROE measures exceed those of firms that capitalize costs (Figure 7-3).

Cash Flow from Operations

Reported *net cash flow*, unlike net income, is immune to accounting alternatives.[4] However, the capitalization decision has a significant impact on the components of cash flow, particularly *cash from operations (CFO).* As discussed in Chapter 3, cash expenditures for capitalized assets are included in investing cash flow and *never* flow through CFO. Firms that expense these outlays, however, include these expenditures in CFO. Thus, CFO will always be higher for the capitalizing firm (Figure 7-4),[5] and the cumulative difference (rather than reversing) increases over time (Figure 7-5).

Thus, the capitalization of long-lived assets results in a permanent shift of expenditures from CFO to cash for investment.

---

[4]Ignoring any income tax effects.

[5]This affects the cash from operations/capital expenditures ratio that measures the degree to which the firm's internally generated funds finance the replacement and expansion of productive capacity.

Leverage Ratios

Expensing firms report lower assets and equity balances.[6] As a result, debt-to-equity and debt-to-assets solvency ratios will appear worse for expensing firms as compared with firms that capitalize the same costs.

Given management discretion as to capitalization, a great deal of care must be exercised when assessing financial performance. The remainder of this chapter considers particular areas where this problem occurs. Some issues are pervasive and cut across all industries; others are industry-specific.

CAPITALIZATION VERSUS EXPENSING: GENERAL ISSUES

Capitalization of Interest Costs

Companies often construct long-lived assets, such as new operating facilities, for their own use and capitalize costs incurred during construction until the assets are ready to be placed in service. How should the firm measure the cost of these self-constructed assets? Should the interest cost on funds used for construction be capitalized or expensed? Should interest capitalization require specific borrowing to finance construction? Should the firm capitalize a return on equity when there is no debt or the firm has borrowed less than the total construction cost? The answers to these questions vary from country to country.

In the United States, SFAS 34 (1979) requires the capitalization of interest costs incurred during the construction period. When a specific borrowing is associated with the construction, the interest cost incurred on that borrowing is capitalized. If no specific borrowing is identifiable, the weighted-average interest rate on outstanding debt (up to the amount invested in the project) is capitalized. When the firm has no interest expense, capitalization of a return on equity is not permitted. SFAS 34 requires the disclosure of the amount of interest capitalized.

The argument for interest capitalization is that the cost of a self-constructed asset should be identical to that of one purchased after completion. In the latter case, the purchase price would presumably include the financing costs of the seller. Capitalization of interest for self-constructed assets, it is argued, replicates this process.

On the other hand, there are strong arguments against the capitalization of interest in general and SFAS 34 in particular. On a conceptual level, interest, as a financing cost, is different from the other costs of getting the asset ready for service. It results from a financing decision rather than an operating decision.

Under SFAS 34, interest is capitalized only for certain assets and then only if the firm is leveraged. But the argument about equating the cost of a self-constructed asset with a purchased asset should apply even when the firm has no debt; in that case, return on equity capital used for construction should be capitalized.

Under SFAS 34, the carrying amount of a self-constructed asset depends on the firm's financing decisions. It seems illogical that two identical assets, one financed by external funds and the other by internally available funds, should be carried at different costs. Further, the capitalization of interest creates differences between earnings and

---

[6]These effects are not shown directly in Box 7-1. However, they can be deduced from the discussion of the return-on-investment (ROA/ROE) measures.

cash flow. Given these arguments, we believe that expensing of all interest is the preferable treatment.

For purposes of analysis, therefore, the income statement capitalization of interest should be reversed, resulting in the following effects:

1. *Capitalized interest should be added to interest expense.* The adjusted interest expense provides a better representation of the level and trend of a firm's financing costs.

2. *Adding capitalized interest to interest expense reduces net income.* Unfortunately, although the amount of interest capitalized in the current year must be disclosed, the amortization of previously capitalized interest (included in the fixed asset account) is not required and rarely disclosed. This amortization must be deducted from depreciation expense. If the amortization amount is unknown, the net effect of interest capitalization on net income is not determinable. *However, if the amount of interest capitalization in previous years is not large and asset lives are long, the amortization (over the asset life) is likely to be immaterial and can be ignored.* If interest capitalization has been large, then the analyst must estimate the amortization.[7]

3. *The capitalization of interest also distorts the classification of cash flows. Interest capitalized as part of the cost of fixed assets will never be reported as CFO, but as an investment outflow. To restore comparability with firms that do not capitalize interest, the amount of interest capitalized should be added back to cash for investment and subtracted from CFO.* The cash flows for capitalized interest are then included with other interest payments.[8]

4. *The interest coverage ratio should be calculated with interest expense adjusted for capitalized interest.* Otherwise, it is overstated.[9]

These adjustments tend to be small relative to cash flows but may be significant for interest expense and net income. The following example illustrates how capitalized interest affects financial statement trends and ratios.

Example: Amerada Hess

As shown below, Amerada capitalized substantial amounts of interest in 1992 and 1993, but none in 1994 (presumably because of a lack of qualifying assets).

---

[7]The amortization of capitalized interest is included in depreciation expense. Thus, one can use the historical ratio of interest capitalized to total capital expenditures to estimate the portion of depreciation applicable to capitalized interest expense.

[8]These interest payments would be deducted from cash from operations, as required by SFAS 95. Alternatively, as we argue in Chapter 3, interest payments should be considered financing cash flows and thus excluded from both CFO and cash for investment regardless of capitalization.

[9]The SFAS 95 requirement for the disclosure of interest paid makes it possible to make this adjustment and compute interest coverage accurately (see Chapter 4) on a cash flow basis. On an accrual basis, the numerator, EBIT (and hence the coverage ratio), will be underestimated if the amortization of previous years' capitalized interest is not removed. However, as noted, this effect is relatively insignificant.

Amerada Hess, Years Ended December 31 ($ in thousands)

	1992	1993	1994	% Change 1992 to 1994
EBIT	$270,584	$ (66,861)	$480,961	78%
Interest expense	147,091	156,615	245,149	67%
Pretax income	$123,493	$(223,476)	$235,812	91%
Interest coverage	1.84X	(0.43)X	1.96X	7%
Interest capitalized	$108,095	$ 92,238	$ 0	

If we ignore the loss year of 1993, it appears that Amerada's interest coverage ratio improved slightly from 1992 to 1994 as EBIT and interest expense rose proportionately.

If we adjust for capitalized interest by adding it back to interest expense, a different pattern emerges[10]:

	1992	1993	1994	% Change 1992 to 1994
EBIT	$270,584	$ (66,861)	$480,961	78%
Adjusted				
Interest expense	255,186	248.853	245,149	(4)%
Pretax income	15,398	(315,714)	235,812	1,431%
Interest coverage	1.06X	(0.27)X	1.96X	85%

After adjustment, the 1994 coverage ratio is almost twice the 1992 ratio. Additionally, the apparent 1994 increase in interest expense disappears. That increase resulted from the effect of capitalization, not a change in interest burden; some interest was capitalized in 1992 but all interest was expensed in 1994. Finally, adjusted pretax income increased fifteenfold over the 1992 to 1994 period; reported pretax income increased approximately 90%.

Interest Capitalization Outside the United States

IAS 23, Borrowing Costs (revised 1993), makes expensing all borrowing costs the benchmark treatment. Alternatively, borrowing costs that are directly attributable to the acquisition, construction, or production of qualifying assets may be capitalized.

Capitalization is permitted, but it is not mandatory in both Australia and Canada. Capitalization is permitted in Germany and Sweden only to the extent that the interest costs are incurred during the manufacturing period.

Although there is no accounting standard on interest capitalization in the United Kingdom, it has gained acceptance in practice. Capitalization of interest is reviewed

---

[10]No adjustment was made for the amortization of interest previously capitalized. Amerada capitalized interest of $8,525, $34,897, and $60,579, in 1989, 1990, and 1991, respectively (all $ in thousands). In 1988, zero interest was capitalized. The capitalized interest in the period 1988 to 1993 seems to be associated with a major expansion of refining facilities. As the amounts in the years prior to 1988 were relatively small (less than $100,000), amortization would not materially affect the analysis.

in the U.K. Accounting Standards Board's October 1996 Discussion Paper, Measurement of Tangible Fixed Assets. The board finds current practice unacceptable and proposes that capitalization should be either mandatory or prohibited.

Intangible Assets

Changes in technology and the growth of the information and service industries have led firms to significantly increase their investment in and use of intangible assets. Licenses, leasehold rights, brand names, copyrights, and patents are among the more familiar examples of assets without tangible, physical substance. As a result, the financial reporting and analysis of such intangible assets have gained importance; they are sometimes important off-balance-sheet revenue producing assets that account for a substantial portion of the value of a firm.

Intangible assets are identifiable, nonmonetary resources controlled by firms.[11] Such assets are sometimes reported on the balance sheet in foreign countries. However, practice is diverse with respect to the recognition, measurement, revaluation, amortization, and impairment of these assets because of a lack of accounting standards.[12]

The capitalize versus expense issue is especially difficult when applied to intangible resources. The variations in legal protection available for intellectual property and other intangible assets in many countries also makes assessments of value more difficult than for tangible assets. We begin with a review of the recognition and measurement issues associated with intangible assets.

Recognition and Measurement Issues

Financial reporting for intangible assets must consider the following stages:

- Initial recognition and measurement at acquisition or creation
- Measurement subsequent to initial recognition
- Amortization
- Impairment
- Retirement and disposal

A discussion of amortization, retirement, disposal, and the impairment of intangible assets is included in Chapter 8.

The cost of acquiring intangible assets from unrelated entities is capitalized at acquisition, measured by the amount paid to acquire them. The market value of such intangible assets is assumed to be accurately reflected given the arm's length transaction.

Intangible assets may also be received through government grants or generated internally by the firm. Few, if any, costs may be incurred in obtaining assets through government grants. Financial statement recognition of such assets would be informative, but in the absence of secondary markets it is difficult to defend any measurement

---

[11]Goodwill is an intangible asset although it is not identifiable. See Chapter 14 for a discussion of acquisition goodwill.

[12]In June 1995, the IASC issued Exposure Draft E50, Intangible Assets, which may bring some consistency to the treatment of such assets. The exposure draft does not address research and development costs, initial recognition of finance leases, financial assets, goodwill recognized in purchase transactions, deferred costs, prepaid expenses, and assets generated in extractive industries.

basis other than cost. When active secondary markets do exist (such as for broadcast properties and cellular licenses), then market value can be a reliable measure of the value of these assets.

Internally generated intangible assets are the most troublesome category because:

- The costs incurred in developing these assets may not be easily separable.
- It is difficult to measure the potential benefits of such expenditures as advertising when they are made, or even later.
- In many cases, it is nearly impossible to determine or establish the economic life of such assets as brand names.

For many internally generated intangible assets, discounted cash flow analysis may be the only way to measure their fair value. However, such measurement is subject to accurate forecasting of the amount and timing of cash flows, and the choice of discount rates.[13]

We now turn to a discussion of capitalization issues for specific intangible assets.

Research and Development

Companies invest in research and development (R&D) because they expect the investment to produce profitable future products. However, absent a resultant commercial product, these expenditures may have no value to the firm. Further, the value of any product may be unrelated to the amount spent on R&D. Due to valuation uncertainties, R&D is generally unacceptable to creditors as security for loans.

SFAS 2, Accounting for Research and Development Costs. Prior to 1975, U.S. firms were permitted to capitalize R&D costs. SFAS 2 (1974), however, requires that virtually all R&D costs be expensed[14] in the period incurred and the amount disclosed. In effect, assets with uncertain future economic benefits are barred from the balance sheet. The impact of SFAS 2 on the financial statements of firms with significant R&D was substantial, and there is some evidence of a decrease in R&D expenditures as a result of this accounting change. Notwithstanding SFAS 2, R&D expenditures are clearly investments in the economic sense, albeit risky ones. Further, empirical evidence[15] suggests that benefits from R&D expenditures last, on average, seven to nine years (depending on the industry), supporting the argument that R&D is an economic asset.

Accounting for Research and Development Costs Outside the United States. IAS 9 (revised in 1993) requires the expensing of research costs but capitalization of

---

[13]E50 of the IASC prohibits the recognition of internally developed goodwill.

[14]The main exception is contract R&D performed for unrelated entities. In this case, R&D is carried as an asset (similar to inventory) until completion of the contract. In addition, certain government-regulated entities (discussed later in this section) capitalize R&D expenses when they are deemed to be recoverable from future revenues.

[15]Research in this area can be found in both the accounting and economics literature. Lev and Sougiannis (1996) provide a brief a review of the literature in this area. See also our discussion of valuation in Box 7-2.

development costs[16] when specific criteria are met. Some foreign countries allow or require the capitalization of qualifying development costs.

Canada, for example, permits deferral of development costs when *all* the following conditions are met:

1. The product (process) is clearly defined.
2. Costs can be clearly identified.
3. Technical feasibility has been established.
4. The firm intends to produce the product (use the process).
5. The market has been clearly defined.
6. The firm has sufficient resources to complete the project.

Capitalized costs must be reviewed periodically to ensure that these conditions are still operable and costs do not exceed net realizable value.

The United Kingdom has rules similar to Canada's GAAP, but few firms capitalize these costs. Expensing is the dominant accounting method worldwide. The financial statements of companies that capitalize R&D must be restated (by expensing all such expenditures) to make them comparable with similar companies that expense these costs. For other analytic purposes, however, it may be desireable to restate a firm's financial statements by capitalizing previously expensed R&D costs (see the Merck example and Box 7-2).

Research and Development Affiliates. Although SFAS 2 does not permit the capitalization of R&D costs, companies have found ways to defer the recognition of such costs. One method is the R&D partnership. Another involves the issuance of "callable common" shares to the public. These and similar arrangements are discussed in Appendix 7-A.

Patents and Copyrights

All costs incurred in developing patents and copyrights are expensed in conformity with the treatment of R&D costs.[17] Only the legal fees incurred in registering internally developed patents and copyrights can be capitalized. However, the full acquisition cost is capitalized when such assets are purchased from other entities.

Patents have a legal life of 17 years under U.S. patent law; copyrights have a legal life of 50 years beyond the creator's life. However, these periods should be viewed as upper limits. Successful patented products invite competition and the development of comparable or improved products that can diminish the value of the patent or make it obsolete. In addition, there is often a gap between the time that a patent is registered and the time the product comes to market.

In the pharmaceutical industry, for example, even after a patent is registered, the product cannot be marketed in most countries until it obtains regulatory approval, which can take a number of years. The analysis of companies that are heavily dependent

---

[16]IAS 9 defines development costs as expenditures incurred to translate research output into the production of materials, devices, products, processes, systems, and services.

[17]However, publishers and motion picture producers capitalize all costs of creating their "inventory."

on patented or proprietary products must consider the remaining legal life of patents on existing products and the number of patents in the "pipeline."

Franchises and Licenses

Companies may sell the right to use their name, products, processes, or management expertise to others for some negotiated time period or market. The franchisee or licensee capitalizes the cost of purchasing these rights.

Brands and Trademarks

The cost of acquiring brands and trademarks in arm's length transactions is capitalized. However, as in the case of other intangibles, U.S. GAAP prohibit recognition of the value of *internally created* brands or trademarks. Companies in a few countries, notably the United Kingdom and Australia, report the value of brand names, whether created or purchased, as balance sheet assets. Many companies in these countries, however, do not capitalize internally generated brands.

Advertising Costs

Successful advertising campaigns can contribute to brand or firm loyalty for many years. However, as with R&D, these benefits are uncertain and difficult to measure, and hence advertising costs are expensed as incurred. Even though there may be economic benefits, no asset is recorded because of measurement problems.

In December 1994, the Accounting Standards Executive Committee (AcSEC) of the AICPA issued Practice Bulletin 13,[18] Direct-Response Advertising and Probable Future Benefits, requiring capitalization of the costs of direct-response advertising that result in probable future benefits.[19] These costs are amortized over the estimated life of the future benefits. Capitalization is not allowed when the advertising produces leads that require additional marketing efforts to convert into sales.

Goodwill

The difference between the cost of an acquired firm and the fair market value of its net assets is accounted for as an intangible asset, goodwill. It represents the amount paid for the acquired firm's ability to earn excess profits, or value that cannot be assigned to tangible assets like property. U.S. and most other GAAP limit the recognition of goodwill to cases where it is acquired in purchase method transactions. (See Chapter 14.)

Asset Revaluation

As discussed in Chapter 17, the balance sheet is more informative when assets and liabilities are stated at market value rather than historical cost. Although the recognition of changes in fixed asset value is generally not permitted under U.S. GAAP, non-U.S. and IASC standards do permit such revaluations. Unfortunately, revaluation is

---

[18]This bulletin provides an interpretation of AICPA SOP 93-7, Reporting on Advertising Costs.

[19]An example would be advertising that results in a telephone response with an order.

applied inconsistently as standards in most countries do not specify either the method(s) to be used for revaluations or the intervals at which they must be made. The resulting balance sheet accounts are not comparable and, in some cases, may be misleading.

Replacement cost is commonly used in the Netherlands, and net realizable value can be used under certain circumstances. Periodic revaluations of fixed assets are common practice in the United Kingdom and Australia and are permitted in France; they are not allowed in Germany or Japan. In Canada revaluations were permitted until December 1, 1990; although subsequent revaluations are not permitted, prior revaluations could remain in use for the balance sheet. Appendix 8-A discusses the impact of changing prices on financial statements and suggests adjustments to fixed assets for these effects.

The October 1996 Discussion Paper, Measurement of Tangible Fixed Assets, issued by the U.K. Accounting Standards Board proposes a modified historical cost-reporting system for tangible fixed assets. This approach would continue predominant current practice in the United Kingdom.

The proposal calls for a full external professional valuation every five years supplemented by less comprehensive interim valuations for revalued properties. Market comparisons and selected indices are proposed for other revalued tangible fixed assets. Firms would be permitted to revalue a fixed asset only if all tangible fixed assets of the same class were revalued.

Gains on revaluation would be recognized in the statement of total recognized gains and losses to the extent that the gain exceeds the depreciated historical cost or reverses previous revaluation losses recognized in the statement of total recognized gains and losses.

Losses on revaluation would be reported as components of the statement of total recognized gains and losses until the carrying value reflected depreciated historical cost. Revaluation losses would be recognized in the income statement in the event they involved impairment of the income-generating assets.

IAS 16 (revised in 1993), Property, Plant, and Equipment, allows firms to report fixed assets at fair value less accumulated depreciation.[20] Revaluations must be made with sufficient regularity to keep them current. All items in an asset class must be revalued if any are. Revaluation decreases that place the asset value below historical cost must be included in reported earnings.

Reported earnings per share is also affected when revalued assets are sold. In the United Kingdom, FRS 3, Reporting Financial Performance, requires a note (memorandum) on historical cost profits and losses, facilitating the comparison of the performance of firms that have revalued assets with reported results of nonrevaluing firms.

When subsequent depreciation charges are based on revalued amounts, the result is lower earnings per share, reducing the incentive for revaluations; some U.K. companies have discontinued the practice. In some countries, depreciation based on revalued amounts can be used for tax purposes.

International comparisons require adjustments to earnings (for depreciation based on other than historical costs) and net worth (for revaluations). These comparisons may be difficult for the reasons mentioned earlier, differential tax effects of revaluations in different countries, and the varying treatment of the revaluation surplus (often added to a reserve account, changes in which are not always fully disclosed).

---

[20]Although historical cost is the benchmark treatment, revaluation is an allowed alternative.

CAPITALIZATION VERSUS EXPENSING: INDUSTRY ISSUES

Regulated Utilities

Even prior to the issuance of SFAS 34, almost all U.S. regulated utilities capitalized interest on construction work in progress. In addition, utilities capitalize many cash outflows that unregulated companies cannot. The reason is that accounting rules have direct economic impact for utilities. Rates charged to customers are largely a function of accounting-generated numbers.[21]

Regulators allow utilities to earn profits equal to a specified allowable rate of return on assets (rate base). Adding expenses to this allowable profit yields the rates they can charge their customers. Revenues are derived as follows:

$$\text{Revenues} = \text{Expenses} + (\text{Rate of Return} \times \text{Rate Base})$$

Using interest for a self-constructed asset as an example, Exhibit 7-1 shows the effects of the capitalization versus expense choice on a utility's revenues. Expensing increases revenue immediately as the interest expense is recovered in the year incurred. Capitalizing results in recovery of the expense over time as depreciation of the additional fixed asset. However, the total allowable profit is increased due to the fact that the asset base has been increased. Hence, although revenues are deferred, the total amount collected over the life of the asset is greater. As the average life of utility fixed assets (mainly generating plants) is quite long, the incentive to capitalize costs in fixed assets (increasing the rate base) is powerful.

In this example, the utility increases total revenues by $3,000 over the five-year life of the asset by capitalizing $5,000 of interest. The $3,000 differential includes an incremental return (12% × $5,000 = $600 × 5 years = $3,000) on the capitalized interest. The net result of the trade-off between getting lower revenue initially but higher total revenue over time depends on the utility's cost of capital. In our example, as long as the appropriate discount rate is less than 30%, it pays to capitalize interest (or other expenditures).[22]

Fairness to customers is often one argument for capitalization; as current customers do not (yet) benefit from investments in capacity growth, they should not bear the cost. Thus, the cost of financing new capacity is capitalized and spread over time, matching the costs with the benefits (service to ratepayers). This logic is also appealing to regulators who prefer (for political reasons) to defer rate increases to future time periods. Logic and fairness aside, utilities have a direct economic incentive to capitalize, as our illustration shows.[23]

---

[21]For this reason, virtually all regulators that set prices also mandate the accounting principles followed by the companies that they regulate. This has given rise to so-called RAP (regulatory accounting principles), which may differ materially from GAAP.

[22]The differential cash flows are: year 1, ($3,400); year 2, $1,600; year 3, $1,600; year 4, $1,600; year 5, $1,600. This cash flow stream has a positive net present value at interest rates below (approximately) 30%. If net assets were used to set rates, the calculations are more complex; the rate base declines as the asset is depreciated. The net present value of this second case is positive at interest rates below 21%.

[23]This discussion assumes that the capitalized interest will, in fact, be recovered from future revenues. In practice, "regulatory lag" often results in actual rates of return below the "allowable" rate of return. In addition, by capitalizing interest, the recovery of that interest is delayed to a later period and thus current period cash flow is reduced. For these reasons, some utilities have successfully petitioned regulators to allow some portion of the interest on construction work in progress (CWIP) to be recovered currently (expensed) rather than capitalized.

EXHIBIT 7-1
Effect of Capitalization of Interest on a Utility's Revenue

Assumptions:
12% rate of return allowed on assets.
$100,000 cost of self-constructed asset.
5-year useful life for asset.
10% interest rate on debt.
$5,000 of first year interest is capitalized.
Utility has no expenses other than depreciation and interest.

A. Effects of Expensing

Asset Base = $100,000
Allowable Profit = 12% × $100,000 = $12,000

Year	Depreciation	Interest	Total Expense	Allowable Profit	Allowable Revenue
1	$ 20,000	$10,000	$ 30,000	$12,000	$ 42,000
2	20,000	10,000	30,000	12,000	42,000
3	20,000	10,000	30,000	12,000	42,000
4	20,000	10,000	30,000	12,000	42,000
5	20,000	10,000	30,000	12,000	42,000
Total	$100,000	$50,000	$150,000	$60,000	$210,000

B. Effects of Capitalization

Asset Base = $105,000
Allowable Profit = 12% × $105,000 = $12,600

Year	Depreciation	Interest	Total Expense	Allowable Profit	Revenue
1	$ 21,000	$ 5,000	$ 26,000	$12,600	$ 38,600
2	21,000	10,000	31,000	12,600	43,600
3	21,000	10,000	31,000	12,600	43,600
4	21,000	10,000	31,000	12,600	43,600
5	21,000	10,000	31,000	12,600	43,600
Total	$105,000	$45,000	$150,000	$63,000	$213,000

Regulatory accounting results in the creation of *regulatory assets* and *regulatory liabilities*. Regulatory assets are expenditures that regulators will permit the utility to recover in future periods, even though these expenditures do not qualify as assets for unregulated companies under GAAP. Examples include:

• Capitalization (as part of fixed assets) of return on equity as well as interest. These are called the allowance for funds used during construction (AFUDC).

• Capitalization (as part of fixed assets) of employee costs and other overhead.

• Demand side management costs (expenditures to reduce demand).

• Costs to buy out coal or gas purchase contracts.

Under SFAS 71, such expenditures can be recorded as regulatory assets (regulatory liabilities) as long as recovery (settlement) is expected. If an adverse regulatory ruling is made, such assets must be written off.

When deregulation occurs, the company must reassess the carrying value of its assets and liabilities under these new circumstances. In the United States, deregulation of the telephone industry has resulted in significant write-offs by companies in that industry as they:

1. Write down fixed assets to reflect shorter economic lives.

2. Write off regulatory assets that are no longer recoverable.

The use of shorter asset lives as a result of the accounting change increases depreciation expense, somewhat offset by the elimination of depreciation on older assets that were fully written off as part of the change.

Effective August 1, 1994, Bell Atlantic discontinued its use of regulatory accounting, recording a "one-time non-cash charge" of $3,648 million ($2,150 million after tax) consisting of:

1. An increase of $3,463 million in accumulated depreciation

2. The elimination of regulatory assets (net of liabilities) of $185 million

The accounting change sharply reduced reported stockholders' equity, increasing the reported debt-to-equity ratio.

Computer Software Development Costs

The growing importance of computer software led the FASB to issue SFAS 86 (1985). SFAS 86 requires that all costs incurred to establish the technological and/or economic feasibility of software be viewed as R&D costs and expensed as incurred. Once economic feasibility has been established, subsequent costs can be capitalized as part of product inventory and amortized based on product revenues or on a straight-line basis.

Although this provision allows software firms to increase reported assets and income, some software firms[24] (most notably, Microsoft) have not taken advantage of the provisions of SFAS 86. Disparate accounting for software hinders the comparison of computer software firms, requiring restatement to the same accounting method. Case 7-1, based on Digital Equipment, provides an example of how restatements can be made.

SFAS 86 disclosures are sufficient to evaluate (and eliminate) the impact of capitalization. For some firms, the effect is considerable, as illustrated by the following example.

Example: IBM

Exhibit 7-2 presents selected financial information from IBM's annual reports. Capitalized software (net) at December 31, 1994, equals 3.6% of IBM's total assets and 12.7%

---

[24]See Amir and Lev (1996), footnote 2.

EXHIBIT 7-2. IBM
Software Capitalization ($ millions)

	1990	1991	1992	1993	1994
Balance Sheet					
Software, gross	$9,972	$11,433	$12,650	$13,846	$13,756
Accumulated amortization	5,873	6,950	8,531	10,143	10,793
Software, net	$4,099	$ 4,483	$ 4,119	$ 3,703	$ 2,963
Statement of Cash Flows					
CFO: "Addback" to net income					
Amortization expense	1,086	1,564	1,466	1,951	2,098
CFI					
New investment in software	$1,892	$ 2,014	$ 1,752	$ 1,507	$ 1,361

Source: IBM, *1990–1994 Annual Reports.*

of stockholders' equity. Although the amortization of capitalized software cost is not broken out in IBM's income statement, such amortization is shown as a line item in the statement of cash flows. The difference between the amount amortized and the new investment in software reflects the impact of capitalization on IBM's income statement.

IBM, Years Ended December 31

($ in millions)	1990	1991	1992	1993	1994
New investment	$1,892	$2,014	$1,752	$1,507	$1,361
Less: Amortization	1,086	1,564	1,466	1,951	2,098
Net pretax effect	$ 806	$ 450	$ 286	$ (444)	$ (737)

The data reveal that the capitalization of software development costs increased through 1991 and then declined each year through 1994. During the period of increase, capitalization (as opposed to expensing) increased IBM's reported pretax income (by $806 million in 1990). As expenditures leveled off and declined, and amortization increased (reflecting past capitalized amounts), the net increase declined to $450 million in 1991 and $286 million in 1992.

Starting in 1993, amortization exceeded new investment and the effect of capitalization was to *decrease* pretax income by $444 million in 1993 and $737 million in 1994. The example illustrates that capitalization tends to increase reported earnings when expenditures are rising, but may decrease reported income when expenditures decline, as amortization exceeds new deferrals.

These disclosures can also be used to illustrate the impact of capitalization on reported cash flows. IBM reported its 1994 investment of $1,361 million in new software as an investing cash flow. If the software costs had been expensed, they would have reduced IBM's operating cash flow. The capitalization of software development costs, therefore, increased IBM's reported CFO by $1,361 million as compared with CFO had those costs been expensed.[25]

Finally, the pattern of IBM's expenditure on capitalized software costs is, itself, noteworthy. The 1994 investment was 28% below the 1990 level. An analyst would want to know, for example, whether this trend reflects *an actual decline in spending or a shift to outflows that cannot be capitalized under SFAS 86.* In a footnote to its *1994 Annual Report,* IBM states that

> software-related [R&D] activities were $793 million, $1,097 million, and $1,161 million in 1994, 1993, and 1992 respectively.

The decline in capitalized software expenditures was accompanied by a decline in (software) expenditures that were expensed as R&D. In fact, IBM's total R&D and engineering expenses were $4.36 billion in 1994, a decline of 22% from the 1992 level.

This analysis illustrates how accounting data can reveal both financial statement and real operating effects.

Accounting for Oil and Gas Exploration

Oil and gas exploration results in drilling both productive wells and dry holes.[26] As failure is an integral part of successful exploration, the cost of dry holes can be considered part of the cost of drilling productive ones. As in the case of R&D, the value of an oil discovery is frequently unrelated to the cost of drilling.

The FASB, in SFAS 19 (1977), required all firms to use the successful efforts (SE) accounting method that expenses all dry hole costs. Like the FASB's R&D reporting standard, this rule was conservative and eliminated assets with uncertain future benefits from the balance sheet. The Securities and Exchange Commission (SEC), fearing that the adoption of this rule would result in the curtailment of oil exploration (especially by smaller companies), forced the FASB to suspend SFAS 19 (SFAS 25, 1979). The SEC (ASR 253, 1978) permits public companies to use either SE or full cost (FC) methods of accounting. The latter permits the capitalization of dry hole costs.

Under current accounting practice, therefore, firms have the option of capitalizing the cost of dry holes (FC method) or expensing them as they occur (SE method). The choice between these two methods has a significant impact on the financial statements of oil and gas exploration companies and on many ratios as well. Exhibit 7-3 illustrates the difference between the SE and FC methods of accounting for oil and gas exploration costs. The balance sheet carrying amount of reserves, $4,000, is higher under the FC method because of the inclusion of the cost of dry holes ($3,000). The SE firm carries its reserves at only $1,000.

The reported profitability (both levels and trends over time) of production is also affected. The SE firm reports a net loss of $250 in year 1 but net income of $2,750 per year for years 2 through 4, for a total net income of $8,000. The FC firm shows constant net income of $2,000 per year, again for a total of $8,000 over the four years.

---

[25]Amortization of previously capitalized costs has no effect on reported cash from operations (it is added back to net income under the indirect method and excluded under the direct method).

[26]Dry holes are wells drilled that do not find commercial quantities of oil or gas.

The effect of the FC method is to defer (capitalize) exploration costs and, therefore, accelerate the recognition of profit.

CFO may also differ. As seen in Box 7-1, although the income difference reverses over time, the difference in CFO does not. The cumulative CFO over the life of the well is higher for the FC firm by the cost of the capitalized dry holes ($12,000 − $9,000 = $3,000).

EXHIBIT 7-3
Comparison of Successful Efforts and Full Cost Impact on Net Income and Cash from Operations

Assumptions:
1. $1,000 cost of drilling well (dry or productive).
2. Four wells are drilled: One is productive, the other three are dry.
3. The productive well has a four-year life, with revenues (net of cost of production) of $3,000 per year.

Successful Efforts Method

The $3,000 cost of dry holes is expensed immediately. Only the $1,000 cost of the productive well is capitalized and amortized over its four-year life.

Year	1	2	3	4	Total
Net revenues	$ 3,000	$ 3,000	$ 3,000	$ 3,000	$12,000
Dry hole expense	(3,000)	0	0	0	(3,000)
Amortization	(250)	(250)	(250)	(250)	(1,000)
Net income	$ (250)	$ 2,750	$ 2,750	$ 2,750	$ 8,000

Cash Flows

Operations*	$ 0	$ 3,000	$ 3,000	$ 3,000	$ 9,000
Investment	(1,000)	0	0	0	(1,000)
Total	$(1,000)	$ 3,000	$ 3,000	$ 3,000	$ 8,000

*Net revenues less dry hole expense.

Full Cost Method

The entire $4,000 drilling cost ($3,000 for dry holes and $1,000 for the productive well) is capitalized and amortized over the four-year life of the productive well.

Year	1	2	3	4	Total
Net revenues	$ 3,000	$ 3,000	$ 3,000	$ 3,000	$12,000
Amortization	(1,000)	(1,000)	(1,000)	(1,000)	(4,000)
Net income	$ 2,000	$ 2,000	$ 2,000	$ 2,000	$ 8,000

Cash Flows

Operations*	$ 3,000	$ 3,000	$ 3,000	$ 3,000	$12,000
Investment	(4,000)	0	0	0	(4,000)
Total	$(1,000)	$ 3,000	$ 3,000	$ 3,000	$ 8,000

*Net revenues.

The differences between the methods cause SE firms to report:

1. Lower carrying costs of oil and gas reserves than FC firms
2. Lower earnings than FC firms when exploration efforts are rising
3. Lower cash from operations than FC firms

In practice, however, some oil and gas firms using the SE method adjust their reported cash flow statements for this difference. They add exploration costs expensed back to net income (assuming use of the indirect method) and include those costs in capital expenditures. This adjustment can be seen in duPont's cash flow statement (Appendix A), where 1994 "dry hole costs and impairment of unproved properties" of $152 million is one adjustment shown in the calculation of "cash provided by operations."

Appendix 7-B contains more detail on these issues as well as the motivation for firms to choose the SE or FC methods. The appendix also provides a more detailed discussion of the disclosures provided by and the analysis of oil and gas companies.

ANALYTIC ADJUSTMENTS FOR CAPITALIZATION AND EXPENSING

Need for Analytic Adjustments

Because the choices between capitalization and expensing discussed in the first part of this chapter affect reported corporate performance, analysts must sometimes adjust reported data to facilitate analysis and comparisons.

The pharmaceutical industry, for example, reports the highest return on assets (ROA) of all U.S. industries. Some suggest that this reflects a higher return for the risks inherent in R&D.[27] Others contend that the industry simply earns excess profits. To some extent, however, high drug industry returns reflect the accounting method used for R&D. Expensing these costs understates investment, the denominator of the ROA ratio. Capitalizing R&D costs (treating them as an investment) would give a more accurate measure of ROA.

The data on Merck in Exhibit 7-4 illustrate this point. Panel A shows how the capitalization of R&D increases profitability, as measured by return on sales. ROA, however, is decreased by up to four percentage points.

The effect on ROA depends on the length of the amortization period used to amortize previously expensed (now capitalized) R&D. The exhibit shows the effect of three-, five-, and seven-year lives.

Ideally, the amortization period should be appropriate for the industry and company in question; it should reflect the duration of the effects of R&D expenditures on the firm's profitability. This length of time is difficult to determine in practice.[28]

Sougiannis (1994) and Lev and Sougiannis (1996), however, describe how to measure the effects of R&D on future profitability empirically. Their analysis suggests

[27]Generally, industries with heavy R&D costs report higher ROAs. The arguments and adjustments suggested for Merck can be extended to other industries as well. Although not illustrated here, solvency ratios for Merck would also be improved as a result of the capitalization of R&D expense.

[28]Indeed, it is precisely this difficulty that prompted the FASB to require the expensing of R&D expenditures.

EXHIBIT 7-4. MERCK & CO.
Recalculation of Profitability Ratios Assuming Capitalization of R&D Expenditures

A. Recalculation of Return on Sales and ROA, 1990 to 1994

Merck's income and total assets are recalculated assuming that R&D is capitalized and amortized over three-, five-, or seven-year periods. Note that return on sales increases as the length of the amortization period increases. The effect on return on assets is the opposite as the denominator effect (higher assets) overwhelms the numerator effect (higher income). Thus, ROA *decreases* with longer amortization periods.*

Return on Sales

Year	R&D Expensed as Reported	R&D Capitalized and Amortized over		
		3 Years	5 Years	7 Years
1990	23.2%	24.0%	24.9%	25.5%
1991	24.7	25.6	26.4	27.1
1992	25.3	26.2	27.0	27.7
1993	20.6	21.2	21.9	22.6
1994	20.0%	20.3%	20.7%	21.2%

Return on Assets

Year	R&D Expensed as Reported	R&D Capitalized and Amortized over		
		3 Years	5 Years	7 Years
1990	24.1%	22.6%	21.6%	20.9%
1991	24.2	22.9	21.9	21.2
1992	23.8	22.4	21.5	20.8
1993	14.0	13.4	13.1	12.9
1994	14.3%	13.8%	13.4%	13.2%

B. Explanation of Recalculation

The recalculation is illustrated for 1994 using three-year amortization.† To adjust income, first calculate the amortization expense if R&D expense was capitalized and then amortized over three years. As the table below indicates, for 1994 (shown in bold), amortization expense equals one-third of (the sum of) R&D expense for 1992 to 1994, or $1,172 million. *As actual R&D expense was $1,231, recalculation increases (pretax) income by ($1,231 − $1,172) = $59.* Because Merck's R&D is growing, the net effect of capitalization and amortization increases income.

	Actual R&D Expense	Annual Amortization of Capitalized R&D						
		1990	1991	1992	1993	1994	1995	1996
1990	$ 854	$285	$285	$285				
1991	988		329	329	$329			
1992	1,112			371	371	**$ 371**		
1993	1,173				391	**391**	$391	
1994	$1,231					**410**	410	$410
						$1,172		

The table shows that, by the end of 1994, all R&D expense through 1992 is fully amortized. The only unamortized portion is one-third of 1993 R&D expense ($391) and two-thirds of 1994 expense ($820). *Thus, the balance sheet adjustment is an increase in assets (and equity) of $1,211.*

EXHIBIT 7-4. *(continued)*

C. *Recomputation of Merck's ROE (1982 to 1991) by Lev and Sougiannis (1996)*

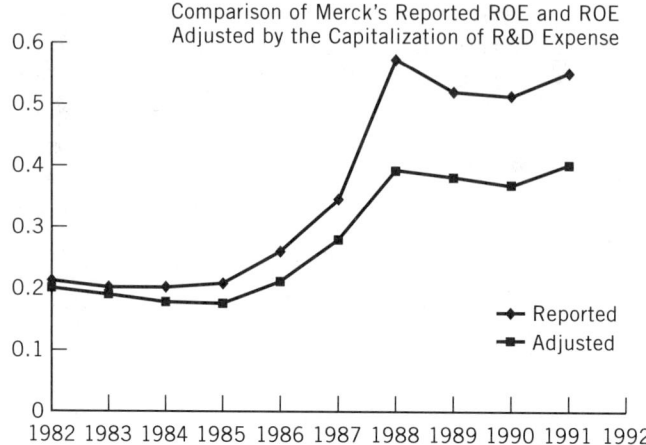

This graph uses data from "The Capitalization, Amortization and Value-Relevance of R&D," *Journal of Accounting and Economics,* Baruch Lev and Theodore Sougiannis, Table 6, Feb. 1996, pp. 107–138.

---

*One can also view these results as the disaggregation of ROA into return on sales and asset turnover. Although return on sales increases, the increased asset base with no change in sales reduces asset turnover and consequently ROA.

†For other amortization periods, the procedure is similar. Using five-year amortization, for 1994, add back to income the R&D expense for that year but subtract one-fifth of the sum of 1990 through 1994 R&D expenditures. Assets are increased by four-fifths of 1994 R&D, three-fifths of 1993 R&D, two-fifths of 1992 R&D, and one-fifth of 1991 R&D.

that R&D has (on average) a seven-year duration for the pharmaceutical industry. Using the implied amortization schedule for Merck,[29] Lev and Sougiannis find a similar downward shift in Merck's ROE. Exhibit 7-4C shows the effects of their conversion process graphically for the period 1982 to 1991.

The Merck example shows the effects of restating by capitalizing an expense. At times, it may be more appropriate to restate capitalized expenditures to expenses. Amerada (capitalized interest) and IBM (capitalized software costs) are examples of such restatements.

Similar adjustments are required for firms that differ in the extent to which they buy operating assets or lease them. Airlines, for example, may buy or lease airplanes. Similarly, retail store chains may own or lease stores. This choice has financial statement effects similar to those stemming from capitalizing or expensing. Reported ROA may

---

[29]The amortization schedule is neither straight-line nor declining balance. Rather, it amortizes capitalized R&D in proportion to the benefits received. As there is a lag between the time of the expenditure and benefits received, amortization increases over the first three years and declines thereafter.

be misleading; adjustments are required for comparability. Chapter 11 discusses leasing and other off balance sheet financing techniques in detail.

Valuation Implications

Expenditures for R&D and advertising are generally expensed because it is difficult, if not impossible, to reliably estimate their future benefits. That does not mean that these expenditures do not affect firm valuation. An outflow that is truly an expense reduces stockholder wealth; an outflow that generates future cash flows may actually increase it.

Chapter 19 discusses two types of valuation models: earnings-based and asset-based. Box 7-2 discusses how the capitalization decision affects these valuation models and presents empirical evidence that the market recognizes the asset characteristics of outflows in categories such as R&D, advertising, and oil and gas wells. These results suggest that the analyst cannot apply either capitalization or expensing mechanically, but must try to forecast the future benefits of these expenditures.

Other Economic Consequences

Although differences in accounting methods are cosmetic, they can have real consequences, as suggested by positive theory.[30]

First, a firm's borrowing ability may be limited by unfavorable profitability or leverage ratios resulting from, for example, expensing R&D expenditures. Second, because of these unfavorable ratios, a firm may curtail these expenditures, effectively scaling back operations. Finally, whether or not managers actually reduce R&D, the fact that the market perceives such a possibility can cause negative market reaction.

Mandated accounting changes is one area where such effects can be examined, as they provide a "laboratory" environment permitting before-and-after comparisons. Box 7-3 reviews empirical evidence regarding mandated accounting changes for R&D and oil and gas accounting.

The research confirms that, even if an accounting change has no direct economic impact, the effects of the change on reported income can have real indirect consequences, such as the curtailment of expenditures and negative market reaction. Indirect effects may also result from debt covenant constraints or the influence of management compensation contracts. Accounting choices may also be motivated by firm characteristics (see Appendix 7-B for a discussion of accounting choices by large and small oil companies).

Additional Analysis of Fixed Asset Data

Changes in the balance sheet cost of fixed assets result from four types of events:

1. Capital spending (acquisition of fixed assets)
2. Sale or retirement (no longer in use) of fixed assets
3. Increases (decreases) in fixed assets due to acquisitions (disposals)
4. Changes due to the effects of foreign currency translation

---

[30]See Chapter 5.

BOX 7-2
Capitalization and Valuation

Consider the following simplified valuation model:

Value = p × Net Inflows

The model can be used to represent a (constant) discounted earnings model, where net inflows represent revenue and expense flows and the coefficient p is simply the price/earnings (P/E) ratio. Disaggregating the net inflows into inflows and outflows yields

Value = p × Inflows − p × Expense Outflows + b × Asset Outflows

where asset outflows represent expenditures for such categories as R&D. If these outflows are actually expenses, then $b = -p$.

From a valuation perspective, the difference between asset and expense outflows should be whether the associated outflow has expected future benefits. The level and sign of the coefficient b measure whether the outflow should be considered an expense. An expense benefits only the period of occurrence, and the outlay reduces value by $-p$ times the outflow.* An asset outflow benefits future periods and, therefore, the coefficient b should be positive.†

Bublitz and Ettredge (1989) compared the market valuation of unexpected changes in advertising, R&D, and other expenses. Advertising was included because, like R&D, it is expected to provide benefits for more than one period, albeit for a shorter term than R&D. They expected the coefficient for R&D to be larger (more positive) than the coefficient for advertising, and both larger than the coefficient for other expenses. The results were mixed, but on balance they found

> the evidence is consistent with a market assessment that advertising is short-lived while R&D is long-lived.‡

Their R&D results are consistent with those of Hirschey and Weygandt (1985) who found that the market valuation of R&D implies it is an asset outflow. Hirschey and Weygandt also found that advertising had characteristics similar to a long-lived asset.

Their valuation model used a discounted earnings-based perspective. Shevlin (1991) used an asset-based valuation model for R&D partnerships. In such a model, the value of the firm is defined as

Value = Assets − Liabilities

Shevlin§ found that when R&D expenditures were considered assets, they contributed to firm value. Moreover, the market weighting given these expenditures was larger than for other assets, indicating that the expected benefit from these expenditures exceeds their book value.

Lev and Sougiannis (1996) and Sougiannis (1994) estimated stock prices and returns as functions of *both* earnings and book values. They also found that the capitalized components of R&D have value relevance** and are associated with current period stock returns. More important, Lev and Sougiannis found a significant association between capitalized R&D and *subsequent* stock returns:

> suggesting either a systematic mispricing of the shares of R&D-intensive companies, or a compensation for an extra-market risk factor associated with R&D.††

Using a sample of oil and gas companies, Harris and Ohlson (1987) found that the market distinguished between SE and FC companies in a rational fashion. Book values of full cost companies were given less weight than those of SE companies. Additionally, they found that FC book values had less explanatory power than those of SE companies. This finding is consistent with a survey that indicated analysts prefer SE.‡‡

---

*The current benefits are reflected in the inflows.

†The asset outflows representing future benefits can be thought of as a growth component. In Chapter 19, we show that for a firm with growth, its value can be expressed as

$$\text{Value} = \frac{E}{r} + \left[\frac{1}{r} \left(\frac{r^* - r}{r - ar^*} \right) \right] aE$$

where E is earnings, r the appropriate discount rate, r^* the amount the firm earns on its investment, and aE the amount the firm reinvests. In our example, $p = 1/r$ and b is the coefficient of the asset investment aE. That is, b is equal to the term in brackets. On the margin, it may be zero (if $r^* = r$) as the firm undertakes zero or break-even net present value investments.

‡Bruce Bublitz and Michael Ettredge, "The Information in Discretionary Outlays: Advertising, Research and Development," *The Accounting Review,* Jan. 1989, pp. 108–124.

§As noted in Appendix 7-A, Shevlin applied option pricing models to the valuation of R&D partnerships.

**Sougiannis, for example, shows that (on average) a one-dollar increase in R&D expenditures produces a five-dollar increase in market value.

††Baruch Lev and Theodore Sougiannis, "The Capitalization, Amortization and Value-Relevance of R&D," *Journal of Accounting and Economics,* Feb. 1996, pp. 107–138.

‡‡Somewhat surprisingly, they found that net book value measures were not only highly significant explanatory variables for the market valuation of oil and gas companies but that the book value measures dominated the other disclosures provided in the footnotes (such as the standardized present value of expected cash flow measures discussed in Appendix 7-B). In a subsequent paper, Harris and Ohlson (1990) questioned whether their result really showed the greater value relevance of historical costs or the market was incorrectly focusing on the book values (functional fixation). If the latter, they really observed a mispricing phenomenon. As preliminary evidence of mispricing, they found that abnormal riskless trading profits could be made from a simple trading filter rule: Rank firms on the basis of market value per barrel of reserves and then create a zero investment portfolio by going long (short) those firms whose ranking fell above (below) the median.

The authors then created a similar trading rule based on the portion of market value not explained by book values. They found that abnormal profits were even greater under this second rule, indicating that, although the market was inefficient in its pricing, the source of the inefficiency was not historical accounting book values. On the contrary, the results indicated that the market would have been more efficient had it paid more attention to the historical cost information.

See also the discussion in Appendix 7-B of Clinch and Margiolo (1992), who further qualify the Harris and Ohlson results.

The effects of acquisitions and foreign currency translation are considered in Chapters 14 and 15, respectively. The following sections discuss capital expenditures and the sale/retirement of assets.

Capital Expenditures

The capital expenditure decision provides information to the investor as to a firm's future profitability and growth prospects. Major capital expenditure plans are often announced separately by management. McConnell and Muscarella (1986) and Kerstein and Kim (1995) provide evidence that there is positive (negative) market reaction to unexpected increases (decreases) in capital expenditures. Similarly, Lev and Thiagarajan (1993) show that firms with higher (lower) changes in capital expenditures than

---

BOX 7-3
Mandated Accounting Changes: Economic Consequences and Market Reaction

---

The capitalization versus expense issue has proved a fruitful area of empirical research. The issues examined provide interesting parallels between R&D (SFAS 2) and oil and gas accounting (SFAS 19). In both cases, mandated accounting changes favored expensing over capitalization (albeit in one case, the standard was suspended). Proponents of capitalization argued that, in each case, the accounting change would lead to a reduction of risk-taking activities such as expenditures for R&D and exploration activities, as the cost of risk taking would increase. Furthermore, preferences were related in a systematic fashion to firm characteristics. The empirical issues examined in this section are:

- Economic consequences of mandated changes—impact on management behavior
- Market reaction to mandated accounting changes

Economic Consequences: Impact on Management Behavior

Any adverse effect of expensing R&D or exploration costs should be directly related to the level of expenditures on these items.

The standards primarily affected smaller firms as, in both cases, larger firms generally used the expensing method.* Smaller companies feared that markets (at least private lenders) would focus on the effects on reported income (both amounts and variability). The change would thus impair their ability to raise capital.

As SFAS 19 was never implemented, the validity of these claims could not be verified. However, for SFAS 2, a number of studies attempted to verify whether or not the new standard curtailed R&D.

Horwitz and Kolodny (1980) reported that

> in response to the question: "Do you believe that small firms reduced planned R&D expenditures as a consequence of SFAS 2?" 66.7 percent of firms with sales less than $10 million and 58.9 percent of firms with sales greater than $10 million answered affirmatively or possibly.†

Using a sample of small high-technology firms, they then found evidence that the actual levels of R&D expenditures dropped following the introduction of SFAS 2. In contrast, Dukes et al. (1980), whose sample consisted of larger companies, found no evidence of curtailment of R&D subsequent to the adoption of SFAS 2.

In a subsequent study, Elliott et al. (1984) confirmed the finding that small companies that had previously capitalized R&D curtailed R&D expenditures after the issuance of SFAS 2. However, they noted that the downward trend in R&D expenditures for these companies had already begun years prior to the issuance of SFAS 2. Comparing the operating performance of the "capitalizers" with a control sample of firms that had always expensed R&D, they found that the operating performance of the capitalizers was worse. They conjectured that financial difficulties, rather than the accounting change, may have caused the curtailment of R&D. In fact, it could be argued that the original decision to capitalize R&D by these firms may have been motivated by an effort to improve reported financial performance in the face of financial stress.

Selto and Clouse (1985) argued that firms would be likely to anticipate the effects of an accounting change such as SFAS 2 and adapt to it. Thus, if divisional managers would be motivated to reduce R&D expenditures because of the effect on their compensation (through earnings-based compensation plans), firms would adjust their compensation plans accordingly or, alternatively, take steps to centralize the R&D decision-making process. They found that although not all firms made such changes, those that did were the ones most likely to be affected by the provisions of SFAS 2. Thus, to the extent accounting changes have economic consequences, they may be manifested internally rather than externally.

Market Reaction

Vigeland (1981) found no market reaction to the mandated accounting change for R&D expenditures. There is little controversy with respect to this mandated accounting change. This is not true with respect to the mandated change(s) affecting accounting for oil and gas exploration. This issue spawned a cottage industry of research with studies examining the reaction to the announcement of:

1. Exposure draft of SFAS 19
2. SFAS 19
3. Accounting Series Release (ASR) 253, issued by the SEC, that suspended SFAS 19

The research examined whether firms using the full cost method (FC) had negative (positive) returns when SFAS 19 (ASR 253) was announced. Generally negative reaction was found around the time of the announcement of the SFAS 19 exposure draft. Not everyone, however, agreed with its significance. Collins and Dent (1979) and Lev (1979) claimed that the results were statistically significant, whereas Dyckman and Smith (1979) argued that the market reaction was not statistically different from that experienced by firms using successful efforts (SE). The results were also found to be sensitive to the exact time period examined. In addition, at the time of the exposure draft announcement, there was "confounding" news affecting the oil industry. Thus, even when negative market reaction was found, its cause was not clear.

With respect to the ASR 253 announcement, Collins et al. (1982), using a "reversal" methodology, compared the market reaction at the time the SFAS 19 exposure draft was announced with the reaction experienced when ASR 253 was announced. They found that there was a significant negative correlation for the FC firms; that is, negative reaction to the first announcement was followed by positive reaction to the subsequent (suspension) announcement.

These studies tested market reaction without considering any factors that might cause differential market reactions across firms due to differential impacts on income and equity. Such factors might include firm size, the relative importance of exploration, firm leverage, and the existence of debt covenants and accounting-based management compensation schemes. Collins et al. (1981) and Lys (1984) tested for such factors with some success. Collins and co-workers, for example, found that the degree of market reaction was related to (1) the size of the reduction in owner's equity that would result from SFAS 19, (2) the existence of debt covenants, and (3) management compensation schemes based on reported income.

---

*See Box 7-1 for a discussion of the differential impact of the capitalize versus expense decision on large and small firms.

†Bertrand N. Horwitz and Richard Kolodny, "The Economic Effects of Involuntary Uniformity in the Financial Reporting of R&D Expenditures," *Journal of Accounting Research*, Supplement 1980, pp. 38–74.

their industry average experience positive (negative) market reaction. Thus, it is important to monitor (changes in) the level of a firm's capital expenditures.

In doing so, note that capital expenditures tend to be seasonal, with the majority of such expenditures being carried out in the fourth quarter. Different theories exist as to whether this phenomenon is tied to a firm's budgetary cycle [Callen et al. (1996)] or the timing is tax-related [Kinney and Trezevant (1993)].

Sale or Retirement of Assets

The sale or retirement of fixed assets removes these assets from the balance sheet. For most firms, sale or retirement also generates gains or losses, included in reported income.

In the case of duPont, gains on asset sales are included in other income (see financial statement Note 2). In 1993, such gains accounted for more than 20% of pretax income. Some companies report gains or losses on a separate line in the income statement, whereas others include them elsewhere. The analyst should examine such gains or losses for several reasons.

First, gains and losses resulting from asset sales are considered nonrecurring and the inclusion of such gains in reported income lowers the quality of earnings. However, if such gains or losses occur in most years, it is difficult to consider them "nonrecurring." As asset sales are to a great extent subject to management discretion, their timing and variation from year to year must be closely monitored as they can be used to distort operating trends. Bartov (1993) reported that gains or losses from asset sales are used by firms to engage in income smoothing.[31] Additionally, highly leveraged firms sell more long-lived assets then less leveraged firms in an effort to improve their reported debt-to-equity ratios.

A second reason for looking at asset sales is more fundamental. Sale of a significant portion of fixed assets is an indicator of change—in product line or production location. The examination of trends in capital spending and fixed asset sales can help the analyst ask perceptive questions regarding changes in future operations.

Finally, a pattern of gains suggests that the company's depreciation method is conservative, understating reported income and the net carrying amounts of fixed assets. A pattern of losses suggests that depreciation expense is understated (income is overstated) and fixed assets are overvalued on the balance sheet. In extreme cases, such losses are recognized as "impairments." Issues relating to depreciation and impairments are discussed in Chapter 8.

SUMMARY

This chapter considers the financial statement effects of the capitalize versus expense decision for long-lived assets. Once the capitalized amount is determined, the firm must choose an appropriate pattern of depreciation or amortization. Analysts must also contend with financial reporting for impairments and disposal of these assets. We discuss these issues in the next chapter.

---

[31]Whether this constitutes "good" or "bad" behavior depends on whether one views income smoothing (see Chapter 2) as "variance reducing" (providing information to investors as to a firm's expected performance) or manipulative behavior that hides a firm's actual performance.

CASE 7-1

Adjustments for Capitalization and Expensing: Digital Equipment

Digital Equipment first began to capitalize computer software development costs in 1987. Its footnote at that time stated:

> During the year, the Company capitalized $35,115,000 of computer software development costs which are included in other assets, net on the balance sheet. These costs are amortized over three years from the date the products are available for general release. Costs amortized during the year were $1,431,000.

Exhibit 7C-1 presents the amount of computer software development costs amortized each year for 1987 to 1995 and the balance of the unamortized computer software development costs; other selected financial information for Digital is provided for the years 1984 to 1995 ($ in millions).

1. Compute Digital's expenditure for computer software development for each year during the period 1987 to 1995.

2. Based on the data provided in the exhibit and your answer to part 1 estimate the lag between the time software is developed and the time it is "available for general release."

3. Digital's other research and engineering costs are expensed as they are incurred.

   (a) Discuss the rationale for expensing these costs while capitalizing computer software development costs.

   (b) Discuss how the different accounting treatment of these costs will affect trends in profitability and solvency ratios, assuming that software becomes a more significant factor in Digital's products.

4. Assuming that Digital expensed computer software development costs as incurred, compare the (adjusted) operating income, return on assets, and return on equity with the amounts reported for 1987 to 1992. (Ignore income tax effects.)

5. Repeat part 4, assuming that Digital capitalized all research and engineering costs (as well as software costs) and amortized them over three years beginning the following year.

6. Digital Equipment's cash from operations was $47 million, $375 million, and $348 million in the years 1993 to 1995, respectively. How would the accounting assumptions made in parts 4 and 5 affect these reported numbers?

EXHIBIT 7C-1. DIGITAL EQUIPMENT
Capitalized Software Costs and Selected Financial Data, Years Ended June 30 ($ millions)

	1984	1985	1986	1987	1988	1989	1990	1991	1992	1993	1994	1995
Capitalized Software Costs												
Amortization expense	$ 0	$ 0	$ 0	$ 1	$ 12	$ 27	$ 37	$ 44	$ 64	$ 69	$ 68	$ 59
Unamortized cost (year-end)	0	0	0	34	66	90	110	112	134	138	125	101
Selected Financial Data												
Research and engineering costs*	$ 631	$ 717	$ 814	$1,010	$ 1,306	$ 1,525	$ 1,614	$ 1,649	$ 1,754	$ 1,530	$ 1,301	$1,040
Operating income†	395	450	829	1,612	1,635	1,336	563	511	(636)	(237)	(790)	108
Total assets (year-end)	5,593	6,369	7,173	8,407	10,112	10,668	11,655	11,875	11,284	10,950	10,580	9,947
Stockholders' equity (year-end)	$3,979	$4,555	$5,728	$6,294	$ 7,510	$ 8,036	$ 8,182	$ 7,624	$ 4,931	$ 4,885	$ 3,280	$3,528

*Assume that research and engineering costs include amortized portion of software costs.
†Operating income calculated prior to restructuring charges taken in 1990 to 1992.
  Source: Digital Equipment, *1987–1995 Annual Reports.*

Chapter 7

Problems

1. [Capitalizing versus expensing; 1996 CFA adapted] Describe the effect of capitalizing versus expensing costs, for a firm growing at a variable growth rate, on:

(i) CFO

(ii) ROA

2. [Capitalizing versus expensing; 1996 CFA adapted] As compared with expensing costs, describe the effect of capitalization on a firm's

(i) Assets

(ii) Equity

3. [Capitalization of interest; 1988 CFA adapted] Rogan Development, a real estate developer, is developing an office building in Charlottesville, Virginia. The average balance of the "building under construction" account for 19X7 was $10 million. Rogan had the following debt outstanding during 19X7 ($ in millions):

	Average Balance	Interest Rate
Development loan	$ 6	11%
Mortgage debt	10	9
Senior debentures	40	10

A. Calculate each of the following for 19X7, assuming that the development loan applied solely to the Charlottesville building:

(i) Interest payable for 19X7

(ii) Capitalized interest for 19X7

(iii) Interest expense for 19X7

B. As a bond analyst, you use the interest coverage ratio to assess Rogan's ability to meet interest payments. Discuss how to calculate that ratio for 19X7.

C. Discuss the impact of the capitalization of interest on the comparison of the following for different firms:

(i) Interest coverage ratios

(ii) Cash flow from operations

(iii) Profitability ratios

Your answer should consider the effects of (1) the availability of internally generated funds for construction, (2) the cost of capital, and (3) amortization periods and methods.

4. [Capitalization of interest] The *1989 Annual Report* of Rohm and Haas, a chemical company, contained the following footnote:

> In 1989, 1988 and 1987, respectively, interest costs of $20 million, $16 million and $11 million were capitalized and added to the gross book value of land, buildings and equipment. Amortization of such capitalized costs included in depreciation expense was $8 million in 1989, $7 million in 1988 and $5 million in 1987.

A. Compute the effect of capitalization of interest on net income for the period 1987 to 1989.

B. Compute the effect of capitalization of interest on the components of cash flow for the period 1987 to 1989.

C. For the year ended December 31, 1989 Rohm and Haas reported interest expense of $39 million and pretax income of $251 million. Calculate the company's times interest earned (coverage ratio) as reported and after adjustment for capitalized interest.

5. [Brand names] "Buildings age and become dilapidated. Machines wear out. Cars rust. But what lives on are brands," argues Sir Hector Laing of Britain's United Biscuits (*The Economist,* December 24, 1988, p. 100).

A. Using this quotation as a point of departure, discuss the advantages and disadvantages (from the point of view of financial analysis) of the balance sheet recognition of brand names.

B. Discuss the advantages and disadvantages (also from the point of view of financial analysis) of the amortization of brand name intangible assets through charges to income.

6. [Capitalization versus expense] The following footnote appeared in the *1991 Annual Report* of Morrison Knudsen Corp.:

Development Costs: Effective April 1, 1991 the Corporation adopted a new accounting policy to defer certain costs related to the design, engineering, construction, and ongoing operation and maintenance of certain major projects in which the Corporation for the first time intends to retain an ownership interest. Such costs include licenses, fees, permits, outside professional consulting costs and engineering and technical labor costs which are expected to benefit future operations. Such costs will be capitalized as part of the project when the project becomes operational. When the commercial success of a particular project becomes doubtful, deferred development costs are written off immediately. Development costs of $4,710 have been deferred during 1991 and are included in the balance sheet caption "Other Investments and Assets."

A. Discuss the impact of this accounting change on reported:

  (i) 1991 income

 (ii) 1991 cash flows

(iii) Income in future years

 (iv) Cash flows in future years

B. Discuss the effect of this accounting change on the level and trend of the following ratios:

  (i) Debt-to-equity

 (ii) Return on assets

7. [Capitalization versus expense] Exhibit 7P-1 contains a footnote from the *1991 Annual Report* of Grant Tensor Geophysical, which gathers, processes, and markets seismic data used by oil and gas exploration companies.

EXHIBIT 7P-1. GRANT TENSOR GEOPHYSICAL CORP.

Proprietary Geophysical Data

Effective January 1, 1991, the Company changed its method of amortizing proprietary geophysical data from the cost recovery method to a method whereby costs are amortized over sales the Company anticipates receiving from the licensing of its proprietary geophysical data. The Company believes the new method of accounting results in a better matching of costs and revenues and more properly reflects the carrying value of the asset.

Under the cost recovery method, equal amounts of revenue and expense were recognized as sales were made until all costs were recovered, postponing any recognition of profit until that time. Costs not recovered through sales were amortized over 36 months. Under the new method of accounting, costs are amortized based on the sales that the Company expects to realize from the licensing of its proprietary geophysical data. Management has established guidelines requiring that a minimum of 40% of the cost be amortized within 12 months from the completion date of a geophysical data program and the remainder, except for a residual of 10%, be amortized ratably over the next 24 months.

The $983,000 cumulative effect of the change on prior years (to December 31, 1990) is included in income for the year ended December 31, 1991. The cumulative effect of the change is shown without a tax effect as the Company has net operating losses available for U.S. federal tax purposes. The effect of the change for the year ended December 31, 1991 is an increase in income before the cumulative effect of the change in accounting principle of $1,720,500 ($0.14 per share—assuming no and full dilution) and an increase in net income applicable to common stock of $737,500 ($0.06 per share—assuming no and full dilution). The *pro forma* amounts on the statement of operations reflect the effect of retroactive application of the change in accounting principle that would have been made for the eleven months ended December 31, 1989 and the year ended December 31, 1990 had the new method been in effect.

Source: Grant Tensor Geophysical Corp., *1991 Annual Report.*

The company reported income for the years ended December 31, 1990 and 1991 ($ in thousands):

	1990	1991
Income before extraordinary item and cumulative effect of change in accounting principle	$(8,640)	$ 2,770
Extraordinary item (debt extinguishment)	—	(504)
Cumulative effect of accounting change	—	983
Dividends on preferred shares	(640)	(2,263)
Net income (loss) applicable to common stock	$(9,280)	$ 986
Pro forma amounts assuming the change in accounting principle is applied retroactively:		
Net income (loss) applicable to common stock	$(8,499)	$ 3

A. Compute income before extraordinary item and cumulative effect of change in accounting principle and net income for 1991, assuming that the accounting change had not been made.

B. Compare *pro forma* net income for 1990 with that originally reported. Explain why that difference does not equal the cumulative effect reported in 1991.

C. The accounting change increased 1991 income (before cumulative effect) by $1,720,000. Discuss the two effects of the accounting change that resulted in that increase.

D. Grant Tensor reports changes in capitalized geophysical costs as part of cash from operations. Given this, explain why the accounting change had no effect on reported cash flows.

E. The balance sheet reports proprietary geophysical data at year-end of $1,739,000 (1990) and $4,092,000 (1991). The cash flow statement shows an increase of $2,943,000 for 1991. Explain the difference and interpret the meaning of the $2,943,000 figure.

F. The third paragraph of the footnote contains an apparent error. Explain.

8. [Change in accounting methods: SE versus FC] In 1991, Sonat changed its accounting method for oil and gas properties from FC to SE. As a result of the switch, the company (in its *1991 Annual Report*) restated its 1990 results to conform with the new accounting method. Selected data from the original and restated reports are reported in columns X and Y below. However, some of the originally reported (FC) numbers have been placed in column X and some in column Y. The same is true for the restated (SE) data. Additionally, some of the data are missing.

($ in millions)	X	Y
Cash flow from operations	$ 361	$382
Cash flow from investing	(325)	?
Cash flow from financing	?	(30)
Net change in cash	?	6
Net income	94	110
Depreciation, depletion, and amortization	$ 200	$193

Using your knowledge of the difference between the two accounting methods:

A. Determine the "missing" data and, for each of the data provided, identify which are the original (FC) numbers and which are the restated (SE) numbers.

B. Given your answer to A, explain why Sonat may have changed its accounting method.

9. [Appendix 7-B; Analysis of oil and gas disclosures] Exhibit 7P-2 contains data from the *1994 Annual Report* of Elf Aquitaine, a French multinational oil company. Elf uses the SE method of accounting for exploration and development.

A. Discuss the 1992 to 1994 trend in Elf's oil and gas reserves (physical quantities).

B. Compute Elf's finding costs for new reserves for 1992 to 1994 and discuss their trend.

C. Discuss the factors that changed the discounted future net cash flows for Elf's reserves over the 1992 to 1994 period. (Be sure to use both Table 6 and Table 7 of Exhibit 7P-2.]

D. Explain how to use the data provided to recalculate Elf's book value per share to reflect the value of the company's reserves.

EXHIBIT 7P-2. ELF AQUITAINE
Selected Footnotes

REPORT OF AUDIT COMMITTEE

The Audit Committee of the Board of Directors of Elf Aquitaine, which was created on June 24, 1994 and is comprised of two Board Members, is responsible for examining and analyzing the accounting principles and internal control procedures, as well as the annual Parent Company financial statements and consolidated financial statements of the Group. The Financial Officers of the Company and the Statutory Auditors report to the Audit Committee.

The Audit Committee held two meetings to examine the annual Parent Company financial statements and the consolidated financial statements for the year ended December 31, 1994, as well as the financial and accounting information included in the Annual Report of Elf Aquitaine. In accordance with the recommendation of the Audit Committee, the Board of Directors approved these documents.

Philippe Pontet
Audit Committee Chairman
March 15, 1995

SUPPLEMENTARY OIL AND GAS INFORMATION (unaudited)

The seven tables included below provide supplemental information concerning oil and gas exploration and production activities in accordance with Statement of Financial Accounting Standards n° 69 "Disclosures about Oil and Gas Producing Activities" ("SFAS 69").

Tables 1 and 2: Oil and Gas reserve quantities

The following tables set forth by geographic zone the Group's estimate of quantities of oil and gas reserves at December 31, 1994, 1993 and 1992.

Quantities shown are:

– proved developed and undeveloped reserves, together with the movements of these reserves during 1994, 1993 and 1992;

– proved developed reserves.

Proved developed and undeveloped reserves are the Group's share of reserves which it intends to produce in the future based on engineering data and tests, and on current prices and economic conditions.

Proved developed reserves are those that can be expected to be recovered through existing wells and with existing equipment and operating methods.

Reserve quantities are shown after deduction of all royalties.

The determination of these reserves is an ongoing process subject to continual revision as additional information becomes available. In many cases it is only after several years of production that a more reliable estimate of reserves can be made.

The reserves shown below do not include quantities that may be produced due to the introduction of new technology or changes in economic conditions.

In 1993, the purchase of reserves in place relates primarily to the acquisition of an additional 5% in the NNPC-Shell joint venture in Nigeria representing 32 million metric tons of oil.

In 1994, the sale of reserves in place relates primarily to the sale of a 34% interest in the Nkossa field in Congo to Chevron and Engen in conjunction with the signing of a new production-sharing agreement.

EXHIBIT 7P-2. (*continued*)

Table 1 (a) - Oil (including natural gas liquids and condensates)

(in millions of metric tons)	France	Rest of Europe	Africa	Rest of world	Total
Proved developed and undeveloped reserves					
At January 1, 1992	**9.4**	**94.5**	**226.7**	**4.7**	**335.3**
Revisions of previous estimates	(0.2)	1.8	8.7	0.2	10.5
Extensions, discoveries and other	0.8	1.8	13.9	4.5	21.0
Acquisitions of reserves in place	–	0.4	–	–	0.4
Sales of reserves in place	–	–	(0.5)	–	(0.5)
Production for the year	(1.2)	(7.6)	(18.7)	(1.1)	(28.6)
At December 31, 1992	**8.8**	**90.9**	**230.1**	**8.3**	**338.1**
Revisions of previous estimates	(0.7)	1.1	5.8	(2.2)	4.0
Extensions, discoveries and other	0.9	–	2.8	1.7	5.4
Acquisitions of reserves in place	–	0.4	32.8	–	33.2
Sales of reserves in place	–	(1.1)	–	(1.5)	(2.6)
Production for the year	(1.1)	(8.7)	(20.3)	(0.8)	(30.9)
At December 31, 1993	**7.9**	**82.6**	**251.2**	**5.5**	**347.2**
Revisions of previous estimates	(0.4)	3.7	9.4	–	12.7
Extensions, discoveries and other	0.3	9.8	2.9	1.7	14.7
Acquisitions of reserves in place	–	–	–	–	–
Sales of reserves in place	(0.1)	(0.5)	(16.5)	–	(17.1)
Production for the year	(1.2)	(10.4)	(22.1)	(0.7)	(34.4)
At December 31, 1994	**6.5**	**85.2**	**224.9**	**6.5**	**323.1**
Proved developed reserves					
At January 1, 1992	5.5	37.3	103.0	2.6	148.4
At December 31, 1992	5.4	40.0	96.9	3.6	145.9
At December 31, 1993	5.1	45.6	108.6	1.4	160.7
At December 31, 1994	**5.1**	**47.1**	**101.1**	**4.7**	**158.0**
Minority interest in proved developed and undeveloped reserves					
At December 31, 1992	–	8.2	37.1	–	45.3
At December 31, 1993	–	7.6	34.7	–	42.3
At December 31, 1994	–	**6.2**	**29.4**	–	**35.6**

EXHIBIT 7P-2. (*continued*)

Table 1 (b) - Oil (including natural gas liquids and condensates)

The reserve information in barrels indicated is presented solely for the convenience of the reader and is converted from metric tons at a rate of 7.3 barrels per metric ton.

(in millions of barrels)	France	Rest of Europe	Africa	Rest of world	Total
Proved developed and undeveloped reserves					
At January 1, 1992	**68**	**690**	**1,655**	**34**	**2,447**
Revisions of previous estimates	(2)	13	65	1	77
Extensions, discoveries and other	7	13	101	33	154
Acquisitions of reserves in place	–	3	–	–	3
Sales of reserves in place	–	–	(4)	–	(4)
Production for the year	(9)	(56)	(137)	(7)	(209)
At December 31, 1992	**64**	**663**	**1,680**	**61**	**2,468**
Revisions of previous estimates	(5)	8	42	(16)	29
Extensions, discoveries and other	7	–	20	12	39
Acquisitions of reserves in place	–	3	239	–	242
Sales of reserves in place	–	(7)	–	(11)	(18)
Production for the year	(8)	(64)	(147)	(6)	(225)
At December 31, 1993	**58**	**603**	**1,834**	**40**	**2,535**
Revisions of previous estimates	(3)	26	69	–	92
Extensions, discoveries and other	2	73	21	12	108
Acquisitions of reserves in place	–	–	–	–	–
Sales of reserves in place	(1)	(3)	(121)	–	(125)
Production for the year	(9)	(77)	(160)	(5)	(251)
At December 31, 1994	**47**	**622**	**1,643**	**47**	**2,359**
Proved developed reserves					
At January 1, 1992	41	272	751	19	1,083
At December 31, 1992	40	292	706	27	1,065
At December 31, 1993	37	333	793	10	1,173
At December 31, 1994	**37**	**343**	**739**	**34**	**1,153**
Minority interest in proved developed and undeveloped reserves					
At December 31, 1992	–	60	271	–	331
At December 31, 1993	–	55	253	–	308
At December 31, 1994	–	45	215	–	260

EXHIBIT 7P-2. (*continued*)

Table 2 (b) - Natural gas

The reserve information in cubic feet indicated below is presented solely for the convenience of the reader and is converted from cubic meters at a rate of 35.3 cubic feet per cubic meter.

(in billions of cubic feet)	France	Rest of Europe	Africa	Rest of world	Total
Proved developed and undeveloped reserves					
At January 1, 1992	**1,066**	**4,667**	**228**	**113**	**6,074**
Revisions of previous estimates	(84)	63	279	1	259
Extensions, discoveries and other	–	133	298	1	432
Acquisitions of reserves in place	1	32	–	–	33
Sales of reserves in place	–	(21)	–	(1)	(22)
Production for the year	(104)	(306)	(9)	(30)	(449)
At December 31, 1992	**879**	**4,568**	**796**	**84**	**6,327**
Revisions of previous estimates	29	21	(1)	12	61
Extensions, discoveries and other	–	24	1	17	42
Acquisitions of reserves in place	–	7	–	–	7
Sales of reserves in place	–	–	–	–	–
Production for the year	(107)	(323)	(13)	(24)	(467)
At December 31, 1993	**801**	**4,297**	**783**	**89**	**5,970**
Revisions of previous estimates	(34)	(14)	(69)	22	(95)
Extensions, discoveries and other	–	348	–	14	362
Acquisitions of reserves in place	–	–	–	–	–
Sales of reserves in place	–	(22)	–	(6)	(28)
Production for the year	(102)	(353)	(16)	(23)	(494)
At December 31, 1994	**665**	**4,256**	**698**	**96**	**5,715**
Proved developed reserves					
At January 1, 1992	658	1,567	227	56	2,508
At December 31, 1992	522	1,479	105	47	2,153
At December 31, 1993	476	1,729	240	39	2,484
At December 31, 1994	**594**	**1,791**	**120**	**34**	**2,539**
Minority interest in proved developed and undeveloped reserves					
At December 31, 1992	–	21	15	–	36
At December 31, 1993	–	19	16	–	35
At December 31, 1994	**–**	**14**	**15**	**–**	**29**

EXHIBIT 7P-2. (*continued*)

Table 3 - Capitalized costs related to oil and gas producing activities

The following table sets forth the capitalized costs for oil and gas exploration and production activities and related accumulated depreciation, depletion and amortization.

(in millions of French francs)	At December 31	
	1994	1993
Capitalized costs		
Proved properties	128,434	125,625
Unproved properties	8,835	12,428
Total	**137,269**	138,053
Accumulated depreciation, depletion and amortization	73,697	67,047
Net capitalized costs	**63,572**	**71,006**

Table 4 - Cost incurred in oil and gas property acquisition, exploration and development activities

The table below presents costs incurred for oil and gas property acquisition and exploration and development activities. These costs comprise both capitalized and expensed amounts.

In 1993, the most important purchase of unproved properties (nearly FF 1 billion) relates to the acquisition of an additional 5% interest in the NNPC-Shell joint venture in Nigeria.

(in millions of French francs)	France	Rest of Europe	Africa	Rest of world	Total
Year ended December 31, 1992					
Costs incurred					
Proved and unproved property acquisition	–	364	167	71	602
Exploration	360	1,677	1,477	1,043	4,557
Development	532	7,270	3,888	237	11,927
Total costs incurred	**892**	**9,311**	**5,532**	**1,351**	**17,086**
Year ended December 31, 1993					
Costs incurred					
Proved and unproved property acquisition	–	(3)	3,329	–	3,326
Exploration	295	897	1,312	1,165	3,669
Development	398	5,401	5,080	401	11,280
Total costs incurred	**693**	**6,295**	**9,721**	**1,566**	**18,275**
Year ended December 31, 1994					
Costs incurred					
Proved and unproved property acquisition	1	(4)	3	1	1
Exploration	176	778	1,012	937	2,903
Development	379	4,334	6,075	678	11,466
Total costs incurred	**556**	**5,108**	**7,090**	**1,616**	**14,370**

EXHIBIT 7P-2. (*continued*)

Table 5 - Results of operations for oil and gas producing activities

The following information summarizes the operating results of oil and gas producing activities. Sales to Group refining and marketing subsidiaries are shown at market values. Income taxes are computed using statutory tax rates after adjusting for permanent tax differences and tax credits and do not purport to represent actual tax expense. The information presented below is restricted to oil and gas activities and does not include by-product sales, mining and associated non-producing activities which are included in the segment information in Note 4 of notes to consolidated financial statements.

(in millions of French francs)	France	Rest of Europe	Africa	Rest of world	Total
Year ended December 31, 1992					
Sales to consolidated companies	878	4,980	12,481	145	18,484
Sales to third-parties	2,137	6,041	418	767	9,363
Total sales	**3,015**	**11,021**	**12,899**	**912**	**27,847**
Production costs	1,036	2,834	2,983	254	7,107
Exploration expensed	210	1,511	1,255	846	3,822
Depreciation, depletion and amortization	545	2,734	2,709	678	6,666
Total costs	**1,791**	**7,079**	**6,947**	**1,778**	**17,595**
Results before taxes	1,224	3,942	5,952	(866)	10,252
Income taxes	428	1,687	4,116	31	6,262
Results after taxes	**796**	**2,255**	**1,836**	**(897)**	**3,990**
Year ended December 31, 1993					
Sales to consolidated companies	831	4,523	13,067	91	18,512
Sales to third-parties	2,098	6,455	356	685	9,594
Total sales	**2,929**	**10,978**	**13,423**	**776**	**28,106**
Production costs	1,165	2,904	3,348	227	7,644
Exploration expensed	445	1,086	1,072	839	3,442
Depreciation, depletion and amortization	355	5,072	3,480	742	9,649
Total costs	**1,965**	**9,062**	**7,900**	**1,808**	**20,735**
Results before taxes	964	1,916	5,523	(1,032)	7,371
Income taxes	305	1,426	3,928	26	5,685
Results after taxes	**659**	**490**	**1,595**	**(1,058)**	**1,686**
Year ended December 31, 1994					
Sales to consolidated companies	912	4,557	12,962	32	18,463
Sales to third-parties	1,302	7,337	286	597	9,522
Total sales	**2,214**	**11,894**	**13,248**	**629**	**27,985**
Production costs	896	2,760	2,945	175	6,776
Exploration expensed	156	831	1,061	1,127	3,175
Depreciation, depletion and amortization	668	7,682	3,791	778	12,919
Total costs	**1,720**	**11,273**	**7,797**	**2,080**	**22,870**
Results before taxes	494	621	5,451	(1,451)	5,115
Income taxes	97	813	3,493	–	4,403
Results after taxes	**397**	**(192)**	**1,958**	**(1,451)**	**712**

EXHIBIT 7P-2. (*continued*)

Table 6 - Standardized measure of discounted future net cash flows

The table below sets forth the standardized measure of future net cash flows relating to proved reserves presented in Tables 1 and 2 computed in accordance with SFAS 69. This standard specifies that the following assumptions be followed when computing the standardized measure.

Current prices: expected revenues are based on oil and gas prices existing at December 31. Future price changes provided for by contracts are included when known at year-end.

Current costs: production and development costs related to future production of proved reserves are based on cost levels existing at year-end and assume continuation of existing economic conditions.

Income taxes: estimated future income taxes are computed using appropriate legislated statutory tax rates on income reflecting permanent differences and future income tax credits.

10% discount: future net cash flows from oil and gas production have been discounted at 10% as required by SFAS 69.

The standardized measure also assumes that all reserves will be produced and sold.

The assumptions used to compute the standardized measure are those required by SFAS 69 and, as such, do not necessarily reflect the Group's expectations of actual revenues to be derived from those reserves nor their present worth.

(in millions of French francs)	France	Rest of Europe	Africa	Rest of world	Total
Year ended December 31, 1992					
Future cash inflows	22,170	130,615	155,481	6,250	314,516
Future production and development costs	(14,396)	(52,734)	(61,593)	(4,159)	(132,882)
Future income tax expense	(1,240)	(37,029)	(62,877)	(98)	(101,244)
Future net cash flows	6,534	40,852	31,011	1,993	80,390
Discount	(1,890)	(15,925)	(17,179)	(879)	(35,873)
Standardized measure of discounted future net cash flows	**4,644**	**24,927**	**13,832**	**1,114**	**44,517**
Year ended December 31, 1993					
Future cash inflows	18,635	107,834	135,713	4,117	266,299
Future production and development costs	(12,811)	(49,558)	(74,385)	(3,911)	(140,665)
Future income tax expense	(941)	(24,287)	(35,918)	–	(61,146)
Future net cash flows	4,883	33,989	25,410	206	64,488
Discount	(1,410)	(12,942)	(14,729)	(71)	(29,152)
Standardized measure of discounted future net cash flows	**3,473**	**21,047**	**10,681**	**135**	**35,336**
Year ended December 31, 1994					
Future cash inflows	14,321	114,011	136,774	4,709	269,815
Future production and development costs	(9,415)	(49,468)	(61,133)	(2,275)	(122,291)
Future income tax expense	(906)	(27,342)	(45,127)	–	(73,375)
Future net cash flows	4,000	37,201	30,514	2,434	74,149
Discount	(1,103)	(14,280)	(13,656)	(619)	(29,658)
Standardized measure of discounted future net cash flows	**2,897**	**22,921**	**16,858**	**1,815**	**44,491**
Minority interest in standardized measure of discounted future net cash flows					
At December 31, 1992	–	1,352	1,987	–	3,339
At December 31, 1993	–	1,322	895	–	2,217
At December 31, 1994	**–**	**1,276**	**2,410**	**–**	**3,686**

EXHIBIT 7P-2. (*continued*)

Table 7 - Principal sources of changes in standardized measure of discounted future net cash flows

The following table explains the sources of changes in the standardized measure of discounted future net cash flows shown in Table 6.

(*in millions of French francs*)	**1994**	1993	1992
Discounted future net cash flows at January 1	35,336	44,517	39,035
Sales net of production costs	(21,209)	(20,462)	(20,740)
Development costs incurred during the period	11,466	11,280	11,908
Revisions in previous quantity estimates	3,243	(3,980)	(5,022)
Changes in prices and production costs	16,494	(26,713)	2,563
Changes in estimated future development costs	54	(4,408)	(538)
Accretion of discount	3,534	4,452	3,904
Extensions, discoveries and improved recovery	2,173	540	2,253
Purchase and sale of reserves in place	(2,851)	5,686	(66)
Net change in income taxes	(3,749)	24,424	11,220
Discounted future net cash flows at December 31	44,491	35,336	44,517

E. If Elf used the FC method of accounting, how would the following be expected to differ from the amounts actually reported:

(i) Finding costs

(ii) Capitalized costs

(iii) Discounted future net cash flow

10. [Revaluation of assets] Exhibit 7P-3 contains excerpts from the fiscal 1995 financial statements issued by The News Corporation Limited, an Australian media company.

A. Discuss the impact of revaluation on the trend of the firm's reported income, return on equity, and cash flow from operations:

(i) At the time of revaluation

(ii) As the revalued assets are used in operations

(iii) At the time they are sold

B. Provide arguments for and against the use of these revalued amounts in the company's financial statements.

C. Evaluate the company's policy of not amortizing these assets.

D. If the company did amortize these assets, how would the revaluation affect News Corporation's reported:

(i) Net income

(ii) Cash flow from operations

EXHIBIT 7P-3. THE NEWS CORPORATION LIMITED
Selected Footnotes

Note 1: Basis of Presentation and Significant Accounting Policies

(d) Other Assets

Publishing Rights, Titles, and Television Licenses

These assets are stated at cost or valuation. No amortization is provided on publishing rights and titles since, in the opinion of the Directors, they do not have a finite useful economic life. Although television licenses in the United States are renewable every five years, the Directors have no reason to believe that they will not be renewed and, accordingly, no amortization has been provided.

(k) Reserves

  (i) Capital

   (c) Asset revaluation reserves are the excess of the valuation of investments, property, plant, and equipment and publishing rights, titles and television licenses over their net book values at the date of revaluation.

(l) Revaluation of Assets

Certain noncurrent assets are revalued periodically. Amounts shown "at valuation" in respect of investments, property, plant, and equipment and publishing rights, titles, and television licenses comprise the historical cost of revalued assets plus the revaluation increment. Increments in the value of a class of assets are taken to the asset revaluation reserve. Decrements are offset against previous increments relating to the same class of assets, or, if there are no such increments, charged against profit.

Noncurrent assets are written down to the recoverable amount where the carrying value of the noncurrent asset exceeds the recoverable amount.

The recoverable amount of property, plant, and equipment, publishing rights, titles, and television licenses and the excess of cost over net assets acquired have been determined by discounting the expected inflow of cash arising from their continued use.

Note 7: Publishing Rights, Titles, and Television Licenses

	June 30 ($ in millions)	
	1994	1995
At cost	$ 2,911	$ 2,971
At valuation June 1990		
Original valuation	6,373	6,513
Revaluation increment	3,878	4,043
	10,231	10,556
	$13,162	$13,527

Note 19: U.S. Generally Accepted Accounting Principles (continued)

Property, plant, and equipment and publishing rights, titles and television licenses, and investments have been revalued at an amount in excess of cost. The major portion of such revaluation was ascribed to publishing rights. Accounting principles generally accepted in the United States do not permit the revaluation of assets in excess of cost.

EXHIBIT 7P-3. (*continued*)

The revaluation of a class of assets in Australian GAAP allows the netting of increments and decrements, with the resultant net increment taken directly to reserves. Under U.S. GAAP, any permanent decrement in value of an asset is expensed.

Note: The Form 20-F reconciliation of Australian GAAP to U.S. GAAP showed the following effects of revaluation of publishing rights, titles, and television licenses. (Various others differences omitted.)

	June 30 ($ in millions)		
	1993	1994	1995
Australian GAAP stockholders' equity (SE)		$14,463	$16,582
Publishing rights, titles, and television licenses			
Revaluation and other		(4,044)	(4,203)
Amortization		(1,258)	(1,491)
U.S. GAAP stockholders' equity		$ 7,353	$ 9,020
Australian GAAP net income	864	1,335	1,365
Amortization	(218)	(228)	(233)
Deferred taxes	(131)	(154)	(35)
U.S. GAAP net income	$ 488	$ 937	$ 1,035

Source: The News Corporation Limited, *1995 Annual Report* and 20-F.

Appendix 7-A

Research and Development Affiliates

RESEARCH AND DEVELOPMENT PARTNERSHIPS

An R&D partnership allows a company to defer the recognition of R&D costs. The partnership raises funds from investors. Those funds are then used to pay the company for research. Any patents or products resulting from that research belong to the partnership, but the company can either purchase the partnership or license the product. Thus, the company controls the technology without reporting the expenses resulting from research costs, as the "revenue" from the partnership offsets the research expense. A typical arrangement is described in Exhibit 7A-1.

This arrangement has many of the attributes of an option; the firm has a call option on the patents or products developed for the partnership, with the purchase price being the exercise or strike price. Shevlin (1991) treats such limited partnerships

EXHIBIT 7A-1. BIOTECH PARTNERS, L.P.
An R&D Partnership

On January 1, 1993, the Biotech Corp. establishes a partnership to conduct biotechnology research with the goal of creating new drugs. The firm raises $10 million by selling partnership units in Biotech Partners, L.P. (BTP).

Biotech Corp. assigns its patents to the partnership and signs a contract to provide research services. BTP agrees to pay 100% of the research costs in return for the right to any drugs developed. Biotech may license any drugs developed by paying BTP a royalty of 10% of the wholesale selling price of drugs sold.

Biotech has the right to purchase the partnership interests during various time periods at a total price (payable in cash or in Biotech Corp. shares) of:

$20 million (January 1–March 31, 1995)
$30 million (January 1–March 31, 1996)
$45 million (January 1–March 31, 1997)

BTP disburses funds to Biotech Corp. at the rate of $5 million per year. Biotech Corp. treats these receipts as revenue and the associated research costs as contract research expenses. The revenue offsets the R&D costs, so that Biotech's reported earnings are not affected.

On February 1, 1995, Biotech Corp. exercises its right to acquire the entire partnership interest for a price of $20 million. That payment is shown as an expense for the quarter ended March 31, 1995.

(LPs) as an option and uses option pricing theory to value the LP:

> The value of the LP call option to the R&D firm may be decomposed into the present value of the underlying project financed by the LP (an asset) less the present value of the payments to the limited partners if the firm exercises its option (liability).[1]

SFAS 68 (1982), Research and Development Arrangements, sets criteria to distinguish true transfers of risk from disguised borrowings. The following are indicators that there has *not* been a true transfer of risk:

1. The company has an obligation to the partnership (or investors) regardless of the outcome of the research. Such obligation may take the form of a guarantee of partnership debt or granting of a "put" option to the investors.

2. Conditions make it probable that the company will repay the funds raised by the partnership. Such conditions include the company's need to control the technology owned by the partnership or relationships between the company and the investors (e.g., top management invests in the partnership).

If there has not been a true transfer of risk, then the company is required to expense the actual research costs and treat funds received from the partnership as borrowings.

When the requirements of SFAS 68 are met, however, the company can recognize revenue from the partnership to offset R&D costs. The result is, in effect, a deferral of research cost until products are sold (and license fees paid) or the partnership is purchased. Such arrangements are disclosed in financial statement footnotes and analysts should be alert to their effects on reported income.

---

[1]Terry Shevlin, "The Valuation of R&D Firms with R&D Limited Partnerships," *The Accounting Review,* Jan. 1991, pp. 1–21.

In recent years, the R&D partnership has been largely superseded by a new vehicle: a separate company that sells "callable common" shares to the public. The shares are usually packaged with warrants of the (parent) company to make the resulting "units" more attractive to investors. The new common shares are callable at prices that promise a high rate of return to investors if the venture is successful. These vehicles are similar to R&D partnerships in their effects on the firm.

Analysis of Firms with R&D Affiliates

The impact of R&D affiliates on reported financial results is favorable as research costs are offset by "revenue" from the affiliate. If these costs were funded by borrowing (or from the firm's own assets), reported income would be lower. Further, obtaining those funds would require additional debt or equity capital. R&D financing arrangements permit the company to conduct research without incurring debt or equity dilution, in addition to avoiding the effects of reporting the research costs as an expense.

There is a cost to this capital, however. When the partnership is purchased or the callable common is called, a substantial cash payment or share issuance is required. Given the risk, investors in R&D affiliates require a high rate of return.

The second cost factor is the impact when the affiliate is purchased. At that time, the entire purchase price must be written off as research costs.[2] The resulting write-off exceeds the amount of funds originally raised. But that write-off is delayed until the partnership is purchased. In effect, these arrangements permit the deferral of research costs, but with the penalty of a high interest factor (cost of capital).

[2]FASB Interpretation 4 (1975) provides that when an acquisition is accounted for under the purchase method of accounting, any portion of the purchase price allocated to R&D must be immediately expensed at the time of the acquisition. Chapter 14 contains more discussion of this issue.

Appendix 7-B

Analysis of Oil and Gas Disclosures

INTRODUCTION

The two acceptable accounting methods used for oil and gas exploration: the *successful efforts* method (SE) and *full cost* method (FC)[1] are illustrated in Exhibit 7-3. The choice between these methods has significant effects on reported financial statements. These differences can be summarized as follows:

1. SE firms, by expensing dry hole costs, have lower carrying costs of oil and gas reserves than FC firms.
2. SE firms have lower earnings than FC firms when exploration efforts are rising.
3. SE firms have lower cash from operations than FC firms (unless explicitly adjusted for, as in the case of duPont).

[1]Both methods are described on pages 340–342.

The objectives of this appendix are to:

- Examine the motivation for accounting choices.
- Discuss the impact of accounting choices in greater detail.
- Review the analysis of mandatory supplementary disclosures regarding oil and gas reserves.

Motivations for Accounting Choice

The differential effects on financial statements demonstrated in Exhibit 7-3 as well as the illustration in Box 7-1 help explain why some firms prefer the SE method and others the FC method. Empirical evidence as to these preferences is provided in Box 7B-1.

Small firms generally prefer the FC method; large firms tend to be indifferent. For larger firms, with relatively stable exploration budgets and relatively constant success ratios (productive to total expenditures) across a "portfolio" of exploration projects, the year-to-year variability of dry hole expense is small. Amortization of past expenditures is large, reflecting a large reserve base. As a result, the difference between the two methods is small.

Additionally, larger oil companies are often diversified into the refining and distribution segments of the oil business. Income from these sources dampens the variability of exploration income. Large oil companies tend to use the SE method as well because it is perceived to be more conservative.[2]

For smaller companies, however, the differential impact of these two accounting methods can be considerable. Year-to-year variations in spending and success ratios mean that dry hole expense can vary greatly. Under SE accounting, this variability is transmitted directly to the income statement. Further, smaller companies (especially if growing rapidly) have small reserve bases and low amortization of past capitalized costs. Dry hole costs from current drilling activities may exceed the amortization of the capitalized costs of past drilling. Smaller companies are also less diversified as they concentrate on exploration. Widely fluctuating patterns of earnings growth are considered a drawback for firms attempting to obtain external (equity or debt) financing. This problem is further exacerbated because, under successful efforts, the balance sheet shows lower assets and equity, thus hurting reported solvency ratios. As a result, smaller companies tend to use the FC method of accounting.

Changing Accounting Methods

The FC method has one drawback, however. When the price of oil causes the value of the reserves to fall below book value, the SEC requires that companies using the FC method write down properties whose carrying cost exceeds the present value of future cash flows of the proved reserves attributable to that property. Companies using the SE method are required to use the less stringent measure of *undiscounted* future cash flows.[3] In the 1980s, when the price of oil fell drastically, some companies that had previously chosen FC accounting (presumably to report higher income) were forced to take large write-offs, reducing reported income.

---

[2]A more detailed analysis of the financial reporting effects of SE versus FC on firms under different environments is provided by Sunder (1976).

[3]See David B. Pariser and Pierre L. Titard, "Impairment of Oil and Gas Properties," *Journal of Accountancy,* Dec. 1991, pp. 52–62.

BOX 7B-1
SE Versus FC Choice of Methods: Empirical Evidence

A number of research studies* have examined characteristics of firms using SE versus FC accounting. Malmquist (1990) tested the relationship between the following characteristics and firm choice.

1. Size

The larger the firm, the less likely it will choose FC for several reasons. First, large firms prefer income-reducing alternatives such as SE to avoid earning "windfall profits," especially when prices are rising, given the political sensitivity of energy prices.

Second, large firms have more drilling activities occurring simultaneously, creating a portfolio effect and thereby decreasing income variability. Third, in addition to the risks associated with exploration, oil companies are subject to the risks associated with marketing and refining. The larger the proportion of the firm's activities in marketing and refining, the lower the impact of SE because its effect is limited to the income associated with exploration. As large firms tend to be more diversified, they have less incentive to opt for FC.

Using sales as a proxy for size (political costs) and the ratio of exploration costs to market value as well as the ratio of production costs to market value to measure the various aspects related to size, Malmquist found them all to be significant in explaining the accounting choice. Higher sales and a larger proportion of production costs made the firm more likely to choose SE. Conversely, the larger the exploration cost proportion, the more likely the firm was to choose FC.

2. Difficulty of Raising Capital in the Equity and Debt Markets

SE companies report lower assets than FC companies. Therefore, securities underwriters may be hesitant (or find it difficult) to sell the securities of firms having low or negative net book value (equity) levels. Borrowing may also be more difficult for firms with high and variable debt/equity ratios. Moreover, for debt already in existence, there is a higher probability of technical violation of debt/equity-related debt covenants. Malmquist's study confirmed that firms with higher debt/equity ratios are less likely to choose SE.

3. Management Compensation Contracts

Earnings-based management compensation contracts are affected by the choice of accounting method. Opportunistic managers may choose full costing to increase the level of their compensation and decrease its variability. Malmquist notes "there are strong disincentives and limits placed on such behavior by the managerial labor market." No apparent relationship between the choice of accounting method and the presence of an earnings-based compensation contract was observed.

These results are consistent with some (but not all) of Deakin's (1989) findings. Analyzing firms that lobbied for FC and the reasons given by those firms for lobbying, Deakin found that, on average, they had characteristics consistent with the stated reasons. The reasons given by the firms were:†

1. The expected impact on cost of capital and access to capital markets
2. The potential of the proposed elimination of the FC method to affect accounting income-based management incentive contracts
3. The perceived effect on future drilling activity
4. The effect on rate regulation‡

To some extent, generalizing from Deakin's sample of companies, which lobbied for a particular accounting method, to the general population of firms, is fraught with danger as the sample may be biased. Taking the time and effort to lobby can be an indication that these firms are the ones most likely to be affected by the choice. Thus, Deakin's finding that the presence of management incentive contracts was associated with firms that lobbied for FC in contrast to Malmquist, who did not find such a relationship, may reflect their different samples.

---

*See, for example, Steven Lilien and Victor Pastena, "Determinants of Intra-Method Choice in the Oil and Gas Industry," *Journal of Accounting and Economics,* 1982, pp. 145–170 and Edward B. Deakin III, "An Analysis of Differences Between Non-Major Oil Firms Using Successful Efforts and Full Cost Methods," *The Accounting Review,* Oct. 1979, pp. 722–734.

†Edward B. Deakin III, "Rational Economic Behavior and Lobbying on Accounting Issues: Evidence from the Oil and Gas Industry," *The Accounting Review,* Jan. 1989, pp. 137–151.

‡The latter reason applied primarily to regulated companies that were required by rate-making authorities to use FC accounting procedures.

One method of avoiding such large write-offs was to change reporting methods from FC to SE, reducing the carrying amount of reserves. The change to or from the FC method is one of those cases where retroactive adjustment for accounting changes is mandatory; all prior years presented must be restated and the cumulative effect reported as an adjustment to the beginning retained earnings. Note that this change does not affect the valuation of the reserves; it only changes the carrying amount on the balance sheet.

Adoption of the SE method of accounting requires the expensing of capitalized exploration expenditures, lowering reported income. On the other hand, the amortization of previously capitalized costs is also reduced, increasing reported earnings. The balance between increased expensing of current year expenditures and reduced amortization of past expenditures determines the net effect on earnings for any given year.

What is the effect of the accounting change on cash flow? There is no effect on actual cash flow as the change to the successful efforts method merely reallocates cash flows for financial reporting purposes. (For income tax purposes, oil and gas companies expense the maximum allowable; the accounting change has no impact on tax return income.)

However, components of reported cash flows may be affected by the accounting change. Lower reported capital expenditures are offset over time by lower reported operating cash flows. Once again, we see how the classification of cash flow components is affected by accounting choice.

SFAS 69: DISCLOSURES REGARDING OIL AND GAS RESERVES

A major drawback of both accounting methods is the lack of correspondence between the reported cost of a producing oil or gas field and its economic value. Although this is true of virtually all fixed assets, it is especially true of oil- and gas-producing assets because, even at the time of drilling, there may be little relationship between the expenditures and results. An expenditure of millions of dollars can result in a dry hole. Alternatively, a small expenditure can result in a discovery of oil or gas worth many times its cost.

Neither method provides truly relevant data as to the value of reserves. This shortcoming is addressed by the disclosure requirements of SFAS 69 (1982), which requires extensive information about the results of operations for oil and gas activities and disclosure of a standardized measure of proved oil and gas reserves. Additional summary disclosures of these activities by equity method investees and minority interests are also required.

Disclosure of Physical Reserve Quantities

DuPont's financial statements contain a section entitled, "Supplemental Petroleum Data" (Appendix A). The second table provides data on the physical quantities of duPont's proved oil and gas reserves, including:

1. Separate disclosure of oil and gas reserves
2. Separate disclosure by geographic area
3. Separate disclosure of the reserves of equity affiliates[4]
4. Reconciliation of the year-to-year change in proved reserves
5. Disclosure of proved developed reserves

These data describe the company's physical reserves at each balance sheet date. The first two features listed help the user understand the nature of the reserves. For example, oil reserves in the United States have different economic characteristics than gas reserves in Algeria. Separate disclosure of the reserves of equity method affiliates aids the evaluation of the investment in such companies.

The reconciliation is one of the most significant features as it enables us to understand how estimated reserves change from year to year as a result of:

1. Production, which reduces reserves
2. Discoveries, which increase reserves
3. Purchases and sales of reserves
4. Revisions of estimates
5. Price changes, which can make reserves economically feasible to produce, or not[5]

Each of these disclosures provides useful data because physical quantities can be related to cash flows. For example, the cost of finding reserves can be derived by comparing exploration expenditures with reserves discovered. This is considered an important measure of management ability.

Revisions, as noted by Clinch and Magliolo (1992),[6] are important indicators of the "quality" of management estimates. Companies reporting predominantly downward

---

[4]See Chapter 13 for a discussion of the equity method.

[5]For example, in 1985, Atlantic Richfield removed 8.3 trillion cubic feet (trillion = billion MCF) of natural gas reserves located in northern Alaska from its estimate of proved reserves, reducing its domestic gas reserves by more than 50%. The company explained that this change was prompted by a review of economic factors, especially the significant drop in oil and gas prices in that year.

[6]Clinch and Magliolo argue that the value-relevance (informativeness) of the SFAS 69 data depends on the reliability investors attach to it. As data are subject to constant revision, reliability suffers. They found that although the market did not find reserve data to be value-relevant, production data were found to be informative. Production data, they argue, are more objective as they reflect actual actions taken by management rather than just estimates. Further, they found, for the subset of firms whose quantity estimates appeared more reliable (less revision of estimates), that proved reserve data were also value-relevant. (Greg Clinch and Joseph Magliolo, "Market Perceptions of Reserve Disclosures Under SFAS No. 69," *The Accounting Review,* Oct. 1992, pp. 843–861.)

revisions are viewed with some skepticism, reflecting the apparent overoptimism of past estimates. Investors prefer positive surprises, that is, upward revisions of estimated reserves.

DuPont's disclosures show that worldwide oil reserves steadily declined over the 1991 to 1994 period, from 1,112 million barrels at December 31, 1991 (beginning of 1992) to 953 million barrels at December 31, 1994. The United States accounted for this decline; European reserves showed little change, and reserves in "other regions" fell slightly. For gas reserves, a large increase in European reserves was partly offset by declining U.S. reserves. These data indicate a shift in duPont's production; U.S. oil production has already declined and U.S. gas production can be expected to follow.

The reconciliations give us additional insights:

• Revisions have generally been positive.
• There was a large purchase of European gas reserves in 1994.

The data can also be used to measure the *reserve life* (end-of-year reserves divided by production) of duPont's reserves, by type and geographic segment. The computations below indicate that duPont's reserve lives are short, with the exception of European gas reserves.

1994 Reserve Life in Years

	World	United States	Europe
Oil	7.22	10.18	6.68
Gas	8.93	5.50	16.10

Disclosure of Capitalized Costs

The supplemental data also contain two additional sets of disclosures: the balance sheet carrying cost of the disclosed reserves and the current year costs incurred.

Analysis of Finding Costs

The "Costs Incurred" table reports duPont's exploration costs. *This table includes all expenditures, regardless of whether they are capitalized or expensed, making the data comparable among companies with different accounting methods.*

These expenditures can be compared with reserves found to compute the actual per unit *finding cost.* Although annual finding costs are volatile, over longer time periods they measure management's proficiency in discovering reserves.

Turning to the capitalized costs at the bottom of that page, note that:

• *Capitalized costs depend on the accounting method followed:* Companies using the FC method will capitalize more exploration cost than companies employing the SE method. Notice that the capitalized costs of equity affiliates are disclosed separately, just as their reserve quantities are disclosed separately.
• Costs are net of accumulated depreciation, amortization, and valuation allowances; *different accounting choices in these areas will affect the net carrying cost.*
• Costs of unproved properties are separately disclosed.
• Capitalized costs are aggregated for oil and gas and for all geographical areas, unlike reserve quantities.

These data give analysts a balance sheet cost to match against the physical reserves with all oil and gas reserves combined into one measure, usually termed barrel of oil equivalent (BOE). Quantities can be combined into units of BOE based on either energy equivalence (1 barrel of oil = 6 MCF of gas)[7] or the basis of relative price.[8]

Once this has been done, the balance sheet cost per BOE can be computed. For duPont, at December 31, 1994, the calculation would be (in millions)

$$\text{No. of BOE} = \text{No. of Barrels of Oil} + \text{BOE Equivalent of Gas Reserves}$$

$$= 953 + \frac{4,330}{6} \text{ BCF (billion cubic feet)}$$

$$= 953 + 722$$

$$= 1,675$$

The capitalized cost per BOE is

$$\frac{\$}{\text{BOE}} = \frac{\$4,884^9}{1,675} = \$2.92$$

Note that since part of the capitalized cost represents outflows for unproved properties (for which no reserves have yet been estimated), those costs are excluded from the calculation.

With three years of data, we can look at the trend of capitalized cost per BOE as well as variations by geographic area:

DuPont's Capitalized Cost per BOE Equivalent,
December 31

	1992	1993	1994
United States	3.16	2.97	2.76
Europe	4.09	4.37	3.54
Worldwide	3.22	3.29	2.92

This table indicates that duPont's unit carrying costs are low and they have been declining. Low capitalized costs are expected, given duPont's use of successful efforts accounting. These amounts represent the costs that duPont must amortize as oil and gas reserves are produced; low capitalized costs equate to low amortization and higher operating earnings. Low capitalized costs also indicate that the risk of impairment write-downs is low.

The capitalized cost per BOE, however, is only a crude means of comparing the cost of reserves for different companies. It reflects both the accounting method used and the "efficiency" in finding oil (the finding cost per BOE). Companies that use the SE method and have low finding costs have a low capitalized cost per BOE. Companies using the FC method or recording higher finding costs have higher capitalized cost per BOE.

---

[7]Natural gas is measured in MCF (thousand cubic feet).

[8]In recent years, in the United States, gas has sold at a lower relative price than its energy equivalent would suggest. Thus, many analysts use a ratio of 1:10 to combine oil and gas reserves.

[9]Gross costs − accumulated depreciation = $11,057 − $6,173 = $4,884.

The capitalized cost per BOE can also be compared with the market value of oil and gas reserves, as revealed by market transactions. If the capitalized cost is higher than transaction prices, this indicates that the balance sheet amount is overstated; if transaction prices are higher, the reverse is true.

However, using the capitalized cost per BOE is, at best, only an approximation of the value of reserves. It is deficient because it fails to recognize the following factors:

1. Reserves in different geographic markets vary in value.

2. Oil reserves have different values from natural gas reserves of equivalent energy content.

3. The cost of producing reserves (bringing them to the surface) may vary with location.

4. A barrel of oil produced today is more valuable (assuming constant pricing) than one produced in five years because of the time value of money.

5. Tax rates vary by jurisdiction and, within jurisdictions, may vary by location and type of resource.

For these reasons, the aggregation of all reserves by physical quantities does not capture the market value of reserves. Fortunately, better data are available.

Disclosure of Present Value Data

Examine the table with the cumbersome title, "Standardized Measure of Discounted Future Net Cash Flows Relating to Proved Oil and Gas Reserves." This table contains data regarding the estimated future cash flows of the specific reserves owned by the firm. The following elements are presented:

1. *Future cash inflows.* Based on a year-by-year schedule of planned unit production, multiplied by current price levels, that is, future gross revenues based on current prices. Companies are not permitted to assume price changes, unless provided for by a firm contract, which may then be incorporated in the computation.

2. *Future production costs.* Also based on current prices. Production costs include all expenditures required to bring the oil or gas to market.

3. *Development costs.* Include the cost at current price levels of additional wells and other production facilities that may be required to produce the reserves.

Future *net* cash flows, which are inflows net of production and development costs, are a forecast of net cash flows from existing oil and gas reserves. After income taxes are subtracted, the data must be adjusted to reflect the time value of money by discounting to present value. SFAS 69 requires that all firms use a discount rate of 10%. The objective is comparability; the "correct" discount rate will vary over time and, perhaps, from firm to firm.

The result is a net present value of the after-tax[10] cash flows expected from the

---

[10]DuPont deducts tax payments from net cash flows (both undiscounted) and then discounts the after-tax cash flows. We can estimate the discounted income taxes by using the ratio of the discounted pretax cash flows to the undiscounted cash flows. (This assumes a constant tax rate.)

Some firms deduct the present value of tax payments from the net present value of pretax cash flows. The result is the same, but this latter case permits more accurate calculation of the pretax net present value.

firm's reserves. Note that these data are provided separately for reserves in different geographic areas.

Companies providing these data routinely state that the standardized measure is not market value and suggest that the data have limited usefulness. Nonetheless, the data are widely used in the analysis of companies with oil and gas reserves and, in practice, are a useful approximation of market values. Despite some limitations, the data are far more representative of market values than the cost shown on the balance sheet, regardless of the accounting method used.

Using Present Value Disclosures

How can the data be used? One simple adjustment is to replace the capitalized cost of reserves with the net present value (standardized measure). This is one step in preparing a current value balance sheet (see Chapter 17) or computing adjusted net worth. Before making this adjustment, the following issues should be considered:

1. Have prices changed since the balance sheet date? If so, the present value data must be adjusted to current prices, for example, a 10% increase in oil prices increases future cash flows by 10%. (Because oil and gas prices do not always move together, use a weighted-average based on the composition of reserves.)

2. Costs may also be adjusted. Although hard data are difficult to come by, industry sources can provide a rough guide as to changes in production and development costs.

3. Do economic or other factors suggest a need for assumptions of future price changes? Some analysts construct their own price scenarios and make their own computations of future cash flows.

4. Is 10% the right discount rate? The discount rate is a function of the general level of interest rates and the relative riskiness of the firm's reserves. Adjustments may be required. A higher discount rate, of course, reduces the net present value calculation; a lower rate increases the present value.

5. Should pretax or after-tax net present values be used? The answer depends on the tax status of the firm and purpose of the analysis.[11] In a liquidation analysis, for example, when all cash flows are evaluated on a pretax basis, pretax present values would be used for consistency.

Example: DuPont

To illustrate, we use the data provided by duPont and the following assumptions:

1. No change in prices or costs

2. A 10% discount rate

3. Pretax net present values for U.S. reserves but after-tax present values for foreign reserves (see footnote 11)

---

[11]Disclosures for firms with significant reserves outside of North America and Europe frequently show very high income tax rates for these reserves. These high rates reflect the fact that royalties in many countries are a percentage of the gross value of the oil or gas produced. Accounting for these royalties as income taxes obtains better income tax treatment in the United States. This suggests that net present value data for such reserves should always be used on an after-tax basis.

DuPont's "other regions" clearly fit the category just described.

The data provided can be used to adjust duPont's equity at December 31, 1994, for the difference between the present value of its oil and gas reserves and the carrying amount (data in $ millions):

United States (pretax)[12]	$ 2,083
Europe (pretax)	4,134
Other regions (after tax)	324
Total	$ 6,541
The carrying value equals[13]	4,884
The difference is	$ 1,657
Stated equity at 12/31/94[14]	12,822
Adjusted equity at 12/31/94	$14,479

This adjustment increases the equity of duPont at December 31, 1994, by 13%. The use of after-tax present value for all reserves would not generate any increase, as the worldwide total of $4,275 million is below the balance sheet carrying amount. Varying the discount rate or making assumptions about changes in prices or costs would also lead to different adjustments.

The adjustment of net worth is not an end in itself, but one step in the analysis of a firm. Although equity after adjustment is not a precise measure of the market value of duPont's net assets, it is a better measure than the historical cost of those assets. Chapter 17 discusses the usefulness of equity adjustments in greater detail.

Changes in Present Values

The standardized measure table is followed by a reconciliation of changes in the standardized measure, akin to the reconciliation of reserve quantities. But these data are richer as they include the impact of such factors as:

- Changes in prices and costs
- Accretion of discount (the passage of time reduces the discount period)
- Expenditures that reduce future required cash flows
- Changes in estimates
- Purchases and sales of reserves
- Effect of production

DuPont's reconciliation provides the following insights:

1. Changing prices and costs were the major factor accounting for the sharp decline in the standardized measure in 1993 and its recovery in 1994.

2. DuPont's quantity revisions were positive, suggesting that the company's estimates have been conservative.

---

[12]Calculated as the net present value ($1,579) plus the estimated present value of income tax payments ($504). The latter is estimated by applying the ratio, $1,579/$2,733 × $873, and assuming a constant tax rate.

[13]Calculated on page 373.

[14]Obtained from duPont's balance sheet.

8

ANALYSIS OF LONG-LIVED ASSETS, PART II
Analysis of Depreciation and Impairment

CHAPTER OUTLINE

CHAPTER OBJECTIVES

INTRODUCTION

THE DEPRECIATION CONCEPT
Depreciation Methods
  Annuity or Sinking Fund Depreciation
  Straight-Line Depreciation
  Accelerated Depreciation Methods
  Units-of-Production and Service Hours Methods
  Group and Composite Depreciation Methods
Depletion
Amortization
Depreciation Method Disclosures
  Depreciation Lives and Salvage Values
Impact of Depreciation Methods on Financial Statements
Accelerated Depreciation and Taxes
The Impact of Inflation on Depreciation
Changes in Depreciation Method

ANALYSIS OF FIXED ASSET DISCLOSURES
Estimating Relative Age and Useful Lives
Estimating the Age of Assets
Example: Forest Products Industry Comparison

IMPAIRMENT OF LONG-LIVED ASSETS
Financial Reporting of Impaired Assets
Financial Statement Impact of Impairments
Effect of SFAS 121 on Analysis of Impairment
Empirical Findings

LIABILITIES FOR CLOSURE AND ENVIRONMENTAL COSTS

SUMMARY

CASE 8-1: ANALYSIS OF FIXED ASSETS IN THE SWEDISH FOREST PRODUCTS INDUSTRY

APPENDIX 8-A: ANALYSIS OF CHANGING PRICES INFORMATION
Introduction
Analysis of General Inflation
  Constant Dollar Method
Analysis of Firm-Specific Inflation
  Current Cost Method
  Adjusting Financial Statements for Changing Prices
  Concluding Remarks

CHAPTER OBJECTIVES

Chapter 8 has the following objectives:

1. Define the characteristics of different depreciation methods.

2. Explain the role of depreciable lives and salvage values in the computation of depreciation expense.

3. Show the effects of different depreciation methods on the financial statements.

4. Discuss how inflation impacts the measurement of economic deprecation.

5. Illustrate the impact of changes from one depreciation method to another.

6. Define the measurement of relative age, useful life, and average age of fixed assets, and the use of these measures.

7. Illustrate the financial reporting of asset impairment and its financial statement effects.

8. Discuss the liability for closure, removal, and environmental effects of long-lived operating assets.

INTRODUCTION

This chapter continues the analysis of long-lived assets begun in the previous chapter where we examined financial reporting and analysis issues arising at acquisition. We now consider the reporting and analysis of long-lived assets:

1. Over their useful lives, with emphasis on
   - Depreciation methods
   - Depreciable lives and salvage values
   - Impact of choices on financial statements

2. When they are disposed of, or written off when impaired, or at the end of their useful lives, with particular attention to the effects of impairment write-downs on financial statements and ratios

Amortization, depletion, and depreciation are all terms used for the systematic allocation of the capitalized cost of an asset to income over its useful life. Depreciation, the most frequently used of these terms, is often used generically in discussions of the concept. Strictly speaking, *depreciation* represents the allocation of the cost of tangible fixed assets, *amortization* refers to the cost of intangible assets, and *depletion* applies to natural resource assets.

THE DEPRECIATION CONCEPT

For accountants, depreciation is an allocation process, not a valuation process. It is important, therefore, for analysts to differentiate between accounting depreciation and economic depreciation. Although the accounting process may be purely allocative, the concept of depreciation also has economic meaning.

In Chapter 2, income was defined as the amount that can be distributed during the period without impairing the productive capacity of the firm. The cash flows

EXHIBIT 8-1
Sinking Fund Depreciation

Year	(1) Opening Balance Asset	(2) Cash Flow	(3) Depreciation Expense	(4) = (2) − (3) Net Income	(5) = (4)/(1) Rate of Return
1	$240	$100	$ 71	$29	12%
2	169	100	80	20	12
3	89	100	89	11	12
Totals		$300	$240	$60	

generated by an asset over its life, therefore, cannot be considered income until a provision is made for its replacement. These cash flows must be reduced by the amount required to replace the asset to determine the earnings generated by that asset.

This is the underlying principle of economic depreciation; profits are overstated if no allowance is made for the replacement of the asset. The periodic depreciation expense, therefore, segregates a portion of cash flows for reinvestment, preserving that sum from distribution as dividends and taxes.[1]

Continuing this conceptual argument, suppose an asset costs $240 and is expected to generate net cash flows of $100 per year over its three-year life. Over the life of the asset, income equals $60 ($300 − $240) as $240 is required to replace the asset (if we assume that the asset is worthless at the end of the three-year period and price levels do not change). As financial statements report income annually, it is necessary to determine how much income (how much depreciation) to report each year. This requires the allocation of a portion of the multiperiod return to each period.

The next section describes the depreciation methods used in financial reporting, followed by a discussion of the impact of depreciation methods on financial statements. A separate analysis of accelerated depreciation methods used for income taxes is followed by a discussion of the interaction of inflation and depreciation methods. Analysis of financial statement depreciation disclosures, changes in depreciation methods, and a comprehensive examination of fixed asset disclosures round out the discussion.

Depreciation Methods

Annuity or Sinking Fund Depreciation

From an economic perspective, the income reported each year should reflect the rate of return earned by the asset. For example, the asset just described generates a return of 12% over its three-year life.[2] To report a 12% return for each year requires the pattern of depreciation shown in Exhibit 8-1.

---

[1]This does not mean that cash equal to depreciation expense is set aside for reinvestment but, rather, that the definition of income requires a subtraction for asset replacement.

[2]The present value of a three-year annuity of $100 per year discounted at 12% is (approximately) equal to $240.

EXHIBIT 8-2
Straight-Line Depreciation with Declining Cash Flows

Year	(1) Opening Balance Asset	(2) Cash Flow	(3) Depreciation Expense	(4) = (2) − (3) Net Income	(5) = (4)/(1) Rate of Return
1	$240	$109	$ 80	$29	12%
2	160	99	80	19	12
3	80	90	80	10	12
Totals		$298	$240	$58	

This pattern, with the amount of depreciation increasing every year, is known as *annuity or sinking fund depreciation*. U.S. GAAP, however, do not permit this form of depreciation. In Canada, increasing charge methods are used for income-producing properties in the real estate industry and by a few utilities, but they are not generally acceptable depreciation methods.

Straight-line and accelerated depreciation (discussed shortly) can also produce a constant rate of return when cash flows generated by the asset decline over time. Exhibit 8-2 illustrates this case; the rate of return is constant and reflects the true return earned by the asset.

Instead of depreciation patterns that generate a constant rate of return, accountants generally use depreciation patterns that result in constant or declining expense. These patterns are sometimes justified by the matching principle. Generally, however, they are arbitrary, their sole purpose being a systematic allocation of the asset cost over time.

Straight-Line Depreciation

Given the same asset and the pattern of cash flows in Exhibit 8-1, accountants (using the matching principle) argue that since the revenues (cash flows of $100) generated by the asset are the same each year, the income shown each year should also be the same. The result of this line of reasoning is the *straight-line method*, the pattern of depreciation expense exhibited in Exhibit 8-3. *Straight-line depreciation is the dominant method in the United States and most countries worldwide.*

Note that the use of this method results in an *increasing* rate of return and does not report the actual rate of return earned over the life of the asset.

Accelerated Depreciation Methods

The matching principle can also justify accelerated depreciation patterns, with higher depreciation charges in early years and smaller amounts in later years. There are two arguments:

1. Benefits (revenues) from an asset may be higher in early years, declining in later years as efficiency falls (the asset wears out). The matching process suggests that depreciation should decline with benefits.

EXHIBIT 8-3
Straight-Line Depreciation with Constant Cash Flows

Year	(1) Opening Balance Asset	(2) Cash Flow	(3) Depreciation Expense	(4) = (2) − (3) Net Income	(5) = (4)/(1) Rate of Return
1	$240	$100	$ 80	$20	8.3%
2	160	100	80	20	12.5
3	80	100	80	20	25.0
Totals		$300	$240	$60	

2. Even if revenues are constant over time, an asset requires maintenance and repairs over time, costs that tend to increase as the asset ages. Accelerated depreciation methods compensate for the rising trend of maintenance and repair costs so that total asset costs are level over the asset's life.

However, both the efficiency and maintenance of an asset are difficult to forecast, and, in any case, accelerated depreciation methods are (like straight-line) arbitrary procedures designed to yield the desired pattern of higher depreciation amounts in earlier years. Accelerated methods have historically been used for tax reporting, where they are justified by the desire to promote capital investment, rather than accounting theory.

The two most common accelerated methods are the *sum-of-years'-digits* (SYD) method and the family of *declining-balance* methods. A comparison of these methods (using the double-declining-balance method) with straight-line (SL) depreciation is presented in Exhibit 8-4. In the example used, the concept of *salvage value*, the estimated amount that the asset can be sold for at the end of its useful life, is introduced into the calculations.

Units-of-Production and Service Hours Methods

These methods depreciate assets in proportion to their actual use rather than as a function of the passage of time. Thus, more depreciation is recognized in years of higher production. Measurement requires an initial estimate of the total number of units of output or service hours expected over the life of the machine. The methods differ in whether asset usage is measured by output or hours used.

Assume that the asset described in Exhibit 8-4 is expected to produce 60,000 units of output over its life and have a service life of 150,000 hours. The actual hours of service and output, and the resultant depreciation schedules, are presented in Exhibit 8-5.

These methods make depreciation expense a variable rather than a fixed cost, decreasing the volatility of reported earnings as compared to straight-line or accelerated methods. Some companies use a hybrid depreciation method, combining features of the units-of-production and straight-line methods.

A significant drawback of these two methods occurs when the firm's productive capacity becomes obsolete as it loses business to more efficient competitors. The units-of-production and service hours methods decrease depreciation expense during periods

EXHIBIT 8-4
Comparison of Straight-Line and Accelerated Depreciation Methods

Original Cost = $18,000
Salvage Value = $3,000
Depreciable Life $n = 5$

A. Straight-Line Depreciation

Depreciation in Year $i = \dfrac{1}{n} \times$ (Original Cost − Salvage Value)

Depreciation expense is constant each year; at the end of the five-year period, the net book value of the asset equals its salvage value of $3,000.

Year	Rate	(Original Cost— Salvage Value)	Depreciation Expense	Accumulated Depreciation	Net Book Value
0					$18,000
1	1/5	$15,000	$ 3,000	$3,000	15,000
2	1/5	15,000	3,000	6,000	12,000
3	1/5	15,000	3,000	9,000	9,000
4	1/5	15,000	3,000	12,000	6,000
5	1/5	15,000	3,000	15,000	3,000
Total			$15,000		

B and C. Accelerated Depreciation Methods

B. Sum-of-Years' Digits (SYD) Method

Depreciation in Year $i = \dfrac{(n - i + 1)}{\text{SYD}} \times$ (Original Cost − Salvage Value)

where SYD $= 1 + 2 + 3 + \cdots + n$ the summation over the depreciable life of n years or simply SYD $= n(n + 1)/2$. For our example, $n = 5$.

$$\text{SYD} = 1 + 2 + 3 + 4 + 5 = 15$$

or, alternatively,

$$\text{SYD} = \frac{(5)(5 + 1)}{2} = 15$$

The rate of depreciation thus varies from year to year (as i varies) in reverse counting order of the years; that is, the pattern is 5/15, 4/15, 3/15, 2/15, and 1/15 and is depicted as follows:

Year	Rate	(Original Cost— Salvage Value)	Depreciation Expense	Accumulated Depreciation	Net Book Value
0					$18,000
1	5/15	$15,000	$ 5,000	$5,000	13,000
2	4/15	15,000	4,000	9,000	9,000
3	3/15	15,000	3,000	12,000	6,000
4	2/15	15,000	2,000	14,000	4,000
5	1/15	15,000	1,000	15,000	3,000
Total			$15,000		

EXHIBIT 8-4 (*continued*)

C. Double-Declining-Balance

Depreciation in Year $i = \dfrac{2}{n} \times$ (Original Cost $-$ Accumulated Depreciation)

or

$\dfrac{2}{n} \times$ (Net Book Value)

The rate of $(2/n)$ is what gives the double-declining-balance (DDB) method its name. The depreciation rate is double* the straight-line rate. The declining pattern occurs because the fixed rate is applied to an ever-decreasing asset balance (net book value),† and in our example it is calculated as

Year	Rate	Net Book Value	Depreciation Expense	Accumulated Depreciation	Net Book Value
0					$18,000
1	2/5	$18,000	$ 7,200	$7,200	10,800
2	2/5	10,800	4,320	11,520	6,480
3	2/5	6,480	2,592	14,112	3,888
4	NA	NA	888	15,000	3,000
5	NA	NA	0	15,000	3,000
Total			$15,000		

Note that in year 4 the DDB procedure is discontinued. This is because depreciation can be taken only until the salvage value is reached. Following DDB in year 4 and beyond would have reduced net book value below salvage. When the DDB method is applied to longer-lived assets, a switch to the straight-line method often occurs in later years, when the latter method results in higher depreciation expense.

NA = not applicable.

*The DDB method is actually only one case of the family of declining-balance methods. The same principle can be applied to other multiples of the straight-line rate (e.g., 150% declining balance). Higher multiples result in more accelerated patterns of depreciation expense.

†Note that salvage value is not used to calculate depreciation under declining-balance methods but acts as a floor for net book value.

of low production. The result is to overstate reported income and asset values at the same time as the asset's economic value declines. This danger is particularly acute for mature industries facing increased competition from new entrants or imports. Competition frequently increases the rate of economic depreciation of fixed assets. However, the corporate response is often to relieve the pressure on earnings by decreasing depreciation expense by changing to a method such as units-of-production. Alternatively, firms may get the same effect by lengthening lives.

Sooner or later, however, the firm will recognize the impairment (see the discussion later in this chapter) of its productive capacity. Once impairment exists, companies report "restructuring" or similar charges to correct the overvaluation of fixed assets. Analysts often exclude such "nonrecurring" charges when evaluating corporate earn-

EXHIBIT 8-5
Service Hours and Units-of-Production Methods

Original Cost − $18,000
Salvage Value = $3,000

| | Service Hours Method
Expected Service Hours = 150,000
Cost/Service Hour = $0.10* | | | Units-of-Production Method
Expected Output = 60,000
Cost/Unit of Output = $0.25† | | |
| | Hours Worked | Depreciation | Net Book Value | Units of Output | Depreciation | Net Book Value |
Year						
0			$18,000			$18,000
1	40,000	$ 4,000	14,000	15,000	$3,750	14,250
2	35,000	3,500	10,500	16,000	4,000	10,250
3	45,000	4,500	6,000	20,000	5,000	5,250
4	20,000	2,000	4,000	10,000	2,250‡	3,000
5	40,000	1,000‡	3,000	12,500	0‡	3,000
Total		$15,000			$15,000	

*($18,000 − $3,000)/150,000.
†($18,000 − $3,000)/60,000.
‡Note that in both cases, the asset is never depreciated below the salvage value even when actual use exceeds estimated use.

ings. But to the extent that these charges represent an adjustment for past underdepreciation of assets, they correct a systematic overstatement of past earnings. As past earnings are used to forecast the future, this issue should not be ignored.

The following footnote from the 1992 financial statements of Brown & Sharpe, a machine tool manufacturer, provides an illustration of this phenomenon:

> In 1992, the Company extended the estimated useful lives of machinery and equipment at its Swiss subsidiary, based upon the current low rate of utilization. The effect of this change was to reduce 1992 depreciation expense and net loss by $921,000 or $.19 per share.

Total depreciation expense for Brown & Sharpe fell from $8 million in 1992 to $6.8 million in 1993; the change in accounting estimate was apparently the major factor in that decline. In 1994, Brown & Sharpe reported restructuring charges that included: "costs . . . for . . . property, plant, and equipment . . . writeoffs . . . due to a plant closing in Switzerland."

Although the corporate temptation to change accounting when business is weak is understandable, that change can mislead investors. Furthermore, on occasion, a company recognizes the impairment of fixed assets gradually, by accelerating depreciation on a group of assets in danger of becoming obsolete. From an analytic point of view, it is preferable to recognize the impairment immediately. Because accounting depreciation is a systematic allocation of cost, its acceleration when the asset is impaired (and its use has declined or it has been temporarily idled) fails to match costs and revenues and misstates the earning power of the company.

Group and Composite Depreciation Methods

Depreciation methods described in the preceding sections apply to single assets; they may be impractical when firms use large numbers of similar assets in their operations. Group (composite) depreciation methods allocate the costs of similar (dissimilar) assets using depreciation rates based on a weighted average of the service lives of the assets.

Gains or losses on the disposal of assets depreciated using group or composite methods are either:

1. Recognized in reported income, or

2. Reported instead as a component of accumulated depreciation[3]

Example: DuPont. DuPont uses group methods for all its assets except for petroleum and coal fixed assets. DuPont's "Summary of Significant Accounting Policies" (Note 1 in Appendix A) is representative of the information provided by companies using group depreciation.

Note the change in accounting. For assets acquired prior to 1991, duPont did not recognize gains or losses from the disposition of fixed assets; the accumulated depreciation account was adjusted to reflect assets retired or sold. Starting in 1991, however, gain or loss (the difference between any proceeds received and the net book value of the assets disposed of) is recognized as part of income. The gains recognized on the sale of assets are disclosed in Note 2.

Depletion

Financial reporting requirements for natural resources are similar to those for tangible assets. The carrying costs of natural resources include the costs of acquiring the land or mines and the costs of exploration and development of the resources. These costs may be capitalized or expensed as a function of the firm's accounting policies (such as successful efforts or full cost for oil and gas exploration).

The carrying costs of natural resources (excluding costs of machinery and equipment used in extraction or production) are allocated to accounting periods using the units-of-production method. This method requires an initial estimate of the units (of oil, coal, gold, or timber) in the resource base to compute a unit cost, which is then applied to the actual units produced, extracted, or harvested.

Amortization

Amortization of intangible assets may be based on useful lives as defined by law (e.g., patents) or regulation, or such assets may be depreciated over the period during which the firm expects to receive benefits from them (computer software). Companies use either straight-line or units-of-production methods. Goodwill and indefinite-term franchises and licenses may be amortized over periods not exceeding 40 years.[4]

---

[3]At the time of the sale, the proceeds are added to cash, the original asset cost is removed from gross PPE, and the accumulated depreciation for the asset is removed from that account. The difference between the cash proceeds and the net book value of the assets sold is then credited/debited to the accumulated depreciation account; no gain or loss is recorded.

[4]See Chapter 14 for an extensive discussion of goodwill.

EXHIBIT 8-6. IBM
Accounting for Computer Software

Significant Accounting Policies

Software

Costs related to the conceptual formulation and design of licensed programs are expensed as research and development. Costs incurred subsequent to establishment of technological feasibility to produce the finished product are capitalized. The annual amortization of the capitalized amounts is the greater of the amount computed based on the estimated revenue distribution over the products' revenue-producing lives, or the straight-line method, and is applied over periods ranging from two to four years. Periodic reviews are performed to ensure that unamortized program costs remain recoverable over future revenues. Costs to support or service licensed programs are charged against income as incurred, or when related revenue is recognized, whichever occurs first.

Management Discussion and Analysis

The 1994 software gross profit dollars and margin were affected by a change in the company's software amortization periods effective January 1, 1994. This change was a result of a continuing review of the company's portfolio of software offerings, software amortization periods, and recoverability of the capitalized investment in software products. The change reduced amortization periods to a maximum of four years to recognize more rapid advances in software technology and thus a shorter period over which to recover capitalized costs. This change resulted in increased amortization costs after tax of $192 million ($.33 per common share).

Source: IBM, *1994 Annual Report.*

Example: IBM. Exhibit 8-6, from IBM's *1994 annual report*, contains the firm's accounting policies for capitalized software development costs. In Chapter 7, we examined the pattern of capitalization; now we discuss amortization.

The accounting policies footnote is typically vague about amortization periods. Curiously, the footnote does not report that IBM changed its policy in 1994; that change in the accounting estimate, reported only in the Management Discussion and Analysis, is also included in Exhibit 8-6.

Although the effect of the change is reported after tax, we can estimate the pretax effect:

After-tax effect:	$192 million
Tax rate:	41% (from tax footnote, not shown)
Pretax effect:	$192/(1 − 0.41) = $325 million

The accounting change explains why IBM's software amortization did not decrease in 1994 despite the declining trend of capitalization in previous years (see the data in Exhibit 7-2 and the related discussion on p. 339).

Depreciation Method Disclosures

As we have shown, the choice of the depreciation method can greatly affect the pattern of reported income. Disclosure of the depreciation method used is required and can usually be found in the footnote listing accounting policies. Most (more than 90%)

American firms use straight-line depreciation, which is also the dominant method used in other countries. The use of accelerated methods has declined in recent years as firms have changed to straight-line depreciation.

Depreciation Lives and Salvage Values

Even when the same depreciation method is used, comparability for a firm over time and among companies at a given point in time may be lacking. The *useful life* (the period over which the asset is depreciated) can vary from firm to firm, and excessively long lives understate reported depreciation expense. Although companies are required to disclose depreciation lives, in practice such disclosures are often vague, providing ranges rather than precise data.[5] In such cases, the analyst must use available data to compute approximate depreciation lives (see the analysis of fixed asset disclosures later in the chapter).

Although usually a less significant factor, *salvage values* also affect comparisons; they (like asset lives) are also management estimates. High estimates reduce the depreciation base (cost less salvage value) and, therefore, reduce depreciation expense. (Note that salvage values are not employed in declining-balance depreciation methods.) In practice, companies rarely disclose data regarding salvage values, except when estimates are changed.[6]

Impact of Depreciation Methods on Financial Statements

The choice of depreciation method impacts both the income statement and balance sheet; for capital-intensive companies, the impact can be significant. As depreciation is an allocation of past cash flows, the method chosen for financial reporting purposes has no impact on the statement of cash flows.[7]

Accelerated depreciation methods, with higher depreciation expense in the early years of asset life, tend to depress both net income and stockholders' equity when compared with the straight-line method. As the percentage effect on net income is usually greater than the effect on net assets, return ratios tend to be lower when accelerated depreciation methods are used. Consequently, these methods are considered more conservative.

Toward the end of an asset's life, however, the effect on net income reverses. In Exhibit 8-4, depreciation expense in years 4 and 5 is lower using accelerated methods than under the straight-line method. This is true for individual assets. However, for companies with stable or rising capital expenditures, the early year impact of new assets acquired dominates, and depreciation expense on a total firm basis is higher under an accelerated method. When capital expenditures decline, however, accelerated depreciation decreases depreciation expense as the later year effect on older assets dominates.

---

[5]See duPont's disclosures, which are typical, in financial statement Note 1.

[6]As discussed in Chapter 1, changes in accounting estimates receive less disclosure than changes in method. APB 20 requires (para. 33) disclosure of the effect of a change that affects future periods, such as changes in depreciable lives.

[7]This assumes that the method chosen for tax purposes is independent of the method chosen for financial statement purposes.

Depreciable lives and salvage values impact both depreciation expense and stated asset values. Shorter lives and lower salvage values are considered conservative in that they lead to higher depreciation expense. These factors interact with the depreciation method to determine the expense; for example, use of the straight-line method with short depreciation lives may result in depreciation expense similar to that obtained from the use of an accelerated method with longer lives. Conservative depreciation practices also increase asset turnover ratios by decreasing the denominator of that ratio.

Accelerated Depreciation and Taxes

Notwithstanding the theoretical arguments and the financial statement effects discussed, the primary reason for accelerated depreciation methods is their beneficial effect on the firm's tax burden. At the onset of an asset's life, the total amount of depreciation expense available is fixed. Depreciation acts as a tax shield by reducing the amount of taxes paid in any given year. Given a positive interest rate, firms are better off using accelerated depreciation methods to obtain the benefit of increased cash flows (from reduced taxes) in the earlier years.

The tax code has long been used by governments to encourage investment, and this was the intent of the U.S. government when it first allowed accelerated depreciation methods for tax purposes in 1954. Many foreign governments also permit the use of accelerated depreciation methods. Since 1954, the U.S. government has frequently changed tax depreciation regulations to increase or decrease investment incentives in certain types of fixed assets or simply to raise revenues. The present system is known as MACRS—modified accelerated cost recovery system—which consists of specified depreciation patterns and depreciable lives (generally shorter than actual useful service lives) for different property classes.

MACRS uses double-declining-balance and 150% declining-balance methods, which few companies use for financial reporting purposes. Thus, in the United States, the depreciation method and lives used for financial statements almost always differ from those used for tax purposes. The implications of these differences are discussed in Chapter 9, which also illustrates the use of tax disclosures to obtain insights into the depreciation practices used for financial reporting.

The Impact of Inflation on Depreciation

Historical cost-based depreciation expense may be used to define income as long as the total expense over the asset's life is enough to replace the asset after it has been fully utilized. If, however, the replacement cost of the asset increases, then depreciation expense based on the original cost will be insufficient.

Returning to the example in Exhibit 8-1, assume that after three years, the firm requires $300 to replace the asset. Now the total economic income earned by the firm is $0, as total cash flows equal the cost to replace. If we use the historical cost basis, however, total depreciation is limited to the original $240 cost, and reported income is overstated. In addition, because firms are only allowed to use historical cost basis depreciation for tax reporting, the resultant taxes are too high. Income taxes become, in effect, a tax on capital rather than a tax on income. Box 8-1 illustrates the resulting disincentives for investment in the context of a simple capital budgeting model.

Accelerated depreciation methods partially compensate for this inflation effect by shortening the (tax) recovery period. Depreciating the asset over a shorter life serves a similar purpose. A number of studies have examined whether accelerated

---

BOX 8-1
Disincentives for Investment Arising from Historical Cost Depreciation

We begin by assuming that the inflation rate p is equal to zero. A project is profitable if the net present value (NPV) of the cash flows of the investment:

$$\text{NPV}_{(p=0)} = -I + (1 - t) \sum \frac{C_i}{(1 + r)^i} + t \sum \frac{d_i I}{(1 + r)^i}$$

is greater than zero (i.e., NPV > 0), where C_i is the pretax (real) cash flow in period i, t is the marginal tax rate, d_i is the rate of depreciation in period i, I is the cost of the original investment, and r is the appropriate real discount rate.* The summation on the right reflects the depreciation tax shelter, and the NPV can be disaggregated into

NPV = − Investment + Present Value (After-Tax Cash Flows)

+ Present Value (Depreciation Tax Shelter)

If we introduce an annual inflation rate of $p > 0$, then the expected (nominal) cash flows in any period will increase. In addition, the discount rate will change to reflect inflation. The depreciation deduction based on historical costs will not change. The expression for net present value now becomes

$$\text{NPV}_{(p>0)} = -I + (1 - t) \sum \frac{(1 + p)^i C_i}{(1 + p)^i (1 + r)^i} + t \sum \frac{d_i I}{(1 + p)^i (1 + r)^i}$$

As the $(1 + p)^i$ terms in the first summation cancel, inflation (when it is expected) will not affect the after-tax cash flows. However, the depreciation tax shelter will now be worth less as

$$t \sum \frac{d_i I}{(1 + r)^i} > t \sum \frac{d_i I}{(1 + p)^i (1 + r)^i}$$

The decline in the depreciation tax shelter will reduce the profitability of the project:

$$\text{NPV}_{(p>0)} < \text{NPV}_{(p=0)}$$

and *ceteris paribus*, there is less likelihood that the project will be undertaken.

---

*Generally, the depreciation tax shelter would be discounted at a rate lower than the cash flows themselves as the tax deduction is "riskless." We do not make the distinction here for the sake of simplification. Alternatively, one can view this problem in the context of certainty, and r is the risk-free rate.

---

methods compensate for inflation and/or reflect economic depreciation (variously defined).

Kim and Moore (1988), for example, report that, for the Canadian trucking industry, tax depreciation exceeded economic depreciation, resulting in a tax subsidy. Most (1984), focusing on reported income, found that in the United States the useful life (used for financial reporting) is generally longer than the economic life of the asset, understating reported depreciation and overstating reported income. Skinner (1982), on the other hand, reported the opposite phenomenon in the United Kingdom.

Beaver and Dukes (1973) examined firm price/earnings ratios and found that market prices, on average

assign a more accelerated form of depreciation than is implied by reported earnings.[8]

They did not attempt to discern the reasons for this result but recognized that it was consistent with either a constant rate of return depreciation model (with declining cash flows) or depreciation based on current costs rather than a historical cost system.

Generalizing these results to other time periods, particularly for studies that examined whether depreciation practices (whether for tax or book purposes) compensated for the actual economic or physical depreciation of assets, requires a great deal of caution, given changing economic environments. These comparisons are a function of the provisions of the tax code, the inflation rate, and varying degrees of technological obsolescence across industries during the comparison period. During the 1980s, the depreciation provisions of the U.S. tax code were changed three times, inflation declined to approximately 4% from double digit rates, and technological change was rapid in many industries. International differences are an additional difficulty.

The benchmark issue emerging from these studies is: How does one determine the "correct" useful life and economic depreciation rate? This is an important question for analytic purposes. Estimates of economic lives on an aggregate industry basis can be derived from Department of Commerce data.

In 1982, the FASB issued SFAS 33 (Changing Prices), which required very large firms[9] to disclose supplementary, unaudited data on the effects of changing prices. Among the required disclosures were:

1. The current cost of fixed assets
2. Depreciation expense on a current cost basis

These disclosures were intended to help financial statement users adjust for the shortcomings of historical cost depreciation discussed earlier. However, studies that examined the informational content of the replacement cost data found that, although historical cost earnings had informational content above and beyond that of current cost data provided by SFAS 33, the reverse did not hold.[10] Inflation-adjusted data did not appear to have any marginal information content above that provided by historical cost data. The reasons offered for this surprising result were that the data were:

1. Too difficult to comprehend, and the market had not yet learned how to use them

---

[8]William H. Beaver and Roland E. Dukes, "Interperiod Tax Allocation and δ-Depreciation Methods: Some Empirical Results," *The Accounting Review*, July 1973, pp. 549–559.

[9]SFAS 33 applied to firms with inventories and gross (before deducting depreciation) property exceeding $125 million (in the aggregate) or with total assets exceeding $1 billion.

[10]Some studies [e.g., Beaver et al. (1980, 1982)] found little information content, focusing on ASR 190 disclosures (see Appendix 8-A). Others [Beaver and Landsman (1983)] examined the SFAS 33 data with similar results. Although the consensus was that these data did not have information content, the conclusions were by no means unanimous [see, e.g., Easman et al. (1979) and Murdoch (1986)].

2. Not new, as the market knew how to adjust historical costs for inflation without SFAS 33 disclosures[11]

3. Irrelevant, either from a conceptual point of view or in the manner in which they were prepared and reported

Whatever the reason, in practice the data were difficult to prepare and use. Facing intense complaints regarding the cost of the disclosures and empirical research that seemed to belie the usefulness of the data, the FASB subsequently made the disclosures voluntary. A detailed discussion of the effects of inflation on fixed assets and depreciation appears in Appendix 8-A.

Changes in Depreciation Method

Companies may change the reported depreciation of fixed assets in different ways:

1. Change in method applicable to newly acquired assets only
2. Change in method applicable to all assets
3. Changes in asset lives or salvage value

Change in Method Applicable to Newly Acquired Assets Only. A company can change its depreciation method only for newly acquired assets and continue to depreciate previously acquired similar assets using the same method(s) as in the past. The impact of the new method will be gradual, increasing as fixed assets acquired after the change grow in relative importance.

DuPont, for example, changed from the sum-of-the-years' digits method (for nonpetroleum properties) to the straight-line method for properties placed in service in 1995 (see Note 1). This is a common method of changing accounting principles, as it does not require the restatement of past earnings.

The company makes the uninformative statement that "the change is not expected to have a material effect on 1995 results." Nonetheless, *the change will increase future reported income* as depreciation charges for new PPE will be lower (depreciation charges on old PPE continue to be computed using the SYD method).

Change in Method Applicable to All Assets. Alternatively, the new method can be applied retroactively so that all fixed assets are depreciated using the new method. In this case, the effect is greater and can be significant in the year of the switch as well as in future years. For a sample of 38 companies that switched to straight-line depreciation, Healy et al. (1987) estimated that the median increase in income was 8% to 10% in the 10-year period following the change. In addition to the effect on current and future depreciation expense (and net income), there is a cumulative effect, given the retroactive nature of the change: the cumulative difference between originally reported depreciation and the restated depreciation for all past periods. When the new method is applied retroactively, companies must also disclose the *pro forma* impact of the new method on prior periods.

---

[11]One example is the work of Angela Falkenstein and Roman L. Weil, "Replacement Cost Accounting: What Will Income Statements Based on the SEC Disclosures Show?—Part I," *Financial Analysts Journal*, Jan.–Feb. 1977, pp. 46–57 and "Replacement Cost Accounting: What Will Income Statements Based on the SEC Disclosures Show?—Part II," *Financial Analysts Journal*, March–April 1977, pp. 48–57.

EXHIBIT 8-7. DELTA AIRLINES
Change in Depreciable Lives

Depreciation and Amortization

Prior to April 1, 1993, substantially all of the Company's flight equipment was being depreciated on a straight-line basis to residual values (10% of cost) over a 15-year period from the dates placed in service. As a result of a review of its fleet plan, effective April 1, 1993, the Company increased the estimated useful lives of substantially all of its flight equipment. Flight equipment that was not already fully depreciated is being depreciated on a straight-line basis to residual values (5% of cost) over a 20-year period from the dates placed in service. The effect of this change was a $34 million decrease in depreciation expense and a $22 million ($0.44 per common share) decrease in net loss for fiscal 1993. Ground property and equipment are depreciated on a straight-line basis over their estimated service lives, which range from three years to thirty years.

Source: Delta Air Lines, *1993 Annual Report.*

A change in depreciation method for all assets is considered a change in accounting principle under APB 20, Accounting Changes. *The cumulative effect of the change must be reported separately and net of taxes.*

Changes in Asset Lives or Salvage Value. Changes in asset lives and salvage values are changes in accounting estimates and are not considered changes in accounting principle. Their impact is only prospective, and no retroactive or cumulative effects are recognized. Estimate changes attract much less notice than do changes in depreciation methods (see footnote 6). They are not, for example, referred to in the auditor's opinion. Thus, it is important to read financial statement footnotes carefully to be sure that no changes in accounting estimates have been made.

Example: Delta Airlines. Exhibit 8-7 contains a footnote from the *1993 Annual Report* of Delta Airlines, which changed *both* the estimated useful lives *and* the salvage values used to compute depreciation on its flight equipment, effective April 1, 1993. Given the asset intensity of airlines, this change had a significant impact on reported earnings, an increase of $22 million or $0.44 per share. Delta reported large losses in 1992 and 1993, perhaps explaining the accounting change.
Note that these are considered changes in accounting estimates. Thus, such changes are not highlighted in the accountant's report or on the face of the income statement; careful reading of footnotes is required to find such changes and understand their impact. Remember that the effect of such changes persists, as depreciation on both old and new fixed assets is stretched out, increasing reported income.
In the case of Delta, the accounting change affected fiscal 1993 earnings (Delta has a June fiscal year) for only one quarter; the effect on fiscal 1994 earnings can be assumed to be approximately four times as great, that is, $136 million (4 × $34 million).
Delta's *reported* operating losses and depreciation declined over this period. However, by adjusting depreciation and operating losses for the change in depreciation methods [increase 1993 (1994) depreciation by $34 ($136) million], we find that the change in lives and salvage value accounted for 60% of the reported improvement in operating results from 1992 to 1994.[12]

---

[12]($34 × 4)/($675 − $447) = 59.6%.

Delta Airlines ($ in millions)
Fiscal Years Ended June 30

	1992	1993	1994
As Reported (with Depreciation Changes)			
Depreciation expense	$635	$735	$678
% Change from previous year	—	16%	(8)%
Operating income (loss)	(675)	(575)	(447)
% Change from previous year	—	15%	22%
After Adjustment for Depreciation Change			
Depreciation expense	635	769	814
% Change from previous year	—	21%	6%
Operating income (loss)	(675)	(609)	(583)
% Change from previous year	—	10%	4%

Increases in asset lives have been common in recent years. The effect of such increases is, of course, to increase reported earnings. Such changes are often made by more than one firm in an industry, as firms "compete" to show higher reported earnings and ROE. For example, in the forest products industry, we find the following progression of firms that lengthened lives:

- 1991   Union Camp
- 1992   Scott Paper
- 1993   Georgia-Pacific
- 1994   Mead

Box 8-2 examines the motivation for and reaction to depreciation changes. Whenever a change in depreciation method or lives is reported, the effect of the change on current year reported earnings should be removed to evaluate operating performance on a comparable basis. The change should also be factored into estimates of future reported income.

ANALYSIS OF FIXED ASSET DISCLOSURES

In practice, firms use varying accounting methods, lives, and residual value assumptions for fixed assets, hampering comparisons between firms. To improve comparability, the analyst must use financial statement disclosures to gain insight into a company's depreciation accounting. Unfortunately, in 1994 the SEC deleted the requirement for firms to disclose details of their property accounts.[13] As a result, only a broad analysis is possible except when detailed data are made available by the company.

---

[13]Financial Reporting Release (FRR) 44 (December 13, 1994) amended Rule 5-04 of Regulation S-X to eliminate Schedule V, Property, Plant and Equipment, and Schedule VI, Accumulated Depreciation, Depletion and Amortization of Property, Plant and Equipment. See FRR 44 for a listing of other schedules eliminated.

BOX 8-2
Changes in Depreciation Methods: Motivation and Reaction

When the Internal Revenue Code of 1954 permitted the use of accelerated depreciation for tax purposes, many firms also adopted these methods for financial statement purposes. Subsequently, many of these firms "switched back" to straight-line depreciation for financial reporting purposes. The effect of the switch-back was to increase the firm's reported net income, (tangible) assets, and retained earnings.

Unlike the FIFO-LIFO switch discussed in Chapter 6, the depreciation switch-back was a "pure accounting" change without any direct cash flow consequences as accelerated depreciation was retained for tax purposes. The phenomenon was originally studied by Archibald (1972) and Kaplan and Roll (1972) as a test of whether the efficient market hypothesis (EMH) or the functional fixation hypothesis prevailed with respect to financial statements; that is, was the market "fooled" by the numbers, or did it see through the accounting change, realizing that it had no economic consequence? As detailed in Chapter 5, the results of these studies (using weekly and monthly data) were consistent with the EMH, finding no market reaction to the switch.

With the advent of positive accounting research, the assumption of no economic consequences to a "pure accounting" change was reexamined. Management compensation contracts as well as debt covenants based on accounting numbers are affected by accounting changes. Holthausen (1981) examined the accounting switch-backs in this framework. He argued that an accounting change that increases reported income, given earnings-based management contracts, should result in negative market reaction, as there would be a wealth transfer from the owners of the firm to the managers. Conversely, the presence of debt covenants should result in a positive market reaction, as the increase in reported earnings and assets would generally increase the slack associated with any leverage constraints. Empirical results did not confirm these hypotheses.

As noted in Chapter 5, studies of market reaction to voluntary accounting changes have generally not found results consistent with the positive accounting framework, as (it is argued that) by the time the change is made, it has been generally anticipated that the firm (or its managers) will make the change to improve reported performance. Thus, although the motivation for the change (compensation, debt convenants) is as specified, the market has already taken it into account.

Evidence consistent with the compensation motivation for depreciation switch-backs is reported by Dhaliwal et al. (1982), who found that management-controlled firms are more likely to adopt straight-line depreciation methods. Furthermore, Healy et al. (1987) found that when firms changed reporting methods to straight-line depreciation,

> the CEO's bonus and salary awards are based on reported earnings both before and after the accounting changes. We find no evidence that subsequent to either the inventory change or the depreciation change, reported earnings are transformed to earnings under the original accounting method for computing compensation awards.*

Generally, however they note that the percentage of the CEO's compensation attributable to the accounting change is small relative to their overall compensation package. On average, these results do not find a debt covenant or (significant) management compensation motivation for the change in depreciation method. For a given company, however, an analyst would be wise to check these factors whenever an income-increasing accounting change is implemented.

---

*Paul H. Healy, Sok-Hyon Kang, and Krishna Palepu, "The Effect of Accounting Procedure Changes on CEO's Cash Salary and Bonus Compensation," *Journal of Accounting and Economics*, 1987, pp. 7–34.

Estimating Relative Age and Useful Lives

Fixed asset data can be used to estimate the relative age of companies' property, plant, and equipment. The relative age as a percentage of depreciable ("useful") life is calculated as

$$\text{Average Age \%} = \frac{\text{Accumulated Depreciation}}{\text{Ending Gross Investment}}$$

As long as straight-line depreciation is used,[14] this is an accurate estimate of asset age as a percentage of depreciable life. Neither changes in asset mix (additions with longer or shorter lives than existing assets) nor the timing of purchases affect the calculation. The relative age is a useful measure of whether the firm's fixed asset base is old or new. Newer assets are likely to be more efficient; when relative age is high, the firm has not been adding to (or modernizing) its capital stock and may find it difficult to compete with firms that have more modern facilities. Remember, however, that this calculation is affected by the firm's accounting methods in the following areas:

- Depreciation lives
- Salvage values[15]

Another useful calculation is the average depreciable life of fixed assets:

$$\text{Average Depreciable Life} = \frac{\text{Ending Gross Investment}}{\text{Depreciation Expense}}$$

This calculation is only a rough approximation as it can be affected by changes in asset mix. During periods of rapid growth in fixed assets, the time (within the year) when assets are placed into service can also affect the ratio. Over longer time periods, however, this ratio is a useful measure of a firm's depreciation policy and can be used for comparisons with competitors.

Estimating the Age of Assets

We can also calculate the approximate age (in years) of a firm's fixed assets by comparing accumulated depreciation with depreciation expense:[16]

$$\text{Average Age} = \frac{\text{Accumulated Depreciation}}{\text{Depreciation Expense}}$$

As in the case of depreciable life, average age calculations may be distorted by changes in asset mix and by acquisitions. Nonetheless, these data are useful for comparison purposes and can suggest a useful line of questioning when meeting with management.

---

[14]The use of accelerated depreciation methods invalidates this analysis. However, since more than 90% of companies use straight-line depreciation, the method has general application.

[15]As noted earlier, depreciable lives and economic lives for reporting purposes are not equivalent. See the earlier reference to Most (1984).

[16]Average age can also be computed as (average age as a percentage of depreciable life) multiplied by depreciable life.

Average age data, either as a percentage of gross cost or in absolute terms, are useful for two reasons. First, older assets tend to be less efficient; inefficient or obsolete fixed assets may make the firm uncompetitive. Second, knowing past patterns of capital replacement helps the analyst estimate when major capital expenditures will be required. The financing implications of capital expenditure requirements may be significant. Furthermore, when forecasting capital expenditures, the data should be compared with benchmark data on the useful (economic) life of fixed assets for that industry.

EXHIBIT 8-8
Fixed Asset Comparison of Forest Products Industry

	Georgia-Pacific	Glatfelter	Mead	Union Camp	Westvaco
Average Age %					
1992	47.5%	40.6%	45.8%	42.0%	42.3%
1993	52.1	39.8	50.5	44.8	39.9
1994	54.9	54.9	50.4	46.4	42.0
Average Depreciable Life in Years					
1992	14.1	20.5	15.9	23.9	21.7
1993	14.9	19.6	16.1	23.8	23.7
1994	15.8	22.7	19.5	23.9	22.1
Average Age in Years					
1992	6.7	8.3	7.3	10.0	9.2
1993	7.8	7.8	8.1	10.7	9.5
1994	8.7	12.5	9.8	11.1	9.3

Note on Computations

As land and construction in progress are not depreciated, these amounts are excluded from gross investment when data are available.

Analysis of Data

Average Age: Trend is rising for all companies except Westvaco. The latter just completed a major capital spending program, lowering its average age. 1994 increase for Glatfelter is caused by impairment write-off.

Average Depreciable Life: Major differences among firms. Georgia-Pacific is low, possibly reflecting the acquisition of Great Northern Nekoosa in 1990 (see Case 14-1). The acquisition added a large amount of used property, with the depreciation balance reset to zero. The useful life of these assets should be lower than the useful life of new fixed assets, decreasing the average depreciable life of the firm's assets.

Note the increase in Mead's average depreciable life in 1994, resulting from the change in useful lives in that year. Union Camp had increased its estimated useful lives in 1991. The reason for Westvaco's high average life may be that it had always used longer lives, or it may be due to differences in asset mix. This question should be posed to management.

Average Age in Years: Georgia-Pacific is lowest, again probably due to acquisition. Westvaco is only firm without rising trend; recent heavy capital spending is probably responsible.

EXHIBIT 8-8 (continued)

WESTVACO
Analysis of Fixed Asset Disclosures by Property Class ($ in millions)

	1992	1993	1994
Machinery and Equipment			
Gross investment	$3,258	$3,785	$3,951
Accumulated depreciation	1,381	1,515	1,667
Net investment	1,877	2,270	2,284
Depreciation expense	155	166	186
Average age %	**42.4%**	**40.0%**	**42.2%**
Average depreciable life years	**21.0**	**22.8**	**21.2**
Average age years	**8.9**	**9.1**	**9.0**
Buildings			
Gross investment	$439.3	$505.6	$526.9
Accumulated depreciation	184.4	197.6	213.8
Net investment	254.9	308.0	313.1
Depreciation expense	14.9	15.9	17.7
Average age (%)	**42.0%**	**39.1%**	**40.6%**
Average depreciable life (years)	**29.5**	**31.8**	**29.8**
Average age (years)	**12.4**	**12.4**	**12.1**

Source: Georgia-Pacific, P.H. Glatfelter, Mead, Union Camp, and Westvaco, *1992–1994 Annual Reports.*

Example: Forest Products Industry Comparison.

Exhibit 8-8 contains average age and average depreciable life statistics for five companies in the forest products industry. Both the levels and trends differ. The exhibit also discusses possible explanations for these differences.

The second part of the exhibit shows the same statistics for Westvaco, broken down by property class. When data are available, analysis by property class is a useful means of gaining insight into the physical and accounting characteristics of a firm's fixed assets. Note the differences in characteristics between the property classes, and the information lost in the aggregation of the data. Although U.S. companies are no longer required to provide data by property class,[17] many non-U.S. companies do report on this basis. These disclosures are required, for example, by IAS 16, Property, Plant and Equipment (revised 1993), and GAAP in Sweden.

Whether this analysis is done for the total firm, or by property class, it is not an end in itself. Although differences between firms and firm trends can sometimes be explained by changes in accounting methods or by major transactions (such as acquisitions or the sale/retirement of assets), an important function of fixed assets analysis is to suggest questions that should be asked of management.

[17]See footnote 13.

IMPAIRMENT OF LONG-LIVED ASSETS

Fixed assets used in continuing operations are carried at acquisition cost less accumulated depreciation. The carrying amount of fixed assets may also be affected by changes in market conditions and technology. These changes may increase or decrease the fair value of fixed assets. Unlike many foreign countries (and the IASC), U.S. GAAP do not allow firms to recognize increases in value.

This section is concerned with the recognition, measurement, and disclosure problems associated with decreases in fair value, often called impairment, of long-lived assets. Impairment means that some portion or all of the carrying cost cannot be recovered through expected levels of operations. Due to unfavorable economic conditions, technological developments, or declines in market demand, firms may temporarily idle, continue to operate at a significantly reduced level, sell, or abandon impaired assets. These economic conditions may also call for fewer employees or those with different skills.

Financial Reporting of Impaired Assets

Impairments are sometimes reported as part of "restructuring" provisions. Such provisions (see Chapter 2 for further discussion) contain elements that fall into two general categories. Some elements, including impairment write-downs, write off past cash flows.[18] Others reflect a major restructuring of the firm and may include current and expected future cash outflows for such items as employee severance and lease payments. Restructuring provisions must, therefore, be separated into impairment (noncash write-downs of past cash outflows) and those with cash flow implications.

With respect to impairments, there is a distinction between assets the firm has decided to dispose of and those it intends to keep and operate, albeit at reduced levels. The disposition decision severs the link between those assets and continuing operations, since the assets are no longer expected to contribute to the ongoing operations of the firm. APB 30, Reporting Results of Operations (1973), governs the financial reporting of the disposal or sale of a business segment; a related AICPA Interpretation extends these rules to the disposition or sale of portions of a segment. The results of operations, net asset values, and gain or loss on sale or disposition of these assets are shown separately.[19]

Impaired assets retained by the firm that are expected to contribute to operations and cash flows at reduced levels were not covered by APB 30. The absence of both reporting guidelines and reliable market prices limited the recognition and disclosure of impairments of these long-lived assets; impairment provisions were subject to enormous management discretion.

SFAS 121 (1995), Accounting for the Impairment of Long-Lived Assets and for Long-Lived Assets to Be Disposed of, established standards for the recognition and measurement of impairments.

The standard requires the recognition of impairment when there is evidence that the carrying amount of an asset or a group of assets can no longer be recovered. Lack of recoverability may be signaled by one or more of the following indicators:

---

[18]However, they may signal departure from a business segment or the need for significant capital expenditures for investments in new and improved technologies.

[19]See Chapter 2 for a discussion of these reporting requirements.

- A significant decrease in the market value, physical change, or use of the assets
- Adverse changes in the legal or business climate
- Significant cost overruns
- Current period operating or cash flow losses combined with a history of operating or cash flow losses and a forecast of a significant decline in the long-term profitability of the asset

SFAS 121 provides a two-step process. First is the recoverability test: Impairment must be recognized when the carrying value of the assets exceeds the *undiscounted* expected future cash flows from their use and disposal. The second stage is loss measurement: the excess of the carrying amount over the fair value of the assets. When fair value cannot be determined, the *discounted* present value of future cash flows (discounted at the firm's incremental borrowing rate) must be used.[20]

The recoverability test and loss measurement are based on assets grouped at the lowest level for which cash flows can be identified independently of cash flows of other asset groups. The impairment loss is reported pretax as a component of income from continuing operations.

The standard prohibits restoration of previous impairments. It requires disclosure of the amount of the loss, segments affected, events and circumstances surrounding the impairment, and how fair value was determined.

SFAS 121 does not require firms to disclose cash flows and discount rates used to measure impairment. Firms do not have to disclose impaired assets (even though one or more impairment indicators are present) as long as their gross *undiscounted* cash flows exceed their carrying amount (even when the discounted cash flows are below the carrying amount). Thus, there is no disclosure of "early warning" signals.

However, the need to evaluate recoverability periodically may result in the review of depreciation methods and estimates. Reported changes in these methods and estimates may precede a firm's reluctant and delayed reporting of asset impairment. It is unclear whether, in practice, the new standard will reduce management discretion over the amount and timing of impairment announcements. In 1996 the FASB began a limited-scope project to consider application of provisions of SFAS 121 to goodwill impairment under APB 17 and to develop a single consistent model for all assets to be disposed of.

Example: P. H. Glatfelter. Exhibit 8-9 provides an example of impairment recognition and disclosure. Glatfelter, a paper manufacturer, reported asset impairments (included in unusual items) in both 1993 and 1994. Although SFAS 121 was not yet effective, the 1994 impairment appears to meet the requirements of that standard. Excerpts from the 1994 income statement and footnotes are reproduced in Exhibit 8-9.

The 1993 "Rightsizing and Restructuring" provision (see Note 3 in Exhibit 8-9) of $16,363,000 includes early retirement and termination costs. The unusual item

---

[20]When the recoverability test is applied to assets acquired in purchase method business combinations, the standard requires the elimination of goodwill before recording write-downs of related impaired tangible and identifiable intangible assets. When only some of the acquired assets are subject to the recoverability test, goodwill must be allocated to the affected assets on a pro rata basis using the relative fair values of all assets acquired.

EXHIBIT 8-9. P. H. GLATFELTER COMPANY AND SUBSIDIARIES
Asset Impairment

A. Consolidated Statement of Income ($ in thousands)

Years ended December 31	1992	1993	1994
Net sales	$540,057	$473,509	$ 478,302
Other income	7,782	8,496	9,201
Total	$547,839	$482,005	$ 487,503
Costs and expenses	457,078	433,393	471,328
Unusual items (Notes 2 and 3)		13,229	208,949
Total costs and expenses	457,708	446,622	680,277
Income (loss) before income taxes and accounting changes	$ 90,761	$ 35,383	$(192,774)
Income tax provision	32,217	14,974	(74,523)
Net income (loss)	$ 56,544	$ 20,409	$(118,251)

B. Balance Sheet Highlights ($ in thousands)

Years Ended December 31	1993	1994
Plant, equipment, and timberlands	$621,113	$460,420
Total assets	842,087	650,810
Deferred income tax liabilities	130,509	60,313
Stockholders' equity	$441,400	$295,734

C. Selected Footnotes

1. Summary of Significant Accounting Policies

(k) Asset Impairment

Assets are reviewed for impairment on an annual basis in conjunction with the preparation of the annual budget or when a specific event indicates that the carrying value of an asset may not be recoverable. Recoverability is assessed based on estimates of future cash flows expected to result from the use and eventual disposition of the asset. If the sum of expected undiscounted cash flows is less than the carrying value of the asset, an impairment loss is recognized. The impairment loss is measured as the amount by which the carrying amount of the asset exceeds its fair value.

2. Writedown of Impaired Assets (Unusual Items)

During the fourth quarter of 1994, the Company recognized a noncash, pre-tax writedown of impaired assets of $208,949,000. Of this amount, $198,189,000 relates to the pretax writedown of the Company's Ecusta Division to its fair value primarily due to writedowns related to property, plant and equipment of $189,441,000 and inventory of $6,406,000.

During 1994, the Company closely monitored the Ecusta Division and continued its efforts to maximize utilization of the Ecusta Division's assets by attempting to direct sales volume to its more profitable grades and by controlling costs. Despite these efforts, the Ecusta Division experienced a 1994 operating loss of $4,921,000 before an unfavorable LIFO inventory charge, unusual items, interest expense and taxes.

Based on 1994 Ecusta Division operating results, and indications that market conditions were unlikely to improve significantly in the near future, the Company determined that its efforts to return the Ecusta Division to an acceptable level of profitability would not be successful. As a result, the Company decided to evaluate other strategic alternatives. As part of its consider-

EXHIBIT 8-9. (*continued*)

ation of such alternatives, the Company solicited offers to buy the Ecusta Division during the fourth quarter of 1994. In January 1995, the Company rejected all offers which it received to buy the Ecusta Division because the offers were less than the Company's valuation of the net assets.

The Company concluded that asset impairment recognition was required as the revised projected undiscounted future cash flows of the Ecusta Division were less than its carrying value. In developing the revised projections, the Company considered 1994 actual results and the Company's conclusions concerning future market conditions and the resulting impact on prices. To determine the fair value of the Ecusta Division net assets, the Company projected the present value of future cash flows using a 13% discount rate. The resulting fair value, which exceeded the offers received, was used to determine the amount of the writedown. The Company plans to continue to operate the Ecusta Division and enhance its profitability and cash generation through additional cost reduction efforts.

During the fourth quarter of 1994, the Company also identified impaired property and equipment at its Spring Grove, Pennsylvania and Neenah, Wisconsin mills, resulting in a pretax charge of $10,760,000. This writedown primarily relates to solid waste disposal assets, specifically, a sludge combustor at the Neenah mill and an unused landfill at the Spring Grove mill. Both of these assets would require significant additional expenditures to receive the required operating permits from the appropriate environmental agencies. During the fourth quarter of 1994, the Company identified more economical means, acceptable to such agencies, by which to dispose of its solid waste at these locations and concluded that the significant additional expenditures necessary to make the assets operational were not prudent, resulting in unusable assets.

The aggregate after tax impact of these charges is $127,981,000 or $2.89 per common share.

3. Rightsizing and Restructuring (Unusual Items)

During 1993, the Company incurred net unusual charges of $13,229,000, including rightsizing and restructuring costs of $16,363,000, partially offset by a gain of $1,492,000 on the disposal of its Ecusta Division's airplane and a credit of $1,642,000 resulting from the updating of estimates relating to SFAS No. 106, subsequent to its adoption on January 1, 1993. The charges primarily include provisions for the accelerated pension, stock awards and postretirement benefit costs of early retirements and other terminations in the second quarter of 1993 and other one-time net costs relating to the rightsizing and restructuring of the Company's operations. The rightsizing and restructuring, which was completed during 1993, resulted in the early retirement of 156 employees and a reduction in annual salaries, wages and benefits of approximately $7,500,000. The after tax impact of these charges was $8,430,000 or $.19 per common share.

Source: P. H. Glatfelter Co., *1992–1994 Annual Reports.*

reported on the income statement is $13,229,000, after deducting a gain of $1,492,000 on the sale of assets and a credit of $1,642,000 due to a change in the accounting estimate. No other breakdown is provided. The reported after-tax cost of $8,430,000 does not separate the tax effects of different components of the charges. It appears that all the "rightsizing and restructuring" costs required cash outflows, although that is not clearly stated.[21]

---

[21]Note 3 discloses the number of employees taking early retirement and specifies the reduction in annual salaries and benefits due to the 1993 charge. This additional information is an example of the improved disclosure of restructuring discussed in Chapter 2.

Disclosures relating to the 1994 write-down (see Note 2 in Exhibit 8-9) are much more detailed and informative. The firm describes the conditions leading to the recognition of impairment, and the methodology followed (projected cash flows discounted at 13%).[22] The affected segments and types of impaired assets are identified as is the noncash nature of the write-down. $198 million of the total write-down of $208 million involved assets of the Ecusta Division, which the firm had attempted to sell.

However, note that the firm's estimate of fair value, used to measure the write-down of Ecusta assets, exceeded the offers received. Glatfelter decided to retain the division and to improve profitability and cash flows through further cost reductions. The assets of the division remain overstated to the extent the new carrying amount exceeds offers received. Whether management can justify this carrying amount by improving profitability remains to be seen.

Financial Statement Impact of Impairments

Impairment write-downs of long-lived assets have pervasive and significant effects on financial statements and financial ratios. We examine these effects using the data in Exhibit 8-9.

The principal balance sheet impacts of the write-downs were reductions in Glatfelter's:

- Carrying value of plant, equipment, and timberland
- Deferred tax liabilities
- Stockholders' equity

The lower level of fixed assets is a direct consequence of the impairment write-down. As a result, Glatfelter's fixed asset and total asset turnover increases, affecting any comparison with firms that have not recognized impairments.

The reduction in deferred tax liabilities reflects the fact that the impairment loss is not recognized for tax purposes until the property is disposed of. However, because Glatfelter (like virtually all firms) depreciates its fixed assets more quickly for tax purposes than for financial reporting, the impairment has the effect of reducing the difference between the tax basis and reporting basis of these assets. Thus, previously established deferred tax liabilities are reduced (see Chapter 9, problem 7).

The reduction in equity is the net effect of the impairment provision. This reduction increases Glatfelter's debt-to-equity ratio and decreases reported book value per share. The price-to-book value ratio is increased.

Glatfelter's future financial statements will also be affected by the write-down. 1995 depreciation expense declined 24% as higher depreciation from other properties was more than offset by the lower depreciation of Ecusta; reported earnings are higher than if no impairment were recognized. With higher earnings and lower assets and equity, return ratios (ROA and ROE) also increase.

The ratios used to evaluate fixed assets and depreciation policy earlier in this chapter are also distorted by the impairment write-down. For example, the average age of Glatfelter's fixed assets increased from about 8 years (1992 to 1993) to 12.5

---

[22]Note 1(k) describes Glatfelter's accounting policies for impairments. The firm follows procedures recommended in SFAS No. 121. Note that the firm annually reviews assets for impairment as part of its budgeting process and when specific events indicate uncertain recoverability.

years in 1994 despite substantial new investment in 1994. In comparison with other firms in Exhibit 8-9, Glatfelter's fixed assets appear older than they really are.

Effect of SFAS 121 on Analysis of Impairment

The lack of reporting guidelines for impairments prior to SFAS 121 resulted in widely divergent timing, measurement, and reporting practices. Fried et al. (FSS) (1989) and two Financial Executives Institute surveys[23] found that a majority of companies used net realizable values (NRV) to measure impairments. However, NRV meant different things to different firms, and the definition used was rarely disclosed.[24] The use of undiscounted cash flows under SFAS 121 reduces the probability of recognition of impairments and overstates asset values because of the failure to recognize the time value of money.

It is difficult to forecast impairment write-downs because managements have so much discretion as to timing. Substandard profitability, especially when persistent, is probably the surest sign of impaired assets. LIFO liquidations and changes in depreciation methods, estimated useful lives, and salvage values provide useful but very imprecise signals. Segment data (see Chapter 13) can help the analyst spot underperforming operations.

The cash flow and tax implications of write-offs are also unclear in some cases. Generally, impairments recognized for financial reporting are not deductible for tax purposes until the affected assets are disposed of. Recognition of the impairment, therefore, leads to a deferred tax asset (a probable future tax benefit), not a current refund. Beneficial cash flow impacts may occur only in the future, when tax deductions are realized.[25] Close attention to the income tax footnote (see Chapter 9) should be helpful, but a complete understanding may require posing questions to management.

Timely recognition of impairments may correct understated past depreciation or permit recognition of the effect of changes in markets or technology on operating assets. Higher frequency of impairment announcements and the absence of reporting guidelines resulted in diverse accounting practices that were not comparable across companies and inconsistently applied within firms over time. The FASB recognized this problem when it placed asset impairment on its agenda. SFAS 121, and SEC efforts to improve disclosures regarding "restructuring" provisions, have improved disclosure.

Empirical Findings

The analysis of the impact of write-offs on companies has been confounded by the existence of an unusually strong set of beliefs about the nature and effects of impairment announcements. Articles in the financial and popular press often talk about the "big bath"—a tendency to take large write-offs during adverse times and of "house cleaning"—large write-offs assumed to accompany changes in senior management. Consequently, write-off announcements often are viewed as a signal that the worst is over, to be followed by an upturn in the firm's fortunes.

---

[23]Financial Executives Institute, Committee on Corporate Reporting, "Survey on Unusual Charges," 1986 and 1991.

[24]The problem is compounded by SFAC 5, in which NRV is defined as a short-term, gross, undiscounted cash flow.

[25]See the discussion of Glatfelter in the previous section.

Elliott and Shaw (1988), Fried et al. (FSS, 1989, 1990), Lindhal and Ricks (1990), and Strong and Meyer (1987) all examined the write-off phenomenon. These studies document a number of recurring characteristics of write-offs. Many of these findings are not consistent with the big bath hypothesis.

1. Studies found an increasing frequency in the number and dollar amount of write-downs. FSS reported that write-offs increased from $1 billion (average write-off of $28 million per company) in 1980 to $24 billion ($117 million per company) before taxes in 1986.[26]

2. The majority of write-offs (approximately 60%) are announced in the fourth quarter. Given the detailed review (both by management and auditors) during preparation of the annual report, it is likely that the fourth quarter will always contain the largest number of write-offs. However, this finding also reflected fundamental problems with financial reporting for impairments, subjectivity in timing of announcements, and measurement uncertainty.

3. Write-offs are usually preceded by poor financial as well as stockmarket performance. Elliott and Shaw (1988) showed that, when compared to industry medians, firms with write-offs had lower earnings, ROA, and ROE and had higher debt-to-equity ratios[27] as well as the three-year period preceding the write-off. FSS (1989), using a control group of firms matched by industry and size, found similar results. Strong and Meyer (1987), however, reported that although the write-off firms were not the best performers in their industry, they were not the worst either, but tended to cluster in the middle quintiles.

4. Consistent with the foregoing, the stockmarket performance of write-off firms tends to be poorer than the control group. Elliott and Shaw found that for three years prior to the write-off, the sample companies had significantly worse returns than the industry. Similar results occur around the time of the write-off itself and for up to 18 months following the write-off. Elliott and Shaw reported that the size of the write-off was directly related to the degree of negative return experienced around the time of the write-off; the larger the write-off, the more negative the reaction.

   In general, these results contradict the popular belief that write-offs result in positive market reaction. Figure 8-1 from FSS (1989) provides some insight into this conclusion. As the period studied was a "bull market," firms that took write-offs still had positive returns. However, they underperformed the control group. Both the sample group (firms with impairments) and the control group underperformed the market as a whole.

   On the other hand, Lindhal and Ricks (1990) indicate that although, in general, market reaction to write-offs was negative, the results depend on whether the event is a write-down or a restructuring. For the latter type of event, they report positive market reaction.

---

[26]The most recent survey of impairments was taken by the Financial Executives Institute (FEI) in 1991. Questionnaires were sent to 523 firms that had recently announced write-offs, updating FEI's 1986 survey of 110 announcers. In 1991 (1986), 109 (55) firms responded with information on write-downs. Unfortunately, it is not possible to determine the numbers or dollar amounts of write-downs announced by either all firms in the sample or survey respondents.

[27]These conditions hold even without taking the write-off into consideration.

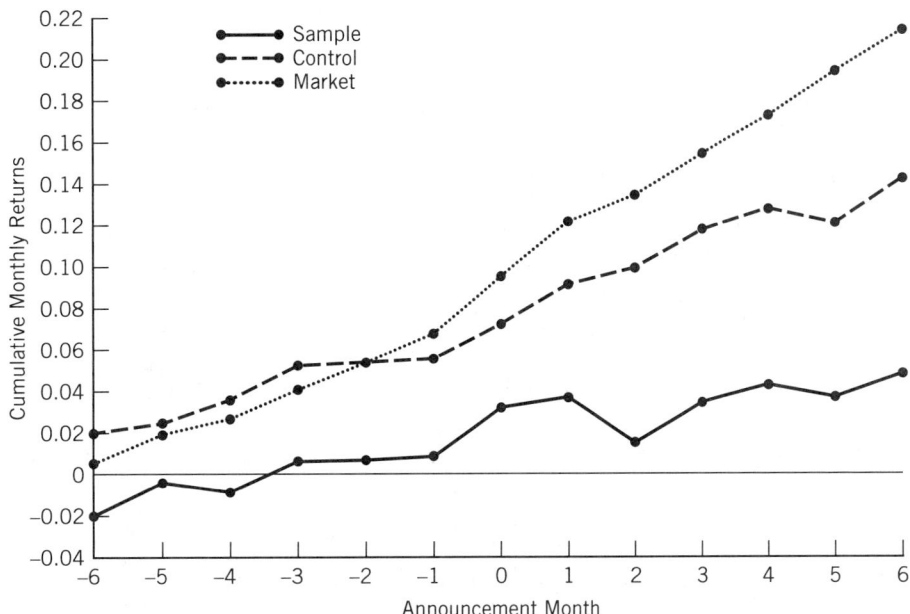

FIGURE 8-1 Cumulative monthly returns of write-off sample, control group, and market.

Source: Dov Fried, Michael Schiff, and Ashwinpaul Sondhi, *Impairments and Writeoffs of Long-Lived Assets* (Montvale, NJ: National Association of Accountants, 1989), Figure 6-9, p. 101.

Bartov et al. (1996) similarly partitioned their write-off sample into:

- *A write-down category* comprising purely accounting decisions to reduce the carrying value of assets with no (apparent) change in operations
- *An operating decision category* that consists of decisions to modify operations (e.g., sell assets, employee layoffs, plant closings)

Their results were similar to those of Lindhal and Ricks in the four-day period surrounding the write-off announcement. However, looking at a longer horizon, they found that stockmarket performance was poor in the three-year period around the write-off date for both categories of write-offs. Results, however, were far worse for the write-down category. In the two-year period preceding the write-off, the cumulative abnormal return was −24 and −34% for the operating decision and write-down categories, respectively. In the year following the write-off, the declines were −6 and −12%, respectively.

5. Economy- and industrywide factors seem to dominate firm-specific factors as impairment signals. FSS (1989) reported that the highest proportion of write-offs were taken in the oil and gas, chemicals, electronics, iron and steel, and machinery industries. These industries suffered from poor operating conditions in the early 1980s. Similarly, as Figure 8-1 shows, FSS's control group (which was matched by industry) consistently underperformed the market as a whole.

6. Problems leading to write-offs are rarely short-lived and generally persist after the write-off. This is confirmed by the poor market reaction persisting up to 18 months following the write-off. In addition, write-offs tend not to be one-

time affairs. FSS reported that firms generally take multiple write-offs. They found that 45% of the companies that take a write-off announce a subsequent one the next year, over 61% do so within two years, and 73% report another write-off within three years.[28] In effect, firms "warehouse" bad news and report it through multiple write-offs. Furthermore, FSS found that subsequent write-offs tend to be larger than previous ones.[29]

The prevalence of multiple write-offs and their increasing size is inconsistent with big bath behavior, usually associated with a "once and for all" write-off. In practice, once a firm has taken a write-off, there is high probability of a second, larger write-off. Given the significance and frequency of impairments, it is unfortunate that indicators of initial write-offs are hard to find. FSS (1989) found that LIFO liquidations and poor financial condition were the most reliable indicators of potential write-offs. Similar results appear in other studies. Better disclosure in financial statements (or the Management Discussion and Analysis) of problems with particular segments would make it easier to predict write-offs.

LIABILITIES FOR CLOSURE AND ENVIRONMENTAL COSTS

Governments often require that owners of operating assets remedy the environmental damage caused by operating those assets or restore land to its preexisting condition. Common examples include:

- Restoration of strip mines after mining is completed
- Removal of toxic wastes caused by production
- Decontamination of site when a nuclear power plant is decommissioned

The current period costs of these activities are normally expensed except that capital expenditures may be capitalized.[30] As no standards have existed for the accrual of future expenditures, practice has been inconsistent with respect to:

1. Whether (or when) accrual takes place
2. Whether accruals increase the carrying amount of the related asset (and whether they must be depreciated)
3. Whether accruals are included in depreciation expense
4. Measurement of the liability (whether or not discounted, and at what rate)
5. Disclosure

Because of inconsistent accounting practice, in February 1996 the FASB issued an exposure draft, Accounting for Certain Liabilities Relating to Closure or Removal of Long-Lived Assets. A final standard is expected before the end of 1997. Box 8-3 is a summary of that exposure draft.

---

[28]Dov Fried, Michael Schiff, and Ashwinpaul Sondhi, "Big Bath or Intermittent Showers? Another Look at Write-offs," working paper, 1990, p. 12.

[29]This result could also explain why FSS (1989) found that the market reaction to the second write-offs tended to be more adverse than for the original write-offs.

[30]For an example, see the breakdown of Mead's capital expenditures in Exhibit 8A-2.

BOX 8-3
FASB Exposure Draft: Accounting for Certain Liabilities Related to Closure or Removal of Long-Lived Assets

The proposed standard would require accrual of liabilities for legal and constructive* obligations stemming from dismantlement, removal, site reclamation, decontamination, and similar activities incurred at any time in the operating life of long-lived assets.

Such liabilities would be reported as an increase in the carrying amount of the underlying long-lived asset and depreciated over the remaining useful life of the asset.

The liability would be measured at the present value of the estimated future cash flows required to settle those obligations. Factors to be considered in the estimation of cash flows include inflation, expected efficiencies from experience with similar activities, unforeseeable circumstances related to projects of similar scope and complexity, direct internal costs (including employee costs), and technological advances expected to be operational in the near term. The estimated cash flows would be discounted at the risk-free rate in effect when the liability is incurred. This discount rate would not be subsequently adjusted.

Changes in estimated liabilities due to changes in assumptions and changes in legal requirements would be accounted for as changes in the estimate of the liability. Depreciation would be revised prospectively over the remaining useful life. Changes in the present value of the liability due to the passage of time would be treated as period costs.

Compliance with assurance provisions (through surety bonds, prepayment, insurance policies, letters of credit, trust funds, or dedicated assets) would not be considered sufficient to reduce or defease the carrying amount of the liability. The liability could not be offset using dedicated assets or securities unless the arrangement satisfies the requirements of FASB Interpretation 39, Offsetting of Amounts Related to Certain Contracts. However, in some cases, companies have offset the liabilities for reclamation activities against refunds expected from state and local governments (see Exhibit 8-10 for an example).

Disclosure requirements include:

1. Description of the long-lived assets and the obligation for closure or removal
2. The liability for closure or removal recognized
3. All assumptions critical to the estimation of the liability
4. The funding policy, if any
5. Income statement impact of recognized costs
6. The effects of changes in the estimated future costs of closure or removal activities

The standard is expected to be effective for financial statements issued for fiscal years beginning after December 15, 1997 (i.e., calendar year 1998), but earlier application is encouraged.

The cumulative effect of initial adoption of the standard would be reported as a change in accounting principle, pursuant to APB 20 (see Chapter 1).

---

*A constructive obligation is one the entity has little or no discretion to avoid.

Exhibit 8-10, from Mobil's annual report, is a good example of current practice. The December 31, 1995 total accrual of $1,054 million equals 5.9% of stockholders' equity. Note that the accrual is undiscounted and offset by expected recoveries from state funds. Although the disclosures indicate the general nature of Mobil's obligations, they are typically vague.

EXHIBIT 8-10. MOBIL
Restoration, Removal, and Environmental Liabilities

---

1. Major Accounting Policies

Restoration, Removal and Environmental Liabilities

The estimated costs of restoration and removal of major producing facilities are accrued on a unit-of-production basis over the life of the property. The estimated future costs for known environmental remediation requirements are accrued when it is probable that a liability has been incurred and the amount of remediation costs can be reasonably estimated. These amounts are the undiscounted, future estimated costs under existing regulatory requirements and using existing technology.

18. Restoration, Removal and Environmental Liabilities

Exploration and producing properties must generally be restored to their original condition when the oil or gas reserves are depleted and/or operations cease. At December 31, 1994 and 1995, $790 million and $835 million, respectively, had been accrued for restoration and removal costs, mainly related to offshore producing facilities.

Mobil accrues for its best estimate of the future costs associated with known environmental remediation requirements at its service stations, marketing terminals, refineries and plants, and at certain Superfund sites. At December 31, 1994 and 1995, the accumulated reserve for environmental remediation costs was $551 million and $519 million, respectively. Of these amounts, $150 million and $100 million were included in current accrued liabilities in the Consolidated Balance Sheet. Accrued remediation costs for the company's U.S. service stations reflect amounts recoverable from certain states under existing programs established to assist companies in clean-up efforts. The expected recoverable costs were $68 million and $47 million at December 31, 1994 and 1995, respectively. Amounts accrued with respect to Superfund waste disposal sites, which are not material, are based on the company's best estimate of its portion of the costs of remediating such sites.

Source: Mobil, 1995 Annual Report.

IAS 16 allows firms to recognize the liability for these costs by *either:*

· Increasing depreciation charges, or
· Recording a separate expense

SUMMARY

The capitalization decision is only the start of the accounting cycle for long-lived assets. Depreciation expense depends on the choice of accounting method and asset life and salvage value assumptions. Thus, the same asset can produce different amounts of depreciation expense, limiting the comparability of reported income. Economic depreciation may be entirely different from accounting depreciation.

Economic changes often result in asset lives that differ from those anticipated by accounting conventions. In such cases asset impairment may require accounting recognition. Although SFAS 121 provides standards for impairment write-downs in the United States, management retains considerable discretion over their timing and amounts. The accrual (if any) for future environmental costs related to long-lived assets is another area where practice is highly inconsistent.

CASE 8-1

Analysis of Fixed Assets in the Swedish Forest Products Industry

Exhibit 8C-1 contains selected data from the financial statements of three major Swedish forest products companies. SCA, MoDo, and STORA depreciate fixed assets on the basis of historical costs and over their estimated useful economic lives. STORA also reports that book depreciation normally corresponds to the maximum allowed for tax purposes. MoDo specifically mentions its use of the straight-line method.

EXHIBIT 8C-1
Fixed Asset Comparison of Forest Products Industry in Sweden

Fixed Asset Disclosures by Property Class

1. SCA (Amounts in SEK millions)

Machinery & Equipment	1992	1993	1994
Gross Investment	SEK 22,151	SEK 23,438	SEK 24,920
Accumulated Depreciation	9,971	11,199	12,559
Net Investment	12,180	12,239	12,361
Depreciation Expense	1,453	1,498	1,569

Buildings	1992	1993	1994
Gross Investment	SEK 5,492	SEK 5,570	SEK 5,381
Accumulated Depreciation	1,608	1,768	1,865
Net Investment	3,884	3,802	3,516
Depreciation Expense	216	220	207

2. STORA (Amounts in SEK millions)

Machinery & Equipment	1992	1993	1994
Gross Investment	SEK 44,587	SEK 49,043	SEK 46,995
Accumulated Depreciation	22,638	26,263	25,997
Net Investment	21,949	22,780	20,998
Depreciation Expense	2,611	2,884	2,749

Buildings	1992	1993	1994
Gross Investment	SEK 10,753	SEK 11,304	SEK 10,412
Accumulated Depreciation	4,484	5,043	4,987
Net Investment	6,269	6,261	5,425
Depreciation Expense	414	440	394

3. MoDo (Amounts in SEK millions)

Machinery & Equipment	1992	1993	1994
Gross Investment	SEK 21,708	SEK 21,761	SEK 22,017
Accumulated Depreciation	8,771	10,503	11,206
Net Investment	12,937	11,258	10,811
Depreciation Expense	982	1,078	1,033

EXHIBIT 8C-1 (*continued*)

Fixed Asset Disclosures by Property Class

Buildings	1992	1993	1994
Gross Investment	SEK 3,494	SEK 3,475	SEK 3,680
Accumulated Depreciation	1,643	1,775	2,013
Net Investment	1,851	1,700	1,667
Depreciation Expense	126	134	137

1. Use Exhibit 8C-1 to compute the following measures for all three firms:
   * Average Age %
   * Average Depreciable Life in Years
   * Average Age in Years
2. Discuss what the ratios computed in question 1 suggest regarding the
   * adequacy of reported depreciation expense
   * expected capital expenditures
   of the three Swedish firms.
3. Compare your answers to question 1 with the data for U.S. firms in Exhibit 8-8. Discuss any differences between the firms from each country as a group as well as differences within each group.
4. **(i)** Discuss the limitations of these comparisons.
   (ii) Describe the additional data required to increase the validity of the conclusions obtained from these comparisons.

Chapter 8

Problems

1. [Depreciation methods; 1996 CFA adapted] A firm pays $20,000 for equipment with an economic life of five years and estimated salvage value of $2,000. Compute depreciation expense for the first and fifth years under *each* of the following methods:
   (i) Straight-line
   (ii) 150% declining-balance
   (iii) Sum-of-years' digits

2. [Effect of depreciation methods; 1996 CFA adapted] Compare the straight-line method of depreciation with accelerated methods with respect to their impact on:
   (i) Trend of depreciation expense
   (ii) Trend of net income
   (iii) Reported return on equity and return on assets
   (iv) Reported cash flows

3. [Effect of depreciation methods] The Jonathan Corp. acquires a machine with an original cost of $9,000 on January 1, 19X3. The machine has a five-year life and

estimated salvage value of $1,000. Compute depreciation for 19X3 and 19X4 under each of the following methods:

  (i) Sum-of-years' digits

  (ii) Double-declining-balance

  (iii) Straight-line

4. [Effect of useful life and salvage value assumptions on depreciation] The Juliet Company acquires a machine with an original cost of $9,000 on January 1, 19X3. Juliet uses the straight-line method of computing depreciation. Compute depreciation expense for 19X3 under the following assumptions:

  (i) Eight-year life, $1,800 salvage value

  (ii) Nine-year life, $1,800 salvage value

  (iii) Eight-year life, $1,080 salvage value

  (iv) Nine-year life, $1,080 salvage value

5. [Depreciation methods and cash flows, courtesy of Professor Stephen Ryan] The Capital Company considers investing in either of two assets. Cash flows of these assets are:

Year	Asset A	Asset B
1	$36	$26
2	23	24
3	11	22

  A. At an interest rate of 10%, how much should Capital be willing to pay for each asset?

  B. Assuming that the amount calculated in part A is paid for each asset, calculate the depreciation schedule for each asset that results in a constant rate of return.

  C. What type of historical cost depreciation is equal to present value depreciation for asset A? asset B?

6. [Change in depreciation method] Exhibit 8P-1 contains the property, plant, and equipment footnote from the *1991 Annual Report* of Cummins Engine. The following data are taken from the income statements of Cummins Engine for years ended December 31, 1989 to 1991 ($ in millions):

	1989	1990	1991
Net sales	$3,520	$3,462	$3,406
Earnings (loss) before extraordinary credit and cumulative effect of accounting change	(6)	(165)	(66)
Extraordinary credit (debt repurchase)	—	27	—
Cumulative effect of accounting changes*	—	—	52
Net earnings (loss)	$ (6)	$(138)	$ (14)
Pro forma net earnings (loss) assuming the accounting changes had been applied retroactively	$ 3	$(124)	$ (66)

*Effect of capitalization of overhead in inventory	$25
Effect of change in method of depreciation	27
Total cumulative effect of accounting changes	$52

EXHIBIT 8P-1. CUMMINS ENGINE

Property, Plant, and Equipment

Property, plant, and equipment are recorded at cost. Effective January 1, 1991, the company changed its method of depreciation for substantially all engine production equipment from straight-line to a modified units-of-production method, which is based upon units produced subject to a minimum level. The company believes that modified units-of-production is preferable to the method previously used because the new method recognizes that depreciation of this equipment is related substantially to both physical wear and the passage of time. This method, therefore, more accurately matches costs and revenues. The change in accounting increased results of operations $18.6 million ($1.26 per share) in 1991, exclusive of the cumulative effect of $26.5 million. Depreciation of all other equipment is computed using the straight-line method for financial reporting purposes. The estimated service lives to compute depreciation range from 20 to 40 years for buildings and 3 to 20 years for machinery, equipment and fixtures. Maintenance and repair costs are charged to earnings as incurred.

Source: Cummins Engine, *1991 Annual Report.*

A. Compute Cummins' net earnings for 1991, assuming that the change in depreciation method had not taken place.

B. The change in depreciation method increased Cummins' net earnings for all three years. What can you infer from these increases about the level of production over the period 1989 to 1991?

C. Discuss the effect of the change in depreciation method on the components of Cummins' 1991 cash flow.

D. Discuss the likely effect of the change in depreciation method on the variability of Cummins' net income in future years. State your assumptions.

7. [Change in depreciation method] The *1989 Annual Report* of Rohm and Haas, a chemical company, contains the following footnotes:

> Land, buildings and equipment are carried at cost. Assets are depreciated over their estimated useful lives. Effective January 1, 1989, the company changed its method of depreciation for newly acquired buildings and equipment to the straight-line method. Buildings and equipment acquired before that date continue to be depreciated principally by accelerated methods. Maintenance and repairs are charged to earnings; replacements and betterments are capitalized.
>
> The change had no cumulative effect on prior years' earnings but did increase net earnings by $9 million, or $.14 per share in 1989.
>
> At December 31, 1989, the gross book values of assets depreciated by accelerated methods totaled $1,449 million and assets depreciated by the straight-line method totaled $682 million.

A. Explain why there was no cumulative effect for the change in depreciation method.

B. Discuss the effect of the change in depreciation method on the trend of future depreciation expense and net income.

8. [Analysis of fixed assets] Exhibit 8P-2 reproduces data from the financial statements of Atlas Copco, a multinational manufacturer based in Sweden.

EXHIBIT 8P-2. ATLAS COPCO
Fixed Asset Disclosures (Data in SEK millions)

Years Ended	12/31/91	12/31/92	12/31/93	12/31/94
Buildings				
Gross	SEK 1,942	SEK 2,320	SEK 2,551	SEK 2,544
Accumulated depreciation	525	715	865	921
Net	1,417	1,605	1,686	1,623
Depreciation expense	SEK 68	SEK 80	SEK 92	SEK 120
Machinery				
Gross	SEK 3,337	SEK 4,513	SEK 5,130	SEK 5,019
Accumulated depreciation	1,830	2,750	3,326	3,385
Net	1,507	1,763	1,804	1,634
Depreciation expense	SEK 348	SEK 381	SEK 479	SEK 491

Source: Atlas Copco, *1991–1994 Annual Reports.*

A. Use the data provided to estimate the following:

 (i) Relative age

 (ii) Average depreciable life

 (iii) Average age

of the company's buildings and machinery.

B. Briefly discuss how you would use this information when analyzing the company.

9. [Impairment] Mobil's *1995 Annual Report* contains the following disclosure:

> In fourth quarter 1995, Mobil adopted SFAS 121, Accounting for the Impairment of Long-Lived Assets and for Long-Lived Assets to Be Disposed of, resulting in a before-tax, $774 million noncash charge to "Depreciation, depletion and amortization" on the Consolidated Statement of Income ($487 million after tax). The charge relates to impairment of upstream producing properties, primarily in the U.S. and Canada.
>
> FAS 121 requires that long-lived assets with book values that cannot be recovered by estimated undiscounted future cash flows be written down to fair value. The fair value of the impaired assets was determined by calculating the net present value of future cash flows; previously, the Company's policy was to write down to breakeven significant properties determined to be permanently impaired.

1995 pretax income for Mobil was $2,376 million.

A. Discuss the cash flow consequences of the impairment charge.

B. Discuss the impact of the impairment charge on the comparison of 1995 income with reported:

 (i) 1994 income

 (ii) 1996 income

EXHIBIT 8P-3. CATERPILLAR TRACTOR
Selected Financial Data ($ in millions)

Year	1989	1990	1991	1992	1993	1994	1995
Depreciation expense	n/a	$ 488	$ 548	$ 591	$ 598	$ 588	$ 580
Capital expenditures	$ 984	926	650	513	415	498	460
Gross property	7,114	7,585	7,790	7,842	7,965	8,230	8,303
Accumulated depreciation	3,609	3,599	3,741	3,888	4,138	4,454	4,659
Net property	$3,505	$3,986	$4,049	$3,954	$3,827	$3,776	$3,644

Source: Caterpillar Tractor, *1989–1995 Annual Reports.*

C. Discuss the impact of the charge on future:

　(i) Return on assets

(ii) Asset turnover ratio

D. What does the charge suggest about prior-year depreciation expense?

10. [Effects of accelerated depreciation methods] Caterpillar's summary of significant accounting policies includes the following:

Depreciation

Depreciation is computed principally using accelerated methods. These methods result in a larger allocation of the cost of buildings, machinery, and equipment to operations in the early years of the lives of assets than does the straight-line method, which allocates costs evenly over the lives of assets.

Exhibit 8P-3 contains data extracted from the company's financial statements.

A. Compute the average age and average depreciable life for Caterpillar for all years presented.

B. Explain why these ratios are especially difficult to interpret in the case of Caterpillar.

C. Discuss the effect of the trend in capital expenditures on Caterpillar's depreciation expense.

D. How would the answer to part C differ if Caterpillar used straight-line depreciation methods?

Appendix 8-A

Analysis of Changing Prices Information

INTRODUCTION

Price changes have pervasive effects on financial statements, and good analysis must recognize those effects and incorporate them into valuation decisions. Before discussing these issues, it is important to distinguish between two types of price change: general inflation and specific price change.

General inflation refers to price changes for an economy as a whole. Indices such as the consumer price index in the United States attempt to measure the impact of price changes on the broad population. Specific price changes refer to the prices of specific goods and services that are the inputs and outputs of firms in a given industry.

The goal of this appendix is to show how price changes impact financial statements and suggest analytical tools that can help the analyst adjust for that impact. We start with general inflation.

ANALYSIS OF GENERAL INFLATION

From the financial analysis point of view, the impact of general inflation is that the purchasing power of capital is continuously eroded. Analytically, there is a well-developed method of dealing with this phenomenon, *constant dollar accounting,* also called *general price level accounting* or *purchasing power accounting.*[1] Its goal is to measure the impact of changes in purchasing power (general inflation) on the *financial capital* of the firm.

In the simple model depicted in Exhibit 8A-1, the firm invests its capital in inventory at the start of the first year and sells that inventory at the end of the year. At the beginning of the next year, it again invests its capital (obtained from the sale of inventory one day earlier) in inventory. For simplicity, we assume that there are no markups and no expenses other than cost of goods sold.

The historical cost (or nominal dollar) model recognizes as income the difference between the proceeds of sale and the cost of inventory for each year. The total income over the three-year period is $331, the difference between beginning capital ($1,000) and ending capital ($1,331).

This model, however, does not recognize the decline in the real value of money or financial capital due to inflation. In this case, the purchasing power of $1,000 declines (at the rate of 25%) to $800 ($1,000/1.25) in one year.

Constant Dollar Method

The constant dollar method recognizes this effect by restating all monetary amounts into units of constant purchasing power at a designated base period, which can be any period of time (all of 1991) or point in time (January 1, 1991). The base fixes the yardstick used to measure purchasing power.

In our example, January 1, 1991 is the base so that all cash flows will be restated into units of January 1, 1991 purchasing power.

The nominal dollar cash flow of $1,100 was received at December 31, 1991. Inflation reduces the purchasing power of those dollars to only 80% (1/1.25) of the purchasing power at the base date of January 1, 1991. Thus, we must divide the cash flow by the relevant index (1.25) to obtain revenues in January 1, 1991 dollars.

$$\textbf{1991 Sales (\$1/1/91)} = \frac{\textbf{\$1,100}}{\textbf{1.25}} = \textbf{\$880}$$

[1]Accounting Principles Board (APB) Statement 4 (1969), Financial Statements Restated for General Price-Level Changes.

EXHIBIT 8A-1
Accounting for Changing Prices

Assumptions: Capital at January 1, 1991, is $1000.
Each January 1, the firm will invest entire capital in inventory.
Each December 31, the firm will sell entire inventory.
Price of inventory is $100 per unit at January 1, 1991, and rises at 10% per annum.
The general price level (CPI-U) rises at 25% per annum. Base period is January 1, 1991 = 100.

Historical Cost Model

Year	Sales	Cost of Goods Sold	Income
1991	$1100	$1000	$ 100
1992	1210	1100	110
1993	1331	1210	121
Total			$ 331

Constant Dollar Model

(January 1, 1991 dollars)

1991	880	1000	$(120)
1992	774	880	(106)
1993	681	774	(93)
Total			$(319)

Current Cost Model

1991	1100	1100	0
1992	1210	1210	0
1993	1331	1331	0
Total			$ 0

CPI-U:	January 1, 1991	100	December 31, 1991	125
	January 1, 1992	125	December 31, 1992	156.25
	January 1, 1993	156.25	December 31, 1993	195.31

Cost of goods sold (COGS) resulted from a cash outflow at January 1, 1991, and, therefore, requires no restatement. In constant dollar terms, therefore, net income for 1991 equals

1991 Income = $880 − $1,000 = $(120)

In purchasing power terms, the firm's capital has declined. This results from the fact that its inventory rose in price by less than the rate of inflation.

For 1992, we compute income in the same manner. The December 31, 1992 cash inflow has lost purchasing power over a two-year period and the January 1, 1992 cash outflow must be adjusted for one year's inflation:

$$\text{1992 Sales (\$1/1/91)} = \frac{\$1,210}{1.5625} = \$774 \qquad \text{COGS} = \frac{\$1,100}{1.25} = \$880$$

Thus

$$\text{1992 Income (\$1/1/91)} = \$774 - \$880 = \$(106)$$

The calculations for 1993 are similar, resulting in

$$\text{1993 Income (\$1/1/91)} = \$681 - \$774 = \$(93)$$

Over the three-year period, the constant dollar method reports a loss of $319 in purchasing power of the firm's capital. At the end of 1993, the firm has $1,331, the proceeds of inventory sold at December 31, 1993. But in units of 1/1/91 purchasing power, the firm's capital is only $681 ($1,331/1.9531), whereas its original capital was $1,000.

Note that these computations use the company's actual cash flows but the price index is for the economy as a whole. The calculations do not take into account the specific price changes faced by the firm. This feature of the constant dollar method is both its strength and its weakness.

Advantages and Disadvantages of Constant Dollar Method

The constant dollar method involves very simple calculations and the erosion of purchasing power is a simple economic concept. The method facilitates audits because it is objective as the only choice involved is that of the inflation index and given the same data, the results will always be the same contributing to ease of verifiability. For these reasons, corporate financial statement preparers and auditors have generally supported use of the constant dollar method to disclose the impact of inflation.

From the standpoint of financial analysis, however, the constant dollar method has a significant drawback: Constant dollar data do not have any apparent usefulness. Although loss of purchasing power is a useful economic concept, it has limited application in the financial world. Stock prices, interest rates, and other financial data are stated in nominal currency units, not real (purchasing power) units.

ANALYSIS OF FIRM-SPECIFIC INFLATION

Contributing to the lack of utility of constant dollar data is their lack of specificity; they treat all companies identically regardless of the composition of their assets and liabilities. For data that relate to specific companies, analysts prefer the current cost method.

Current Cost Method

The current cost[2] method ignores general inflation in favor of the specific price and cost changes faced by the individual firm. It starts with the idea that income, when properly measured, must include a provision for the replacement of capacity used during the period.[3] Otherwise, income is overstated as it includes the consumption of capacity.[4]

It follows that the provision for the cost of replacing capacity must be made at current prices. Although application of this principle is difficult in practice, it is essential in theory. If a firm has used up a machine and must replace it to remain in business, it is the cost of buying the new machine that is relevant, not the original cost of the worn-out one.

The current cost method, therefore, measures income by matching revenues with operating costs, including the cost of replacing inventory sold and fixed assets used up during the period.

Exhibit 8A-1 applies this principle to our model company. At the end of 1991, the firm has $1,100 as proceeds of sales. To remain in business, the firm must purchase new inventory on January 1, 1992. The cost of that new inventory will be 1,100 (10 @ $110 per unit), as prices have risen by 10% since January 1, 1991. Under the current cost method, therefore, there was no income earned in 1991:

$$\text{1991 Income} = \$1,100 - \$1,100 = 0$$

The firm can purchase 10 units of inventory, the same as its "capacity" one year earlier. The firm has neither a profit nor a loss for 1991 but has simply maintained its *physical capital* (capacity to do business). This contrasts with the constant dollar method, which is concerned with maintaining *financial capital.*

1992 and 1993 results are the same. There is no income in current cost terms because the firm has simply maintained its physical capital.

Disadvantages of Current Cost

As compared with the constant dollar method, the current cost method is more complex: the firm must estimate the cost to replace each type of inventory and each category of fixed assets. We discuss the difficulty of estimating current costs shortly. These estimates require judgements about how the firm will replace used up capacity adding subjectivity and a lack of reliability to the results. Because of these factors, current cost data are more expensive and time-consuming to prepare and audit than constant dollar data. For all these reasons, financial statement preparers and auditors have mostly opposed the presentation of current cost data in financial statements. In some cases, however, corporations have stated that they find such data useful when managing their business.[5]

---

[2]Current cost is the term used in SFAS 33 and other FASB standards. Previous accounting literature used such terms as replacement cost, current value, and fair value. The distinction among these terms is often more theoretic than real and varies with the user. For simplicity, we ignore these distinctions throughout the appendix.

[3]J. R. Hicks, *Value and Capital,* 2nd ed. (Oxford: Chaundon Press, 1946), p.176.

[4]This concept was more fully developed in Chapter 2.

[5]See, for example, Kenneth R. Todd, Jr., "How One Financial Officer Uses Inflation-Adjusted Accounting Data," *Financial Executive,* Oct. 1982. Todd was vice president and controller of American Standard, Inc.

For financial analysis, however, current cost data are greatly preferred to constant dollar data. The main reason is the relevance of such data to the operations of specific firms.

Accounting Series Release 190

The high rate of inflation in the 1970s and large specific price changes in some industries led the Securities and Exchange Commission to issue Accounting Series Release (ASR) 190 (1976) requiring large firms to disclose the replacement cost of inventory and fixed assets as well as cost of goods sold and depreciation expense computed on a replacement cost basis. Disclosures were first required in 1976.

At about the same time, the FASB placed inflation accounting on its agenda and issued SFAS 33 in 1979, at which time the SEC withdrew ASR 190.

SFAS 33 Requirements

SFAS 33, Financial Reporting and Changing Prices, the first U.S. accounting standard to require disclosure of the impact of changing prices was a hybrid; it attempted to combine both the current cost and constant dollar methods into one standard. In theory, the two approaches can be combined. Data adjusted for specific price changes can then be further adjusted for changes in purchasing power. The resulting complexity, however, made use of this data difficult for financial analysts.

SFAS 33 provided for review after five years. SFAS 89 (1989) made the SFAS 33 disclosure requirements voluntary. This action resulted from three factors. First, the rate of inflation subsided greatly in the 1980s, making the issue of general inflation effects less important. Second, preparers and auditors complained that the costs of compliance with SFAS 33 were too high. Finally, little or no benefit could be traced to the disclosures. Because of the voluntary nature of SFAS 89, the disclosures are rarely provided.

Problems with SFAS 33 Disclosures

The data disclosed under the provisions of SFAS 33 received little use, we believe, for the following reasons:

1. It was unclear whether companies should attempt to measure the market value, the reproduction cost, or the replacement cost of existing capacity. Each of these choices results in a different measure of cost and a different set of problems.

2. Market value is often difficult to estimate because many productive assets are customized or unique. Although market values can be estimated for office buildings, for example, there is no active market for steel mills. Curiously, the FASB did not permit the disclosure of market values in lieu of current cost for such assets as oil and gas properties, timberland, and real estate, for which active markets do exist.[6]

3. Reproduction cost is an estimate of the cost to build existing facilities at current prices. However, it is hard to price machines that are no longer being manufactured (having been replaced by newer models or machines using different

---

[6]SFAS 39, Mining and Oil and Gas, SFAS 40, Timberlands, and SFAS 41, Income Producing Real Estate, were all issued in 1980 as supplements to SFAS 33.

production processes). Use of reproduction cost also assumes that the firm would replace its existing capacity with exactly the same mix of factory sizes and locations.

Replacement cost is, in theory, the cost of replacing existing productive capacity. Such an estimate must, first, define whether capacity should be measured in physical units (tons of steel or pairs of shoes) or financial units (dollars of revenue). Second, the firm must decide what mix of geographic locations and plant capacities it would construct if it were to replace its facilities today. Finally, the firm must estimate what production processes, raw and intermediate materials, and markets it would pursue if it could "start from scratch."

The computations become increasingly speculative as one moves from the market value of assets to reproduction cost to replacement cost. In many cases, companies complied with SFAS 33 by simply applying construction and machinery cost indices to the historical cost of fixed assets.

Problems with Current Cost Depreciation

SFAS 33 also required that companies providing current cost data disclose depreciation expense on a current cost basis. At first glance, this is a simple exercise; companies simply apply their existing depreciation methods and lives to their estimated current cost of fixed assets.

The difficulties in defining current cost carry over to the definition of current cost depreciation expense. In addition the interpretation of current cost depreciation expense is subject to another problem. Replacement of historical cost depreciation with current cost depreciation assumes that the operating costs of the firm are unaffected by the "replacement" process. It assumes that more expensive new machines and processes are no more cost efficient than the original machines and processes.

That assumption is, of course, absurd in most cases. In theory, therefore, the operating costs of the firm should be adjusted to reflect the greater efficiency of the new equipment. Such adjustments are subjective when made by the firm; a financial analyst outside the firm cannot begin to make them.

Because of the subjectivity of the data, lack of comparability of disclosures by competing firms, difficulty of interpreting the data, and lack of a well-defined way of incorporating the data into investment decision models, use of the current cost data provided by SFAS 33 was limited. Perhaps for that reason there is little evidence that current cost data impacted financial markets.

Adjusting Financial Statements for Changing Prices

Given the voluntary nature of changing prices disclosures under SFAS 89, the analysis of the impact of changing prices must be done by each analyst. As we believe that constant dollar calculations are of use only under limited circumstances (see the following section), we devote our attention to adjustments for specific price changes. As the effects of changing prices on inventories are dealt with in Chapter 6, we concern ourselves here only with the effects on fixed assets.

Changing prices for fixed assets have two primary effects on financial statements:

1. Since fixed assets are carried at cost (net of accumulated depreciation), their carrying amount does not reflect the current cost. Thus, the assets and the net worth are understated if prices have risen (the normal case).

2. Depreciation expense is also understated because it is based on the understated carrying amount of the fixed assets. Depreciation expense, which should be a measure of the capacity used up during the period, is instead just an arbitrary allocation of past cash flows. Understatement of depreciation expense results in the overstatement of reported earnings.

Adjustments to Fixed Assets

In the absence of company-provided data, the analyst must use other sources of information to make adjustments. In some cases, data on the cost of capacity are available from industry sources; this is more likely to be true for relatively homogeneous industries such as paper, oil refining, and chemicals. Cost per ton of capacity data for such industries is frequently cited in trade publications or can be gleaned from company contacts.

Another possible source of data is actual construction. Companies frequently report the cost and capacity of new plants. Such data from the company or its competitors can be used to estimate the current cost of existing facilities.

Yet another approach is the use of construction cost statistics. If the year of construction of a plant is available, the historical cost can be indexed to estimate the current construction cost of the same facility.

For real estate assets, current land and construction cost data are frequently included in industry publications. The analyst can use this data to estimate the current cost of construction for factories, warehouses, and so forth. For some categories of real estate, especially income-producing properties (office buildings, shopping centers, hotels), publicly available market value estimates should be used as the measure of current costs as market value is more relevant than reproduction cost. Acquisitions accounted for under the purchase method result in the restatement of acquired fixed assets to their fair value or current cost.

In some cases, industry-specific disclosures are available. For example, see the discussion of the disclosures of the net present value of oil and gas reserves discussed in Appendix 7-B.

All these approaches require estimates. The lack of precision does not mean that the exercise is not worthwhile. Remember that estimates are present in the reported financial statements as well.

Using Current Cost Asset Values

The main use for current cost asset data is to prepare a current cost balance sheet. The historical cost of all assets and liabilities should be replaced with the current cost (market value) of those assets. As compared with the historical cost balance sheet, a current cost balance sheet provides a better measurement of the net assets available to management. These data can be used to make a better evaluation of management's use of available resources, the borrowing capacity of the firm, security for creditors, and the liquidation value of the company. These issues will be discussed more fully in Chapter 17.

Estimating Current Cost Depreciation

Once the current cost of fixed assets is estimated, the next step is to estimate depreciation on a current cost basis. The current cost of fixed assets should be amortized over the estimated economic life of the assets, allowing for salvage values. The arbitrarily

EXHIBIT 8A-2. MEAD CORP.
Capital Expenditures Analysis

($ in millions)	1995	1994	1993	1992	1991
Growth (including related environmental expenditures)	$ 81.8	$ 18.1	$ 29.2	$ 63.6	$ 75.6
Maintenance	75.1	91.9	136.8	85.9	74.7
Cost-effectiveness	91.7	189.1	126.4	44.5	68.6
Environmental projects	14.4	16.5	13.7	24.0	12.3
Total	$263.0	$315.6	$306.1	$218.0	$231.2

Source: Mead Corp., 1995 Annual Report.

chosen depreciation method and lives used for financial reporting purposes may not be adequate for this purpose. For analysis purposes, the choice of depreciation method, lives, and salvage values should be carefully considered.

It is important to look at overall corporate trends. If real output is static, then one can argue that *all* capital expenditures have been made to replace used up capacity. As SFAS 14 requires (see Chapter 13) the disclosure of capital expenditures and depreciation expense for each reportable segment, this analysis can be done for each segment of a multiindustry company.

Some companies disclose the cost of major capital projects, allowing the analyst to "back into" an estimate of "maintenance" expenditures. Other firms provide approximate data regarding the purpose of current capital expenditures. The portion allocated to the "maintenance of existing capacity" may be a good proxy for current cost depreciation.[7] Remember that the goal is to estimate the cost to replace capacity used up during the accounting period.

Example: Mead. Exhibit 8A-2 is an excerpt from the 1995 financial statements of Mead, a major paper producer. This capital expenditures analysis breaks out the components of capital spending: growth, maintenance, cost-effectiveness, and environmental. When growth is excluded, capital spending for 1995 approximates 1995 depreciation of $191 million. However, over the 1991-1995 period, average capital spending (ex-growth) of $213 million slightly exceeds average depreciation expense of $203 million.[8] As Mead has made significant "cost-effectiveness" investments during this period, cost reductions are presumably being realized currently, whereas depreciation is understated by the use of historical cost.

Use of Current Cost Depreciation

Estimates of current cost depreciation should be used to adjust reported income to current cost. Along with the adjustment to last-in, first-out (LIFO) when applicable

---

[7]In IAS 7, Cash Flow Statements, the IASC recommends that companies disclose the portion of capital expenditures required to maintain capacity.

[8]In 1994, Mead lengthened its depreciation lives, as discussed in Chapter 8, reducing depreciation expense for 1994 and 1995. Average depreciation expense for 1991 to 1995 would be $12 million higher if no change had taken place, approximately equal to average capital spending. This is another illustration of why the analysis of corporate time series data *must* adjust for any accounting changes.

(see Chapter 6), the replacement of historic cost depreciation by current cost will produce a better measure of sustainable income.[9]

Current cost data should also be used to adjust ratios so that they are better measures of management performance. When prices are increasing, the use of current cost data reduces the computed return on equity (ROE) as income is reduced (higher depreciation) and equity is increased (higher asset values). If the current cost ROE is very low, for example, it tells us that the company might be better off selling its assets and either reinvesting the proceeds in other assets, providing higher returns, or distributing them to stockholders for reinvestment.

Using Constant Dollar Data

Although we have stated that constant dollar data are generally not useful for financial analysis, there are some applications. Constant dollar data can be used to look at investment returns from the investor point of view.

An investor should measure the performance of an investment relative to inflation, not in absolute terms. Investors defer current consumption to obtain higher future consumption. In highly inflationary societies, the instinct to save is stifled if nominal rates of return are below the inflation rate. Under these conditions, consumption deferred is consumption reduced.

To measure the impact of changing prices on the investor, deflate returns by a measure of purchasing power such as the consumer price index. The index for the investor, not the investment, should be used. For example, an investment in General Motors shares by a Canadian investor must be evaluated by deflating the returns (translated into Canadian dollars) by the Canadian consumer price index. This can be done using the constant dollar method illustrated in Exhibit 8A-1.

The constant dollar method is also widely used in highly inflationary economies, especially when their financial systems are indexed to inflation. In many cases, the constant dollar method (sometimes in modified form) is used to produce the primary financial statements for financial and/or tax reporting.

Although the analysis of such statements is beyond the scope of this text, we will provide one caveat. Unless the input and output prices of the firm subjected to analysis are fully indexed, the constant dollar method will not provide a satisfactory basis for analysis. Sound investment decisions require an understanding of the effects of the specific price changes faced by the firm.

Concluding Remarks

With the adoption of SFAS 89, changing prices disappeared as an accounting issue. Yet prices continue to change. While general inflation has remained at low levels in virtually all industrialized countries, the prices of specific commodities continue to fluctuate.

Thus, financial analysis requires identification of the effects of significant price changes. Some of these effects can be dealt with summarily. For example, it is relatively easy to use an index of retail prices to compute the effect of inflation on department store sales. It is more complex (and more difficult) to discern the effect of a change in oil prices on an oil refiner's profit margins, turnover ratios, and return on equity. The objective of this appendix, and the material on the effect of price changes in Chapters 6 through 8, was to provide tools to permit such analysis.

[9]Sustainable income is defined and discussed in Chapter 2.

9

ANALYSIS OF INCOME TAXES

CHAPTER OUTLINE

CHAPTER OBJECTIVES

INTRODUCTION

ACCOUNTING FOR INCOME TAXES: BASIC ISSUES
Deferred Tax Assets and Liabilities
  Deferred Tax Liabilities
  Deferred Tax Assets

SFAS 109: THE LIABILITY METHOD
Effect of Tax Rate and Tax Law Changes
Treatment of Operating Losses
Deferred Tax Assets and the Valuation Allowance
Financial Statement Presentation and Disclosure Requirements
  Effective Date and Transition Method

DEFERRED TAXES: ANALYTICAL ISSUES
Factors Influencing the Level and Trend of Deferred Taxes
  Effects of Changes in Tax Laws and Accounting Methods
  Effect of the Growth Rate of the Firm
  Effects of Nonrecurring Items and Equity Adjustments
Liability or Equity?
Analysis of Deferred Tax Assets
Effective Tax Rates

ACCOUNTING FOR TAXES: SPECIALIZED ISSUES
Temporary Versus Permanent Differences
Indefinite Reversals
Accounting for Acquisitions

ANALYSIS OF INCOME TAX DISCLOSURES: DUPONT
Analysis of the Effective Tax Rate
Analysis of Deferred Income Tax Expense
Using Deferred Taxes to Estimate Taxable Income
Analysis of Deferred Tax Assets and Liabilities
Other Issues in Income Tax Analysis

FINANCIAL REPORTING OUTSIDE THE UNITED STATES
IASC Standards
Non-U.S. Standards

SUMMARY

CASE 9-1: ANALYSIS OF INCOME TAX DISCLOSURES OF DOW AND ICI

APPENDIX 9-A: DEFERRAL METHOD OF INCOME TAX ACCOUNTING

CHAPTER OBJECTIVES

As all business enterprises are subject to income tax, its analysis is an essential part of an overall firm analysis. In this chapter, we:

1. Examine the methods used to account for income tax.
2. Show how temporary differences between tax and financial reporting affect the balance sheet and income statement.
3. Review the impact of tax law and rate changes on deferred tax assets and liabilities.

4. Discuss the importance of the valuation allowance under SFAS 109.
5. Show how disclosures can be used to analyze and forecast the firm's effective tax rate.
6. Examine the relationship between deferred taxes and cash outflows for tax payments.
7. Evaluate the relevance of deferred tax assets and liabilities to firm valuation.

INTRODUCTION

Income taxes are a troublesome issue in financial reporting. The difference in the objectives of financial and tax reporting is an important reason for this difficulty. The objective of financial reporting is to provide users with information needed to evaluate a firm's financial position, performance, and cash flows. At the same time, the accrual basis of financial reporting allows management to select revenue and expense recognition methods that permit it to smooth or otherwise manage (maximize or minimize) reported net income. As discussed throughout the text, management incentives to manage reported income result from management compensation, bond covenants, political considerations, and the (presumed) effect on financial markets.

Tax reporting, in contrast, is the product of political and social objectives. The current period taxable income is measured using the modified cash basis; revenue and expense recognition methods used in tax reporting often differ from those used for financial reporting as the firm has strong incentives to select methods allowing it to minimize taxable income and, therefore, taxes paid, maximizing cash from operations.[1]

Thus, differences between taxes payable for the period and the tax expense recognized in the financial statements result from:

- The difference between accrual and modified cash bases of accounting
- Differences in reporting methods and estimates

These differences create deferred tax liabilities (credits) and deferred tax assets (debits or prepaid taxes) that are difficult to interpret. There is disagreement as to whether

---

[1]In countries such as Japan, Germany, and Switzerland, statutory financial reporting is required to conform to tax reporting. In these countries, the problems discussed in this chapter do not occur for statutory (usually, parent company only) statements. However, consolidated financial statements, for example, those prepared under IASC GAAP, do not conform with tax reporting and deferred tax issues must be dealt with. See the discussion of financial reporting practices outside the United States later in this chapter.

they are true assets or liabilities and their usefulness as indicators of future cash flows. When these deferrals become very large, their interpretation can have a significant effect on the financial analysis of a firm or group of firms.

Note: Terminology related to income tax accounting can be confusing as two terms that may seem similar to the reader can have very different meanings. A glossary of terms used in this chapter is therefore provided in Box 9-1. Each term in the glossary is shown in italics when first used in the chapter.

BOX 9-1
Glossary: Income Tax

Based on Tax Return

Taxable income	Income subject to tax.
Taxes payable (current tax expense)	Tax return liability resulting from current period taxable income. SFAS 109 calls this "current tax expense or benefit."
Income tax paid	Actual cash flow for income taxes, including payments (refunds) for others years.
Tax loss carryforward	Tax return loss that can be used to reduce taxable income in future years.

Based on Financial Reporting

Pretax income	Income before income tax expense.
Income tax expense	Expense resulting from current period pretax income; includes taxes payable and deferred income tax expense.
Deferred income tax expense	Accrual of income tax expense expected to be paid (or recovered) in future years; difference between taxes payable and income tax expense. Under SFAS 109, this results from changes in deferred tax assets and liabilities.
Deferred tax asset	Balance sheet amounts expected to be recovered from future operations.
Deferred tax liability	Balance sheet amounts expected to result in future cash outflows.
Valuation allowance	Reserve against deferred tax assets based on likelihood that those assets will be realized.
Timing difference	The result of tax return treatment (timing or amount) of transaction that differs from financial reporting treatment.
Temporary difference	Differences between tax reporting and financial reporting that will affect taxable income when those differences reverse. Similar to but slightly broader than timing differences (see footnote 6).

Note: SFAS 109 contains a more technical glossary of terms used in that standard.

ACCOUNTING FOR INCOME TAXES: BASIC ISSUES

The central accounting issue is whether the tax effects of transactions for which GAAP-based and tax-based accounting rules differ should be recognized in the period(s) in which they affect *taxable income* or in the period(s) in which they are recognized in the financial statements. These alternatives produce different measures of operating and financial performance, affecting the evaluation of a firm's operating performance and earning power. Cash flows for taxes are not affected by financial reporting choices except when conformity between tax and financial reporting is required.

Exhibit 9-1 uses a simplified example to illustrate the issues faced when tax accounting differs from accounting for financial statements. In this example, depreciation is the only item of expense.

EXHIBIT 9-1
Alternative Approaches to Tax Expense and Taxes Payable

Assumptions

- A firm purchases a machine costing $6,000 with a three-year estimated service life and no salvage value.
- For financial reporting purposes, the firm uses straight-line depreciation with a three-year life.
- For income tax reporting, the machine is depreciated straight-line over two years.
- The machine is used to manufacture a product that will generate annual revenue of $5,000 for three years.
- The tax rate is 40% in all three years.

A. Income Tax Reporting: Straight-Line Depreciation over Two Years

	Year 1	Year 2	Year 3	Total
Revenue	$5,000	$5,000	$5,000	$15,000
Depreciation	3,000	3,000	0	6,000
Taxable income	$2,000	$2,000	$5,000	$ 9,000
Taxes payable @ 40%	800	800	2,000	3,600
Net income	$1,200	$1,200	$3,000	$ 5,400

B. Financial Statement Reporting: Straight-Line Depreciation over Three Years

B1. Method Rejected by APB and FASB

- No recognition of deferred taxes
- Tax expense defined as taxes payable

	Year 1	Year 2	Year 3	Total
Revenue	$5,000	$5,000	$5,000	$15,000
Depreciation	2,000	2,000	2,000	6,000
Pretax income	$3,000	$3,000	$3,000	$ 9,000
Tax expense = payable	800	800	2,000	3,600
Net income	$2,200	$2,200	$1,000	$ 5,400

EXHIBIT 9-1 (*continued*)

B2. Required Presentation Under GAAP (SFAS 109)

- Recognition of deferred taxes
- Tax expense differs from taxes payable

	Year1	Year 2	Year 3	Total
Revenue	$5,000	$5,000	$5,000	$15,000
Depreciation	2,000	2,000	2,000	6,000
Pretax income	$3,000	$3,000	$3,000	$ 9,000
Tax expense @ 40%	1,200	1,200	1,200	3,600
Net income	$1,800	$1,800	$1,800	$ 5,400
Taxes payable (from part A)	800	800	2,000	3,600
Deferred tax expense	400	400	(800)	0
Deferred tax credit (on balance sheet)	400	800	0	0

Journal Entries

Years 1 and 2

Tax expense	$1,200	
Deferred tax liability		$ 400
Taxes payable		800

Year 3

Tax expense	$1,200	
Deferred tax liability	800	
Taxes payable		$2,000

Part A depicts the income tax reporting choice. The company depreciates a $6,000 asset over two years, giving rise to *taxes payable* of $800, $800, and $2,000 over the three-year period.

For financial reporting (part B), the firm depreciates the asset over three years. *Pretax income* exceeds taxable income in the first two years; taxable income is higher in year 3.[2] What *tax expense* should the company report in its financial statements?

One approach (not permitted under U.S. GAAP) would make tax expense equal to taxes payable. Part B1 shows tax expense equal to taxes payable for each year. As a result, the relationship between tax expense and pretax income is inconsistent over time and with the prevailing tax rate. Pretax income is the same for all three years, but tax expense differs as the tax deferred in earlier years is paid in year 3. For example, although the statutory tax rate is 40%, the tax rate reported in part B1 is 26.7% for the first two years and 66.7% for year 3.

Part B2 illustrates the U.S. GAAP treatment. At the end of year 1, it is recognized that the tax on the deferred $1,000 *timing difference* will be paid in year 3. Consequently, a *deferred tax liability* of $400 is created equal to the $1,000 timing difference multiplied

---

[2]Of the $3,000 pretax income reported in years 1 and 2, $1,000 (the excess tax depreciation) is not subject to taxes in those years. The $2,000 (2 × $1,000) deferred in the first two years becomes subject to taxation in the third as taxable income ($5,000) exceeds pretax income ($3,000) by $2,000.

by the 40% tax rate. This liability is recognized in year 1 and becomes a portion of that year's tax expense. Thus, total income tax expense equals $1,200: taxes payable ($800) plus *deferred income tax expense* ($400). The matching principle is satisfied as the relationship between revenues and expenses (40% tax rate) is maintained. From the balance sheet perspective, a liability is recorded equal to the amount of tax that will be paid in year 3 when the difference in accounting methods reverses. In year 2, a similar deferred tax is recognized. At the end of year 2, the cumulative timing difference is $2,000 and the aggregate deferred tax liability is $800.

No tax depreciation remains to be recorded in year 3, but book depreciation expense equals $2,000. At the end of year 3, there is no remaining timing difference as the machine is fully depreciated for both tax and financing reporting purposes. Thus, year 3 income tax expense equals taxes payable ($2,000) *less* the reversal of the deferred tax liability of $800 accumulated over the first two years for a net amount of $1,200.

Deferred Tax Assets and Liabilities

Deferred tax liabilities are required when future taxable income is expected to exceed pretax income, as illustrated in Exhibit 9-1. Pretax income exceeds taxable income in years 1 and 2, but year 3 taxable income is expected to exceed pretax income by $2,000. Differences between financial accounting and tax accounting can also give rise to *deferred tax assets* when future pretax income is expected to be less than taxable income.

Exhibit 9-2 extends our example of Exhibit 9-1 by introducing warranty expense, a timing difference that gives rise to a deferred tax asset in years 1 and 2. As warranty

EXHIBIT 9-2
Basic Example: Accounting for Income Taxes

Assumptions

Identical to Exhibit 9-1

- A firm purchases a machine costing $6,000 with a three-year estimated service life and no salvage value.
- For financial reporting purposes, the firm uses straight-line depreciation with a three-year life.
- For income tax reporting, the machine is depreciated straight-line over two years.
- The machine is used to manufacture a product that will generate annual revenue of $5,000 for three years.
- The tax rate is 40% in all three years.

Additional for Exhibit 9-2

- Warranty expenses are estimated at 10% of revenues each year; all repairs are provided in year 3.

A. Deferred Tax Assets and Liabilities

In years 1 and 2, the difference in depreciation lives generates a temporary difference of $1,000 (pretax income *exceeds* taxable income), resulting in a deferred tax liability of $400 ($1,000 × 0.40) each year. At the end of the second year, the cumulative temporary difference is $2,000, and the cumulative deferred tax liability is $800.

No tax depreciation remains to be recorded in year 3, but a book depreciation of $2,000 is recognized. Pretax income is *less than* taxable income, resulting in a temporary difference in

EXHIBIT 9-2 (*continued*)

the opposite direction and the elimination of the deferred tax liability accumulated during the first two years.

Warranty expense of $500 is recognized each year. Since no expenditures are incurred in years 1 and 2, no expense can be recognized on the tax return for those years. The temporary difference (pretax income is *less than* taxable income) results in a deferred tax asset of $200 for each year. In year 3, an expense of $500 is recognized in the financial statements, but tax-deductible expenditures of $1,500 are made for repairs; pretax income *exceeds* taxable income by $1,000, and the cumulative deferred tax assets are eliminated.

Journal Entries

Years 1 and 2

Tax expense	$1,000	
Deferred tax asset	200	
Deferred tax liability		$ 400
Taxes payable		800

Year 3

Tax expense	$1,000	
Deferred tax liability	800	
Deferred tax asset		$ 400
Taxes payable		1,400

Each year, the deferred tax assets and liabilities have been shown separately to highlight their different sources and expected cash consequences. Note that over the entire three-year period, tax expense and taxes payable are identical. By the end of the third year, all temporary differences have reversed so that all deferred tax assets and liabilities have been offset.

B. Financial Statements

Year	Gross Revenues	Total Expense	Pretax Income	Tax Expense*	Net Income
1	$ 5,000	$2,500†	$2,500	$1,000	$1,500
2	5,000	2,500†	2,500	1,000	1,500
3	5,000	2,500†	2,500	1,000	1,500
	$15,000	$7,500	$7,500	$3,000	$4,500

*Tax expense is 40% (tax rate) × pretax income.
†Depreciation expense is $2,000 ($6,000/3); warranty expense is $500 ($5,000 × 10%).

C. Tax Return

Year	Gross Revenues	Total Expense	Taxable Income	Taxes Payable*	Posttax Income
1	$ 5,000	$3,000†	$2,000	$ 800	$1,200
2	5,000	3,000†	2,000	800	1,200
3	5,000	1,500‡	3,500	1,400	2,100
	$15,000	$7,500	$7,500	$3,000	$4,500

*Taxes payable are 40% (tax rate) × taxable income.
†Annual depreciation expense is $6,000/2 = $3,000; no expenditures are incurred for warranties during the first two years.
‡There is no depreciation expense, as equipment is fully depreciated at the end of year 2; repair expenditures of $1,500 are incurred.

payments are tax-deductible when paid rather than when accrued, the amount charged to warranty expense for financial statement purposes is generally larger than that allowed for tax purposes.

As shown in Exhibit 9-2A, the firm recognizes a warranty expense of $500 in each of years 1 and 2, but receives no tax deduction. As pretax income exceeds taxable income (for this expense only), a deferred tax asset must be created.

Thus, the tax computations for each year must reflect both the deferred tax liability resulting from depreciation and the deferred tax asset resulting from warranty expense. The journal entries in part A, financial statements in part B, and tax return data in part C incorporate both. In practice, firms have many deferred tax assets and liabilities, resulting from different timing differences.

Income tax expense is based on pretax income, which reflects the use of machinery (financial statement depreciation) and estimated warranty expense for products sold. Taxes payable are measured as the tax rate times taxable income and reflect the effects of tax depreciation and allowable warranty deductions on the tax return. Over the three-year period, total revenues are $15,000, total depreciation expense is $6,000, and total warranty expense is $1,500 for both financial and tax reporting. The timing of expense recognition differs, but the total amount is the same.[3]

Deferred Tax Liabilities

The calculation of the deferred tax liability is identical to that shown in Exhibit 9-1.

Deferred Tax Assets

Warranty expenses of $500 are accrued each year. Since no expenditures are incurred in years 1 and 2, no deductions can be taken on the tax return for those years. The higher taxable income results in a prepayment of taxes; tax expense in the financial statements reflects lower pretax income. The difference of $500 in each of the first two years generates a deferred tax asset of $200 ($500 × 0.40) each year and increases tax expense by that amount each year. At the end of year 2, there is a deferred tax asset of $400.

In year 3, tax-deductible expenditures of $1,500 are incurred for repairs, reducing taxable income and tax payments. These expenditures exceed year 3 expense ($500) by $1,000, equal to the total additional expense recognized in years 1 and 2. The temporary difference reverses, deferred income tax expense is reduced by $400 ($1,000 × 0.40), and the deferred tax asset generated during the first two years is eliminated.[4]

Do the deferred tax liabilities at the end of years 1 and 2 actually represent a liability for tax payments due in year 3? Similarly, does the deferred tax asset qualify as an asset? In this simple case, they do, as the forecast reversals occur as expected. In the real world, the answer is not so clear; these are important issues from an analytical perspective and we will return to them shortly.

---

[3]Warranty expense and actual repair costs are assumed to be identical for illustration only; it is difficult to predict the frequency and level of repair costs perfectly. Bad debt expenses and litigation losses are other examples of timing differences where predictions are uncertain.

[4]In the examples of Exhibit 9-1 and 9-2, income tax expense could also have been computed by applying the income tax rate of 40% directly to pretax income in each year. However, in more complex situations, discussed in the next section, this approach would produce a different result.

SFAS 109: THE LIABILITY METHOD

Accounting for taxes in the United States is based on SFAS 109 (1992), whose two objectives are to recognize:

1. Taxes payable or refundable for the current year
2. The deferred tax liabilities and assets (adjusted for recoverability) measured as the future tax consequences of events that have been recognized in financial statements or tax returns

Statement 109 replaced APB 11 and shifted the emphasis from the deferral method to the liability method.[5] The deferral method has an income statement focus; balance sheet deferred tax assets and liabilities result from the calculation of deferred tax expense. The focus of the liability method is the balance sheet, as deferred tax assets and liabilities are calculated directly; deferred tax expense used to determine reported income is a consequence of the balance sheet calculations. As the deferral method is now used only in a few countries, we defer further discussion of that method to the section entitled, "Financial Reporting Outside the United States" and Appendix 9-A.

SFAS 109 recognizes the deferred tax consequences of temporary differences.[6] *The standard mandates the recognition of deferred tax liabilities for all temporary differences expected to generate net taxable amounts in future years.*

The FASB argues that deferred tax consequences of temporary differences that will result in net taxable amounts in future years meet the SFAC 6 definition of liabilities.[7] The board contended that deferred taxes are legal obligations imposed by tax laws and temporary differences will affect taxable income in future years as they reverse.

The expected reversal of the temporary difference is confirmed by the firm's decision to report the machine (in Exhibit 9-1) on its balance sheet; use of the machine in operations suggests continued depreciation on the financial statements and therefore a reversal of that difference. These considerations are the basis of the FASB view that the only question is when, not whether, the use of the machine will generate taxable income in future periods.

The financial statement effects of the liability method can best be highlighted by examining its treatment of tax rate changes.

---

[5]SFAS 96 (1987) was an interim step in this process. As that standard, which used the liability method, was superseded by SFAS 109, we do not discuss it here.

[6]This concept is broader than the timing difference concept used in APB 11, as it also considers other events that result in differences between the tax bases of assets and liabilities and their carrying amounts in financial statements. Such differences arise when (1) the tax basis of an asset is reduced by tax credits, (2) investment tax credits are accounted for under the deferred method, (3) the tax basis of a foreign subsidiary's assets is increased as a result of indexing, and (4) carrying amounts and tax bases of assets differ in purchase method acquisitions.

[7]The temporary difference in Exhibit 9-1 derives from the firm's use of different depreciation lives for financial reporting than for tax return reporting, creating a difference between the carrying amount of the asset and its tax basis. Use of the asset in operations will result in taxable income in year 3, when no depreciation can be recorded on the tax return. The board acknowledged that other events may offset the net taxable amounts that would be generated when temporary differences reverse, but because those events have not yet occurred, and they are not assumed in the financial statements, their tax consequences should not be recognized. See para. 75 to 79, SFAS 109, for more discussion of this issue.

Effect of Tax Rate and Tax Law Changes

Exhibit 9-3 depicts the impact of a change in tax rates using the example in Exhibit 9-2. The corporate tax rate is assumed to decrease from 40% to 35% at the beginning of year 2.

In panel A, we assume that the upcoming tax decrease *was enacted before* the year 1 financial statements were prepared. In panel B, however, we assume that the year 2 tax decrease *was enacted after* year 1 financial statements were prepared.

EXHIBIT 9-3
Impact of Tax Rate Change: The Liability Method

Assumptions

Identical to Exhibit 9-2

- A firm purchases a machine costing $6,000 with a three-year estimated service life and no salvage value.
- For financial reporting purposes, the firm uses straight-line depreciation with a three-year life.
- For income tax reporting, the machine is depreciated straight-line over two years.
- The machine is used to manufacture a product that will generate annual revenue of $5,000 for three years.
- Warranty expenses are estimated at 10% of revenues each year; all repairs are provided in year 3.

A. Year 2 Tax Rate Change Enacted in Year 1

Year 1: Tax Rate = 40%

Year 2 Tax Rate Will Be 35%

Selected T-Accounts

			Deferred Tax Asset		Deferred Tax Liability	
Income tax expense	975					
Deferred tax asset	175		$175			$350
Deferred tax liability		350	$175			$350
Taxes payable		800				

Year 2: Tax Rate = 35%

			Deferred Tax Asset		Deferred Tax Liability	
			$175			$350
Income tax expense	875		175			
Deferred tax asset	175					$350
Deferred tax liability		350	$350			$700
Taxes payable		700				

Year 3: Tax Rate = 35%

			Deferred Tax Asset		Deferred Tax Liability	
			$350			$700
Income tax expense	875				700	
Deferred tax liability	700			350		
Deferred tax asset		350	$ 0			$ 0
Taxes payable		1,225				

EXHIBIT 9-3 (*continued*)

Calculations

Temporary Differences

	Depreciation (Liability)	Warranty (Asset)	Taxes Payable	Income Tax Expense
Year 1	35% × $1,000	35% × $(500)	40% × $2,000	$350 − $175 + 800
Year 2	35% × 1,000	35% × (500)	35% × 2,000	$350 − $175 + 700
Year 3	35% × (2,000)	35% × 1,000	35% × 3,500	−$700 + $350 + $1,225

B. Year 2 Tax Rate Change Enacted in Year 2

Year 1: Tax Rate = 40%

Selected T-Accounts

			Deferred Tax Asset	Deferred Tax Liability
Income tax expense	1,000			
Deferred tax asset	200		$200	$400
Deferred tax liability		400		
Taxes payable		800	$200	$400

Year 2: Tax Rate Reduced to 35%

(i) *Adjustment of Prior-Year Deferrals*

			Deferred Tax Asset	Deferred Tax Liability
Deferred tax liability	50			
Deferred tax asset		25	$200	$400
Income tax expense		25	25	50
			$175	$350

(ii) *Current Year Operations*

			Deferred Tax Asset	Deferred Tax Liability
Income tax expense	875			
Deferred tax asset	175		$175	$350
			175	
Deferred tax liability		350		350
Taxes payable		700		
			$350	$700

Year 3: Tax Rate = 35%

			Deferred Tax Asset	Deferred Tax Liability
			$350	$700
Income tax expense	875			700
Deferred tax liability	700			
Deferred tax asset		350	350	
Taxes payable		1,225	$ 0	$ 0

Calculations

Temporary Differences

	Depreciation (Liability)	Warranty (Asset)	Taxes Payable	Income Tax Expense
Year 1	40% × $1,000	40% × $(500)	40% × $2,000	$400 − $200 + $800
Year 2	(5%) × 1,000	(5%) × (500)		−$50 + $25
	35% × 1,000	35% × (500)	35% × 2,000	$350 − $175 + $700
Year 3	35% × (2,000)	35% × 1,000	35% × 3,500	−$700 + $350 + $1,225

Panel A: Future Tax Rate Change Enacted in Current Year. The balance sheet orientation of SFAS 109 requires adjustments to deferred tax assets and liabilities to reflect the impact of a change in tax rates or tax laws. Thus, in panel A for year 1, although taxes payable are based on the current tax rate of 40%, the calculation for deferred tax assets and liabilities is based on the tax rate expected to be in effect when the differences reverse, 35%.

Calculation of Year 1 Income Tax Expense

Taxes payable = $2,000 taxable income × 40%	= $ 800
Deferred tax asset = $500 temporary difference × 35%	= (175)
Deferred tax liability = $1,000 temporary difference × 35%	= 350
Total income tax expense	= $ 975

Note that year 1 tax expense as a percentage of pretax income (the effective tax rate) is 39%: a weighted average of the current tax rate of 40% and the 35% rate that will be in effect when the timing differences that gave rise to the deferred taxes reverse. There is no attempt to match income tax expense directly with pretax income, and one cannot calculate tax expense directly by multiplying pretax income by the current tax rate.

For years 2 and 3, the calculations are similar to those in Exhibit 9-2 except that the new tax rate of 35% (rather than 40%) is used for all calculations.

Panel B: Future Tax Rate Change Enacted Subsequently. In panel B, we assume that the tax rate decrease for year 2 is enacted after year 1 statements have been prepared. Calculations for year 1 tax expense, taxes payable, and deferred taxes therefore use the year 1 tax rate of 40% and are identical to those in Exhibit 9-2. A deferred tax asset of $200 and a deferred tax liability of $400 are created.

In year 2, when the rate decrease is effective, two steps are necessary to calculate the current year's tax expense:

1. The deferred tax asset and liability balances at the end of year 1 must be restated at the new (lower) tax rate of 35% (assumed to be in effect when the deferred taxes will be paid). This calculation is shown in Exhibit 9-3B. Year 2 tax expense is reduced (income is increased) since the lower rate reduces the expected tax payment when the depreciation difference reverses, partially offset by a lower expected tax benefit when the warranty expense difference reverses. The adjustment results in a deferred tax asset of $175 and liability of $350.[8]

2. The taxes payable and deferred taxes arising from current year operations are calculated using the new rate of 35%.

[8]These balances are now identical to those shown in panel A of the exhibit when the tax law change was known prior to the issuance of the year 1 financial statements. The only difference between the two panels is the timing of the restatement at the lower rate.

Tax expense for year 2 is calculated as follows:

Adjustment of Year 1 Balances to New Rate

Deferred tax asset of $200 restated to $175	$ 25
Deferred tax liability of $400 restated to $350	(50)

Year 2 Taxes Payable and Temporary Differences

Taxes payable = $2,000 taxable income $\times$ 35%	700
Deferred tax asset = $500 temporary difference $\times$ 35%	(175)
Deferred tax liability = $1,000 temporary difference $\times$ 35%	350
Income tax expense	$ 850

Note that, as in panel A, the income tax expense of $850 is affected by changes in the deferred tax liability and asset accounts and there is no attempt to directly match the relationship of tax expense to pretax income.[9]

Under SFAS 109, the liability method requires that changes in tax rates (or other tax regulations) that affect the estimated future tax liability are recognized in reported income in the year the change is enacted.

Treatment of Operating Losses

Operating losses are due to an excess of tax deductions over taxable revenues. Tax losses can be carried back and applied to prior years to obtain refunds of taxes paid; the impact of the carryback on income tax expense is recognized in the loss period because it can be measured and is recoverable.

Tax losses may also be carried forward to future periods if insufficient taxes were paid during the carryback period or the firm would lose valuable tax credits if losses were carried back to that period. Because the realization of *tax loss carryforwards* depends on future taxable income, the expected benefits are recognized as deferred tax assets. Under SFAS 109, such assets are recognized in full but a *valuation allowance* may be required if recoverability is unlikely.

Deferred Tax Assets and the Valuation Allowance

SFAS 109 is permissive regarding the recognition of deferred tax assets. The standard permits recognition of a deferred tax asset whenever a deductible temporary difference results in an operating loss or tax credit carryforward. However, management (and its auditors) must defend recognition of all deferred tax assets. A valuation allowance reducing the deferred tax asset is required if an analysis of the sources of future taxable

---

[9]Under the deferral method, however, the change in tax rates is ignored until the year when the reversal occurs and current year tax expense is simply the current tax rate times pretax income (see Appendix 9-A).

income suggests that it is more likely than not that some portion or all of the deferred tax asset will not be realized.[10]

Tax-planning strategies can be used to reduce required valuation allowances, but they must be disclosed. SFAS 109 provides examples of positive and negative evidence that must be weighed to determine the need for a valuation allowance and to measure the amount of the allowance.[11] *Changes in the valuation allowance are included in income from continuing operations except when they are generated by unrecognized changes in the carrying amount of assets or liabilities.*[12]

Financial Statement Presentation and Disclosure Requirements

The disclosure requirements of SFAS 109 incorporated U.S. Securities and Exchange Commission disclosure requirements that had been in effect for many years.

Large multinational companies operate in dozens of tax jurisdictions and their financial reports must summarize their tax position for all consolidated entities. Such firms often generate deferred tax assets and liabilities in different tax jurisdictions. *Statement 109 permits offsets of deferred tax effects only within each tax-paying component and tax jurisdiction of the firm.*

Deferred tax assets and liabilities must be separated into current and noncurrent components based on the classification of the assets and liabilities generating the deferral. However, deferred tax assets due to carryforwards are classified by reference to expected reversal dates. SFAS 109 specifically requires:

1. Separate disclosure of all deferred tax assets and liabilities, any valuation allowance, and the net change in that allowance for each reporting period.

2. Disclosure of any unrecognized deferred tax liability for the undistributed earnings of domestic or foreign subsidiaries and joint ventures. These disclosures should facilitate the comparison of the operating results of firms that have different policies with respect to deferred tax recognition or the remission of income from such affiliates.

3. Disclosure of the current year tax effect of each type of temporary difference.

4. Disclosure of the components of income tax expense.

5. Reconciliation of reported income tax expense with the amount based on the statutory income tax rate (the reconciliation can use either amounts or percentages of pretax income).

6. Disclosure of tax loss carryforwards and credits.

[10]Sources of future taxable income include existing taxable temporary differences, future taxable income net of reversing temporary differences, taxable income recognized during qualifying carryback periods, and applicable tax-planning strategies.

[11]Existing contracts or backlogs expected to be profitable, appreciated assets, earnings over the past few years, and the nature (nonrecurring) of the loss would suggest that a valuation allowance is not needed. Examples of negative evidence include cumulative losses in recent years and the past inability to use loss or tax credit carryforwards.

[12]The most common example is the deferred tax assets that arise when the market value of "available-for-sale" securities is less than cost; the unrealized loss is included in equity, under SFAS 115, net of the related deferred income tax asset. See Chapter 13 for further discussion.

These requirements determine the income tax disclosures in duPont's Note 7 (see Appendix A). These disclosures are the raw material for the analysis provided later in this chapter.

Effective Date and Transition Method

SFAS 109 was effective for fiscal years beginning after December 15, 1992. The standard allowed significant flexibility with respect to adoption methods and effective dates. Firms adopting SFAS 109 could do so either retroactively or prospectively.[13]

DuPont adopted the new standard effective January 1, 1992 (see Note 7). Adoption increased deferred tax liabilities by $1,045 million, mainly due to required adjustments (discussed later in this chapter) to purchase method acquisitions.

DEFERRED TAXES: ANALYTICAL ISSUES

Estimates of the firm's future cash flows and earning power, and the analysis of financial leverage must consider changes in deferred tax assets and liabilities, deferred tax expense, and any changes in the valuation allowance. *The key analytic issue is whether the deferred tax assets and liabilities will reverse in the future. If they will not, then it is highly debatable whether to classify deferred taxes as assets or liabilities; it may be more appropriate to consider them as decreases or increases to equity.*

To resolve that issue, we need to understand the factors that determine the level of and trends in reported deferred taxes, to decide whether they are assets (or liabilities) and to evaluate their expected cash consequences.

Factors Influencing the Level and Trend of Deferred Taxes

In general, temporary differences originated by individual transactions will reverse and offset future taxable income and tax payments. However, *these reversals may be offset by other transactions, for example, newly originating temporary differences.* The cash consequences of deferred tax debits and credits depend on the following factors:

- Future tax rates and tax laws
- Changes in accounting methods
- The firm's growth rate
- Firm-specific and general price level changes
- Nonrecurring items and equity adjustments

We discuss these factors next.

Effects of Changes in Tax Laws and Accounting Methods

Management incentives for choosing revenue and expense recognition methods on the tax return and financial statements differ, as mentioned previously. Choices (and subsequent changes) of tax and/or accounting methods determine taxes payable, income tax expense, and both the amounts and rate of change of reported deferred tax balances.

---

[13]For firms that had adopted SFAS 96, the effect of adopting SFAS 109 was often immaterial.

Under the liability method, as seen in Exhibit 9-3, when a new tax law is enacted, its effects must be recognized immediately. Thus, lower tax rates will reduce deferred tax liabilities and assets, increase equity (if we assume net deferred tax liabilities), and affect income tax expense for the year. The larger the net deferred tax liability, the greater the impact of the tax cut, as previous-year deferrals are adjusted to the lower rate. For analytic purposes, one need not wait for the actual tax change to be enacted; estimates can be made when legislation is proposed.

Changes in GAAP can also significantly impact deferred taxes. For example, in 1992 duPont adopted SFAS 106, Accounting for Postretirement Benefits Other Than Pensions. The standard (see Chapter 12) required accrual accounting for postretirement costs (mainly medical benefits for current employees after retirement) rather than cash basis accounting. As cash basis accounting was used for income tax purposes, there was no temporary difference associated with these benefits prior to the adoption of SFAS 106.

Upon adoption, duPont recognized a postretirement benefit liability of $5.9 billion and deferred tax asset of $2.1 billion. Is this $2.1 billion an asset? Can it be used to reduce future taxes? That depends on the $5.9 billion liability associated with it. As postretirement benefits are paid, future taxes payable will be reduced, but the amounts are uncertain. If, for example, duPont reduces future medical benefits and payments are below the estimated liability, then the deferred tax asset of $2.1 billion will not fully materialize. Thus, *realization of a deferred tax asset or liability depends on the realization of the temporary difference that created it.*

Effect of the Growth Rate of the Firm

For most firms, the deferred tax liability grows over time; temporary differences do not reverse on balance.[14] For growing firms, increased or higher-cost investments in fixed assets result in ever-increasing deferred tax liabilities due to the use of accelerated depreciation methods for tax reporting.

Exhibit 9-4 extends the Exhibit 9-1 example by focusing on the deferred tax consequences of depreciation differences. Assume that the firm acquires one machine each year and it continues to use the depreciation lives in Exhibit 9-1. The depreciation differences will produce a deferred tax expense of $400 in each year during the first two years of each machine's operation, with a reversal of $800 in its third year to eliminate the deferred tax liability generated over the first two years.

The $400 deferred tax liability at the end of the first year represents the effect of the temporary difference from the single machine in use. In year 2, machine 1 adds an additional deferred tax liability of $400. The acquisition of a second machine in year 2 adds another difference of $400; there is now an accumulated deferred tax liability of $1,200 at the end of year 2.

---

[14]A similar analysis can be made for deferred tax assets. We focus on deferred tax liabilities because they are generally larger. Deferred tax assets (more precisely, prepaid taxes) stem from both recurring transactions (such as warranty expenses, management compensation, employee benefits, and bad debt reserves), and from more irregular events (such as restructuring costs, impairments, environmental remediation obligations, and provisions for litigation losses) that are accrued on the financial statements prior to their deduction on the tax return.

Management often has substantial discretion over the amount and timing of the origination of these debit balances as it controls the recognition of these expenses. However, the amount and timing of their reversal may not be as discretionary or predictable as the temporary differences (such as depreciation differences) that generate deferred tax liabilities.

EXHIBIT 9-4
Impact of Growth on Deferred Tax Liability

Assumptions

A firm purchases one machine during each year of operation. All other assumptions are identical to those used in Exhibit 9-1. Most important, temporary differences are originated and reversed as in Exhibit 9-1 and at the same tax rate, which is assumed to remain constant over time.

Deferred Tax Liability

Year 1	$ 400	Machine 1 (origination)
Year 2	400	Beginning balance
	400	Machine 1 (origination)
	400	Machine 2 (origination)
Year 3	$1,200	Beginning balance
	(800)	Machine 1 (reversal)
	400	Machine 2 (origination)
	400	Machine 3 (origination)
Year 4	$1,200	Beginning balance
	(800)	Machine 2 (reversal)
	400	Machine 3 (origination)
	400	Machine 4 (origination)
Year 5	$1,200	Beginning balance

Note: The balance stabilizes at $1,200 in this example at the end of year 3, with the originations exactly offset by the reversals. This result assumes constant levels of asset acquisitions, price levels, tax rates, and regulations. Increases in either price levels or acquisitions would result in rising balances of deferred tax liabilities.

In year 3, the firm acquires and uses the third machine that generates its first year temporary difference, and the asset acquired in year 2 originates its second year difference. However, the machine acquired in year 1 now generates a reversal of temporary difference; whereas depreciated in the financial statements, no depreciation remains to be recorded for the asset on the tax return. The originating temporary differences from the second and third machine offset the reversal due to the first machine; there is no change in the net deferred tax liability.

Note that the deferred tax consequences of one asset have reversed, generating taxable income that is offset by other originating differences. The deferred tax liability remains $1,200 and *stabilizes at that level* if asset acquisitions, depreciation methods, and tax rates and tax laws remain unchanged. Increased asset purchases above present levels (either in physical quantity or due to higher prices) will result in a growing deferred tax liability as originations exceed reversals. Thus, as a result of growth, either in real or nominal terms, the net deferred tax liability will increase over time; *in effect, it will never be paid*.

If the firm reduces its acquisition of fixed assets and reversals exceed originations, the related deferred tax liability will decline. The cash consequences of this scenario, however, are uncertain. If the decrease in asset acquisitions results from declining product demand, then lower asset acquisitions may be accompanied by poor profitability. Without taxable income, the deferred taxes will never be paid. Alternatively, the firm may originate other temporary differences that offset depreciation reversals; in the aggregate, deferred tax liabilities may not decline.

The cash consequences of reversing temporary differences, therefore, depend on both future profitability and other activities of the firm that affect future taxable income.

Effects of Nonrecurring Items and Equity Adjustments

The following may also affect income tax expense, taxes paid, and deferred tax assets and liabilities:

- Nonrecurring items
- Extraordinary items
- Accounting changes
- Equity adjustments

Nonrecurring items (such as restructuring charges) may have future as well as current period tax consequences, and complicate the analysis of the firm's tax position. DuPont, for example, had restructuring changes in 1992 and 1993, partly reversed in 1994, as detailed in Note 6. These charges generated significant deferred tax assets, as discussed later in this chapter.

Extraordinary items, such as duPont's loss from the early retirement of debt (Note 8), are reported after tax; the tax effect is shown separately in duPont's tax footnote. Transition effects of accounting changes often generate deferred tax effects, especially when the new method is not a permitted method of tax reporting. The large deferred tax asset resulting from duPont's adoption of SFAS 106 (postretirement benefits other than pensions) is a typical example.

Finally, equity adjustments that bypass the income statement may have current and deferred tax consequences. Common examples include:

- Unrealized gains or losses on marketable securities (see Chapter 13)
- Currency translation adjustments (see Chapter 15)

The cash and deferred tax effects of continuing operations may be obscured by the items discussed above. Although firms generally disclose their associated tax effect, discerning their cash and deferred tax impact may require careful reading of the tax footnote supplemented by discussions with management.

Liability or Equity?

How should analysts treat deferred tax liabilities in the analysis of a firm's solvency?

As indicated above, changes in a firm's operations or tax laws may result in deferred taxes that are never paid (or recovered). Moreover, a firm's growth may continually generate deferred tax liabilities. Even if temporary differences do reverse, future losses may forestall tax payments. These factors suggest that, in many cases, deferred taxes are unlikely to be paid.

Even if deferred taxes are eventually paid, the present value of those payments is considerably lower than the stated amounts. Thus, the deferred tax liability should be discounted at an appropriate interest rate.[15]

These arguments suggest that the components of the deferred tax liability should be analyzed to evaluate the likelihood of reversal or continued growth. Only those components that are likely to reverse should be considered a liability.[16] In addition, the liability should be discounted to its present value based on an estimate of the year(s) of reversal. If the temporary differences giving rise to deferred tax liabilities are not expected to reverse, those amounts should not be considered liabilities.

SFAS 109 requires disclosure of the components of the deferred tax liability at each year-end. These components should be examined over time to see which tend to reverse and which do not. For example, the effect of using accelerated depreciation methods for tax reporting tends not to reverse.[17] If reversal occurs gradually, as capital expenditures decline, the liability should be discounted to present value. Similar analysis can be applied to other major differences, keeping in mind any changes in the tax law.

To the extent that deferred taxes are not a liability, then they are stockholders' equity. Had they not been recorded, prior-period tax expense would have been lower and net income higher. Thus, equity should be increased. This adjustment reduces the debt-to-equity ratio, in some cases considerably.[18]

In some cases, however, deferred taxes are neither liability nor equity. For example, if tax depreciation is a better measure of economic depreciation (see Chapter 8) than financial statement depreciation, adding the deferred tax liability to equity overstates the value of the firm. However, if the deferred tax liability is unlikely to result in a cash outflow, it is not a liability either. Ultimately, the financial analyst must decide on the appropriate treatment of deferred taxes on a case-by-case basis.

In practice, the analytic treatment of deferred tax liabilities varies. Some creditors, notably banks, do not consider them to be liabilities (but neither do they include them as part of equity). In calculating solvency and other ratios, most analysts ignore deferred taxes altogether.

Standard and Poor's, a major U.S. rating agency, includes noncurrent deferred taxes in permanent capital for its computation of pretax return on permanent capital. However, it does not consider deferred tax liabilities as debt.[19]

---

[15]Discounting of deferred taxes is not allowed under U.S. GAAP and is rare elsewhere. It is currently allowed in the Netherlands; however, few firms discount. The most recent proposal from the U.K. Accounting Standards Board calls for discounting under certain conditions.

[16]The United Kingdom allows partial allocation and deferred taxes are recognized only when reversal is expected within the foreseeable future (see Exhibit 9-7 and related discussion).

[17]However, the recognition of fixed asset impairment (see the discussion in Chapter 8) may instantaneously offset many years of accelerated depreciation. Such write-downs do not affect tax reporting until the affected assets are sold. As a result, previously established deferred tax liabilities relating to these assets reverse. If the carrying value of the impaired assets is reduced below their tax basis, deferred tax assets must be established. But this reversal has no effect on taxable income or, therefore, taxes payable. This is another case where the reversal of temporary differences may not generate income tax cash outflows. For an example, see the discussion of Glatfelter's impairment provision in Chapter 8. Problem 7 in Chapter 9 considers the income tax consequences of that write-down.

[18]Some creditors treat deferred tax liabilities as debt. In this case, there is a double effect; debt is decreased and equity increased by the same amount, with an even greater decrease in the debt-to-equity ratio.

[19]See Standard and Poor's "Formulas for Key Ratios," *Corporate Finance Criteria* (New York: McGraw-Hill, 1994), p. 75.

Box 9-2 discusses evidence provided by market research regarding the relevance of deferred taxes to securities valuation. The evidence indicates that the market does consider firm growth rates, the probability of reversal, and present value factors in assessing whether to treat deferred taxes as liability or equity.

Analysis of Deferred Tax Assets

Deferred tax assets may be indicators of future cash flow, reported income, or both. Therefore, as with liabilities, one should examine the source of those assets and evaluate the likelihood and timing of reversal. Any valuation allowance should also be reviewed. To the extent that deferred tax assets have been offset by a valuation allowance, realization of those assets will increase reported income (and stockholders' equity) as well as generate cash flow. If no valuation allowance has been provided, then realization will have no effect on reported income or equity, although cash flow will still benefit.

Conversely, when deferred tax assets are no longer realizable, if no valuation allowance had been provided, then the establishment of such an allowance reduces reported income and equity.

Given management discretion, the valuation allowance has become another factor used to evaluate the quality of earnings. Some firms are conservative, offsetting most or all deferred tax assets with valuation allowances. Other firms are more optimistic and assume that no valuation allowance is necessary.

BOX 9-2
Market Valuation of Deferred Taxes

Surprisingly, there have not been many empirical studies that examined whether the market as a whole treats deferred tax liabilities as debt. Earlier discussion noted that the extent to which deferred tax liabilities should be treated as debt is a function of the probability that the deferrals will be reversed and the debt (if considered) should be discounted to its present value.

Givoly and Hayn (1992) examined these issues in the context of the Tax Reform Act (TRA) of 1986. The TRA cut the statutory tax rate for U.S. corporations from 46 to 34%. This affected a firm's current tax position as well as the amount that would have to be repaid if and when future reversals of temporary differences occurred.

The TRA was debated for over two years in Congress. Givoly and Hayn examined the effects on stock prices of events that indicated an improved chance of the measure passing as well as events that indicated a decreased chance of the measure passing. After controlling for the effects on current tax payments,* they argued that if the market treated the deferred tax as a liability:

1. The larger the deferred taxes, the more positive the impact of the TRA on the firm's market price.

2. No matter how large the firm's deferred tax account is, if temporary differences will not be reversed or future tax losses will result in nonpayment of the tax at reversal, the effects of the TRA should be minimal. Thus, they argued that the larger the growth rate in the deferred tax account and the greater the probability of tax losses,† the less likely there would be a positive impact on stock prices.

If the market ignored the deferred tax liability, there would be no impact of any of these factors. Overall, their results confirmed that the market incorporated the deferred tax liability into valuation.

When chances of the TRA being adopted increased (decreased), then:

1. The larger the deferred tax account, the more positive (negative) the market reaction.
2. A large growth rate and increased probability of losses decreased (increased) the abnormal return.

A by-product of their study was the indication that the market incorporated a discount factor in valuing the deferred tax liability. The deferred tax accounts of high-risk‡ firms tended to affect market valuation less than low-risk firms. This result is consistent with a higher discount rate being applied to the higher-risk firms.

The Givoly and Hayn study focused on the deferred tax account in the balance sheet. It found that deferred tax accounting is incorporated in balance sheet valuation. Focusing on earnings, an earlier study by Beaver and Dukes (1972) also found that the market "favors" the deferral process. They found market reaction tended to be more closely associated with income that incorporated deferrals than with income that ignored deferrals and calculated taxes on the basis of current tax expense.§ Rayburn (1986), however, found that the association between deferred tax accruals and security returns was dependent on the expectations model assumed.

---

*Givoly and Hayn also controlled for other factors such as the present stock and age of machinery and equipment.

†The probability of losses was estimated using the frequency of losses that occurred in the previous five years.

‡High risk was determined on the basis of the firm's market beta.

§The authors found this result surprising as they expected the number closer to cash flows (earnings without deferral) to be more closely associated with security prices. In a subsequent paper (Beaver and Dukes, 1973), the authors offered a different explanation. They demonstrated (see the discussion in Chapter 8) that the market generally imputes a more accelerated form of depreciation than straight-line depreciation. As deferred taxes increase expense shown for firms using straight-line depreciation, they argued that the observed results with respect to deferred taxes may be a function of deferred taxes masking as a form of accelerated depreciation.

The important point is that changes in the valuation allowance often affect reported earnings and can be used to manage them.

DuPont's reported valuation allowance declined by $88 million in 1994, from $445 million at December 31, 1993 to $357 million at December 31, 1994. A change in the tax status of some affiliates reduced the allowance by $105 million. That reduction was partly offset by an unexplained $17 million net increase. The $88 million net change in the valuation allowance ($0.13 per share) increased reported income.

Effective Tax Rates

Valuation models that forecast future income or cash flows use the firm's effective tax rate as one input. Moreover, trends in effective tax rates over time for a firm and the relative effective tax rates for comparable firms within an industry can help assess operating performance and the income available for stockholders. Several alternative measures can be used to assess the firm's effective tax rate.

The *reported* effective tax rate is measured as:

$$\frac{\textbf{Income Tax Expense}}{\textbf{Pretax Income}}$$

EXHIBIT 9-5. DUPONT
Effective Tax Rates

	1992	1993	1994	1992 to 1994
Taxes payable	$ 896	$1,100	$1,407	$3,403
Deferred tax expense	(221)	(737)	306	(652)
Other	161	29	(58)	132
Income tax expense	$ 836	$ 392	$1,655	$2,883
Income tax paid	$1,213	$ 896	$1,344	$3,453
Pretax income	$1,811	$ 958	$4,382	$7,151
Statutory tax rate	34%	35%	35%	34.7%
Income tax expense/pretax income	46.2%	40.9%	37.8%	40.3%
Taxes payable/pretax income	49.5%	114.8%	32.1%	47.6%
Income tax paid/pretax income	67.0%	93.5%	30.7%	48.3%

Both reported tax expense and pretax income, however, are affected by management choices of revenue and expense recognition methods. Although it is useful to retain pretax income, a key indicator of financial performance, as the denominator, other numerators generate tax rates that provide additional information.[20]

The first alternative tax rate uses taxes payable (current tax expense) for the period, based on revenue and expense recognition methods used on the tax return:

$$\frac{\text{Taxes Payable}}{\text{Pretax Income}}$$

This ratio may also be used with cash taxes paid instead of taxes payable. The resulting ratio focuses more on cash flows:

$$\frac{\text{Income Tax Paid}}{\text{Pretax Income}}$$

The amount of cash taxes paid can be easily obtained as SFAS 95, Statement of Cash Flows, requires separate disclosure of this amount. Due to interim tax payments and refunds, cash taxes paid may be quite different from taxes payable.

Exhibit 9-5 calculates these differing measures of an effective tax rate for duPont.

The first calculation is the reported effective tax rate (income tax expense/pretax income). DuPont's effective tax rate decreased from 46.2% in 1992 to 37.8% in 1994; the three-year average rate is 40.3%. All these rates exceed the U.S. statutory rate for the period.[21]

---

[20]Some empirical evidence (see Zimmermann, 1983) indicates that effective tax rates calculated using income tax paid and/or current tax expense tend to be higher for large firms. This is cited as evidence of the political cost hypothesis as large firms, being more politically sensitive, are required to make (relatively) larger wealth transfers than smaller firms. As the research results are largely due to the oil and gas industry, it is difficult to tell whether the political costs result from size or industry classification. Wang (1991) notes that smaller firms are more likely to have net operating losses than larger firms, at which time their effective tax rate is zero. Ignoring these losses may bias the research results.

[21]The average statutory rate for a multiyear period should be a weighted average, with pretax income providing the weights.

Two questions are suggested by these data:

1. Why is duPont's effective tax rate above the statutory rate?
2. What is duPont's effective tax rate likely to be in the future?

We seek answers to these questions shortly.

The second effective tax rate (taxes payable/pretax income) calculated in Exhibit 9-5 is highly variable over the 1992 to 1994 period, ranging from a high of 114.8% in 1993 to a low of 32.1% in 1994. The average rate is 47.6% over the three-year period, well above *both* the first effective rate and the statutory rate. Again, we will try to understand the factors in this high rate and the likelihood that they will persist in the future.

The third measure of effective tax rate, which compares income tax paid with pretax income, is also variable over the three-year period. The average rate of 48.3% is close to the average rate for taxes payable. This congruence should be expected as the timing of taxes paid is affected by technical payment requirements and by errors in management's forecast of tax liability in each jurisdiction. Over time, these factors should cancel out.

We return to the analysis of duPont's income tax position shortly. To provide additional background for that analysis, we must first discuss the effect of temporary versus permanent differences on effective tax rates and other specialized issues that highlight differences between tax and financial reporting.

ACCOUNTING FOR TAXES: SPECIALIZED ISSUES

Temporary Versus Permanent Differences

The different objectives of financial and tax reporting generate temporary differences between pretax financial income and taxable income. Some differences, however, are permanent because they result from revenues and expenses that are reportable on either tax returns or in financial statements but not both. In the United States, for example, interest income on tax-exempt bonds, premiums paid on officers' life insurance, and amortization of goodwill (in some cases) are included in financial statements but are never reported on the tax return. Similarly, certain dividends are not fully taxed, and tax or statutory depletion may exceed cost-based depletion reported in the financial statements.

Tax credits are another type of permanent difference. The alternative fuels credit reported by duPont is one example. Such credits directly reduce taxes payable and are different from tax deductions that reduce taxable income.

No deferred tax consequences are recognized for *permanent differences*; however, they result in a difference between the effective tax rate and the statutory tax rate that should be considered in the analysis of effective tax rates.

Indefinite Reversals

The amount and timing of the reversal of some temporary differences are subject to management influence or control. Some differences may never reverse at all. The accounting for these differences is especially troublesome. The uncertainty as to the amount and timing of their cash consequences affects the estimation of cash flows and firm valuation.

The undistributed earnings of unconsolidated subsidiaries and joint ventures are the most common example of this problem. The U.S. tax code requires 80% ownership to consolidate for tax purposes, ruling out joint ventures and many subsidiaries that are consolidated for accounting purposes. In addition, foreign subsidiaries are not consolidated in the U.S. tax return.[22]

As a result, the income of these affiliates is taxable on the parent's (U.S.) tax return only when dividends are received or the affiliate is sold, not when earnings are recognized. There is a difference between (tax return) taxable income and (financial reporting) pretax income. If the affiliate earnings are permanently reinvested, then affiliate earnings may never be taxable on the parent company tax return.

APB 23 permitted firms to omit deferred tax provisions on the reinvested earnings of affiliates that met the "indefinite reversal" criteria of that standard.[23] APB 24 provided different reporting rules for equity method investments (other than controlled subsidiaries and joint ventures) as the assumption of permanent reinvestment of undistributed earnings could be justified only when the parent controls the investee. The deferred tax effects of undistributed earnings were computed based on whether they were expected to be received as dividends or capital gains.[24]

SFAS 109 superseded APB 23[25] by requiring the recognition of deferred tax liabilities for temporary differences due to the undistributed earnings of essentially permanent domestic subsidiaries and joint ventures for fiscal years beginning on or after December 15, 1992.[26] However, SFAS 109 maintained the APB 23 exemption from the provision of deferred tax liabilities in the following cases:

- Undistributed earnings of a foreign subsidiary or joint venture that are considered to be permanently reinvested.
- Undistributed earnings of a domestic subsidiary or joint venture for fiscal years prior to December 15, 1992.

In its income tax note (Note 7), duPont reports that the firm has not recorded deferred taxes on undistributed earnings of foreign affiliates in the amount of $4,333 million (59% of the reported retained earnings of $7,406 million) at December 31, 1994. If the indefinite reversal assumption had not been applicable, the firm would have reported an additional unspecified deferred tax liability.

---

[22]In some cases, even wholly owned U.S. subsidiaries may not be consolidated for tax purposes. Insurance subsidiaries, which are governed by special tax regulations, are one example.

[23]Criteria for "indefinite reversal" included a history of reinvestment (lack of dividend payments) and operational budgets (showing the intent to reinvest earnings).

[24]Since dividends from qualifying investments are eligible for an 80% dividends received exclusion in the US, the effective tax rate is much lower than the rate applicable to income received as capital gains.

[25]SFAS 109 also amended APB 23 as follows: Deferred taxes must be provided on bad debt reserves of U.S. thrift lenders originating after 1987, on deposits in statutory reserve funds of U.S. steamship enterprises, and on post-1992 policyholders' surplus of stock life insurance companies; these issues are beyond the scope of this book.

[26]But if the parent has the statutory ability to realize those earnings tax free, no deferred tax provision is required (para. 33, SFAS 109).

Accounting for Acquisitions

SFAS 109 requires separate recognition of the deferred tax effects of any differences between the financial statement carrying amounts and tax bases of assets and liabilities recognized in purchase method acquisitions (see Chapter 14). APB 16 required firms to record acquired assets and liabilities *net* of related deferred taxes. As a result, many firms that had made purchase method acquisitions had to record additional deferred tax liabilities when adopting SFAS 109. DuPont reports that this requirement was the principal reason why the adoption of the new standard increased deferred tax liabilities by more than $1 billion (see duPont's Note 7).

In some cases, a valuation allowance must be recorded for deferred tax assets due to the acquired firm's temporary differences or its operating loss or tax credit carryforwards. The tax benefits of subsequent reversals of the valuation allowance must be used, first, to reduce all related goodwill, second, to eliminate all other related noncurrent intangible assets, and third, to reduce reported income tax expense.

ANALYSIS OF INCOME TAX DISCLOSURES: DUPONT

Accounting for income taxes is complex; a large company may have many permanent and temporary differences between financial statement income and taxable income. A large multinational pays taxes in a number of jurisdictions, further complicating the process. From an analyst's perspective, unraveling these layers can seem daunting indeed.

Some analysts respond to this complexity by ignoring the issues. They analyze corporate performance on a pretax basis and simply accept that variations in the reported tax rate occur. We agree that analysis on a pretax basis is sound, but also believe that a firm's income tax accounting is too important to ignore.

The goals of income tax analysis are to:

1. Understand why the firm's effective tax rate differs (or does not differ) from the statutory rate in its home country.
2. Forecast changes in the effective tax rate, improving forecasts of earnings.
3. Review the historical differences between income tax expense and income taxes paid.
4. Forecast the future relationship between income tax expense and income tax payments.
5. Examine deferred tax liabilities and assets, including any valuation allowance, for

   - Possible effects on future earnings and cash flows.
   - Their relevance to firm valuation.
   - Their relevance in assessing a firm's capital structure.

We pursue these goals, using duPont as an example, and illustrate the insights regarding a firm that can be derived from its income tax disclosures.

Analysis of the Effective Tax Rate

The first step is an examination of the firm's tax rate, the trend in that rate, and the rate relative to similar companies. Variations are generally the consequence of:

1. Different statutory tax rates in different jurisdictions; analysis can offer important clues as to the sources of income.

2. Tax holidays that some countries offer; earnings from such operations usually cannot be remitted without payment of tax. Be alert to possible changes in the operations in such countries or the need to remit the accumulated earnings.

3. Permanent differences between financial and taxable income: tax-exempt income, tax credits, and nondeductible expenses.

4. The effect of tax rate and other tax law changes that, under SFAS 109, are included in income tax expense (a separate disclosure of this effect is required).

5. Deferred taxes provided on the reinvested earnings of foreign affiliates and unconsolidated domestic affiliates.

As noted earlier, duPont's effective tax rate averaged 40.3% over the 1992 to 1994 period. DuPont's tax footnote provides the required reconciliation between its statutory rate and effective rate for each year.[27] Because of the significance of some of these differences and variation in pretax income over the period, the rate-based disclosures are difficult to analyze. For that reason, Exhibit 9-6 converts them to dollar-based disclosures.

Starting with the three-year totals, we see that a higher tax rate on non-U.S. earnings is the largest single factor in duPont's high effective tax rate, adding $1.3 billion or 18 percentage points for the three-year period. DuPont's petroleum operations accounted for 43% of revenues and 26% of operating profit in 1994. Three-quarters of those operations are outside the United States, mostly in Europe.[28] Under U.S. tax law, oil royalties are tax-deductible expenses, whereas foreign income tax payments are tax credits. For that reason, foreign countries generally structure royalties as "income taxes" and U.S. companies with foreign petroleum operations report high effective tax rates. Thus, duPont's high effective tax rate is largely a function of its non-U.S. petroleum operations. Forecasting future effective tax rates, therefore, requires explicit forecasts of the earnings of these operations.

Partly offsetting this effect is lower tax rates paid by duPont operations in (unspecified) U.S. possessions. This factor reduced the composite three-year tax rate by two percentage points, adding an average of nearly $50 million to net income. No further data are provided regarding these operations. Another continuing benefit is the alternative fuels credit, whose dollar amount grew each year. Discussion with management should result in a better understanding of the source and likelihood of continuation of these benefits.

Several factors in duPont's effective tax rate are nonrecurring in nature. One is the benefit ($274 million) from 1993 changes in the U.K. Petroleum Revenue Tax law. Another is the 1994 benefit ($105 million) from "tax status changes" affecting the valuation allowance.

---

[27]The reconciliation can be done in either percentages (relative to the statutory tax rate) or monetary amounts (relative to "statutory" income tax expense equal to pretax income multiplied by the statutory rate).

[28]Based on duPont's reported segment data, discussed in detail in Chapter 13.

EXHIBIT 9-6. DUPONT
Reconciliation of Effective and Statutory Tax Rates

	1992	1993	1994	1992 to 1994 Total	Rate
Pretax income	$1,811	$958	$4,382	$7,151	
Statutory rate	34%	35%	35%		
Variations from Statutory Rate					
Non-U.S. income	20.5	51.9	9.9		
U.S. possessions	(2.4)	(5.6)	(1.1)		
Alternative fuels	(2.0)	(6.9)	(2.1)		
Tax rate changes	—	(28.6)			
Tax status change	—		(2.4)		
Other—net	(3.9)	(4.9)	(1.5)		
Net effect	12.2	5.9	2.8		
Effective tax rate	46.2	40.9	37.8		
Tax in Millions of Dollars = Rate × Pretax Income					
At statutory rate	$ 616	$335	$1,534	$2,485	34.8%
Effect of					
Non-U.S. income	$ 371	$497	$ 434	$1,302	18.2%
U.S. possessions	(43)	(54)	(48)	(145)	−2.0
Alternative fuels	(36)	(66)	(92)	(194)	−2.7
Tax rate changes	—	(274)	—	(274)	−3.8
Tax status change	—	—	(105)	(105)	−1.5
Other—net	(71)	(47)	(66)	(183)	−2.6
Net effect	$ 221	$ 57	$ 123	$ 400	5.6%
Income tax expense	$ 837	$392	$1,656	$2,885	40.3%

Source: Adapted from duPont Note 7, *1994 Annual Report.*

Now that we understand the reasons for duPont's high effective tax rate in the past, we turn to the future. A forecast of future income tax expense should start with estimated pretax income and apply the statutory rate of 35%. The analyst should then adjust for the effects of the:

• Higher tax rate on petroleum income
• Lower tax rate on U.S. possession operations
• Alternative fuels credit
• "Other" effects

These adjustments may require input from duPont management or trade publications. Some firms provide periodic forecasts of their tax rate because of the difficulty of making such forecasts externally.

Analysis of Deferred Income Tax Expense

We now examine the effects of temporary differences on income tax expense. Companies are required to provide details of these differences, although formats vary. DuPont's disclosure is typical, showing a breakdown in dollars for each year.

Temporary differences are generally the result of the use of different accounting policies or estimates for tax purposes than for financial reporting differences. Some of these differences are systematic; others are transaction-specific. Frequent examples include:

1. *Depreciation.* Different methods and/or lives results in different measures of depreciation expense.

2. *Impairment.* Financial reporting write-downs do not generate tax deductions until assets are sold.

3. *Restructuring costs.* Usually tax-deductible when paid rather than when accrued.

4. *Inventories.* Companies using last-in, first-out (LIFO) accounting for tax purposes in the United States must also use LIFO for reporting purposes, but when other methods are used, differences may occur.

5. *Postemployment benefits.* The accruals required by SFAS 87 (pensions), SFAS 106 (other retiree benefits), and SFAS 112 (other postemployment benefits) are discussed in Chapter 12. Tax treatment of these costs is generally cash-based, generating deferred tax effects.

6. *Deferred compensation.* Tax-deductible only when payments are made.

On a cumulative basis, duPont generated negative deferred tax expense (taxes payable > income tax expense) over the 1992 to 1994 period, although deferred tax expense was positive in 1994.[29] Depreciation was the only factor generating positive deferred tax expense over this period. Although duPont used accelerated depreciation methods for most property (see the discussion in Chapter 8), its tax depreciation is higher still. This effect may be due to petroleum property (depreciated using the straight line method) or to the use of shorter lives for tax accounting. As duPont switched to the straight-line method for all property effective January 1, 1995, deferred tax expense from this source should increase.

Note, however, that in 1993 depreciation generated negative deferred tax expense. As reported in Note 6, duPont wrote down fixed assets in that year, reversing a portion of the excess tax depreciation from prior years.

The 1993 restructuring charges had other deferred tax effects. Although the disclosure is not clear, the "other accrued expenses" line in the deferred income tax disclosure probably reflects charges that did not generate tax deductions in that year. *When a large restructuring charge is taken, the tax effects generally occur as expenditures are made, with significant effects on deferred tax expense both in the year of the charge and the year(s) of payment.*

The two nonrecurring adjustments for tax rate and tax status changes (both discussed above) affected deferred tax expense. Neither adjustment had any effect on cash flow.

---

[29]See Note 7 to duPont financial statements and data in Exhibit 9-5.

Because duPont's deferred tax expense was negative over the 1992 to 1994 period, taxes payable (and income tax paid) exceeded income tax expense. Absent write-offs or other "restructuring" charges and given the 1995 change in depreciation method, it appears unlikely that deferred tax expense will be negative in the future.

Using Deferred Taxes to Estimate Taxable Income

Deferred tax expense reflects the difference between taxable income reported to tax authorities and pretax income reported to shareholders. This relationship can be used to estimate components of taxable income. The difference between taxable income and pretax income equals

$$\frac{\text{Deferred Tax Expense}}{\text{Statutory Tax Rate}}$$

For example, duPont's 1994 depreciation expense (financial reporting) was $2,976 million. Deferred tax expense related to depreciation was $144 million in 1994 (Note 7). Using that amount and the statutory tax rate of 35%, we estimate that the additional depreciation expense under tax reporting was $411 million ($144 million divided by 0.35) and tax basis depreciation was $3,387 million ($2,976 + $411).

These calculations should be viewed as estimates. They are most reliable when they relate to a single tax jurisdiction as the appropriate tax rate and the difference between tax and financial reporting rules are clear. Although this method can, in theory, be used to calculate taxable income for the entire firm, such calculations for large multinationals are less reliable.

Similar calculations can be made for the cumulative financial reporting-tax differences using deferred tax asset and liability data. The calculation for duPont's fixed assets is shown in the next section of this chapter.

Deferred tax disclosures can also be used, in some cases, to estimate the taxes paid associated with components of income and expense. Problem 11B applies this approach to the gain on an asset sale by Honda.

Analysis of Deferred Tax Assets and Liabilities

Our final step is an examination of the balance sheet consequences of duPont's income tax accounting. As required by SFAS 109, Note 7 contains a table of significant deferred tax assets and liabilities, as well as the valuation allowance, at each balance sheet date.

The most significant deferred tax asset relates to accrued employee benefits. As previously discussed, the adoption of SFAS 106 (postretirement benefits) generated a large deferred tax asset.

The second largest asset results from "other accrued expenses," presumably accruals that have not yet generated tax deductions. Possible sources include deferred compensation, accruals for the fungicide recall (see Note 3) and restructuring charges. Note 18 lists duPont's "other accrued liabilities."

Tax loss and tax credit carryforwards are a third significant source of deferred tax assets. Although duPont does not say so, it is likely that this source has generated the valuation allowance.

DuPont's largest single source of deferred tax liabilities, as for most firms, is depreciation. This difference usually reflects the use of accelerated methods and shorter lives for tax return depreciation calculations.

If we assume a 35% tax rate for all depreciation-related deferred tax assets, the reporting difference can be estimated as $8.4 billion ($2.94/0.35) or 30% of accumulated depreciation of $27.7 billion. Given duPont's use of accelerated methods for nonpetroleum property, this large difference is surprising. Although much of this difference may relate to petroleum property, some may reflect the use of shorter lives for tax reporting.

Although the remaining deferred tax liabilities are small, several deserve comment. While duPont uses the LIFO inventory method for "substantially all" inventories, there is a $310 million deferred liability from this source. This liability may reflect obsolescence write-downs that cannot be recognized for tax purposes under LIFO or different varieties of LIFO used for financial and tax reporting.[30]

Although duPont has several significant affiliates accounted for by the equity method (see Note 14 and Chapter 13), there is only a small deferred tax liability from this source. Note 14 indicates that virtually all of duPont's share of earnings is paid out as dividends, which are taxed currently.

DuPont reported a valuation allowance of $357 million at December 31, 1994 ($445 million at December 31, 1993). Although there is no discussion in the financial statements, the tax loss/tax credit carryforwards are the most likely reason for that allowance.

If we put together all these pieces, duPont's net balance sheet liability for income tax is:

Deferred tax assets	$ 4,592
Less: Valuation allowance	(357)
Less: Deferred tax liability	(5,152)
Net liability	$ (917)

Where does this liability appear on duPont's balance sheet? The answer is—in several places. Fortunately, SFAS 109 requires the disclosure of all deferred tax components on the balance sheet. In the case of duPont, these are ($ in millions):

Assets		Liabilities	
Deferred income taxes	$558	Income taxes	$ 63
Other assets	82	Deferred income taxes	1,494
Totals	$640	Totals	$1,557
		Net liability	$ 917

Is this $917 million a real liability? Or, to rephrase the question, what are the likely future cash flow effects of duPont's deferred tax assets and liabilities?

Given its large size, the deferred tax liability associated with accumulated depreciation is the logical starting point. On the one hand, capital expenditures have been declining (41% since 1990), although the Management Discussion and Analysis forecasts an increase for 1995. In addition, the switch to straight line depreciation for nonpetroleum property will tend to increase the deferred tax liability from this source. Thus, unless there are further decreases in capital spending, it seems unlikely that the deferred tax liability from depreciation will decline over the next few years. The trend

---

[30]Appendix 6-A contains a discussion of the different varieties of LIFO.

in capital spending must, however, be monitored. Based on data available in the annual report, no other deferred tax liability seems likely to reverse.

On the other hand, duPont's largest deferred tax asset, related to accrued employee benefits, may start to reverse at some point. As retiree benefit payments increase, they may exceed the accrual for additional benefits earned. Trends in these amounts can be monitored using the analytic techniques in Chapter 12.

In total, therefore, it appears unlikely that duPont's deferred tax accruals will generate any significant cash outflow over the next few years. In addition, given the unlikelihood of near-term reversal, the net liability should be discounted for the time value of money. The combination of these factors suggests that a liability should not be recognized for valuation purposes.

Other Issues in Income Tax Analysis

The following issues, although not relevant to an analysis of duPont, occur frequently enough to warrant brief mention:

- Watch for companies that report substantial income for financial reporting purposes but little or no taxes payable (implying little or no taxable income). Such differences often reflect aggressive revenue and expense recognition methods used for financial reporting, and low quality of earnings. In such cases, caution is indicated as the methods used for financial reporting purposes may be based on optimistic assumptions.

- Look for current or pending reversals of past temporary differences. For example, a decline in capital spending may result in a greater proportion of depreciation coming from old assets that have already been heavily depreciated for tax purposes. Thus, financial reporting depreciation may exceed tax depreciation, generating a tax liability.

- Remember that deferred tax assets and liabilities may point to near-term cash consequences. Restructuring provisions often generate little cash or tax effect in the year they occur, but substantial effects in following years.

- Tax law changes may also result in the reversal of past temporary differences. In the United States, tax law changes in recent years have curtailed the use of the completed contract and installment methods for tax purposes, generating substantial tax liabilities for affected companies.

FINANCIAL REPORTING OUTSIDE THE UNITED STATES

As already noted, many foreign jurisdictions require conformity between financial reporting and tax reporting in separate (parent company) financial statements. In such cases, the issues discussed in this chapter do not occur. That statement is no longer true, however, once consolidated statements include subsidiaries that are not consolidated for tax purposes. Given the worldwide tendency toward consolidated reporting, even firms in tax conformity countries must grapple with the question of deferred tax accounting.

IASC Standards

The IASC revised IAS 12 in 1996. It requires use of the liability method but permits companies to use "indefinite reversal" criteria to avoid recognizing deferred taxes on the reinvested earnings of subsidiaries, associates, and joint ventures, when all the following conditions are met:

- The parent, investor, or venturer can control the manner and timing of the reversal of the temporary difference.
- It is probable that the temporary difference will not reverse in the foreseeable future.
- It is impractical to estimate applicable taxes when the reversal ultimately occurs.

As a result, there are significant differences in the recognition of deferred tax liabilities among firms using IASC and U.S. GAAP; the latter group must record deferred taxes for the reinvested earnings of domestic affiliates, whereas, under certain conditions, IASC standards permit nonrecognition.

Non-U.S. Standards

Virtually all countries require the recognition of deferred taxes on temporary differences. Germany and the United Kingdom use the liability method, whereas France and Japan allow either the deferred or liability method. Most countries limit the recognition of deferred tax liabilities and few address the issue of deferred tax assets.

U.K. tax accounting rules are based on a partial allocation approach that is quite different from the comprehensive allocation method used in the United States (and required by the IASC). Under U.K. GAAP, deferred taxes must be provided only to the extent it is considered probable that a tax liability or benefit will occur in the foreseeable future. Forecasts of the probability of realization of deferred amounts must take into consideration planned capital expenditures and other financial plans.

Example: Cadbury Schweppes. Exhibit 9-7 presents the deferred tax footnote taken from Cadbury Schweppes 1995 Form 20-F, which includes financial statements prepared using U.K. GAAP. The company uses the partial allocation method and excludes an additional 92 million pound deferred tax liability that it would have reported under the comprehensive allocation method. Most (73 million pounds) of that unrecorded liability results from the use of accelerated tax depreciation. As this timing difference is not expected to reverse, no deferred tax liability is required.[31]

Although partial allocation is a logical alternative to the comprehensive allocation method required elsewhere, it presents two analytical problems. First, it makes Cadbury financial statements not comparable with those of firms using comprehensive allocation. To restore comparability, the analyst must either create the deferred tax liability for Cadbury (and reduce equity by the same amount) or adjust the financial statements of the other firms to a partial allocation method. Income statement adjustments are also required as Cadbury's income tax expense excludes the changes in unrecognized deferred tax liabilities.

The second problem is the management discretion that partial allocation permits. As is the case for the valuation allowance under SFAS 109 (in effect, partial allocation applied to deferred tax assets), this discretion can be used to manage earnings.

U.K. GAAP limits the recognition of net deferred tax assets to the amounts expected to be recovered without the assumption of future taxable income. However,

---

[31]This is similar to the approach suggested in the section, ''Liability or Equity'': Deferred tax assets and liabilities should be recognized (for analysis) only for timing differences expected to reverse.

EXHIBIT 9-7. CADBURY SCHWEPPES PLC
Deferred Taxes: Partial Allocation

The deferred tax asset of the Company is net of a deferred tax liability of £56 million. The deferred liability of the Company in 1994 was net of a deferred tax asset of £28 million. The total potential liability of the Company for deferred tax at December 31, 1994 and December 30, 1995 was as follows:

	(Pounds in millions)	
	1994	1995
Included in accounts		
Timing differences		
United Kingdom	£ 2	£ 22
Overseas	5	(62)
	£ 7	£(40)
Not accounted for		
Accelerated tax depreciation:		
United Kingdom	£42	£ 49
Overseas	20	24
U.K. finance leases	16	14
U.K. property valuations	8	7
Other timing differences	—	(2)
	£86	£ 92

To the extent that dividends from overseas companies are expected to result in additional taxes, appropriate amounts have been provided. No taxes have been provided for other unremitted earnings since such amounts are considered permanently reinvested by subsidiaries and in the case of associated companies the taxes would not be material. Earnings retained by overseas subsidiaries and the principal overseas associated companies totalled approximately £557 million at December 30, 1995; the remittance of these amounts would incur tax at substantially lower than normal rates after giving effect to foreign tax credits.

Source: Cadbury Schweppes, 1995 Form 20-F.

firms may elect to use either comprehensive or partial allocation to account for the deferred tax consequences of pensions and other postretirement benefits accounted for under SSAP 24, Accounting for Pension Costs, and UITF 6, Accounting for Post-Retirement Benefits other than Pensions. Firms are required to disclose the method selected.

German GAAP permits the recognition of deferred tax assets for the elimination of intercompany profits. In general, deferred taxes are computed under the liability method, but the amounts recognized are limited to the excess of consolidated deferred tax liabilities over consolidated deferred tax assets.

The accounting differences among U.S., IASC, and foreign GAAPs affect reported net income and stockholders' equity (generally higher under partial allocation but lower when deferred tax assets are unrecognized or offset by a valuation allowance). However, firms in different countries may use similar revenue and expense recognition methods. Exhibit 9-8 compares the effects of accounting variations (partial versus

EXHIBIT 9-8
Comparison of Alternative Methods of Reporting Deferred Taxes

Assumptions

Income Before Temporary Differences = 100

The following are temporary differences between tax and financial reporting (FR):

	Tax	FR	Difference
Depreciation	20	12	8
Bad debt expense	0	3	−3
Total	20	15	5

Current Tax Rate = 40%
Future Tax Rate (expected to be in effect when differences reverse) = 20%

It is expected that the difference due to depreciation will not reverse, but the difference due to bad debt expense will reverse.

Taxable Income and Taxes Payable on the Tax Return

Income before expenses creating differences	$100
Depreciation and bad debt expense	20
Taxable income	$ 80
Taxes payable (40% × $80)	$ 32

For financial statements, there are four different methods of reporting income tax expense and net income. There are two allocation methods (comprehensive and partial) and two recognition methods (deferral and liability). The deferred tax expense for each method differs:

Choice	Allocation	Recognition	Deferred Tax Expense
(1)C-D	**Comprehensive**	**Deferral**	
	All temporary differences	Current tax rate	
	$5	40%	$2 credit
(2)C-L	**Comprehensive**	**Liability**	
	All temporary differences	Future tax rate	
	$5	20%	$1 credit
(3)P-D	**Partial**	**Deferral**	
	Reversing differences	Current tax rate	
	$−3	40%	$−1.2 debit
(4)P-L	**Partial**	**Liability**	
	Reversing differences	Future tax rate	
	$−3	20%	$−0.6 debit

Taxes payable are $32 for each case as financial reporting choices do not affect the tax return. *Because of the different calculations of deferred tax expense, income tax expense (current and deferred) differs for each case, resulting in different measures of net income and different effective tax rates:*

Case	(1)C-D	(2)C-L	(3)P-D	(4)P-L
Income before expenses creating differences	$100.0	$100.0	$100.0	$100.0
Depreciation and bad debt expense	(15.0)	(15.0)	(15.0)	(15.0)
Pretax income	$ 85.0	$ 85.0	$ 85.0	$ 85.0
Income tax expense	(34.0)	(33.0)	(30.8)	(31.4)
Net income	$ 51.0	$ 52.0	$ 54.2	$ 53.6
Effective tax rate	40.0%	38.8%	36.2%	36.9%

comprehensive allocation and deferred versus liability methods) on reported tax expense.

Another difficulty when comparing firms using different GAAPs is the paucity of disclosure requirements in many cases. Both the United States (SFAS 109) and IASC (IAS 12) have substantial disclosure requirements; similar information is rarely available in the financial statements of most foreign countries. U.K. firms, however, often provide data on deferred tax liabilities that are not expected to have cash consequences in the foreseeable future (see Exhibit 9-7).

Form 20-F reconciliations of reported net income and stockholders' equity show the adjustments due to differences in deferred tax accounting. These differences can be used to restore comparability between U.S. firms and foreign firms (such as Cadbury) that file Form 20-F. In some cases, these adjustments can be used to approximate adjustments for firms not providing Form 20-F reconciliations, when they are similar to firms that do provide them.

SUMMARY

In this chapter, we have seen how income tax expense and deferred tax assets and liabilities are affected by the accounting method used and by management choices and assumptions. As all business enterprises are subject to income tax, no financial analysis is complete until the issues raised in this chapter have been examined. Analysts must examine, in particular, the effective tax rate, cash flow effects of deferred tax accruals, and the relevance of such accruals for valuation.

CASE 9-1

Analysis of Income Tax Disclosures of Dow and ICI

Dow Chemical and ICI operate in and compete with duPont in certain markets. Appendices B and C contain the financial statements of Dow Chemical and ICI, respectively for the year ended December 31, 1994.

1. Effective January 1, 1992, Dow adopted SFAS 106, Accounting for Postretirement Benefits Other Than Pensions. Dow recorded a charge to income of $994 million. Reported deferred tax assets related to postretirement benefits other than pensions are depicted in the following table ($ in millions):

Year-end	Deferred Tax Assets	Deferred Tax Liabilities
1992	$582	$–0–
1993	$625	$–0–
1994	$624	$ 9
1994*	$673	
1995	$596	

*Restated in 1995 statements.

Use applicable effective tax rates and other relevant data to:
   (i) compute the difference between the benefits accrued and amounts deducted for taxes for the years 1993 and 1994.

    (ii) explain potential causes of the reported deferred tax liability of $9 for postretirement benefits in 1994.

    (iii) explain the decrease in the deferred tax asset during 1995.

2. The balance in Dow's valuation allowance over the 1992–1995 period was:

1992	$64 million
1993	$60
1994	$23
1995	$16

Discuss the impact of these changes on the reported income and cash flows.

3. Exhibit 9C-1 provides required additional data from the 1993 annual report issued by ICI and the tax footnote from the 1992 Annual Report of Dow. Use these data and

EXHIBIT 9C-1
Excerpts from the Dow and ICI Financial Statements
(in millions of U.S. dollars and Pounds)

A. ICI Income Statement

	1992			
	Continuing Operations			
	Before Exceptional Items	Exceptional Items	Discontinued Operations	Total
Profit (loss) on ordinary activities before taxation	163	−595	48	−384
Taxes	−124	−63	4	−183
Profit (loss) on ordinary activities after taxation	39	−658	52	−567
Attributable to minorities	−16	14	−1	−3
Net profit (loss) for the financial year	23	−644	51	−570

B. ICI Footnote 8: Tax on Profit (Loss) on Ordinary Activities

ICI and Subsidiaries

United Kingdom taxation				
Corporation tax	89	−21	89	157
Double taxation relief	−38	0	−68	−106
Deferred taxation	−14	72	−58	0
	37	51	−37	51
Overseas Taxation				
Overseas taxes	51	27	91	169
Deferred taxation	27	−15	−59	−47
	78	12	32	122
	115	63	−5	173
Associated undertakings	9	0	1	10
Tax on profit (loss) on ordinary activities	124	63	−4	183

UK Corporation tax has been provided at 33 percent.

EXHIBIT 9C-1 (continued)

C. Deferred Taxation (ICI)

	1992
Accounted for at Balance Sheet Date	
Timing differences on UK capital allowances and depreciation	212
Miscellaneous timing differences	−157
	55
Not Accounted for at Balance Sheet Date	
UK capital allowances utilized in excess of depreciation charged	108
Miscellaneous timing differences	−116
	8
Full potential deferred taxation	47

D. Taxes on Income (Dow Chemical)

Domestic and Foreign Components of Income before
Taxes on Income and Minority Interests

	1993	1992	1991
Domstic	**$1,099**	$632	$1,274
Foreign	**426**	240	414
Total	**$1,525**	$872	$1,688

Provision (Credit) for Taxes on Income

	1993			1992			1991		
	Current	**Deferred**	**Total**	Current	Deferred	Total	Current	Deferred	Total
Federal	**$404**	**$(8)**	**$396**	$381	$(158)	$223	$400	$ (68)	$332
State and local	**63**	**—**	**63**	39	—	39	44	—	44
Foreign	**115**	**32**	**147**	149	(137)	12	243	(109)	134
Total	**$582**	**$24**	**$606**	$569	$(295)	$274	$687	$(177)	$510

Reconciliation to U.S. Statutory Rate

	1993	1992	1991
Taxes at U.S. statutory rate	**$534**	$296	$574
Amortization of nondeductible intangibles	**45**	43	36
Taxes on foreign operations at rates different from U.S. statutory rate (including FSC)	**29**	37	(8)
Nontaxable Destec IPO gain	**—**	—	(72)
Other—net	**(2)**	(102)	(20)
Total tax provision	**$606**	$274	$510
Effective tax rate	**39.7%**	31.4%	30.2%

EXHIBIT 9C-1 (*continued*)

At December 31, 1993, the valuation allowance to offset deferred tax assets which may not be realized was $60. The movement in the valuation allowance during 1993 was a net reduction of $4.

Operating loss carryforwards at December 31, 1993 amounted to $943 of which $3 is subject to expiration in 1994, $40 in 1995, $107 in 1996, $111 in 1997, and $149 in 1998. The remaining balances expire in years beyond 1998 or have an indefinite carryforward period.

Tax credit carryforwards at December 31, 1993 amounted to $202 of which $20 is subject to expiration in 1994, $3 in 1995, $3 in 1996, $45 in 1997 and $20 in 1998. The remaining balances expire in years beyond 1998 or have an indefinite carryforward period.

Unremitted earnings of subsidiaries and related companies which are deemed to be permanently invested amounted to $1,782 and $1,989 at December 31, 1993, and 1992, respectively. It is not practicable to calculate the unrecognized deferred tax liability on those earnings.

Deferred Tax Balances Consisted of the Following Temporary Differences:

	1993		1992	
	Deferred Tax Assets	**Deferred Tax Liabilities**	Deferred Tax Assets	Deferred Tax Liabilities
Property	$ 94	$ (732)	$ 88	$(683)
Inventory	103	(95)	59	(27)
Accounts receivable	47	(29)	38	(3)
Pension and other compensation accruals	127	(47)	165	(57)
Tax loss and credit carryforwards	355	—	280	—
Long-term debt	66	(16)	166	(18)
Alternative minimum tax	102	—	68	—
Accrual for postretirement benefit obligations	625	—	582	—
Investments	76	(96)	—	—
Amortization of intangibles	15	(37)	—	—
Other accruals and reserves	305	(10)	308	(17)
Other	141	(115)	83	(95)
Subtotal	$2,056	$(1,177)	$1,837	$(900)
Less: Valuation allowance	60	—	64	—
Total	$1,996	$(1,177)	$1,773	$(900)

Appendices B and C to compute the following effective tax rates for Dow and ICI for the 1992 to 1994 period:

  (i) reported effective tax rate

  (ii) alternative effective tax rate based on taxes payable and

  (iii) another alternative effective tax rate based on taxes paid.

  (iv) Explain your treatment of timing differences not accounted for at Balance Sheet date by ICI. (See Note 9 in ICI's 1994 annual report).

4. Discuss why Dow reports an effective tax rate above the statutory rate.

5. Dow has recorded asset writedowns and increasing deferred tax assets for Property in both 1992 and 1993. However, the deferred tax asset declined in 1994. Explain the increase (decline) in the deferred tax asset balance at the end of 1993 (1994).

6. (i) Did Dow report higher or lower tax depreciation compared to financial statement depreciation expense of $1,552 and $1,525 million in 1993 and 1994? Compute the difference in depreciation expense and the tax deduction.

(ii) Why does Dow report increasing deferred tax credits related to property despite its use of accelerated depreciation methods for financial reporting?

7. Explain the reason for and the changes in deferred tax asset and liability balances reported by Dow for inventory and long-term debt.

Chapter 9

Problems

1. [Deferred tax classification; 1990 CFA adapted] Explain in which of the following categories deferred taxes can be found? Provide an example for each category in your answer.

(i) Current liabilities

(ii) Long-term liabilities

(iii) Stockholders' equity

(iv) Current assets

(v) Long-term assets

2. [Deferred taxes; 1990 to 1996 CFA adapted] State which of the following statements are correct under SFAS 109. Explain why.

(i) The deferred tax liability account must be adjusted for the effect of enacted changes in tax laws or rates in the period of enactment.

(ii) The deferred tax asset account must be adjusted for the effect of enacted changes in tax laws or rates in the period of enactment

(iii) The tax consequences of an event must not be recognized until that event is recognized in the financial statements.

(iv) Both deferred tax liabilities and deferred tax assets must be accounted for based on the tax laws and rates in effect at their origin.

(v) Changes in deferred tax assets and liabilities are classified as extraordinary items in the income statement.

3. [Permanent versus temporary differences; 1991 CFA adapted] Define *permanent differences* and describe two events or transactions that generate such differences. Describe the impact of permanent differences on a firm's effective tax rate.

4. [Treatment of deferred tax liability; 1996 CFA adapted]

A. When computing a firm's debt-to-equity ratio, describe the conditions for treating the deferred tax liability:

(i) As equity

(ii) As debt

B. Provide arguments for excluding deferred tax liabilities from both the numerator and the denominator of the debt-to-equity ratio.

C. Describe the arguments for including a portion of the deferred taxes as equity and a portion as debt.

5. [Depreciation methods and deferred taxes] The Incurious George Company acquires assets K, L, and M at the beginning of year 1. Each asset has the same cost, a five-year life, and an expected salvage value of $3,000. For financial reporting, the firm uses the straight-line, sum-of-the-years'-digits, and double-declining-balance depreciation methods for assets K, L, and M, respectively. It uses the double-declining-balance method for all assets on its tax return; its tax rate is 34%. Depreciation expense of $12,000 was reported for asset L for financial reporting purposes in year 2. Using this information:

A. Calculate the tax return depreciation expense for each asset in year 2.

B. Calculate the financial statement depreciation expense for assets K and M in year 2.

C. Calculate the deferred tax credit (liability) or debit (asset) for each asset at the end of:

(i) Year 2

(ii) Year 5

6. [Analysis of deferred tax; 1988 CFA adapted] On December 29, 1996, Mother Prewitt's Handmade Cookies Corp. acquires a numerically controlled chocolate chip milling machine. Due to differences in tax and financial accounting, depreciation for tax purposes is $150,000 more than depreciation in the financial statements, adding $51,000 to deferred taxes. At the same time, Mother Prewitt's sells $200,000 worth of cookies on an installment contract, recognizing the $100,000 profit immediately. For tax purposes, however, $80,000 of the profit will be recognized in 1997, requiring $27,200 of deferred taxes.

A. Compare the expected cash consequences of the two deferred tax items just described. When calculating Mother Prewitt's solvency and leverage ratios, how should you treat the deferred tax liability?

B. In 1997, Mother Prewitt's tax rate will be 40%. Briefly discuss the adjustments to *each* of the two deferred tax items in 1997 because of the change in the tax rate, assuming the use of:

(i) The deferral method

(ii) The liability method (SFAS 109)

C. Under what conditions will Mother Prewitt need to recognize a valuation allowance for any deferred tax assets?

7. [Tax effect of restructuring; follow-up to Chapter 8] In 1994, Glatfelter recognized impairments including a $189 million write-down of the fixed assets of its Ecusta Division. The income tax footnote for 1994 reports the following deferred tax liability ($ thousands):

Year Ended December 31	1993	1994
Property	$131,667	$60,438

A. Explain the likely origin of the 1993 deferred tax liability.

B. Explain why the impairment write-down in 1994 would reduce the deferred tax liability.

C. Using the U.S. federal tax rate of 35%, estimate the amount of the reduction of the deferred tax liability resulting from the Ecusta write-down.

D. Explain why your answer to part C does not equal the actual reduction in the liability during 1994.

8. [Tax effect of permanently reinvested earnings] Brown-Forman reports, in the tax footnote to its *1995 Annual Report,* that

> deferred taxes were not provided on certain undistributed earnings ($58,980,000 at April 30, 1995) of certain foreign subsidiaries because such undistributed earnings are expected to be reinvested indefinitely overseas. If these amounts were not considered permanently reinvested, additional deferred taxes of approximately $20,173,000 would have been provided.

A. Explain how Brown-Forman's treatment of the undistributed earnings of these foreign subsidiaries has affected its reported:

(i) Income tax expense

(ii) Income tax paid

(iii) Effective tax rate

(iv) Earnings per share

(v) Book value per share

B. If the company remitted these earnings to the United States, describe the effect on the following reported amounts in that year:

(i) Pretax income

(ii) Income tax expense

(iii) Income tax paid

(iv) Effective tax rate

(v) Earnings per share

(vi) Book value per share

C. State whether an analyst should adjust Brown-Forman's reported financial data for the tax effect of the undistributed earnings. Justify your answer.

D. Brown-Forman recognized a deferred tax liability of $17,318,000 at April 30, 1995 for undistributed foreign earnings. Suggest why this liability was established given the statement quoted at the beginning of this question.

9. [Effect of foreign operations on income tax rate] PepsiCo reported the following tax rate reconciliation in its *1994 Annual Report:*

	1992	1993	1994
Statutory rate	34.0%	35.0%	35.0%
Effect of lower foreign tax rate	(5.0)	(3.3)	(5.4)
Other effects (net)	2.4	2.8	3.4
Effective tax rate	31.4%	34.5%	33.0%

PepsiCo's pretax earnings were ($ in millions):

	1992	1993	1994
United States	$1,197	$1,633	$1,762
Foreign	702	790	902

A. Using this data, calculate the following:

  (i) U.S. dollar reduction in income tax expense in 1992 to 1994 due to lower foreign tax rates

  (ii) Effective tax rate on foreign income for each year

  (iii) Net foreign income (after tax) for each year

  (iv) Effective tax rate on U.S. income for each year

  (v) Net U.S. income (after tax) for each year

B. Using your answers to part A, calculate the percentage changes in foreign and U.S. income for 1993 and 1994:

  (i) Pretax

  (ii) After tax

C. Discuss the differences in the pretax and after-tax growth of income calculated in part B.

D. List and justify the questions you would want to ask PepsiCo management about their tax position based on your answers to parts A through C.

10. [Tax effect of zero coupon debt] PepsiCo reported a deferred tax asset of $110.6 million at December 31, 1994 resulting from outstanding zero coupon debt.

A. Explain why zero coupon debt might generate deferred tax assets.

B. Describe the expected trend of these deferred tax assets over the life of the debt. *Note:* Do not forget to consider what happens when the debt matures.

11. [Analysis of income tax footnote data] Exhibit 9P-1 contains the income tax footnote from the *1994 Annual Report* of Honda, a multinational automobile manufacturer based in Japan. *Note that these data are adjusted to U.S. GAAP.*

A. Calculate the differences (in yen) between Honda's income tax expense and that expense based on the statutory rate.

B. Using your answer to part A, calculate the effective tax rate on the 14,654 million yen gain from the sale of Honda's investment in Rover.

(9) Income Taxes

Total income taxes for each of the years in the three-year period ended March 31, 1995 were allocated as follows:

	Yen (millions)			U.S. dollars (thousands) (note 2)
	1993	1994	1995	1995
Income..	¥53,208	¥33,719	**¥44,904**	**$502,563**
Stockholders' equity, for adjustment from foreign currency translation	(2,917)	(2,149)	**(6,506)**	**(72,815)**
Stockholders' equity, for net unrealized gains on marketable equity securities ...	—	—	**46,350**	**518,747**
	¥50,291	¥31,570	**¥84,748**	**$948,495**

Income tax expense for each of the years in the three-year period ended March 31, 1995 consists of the following:

	Yen (millions)		
	Current	Deferred	Total
1993:			
Japanese..	¥33,459	¥ 4,147	¥37,606
Foreign..	12,562	3,040	15,602
	¥46,021	¥ 7,187	¥53,208
1994:			
Japanese..	¥24,531	¥ 3,600	¥28,131
Foreign..	(2,789)	8,377	5,588
	¥21,742	¥11,977	¥33,719
1995:			
Japanese..	**¥23,538**	**¥ (3,972)**	**¥19,566**
Foreign..	**21,862**	**3,476**	**25,338**
	¥45,400	**¥ (496)**	**¥44,904**

	U.S. dollars (thousands) (note 2)		
	Current	Deferred	Total
1995:			
Japanese..	**$263,436**	**$(44,454)**	**$218,982**
Foreign..	**244,678**	**38,903**	**283,581**
	$508,114	**$ (5,551)**	**$502,563**

The significant components of deferred income tax expense for each of the years in the three-year period ended March 31, 1995 are as follows:

	Yen (millions)			U.S. dollars (thousands) (note 2)
	1993	1994	1995	1995
Deferred tax expense (exclusive of the effects of other components listed below)..	¥7,768	¥11,485	**¥ 9,949**	**$111,349**
Adjustments to deferred tax assets and liabilities for enacted changes in tax laws and rates..	(581)	1,257	**(55)**	**(616)**
Decrease in beginning-of-the year balance of the valuation allowance for deferred tax assets..	—	(765)	**(10,390)**	**(116,284)**
	¥7,187	¥11,977	**¥ (496)**	**$ (5,551)**

The Company and its domestic subsidiaries are subject to a number of taxes based on income, which in the aggregate resulted in normal tax rates of approximately 52% for the years ended March 31, 1993, 1994 and 1995. The foreign subsidiaries are subject to taxes based on income at rates ranging from 30% to 60%.

EXHIBIT 9P-1. (*continued*)

The effective tax rate of the companies for each of the years in the three-year period ended March 31, 1995 differs from the normal Japanese income tax rate for the following reasons:

	1993	1994	1995
Normal income tax rate	52.0%	52.0%	**52.0%**
Expenses not deductible for tax purposes	2.2	5.0	**2.6**
Valuation allowance provided for current year operating losses of subsidiaries	10.9	14.9	**5.2**
Difference in normal tax rates of foreign subsidiaries	(5.1)	(3.6)	**(1.4)**
Adjustments to deferred tax assets and liabilities for enacted changes in tax laws and rates	(0.7)	2.7	**(0.1)**
Gain on sale of Rover Group Limited shares	—	—	**(6.4)**
Reversal of valuation allowance due to utilization of operating loss carryforwards	—	(0.9)	**(4.1)**
Other	0.8	1.8	**(0.2)**
Effective tax rate	60.1%	71.9%	**47.6%**

The tax effects of temporary differences that give rise to significant portions of the deferred tax assets and deferred tax liabilities at March 31, 1994 and 1995 are presented below:

	Yen (millions)	
	1994	1995
Deferred tax assets:		
Inventory valuation	¥ 59,640	**¥ 62,510**
Allowance for dealers and customers	47,398	**45,071**
Alternative minimum tax credit	10,882	**9,541**
Operating loss carryforwards	28,609	**29,715**
Other	36,234	**34,365**
Total gross deferred tax assets	182,763	**181,202**
Less valuation allowance	(44,123)	**(33,424)**
Net deferred tax assets	138,640	**147,778**
Deferred tax liabilities:		
Inventory valuation	(16,211)	**(14,827)**
Depreciation and amortization, excluding lease transactions	(18,056)	**(14,524)**
Lease transactions	(34,629)	**(38,146)**
Undistributed earnings of subsidiaries and affiliates	(19,657)	**(22,659)**
Net unrealized gains on marketable equity securities	—	**(46,350)**
Other	(5,730)	**(6,263)**
Total gross deferred tax liabilities	(94,283)	**(142,769)**
Net deferred tax asset	¥ 44,357	**¥ 5,009**

The valuation allowance for deferred tax assets as of March 31, 1993 was ¥38,073 million. The net change in the total valuation allowance for the years ended March 31, 1994 and 1995 was an increase of ¥6,050 million and a decrease of ¥10,699 million ($119,743 thousand), respectively.

In assessing the realizability of deferred tax assets, management considers whether it is more likely than not that some portion or all of the deferred tax assets will not be realized. The ultimate realization of deferred tax assets is dependent upon the generation of future taxable income during the periods in which those temporary differences become deductible. Management considered the scheduled reversal of deferred tax liabilities, projected future taxable income and tax planning strategies in making this assessment. Based upon the level of historical taxable income and projections for future taxable income over the periods which the deferred tax assets are deductible, management believes it is more likely than not that the companies will realize the benefits of these deductible differences, net of the existing valuation allowances at March 31, 1994 and 1995.

EXHIBIT 9P-1. (*continued*)

At March 31, 1995, certain of the Company's subsidiaries have operating loss carryforwards for income tax purposes of approximately ¥63,531 million ($711,035 thousand) which are available to offset future taxable income, if any. Periods available to offset future taxable income vary in each tax jurisdiction and range from one year to an indefinite period as follows:

	Yen (millions)	U.S. dollars (thousands) (note 2)
Within 1 year	¥ 5,205	$ 58,254
1 to 5 years	35,214	394,113
5 to 15 years	6,472	72,434
Indefinite periods	16,640	186,234
	¥63,531	$711,035

In addition, certain of the Company's subsidiaries have tax credit carryforwards of approximately ¥9,541 million ($106,782 thousand) which are available to reduce future income taxes, if any, over an indefinite period.

As of March 31, 1994 and 1995, the Company did not recognize deferred tax liabilities of ¥47,052 million and ¥41,879 million ($468,707 thousand), respectively, for certain portions of the undistributed earnings of the Company's subsidiaries because such portions were reinvested or were determined to be reinvested. As of March 31, 1994 and 1995, the undistributed earnings not subject to deferred tax liabilities were ¥558,317 million and ¥554,161 million ($6,202,138 thousand), respectively. The Company has recognized deferred tax liabilities for undistributed earnings for which decisions of reinvestment have not been made.

Deferred income taxes at March 31, 1994 and 1995 are reflected in the consolidated balance sheets under the following captions:

	Yen (millions) 1994	Yen (millions) 1995
Prepaid expenses and other current assets	¥75,766	**¥78,227**
Other assets	12,284	**19,683**
Other current liabilities	(22,652)	**(21,335)**
Deferred income taxes	(21,041)	**(71,566)**
Net deferred tax asset	¥44,357	**¥ 5,009**

Source: Honda Motor, *1995 Annual Report.*

C. Using your answer to part A, discuss the impact on Honda's income tax expense over the 1993 to 1995 period of:

(i) Nondeductible expenses

(ii) Changes in the valuation allowance

(iii) Tax law changes

D. Lower non-Japanese tax rates reduced Honda's tax expense in each year, 1993 to 1995.

(i) Discuss the trend in that reduction.

(ii) Discuss the likely explanation for that trend.

E. Compute the effective tax rate on the unrealized gain on equity securities of 89,134 million yen. What information is conveyed by that rate?

F. Discuss the factors that an analyst must consider when forecasting Honda's effective tax rate for 1996.

12. [Deferred taxes and interim reports] State Auto Financial reported the following operating results for the first three quarters of 1991 and 1992 ($ in thousands):

	1991			1992		
	Q1	Q2	Q3	Q1	Q2	Q3
Pretax income	$4,797	$2,600	$3,244	$1,123	$3,723	$ 98
Income tax expense	(1,224)	(624)	(848)	(232)	(934)	583
Net income	$3,573	$1,976	$2,396	$ 891	$2,789	$681

State Auto's 1992 third-quarter 10-Q reported that

> the estimated annual effective tax rate was revised during the third quarter of 1992 from 25% to 17% to reflect the estimated tax impact of a decrease in taxable earnings, as prescribed by generally accepted accounting principles. The effect of this adjustment in the current quarter was a benefit of approximately $600,000.

A. Compute the tax rate used to compute net income for each quarter.

B. Using the data given, show how the change in estimated tax rate increased third-quarter 1992 income by approximately $600,000.

C. Describe how the changed tax rate assumption distorted the comparison of third-quarter net income for 1991 and 1992.

D. Suggest two ways by which analysis can offset the distortion discussed in part C.

E. Assume that State Auto had estimated a tax rate of 17% for the first two quarters of 1992.

    (i) Compute the effect of that assumption on reported net income for those quarters.

    (ii) Discuss how that assumption would have affected the year-to-year comparison of operating results for the first two quarters.

Appendix 9-A

The Deferral Method of Income Tax Accounting

The income statement is the focus of the deferral method, with the objective of matching income tax expense with current year pretax income. Under the liability method, income tax expense is a by-product of the calculation of deferred tax assets and liabilities: Under the deferral method, the process is reversed. Income tax expense is calculated first and deferred tax assets and liabilities are the by-product. The difference between the two methods is illustrated in Exhibit 9A-1, which uses the example of Exhibit 9-3 (impact of tax rate changes).

Under the deferral method, deferred tax expense is computed at the tax rates in effect in the periods of origination, and the resulting balance sheet amounts are not adjusted to reflect subsequent changes in tax rates or laws. When reversals occur, payments are made (or received) at current tax rates. But the reversal of the deferred

EXHIBIT 9A-1
Impact of Tax Rate Change Under Deferral Method (Basic assumptions as in Exhibit 9-3)

Year 1: Tax rate is 40%

Journal Entries			Selected T-Accounts	
			Deferred Tax Asset	Deferred Tax Liability
Tax expense	$1,000			
Deferred tax asset	200		$200	
Deferred tax liability		$ 400		
Taxes payable		800		$400
			$200	$400

Year 2: Tax rate changes to 35%			Deferred Tax Asset	Deferred Tax Liability
Tax expense	$ 875*		$200	$400
Deferred tax asset	175†		$175	
Deferred tax credit		$ 350‡		$350
Taxes payable		700§	$375	$750

*$2,500 × 0.35 = $875 (pretax income × tax rate).
† $500 × 0.35 = $175 (deferral due to warranty expense).
‡$1,000 × 0.35 = $350 (deferral due to depreciation).
§§$2,000 × 0.35 = $700 (tax return).

Year 3: Tax rate remains at 35%			Deferred Tax Asset	Deferred Tax Liability
Tax expense	$ 850*		$375	$750
Deferred tax liability	750†			750
Deferred tax asset		$ 375‡		
Taxes payable		1,225§	375	
			$ 0	$ 0

*$2,500 × 0.35 = $875 − $25 (benefit of rate change, see text).
†$2,000 × 0.375 = $750 (reversals at average origination rates).
‡$1,000 × 0.375 = $375 (reversals at average origination rates).
§§$3,500 × 0.35 = $1,225 (tax return).

The computations for year 3 are made under the gross change method, which assumes that each temporary difference is treated separately. Under the net change method, the year 3 effect on the deferred tax asset would be $350 ($1,000 × 0.35), where $1,000 is the net effect of the two temporary differences (depreciation and warranty). Under this method, a deferred tax asset of $25 and a deferred tax liability of $50 would remain on the balance sheet at the end of year 3 even though both temporary differences have reversed! Although the gross change method is considered preferable, the net change method is frequently used in practice.

tax accrual is recorded at the tax rates in effect when the deferrals originated. The difference between the cash flow and the asset or liability reversal is included in tax expense in the current period.[1]

Exhibit 9A-1 depicts the impact of a change in tax rates on the deferred tax balances reported under the deferral method. Tax rates are assumed to change at the beginning of year 2. All computations for year 1 are unchanged from Exhibit 9-3B. Even though the actual reversal will occur at a lower rate, no adjustment is made to the liability or asset. The new tax rate of 35% only affects temporary differences originating in year 2. Reversals in year 3 (of year 1 differences) are, however, effected at the same 40% rate at which they were originated, if we assume the use of the gross change method (explained in Exhibit 9A-1).

If, however, the net change method were used, the differences originated in year 1 at 40% would reverse at the current lower rate of 35%, leaving a balance in both the deferred tax asset and credit accounts. This balance would remain in the financial statements until partially or fully eliminated by the impact of future tax rate changes on tax expense.[2]

---

[1]Under the deferral method, it does not matter when the tax law was enacted. Changes in tax rates are reflected only when differences reverse.

[2]Under the deferral method, firms may use either the gross change method or the net change method. As the choice is generally not disclosed, the impact on deferred tax balances is obscured.

10

ANALYSIS OF FINANCING LIABILITIES

CHAPTER OUTLINE

CHAPTER OBJECTIVES

INTRODUCTION

BALANCE SHEET DEBT
Current Liabilities
Long-Term Debt
  Financial Statement Effects
  Zero-Coupon Debt
  Variable-Rate Debt
  Fixed- Versus Variable-Rate Debt and Interest Rate Swaps
  Debt Denominated in a Foreign Currency
  Project Debt
Debt with Equity Features
  Convertible Bonds and Warrants
  Commodity Bonds
  Perpetual Debt
  Preferred Stock
Effects of Changes in Interest Rates
  Estimating the Market Value of Debt
  Complexities in Market Value Estimation
  Debt: Market or Book Value?

Debt of Firms in Distress
  Accounting for Restructured and Impaired Debt
Retirement of Debt Prior to Maturity
  Accounting for Debt Retirement
  Callable Bonds
  Defeasance

BOND COVENANTS
Nature of Covenants
Calculation of Accounting-Based Constraints
  Costs and Effects of Covenant Violations

INTERNATIONAL ACCOUNTING AND REPORTING PRACTICES

SUMMARY

CASE 10-1: COMPARATIVE ANALYSIS OF THE FINANCING LIABILITIES OF DUPONT, DOW CHEMICAL, AND IMPERIAL CHEMICAL INDUSTRIES PLC (ICI)

CHAPTER OBJECTIVES

This chapter concerns debt obligations that are recognized on the firm's balance sheet. The following major issues are discussed:

1. The effect on reported financial statements, including the pattern of income and cash flow, of:
   - Zero-coupon debt
   - Fixed- and variable-rate debt
   - Debt denominated in foreign currencies
   - Debt with equity features
2. The different effects of changes in interest rates on both the interest payments and market value of fixed- and variable-rate debt

3. The use of interest rate swaps to change the firm's risk exposure to changing interest rates
4. The circumstances under which preferred stock should be treated as debt, or debt as equity for financial analysis
5. The economic and accounting effects (often different) related to debt retirement or refinancing
6. The role of debt covenants in protecting creditors by limiting the firm's freedom to invest or pay dividends

INTRODUCTION

The assessment of a firm's liabilities is crucial to the analysis of its long-run viability and growth. A firm can incur obligations in myriad ways; some are a consequence of the firm's operating activities, whereas others result from its financing decisions. The former are characterized by exchanges of goods and services for the later payment of cash (or vice versa), whereas debt arising from financing decisions generally involves current receipts of cash in exchange for later payments of cash. Both forms of debt are generally reported "on balance sheet," and our focus in this chapter is on their measurement, interpretation, and analysis.

More complex arrangements, often based on contracts rather than immediate cash exchanges, involve promises to purchase (or use) products, services, or distribution systems in return for specified future payments of cash or equivalent resources. Such contractual arrangements are usually not recorded on the firm's balance sheet but may receive footnote disclosure. A thorough analysis of the firm's financial structure requires recognition of these liabilities as well. Such "off-balance-sheet" debt must first be identified, then measured, interpreted, and analyzed.

The analysis of a firm's short-term liquidity and long-term solvency position requires evaluation of both on- and off-balance-sheet debt. Debt-to-equity and interest coverage ratios based on reported financial data, for example, are affected by the form of transactions (rather than their substance), which determines whether they are recognized and how they are accounted for. This analysis must also consider incentives for management decisions regarding the proportion of on- versus off-balance-sheet debt.

An additional focus of analysis is debt covenants, used by creditors to protect themselves. These restrictions limit the firm's operations, its distributions to shareholders, and the amount of additional debt or leverage the firm can assume. Firms may alter their operating and financing activities and change accounting policies in an effort to operate within the confines of these covenants.

This chapter is the first of a series of chapters that deal with these issues. It primarily examines liabilities resulting from financing activities, the nature of various debt instruments, the impact of market rate (and credit) changes on reported and economic liabilities, and the nature and effect of covenants imposed by creditors. Liabilities arising from contractual obligations such as leases (a combined financing and investment activity) and other off-balance-sheet debt, debt guarantees, and obligations of the firm's affiliates are the subject of Chapter 11. Chapter 12 covers pensions and other postemployment benefits that arise from dealings between a firm and its employees. The effects of hedging or speculative activities in options, futures, and other derivatives on a firm's liability position are included in Chapter 16.

BALANCE SHEET DEBT

The liability amount reported on the balance sheet does not equal the total cash outflow required to satisfy the debt. Only the principal portion, that is, the present value of the future cash flow, is recorded. For example, if a firm borrows $100 at an interest rate of 10%, the actual amount payable at year-end is $110. The balance sheet liability equals the present value of the future payment or $100.

Current Liabilities

Current liabilities are defined as those due within one year[1] or one operating cycle; they result from both operating and financing activities. Analysis must distinguish among different types of current operating and financing liabilities:

Consequences of Operating Activities

1. *Operating and trade liabilities*, the most frequent type, are the result of credit granted to the company by its suppliers and employees.

2. *Advances from customers* arise when customers pay in advance for services to be rendered by the company. The firm is obligated to render the service and/or deliver a product to the customer in the near future.

Consequences of Financing Activities

3. *Short-term debt* represents amounts borrowed from banks or the credit markets that are expected to be repaid within one year or less.

4. *Current portion of long-term debt* identifies the portion of long-term debt that is payable within the next year; it is excluded from the long-term liability section of the balance sheet.

Operating and trade debt is reported at the expected (undiscounted) cash flow and is an important exception to the rule that liabilities are recorded at present value. A purchase of goods for $100 on credit, to be paid for within the normal operating cycle of the firm, is recorded at $100 even though its present value is lower. This treatment is justified by the short period between the incurrence of the debt and its payment, rendering the adjustment to present value immaterial.

---

[1]The one-year classification rule is not universal; some non-U.S. GAAPs classify debt with maturities of up to three years as current.

When analyzing a firm's liquidity, advances from customers should be distinguished from other payables. Payables require a future outlay of cash. Advances from customers, on the other hand, are satisfied by delivery of goods or services,[2] requiring a cash outlay lower[3] than the advances recorded; otherwise, the firm would be selling below cost. Increases in advances should be viewed favorably as *advances are a prediction of future revenues rather than cash outflows.*

Short-term debt and the current portion of long-term debt are the result of prior financing cash inflows. They indicate the firm's need for either cash or a means of refinancing the debt. The inability to repay short-term credit is a sign of financial distress.

It is important to monitor the relative levels of debt from operating as compared to financing activities. The former arise from the normal course of business activities and represent the required operating capital for a given level of production and sales: *A shift from operating to financing liabilities may signal the beginning of a liquidity crisis.*

Long-Term Debt

Firms obtain long-term debt financing from public issuance; from private placements with insurance companies, pension plans, and other institutional investors; or from long-term bank credit agreements. Creditors may receive a claim on specific assets pledged as security for the debt (e.g., mortgages), or they may have only general claims on the assets of the firm. Some debt, known as *project financing*, is repaid solely from the operations of a particular activity (e.g., a coal mine or office building). Some creditor claims are *subordinated,* in that they rank below those of *senior* creditors, whose claims have priority.

Long-term liabilities are interest-bearing in nature, but the structure of interest and principal payments varies widely. The different payment terms are, however, conceptually identical. As the subtleties of the financing equation(s) can be overwhelming and obscure the sight of the forest for the trees, *we suggest that the reader keep two basic principles in mind:*

1. Debt equals the present value of the remaining future stream of (interest and principal) payments. The book value reported in the financial statements uses the discount rate (market interest rate) in effect when the debt was incurred. Market value measurements use the current market interest rate.

2. Interest expense is the amount paid by the debtor to the creditor in excess of the amount borrowed. The *total* amount of interest paid over time is known; its allocation to individual time periods (both cash outflows and accrual of expense in periodic income statements) may vary.

These points seem simplistic but reference to them from time to time may help focus the discussions that follow.

Although bonds are only part of the debt universe, they are used for convenience to illustrate the accounting and analysis issues.

A bond is a "contract" or written agreement that obligates the borrower (bond issuer) to make certain payments to the lender (bondholder) over the life of the bond.

---

[2]The firm will have a cash obligation only if the goods and services are not delivered. Thus, the primary liability does not require cash.

[3]This is especially true in industries with high fixed/low variable cost structures. The marginal cost for any individual customer is low relative to the selling cost.

A typical bond promises two types of payments: periodic interest payments (usually semiannual in the United States) and a lump-sum payment when the bond matures.

The *face value* of the bond is the lump-sum payment due at maturity. The *coupon rate* is the stated cash interest rate (but not necessarily the actual rate of return).

Periodic Payment = "Coupon Rate" × Face Value

The coupon rate is in quotation marks because it is stated on an annual basis, whereas payments are made semiannually. The coupon rate (CR) used for the payment calculation is therefore equal to one-half the stated coupon rate.

The example in Exhibit 10-1 is based on a three-year bond[4] with the following terms:

Face value (FV):	**$100,000**
Coupon:	**10%**
Interest payment:	**Semiannual**

The purchaser of the bond expects six payments of interest (each payment is $5,000) and a final principal payment of $100,000 for a total of $130,000. Note that this stream of payments does not uniquely determine the principal amount borrowed by the bond issuer. *The amount borrowed (the proceeds received on issuance) depends on the market rate of interest for bonds of a similar maturity and risk as well as the payment stream.*

The market rate may be less than, equal to, or greater than the coupon rate. *It is the current market interest rate that allocates payments between interest and principal.*

Exhibit 10-1, parts A through C, shows how the economics of the bond and the accounting treatment of the payments are affected by the relationship between the market and coupon rates. The following points should be noted:

1. The initial liability is the amount paid to the issuer by the creditor (present value of the stream of payments discounted at the market rate), not necessarily the face value of the debt.

2. The *effective interest rate* on the bond is the market (not the coupon) rate at the time of issuance, and interest expense is that market rate times the bond liability.

3. The coupon rate and face value determine the actual cash flows (stream of payments from the issuer).

4. Total interest expense is equal to the payments by the issuer to the creditor in excess of the amount received. (Thus, total interest expense = $130,000 − initial liability.)

5. The balance sheet liability over time is a function of (a) the initial liability and the relationship of (b) periodic interest expense to (c) the actual cash payments.

6. The balance sheet liability at any point in time is equal to the present value of the remaining payments, discounted at the market rate in effect at the time of the issuance of the bonds.

---

[4]Bonds issued for periods of 10 years or less are usually called *notes*. There is no analytic distinction, and we call all debt issues bonds for convenience.

EXHIBIT 10-1
Comparison of Bond Issued at Par, Premium, and Discount

Face Value (FV) of bond = $100,000
Coupon (CR) = 5% (semiannual payment; 10% annual rate)
Maturity = 3 years
Semiannual payments of $5,000 (0.5 × 10% × $100,000)

A. Bond Issued at Par: Market Rate = 10% (MR = 5%)

Period Ending	(1) Liability Opening	(2) (1) × MR Interest Expense	(3) FV × CR Coupon Payment	(4) (2) − (3) Change in Liability	(5) (1) + (4) Liability Closing	(6) FV Face Value of Bond
1/1/X1	Proceeds (see below)				$100,000	$100,000
6/30/X1	$100,000	$ 5,000	$ 5,000	$0	100,000	100,000
12/31/X1	100,000	5,000	5,000	0	100,000	100,000
6/30/X2	100,000	5,000	5,000	0	100,000	100,000
12/31/X2	100,000	5,000	5,000	0	100,000	100,000
6/30/X3	100,000	5,000	5,000	0	100,000	100,000
12/31/X3	100,000	5,000	5,000	0	100,000	100,000
Totals		$30,000	$30,000			

Calculation of Proceeds

Present value of annuity of $5,000 for 6 periods, discounted at 5%:
$5,000 × 5.0756 = $ 25,378
Present value of $100,000 in 6 periods, discounted at 5%:
$100,000 × 0.74622 =   74,622
Total $100,000

B. Bond Issued at Premium: Market Rate = 8% (MR = 4%)

Period Ending	(1) Liability Opening	(2) (1) × MR Interest Expense	(3) FV × CR Coupon Payment	(4) (2) − (3) Change in Liability	(5) (1) + (4) Liability Closing	(6) FV Face Value of Bond	(7) (5) − (6) Closing Premium
01/01/X1	Proceeds (see below)				$105,242	$100,000	$5,242
06/30/X1	$105,242	$ 4,210	$ 5,000	$ (790)	104,452	100,000	4,452
12/31/X1	104,452	4,178	5,000	(822)	103,630	100,000	3,630
06/30/X2	103,630	4,145	5,000	(855)	102,775	100,000	2,775
12/31/X2	102,775	4,111	5,000	(889)	101,886	100,000	1,886
06/30/X3	101,886	4,075	5,000	(925)	100,961	100,000	961
12/31/X3	100,961	4,039	5,000	(961)	100,000	100,000	0
Totals		$24,758	$30,000	$(5,242)			

Calculation of Proceeds

Present value of annuity of $5,000 for 6 periods, discounted at 4%:
$5,000 × 5.2421 = $ 26,211
Present value of $100,000 in 6 periods, discounted at 4%:
$100,000 × 0.79031 =   79,031
Total $105,242

EXHIBIT 10-1 (*continued*)

C. *Bond Issued at Discount: Market Rate = 12% (MR = 6%)*

	(1)	(2) (1) × MR	(3) FV × CR	(4) (2) − (3) Change	(5) (1) + (4)	(6) FV Face	(7) (5) − (6)
Period Ending	Liability Opening	Interest Expense	Coupon Payment	in Liability	Liability Closing	Value of Bond	Discount
1/1/X1	Proceeds (see below)				$95,083	$100,000	$(4,917)
6/30/X1	$95,083	$ 5,705	$ 5,000	$ 705	95,788	100,000	(4,212)
12/31/X1	95,788	5,747	5,000	747	96,535	100,000	(3,465)
6/30/X2	96,535	5,792	5,000	792	97,327	100,000	(2,673)
12/31/X2	97,327	5,840	5,000	840	98,167	100,000	(1,833)
6/30/X3	98,167	5,890	5,000	890	99,057	100,000	(943)
12/31/X3	99,057	5,943	5,000	943	100,000	100,000	0
Totals		$34,917	$30,000	$4,917			

Calculation of Proceeds

Present value of annuity of $5,000 for 6 periods, discounted at 6%:
$5,000 × 4.9173 = $24,587

Present value of $100,000 in 6 periods, discounted at 6%:
$100,000 × 0.70496 =   70,496

Total $95,083

Exhibit 10-1A: Market Rate = Coupon Rate. When the market rate equals the coupon rate of 10% (compounded semiannually), the bond is issued at par; that is, the proceeds equal the face value.[5] The creditor is willing to pay $100,000, the present value of the stream of payments and the face value of the bond. In this case, the initial liability equals the face value.

Since the debt has been issued at the market rate of 10%, periodic interest expense (Exhibit 10-1A, column 2) equals the periodic cash payments (column 3). The liability remains $100,000 (column 5) throughout the life of the bond.

Exhibit 10-1B: Market Rate < Coupon Rate. When the market rate is less than the coupon rate, the creditor is willing to pay (and the bond issuer will demand) a premium above the face value of $100,000.[6] If we assume a market rate of 8%, the proceeds and initial liability (Exhibit 10-1B) equal $105,242 (face value of $100,000 plus premium of $5,242).

After six months, the bondholder earns interest of $4,210 (4% × $105,242) but receives a payment of $5,000 (coupon rate times face value). This $5,000 payment includes interest expense of $4,210 and a $790 principal payment, reducing the liability to $104,452. For the second period, interest expense is $4,178 (4% × $104,452), lower

[5]We ignore, for simplicity, the underwriting costs and expenses associated with the bond issuance. These costs are generally capitalized and amortized over the life of the bond issue.

[6]Assuming a market interest rate of 8%, the bond issuer could find an investor willing to lend $100,000 in exchange for a semiannual annuity stream of $4,000 (4% × $100,000) in addition to the lump-sum payment at maturity. For the borrower to obligate itself to pay the higher annuity of $5,000 requires additional proceeds above the face value.

than the first period expense since the liability has been reduced. After the second payment of $5,000, the liability is further reduced. This process is continued until the bond matures. At that time, as shown in Exhibit 10-1B, the liability is reduced to $100,000, the face value of the bond, which is repaid at maturity.

The process by which a bond premium (or discount) is amortized over the life of the bond is known as the *effective interest method*. This process, which results in a constant rate of interest over the life of the obligation, is widely used in financial reporting.[7]

Exhibit 10-1C: Market Rate > Coupon Rate. When the market rate exceeds the coupon rate, the bondholder is unwilling to pay the full face value of the bond.[8] At a market rate of 12%, the bond would be issued at a discount of $4,917, and the proceeds and initial liability equal $95,083.

Interest expense for the first six months is $5,705 (6% × $95,083), but cash interest paid is only $5,000; the shortfall of $705 is added to the balance sheet liability. As a result, a higher liability is used to calculate interest expense for the second period, increasing interest expense, increasing the shortfall, and further increasing the liability. This cycle is repeated for all remaining periods until the bond matures. At that point, the initial principal of $95,083 plus the accumulated (unpaid) interest of $4,917 equals $100,000, the face value payment that retires the debt. The zero-coupon bond, discussed shortly, is the extreme case; all interest is unpaid until the bond matures.

Financial Statement Effects

Interest expense reported in the income statement (column 2 of Exhibit 10-1) is the effective interest on the loan based on the market rate in effect at issuance times the balance sheet liability at the beginning of the period. The actual cash payments (column 3) may not equal interest expense, but do equal the reduction in cash from operations (CFO). The balance sheet liability is shown in column 5. The initial cash received and the final face value payment of $100,000 are both treated as cash from financing (CFF). The financial statement effects on an annual basis (if we assume a December fiscal year-end) are summarized in Exhibit 10-2. Note that for bonds issued at a premium (discount), the interest expense decreases (increases) over time. This is a direct function of the declining (rising) balance sheet liability; for each period, interest expense is the product of the beginning liability and the effective interest rate. At any point in time, the balance sheet liability equals the present value of the remaining payments discounted at the effective interest rate at the issuance date.[9,10]

---

[7]Alternative approaches used internationally are discussed at the end of the chapter.

[8]The bondholder can purchase a 12% bond and receive periodic payments of $6,000. The periodic payments from this bond are only $5,000. Thus, an investor would only purchase this bond at a *discount*.

[9]To illustrate this property, compute the balance sheet liability of $96,535 at December 31, 1991, for the bond issued at a discount. The present value of the remaining four periodic payments and lump-sum payment equals:

Present value of annuity of $5,000
    for 4 periods discounted at 6%: $5,000 × 3.46511   = $17,326
Present value of $100,000
    for 4 periods discounted at 6%: $100,000 × 0.79209 =   79,209
                                                          $96,535

[10]The *market* value of the debt, however, is equal to the present value of all remaining payments discounted at the *current market* interest rate.

EXHIBIT 10-2
Comparison of Financial Statement Effects of Bonds Issued at Par, Premium, and Discount

Bond Face Value = $100,000
Maturity = 3 years
Coupon Rate = 10% (semiannual payments)

Premium Case: Market Rate = 8%
Discount Case: Market Rate = 12%

| | Interest Expense Bond Issued at | | | Balance Sheet Liability Bond Issued at | | | Cash Flow from | |
Year	Par	Premium	Discount	Par	Premium	Discount	Operations	Financing (for all cases)
19X1	$10,000	$ 8,388	$11,452	$100,000	$103,630	$ 96,535	$10,000	
19X2*	10,000	8,256	11,632	100,000	101,886	98,167	10,000	
19X3*	10,000	8,114	11,833	100,000	100,000	100,000	10,000	$100,000
Totals	$30,000	$24,758	$34,917				$30,000	$100,000

*Interest expense and cash flow total of June 30 and December 31 amounts for each year. All data from Exhibit 10-1.

The reported cash flows for each period over the life of the bond (Exhibit 10-2) are identical across all three scenarios; the $100,000 face value payment is treated as cash from financing, and the periodic cash payments of $5,000 are reported as reductions in CFO.[11] For bonds issued at a premium or discount, however, these cash flows *incorrectly* describe the economics of the bond transaction.

The misclassification of cash flows results from reporting coupon payments as CFO. For bonds sold at a premium, part of the coupon payment is a reduction of principal and should be treated as a financing cash (out)flow. CFO is understated and financing cash flow is overstated by an equal amount. Similarly, when bonds are issued at a discount, part of the discount amortization represents additional interest expense. Consequently, CFO is overstated and financing cash flow is understated by that amount.

In summary, the cash flow classification of the debt payments depends on the coupon rates, not the effective interest rate. When these differ, CFO is misstated.

Exhibit 10-3 presents two cash flow reclassifications. The first correctly allocates cash outflows based on interest expense. After reallocation, the cash flows reflect the economics of the debt rather than the coupon payments alone.

The second reclassification, however, goes much further. In Chapter 3, we argue that all debt-related cash flows should be separated from operating cash flows. The "functional" reclassification in Exhibit 10-3 makes that separation so CFO is unaffected by borrowing. All debt-related cash flows are included in financing cash flow regardless of the coupon or effective interest rates.

Most debt is issued at or close to par (face value), making the distortion from bond premium or discount immaterial. However, when the discount is large, for example, with zero-coupon bonds, the difference between coupon and effective interest rates leads to the significant distortion of reported cash flows.

[11]Under the indirect method, this is accomplished by adding to or deducting from income the change in bond discount/premium (the periodic amortization of the bond/discount premium) to derive CFO. Thus for the first year, the cash flow statement will show an addback of $1,612 in the premium case and a deduction of $1,452 in the discount case.

EXHIBIT 10-3
Reclassification of Cash Flows for Bonds in Exhibits 10-1 and 10-2

Year	Actual Cash Flow	SFAS 95 Cash Flow for All Bonds		Reclassification Based on Interest Expense Premium Bond		Discount Bond		Functional Reclassification for All Bonds	
		Operations	Financing	Operations	Financing	Operations	Financing	Operations	Financing
19X1	$ 10,000	$10,000	0	$ 8,388	$ 1,612	$11,452	$(1,452)	0	$ 10,000
19X2	10,000	10,000	0	8,256	1,744	11,632	(1,632)	0	10,000
19X3	110,000	10,000	100,000	8,114	101,886	11,833	98,167	0	110,000
Totals	$130,000	$30,000	$100,000	$24,758	$105,242	$34,917	$95,083	0	$130,000

SFAS 95 requires that cash flows be allocated between operations and financing based on the coupon interest rate.

The first reclassification allocates cash outflows based on interest expense. In 19X1, for the premium case, $8,388 is shown as operating cash flow and the balance of $1,612 ($10,000 − $8,388) as financing. The interest expense reported for the discount issue, $11,452, is shown as operating cash flow and the excess over interest paid, $1,452, ($11,452 − $10,000) is reported as a financing cash inflow. The 19X3 financing cash flow for the discount issue, therefore, equals the outflow of $100,000 to repay the debt less $1,833 (interest expense in excess of interest paid).

The second reclassification is based on the authors' view that financing cash flow should include both principal and interest paid. Regardless of whether debt is issued at par, premium, or discount, financing cash flow reflects all payments made in the year of the actual payments.

Zero-Coupon Debt

A zero-coupon bond has no periodic payments (coupon = 0).[12] For that reason, it must be issued at a deep discount to face value. The lump-sum payment at maturity includes all unpaid interest (equal to the face value minus the proceeds) from the time of issuance.

The proceeds at issuance equal the present value of the face amount, discounted at the market interest rate. Thus, at a market rate of 10%, a $100,000 face value zero-coupon bond payable in three years will be issued at $74,622.

Exhibit 10-4 shows the income statement, cash flow, and balance sheet effects for this bond. Note that the repayment of $100,000 includes $25,378 of interest that is never reported as CFO; the full $100,000 payment is treated as cash from financing. The contrast with the bond issued at par (Exhibit 10-1A) is striking.

The interest on a zero-coupon bond never reduces operating cash flow. This surprising result has important analytic consequences. *One is that reported CFO is systematically "overstated" when a zero-coupon (or deep discount) bond is issued.* Furthermore, solvency ratios, such as cash-basis interest coverage, are improved relative to the issuance of par bonds. Finally, the cash eventually required to repay the obligation may become a significant burden.[13]

EQK Realty Investors (EQK), a real estate investment trust, illustrates this phe-

[12]The following discussion also applies to bonds sold at deep discounts, that is, with coupons that are far below market interest rates.

[13]In fact, interest expense increases cash flow by generating income tax deductions. (Zero-coupon bond interest is tax-deductible even though it is not paid.) This result can have real-world consequences. When valuing a company for leveraged buyout (LBO) purposes, the use of zero-coupon or low-coupon debt (issued at a discount) can result in the following anomaly: The higher the interest rate, the higher the cash flow, mistakenly resulting in a higher price for the company. An investment banker commented to one of the authors that this factor contributed to overbidding in the late 1980s. Of course when the zero-coupon bond comes due, the cash must be found to repay the (much higher) face amount.

EXHIBIT 10-4
Zero-Coupon Bond Analysis

Bond: Face Value (FV) = $100,000 Coupon 0%
Maturity = 3 years
Market Rate = 10% (MR = 5%)

	(1) Liability Opening	(2) (1) × MR Interest Expense	(3) FV × CR Coupon Payment	(4) (2) − (3) Change in Liability	(5) (1) + (4) Liability Closing	(6) FV Face Value of Bond	(7) (5) − (6) Discount
01/01/X1	Proceeds (see below)				$ 74,622	$100,000	$(25,378)
06/30/X1	$74,622	$ 3,731	$0	$ 3,731	78,353	100,000	(21,647)
12/31/X1	78,353	3,917	0	3,917	82,270	100,000	(17,730)
06/30/X2	82,270	4,114	0	4,114	86,384	100,000	(13,616)
12/31/X2	86,384	4,319	0	4,319	90,703	100,000	(9,297)
06/30/X3	90,703	4,535	0	4,535	95,238	100,000	(4,762)
12/31/X3	95,238	4,762	0	4,762	100,000	100,000	(0)
Totals		$25,378	$0	$25,378			

Calculation of Proceeds

Present value of $100,000 in 6 periods, discounted at 5%:

$100,000 × 0.74622 = $74,622

Cash flow from operations: Zero in all periods

Cash flow from financing: $74,622 inflow at 1/1/X1; $100,000 outflow at 12/31/X3

nomenon. The company issued zero-coupon mortgage notes in 1985 and 1988. Adjustment of reported cash flow for the effect of interest on these zero-coupon bonds results in a quite different CFO trend.

Exhibit 10-5 presents excerpts from EQK's 1992 Balance Sheet, Cash Flow Statement, and Financial Statement Notes. The zero-coupon notes were retired in December 1992, using cash and a new (conventional) mortgage bond.

Given the opening (January 1, 1992) balance of $89,410 on the zero-coupon bond and the issuance of a mortgage bond having a face value of $75,716 ($75,324 + $392 debt discount), the cash required to retire the bond should have been $13,694 ($89,410 − $75,716). Why then did EQK report a cash payment of $23,038, an excess of $9,344, as cash from financing?

The answer can be found in the cash flows from operating activities section of the statement of cash flows. "Amortization of discount on zero-coupon mortgage notes" of $9,344 appears as an addback to net income, thereby *removing it from CFO*. $9,344 is the amount of interest that accrued on the zero-coupon bond from January 1992 through its retirement in December 1992. This interest, paid in 1992, was treated as a financing rather than an operating cash outflow. The impact of this misclassification on CFO is significant. Reclassifying the interest expense as CFO turns a positive cash flow of over $8 million into a negative $1.276 million:

Reported CFO	$8,068
Reclassify 1992 interest portion	(9,344)
Adjusted CFO	($1,276)

EXHIBIT 10-5. EQK REALTY
Zero Coupon Financing, Financial Statement Excerpts

Balance Sheet

Year Ended December 31	1991	1992
Liabilities		
Mortgage note payable, net of debt discount of $392	—	$ 75,324
Zero-coupon mortgage notes, net of unamortized discount of $9,574	$89,410	—

Statement of Cash Flows

Year Ended December 31	1992
Cash flows from operating activities	
Net loss	$ (8,850)
Adjustments to reconcile net loss to net cash provided by operating activities	
Amortization of discount on zero-coupon mortgage notes	9,344
Other adjustments	7,574
Net cash provided by operating activities	$ 8,068
Cash flows from financing activities	
Prepayment of zero-coupon note	$(23,038)
Other adjustments	1,572
Net cash provided by (used in) financing activities	$(21,466)

Note 2: Debt Restructuring

In December 1992, the Company refinanced $75,689,000 representing the balance of its zero-coupon mortgage note that remained after reducing this indebtedness with the proceeds from the sale of properties. . . . The new financing, which is collateralized by first mortgage liens . . . matures in December 1995.

Source: EQK Realty Investors, *1992 Annual Report.*

Similar reclassification can be extended to previous years, when the company accrued (but did not pay) interest cost (amortization of discount) on these notes. Reported CFO ignores the fact that at some point the accrued interest must be repaid.[14] As the maturity of the debt approaches, the company could face a liquidity crisis.[15]

The table below presents reported and adjusted CFO for the period 1989 to 1994. The treatment of the interest on the zero-coupon bond causes significant distortions both prior to and following the 1992 refinancing.[16]

---

[14]The 1992 payment, in fact, was all accrued interest but only a small portion of the total accrued since issuance.

[15]Indeed, in 1991 EQK's auditors issued a "going concern qualification" due to the impending maturity of the zero-coupon bond.

[16]The adjustment ignores small amounts of amortization of other discount notes.

EQK Realty Investors
Adjustment of Operating Cash Flow (CFO),
Years Ending December 31, 1989 to 1994
($ in thousands)

	1989	1990	1991	1992	1993	1994
Reported CFO	$10,458	$9,795	$ 5,728	$ 8,068	$4,087	$2,184
Less: Zero-coupon interest	7,486	8,318	9,229	9,344	0	0
Adjusted CFO	$ 2,972	$1,477	$(3,501)	$(1,276)	$4,087	$2,184

After adjustment, the 1989 to 1991 deterioration in CFO is even more striking as 1991 CFO is negative.[17] The 1992 recovery is less impressive as adjusted CFO remains negative. In 1993, CFO rises despite the burden of full-coupon debt; the unadjusted data obscure this improvement. The adjusted CFO data provide better information regarding the cash flow trend.

Variable-Rate Debt

Some debt issues do not have a fixed coupon payment; the periodic interest payment varies with the level of interest rates. Such debt instruments are generally designed to trade at their face value. To achieve this objective, the interest rate "floats" above the rate on a specified-maturity U.S. Treasury obligation or some other benchmark rate such as the prime rate or LIBOR (London InterBank Offered Rate). The "spread" above the benchmark depends on the credit rating of the issuer.

Fixed- Versus Variable-Rate Debt and Interest Rate Swaps

Borrowers can issue fixed-rate or variable-rate debt directly; alternatively, they can enter into interest rate swap agreements that convert a fixed-rate obligation to a floating-rate obligation or vice versa.

Whether a firm prefers to incur fixed-rate or variable-rate debt depends on a number of factors. Variable-rate debt exposes the firm's interest expense, cash flows, and related ratios to higher volatility due to interest rate changes.[18] On the other hand, when the firm's operating cash flows are correlated with movements in interest rates, variable-rate debt minimizes risk. The common notion that fixed rates minimize risk by reducing the volatility of a firm's income and cash flows is, thus, only a half-truth.[19]

Financial institutions (banks, finance companies) generally issue a high proportion of variable-rate debt, as their assets tend to be variable-rate in nature. Thus, they match the variability of their assets and liabilities (see the detailed discussion of hedging in Chapter 16).

---

[17]Note the increasing trend of interest expense on the zero-coupon debt, similar to the trend in Exhibit 10-4.

[18]The impact of interest rate changes can, of course, be either positive or negative.

[19]The investor point of view, however, is different. Variable-rate debt has low price risk; interest rate changes should have minimal impact on its market price. Significant market fluctuation should result only from perceived changes in credit quality. However, the variability of income is higher than for fixed-rate debt.

However, a nonfinancial firm may also view variable-rate debt as hedging variable operating cash flows. For example, the 1994 financial statements of AMR (American Airlines) state:

> Because American's operating results tend to be better in economic cycles with relatively high interest rates and its capital instruments tend to be financed with long-term fixed-rate instruments, interest rate swaps in which American pays the floating rate and receives the fixed rate are used to reduce the impact of economic cycles on American's net income.[20]

Alternatively, a firm may prefer to issue variable-rate debt because management believes that interest rates will fall or short-term rates (the usual basis for variable debt) will remain below long-term rates charged on fixed-rate loans. The analysis of a firm's debt should include a consideration of whether management's choice of financing alternatives is based on the inherent economics of the business or management is speculating on future interest rate changes.

Debtors use interest rate swaps to manage the fixed- and variable-rate mix of total borrowings. Box 10-1 presents the mechanics of interest rate swaps.

Exhibit 10-6, from the financial statements of Glatfelter (PHG), discloses the terms of interest rate swaps entered into by the company. These disclosures allow us to discuss the effect of the swaps on the company's risk exposure.

Glatfelter borrowed $150 million at a fixed rate of 5.875%. The company then "swapped" payments on $50 million of notional principal, receiving 5.875% and paying LIBOR + 0.6%. Note that the entire $150 million debt remains the obligation of PHG, which is liable for the original principal and interest payments (see Box 10-1).

At the inception of the swap, no accounting recognition is required although PHG has altered its debt obligation. Presumably at that time, the swap was "fair," that is, the net present value of the swap payments was zero. The transaction is an *off-balance-sheet contract.*

Exhibit 10-6 states that PHG includes the net difference in payments made and received under the swap in interest expense. In 1994, the company paid $2,505,000 (implying an average floating rate of approximately 5%), but received the fixed-rate payments of $2,938,000 (5.875% × $50 million); the net receipt of $433,000 decreased interest expense.[21] Note that the floating rate for the six months ending March 1, 1995 is 5.9125% (above the fixed rate), implying that PHG will make net payments in 1995, increasing interest expense. Although PHG benefited from low rates in 1994, higher 1995 rates increased interest expense.[22]

Exhibit 10-6 also discloses the *fair value* of the swap, equivalent to the cost of termination, of $4 million. Since the inception of the swap, interest rates had risen. PHG's counterparty profited by assuming fixed-rate debt in exchange for variable-rate debt. If PHG terminated the swap, the counterparty would have to pay a higher rate to obtain fixed-rate debt to replace Glatfelter's debt. PHG must compensate the counterparty for that higher cost. The fair value[23] depends on interest rate levels at

---

[20]AMR Corporation, 1994 Financial Statements, Note 6.

[21]As the differential can be positive at times and negative at other times, depending on interest rate levels, some firms account for the differentials by amortizing them over the remaining life of the swap.

[22]Glatfelter's *1995 Annual Report* states that the swap increased 1995 interest expense by $453,000 as the floating rate rose to more than 6.5% for the six months ended February 29, 1996. On the other hand, operating earnings increased sharply in 1995 so that net income rose despite higher interest expense. If PHG management intended the swap as a hedge, it has been an effective one.

[23]Problem 14 requires the reader to estimate the $4 million fair value.

BOX 10-1
Interest Rate Swaps

Firms use interest rate swaps* to exchange variable- (floating-) rate debt for obligations with fixed interest rates or, alternatively, to exchange fixed-rate debt for obligations with variable rates.

Swaps are contractual obligations that supplement existing debt agreements. Each firm remains liable for its original debt, makes all payments on that debt, and carries that debt on its books. The firm with variable-rate debt agrees to pay, at specified intervals, amounts equal to a fixed rate times the *notional principal amount*. In return, the counterparty pays variable amounts equal to the variable interest rate (pegged to a specified rate or index) times that same notional principal amount.

Because firms wish to minimize credit risk, they do not engage in swaps with other industrial firms, even when a swap would meet the objectives of both parties. The counterparty is normally a bank or other financial institution with a high credit rating. Money center banks, as a result, have large portfolios of swaps.†

Given that some firms prefer variable-rate debt and others fixed-rate debt, why do they not arrange their preferred form of financing directly with their creditors? Why incur the additional costs and/or risks of swaps? Frictions in the credit markets and/or the institutional setting of the firm may result in differential borrowing costs that make it cheaper to borrow in the nonpreferred mode and swap into the preferred mode of borrowing rather than borrowing directly in the preferred mode. For example, some "household name" American firms can borrow at very low rates in certain foreign markets. A second factor leading to swaps is that preferences change over time. This is especially true of firms that use swaps to "match" assets and liabilities (see Chapter 16 for a discussion of hedging activities).

Illustration

The Triple A and Triple B companies each want to borrow $100 million. Assume that the Triple A company prefers variable-rate debt, whereas the Triple B company prefers fixed-rate debt. The companies' respective borrowing rates and preferences are:

Company	Fixed-Rate	Variable-Rate	Preferred Mode
Triple A	8%	Prime	Variable
Triple B	10%	Prime + 1%	Fixed

The Triple-A company is considered to be more creditworthy than the Triple B company and, hence, is offered more favorable borrowing terms. Note that the rate differential on fixed-rate debt (2%) is greater than the differential (1%) on floating-rate debt. This discrepancy makes it profitable for firms to enter into swaps.

Based on these rates, we demonstrate that the combined borrowing cost for the two firms is 1% lower when each company *borrows in its nonpreferred mode*. This 1% difference is independent of changes in the prime rate.

Company	Borrow Preferred Mode	Borrow Nonpreferred Mode
Triple A	Prime	8%
Triple B	10%	Prime + 1%
Total cost	Prime + 10%	Prime + 9%

The two firms are both better off borrowing in their nonpreferred mode, "swapping" the debt and splitting the 1% savings. The swap agreement requires the following payments:

- The Triple A company pays the Triple B company the prime rate (times the notional amount of $100 million).

- The Triple B company pays the Triple A company 8.5% (times the notional amount of $100 million).

The net cost of the original borrowing and the swap for each company is

	Original Loan +	To Swap Counterparty −	From Swap Counterparty =	Net Cost
Triple A	8%	Prime	(8.5%)	Prime − 0.5%
Triple B	Prime + 1%	8.5%	(Prime)	9.5%

Each company has obtained debt in its preferred mode at a rate one-half percent below the rate available on its preferred mode of borrowing.

Economic Effects of the Swap

Assume that the swap illustrated has a five-year term, the prime rate is 6% at inception, payments are made semiannually, and adjustments for changes in the prime rate are also semiannual. The first semiannual assessment results in a net payment of $1.25 million [0.5 × (8.5% − 6%) × $100 million] from Triple B to Triple A. If, for the second semiannual period, the prime rate increases to 7%, then the second scheduled payment will be $0.75 million [0.5 × (8.5% − 7%) × $100 million]. *Although Triple B has borrowed at a variable rate, increases in that rate are passed on to Triple A as Triple B's payments decline. Thus, Triple B's economic cost is the fixed rate of 9.5%. Conversely, Triple A is exposed to rising interest rates although it has incurred only fixed-rate debt. The swap has changed the economic position of both firms.*

Economic Effects of Termination

Now assume that Triple A, expecting increases in interest rates, wishes to terminate the swap agreement after the first payment. How much should Triple A pay to do so? The required payment should equal the fair value of the swap agreement, calculated as follows.‡

Triple B is liable for 9 semiannual payments of $4.25 million (0.5 × 8.5% × $100 million). If Triple B enters into another swap agreement, it would be based on current interest rates. If the fixed rate has increased by 0.5% (while the prime rate has increased by 1%), Triple B would have to make 9 payments of $4.5 million (0.5 × 9% × $100 million), an increase of $250 thousand. The present value of the increase discounted at the *new* rate of 9% is equal to approximately $1.8 million. Thus, to terminate the swap, Triple A must pay Triple B that amount.

---

*For a further elaboration of these issues, see James Bicksler and Andrew Chen, "An Economic Analysis of Interest Rate Swaps," *Journal of Finance,* July 1986 and John Hull, *Introduction to Futures and Options Markets* (Englewood Cliffs, NJ: Prentice-Hall, 1995), Chapter 6.

†See Chapter 16 for further discussion of derivatives held by financial institutions.

‡In our simplified example, we assume that the swap is terminated at the same time when the floating rate is reset. Were this not the case, then a similar calculation would have to be made for the variable-rate bond to compensate for the fact that if Triple B entered into a new swap agreement, while it is true that it would pay a higher fixed rate, it would receive immediately floating-rate payments based on the higher floating rate and not have to wait for the next adjustment date. This calculation, however, is usually not very material; it is for only one payment and the discounting period is less than six months (from the termination date to the interest rate adjustment date).

December 31, 1994. *Note that $4 million is the present value of PHG's obligation given current market rates; the fair value will fluctuate as rates change. By entering into the swap, Glatfelter changed its risk exposure.*

PHG has also assumed *counterparty risk*, the risk that the other party will default. This risk is not important if PHG must make net payments, as default would relieve

EXHIBIT 10-6. P. H. GLATFELTER
Interest Rate Swap

---

13. Borrowings

In March 1993, the Company issued $150,000,000 principal amount of its 5⅞% Notes. These Notes will mature on March 1, 1998 and may not be redeemed prior to maturity. Interest on the Notes is payable semiannually on March 1 and September 1. The Notes are unsecured obligations of the Company.

In March 1993, the Company entered into an interest rate swap agreement having a total notational principal amount of $50,000,000. Under the agreement, the Company receives a fixed rate of 5⅞% and pays a floating rate (London Interbank Offered Rate (LIBOR) plus sixty basis points), as determined at six month intervals. The floating rate is 5.9125% for the six month period ending March 1, 1995. The agreement converts a portion of the Company's debt obligation from a fixed rate to a floating rate basis. During 1994, the Company recognized $2,938,000 of interest income and $2,505,000 of interest expense under the agreement, resulting in a net credit of $433,000. This net amount is included in "Interest on debt" on the Company's Consolidated Statements of Income and Retained Earnings. The Company has pledged $6,500,000 of its other assets as security under the swap agreement. Although the Company can pay to terminate the swap agreement at any time, the Company intends to hold the swap agreement until its March 1, 1998 maturity. The cost to the Company to terminate the agreement fluctuates with prevailing market interest rates. As of December 31, 1994, the cost to terminate the swap agreement was approximately $4,000,000.

The Company has approximately $9,300,000 of letters of credit outstanding as of December 31, 1994. The Company bears the credit risk on this amount to the extent that the Company does not comply with the provisions of certain agreements. The letters of credit do not reduce the amount available under the Company's lines of credit.

Source: P. H. Glatfelter, *1994 Annual Report.*

the company of a burden. However, if the swap results in net payments to Glatfelter and the counterparty defaults, then PHG will lose out. Exhibit 10-6 states that PHG provided collateral of $6.5 million to protect the counterparty against default by Glatfelter. If we assume that the counterparty is a highly rated financial institution, it would not provide collateral to protect PHG against default. *When a company enters into swaps that are material to its financial position, the analyst should ensure that the counterparties are sufficiently strong so that the likelihood of default is insignificant.*

Debt Denominated in a Foreign Currency

Companies sometimes issue debt for which all interest and principal payments are made in a foreign currency. There are two motivations for such issuance:

1. More favorable terms in foreign markets than domestic ones
2. Assets denominated in the foreign currency and debt denominated in that currency can hedge[24] against exchange rate movements

The carrying value of foreign currency debt is adjusted for changes in exchange rates.

---

[24]If the dollar strengthens relative to the foreign currency, then the dollar value of assets denominated in foreign currencies decreases. This decrease is offset by the decrease (in dollars) of the debt to be repaid.

For example, Pepsico had $5\frac{1}{4}$% bonds outstanding denominated in Swiss francs. The liability for these bonds was reported as $90.1 million at December 31, 1993, but $99.7 million at December 31, 1994. The exchange value of the Swiss franc rose 11% over this period. Thus, although the amount of the debt (in Swiss francs) did not change, the carrying value of the debt (in dollars) increased.

This adjustment for exchange rate changes is separate from any adjustment to current market value. Market value adjustments are based on changes in interest rates.[25] The market value of this debt in Swiss francs may have increased if interest rates declined since the debt was issued; this change is *not* reflected on the balance sheet. *Thus, the balance sheet liability has been adjusted for exchange rate changes but not interest rate changes.*

Project Debt

Some debt is issued to finance a single project, such as a factory, pipeline, or real estate. In these cases, the debt terms are tailored to the expected cash flows generated by the project. Project debt may be *nonrecourse*, meaning that the lender will be paid only from project cash flows and cannot demand payment from the debtor if the project is unsuccessful. Mortgages on real estate are the major example of nonrecourse debt. Even though such debt is shown on the debtor's balance sheet, the debt is a claim only against the project cash flows and assets. Some project debt is incurred by joint ventures, discussed in Chapter 11.

Debt with Equity Features

Convertible Bonds and Warrants

To reduce borrowing costs, many companies issue debt convertible into their common shares or issue a combination of bonds and warrants to purchase common shares. Although conceptually these two types of "equity-linked" debt are identical, their accounting consequences differ.[26]

Convertible Bonds. Under APB 14 (1969), the convertibility feature of a bond is completely ignored when the bond is issued. Thus, the entire proceeds of the bond are recorded as a liability, and interest expense is recorded as if the bond were nonconvertible. However, the conversion feature lowers interest expense. When the convertible bond is converted into common stock by the bondholder, the entire proceeds are reclassified from debt to equity.

From an analytic perspective, however, recognition should be given to the equity feature prior to the conversion. When the stock price is (significantly) greater than

---

[25] In theory, exchange rates are also affected by interest rates. However, that influence is based on the *difference* in interest rate levels between the two countries, *not the level* of interest rates.

[26] A convertible bond can be disaggregated into a bond plus an option to convert the bond into common shares. An important difference between a convertible and a debt-plus-warrant issue is that, in the former case, the bond must be surrendered to exercise the option, whereas in the latter case, the bond and warrant are not linked. Thus, the issuer can use the proceeds of exercised warrants for purposes other than the retirement of the associated debt. (In the 1960s, some U.S. companies permitted warrantholders to use the associated bond to exercise the warrant; this provision protected bondholders as the bond was valued at face value regardless of its market value.) Another difference is their impact on earnings per share calculations. The interest expense on the convertible issue is eliminated when the issue is considered a common stock equivalent and is dilutive, whereas the interest on the debt component of the bond plus option alternative will never affect earnings per share calculations.

the conversion price, it is likely that the debt will not have to be repaid, and the convertible bond should be treated as equity rather than debt when calculating solvency ratios such as debt-to-equity. When the stock price is significantly below the conversion price, the bond should be treated as debt. At levels close to the conversion price, the instrument has both debt and equity features, and its treatment becomes a more difficult issue.

One possibility is to separate the debt and equity values of the convertible bond, using option pricing models. This analysis is complex, however, and beyond the scope of this book.[27] Alternatively, the analyst can examine the sensitivity of key ratios to bond classification, first treating the bond as debt and then as equity to see whether the differences are significant. If they are, then the question of whether the debt will ultimately be converted becomes a key issue, which may depend on the purpose of the analysis.[28]

Hercules, for example, reported the following capital structure at December 31, 1994:

	$ in millions	% Total
Short-term debt	$ 188.3	10.5%
Long-term debt	307.2	17.2
Equity	1,294.7	72.3
Total capital	$1,790.2	100.0%

However, Hercules' long-term debt includes the following convertible bond issues:

- 6.5% due 1999, convertible at $11.67
- 8% due 2010, convertible at $14.90

As the price range of Hercules common was $32\frac{1}{8}$ to $40\frac{1}{2}$ during 1994, there is no doubt that these issues represent equity rather than debt. Significant portions of both issues were converted to common during 1994 and the firm could force conversion of the balance by calling them.

For this reason, the reported capital structure should be adjusted by shifting the total principal amount of these bonds ($71.1 million) from long-term debt to equity. The resulting capital structure is

	$ in millions	% Total
Short-term debt	$ 188.3	10.5%
Long-term debt	236.1	13.2
Equity	1,365.8	76.3
Total capital	$1,790.2	100.0%

---

[27]For a discussion of the option features of convertible bonds (and warrants) and the difficulty in pricing them, see Frank J. Fabozzi, *Bond Markets, Analysis and Strategies*, 3rd ed. Upper Saddle River, NJ: Prentice-Hall, 1996 (p. 380).

[28]For example, in takeover analysis, the intended purchase price will determine whether convertible bonds will be converted to common or remain outstanding debt.

Exchangeable Bonds. Some bond issues are convertible into shares of another firm rather than those of the issuing firm. The analysis of such issues is more complex than the analysis of convertible debt. Exercise of the conversion privilege results in:

- Extinguishment of the debt
- Elimination of the investment in the underlying shares
- Recognition of gain or loss from the "sale" (via debt conversion) of the underlying shares

The motivation for such debt issues may include:

1. The desire to obtain cash while retaining the underlying shares for strategic reasons.
2. Minimizing the market effect of sales; the underlying shares are sold over time as bonds are exchanged.
3. Financial benefits: The interest rate on the exchangeable bonds will be lower (because of the exchange feature) than on straight debt, and the exercise price will contain a premium over the current market price.
4. Delayed recognition of a large unrealized gain; recognition is postponed until the exchange privilege is exercised. This delays the income tax recognition of the gain and may permit management some control over the timing of the gain (it can call the bonds, forcing exchange, when it wishes to report the gain).

One example is the March 1996 sale by Times Mirror (TMC) of 1.3 million shares of Premium Equity Participating Securities (PEPS) redeemable for shares of Netscape. TMC had purchased Netscape shares less than one year earlier, before Netscape's initial public offering, at a price of $2.25 per share. TMC's Netscape shares were restricted from public sale. The PEPS were sold at a price of $39.25 with a 4.25% coupon and a March 15, 2001 maturity. At that date, each PEPS is redeemable for the cash equivalent of:

- One Netscape share if that share's price is below $39.25
- .87 Netscape share if its price is $45.15 or higher
- $39.25 cash if Netscape's share price is between $45.15 and $39.25

The advantages to TMC of offering PEPS were that TMC:

1. Received the fair market value of its Netscape shares, at a low interest rate of 4.25%, despite the fact that the shares could not be legally sold.
2. Hedged its investment; if Netscape shares decline, the PEPS holders receive less payment at maturity.
3. Maintained part of the upside potential given the reduced conversion rate if Netscape shares exceeded $45.14 in price at maturity.
4. Postponed capital gains tax on the sale of Netscape shares.

Bonds with Warrants. When warrants and bonds are issued together, the accounting treatment differs from that of convertible bonds. The proceeds must be allocated between the two financial instruments.[29] The fair value of the bond portion is the recorded liability. As a result, the bond is issued at a discount, and interest expense includes amortization of that discount. The fair value of the warrants is included in equity and has no income statement impact. When warrants are exercised, the additional cash increases equity capital.

Roche, the Swiss drug multinational, has made extensive use of bonds with equity features. Problem 21 describes these issues and explores their accounting and analytic consequences.

Comparison of Convertible Bonds and Bonds with Warrants. As bonds with warrants are accounted for as if they were issued at a discount, the reported liability is lower (but increases as the discount is amortized) as compared to that of a convertible bond. However, reported interest expense is higher.[30] As discussed earlier in this chapter, reported cash flow from operations is the same, equal to the coupon interest.

These differences are summarized in the list below, which also includes a comparison with a conventional bond. Note that issuing debt with equity features lowers interest expense, increases operating cash flows, and results in a balance sheet liability equal to or below that of a conventional bond. In all respects, such debt appears less costly.

Interest Expense	Balance Sheet Liability	Operating Cash Flow
Conventional bond	Conventional bond	Conventional bond
greater than	*equal to*	*less than*
Bond with warrants	Convertible bond	Convertible bond
greater than	*greater than*	*equal to*
Convertible bond	Bond with warrants	Bond with warrants

However, this comparison is misleading as the cost of the equity feature is ignored. When convertible debt is issued, there is a systematic understatement of interest expense. Moreover, the impact of equity-linked bonds on earnings per share must always be taken into consideration (see Chapter 4).

Commodity Bonds

The interest and principal payments on bond issues are sometimes tied to the price of a commodity, such as gold, silver, or oil. Such bonds may be issued by firms producing the commodity, as part of a hedge strategy. A higher commodity price increases the payments to bondholders but is offset by higher operating profitability. These bonds, therefore, convert interest from a fixed to a variable cost.

For example, Freeport-McMoRan, a mining firm, has issued securities with returns denominated in ounces of gold and silver, both of which it produces. The off-balance-sheet financing and hedging aspects of such bond issues are discussed in Chapters 11 and 16, respectively.

---

[29]The FASB has proposed extending this accounting treatment to convertible bonds as well.

[30]Because of the accounting difference, American companies rarely issue debt/warrant combinations. However, such issues are common outside of the United States.

EXHIBIT 10-7. THE SAS GROUP
Excerpts from the Balance Sheet and Footnotes to the Financial Statements (in millions of Swedish Kroner)

Footnote 26: Subordinated Debenture Loan

A perpetual 200 million Swiss franc subordinated loan was issued during the 1985/86 fiscal year. There is no set maturity date on the loan. The SAS Consortium has the exclusive right to terminate the loan once every five years. The interest rate, fixed for periods of 10 years, at present amounts to 5¾ p.a. During the year, SAS repurchased bonds for a nominal 55.3 million Swiss francs of the outstanding loan, following which the loan amounts to 144.7 million Swiss francs.

The SAS Group	1994	1993
Current portion of long-term debt	SEK 1,845	SEK 1,579
Bond issues	5,587	8,594
Other loans	7,514	10,896
Total debt	SEK14,946	SEK21,069
Subordinated debenture loan	823	1,136
Total equity	9,915	8,631
Ratio Analysis		
Debt plus subordinated debenture loan	SEK15,769	SEK22,205
Equity plus subordinated debenture loan	SEK10,738	SEK 9,767
Debt (including subordinated loan) to equity	1.59X	2.57X
Debt to equity (including subordinated loan)	1.39X	2.16X

Source: The SAS Group, *1994 Annual Report.*

Perpetual Debt

Some debt issues have no stated maturity. When debt does not have a maturity date, it may be considered preferred equity rather than a liability for analytic purposes. An exception would be cases where debt covenants are likely to force repayment or refinancing of the debt.

Exhibit 10-7 reproduces Footnote 26 and excerpts from the 1994 financial statements of SAS (Scandinavian Airlines). The firm issued a perpetual 200 million Swiss franc-denominated subordinated loan, with the interest rate fixed for 10 years and no set maturity date. SAS has the exclusive right to terminate the loan once every five years.

The loan reflects a 5.75% interest rate in 1994, compared to rates of 5.00 and 7.00% on other Swiss-franc-denominated debt reported by the firm. These rates are significantly lower than those paid by SAS on debt issued in other currencies. In 1994, the reported debt-to-equity ratio declines to 1.39X (2.16X in 1993) from 1.59X (2.57X in 1993) when this perpetual debt is treated as equity.

Problem 19 discusses the analytical issues raised by a perpetual bond issued by Pepsico.

With long-term interest rates at low levels, some firms have issued debt with a maturity of 100 years. Although such issues are technically debt, their long maturity suggests that, for all practical purposes, they represent permanent capital and should be treated as equity when computing the debt-to-equity ratio. ABN Amro, BellSouth, Coca-Cola, Columbia/HCA Healthcare, and Walt Disney have all issued 100-year bonds.[31]

Preferred Stock

Many companies issue more than one class of shares. Preferred (or preference) shares have priority over common shares with respect to dividends and entitlement to the proceeds of sale or liquidation. In exchange for this privileged position, preferred shareholders usually give up their right to participate fully in the success of the company.

Preferred shares generally have a fixed dividend payment and a fixed preference on liquidation. Dividend payments are almost always *cumulative*; if not paid when due, they remain a liability (but one that is not recorded). Dividend arrears must be paid before any dividend can be paid to common shareholders. When calculating the net worth of a company with preferred shares outstanding, the analyst should:

1. Subtract the liquidating value of the preferred, not the stated value, which may be lower.

2. Subtract any cumulative dividends that are in arrears.

Some preferred shares have a variable interest rate. "Auction rate" preferred shares have interest rates that change frequently, making them attractive to buyers seeking "money-market"-type investments.[32] From an analytic perspective, these preferred shares function as short-term liabilities and should be treated as such. They are often called when market conditions change, making them a less permanent source of funds.

Preferred shares are almost always callable by the issuer. Many issues are, however, redeemable by the preferred shareholder, often over a period of years.[33] Because of these "sinking fund" provisions, redeemable preferreds should be treated as debt for analysis; they should be included as debt in solvency ratios, and dividend payments should be treated as interest.

Consistent with this view, the SEC requires that redeemable preferred shares be excluded from stockholders' equity. However, at the same time, the SEC does not require their classification as debt. The argument against debt classification is that, ultimately, *firms cannot be forced to pay the dividends or redeem the preferred shares. Unlike creditors, preferred shareholders do not have the power to force the firm into bankruptcy for noncompliance* with the terms of the agreement.[34] Often, when dividends are in arrears, they do gain representation on the board of directors.

[31] In December 1995 the U.S. Treasury proposed that bond issues in excess of 40 years not be treated as debt for tax purposes, making interest payments not tax-deductible.

[32] For U.S. corporate buyers, preferred dividends are 80% tax-free, making these issues more attractive on an after-tax basis than many other short-term investments. The U.S. Treasury has proposed the reduction of that exclusion to 50%.

[33] These provisions provide preferred shareholders with a guaranteed future value for the shares.

[34] In many states, a firm cannot pay dividends or redeem shares if such payments will jeopardize the company's survival.

The ambiguity as to whether these shares are debt or equity was shown in two studies by Kimmel and Warfield (1993, 1995). They found that only 60% of redeemable preferred shares are actually redeemed; the other 40% are eventually converted to common shares, arguing against treating these hybrids as debt. Furthermore, as a firm's systematic risk (its beta) is related to a firm's debt-to-equity ratio,[35] they tested whether the relationship had a better "fit" with the redeemables treated as debt or equity. They found that they *did not fit into either category unless the redeemables had voting rights and were convertible.* Only when these attributes were present, did the securities exhibit equitylike qualities. Thus, on average, one cannot generalize as to the nature of these hybrid securities.

The line between debt and equity has become increasingly blurred in recent years. Companies prefer to issue securities that minimize the after-tax cost of financing yet provide maximum flexibility. Some issues are designated preferreds but are really debt; others are called debt but are functionally equity. Although help from accounting standards setters may eventually arrive,[36] analysts must evaluate such instruments on a case-by-case basis and decide whether to treat them as debt or equity.

Effects of Changes in Interest Rates

Debt reported on the balance sheet is equal to the present value of future cash payments discounted at the *market rate on the date of issuance.* Increases (decreases) in the *current market rate* decrease (increase) the *market value* of the debt. A company that issued fixed-rate debt prior to an increase (decrease) in market rates experiences an economic gain (loss) as a result of the rate change. This economic gain or loss is not reflected in either the income statement or balance sheet.

For some analytic purposes, however, the market value of a company's debt may be more relevant than its book value. It better reflects the firm's economic position and is as important as the current market values of a firm's assets. Analysis of a firm's absolute and relative level of debt and borrowing capacity should be based on current market conditions. Consider two firms reporting the same book value of debt. One firm issued the debt when interest rates were low; the other at higher current interest rates. Debt-to-equity ratios based on book values may be the same. However, the firm that issued the bonds at the lower interest rate has higher borrowing capacity as the economic value of its debt is lower.[37] Ratios calculated using the market value of debt will reflect the stronger solvency position.

Furthermore, in valuation models[38] that deduct the value of debt from the value of the firm (or of its assets), that debt should be measured at market value rather than book value. Firms that issued debt at lower rates are relatively better off when interest rates increase, and this advantage should increase the equity value of the firm.

In the United States, SFAS 107, Disclosures about Fair Value of Financial Instruments, requires that firms report the fair value of outstanding debt. The next section

---

[35]See the discussion of beta in Chapter 18.

[36]The FASB issued a discussion memorandum, Distinguishing Between Liability and Equity Instruments and Accounting for Instruments with Characteristics of Both, in August 1990. This project is inactive, but some of its issues are under consideration in various projects on financial instruments.

[37]Theoretically, it could refinance its current debt at the same interest rate as the other firm, lowering the book value of debt.

[38]Similarly (as discussed in Chapter 19), in discounted cash flow valuation analysis, the calculation of a firm's (weighted-average) cost of capital is based on market rather than book values of debt (and equity).

restates the debt of Boeing from book to market value. This exercise is useful for several reasons.

First, financial statement disclosures are based on year-end (or quarter) prices. When interest rates have changed significantly since the last report date, the analyst may need to recalculate the market value of the firm's debt. Second, most non-U.S. firms, and firms in the United States that are not subject to FASB disclosure requirements, do not provide market value disclosures; analysts must know how to estimate the market value of debt for such firms. Finally, market valuation requires assumptions and (especially for firms with complex financial instruments) often there are competing valuation methods. In some cases, analysts may want to perform their own market value calculations. To do so, they must disaggregate management's aggregate fair value disclosure; this requires an understanding of how market values are estimated.

Estimating the Market Value of Debt

In many cases, the replacement of book value with market value is simple. For publicly traded debt, market values are readily available.[39] If the debt is not publicly traded, its present value can be calculated by applying the current market rate to the original debt terms. The maturity, coupon rate, and other terms of long-term debt are generally disclosed for each debt security issued.

The appropriate current market rate can be obtained from:

1. Other publicly traded debt of the company having approximately the same maturity; estimate the rate used by the market to discount that debt.

2. Publicly traded debt of equivalent companies in the same industry; estimate the rate used to discount that debt.

3. Estimating the risk premium over the rate on government debt of the same maturity. The risk premium depends on the bond-rating "risk" class of the company's bonds. (See Exhibit 10P-1 in the problems section of this chapter.)

Calculating the Market Value of Boeing's Long-term Debt. Exhibit 10-8 shows the restatement of Boeing's long-term debt from book to market value.[40] Boeing states, as part of its SFAS 107 disclosure, that

> the carrying amount of long-term debt was $2,609 and $2,630, as of December 31, 1994 and 1993. The fair value of long-term debt based on current market rates for debt of the same risk and maturities was estimated at $2,486 and $2,870 as of December 31, 1994 and 1993.

The maturities, coupon rates, and book values are taken directly from Boeing's long-term debt footnote. Except for the 7.50% debt maturing in 2042 and the debt listed as "other," Boeing's listed debt is publicly traded.

The publicly traded debt was valued using market prices (expressed as a percentage of face value) obtained from Standard & Poor's *Bond Guide*, which also provides the

---

[39]Sources include rating service publications (such as Standard & Poor's Bond Guide used for Boeing), newspapers, and electronic quotation services.

[40]The current portion of long-term debt is included in the calculation.

EXHIBIT 10-8. BOEING
Market Valuation of Long-Term Debt at December 31, 1994

Coupon		Maturity	Book Value ($ in millions)	Face Value ($ in millions)	Market Price	Market Value ($ in millions)	Market Yield to Maturity
Debt for Which Market Prices Are Available							
8.375%	March 1	1996	$ 250	$ 250	100.75	$ 252	7.68%
6.350%	June 15	2003	299	300	88.25	265	8.31%
8.100%	November 15	2006	175	175	97.75	171	8.40%
8.750%	August 15	2021	398	400	101.13	405	8.64%
7.950%	August 15	2024	300	300	96.13	288	8.30%
7.250%	June 15	2025	247	250	85.13	213	8.64%
8.750%	September 15	2031	248	250	100.88	252	8.67%
8.625%	November 15	2031	173	175	99.63	174	8.66%
7.875%	April 15	2043	173	175	90.38	158	8.73%
6.875%	October 15	2043	125	125	79.50	99	8.68%
	Subtotal		$2,388	$2,400		$2,277	
Debt for Which Market Prices Are Not Available							
7.500%	August 15	2042	100	100	86.64	87	8.68%
Other notes			121	121	100.00	121	
	Grand total		$2,609	$2,621		$2,485	

Source: Standard & Poor's, *Bond Guide,* and Boeing, *1994 Annual Report.*

balance (face value) outstanding for each debt issue.[41] These face values were multiplied by market prices to obtain market values. The *Bond Guide* also provides the yield-to-maturity (YTM), the implicit market rate of interest used to discount the bonds to market value.

The bonds have been arranged in order of maturity. Note that YTM (with some aberrations[42]) increases for longer maturities, implying a (conventional) upward-sloping yield curve. For the 7.50% debt, fair value was estimated by discounting the cash flows at an assumed YTM of 8.68%, based on the YTM of Boeing's debt of similar maturity (2043). Finally, for the "other" debt, we chose (lacking any data) to assume a market value equal to book value.

These calculations yield an estimated market value of $2,485 million, virtually identical to the fair value disclosed by Boeing.

Complexities in Market Value Estimation

Because of the conventional nature of Boeing's debt, the calculation of its market value was straightforward. Boeing's debt is all fixed-rate and dollar-denominated.

[41] These amounts may differ from the carrying value of the debt if the debt was originally issued at a premium or discount. For Boeing, the differences are minor.

[42] The major aberration occurs for the bonds due August 15, 2024, where the YTM drops to 8.30%. Since the bond can be redeemed by the bondholders at their option starting in the year 2012, the relevant maturity date is 2012 not 2024. This reduces the YTM. Furthermore, the option privilege also serves to reduce the required YTM.

Simple debt structures, however, are becoming the exception rather than the rule for large companies, given globalization and the increased sophistication of financial markets.

Some complexities make the calculation of market values almost impossible as the requisite information is lacking. A few of the complexities summarized below have been discussed earlier, others will be addressed in later sections of the text, and some remain beyond the scope of our book.

Convertible Bonds. Market prices are readily available for most convertible debt issues. However, these prices incorporate both the debt and equity features of the security. Only the appropriate portion of the market value should be included as part of debt.

Variable-Rate Debt. Variable-rate debt usually requires no market value adjustment. Because of the continuous adjustment of the interest rate on the debt, market value approximates book value.[43]

Debt Denominated in a Foreign Currency. For debt denominated in a foreign currency, the present value calculations should be based on current interest rates on the currency in which the debt is denominated.

Hedges and Derivatives. Firms can protect themselves against changes in interest rates and/or currency exchange rates using instruments such as options or forward contracts (including swap agreements). We defer a discussion of the accounting treatment and economic impact of these instruments on the value of a firm's debt, for the most part, to Chapter 16. In this chapter we confine ourselves to a discussion of *interest rate swaps.*

As previously discussed, *the original debt instrument with its original parameters remains in effect and is reported in the firm's financial statements; if publicly traded, market prices are available.* However, the estimated market value of the underlying debt instrument must reflect any interest rate swap.

When fixed-rate debt has been converted to floating-rate debt with an interest rate swap covering its full term, no adjustment to market value is required. Thus, for the Glatfelter example, the economic gain on the $50 million of debt that has been swapped accrues to the counterparty; there should be no adjustment to market value. The remaining $100 million should be adjusted for the increase in interest rates.

If a swap does not cover the full term of fixed-rate debt, changes in interest rates after the end of the swap term will affect market values. Thus, it is important to discern the terms of any swaps by careful reading of footnotes.

When a swap converts floating-rate debt to fixed-rate debt, however, the market value is exposed to changes in interest rates. Even though the market value of the original obligation does not change, the fair value of the effective (because of the swap) obligation does and should be calculated.

Given the effort and assumptions required to estimate market values when they are not provided, we must consider the factors that determine whether the adjustment from book value to market value is worthwhile. The next section discusses these factors.

---

[43]This is not precisely accurate. The variable-rate adjustment may lag the interest rate change. Nevertheless, given the short period until adjustment, the effect of any lag on present value is usually immaterial. Because of this, SFAS 107 states that, for variable-rate debt, the book value can be used to approximate the market or fair value.

Debt: Market or Book Value?

The book value of Boeing's long-term debt was $2,630 at December 31, 1993; its market value was $2,870, or 9% *higher*. The December 31, 1994 book value was $2,609; its market value was $2,486, or 5% *lower*. Thus, during 1994, market value relative to book value declined 14%. This decline was significant, but in many ways was unique to:

- The year(s) in question. At year-end 1993, interest rates were at recent historical lows but rose significantly during 1994. The interest rate on AA bonds (Boeing's rating) rose from approximately $7\frac{1}{4}\%$ (lowest in over 20 years) to more than $8\frac{1}{2}\%$.[44]
- The structure of Boeing's debt. Boeing has fixed-rate debt with long maturities (25 to 50 years) but little variable-rate debt.

These factors (confirmed by empirical results discussed in Box 10-2) suggest the conditions to be considered before deciding whether the restatement of debt to market value is a useful exercise. All the following factors should be considered.

Debt Maturities. The effect of interest rate changes on the market value of debt increases with the maturity of the debt. If a firm's debt is mostly short-term, changes in interest rates will not appreciably affect its market value.[45] For example, no adjustment is required for trade debt whose maturity is a few months rather than many years.

Interest Rates on Debt. For adjustable rate debt, whose interest rate varies with the market rate of interest, book value approximates market value and no adjustment is required. Similarly, when the firm has swapped its fixed debt for floating-rate debt, there should be no adjustment as the value of that debt is no longer exposed to interest rate changes.

On the other hand, the market value of fixed-rate debt issues does change with interest rates. This is especially true of zero-coupon and other discount debt, due to their longer duration relative to debt issued at par.

Changes in Market Interest Rates. The adjustment to market value depends on changes in the market rate of interest. In 1994, interest rates increased sharply and, therefore, there was a large market value adjustment for Boeing's debt. As long as there is no long-term trend, these fluctuations tend to offset, leaving the difference between book and market values small. However, when rates rise or fall greatly over several years, the differences between book and market value can be significant.

Imbedded Interest Rate. Boeing issued debt at various times and its (weighted) average outstanding coupon rate (*imbedded rate*) was approximately 7.85%, within the range of interest rates over 1993 to 1994. The adjustment from book value does not depend on the change in interest rates itself, but rate changes relative to the imbedded rate. Unless there are limits on the firm's ability to refinance (noncallable debt or deterioration in credit quality), the imbedded rate should decline (with some lag) as interest rates fall. The reverse is not true; firms with long-term fixed-rate debt can enjoy low interest costs for many years even though interest rates in general have risen.

---

[44]Similarly, over this time period, the rate on the U.S. 30-year Treasury Bond rose from just below $6\frac{1}{4}\%$ (the lowest rate in over 20 years) to 8%.

[45]Thus, even if its long-term debt is adjusted by 10%, total debt will only be affected by 10% times the percentage of long-term debt. The lower the percentage of long-term debt, the smaller the overall adjustment.

BOX 10-2
Market or Book Values: Empirical Evidence

Bowman (1980) examined the relationship between firms' market betas and the debt-to-equity ratio. Finance theory predicts (see Chapter 18) that the higher a firm's debt-to-equity ratio (using market values), the higher the firm's beta.

Letting the superscripts M and B refer to the market and book value, respectively, Bowman examined which of the following four measures of the debt-to-equity ratio, D^M/E^M, D^M/E^B, D^B/E^M, and D^B/E^B, were more closely associated with the firm's beta.

Bowman obtained the best results when he used the market value of equity in the denominator. Whether debt was measured on a market basis or debt basis made little difference as the ratios D^B/E^M and D^M/E^M yielded similar results. The pure book value ratio D^B/E^B did not perform as well; the measure of the market value of the debt-to-book value of equity (D^M/E^B) performed the poorest.

These results can be partly attributable to the fact that for close to 60% of the debt in Bowman's sample, book value and market value were equivalent. Furthermore, the correlation between the market value of debt and the book value of debt was close to 100%. As the study ranked debtors by relative rather than absolute levels of debt, changes in the market rates of interest shifted debt valuations without changing ranks.

Mulford (1986) replicated Bowman's study using a later time period. Bowman's analysis was based on 1973 data, predating the dramatic rise in market interest rates of the late 1970s. Mulford, referring to Bowman's study, noted:

> His failure to find evidence of superior performance for a debt-to-equity ratio based on market values of debt may have been due to small differences between the book and market values of debt which accompanied the general level of interest rates at that time.*

To remedy this deficiency, Mulford focused on 1980, when market rates of interest were historically high. In addition, to alleviate potential measurement problems arising from the conversion of book to market values, he examined the performance of portfolios of firms in addition to individual firms. Mulford's results were more in line with theory, but only on a portfolio basis. No matter which variation was used to measure the relationship between beta and debt-to-equity, the market-based debt-to-equity ratio was always the most closely associated with beta on a portfolio basis. On an individual basis, D^M/E^M did not always perform as well, but the differences between it and the best performing ratio were minimal.

These results suggest, not surprisingly, that the market value of debt is not superior to book value when the difference between the stated and market rates of interest is small; the additional cost of obtaining market values is not worthwhile.† Adjustment is necessary only when the gap between the historic and market rates of interest is large. Even then, potential measurement problems‡ in estimating market values may offset any benefits from the adjustment process.

---

*Charles W. Mulford, "The Importance of a Market Value Measurement of Debt in Leverage Ratios: Replications and Extensions," *Journal of Accounting Research,* Autumn 1985, pp. 897–906.

†Given the high correlation between market and book values of debt, this is especially true for analyses that focus on relative rather than absolute debt burdens.

‡The issue of a measurement problem also calls into question the results of both Bowman and Mulford from a different perspective. They adjusted only on-balance-sheet debt, ignoring any "off-balance-sheet" debt. As Chapter 11 will make clear, the latter can be significant.

Debt of Firms in Distress

When the credit quality of a firm changes significantly (in either direction), the market price of debt will follow, independent of interest rate trends. When credit quality and the market value of debt decline, there appears to be a gain to the firm, yet it is difficult to argue that shareholders are better off. This apparent paradox reflects simultaneous changes in the value of assets as credit quality changes. It is reasonable to assume that some assets of such troubled companies are impaired (see the discussion in Chapter 8).

Accounting for Restructured and Impaired Debt

When a debtor is in financial difficulty, creditors may agree to accept assets in payment of the debt or to "restructure" the obligation by modifying its terms (e.g., reducing the interest rate or deferring principal payments). When debt is extinguished, both the debtor and creditor will recognize gain or loss measured as the difference between the fair value of the assets (cash or other assets) used to repay the debt and its carrying amount. This accounting treatment raises neither accounting nor analysis issues.

When the obligation is restructured, however, different accounting rules apply to creditors and debtors. Creditors adhere to SFAS 114 (1993), as amended by SFAS 118 (1994), whereas debtors use SFAS 15 (1977) to account for these transactions.

Under SFAS 114, the creditor must recognize a loss equal to the difference between the carrying value of the loan and the present value of the restructured payment stream *discounted at the original discount rate* (effective interest rate). Thus, if a 12% coupon loan with a face value of $100,000 and three years remaining to maturity is restructured by reducing the interest rate to 8%, the creditor recognizes a loss of $9,610 as the new carrying value of the loan is $90,390.[46] The loan impairment may also be measured using the observable market price of the loan or the fair value of collateral when the loan is collateral-dependent.[47]

The FASB was reluctant, however, to allow debtors to record gains resulting from financial distress. SFAS 15 provides that the debtor's carrying amount of the debt be compared with the *undiscounted gross cash flows* (principal and interest) due after restructuring. As long as the gross cash flows exceed the carrying amount, no gain is recognized by the debtor. In our example, the future payments are ($100,000 + 3 × $8,000) = $124,000. No gain is recognized.[48]

However, the present value of the cash flows has been reduced; in economic terms, the debtor has gained at the expense of the creditor. The accounting mandated by SFAS 15 recognizes this transfer only over the life of the loan as payments are made; the debtor will show lower interest expense as the loan is amortized at the implicit interest rate of the loan. In our example, interest expense is now calculated at an interest rate of 8% rather than 12%.

---

[46]If we assume annual payments, the present value of a three-year annuity of $8,000 discounted at 12% + present value of $100,000 in three years discounted at 12% equals $90,390.

[47]SFAS 118 amended SFAS 114 to allow creditors to continue income recognition methods for impaired loans that had been used prior to the adoption of SFAS 114. For example, cost-recovery or cash-basis methods report investments in impaired loans at less than the present value of expected future cash flows. In these cases, no additional impairment needs to be recognized under SFAS 118. SFAS 114 was also amended to require additional disclosures regarding the investment in certain impaired loans and the recognition of interest income on those loans.

[48]If the payments do not exceed the carrying value, then the gain is limited to the difference between those amounts; the debt is discounted at an implicit interest rate of zero.

A similar approach is mandated by the FASB for loans considered to be "impaired." Creditors are required to recognize the probable loss, but recognition of gains by debtors is not allowed. Under SFAS 114, creditors are required to carry impaired loans at the present value of cash flows expected after modification of the loan terms, *discounted at the original effective interest rate*. For the debtor, however, no gain recognition is permitted.

For purposes of analysis, however, both impaired and restructured debt should be restated to fair market value using a *current market interest rate* to discount the cash flows required by the (actual or expected) restructured obligation. However, as noted earlier, debtor "gains" should be viewed warily; gains resulting from an inability to repay loans are almost certainly offset by asset impairment.

Retirement of Debt Prior to Maturity

Firms generally choose the initial debt maturity of their obligations based on such considerations as cost and investment horizon (when projects funded with debt are expected to generate cash flows). Subsequently, conditions may change and a firm may wish to refinance or retire debt prior to the original maturity. Examples include:

- Declining interest rates permit the reduction of interest cost.
- Increasing cash from operations permits debt retirement earlier than expected.
- Sale of assets or additional equity generates funds and the firm decides to reduce financial leverage.

In such cases, the firm can reduce bank debt, commercial paper, and other short-term debt quickly and at small expense. For longer-maturity debt, the firm may exercise call provisions, use tender offers, or in-substance defeasance. We examine the economic and accounting effects of these choices shortly.

Accounting for Debt Retirement

When firms retire debt prior to maturity, the difference between the book value of the liability and the amount paid at retirement is treated as an extraordinary gain or loss in the income statement.[49]

Using the par bond example in Exhibit 10-1A (see p. 478), assume that on December 31, 19X1, the market interest rate for the firm is 12%. As a result, the market price of the bonds should be $96,535.[50] If the firm paid $96,535 to retire the bond, the resulting gain on the bond retirement is $3,465 since the book value is $100,000.[51] This gain must be recognized as an extraordinary item. The logic for this treatment is:

- In reality, the firm is no better off as a result of the refinancing. To finance the retirement of the bond, it must issue new debt[52] bearing at least the same effective

---

[49]SFAS 4 (1975), which mandates this treatment, exempts gains from normal sinking fund repurchase from extraordinary designation.

[50]This can be seen from Exhibit 10-1C as the carrying amount of the discount bond is the present value at the (original) 12% interest rate.

[51]We have ignored unamortized debt issuance costs. When bonds are retired, the firm must write off these costs that were capitalized when the bonds were issued. This write-off becomes a component of the gain or loss on retirement.

[52]Even if it did not issue new debt to retire the bond but rather used internal funds, the firm would experience an opportunity cost equal to the forgone interest revenue.

interest rate (and must incur transaction costs). Effectively, over the remaining life of the original bond, the net borrowing cost would be identical; the company has simply replaced 10% coupon debt with 12% coupon debt. In economic terms, the gain took place as interest rates rose, not when the refinancing took place. Because of the use of historical cost as a measure of the bond liability, however, only refinancing results in a recognized gain.

- The decision to refinance is a function of the change in market interest rates.[53] As its impact is not part of normal operations, segregation of the gain or loss as extraordinary is appropriate.

In the early 1970s, interest rates rose sharply at the same time the U.S. economy entered recession. Firms found their outstanding low-coupon bonds selling at deep discounts. Many of these firms had poor operating profitability, but were able to increase reported income by retiring bonds. The issuance of SFAS 4 in 1975 was partially a response to this income manipulation activity.

Recent refinancings more often retire high-coupon debt issued when interest rates were higher. For example, in 1992 to 1993, as interest rates fell sharply, monthly corporate refundings approached $30 to $35 billion; in 1991, they had been below $5 billion. Such refinancing results in a recognized loss. That loss should be viewed, however, as a signal of lower future interest expense, as high-coupon debt is replaced by lower-coupon debt (also see the following discussion of callable bonds).

DuPont, for example, reported extraordinary losses from the early extinguishment of debt in both 1992 and 1993 (see Note 8 for details). The company issued substantial amounts of new debt in both years.

Bond retirements are normally accomplished by paying cash, although new debt issues may take place at the same time. In the past, new debt securities or equity (or some combination thereof) were sometimes offered in exchange for outstanding debt. Prior to 1980, the capital gain on exchange transactions could be treated, for tax purposes, in a manner that made them essentially tax-free. After 1980, however, only certain debt-equity swaps were tax-exempt.[54] The Deficit Reduction Act of 1984 eliminated this last loophole.

The change in tax status virtually ended these transactions. According to one estimate (Hand, 1989), only two debt-equity swaps were completed after July 1984, as compared to 291 between August 1981 and July 1984.

Our discussion of discretionary debt retirements indicates that the amounts and timing of the accounting gain and the economic gain from debt retirement are quite different. This especially applies to callable bonds, whose retirement may give rise to economic profit (even in nominal terms) but may generate a loss for accounting purposes.

Callable Bonds

When a bond is callable, the issuer has the option to buy back (call) the bond from bondholders at predetermined dates and prices. This differs from the case in which

---

[53]If the gain or loss is recognized at all, it should be in the period in which interest rates change, not in the year in which the refinancing takes place. In our example, the year is the same, but that coincidence is rare in practice.

[54]See Hand (1989) for a discussion of the tax status of these transactions in the pre-1980, 1981 to 1984, and post-1984 periods.

EXHIBIT 10-9
Analysis of Callable Bond

On January 1, 19X1, Cole issues the following bond:

Face value:	$100,000
Coupon:	10% (annual payments assumed for simplicity)
Maturity:	5 years
Call provision:	Callable at any time after one year at 102

If the market interest rate applicable to Cole is 10%, then the bonds will be issued at par.

Reported Liability = $100,000
Annual Interest Expense = $10,000 (10% × $100,000)

Assume that, on December 31, 19X1, the market rate applicable to Cole has declined to 8%. The rate change has no accounting impact on the company. However, the present value of the cash flows associated with the debt rises to $106,624 (discounted at 8%). Absent the call provision, the expected market price of the bonds is 106.624.

By calling the bonds at a price of 102, Cole realizes an economic gain of $4,624 [(106.624 − 102) × ($100,000)].

However, the call results in an accounting loss of $2,000 [(100 − 102) × ($100,000)].

the issuer retires the old bond at a market price equal to the present value of the future payment stream. The call price is usually set at a premium over the face value of the bond, but is independent of the present value of the payment stream at the time the call is made. However, the actual exercise does depend on the relationship of the call price to that present value.

Exhibit 10-9 contains an analysis of a callable bond. The decline in interest rates constitutes an economic loss at the time of the rate change, as the market value of the bond rises. In the absence of the call provision, a decision to refinance would not impact Cole, which would incur new debt equal to $106,624 to refinance the debt at market rates. However, the call provision permits the firm to retire the bonds for only $102,000; the economic gain is the difference.[55]

Economically, it is beneficial to refinance the debt, but the income statement reports a loss. One can only speculate as to how many firms have not refinanced under such conditions because of the financial statement impact. This is yet another reason why analysts should ignore gains and losses from the retirement of debt.

Defeasance

In some cases, the firm wishes to retire debt but is unable to do so because the debt is noncallable. *In-substance defeasance* involves setting aside riskless securities sufficient to pay all remaining installments of principal and interest. The cash flow characteristics of the securities used must match those of the debt being defeased and must be placed in a trust fund restricted for that purpose.

Although the original debt remained outstanding, U.S. GAAP permitted debtor

---

[55]When bonds are issued, the call provisions are often an important ingredient in the market reception. As call provisions benefit only the issuer, bond buyers will bargain against them. Option-adjusted bond analysis is now routine. Many shorter-term issues are noncallable.

firms to derecognize the defeased obligations through December 31, 1996.[56] However, SFAS 125 (1996)[57] disallows in-substance defeasance and debt may be extinguished only on repayment or when the debtor is legally released from being the primary obligor.

Example: Roche. The *1994 Annual Report* of Roche contains the following footnote disclosure of defeased debt:

> The repayment at maturity of zero-percent subordinated bonds with nominal value of 250 million Swiss francs was fully provided for during 1992. To this end the necessary amount of high-quality securities was fully irrevocably deposited with a bank. The bank was instructed to apply the proceeds from the sale of these securities to the repayment of the bondholders at maturity in 1997. The Group has recognized this transaction as an extinguishment of debt although the Group is not released from the debt obligation.

BOND COVENANTS

Creditors use debt covenants in lending agreements to protect their interests by restricting activities of the debtor that could jeopardize the creditor's position. Auditors and management must certify that the firm has not violated the covenants. If any covenant is violated, the firm is in *technical default* of its lending agreement, and the creditor can demand repayment of the debt after the stated grace period. Generally, however, as we shall see, the terms are renegotiated but at a cost to the debtor as the lender demands concessions. The analysis of a firm's debt position must therefore take into consideration the nature of these covenants and the risk that the firm may violate them.

Information on debt covenants is important both to evaluate the firm's credit risk as well as to understand the implications of such restrictions for the firm's dividend and growth (investment) prospects. In addition, to the extent these covenants are accounting-based, they may affect the choice of accounting policies.

Nature of Covenants

Smith and Warner (1979) characterize debt covenants as placing limits on one or more of the following activities:

1. Payment of dividends (includes share repurchases)
2. Production and investment (includes mergers and acquisitions, sale and leaseback, or outright disposal of certain assets)
3. Issuance of new debt (or incurrence of other liabilities)
4. Payoff patterns (includes sinking fund requirements and the priorities of claims on assets)

In addition to direct restrictions on activities, covenants may require maintenance of certain levels of such accounting-based financial variables as retained earnings, working capital, net assets, and debt-to-equity ratios. These levels are often related to the four types of activities listed above by restricting a certain activity if the accounting variable

---

[56]See SFAS 76 (1983) and FASB Technical Bulletin 84-4 for accounting and disclosure requirements related to defeasance.

[57]See SFAS 125, Accounting for the Transfers and Servicing of Financial Assets and Extinguishments of Liabilities.

EXHIBIT 10-10
Common Accounting-Based Debt Covenant Restrictions

Attribute:	Retained earnings
Measured as:	Restricted retained earnings
Limits:	Payments of dividends or stock repurchase below minimum level of restricted retained earnings
Attribute:	Net assets
Measured as:	Net tangible assets or net assets
Limits:	Investments, dividend payments, and new debt issues if net assets fall below a certain level
Attribute:	Working capital
Measured as:	Minimum working capital or current ratio
Limits:	Mergers and acquisitions, dividend payments, and new debt issues if the working capital or the current ratio fall below a certain level
Attribute:	Debt-to-equity
Measured as:	Debt divided by net tangible assets or debt divided by net assets
Limits:	Issuance of additional debt

Source: Joanne C. Duke and Herbert G. Hunt III, "An Empirical Examination of Debt Covenant Restrictions and Accounting-Related Debt Proxies," *Journal of Accounting and Economics,* Jan. 1990, adapted from Table 1, p. 52.

violates the specified target level. In some cases, the violation itself may signal a breach of the covenant even without any subsequent firm activity.

Exhibit 10-10 contains a summary of the nature of these accounting-based debt covenant restrictions, adapted from Duke and Hunt (1990). *Restricted retained earnings* as a constraint on dividend payments, one of the most common forms used, are outlined in Exhibit 10-11.

Information regarding these covenants was obtained by Smith and Warner (1979) and Duke and Hunt (1990) from the American Bar Foundation's *Commentaries on Debentures*, which summarizes typical covenants found in lending agreements. A cursory examination of these restrictions makes it clear that creditors seek to limit the firm's level of risk (investment and debt restrictions) and preserve the assets of the firm to ensure that debts are repaid (payment restrictions). Thus, covenants attempt to limit shareholders' ability to transfer assets to themselves (dividend restrictions), new shareholders (merger and acquisition restrictions), or new creditors (debt restrictions).

The information provided in the *Commentaries* is of a general nature. The best source of information on specific covenants (and other terms of the bond issue) for publicly issued bonds is the bond indenture, the legal document created when the bond is issued and filed with the registration statement filed with the SEC. The trustee (normally a bank) will have a copy of the indenture and is responsible for the enforcement of its terms. The bond prospectus should contain a good summary of these terms.

For all debt issues, summarized data can be found in:

• Services such as Moody's Industrial Manual

• Annual reports

• SEC filings by debtors

EXHIBIT 10-11
Unrestricted Retained Earnings: Inventory of Payable Funds

The most frequent accounting-based restriction specified is the dividend constraint. Dividends cannot be paid out of restricted retained earnings. Only unrestricted retained earnings, often referred to as the inventory of payable funds (IPF), are available for dividends. The general formulation of IPF is defined (see Smith and Warner, 1979) as the sum of:

1. A specified percentage k of earnings E from the date of the debt issuance to the present period, plus
2. Proceeds from the sale of common shares CS from the date of the debt issuance to the present period, plus
3. A prespecified constant F, less
4. The sum of dividends DV and stock repurchases from the date of the debt issuance to the present period

Algebraically, this is equal to

$$\text{IPF}_t = k \sum_{i=0}^{t} E_i + \sum_{i=0}^{t} CS_i + F - \sum_{i=0}^{t} DV_i$$

where period 0 represents the date of the debt issuance and period t refers to the current date. The prespecified constant F is usually set at approximately one year's earnings.* This builds some slack into the system in the event the firm has a loss.

---

*See Smith and Warner (1979), Note 36.

Press and Weintrop (1990 and 1991) contend that information obtained from annual reports and Moody's is not comprehensive, especially with respect to covenants relating to privately placed debt, and that in these cases, it is necessary to access the original SEC filings.

Calculation of Accounting-Based Constraints

Each type of constraint is defined in the covenants. In addition, the covenants specify:

- Whether GAAP definitions are to be used or GAAP is to be modified. (For examples, see Exhibit 10-12.) Leftwich (1983) noted that such modifications are most often associated with private rather than public debt indentures.
- Whether GAAP in effect at the time of the debt issuance is maintained throughout the life of the bond ("frozen" GAAP), or calculations in subsequent years are to be based on GAAP in effect at the date of the calculation ("rolling" GAAP). This is important when important new accounting standards are adopted. In September 1991, for example, Westinghouse Electric announced that it was asking its bank lenders to change the terms of its loan agreement in anticipation of adopting SFAS 106 (see Chapter 12).

Mohrman (1996) examined a sample of 174 lending agreements that contained covenants based on financial statement information. She found that over half (90) the covenants were based on *fixed* GAAP specified in the agreements. That is, the covenants were not affected by voluntary or FASB mandated accounting changes, nor

EXHIBIT 10-12
Summary of Negotiated Accounting Rules That Are Entirely Outside GAAP (Group 1)

Category	Negotiated Accounting Rule
(i) Business combinations	Retained earnings of an acquired firm do not relax the negotiated restrictions on funds available for dividends even if pooling is used. Some upward revaluation of the acquired assets is allowed, but only if the assets are independently appraised. If upward asset revaluation is allowed, the amount of any revaluation, even if classed as goodwill, can be included in tangible assets.
(ii) Contingencies	All charges for contingencies must be made against income, not against reserve accounts. Specific contingent liabilities, particularly guarantees of third-party indebtedness, are included in balance sheet liabilities.
(iii) Equity investments	Investments, especially short-term investments, are valued primarily at the lower of cost or market. Investments are frequently excluded from the asset base against which firms may borrow. Income from unconsolidated investments is not recognized until it is received; that is, the equity method is not used.
(iv) Foreign subsidiaries	Foreign subsidiaries are seldom consolidated. Income from foreign investments is recognized only when it is actually received.
(v) Goodwill and intangibles	Goodwill and intangibles are frequently excluded from the asset base against which firms may borrow. The accounting double entry is not preserved—goodwill is eliminated from balance sheet numbers but amortization is required in the income statement.
(vi) Income tax	Deferred tax credits are not always classified as a liability. Deferred tax debits are excluded from the firm's asset base.
(vii) Stock dividends and stock splits	No distinction is made between stock dividends and stock splits.

Summary of Negotiated Accounting Rules That Are Consistent with GAAP but
Exclude One or More of the Generally Accepted Alternatives (Group 2)

Category	Negotiated Accounting Rule
(i) All-inclusive income statements	Specific income-increasing items (e.g., transfers to income from contingency reserves) are excluded from income, and specific income-decreasing items (e.g., depreciation of lease-hold improvements) are charged against income.
(ii) Convertible bonds	An issue of stock for debt conversion is valued at the face value of the converted debt.
(iii) Gain or loss on debt redemption	There is no attempt to classify the gain or loss as an ordinary or extraordinary item.
(iv) Leases	Capitalization of most leases is required.
(v) Ratio of earnings to fixed charges	All fixed charges (e.g., sinking fund and lease payments) are included, not just the imputed interest component.
(vi) Treasury stock	Stock repurchases are treated as cash dividends and treasury stock sales as new issues of common.
(vii) Valuation of fixed assets	Fixed assets are valued at depreciated historical cost. Upward revaluations are prohibited, except in some business combinations. Current-cost data are ignored.

Source: Richard Leftwich, "Accounting Information in Private Markets: Evidence from Private Lending Agreements," *The Accounting Review,* Jan. 1983, pp. 23–42, Table 2 (p. 39).

were they originally designed to mimic GAAP in effect at the time the contract was signed. Additionally, she found that contracts that contained more accounting-based covenants were more likely to specify fixed GAAP provisions and the use of such provisions in contracts was increasing over time.

Leftwich (1983) examined a number of private lending agreements to see the extent to which they "followed" GAAP. Exhibit 10-12 summarizes those situations where GAAP is totally or partially modified.

These modifications are interesting for two reasons. Most important, they show how one set of financial statement users, creditors, modify GAAP for their own purposes. The second reason is that they suggest adjustments that can be made when financial statements are used for other purposes. Some of these modifications have been discussed earlier, and some will be discussed in later chapters. We highlight them now for reference purposes:

1. Deferred tax credits not included as liability (see Chapter 9)
2. Inclusion of off-balance-sheet debt and capitalization of all leases (see Chapter 11)
3. Ignoring the equity method of accounting by including only dividends from unconsolidated domestic and foreign subsidiaries (see Chapter 13)
4. Restrictions on income effects of pooling and balance sheet effects of purchase accounting (see Chapter 14)

Costs and Effects of Covenant Violations

Although creditors have a right to demand immediate payment when an accounting-based debt covenant is violated, they do not usually do so. This does not mean that violating such covenants is costless. Waivers of such violations often come with strings attached. Creditors may renegotiate the terms of the debt to demand:

- Accelerated principal payments
- An increased interest rate
- Liens on assets (such as accounts receivable)
- New covenants increasing restrictions on the firm's investing, borrowing, and dividend-paying ability

Chen and Wei (1993) examined a sample of 128 companies that disclosed violations of their accounting-based debt covenants. For 71 of these firms, the creditors did not waive the violation but demanded accelerated payments or higher interest rates. Beneish and Press (1993) found the median interest rate increase to be 80 basis points; they estimated that the overall cost of such renegotiations averaged from 1 to 2% of the market value of the firm's equity or 4 to 7% of the balance on the loan.

When waivers were granted, not surprisingly, they were more often granted for secured debt and for smaller size loans. Similarly, waivers were more likely to be granted to "healthier" firms considered less likely to become bankrupt. When waivers were granted, they were often (24 of the 57 companies) given only for limited time periods.

Successful renegotiation of the debt terms or receipt of a waiver may not be the last word. Chen and Wei found that by the following year creditors demanded payment of the debt for 39 companies (30% of the sample), forcing 13 companies into bankruptcy.

Beneish and Press found that accounting-based covenants were often relaxed as a result of renegotiation. However, they were supplanted with more direct covenants restricting capital expenditures, mergers, assets sales, stock repurchases, and future borrowings.

These results indicate the importance of monitoring debt covenants to ensure that the firm is not close to violating them. Such violations can expose the firm to direct out-of-pocket costs in the form of higher borrowing costs and/or limit the scope of a firm's investing and financing choices.[58] The following illustration shows a firm "treading the line" with respect to its covenants.

Example: NorAm Energy. NorAm Energy reported debt covenants restricting new borrowings and dividend payments. The dividend restriction is similar to the "restricted retained earnings" provision discussed in Exhibit 10-11 except that it is based on total stockholders' equity. Exhibit 10-13 contains data from NorAm's *1994 Annual Report* regarding debt covenants.

In 1993 and 1994, the firm paid dividends of approximately $42 million ($7.8 preferred + $34.2 common) each year. The company states that its dividend capacity as of December 31, 1994 is $43.3 million. This can be calculated as follows:

Minimum shareholders' equity, December 31, 1993	$650.0 million
50% of 1994 Net income (0.5 × $ 48 million)	24.0
Minimum shareholders' equity, December 31, 1994	$674.0 million
Actual shareholders' equity, December 31, 1994	717.3 million
Unrestricted amount	$ 43.3 million

As this capacity is calculated after payment of the 1994 dividend and does not include 1995 earnings, it appears that the firm can maintain its current level of dividends in the future.

A more careful analysis, however, indicates that without any increase in income, the current dividend can be maintained only for two years. As panel A, below shows, by 1997 the minimum equity requirement will be violated. Income will have to increase dramatically to maintain dividend payments at the 1994 level.

	A. Current Income Level			B. Required Level	
	1995	1996	1997	1997	1998
Estimated Stockholders' Equity					
Opening	$717.3	$723.3	$729.3	$729.3	$756.7
Income	48.0	48.0	48.0	69.4	84.0
Dividend	(42.0)	(42.0)	(42.0)	(42.0)	(42.0)
Closing	$723.3	$729.3	$735.3*	$756.7	$798.7
Minimum Stockholders' Equity					
Opening	$674.0	$698.0	$722.0	$722.0	$756.7
Addition (50% of income)	24.0	24.0	24.0	34.7	42.0
Closing	$698.0	$722.0	$746.0	$756.7	$798.7

*Below minimum stockholders' equity required.

[58]Given these costs, one can understand why DeFond and Jiambalvo (1994) reported that managements engage in (accounting) manipulations in an effort to satisfy the covenants.

EXHIBIT 10-13. NORAM ENERGY CORP.
Stockholders' Equity and Debt Covenants

Condensed Shareholders' Equity

	1994	1993
Capital Stock		
Preferred	$ 130,000	$ 130,000
Common stock including paid-in capital	944,870	944,118
	$1,074,870	$1,074,118
Retained Deficit		
Balance at beginning of year	(366,080)	(360,121)
Net income (loss)	48,066	36,087
Cash dividends		
Preferred stock, $3.00 per share	(7,800)	(7,800)
Common stock, $0.28 per share in 1994 and		
$0.28 per share in 1993	(34,265)	(34,246)
Balance at end of year	$ (360,079)	$ (366,080)
Unrealized gain on Itron investment, net of tax	2,586	
Total stockholders' equity	$ 717,377	$ 708,037

Note 5: Restrictions on Stockholders' Equity and Debt

Under the provisions of the Company's revolving credit facility as described in Note 3, and under similar provisions in certain of the Company's other financial arrangements, the Company's total debt capacity is limited and it is required to maintain a minimum level of stockholders' equity. The required minimum level of stockholders' equity was initially set at $650 million at December 31, 1993, increasing annually thereafter by (1) 50% of positive consolidated net income and (2) 50% of the proceeds (in excess of the first $50 million) of any incremental equity offering made after June 30, 1994. The Company's total debt is limited to $2,055 million. Based on these restrictions, the Company had incremental debt issuance and dividend capacity of $321.2 million and $43.3 million, respectively, at December 31, 1994. The Company's revolving credit facility also contains a provision which limits the Company's ability to reacquire, retire or otherwise prepay its long-term debt prior to its maturity to a total of $100 million.

Source: NorAm Energy, *1994 Annual Report.*

Under the provisions of the covenant agreement minimum stockholders' equity must increase by 50% of income each year. But the current dividend payout is close to 100% of current income levels, limiting the growth of retained earnings. As panel B indicates, only if income grows to $84 million, a 75% increase over the current level, will the company be able to maintain the current dividend level.[59]

---

[59]This ignores the effects of any equity offerings that increase the required and actual stockholders' equity. Given its covenant provisions, the company may be able to maintain dividend levels by issuing more shares, diluting existing stockholders. See Problem 12, where this issue is addressed further.

INTERNATIONAL ACCOUNTING AND REPORTING PRACTICES

International accounting rules for on-balance-sheet debt do not differ materially from U.S. GAAP. Accounting methods are generally similar to those discussed in this chapter with the following exceptions:

- Amortization of bond premium and discount
- Classification of balance sheet debt and related footnote disclosures
- The role of debt in firms' overall capital structure

Bonds Issued at a Premium or Discount. In the United States, discounts and premiums are amortized using the effective interest method. Some countries use straight-line amortization. Others write off the premium or discount to interest expense immediately; in subsequent years, interest expense equals actual interest payments. Thus, for the example in Exhibit 10-1C (p. 479), issuance of the bond at a discount of $4,917 produces the following differing patterns of interest expense:

	U.S. Practice	International Alternatives	
	Effective Method	Straight-Line	Immediate Write-off
19X1	$11,452	$11,639	$14,917
19X2	11,632	11,639	10,000
19X3	11,833	11,639	10,000
	$34,917	$34,917	$34,917

Classification and Disclosure. As noted earlier, fair value disclosures required by SFAS 107 are confined to the United States. Although foreign firms filing Form 20-F must comply with SFAS 107, in most cases analysts must estimate the fair values of foreign firm debt. However, non-U.S. firms generally do not provide detailed disclosures regarding long-term debt; they show aggregate data instead of specific yields and maturity dates.

For example, Exhibit 10-14 contains the 1993 debt disclosures of Philips Electronics, which follows Netherlands GAAP. Philips provides average interest rates and remaining terms. Treating each debt group as one debt instrument, analysts can use the average rate and maturity to estimate fair value. Some companies, however, do not provide even this level of interest rate and maturity data, making fair value estimates difficult.

Lack of disclosure of maturity data also makes it more difficult to estimate non-U.S. firms' future (near- and long-term) cash flow and financing requirements. Such analysis is further complicated by varying debt classification practices. Current debt can include debt with maturities of up to three years as opposed to one year in the United States. Another problem is that many firms (both U.S. and foreign) include bank overdrafts in accrued liabilities rather than as short-term bank debt, understating reported debt levels.

Debt Versus Equity Financing. A firm's capital structure is greatly influenced by local financial market conditions, which differ from country to country. In countries

EXHIBIT 10-14. PHILIPS ELECTRONICS N.V.
1993 Long-Term Debt Disclosure (millions of Dutch guilders)

	Range of Interest Rates (%)	Average Rate of Interest (%)	Amount Outstanding	Due Within One Year from Balance Sheet Date	Due After One or More Years from Balance Sheet Date	Due After Five or More Years from Balance Sheet Date	Average Remaining Term (Years)
Convertible debentures	4.1–7.1	5.6	217	53	164	—	2.2
Other debentures	4.0–9.5	6.2	3,377	422	2,955	1,456	6.7
Private financing	4.5–11.0	7.1	167	7	160	63	8.0
Institutional financing	3.0–11.0	6.5	4,842	846	3,996	421	2.5
Other long-term debt	4.5–12.8	8.2	771	233	538	125	4.0
Total			9,374	1,561	7,813	2,065	
Total previous year			12,692	2,670	10,022	1,348	

Source: Philips Electronics N.V., *1993 Annual Report.*

such as Germany and Japan, firms historically have been financed primarily by bank debt rather than equity. As a result, firms in those countries have higher debt-to-equity ratios than comparable U.S. firms.

Further, although a low debt-to-equity ratio for a U.S. firm is viewed positively, a low ratio may be a negative signal in countries where banks are the main source of financing. *Low debt-to-equity ratios may indicate that the banks do not view the company favorably and are not willing to provide credit.*

The proportion of current and noncurrent debt can also depend on the lending environment. In Japan, firms have a relatively high proportion of short-term debt. Many public companies belong to *keiretsu*, characterized by high levels of intercompany shareholdings. Each *keiretsu* has a core bank that provides financing for member firms. Although debt is usually structured as a short-term loan, it is routinely rolled over, even when credit quality deteriorates. Given the close relationship of the bank to *keiretsu* firm(s), the debt is really a long-term liability.

These historical patterns, however, are changing as financial markets become more international. Enormous bank loan losses in Japan and changing views of the appropriate bank role in Germany are weakening the dominance of banks in providing financing for large public companies, who are accessing international capital markets to a much greater extent than in the past.

Government subsidies also play a significant role in the financing practices in some foreign countries. Repsol, a Spanish multinational oil, gas, and chemical firm, reported 7.3 billion pesetas of "State Financing of Investments in Exploration" at December 31, 1994.

Prior to 1990, the Spanish Government financed a portion of the firm's exploration investments. Subsidized successful exploration activities were capitalized, and government loans repaid from net cash flows generated by the sale of reserves. Unsuccessful expenditures were not recognized as assets,[60] and government loans that financed them were forgiven. The state continues to subsidize research and development and various pipeline and network construction projects.

Subsidies distort performance measures. It is impossible to know how much of the "state financing" will have to be repaid and the timing of repayment. Subsidies

---

[60]Repsol uses the successful efforts accounting method, described in Chapter 7.

thus postpone the recognition of debt and related interest expense, understating the debt-to-equity ratio, overstating interest coverage ratios, and providing misleading information about available cash flows and future cash flow needs.

SUMMARY

In this chapter, we have examined the different forms that debt financing can take. The choice of debt issue can have significant effects on the pattern of reported income, cash flows, and financial position. In addition, different debt instruments respond differently to changes in interest rates.

Moreover, debt can take forms that do not require recognition on the balance sheet. Such off-balance-sheet debt is the subject of the next chapter.

CASE 10-1

Comparative Analysis of the Financing Liabilities of duPont, Dow Chemical, and Imperial Chemical Industries PLC (ICI)

Dow Chemical and ICI operate in and compete with duPont in certain markets. Appendices B and C contain the financial statements of Dow Chemical and ICI, respectively, for the year ended December 31, 1994.

Case 4-1 involves an integrated analysis of duPont, Dow Chemical, and ICI. Among other requirements, it calls for the preparation of leverage and solvency ratios for these three firms. The objective of this case is to extend the analysis of their financing liabilities.

Note that the ICI statements are presented in British pounds and prepared according to U.K. GAAP. One consequence of this is the absence of market value data for the debt of ICI.

1. In 1993, ICI provides separate disclosure of interest related to discontinued operations. Discuss whether you should include this component of interest costs in the measurement of interest coverage.

2. The market prices of selected issues of ICI's long-term debt are listed below. The market prices were obtained from Standard & Poor's and Bloomberg and reflect prices on the last trading day in 1994.

Type and Coupon	Coupon	Maturity Date	Face Amount ($ millions)	Market Price (on 12/31/94)	Market YTM
U.S. $ debt*					
	7.625%	03/15/1997	225.00	98.625	8.31%
	9.500%	11/15/2000	300.00	104.500	8.51%
	8.750%	05/01/2001	250.00	101.250	8.49%
	7.500%	01/15/2002	200.00	95.625	8.33%
	8.875%	11/15/2006	250.00	102.000	8.60%
Eurodollar†					
	8.000%	07/01/1996	100.00	99.250	?

*All U.S. dollar denominated borrowings are semiannual coupon debt.
†The Eurodollar issue carries an annual coupon.

(a) Compute the market yield-to-maturity (YTM) for the 8.00%, annual coupon Eurodollar issue.

(b) Compute the market value of ICI's debt. For this computation, assume that the market value of the following securities is equal to the carrying amount reported in Footnote 20:

- All secured loans
- All unsecured loans
- The 7.83 to 8.9% medium-term notes
- The Australian dollar, Swiss franc, and debt denominated in other currencies

(c) All the U.S. dollar debt issues were rated A+ by S&P. Use Exhibit 10P-1 to discuss whether the market YTM is consistent with the yields suggested by the ratings.

3. The December 31, 1994 market prices of selected issues of Dow Chemical's long-term debt are listed below. The market prices were obtained from Standard & Poor's and Bloomberg and reflect prices on the last trading day in 1994.

Type and Coupon		Coupon	Maturity Date	Face Amount ($ millions)	Market Price	Market YTM
U.S. $ debt		4.630%	1995	150.00	98.000	7.26%
		8.250%	1996	150.00	100.250	8.00%
	Convertible*	5.750%	2001	150.00	100.50	5.65%
		7.380%	2002	150.00	94.500	8.40%
		9.350%	2002	200.00	103.250	8.73%
		7.130%	2003	150.00	92.625	8.40%
		8.630%	2006	200.00	100.500	8.55%
		9.000%	2010	150.00	101.875	8.77%

*These bonds were convertible to shares of Magma Power Company at $37.50 per share. On December 31, 1994, Magma shares traded at $37.00 per share.

(a) All issues (except the convertible bond, which is rated A−) are rated A by S&P. Use Exhibit 10P-1 to discuss potential reasons for the difference between the market YTM and the yields suggested by the rating.

(b) Explain why the market YTM of the 5.75% convertible issue and the 9.35% issue is not consistent with an upward-sloping yield curve.

(c) The firm also reports that the average rate on long-term debt has fallen from 7.43% in 1993 to 6.64% in 1994. Provide possible explanations for the decline.

(d) Footnote J provides the following information on the fair value of debt:

Long-term Debt	December 31, 1994	December 31, 1993
Carrying cost	$5,303	$5,902
Fair value	5,270	6,293
Gain (loss)	$ 33	$ (391)

Explain why the market value of debt fell from the December 31, 1993 to December 31, 1994 period.

4. (a) The debt of duPont is rated AA by S&P. However, the 8.125% issue maturing in 2004 trades at a YTM of 8.28%. Explain why this yield is not consistent with that implied by Exhibit 10P-1.

(b) Average interest rates on duPont's long-term debt rose to 7.5% in 1994 from 6.8% in 1993. Provide possible explanations for the increase.

(c) Note 19 provides the following information on the market value of duPont's debt:

Long-term Debt	December 31, 1994	December 31, 1993
Carrying cost	$6,376	$6,531
Fair value	6,600	7,500
Gain (loss)	$ (224)	$ (969)

Explain the decline in market value of debt over the 1993 to 1994 period.

5. Compare the relative sensitivity of the market values of debt and interest expense of duPont, Dow, and ICI to changes in interest rates.

EXHIBIT 10P-1
Bond Yields by Rating Category

Standard & Poor's Corporate & Government Bond Yield Index: By Ratings

	Industrial						U.S. Government			
	AAA	AA	A	BBB	BB	B	Long-Term	Intermediate	Short-Term	Municipals
Monthly Averages										
1994										
December	8.30	8.52	8.90	9.47	10.34	11.74	7.97	7.76	7.55	6.76
November	8.43	8.60	8.98	9.67	10.07	11.70	8.18	7.49	7.14	6.96
October	8.35	8.54	8.92	9.55	9.84	11.70	8.07	6.90	6.76	6.50
September	8.07	8.35	8.76	9.27	9.89	11.49	7.83	6.69	6.42	6.33
August	7.80	8.07	8.47	8.92	9.84	11.10	7.54	6.55	6.21	6.19
July	7.97	8.19	8.59	9.03	9.89	10.93	7.68	6.69	6.29	6.19
June	7.81	8.05	8.52	8.83	9.76	10.53	7.47	6.48	6.11	6.41
May	7.96	8.10	8.64	8.79	9.76	10.64	7.50	6.62	6.20	6.26
April	7.79	7.92	8.50	8.57	9.54	10.62	7.32	6.29	5.85	6.28
March	7.39	7.59	8.21	8.35	9.12	10.31	6.89	5.78	5.30	5.93
February	6.94	7.33	7.97	8.19	8.91	10.50	6.44	5.23	4.74	5.44
January	6.80	7.26	7.91	8.28	9.01	10.29	6.28	5.02	4.01	5.30
1993										
December	6.79	7.28	7.83	8.28	9.06	10.45	6.23	5.08	3.87	5.35
November	6.77	7.27	7.82	8.27	9.16	10.40	6.21	5.08	3.87	5.47
October	6.47	7.11	7.66	8.16	9.04	10.45	5.87	4.73	3.68	5.29
September	6.35	7.18	7.62	8.01	9.05	10.67	5.91	4.78	3.70	5.31
August	6.68	7.32	7.80	8.45	9.11	10.57	6.19	5.08	3.88	5.50
July	6.90	7.36	7.97	8.63	9.17	10.55	6.34	5.16	3.99	5.60
June	7.25	7.70	8.10	8.72	9.33	10.55	6.56	5.30	4.09	5.73
May	7.63	8.11	8.20	8.84	9.39	10.59	6.69	5.34	3.93	5.81
April	7.65	7.77	8.11	8.79	9.36	10.57	6.66	5.35	3.86	5.78
March	7.61	7.65	8.00	8.73	9.39	10.65	6.69	5.41	4.00	5.65
February	7.82	7.87	8.28	8.81	9.58	10.85	6.96	5.75	4.24	5.87
January	7.99	8.13	8.48	8.94	9.81	11.07	7.25	6.06	4.35	6.18

Source: Standard & Poor's *Bond Guide,* Jan. 1995.

Chapter 10

Problems

Exhibit 10P-1 is provided for use in answering many Chapter 10 problems.

1. [Zero-coupon debt; 1996 CFA adapted] A firm decides to issue zero-coupon debt rather than full-coupon debt. Describe the effect on:

> **(i)** Cash flow from operations over the life of the debt
>
> **(ii)** Cash flow from financing in the year of issuance, in the year of maturity, and over the life of the debt
>
> **(iii)** Net income over the life of the debt

2. [Variable- vs. fixed-rate debt; 1996 CFA adapted] Assuming that a firm has variable-rate debt and interest rates rise, describe the effect of the rise on:

> **(i)** Net income
>
> **(ii)** The market value of the firm's debt

3. [Effect of interest rate changes on leverage; 1996 CFA adapted] Assume that Firm A issued $10 million of long-term debt when interest rates were low and Firm B issued $10 million of long-term debt when interest rates were high. Assuming that interest rates remain high:

> **(i)** Discuss whether the book value or market value of debt should be used to compute leverage ratios.
>
> **(ii)** Describe which firm will have the higher computed leverage ratio under each method. (Assume no other debt and identical equity.)

4. [Debt retirement; 1996 CFA adapted] Assuming that a firm retires long-term debt prior to maturity, describe how the firm must account for the difference between the book value of the debt and the amount paid to retire it.

5. [Current liabilities, customer advances] Exhibit 10P-2 contains selected balance sheet accounts and the net revenues of American Airlines for 1987 and 1988.

A. Calculate the company's reported working capital and its current, quick, and cash ratios for both years.

B. The air traffic liability primarily reflects tickets sold in advance. Discuss any differences between the air traffic liability and other liabilities.

C. Eliminate the air traffic liability and recompute the ratios in part A. Discuss any differences from the ratios calculated in part A.

D. Exhibit 10P-2 also presents data for Eastern Airlines. At December 31, 1988, Eastern was just months away from bankruptcy. Compare Eastern's short-term liquidity position with that of American Airlines at December 31, 1988.

E. The chapter states that accounts such as the air traffic liability may be better viewed as indicators of future profitability than as liabilities. Evaluate this statement using the data in Exhibit 10P-2.

6. [Understanding bond relationships, coupon versus effective interest] The Walk & Field Co. has outstanding bonds originally issued at a discount. During 19X2, the unamortized bond discount decreased from $8,652 to $7,290. Annual interest paid was $7,200. The market rate of interest was 12% when the bond was issued.

EXHIBIT 10P-2
Selected Balance Sheet Data, December 31, 1987 to 1988 ($ in millions)

	American Airlines		Eastern Airlines	
	1987	1988	1987	1988
Cash and short-term investments	$1,012.4	$1,286.6	$ 332.9	$ 402.3
Net receivables	729.2	833.6	463.1	396.5
Inventories	299.4	375.1	182.1	163.7
Other current assets	105.3	119.7	44.3	37.4
Current assets	$2,146.3	$2,615.0	$1,022.4	$ 999.9
Accounts payable	560.4	710.4	267.2	242.7
Accrued liabilities	728.5	1,072.0	344.9	455.7
Air traffic liability*	577.0	800.0	390.5	302.4
Notes payable and current portion long-term debt	205.1	213.2	190.1	153.0
Current liabilities	$2,071.0	$2,795.6	$1,192.7	$1,153.8
Net revenues	$7,198.0	$8,824.3	$4,447.5	$3,806.1

*For Eastern Air Lines includes $7.8 million and 19.2 million in frequent flier miles for 1987 and 1988, respectively.
Source: American Airlines and Eastern Airlines, *1988 Annual Reports.*

Using the data provided, calculate:

(i) Interest expense for 19X2.

(ii) The face value of the bond.

(iii) The coupon rate of the bond.

Note: You do not need present value calculations or tables to solve this problem.

7. [Zero-coupon bonds] The Null Company issued a zero-coupon bond on January 1, 1996, due December 31, 2000. The face value of the bond was $100,000. The bond was issued at an effective rate of 12% (compounded annually).

A. Calculate the cash proceeds of the bond issue.

B. Complete the following table on a *pretax* basis, assuming that all interest is paid in the year it is due:

	1996	1997	1998	1999	2000
Earnings before interest and taxes	$50,000	$50,000	$50,000	$50,000	$50,000
Cash flow from operations before interest and taxes	60,000	60,000	60,000	60,000	60,000
Interest expense					
Cash flow from operations					
Times interest earned					
Times interest earned (cash basis)					

C. Assume that Null had raised the same cash proceeds with a conventional bond issued at par, paying interest annually and the principal at maturity. Complete the following table, under the assumptions in part B:

	1996	1997	1998	1999	2000
Earnings before interest and taxes	$50,000	$50,000	$50,000	$50,000	$50,000
Cash flow from operations before interest and taxes	60,000	60,000	60,000	60,000	60,000
Interest expense					
Cash flow from operations					
Times interest earned					
Times interest earned (cash basis)					

D. Using the results of parts B and C, discuss the impact on reported cash flow from operations and interest coverage of Null's choice of bond.

E. How would the consideration of income taxes change your answers to parts B through D?

8. [Issue and repurchase of debt] On January 1, 1994, Derek Corporation issues $20 million (face value) bonds due January 1, 2004. Interest is payable semiannually on January 1 and July 1 at a coupon rate of 10%. The market (effective interest) rate on the date of issuance is 8%.

A. Compute the impact of the bond issuance on Derek's balance sheet, income statement, and statement of cash flows for 1994 and 1995.

B. Calculate the gain or loss recorded by Derek if it repurchases the entire bond issue on July 1, 1997 at an effective interest rate of 10%.

C. Discuss whether this gain (loss) should be considered a component of continuing operating income.

D. Discuss two reasons why Derek might choose to refinance its 8% debt at a higher interest rate.

9. [Evaluation of convertible debt] Conner Peripherals, a disk drive manufacturer, had two issues of convertible subordinated debentures outstanding at December 31, 1994:

(i) 6.75%, due 2001, convertible at $29.00 per share

(ii) 6.50%, due 2002, convertible at $24.00 per share

The market price of Conner's common shares was $9.50 on December 31, 1994. Conner's *1994 Annual Report* reports the following balance sheet data:

	$ in millions
Current portion of long-term debt	$ 35
6.75% convertible debt	230
6.50% convertible debt	345
Other long-term debt	52
Total debt	$662
Stockholders' equity	337
Total capital	$999

A. Compute the debt-to-equity ratio of Conners assuming:

(i) Both convertible debt issues are treated as debt.

(ii) Both convertible debt issues are treated as equity.

B. Discuss whether Conner convertible bonds should be classified as debt or equity at December 31, 1994.

On December 11, 1995 Conner common shares traded at $24 per share following the announcement that the company would merge with Seagate Technology, with Conner shareholders receiving Seagate shares in exchange.

C. Discuss whether Conner convertible bonds should be classified as debt or equity, based on the situation at December 11, 1995.

D. Based on your conclusion in part C, recalculate Conner's debt-to-equity ratio.

10. [Zero-coupon bonds] Sonat issued zero-coupon notes due September 6, 2005, with a face value of $661.25 million and an effective yield of 7.25%. Sonat's reported balance sheet liability on December 31, 1992 was $268 million. On March 15, 1993, the company redeemed the notes for $272 million.

A. Calculate interest expense on the notes for 1992 and 1993.

B. Calculate Sonat's balance sheet liability (to the nearest million $) for the notes on December 31, 1991.

C. Estimate the gain or loss that Sonat recognized upon redemption.

D. Compare the impact of these notes with that of conventional notes with the same interest rate on cash flow from operations *and* cash flow from financing:

(i) In 1992

(ii) In 1993

(iii) Over the life of the notes

11. [Preferred shares, debt ratios, book value; 1989 CFA adapted] The balance sheet of Mother Prewitt's Handmade Cookies (MPH) follows:

	December 31, 19X1
Assets	
Cash	$15,000,000
Plant and equipment (net)	17,000,000
Total	$32,000,000
Liabilities	
Long-term debt	$4,000,000
Stockholders' equity	
Preferred stock, issued 100,000, par value $150, 5% cumulative, liquidation value $160, callable at $165	$15,000,000
Common stock, issued 200,000 shares, par value $75	15,000,000
Capital contributed in excess of par value	100,000
Retained earnings (deficit)	(2,100,000)
	$28,000,000
Total liabilities and equity	$32,000,000

Note: Preferred dividends are two years in arrears.

A. Calculate the debt-to-equity ratio of MPH, assuming that preferred shares are:

(i) Nonredeemable

(ii) Redeemable by stockholders at $160 per share

B. Calculate the book value per share of MPH common stock assuming that preferred shares are:

(i) Nonredeemable

(ii) Redeemable by stockholders at $160 per share

C. Discuss whether the preferred shares should be considered debt or equity, making reference to your answers to parts A and B.

12. [Implications of bond covenants] Prior to its stockholders' meeting in mid-1995, NorAm Energy sent the following proposal to its stockholders:

> Stockholders will be asked to consider and vote on a proposal to amend the Company's Restated Certificate of Incorporation to increase the number of authorized shares of Company Common Stock, $0.625 par value (the "Common Stock") from 150,000,000 shares to 250,000,000 shares. If such proposal is not adopted, approximately 11,387,682 of the currently authorized 150,000,000 shares of Common Stock will be available for future issuances and approximately 138,612,318 will be issued and outstanding or re-served for issuance in connection with existing employee benefit plans, the Direct Stock Purchase and Dividend Reinvestment Plan and the Company's $3.00 Convertible Ex-changeable Preferred Stock. If the amendment to the Restated Certificate of Incorpora-tion is not approved, it is expected such a proposal will be made again at a later date.

Considering the information provided in Exhibit 10-13 and the related text discussion of NorAm:

A. Provide two reasons why the company might issue new shares.

B. Discuss whether this proposal could have been anticipated.

C. Discuss whether, as a shareholder of the company, you would support the proposal.

13. [Market versus book value; convertible securities] Community Psychiatric Centers provided the following long-term debt footnote in its fiscal 1994 financial statements. In its SFAS 107 disclosures, the company stated that fair value approximated book value. The company's share price on that date was approximately $12 per share.

	November 30, 1994 ($ in thousands)
Borrowings under revolving credit agreements	$55,169
$5\frac{3}{4}$% convertible subordinated debentures due 2012, convertible into common stock of the company at $35.89 per share, may be redeemed at 103.75% of face value as of October 15, 1992, declining annu-ally to 100% of face value on or after October 15, 1999	7,366
$8\frac{1}{4}$% subordinated guaranteed debentures due 1996 (net of unamortized discount of $44)	4,956

8½% subordinated guaranteed debentures due 1995 (net of unamortized discount of $22)	10,840
Notes payable, collateralized by deeds of trust on land, buildings, and equipment with a cost of approximately $8,051, payable in installments to 2004 including interest ranging from 7 to 10½%	1,903
Note payable due December 31, 1994, interest payable quarterly at the LIBOR rate plus 2%	1,485
Other	595
Total	$82,314
Less current portion	(13,224)
Long-term debt	$69,090

A. Discuss whether you would treat the 5¾% convertible debentures as debt or equity.

B. Discuss the factors in the company's debt structure that contributed to the fact that the fair value of long-term debt approximated book value.

14. [Interest rate swaps, estimating market value] Exhibit 10-6 discusses the fixed-rate debt issue and interest rate swap agreement that Glatfelter entered into in March 1993. The company stated that, as of December 31, 1994, it would cost $4,000,000 to terminate the swap agreement.

A. Estimate the spread on the fixed-rate noted issued March 1993 relative to a Treasury Bond of intermediate maturity. (Use Exhibit 10P-1.)

B. Estimate the market interest rate on that obligation as of December 31, 1994.

C. Calculate the $4,000,000 cost to terminate the swap agreement, using the information in part B. (To simplify the calculation, ignore the last two months and assume that the next payment is on January 1, 1995 and the swap maturity to be January 1, 1998.)

15. [Bond covenants and financing options] The Sleepman Company wishes to acquire plant and equipment worth $1 million. The purchase must be financed by issuing preferred shares or debt (in any combination, including zero-coupon). The only constraint is that the company not violate *any* of the following bond covenants:

  (i) Times interest earned (cash basis) calculated as

$$\frac{\text{Cash from Operations before Interest}}{\text{Interest Payments}} \text{ must be at least 1.8.}$$

  (ii) Fixed charge coverage ratio (cash basis) calculated as

$$\frac{\text{Cash from Operations before Interest}}{\text{Interest Payments} + \text{Preferred Dividends}} \text{ must be at least 1.4.}$$

  (iii) Debt to gross tangible assets calculated as

$$\frac{\text{Long-Term Debt}}{\text{Gross Tangible Fixed Assets}} \text{ must not exceed 0.50.}$$

Sleepman has made the following financial projections for the coming year:

Interest expense (= interest paid)	$200,000
Preferred dividends	0
Cash flow from operations before interest	390,000
Long-term debt	2,000,000
Tangible fixed assets (gross)	$5,000,000

These amounts include the operating results generated by the new plant and equipment. They exclude, however, the accounting impacts of the purchase (depreciation and interest expense) as well as the assets and liabilities arising from the purchase.

For simplicity, assume that all financing is available at an interest rate of 10% with a maturity of 10 years. Similarly, any required depreciation or amortization should assume an asset life of 10 years using the straight-line method and zero residual value. Ignore income taxes.

A. Assume that there are three alternatives to finance the asset purchase:

(i) Issue preferred shares

(ii) Issue conventional (full-coupon) bonds

(iii) Issue zero-coupon bonds

Calculate the three ratios in the bond covenants for *each* alternative for the *first year*. Discuss which of the alternatives would permit Sleepman to acquire the assets without violating at least one of the covenants.

B. Assume that the assets are divisible (you can acquire any amount using any financing mode). Calculate a combination of financing modes that enables Sleepman to acquire the assets without violating any of the covenants.

16. [Effect of interest rate changes on market value of bonds] Excerpts from the Illinois Tool Works long-term debt footnote are provided below:

Long-Term Debt at December 31, 1994

$ in thousands	1994
$7\frac{1}{2}$% notes due December 1, 1998	$125,000
$5\frac{7}{8}$% notes due March 1, 2000	125,000
Commercial paper	—
Other, including capitalized lease obligations	24,996
	$274,996
Current maturities	(2,009)
	$272,987

In December 1991, the Company issued $125,000,000 of $7\frac{1}{2}$% notes due December 1, 1998 at 99.892% of face value. The notes may not be redeemed by the Company prior to maturity. The effective interest rate of the notes is 7.6%. In March 1993, the Company issued $125,000,000 of $5\frac{7}{8}$% notes due March 1, 2000 at 99.744% of face value. The notes may not be redeemed by the Company prior to maturity. The effective interest rate of the notes is 5.9%.

At December 31, 1994, the carrying values of the $7\frac{1}{2}\%$ and $5\frac{7}{8}\%$ notes exceeded the quoted market prices by approximately $14,000,000.

When answering parts A through C, use Exhibit 10P-1.

A. Explain why the company was able to issue notes in March 1993 at an effective rate of 5.9% when in December 1991 it issued notes of similar size and maturity at an effective rate of 7.6%.

B. Estimate the rate the company would have offered to issue similar notes on December 31, 1994.

C. Calculate the $14,000,000 difference between fair value and the carrying value of long-term debt at December 31, 1994. Show calculations for each note issue separately.

Problem 17 is based on data from the 1994 financial statements of Ashland Coal in Exhibit 10P-3. Related problems on Ashland Oil, parent of Ashland Coal, appear in Chapter 11.

17. (Capitalization table, bonds, preferred shares, debt and coverage ratios)

A. Prepare a capitalization table for Ashland Coal listing its financial obligations and equity. Using this table, calculate the firm's debt-to-equity ratio at December 31, 1994.

B. Calculate Ashland Coal's times interest earned ratio for 1994.

C. Exhibit 10P-3 includes Ashland Coal's Note 16, Fair Values of Financial Instruments. The firm has no publicly rated debt; its parent is rated BBB. From the data provided, assess whether Ashland Coal's rating should be higher, the same, or lower than BBB.

18. [Foreign currency convertible debt issued at discount] PSA Peugeot Citroen prepares its financial statements using French GAAP. It reported convertible bond debentures of FF 3,980 at December 31, 1994. A footnote discloses the following:

Note 13: Convertible Bond Debenture

In March 1994, Peugeot S. A. issued convertible debentures for a total of FF 3,960 million. The four million bonds were issued at a price of FF 990 and are convertible at any time on the basis of one share per bond.

The bonds pay interest at a nominal rate of 2% and a premium of FF 234 will be paid on any unconverted bonds redeemed at maturity, on January 1, 2001, corresponding to a yield to maturity of 5%.

The estimated cost of the redemption premium is being provided for over the life of the debentures.

On March 7, 1994, just prior to the bond issue, PSA common shares traded at FF 880. The closing price on December 31, 1994 was FF 732.

A. Discuss whether the debentures should be classified as debt or equity on December 31, 1994.

B. The bonds initially paid interest of FF 15.7 per bond on January 1, 1995, with annual interest payments thereafter. Calculate the expected cash payment and any adjustment to the carrying amount of the bonds on January 1, 1995.

EXHIBIT 10P-3. ASHLAND COAL, INC.
Selected Financial Statement Data ($ in thousands)

	Year Ended December 31	
	1994	1993
Income Statement		
Operating income	$54,720	$ 5,157
Interest income	366	1,057
Interest expense	−22,238	−25,342
Pretax income	$32,848	$(19,128)
Income tax (expense) benefit	−628	64,502
Net income	$32,220	$ 45,374

	Year Ended December 31	
	1994	1993
Balance Sheet		
Total Assets	$838,392	$835,991
Liabilities and Stockholders' Equity		
Accounts payable and accrued expenses	$ 69,645	$ 55,338
Current portion of debt	43,963	37,260
Current liabilities	$113,608	$ 92,598
Long-term debt	$200,000	$244,342
Deferred gain on sale and leaseback	3,051	3,624
Other liabilities	152,750	152,000
Total liabilities	$469,409	$492,564
Stockholders' equity		
Convertible preferred stock	$ 67,841	$ 67,841
Common stock and paid-in-capital	108,848	107,223
Retained earnings	192,294	168,363
Total liabilities and stockholders' equity	$838,392	$835,991

Source: Ashland Coal, Inc., *1994 Annual Report.*

Note 1: Other

Cash equivalents (none at December 31, 1994 and 1993) represent highly liquid investments with a maturity of three months or less when purchased. Cash equivalents are recorded at cost, plus accrued interest, which approximates market.

Interest costs on borrowed funds are capitalized for significant asset construction projects. Capitalized interest costs were $176,000 in 1994 and $4,911,000 in 1992. No interest was capitalized in 1993.

EXHIBIT 10P-3. (*continued*)

Note 7: Debt and Financing Arrangements

Debt at December 31, 1994 and 1993, consists of the following:

($ in thousands)	1994	1993
9.78% senior unsecured notes, payable in four equal annual installments beginning September 15, 1997	**$100,000**	$100,000
9.66% senior unsecured notes, payable in six equal annual installments beginning May 15, 2001	**52,900**	52,900
8.92% senior unsecured notes, due May 15, 1996	**22,100**	22,100
Indebtedness to banks under revolving credit agreement (rate at December 31, 1994— 6.51%; 1993—3.62%)	**25,000**	50,000
Indebtedness to banks under lines of credit (weighted average rate at December 31, 1994—6.74%; 1993—3.60%)	**43,858**	56,332
Other	**105**	270
	243,963	281,602
Less current portion	**43,963**	37,260
Long-term debt	**$200,000**	$244,342

Ashland Coal has a revolving credit agreement, which terminates in 1999, with a group of banks providing for borrowings of up to $500,000,000. The rate of interest on borrowings under this agreement is, at Ashland Coal's option, a money market rate determined by a competitive bid process, the National Westminster Bank PLC reference rate, a rate based on LIBOR, or a rate based on an average market certificate of deposit rate. The provisions of the revolving credit agreement require a facility fee, which is currently computed at the rate of 0.225% per annum on the amount of the commitment. The rate used to compute the facility fee is redetermined quarterly based upon the Company's ratio of debt to equity and may vary from 0.15% to 0.35% per annum. Amounts borrowed under the revolving credit agreement are classified as long-term as the Company has the intent and ability to maintain these borrowings on a long-term basis.

Ashland Coal periodically establishes uncommitted lines of credit with banks. These agreements generally provide for short-term borrowings at market rates. At December 31, 1994, there were $237,900,000 of such agreements in effect.

Aggregate maturities of debt at December 31, 1994, are $43,963,000 in 1995, $47,100,000 in 1996, $25,000,000 in each of 1997, 1998, and 1999, and $77,900,000 thereafter. Included in these maturities are discretionary prepayments of $25,000,000 in 1996.

The credit agreements contain, among other covenants, provisions setting forth certain requirements for current ratio and consolidated net worth and restrictions on the payment of dividends and the creation of additional debt. At December 31, 1994, retained earnings of $54,467,000 were available for dividends.

EXHIBIT 10P-3. (*continued*)

Note 16: Fair Values of Financial Instruments

The following methods and assumptions were used by Ashland Coal in estimating its fair value disclosures for financial instruments:

Cash and Cash Equivalents

The carrying amount reported in the consolidated balance sheets for cash and cash equivalents approximates its fair value.

Debt

The carrying amounts of Ashland Coal's borrowings under its revolving credit agreement and under lines of credit approximate their fair value. The fair values of Ashland Coal's senior notes are estimated using discounted cash flow analyses, based on Ashland Coal's current incremental borrowing rates for similar types of borrowing arrangements.

The carrying amounts and fair values of Ashland Coal's financial instruments at December 31, 1994 and 1993, are as follows (in thousands):

	1994		1993	
	Carrying Amount	Fair Value	Carrying Amount	Fair Value
Cash and cash equivalents	$ 1,120	$ 1,120	$ 556	$ 556
Lines of credit	43,858	43,858	56,332	56,332
Revolving credit agreement	25,000	25,000	50,000	50,000
Senior notes	175,000	188,000	175,000	197,000

C. Assuming that the bonds are not converted to common but are redeemed on January 1, 2001:

 (i) Calculate the redemption premium *per bond* using *only* the coupon and yield to maturity (effective rate).

 (ii) Calculate the redemption premium for the entire bond issue.

 (iii) Discuss the income statement classification of the redemption premium.

 (iv) Discuss the cash flow statement classification of the redemption premium.

D. Discuss why PSA may have chosen to issue:

 (i) Convertible debentures rather than either common shares or straight debt

 (ii) Discount debt rather than full-coupon debt.

19. [Perpetual debt] PepsiCo issued 400 million Swiss franc bonds with no maturity date. At the end of each 10-year period, PepsiCo and the bondholders each have the right to cause redemption of the bonds. If not redeemed, the coupon rate is adjusted based on the yield of 10-year U.S. Treasury securities. Interest payments are calculated by applying the coupon rate to the initial U.S. dollar proceeds of $214 million.

A. Discuss the conditions under which the bonds are likely to be redeemed. Be sure to consider both the PepsiCo and investor points of view.

B. Discuss whether these bonds should be classified as debt or equity when analyzing PepsiCo's capital structure.

20. [Foreign currency debt] DuPont has outstanding 150 million Swiss franc $6\frac{3}{4}\%$ notes, due in 2000. The Swiss franc appreciated by 11% against the $U.S. during 1994.

A. Calculate the U.S. dollar equivalent of the debt based on the following exchange rates:

   (i) 1993: $U.S. = SFR 1.48

   (ii) 1994: $U.S. = SFR 1.31

B. Explain why this debt is carried at $103 million (shown in Note 19), both at the end of 1993 and 1994 despite the actual exchange rate.

21. [Foreign currency debt with warrants] In 1991, Roche issued $1 billion of $3\frac{1}{2}\%$ bonds with equity warrants. The proceeds were allocated between the bonds and warrants based on fair market value. The discount represented by the difference between the principal amount and the net proceeds ($U.S. 639 million) is being charged to interest expense over the life of the bonds.

The bonds are shown on Roche's balance sheet in Swiss francs net of the unamortized discount:

Swiss franc millions	12/31/93	12/31/94
Net amount	1,069	989
Unamortized discount	411	321
Swiss francs per $U.S.	1.48	1.31

A. Calculate the following $U.S. amounts:

   (i) Gross debt

   (ii) Unamortized discount

   (iii) Net debt

B. Using the answers to part A, calculate (in $U.S.)

   (i) Discount amortization for 1994

   (ii) Effective interest rate on the bonds

C. Compare the effects of issuing bonds with warrants as opposed to convertible debt on Roche's:

   (i) Balance sheet

   (ii) Income statement

   (iii) Statement of cash flows

22. [Debt and equity at market value versus book value] In its *1994 Annual Report*, Pepsico states that

> PepsiCo believes that market leverage (defined as net debt as a percent of net debt plus the market value of equity, based on the year-end stock price) is an appropriate measure of PepsiCo's financial leverage. Unlike historical cost measures, the market value of equity primarily reflects the estimated net present value of expected future cash flows that will both support debt and provide returns to shareholders. The market net debt ratio was 26% at year-end 1994 and 22% at year-end 1993. The increase was due to a 13% decrease in PepsiCo's stock price as well as an 8% increase in net debt. PepsiCo has established a long-term target range of 20–25% for its market net debt ratio to optimize its cost of capital.

As measured on an historical cost basis, the ratio of net debt to net capital employed (defined as net debt, other liabilities, deferred income taxes and shareholders' equity) was 49% at year-end 1994 and 50% at year-end 1993. The decline was due to a 9% increase in net capital employed, partially offset by the increase in net debt.

A. Explain why Pepsico's debt-to-equity ratio rose during 1994 using market values but declined using book values.

B. What do the relative ratios for 1994 tell us about the price-to-book value ratio of Pepsico shares?

C. Discuss why the market-based ratio is superior to the book value–based ratio as an indicator of Pepsico's financial conditions.

D. Discuss why the book value–based ratio is superior to the market-based ratio as an indicator of financial leverage.

11

LEASES AND OFF-BALANCE-SHEET DEBT

CHAPTER OUTLINE

CHAPTER OBJECTIVES

INTRODUCTION

LEASES
Incentives for Leasing
Lease Classification: Lessees
  Capital Leases
  Operating Leases
Financial Reporting by Lessees: Capital Versus
Operating Leases
  Comparative Analysis of Capitalized and
  Operating Leases
Analysis of Lease Disclosures
  Lease Disclosure Requirements
  Financial Reporting by Lessees: An Example
  Impact of Operating Lease Adjustment

OFF-BALANCE-SHEET FINANCING ACTIVITIES
Take-or-Pay and Throughput Arrangements
Sale of Receivables
Finance Subsidiaries

Joint Ventures and Investment in Affiliates
Other Off-Balance-Sheet Activities
  Commodity-Linked Bonds
  Bonds Tied to Investments

ANALYSIS OF OBS ACTIVITIES: ASHLAND OIL

**INTERNATIONAL ACCOUNTING AND
REPORTING PRACTICES**
Lease Accounting Outside the United States

SUMMARY

**CASE 11-1: OFF-BALANCE-SHEET FINANCING
TECHNIQUES FOR TEXACO AND CALTEX**

**APPENDIX 11-A: FINANCIAL REPORTING BY
LESSORS AND FOR SALE LEASEBACKS**

CHAPTER OBJECTIVES

In this chapter, we:

1. Discuss the motivations for leasing assets as opposed to buying them and the incentives for reporting the leases as *operating leases* rather than *capital leases*.

2. Compare the financial statement effects of *operating leases* and *capital leases*.

3. Demonstrate how operating leases keep substantial portions of a firm's operating capacity and debt off the balance sheet.

4. Adjust reported leverage, profitability, and cash flows for off-balance-sheet (OBS) leases.

5. Discuss the similarity between OBS leases and other OBS activities such as *take-or-pay and throughput arrangements* and adjust reported financial statements and ratios for these activities.

6. Explain the impact of *transfers of receivables* on reported cash flow from operations and short-term debt and how to undo those effects.

7. Illustrate the analysis of the OBS *debt of the subsidiaries and affiliates of a firm.*

INTRODUCTION

Rapid changes in manufacturing and information technology and expanding international trade and capital markets have resulted in the growth of multinational corporations that must cope with increasingly mobile capital, labor, and product markets. These changes have been accompanied by volatile commodity and other factor price levels, fluctuating interest and foreign currency exchange rates, and a frenzy of domestic and international tax and regulatory changes. In addition, general inflation and industry-specific price changes have raised most asset prices and have increased the risks of operations and investments.

This economic climate has required increasing amounts of capital as firms acquire operating capacity (both for expansion and replacement purposes) at ever higher prices. Because of the volatility of prices and cash flows, the risks of owning operating assets have also increased. These trends have driven firms to seek methods of:

1. Acquiring the rights to assets through methods other than traditional direct purchases (financed by debt)

2. Controlling the risks of operations through derivative and hedging transactions

"Executory contracts" are the primary alternative form of transactions used by firms to acquire operating capacity, supplies of raw materials, and other inputs. Such contracts or arrangements are the subject of this chapter. Hedging transactions will be discussed in Chapter 16.

The trend toward these financing techniques and hedging transactions has been encouraged by drawbacks in the historical cost-based financial reporting system, in which recognition and measurement depend primarily on actual transactions. As contracts are considered legal promises, and neither cash nor goods may be exchanged at the inception of these contracts, accounting recognition is not required in many cases. The emphasis on accounting assets and liabilities rather than the recognition of economic resources and obligations further encourages firms to keep resources and *obligations* off the balance sheet.

Firms may engage in these transactions to avoid reporting high debt levels and leverage ratios and to reduce the probability of technical default under restrictive covenants in debt indentures. Off-balance-sheet transactions may also keep assets and potential gains out of the financial statements but under the control of management, which can orchestrate the timing of gain recognition to offset periods of poor operating performance.

Footnote disclosures constitute the best source of information about off-balance-sheet activities. Additional information may be available from disclosures in 10-K filings and from other company publications. In some cases, the economic meaning behind the disclosures requires explanation from management. Thus, a complete analysis of the firm must include a review of all financial statement disclosures to obtain data on off-balance-sheet activities. In many cases, straightforward adjustments can be used to reflect off-balance-sheet assets and liabilities on the balance sheet. Such adjustments result in a balance sheet that presents a more complete portrait of the firm's resources and obligations and financial ratios that are more comparable to those of competitors whose use of off-balance-sheet techniques is different.

The chapter begins with a discussion of leases, the most common form of executory contract entered into by firms. The methods used to analyze and adjust for leases serve as a model for the analysis of other off-balance-sheet activities that comprise the second part of the chapter.

LEASES

Accounting policy makers have grappled with leases for years to develop reporting requirements that emphasize the economic substance rather than the legal form of the leasing transaction. We begin our discussion of leases with a review of incentives for leases. A discussion of reporting requirements and the analysis of leases complete this section of the chapter.

Incentives for Leasing

Firms generally acquire rights to use property, plant, and equipment by outright purchase, partially or fully funded by internal resources or externally borrowed funds. In a purchase transaction, the buyer acquires (and the seller surrenders) ownership, which includes all the benefits and risks embodied in the asset. A firm may also acquire the use of property, including some or all of the benefits and risks of ownership, for specific periods of time and stipulated rental payments through contractual arrangements called leases.

Short-term, or *operating,* leases allow the lessee to use leased property for only a portion of its economic life. The lessee accounts for such leases as contracts reporting (as rental expense) only the required rental payments as they are made. Because the lessor retains substantially all the risks of ownership of leased property, the leased assets remain on its balance sheet and are depreciated over their estimated economic lives; rental payments are recognized as revenues over time according to the terms of the lease.

Alternatively, longer-term leases may effectively transfer all (or substantially all) the risks and rewards of the leased property to the lessee. Such leases are the economic equivalent of sales with financing arrangements designed to effect the purchase (by the lessee) and sale (by the lessor) of the leased property. *Such leases, referred to as finance or capital leases, are treated for accounting purposes as sales.* The asset and associated debt are carried on the books of the lessee, and the lessor records a gain on "sale" at the inception of the lease. The lessee depreciates the asset over its life, and treats lease payments as payments of principal and interest. The financial reporting differences between accounting for a lease as an operating or capital lease are far-reaching and affect the balance sheet, income statement, cash flow statement, and associated ratios.

One motivation for leasing rather than borrowing and buying an asset is to avoid recognition of the debt and asset on the lessee's financial statements. Lease capitalization eliminates this advantage. Whether a lease is reported as operating or capitalized depends, as we shall see, on the terms of the lease and their relationship to criteria specified by SFAS 13.

Notwithstanding these financial reporting requirements, leases may be structured to qualify as operating leases to achieve desired financial reporting effects and capital structure benefits. Operating leases allow lessees to avoid recognition of the asset and report higher profitability ratios and indicators of operating efficiency. Reported leverage is also lower because the related liability for contractual payments is not recognized.

Extensive use of operating leases needs careful evaluation and the analyst must adjust financial statements (to reflect unrecognized assets and liabilities) and the leverage, coverage, and profitability ratios for the effects of operating leases.

Box 11-1 reviews the finance literature on the competing incentives of the lease versus purchase decision. The impact of the financial reporting alternatives (operating vs. capitalization) on this decision is also discussed.

Lease Classification: Lessees

The preceding discussion suggests that lessees generally structure and report leases as operating leases. Their counterparts, lessors, however, prefer to structure leases as capital leases. This allows earlier recognition of revenue and income by reporting transactions that are in substance installment sales or financing arrangements as completed sales. The resulting higher profitability and turnover ratios are powerful incentives for lessors. Appendix 11-A is devoted to a discussion of lease accounting from the perspective of the lessor. The chapter itself retains the lessee perspective.

Lease classifications are not intended to be alternative reporting methods. However, management actively negotiates the provisions of lease agreements and the preferred accounting treatment is an important element of these contractual negotiations.

SFAS 13 attempted to promulgate "objective" and "reliable" criteria that facilitate the evaluation of the economic substance of lease agreements. One goal was to discourage off-balance-sheet financing by lessees and front-end loading of income by lessors. The criteria were designed to ensure that either the lessee or lessor recognize the leased assets on their books.

Capital Leases

A lease that, in economic substance, transfers to the lessee substantially all the risks and rewards inherent in the leased property is a financing or capital lease and should be capitalized. A lease meeting *any one* of the following SFAS 13 criteria at the inception of the lease must be classified as a capital lease by lessees:

1. The lease transfers ownership of the property to the lessee at the end of the lease term.
2. The lease contains a bargain purchase option.
3. The lease term is equal to 75% or more of the estimated economic life of the leased property (not applicable to land or when the lease term begins within the final 25% of the economic life of the asset).

BOX 11-1
Incentives for Leasing and Their Effect on the Capital Versus Operating
Lease Choice

Management may have a number of reasons to prefer leasing compared to outright asset purchases. The choice may be a function of strategic investment and capital structure objectives, the comparative costs* of leasing versus equity or debt financing, the availability of tax benefits, and perceived financial reporting advantages. Some of these reasons influence whether the lease will be treated as an operating or capital lease; others are unrelated to the accounting choice.

Tax Incentives

The tax benefits of owning assets can be exploited best by transferring them to the party in the higher marginal tax bracket. Firms with low effective tax rates more readily engage in leasing than firms in high tax brackets as the tax benefits can be passed on to the lessor. El-Gazzar et al. (1986) provide evidence consistent with this hypothesis; firms with lower effective tax rates had a higher proportion of lease debt to total assets than did firms with higher effective tax rates. Moreover, El-Gazzar et al. argue that tax effects also influence the choice of accounting method as the lessee attempts to influence the tax interpretation (by the IRS) of lease contracts. That is, it is more difficult to argue for capital lease treatment for tax purposes if the lease is treated as an operating lease for book purposes. Citing evidence by Mellman and Bernstein (1966) of substantial conformity (pre-SFAS 13)† between tax and book accounting for lessees, they note that

> apparently, a high-tax-rate lessee's claim of material equity on the tax return could be enhanced by showing ownership for reporting purposes.‡

Their sample of firms confirmed this finding as firms with high effective tax rates tended to capitalize their leases.

Nontax Incentives

Smith and Wakeman (1985) analyzed nontax incentives related to the lease versus purchase decision. Their list of eight nontax factors that make leasing more likely than purchase is presented here. Some of these factors are not directly related to the lessee's choice, but are motivated by the manufacturer or lessor and/or the type of asset involved. We have sorted these conditions by their potential impact on the operating versus capitalization accounting choice.

Nontax Incentives for Leasing Versus Purchase: Incentives Classified by Potential Impact on Operating Versus Capital Lease Choice

Favors Operating Lease as per SFAS 13

1. Period of use is short relative to the overall life of the asset.
2. Lessor has comparative advantage in reselling the asset.

Favors Structuring Lease as Operating Lease

3. Corporate bond covenants contain specific covenants relating to financial policies that the firm must follow.
4. Management compensation contracts contain provisions expressing compensation as a function of returns on invested capital.

Not Relevant to Operating Versus Capital Lease Decision

   5. Lessee ownership is closely held so that risk reduction is important.

   6. Lessor (manufacturer) has market power and can thus generate higher profits by leasing the asset (and controlling the terms of the lease) than selling it.

   7. Asset is not specialized to the firm.

   8. Asset's value is not sensitive to use or abuse (owner takes better care of asset than lessee).

Based on Smith and Wakeman (1985).

Short periods of use and the resale factor favor the use of operating leases, and under GAAP, these conditions would lead to lease agreements consistent with operating leases. The bond covenant and management compensation incentives also favor the *negotiated structuring of* the agreement as an operating lease.

Consistent with the foregoing, both Abdel-Khalik (1981) and Nakayama et al. (1981) note that the expected covenant violations resulting from SFAS 13 influenced firms to lobby against its adoption. Furthermore, Abdel-Khalik notes that firms renegotiated the terms of their leases during SFAS 13's transition period to make them eligible for treatment as operating leases. Imhoff and Thomas (1988) found that subsequent to SFAS 13, there was a general decline in leases as a form of financing. Further evidence with respect to the choice of accounting method is provided by El-Gazzar et al., who note that in the pre-SFAS 13 period, firms that had high debt-to-equity ratios and/or had incentive-based contracts based on income after interest expense were more likely to have leases classified as operating leases. Taken together, these results confirm that debt covenant and compensation factors affect both the choice of leasing as a form of financing as well as the choice of accounting treatment of the lease.

---

*Related to these costs are the risks related to residual values and obsolescence.

†Prior to SFAS 13, GAAP also required that certain leases be treated as capital leases. The effect of SFAS 13 was to tighten the requirements, making more leases qualify as capital leases.

‡Samir El-Gazzar, Steven Lilien, and Victor Pastena, "Accounting for Leases by Lessees," *Journal of Accounting and Economics,* 1986, pp. 217–237.

   4. The present value[1] of the minimum lease payments [2] (MLPs) equals or exceeds 90% of the fair value of leased property to the lessor.

The ownership and bargain purchase criteria imply a transfer of all the risks and benefits of the leased property to the lessee; in economic substance, such leases are financing arrangements. Lease terms extending to at least 75% of the economic life of the leased asset are also considered to achieve such a transfer; there is an implicit assumption that most of the value of an asset accrues to the user within that period. Finally, a lease must be capitalized when the present value of the minimum lease payments is equal to or exceeds 90% of the fair value of the leased property at the inception of the lease. In effect, the lessee has contractually agreed to payments ensuring that the lessor will recover its investment along with a reasonable return.

---

[1]The discount rate used to compute the present values should be the lessee's incremental borrowing rate or the implicit interest rate of the lessor, whichever is lower. The use of the lower rate generates the higher of two present values, increasing the probability that this criterion will be met and the lease capitalized.

[2]MLPs include residual values when they are guaranteed by lessees since the guarantee results in a contractually fixed residual value and effectively transfers the risk of changes in residual values to the lessee.

The transaction is, therefore, an installment purchase for the lessee financed by the lessor, and capitalization reflects this economic interpretation of the leasing transaction.[3]

Operating Leases

Leases not meeting any of the four criteria listed above are not capitalized and no asset or obligation is reported in the financial statements since no purchase is deemed to have occurred. Such leases are classified as operating leases, and payments are reported as rental expense. SFAS 13 mandates the use of the straight-line method of recognizing periodic rental payments unless another, systematic basis provides a better representation of the use of leased property. As a result, for leases with rising rental payments, lease expense and cash flow will not be identical.

Financial Reporting by Lessees: Capital Versus Operating Leases

Financial reporting by lessees will be illustrated using a noncancellable lease beginning December 31, 19X0, with annual MLPs of $10,000 made at the end of each year for four years. Ten percent is assumed to be the appropriate discount rate.

Operating Lease. If the lease does not meet any criteria requiring capitalization:

- No entry is made at the inception of the lease.
- Over the life of the lease, only the annual rental expense of $10,000 will be charged to income and CFO.

Capital Lease. If the lease meets any one of the four criteria of a capital lease, then:

- At the inception of the lease, an asset (leasehold asset) and liability (leasehold liability) equal to the present value of the lease payments, $31,700, is recognized.
- Over the life of the lease:
  1. The annual rental expense of $10,000 will be allocated between interest and principal payments on the $31,700 leasehold liability according to the following amortization schedule:

Year	Opening Liability	Allocation of Payment of $10,000 Interest*	Principal	Closing Liability†
X0				$31,700
X1	$31,700	$3,170	$6,830	24,870
X2	24,870	2,487	7,513	17,357
X3	17,357	1,735	8,265	9,092
X4	9,092	909	9,092	0

*10% of the opening liability.
†Equals the opening liability less the periodic amortization of the lease obligation. Also equals the present value of the remaining MLPs.

[3]Leases are classified at the inception of the lease; the classification is not changed when the lessee or lessor is acquired unless the provisions of the lease agreement are changed. See FASB Interpretation 21 (1978).

2. The cost of the leasehold asset of $31,700 is charged to operations (annual depreciation is $7,925) using the straight-line method over the term of the lease.[4]

Comparative Analysis of Capitalized and Operating Leases

Balance Sheet Effects. No assets or liabilities are recognized if the lease is treated as an operating lease. When leases are capitalized, there is a major impact on a firm's balance sheet at inception and throughout the life of the lease. At the inception of the lease, an asset and a liability equal to the present value of the lease payments are recognized.

Balance Sheet Effect of Lease Capitalization

	19X0	19X1	19X2	19X3	19X4
Assets					
Leased assets	$31,700	$31,700	$31,700	$31,700	$31,700
Accumulated depreciation	0	7,925	15,850	23,775	31,700
Leased assets, net	$31,700	$23,775	$15,850	$ 7,925	0
Liabilities					
Current portion of lease obligation	6,830	7,513	8,265	9,092	0
Long-term debt: lease obligation	24,870	17,357	9,092	0	0
	$31,700	$24,870	$17,357	$ 9,092	0

The gross and net (of accumulated depreciation) amounts are reported at each balance sheet date. The current and noncurrent components of the lease obligation are reported as liabilities under capitalization. The current component is the principal portion of the lease payment to be made in the following year. Note that, at the inception of the lease, the leased asset and liability are equal at $31,700. Since the asset and liability are amortized using different methods, this equality is not again observed until the end of the lease term when both asset and liability are equal to zero.

Effect on Financial Ratios. Lease capitalization increases asset balances, resulting in lower asset turnover and return on asset ratios, as compared with the operating lease method, which does not record leased assets.

The most important effect of lease capitalization, however, is its impact on leverage ratios. As lease obligations are not recognized for operating leases, leverage ratios are understated. Lease capitalization adds both current and noncurrent liabilities to debt, resulting in a corresponding decrease in working capital and increases in the debt-to-equity and other leverage ratios.

Income Statement Effects. The income statement effects of lease reporting are also significant and impact operating income as well as net income. The operating

---

[4]Generally, depreciation methods used for similar purchased property are applied to leased assets over their estimated economic lives when one of the transfer of ownership criteria (1 and 2) is met and over the lease term when one of the other capitalization criteria (3 and 4) is satisfied.

lease method charges the periodic rental payments to expense as accrued, whereas capitalization recognizes depreciation and interest expense over the lease term.

Income Effects of Lease Classification

| | Operating Lease | Capital Lease | | |
| | Operating = Total Expense | Operating Expense | Nonoperating Expense | |
Year	Rent	Depreciation	Interest	Total Expense
X1	$10,000	$ 7,925	$3,170	$11,095
X2	10,000	7,925	2,487	10,412
X3	10,000	7,925	1,735	9,660
X4	10,000	7,925	909	8,834
	$40,000	$31,700	$8,300	$40,000

Operating Income. Capitalization results in higher operating income (earnings before interest and taxes, or EBIT) since an annual straight-line depreciation expense of $7,925 is lower than the annual rental expense of $10,000 reported under the operating lease method. For an individual lease, this difference is never reversed and remains constant over the lease term given use of the straight-line depreciation method. Accelerated depreciation methods would generate smaller differences in early years, with an increasing difference as depreciation declines, increasing both the level and trend of EBIT.

Total Expense and Net Income. Under capitalization, lease expense includes interest expense and depreciation of the leased asset. Initially, total expense for a capital lease exceeds rental expense reported for an operating lease, but declines over the lease term as interest expense falls.[5] In later years, total lease expense will be less than rental expense reported for an operating lease.

Note that total expense (interest plus depreciation) for a capital lease must equal total rental expense for an operating lease over the life of the lease.[6] Consequently, although total net income over the lease term is not affected by capitalization, the timing of income recognition is changed; lower net income is reported in the early years, followed by higher income in later years. This relationship holds for individual leases, but the effect on a firm depends on any additional leases entered into in subsequent periods. The effect of inflation on asset prices (and lease rentals) means that the impact of old leases nearing expiration may be swamped by the impact of new leases. If a firm enters into new leases at the same or increasing rate over time, reported net income will remain lower under capitalization.

Effect on Financial Ratios. In general, firms with operating leases report higher profitability, interest coverage (as interest expense is lower), return on equity, and return on assets ratios. The higher ROE ratios are due to the higher profitability

[5]If the company uses accelerated depreciation, then the difference in earlier years will be greater but the subsequent decline will also be rapid.

[6]This equality does not hold when the residual value is not zero.

(numerator effect), whereas the higher ROA is due primarily to the lower assets (denominator effect).

Cash Flow Effects of Lease Classification. Lease classification provides another example where accounting methods affect the classification of cash flows.[7] Under the operating lease method, all cash flows are operating and there is an operating cash outflow of $10,000 per year. However, lease capitalization results in both operating and financing cash flows as the rental payments of $10,000 are allocated between interest expense (treated as CFO) and amortization of the lease obligation (reported as cash from financing).

Cash Flow Effect of Lease Classification

	Operating Lease	Capital Lease	
Year	Operations	Operations	Financing
X0			
X1	$10,000	$3,170	$6,830
X2	10,000	2,487	7,513
X3	10,000	1,735	8,265
X4	10,000	909	9,091

In 19X1, for example, CFO differs between the two methods by $6,830, the amortization of the lease obligation. Because interest expense declines over the lease term and an increasing proportion of the annual payment is allocated to the lease obligation, the difference in CFO increases over the lease term. Thus, lease capitalization systematically decreases the operating cash outflow while increasing the financing cash outflow.

Therefore, although the capital lease method adversely affects some financial statement ratios, it allows firms to report higher operating cash flows compared to those reported using the operating lease method.

Before proceeding, it is important to point out that *at the inception of the lease (year X0), no cash flows are reported.* This is true even though a capital lease implies the purchase of an asset (cash outflow for investment) financed by the issuance of new debt (cash inflow from financing). Disclosure of the event is reported as part of the "significant noncash financing and investing activities." Analysts attempting to estimate a firm's cash flow requirements for operating capacity should however include the present value of such leases as a cash requirement. Moreover, free cash flow calculations for valuation purposes should incorporate the present value of leases as a cash outflow for investment at the inception of the lease (see Chapter 19).

Analysis of Lease Disclosures

A noncancellable lease, whether reported as a capital or operating lease, in effect, constitutes debt and the right to use an asset. If the lease is reported as a capital lease,

---

[7]We discuss only the classification of cash flows. After-tax cash flows are not affected by lease classification as *generally* even firms that use the capital lease method for financial reporting purposes are required to use the operating lease method for tax purposes. Tax payments and actual cash flows are therefore identical. Under the capital lease method, the lease expense under financial reporting exceeds the lease expense reported for tax purposes, resulting in a deferred tax asset.

this information is on-balance-sheet. If it is reported as an operating lease, then the debt and asset are off-balance-sheet and the analyst must adjust accordingly.

This is especially true in industries such as airlines and retail department stores where some firms own operating assets (i.e., airplanes or stores), other firms lease them and report the leases as capital leases, and still other lessees account for them as operating leases. Given the same conditions, the firms using operating leases may report the "best" results as they will show minimal debt and their higher profits will appear to be generated by a relatively smaller investment in assets.

However, the disclosure requirements of firms with leases, capital or operating, are sufficiently detailed to provide the information required for adjustments.

Lease Disclosure Requirements

SFAS 13 requires the disclosure of gross amounts of capitalized lease assets as of each balance sheet date, by major classes or grouped by their nature or function; they may be combined with owned assets.

Lessees must also disclose future MLPs for each of the five succeeding fiscal years and the aggregate thereafter as well as the net present value of the capitalized leases. Separate disclosure of minimum sublease rentals receivable from noncancellable subleases is also required.

Lessees using operating leases must also disclose future MLPs for each of the five succeeding fiscal years and in the aggregate thereafter. The present value of the MLPs is not required but may occasionally be provided. The rental expense under operating leases (classified as to minimum, contingent, and sublease rentals) for each period for which an income statement is presented must be disclosed as of the balance sheet date.[8]

For both operating and capital leases, lessees must also disclose aggregate minimum rentals receivable under noncancellable subleases. Information regarding renewal terms, purchase options, contingent rentals, any escalation clauses, and restrictions on dividends, additional debt, and leasing is also required. Such disclosure is usually general in nature.

Financial Reporting by Lessees: An Example

Exhibit 11-1 contains the lease disclosure of AMR (the parent of American Airlines). From the balance sheet alone, it would seem that AMR is inclined to purchase rather than lease its airplanes. The carrying value of purchased equipment is over six times that of leased equipment.

The footnote paints an entirely different picture. AMR engages heavily in leasing, but the leases are mostly structured as operating leases. Capital lease obligations and operating leases are shown separately. Future MLPs for the next five years, and the aggregate thereafter, are disclosed for both capital and operating leases. For capital leases, interest has been deducted to report their present value of $2,403 million ($128 million is reported as current and $2,275 million as long-term debt).

Note that the (aggregate) operating lease payments of $20,011 million are more than five times the capital lease payments ($3,839 million). Moreover, the data suggest that the operating leases are of longer term than the capital leases.

Aggregate MLPs of the capital leases for the next five years are about 36% of total future MLPs or $1,399 million. Total MLPs for the remaining years are $2,440

---

[8]Unlike the case of capital leases, disclosure of the interest component of operating lease MLPs and their present value is not mandated by SFAS 13; it is occasionally provided.

EXHIBIT 11-1. AMR
Excerpts from Balance Sheet and Lease Footnotes

	December 31, 1994
Assets	
Equipment and property (net of accumulated depreciation of 5,465)	$12,020
Equipment and property under capital leases (net of accumulated amortization of 1,166)	1,878
Total assets	19,486
Liabilities	
Long-term debt	
Current maturity	590
Noncurrent	5,603 6,193
Capital lease obligations	
Current	128
Noncurrent	2,275 2,403
Total long-term debt and capital lease obligations	8,596
Shareholders equity	$ 3,380

Leases

AMR's subsidiaries lease various types of equipment and property, including aircraft, passenger terminals, equipment, and various other facilities. The future minimum lease payments required under capital leases, together with the present value of net minimum lease payments, and future minimum lease payments required under operating leases that have initial or remaining noncancelable lease terms in excess of one year as of December 31, 1994, were ($ in millions):

Year Ending December 31	Capital Leases	Operating Leases
1995	$ 273	$ 946
1996	300	924
1997	280	920
1998	276	931
1999	270	912
2000 and subsequent	2,440	15,378
	$3,839	$20,011
Less amount representing interest	1,436	
Present value of minimum lease payments	$2,403	

At December 31, 1994, the Company had 216 jet aircraft and 123 turboprop aircraft under operating leases and 82 jet aircraft and 63 turboprop under capital leases.

Source: AMR, *1994 Annual Report.*

million or 64% of the total MLPs of $3,839 million over the lease terms. The capitalized MLPs generally decline slowly over time, and a substantial proportion of the payments occurs after the initial five years, suggesting long-term leases. The average lease term of the capitalized leases can be estimated by computing the number of payments included in the "later years" amount of $2,440 million; that is, ($2,440 million/$270 million) if we assume that annual payments remain at the 1999 level. This suggests a lease term of approximately 14 (initial five plus the estimated nine) years.

For operating leases, the proportion of payments after the first five years is ($15,378/$20,011) 77% of total payments. This suggests a longer term than for the capital leases. Dividing the remaining payments of $15,378 by the 1999 payment of $912 yields 17, suggesting a lease term of 22 years (5 plus 17) or 50% longer than for the capital leases.

The note indicates that 216 jet aircraft and 123 turboprops are under operating leases. *Neither these assets nor the debt associated with them appear on the balance sheet.*

Investors and analysts can use the lease disclosures to adjust the balance sheet appropriately. The present value of the operating leases can be estimated by discounting the future cash flows. This estimate requires assumptions about the pattern of MLPs after the first five years and the discount rate. This estimation procedure is "robust," with the calculated present value relatively invariant to the assumptions.

Assumed Pattern of MLPs. Footnote disclosures reflect the payments to be made over each of the next five years and the total payments thereafter. The present value computation requires an estimate of the number of payments implicit in the latter lump sum. Either the rate of decline suggested by the cash outflows for the next five years or a constant amount over the remaining term may be used to derive the present value of the operating lease payments.

Discount Rate. The discount rate should reflect the risk class of the leased assets as well as the company being analyzed. The interest rate implicit in the reported capital leases is a good approximation of that rate.[9]

Box 11-2 uses AMR to illustrate the estimation method(s). The procedure yields a rate of between 6 and 7% depending on the assumptions made; we use 6.5%. The two assumptions regarding pattern of cash flows over the lease term generate present value estimates of $10.5 and $10.2 billion, a difference of only 3%.

Impact of Operating Lease Adjustments

Liabilities. The impact of the adjustment is highly significant. AMR's reported long-term debt and capital leases total $8.6 billion. Adding approximately $10.5 billion for off-balance-sheet operating leases more than doubles debt to approximately $19 billion. *AMR has more debt off the balance sheet than on the balance sheet.* With equity of $3.4 billion, an already high debt-to-equity ratio of 2.5 increases to 5.6.

AMR: Effects of Operating Lease Adjustment ($ in billions)

	As Reported	+ Operating Leases	= Adjusted
Debt	$ 8.6	$10.5	$19.1
Equity	3.4		3.4
Debt/equity	2.5X		5.6X
Assets	$19.5	$10.5	$30.0

[9]Because the implicit rate is an average rate based on terms at inception, it may be significantly different from either the reported or marginal long-term borrowing rate the company faces in the capital markets and it may not reflect the market value of equivalent debt. The analyst may want to use an estimated (from the debt footnote or based on current market conditions) long-term borrowing rate.

BOX 11-2
Estimation of the Present Value of Operating Leases

A. The Implicit Discount Rate of a Firm's Capital Leases

Two approaches may be employed to estimate the average discount rate used to capitalize a firm's capital leases. The first uses only the next period's MLP; the second incorporates all future MLPs in the estimation procedure.

1. Using Next Period's MLP

The 1995 MLP for AMR's capital leases is $273 million. That payment includes interest and principal. The principal portion is shown in AMR's current liabilities section as $128 million. The difference between the two, $145 million, represents the interest component of the MLP. As the present value of AMR's capital leases equals $2,403, the interest rate on the capitalized leases can be estimated as ($145/$2,403) 6.03%.

This calculation assumes that the principal payment of $128 million will be made at the end of the year. If it is made early in the year, then the interest expense is based on the principal outstanding after payment of the current portion. If the current portion is a significant portion of the overall liability, then the results can be biased. An alternative estimate of the implicit interest rate may be derived using the average liability balance; that is, $145/[0.5 × ($2,403 + $2,275)] = 6.2%.

2. Using All Future MLPs

The interest rate can also be estimated by solving for the implicit interest rate (internal rate of return) that equates the MLPs and their present value. This calculation requires an assumption about the pattern of MLPs after the first five years. As discussed further in the next section (with reference to operating leases), the simplest assumption is that the payment level ($270 million) in the fifth year (1999) continues to the future, implying the following payment stream:

Year	Payments
1995	$ 273
1995	300
1997	280
1998	276
1999	270
2000–2008	270
2009 (residual)	10
	$3,839

The internal rate of return that equates this stream to the present value of $2,403 is 7.0%.

Alternatively, one can assume a declining rate of payments with a decline rate based on the payment pattern of the first five years. In AMR's case, payments increase initially and then decline slowly as the payment levels of 1998 and 1999 are approximately 98% of the previous year. Using this pattern and assuming payments of

$$(0.98 \times \$270) = \$264 \text{ in the year } 2000$$
$$(0.98 \times \$264) = \$256 \text{ in the year } 2001$$

and so on result in an internal rate of return of 6.9%, very close to the 7.0% based on the constant rate assumption. Generally, the differences are not significantly different, and unless the rate of decline is very steep, the constant rate assumption simplifies the computation.

The first procedure yields an estimate of 6.0 to 6.2%; the second yields estimates of 6.9 to 7.0%. Based on these estimates, we use 6.5% for our analysis of AMR's operating leases.

B. Assumed Pattern of MLPs

The MLPs for the first five years (1995 to 1999) are given. From the year 2000 and on, two assumptions are possible:

1. Constant rate, or
2. Declining rate

Under the constant rate assumption, it is assumed that MLPs from the year 2000 and on equal the 1999 payment of $912. Alternatively, and more realistically, one would expect the payments to decline over time. The rate of decline implicit in the MLPs reported individually for the first five years may be used to estimate the payment pattern after the initial five years. Based on that payment pattern,* we use a decline rate of 1.8%. The assumed patterns and the resultant present values are presented below.

Assumed Pattern of MLPs for Operating Leases

Initial five-year given payments

Year	MLPs
1995	$946
1996	924
1997	920
1998	931
1999	$912

	Assumed Payment Rate	
Year	Constant Amount	Declining Rate (1.8%)
2000	$912	$896
2001	912	879
2002	912	864
2003	912	848
2004	912	833
2005	912	818
2006	912	803
2007	912	789
2008	912	774
2009	912	760
2010	912	747
2011	912	733
2012	912	720
2013	912	707
2014	912	694

| | Assumed Payment Rate | |
Year	Constant Amount	Declining Rate (1.8%)
2015	912	682
2016	786†	670
2017		658
2018		646
2019		634
2020		224†
Aggregate	$20,011	$20,011
Present value at 6.5%	**$10,515**	**$10,212**

---

†Residual to arrive at aggregate MLPs of $20,011.

Note that the two present value estimates of $10.5 billion and $10.2 billion are within 3% of each other.

C. Executory Costs

Reported MLPs include such executory costs as maintenance, taxes, and insurance on the leased assets. These costs are not financing costs and should be excluded from the calculation of the lease present value. However, because footnote disclosures generally do not reduce MLPs by executory costs, the present value calculation described above is biased.

In most cases that bias is small and can be ignored. However, the estimation method can be modified to adjust for this bias. When the firm discloses the total of the executory costs, we can assume that the pattern of the executory costs follows that of the MLPs. If we define p as the proportion of total executory costs to total MLPs,

$$p = \frac{\text{Total Executory Costs}}{\text{Total MLPs}}$$

then the procedures described above can be applied‡ to a pattern of *adjusted MLPs*, where the

$$\text{Adjusted MLP (for any year)} = (1 - p) \times \text{Unadjusted MLP (for that year)}$$

---

*From 1995 through 1999, the MLPs declined by about 3.6% or on average about 0.9% per year. In 1999 itself, the rate of decline was just over 2%. Thus, we decided on a rate between 0.9 and 2%, with a greater weighting given the last year, bringing us to a decline rate of 1.8%.

‡Alternatively, one can use the unadjusted MLPs and make the following two adjustments:
1. In calculating the implicit interest rate of the capital leases, "gross up" the present value of the capital leases by *dividing* by $(1 - p)$.
2. Using the interest rate calculated in step 1, find the present value of the unadjusted MLPs. *Multiply* that present value by $(1 - p)$.

Assets. Exhibit 11-1 reports total assets of $19.5 billion. Capitalization of the operating leases increases total assets by $10.5 billion. AMR is operating 50% more assets than reported on its balance sheet. Efficiency measures such as turnover or ROA use total assets in the denominator and are highly overstated; adjusted ratios more accurately portray AMR's asset efficiency.

Income and Cash Flow Effects. Adjustments for operating leases also affect the income and cash flow statement (as well as related ratios). These effects can be illustrated by using the 1995 MLP of $946 million as an example. Under the operating lease method, both rent expense and the CFO outflow equal $946 million. Capitalization results in allocation of that $946 million between interest expense and principal payments; in addition, the leased asset must be depreciated. These changes reduce reported income but increase CFO.

AMR: Effects of Operating Lease Adjustment, 1995 ($ in millions)

	As Reported	Adjusted
Income Statement		
Rent expense	$946	
Interest expense		$ 683*
Amortization expense		477†
		$1,160
Cash Flow Statement		
If interest payments are treated as CFO (per SFAS 95)		
CFO outflow	$946	$ 683
CFF outflow	0	$ 263
If interest payments are treated as CFF (per Chapter 3)		
CFO outflow	$946	0
CFF outflow	0	$ 946

*Interest Expense = Interest Rate × PV of Leases = 0.065 × $10.5 billion = $683
†Amortization Expense = PV of Lease Divided by Lease Term = $10.5/22 = $477

OFF-BALANCE-SHEET FINANCING ACTIVITIES

Leases are but one example of contractual arrangements that give rise to off-balance-sheet debt. In this section, we discuss other such arrangements and show how financial statements should be adjusted to reflect the underlying economic consequences. Like leases, some of these off-balance-sheet activities are commonplace and can be found in many firms and industries. Others tend to be industry-specific or are the product of specific market conditions.

Take-or-Pay and Throughput Arrangements

Firms use take-or-pay contracts to ensure the long-term availability of raw materials and other inputs necessary for operations.[10] These agreements are common in the natural gas, chemical, paper, and metal industries. Under these arrangements, the purchasing firm commits to buy a minimum quantity of an input over a specified time period. Input prices may be fixed by contract or may be related to market prices. Natural resource companies use throughput arrangements with pipelines or processors (such as refiners) to ensure future distribution or processing requirements.

These contracts are often used as collateral for bank or other financing by unrelated suppliers or by investors in joint ventures. The contract serves as an indirect guarantee of the related debt. However, neither the assets nor the debt incurred to obtain (or guarantee availability of) operating capacity are reflected on the balance sheet of the purchaser. SFAS 47 (1981) requires that, when a long-term commitment is used to obtain financing, the purchaser must disclose the nature of the commitment and the minimum required payments in its financial statement footnotes.

As take-or-pay contracts and throughput agreements effectively keep some operating assets and liabilities off the balance sheet, the analyst should add the present value of minimum future commitments to both property and debt.

Exhibit 11-2 contains the commitments and contingencies footnote from Alcan's *1994 Annual Report,* disclosing take-or-pay and similar obligations. Note that the disclosure is similar to that required for (capital and operating) leases. We can apply the method used earlier to compute the present value of the debt. The calculation is shown in panel B of the exhibit.

The take-or-pay contracts reported by Alcan represent $750 million of off-balance-sheet assets and debt. The impact of this adjustment on the leverage ratio is

Alcan Balance Sheet, at December 31, 1994 (Canadian $ in millions)

	Reported	Adjusted	Increase in Debt
Total debt	$2,471	$3,221	30%
Stockholders' equity	$4,308	$4,308	
Debt-to-equity ratio	0.57X	0.75X	

Sale of Receivables

Receivables are sometimes financed by their sale (or securitization) to unrelated parties. That is, the firm sells the receivables to a buyer (normally a financial institution or investor group).[11] The seller uses the proceeds from the sale for operations or to reduce existing or planned debt. The firm continues to service the original receivables; it receives payment from its customers but transfers those funds to the new owner of

---

[10]Inventories can also be financed through product financing arrangements under which inventories are sold and later repurchased. SFAS 49 (1981) requires that such arrangements that do not effectively transfer the risk of ownership to the buyer must be accounted for as debt financing rather than sale of inventory. In such cases, the cost of holding inventories (storage and insurance) and interest cost on the imputed debt must be recognized as incurred. Prior to SFAS 49, companies sometimes used these arrangements to defer these costs and accelerate the recognition of profit. Product financing arrangements are still accounted for as sales outside of the United States.

[11]Depending on the interest (if any) paid by customers and the effective interest rate on the sale transaction, the seller may recognize a gain or loss on the receivables sold.

EXHIBIT 11-2. ALCAN
Analysis of Take-or-Pay Contracts

A. Footnote: Commitments and Contingencies

To ensure long-term supplies of bauxite and access to alumina and fabricating facilities, Alcan participates in several long-term cost sharing arrangements with related companies. Alcan's fixed and determinable commitments, which comprise long-term debt service and "take-or-pay" obligations are estimated at $115 in 1995, $95 in 1996, $155 in 1997, $91 in 1998, $91 in 1999, and $222 thereafter. Total charges from these related companies were $132 in 1994, $280 in 1993, and $309 in 1992. In addition, there are guarantees for the repayment of approximately $23 of indebtedness by related companies. Alcan believes that none of these guarantees is likely to be invoked. Commitments with third parties for supplies of other inputs are estimated at $44 in 1995, $17 in 1996, $12 in 1997, $33 in 1998, $30 in 1999, and $189 thereafter. Total fixed charges from these third parties were $44 in 1994, $28 in 1993, and $35 in 1992.

Minimum rental obligations are estimated at $48 in 1995, $40 in 1996, $24 in 1997, $21 in 1998, $20 in 1999, and $57 thereafter. Total rental expenses amounted to $94 in 1994, $112 in 1993, and $114 in 1992.

B. Analysis: Fixed and Determinable Payments, 1995 to 1999 and Beyond
(in $ millions)

	Long-Term Debt Service and Take-or-Pay Obligations	To Third Parties
1995	$115	$ 44
1996	95	17
1997	155	12
1998	91	33
1999	91	30
Thereafter	222	189

Using the technique for capitalizing operating leases discussed earlier in the chapter, these payment streams can be discounted to their present value. Estimated payments continue after 1999 (using, for simplifying purposes, the constant rate assumption) for

$$\frac{\$222 \text{ million}}{\$91 \text{ million}} = 2.45 \text{ years}, \qquad \frac{\$189 \text{ million}}{\$30 \text{ million}} = 6.3 \text{ years}$$

Given these payment streams, the present values can be estimated using an estimated cost of debt (based on capitalized lease disclosures or other long-term debt). For Alcan, we estimate an interest rate of 9%. When applied to the minimum payments shown above, the resulting present value equals $553 million for long-term debt service and take-or-pay obligations and $197 million for the obligations to third parties. The total of $750 million should be used to adjust Alcan's property and total debt.

Source: Alcan, *1994 Annual Report.*

the receivables. Some arrangements are revolving in nature as collected receivables are periodically replaced by new ones.

Such transactions are generally recorded as sales under U.S. GAAP.[12] The sale

[12]SFAS 77, Reporting by Transferors for Transfers of Receivables with Recourse (1983), permits sales treatment when the risks and rewards have been substantially transferred to the buyer, even when the buyer has limited recourse to the seller for nonpayment. The primary requirement is that the recourse obligation (probability of nonpayment) can be estimated, permitting the seller to provide an adequate reserve for bad debts.

decreases accounts receivable, increasing cash from operations. However, most sales of receivables provide that the buyer has *limited recourse* in the event some customers do not pay. As the recourse provision is generally well above the expected loss ratio on the receivables, the seller retains the entire expected loss experience. These transactions are therefore effectively collateralized borrowings with the receivables serving as collateral. Sales of receivables are another form of off-balance-sheet financing and should be adjusted as follows:

- Both accounts receivable and current liabilities should be increased by the amount of receivables sold that have not yet been collected.

BOX 11-3
SFAS 125, Accounting for Transfers and Servicing of Financial Assets and Extinguishments of Liabilities

This statement contains accounting and reporting standards for transfers and servicing of financial assets and extinguishments of liabilities. It supersedes SFAS 77, Reporting by Transferors for Transfers of Receivables with Recourse (FASB, 1983), and SFAS 76, Extinguishment of Debt (FASB, 1983). It is effective for transactions occurring after December 31, 1996. It must be applied prospectively and early or retroactive application is prohibited.

SFAS 77 allowed sales treatment for transfers of receivables when the risks and rewards were substantially transferred to the buyer, even when the buyer retained "limited recourse" to the seller for noncollection.*

Transfers of financial assets have become considerably more complex since the issuance of SFAS 77. Sales treatment for transfers where the transferor has no continuing involvement with either the transferred asset or the transferee creates no accounting or analytic problems. However, SFAS 77 did not provide adequate guidance for transfers with continuing involvement (e.g., recourse, servicing, agreements to repurchase, options written or held, and pledges of collateral).

Under SFAS 125, transfers of financial assets (primarily securitizations) in which the transferor surrenders control† over the assets must be reported as sales to the extent that consideration other than beneficial interests in those assets is received in exchange. Transfers not meeting these criteria must be reported as secured borrowings with a pledge of collateral.

However, SFAS 125 does not continue the disclosure requirements of SFAS 77. As a result, some firms may no longer report data about receivables sold. Financial statement users will need to watch for clues regarding such sales and request the information needed for the required adjustments.

SFAS 125 also supersedes SFAS 76, allowing derecognition of liabilities only when the debtor pays the creditor and is legally released from being the primary obligor for the liability.

The standard also amends SFAS 115, Accounting for Certain Investments in Debt and Equity Securities, to prohibit the classification of debt securities in the held-to-maturity portfolio if it can be prepaid or settled in an amount less than the carrying amount of the investment. Reclassifications of qualifying held-to-maturity debt securities due to this amendment will not prejudice a company's intent to hold other debt securities to maturity. See Chapter 13 for a further discussion of SFAS 115.

---

*The primary requirement is the ability to estimate the recourse obligation, enabling the accrual of an adequate reserve for bad debts.

†Surrender of control criteria are very stringent and essentially legalistic. They are designed to ensure that the transferor is legally unable to benefit from the transferred assets. See para. 9(a)–(c).

• CFO must be adjusted; the increase in uncollected amount should be classified as cash from financing rather than CFO. SFAS 125, Accounting for Transfers and Servicing of Financial Assets and Extinguishment of Liabilities (1996), confirmed the current accounting treatment of receivable sales. Box 11-3 summarizes the financial reporting requirements of this standard.

■ Example: AMR and Delta Airlines

Exhibit 11-3 presents excerpts from the financial statements and footnotes of AMR and Delta Airlines describing their sales of receivables. AMR has engaged in sales of receivables since 1991 and reported a balance of $300 million of outstanding uncollected receivables in 1992 and 1993, with a decline to $112 million in 1994.

Delta sold $489 million of accounts receivable in 1994 and received two notes (one for $300 million and the other for $189 million) in return. The $300 million note was sold for cash; the $189 million note (the effective recourse obligation) remains on Delta's balance sheet as accounts receivable. The Delta sale is slightly more complex than AMR's as Delta sold receivables to one party and received cash from another. Nonetheless, the effects of the transaction and the required adjustments are similar.

Balance Sheet. Both companies report an allowance for doubtful accounts that includes estimated losses on the receivables sold. Delta states explicitly, "the Company has substantially the same credit risk as if the receivables had not been sold." The sale proceeds should therefore not be viewed as a reduction of accounts receivable, but rather as an increase in (short-term) borrowing. Delta's 1994 accounts receivable and current liabilities should both be increased by $300 million. AMR's 1994 (1993) accounts receivable and current liabilities should be increased by $112 ($300) million.

Adjustments to Balance Sheet for Sales of Receivables

	Increase Accounts Receivable and Current Liabilities by			
	AMR		DELTA	
	$112 in 1994 and $300 in 1993		$300 in 1994	
Adjusted Data	1994	1993	1994	1993
Cash and short-term investments	$ 777	$ 586	$1,710	$1,180
Accounts receivable, net of allowance	1,318	1,210	1,186	1,055
Quick assets	$2,095	$1,796	$2,896	$2,235
Current liabilities	$5,026	$4,717	$3,836	$3,019

Cash Flow Classification. Accounting for these transactions as sales distorts the amount and timing of CFO as the firm receives cash earlier than if the receiv-

EXHIBIT 11-3. AMR AND DELTA
Sale of Receivables

Excerpts from Footnotes and Balance Sheet

	AMR		DELTA	
	1994	1993	1994	1993
Cash and short-term investments	$ 777	$ 586	$1,710	$1,180
Accounts receivable, net	1,206	910	886	1,055
"Quick assets"	$1,983	$1,496	$2,596	$2,235
Current liabilities	4,914	4,417	3,536	3,019
Cash from operations	$1,609	$1,377	$1,324	$ 677

From AMR's 1994 Annual Report

Commitment and Contingencies Footnote

In July 1991, American entered into a five-year agreement whereby American transfers, on a continuing basis and with recourse to the receivables, an undivided interest in a designated pool of receivables. Undivided interests in new receivables are transferred daily as collections reduce previously transferred receivables. At December 1994 and 1993, receivables are presented net of approximately $112 million and $300 million, respectively, of such transferred receivables. American maintains an allowance for uncollectible receivables based upon expected collectability of all receivables, including the receivables transferred.

From AMR's 1993 Annual Report

Commitment and Contingencies Footnote

. . . At December 1993 and 1992, receivables are presented net of approximately $300 million of such transferred receivables. . . .

From Delta's 1994 Annual Report

Sale of Receivables Footnote

On June 24, 1994, Delta entered into a revolving accounts receivable facility (Facility) providing for the sale of $489 million of a defined pool of accounts receivable (Receivables) through a wholly-owned subsidiary to a trust in exchange for a senior certificate in the principal amount of $300 million (Senior Certificate) and a subordinate certificate in the principal amount of $189 million (Subordinate Certificate). The subsidiary retained the Subordinate Certificate and the Company received $300 million in cash from the sale of the Senior Certificate to a third party. The principal amount of the Subordinate Certificate fluctuates daily depending upon the volume of receivables sold, and is payable to the subsidiary only to the extent the collections received on the Receivables exceed amounts due on the Senior Certificate. The Facility, which replaced an interim facility established in March 1994, is scheduled to terminate in July 1995, subject to earlier termination in certain circumstances

At June 30, 1994, the $300 million net proceeds from the sale were reported as operating cash flows in the Company's Consolidated Statements of Cash Flows and as a reduction in accounts receivable on the Company's Consolidated Balance Sheets. The Subordinate Certificate is included in accounts receivable on the Company's Consolidated Balance Sheets. The full amount of the allowance for doubtful accounts related to the receivables sold has been retained, as the Company has substantially the same credit risk as if the receivables had not been sold.

Source: AMR and Delta, 1993–1994 Annual Reports.

ables had been collected in due course. An adjustment is required that reclassifies *the change in the uncollected receivables sold*[13] from CFO to cash from financing.

If the balance of uncollected receivables stays the same each year, there is no distortion. Any variation, however, affects the year-to-year comparison of cash flows.

Delta's footnote points out the $300 million increase in cash from operations in 1994. This amount should be transferred from CFO to cash from financing. For AMR, there is no adjustment required for 1993 as the uncollected receivables were $300 million in both 1992 and 1993. In 1994, the uncollected receivables decreased by $188 million. Thus, *1994 CFO is understated* by this amount as AMR reported this cash as part of CFO in earlier years.

Adjusting CFO for Sale of Receivables

	Deduct (Add) Net Proceeds from (to) CFO			
	AMR		DELTA	
	$188 in 1994		$300 in 1994	
	1994	1993	1994	1993
Cash from operations	$1,797	$1,377	$1,024	$677

Effects of Adjustments. The effects of these adjustments can be demonstrated using selected data.

Comparison of Selected Data

	As Reported (%)		After Adjustment (%)	
	AMR	DELTA	AMR	DELTA
% Change in receivables, 1994	32.3	(16.0)	8.9	12.4
Quick ratio (%)	40.3	73.4	41.7	75.5
% Change in CFO, 1994	16.8	95.6	30.5	51.2
CFO/current liabilities				
1994	32.7	37.4	35.8	26.7
1993	31.2	22.4	29.2	22.4

AMR's reported accounts receivable increased 32.3% in 1994 (from $910 to $1,206 million), whereas Delta's decreased by 16% (from $1,055 to $886 million). Given their similar revenue increase, the difference is notable. However, after adjustment for receivables sold, the percentage change in receivables is quite similar; Delta's receivables increased by approximately 12% and AMR's by 9%.

---

[13] In Chapter 3, it was shown that the change in accounts receivable is an adjustment to net income when deriving CFO. Because the uncollected balance of the receivables sold must be added to the reported balance of accounts receivable, calculation of the adjusted CFO requires exclusion of any change in the balance of uncollected receivables sold.

With respect to CFO, the adjustment procedure has a similar effect. For Delta, reported CFO nearly doubled, showing an increase of 95.6%, whereas AMR reported an increase of only 16.8%. When the effects of the transfers of receivables are removed, we find that the increase in CFO was a more modest 51% for Delta and a more comparable 30.5% for AMR.

Finally, Delta's reported CFO/current liabilties (liquidity) ratio improved by 50%, from 22.4% in 1993 to 37.4% in 1994; AMR's reported ratio remained basically unchanged at about 31 to 32%.[14] After adjustment for receivables sold, Delta's 1994 ratio of 26.7% was closer to its 1993 level; AMR's ratio also rose, from 29.2 to 35.8%.

The upward adjustment to receivables and short-term debt for receivables sold decreases the firm's accounts receivable turnover (increased A/R) and leverage ratios (increased debt). It may also reduce reported short-term liquidity. Similarly, when the level of sold receivables increases (the uncollected receivables rise), the adjustment reduces CFO and its related ratios. Interestingly, in this example, as the quick ratio is less than 1 for both companies, the adjustment increases that ratio as the same amount was added to both the numerator and denominator. ■

Finance Subsidiaries

Many firms have long used legally separate (but wholly owned) finance subsidiaries to borrow funds to finance parent company receivables. Such debt is often lower-cost than general-purpose borrowings because of the well-defined collateral. Finance subsidiaries enable the parent to generate sales by granting credit to dealers and customers for purchases of its goods and services.

Until 1987, most firms used the equity method to account for finance subsidiaries; the consolidated balance sheet reported only the parent's net investment, suppressing the debt used to finance the receivables. As shown by Livnat and Sondhi (1986), the exclusion of subsidiary debt allowed firms to report higher coverage and lower leverage ratios, stabilized reported debt and debt ratios over time, and reduced the probability of a technical violation of bond covenants.

Heian and Thies (1989) identified 182 companies (in 35 industry groups) reporting unconsolidated finance subsidiaries in 1985. Supplementary disclosures provided by 140 of these companies indicated a total of $205 billion in subsidiary debt that had not been reported on the parent's balance sheet. The authors also computed debt-to-capital ratios on the basis of *pro forma* consolidation and compared them to the preconsolidation ratios; the average increase in the ratio for the sample was 34%, but nearly 90% for the firms with the 21 largest finance units.

The FASB eliminated the nonconsolidation option (SFAS 94)—and all firms must now consolidate the assets and liabilities of controlled financial subsidiaries. Some parent firms have reduced their ownership of finance subsidiaries below 50% and account for these units using the equity method (discussed in Chapter 13). The balance sheet reports the firm's net investment in the subsidiary and the parent's income (and equity) includes its proportionate share of the subsidiary's income (and equity).

Because the net investment in the finance subsidiary reflects the parent's proportionate share of the assets minus the liabilities of the subsidiary, the parent's financial statements do not report its share of the debt of its finance subsidiary. However, from

---

[14]The CFO/current liabilities ratio is affected by adjustments to both the numerator and denominator.

EXHIBIT 11-4. GEORGIA-PACIFIC
Joint Venture Financing

Note 11: Related Party Transactions

The Corporation is a 50% partner in a joint venture (GA-MET) with Metropolitan Life Insurance Company (Metropolitan). GA-MET owns and operates the Corporation's office headquarters complex in Atlanta, Georgia. The Corporation accounts for its investment in GA-MET under the equity method.

At December 31, 1994, GA-MET had an outstanding mortgage loan payable to Metropolitan in the amount of $158 million. The note bears interest at 9½%, requires monthly payments of principal and interest through 2011 and is secured by the land and building of the Atlanta headquarters complex. In the event of foreclosure, each partner has severally guaranteed payment of one-half of any shortfall of collateral value to the outstanding secured indebtedness. Based on the present market conditions and building occupancy, the likelihood of any obligation to the Corporation with respect to this guarantee is considered remote.

Source: Georgia-Pacific, *1994 Annual Report.*

an overall economic entity (parent firm plus share in the affiliate) perspective, the debt of finance subsidiaries should be considered explicitly because it is clearly required to maintain the parent's operations. Additionally, the parent firm generally supports finance subsidiary borrowings through extensive income maintenance agreements and direct or indirect guarantees of debt.

The analyst should compute (proportionately) consolidated debt-to-equity, receivables turnover, and interest coverage ratios. This requires the addition of the parent's proportionate share of the assets and liabilities of the finance subsidiary to the assets and liabilities of the parent.[15]

The information required for these adjustments to reported receivables and debt, and the turnover, interest coverage, and leverage ratios can be obtained from the footnotes, which may disclose the assets, liabilities, and results of operations of finance subsidiaries in a summarized format.[16]

Joint Ventures and Investment in Affiliates

Firms may acquire manufacturing and distribution capacity through investments in affiliated firms, including suppliers and end users. Joint ventures with other firms may offer economies of scale and provide opportunities to share operating, technological, and financial risks. To obtain financing for the venture, the investors often enter into take-or-pay or throughput contracts with minimum payments designed to meet the venture's debt service requirements. Direct or indirect guarantees of the joint venture debt may also be present.

Exhibit 11-4 contains an excerpt from the footnote on commitments and contingencies in the *1994 Annual Report* issued by Georgia Pacific (GP). It discloses a joint venture with Metropolitan Life. GP is clearly liable for one-half of this off-balance-sheet debt, and $79 million should be added to GP's (property and) debt.

---

[15]The net investment in affiliates must be eliminated against the equity accounts. See Chapter 13 for a discussion of the proportionate consolidation accounting method.

[16]When the finance subsidiary issues publicly traded debt, then full financial statements are available and can be used for more accurate adjustments.

In the GP example, the parent explicitly guaranteed the debt of the affiliate. Even in the absence of such guarantees, the proportionate share of the affiliate's debt should be added to the reported debt of the investor. Generally, firms account for their investments in joint ventures and affiliates (where they have 20 to 50% ownership) using the equity method. These adjustments will be illustrated shortly in the analysis of Ashland Oil and Exhibits 11-7 and 11-8. Case 11-1 examines Texaco and its 50% owned affiliate, Caltex, to explore the use of off-balance-sheet activities in a more complex setting.

Other Off-Balance-Sheet Activities

The activities discussed to this point are those most commonly found. However, given volatile economic conditions faced by some firms, other off-balance-sheet techniques are sometimes observed. Two such activities are illustrated in this section. They are reminders of the need to be alert when reviewing firm disclosures as new techniques are always being invented.

Commodity-Linked Bonds

Natural resource firms may finance operations with commodity-indexed debt, with interest and/or principal repayments that depend on the price of underlying commodities. Changing commodity prices should be monitored to determine their impact on the related debt and debt-to-equity ratios. Exhibit 11-5 contains one such disclosure.

The LAC bonds were denominated in Swiss francs and exchangeable for a specified amount of gold. As the firm is a gold producer, these bonds can be viewed as a hedge. If the price of gold rose, bondholders would take gold (which would have a higher value than the face amount of the bonds). This loss (LAC would have less gold to sell at higher prices) would partly offset the earnings gain from the higher gold price. If the price of gold remains low, LAC benefits from the low stated interest rate on the bonds (which investors accept because of the imbedded option to convert to gold). Issuing these bonds, therefore, reduces the sensitivity of reported earnings to the price of gold.

In 1991, LAC retired most of the bonds four years prior to maturity, taking advantage of the low price of gold at that time. The company recognized a small gain from that retirement and increased its sensitivity to future changes in the price of gold.

When the issuer can force conversion or redemption, or when economic conditions suggest that the holder would benefit from conversion or redemption, the analyst should compute the potential gain or loss to the issuer assuming conversion. If, for

---

EXHIBIT 11-5. LAC MINERALS
Commodity-Linked Bonds

Swiss franc 14,505,000 (1990—92,035,000) gold equivalent convertible bonds, due November 1995, bearing interest at 4 percent. Each Swiss franc 5,000 bond entitles the holder to exchange it at any time for the cash equivalent in U.S. dollars of 6.835 troy ounces of gold, based on the market price of gold on the day of the investor election. During the year, the Company made an offer to the bond holders to acquire all bonds outstanding at a discount to the par value of the bonds. Pursuant to this offer, the company retired Swiss franc 77,530,000 bonds for cash consideration totalling $44,685,000 and recorded a gain on retirement of $2.8 million.

Source: LAC Minerals, *1991 Annual Report.*

EXHIBIT 11-6. PANHANDLE EASTERN
Exchangeable Bonds

In May 1985, Panhandle issued $105,750,000 of 12% subordinated debentures due 2010 which were exchangeable for 3,000,000 shares of common stock of Quantum Chemical Corporation owned by Panhandle. At December 31, 1987, $104,623,000 principal amount of the debentures were outstanding and were exchangeable for 2,968,036 shares of the Quantum stock. Beginning May 1, 1988, these debentures are callable by Panhandle upon not less than thirty days' notice at 108.4% of face amount unless exchanged prior to the redemption date.

Source: Panhandle Eastern, *1987 Annual Report.*

example, the price of gold rises, Lac's debt should be valued at the conversion value and not its face.

Bonds Tied to Investments

Some firms issue long-term debt exchangeable (at the option of the bondholder) for the common stock of another publicly traded firm held as an investment. Motives for these transactions include lower borrowing costs, the deferral of capital gains tax liability, tax benefits related to the low corporate tax rates on dividends to corporations in the United States, and the desire to maintain an investment while having the use of cash. Exhibit 11-6 describes an exchangeable bond issued by Panhandle Eastern.

When the bonds were originally issued by Panhandle, it obtained $105 million of cash while maintaining its strategic investment in Quantum Chemical. Because of the low cost of the stock investment ($7.42 million), the bond sale allowed Panhandle to defer the capital gains tax on the unrealized gain of $98.33 million ($105.75 million − $7.42 million). In 1988, at the time of Panhandle's choosing, the bonds were called, forcing an exchange of the bonds for the Quantum Chemical shares. Possible reasons for the call were the desire to recognize the capital gain for both tax purposes (corporate capital gains taxes had been reduced) and financial reporting purposes. The decline in corporate tax rates had also made the tax deduction for interest expense less valuable.

As in the case of commodity-linked bonds, conversion should be assumed when it can be forced by the issuer or when it is advantageous to holders. The conversion assumption depends on the terms of the issue, as disclosed in the issuer's footnotes. Leverage, interest coverage, and profitability ratios should then be adjusted.

ANALYSIS OF OBS ACTIVITIES: ASHLAND OIL

Ashland Oil is a major refiner, marketer, and distributor of oil whose other interests include coal (through a 50% interest in Arch Mineral and a 39% ownership of Ashland Coal in 1994) and natural gas. Ashland Oil's distribution system includes interests of 18.6 to 20.4% in LOOP and LOCAP, joint ventures operating deepwater offshore port and pipeline facilities. Exhibit 11-7 contains excerpts from footnotes to Ashland Oil's 1994 financial statements. The footnotes disclose that firm's unconsolidated subsidiaries, leases, and commitments and contingencies.

Exhibit 11-8 provides an illustration of the adjustments for off-balance-sheet financing activities discussed in this chapter. Ashland's reported debt is adjusted for (the present value of) operating leases, debt of equity method subsidiaries, and its

EXHIBIT 11-7. ASHLAND OIL, INC.
Off-Balance-Sheet Activities

Excerpts from 1994 Notes to Financial Statements

Note D: Unconsolidated Affiliates

Affiliated companies accounted for under the equity method include: Arch Mineral Corporation (a 50% owned coal company); Ashland Coal, Inc. (a 39% owned publicly traded coal company); LOOP INC. and LOCAP INC. (18.6% and 21.4% owned corporate joint ventures operating a deepwater offshore port and related pipeline facilities in the Gulf of Mexico); and various other companies. Summarized financial information reported by these affiliates and a summary of the amounts recorded in Ashland's consolidated financial statements follow.

($ in millions)	Arch Mineral Corporation	Ashland Coal, Inc.	LOOP INC. and LOCAP INC.	Other	Total
September 30, 1994					
Financial position					
Current assets	$ 173	$ 119	$ 36	$ 204	
Current liabilities	(132)	(110)	(86)	(123)	
Working capital	41	9	(50)	81	
Noncurrent assets	797	721	638	203	
Noncurrent liabilities	(713)	(373)	(525)	(96)	
Stockholders' equity	$ 125	$ 357	$ 63	$ 188	
Results of operations					
Sales and operating revenues	$ 641	$ 561	$ 149	$ 701	
Gross profit	60	71	54	172	
Net income	14	17	15	14	
Amounts recorded by Ashland					
Investments and advances	70	138	12	71	$291
Equity income	7	6	3	6	22
Dividends received	—	3	—	5	8

Note G: Leases and Other Commitments

Leases

Ashland and its subsidiaries are lessees in noncancelable leasing agreements for office buildings, warehouses, pipelines, transportation and marine equipment, storage facilities, retail outlets, manufacturing facilities and other equipment and properties which expire at various dates. Capitalized lease obligations are not significant and are included in long-term debt. Future minimum rental payments at September 30, 1994, and rental expense under operating leases follow.

($ in millions)

Future Minimum Rental Payments		Rental Expense	1994	1993	1992
1995	$ 63				
1996	50	Minimum rentals			
1997	41	(including rentals under			
1998	40	short-term leases)	$113	$111	$104
1999	35	Contingent rentals	12	11	12
Later years	222	Sublease rental income	(12)	(17)	(13)
	$451		$113	$105	$103

EXHIBIT 11-7. (*continued*)

Other Commitments

Under agreements with LOOP and LOCAP (see Note D), Ashland is committed to advance funds against future transportation charges if these corporate joint ventures are unable to meet their cash requirements. Such advances are limited to Ashland's share, based on its equity interests, of the total debt service and defined operating and administrative costs of these companies. Such advances, however, are reduced by (1) transportation charges Ashland paid, (2) a pro rata portion of transportation charges paid by other equity participants in excess of their required amounts, and (3) a pro rata portion of transportation charges paid by third parties who are not equity participants. At September 30, 1994, all advances made to LOOP and LOCAP by Ashland had been applied against transportation charges. Transportation charges incurred amounted to $24 million in 1994, $22 million in 1993 and $25 million in 1992. At September 30, 1994, Ashland's contingent liability for its share of the indebtedness of LOOP and LOCAP secured by throughput and deficiency agreements amounted to approximately $100 million.

Ashland is contingently liable under guarantees of certain debt and lease obligations of Ashland Coal, Inc., an unconsolidated affiliate. At September 30, 1994, such obligations have a present value of approximately $16 million. Ashland is also contingently liable for up to $16 million of borrowings under a revolving credit agreement of AECOM Technology Corporation, an unconsolidated affiliate. Ashland's guaranteed portion of outstanding borrowings under this agreement amounted to $9 million at September 30, 1994.

Source: Ashland Oil, *1994 Annual Report.*

contingent obligation for the debt of these units. The result is a more comprehensive measure of the firm's leverage.

Also given in Exhibit 11-8 are the reported and adjusted leverage data for Ashland for the period 1990 to 1993, in addition to 1994. Data for previous years are provided for comparison purposes as the footnote disclosures in Exhibit 11-7 are insufficient to adjust for those years.

Adjustments to 1994 Debt. Since Ashland Oil owns 50% of Arch Minerals and 39% of Ashland Coal, proportionate amounts (0.50 × $713 and 0.39 × $373) of noncurrent liabilities of those two units were added to its reported debt. Current liabilities may include financing obligations, but they are excluded as no disclosures were provided. Similarly, we use 20% (the average percentage) of LOOP (18.6%) and LOCAP's (20.4%) noncurrent liabilities giving a share of debt of (0.2 × $525) $105. As the footnote does not disclose Ashland's percentage of ownership of its other affiliates, we have approximated the share using the ratio of $71 recorded as its investments and advances in these other affiliates to the reported total equity of $188, implying an average ownership of ($71/$188) 38% and a proportionate share of debt of (0.38 × $96) $36 million.

The contingent liability for the debt of LOOP, LOCAP, Ashland Coal, and AECOM Technology (discussed in the section entitled "Other Committments") is not added in separately because it has already been included in the adjustments made for Ashland's share of the debt of its affiliates.

The capitalization of operating leases is straightforward in 1990 to 1992. However, capital leases declined substantially in 1993 and are not separately reported in 1994. The implicit interest rate in the 1993 capital leases is 15.5%, significantly higher than the firm's indicated cost of debt (ranging from 7.7 to 8.4%) at any time over the 1990 to 1994 period. We have used 8.5%, the rate implicit in the 1992 disclosures.

Adjusted debt is 54% higher than reported debt in 1994 and 53% higher on average over the five-year period analyzed. Similar patterns emerge for the adjusted debt-to-

EXHIBIT 11-8. ASHLAND OIL, INC.
Adjusted Long-Term Debt and Solvency Analysis and Adjusted Capitalization

	($ in millions)					
	9/30/90	9/30/91	9/30/92	9/30/93	9/30/94	Average
Short-term debt	170	196	306	159	**133**	193
Long-term debt	1,180	1,289	1,403	1,398	**1,391**	1,332
Capitalized leases	55	48	41	1	—	29
Insurance reserves*	118	141	159	173	**173**	153
Total debt	1,523	1,673	1,910	1,731	**1,697**	1,707
Preferred Shares	—	—	—	293	**293**	117
Common equity†	1,364	1,515	1,137	1,211	**1,346**	1,315
Stockholders' equity (BV)	1,364	1,515	1,137	1,504	**1,639**	1,432
Total capital (BV)	2,886	3,188	3,047	3,235	**3,336**	3,139
Stockholders' equity (MV)‡	1,777	1,819	1,491	2,347	**2,504**	1,988
Total capital (MV)	3,300	3,492	3,401	4,079	**4,201**	3,694
Adjustments to debt						
50% of Arch Mineral's non-current liabilities	217	206	283	318	**357**	276
Ashland Coal's liabilities and redeemable preferred	124	132	264	177	**145**	168
LOOP and LOCAP debt	123	124	119	114	**105**	117
Other noncurrent liabilities	59	57	47	37	**36**	47
Capitalization of operating leases§	260	275	297	311	**296**	288
Adj. total debt	2,305	2,467	2,919	2,688	**2,636**	2,603
Adj. total capital (BV)	3,669	3,983	4,057	4,192	**4,275**	4,035
Adj. total capital (MV)	4,083	4,286	4,410	5,036	**5,140**	4,591
Debt						
To equity (BV)	1.12	1.10	1.68	1.15	**1.04**	1.19
To capital (BV)	0.53	0.52	0.63	0.54	**0.51**	0.54
Debt						
To equity (MV)	0.86	0.92	1.28	0.74	**0.68**	0.86
To capital (MV)	0.46	0.48	0.56	0.42	**0.40**	0.46
Adj. debt						
To equity (BV)	1.69	1.63	2.57	1.79	**1.61**	1.82
To adj. capital (BV)	0.63	0.62	0.72	0.64	**0.62**	0.65
Adj. debt						
To equity (MV)	1.30	1.36	1.96	1.15	**1.05**	1.31
To adj. capital (MV)	0.56	0.58	0.66	0.53	**0.51**	0.57

Footnotes (applicable to 1994 computations):
*Reflects obligations of captive insurance companies.
†Includes common stock, paid-in-capital, and retained earnings.
‡Includes equity at market value based on number of shares outstanding at year-end and market price on September 30, 1994 and the common stock equivalent (at market value) of the convertible preferred stock.
§From Note G, Present Value of Future Rental Payments Under Operating Lease. See text for an explanation of the discount rate used.

equity and debt-to-capital ratios (at both book and market values of equity) as they are significantly higher than reported ratios. Reported debt has declined relative to the level reached in 1992 and the average over time. Adjusted debt is also lower compared to the 1992 level but it is slightly higher than the average, although both have declined relative to the 1992 and five-year average ratios.

Exhibit 11-8 shows that both reported and adjusted leverage reached a peak in 1992 and since that time Ashland has been able to significantly reduce the amount of leverage in its capital structure. The 1993 improvement resulted from Ashland's issuance of preferred shares, which increased equity. Additionally, the issuance proceeds were used to reduce outstanding debt in 1993. The lower cost of the preferred issue was due to its conversion feature and the tax advantage (to corporate investors) of the 80% dividend exclusion.

INTERNATIONAL ACCOUNTING AND REPORTING PRACTICES

Lease Accounting Outside the United States

U.S. financial reporting standards for leases are the most detailed and comprehensive in the world. Lessee and lessor reporting standards in Canada, the Netherlands, and the United Kingdom are similar to those in the United States, but they are more general, and disclosure requirements are substantially poorer.

International Accounting Standards are representative; IAS 17 requires capitalization when substantially all the risks and rewards of ownership are transferred, based on four criteria similar to those used in the United States.[17] However, capitalization is required:

1. When the lease term is for a major portion of the asset's life; it does not specify 75% as in the United States.
2. The present value of the MLPs is equal to or greater than the fair value of the asset, unlike the 90% test specified in the United States.

Capitalization is less likely under these two criteria than under U.S. standards. The two standards also have significant differences with respect to the interest rate used to capitalize leases, treatment of sublease and contingent rentals, and the reporting of sale leasebacks. Finally, disclosure requirements in the United States are substantially more comprehensive. The paucity of disclosures in IAS 17 makes it difficult to capitalize the more numerous operating leases.

In Germany and Japan, lease capitalization is uncommon since lease accounting follows tax rules. In Germany, capitalization is required when the basic lease term is less than 40% or more than 90% of the economic life and/or bargain purchase and renewal options exist; the present value of minimum lease payments criterion is not used. Few countries provide detailed criteria for lessor capitalization or financial reporting standards for sale leasebacks, real estate, and leveraged leases. Sale leasebacks result in higher profits than allowed in the United States and should be analyzed with care.

As discussed earlier, U.S. GAAP footnote disclosures of lease payments can be used to capitalize operating leases and develop adjusted ratios. Footnote disclosures

[17]In 1996, the IASC started a project to reconsider IAS 17.

provided by foreign firms are rarely adequate to permit capitalization and other adjustments.

For example, in its Form 20-F for 1990, Beazer discloses that profit on a sale leaseback was £6.6 million, accounting for nearly 10% of net income before extraordinary items under U.K. GAAP. A footnote states that, under U.S. GAAP, this gain would be deferred and recognized only over the life of the lease. No further disclosures are made regarding leases.

As non-U.S. financial statements generally lack detailed lease data, the analyst must look for indirect disclosures or question management regarding lessee or lessor activities. To the extent that non-U.S. firms engage in other off-balance-sheet activities, the problems with respect to lack of detailed disclosures are further magnified. The analyst is forced to go to secondary sources or question management to receive any information at all.

SUMMARY

Financial liabilities can take many forms, from simple, full-coupon debt to leasing and other more esoteric forms of off-balance-sheet activities. This chapter and the previous one illustrated the far-reaching effects of such transactions on a firm's income, cash flow, and capital structure.

The discussion and analysis are as yet not complete. Chapter 12 contains an analysis of employee benefit plans, an important form of off-balance-sheet financing. Hedging activities are covered in Chapter 16. Many of these strands are brought together in Chapter 17 that provides a detailed summary of the effects of various forms of debt financing.

CASE 11-1

Off-Balance-Sheet Financing Techniques for Texaco and Caltex

Texaco is a worldwide oil and gas firm, with 1994 revenues of approximately $33 billion. Caltex is a joint venture between Texaco and Chevron (another oil multinational); each partner owns 50%.

The objective of the case is the analysis of the off-balance-sheet financing activities of both Texaco and its affiliates, and the adjustments to reported financial statements required to reflect these activities.

Exhibit 11C-1 contains the 1994 condensed balance sheet, income statement, and selected footnotes from Texaco's 1994 Annual Report. Exhibit 11C-2 includes the condensed balance sheet, income statement, and selected footnotes of Caltex as well as general information, all extracted from Texaco's 10-K report filed with the SEC.

1. a. Using the Texaco reported balance sheet and income statement (without any adjustments), prepare a capitalization table for the years ended December 31, 1993, and December 31, 1994.

   b. Compute the following ratios for both years:

   • Debt-to-equity

   • Return on assets (total assets at December 31, 1992 = $25,992 million)

   • Times interest earned

EXHIBIT 11C-1. TEXACO, INC.
Excerpts from Annual Report

Statement of Consolidated Income (Condensed) ($ in millions)

For the years ended December 31	1994	1993
Revenues		
Sales and services (includes transactions with significant affiliates of $2,561 in 1994 and $3,027 in 1993)	$32,540	$33,245
Equity in income of affiliates, income from dividends, interest, asset sales, and other	813	826
	$33,353	$34,071
Deductions		
Purchases and other costs (includes transactions with significant affiliates of $1,679 in 1994 and $1,709 in 1993)	$23,931	$24,667
Operating expense	3,069	3,086
Selling, general, and administrative expenses	1,679	1,783
Maintenance and repairs	390	418
Exploratory expenses	307	352
Depreciation, depletion, and amortization	1,735	1,568
Interest expense	498	459
Taxes other than income taxes	496	549
Minority interest	44	17
Total	$32,149	$32,899
Income from continuing operations	$1,204	$1,172
Provision for (benefit from) income taxes	225	(87)
Income from continuing operations	$ 979	$ 1,259

Consolidated Balance Sheet (Condensed)

December 31	1994	1993
Assets		
Current assets	$ 6,019	$ 6,865
Investments and advances	5,336	4,984
Net property, plant, and equipment	13,483	14,171
Deferred charges	667	606
Total assets	$25,505	$26,626
Liabilities and Owner's Equity		
Notes payable, commercial paper and current portion of long-term debt	$ 917	$ 669
Accounts payable and accrued liabilities	3,297	3,324
Taxes payable	801	763
Current liabilities	$ 5,015	$ 4,756
Long-term and capital lease obligations	$ 5,564	$ 6,157
Deferred income taxes	879	1,162
Other noncurrent liabilities	3,688	3,740
Minority interest	610	532
Total liabilities	$15,756	$16,347
Stockholders' equity	9,749	10,279
Total liabilities and equity	$25,505	$26,626

Source: Texaco, *1994 Annual Report.*

EXHIBIT 11C-1 (*continued*)

NOTE 6. INVESTMENTS AND ADVANCES

Investments in affiliates, including corporate joint ventures and partnerships, owned 50% or less are accounted for on the equity method. Texaco's total investments and advances are summarized as follows:

(Millions of dollars) As of December 31	1994	1993
Affiliates accounted for on the equity method		
Caltex group of companies		
Exploration and production	$ 494	$ 500
Manufacturing, marketing		
and distribution	1,873	1,647
Total Caltex group of companies	2,367	2,147
Star Enterprise	830	863
Other affiliates	709	731
	3,906	3,741
Miscellaneous investments, long-term receivables, etc., accounted for at		
Fair value	631	699
Cost, less reserve	799	544
Total	$5,336	$4,984

Texaco's equity in the net income of affiliates accounted for on the equity method, adjusted to reflect income taxes for partnerships whose income is directly taxable to Texaco, is as follows:

(Millions of dollars) For the years ended December 31	1994	1993	1992
Equity in net income			
Caltex group of companies			
Exploration and production	$136	$134	$154
Manufacturing, marketing			
and distribution	210	227	180
Total Caltex group of companies	346	361	334
Star Enterprise	37	61	7
Cumulative effect of accounting changes—Caltex and Star	—	—	(11)
Other affiliates	111	108	125
Total	$494	$530	$455
Dividends received from these companies	$467	$366	$351

2. a. Using the footnote data from Exhibit 11C-1, compute the appropriate adjustments to Texaco's debt for its off-balance-sheet obligations.
   b. Using the result of part (a), recompute the ratios in question 1(b).
   c. Discuss the significance of your results.

3. a. Using the Caltex reported balance sheet and income statement (without any adjustments), prepare a capitalization table for the year ended December 31, 1994.
   b. Compute the following ratios:

   • Debt-to-equity

   • Return on assets

   • Times interest earned

EXHIBIT 11C-1 (*continued*)

(Millions of dollars)	Caltex group			Star Enterprise			Other equity affiliates			Texaco's share		
	1994	1993	1992	1994	1993	1992	1994	1993	1992	1994	1993	1992
For the years ended December 31:												
Gross revenues	$15,148	$15,648	$17,527	$ 6,100	$ 6,399	$ 6,965	$ 3,058	$ 3,233	$ 2,891	$11,766	$12,224	$13,299
Income before income taxes and cumulative effect of accounting changes	$ 1,111	$ 1,178	$ 1,178	$ 101	$ 194	$ 29	$ 639	$ 633	$ 634	$ 780	$ 852	$ 781
Net income (loss)*	$ 689	$ 720	$ 720	$ 66	$ 126	$ (53)	$ 410	$ 406	$ 416	$ 494	$ 530	$ 455
As of December 31:												
Current assets	$ 2,421	$ 2,123	$ 2,378	$ 928	$ 1,015	$ 1,081	$ 641	$ 635	$ 675	$ 1,711	$ 1,637	$ 1,826
Noncurrent assets	7,389	6,266	5,485	3,247	3,188	3,097	3,351	3,481	3,464	6,453	5,888	5,463
Current liabilities	(3,072)	(2,411)	(2,453)	(748)	(647)	(717)	(759)	(755)	(774)	(2,213)	(1,835)	(1,862)
Noncurrent liabilities and deferred credits.....	(1,853)	(1,537)	(1,453)	(1,109)	(1,161)	(1,170)	(1,835)	(1,928)	(1,979)	(1,969)	(1,876)	(1,890)
Minority interest in subsidiary companies	(152)	(146)	(138)	—	—	—	—	—	—	(76)	(73)	(69)
Net assets (or partners' equity)**	$ 4,733	$ 4,295	$ 3,819	$ 2,318	$ 2,395	$ 2,291	$ 1,398	$ 1,433	$ 1,386	$ 3,906	$ 3,741	$ 3,468

*Net income (loss) for 1992 includes the cumulative effect of accounting changes. For the Caltex group, this represents an after-tax charge of $26 million for SFAS 106 and a benefit of $77 million for SFAS 109. For Star Enterprise, adoption of SFAS 106 resulted in an after-tax charge of $72 million.

**Net assets for the Caltex group includes the cumulative effect at January 1, 1994 of the adoption of SFAS 115, resulting in an increase in stockholders' equity of $70 million and an additional increase of $9 million during 1994.

NOTE 9. LEASE COMMITMENTS AND RENTAL EXPENSE

The company has leasing arrangements involving service stations, tanker charters, a manufacturing plant and other facilities. Amounts due under capital leases are reflected in the company's balance sheet as obligations, while Texaco's interest in the related assets is principally reflected as properties, plant and equipment. The remaining lease commitments are operating leases, and payments on such leases are recorded as rental expense.

As of December 31, 1994, Texaco Inc. and its subsidiary companies (excluding discontinued operations) had estimated minimum commitments for payment of rentals (net of noncancelable sublease rentals) under leases which, at inception, had a noncancelable term of more than one year, as follows:

(Millions of dollars)	Operating leases	Capital leases
1995...	$ 193	$ 46
1996...	128	38
1997...	564	21
1998...	72	19
1999...	52	20
After 1999...................................	415	88
Total lease commitments.......................	$1,424	232
Less amounts representing Executory costs		37
Interest		100
Add noncancelable sublease rentals netted in capital lease commitments above		54
Present value of total capital lease obligations		$149

Rental expense (excluding discontinued operations) relative to operating leases, including contingent rentals based on factors such as gallons sold, is provided in the table below. Such payments do not include rentals on leases covering oil and gas mineral rights.

(Millions of dollars)	1994	1993	1992
Rental expense			
Minimum lease rentals	$205	$238	$252
Contingent rentals	15	20	24
Total........................	220	258	276
Less rental income on properties subleased to others	40	36	36
Net rental expense................	$180	$222	$240

In 1992, Texaco as lessee entered into a five year agreement for the leasing of a chemical manufacturing plant to be constructed in Port Neches, Texas. As of December 31, 1994, construction was largely completed. The lease provides for a substantial residual value guarantee by the lessee at the termination of the lease. Both the lease payment amount and the residual value guarantee amount for this operating lease are included in the preceding table of minimum rental commitments.

NOTE 16. COMMITMENTS

Financial Guarantees

The company has guaranteed the payment of certain debt and other obligations of third parties and affiliates. These guarantees totaled $176 million and $154 million at December 31, 1994 and 1993, respectively.

Exposure to credit risk in the event of non-payment by the obligors is represented by the contractual amount of these instruments. No loss is anticipated under these guarantees.

Throughput Agreements

Texaco Inc. and certain of its subsidiary companies have entered into certain long-term agreements wherein they have committed either to ship through affiliated pipeline companies and an offshore oil port, or to refine at an affiliated refining company a sufficient volume of crude oil or petroleum products to enable these affiliated companies to meet a specified portion of their individual debt obligations, or, in lieu thereof, to advance sufficient funds to enable these affiliated companies to meet these obligations. Additionally, Texaco has entered into long-term purchase commitments with third parties for take or pay gas transportation. The company's maximum exposure to loss was $726 million and $765 million at December 31, 1994 and 1993, respectively.

However, based on Texaco's right of counterclaim against third parties in the event of nonperformance, Texaco's net exposure was approximately $561 million and $590 million at December 31, 1994 and 1993, respectively.

No losses are anticipated as a result of the above obligations.

EXHIBIT 11C-2. CALTEX GROUP OF COMPANIES
Excerpts from Annual Report

Consolidated Income Statement (Condensed)

	1994
Sales and other operating revenue	$14,751
Cost of sales and operating expenses	$12,801
Selling, general, and administrative expenses	568
Depreciation, depletion, and amortization	331
Maintenance and repairs	160
Total operating charges	$13,860
Operating income	891
Other income (Deductions)	
Equity in net income of nonsubsidiary companies	263
Dividends, interest, and other income	134
Foreign exchange, net	(73)
Interest expense	(101)
Minority interest in subsidiary companies	(3)
	$ 220
Income before provision for income taxes	$ 1,111
Provision for income taxes	422
Net income	$ 689

Consolidated Balance Sheet (Condensed)

	1994	1993
Assets		
Current assets	$2,421	$2,123
Investments and advances	2,370	1,796
Net property, plant, and equipment	4,612	4,038
Other	407	432
Total assets	$9,810	$8,389
Liabilities and Owner's Equity		
Notes payable, commercial paper and current portion of long-term debt	$1,386	$1,017
Accounts payable	1,440	1,203
Other	246	191
Current liabilities	$3,072	$2,411
Long-term debt and capital lease obligations	$ 715	$ 530
Deferred income taxes	236	263
Other noncurrent liabilities	902	744
Minority interest	152	146
Long-term liabilities	$2,005	$1,683
Stockholders' equity	4,733	4,295
Total liabilities and equity	$9,810	$8,389

EXHIBIT 11C-2 *(continued)*

4. Nonsubsidiary Companies at Equity

Investments in and advances to nonsubsidiary companies at equity at December 31 include the following ($ in millions):

	Equity Share	1994	1993
Nippon Petroleum Refining Company, Ltd.	50%	$ 997	$ 829
Koa Oil Company, Ltd.	50%	448	310
Honam Oil Refinery Company, Ltd.	50%	557	423
All other	Various	368	234
		$2,370	$1,796

Shown below is summarized combined financial information for these nonsubsidiary companies:

	100%		Equity Share	
	1994	1993	1994	1993
Current assets	$ 5,352	$ 4,680	$2,651	$2,316
Other assets	7,821	6,147	3,858	2,975
Current liabilities	4,940	4,900	2,363	2,349
Other liabilities	3,504	2,306	1,776	1,146
Net worth	4,729	3,621	2,370	1,796

	100%		Equity Share	
	1994	1993	1994	1993
Operating revenues	$10,886	$10,679	$5,418	$5,304
Operating income	770	494	381	242
Net income	526	281	263	140

Retained earnings at December 31, 1994, includes $1.4 billion representing the group's share of undistributed earnings of nonsubsidiary companies at equity.

Cash dividends received from these nonsubsidiary companies were $43 million, $37 million, and $30 million in 1994, 1993, and 1992, respectively.

Sales to the other 50 percent owner of Nippon Petroleum Refining Company, Ltd. of products refined by Nippon Petroleum Refining Company, Ltd. and Koa Oil Company, Ltd. were approximately $2 billion, $1.9 billion, and $2 billion in 1994, 1993, and 1992, respectively.

8. Operating Leases

The Group has various operating leases involving service stations, equipment and other facilities for which net rental expense was $121 million, $110 million, and $95 million in 1994, 1993, and 1992, respectively.

Future net minimum rental commitments under operating leases having noncancelable terms in excess of one year are as follows (in millions): 1995—$55; 1996—$67; 1997—$52; 1998—$47; 1999—$44; 2000 and thereafter—$106.

9. Commitments and Contingencies

. . . Unconditional purchase obligations in 1992 and 1993 were not considered material. However, in April 1994, a Group subsidiary entered into a contractual commitment, effective

EXHIBIT 11C-2 (*continued*)

October 1996, for a period of eleven years, to purchase refined products in conjunction with the financing of a refinery that is presently under construction by a nonsubsidiary company. Total future estimated commitments (in billions) for the Group under this and other similar contracts, based on current pricing and projected growth rates, are: 1995—$.6, 1996—$.9, 1997—$1.1, 1998—$1.3, 1999—$1.5, and 2000 to expiration of contracts—$9.6. Purchases (in billions) under similar contracts were $.5, $.6, and $.4 in 1994, 1993, and 1992, respectively. . . .

General Information

The Caltex Group of Companies (Group) is jointly owned 50% each by Chevron Corporation and Texaco Inc. The private joint venture was created in Bahrain in 1936 by its two owners to produce, transport, refine and market crude oil and refined products. The Group is comprised of the following companies:

- Caltex Petroleum Corporation, a company incorporated in Delaware, that through its many subsidiaries and affiliates, conducts refining, marketing and transporting activities in the Eastern Hemisphere;
- P. T. Caltex Pacific Indonesia, an exploration and production company incorporated and operating in Indonesia;
- American Overseas Petroleum Limited, a company incorporated in the Bahamas, that, through its subsidiaries, manages certain exploration and production operations in Indonesia in which Chevron and Texaco have interests, but not necessarily jointly or in the same properties.

Environmental Activities

The Group's activities are subject to environmental, health and safety regulations in each of the countries in which it operates. Such regulations vary significantly in degree of scope, standards and enforcement. The Group's policy is to comply with all applicable environmental, health and safety laws and regulations. The Group has an active program to ensure its environmental standards are maintained, which includes closely monitoring applicable statutory and regulatory requirements, as well as enforcement policies, in each of the countries in which it operates, and conducting periodic environmental compliance audits. At December 31, 1994, the Group had accrued $12 million for various remediation activities. The environmental guidelines and definitions promulgated by the American Petroleum Institute provide the basis for reporting the Group's expenditures. For the year ended December 31, 1994, the Group, including its equity share of nonsubsidiary companies, incurred capital costs of $233 million and nonremediation related operating expenses of $132 million. The major component of the Group's expenditures is for the prevention of air pollution. In addition, as of December 31, 1994, reserves relative to the future cost of restoring and abandoning existing oil and gas properties were $27 million. Based upon existing statutory and regulatory requirements, investment and operating plans and known exposures, the Group believes environmental expenditures will not materially affect its liquidity, financial position or results of operations.

Source: Texaco, 1994 Form 10-K.

4. a. Using the footnote data from Exhibit 11C-2, compute the appropriate adjustments to Caltex's debt for its off-balance-sheet obligations.
   b. Using the result of part (a), recompute the ratios in question 3(b).
   c. Discuss the significance of your results.

5. Use the results of Questions 3 and 4 to further adjust Texaco's debt, equity, and ratios calculated in Questions 1 and 2.

6. Describe the information *not* contained in the Texaco and Caltex financial data that would help you evaluate the impact of their off-balance-sheet obligations on future cash flows. (Your discussion should include both financial and operational factors.)

Chapter 11

Problems

1. [Analysis of lessee; 1992 CFA adapted] If a lease is capitalized, as compared to being treated as an operating lease, describe the first-year impact on:

    (i) The current ratio

    (ii) The debt-to-equity ratio

    (iii) Operating income

    (iv) Net income

    (v) Cash flow from operations

2. [Leases, effect of interest rate] For assets under capital leases, lease expense has two components: interest and amortization (depreciation). Assume that a lease can be capitalized at either 9 or 10%. Compare the effects of this choice on the lessee in the first year and over the life of the lease on:

    (i) Interest expense

    (ii) Amortization expense

    (iii) Total lease expense

    (iv) Cash flow from operations

    (v) Average assets

    (vi) Average liabilities

3. [Analysis of lessee; 1992 CFA adapted] Dale Mail leases a computer from Gray Computing Services for 10 years at an annual rental of $2,400. Dale guarantees that the residual value will be $4,000 at the end of the lease. Dale uses the straight-line method of depreciation. Assume that the lease is accounted for by Dale as a capital lease.

    A. Calculate the present value of the lease using a 9% interest rate.

    B. Calculate total lease expense in the first year of the lease.

    C. Describe the trend of total lease expense over the lease term.

4. [Analysis of lease terms] The Pallavi Company leases equipment (fair market value of $125,000) from Priyanka Corp. The lease contains a bargain purchase option and requires 15 annual minimum lease payments of $15,000 payable at the end of each year. The economic life of the equipment is 20 years. The lessee's borrowing rate is 10%, and the lessor's implicit rate is 8%.

A. Pallavi will capitalize this lease. Why?

B. Compute the amount at which Pallavi should capitalize the lease.

C. Select the number of years over which Pallavi should depreciate the leased equipment.

D. Discuss whether the absence of a bargain purchase option would change your answer to part C.

5. [Analysis of lessee] The Tolrem Company has decided to lease an airplane on January 1, 1997. The firm and its lessor have not yet decided the terms of the lease. Assume that the terms can be adjusted to permit Tolrem to either capitalize the lease or record it as an operating lease.

A. State the effect (higher, lower, or equal) of the choice of capitalizing the lease on the following for 1997 (the initial year of the lease):

- **(i)** Cash flow from operations
- **(ii)** Financing cash flow
- **(iii)** Investing cash flow
- **(iv)** Net cash flow
- **(v)** Debt-to-equity ratio
- **(vi)** Interest coverage ratio
- **(vii)** Operating income
- **(viii)** Net income
- **(ix)** Deferred tax asset or liability
- **(x)** Taxes paid
- **(xi)** Pre- and posttax return on assets
- **(xii)** Pre- and posttax return on equity

B. You recall that the difference between net income under the two methods changes direction at some point during the lease term. State which answers to part A will change in the year after the switch occurs and describe the change.

C. Assume that Tolrem enters into new aircraft leases at a constant annual rate. Describe the effect of the choice of accounting method on the items in part A.

6. [Leases, tax effects, cash flows and deferred taxes] On January 1, 1993, two identical companies, Caramino Corp. and Aglianico, Inc., lease similar assets with the following characteristics:

- **(i)** Economic life is eight years.
- **(ii)** Lease term is five years.
- **(iii)** Lease payments of $10,000 per year are payable at the beginning of each year, with the first payment due on January 1, 1993.
- **(iv)** Fair market value is $48,000.
- **(v)** Each firm has an incremental borrowing rate of 8% and a tax rate of 40%.

Caramino capitalizes the lease, whereas Aglianico uses the operating lease method. Both firms use straight-line depreciation for all assets on their financial statements. Assume that both firms treat the lease as an operating lease on their tax returns. Assume that each firm generates income before lease-related expense and income taxes of $20,000 in 1993.

A. Compute earnings before interest and taxes and earnings before taxes for 1993 for each firm. Identify the sources of the difference.

B. Compute the deferred taxes resulting from the lease for each firm in the first year of the lease.

C. Compute the effect of the lease on the 1993 reported cash flow from operations for both firms. Explain the difference.

D. Compute the impact of the lease on the 1993 reported financing cash flows of both firms. Explain the difference.

E. Compute the impact of the lease on the 1993 reported cash flow for investing of both firms. Explain the difference.

F. Using your answers to parts C through E, compute the effect of the lease on the 1993 reported net cash flow of both firms. Explain why they are identical.

G. Using your answers to parts A through F, discuss the reasons why Caramino and Aglianico may have wished to use different accounting methods for the same transaction.

7. [Effect of leases] Exhibit 11P-1 presents information provided by The Limited Company in its 1994 annual report, MD&A, and 10-K report.

A. In its 10-K filing, The Limited provides an adjusted "earnings to fixed charge coverage" ratio. What is the nature of the adjustment? What would the ratio be without the adjustment?

B. In its MD&A, the company provides a capitalization table as well as "several measures of liquidity and capital resources." These measures are not adjusted as in part A. Prepare an adjusted capitalization table and (to the extent possible) adjusted measures of liquidity and capital resources. Compare the adjusted capitalization table and ratios with those reported by The Limited. *Note:* Use 8% as the appropriate interest rate for present value calculations.

8. [Sale of receivables, CFO and liquidity] The Wackenhut Corporation's interim report included the following information (in thousands) for the three-month periods ended April 2, 1995 and April 2, 1994:

	Three Months Ended	
	4/2/1995	4/2/1994
CFO	$ 34,649	$ 6,747
Current assets	108,355	137,645
Current liabilities	66,195	65,570

A. Compare the 1995 first quarter's reported CFO, current ratio, and CFO/current liabilities ratio with that reported in the first quarter of 1994.

EXHIBIT 11P-1. THE LIMITED INC.
Selected Information from MD&A, Annual Report, and 10-K

Liquidity and Capital Resources (From the MD&A)

Cash provided from operating activities, commercial paper backed by funds available under committed long-term credit agreements, and the Company's capital structure continue to provide the resources to support operations, including projected growth, seasonal requirements, and capital expenditures. A summary of the Company's working capital position and capitalization follows ($ in thousands):

	1994
Cash provided by operating activities	$ 361,078
Working capital	1,750,111
Capitalization	
Long-term debt	650,000
Deferred income taxes	306,139
Shareholders' equity	2,760,956
Total Capitalization	$3,717,095

The Company considers the following to be several measures of liquidity and capital resources:

	1994
Debt-to-equity ratio (long-term debt divided by shareholders' equity)	24%
Debt-to-capitalization ratio (long-term debt divided by total capitalization)	17%
Interest coverage ratio (income before interest expense, depreciation, amortization, and income taxes divided by interest expense)	16X
Cash flow to capital investment (net cash provided by operating activities divided by capital expenditures)	113%

5. Leased Facilities and Commitments (Notes to Financial Statements)

Annual store rent is comprised of a fixed minimum amount, plus contingent rent based on a percentage of sales exceeding a stipulated amount. Store lease terms generally require additional payments covering taxes, common area costs, and certain other expenses.

A summary of rent expense for 1994 and 1993 . . . follows ($ in thousands):

	1994	1993
Store rent		
Fixed minimum	$586,437	$540,381
Contingent	17,522	19,727
Total store rent	$603,959	$560,108
Equipment and other	27,710	31,897
Total rent expense	$631,669	$592,005

EXHIBIT 11P-1 (*continued*)

A summary of minimum rent commitments under noncancelable leases follows ($ in thousands):

1995	$ 617,645
1996	606,120
1997	587,825
1998	565,999
1999	539,742
Thereafter	$2,802,487

Ratio of Earnings to Fixed Charges (From 10-K)

	Year Ended January 28, 1995
Adjusted Earnings	
Pretax earnings	$ 744,343
Portion of minimum rent ($614,147) representative of interest	204,716
Interest on indebtedness	65,381
Total earnings as adjusted	$1,014,440
Fixed Charges	
Portion of minimum rent representative of interest	$ 204,716
Interest on indebtedness	65,381
Total fixed charges	$ 270,097
Ratio of earnings to fixed charges	3.76X

Source: The Limited 1994 Annual Report.

B. Redo A, taking into consideration the information provided by Wackenhut in the following footnote in their interim report:

> In January 1995, the corporation entered into a $40,000,000, three-year, revolving trade receivable securitization facility agreement to sell undivided fractional interests in a pool of eligible receivables. At April 2, 1995, $28,940,000 had been sold, and is presented as a reduction in accounts receivable in the accompanying balance sheet and as providing operating cash flow in the Consolidated Statement of Cash Flows. The costs associated with this program are based on the purchasers' level of investment and cost of issuing commercial paper plus predetermined fees. The corporation will retain substantially the same risk of credit loss as if the receivables had not been sold. Such costs are included in "Interest and receivable discount expense," in the Consolidated Statement of Income.

9. [Sale of receivables] The following footnote appeared in Arkla Inc.'s March 31, 1995 10-Q interim report:

> Under a March 1994 agreement (the "Agreement"), the Company sells an undivided interest (currently limited to a maximum of $235 million) in a designated pool of accounts receivable with limited recourse. The Company has retained servicing responsibility

under the program, for which it is paid a fee which does not differ materially from a normal servicing fee. Total receivables sold under the Agreement but not yet collected were approximately $167.2 million, $192.8 million and $118.7 million, respectively, at March 31, 1995, December 31, 1994 and March 31, 1994, which amounts have been deducted from "Accounts and notes receivable" in the accompanying Consolidated Balance Sheet and, at March 31, 1995, $42.9 million of the Company's remaining receivables were collateral for receivables which had been sold. During the three months ended March 31, 1995 and 1994, the Company experienced cash outflows of $25.6 million and $107.7 million, respectively, under the program. In accordance with authoritative accounting guidelines, cash flows related to these sales of accounts receivable are included in the accompanying Statement of Consolidated Cash Flows within the category, "Cash flows from operating activities."

A. Explain Arkla's statement that it experienced a *cash outflow* of $25.6 million during the three months ended March 31, 1995.

B. State the amount of receivables sold but uncollected at December 31, 1993.

C. Compute the appropriate adjustments (for receivables sold) to Arkla's CFO for the quarters ended:

  (i) March 31, 1995

  (ii) March 31, 1994

10. [Sale of receivables] The accounts receivable footnote from the *1993 Annual Report* of Morrison Knudsen is reproduced below:

The Corporation has a three year agreement with banks (expiring in December 1994) to sell, with limited recourse, up to $60,000 of undivided interests in a designated pool of accounts receivables. As collections reduce previously sold undivided interests, new receivables can be sold up to the $60,000 level. In addition, accounts receivable were sold to a bank under an agreement which ends in February 1994. Accounts receivable totaling $713,804 and $651,030 have been sold under the agreements in 1993 and 1992, respectively. At December 31, 1993 and 1992, accounts receivable in the accompanying balance sheet are net of receivables sold under the agreements of $75,937 and $87,264, respectively.

Selected reported financial data follow:

The Company initially sold receivables in 1991, with a year-end balance of $66,796.

	Year Ended December 31 ($ in thousands)			
	1993	1992	1991	1990
Sales	$2,722,543	$2,284,931	$2,024,791	$1,758,758
Earnings before interest and taxes	66,075	36,690	74,610	75,306
Accounts receivable	231,021	160,196	135,253	182,283
Current assets	793,221	681,412	658,200	645,440
Current liabilities	689,534	608,730	379,121	404,795
Short-term debt	37,238	5,757	1,226	3,143
Long-term debt	9,768	457	195,232	194,215
Stockholders' equity	406,967	375,771	385,725	281,940
Cash flow from operations	$ (64,302)	$ 173,905	$ 94,652	$ 72,679

A. Compute the impact of the sale of receivables on the current ratio, cash cycle, and receivable turnover ratio for 1992 to 1993.

B. Compute the reported and adjusted (for the sale of receivables) debt-to-equity and return on total capital ratios for 1992 to 1993.

C. Discuss the impact of the sale on the trend of the firm's cash flow from operations over the period 1990 to 1993.

11. [Sale of receivables] The W.R. Grace company entered into arrangements to sell receivables in 1993 and 1994. The accounts receivable footnote in the firm's *1994 Annual Report* noted that as of

> December 31, 1994 and 1993, $296.8 (million) and $263.8 (million), respectively, had been received pursuant to those sales; these amounts are reflected as reductions to trade receivables.

Selected reported financial data follow:

	Year Ended December 31 ($ in millions)	
	1994	1993
Sales	$5,093	$4,408
Earnings before interest and taxes	249	306
Accounts receivable	742	546
Current assets	2,229	2,078
Current liabilities	2,232	1,993
Short-term debt	431	533
Long-term debt	1,099	1,174
Stockholders' equity	1,505	1,518
Cash flow from operations	$ 454	$ 243

A. Compute the impact of the sale of receivables on the current ratio, cash cycle, and receivable turnover ratio for 1994.

B. Compute the reported and adjusted (for the sale of receivables) debt-to-equity and return on total capital ratios for 1994.

C. Discuss the impact of the sale on the firm's cash flow in 1994.

12. [Take-or-pay agreements] The following paragraphs were extracted from an article in the *Financial Times* on March 4, 1993:

Brazilians Cannot Afford to Cut Aluminum Losses

Any hopes that Brazil will this year relieve the pressure of oversupply on the languishing aluminum market by cutting its output seem destined to be disappointed. Despite a combination of low international prices and what local industry considers high domestic energy costs, the country registered record production of aluminum in 1992, and output is expected to remain at a similar level this year.

Many energy contracts are "take-or-pay" agreements. . . . Some bauxite supply contracts run on a "take-or-pay" basis, meaning that [aluminum] producers must withdraw their share of raw material whether or not they intend to use it.

Explain the relationship between these two paragraphs. (*Note:* Aluminum is refined from bauxite using large amounts of energy.)

13. [Exchangeable debt] The long-term debt of Alleghany Corp. at December 31, 1990, included $59,600,000 debentures (6.50%, due 2014) exchangeable for common shares of American Express (at a rate of 22.8833 shares for each $1,000 bond). A portion of Schedule I (Marketable Securities) from the firm's 10-K filing is reproduced below:

Schedule I, Marketable Securities, December 31, 1990 ($ in thousands)

	Number of Shares	Cost	Market Value	Carrying Value
American Express Company	1,366	$22,033	$28,182	$28,182
Armco, Inc.	3,000	21,137	15,375	15,375
Other	1,677	17,490	10,330	10,330
Total Alleghany equity securities	6,043	$60,660	$53,887	$53,887

Source: Alleghany Corporation, 1990 10-K.

A. Determine the gain or loss that would be recorded by Alleghany if the debenture holders exchange their bonds for American Express stock.

B. Compute the effective interest cost of this debt (net of dividend income on the American Express shares) for 1991. (American Express common stock paid 1991 dividends of $0.94 per share; assume a tax rate of 36%.)

C. Discuss why Alleghany may have chosen to issue the exchangeable bonds rather than simply to sell its shares of American Express.

14. [Off-balance-sheet obligations; 1990 CFA adapted] Extracts from The Bowie Company's December 31, 1993, balance sheet and income statement are presented in the following schedule, along with its interest coverage ratio:

Debt	$12 million
Equity	20
Interest expense	1
Times interest earned	5.0X

The Bowie Corporation's financial statement footnotes include the following:

(i) At the beginning of 1993, Bowie entered into an operating lease with total future payments of $40 million ($5 million/year) with a discounted present value of $20 million.

(ii) Bowie has guaranteed a $5 million, 10% bond issue, due in 1999, issued by Crockett, a nonconsolidated 30%-owned affiliate.

(iii) Bowie has committed itself (starting in 1994) to purchase a total of $12 million of phosphorous from PEPE, Inc., its major supplier, over the next five years. The estimated present value of these payments is $7 million.

A. Adjust Bowie's debt and equity and recompute the debt-to equity ratio, using the information in footnotes (i) to (iii).

B. Adjust the times interest earned ratio for 1993 for these commitments.

C. Discuss the reasons (both financial and operating) why Bowie may have entered into these arrangements.

D. Describe the additional information required to evaluate fully the impact of these commitments on Bowie's current financial condition and future operating trends.

Problems 15 and 16 are based on data from the financial statements of duPont presented in Exhibit 11P-2. The questions pertain to various aspects of leases and off-balance-sheet analysis. These questions may be assigned separately or together.

15. [Analysis of lessee] Note 20 in Exhibit 11P-2 discloses future minimum lease payments for duPont's capital and operating leases.

A. Estimate the interest rate implicit in the capital leases:
 (i) Based on 1995 lease interest expense
 (ii) Based on minimum lease payments over the life of the leases

B. The rates calculated by the two methods are not similar. Explain why, based on the pattern of capital lease payments.

C. Compute the present value of the minimum lease payments for duPont's operating leases. Use the higher of the interest rates calculated in part A.

D. Compute the impact of capitalizing the operating leases on duPont's leverage and interest coverage ratios.

16. [Off-balance-sheet activities] Using the information provided in Exhibit 11P-2, calculate the effects of including all off-balance-sheet debt on duPont's leverage ratios.

17. [Off-balance-sheet obligations; extension of Problem 10-17] Exhibit 10P-3 (p. 526) provides financial statement data for Ashland Coal from its *1994 Annual Report.* Exhibit 11P-3 contains excerpts from footnotes in the *1994 Annual Report.*

A. Using the data provided by these exhibits, adjust Ashland Coal's debt for its off-balance-sheet obligations and recompute its debt-to-equity, return on assets, and times interest earned ratios. Assume a 9% interest rate.

B. Discuss the significance of your results.

C. Exhibit 11-7 contains excerpts from the 1994 Notes to Financial Statements of Ashland Oil (Ashland), 39% owner of Ashland Coal (Coal). Exhibit 11-8 depicts the adjusted long-term debt and solvency analysis of Ashland. Use the results of part A to further adjust Ashland's debt, equity, and ratios calculated in Exhibit 11-8.

D. Describe the additional information you would need to better evaluate the financial and operational impact of Coal's off-balance-sheet obligations on Coal and Ashland.

18. [Appendix 11-A; analysis of lessor] Carignane Corp., a manufacturer/lessor, enters into a sales-type lease agreement with Mourvedre, Inc., as lessee. The lessor capitalizes the lease rather than reporting it as an operating lease.

EXHIBIT 11P-2. DUPONT
Selected Notes: Leases and Off-Balance-Sheet

20. Leases

The company uses various leased facilities and equipment in its operations. The company's future minimum lease payments under operating and capital leases, together with the present value of the net minimum capital lease payments at December 31, 1994, are as follows:

	Capital Leases	Operating Leases
Minimum lease payments for years ending December 31		
1995	$ 20	$ 290
1996	16	224
1997	11	182
1998	11	156
1999	11	124
Remainder	104	673
	$173	$1,649
Less: Estimated executory costs	7	
Net minimum lease payments	$166	
Less: Imputed interest	72	
Present value of net minimum lease payments	$ 94	
Due in 1995	8	
Due after 1995	$ 86	

Rental expense under operating leases was $355 in 1994, $429 in 1993, and $453 in 1992.

From Note 14. Summarized Financial Information for Affiliated Companies

Summarized combined financial information for affiliated companies for which duPont uses the equity method of accounting:

	December 31	
Financial position	1994	1993
Current assets	$ 3,254	$2,703
Noncurrent assets	8,147	6,813
Total assets	$11,401	$9,516
Short-term borrowings*	$ 648	$ 475
Other current liabilities	2,065	1,820
Long-term borrowings*	2,590	2,220
Other long-term liabilities	2,934	2,847
Total liabilities	$ 8,237	$7,362
DuPont's investment in affiliates (includes advances)	$ 1,662	$1,607

*DuPont's pro rata interest in total borrowings was $1,220 in 1994 and $985 in 1993, of which $599 in 1994 and $388 iin 1993 were guaranteed by the company.

EXHIBIT 11P-3. ASHLAND COAL
Off-Balance-Sheet Disclosures

---

3. Dominion Terminal Associates

Ashland Coal holds a 17.5% general partnership interest in Dominion Terminal Associates (DTA), which operates a ground storage-to-vessel coal transloading facility in Newport News, Virginia. DTA leases the facility from Peninsula Ports' Authority of Virginia (PPAV) for amounts sufficient to meet debt service requirements. Financing is provided through $132,800,000 of tax-exempt bonds issued by PPAV which mature July 1, 2016.

Under the terms of a throughput and handling agreement with DTA, each partner is charged its share of cash operating and debt service costs in exchange for the right to use its share of the facility's loading capacity and is required to make periodic cash advances to DTA to fund such costs. On a cumulative basis, costs exceeded cash advances by $6,933,000 and $6,497,000 at December 31, 1994 and 1993, respectively (included in other long-term liabilities). Costs and cash advances for the last three years follow:

(In thousands)	1994	1993	1992
Operating and debt service costs charged to costs and expenses	**$3,316**	$3,158	$3,849
Cash advances	**2,880**	2,705	3,139

Future payments for fixed operating costs and debt service are estimated to approximate $3,000,000 annually through 2015 and $26,000,000 in 2016.

17. Sale and Leaseback

On January 29, 1993, Ashland Coal sold mining equipment valued at approximately $64,000,000 and leased back the equipment under an operating lease with a term of three years. The proceeds of this transaction were used to repay borrowings under Ashland Coal's revolving credit agreement. The lease provides for annual rental payments of approximately $10,500,000 in 1995 and approximately $2,500,000 in 1996. At the end of the lease term, the Company has the option to purchase the equipment for $43,200,000. Alternatively, the equipment may be sold by the lessor to a third party. In the event of such a sale, the Company will be required to make payment to the lessor in the event, and to the extent, that the proceeds are below $35,600,000.

19. Commitments and Contingencies

Ashland Coal leases office space, mining equipment, land, and various other properties under noncancellable long-term leases, expiring at various dates. Rental expense related to these operating leases amounted to $14,088,000 in 1994, $10,772,000 in 1993, and $3,510,000 in 1992. Minimum annual rentals due in future years under lease agreements in effect at January 1, 1995, are approximately $14,012,000 in 1995, $6,077,000 in 1996, $3,518,000 in 1997, $3,187,000 in 1998, $3,118,000 in 1999, and additional amounts thereafter aggregating $13,107,000 through 2011.

Source: Ashland Coal, *1994 Annual Report.*

Describe the effect (lower, higher, or none) of this choice on the following accounts and ratios of Carignane (the lessor) in the first and ninth years of a 10-year lease:

(i) Total assets	**(vii)** Net income
(ii) Revenues	**(viii)** Retained earnings
(iii) Expenses	**(ix)** Income taxes paid
(iv) Asset turnover ratio	**(x)** Posttax return on assets
(v) Interest income	**(xi)** Cash flow from operations
(vi) Cost of goods sold	**(xii)** Investment cash flow

19. [Appendix 11-A; analysis of lessor and lessee] On January 1, 1994, The Malbec Company leases a Willmess winepress to the Baldes Group under the following conditions:

- **(i)** Annual lease payments are $20,000 for 20 years.
- **(ii)** At the end of the lease term, the press is expected to have a value of $5,500.
- **(iii)** The fair market value of the press is $185,250.
- **(iv)** The estimated economic life of the press is 30 years.
- **(v)** Malbec's implicit interest rate is 12%; Baldes' incremental borrowing rate is 10%.
- **(vi)** Malbec reports similar presses at $150,000 in finished goods inventory.

A. Based on the data given, state whether Baldes should treat this lease as an operating or a capital lease. Justify your answer. What additional information would help to answer the question?

B. Assume that Baldes capitalizes the lease. List the financial statement accounts affected (at January 1, 1994) by that decision and calculate each effect.

C. Assume that Baldes uses straight-line depreciation for financial reporting purposes. Compute the income statement, balance sheet, and statement of cash flows effects of the lease for 1994 and 1995 under each lease accounting method.

D. Based on the data given, state whether Malbec should treat this lease as an operating or a sales-type lease. Justify your answer. What additional information would help to answer the question?

E. Assume that Malbec treats the lease as an operating lease. List the financial statement accounts affected (at January 1, 1994) by that decision and calculate each effect.

F. Assume that Malbec treats the lease as a sales-type lease and the residual value of the winepress is not guaranteed by the lessee. List the financial statement accounts affected (at January 1, 1994) by that decision and calculate each effect.

G. Assume that Malbec uses straight-line depreciation for financial reporting purposes. Compute the income statement, balance sheet, and statement of cash flows effects of the lease for 1994 and 1995 under each lease accounting method.

Appendix 11-A

Financial Reporting by Lessors and for Sale Leasebacks

INTRODUCTION

Many manufacturers and dealers offer customers leases to market their products. Such *sales-type leases* include both a manufacturing or merchandising profit (the difference between the fair value at the inception of the lease and the cost or carrying value of the leased property) and interest income due to the financing nature of the transaction.

Financial institutions and leasing intermediaries offer direct financing leases that generate interest income only. Operating leases may be created by either class of lessors.

This appendix discusses the accounting by lessors for sales-type and direct financing leases. Leveraged leases are beyond the scope of this text. Lessor financial reporting is illustrated using the lessee example from the chapter, with the additional assumptions that the leased equipment cost $20,000 to manufacture and the expected residual value (not guaranteed by the lessee) is $2,500 after four years.

LEASE CLASSIFICATION: LESSORS

Lease capitalization by lessors is required when the lease meets *any one* of the four criteria specified for capitalization by lessees and *both* of the following revenue recognition criteria:

1. Collectibility of the MLPs is reasonably predictable.
2. There are no significant uncertainties regarding the amount of unreimbursable costs yet to be incurred by the lessor under the provisions of the lease agreement.

Leases not meeting these criteria must be reported as operating leases since either the risks and benefits of leased assets have not been transferred, or the earnings process is not complete.

Sales-Type Leases

Exhibit 11A-1 presents financial reporting by a lessor for a sales-type lease using the lessee example. Part A illustrates the accounting recognition at inception and the determination of gross and net investment in the lease; part B provides the lessor's amortization schedule for the sales-type lease.

The lessor recognizes sales revenue of $31,700, the present value of the MLPs. The cost of goods sold is the cost or carrying amount of the leased property. The present value of the unguaranteed residual value of the leased property constitutes continuing investment by the lessor and is not included in costs charged against income; that is, it is deducted from cost to manufacture.

The lessor's gross investment in the lease is $42,500, the sum of the MLPs and the unguaranteed residual value. Net investment in the lease is $33,407, determined by discounting the MLPs and the unguaranteed residual value at the interest rate implicit in the lease (10%), as shown in part A.

The difference between the gross and net investment represents unearned income, the interest component of the transaction. Unearned income is systematically amortized to income over the lease term, using the interest method that reports a constant rate of return of 10% on the net investment in the lease. The lessor reports its net investment in the lease on the balance sheet (see the next section). Contingent rentals, if any, are reported as they are earned. SFAS 13 requires an annual review of the estimated residual value. Nontemporary declines must be recognized; however, increases in value or subsequent reversals of declines cannot be reported.

Balance Sheet Effects (Exhibit 11A-1C)

The lessor reports the current and noncurrent components of its net investment in sales-type leases. Lessors using the operating lease method do not report any investment

EXHIBIT 11A-1
Lessor Financial Reporting

A. Sales-Type Lease

Lessor's Gross Investment in Leased Equipment

MLPs: $10,000 × 4	$40,000
Unguaranteed residual value	2,500
	$42,500

Lessor's Net Investment in Leased Equipment

Present value at 10% of an annuity of 4 payments of $10,000	$31,700
Present value at 10% of $2,500, 4 periods hence	1,707
	$33,407

Unearned Income

Gross investment in lease	$42,500
Less: Net investment	33,407
	$ 9,093

Accounting Recognition at Lease Inception

Sales revenue*	$ 31,700	
Cost of goods sold†	(18,293)	
Gross profit on sale		$13,407
Gross investment in lease	$ 42,500	
Unearned income	(9,093)	
Net investment in lease		$33,407

*Present value of lease payments, excluding residual value.
†Cost to manufacture (assumed to be $20,000) less PV of residual value.

B. Lessor Amortization Schedule: Sales-Type Lease

Year	Annual Payment Received (A)	Interest Income (B)	Reduction in Investment (C) = (A) − (B)	Net Investment (D)
X0				$33,407
X1	$10,000	$3,340	$ 6,660	26,747
X2	10,000	2,675	7,325	19,422
X3	10,000	1,942	8,058	11,364
X4	10,000	1,136	8,864	2,500
Totals	$40,000	$9,093	$30,907	

EXHIBIT 11A-1 (*continued*)

C. Balance Sheet

	Capital (Sales-Type) Lease			Operating Lease		
	Net Investment in Leases			Assets Under	Accumulated	
Year	Current	Long-Term	Total	Lease	Depreciation	Net
X0	$6,660	$26,747	$33,407	$20,000	$ 0	$20,000
X1	7,325	19,422	26,747	20,000	4,375	15,625
X2	8,058	11,364	19,422	20,000	8,750	11,250
X3	8,864	2,500	11,364	20,000	13,125	6,875
X4	2,500	0	2,500	20,000	17,500	2,500

D. Income Statement Effect

	Capital (Sales-Type) Lease		Operating Lease		
			Rental		
Year		Income	Revenue	Depreciation	Income
X0	Gain on Sale	$13,407			
X1	Interest	3,340	$10,000	$ 4,375	$ 5,625
X2	Interest	2,675	10,000	4,375	5,625
X3	Interest	1,942	10,000	4,375	5,625
X4	Interest	1,136	10,000	4,375	5,625
		$22,500	$40,000	$17,500	$22,500

E. Cash Flow Statement Effect

	Capital (Sales-Type) Lease			Operating Lease
		Cash from		
Year	CFO	Investment	Total	CFO
X0	$13,407	$(13,407)	$ 0	$ 0
X1	3,340	6,660	10,000	10,000
X2	2,675	7,325	10,000	10,000
X3	1,942	8,058	10,000	10,000
X4	1,136	8,864	10,000	10,000
Totals	$22,500	$ 17,500	$40,000	$40,000

in leases, but they continue to report the assets on the balance sheet as long-term assets, net of accumulated depreciation. These amounts assume straight-line depreciation over four years of the original cost of the asset less estimated residual value ($20,000 − $2,500). Note that the operating lease method reports lower net assets each year and, ignoring income effects, tends to increase return on assets relative to the sales-type lease method.

Income Statement Effects (Exhibit 11A-1D)

For the sales-type lease, the lessor records profit at inception of $13,407. The annual rental of $10,000 is allocated to interest income and return of principal. Reported interest income reflects a constant 10% return on the declining net investment in the lease. The balance of the rental payment is applied to amortize (reduce principal) the net investment systematically over the lease term.

The operating lease method reports constant income over the lease term as straight-line depreciation is charged against the constant annual rental. The use of accelerated depreciation would result in a pattern of increasing income over the lease term as depreciation declines.

The sales-type lease reports substantially higher income in the first year of the lease due to recognition of manufacturing profit at the inception of the lease. However, reported income declines thereafter due to declining interest income over the remainder of the lease term, relative to constant or increasing income under the operating lease method. In our example, reported net income is higher under the operating lease method after the initial year. *Over the lease term, the total net income is the same under both methods.*

Cash Flow Effects (Exhibit 11A-1E)

At the inception of the lease, no cash changes hands. The operating lease method reports no cash flow effects on the Statement of Cash Flows. In contrast, the sales-type lease method reports 19X0 operating cash flow of $13,407, equal to the sales profit at the inception of the lease. This cash inflow is offset by a net cash outflow for investment equal to $13,407 (the investment of $33,407 less the $20,000 prior carrying amount of the leased property). Net cash flow remains zero.

In subsequent years, under the operating lease method, CFO is equal to the rental payment of $10,000/year. Under the sale-type lease method, the $10,000 payment is allocated between CFO and cash from investment; CFO is equal to interest income and cash from investment is equal to the reduction in the net investment. Thus, after inception, the operating lease method reports higher CFO and, since interest income declines over the lease term, this difference in CFO increases. Simultaneously, a correspondingly larger reduction in net investment is reported in investment cash flow.

Note that total cash flow (operating plus investing) is unaffected by the method of lease accounting. The actual cash flow in each year is $10,000, the lease payment received. Only under the operating lease method does CFO record faithfully the cash flows associated with the lease. Capitalization of the lease by the lessor reclassifies reported cash flows between operating and investing activities.

The use of sales-type lease accounting allows firms to recognize income earlier than the operating lease method. Lease capitalization also allows firms to report higher CFO at the inception of the lease. This aggressive recognition of income and cash flows ("front end loading") improves financial ratios; it accurately reflects the firm's operations only if the risks and benefits of leased property have been fully transferred to the lessee and the lessor has no further performance obligation.

Footnote Disclosures

Footnote disclosure for lessors is similar to that of lessees. The sales-type lease method requires the disclosure of gross MLPs receivable, unearned income, and the current and noncurrent components of the net investment in leases. Lessors must also provide information on lease terms, future MLPs receivable over the next five years, and the aggregate thereafter. Disclosure for operating leases is limited to MLPs receivable over the next five years and the aggregate thereafter.

Direct Financing Leases

In a direct financing lease, the lessor's original cost or carrying value (prior to the lease) of the asset approximates the market value of the leased asset (the present value of the MLPs). Such leases are pure financing transactions and financial reporting for direct financing leases reflects this fact. *No sale is recognized at the inception of the lease, and there is no manufacturing or dealer profit. Only financing income is reported.*

Unearned income is the difference between the gross investment in the lease and the cost or carrying amount of the leased property. It is amortized to report a constant periodic return (effective interest method) on the net investment in the lease (gross investment plus initial direct costs less unearned income). Thus, in our example, the lessor would report (interest) income and cash flows similar to those reported for the sales-type lease over the period 19X1-19X4. There are no income or cash flow consequences at the inception of the lease in 19X0.

Disclosure requirements for financing leases are similar to those for sales-type leases. Lessors must disclose MLPs receivable over the next five fiscal years and the aggregate thereafter. Any allowance for uncollectibles, executory costs, unguaranteed residual value, and unearned income must also be reported.

Financial Reporting by Lessors: An Example

Exhibit 11A-2 contains IBM Credit Corp.'s footnote on its activities as lessor. The company finances customer purchases of information-handling equipment through direct financing leases; shorter-term leases of such equipment are treated as operating leases.

IBM discloses aggregate MLPs receivable and reports the periodic payments in each of the next five years and in the aggregate thereafter as a percentage of this total. The terms of the direct financing leases range from three to five years and operating leases span two to four years. Note that both types of leases have similar terms, but nearly 50% of the direct financing leases are due within one year, higher than the 37% of operating leases due within 12 months of the financial statement date. We can assume that the operating leases do not meet the capitalization requirements of SFAS 13.

Additional disclosures are required for the capitalized direct financing leases: current and noncurrent components, allowance for uncollectibles, estimated unguaranteed residual values, and unearned interest. IBM Credit Corp. provides most applicable disclosures. No contingent rentals are reported; they may not be significant. However, the current and noncurrent components have not been reported separately. Computation of the implicit interest rate requires additional assumptions.

The footnote includes a reconciliation of the allowance for losses and other disclosure pertaining to the securitization of direct financing lease receivables.

Going beyond the financial effects of IBM's lessor activities, the footnote data provide some insight into changes in the company's operations. Direct financing leases declined by 17% (using MLPs) during 1994. Operating leases rose slightly in gross dollars but the depreciated amount fell. This suggests that new leases are low relative to the existing lease base.

These declines may represent lower lease prices, a shift from leases to sales (reflecting changes in relative prices or customer preferences) or reduced leases of a

EXHIBIT 11A-2. IBM CREDIT CORP.
Net Investment in Capital Leases

The Company's capital lease portfolio includes direct financing and leveraged leases. The Company originates financing for customers in a variety of industries and throughout the United States. The Company has a diversified portfolio of capital equipment financings for end users.

Direct financing leases consist principally of IBM information handling equipment with terms generally from three to five years. The components of the net investment in direct financing leases at December 31, 1994 and 1993, are as follows ($ in thousands):

	1994	1993
Minimum lease payments receivable	$3,735,154	$4,500,304
Estimated unguaranteed residual values	287,511	366,356
Deferred initial direct costs	30,076	30,932
Unearned income	(547,685)	(622,410)
Allowance for receivable losses	(24,389)	(47,398)
	$3,480,667	$4,227,784

The scheduled maturities of minimum lease payments outstanding at December 31, 1994, expressed as a percentage of the total, are as follows:

	1994
Due within 12 months	46.0%
13 to 24 months	33.0
25 to 36 months	14.2
37 to 48 months	6.0
After 48 months	0.8
	100.0%

The following is a reconciliation of the direct financing lease allowance for receivable losses ($ in thousands):

	1994	1993	1992
Beginning of year	$ 47,398	$ 74,548	$ 42,089
Additions	32,395	24,793	66,665
Accounts written off (net of recoveries)	(54,610)	(45,336)	(34,206)
Transfers to allowance for losses on receivables sold	(794)	(6,607)	—
End of year	$ 24,389	$ 47,398	$ 74,548

Included in the net investment in capital leases is $252.8 million and $335.0 million of seller interest at December 31, 1994 and 1993.

EXHIBIT 11A-2 (*continued*)

Equipment on Operating Lease

Operating leases consist principally of IBM information-handling equipment with terms generally from two to four years. The components of equipment on operating lease at December 31, 1994 and 1993, are as follows ($ in thousands):

	1994	1993
Cost	$ 3,135,364	$ 2,853,672
Accumulated depreciation	(1,562,122)	(1,100,551)
	$ 1,573,242	$ 1,753,121

Minimum future rentals were approximately $1,494.6 million at December 31, 1994. The scheduled maturities of the minimum future rentals at December 31, 1994, expressed as a percentage of the total, are as follows:

	1994
Due within 12 months	37.1%
13 to 24 months	29.4
25 to 36 months	20.4
37 to 48 months	9.3
After 48 months	3.8
	100.0%

Source: IBM Credit Corp., *1994 Annual Report.*

particular equipment class. This is another example of how attention to footnote detail can suggest worthwhile questions about changes in operations to ask management.

FINANCIAL REPORTING FOR SALES WITH LEASEBACKS

Sale leaseback transactions are sales of property by the owner who then leases it back from the buyer-lessor. Financial reporting for these transactions is governed by SFAS 28, Accounting for Sales with Leasebacks (1979), as amended by SFAS 66, Accounting for Sales of Real Estate (1982).

The amount and timing of profit (or loss) recognized on a sale leaseback transaction are determined by the proportion of the rights to use the leased property retained by the owner-lessee after the sale. If all or substantially all the use rights are retained by the owner-lessee, it is a financing transaction, and no profit or loss on the transaction should be recognized.

The extent of continuing use is determined by the proportion of the present value of reasonable rentals relative to the fair value of assets sold and leased back. This proportion is used to assign sale leaseback transactions to the following financial reporting categories.

Minor Leasebacks. Present value of reasonable rentals is less than 10% of the fair value of the leased property; the buyer-lessor obtains substantially all the rights to use the leased property. Any gain (or loss) on the transaction is recognized in full at the inception of the lease.

More than Minor but Less than "Substantially All" Leasebacks. Present value of reasonable rentals exceeds 10% but is less than 90% of the fair value of the asset sold; depending on specific criteria, some or all of the gain or loss must be deferred and amortized over the lease term.

Substantially All Leasebacks. Present value of MLPs equals or exceeds 90% of the fair value of property sold; the total gain (loss) must be deferred and amortized over the lease term. The leaseback is a financing transaction, and the gain (loss) is recognized as the leased property is used.

12

PENSIONS AND OTHER EMPLOYEE BENEFITS

CHAPTER OUTLINE

CHAPTER OBJECTIVES

INTRODUCTION

PENSION PLANS
Defined Contribution Plans
Defined Benefit Plans

DEFINED BENEFIT PENSION PLANS
Estimating Benefit Obligations
Factors Affecting Benefit Obligations
Service Cost
Interest Cost
Actuarial Gains and Losses
Prior Service Cost from Plan Amendments
Benefits Paid
Factors Affecting Plan Assets
Employer Contributions
Return on Assets
Benefits Paid
Funded Status of Pension Plan

ACCOUNTING FOR PENSIONS: SFAS 87
Pension Cost: Components and Measurement
Service Cost and Interest Cost
Expected Return on Assets
Amortization of Gains or Losses
Amortization of Prior Service Cost

Amortization of Transition Asset or Liability
Disclosure of Plan Status

ANALYSIS OF PENSION COSTS AND LIABILITY
Importance of Assumptions
Impact of Assumptions on Pension Obligations
Impact of Assumptions on Pension Cost
Analysis of Plan Status, Costs, and Cash Flows
Motivation for Adjustments to Liability and Cost
Analysis of duPont Pension Plan Disclosures
Analysis of duPont's Pension Trends
Estimating Future Pension Cost

IMPACT OF DISCONTINUITIES
Acquisitions and Divestitures
Curtailments and Settlements

NON-U.S. REPORTING REQUIREMENTS

OTHER POSTEMPLOYMENT BENEFITS
Estimating Health Care Benefits
Computing Postretirement Benefit Cost
Disclosure of Plan Status
Importance of Assumptions
Effect of Assumptions
Effects of Transition Methods
Analysis of duPont's Postretirement Health Care Costs

591

Using SFAS 106 Disclosures
Postretirement Benefits Outside the United States

PRERETIREMENT BENEFITS

STOCK COMPENSATION PLANS
   Example: Foster Wheeler
Using SFAS 123 Disclosures

SUMMARY

CASE 12-1: Analysis of Pension Plan Disclosures: GM

Introduction and Case Objectives
The GM Pension Plan
   Minimum Liability Provision
Analysis of GM's Pension Status
   Adjustments to GM's Balance Sheet
   GM's Pension Costs
Analysis of GM Pension Trends
   Trends in Pension Obligations and Assets
   Trends in Pension Cost
   Investment Performance Trends
   Cash Flow Trends
GM's Pension Plans: Concluding Comments

CASE 12-2: DBP Corp Defined Benefit Plan Example

CHAPTER OBJECTIVES

The motivation of employees almost always requires that cash compensation be supplemented by other benefits. Benefits may be received:
- During the period of employee service
- After service ceases but before retirement
- During retirement

The objectives of this chapter are to examine the accounting methods used to record the employer's obligation to provide such benefits, with particular emphasis on defined benefit pension and postretirement medical plans. It shows how to:

1. Examine the components of pension cost, determine their significance, and forecast their trend.
2. Determine the funded status of a defined benefit pension plan, the reasons why the balance sheet does not fully report that status, and the balance sheet adjustments required to reflect the actual plan status.
3. Evaluate the investment performance of pension fund assets.

4. Unravel the smoothing and lagging provisions of pension plan accounting under SFAS 87.
5. Understand the role of assumptions and accounting choices on pension cost and the recognition of changes in plan status.
6. Discern the effect on pension plan status of benefit curtailments and settlements as well as acquisition and divestiture of operating units of the firm.
7. Review the reporting requirements for pension plans outside the United States.
8. Understand the similarities and differences between pension plans and postretirement medical and life insurance plans.
9. Apply the analysis used for pension plans to postretirement benefit plan status and costs.
10. Review the disclosure provisions of SFAS 123 regarding stock compensation plans and use those disclosures to adjust reported financial data.

INTRODUCTION

This chapter discusses the analysis of pension and other employee benefits. Such plans include pension or profit-sharing plans, postemployment life and health insurance benefits, and stock compensation plans. As such plans grew significantly, especially for large (often unionized) companies with generous benefits, the accounting for these

---

BOX 12-1
Glossary

Accumulated benefit obligation (ABO)	The present value of pension benefits earned to date based on employee service and compensation to that date
Accumulated postretirement benefit obligation (APBO)	The present value of postretirement benefits earned to date based on employee service to that date
Assumed per capita cost claims (by age)	Estimated cost of health care benefits at specific ages, based on current costs but adjusted using the assumed health care cost trend rates
Discount rate	The interest rate used to compute the present value of the benefit obligation
Expected long-term rate of return on plan assets	The assumed rate of return on pension and other postretirement benefit funds
Fair value of plan assets	Current market value of all plan assets
Gain or loss	Differences between expectation and actual experience in the investment performance of plan assets or calculation of the benefit obligation
Health care cost trend rate	Assumed inflation rate for health care costs resulting from cost increases as well as changes in utilization and technology
Market-related value of plan assets	A smoothed measure of plan assets that incorporates changes in market values over not more than five years; can be used to compute the expected return on plan assets
Medicare reimbursement rates	Payments due to retirees from Medicare under current legislation
Prior service cost	A change in the benefit obligation due to plan amendment
Projected benefit obligation (PBO)	The present value of pension benefits earned to date based on past service and an estimate of future compensation levels for pay-related plans
Rate of compensation increase	The expected growth rate of employee compensation; used to compute the projected benefit obligation, as well as measures of the postretirement benefit obligation
Service cost	The present value of benefits earned during the current period
Vested benefit obligation (VBO)	The portion of the pension benefit obligation that does not depend on future employee service

benefits became more significant. The FASB issued five new standards on accounting for employee benefits in recent years.

Box 12-1 contains a glossary of specialized terms used in this chapter.

PENSION PLANS

A pension plan is an agreement under which an employer agrees to pay monetary benefits to employees on their retirement from active service. Employees earn benefits based on predetermined factors such as age and years of service. The deferred compensation nature of pension plans may motivate employees to stay with a firm for a longer period of time, at least until they are vested. Some labor economists therefore consider pensions as "implicit contracts" between the firm and its employees.[1]

In the United States, pension plans are virtually always funded because of the requirements of the Employee Retirement Income Security Act of 1974 (ERISA), tax deductibility of the employer's contribution, and tax-exempt status of earnings on fund investments. Outside the United States, pension obligations are often unfunded.

Box 12-2 discusses incentives for the creation and funding of pension plans. It provides a framework for the analysis discussed in the chapter.

A pension fund may be used as an intermediary to satisfy the employer's pension obligations. Employer contributions to the fund[2] are invested; the earnings on these investments are used to pay pension benefits to employees. The relationship among employer, employees, and fund is shown in the following diagram:

Employer
(makes contributions to)
↓
Pension Fund
(invests contributions and pays benefits to)
↓
Eligible Retired Employees

Pension plans differ across industries and countries. Companies may offer different plans to unionized and nonunion employees; salaried employees may receive yet other plans. In addition, some firms provide (typically unfunded) plans to senior management. However, two general types of pension plan exist: defined contribution and defined benefit. A brief discussion of the critical features of these plans follows.

---

[1]The implicit contract argument that pensions tie employees to the firm is further supported by evidence that, given an equal level of deferred compensation, the present value of that compensation is lower for younger workers than for older workers. Thus, defined benefit plans generally undercompensate employees many years from retirement and overcompensate them in later years. On average, the over- and undercompensation should even out. However, for young employees to obtain the average fair wage, they must work until retirement to make up for the early period of undercompensation.

The implicit contract argument has further implications (discussed in later sections) for measuring the pension liability and explaining motivations for plan terminations. It should be noted that the implicit contract view of pensions is by no means unanimous [see Bulow (1982)].

[2]Firms may contribute (subject to certain limitations) their own securities to the pension fund. For example, on December 31, 1994, General Motors' pension plan assets included GM preferred stock (2.4% of total assets) and GM Class E common stock (2.0%).

BOX 12-2
Incentives for Creating and Funding Pension Plans

Tax incentives are a powerful motivation for firms to both create pension plans and to overfund them. Contributions to pension plans are tax-deductible (subject to IRS limits) and the income earned by the funds is tax-exempt. This enables funds in pension plans to grow at a faster rate (compounded tax-free) than if they were held by firms or their employees. Employees pay taxes on benefits after retirement, when their marginal tax rate is expected to be lower than during their working years. *Ceteris paribus,* firms with higher tax rates should have greater incentives to fund pension plans than those with lower tax rates or tax loss carryforwards.

Firms facing a temporary decline in cash flows must reduce capital spending, cut dividends, or obtain external financing. Myers and Majluf (1984) argued that managements prefer to use internal resources to fund investments rather than to cut dividends or obtain costly external financing. When management has better information than potential investors or creditors as to the desirability of investment projects, any new securities issued would be underpriced. Therefore, managers build up financial slack, that is, an inventory of internal resources to avoid diluting the value of extant shareholders' claims. Pension plans (with the added benefits of favorable tax treatment) can be used to store this slack. When needed, the firm can draw on it by reducing future contributions (by changing actuarial methods or assumptions) or by terminating the pension plan.

In addition to the bonding mechanism implied by the implicit contract view of pensions, employees become creditors of the firm when their pension plans are underfunded. This relationship may be an effective control mechanism with respect to both management (also beneficiaries of the pension plans) as well as lower-level employees.

When managers are also creditors, they have additional incentives to avoid actions that might hurt the firm in the long run. External bondholders are also less fearful of actions that might benefit shareholders at the expense of creditors, reducing their monitoring costs and thereby lowering the cost of debt to the firm. Underfunding may also constrain employees who might otherwise make greater economic demands at the expense of shareholders.

Francis and Reiter (1987) examined the 1980 and 1981 pension plan status of a sample of 255 firms. They found that a plan's funded status was directly related to the firm's tax status and capital availability; the higher the tax rate and the greater the available financial slack, the higher the funded status. In addition, separate pension plans for unions and higher benefits per employee were significantly related to the level of underfunding of plans. This result is consistent with the use of underfunding as a control mechanism.

> The support for labor underfunding incentives suggests that for some firms a long-term or implicit contract is evidenced. Other firms may choose, as a policy matter, to adopt the view that pension plans could be terminated at any time and overfund them. Tax and financial slack motivations are consistent with this point of view. Therefore it is not possible to reach an unambiguous conclusion as to which view of the pension contract is "correct." Both views of pensions appear to co-exist in our sample and this is one of the choices or tradeoffs firms can make.*

Thus, the role of a pension plan and its funded status depends on the specific situation of the firm and its relationship with its employees.

Francis and Reiter used a "zero-one" dichotomy to classify the sample firms by their tax status; firms were placed in the zero group if they reported tax-loss carryforwards and in the one subsample if they did not. The zero tax status was consistent with underfunding and the one classification implied overfunding. However, when tax status was based on the firm's actual average tax rate, higher tax rates were associated with underfunding! Francis and Reiter provide the following explanation for the inconsistent outcomes:

One reason for this apparent anomaly is a connection between profitability and average tax rate. Highly profitable firms in the sample face higher average tax rates (correlation of $r = 0.36$). *If highly profitable firms are able to earn higher after-tax returns on internal investments than on tax-free pension fund investments, then the incentive is to minimize rather than maximize pension funding.*†

In addition to the pension-specific variables examined, they also found that firms with higher debt-to-equity ratios tend to underfund their plans, consistent with the debt covenant hypothesis that firms are reluctant to lower income and net worth if it could affect the status of their debt covenants.‡

---

*Jere R. Francis and Sara Ann Reiter, "Determinants of Corporate Pension Funding Strategy," *Journal of Accounting and Economics,* April, 1987, p. 35.
†Ibid., p. 54 (emphasis added).
‡Prior to SFAS 87, a firm's funding policy and its method of recognizing pension expense were equivalent.

Defined Contribution Plans

Employer payments to defined contribution plans may be contractually fixed or variable (e.g., profit-sharing plans). The employer does not promise a specific level of future benefits. The employees bear the risk of investment performance: Benefits will be high if the contributions are invested well; poor investments result in lower benefits.

The accounting for a defined contribution plan is quite simple. The recognized cost equals the required contribution. The employer's balance sheet asset or liability for pensions reflects the excess or shortfall of payments relative to the specified contribution. Because of their simple nature, defined contribution plans do not present significant analytical issues. The remaining discussion of pension plan accounting will deal solely with defined benefit plans.

Defined Benefit Plans

Defined benefit plans specify the benefit to be received on retirement. "Flat benefit" plan payments are fixed (e.g., $50 per month for each year worked). More common, "pay-related" plans tie the benefit to the level of employee earnings, either final salary (e.g., final year or highest three of last five years' compensation) or "career average" earnings. The difficulty of predicting future employee earnings makes the accounting for pay-related plans more complicated than that for flat benefit plans.

All defined benefit plans share one essential characteristic: The plan sponsor (employer) bears the investment risk. By promising a specific benefit, the employer has agreed to make whatever contributions are necessary to provide the promised benefits. As discussed shortly, the employer needs an estimate of future benefit payments to determine the contributions necessary to make those payments.

Defined benefit plans present difficult accounting and analysis issues. Our discussion of these plans will be divided into three stages:

1. Discussion of the mechanics and underlying economics of the plans
2. Review of the accounting rules and footnote disclosures required by SFAS 87
3. The analysis of employer disclosures to discern the underlying economic liability, pension cost, investment performance, and cash flows of the plan

The first step toward understanding pension plan accounting is the mechanics of pension plans themselves. We illustrate the mechanics using simple examples and the duPont pension footnote. *Case 12-2 is an extended example of a defined benefit plan for the hypothetical DBP Co. The example spans four years with additional complexities added each year.*

DEFINED BENEFIT PENSION PLANS

The principal elements of a defined benefit pension plan are:

- The obligation for benefits to be paid to retirees
- The plan assets that are invested to meet that obligation

Figure 12-1 illustrates the relationship between these two elements and the factors that affect them. The link between the two elements is the use of plan assets to pay plan benefits.

Estimating Benefit Obligations

Employers must forecast the cash outflows required by the plan by developing complex actuarial estimates of future benefits. They require assumptions regarding such employee variables as turnover, mortality, quit rates, and retirement dates. For pay-related plans, future salary increases must also be estimated. These assumptions are combined with the terms of the plan to produce a forecast of required future cash

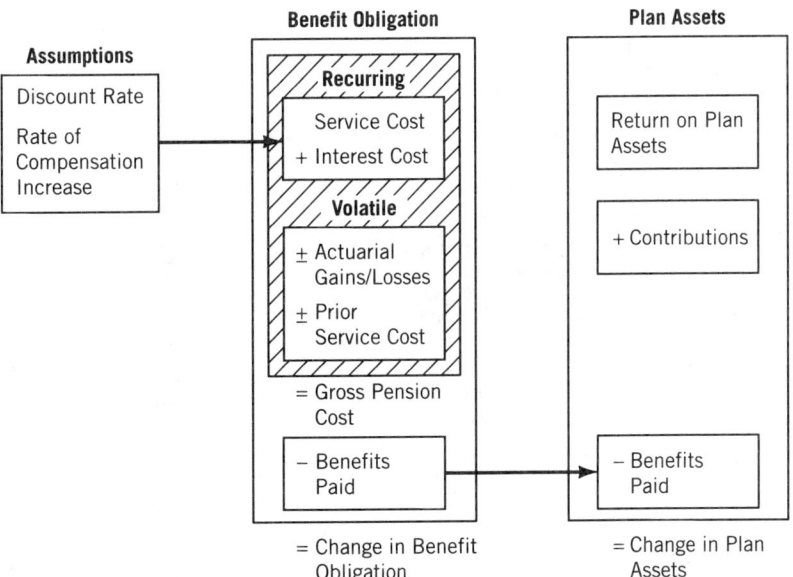

FIGURE 12-1 Components of benefit obligation and plan assets.

outflows (benefit payments) stretching decades into the future. *The pension obligation is the present value of these forecasted benefits.*

Three measures of the pension obligation must be disclosed under current accounting rules. All these measures are based on the same assumptions and discount rate. However, they provide different views of the obligation. The *accumulated benefit obligation (ABO)* is the present value of pension benefits earned as of the balance sheet date based on current salaries. The *projected benefit obligation (PBO)* includes projected salary increases for career average or final pay plans.

The ABO and PBO differ only with respect to the treatment of future compensation growth; they are identical for flat benefit (non-pay-related) plans. Both measure benefits that, although earned, require future employee service; the third measure, the vested benefit obligation (VBO), includes only the portion of benefit obligations that is not contingent on future service.

SFAS 87 mandates use of the PBO to measure the pension obligation. The PBO is consistent with a going concern assumption as it is the present value of the benefits that will be paid if the pension plan and the firm continue. If, however, the pension plan were dissolved, the firm would be able to satisfy its employee obligations by paying only the (vested) ABO.

The benefit obligation is highly sensitive to the assumptions (see Figure 12-1) used to estimate future benefits. The most significant assumption is the *discount rate* used to compute the present value of the benefit obligation. It is intended to be a current interest rate (such as the rate at which the pension obligation could be settled).[3] Companies change the discount rate as market conditions change, and financial statement users must be alert as such changes may significantly affect the computed benefit obligation and pension cost, as discussed shortly.

The *rate of compensation increase* is another key assumption under SFAS 87.

Illustration. For each year of service, a firm promises to pay an employee at retirement an amount equivalent to one week's salary for 15 years. Our assumptions are:

Employee's age = 30 years	Retirement age = 65
Current salary level = $1,500/week	Discount rate = 10%
Projected salary at retirement = $2,000/week	

Obligation Based on Current Salary Levels. Accumulated benefit obligation (ABO) after the first year of service equals the present value of a 15-year annuity of $1,500, discounted for 35 years. Using Table 4 and Table 2 (see Present Value Tables at the end of the book) for an interest rate of 10% yields

$$\textbf{ABO} = \$1,500 \times 7.606 \times 0.03558 = \textbf{\$406}$$

Obligation Based on Projected Salary Levels. Projected benefit obligation (PBO) after the first year of service equals the present value of a 15-year annuity of $2,000, discounted for 35 years.

$$\textbf{PBO} = \$\,2,000 \times 7.606 \times 0.03558 = \textbf{\$541}$$

---

[3]Settlement means transfer of the obligation to another entity (such as an insurance company) in return for a cash payment from the employer (or plan).

Firms are expected to choose a rate of compensation increase that is economically consistent with other assumptions made. For example, a high inflation scenario is not compatible with a very low compensation growth rate. Except for the general guidance indicated, SFAS 87 does not limit an employer's choice of compensation growth rate and discount rate. In an AICPA survey[4] as of December 31, 1995, 471 firms (of 600 surveyed) with defined benefit pension plans reported discount rates ranging from 6.0% to 9.0%, with 89% using a discount rate of 7.0% to 8.0%. The same survey group showed rates of compensation growth ranging from 4.5% or less to 7.0%, with 74% reporting compensation growth rates of 5% or lower.

Factors Affecting Benefit Obligations

There are five factors that can affect the periodic measurement (change) of both ABO and PBO. As SFAS 87 requires the use of projected salaries to compute pension cost,[5] our discussion of these factors pertains primarily to the PBO. The PBO balance is derived as follows:

	PBO Opening Balance
$+$	Service cost
$+$	Interest cost
$+/-$	Actuarial gains/losses
$+/-$	Prior service cost
$-$	Benefits paid
$=$	PBO Closing Balance

Service Cost

The present value of benefits earned during the current period, or the *service cost*, is sensitive to all the assumptions used to compute the pension obligation, most particularly the discount rate. Service cost trends should generally track employee age and compensation trends, except when assumptions are changed. The service cost is a principal component of pension cost under SFAS 87.

> The $541 in our illustration is the first-year *service cost*, the PBO increase that results solely from this year's service.

Interest Cost

This factor is the increase in future pension payments (the benefit obligation) due to the passage of time. *Interest cost* represents the accretion of discount for that period and equals the product of the beginning projected benefit obligation and the discount rate. The discount rate used is the same as the one used to compute the PBO at the

[4]American Institute of Certified Public Accountants (AICPA), *Accounting Trends and Techniques* (New York: AICPA, 1996), p. 313.

[5]SFAS 87 governs the determination of pension cost. For most companies, that cost will be pension expense as well. In some cases, however, part of the cost is capitalized. For example, Sierra Pacific Resources disclosed in its *1995 Annual Report* that 65% of pension cost was charged to operations; the remainder was capitalized as part of utility plant.

previous year-end. For mature firms, interest cost can be the most significant component of pension cost (see the analysis of GM in Case 12-1).

After the second year,[6] if we ignore compensation for the second year's service, the PBO
increases as retirement is one year closer. That increase is

Interest cost = discount rate × opening PBO = 10% × $541 = $54.

Actuarial Gains and Losses

Changes in one or more actuarial assumptions, such as quit rates, retirement dates,
mortality, and discount rates require recalculation of the PBO, generating *actuarial
gains* (decreases in PBO) *or losses* (increases in the obligation).

Assume that, in the second year, the projected retirement salary increases by 10%; it is now
expected that, at retirement, the employee will earn $2,200 per week. Therefore, the annuity
to be paid is $4,400: $2,200 as a result of first year's service and $2,200 as a result of the second
year's service.

The PBO[7] for *each of these $2,200 annuities* is the present value of a 15-year annuity of
$2,200 discounted for 34 years:

$$\$2,200 \times 7.606 \times 0.03914 = \$655$$

Without the estimate revision, the PBO resulting from the first year's service was $595. The
change is a result of a revision in actuarial assumption, yielding an

Actuarial Loss = $60

Prior Service Cost from Plan Amendments

Pension plan amendments may increase (or decrease) previously specified pension
benefit obligations. Prior service cost is the increase in the PBO allocated to periods
of employment prior to the amendment.

---

[6]Note that after the second year, the annuity amount to be paid is $4,000; $2,000 as a result of first
year's service and $2,000 as a result of the second's year's service. The total PBO at the end of year 2 is
the present value of a 15 year annuity of $4,000 discounted for 34 years:

$$\$4,000 \times 7.606 \times .03914 = \$1,190$$

This is a $649 change from the previous year ($1,190 − $541). This increase is the sum of:

Interest Cost in year 2	$ 54
Service Cost for year 2's work (PBO of $2,000 benefit earned this year)	595
	$649

[7]Note that the total PBO at the end of year 2 is $1,310 (2 × $655), an increase of $769 from the
previous year. This increase is the sum of:

Interest cost in year 2	$ 54
Service cost for year 2 service (present value of $2,200 benefit earned this year)	655
Actuarial loss	60
Total increase	$769

> Assume now that there was no revision in the estimated rate of compensation increase; that is, estimated weekly salary at retirement remains $2,000. Instead, assume that, as a result of a renegotiation of the union contract, the benefit payable now is 110% of the weekly salary per year of service. If we use the same calculations as above,[8] the PBO resulting from the first year's service increases (by $60) because of the revised benefit formula. Therefore,
>
> **Prior Service Cost = $60**

Benefits Paid

Benefits paid to retired employees reduce the PBO as a portion of the obligation has been met.

Factors Affecting Plan Assets

The assets of the pension fund (see Figure 12-1) are affected by three factors:

	Plan Assets Opening Balance
+	Employer contributions
+	Return on assets
−	Benefits paid
=	Plan Assets Closing Balance

Employer Contributions

Employers make periodic contributions to the pension fund to fund their benefit obligations. Funding policy may be governed by income tax and ERISA rules, as well as employer cash flow considerations. Although prior to SFAS 87, firms used the same actuarial cost method to determine both pension cost and the amount contributed to the pension plan, that is no longer the case.

Return on Assets

The pension fund is (usually) managed by an independent trustee or investment advisor. The return on assets (ROA) is the actual return (capital gains plus dividends and interest) earned during the year, which can fluctuate from year to year.[9]

Benefits Paid

The benefits paid from plan assets are, of course, the same amounts discussed in the section on the pension obligation. This linkage facilitates reconciliation of the PBO and plan assets.

---

[8]Parenthetically, we should note that renegotiation of the contract will affect the ABO; revision in the rate of compensation increase will not.

[9]Because of this fluctuation, the expected long-term rate of return on plan assets (the forecasted rate of return) is used for accounting purposes.

Funded Status of Pension Plan

The funded status is a comparison of plan assets with the plan liability (e.g., the PBO). When plan assets are greater, the plan is overfunded and the firm has a net asset position. If plan assets are less than the PBO, the plan is underfunded and the firm has a net liability position with respect to its pension plan.

Nonsmoothed pension cost is comprised of four labor-related cost components (service, interest, actuarial gains and losses, and prior service cost) offset by one investment component (return on assets):

Nonsmoothed Pension Cost

	(1) Service cost
+	(2) Interest cost
+/−	(3) Actuarial gains and losses
+/−	(4) $\dfrac{\text{Prior service cost}}{\text{Gross pension cost}}$
+/−	(5) Return on assets

Nonsmoothed pension cost

The change in the pension plan status reflects both the nonsmoothed pension cost and the actual cash flows of the plan (contributions and benefits paid). Figure 12-2a demonstrates these relationships in T-account format.

FIGURE 12-2 Comparison of economic position and accounting for pension plans.

ACCOUNTING FOR PENSIONS: SFAS 87

SFAS 87, adopted in 1985, requires that all companies use the same actuarial cost method and requires disclosure of the key assumptions used to compute the pension obligation and pension cost. These assumptions, combined with other detailed disclosure requirements of SFAS 87, permit users of financial statements to analyze the status of the pension plan and the performance of the pension fund.

Under SFAS 87, however, the accounting impacts of economic events are smoothed to avoid volatility in the reporting of pension costs. As a result of this smoothing, accounting measures of periodic pension cost and pension plan status are often not reflective of economic reality. To evaluate the underlying cash flows and consequences of operating events, the analyst must unravel the smoothing and aggregating process.

Pension Cost: Components and Measurement

Under SFAS 87, reported pension cost includes both components reflecting actual events and elements (some aggregated) that smooth the effects of other events:

Components of Reported Pension Cost

Actual events	Service cost
	Interest cost
Smoothed events	Expected return on assets
	Amortization of gains and losses
	Amortization of prior service cost
	Amortization of transition asset or liability
Total	Reported pension cost

Figure 12-3 illustrates the interrelationship among these elements; Figures 12-2*a* and 12-2*b* show their correspondence in T-account format. Other than amortization of the transition asset or liability (not shown), each component corresponds to one pension plan factor already discussed.

Service Cost and Interest Cost

Service cost and interest cost are the actual amounts originating during the period as previously defined. Recall that pension cost is calculated using projected benefits rather than accumulated benefits.

Expected Return on Assets

To compute this component, firms estimate the expected long-term rate of return on plan assets. This is intended to be a more stable assumption than the discount rate, although firms can change this assumption. The 1995 AICPA survey[10] shows a median return assumption of 9% and a range of 6% to 11.5% or greater.

To dampen the effect of volatile investment returns on pension cost, the *expected ROA* (expected long-term rate of return times the opening fair value or market-related value of the plan assets) is the offset to other elements of pension cost. *As a*

---

[10] AICPA, *Accounting Trends and Techniques,* 1996, p. 314.

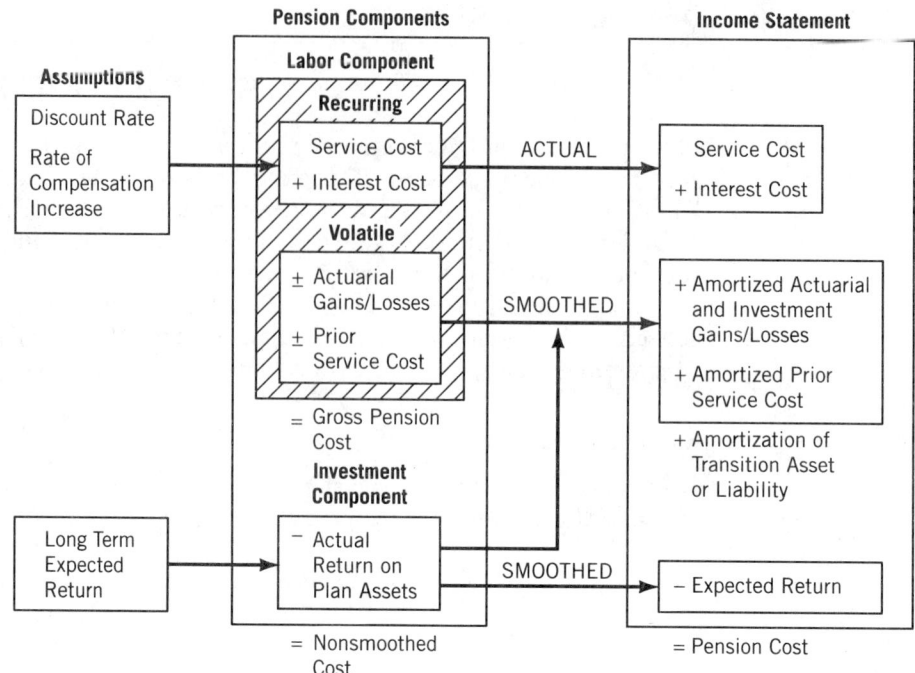

FIGURE 12-3 Relationship between actual pension components and income statement presentation.

result, pension cost reflects the expected return on assets rather than the actual return. The difference between the expected and the actual return on assets is deferred and accumulated on the assumption that the unexpected returns will balance out over time.

Amortization of Gains or Losses

Actuarial gains and losses and the difference between expected and actual ROA are deferred and accumulated. Total deferrals in excess of 10% of the larger of the PBO and the fair value of plan assets must be amortized over the average remaining employee service life.[11] Amortization of deferred amounts starts, when required, in the year following the year in which the deferrals originate. Any amortization of these combined deferrals becomes an additional element of pension cost.

Amortization of Prior Service Cost

Prior service cost is not expensed as incurred, but is amortized over the average remaining service life of employees as an additional component of pension cost.

Amortization of Transition Asset or Liability

The initial adoption of SFAS 87 generated either a transition asset or liability. Prior to adoption, firms recorded pension plan accruals based on their previous accounting

---

[11]This is the "corridor method" permitted by SFAS 87. The corridor method is an arbitrary means of deferring recognition of "temporary" gains and losses (which are expected to equalize over time) unless they become so large that there is reason to question their eventual reversal. Note that the amount to be amortized is recomputed each year.

method. The difference between the previous balance sheet accrual and the economic (funded) status of the plan (PBO less fair value of plan assets) was the transition asset or liability. This transition asset or liability remains "off balance sheet" but must be amortized over the average remaining service life of employees.[12] This amortization is yet another component of pension cost.

Disclosure of Plan Status

SFAS 87 requires disclosure of the:

- Components of pension cost
- Plan status and detailed reconciliation with the balance sheet accrual
- Assumptions used to calculate pension cost and obligations

The footnote disclosures allow analysts to differentiate between changes in pension cost due to operational factors and those due to changes in assumptions or the effects of prior period misestimation.

We discuss these disclosures using Exhibit 12-1, which presents duPont's 1994 pension footnote.

Pension Cost. DuPont reported pension cost for 1994 of $42 million. SFAS 87 requires that firms disclose the components of pension cost. Service cost ($380 million) and interest cost ($1,079 million) are the actual PBO increases for the year due to employee service and the passage of time. The relatively high interest cost indicates a mature plan. The interest cost of $1,079 million can be approximated by multiplying the opening PBO of $14,195 million by the discount rate of 7.25% (the rate in effect when the opening PBO was calculated), yielding $1,024 million.

The remaining components of pension cost are smoothed amounts rather than the actual amounts originating during the year. The actual return on assets was a negative $214 million. DuPont, however, reports a positive return of $1,326 million. This amount is computed using the assumed long-term rate of return on plan assets of 9% and average plan assets [$0.5 \times (\$14,223 + \$15,250) = \$14,737$] or $1,326 million.

Net amortization of $91 million is the sum of the amortization of the smoothed components of pension cost: prior service cost, actuarial and deferred investment gains/losses, and the transition asset.

Plan Status. SFAS 87 requires a detailed reconciliation of the funded status of defined benefit pension plans and disclosure of the:

- Projected benefit obligation
- Accumulated benefit obligation
- Vested benefit obligation
- Fair value of plan assets

---

[12]An amortization period of 15 years may be used when this average is less than 15 years.

EXHIBIT 12-1. DUPONT
Pension Plan Footnote

26. Pensions

The company has noncontributory defined benefit plans covering substantially all U.S. employees. The benefits for these plans are based primarily on years of service and employees' pay near retirement. The company's funding policy is consistent with the funding requirements of federal law and regulations.

Pension coverage for employees of the company's non-U.S. consolidated subsidiaries is provided, to the extent deemed appropriate, through separate plans. Obligations under such plans are systematically provided for by depositing funds with trustees, under insurance policies or by book reserves.

Net pension cost/(credit) for defined benefit plans includes the following components:

For U.S. plans, the projected benefit obligation was determined using a discount rate of 9 percent at December 31, 1994 and 7.25 percent at December 31, 1993, and an assumed long-term rate of compensation increase of 5 percent. The assumed long-term rate of return on plan assets is 9 percent. Plan assets consist principally of common stocks and U.S. government obligations. For non-U.S. plans, no one of which was material, similar economic assumptions were used.

The Omnibus Budget Reconciliation Act of 1990 permits employers to transfer some of the excess funds from an overfunded pension trust to pay the company portion of certain postretirement health care benefits. The company transferred $260 during 1993 to a special retiree health care account to be used toward the payment of these benefits. This transfer had no impact on earnings (see Note 25).

	1994		1993		1992	
Service cost—benefits earned during the period		$ 380		$ 301		$ 283
Interest cost on projected benefit obligation		1,079		1,038		980
Return on assets:						
Actual (gain)/loss	$ 214		$(1,880)		$(1,055)	
Deferred gain/(loss)	(1,540)	(1,326)	617	(1,263)	(164)	(1,219)
Amortization of net gains and prior service cost		(91)		(123)		(127)
Net pension cost/(credit)		$ 42		$ (47)		$ (83)

The change in the annual pension cost/(credit) was primarily due to the discount rate used to determine the present value of future benefits and the return on pension trust assets.

The funded status of these plans was as follows:

December 31	1994		1993
Actuarial present value of:			
Vested benefit obligation	$(10,342)		$(11,681)
Accumulated benefit obligation	$(10,744)		$(12,177)
Projected benefit obligation		$(12,303)	$(14,195)
Plan assets at fair value		14,223	15,250
Excess of assets over projected benefit obligation		1,920	1,055
Unrecognized net (gains)[1]		(877)	(35)
Unrecognized prior service cost		459	364
Prepaid pension cost[2]		$ 1,502	$ 1,384

1 Includes the unamortized balance of $(1,339) and $(1,513) at December 31, 1994 and 1993, respectively, of unrecognized net gain at January 1, 1985, the initial application date of Statement of Financial Accounting Standards No. 87, "Employers' Accounting for Pensions."
2 Excludes the pension liability for unfunded plans of $820 and $744 and the related projected benefit obligation of $1,213 and $1,228 at December 31, 1994 and 1993, respectively.

Source: DuPont, *1994 Annual Report.*

These data permit the analyst to see the plan status at a glance. However, a plan may appear to be overfunded (assets exceeding benefit obligation) if an unrealistically high discount rate is used (reducing the present values of pension obligations) or appear underfunded (assets less than benefit obligation) if a very low discount rate is employed.

SFAS 87 requires that all pension plan assets (other than operating assets such as office furniture) be carried at fair value. For assets without market quotations (such as nonpublic investments, real estate, and venture capital), current appraisals should be made.[13]

In addition, employers must reconcile the plan status with their balance sheet accruals. Accruals reflect the difference between reported pension cost and contributions.

DuPont's ABO equals $10,744 million. Most of this is vested as the VBO is $10,342 million. The PBO of $12,303 million includes the effect of projected salary increases. As plan assets are $14,223 million, duPont's pension plans are overfunded by $1,920 million in 1994 ($1,055 in 1993). On the balance sheet, however, duPont reported a pension asset of only $1,502 million, *understating* the economic status of the plan by $418 million. In 1993, duPont reported an asset of $1,384 million, *overstating* the net economic position by $329 million. For both years, the footnote reconciles the amounts reported on the balance sheet and the economic status of the plans. The difference is a result of *unrecognized* net (actuarial and investment) gains, prior service cost, and the transition asset. These are the components of nonsmoothed pension cost that are *smoothed* and recognized only over time.

The reconciliation of the plan status with the amounts reported on duPont's balance sheet reveals an unamortized transition gain and deferred losses and prior service cost.

Minimum Liability Adjustment. For plans where the sum of balance sheet accruals and the fair value of assets is less than the accumulated benefit obligation, that shortfall must be recognized on the balance sheet as a minimum liability. An example of the minimum liability is provided in Case 12-1, where GM's pension plan is analyzed.

Rates Used. SFAS 87 requires disclosure of the:

• Discount rate
• Rate of compensation increase (used to calculate the PBO)
• Long-term expected rate of return

DuPont discloses its rates as 9%, 5%, and 9%, respectively. Note that the 1994 discount rate of 9% is higher than the 7.25% used for 1993. The next section shows how these data can be used to further analyze a pension plan.

---

[13]We believe that, in practice, some employers smooth the recognition of value changes for assets with no clearly defined market value. As already noted, the market-related asset valuation can be used to compute the expected return-on-assets component of pension cost.

ANALYSIS OF PENSION COSTS AND LIABILITY

As already discussed, pension plan accounting defers and smoothes the underlying plan economics. Analysis of reported pension costs and liabilities requires focus on the:

1. Effect of the assumptions used
2. Underlying status of the pension plan
3. Calculation of nonsmoothed pension cost and cash flows

Importance of Assumptions

The SFAS 87 requirement that all enterprises use the same actuarial method to calculate benefit obligations and pension cost enhances interfirm comparability. However, companies are free to choose actuarial assumptions within a wide range.

The choice of assumptions affects the reported pension plan status and pension cost in a number of ways. The most immediate impact of assumptions is on the benefit obligation and, hence, the plan status. There is an indirect impact on the balance sheet as assumptions affect pension cost. However, because pension obligations may remain largely "off balance sheet," the full impact of variations in pension assumptions may not be reflected in balance sheet ratios using reported data.

Assumptions about the employee population are undisclosed; we must assume that the company's estimates of such factors as mortality, quit rates, and retirement ages are realistic. However, three key assumptions, the discount rate, rate of compensation increase, and expected long-term rate of return on plan assets, are disclosed.

Assumptions made by a company should be compared to those of its domestic and foreign competitors. One might expect that companies in the same industry, dealing with the same unions or employment market conditions, will have similar assumed rates of compensation increase. In practice, of course, companies do use different rates, just as they use different depreciation methods and lives for similar assets. These differences can be used to make comparative analyses more informative. Problem 16 examines differing assumptions in the chemical industry.

Exhibit 12-2 compares the three key assumptions—discount rate, rate of compensation increase, and expected long-term rate of return on plan assets—for the U.S. and non-U.S. pension plans of three U.S. automakers, General Motors, Ford, and Chrysler, with Honda, a major Japanese auto manufacturer.[14]

Examining the discount rate first, Ford uses the lowest and Chrysler the most aggressive rates. As Honda's "non-U.S." plans are wholly within Japan (see footnote 14), low rates reflect the low interest rates in that country. Note that all four firms raised their discount rate in 1994 and reduced it in 1995, mirroring changes in interest rates. The exception is Honda's Japanese discount rate, which was unchanged in 1994 and decreased in 1995, consistent with trends in Japanese interest rates.

The discount rate assumption, which drives the benefit obligation and hence the funded status (assets versus obligation), should, in theory, be identical for all U.S. companies.[15] Yet, in practice, discount rates vary from company to company. The differences may be a function of either corporate personality (some companies are

---

[14]Although Honda data are prepared in accordance with SFAS 87, they are not completely comparable. For years prior to fiscal 1995, its non-Japanese disclosures included only its U.S. plan; other non-Japanese plans were added in fiscal 1995. Honda's "domestic" (i.e., Japanese) plans are disclosed separately.

[15]Different discount rates for plans in foreign jurisdictions, however, should be expected. See Exhibit 12-2 for an auto industry comparison.

EXHIBIT 12-2
Comparison of Pension Plan Assumptions for Auto Industry

Assumption	Chrysler			Ford			General Motors			Honda*		
	1993	1994	1995	1993	1994	1995	1993	1994	1995	1993	1994	1995
Weighted-Average Discount Rate												
U.S. Plans	7.38%	8.63%	7.00%	7.00%	8.25%	7.00%	7.10%	8.50%	7.00%	7.50%	8.50%	8.00–8.50%
Non-U.S. Plans	8.25%	9.75%	8.25%	7.20%	8.30%	7.60%	8.00%	9.00%	8.00%	5.50%	5.50%	4.50%
Rate of Increase in Future Compensation												
U.S. Plans	6.00%	6.00%	6.00%	5.50%	5.50%	5.50%	5.20%	5.20%	5.10%	5.00–6.00%	5.00–6.00%	5.00–6.00%
Non-U.S. Plans	6.00%	6.00%	6.00%	5.10%	5.20%	5.10%	5.00%	4.80%	4.50%	3.00%	3.00%	3.00%
Expected Long-term Rate of Return on Assets												
U.S. Plans	10.00%	10.00%	10.00%	9.50%	9.00%	9.00%	10.10%	10.00%	10.00%	7.00–10.00%	8.50–9.00%	8.00–9.50%
Non-U.S. Plans	9.00%	9.00%	9.00%	9.50%	9.00%	9.00%	10.00%	9.80%	9.90%	6.00%	5.50%	4.00%

*Years end March 31 of following year.
"U.S. Plan" data consist of Honda's non-Japanese pension plans.
"Non-U.S." data consist of Honda's Japanese pension plans.

more conservative than others) or the plan status itself (a company with an underfunded plan may be tempted to use a higher discount rate to minimize the reported underfunding).

Chrysler assumes the highest expected compensation growth rate. Honda's low rate for its Japanese plans reflects that country's low inflation. The higher rates for Chrysler should affect its relative actuarial gains and losses and changes in pension plan status. GM's low assumed rate (relative to its competitors) is surprising given that it negotiates with the same union.

Ford reports the lowest expected return on assets (9.00%) in 1995, with both GM and Chrysler using 10.00%. Honda uses a range of rates for its non-Japanese plans; the low assumed rate in Japan reflects that country's low interest rates. These differences should be compared with the actual returns earned by the plans over time. The expected ROA impacts reported pension cost only; the higher the expected rate, the lower the cost. Again, theory says that all companies should have the same long-term expected rate available to them in the marketplace. However, in practice, the choice of rate varies. Companies have an incentive to choose a high assumed rate, to report lower pension cost, but an unrealistically high rate will create deferred losses that will, eventually, have to be amortized as a component of future pension cost.

Impact of Assumptions on Pension Obligations

The discount rate assumption has the greatest impact on the reported pension plan status as it is used to compute the present value of the various benefit obligation measures. *A higher (lower) discount rate decreases (increases) the calculated PBO.* As companies are required to disclose the choice of discount rate, the effect of that choice can be examined, and choices of different employers can be compared. Because of the mathematics of present value, adjustments for different rates are difficult to make. Increasing the discount rate from 10% to 11% does not, for example, change the calculated PBO by exactly one-tenth.

Blankley and Swanson (1995) provide evidence that firms do not change discount rates as often as would be warranted by movements in general interest rate levels. Furthermore, they note that this lack of conformity is greatest when rates are declining as firms want to avoid increases in the PBO and pension costs.

The rate of compensation growth also affects the PBO, but less than the discount rate. A higher rate (employee compensation increases more rapidly) increases the calculated PBO, whereas a lower rate decreases the PBO. (The assumed rate is zero for non-pay-related plans.) The reported ABO is not affected by this choice since it excludes the impact of future pay increases; an increase in the assumed rate of compensation growth therefore increases the difference between the ABO and PBO.

Comparisons of the PBO and ABO with the market value of plan assets require consideration of the choice of discount rate and rate of compensation growth. Aggressive assumptions (high discount rate, low rate of compensation increase) improve the reported status of the plan, whereas conservative assumptions (low discount rate, high rate of compensation increase) make the plan appear less well funded.

Impact of Assumptions on Pension Cost

The discount rate has a direct effect on the calculation of service cost as it is used to compute the present value of benefits earned in the current year. The impact is similar to the effect on the pension obligation: A higher rate reduces service cost, a lower rate increases that cost.

Calculation of the interest component of pension cost (the product of the PBO and discount rate) is also affected by the discount rate because both elements of the computation change. Although the effects are opposite (higher discount rate reduces the PBO), the net result of increasing the discount rate is an increase in interest cost.[16] Although the interest cost effect offsets part of the service cost effect, the effect on service cost is normally much greater. Thus, in most cases, a higher discount rate reduces reported pension cost.[17]

The effect of a change in the rate of compensation increase is easier to predict. A higher rate increases both the service cost and interest cost (by increasing the PBO). Conversely, a lower rate of compensation increase decreases all present value calculations and therefore pension cost. Finally, higher assumed rates of return on assets lower pension cost, since the expected return on assets is an offset to other components of that cost.[18]

Summing up, we see that both a low rate of compensation increase and high assumed rate of return on assets decrease pension cost and, therefore, increase reported earnings. Higher discount rates lower the obligation and pension cost. From a quality of earnings viewpoint, these choices are aggressive and result in higher income, but lower quality earnings. Ultimately, however, overly aggressive choices are likely to result in experience (actuarial) losses that will have to be amortized and increase pension cost in the future.

Analysis of Plan Status, Costs, and Cash Flows

Given that pension cost under SFAS 87 contains accruals that depend on managers' accounting choices and the liability shown on the balance sheet reflects the interaction of this calculated cost with pension contributions, we need other measures of a firm's pension cost and liability. It is essential to go beyond the amounts recognized in the financial statements to obtain a better understanding of the impact of the pension plan on the firm. The following issues need to be addressed:

1. What is the firm's actual economic liability?
2. What are the cash flows (contributions and benefit payments) and what do trends in these cash flows mean?
3. What are the elements of (nonsmoothed) pension cost? How are they affected by smoothing? Which economic events have not been recognized for accounting purposes?
4. How can analysts separate the employee service components of pension cost from those related to the investment performance of plan assets?

---

[16]This is analogous to the effect of rising interest rates on bond prices; they fall but the interest cost of subsequent borrowings increases.

[17]In a very mature plan, with very high interest cost relative to service cost, the effect of the discount rate on interest cost may dominate the analysis.

[18]When a company uses the market-related value of plan assets rather than actual asset value, the return on assets calculation is slower to reflect changes in market value. When asset values are rising, therefore, this choice will result in higher pension cost.

Balance Sheet Adjustments. The reported balance sheet liability should be replaced by a measure of the actual plan status. Possible measures of the obligation are the:

- PBO less fair value of plan assets
- ABO or VBO less fair value of plan assets
- PBO
- ABO or VBO

Depending on the purpose of the analysis and the firm's tax status, the measurements may be made either pretax or after tax.

Analysis of Components of Pension Cost and Cash Flows. The following alternative pension cost measures should be computed and their trends analyzed. These alternative measures are not used for accounting purposes but, as in the case of the alternative liability measures, may be more relevant for analysis. These measures eliminate the smoothing imposed by SFAS 87 and reflect the underlying economics of the plan as described earlier and illustrated in Figures 12-2 and 12-3:

1. *Service cost* measures only the benefits earned in the current period. It ignores interest cost and other adjustments (actuarial) to previously earned benefits. The trend in service cost reflects the trend in payroll cost and employee age. Sharp drops (or increases) in this item may result from significant restructuring or other indicators of employee changes.[19]

2. *Recurring cost,* the sum of service and interest costs, excludes actuarial gains or losses and adjustments for prior service.

3. *Gross pension cost* equals the change in PBO excluding benefits paid, but encompassing all labor-related cost factors (including the gross actuarial gains and losses and prior service cost).[20]

4. *Nonsmoothed pension cost* equals gross pension cost less actual investment returns; it measures pension cost without the smoothing effects of SFAS 87. This cost is more volatile because it includes actual investment performance rather than expected returns, and the total amounts of actuarial gains or losses and prior service cost rather than only the net amortization of these amounts.

None of these measures reports the actual cash flows related to the plan. The analysis of the plan is, however, incomplete without examining contributions and benefits paid:

5. *Employer contribution* is the actual cash flow from the company to the plan. The plan status can help the estimation of future cash flows: A growing plan

---

[19]Trends in service cost should be evaluated carefully following the firm's announcement of significant layoffs. For example, service cost reported by IBM grew 27% from 1987 to 1991 ($545 to $691 million) and then declined 22% to $542 million in 1994. The firm began restructuring its workforce in 1989 with the most significant charges, $11.4 billion, taken in 1992 and 1993. Through 1994, 98,000 employees had left IBM.

[20]It can also be calculated using the ABO as the change in the ABO plus the benefits paid.

deficit (PBO less plan assets) suggests that higher contributions will be required in the future; a surplus suggests that future contributions can be reduced.

6. *Benefits paid* are the actual payments made by the plan to retirees.

We illustrate this analysis using the duPont example after a brief discussion of the merits of the alternative measures of pension liability and cost.

Motivation for Adjustments to Liability and Cost

The research discussed in Box 12-3 indicates that the market incorporates the "off-balance-sheet" pension liability in its assessment of a firm's debt position. The market tends to ignore the smoothed elements of cost but, instead, focuses on nonsmoothed cost. Specific adjustments depend on the interpretation of two issues defining the relationship of a firm to its pension plan. The finance and labor economics literature discuss these issues in great detail. This section provides a general discussion of the issues.

The first issue deals with measurement of the firm's liability (and hence expense) to its employees. Is the appropriate measure of the liability the PBO, the ABO, or VBO? In theory, firms can terminate the plan or individual employees at any time. Upon termination, the firm's obligation would be measured by either the ABO or VBO, depending on the circumstances.

SFAS 87 requires that pension cost be measured using the PBO, making the implicit assumption that the firm will *not:*

- Terminate employees before they reach vested status (other than normal turnover, one of the actuarial assumptions).
- Terminate employees in their intermediate or later work years (excluding normal turnover) when the projections on which the PBO are based come to fruition.
- Fail to grant pay raises.
- Terminate the plan and satisfy the obligation early.

These assumptions stem from the going concern assumption that underlies the preparation of financial statements. That is why, in most cases, projected benefits data should be used to analyze a company's pension plan. The ABO is the appropriate measure of the pension obligation only if we assume termination of the plan (perhaps in takeover analysis). Assuming termination of the plan, however, also requires analysis of the impact of such termination on the workforce of the company.

If the going concern assumption is not valid (in bankruptcy, e.g.), then the ABO or VBO should be used to measure the pension obligation.[21] Under these circumstances, however, all assets and liabilities of the firm need to be evaluated for the impact of this event.

Another issue is whether the pension plan should be considered an integral part of the firm or viewed as an independent entity. Under defined benefit plans, employers bear the risk of investment performance. If the pension fund is insufficient to meet the obligations of the pension plan, the firm must cover the shortfall. Conversely, the firm can capture any excess assets by either lowering future contributions or terminat-

---

[21]However, in bankruptcy, regulations of the Pension Benefit Guaranty Corp. (PBGC) may limit the firm's obligation to 40% of stockholders' equity.

BOX 12-3
Market Valuation of Pension Liability and Costs

Research on the market's view of corporate pension liabilities has focused on three issues:

1. Does the market value a dollar of pension liability in the same manner as it values a dollar of other liabilities of a firm?

2. What is the most appropriate basis for measurement of the liability: the PBO, ABO, or VBO?

3. Does the market evaluate the pension liability (however measured) on a gross basis or net of the pension fund's assets?

The first issue is complicated by the argument that the pension liability *should differ* from other liabilities by virtue of its tax deductibility. Unlike other debt where the payment of principal is not tax-deductible, reductions in the liability due to firm contributions are usually tax-deductible. Thus, if the market reduces its valuation of a firm by $1 for each dollar of debt, $1 of pension liability should reduce valuation by only $\$(1 - t)$, where t represents the firm's marginal tax rate.

The second question relates to the going concern assumption underlying pension measurements. This assumption is consistent with the view that pensions are a form of implicit contract between the firm and its employees. Use of the PBO measure recognizes that an implicit contract exists whereby the firm will continue to adjust salaries upward with inflation. Moreover, the firm will not terminate the plan early, thereby ultimately redressing the undercompensation of younger workers relative to older ones.

The third issue implicitly addresses the ownership of the underlying property rights of the pension assets. Landsman (1986) studied pension assets separately from the pension liabilities, and

> disaggregated corporate assets into pension and non-pension assets and corporate liabilities into pension and non-pension liabilities. This procedure does two things. First, it allows for the possibility that pension assets represent assets to which the firm has claim, and that pension liabilities represent a debt obligation of the firm. Second, if in fact pension assets are corporate assets and pension liabilities are corporate obligations, it also permits the pension and non-pension components of corporate assets and liabilities to be differentially priced by the securities markets.*

Prior to SFAS 87, pension accounting was based on APB 8, under which the only disclosure required was the *unfunded portion of the VBO.* SFAS 36, issued in 1980, required disclosure of the entire ABO but not the PBO. Hence, many researchers were constrained by the lack of data as to the total ABO, PBO, and value of pension assets.

Beta and the Pension Liability

One of the determinants of a firm's risk is its financial leverage, with a leveraged firm being riskier than an unleveraged one. Using beta (β) to measure the systematic risk of the firm Dhaliwal (1986) found that adjusting the debt-to-equity ratio by including unfunded (vested) pension liabilities improved the explanatory power of his predictive model. Market participants view unfunded (vested) pension liabilities in much the same way as they view other debt in assessing a firm's systematic risk. This conclusion reinforces our view that financial statements adjusted for pension plan status are more useful for financial analysis.

Market Valuation of Liability

Feldstein and Morck (1983) examined the market's valuation of a firm's pension liability. Using 1979 data for 132 companies, they were limited insofar as only the unfunded ABO and unfunded vested ABO information was available. They hypothesized that these liabilities should reduce the value of the firm on a dollar-for-dollar basis. Thus, a market valuation equation that includes pension liabilities as one of its explanatory variables should yield a coefficient of −1 for the pension liabilities. They found that one could not reject the hypothesis that the coefficient was equal to −1. Results for the vested and total ABO were similar. Additionally, they found that interest rate assumptions varied widely among firms. When an average rate† was used, they found a better fit for their equations, suggesting that the market adjusts the rates used by firms to some overall average.

Daley (1984) argued that the pension liability should not be valued on a dollar-for-dollar basis but rather on an after-tax basis. Only for an adjusted liability, that is, the liability multiplied by $(1 - t)$ would the expected coefficient be −1. Daley, however, found that for his sample, the unfunded vested pension benefit (UVB), adjusted for taxes, had coefficients ranging from −1.5 to −3 and that these variables were significantly different than −1. He does however note that

> this result is consistent with prior research, once an adjustment for the average marginal tax rate is imposed. In Oldfield (1976) and Feldstein and Seligman (1981), no tax adjustment was used and the coefficients associated with UVB measure are approximately −1.0 to −1.5. Impounding the tax rate of $(1 - t)$ tax adjusted values of these coefficients would be −1.92 to −2.88 (assuming a .48 marginal tax rate). Thus, the results here are at least partially supported by earlier research.‡

Daley also examined the effects of using pension expense rather than UVB in the valuation model and found that the pension expense had more explanatory power than the UVB.

An explanation for the finding that the absolute value of the coefficient is greater than −1 might be that these studies were limited to the use of liabilities based on the ABO. The PBO is greater than the ABO. Thus, it is possible that the market based its valuation of the PBO by adjusting each ABO dollar by an amount greater than 1. Alternatively, misspecified coefficients may result if there are missing variables that are systematically related to those variables used in the equation. This raises the intriguing possibility that pension liabilities were acting as a surrogate for postretirement health benefits not contained in these equations. They are off-balance-sheet and would be expected to be systematically related to pension obligations.

Subsequent studies, however, do not seem to support these explanations. Gopalakrishnan and Sugrue (1993) used 1987 and 1988 PBO data and confirmed Landsman's findings that the market viewed pension plan assets and the PBO as assets and liabilities of the firm. However, they found that only the 1988 coefficient on the PBO (−0.98) was close to its theoretical value of −1; in 1987 it was −1.78. Amir (1996) included the unfunded PBO as well as the postretirement health benefit liability and found both to be value-relevant. However, his results also indicated that the coefficient on the pension liability was greater than the theoretical value of −1.

Market Valuation of Pension Cost Components

Barth et al. (1992) using SFAS 87-based data compared the market valuation of various components of pension expense with nonpension expense items. Market valuation of a revenue or expense item reflects the extent to which the market discounts the future stream of this component. Therefore, a higher valuation means that the market uses a lower discount rate for that item. They found that pension expense was more heavily valued than other nonpension items. The reason for this higher valuation may be that the market views pension expense as less risky; hence, a lower discount rate is appropriate. The fact that pension expense includes the return on plan assets, which are usually invested in less risky assets such as bonds, is consistent with this result. Moreover, the interest component of pension expense is also relatively predictable and hence less "risky."

With respect to the components of pension expense, they found the interest component as well as the expected and actual return on plan assets to have the highest valuation. A "zero" valuation for the three amortization components was found. This is to be expected as these items reflect no new information. The most surprising result was that the service cost component seemed to be valued "incorrectly" by the market (i.e., the higher the component, the higher the firm's value). The authors attributed this result to correlations among the various components.

Notwithstanding this anomalous finding, the study also found that the income components as well as the balance sheet elements of the pension costs were incrementally informative when included in a firm's valuation model. Again, this suggests that detailed analysis of a firm's pension plan contributes to better investment and credit decisions.

---

*Wayne Landsman, "An Empirical Investigation of Pension and Property Rights," *The Accounting Review,* Oct. 1986, p. 664.

†They used the average rate calculated over all firms in the sample. The adjustment procedure was approximate; they multiplied the ABO by the ratio of the firm's assumed interest rate to the average rate.

‡Lane A. Daley, "The Valuation of Reported Pension Measures for Firms Sponsoring Defined Benefit Plans," *The Accounting Review,* April 1984, p. 194.

ing the plan. There are some restrictions (mainly ERISA) affecting the level of contributions and the ability of the firm to utilize the assets of the plan.[22]

If the pension plan is considered to be an integral part of the firm, then its balance sheet should be adjusted by adding pension plan assets to the firm's assets and the PBO to the firm's liabilities. The difference between plan assets and the liability (PBO) should be added to stockholders' equity. Pension cost should be the "gross pension cost" defined earlier. The return on plan assets should be included in the income statement as investment income. The only cash flow effect of the pension plan would be the benefits paid; contributions to the plan would be transfers of cash from one "subsidiary" of the firm to another.

However, if we see the pension plan as independent of the firm, then only the net difference between the plan assets and the PBO should be added to the firm's liabilities (or assets, if pension assets exceed PBO). The offset to this adjustment would again be a component of stockholders' equity. This approach recognizes that retirees have first claim against pension assets; only the residual is an asset or liability of the employer. In this case, pension cost would be net of the actual returns on the pension plan; that is, the nonsmoothed amount shown earlier and the cash flow effect would be the contributions from the firm to the pension plan.

SFAS 87 treats the pension plan as a separate entity. Only the net asset or liability and the net pension cost (to the extent there is recognition) are reflected in the financial statements. Generally speaking, we concur with this view. Thus, based on the going concern view, we believe that under most circumstances, the PBO less the plan assets should be used to measure the liability.

Analysis of DuPont Pension Plan Disclosures

We now apply our analysis to the pension plan of duPont, whose pension note is shown in Exhibit 12-1 (p. 606).

---

[22]For companies in regulated industries, such as public utilities, any surplus may belong to the ratepayers rather than the employer. Similarly, there is some question as to the "ownership" of surplus pension assets of defense contractors, whose profits are regulated by the U.S. government. For example, the pension footnote from the *1990 Annual Report* of McDonnell Douglas states that the U.S. government indicates that it is "entitled to its equitable share of pension fund reversions to the extent that the Government participated in pension costs through their contracts." Yet McDonnell Douglas was able to recognize a substantial settlement gain in 1990 (see discussion later in this chapter).

Balance Sheet Adjustments. The economic status of duPont's plan is the difference between plan assets and its benefit obligations. *On a going concern basis, the PBO is the appropriate measure of the obligation.* DuPont's plans were overfunded by $1,920 million, as plan assets of $14,223 exceed the PBO of $12,303 million. As the balance sheet reports a pension asset of only $1,502 million, *duPont's assets and equity should each be increased by $418 million.*

For liquidation analysis, the ABO would be the appropriate measure. On that basis, the overfunding is $3,479 million ($14,223 − $10,744). If we use the ABO to measure the pension obligation, *duPont's assets and equity should be increased by $1,977 million ($3,479 − $1,502).*

The above adjustments suffice when a firm has not recorded a minimum liability. When a minimum liability is recorded, an additional adjustment to the firm's balance sheet may be required. This adjustment is illustrated in Case 12-1 (GM), which also discusses deferred income tax effects.

Cash Flow and Income Analysis. The footnote disclosures allow us to calculate the actual expense and cash flows associated with the pension plan. The following steps should be taken in sequence. For each step, we note which information is provided in duPont's footnote (or derived in the preceding step) and which item (shown in bold type) must be computed.

Step 1: **Calculate contributions** made to the plan by firm.
Use the relationship between the opening and closing balance sheet liability and the reported pension cost:

Opening balance sheet liability (asset)	$(1,384)	Given
+ Pension cost (benefit)	42	Given
− Contributions	**160**	**Plug**
= Closing balance sheet liability (asset)	$(1,502)	Given

Contributions = Pension Cost − Change in Balance Sheet Liability
$$\textbf{\$160} = \textbf{\$42} − \textbf{[\$(1,502) − (\$1,384)]}$$

Step 2: **Calculate benefits paid** to employees.
Use the relationship between the opening and closing balances in the plan assets, the actual ROA, and contributions (derived in Step 1):

Opening plan assets	$15,250	Given
+ ROA	(214)	Given
+ Contributions	160	Derived in Step 1
− Benefits paid	**973**	**Plug**
Closing plan assets	$14,223	Given

Benefits Paid = Contributions + ROA − Change in Plan Assets
$$\textbf{\$973 = \$160} \quad \textbf{+ \$(214) − (\$14,223 − \$15,250)}$$

Step 3: Calculate gross pension cost.
Use the relationship between the opening and closing balances in the PBO and benefits paid (derived in Step 2):

Opening PBO	$14,195	Given
+ Gross pension cost	**(919)**	**Plug**
− Benefits paid	973	Derived in Step 2
Closing PBO	$12,303	Given

Gross Pension Cost = Benefits Paid + Change in PBO
$$\textbf{\$(919)} \qquad\qquad = \textbf{\$973} \qquad + (\textbf{\$12,303} - \textbf{\$14,195})$$

Note that gross pension cost includes recurring costs (service and interest) plus actuarial gains/losses and prior service cost. *However, we are able to calculate gross pension cost without having to derive actuarial gains and losses and prior service cost separately.* The total of these two components equals the difference between the recurring cost and gross pension cost (see below); here, a gain of ($2,378) million. In Box 12-4, we disaggregate the individual components. In duPont's case, we find that the $2,378 is primarily a result of actuarial gains from the discount rate change.

The actual (nonsmoothed) measures of pension cost and cash flows associated with the plan can now be summarized:

Measures of Pension Cost ($ in millions)

(a) Service cost	**$ 380**	Given
Interest cost	1,079	Given
(b) Recurring pension cost	**$ 1,459**	
Nonrecurring costs (actuarial gains and losses + prior service costs)	(2,378)	Plug
(c) Gross pension cost (benefit)	**$ (919)**	Step 3
Actual ROA loss	214	Given
(d) Nonsmoothed cost (benefit)	**$ (705)**	

Pension Plan Cash Flows

(e) Contributions	**$ 160**	Step 1
(f) Benefits paid	**$ 973**	Step 2

DuPont reported pension cost of $42 million in 1994. Our analysis, however, shows that the firm actually realized a benefit of $705 million from its plan during the year and that the benefit emanated from the employee service-related costs not the investment returns (ROA). Furthermore, that benefit largely reflected an actuarial gain from increasing the discount rate used to calculate the PBO.

Prior service cost and actuarial gains and losses have different origins and, therefore, different implications for analysis. In most cases, separating the two requires simplifying and sometimes arbitrary assumptions. As errors caused by faulty assumptions tend to be small, approximations usually provide the insights needed.

Estimation Procedure

The following templates can be used to estimate both amortization and newly originating actuarial gains and losses and prior service cost. We use data from duPont's 1994 pension footnote to illustrate:

Net (Gains) and Losses		Prior Service Cost	
Opening balance*	$1,478	Opening balance	$364
Less: amortization	?	Less: amortization	?
Plus:		Plus	
Deferred investment (gains) losses	1,540	**New prior service cost**	**?**
New actuarial (gains) losses	**?**	Ending balance	$459
Ending balance*	$ 462		

*DuPont (unlike most companies) includes the transition asset in net gains/losses. Removing the transition asset from net gains/losses yields the opening balance of $1,478 [($35) − ($1,513)] and closing balance of $462 [($877) − ($1,339)].

DuPont reports net amortization of ($91) million, including amortization of:

- Actuarial and investment gains (or losses)
- Transition asset
- Prior service cost

Amortization of the transition asset equals the change in the unamortized balance (disclosed in the footnote):

$$\$(1,513) \text{ million} - \$(1,339) \text{ million} = \$(174) \text{ million}$$

Subtracting this amount from net amortization of $(91) million leaves $83 million [$(91) − $(174)] amortization of:

- Actuarial and investment (gains) losses
- Prior service cost

Allocation of this amount between the two sources requires an assumption. When the corridor method (see footnote 11 on p. 604) is used, amortization of the net gains/losses can be estimated. For duPont, 10% of plan assets (larger than the PBO) at year-end 1993 was $1,520 million. As the opening balance of net losses was below that amount, we can assume zero amortization; therefore, the $83 million amortization must relate entirely to prior service cost. With this assumption, we can derive the missing amounts in the two templates:

Net (Gains) and Losses		Prior Service Cost	
Opening balance	$ 1,478	Opening balance	$364
Less: amortization	0	Less: amortization	83
Plus:		Plus	
Deferred investment (gains) losses	1,540	**New prior service cost**	**178**
New actuarial (gains) losses	**(2,556)**	Ending balance	$459
Ending balance	$ 462		

EXHIBIT 12-3. DUPONT
Analysis of Pension Plans, 1990 to 1995 ($ in millions)

Pension Plan Status	1990	1991	1992	1993	1994	1995	
Pension plan assets	$12,809	$14,999	$14,648	$15,250	$14,223	$16,691	
Projected benefit obligation	8,792	11,550	11,815	14,195	12,303	15,404	
Excess assets over PBO	$ 4,017	$ 3,449	$ 2,833	$ 1,055	$ 1,920	$ 1,287	
Prepaid pension cost	2,099	1,534	1,448	1,384	1,502	1,724	

	1990	1991	1992	1993	1994	1995	Cumulative
Pension Cost							
Service cost	$ 274	$ 259	$ 283	$ 301	$ 380	$ 292	$ 1,789
Interest cost	810	860	980	1,038	1,079	1,140	5,907
Recurring cost	$ 1,084	$ 1,119	$ 1,263	$ 1,339	$ 1,459	$ 1,432	$ 7,696
Prior service cost	281	24	82	12	178	114	691
Actuarial losses (gains)	(334)	1,626	157	2,196	(2,556)	2,715	3,804
Gross pension cost	$ 1,031	$ 2,769	$ 1,502	$ 3,547	$ (919)	$ 4,261	$12,191
Actual ROA (gain)	140	(2,937)	(1,055)	(1,880)	214	(3,417)	(8,935)
Nonsmoothed pension cost	$ 1,171	$ (168)	$ 447	$ 1,667	$ (705)	$ 844	$ 3,256
Service cost	$ 274	$ 259	$ 283	$ 301	$ 380	$ 292	$ 1,789
Interest cost	810	860	980	1,038	1,079	1,140	5,907
Expected ROA	(1,226)	(1,148)	(1,219)	(1,263)	(1,326)	(1,335)	(7,517)
Net amortization	(166)	(142)	(127)	(123)	(91)	(108)	(757)
Reported pension cost (credit)	$ (308)	$ (171)	$ (83)	$ (47)	$ 42	$ (11)	$ (578)
Cash Flows							
Contributions	$ 116	$ (736)	$ (169)	$ (111)	$ 160	$ 211	$ (529)
Benefits paid	734	11	1,338	1,167	973	1,268	5,491
Discount rate	9.75%	8.50%	8.50%	7.25%	9.00%	7.25%	

Source: DuPont Annual Reports (1990–1995) and analysis thereof.

Analysis of duPont's Pension Trends

Exhibit 12-3 provides an analysis of duPont's pension plan disclosures over the 1990 to 1995 period. Data for the 1990 to 1993 period and for 1995 were based on those years' financial statements.

The data indicate these plans have been overfunded (plan assets exceed PBO) throughout the 1990 to 1995 period.[23] The degree of overfunding, however, declined considerably over that period as the 1990 overfunding of $4,017 million declined by over two-thirds to $1,287 million in 1995.

---

[23]Note, however, that these disclosures exclude data relating to unfunded plans. These unfunded plans, for senior management, are not analyzed here. The PBO for these plans was $1,213 million at December 31, 1994. Including these plans, duPont's pensions are barely overfunded. As discussed in Chapter 17, adjusted balance sheets should consider all plans.

This decline can be explained by examining the components of the PBO and plan assets separately. The PBO grew from $8.8 to $15.4 billion, an increase of more than 80%, whereas plan assets have increased by only 30% (from $12.8 to $16.7 billion).

An analysis of the components of the PBO provides some explanation for its faster growth. Service cost remained relatively steady over the period and decreased to $292 million in 1995, reflecting the 1993 restructuring. Interest cost increased steadily over this time period and had a much larger cumulative impact on the PBO than service cost.

Prior service cost was not a major factor; actuarial losses were. Over the 1990 to 1995 period, such losses accounted for $3,804 million (nearly 60%) of the PBO increase. Note that actuarial (gains) losses coincide with discount rate changes.

Investment Performance Trends. The actual return on plan assets has fluctuated widely from year to year. Over the six-year period, the arithmetic average rate of return was approximately 10%. In 1995, the plan earned a 24% return (ROA of $3,417 on assets of $14,223 million). Excluding this return brings the average rate (1990 to 1994) to 8.5%. DuPont's use of a long-term expected ROA of 9% therefore seems reasonable.

Analysis of Trends in Pension Costs. With the (minor) exception of 1994, duPont reported a pension credit each year, but with a declining trend. The primary causes were the expected return on plan assets and the amortization reported each year. The expected return on plan assets offset the increasing interest cost.

Alternative measures of pension cost suggest a very different trend. Recurring cost (the sum of service and interest costs) increased nearly 40% from $1,084 in 1990 to $1,432 million in 1995. The cumulative nonsmoothed pension cost presents a startlingly different picture than the reported pension cost. *Over the six-year period 1990 to 1995, duPont's nonsmoothed pension cost totaled $3.3 billion, in contrast to the total reported credit of $0.6 billion.* Under SFAS 87, duPont was able to defer the large actuarial losses.

Cash Flow Trends. As discussed in the next section, discontinuities such as acquisitions and divestitures may distort cash flow data (contributions and benefits paid). This seems to be the case for duPont as the calculated contributions indicate that duPont received "refunds" in the 1991 to 1993 period. We can surmise, however, that any contributions were small as, otherwise, the distortions would not convert contributions into refunds. Benefits paid, however, have remained high. The low level of contributions and high benefit payments are factors in the decline of duPont's overfunded status. The firm may have to increase contributions in the future depending on the rate of growth in benefits and return on plan assets.

Overall, duPont provides an example of a relatively healthy plan. Recurring costs seem to be under control. Actuarial losses were driven by declining discount rates.[24] Investment returns are in line with the expected rate of 9%. In Case 12-1, where GM's pension plans are examined, a different picture emerges.

---

[24]Those declines, it must be noted, contributed to the high actual ROA over the period. The disclosure requirements of SFAS 87 mark to market both sides of the pension plan balance sheet.

Estimating Future Pension Cost

We have examined duPont's pension costs for the period 1990 to 1995. The provisions of SFAS 87 make it possible to forecast future (reported) pension cost. In this section, we use these data to forecast duPont's 1996 pension cost.

The first element, service cost, may be difficult to forecast. 1995 service cost declined to $292 million, partly because of the restructuring and partly because of the higher interest rate assumption at year-end 1994. The restructuring is complete and the discount rate decreased in 1995; both factors should increase 1996 service cost. We must also consider the effects of inflation and the aging workforce as it nears retirement. Overall, therefore, we project a 20% increase in service cost to $350 million, mainly due to the effect of the lower discount rate.

Interest cost is easier to forecast. It can be estimated as the PBO at year-end 1995 multiplied by the discount rate in effect at that time or $7.25\% \times \$15,404 = \$1,117$ million.

Similarly, the expected return on assets can be estimated as plan assets at year-end 1995 times the long-term expected rate of return, or $9\% \times \$16,691 = \$1,502$ million.

We assume that net amortization remains at its current level of $108 million for the following reasons:

- Actuarial gains/losses are not amortized due to application of the corridor method.
- Prior service costs have not increased significantly.
- DuPont continues to amortize its transition asset.

These assumptions result in the following forecast:

**Forecast of DuPont's 1996
Pension Cost**

Service cost	$ 350 million
Interest cost	1,117
Expected ROA	(1,502)
Net amortization	(108)
Net pension cost	$ (143)

For 1995, duPont reported a pension credit of $11 million. In 1996, that credit is forecasted to increase considerably. The lower discount rate (reducing interest cost) and high 1995 (actual) return on assets (increasing the expected ROA) are the major contributors to the forecasted increase.

How good was this forecast? At the time this forecast was made,[25] duPont had as yet not issued its *1996 Annual Report*. Thus, we provide the forecast without the benefit of hindsight. We leave it to the reader to evaluate its accuracy.

---

[25]The manuscript was submitted in November 1996.

IMPACT OF DISCONTINUITIES

The preceding sections have considered pension plans without significant changes in the firm or the plan. This section discusses the effect of departures from these assumptions.

Acquisitions and Divestitures

Acquisitions and divestitures often create discontinuities in financial data that hamper financial analysis (see Chapter 14). The acquisition or divestiture of an entity with a defined benefit pension plan impacts the balance sheet, and related footnotes, and therefore, the analysis of the merged or surviving entity. This effect is a function of the accounting method used to report the acquisition.

Under the pooling of interests method, the financial statements of the newly acquired entity are simply added to those of the acquiring company, and past statements are restated. Postacquisition pension and other postretirement benefits footnotes include plan data of the acquired enterprise. If the plan data for the previous year are restated, then the analysis discussed in this chapter will be possible for the latest year. However, the data will no longer be consistent with those of earlier years.

If data for previous years have not been restated, or if the purchase method of accounting is used,[26] lack of separate data for the benefit plan obligations and assets of the acquired firm makes reconciliation of footnote data and meaningful analysis difficult and, at times, impossible.[27]

SFAS 87 requires explicit recognition of the funded status of an acquired firm's plan as part of accounting for a purchase method acquisition. The excess of plan assets over the projected benefit obligation at the acquisition date is treated as a purchased asset; any deficit is reported as a liability. This asset or liability is reported on the balance sheet although the plan status of the acquiring entity remains off balance sheet.

Divestitures of subsidiaries with benefit plans create a similar problem. The assets and obligation of the divested plan may be removed from those of the divesting firm without providing separate disclosure of those assets and liabilities, complicating the analysis of footnote data for that year.[28]

Curtailments and Settlements

SFAS 88 created new standards of accounting for curtailments and settlements.[29] A plan *curtailment* due to plan termination in total or as a result of closing down a division effectively freezes the benefits of the affected employees, changing the pension obligation. Any gain or loss due to a plan curtailment must be recognized in current period income.

---

[26]The financial statements of the acquired entity are added to those of the acquiring firm as of the acquisition date (see Chapter 14 for a further explanation of the purchase method).

[27]The analysis demonstrated in the previous section results in miscalculation of the contributions and benefits paid. Specifically, calculated contributions equal actual contributions less the unfunded portion of the new pension plans acquired (PBO − plan assets) and calculated benefits equal actual benefits paid less the fair value of the assets of the new pension fund acquired. *Gross pension cost and nonsmoothed costs, however, are not distorted as the errors cancel out.*

[28]However, in some cases, the postemployment benefit obligations for retirees of the divested unit may be retained by the selling entity.

[29]SFAS 106 prescribes similar principles for settlements of other postemployment benefits.

A plan *settlement* shifts the obligation to an outside entity; for example, an employer may pay an insurance company to assume the pension obligation for a group of employees. Any difference between the amount paid and the PBO "sold" is recognized as a gain or loss from settlement of the plan.

Settlements and curtailments hamper the analysis of retirement plan disclosures, unless the gross amounts are provided. Analyses of pension data misstate benefits paid, as these transactions reduce both the benefit obligation and plan assets by the amount (generally undisclosed) paid; the benefit obligation is further reduced by the amount of the recognized gain.

For example, in 1990, McDonnell Douglas transferred its benefit obligation for approximately 37,000 retirees to two insurance companies. The settlement generated an after-tax gain of $376 million, or $9.82 per share, which exceeded the company's 1990 earnings from continuing operations of $7.18 per share; there would have been a reported loss if not for the settlement. There was no immediate cash flow consequence to McDonnell; the company simply recognized a portion of the excess of pension plan assets over the PBO. Both plan assets and the PBO declined sharply during 1990, reflecting the transfer of pension plan assets to the insurance companies that assumed the pension liability.[30] Because the firm did not disclose the gross amounts involved and it divested a subsidiary during 1990, the disclosures mandated by SFAS 87 are insufficient to analyze fully the pension plan.

When a plan curtailment or settlement occurs as part of a plan to dispose of a segment or line of business, the effect must be included in the gain or loss from discontinued operations. For example, in April 1993, General Electric transferred its discontinued Aerospace business segment to a new company controlled by shareholders of Martin Marietta Corporation. It reported a gain of $753 million on the transfer. Footnote disclosures stated that this gain on transfer included a pretax retiree health and life plan settlement/curtailment gain of $245 million.

The potential for settlements and/or curtailments of pension plans is an important consideration for analysts. Recovery of excess plan assets can greatly increase a firm's liquidity. The excess can be obtained immediately by termination[31] or gradually by reducing future contributions. Settlements, which are transactions between the plan and an outside party, generally have no immediate cash flow consequences for the firm, despite the gain recognized in reported income. Box 12-5 reviews some of the research on the termination of pension plans.

NON-U.S. REPORTING REQUIREMENTS

U.S. financial reporting requirements for pension plans are the most comprehensive and detailed of all international standards. Reporting standards in Canada and the United Kingdom are the closest, with rules in France, Germany, the Netherlands, and Japan considerably less well specified. In these countries, plans are rarely funded. In France, there are no specific standards, and most firms use the cash basis to recognize pension payments. Plans are normally unfunded, with no liability reported on or off the balance sheet.

---

[30]The only cash consequences are the effects of the settlements or curtailments on future contributions. The firm has immediate access to the surplus only when a plan is terminated.

[31]Recent tax law changes have made it less attractive for firms to withdraw excess assets from pension plans.

BOX 12-5
The Termination of Overfunded Plans

For the same year of work, the cost of the pension plan to the firm is much smaller for the younger worker as compared to the older one. In other words, the deferred compensation earned by the younger worker is much less than the amount earned by the older one.* Thus, defined benefit plans generally undercompensate employees in the initial stages of employment and overcompensate them in the later years. On average, the over- and undercompensation even out.

However, young employees must work the "full" term to make up for the early period of undercompensation to obtain the average fair wage. A termination would amount to a breach of the "implicit contract" as young, undercompensated employees would never have the chance to "get even." The resultant transfer of wealth from employees to shareholders would be greatest at an intermediate stage of their careers as the cumulative undercompensation would be greatest at that point.

Thomas (1989) examined two methods used by firms to extract funds from overfunded pension plans. The first is a slow withdrawal using changes in actuarial assumptions to lower contributions. The second type involves termination of the pension plan. The excess funds revert to the sponsoring firm, and the liabilities are rolled over into a new defined benefit or defined contribution plan. Thomas hypothesized that the motivation for terminations depends on (1) whether there was a change in control of the firm and (2) whether the change in control was a result of a friendly or hostile takeover.

Thomas compared selected pension and financial attributes of firms that:

1. terminated their pension plans without a change in control of the firm,

2. terminated their pension plans with a change in control of the firm,

3. opted for slow withdrawal

with one another as well as with a benchmark no-withdrawal control group. He also examined time-series data for firms that terminated their plans to see if there was anything significant (or "optimal") about the timing of the termination decision.

Three competing hypotheses were offered:

1. *Liquidation of financial slack.* This motivation has been explained previously in our discussion of incentives for over/underfunding pensions (see Box 12-2).

2. *Wealth transfer from bondholders to shareholders.* If a firm were to become insolvent, the excess pension assets could be used to pay the firm's bondholders. Terminations would funnel money out of such a firm to its shareholders.

3. *Breach of implicit contracts.* The motivation here is seen as not honoring previous implicit agreements between employees and the owners. The bondholders/shareholders gain at the expense of the employees.

In addition, Thomas examined whether a decline in tax status was associated with terminations or withdrawal behavior. He found that on the whole

both slow withdrawal and terminating groups are associated with unusually high proportions of low tax status firms (currently not paying taxes or carrying forward NOLs and ITCs), relative to the benchmark group. Similarly, time series analyses indicated that tax status declined for both groups.†

However, the tax status argument did not explain why some firms chose to terminate and others used the slow-withdrawal route.

Thomas found little difference between the terminating group with control changes and the benchmark no-withdrawal group. On the other hand, the terminating group without control changes "is significantly less profitable, is more highly levered, and has lower amounts of funds from operations than the no-withdrawal benchmark group." The slow-withdrawal group is positioned in between the benchmark no-withdrawal group and the terminating/no-control-change group.

Further examination of the terminating/no-control-change group indicated that in the years immediately preceding the termination, the firms suffered declines in funds flows, cut back on new investment, and reduced contributions to pension plans. The firms did not raise new equity or debt to make up for the shortfalls in working capital. These patterns are consistent with the financial slack hypothesis and also suggest that slow withdrawals take place prior to terminations.‡

Thomas could not find convincing support for the wealth transfer from debtholders hypothesis. Although the low-profitability results for the terminating/no-control-change firms are consistent with firms facing financial distress, Thomas found that this group of firms repaid some long-term debt as well as cut dividends in the years leading up to the termination. This behavior is inconsistent with wealth transfers from bondholders to shareholders.

Vested employees tend to be in the intermediate stage of their employment lives and hence are significantly affected by a plan termination; they lose the additional benefits that depend on salary increases prior to retirement. On the other hand, employees whose benefits are not vested (or partially vested) lose some or all of the benefits already earned. As it is unclear which conditions result in the maximum wealth transfer from employees to bondholders/shareholders, the vesting argument cannot be used to support the breach of contract hypothesis. Not surprisingly, the proportion of vested employees did not differ among the categories of firms.

An examination of 63 of the 88 terminating/no-control-change firms indicated that 62% of the firms (by number) replaced their defined benefit plans with a defined contribution plan. This lends some support to the breach of contract hypothesis, as by switching to a defined contribution plan, the later promised payments will not materialize. However, it was found that 61% of the plans (in dollar terms) were replaced by another defined benefit plan.

An examination of the 29 terminating/control-change firms indicate that 11 were the result of friendly takeovers. These terminations were motivated by the wish to consolidate the various plans of the merging firms into one overall plan. The remaining control-change firms were unfriendly takeovers. Thomas suggests that such takeovers are often characterized by financial restructuring, leaving the firms highly leveraged and suffering stringent financial conditions. The termination could therefore be motivated by a desire to obtain additional funds to finance the takeover and alleviate the financial constraints much the same way firms engage in asset sales following costly takeovers.

---

*This point can perhaps be better understood if one considers what happens if the firm terminated the plan after one year. Each employee would be paid the present value of his or her future benefits. The amount that would be paid the younger worker is much less than that paid to the older worker.

†Thomas (1989), p. 374

‡These results are consistent with those of Ghicas (1990), who also found that firms reduced their funding on a step-by-step basis: "The reduction in pension funding is accomplished first by the use of higher interest rates that decrease pension liabilities, and then by the switch into a benefit-allocation method. It is suggested that the last change is adopted if firms have limited freedom to make further changes in actuarial assumptions. To this extent, the study provides preliminary evidence on the *pecking order* of actuarial choices by firms attempting to reduce pension funding." Dimitrios C. Ghicas, "Determinants of Actuarial Cost Method Changes for Pension Accounting and Funding," *The Accounting Review*, April 1990, p. 401.

Lump-sum or severance payments on retirement are the norm in Japan, and these are recognized systematically in income and on the balance sheet. However, the liability recognized rarely exceeds 40% of the obligation to date. The obligation approximates the accumulated benefit obligation as defined under U.S. GAAP, although it may not be discounted at a "settlement" (current) rate as in the United States. The obligations generally not funded as contributions are not deductible for taxes.

Pension plans in Germany and the Netherlands are also generally unfunded. Pension expense is based on the benefits as of the balance sheet date, discounted at the rate allowed for taxes. Prior service costs are expensed immediately or over the three-year period allowed for taxes. Japanese, French, German, and Dutch firms are thus likely to report higher pension expense but lower pension liabilities compared to those of similar U.S. firms. The understatement of obligations by these firms is compounded by higher risk, since the plans are normally unfunded.

The Canadian, International Accounting Standards Committee (IASC) 29, and U.K. standards are the closest to SFAS 87. There are, however, several important differences. The interest rate used in these standards is a more stable, long-term rate, adjusted for actual experience, compared with the more volatile, short-term, settlement rate used in the United States. Actuarial methods are not limited to the projected unit credit method as in the United States, and there are no requirements to recognize liabilities due to a plan's underfunded status (minimum liability under SFAS 87).

The IASC issued an exposure draft (E 54) in October 1996 that would amend IAS 29 and largely eliminate the differences between that standard and SFAS 87.

In the United Kingdom, pension cost is the sum of regular cost and variations (including experience gains and losses) to regular cost. SSAP 24 defines regular cost as the consistent ongoing cost recognized under the actuarial method used. In practice, it may differ from service cost under SFAS 87, even when the same actuarial method is used. Experience gains and losses are amortized over the remaining employee service life. Their impact on pension cost is greater and earlier than under SFAS 87 as the corridor method cannot be used.

Most foreign standards mandate significantly less disclosure than SFAS 87; in particular, foreign rules either mandate immediate recognition of prior service costs or permit amortization without specifying a method and provide limited or no disclosure of the ABO and little, if any, information on plan assets. This difference may be the most critical given the nature of these liabilities and the uncertainties in their measurement.

Under U.K. GAAP, a change in accounting policy for postretirement benefits other than pensions may be treated as a prior period adjustment requiring restatement of comparatives.

In sum, accounting standards for pension plans outside the United States permit a wider choice of methods with less disclosure. Careful attention to disclosures provided, supplemented by discussions with management, may permit the analyst to obtain a rough understanding of the extent to which the balance sheet reflects the true plan status.

Example: British Petroleum. Exhibit 12-4 contains the pension footnote from the *1994 Annual Report* of British Petroleum (BP), prepared using U.K. GAAP. Note the following differences from SFAS 87:

1. The disclosures are highly summarized.
2. Although BP's plans are apparently overfunded, the data are one year out of date.
3. Some plans are unfunded and only partly accrued on the balance sheet.

EXHIBIT 12-4. BRITISH PETROLEUM
Pension Footnote

---

24 Pensions

Most group companies have pension plans, the forms and benefits of which vary with conditions and practices in the countries concerned. The main plans provide benefits that are computed based on an employee's years of service and final pensionable salary. In most cases group companies make contributions to separately administered trusts, based on advice from independent actuaries using actuarial methods, the objective of which is to provide adequate funds to meet pension obligations as they fall due. In certain countries the plans are unfunded and the obligation for pension benefits is included within other provisions.

The charge to income for pensions in 1994 of £120 million (£156 million) was assessed in accordance with independent actuarial advice using the projected unit method for the group's major pension plans.

The principal assumptions used in calculating the charge were:

	1994	1993
Rate of return on assets/discount rate	**7% to 9%**	7% to 10%
Future salary increases	**4% to 6%**	4% to 7%
Future pension increases	**nil to 4%**	nil to 5%

At 1 January 1994, the date of the latest actuarial valuations or reviews, the market value of assets in the group's major externally funded pension schemes was £8,083 million (£6,748 million). The assets of these plans covered 122% (119%) of the benefits accrued to members of those plans, after allowing for expected future increases in salaries.

At 31 December 1994 the obligation for accrued benefits in respect of the principal unfunded schemes was £1,049 million (£888 million). Of this amount, £797 million (£726 million) has been provided in these accounts.

Source: British Petroleum, *1994 Annual Report.*

Example: Hoechst. Exhibit 12-5 contains the pension footnote from the *1995 Annual Report* of Hoechst, a German firm that complies with IASC standards as well as German GAAP. The following disclosures are noteworthy:

1. The discount rate, compensation growth rate, and assumed benefit growth rate are disclosed for the German plan. No return on assets assumption is provided for this (unfunded) plan.

2. The German plan is unfunded, but nearly all the obligation is accrued on the balance sheet. There is a small unrecognized transition liability required by IAS 19.

3. Hoechst notes that the sale of an affiliate reduced the benefit obligation but provides no detail.

4. Non-German plans are mostly funded, with a transition obligation apparently the only difference between the actuarial present value (benefit obligation) and the total of plan assets and accruals. Assumptions for the Celanese plan are provided.

5. Although 1995 pension cost data are provided, the components are not, and 1994 data are not presented either.

OTHER POSTEMPLOYMENT BENEFITS

Many employers, especially large companies with unionized workforces, have historically provided other benefits to retirees in addition to pension benefits. Most significant are life insurance and health care, often provided for dependents as well as retirees. In the past, almost all companies accounted for such benefits on a "pay-as-you-go" basis, expensing actual payments when made.

The rapid growth in the cost of medical care resulted in increasing concern that employers providing these benefits were systematically overstating reported earnings and net worth by not accruing the cost of these benefits during employees' periods of active service, when the right to benefits is earned. Advances in medical technology,

EXHIBIT 12-5. HOECHST
Pension Footnote

(31) Provisions for pensions and similar obligations

	Dec. 31, 1995	Dec. 31, 1994
Pension commitments	5 110	5 171
Similar obligations	1 438	1 282
	6 548	6 453

Provisions for pension commitments are set up in respect of benefits payable in the form of old-age, disability and surviving dependent pensions. The benefits vary according to the legal, fiscal and economic conditions of each country. The commitments result from defined-contribution and defined-benefit plans and are dependent on years of service and the employee's compensation. Provisions for similar obligations relate mainly to the liabilities incurred in respect of health care benefits for retired employees and eligible dependents, company or statutory severance payments and agreements on early retirement benefits.

The pension plans in Germany largely consist of a basic defined-contribution pension plan which is financed by a legally independent pension fund within the scope of its business plans, and of defined-benefit type of commitments for which provisions are set up. In line with IAS 19, the commitments that are funded by the Company Pension Fund are not subject to separate actuarial valuation (defined-contribution plan).

In accordance with IAS 19, the company's contributions to defined-contribution plans, e.g. the Company Pension Fund in Germany, are recognized as an expense in the period. In principle, the company's obligation resulting from defined-benefit type pension plans in Germany and abroad is determined using the projected unit credit method in accordance with IAS 19, taking into consideration future salary and pension increases. Extraordinary gains or losses as laid out in IAS 19 due to plan terminations, curtailments or settlements were not incurred in the reporting period. The transition obligation of DM 148 million, which has not yet been recognized as an expense, is the difference between the net actuarial present value and provisions and has resulted primarily from actuarially determined losses. In accordance with IAS 19, this amount will be recognized as an expense over the expected remaining working lives of the participating employees.

As in the previous year, the actuarial assumptions used to determine the pension obligations in Germany are based on a discount rate of 7 %, wage and salary increases of 3.5 %, retirement benefit increases of 2.5 % and average employee turnover of 2 %. An average fair market value determined over a three-year period is used in the assets valuation of the German pension funds.

EXHIBIT 12-5. (*continued*)

Obligations, assets and provisions of the pension plans in Germany

	Dec. 31, 1995	Dec. 31, 1994
Actuarial present value of retirement benefit obligations	4 672	4 916
Assets of benefit funds at fair value	281	275
Net actuarial present value	4 391	4 641
Transition obligation	- 148	14
Provision in accordance with IAS 19	4 243	4 655

The decline in the actuarial present value is due in particular to the sale of affiliates.

The provision allocation made in accordance with IAS 19 as at Dec. 31, 1995 compares with a corresponding valuation made in accordance with Art. 6a of the German Income Tax Law of DM 4 003 million (DM 4 250 million in 1994), which is the minimum accrual as stipulated under the German Commercial Code.

Besides Germany, defined-benefit pension plans mainly exist at the larger subsidiaries in Europe and in Japan as well as in the US. The commitments are largely covered by external funds or insurance policies. The Hoechst Celanese Group has various pension plans that are recognized under tax law and financed externally. The actuarial assumptions used are a discount rate of 7.25 % (8.25 % in 1994), a rate of return on assets of 9.0 % (9.0 % in 1994) and a rate of increase in compensation levels of 4.5 % (5.0 % in 1994). The assets of the company's pension plans consist of real estate, equity and fixed income securities. The company has various defined-contribution savings plans for certain employees. Supplemental retirement benefits that are provided to certain employees and do not qualify under tax law are financed internally by the company.

Obligations, assets, provisions of the pension plans of the Hoechst Corporation Group

	Dec. 31, 1995	Dec. 31, 1994
Actuarial present value	2 800	2 207
Plan assets at fair value	2 102	1 708
Net actuarial present value	698	499
Transition obligation	- 119	- 236
1995 provision in accordance with IAS 19	579	263

Expenses related to all pension plans in the Group

	1995
Expenses related to defined-benefit plans	892
Expenses related to defined-contribution plans	228
of which company contributions to the Company Pension Fund	(69)
	1 120

Actuarial valuations of the afore-mentioned obligations resulting from the major pension plans as well as of existing funds are carried out annually. The remaining funds and commitments are valued on a regular basis at least every three years.

Source: Hoechst, *1995 Annual Report.*

increased utilization of health care, and general inflation drove benefit costs to increasingly high levels. According to a survey by A. Foster Higgins & Co., total health benefit costs per employee exceeded \$3,200 in 1990, having doubled since 1985.[32] For GM, for example, the 1994 cost of providing such benefits to retirees was more than \$4.1 billion! However, the increases moderated to some extent over the last five years.

Postemployment benefits other than pensions remain substantially unfunded as well. The lack of funding reflects the fact that (in contrast to pension plans) contributions to retiree medical plans are generally not tax-deductible for U.S. income tax purposes.[33] Employers have no incentive to fund these plans because only payments for actual benefits are deductible. In addition, the earnings of such plans are not tax-exempt.

SFAS 106 (1990) mandated new accounting for postemployment benefits other than pensions. Although the provisions of this standard follow the format of SFAS 87, there are some differences, reflecting the different nature of these other benefits. We discuss the provisions of SFAS 106 mainly with reference to health care benefits as these benefits are generally the most significant.

Health care benefits are different from pension benefits in one important respect. Pension benefits are monetary amounts; medical benefits entitle retirees (and, in many cases, their dependents) to coverage under which the cost may range from zero to a very large sum. Entitlement benefits are, therefore, much harder to estimate. As a result, the cash flow consequences (to employers) of these plans are much more difficult to predict.

Estimating Health Care Benefits

A significant portion of the estimation process is identical to that for pensions: The employer must forecast how many employees will become eligible for benefits and over what time period retirees (and, in many cases, their dependents) will be eligible to receive them. Such variables as employee turnover, mortality, and retirement ages must also be predicted.

Estimation of the *accumulated postretirement benefit obligation* (APBO), however, requires additional assumptions not needed to forecast pension benefits. Among the most significant of these are the *health care cost trend rate*, the *assumed per capita claims cost* (by age), and *Medicare reimbursement rates*. Also required are estimates of any required employee contributions (or cost sharing) and the effect of any cost limitations (caps) that are part of the benefit plan.

Forecasting health care cost is the most difficult aspect of estimating postretirement health care benefits. Health care costs (both direct reimbursement and insurance) have grown rapidly in recent years, outstripping the rate of inflation. Under the provisions of SFAS 106, employers have some latitude in making these estimates. Companies whose plans have cost-sharing provisions (employee contributions, coinsurance provisions, deductibles, etc.) are permitted to take such provisions into account when forecasting benefits.

The APBO is the present value of expected postretirement benefits earned to date. As in the case of pension benefits, the discount rate is an important determinant of the present value and may be changed by the employer from time to time. However,

---

[32]See Ron Winslow, "Medical Costs Soar, Defying Firms' Cures," *Wall Street Journal,* Jan. 29, 1991.

[33]See, however, the last paragraph of duPont's financial statement footnote 26 concerning funds transferred from its overfunded pension plan to be used to pay postretirement medical benefits.

in contrast to SFAS 87, the discount rate is defined as a current rate, not a settlement rate, as it is not possible, in practice, to settle (sell to another entity such as an insurance company) obligations to provide health care benefits.

Computing Postretirement Benefit Cost

The elements of net postretirement benefit cost are identical to the components of net pension cost previously discussed:

- Service cost
- Interest cost
- Return on plan assets
- Amortization of gains and losses
- Amortization of unrecognized prior service cost
- Amortization of transition asset or liability

The computation of these elements is, for the most part, the same as the corresponding elements of net pension cost. Service cost is the portion of the expected postretirement benefit obligation resulting from employee service during the period, the present value of benefits earned during the period.

Interest cost reflects the passage of time. The discount rate used to compute both service cost and interest cost is, as in SFAS 87, almost always the rate used to compute the benefit obligation at the previous year-end.

The other elements are also analogous to the elements of net pension cost. Once again, the difference between the actual return on assets and the expected return is deferred. When a postretirement health care plan is unfunded, however, there is no return-on-assets component, and the net cost does not depend on an assumed rate of return on assets.[34]

Because of the absence of plan funding, the transition liability was large for most employers. As a result, the amortization of this liability (for those companies adopting the standard prospectively) is usually more significant for postretirement health care plans than pension plans. SFAS 106 permits amortization of the transition liability over 20 years rather than the average remaining service period of active employees. This extended amortization period mitigates the impact of this element on reported earnings. On the other hand, companies adopting the standard using the cumulative adjustment method reported a large one-time reduction of net income.

Disclosure of Plan Status

Employers with nonpension postretirement benefit plans are required to disclose the plan status in a manner similar to the disclosures required for pension plans by SFAS 87. The accumulated postretirement benefit obligation (APBO), which reflects service to date, must be disclosed separately for retirees, eligible nonretirees,[35] and other active plan participants.

---

[34]When a postretirement benefit plan is funded and the earnings of the fund are taxable, fund earnings must be recognized on an after-tax basis.

[35]Eligible nonretirees have met all the age and service requirements to receive benefits but are not yet receiving them (generally because they have not reached retirement age or have not retired).

The fair value of plan assets and any accrual on the employer's balance sheet must be disclosed for funded plans. The difference between the plan status (accumulated benefit obligation less plan assets) and the accrual consists of the following:

- Unrecognized prior service cost
- Unrecognized net gain or loss
- Unrecognized transition obligation (if the standard was adopted prospectively)

These unrecognized amounts have the same origin and meaning as those arising for pension plans, which were previously discussed. The duPont example that follows illustrates the first two of these differences.

Importance of Assumptions

SFAS 106 requires disclosure of the assumptions used to compute the postretirement benefit obligation. These assumptions significantly affect the stated obligation as well as the net postretirement benefit cost.

A higher discount rate reduces the present value of the benefit obligation and results in an improvement in the reported plan status (benefit obligation compared with plan assets). A higher rate also reduces service cost but increases the interest cost.

The health care cost trend rate also directly affects the measured obligation. A lower cost trend rate reduces the estimated benefit obligation and improves the reported plan status. A lower cost trend rate also reduces benefit cost by decreasing both service and interest cost.

Because of the importance of the assumed health care cost trend rate, companies with postretirement health care plans are required to disclose the rate used for the next year as well as the pattern of rates assumed thereafter. This disclosure is intended to help financial statement users understand the assumptions made by the employer in measuring its benefit obligation. For example, duPont discloses (see Exhibit 12-6) that

> the health care accumulated postretirement benefit obligation was determined at December 31, 1994 using a health care cost escalation rate of 8 percent decreasing to 5 percent over 8 years and at December 31, 1993 using a health care cost escalation rate of 10 percent decreasing to 5 percent over 10 years.

Note both the decline in level of the health care trend rate (8 versus 10%) and the change in the rate of decline; the trend rate was expected to decrease to 5% in 10 years in 1993 but in 1994 that estimate has fallen to 8 years.[36]

Employers are also required to disclose the impact of a one-percentage-point increase in the assumed health care trend rate for each future year on:

- The accumulated postretirement benefit obligation
- The combined service and interest cost components of the net postretirement health care benefit cost

These disclosures help analysts to compare the cost and benefit obligations of different employers when they are computed under different assumptions. They also

---

[36]In 1995, du Pont retained the trend rate used in 1994.

EXHIBIT 12-6. DUPONT
Excerpts from Note 25: Health Care Benefits

	1992	1993	1994
Components of Health Care Cost			
Service cost	$ 82	$ 55	$ 56
Interest cost on APBO	431	305	288
Amortization of net gains and prior service credit	0	(94)	(78)
Postretirement health care cost	$513	$ 266	$ 266

		1993	1994
Balance Sheet Reconciliation			
Accumulated health care benefit obligation		$4,073	$3,179
Unrecognized net loss (gain)		285	1,267
Unrecognized prior service credit		1,139	1,059
Accrued health care benefit cost		$5,497	$5,505

The lower health care costs in 1994 and 1993 versus 1992 were due to changes in the company's health care benefits programs in the United States, which were announced on December 31, 1992. These changes provide for increased cost control through prevention and managed care, and for increased cost sharing by employees and pensioners. The impact of these changes resulted in an unrecognized prior service credit of $1,219 at the beginning of 1993; the accumulated postretirement benefit obligation was reduced by a similar amount.

The health care accumulated postretirement benefit obligation was determined at December 31, 1994 using a health care cost escalation rate of 8 percent decreasing to 5 percent over 8 years and at December 31, 1993 using a health care cost escalation rate of 10 percent decreasing to 5 percent over 10 years.

A one-percentage-point increase in the health care cost escalation rate would have increased the accumulated postretirement obligation by $251 at December 31, 1994 and the 1994 other postretirement benefit cost would have increased by $44.

The discount rate was 8 percent at December 31, 1994 and 7.25 percent at December 31, 1993.

Source: DuPont, *1994 Annual Report.*

reveal the sensitivity of the measured benefit obligation to the trend rate assumption. Plans with a high degree of cost sharing can be expected to have a lower degree of sensitivity to the trend rate of health care costs. In other words, the plan will pass on some of the cost to retirees when it exceeds expectations.

Effect of Assumptions

DuPont, for example, discloses (Exhibit 12-6) that a one-percentage-point increase in trend rates for each future year would increase the APBO by approximately $251 million (7.9%) and the combined service and interest cost by approximately $44 million (12.8%). General Electric (GE), however, states that a 1% increase in trend rates would not have had a material effect on the December 31, 1995 APBO or annual cost of retiree health plans.

The different degree of sensitivity to changes in the trend rate is dramatic. The very low sensitivity of GE suggests that it has substantial cost-sharing provisions in its plan that limit the impact of unexpected inflation in health care costs. These provisions may include employee contributions and plan limits (caps). DuPont appears to be much more at risk should health care costs exceed those assumed.

Assumptions about the effectiveness of the cost-sharing provisions of the employer plan thus have an important impact on the benefit obligation and benefit cost. Some employers will be tempted to be overly optimistic about the effect of such provisions on their benefit costs. Overoptimism with respect to any assumptions will, however, result in actuarial losses that will eventually require amortization and increase the benefit cost.

Effects of Transition Methods

Companies adopting SFAS 106 could take either of two paths. They could recognize the transition obligation (cumulative effect of the standard) immediately, as a charge against net income in the year of adoption. Alternatively, they could delay recognition of the transition obligation and amortize that obligation over the greater of the average remaining service life of active plan participants or 20 years (prospective adoption).

Because few postretirement health care plans are funded, and because of the size of the unrecognized benefit obligation for many companies, financial analysts need to make adjustments to compare the financial statements of companies that have taken different roads to adopting the standard.

The choice between immediate recognition and delayed recognition may, however, be more complex than meets the eye as the following considerations needed to be evaluated:

- The ability to minimize the effects of the transition liability by recording it on an after-tax basis. For this reason, some companies delayed adoption of SFAS 106 until SFAS 109 was adopted.[37]
- The effect on debt agreements.[38]
- Management's ability to amend postretirement plans and reduce the size of the liability prior to adoption of the standard.

Amir and Livnat (1996) support the third factor as they found that firms adopting SFAS 106 in 1992 and 1993 were more likely than 1991 adopters to amend postretirement benefit plans to reduce benefits. They also found that 1991 adopters reported postretirement benefit obligations that were smaller than those expected by the market. In addition, firms generally announced adoption of SFAS 106 in the period (year and quarter) with lowest pre-SFAS 106 earnings, suggesting a "big bath" effect.

In a similar vein, Mittelstaedt et al. (1995) found that firms with larger APBOs tended to reduce postretirement benefits. However, they conclude that SFAS 106 was not the primary cause of these reductions; firm-specific increases in retiree health care costs as well as the financial condition of the firm were also important factors.

---

[37]For example, Westinghouse Electric adopted both standards in the first quarter of 1992. It recorded an after-tax charge (cumulative adjustment) of $742 million for postretirement benefits and a $404 million credit (deferred tax asset) under SFAS 109. The net effect of the simultaneous adoption of both standards was $338 million. If SFAS 109 had not been adopted (and if we assume that Westinghouse would not have been able to tax effect the cumulative effect of SFAS 106 otherwise), the cumulative effect would have been recorded pretax and would have been more than $1 billion.

[38]In September 1991, Westinghouse Electric announced that it was asking bank lenders to change the terms of its loan agreement in anticipation of adopting SFAS 106.

In practice, virtually all companies with postretirement benefits adopted the new standard by charging the transition liability against earnings in the year of adoption. This method has the benefit of getting the charge behind the company and reducing the impact on future earnings (because there is no transition liability requiring amortization). Paradoxically, this latter reason also provided an incentive for companies with large transition liabilities to adopt the standard with a cumulative charge to earnings in the year of adoption. Although the immediate effect was large, the alternative of amortizing the transition liability over time would adversely affect income for the next 20 years.

IBM, for example, adopted SFAS 106 in the first quarter of 1991. It reported a charge against first-quarter earnings of $2,263 million after tax effects of $350 million. This charge reduced stockholders' equity by approximately 5%. IBM had previously been accruing such benefits at retirement. Cost under this method was $96 million in 1990; cost under SFAS 106 was $394 million in 1991.

If IBM had chosen to amortize the transition liability over 20 years, earnings would have been reduced by $130 million pretax ($2,263 million/20) in each future year. Charging off the liability immediately therefore increased the computed return on equity of IBM as future earnings are higher (without amortization) and equity is lower.

GE also adopted SFAS 106 effective with the first quarter of 1991. Like IBM, GE charged its transition liability ($2.7 billion pretax and $1.8 billion after tax, or $2.07 per share) against first-quarter 1991 earnings. The charge reduced stockholders' equity by 8.3%.

GE paid $374 million in benefits during 1991; the cost of benefits under SFAS 106 was $279 million, 25% lower than the alternative method. However, if GE had chosen to amortize its transition liability over 20 years, it would have reported a charge of $415 million under SFAS 106 (adding $2,710/20 or $136 to the reported $279 million). Its choice of transition method has continued to provide benefits through 1995; GE reported total health care and life insurance costs of $242, $280, and $249 for 1993, 1994, and 1995, respectively.

In contrast to these examples are those companies that adopted the standard prospectively, meaning that the transition liability is amortized over the next 20 years. For that entire time period, financial analysts need to remember that a (perhaps significant) element of cost is completely unrelated to current operations, but is a result of the past failure to accrue postretirement benefit cost.

One example is Noland, a wholesale distributor of mechanical equipment and supplies to contractors and manufacturers. Noland adopted SFAS 106, prospectively, effective January 1, 1993, and amortizes the transition APBO over 20 years. Noland reported an unrecognized transition obligation of:

December 31, 1993	$3,863,000
December 31, 1994	3,660,000
December 31, 1995	3,457,000

indicating annual amortization of $203,000. Net postretirement benefit cost for 1995 was $564,000.

If Noland had adopted SFAS 106 using the cumulative change method, its 1995 stockholders' equity would be reduced by $2,074,000 [$3,457,000 × (1 − 0.40)] as

Noland's tax rate is 40%. On the other hand, net income *in each year* would be higher by $122,000 [$203,000 × (1 − 0.40)]. The effect of the accounting choice can be seen from the following table based on 1995 data:

$ in Thousands	Reported	Adjusted
Stockholders' equity	$111,688	$109,614
Net income	4,947	5,069
Return on year-end equity	4.42%	4.62%

This comparison should make it clear why the overwhelming majority of firms chose to recognize the transition obligation immediately.

Analysis of DuPont's Postretirement Health Care Costs

Exhibit 12-6 reproduces the portion of duPont's Note 25 concerning postretirement health care benefits. The plan is unfunded but, as of December 31, 1994, duPont had recorded a liability of $5,505 million for postretirement health plans. The economic liability, as measured by the APBO, however, is only $3,179 million. Thus, *duPont's balance sheet should be adjusted by decreasing the liability and increasing equity by $2,326 million ($5,505 − $3,179).*

This difference represents unrecognized prior service *credits* and net (actuarial) gains.[39] The prior service benefit arose in 1992 when duPont (after adopting SFAS 106) reduced the health care benefits available to its employees.[40] The unrecognized actuarial gain increased from $285 million to $1,267 million in 1994. This large actuarial gain (as in the case of pensions) was due to the increase in the discount rate from 7.25 to 9%.

DuPont recognized postretirement health care expense of $266 million in 1994, similar to the amount recognized in 1993, but a sharp drop from the 1992 expense. Both service cost and interest costs decreased as the reduction of health care benefits impacted future benefits (service cost) as well as benefits earned previously, reducing the APBO and consequent interest cost.

The 1994 health care expense of $266 million includes service cost of $56 million and interest cost of $288 million (approximately 7.25% of the 1993 APBO of $4,073) less smoothed actuarial gains and prior service credits.

Using analysis similar to that for pension plans earlier in the chapter, we can calculate the nonsmoothed postretirement health care expense as well as the actual benefit payments. However, as postretirement benefits are (usually) not funded, *cash payments by the firm are benefit payments*; there is no need to calculate fund contributions. Additionally, as there is no ROA, gross pension cost and nonsmoothed cost are identical.

---

[39] As the plan is not funded, the only component of gains/losses is actuarial. There is no deferred investment gain or loss to be amortized. Additionally, as there is no transition liability, we know that duPont used the cumulative method when it adopted SFAS 106.

[40] See Problem 8 in Chapter 5 that examines the posssible effects of SFAS 106 on changes in health care benefits.

Calculation of Nonsmoothed Cost and Cash Flows. The following steps should be taken in sequence. In each step, we note which information is provided in duPont's footnote (or derived in the preceding step) and bold the item computed.

Step 1: Calculate benefits paid.

Use the relationship between the opening and closing balance sheet liability and the reported postretirement benefits cost:

Opening balance sheet liability	$5,497	Given
+ Postretirement (health care) cost	266	Given
− **Benefits paid**	**258**	**Plug**
= Closing balance sheet liability	$5,505	Given

Benefits Paid = Postretirement Cost − Change in Balance Sheet Liability
$258 = $266   −   ($5,505 − $5,497)

Step 2: Calculate gross benefit cost (nonsmoothed cost).

Use the relationship between the opening and closing balances in the APBO and benefits paid (derived in Step 1):

Opening APBO	$4,073	Given
+ **Gross benefit cost**	**(636)**	**Plug**
− Benefits paid	258	Derived in Step 1
Closing APBO	$3,179	

Gross Benefit Cost = Benefits Paid + Change in APBO
$(636)   = $258   + ($3,179 − $4,073)

Analysis of duPont's Postretirement Health Care Cost
($ in millions)

(a) Service cost	**$56**	Given
Interest cost	288	Given
(b) Recurring cost	**$ 344**	
Nonrecurring costs:		
(actuarial gains and losses		
+ prior service costs)	(980)	Plug
(c) Gross benefit cost	**$(636)**	Step 2
= (d) Nonsmoothed cost		

It is easy to verify that the $980 nonrecurring benefit is an actuarial gain as the balance of unrecognized net (actuarial) gain increased from $285 million to $1,267 million, an increase of $982 million.[41] As noted, this gain was due to the discount rate increase.

Using SFAS 106 Disclosures

As the accounting for postretirement benefits other than pensions parallels the accounting for pension benefits, the analytical adjustments are the same. On the balance sheet, the accrued amount should be replaced by the excess of the APBO over plan assets (if any). For duPont, the pretax adjustment equals $2,326 million as previously computed. For companies adopting SFAS 106 on a prospective basis, such as Noland, the unamortized transition liability may be a significant factor.

Companies with postretirement benefits have argued that they can reduce or eliminate benefits, although this argument is more difficult to accept when benefits are mandated under union contracts. The result of recent litigation suggests that benefits for retirees cannot be summarily discontinued, even in cases of severe financial distress. In recent years, however, companies have made considerable efforts to limit their exposure to health care costs. Note the duPont plan amendment discussed earlier.

Nonetheless, on a "going concern" basis, these benefits must be considered, as are pension benefits, a corporate liability. Thus, unless there is evidence that benefits will be curtailed or discontinued, financial analysis must take any unrecognized liability into account. Although SFAS 106 does not change cash flow, the APBO does represent a forecast of future cash outflows that will require the use of firm resources.[42]

Adjustment of the income statement may also be necessary. Companies that adopted SFAS 106 prospectively include amortization of the transition liability in postretirement benefit expense. However, this liability represents prior period costs. Current period earnings, one can argue, should not be burdened with these costs. The matching principle suggests that amortization of the transition liability should, therefore, be removed from postretirement benefit cost when evaluating a firm's earning power. This adjustment, whatever its theoretic justification, is required when comparing such a firm with one that fully recognized the transition obligation upon adoption of SFAS 106.

Postretirement Benefits Outside the United States

Health care and life insurance benefits are rarely provided in other countries, accounting for the absence of related reporting standards. SSAP 24 in the United Kingdom, for example, does not contain any specific disclosure requirements; the cash basis remains an acceptable method.[43] To the extent that a foreign firm provides these benefits, such as for U.S. employees, reported income and equity are overstated.

The IASC's E 54 (1996) would amend IAS 19 and make the accounting for postretirement benefits similar to that required by SFAS 106.

---

[41]Note also that the balance in the unrecognized prior service credit decreased from $1,139 million to $1,059; this $80 million decrease approximated the $78 million amortization of net gains and prior service credit.

[42]Thus satisfying the FASB definition of a liability (see Chapter 1).

[43]Another problem in the United Kingdom is its tax standard that would disallow recognition of a deferred tax asset for these liabilities because no net reversal can be assumed in the absence of funding.

PRERETIREMENT BENEFITS

Some employee benefits apply to periods of active service or periods following active service but prior to retirement. Such benefits include:

1. Insurance benefits (mainly health and life)
2. Vacations, holidays, and sick days
3. Severance benefits (including salary and benefit continuation costs)
4. Supplemental unemployment, disability, and similar benefits

The first class of benefits listed is accounted for on a pay-as-you-go basis; life and health insurance benefits are period costs. The second category is covered by SFAS 43 (1980), Accounting for Compensated Absences. That standard requires employers to accrue the cost of these benefits when that cost can be reasonably estimated and employees have earned the right to receive them.

SFAS 112 (1992) extends the reasoning of SFAS 43 to the third and fourth benefit groupings listed above. Previous practice was varied, with some firms using the pay-as-you-go method, some recognizing benefit cost only under certain conditions (e.g., disability of worker), and others accruing benefit cost over the period of active service. SFAS 112 was intended to unify practice.

The new standard was effective for fiscal years beginning after December 15, 1993 and adoption using the cumulative effect method was required. GE, for example, adopted the new standard effective January 1, 1993; the cumulative effect was $862 million or $0.51 per share (net of $444 million of income tax benefit). GE reported $2.45 per share in earnings from continuing operations before the accounting change. Depending on the benefits provided and the prior method of accounting, the effect of SFAS 112 on other companies varied.

STOCK COMPENSATION PLANS

In addition to salary and such traditional employee benefits as retirement and medical plans, some firms also offer employees the opportunity to benefit from increases in the value of the firm. Such plans may take the form of restricted stock or arrangements (phantom stock) under which the employee receives amounts that depend on the performance of a specified number of shares. Often, however, they use employee stock options.

Traditionally, the issuance of stock options to employees receives no accounting recognition when the exercise price equals the market price at the date the options are granted. Some argue that such options have no value at that date, as they have no intrinsic value. However, as option pricing models are increasingly used in the financial world, that view has become harder to justify.

SFAS 123 (1995) was issued by the FASB after a long battle over whether the issuance of stock options should result in employee compensation expense.[44] Strong

---

[44]SFAS 123 also covers options issued to suppliers or for other consideration. In such cases, the standard requires recognition of the fair value of the options granted.

objections from the corporate community resulted in a standard that requires the following disclosures:

1. Detailed data regarding the number of options outstanding, their exercise prices, and whether or not they are exercisable.

2. The grant-date fair value of options granted during the year, with options issued at, above, or below market price disclosed separately.

3. A description of the method and significant assumptions used to determine the grant-date fair value. Specific assumptions that must be disclosed are the:

   • Risk-free interest rate
   • Expected option life
   • Expected stock volatility
   • Expected dividends

4. Any compensation cost recognized during the period.

5. Data regarding the modification of outstanding stock options (e.g., repricing options after a significant decline in stock price).

6. Data regarding other equity instruments (such as restricted stock) issued to employees.

The recognition of compensation cost for stock option plans is not mandatory. Firms that do not recognize such cost, however, are required by the standard to disclose the pro forma *effect (on net income and earnings per share) of doing so.*

SFAS 123 was effective for fiscal years beginning after December 15, 1995 (i.e., calendar 1996).

Example: Foster Wheeler

Foster Wheeler, a multinational engineering and construction firm, adopted SFAS 123 in its *1995 Annual Report*. Exhibit 12-7 contains Note 14 from that report.

The note reports that, if Foster Wheeler had recognized stock compensation expense, its 1995 net income would have been reduced by more than 14%. As 1995 net income included restructuring charges, the effect on 1996 income (which increased sharply from the 1995 level) would have been somewhat smaller.

Note 14 also states that Foster Wheeler used the Black-Scholes option pricing model and provides the assumptions used. We expect that Black-Scholes will be the model of choice when applying SFAS 123.

The footnote also reveals that:

1. The number of options granted increased considerably in 1995, to more than twice the 1994 level and nearly four times the 1993 level. Relatively few options were exercised in that year, however, perhaps because the stock fell in 1994.

2. The 1995 options were issued with a lower exercise price than 1994 options, reflecting the lower market price.

3. With Foster Wheeler shares trading at a price approaching $40 in mid-1996, all outstanding options are "in the money." Other than those granted in 1995, it appears that all options are exercisable.

EXHIBIT 12-7. FOSTER WHEELER
Stock Compensation Footnote

---

14. STOCK OPTION PLANS

The Corporation has two fixed option plans which reserve shares of common stock for issuance to executives, key employees and directors. The Corporation has adopted the disclosure-only provisions of Statement of Financial Accounting Standards No. 123, "Accounting for Stock-Based Compensation." Accordingly, no compensation cost has been recognized for the stock option plans. Had compensation cost for the Corporation's two stock option plans been determined based on the fair value at the grant date for awards in 1995 consistent with the provisions of SFAS No. 123, the Corporation's net earnings and earnings per share would have been reduced to the pro forma amounts indicated below:

	1995
Net earnings - as reported	$ 28,534
Net earnings - pro forma	$ 24,434
Earnings per share - as reported	$0.79
Earnings per share - pro forma	$0.67

The assumption regarding the stock options issued to executives in 1995 was that 100% of such options vested in 1995, rather than 1/3 as required by the Plan, since 1/3 of 1993 and 1994 would have vested in 1995.

The fair value of each option grant is estimated on the date of grant using the Black-Scholes option-pricing model with the following weighted-average assumptions used for grants in 1995: dividend yield of 2.21%; expected volatility of 0.3720%; risk-free interest rate of 7.68%; and expected lives of 7.5 years.

Under the plan approved by the stockholders in April 1995, the total number of shares of common stock that may be granted is 1,500,000. In April 1990, the stockholders approved a Stock Option Plan for Directors of the Corporation. This plan authorizes the granting of options on 150,000 shares of common stock to directors who are not employees of the Corporation, who will automatically receive an option to acquire 2,000 shares each year.

These plans provide that shares granted come from the Corporation's authorized but unissued or reacquired common stock. The price of the options granted pursuant to these plans will not be less than 100 percent of the fair market value of the shares on the date of grant. An option may not be exercised within one year from the date of grant and no option will be exercisable after ten years from the date granted. Under the Executive Compensation Plan, the long-term incentive segment provides for stock options to be issued. Participants may exercise approximately one-third of the stock option shares after the end of each year of the cycle.

EXHIBIT 12-7. (*continued*)

Information regarding these option plans for 1995, 1994 and 1993 is as follows:

	1995		1994	1993
	Shares	Weighted-Average Exercise Price	Shares	Shares
Options outstanding, beginning of year	546,462	$28.12	493,810	417,596
Options exercised	(45,817)	13.49	(125,682)	(50,786)
Options granted	490,700	30.10	178,334	127,000
Options outstanding, end of year	991,345	$29.78	546,462	493,810
Option price range at end of year	$14.50 to $40.0625		$12.25 to $40.0625	$12.25 to $28.75
Option price range for exercised shares	$12.25 to $13.6875		$12.25 to $28.75	$12.25 to $22.0625
Options available for grant at end of year	1,543,000		539,578	717,912
Weighted-average fair value of options, granted during the year	$13.12			

The following table summarizes information about fixed-price stock options outstanding at December 29, 1995:

	Options Outstanding			Options Exercisable	
Range of Exercise Prices	Number Outstanding at 12/29/95	Weighted-Average Remaining Contractual Life	Weighted-Average Exercise Price	Number Exercisable at 12/29/95	Weighted-Average Exercise Price
14.50	9,158	4 years	14.50	9,158	14.50
21.3125 to 22.125	33,986	5 years	21.50	33,986	21.50
22.0625 to 28.6875	61,500	6 years	23.03	61,500	23.03
26.9375 to 27.4375	98,000	7 years	27.35	98,000	27.35
27.4375 to 28.75	119,667	8 years	28.55	85,778	28.47
32.9375 to 40.0625	178,334	9 years	35.73	72,778	36.53
29.75 to 35.25	490,700	10 years	30.10	—	—
14.50 to 40.0625	991,345			361,200	

Source: Foster Wheeler, *1995 Annual Report.*

Using SFAS 123 Disclosures

Based on our view that stock compensation should be recognized as part of employee compensation, the following analytic adjustments should be made for firms that choose the disclosure-only option:[45]

---

[45]Although the text went to press prior to any meaningful number of companies adopting SFAS 123, we believe that only an insignificant number of companies will recognize compensation expense.

1. Use the *pro forma* net income to compute such valuation measures as the price-to-earnings ratio. When computing normalized net income (see Chapter 17), the *pro forma* adjustment for stock compensation expense should be part of recurring income.

2. The balance sheet can be left unchanged. Recognition of stock compensation has some effect on assets (creation of a deferred tax asset); its major impact is a reclassification between retained earnings and paid-in capital. Such effects will be insignificant in virtually all cases.

3. The grant of stock options has no direct cash flow effect. The exercise of options provides cash (included in financing cash flow) and (under U.S. tax law) a tax deduction (included in cash from operations). These effects are insignificant in most cases.

The SFAS 123 disclosure requirements have little effect on the analysis of most firms. In the case of technology and startup companies, who grant sizable stock options in lieu of cash salaries, measures that fail to recognize the real cost of stock options overstate corporate performance. SFAS 123 disclosures should be used, in these cases, to correct such overstatement.

SUMMARY

Current accounting practices for pensions and other postemployment benefits result in an amalgam of smoothed and unsmoothed costs appearing in net income. The actual obligations are disguised and partly or wholly off balance sheet. In this chapter, we show how to use footnote disclosures to unravel the underlying events that occurred during the period. This permits calculation of the actual components of benefit costs, cash flows, and benefit obligations, and the examination of trends in these components. The chapter suggests alternative measures of benefit cost and obligations. Finally, it reviews the motivation for firms to over- or underfund their pension plans and the potential for plan termination.

CASE 12-1

Analysis of Pension Plan Disclosures: GM

INTRODUCTION AND CASE OBJECTIVES

General Motors (GM) adopted SFAS 87 in 1986. At that time, its U.S. pension plans were overfunded by $1.55 billion. By 1992, the plans were underfunded (PBO exceeded assets) by $12.1 billion, a deterioration of over $13.5 billion. What caused this change? How much of this deterioration was recognized in GM's financial statements? What can the analysis of these questions tell us about GM's future cash contributions to its pension plans?

This case uses the analytic tools developed in the chapter to examine GM's pension plans. The analysis focuses first on 1992 and the adjustments to GM's financial statements required to reflect the funded status of the plans. Then, we compare the actual costs and cash flows for GM's pension plans with reported amounts over the period 1986 to 1992, to:

1. Demonstrate the extent to which the smoothing process mandated by SFAS 87 can distort and lag economic reality.

2. Discuss forecasts of the near-term effects of GM's pension plans on the resources of the firm.

3. Illustrate the analysis required when the minimum liability provision is required by SFAS 87.

THE GM PENSION PLAN

Exhibit 12C-1 contains the pension footnote from GM's *1992 Annual Report.*[1] As required by SFAS 87, it provides separate disclosure of the status of U.S. and non-U.S. plans. SFAS 87 also requires that, when pension assets and accruals are lower than the accumulated benefit obligation, the difference must be immediately recognized. In Exhibit 12C-1, the underfunded plans[2] are disclosed separately from those with assets exceeding the ABO.[3] For these underfunded plans, the firm must recognize the minimum liability.

Minimum Liability Provision

We compute the underfunding for these plans as follows:

Accumulated benefit obligation	$ 29,215.8 million
Plan assets	(17,400.4)
ABO excess over assets	$ 11,815.4 million

Because of the delayed recognition of actuarial losses, prior service cost, and the transition liability related to these plans, without the minimum liability adjustment GM's accrued (balance sheet) liability for these plans equals $2,921.1 million:

PBO in excess of plan assets	$(11,919.5)
Less unamortized	
Net losses (gains)	4,447.0
Prior service cost	3,475.1
Transition obligation	1,076.3
Balance sheet accrual	$ (2,921.1)

GM is required under SFAS 87 to increase the accrued liability to the ABO excess of $11,815.4 million, by recognizing a minimum liability of $8,894.3 million ($11,815.4 million − $2,921.1 million).

Because, as Exhibit 12C-1 indicates, the difference between the PBO and ABO for GM's underfunded plans is very small (less than 0.5%), the minimum liability provision eliminates most of the gap between plan assets and the PBO. For firms whose PBO is much greater than the ABO, the minimum liability will not cover the gap between plan assets and the PBO.

Although it is useful to know that some plans are underfunded, we cannot analyze these plans separately because the pension cost components (Exhibit 12C-1) are disclosed on a combined basis. Therefore, we must combine the plan status data for underfunded and overfunded plans; the result, shown in Exhibit 12C-2, is the basis for our analysis.

[1] GM reports plan data for years ending (measurement dates) October 1 and December 1; up to a three-month lag behind the balance sheet date is permitted by SFAS 87.

[2] Note that although the definition of underfunded for purposes of the minimum liability provision is based on the ABO, the components of pension cost are still based on the PBO. Similarly, in keeping with our approach in this chapter, we consider the PBO to be the firm's economic liability.

[3] Note that plans can migrate between categories from year to year.

EXHIBIT 12C-1. GM
Pension Plan Footnote

NOTE 6. Pension Program

The Corporation and its subsidiaries have a number of defined benefit pension plans covering substantially all employes. Plans covering U.S. and Canadian represented employes generally provide benefits of negotiated stated amounts for each year of service as well as significant supplemental benefits for employes who retire with 30 years of service before normal retirement age. The benefits provided by the plans covering its U.S. and Canadian salaried employes, and employes in certain foreign locations, are generally based on years of service and the employe's salary history. The Corporation and its subsidiaries also have certain nonqualified pension plans covering executives which are based on targeted wage replacement percentages and are unfunded.

Total pension expense of the Corporation and its subsidiaries amounted to $1,981.5 million in 1992, $1,520.0 million in 1991, and $368.9 million in 1990. Net periodic pension cost for 1992, 1991, and 1990 of U.S. plans and plans of subsidiaries outside the United States included the components shown in the table below.

(Dollars in millions)	1992 U.S. Plans	1992 Non-U.S. Plans	1991 U.S. Plans	1991 Non-U.S. Plans	1990 U.S. Plans	1990 Non-U.S. Plans
Benefits earned during the year	$ 859.9	$135.1	$ 772.4	$109.9	$ 713.6	$105.5
Interest accrued on benefits earned in prior years	4,089.9	469.2	3,906.4	423.6	3,389.4	373.0
Return on assets —Actual (gain) loss	($2,770.9)	($147.6)	($7,393.3)	($532.0)	$2,117.1	$159.9
—Less deferred gain (plus deferred loss)	(1,320.9) (4,091.8)	(217.0) (364.6)	3,565.3 (3,828.0)	194.0 (338.0)	(6,153.9) (4,036.8)	(517.0) (357.1)
Net amortization	403.9	39.0	390.3	22.5	93.2	7.9
Net periodic pension cost	$1,261.9	$278.7	$1,241.1	$218.0	$ 159.4	$129.3

The table below reconciles the funded status of the Corporation's U.S. and non-U.S. plans with amounts recognized in the Corporation's Consolidated Balance Sheet at December 31, 1992 and 1991.

(Dollars in millions)	U.S. Plans 1992 Assets Exceed Accum. Benefits	U.S. Plans 1992 Accum. Benefits Exceed Assets	U.S. Plans 1991 Assets Exceed Accum. Benefits	U.S. Plans 1991 Accum. Benefits Exceed Assets	Non-U.S. Plans 1992 Assets Exceed Accum. Benefits	Non-U.S. Plans 1992 Accum. Benefits Exceed Assets	Non-U.S. Plans 1991 Assets Exceed Accum. Benefits	Non-U.S. Plans 1991 Accum. Benefits Exceed Assets
Actuarial present value of benefits based on service to date and present pay levels								
Vested	$19,374.6	$23,235.4	$16,975.0	$21,073.8	$1,501.5	$2,910.4	$2,684.8	$1,668.9
Nonvested	1,037.7	5,980.4	665.6	5,240.6	66.8	168.3	194.7	39.7
Accumulated benefit obligation	20,412.3	29,215.8	17,640.6	26,314.4	1,568.3	3,078.7	2,879.5	1,708.6
Additional amounts related to projected pay increases	1,939.3	104.1	1,824.1	107.4	167.9	354.6	175.2	341.6
Total projected benefit obligation based on service to date	22,351.6	29,319.9	19,464.7	26,421.8	1,736.2	3,433.3	3,054.7	2,050.2
Plan assets at fair value	22,171.2	17,400.4	21,100.5	17,802.1	1,947.8	1,311.7	3,626.7	59.7
Projected benefit obligation (in excess of) less than plan assets	(180.4)	(11,919.5)	1,635.8	(8,619.7)	211.6	(2,121.6)	572.0	(1,990.5)
Unamortized net amount resulting from changes in plan experience and actuarial assumptions	3,731.8	4,447.0	1,784.7	1,520.5	629.6	172.9	574.0	(170.7)
Unamortized prior service cost	1,019.1	3,475.1	764.4	3,917.8	193.4	319.3	423.1	194.8
Unamortized net obligation (asset) at date of adoption	(1,364.6)	1,076.3	(1,558.9)	1,210.8	(381.4)	254.6	(610.3)	398.8
Adjustment for unfunded pension liabilities	—	(8,894.3)	—	(6,541.7)	—	(436.3)	—	(111.8)
Net prepaid pension cost (accrued liability) recognized in the Consolidated Balance Sheet	$ 3,205.9	($11,815.4)	$ 2,626.0	($ 8,512.3)	$ 653.2	($1,811.1)	$ 958.8	($1,679.4)

(continued)

EXHIBIT 12C-1. (*continued*)

Plan assets are primarily invested in United States Government obligations, equity and fixed income securities, commingled pension trust funds, GM preference stock (converted in November 1992 into GM Class E common stock) valued at approximately $343.7 million as of the October 1 measurement date in 1992, GM $1-2/3 par value common stock contributed to the U.S. plans in 1992 valued at $500.0 million, and insurance contracts. The Corporation's funding policy with respect to its qualified plans is to contribute annually not less than the minimum required by applicable law and regulation nor more than the maximum amount which can be deducted for Federal income tax purposes.

The unfunded liability in excess of the unamortized prior service cost and net transition obligation was recorded as a reduction in Stockholders' Equity of $2,925.3 million and $936.8 million at December 31, 1992 and 1991, respectively. The remaining portion of the unfunded liability of $6,401.7 million and $5,716.7 million at December 31, 1992 and 1991, respectively, was recorded as intangible assets and deferred taxes.

Measurement dates used for the Corporation's principal U.S. plans are October 1 for GM's plans (including Delco Electronics Corporation) and EDS, and December 1 for Hughes plans. For non-U.S. plans, the measurement dates used are October 1 for certain foreign plans and December 1 for Canadian plans.

The weighted average discount rate used in determining the actuarial present values of the projected benefit obligation shown in the table on the preceding page for U.S. plans was 8.6% at December 31, 1992 and 9.3% at December 31, 1991 and for non-U.S. plans was 9.6% at December 31, 1992 and 10.0% at December 31, 1991. The rate of increase in future compensation levels of applicable U.S. employes was 4.9% at December 31, 1992 and 5.0% at December 31, 1991 and of applicable non-U.S. employes was 4.9% at December 31, 1992 and 5.5% at December 31, 1991. Benefits under the hourly plans are generally not based on wages and therefore no benefit escalation beyond existing negotiated increases was included. The expected long-term rate of return on assets used in determining pension expense for U.S. plans was 11.0% for both 1992 and 1991, and for non-U.S. plans was 10.7% for 1992 and 10.8% for 1991. The assumptions for non-U.S. plans were developed on a basis consistent with that for U.S. plans, adjusted to reflect prevailing economic conditions and interest rate environments.

Certain changes in actuarial assumptions had the effect of reducing the 1990 consolidated net loss by $289.8 million or $0.48 per share of $1-2/3 par value common stock.

Programs for early retirement were offered to certain employes during 1992. The total cost of these programs was $564.1 million of which $359.5 million was expensed during 1992 with the remainder charged to expense in prior restructurings.

Source: GM, *1992 Annual Report.*

ANALYSIS OF GM'S PENSION STATUS

Exhibit 12C-2 shows that the combined PBO exceeds plan assets by $12.1 billion at December 31, 1992, an increase of $5 billion or 70% from the previous year. If not for the minimum liability requirement, none of this shortfall would be recognized on the balance sheet. GM would record an asset of $284.8 million! Because of the minimum liability requirement, however, $8.6 billion of the $12.1 PBO shortfall is recognized.[4]

GM's footnote states that benefits under the hourly plans are generally not based on wages and, therefore, no benefit escalation beyond existing negotiated increases is included. That is, the hourly plans have essentially flat benefits, which make the difference between the PBO and ABO close to zero. Earlier we noted that it is those plans that are significantly underfunded; the minimum liability provision is most likely related to the plans covering (unionized) hourly workers. Presumably, the union leaders also know the plan status, as they receive financial statements of the plan itself (with the same information regarding the benefit obligation and plan assets).

These plans have an unrecognized prior service cost of close to $4.5 billion. As we shall see (in Exhibit 12C-4), prior service cost (resulting from plan amendments) originated in 1987 and 1990 corresponding to the three-year period between successive labor contracts in the auto industry. This suggests a pattern of periodic benefit increases due to inflation. These benefit increases do not affect GM's pension obligation until they are granted. However, the analysis does suggest that the obligation to provide pensions is understated in GM's financial statements. This issue is not discussed by GM in its annual report.

GM also has substantial unamortized losses that grew considerably in 1992. As we shall see, these losses are at least partly due to GM's liberal actuarial assumptions used to calculate its PBO.

[4]As will be discussed, only the liability section fully reflects the minimum liability as just a portion of the minimum liability is generally charged to equity; the rest is offset by an intangible asset.

EXHIBIT 12C-2. GM
Status of U.S. Pension Plans, 1991 to 1992 (data in $ millions)

	1991		
	Assets > ABO	Assets < ABO	Total
Accumulated benefit obligation	$17,640.6	$26,314.4	**$43,955.0**
Projected benefit obligation	19,464.7	26,421.8	**45,886.5**
Plan assets at fair value	21,100.5	17,802.1	**38,902.6**
PBO (in excess of) less than plan assets	$ 1,635.8	$(8,619.7)	**$(6,983.9)**
Unamortized losses	$ 1,784.7	$ 1,520.5	**$ 3,305.2**
Unamortized prior service cost	764.4	3,917.8	**4,682.2**
Unamortized transition (asset) obligation	(1,558.9)	1,210.8	**(348.1)**
Prepaid cost (liability) before adjustment for minimum liability	$ 2,626.0	$(1,970.6)	**$ 655.4**
Minimum liability recognized		(6,541.7)	**(6,541.7)**
Net liability recognized	$ 2,626.0	$(8,512.3)	**$(5,886.3)**

	1992		
	Assets > ABO	Assets < ABO	Total
Accumulated benefit obligation	$20,412.3	$ 29,215.8	**$ 49,628.1**
Projected benefit obligation	22,351.6	29,319.9	**51,671.5**
Plan assets at fair value	22,171.2	17,400.4	**39,571.6**
PBO (in excess of) less than plan assets	$ (180.4)	$(11,919.5)	**$(12,099.9)**
Unamortized losses	$ 3,731.8	$ 4,447.0	**$ 8,178.8**
Unamortized prior service cost	1,019.1	3,475.1	**4,494.2**
Unamortized transition (asset) obligation	(1,364.6)	1,076.3	**(288.3)**
Prepaid cost (liability) before adjustment for minimum liability	$ 3,205.9	$ (2,921.1)	**$ 284.8**
Minimum liability recognized		(8,894.3)	**(8,894.3)**
Net liability recognized	$ 3,205.9	$(11,815.4)	**$ (8,609.5)**

Adjustments to GM's Balance Sheet

As SFAS 87 does not require the balance sheet to reflect the actual funded status of pension plans, two adjustments are required. The first, as discussed in this chapter, replaces the balance sheet liability of $8.6 billion with the PBO shortfall of $12.1 billion. For GM, the adjustment is:

	Pretax	After Tax Assumes 37% tax rate[5]
Increase deferred tax asset	0	$1.3 billion
Increase liability	$3.5 billion	$3.5 billion
Decrease equity	$3.5 billion	$2.2 billion

[5]Exhibit 12C-1 notes that stockholders' equity was charged $2,925.3 million for the minimum liability provision. This charge is after tax. Below we note that $1,730.6 million was recorded as a deferred tax asset for this charge. This implies a 37% tax rate [$1,730.6/($2,925.3 + $1,730.6)].

EXHIBIT 12C-3. GM
Calculation of 1992 Pension Costs and Cash Flows (all amounts are in $ millions)

Step 1: **Calculate contributions** made to the plan by firm:

Contributions = Pension Cost − Change in the Balance Sheet (Asset) Liability
$891.3 = $1,261.9 − [($284.8) − ($655.4)]

Reconciliation

Opening balance sheet (asset) liability (before minimum liability provision)	$ (655.4)	Exhibit 12C-2
+ Pension cost	1,261.9	Exhibit 12C-1
− Contributions	**891.3**	**Plug**
= Closing balance sheet (asset) liability (before minimum liability provision)	$ (284.8)	Exhibit 12C-2

Step 2: **Calculate benefits paid** to employees:

Benefits Paid = Contributions + ROA − Change in Plan Assets
$2,993.2 = $891.3   + $2,770.9 − [($39,571.6 − $38,902.6)

Reconciliation

Opening plan assets	$38,902.6	Exhibit 12C-2
+ ROA	2,770.9	Exhibit 12C-1
+ Contributions	891.3	Derived in Step 1
− Benefits paid	**2,993.2**	**Plug**
= Closing plan assets	$39,571.6	Exhibit 12C-2

Step 3: **Calculate gross pension cost:**

Gross Pension Cost = Benefits Paid + Change in PBO
$8,778.1 = $2,993.2 + ($51,671.5 − $45,886.6)

Reconciliation

Opening PBO	$45,886.6	Exhibit 12C-2
+ Gross pension cost	**8,778.1**	**Plug**
− Benefits paid	2,993.2	Derived in Step 2
Closing PBO	$51,671.5	Exhibit 12C-2

Step 4: **Calculate prior service cost and actuarial gains or losses:**
The sum of actuarial gains/losses and prior service cost equals

Gross Pension Cost − Recurring Cost
$8,778.1 − ($859.9 + $4,089.9) = $3,828.3

As the unamortized prior service cost (Exhibit 12C-2) has decreased slightly during the year, we can assume that the $3,828.3 is due primarily to actuarial losses.

To estimate each amount, first disentangle the $(403.9) "net amortization" element of pension cost, which contains the amortization of the transition asset, prior service cost, and unamortized deferred gains and losses. (All appear in the plan reconciliation in Exhibit 12C-2.) Start with the transition asset, which GM calls "unamortized net obligation (asset) at the date of adoption":

EXHIBIT 12C-3. (*continued*)

Change in Unamortized Asset = Amortization
$288.3 − $348.1 = $59.8

As total net amortization equals $(403.9), the amortization of prior service costs and/or deferred gains and losses must equal $463.7 ($403.9 + $59.8).

As GM uses the corridor method,* we assume that the amortization of gains and losses is zero and the $463.7 million is entirely amortization of prior service cost. From Exhibit 12C-1, we know that GM deferred investment losses of $1320.9 million. The new prior service costs and actuarial gains/losses can now be deduced as follows:

Deferred Gains and Losses		Prior Service Cost	
Opening balance	$3,305.2	Opening balance	$4,682.2
Less: Amortization	—	Less: Amortization	(463.7)
Plus: Deferred investment (gains) losses	1,320.9	Plus: **New prior service cost**	**275.7**
New actuarial (gains) losses	**3,552.7**	Ending balance	$4,494.2
Closing balance	$8,178.8		

*See footnote 11 for a definition of the corridor method.

The second step considers that *when the minimum liability adjustment was made, it was not fully reported either in net income or stockholders' equity.* As required by SFAS 87, the offset for the minimum liability adjustment is:

1. An intangible asset up to the sum of the unamortized prior service cost and unamortized transition liability
2. A charge to stockholders' equity for the remainder (after tax)

GM's footnote in Exhibit 12C-1 states that $6,401.7 of the minimum liability was recorded as intangible assets and deferred taxes. GM's tax footnote (not provided) reports that a deferred tax asset of $1,730.6 million was recorded due to the minimum liability adjustment. Therefore, $4,671.1 million ($6,401.7 − $1,730.6) was recorded as an intangible asset rather than charged to equity. If the pension intangible, a means of deferring recognition, was fully charged to equity, the effect would be to lower equity further. This second adjustment to GM's balance sheet is the removal of these questionable assets:

	Pretax	After Tax Assumes 37% tax rate
Decrease intangible asset	$4.7 billion	$4.7 billion
Increase deferred tax asset	—	$1.7 billion
Decrease equity	$4.7 billion	$3.0 billion

The net effect of these two adjustments reduces GM's $6.2 billion equity by $5.2 billion (after tax):

	Pretax	After Tax Assumes 37% tax rate
Decrease intangible asset	$4.7 billion	$4.7 billion
Increase deferred tax asset	—	$3.0 billion
Increase liability	$3.5 billion	$3.5 billion
Decrease equity	$8.2 billion	$5.2 billion

GM's Pension Costs

Exhibit 12C-1 reports 1992 pension cost for U.S. plans of $1,261.9 million. The interest component of pension cost is high relative to the service component, a sign of a mature plan. Actual ROA of $2,770.9 million was below the expected long-term ROA of $4,091.8 million; GM recognized a deferred loss of $1,320.9 million.

The method used in the chapter to compute nonsmoothed costs and cash flows can be applied to the GM plans. The details are shown in Exhibit 12C-3:

1. Calculate the contribution by deducting the change in the balance sheet liability from pension cost. *Note that this change is calculated using the balance sheet asset or liability excluding the minimum liability,* as that provision has no direct cash flow or income statement consequences.
2. Compute benefits paid by subtracting the change in plan assets from the contributions to the plan and the actual ROA.
3. Calculate gross pension cost by adding the change in the PBO to benefits paid.
4. Disentangle the net amortization and estimate the new prior service cost and actuarial gains and losses. The results of this analysis follow:

Nonsmoothed Pension Cost

Service cost	$ 859.9 **million**
Interest cost	4,089.9
Recurring cost	**$ 4,949.8**
Prior service cost	275.7
Actuarial loss	3,552.7
Gross pension cost	**$ 8,778.2**
Actual ROA	(2,770.9)
Nonsmoothed cost	**$ 6,007.3 million**

Pension Cash Flows

Contributions	$ 891.3 **million**
Benefits paid	2,993.2

Income Statement

Reported pension cost	**$ 1,261.9 million**

Reported pension cost is only 20% of the nonsmoothed cost. Approximately 60% of the nonsmoothed cost is due to actuarial losses. However, even if these losses are removed, reported cost is still less than half of actual cost. GM's pension plan contribution is low relative to both actual and reported cost. Benefits paid, on the other hand, are more than twice reported pension cost and more than three times plan contributions.

To sum up, 1992 pension cost was a small fraction of nonsmoothed cost and GM's plan contribution was a small fraction of benefits paid. As discussed in the previous section, GM's balance sheet understated the underfunded status of its U.S. plans. These conditions signal that future profitability and cash flows will be adversely affected by the plan.

Exhibit 12C-4 applies the analysis to the entire 1986 to 1992 period, providing a detailed picture of GM's U.S. plans since the adoption of SFAS 87 in 1986. These data help us understand the impact of these plans on past, present, and future net income and cash flows. We can consider whether the conclusions based on only 1992 data are truly valid.

ANALYSIS OF GM PENSION TRENDS

As noted in the introduction, the funded status of GM's pension plans declined dramatically over the seven-year period 1986 to 1992. The elements of the change in PBO and plan assets in Exhibit 12C-4 explain this deterioration.

Trends in Pension Obligations and Assets

The combined PBO for GM's U.S. plans more than doubled over the seven-year period ending December 31, 1992. Plan assets, on the other hand, only grew by 53% over the same period.

Service cost (discussed under pension cost trends shortly) showed little growth. Interest cost, on the other hand, rose sharply as the PBO increased.

Two other factors are worthy of mention. Prior service cost, resulting from benefit increases in 1987 and 1990, accounts for nearly one-quarter of the PBO increase over the seven-year period. The fact that the hourly plans provide flat benefits, leaving pensioners exposed to inflation, makes benefit improvements an important objective when labor contracts are renegotiated. *Analysts should be wary of flat benefit plans that show periodic amendments generating large prior service cost since the PBO may significantly understate the effective pension obligation by excluding benefit increases that are likely to occur.*

Actuarial losses, when summed over the seven-year period, equal about 45% of the net increase in the PBO. Part of the actuarial loss reflects changes in assumptions. The January 1, 1986, PBO was based on a discount rate of 10.9%. The large 1986 "loss" was primarily due to the change in discount rate to 8.5%. The 1987 increase to 10.4% recovered much of the 1986 loss. GM has changed its discount rate every year, resulting in gains and losses in subsequent years as well. Overall, the result has been losses as GM has reduced its high discount rate assumption.

GM changed the assumed compensation growth rate in almost every year as well. This affects those plans that do take salaries into account. In Exhibit 12C-1, note that the "overfunded" plans have a PBO nearly 10% above the ABO, indicating that some plans are pay-related. The gradual decreases in the assumed compensation growth rate helped reduce the growth of the PBO for these plans. Over the seven-year period, the effects of changing assumptions may not, however, fully explain the aggregate actuarial loss of more than $12 billion. It appears likely, although we do not have the data to be certain, that GM's employee-related assumptions (mortality, quit rates, etc.) proved to be optimistic.

Trends in Pension Cost

Pension cost for 1986 was $735 million. After increasing to $810 million in 1987, it declined steadily, reaching $159 million in 1990. In 1991 and 1992, however, pension cost increased considerably. What factors contributed to this change in trend?

Exhibit 12C-4 provides some answers. Service cost was little changed. It appears that the effects of higher wages and salaries (and the advancing age of the workforce) were offset by declining employment levels. Additionally, relatively aggressive (high) discount rate assumptions helped keep service cost low.

EXHIBIT 12C-4. GM
U.S. Pension Plan Data, 1986 to 1992 ($ in millions)

	At Adoption	1986	1987	1988	1989	1990	1991	1992	Change
Pension Plan Status									
Plan assets	$25,810.0	$32,084.8	$38,521.5	$36,410.3	$40,051.9	$34,888.5	$38,902.6	$39,571.6	$ 13,761.6
PBO	24,259.7	32,916.7	31,822.1	34,785.9	37,227.2	40,726.8	45,886.5	51,671.5	27,411.8
Over- (under-)funded	$ 1,550.3	$ (831.9)	$ 6,699.4	$ 1,624.4	$ 2,824.7	$(5,838.3)	$(6,983.9)	$(12,099.9)	$(13,650.2)
Computation of Pension Cost									*Cumulative*
Service cost		$ 622.3	$ 798.2	$ 616.6	$ 661.2	$ 713.6	$ 772.4	$ 859.9	$ 5,044.2
Interest cost		2,517.7	2,718.0	3,190.3	3,331.6	3,389.4	3,906.4	4,089.9	23,143.3
Actual return		(6,711.2)	(7,436.6)	56.1	(6,443.9)	2,117.1	(7,393.3)	(2,770.9)	(28,582.7)
Deferred return		4,365.8	4,608.4	(3,420.2)	3,025.6	(6,153.9)	3,565.3	(1,320.9)	4,670.1
Expected return		$(2,345.4)	$(2,828.2)	$(3,364.1)	$(3,418.3)	$(4,036.8)	$(3,828.0)	$(4,091.8)	$(23,912.6)
Amortization of prior service cost		—	182.0	134.7	146.3	152.8	448.7	463.7	1,528.2
Transition asset		(59.9)	(59.5)	(59.8)	(59.3)	(59.6)	(58.4)	(59.8)	(416.3)
Net pension cost		**$ 734.7**	**$ 810.5**	**$ 517.7**	**$ 661.5**	**$ 159.4**	**$ 1,241.1**	**$ 1,261.9**	**$ 5,386.8**
Assumptions (%)									*Average*
Discount rate	10.9	8.5	10.4	10.0	9.5	10.0	9.3	8.6	9.7
Compensation increase	n/a	5.6	5.5	5.6	5.4	5.4	5.0	4.9	5.3
Assumed ROA	n/a	10.0	10.0	10.0	10.1	11.0	11.0	11.0	10.4
Actual ROA	n/a	**24.3**	**23.2**	**-0.1**	**17.7**	**-5.3**	**21.2**	**7.1**	**12.6**
Alternative Measures of Pension Cost									*Cumulative*
(1) Service cost		**$ 622.3**	**$ 798.2**	**$ 616.6**	**$ 661.2**	**$ 713.6**	**$ 772.4**	**$ 859.9**	**$ 5,044.2**
Interest cost		2,517.7	2,718.0	3,190.3	3,331.6	3,389.4	3,906.4	4,089.9	23,143.3
(2) Recurring cost		**$ 3,140.0**	**$ 3,516.2**	**$ 3,806.9**	**$ 3,992.8**	**$ 4,103.0**	**$ 4,678.8**	**$ 4,949.8**	**$ 28,187.5**
Prior service cost			2,085.6	(2.4)	8.8	3,648.4	6.0	275.7	6,022.1
Actuarial (gains)/losses		7,559.5	(4,241.7)	2,070.0	1,183.2	(1,172.2)	3,897.5	3,552.7	12,849.0
(3) Gross pension cost		**$10,699.5**	**$ 1,360.1**	**$ 5,874.5**	**$ 5,184.8**	**$ 6,579.2**	**$ 8,582.3**	**$ 8,778.2**	**$ 47,058.6**
Actual ROA		(6,711.2)	(7,436.6)	56.1	(6,443.9)	2,117.1	(7,393.3)	(2,770.9)	(28,582.7)
(4) Nonsmoothed pension cost		**$ 3,988.3**	**$(6,076.5)**	**$ 5,930.6**	**$(1,259.1)**	**$ 8,696.3**	**$ 1,189.0**	**$ 6,007.3**	**$ 18,475.9**
(5) Contributions		1,606.2	1,455.0	855.6	(58.8)	33.3	43.4	891.3	4,826.0
(6) Benefits paid		2,042.6	2,454.9	2,910.7	2,743.5	3,079.6	3,422.6	2,993.2	19,647.1

Source: Based on data from GM Annual Reports, 1986 to 1992.

From 1986 to 1990, interest cost increased 35%, an average of 8% per year. Expected return on assets grew even faster, 72% from 1986 to 1990. The 60% increase in plan assets from January 1, 1986, to December 31, 1989, accounted for most of the growth; the increase in the return-on-assets assumption to 11% in 1990 accounted for the rest (see the upcoming discussion of investment performance). As the expected return grew faster than service cost and interest cost, the net of these three components fell from a cost of $795 million in 1986 to $66 million in 1990! Amortization components only partly offset this trend.

In 1991, the trend of reported pension cost reversed, because of the $3.6 billion of prior service cost originating in 1990. Interest cost increased 15% because of the higher PBO. Net amortization increased more than 300% due to amortization of the higher prior service cost.

Reported pension cost, however, continued to lag economic events. Cumulative net pension cost over the 1986 to 1992 period was $5.4 billion; cumulative nonsmoothed cost was $18.5 billion, a difference of $13.1 billion. The deferral of actuarial losses and prior service cost account for most of the difference. SFAS 87 does reduce pension cost volatility; net pension cost was less volatile than nonsmoothed cost. However, pension accounting postpones recognition of economic events over long time periods

Investment Performance Trends

The analysis of the data in Exhibit 12C-4 also allows us to examine the actual investment performance of GM's pension plans. The exhibit shows the computation of actual investment returns for each year; 1988[6] and 1990 were poor, but the other years were excellent. Although we cannot compute performance exactly (because we lack data on the timing of contributions), the mean return for the seven-year period was just under 12%; the time-weighted return would be slightly lower.

Over the seven-year period, therefore, the investment performance of GM's plan assets exceeded its assumed rates. However, the use of a high assumed rate meant that relatively little deferral was left to absorb future shortfalls. If we sum the deferred return elements of pension cost, we find that the cushion is $4.7 million or approximately 12% of December 31, 1992, pension plan assets. If GM had used a lower assumed rate, the cushion would be greater.

Cash Flow Trends

Exhibit 12C-4 also shows the cash flows of the plan. Benefit payments grew by 50% over the 1986 to 1992 period to $3 billion per year. Cash contributions did not keep pace. GM's contributions dropped from $1.6 billion for 1986 (twice pension cost) to half of that in 1992. In three (1989 to 1991) of the seven years examined, contributions were nominal or nonexistent.[7] Although net cash outflows are characteristic of mature pension plans, this trend is cause for concern. Over the seven-year period, cumulative cash contributions were $4.8 billion, nonsmoothed pension cost was $18.5 billion. The gap of $13.7 billion accounts for the deterioration in the plan status. It appears that future company contributions must rise.

GM'S PENSION PLANS: CONCLUDING COMMENTS

In conclusion, we draw a number of inferences from our analysis of GM's U.S. pension plans:

1. The benefit obligation grew substantially over the 1986 to 1992 period, fueled by higher wages, plan improvements, and the effects of an aging workforce. Frequent plan amendments and use of a high discount rate suggest that the obligation was understated. GM apparently substituted future benefits for current wages; the latter must be recognized immediately, whereas the cost of benefits can be deferred to future periods.
2. The minimum liability provision did not recognize all the pension obligation. Some of

[6]As most of GM's plans use an October 1 measurement date, the October 1987 market crash did not impact reported returns for 1987, but was reflected in the 1988 performance.

[7]In 1989, it appears that GM received a refund, possibly due to a plan termination.

EXHIBIT 12C-5. GM
U.S. Pension Plan Data, 1993 to 1995 (data in $ millions)

Years Ended December 31	1993	1994	1995
ABO	$ 63,025.2	$ 57,574.0	$ 68,311.5
PBO	65,428.0	59,751.9	71,284.1
Assets	46,949.9	50,407.6	68,281.3
Excess PBO over assets	$(18,478.1)	$ (9,344.3)	$ (3,002.8)
Unamortized losses	$ 13,062.5	$ 9,747.5	$ 13,160.1
Unamortized prior service cost	7,769.6	7,244.7	6,442.6
Unamortized transition (asset)	(226.2)	(411.4)	(324.4)
Subtotal	$ 20,605.9	$ 16,580.8	$ 19,278.3
Accrual before minimum liability	$ 2,127.8	$ 7,236.5	$ 16,275.5
Minimum liability	(14,992.4)	(11,886.5)	(12,716.8)
Accrued pension cost (liability)	$(12,864.6)	$ (4,650.0)	$ 3,558.7
Pension Cost Components			
Service cost	$ 939.9	$ 1,207.0	$ 989.2
Interest cost	4,258.9	4,466.6	4,916.4
Actual return	(7,159.0)	(1,161.3)	(12,156.3)
Deferred return	3,329.1	(3,312.0)	6,624.7
Expected return	$ (3,829.9)	$ (4,473.3)	$ (5,531.6)
Net amortization	647.7	1,323.5	1,054.0
Net pension cost	**$ 2,016.6**	**$ 2,523.8**	**$ 1,428.0**
Minimum Liability (Includes Non-U.S. Plans) Charged to			
Pension intangible asset	$ 11,793.9	$ 7,373.8	$ 6,500.9
Deferred tax for minimum liability	3,209.2	2,213.4	2,926.8
Stockholders' equity	5,311.2	3,548.4	4,736.3
Total minimum liability	$ 20,314.3	$ 13,135.6	$ 14,164.0
Assumptions at Year-End			
% Discount rate	7.1	8.5	7.0
% Assumed ROA	10.0	10.0	10.0
% Compensation growth	5.0	5.2	5.1

Source: GM, *1993–1995 Annual Reports.*

that obligation remains off balance sheet. Adjusting the balance sheet fully for the pension obligations increases GM's liabilities and reduces stockholders' equity significantly.

3. Investment performance has been good, but the use of an aggressive return assumption left little cushion for future disappointments.

4. Favorable investment performance and the use of aggressive assumptions resulted in low pension cost despite the deterioration of the plan status. Contributions also were reduced, possibly reflecting the difficult operating environment faced by the company.

5. Future pension cost is expected to rise sharply as previously deferred costs are amortized and will remain at higher levels unless asset growth accelerates.

6. These same factors suggest that GM must increase its contributions to its pension plans. The fact that the underfunded plans are for unionized employees may result in union pressure on the company to accelerate funding sooner rather than later.

Required:

(a) Using only the information provided in the case thus far (ignore Exhibit 12C-5), estimate GM's reported and nonsmoothed pension costs for 1993. (State any assumptions made.)

(b) Exhibit 12C-5 reports GM's pension cost and plan status for the years 1993 through 1995. Using that information, update Exhibit 12C-4 for those years.

(c) Show the adjustments to GM's 1995 balance sheet required to reflect the economic status of its U.S. plans.

(d) The case makes some predictions as to GM's future pension costs and cash flows. Evaluate these predictions using the information provided in Exhibit 12C-5 and your answer to part (b).

(e) Using the data in Exhibit 12C-5 and your updated version of Exhibit 12C-4, discuss the future impact of its U.S. plans on GM. You should specifically address the likely future trend of:

• Funded status of the plans

• Pension expense

• Cash contributions

CASE 12-2

DBP Corp.

DEFINED BENEFIT PLAN EXAMPLE

This case presents a simple example of a defined benefit plan, using the hypothetical DBP Co. Our objective is to provide a detailed review of the mechanics of defined benefit pension plans and the accounting for such plans.

The DBP Co. has adopted a pension plan covering its two employees, JR and SR, effective at the beginning of year 1. The plan provides for pension payments calculated as follows:

Retirement age: 65

Annual pension: one month's salary × number of years of service

Benefits based on salary at retirement

Pension benefits vest immediately

Currently, each employee earns $1,000 per month under a contract with five years remaining:

SR is expected to retire at the end of year 3, at age 65.

JR is expected to retire at the end of year 26, at age 65. At that time, JR's monthly salary is expected to be $1,500.

Each employee has a life expectancy of 15 years following retirement, collecting pension benefits until age 80.

Assume the following events:
DBP contributes $6,500 to the pension fund at the beginning of years 1 to 3, and $1,500 at the beginning of year 4. The actual return on fund assets for each year is

Year 1	$ 780
Year 2	1,378
Year 3	3,032
Year 4	3,143

Year 3: SR retires at the end of the year.
Actuaries revise JR's life expectancy and now assume that he will live to age 85.

Year 4: SR collects her pension of $3,000.
The pension plan is amended; the annual benefit is now 1.1. times the monthly salary, retroactive to the beginning of the plan for all current employees (JR).

Required:

1. For each of years 1 to 4, calculate the ABO and PBO for each employee, and for the company as a whole. Assume a discount rate of 10%.

2. For each of years 1 to 4, reconcile the change in ABO and PBO (calculated in question 1) using the following format:

> Opening balance
> + Service cost
> + Interest cost
> + Actuarial (gains) or losses
> + Prior service cost
> − Benefits paid
> = Closing balance

3. For each of years 1 to 4, reconcile the change in plan assets using the following format:

> Opening balance
> + Contributions
> + Return on assets
> − Benefits paid
> = Closing balance

4. Assuming that DBP adopts SFAS 87 at the beginning of year 3:

   (a) Calculate the transition liability at the end of year 2

   (b) Prepare DBP's pension plan footnote at the end of year 4. That footnote should include year 3 net pension cost and a reconciliation of pension plan status for year 3. DBP assumes a 12% ROA.

5. Using *only* the result of question 4, compute *each* of the following for year 4:

   i. Contributions
   ii. Benefits paid
   iii. Recurring cost
   iv. Gross pension cost
   v. Nonsmoothed pension cost

Chapter 12

Problems

Exhibit 12P-1 provides information taken from Deere's pension plan footnotes. Problems 1 through 5 involve the analysis of these pension plan disclosures.

1. [Effect of assumptions, discount rate]

A. For 1994, Deere *increased* the discount rate used to calculate pension obligations, but *decreased* the discount rate used to calculate pension expense. Explain how this is possible.

B. Explain the effect of the 1994 discount rate changes on 1994 and 1995:

(i) Service cost

(ii) Interest cost

(iii) Net pension cost

(iv) PBO

C. Calculate Deere's reported interest cost of $286 for 1994 using the PBO.

2. [Effect of assumptions, expected long-term rate of return]

A. Deere used an assumed rate-of-return on plan assets of 9.7% for each year. Explain how an increase in the assumed rate would affect the following in the year of the change:

(i) Pension cost

(ii) Actual plan status

(iii) Balance sheet pension asset or liability

B. Exhibit 12P-1 reports a sharp drop in the pension fund's 1994 actual investment performance. Discuss the likely impact of this adverse investment performance on pension cost and plan status for both 1994 and future years.

C. Show how the deferred investment loss of $(218) million in 1994 was arrived at.

3. [Minimum liability adjustment, balance sheet adjustments] Deere recorded a minimum liability in 1993 and 1994.

A. Explain what the minimum liability represents.

B. Show how the minimum liability adjustments of $545 million and $515 million at October 31, 1994 and 1993, respectively, were arrived at.

C. Discuss the impact of the minimum liability on Deere's 1994 balance sheet, income, and cash flow statements.

D. What adjustments should you make to Deere's 1994 balance sheet to reflect the economic status of its pension plans? How would the adjustment amounts depend on the purpose of your analysis?

EXHIBIT 12P-1. DEERE CO.
Pension Benefits

The company has several pension plans covering substantially all of its United States employees and employees in certain foreign countries. The United States plans and significant foreign plans in Canada, Germany and France are defined benefit plans in which the benefits are based primarily on years of service and employee compensation near retirement. . . .

. . . Provisions of FASB Statement No. 87 require the company to record a minimum pension liability relating to certain unfunded pension obligations, establish an intangible asset relating thereto and reduce stockholders' equity. At October 31, 1994, this minimum pension liability was remeasured, as required by the statement. As a result, the adjustment to recognize the minimum pension liability was increased from $515 million at October 31, 1993 to $545 million at October 31, 1994; the related intangible asset was adjusted from $181 million to $158 million; and the amount by which stockholders' equity had been reduced was adjusted from $215 million to $248 million (net of applicable deferred income taxes of $119 million in 1993 and $139 million in 1994).

The components of net periodic pension cost and the significant assumptions for the United States plans consisted of the following in millions of dollars and in percents:

	1994	1993	1992
Service cost	$ 79	$ 74	$ 63
Interest cost	286	283	259
Return on assets:			
Actual gain	(86)	(590)	(157)
Deferred gain (loss)	(218)	324	(87)
Net amortization	43	32	18
Net cost	$ 104	$ 123	$ 96
Discount rates for obligations	8.0%	7.25%	8.0%
Discount rates for expenses	7.25%	8.0%	8.25%
Assumed rates of compensation increases	5.0%	5.0%	5.7%
Expected long-term rates of return	9.7%	9.7%	9.7%

A reconciliation of the funded status of the United States plans at October 31 in millions of dollars follows:

	1994		1993	
	Assets Exceed Accumulated Benefits	Accumulated Benefits Exceed Assets	Assets Exceed Accumulated Benefits	Accumulated Benefits Exceed Assets
Actuarial present value of benefit obligations				
Vested benefit obligation	$(1,522)	$(1,693)	$(1,555)	$(1,689)
Nonvested benefit obligation	(73)	(270)	(94)	(276)
Accumulated benefit obligation	(1,595)	(1,963)	(1,649)	(1,965)
Excess of projected benefit obligation over accumulated benefit obligation	(340)	(20)	(378)	(21)
Projected benefit obligation	(1,935)	(1,983)	(2,027)	(1,986)
Plan assets at fair value	1,756	1,767	1,805	1,510
Projected benefit obligation in excess of plan assets	(179)	(216)	(222)	(476)
Unrecognized net loss	35	415	114	373
Prior service cost not yet recognized in net periodic pension cost	9	154	3	176
Remaining unrecognized transition net asset from November 1, 1985	(73)	(10)	(83)	(13)
Adjustment required to recognize minimum liability		(545)		(515)
Pension liability recognized in the consolidated balance sheet	$ (208)	$ (202)	$ (188)	$ (455)

Source: Deere, *1994 Annual Report.*

4. [Pension plans, cash flows and alternative cost measures)

A. Calculate Deere's 1994 contributions to its pension fund.

B. Calculate 1994 pension benefits paid to Deere's employees.

C. Estimate (without disaggregating prior service costs and actuarial gains and losses) recurring, gross, and nonsmoothed pension cost for fiscal 1994 for Deere's pension plans.

D. Explain and quantify the major differences between Deere's 1994 gross and recurring pension cost.

5. [Forecasting pension costs] Using only the data in Exhibit 12P-1, forecast the components of Deere's 1995 pension cost.

6. [Pension plans, comprehensive analysis] The following information was abstracted from the footnotes of the CC Company:

	Year 2
Service cost	$ 14,459
Interest cost	50,009
Actual return on assets	(35,720)
Net amortization and deferral	(8,873)
Net pension cost	$ 19,875

	Year 2	Year 1
ABO	$520,065	$ 456,582
PBO	620,993	537,608
Plan assets	588,182	583,819
Excess assets over PBO	$(32,811)	$ 46,211
Less: Unamortized prior service cost	25,815	28,551
(Gains) and losses	(36,678)	(100,428)
Transition obligation (asset)	(17,909)	(19,472)
Accrued pension liability	$ (61,583)	$ (45,138)

A. Use the information above to calculate:

(i) CC's contribution to its pension plan

(ii) Benefits paid to employees

B. Calculate:

(i) Recurring pension cost

(ii) Gross pension cost

(iii) Nonsmoothed pension cost

(iv) Net pension cost recognized in income statement

C. Calculate and justify the adjustments you would make to CC's balance sheet to reflect the economic position of its pension plan, assuming:

(i) A "liquidation" perspective

(ii) A "going concern" perspective

7. [Pension plan, comprehensive analysis with minimum liability] The following information relating to its pension plan was taken from the 1993 financial statement footnotes of EDS:

	1993
Service cost	$ 72.6 million
Interest cost	69.8
Actual ROA	(121.3)
Net amortization and deferral	75.2
Net pension cost	$ 96.3

Reconciliation of the pension plans funded status:

	1993	1992
Plan assets	$ 677.1	$ 499.7
Accumulated benefit obligation	610.4	376.2
Projected benefit obligation	1,023.1	729.5
Excess PBO over plan assets	$(346.0)	$(229.8)
Unrecognized		
Net (gain) loss	145.1	36.6
Transition obligation	19.7	21.0
Prior service cost	33.7	37.0
Additional minimum liability	(3.7)	(1.4)
Net accrued pension cost	$(151.2)	$(136.6)
Additional information		
Discount rate	7.7%	9.1%
Rate of compensation increase	5.9%	5.3%
Long-term rate of return on assets	9.8%	9.7%

Reminder: When solving parts A and B, you should remove the minimum liability from the net accrued pension cost.

A. Calculate 1993:

  (i) Contributions to the plan

 (ii) Benefits paid

B. Calculate the following measures of pension cost:

  (i) Recurring cost

 (ii) Gross pension cost

(iii) Nonsmoothed cost

(iv) Net pension cost recognized in income statement

C. Assuming that the minimum liability was recorded by EDS as an intangible asset, what adjustments should be made to EDS's balance sheet to reflect the actual economic status of its plans?

D. Estimate the amount of ROA deferred and included in unrecognized net (gain) loss.

E. Explain and quantify the major contributing factor to the 1993 increase in EDS's PBO.

F. Disaggregate (using estimates as needed) the components of the net amortization and deferral of $75.2 million.

8. [Pension plans, comprehensive analysis] The following defined benefit pension plan data were reported by Delta:

	($ in thousands)	
	Year 2	Year 1
Accumulated benefit obligation	$3,347,521	$3,048,414
Projected benefit obligation	4,900,555	4,421,453
Plan assets at fair value	4,350,316	3,783,019
PBO in excess of plan assets	$ (550,239)	$ (638,434)
Unrecognized net loss	348,943	504,525
Unrecognized transition obligation	71,713	71,962
Unrecognized prior service cost	9,816	10,382
Accrued pension cost	$ (119,767)	$ (51,565)

For all periods presented, an 8.5% weighted-average discount rate and a 4.9% rate of increase in future compensation levels were used in determining the actuarial present value of the projected benefit obligation. The expected long-term rate of return on assets was 9%.

The net periodic cost of defined benefit pension plans for fiscal years 1 and 2 included the following components:

	($ in thousands)	
	Year 2	Year 1
Service cost	$ 216,867	$ 184,893
Interest cost	389,333	343,694
Actual return on plan assets	(493,703)	(185,356)
Net amortization and deferral	152,888	(130,363)
Net periodic pension cost	$ 265,385	$ 212,868

A. Calculate the year 2:

(i) Contributions

(ii) Benefits paid

B. Calculate the following alternative measures of pension cost for year 2:

(i) Recurring cost

(ii) Gross pension cost

(iii) Nonsmoothed cost

C. Compare the year 2 change in Delta's balance sheet liability with the change in Delta's economic liability. Explain the primary cause of the difference in trend of these two liability measures.

EXHIBIT 12P-2. BF GOODRICH
Note F: Postretirement Benefits Other than Pensions

The Company sponsors several unfunded defined benefit postretirement plans that provide certain health-care and life insurance benefits to eligible employees. The health-care plans are contributory, with retiree contributions adjusted periodically, and contain other cost-sharing features such as deductibles and coinsurance. The life insurance plans are generally noncontributory.

The following table sets forth the combined status of the plans as recognized in the Consolidated Balance Sheet at December 31, 1994 and 1993:

($ in millions)	1994	1993
Accumulated postretirement benefit obligation (APBO):		
Retirees	$281.7	$315.4
Fully eligible active plan participants	24.7	26.2
Other active plan participants	38.3	40.4
Unrecognized gain (loss)	34.4	(9.5)
Unrecognized prior service credit	—	2.2
Accrued postretirement cost	$379.1	$374.7

Net periodic postretirement benefit expense (including $9.9 million allocated to the former Geon Vinyl Division in 1992) included the following components:

($ in millions)	1994	1993	1992
Service cost for benefits earned	$ 2.9	$ 2.4	$ 2.8
Interest cost on APBO	27.0	30.4	37.6
Net amortization and deferral		(.1)	—
Net periodic postretirement cost	$29.9	$32.7	$40.4

For measurement purposes, the annual rate of increase in the per capita cost of covered health-care benefits of 9 percent was assumed for 1995, decreasing gradually to 5.75 percent through the year 2002 and remaining at that level thereafter. The health-care cost trend rate assumption has a significant effect on the amount of the obligation and periodic cost reported. An increase in the assumed health-care cost trend rate by 1 percentage point in each year would increase the APBO as of December 31, 1994, by $27.3 million and the aggregate of the service and interest cost components of net periodic postretirement benefit cost for 1994 by $2.7 million. The weighted average discount rates used in determining the APBO were 8.75 percent, 7.4 percent and 9 percent as of December 31, 1994, 1993 and 1992, respectively.

Source: B.F. Goodrich 1994 Annual Report

9. [Postretirement plans (unfunded), comprehensive analysis] Exhibit 12P-2 presents information taken from BF Goodrich's postretirement plan footnote for 1994.

A. Calculate the firm's APBO at December 31, 1993 and 1994.

B. Calculate the 1994 reported interest cost of $27 million using the APBO.

C. Calculate the postretirement benefits actually paid to employees in 1994.

D. Calculate recurring, gross, and nonsmoothed postretirement costs for 1994.

E. Explain the differences between the postretirement cost reported by Goodrich and the amounts calculated in part D.

F. How should Goodrich's balance sheet at December 31, 1993 and 1994, be adjusted to reflect the economic status of the plan?

G. Explain why the adjustments in part F are so different in 1993 and 1994. How is this difference related to your answer to part E?

Problems 10 through 12 relate to the nonpension postretirement benefit plans of IBM. The nonpension postretirement benefits footnote from IBM's 1994 Annual Report is reproduced in Exhibit 12P-3.

10. [Postretirement plans, motivations for funding]

A. Although IBM has partially funded its nonpension postretirement benefits, most companies do not. Other than any legal requirement to do so, suggest why firms may be motivated to fund their pension but not their nonpension postretirement benefit plans.

B. Discuss the possible motivations for IBM to fund its nonpension postretirement benefits despite your answer to part A.

C. IBM's pension footnotes show significant foreign pension plans. However, the postretirement benefits footnote does not report any data for foreign plans. Explain why.

11. [Postretirement plans (funded plans), comprehensive analysis]

A. Calculate the 1994 interest cost of $512 million using the APBO.

B. IBM shows a deferred return on plan assets of $(125) million. What does this deferral reflect and how was it calculated (approximately)?

C. Calculate the following 1994 cash flows associated with IBM's nonpension postretirement plans:

  (i) Contributions

  (ii) Benefits paid

EXHIBIT 12P-3. IBM
Nonpension Postretirement Benefits

S } n o n p e n s i o n   p o s t r e t i r e m e n t   b e n e f i t s

The company and its U.S. subsidiaries have defined benefit postretirement plans that provide medical, dental, and life insurance for retirees and eligible dependents. In 1993, the company applied plan cost maximums to those who retired prior to January 1, 1992. These maximums will take effect beginning with the year 2001. Plan cost maximums were established in 1990 for those employees retiring after December 31, 1991.

The accumulated postretirement benefit obligation was determined by application of the terms of medical, dental, and life insurance plans, including the effects of established maximums on covered costs, together with relevant actuarial assumptions. These actuarial assumptions include healthcare cost trend rates projected ratably from 12.0 percent in 1995 to 6 percent in the year 2007.

The effect of a 1 percent annual increase in these assumed cost trend rates would increase the accumulated postretirement benefit obligation by approximately $52 million; the annual costs would not be materially affected.

EXHIBIT 12P-3. (*continued*)

Net periodic postretirement benefit cost for the years ended December 31 included the following components:

	1994	1993	1992
Expected long-term rate of return on plan assets	9.5%	9.5%	9.5%
(*Dollars in millions*)			
Service cost:			
Benefits attributed to service during the period	$ 51	$ 53	$ 78
Termination incentive expenses	–	–	71
Interest cost on the accumulated			
postretirement benefit obligation	512	566	485
Return on plan assets:			
Actual	22	(201)	(67)
Deferred	(125)	84	(59)
Net amortizations and other	(38)	29	(61)
Curtailment loss	–	732	–
Net periodic postretirement benefit cost	$ 422	$ 1,263	$ 447

In the Consolidated Statement of Operations, the curtailment loss and termination expenses referred to above are included in restructuring charges.

The table below provides information on the status of the plans.

The funded status at December 31 was as follows:

	1994	1993
Assumed discount rate	8.25%	7.25%
(*Dollars in millions*)		
Accumulated postretirement benefit obligation:		
Retirees	$ (5,411)	$ (5,761)
Fully eligible active plan participants	(567)	(673)
Other active plan participants	(530)	(927)
Total	(6,508)	(7,361)
Plan assets at fair value	1,028	1,366
Accumulated postretirement benefit obligation in		
excess of plan assets	(5,480)	(5,995)
Unrecognized net loss	505	1,431
Unrecognized prior service cost	(744)	(828)
Accrued postretirement benefit cost recognized		
in the statement of financial position	$ (5,719)	$ (5,392)

Source: IBM, 1994 Annual Report.

D. Calculate the following alternative measures of postretirement benefit cost:

  (i) Recurring cost

  (ii) Gross cost

  (iii) Nonsmoothed cost

E. Calculate the adjustment to IBM's balance sheet required to reflect the economic status of the nonpension postretirement plans.

F. Both plan assets and APBO declined considerably in 1994. This decline was not the result of curtailments or terminations referred to in the note as these were completed in 1993. Explain the factors that led to these declines.

12. [Forecasting postretirement benefit costs] Forecast IBM's 1995 postretirement benefits cost.

13. [Postretirement plans, adoption method, comparison with pay-as-you-go] Exhibit 12P-4 contains information from Deere's postretirement benefits footnote. As the exhibit notes, Deere adopted SFAS 106 effective November 1, 1992, and elected to record the obligation as a one-time charge to earnings in fiscal 1993. In its *1992 Annual Report,* Deere disclosed the expected impact of different methods of adopting SFAS 106:

> Although Deere & Company continues to evaluate the impact of this new standard, the company's current estimates of the transition obligation range from $.8 billion to $1.2 billion. Current estimates of incremental annual expense for Deere & Company following adoption range from $40 million (if the entire transition obligation were recognized in the year of adoption) to $100 million if the transition obligation were accrued over a 20-year period. The foregoing amounts have been reduced by income tax benefits expected to be recognized in accordance with FASB Statement No. 109.

A. Explain whether the chosen adoption method allowed Deere to report higher or lower pretax earnings in 1993 and 1994 than the alternative method.

B. Using the information in Exhibit 12P-4, calculate the amount that Deere would have expensed in 1994 on a "pay-as-you-go" basis for its postretirement benefits. Assume a 35% tax rate.

C. Explain the factors that may have contributed to the differences between the estimates provided in 1992 and the answer you arrived at in part B.

14. [Analysis of benefit plans]

The 1994 financial statements of Dow Chemical are shown in Appendix B. Notes O and P contain data on Dow's pension and other postretirement benefits, respectively.

A. Compute the 1993 and 1994 funded status of Dow's pension plans by combining the amounts shown for "fully funded" and "partially funded" plans in Note O.

B. Using your answer to part A, discuss the factors that caused the 1994 change in funded status.

C. To what extent was the change in funded status reflected in Dow's financial statements?

D. Explain why Dow reports negative prior service cost for its postretirement benefit plans.

EXHIBIT 12P-4. DEERE
Postretirement Benefits Other than Pensions

POSTRETIREMENT BENEFITS OTHER THAN PENSIONS

The company generally provides defined benefit health care and life insurance plans for retired employees in the United States and Canada. Provisions of the benefit plans for hourly employees are, in large part, subject to collective bargaining. The plans for salaried employees include certain cost-sharing provisions. It is the company's policy to fund a portion of its obligations for the United States postretirement health care benefit plans under provisions of Internal Revenue Code Section 401(h). Plan assets consist primarily of common stocks, common trust funds, government securities and corporate debt securities.

The components of net periodic postretirement benefits cost and the significant assumptions for the United States and Canadian plans consisted of the following in millions of dollars and in percents:

	1994	1993
Health Care		
Service cost	$ 54	$ 28
Interest cost	117	120
Return on assets:		
Actual gain	(4)	(21)
Deferred gain (loss)	(10)	11
Net amortization	(44)	(12)
Net cost	113	126
Life Insurance		
Service cost	3	3
Interest cost	15	13
Net cost	18	16
Total net cost	$131	$142
Discount rates for obligations	8.25%	7.5%
Discount rates for expense	7.5%	8.25%
Expected long-term rate of return	9.7%	9.7%

Postretirement benefits cost was $86 million in 1992 under the previous accounting principle.

A reconciliation of the funded status of the United States and Canadian plans in millions of dollars follows:

	1994		1993	
	Health Care	Life Insurance	Health Care	Life Insurance
Accumulated postretirement benefit obligations				
Retirees	$(1,120)	$(112)	$(1,042)	$(117)
Fully eligible active plan participants	(167)	(24)	(209)	(24)
Other active plan participants	(302)	(46)	(279)	(52)
Total	(1,589)	(182)	(1,530)	(193)
Plan assets at fair value	153		129	
Accumulated postretirement benefit obligation in excess of plan assets	(1,436)	(182)	(1,401)	(193)
Unrecognized net loss	106		125	20
Prior service credit not yet recognized in net periodic postretirement benefits costs	(175)		(222)	(1)
Postretirement benefit liability recognized in the consolidated balance sheet	$(1,505)	$(182)	$(1,498)	$(174)

The annual rate of increase in the per capita cost of covered health care benefits (the health care cost trend rate) used to determine 1994 cost was assumed to be 8.2 percent for 1995 decreasing gradually to 4.5 percent by the year 2001. The annual rate of increase in the health care cost trend rate used to determine 1993 cost was assumed to be 1.3 percent for 1994 increasing to 9.0 percent in 1995 and decreasing gradually to 4.3 percent by the year 2001. The 1994 rate was lower than normal due to the effects of plan changes, particularly the migration of employees to managed care programs and company-operated clinics. An increase of one percentage point in the assumed health care cost trend rate would increase the accumulated postretirement benefit obligation as of October 31, 1994 by $163 million and the aggregate of the service and interest cost components of net periodic postretirement benefits cost for the year then ended by $23 million.

Source: Deere, *1994 Annual Report.*

E. Calculate the adjustments required to conform Dow's balance sheet accruals to the funded status of its:

(i) Pension plans

(ii) Other postretirement benefit plans

15. [Analysis of non-U.S. benefit plan disclosures]

The 1994 financial statements of Imperial Chemical Industries (ICI) are shown in Appendix C. Notes 33 and 34 contain data on ICI's pension and health care benefits, respectively.

A. Compare ICI's pension plan assumptions with those shown in Exhibit 12P-5. What factors might explain the differences between ICI's assumptions and those of the firms shown in that exhibit?

B. What adjustment to ICI's balance sheet is required to fully reflect the funded status of its pension plan?

C. What additional disclosures would be helpful in assessing the long-term outlook for ICI's pension plan?

EXHIBIT 12P-5
Chemical Industry Comparison of Pension Plan Assumptions

	Air Products			Dow Chemical			DuPont		
A. Assumptions	1992	1993	1994	1992	1993	1994	1992	1993	1994
Discount rate	8.50%	7.63%	8.80%	8.25%	7.25%	7.75%	8.50%	7.25%	9.00%
Rate of compensation increase	5.13%	5.13%	5.00%	6.00%	5.50%	5.50%	5.00%	5.00%	5.00%
Long-term rate of return on plan assets	11.40%	11.00%	10.60%	9.00%	9.00%	9.00%	9.00%	9.00%	9.00%

	Georgia Gulf			B. F. Goodrich			Monsanto		
	1992	1993	1994	1992	1993	1994	1992	1993	1994
Discount rate	8.00%	8.00%	7.00%	8.50%	7.40%	8.75%	8.50%	7.25%	8.50%
Rate of compensation increase	6.50%	6.50%	5.50%	5.00%	4.50%	5.00%	6.00%	4.25%	5.00%
Long-term rate of return on plan assets	8.00%	8.00%	9.00%	9.50%	9.00%	9.00%	9.50%	9.50%	9.50%

	Quaker Chemical			Rohm and Haas			Union Carbide		
	1992	1993	1994	1992	1993	1994	1992	1993	1994
Discount rate	8.00%	7.50%	8.00%	8.50%	7.00%	8.00%	8.00%	7.00%	8.50%
Rate of compensation increase	6.00%	5.50%	5.50%	6.00%	5.00%	5.00%	4.25%	4.25%	5.75%
Long-term rate of return on plan assets	9.50%	9.50%	9.25%	8.50%	8.50%	8.50%	8.25%	8.25%	8.50%

	Industry Average		
	1992	1993	1994
Discount rate	8.31%	7.36%	8.26%
Rate of compensation increase	5.54%	5.07%	5.25%
Long-term rate of return on plan assets	9.18%	9.08%	9.15%

Source: Annual reports of included companies.

D. What adjustment to ICI's balance sheet is required to fully reflect the funded status of its nonpension benefit plans?

16. Exhibit 12P-5 depicts the three key assumptions: discount rate, rate of compensation increase, and the expected long-term rate of return on plan assets for nine U.S. chemical companies, and industry averages.

A. DuPont used the highest discount rate for 1994. Explain the effect of that choice on the funded status of duPont's plan relative to its competitors.

B. The choice of the long-term rate of compensation increase reflects expected inflation, which also affects the discount rate.

  (i) Which chemical firm has the greatest spread between these two assumptions?

  (ii) Explain the effect of that large spread on the funded status of the firm relative to its competitors.

C. Which chemical firm has the highest assumed rate of return on plan assets? Explain the effect of that high rate on:

  (i) Plan status relative to its competitors

  (ii) Pension cost relative to its competitors

  (iii) The likelihood of future actuarial gains or losses relative to its competitors.

13

ANALYSIS OF INTERCORPORATE INVESTMENTS

CHAPTER OUTLINE

CHAPTER OBJECTIVES

INTRODUCTION

INVESTMENTS IN SECURITIES
Cost Method
Market Method
Lower of Cost or Market Method
U.S. Accounting Requirements
    Classification Criteria

ANALYSIS OF MARKETABLE SECURITIES
Separation of Operating from Investment Results
Effects of Classification of Marketable Securities
Under SFAS 115
    Effect on Reported Performance
    Effect on Investment and Financing Decisions
Analysis of Investment Performance
    Mark-to-Market Accounting
Summary of Analytical Procedures
Financial Reporting for Marketable Securities
Outside the United States

EQUITY METHOD OF ACCOUNTING
Conditions for Use
Illustration of the Equity Method
Comparison of the Equity Method and SFAS 115
Equity Accounting and Analysis

CONSOLIDATION
Conditions for Use
Illustration of Consolidation

**COMPARISON OF CONSOLIDATION WITH
THE EQUITY METHOD**
Consolidation Versus the Equity Method:
Analytic Considerations
    Nonhomogeneous Subsidiaries
    Joint Ventures
Proportionate Consolidation
    *Comparison of Proportionate Consolidation
    and the Equity Method*
    Use of Proportionate Consolidation in Practice
Significance of Consolidation: Summary

ANALYSIS OF MINORITY INTEREST

**CONSOLIDATION PRACTICES OUTSIDE THE
UNITED STATES**

ANALYSIS OF SEGMENT DATA
Illustration of Industry Segments: DuPont
Illustration of Geographic Segments: DuPont
Management Discussion and Analysis
Uses and Limitations of Segment Data

Proposed Changes in Segment Reporting
Using Segment Data to Estimate Consolidated
Earnings and Risk
Segment Reporting Outside the United States

SUMMARY

CASE 13-1: COCA-COLA
Consolidation Versus Equity Method

CHAPTER OBJECTIVES

The goal of this chapter is to enhance the understanding of the accounting and analysis issues related to intercorporate investments. Specific issues include:

1. Differences between the return earned on investments in marketable securities and the recognition of that return in financial statements
2. The financial statement effects of the equity method of accounting for investments in other firms

3. The financial statement effects of consolidation and differences between that method and the equity method of accounting
4. Proportionate consolidation as an accounting method and tool for analysis
5. The use of segment data to enhance the understanding of firms with operations in more than one industry

INTRODUCTION

The modern company rarely consists of a single corporate entity. The larger the enterprise, the more likely that it will contain more than one unit; large multinationals may have hundreds of subsidiaries in dozens of jurisdictions. In addition, large enterprises frequently invest in other entities, including joint ventures and partnerships. In this chapter, we examine the accounting principles applicable to intercorporate investments, evaluate the impact of the reporting choice on the financial statements, and discuss applicable analytical techniques.

Enterprises invest in the securities of other companies for various reasons. Intercorporate investments may involve temporary purchases of equity or debt securities to capture dividends, interest income, or capital gains. Investments may also be motivated by risk-sharing or participation in new markets or technologies. Finally, the investment may be a precursor to an acquisition.

Financial reporting of intercorporate investments depends primarily on the degree of investor influence or control over the investee. Percentage of ownership[1] in the investee firm is often used as a practical guideline to measure significant influence or control:

Ownership Level	Degree of Influence	Reporting Method
<20%	No significant influence	Cost or market
20–50%	Significant influence	Equity method
>50%	Control	Consolidation

[1]Percentage ownership may be defined by either ownership or voting control of investee common stock.

These ownership percentages, however, are merely guidelines. If significant influence exists with ownership below 20%, the equity method may be used. Similarly, if control does not exist even with ownership of above 50%, consolidation is not appropriate. The FASB exposure draft, Consolidated Financial Statements: Policy and Procedures (1995), proposes a modified definition of control, *effective rather than legal control,* paving the way for consolidation even when the investor owns less than 50% of the investee. See Box 13-3 for a discussion of this exposure draft.

The primary conceptual distinction among the different reporting requirements is the extent to which the investee (affiliate) constitutes an integral part of the investor (parent) company. Under the cost and market methods, the two firms are treated as separate entities and the parent's income from its investment is based on actual dividends received and any changes in market value of the investment.

The parent's ability to exercise significant influence over the operating and strategic activities of the affiliate provides the rationale for the equity method: Income reported by the parent includes its share (in proportion to ownership) of the income reported by the affiliate. The parent's proportionate share of dividends declared by the affiliate is reported as a reduction in the carrying amount of the investment to reflect the corresponding decline in the net assets of the affiliate. Reported income under the equity method is not affected by changes in market prices, unless the price decline is considered permanent or the investment is sold.

Finally, consolidated reporting views the two companies as a unified economic entity even when they are legally separate. The entire income of the affiliate (net of intercompany transactions) is added to that of the parent.

INVESTMENTS IN SECURITIES

Enterprises often invest in the common and preferred shares, bonds, or other securities of other entities. Generally, when such investments are small relative to the capital of the investee (measured by the amount of outstanding voting common stock held), the investor is unable to influence the activities of the investee.

Over the life of the investment, the total return earned on the investment equals

Dividends and Interest Received + Capital Gain or Loss

The following accounting methods used to report the investments in securities of other entities recognize dividends and interest as part of income in the year they are earned; they differ as to when changes in the market value of the asset are recognized:

- The cost method recognizes price changes only in the period they are sold.
- The market method mirrors the actual economic performance of the security and recognizes price changes in the period they occur.
- Lower of cost or market (LOCOM) recognizes price changes prior to sale only when the market value *declines below original cost.*

These three methods are illustrated using the following data:

- Company P purchases 1 share (out of 100 shares outstanding) of Company S for $100.

- Company S reports net income of $25 per share for period 1 and declares dividends of $10 per share on its common stock.
- The market value of the shares of Company S rises to $135 per share at the end of period 1.
- Company P sells its share of Company S for $120 during period 2.

Cost Method

Under the cost method, assets are reported at their amortized cost.[2] Market value changes are not recognized until there is an actual transaction (sale). Only dividends and interest received from the investee and realized gains and losses are recognized.

At acquisition, Company P reports the purchased asset on its balance sheet at the acquisition cost as follows[3]:

Investment in Company S   **$100**

For period 1, Company P's income statement would include (as other income) the following:

Dividend received   **$10**

At the end of period 1, the increase in market price of the shares of Company S is not recorded by Company P. When the security is sold, Company P recognizes the realized gain or loss equal to the difference between the proceeds of the sale and the original cost, $120 − $100, or $20 in our example, yielding a total two-period return (dividend + capital gain) on the investment of $30.

In the absence of a dividend, sale, or write-down of the investment, the operating, financing, and investing activities of Company S have no impact on the financial statements of Company P. The carrying value of the investment remains $100 until the investment is sold. A write-down of the investment to its estimated market value is required only when Company P determines that it has been permanently impaired (e.g., due to financial problems of Company S). In that case, the write-down is recognized in current period income. The estimated market value becomes the new carrying amount. Upon subsequent sale of the investment, gain or loss would be determined by comparing the proceeds of sale with this new carrying amount, not the original cost. Write-downs cannot be restored under U.S. GAAP, regardless of future circumstances.

Market Method

Under the market method, securities with a public market are carried at their current market value. Unrealized changes in market value (from period to period) are included in net income along with dividends, interest, and realized gains and losses.

In our example, the carrying value on Company P's books increases to $135 and an (unrealized) capital gain of $35 is reported to recognize the increase in the market value of Company S shares to $135 at the end of period 1. Total return (dividend +

---

[2]Premiums or discounts from the face amount are amortized over the life of the debt issue using the interest method (see Chapter 10 for a discussion from the point of view of the debt issuer).

[3]The account title may not identify a specific company but may use a more general term such as marketable securities or investments in affiliate(s).

capital gain) in period 1 is $45. When the investment is sold for $120 in period 2, a loss of $15 is recognized. The total (two period) return remains $30 as under the cost method. However, the returns recognized each period differ considerably. *The market method reflects the actual economic return earned on the investment in each time period.*

Lower of Cost or Market Method

LOCOM takes a conservative approach and recognizes unrealized losses (but not gains) and recoveries of previously recognized unrealized losses. In our example, market value is higher than cost at the end of period 1; therefore, no market value change is recognized. When market value is below cost, LOCOM produces the same result as the market method.

The methods can be summarized as follows:

Method	Balance Sheet (Carrying Value)	Income Statement (Recognized as Income)
Cost	Cost	Dividends and interest Realized gains and losses
Market	Market value	Dividends and interest Realized and unrealized gains and losses
LOCOM	LOCOM	Dividends and interest Realized gains and losses Unrealized losses and recoveries

U.S. Accounting Requirements

Outside the United States, the cost and LOCOM[4] methods prevail. In the United States, the provisions of SFAS 115 (1993) require a hybrid of the cost and market methods.

The cost method is used for securities with no readily available market price (i.e., they are not publicly traded). Securities that have a public market or readily determined fair value must be classified into three categories:

1. *Debt securities held-to-maturity.* The cost method is used to report these securities as current or noncurrent assets at amortized cost. Interest income and realized gains and losses are reported in income.

2. *Debt and equity securities available-for-sale.* The market method is applied to record current or noncurrent investments in this category at fair market value.

---

[4]The LOCOM method is no longer used in the United States. However, SFAS 12 (1975), which was replaced by SFAS 115, applied the LOCOM method (on a portfolio basis) to marketable equity securities (MES). Under the provisions of SFAS 12, the accounting treatment of unrealized gains and losses on investments in MES depended on whether the securities were classified as current or noncurrent assets. The classification was determined by management intent; if the securities were to be sold within one year or the operating cycle, whichever is longer, they were current assets. A longer expected holding period required classification as noncurrent assets.

For MES reported as current assets, unrealized gains and losses were included in current period operating results on the income statement. For MES classified as noncurrent assets, all market value changes were excluded from operating results; these changes were accumulated in a securities valuation account, a component of stockholders' equity.

Under SFAS 12, fixed-income investments were carried at amortized cost, except for trading portfolios.

However, the cost method is used to report dividends, interest income, and realized gains and losses in income; unrealized gains and losses are reported (net of deferred income tax) as a separate component of stockholders' equity.

3. *Debt and equity trading securities.* The market method is used to report these investments as current assets at fair market value on each reporting date. Dividends, interest income, and all gains and losses (realized and unrealized) are reported in income.

These classifications result in the use of the cost method for debt securities held-to-maturity and the market method for trading securities. *For available-for-sale debt and equity investments, the balance sheet follows the market method and the income statement the cost method.*

The financial statement effects of classification are summarized below:

Portfolio	Balance Sheet (Carrying Value)	Income Statement (Recognized as Income)
Held-to-maturity	Cost	Interest Realized gains and losses
Available-for-sale	Market value	Dividends and interest Realized gains and losses
Trading	Market value	Dividends and interest Realized gains and losses Unrealized gains and losses

Classification Criteria

The classification decision depends on management intent, an inherently subjective standard. However, it is not a completely free choice. SFAS 115 establishes criteria governing the designation of securities among the three portfolio categories. These criteria are intended to ensure that portfolio holdings conform to the conceptual basis for the accounting principles used and to preclude arbitrary transfers among portfolios intended to circumvent those accounting principles.

To classify debt securities as held-to-maturity, the firm must have *both the intent and the ability* to do so. The intent requirement means that held-to-maturity securities cannot be sold prior to maturity except in exceptional circumstances.[5] Portfolios that are actively managed, therefore, must be classified as available-for-sale.

Transfers between portfolios are subject to special rules:

- Securities are transferred to the trading portfolio at fair market value; any unrealized gain or loss must be included in income.

- Debt securities from the held-to-maturity category are transferred to the available-for-sale portfolio at fair market value; any unrealized gain or loss is included in equity.

- Available-for-sale debt securities are transferred to held-to-maturity at fair market value; any unrealized gain or loss remains in equity but must be amortized over the remaining life of the bond.

---

[5]SFAS 115 (para. 8) identifies the following *exceptional* changes in circumstances: significant deterioration in credit rating, change in tax law or regulatory requirements, or a major acquisition or disposition.

EXHIBIT 13-1
Comparison of Accounting Methods for Intercorporate Investments

Assumptions

Year	Shares Purchased (Sold)	Price/Share
19X1	100	$80
19X2	(30)	60
19X3	40	70

Note: All sales and purchases assumed to occur on January 1. Price may vary from previous day's (December 31) price.

	19X1	19X2	19X3
Investee earnings per share	$7	$8	$7
Investee dividend per share	2	2	2

Year-End Holdings Valued at Cost and Market

	No. of Shares	Cost/ Share	Total Cost	Price/ Share	Market Value
19X1	100	$80	$8,000	$70	$7,000
19X2	70	80	5,600	80	5,600
19X3	70	80	$5,600	90	$6,300
	40	70	2,800	90	3,600
	110		$8,400		$9,900

Accounting Methods

Classification	Carried at	Balance Sheet Carrying Amount		
		19X1	19X2	19X3
Held-to-maturity	Amortized cost	$8,000	$5,600	$8,400
Trading	Market value	7,000	5,600	9,900
Available-for-sale	Market value	7,000	5,600	9,900
Equity method	Cost plus equity in reinvested earnings	8,500	6,370	9,720

The intent of the transfer rules is to prevent selective recognition of gains or losses merely by reclassifying securities among portfolios. As discussed shortly, some scope for manipulation remains.

Exhibit 13-1 compares the accounting for marketable securities (trading and available-for-sale) to that of securities carried at cost.[6] Note the dichotomy in the accounting for available-for-sale securities. Market value is used on the balance sheet, as it is for the trading portfolio; both differ markedly from the cost method used for held-to-maturity investments. *However, on the income statement, available-for-sale securities use the cost method, ignoring market values.* Only the trading portfolio is market-based (i.e., marked to market) for both income and balance sheet purposes. Finally, the operating performance of the investee (earnings or cash flow) does not affect the accounting in any of these cases.

[6]The exhibit also shows results for the "equity method" covered later in the chapter.

EXHIBIT 13-1 (*continued*)

Total Investment Income

Classification	Measurement	19X1	19X2	19X3
Held-to-maturity	Dividends + realized G/L	$ 200	$(460)	$ 220
Trading	Dividends + all G/L	(800)	540	1,720
Available-for-sale	Dividends + realized G/L	200	(460)	220
Equity method	Share of investee earnings + realized G/L	700	(190)	770

Components of Investment Income

Classification		19X1	19X2	19X3
Dividend income				
All methods except equity method		$ 200	$ 140	$ 220
Equity method			Not Relevant	
Equity in earnings of investee				
Equity method only (EPS × number of shares held)		$ 700	$ 560	$ 770
Recognized gains and losses				
Held-to-maturity	Realized only	$ 0	$(600)	$ 0
Trading	Realized and unrealized	(1,000)	400*	1,500
Available-for-sale	Realized only	0	(600)	0
Equity method	Realized only	0	(750)†	0

*$(600) Realized + $1,000 Unrealized.

†Loss on shares sold = 30 × ($80 + $5 − $60) as sales proceeds must be compared with carrying value at date of sale.

ANALYSIS OF MARKETABLE SECURITIES

The following issues are important to the analysis of marketable securities:

1. The need to segregate the operating results of the firm from its investment results[7]
2. The differential effects of portfolio classification
3. The assessment of investment results

Separation of Operating from Investment Results

Although the success of corporate investments enhances the value of the enterprise, investment results and operating results must be clearly segregated and analyzed separately. Reported income from investments can distort operating trends. It is important to know how the firm's "core" business performs apart from investment results.

Helmerich & Payne, an oil and gas company, has extensive holdings (approximately 20% of total assets) of marketable securities. Helmerich & Payne's condensed

[7]See the footnote 39 reference to Foster (1975).

EXHIBIT 13-2. HELMERICH & PAYNE
Marketable Securities: Disaggregation of Operating and Investment Results,
1990 to 1992 ($ in millions)

Condensed Income Statements

	1990	1991	1992
Sales and operating revenues	$ 199.2	$ 190.4	$ 230.5
Investment income	38.8	23.1	8.6
Total revenues	$ 238.0	$ 213.5	$ 239.1
Operating costs	(168.2)	(178.5)	(215.0)
Pretax income	$ 69.8	$ 35.0	$ 24.1
Year-to-year change		−34.8	−10.9
Percentage change		−50%	−31%

Disaggregation of Operating and Investment Results

	1990	1991	1992
Operating income	$31.0	$11.9	$15.5
Year-to-year change		−19.1	+3.6
Percentage change		−62%	+30%
Investment income	$38.8	$23.1	$ 8.6
Year-to-year change		−15.7	−14.5
Percentage change		−40%	−63%

Source: Helmerich & Payne 1991–1992 Annual Reports

income statements for the years 1990 to 1992 are shown in Exhibit 13-2. The company's aggregate pretax income declined substantially in 1991 and 1992. However, when we separate operating results from investment income, we find that 1992 operating income *increased*. The overall decline was due to investment performance.

Segregation of operating from investment performance facilitates the analysis of:

1. The firm's *operating performance* relative to other firms in its industry (oil and gas)
2. Its *investment performance* compared to investment benchmarks

However, reported data should *not* be used to analyze investment performance. Reported results are a function of accounting classifications and a hybrid of cost/market measurement bases that may distort the actual portfolio performance as discussed below.

Effects of Classification of Marketable Securities Under SFAS 115

The classification choice under SFAS 115 can affect *both*:

1. The firm's *reported* financial performance
2. The firm's financing and investment decisions

Effect on Reported Performance

Unrealized market value changes do not affect reported income for securities in the available-for-sale and held-to-maturity portfolios. On the other hand, such changes are components of reported income for trading securities, regardless of whether they are sold. SFAS 115 requires that transfers from trading to other categories take place at current market prices. This provision is designed to ensure that firms cannot avoid reporting unrealized losses by reclassification.

Notwithstanding that provision, it is still possible for managers to manipulate reported earnings through reclassification. Consider the case of unrealized gains in the available-for-sale portfolio. Reclassifying securities from available-for-sale to trading results in reporting the (still unrealized) gain as part of income.

Balance sheet carrying values of debt securities can be insulated from market value changes by classifying these securities as held-to-maturity. To guard against abuse of this provision, the FASB restricted such classification as previously discussed.

EXHIBIT 13-3. THE CHUBB CORPORATION
Analysis of Investment Portfolio

A. Selected Balance Sheet and Income Statement Information ($ in millions)

Balance Sheet, Years Ended December 31

	1992	1993	1994
Fixed maturities			
Held-to-maturity (at amortized cost)*	$ 7,740	$ 8,058	$ 3,769
Available-for-sale (1992 to 1993 at amortized cost; 1994 at market)†	1,998	2,129	6,954
Subtotal	$ 9,738	$10,187	$10,723
Equity securities			
Available-for-sale (at market)‡	738	930	642
Total	$10,476	$11,117	$11,365

Note: Preferred shares with fixed redemption dates are included in fixed maturities; all other preferred shares included in equities.

Income Statement, Years Ended December 31

	1993	1994
Fixed maturities		
Interest income	$734	$741
Realized gains (losses)	173	(62)
Subtotal	$907	$679
Equity securities		
Dividend income	$ 24	$ 27
Realized gains (losses)	59	125
Subtotal	$ 83	$152
Total investment income	$990	$831

*Market values: $8,212, $8,775, and $3,781.
†Market values 1992: $2,048; 1993: $2,149; 1994 cost: $7,128.
‡Cost: $592, $710, and $610.

EXHIBIT 13-3. (*continued*)

B. Accounting Method Used in 1992 and 1993, Prior to SFAS 115 Adoption

- Fixed-income securities that management intended to hold to maturity were carried at amortized cost.
- Fixed-income securities considered available-for-sale were carried at lower of cost or market.
- The entire portfolio of equities was carried at market value.
- Only realized gains and losses were included in reported income.
- Unrealized gains and losses for the equity portfolio and the available-for-sale fixed income portfolio were not included in reported income, but were charged directly (net of deferred taxes) to stockholders' equity.

C. Reported Investment Income and ROA, 1993 to 1994 ($ in millions)

	1993	1994
Fixed maturities		
Investments (opening balance)	$ 9,738	$10,187
Investment income	907	679
Return on assets	9.3%	6.7%
Equity securities		
Investments (opening balance)	$ 738	$ 930
Investment income	83	152
Return on assets	11.2%	16.3%
Total		
Investments (opening balance)	$10,476	$11,117
Investment income	990	831
Return on assets	9.5%	7.5%

D. Mark-to-Market Income and ROA, 1993 to 1994 ($ in millions)

	1993	1994
Fixed maturities		
Investments (opening balance)	$10,260	$10,924
Investment income	1,121	(219)
Return on assets	10.9%	(2.0%)
Equity securities		
Investments (opening balance)	$ 738	$ 930
Investment income	157	(36)
Return on assets	21.3%	(3.9%)
Total		
Investments (opening balance)	$10,998	$11,854
Investment income	1,278	(255)
Return on assets	11.6%	(2.2%)

Source: Based on data from Chubb 1993–1994 Annual Reports

Exhibit 13-3 illustrates the effect of reclassification using data from the Chubb Corporation's 1993 and 1994 annual reports. Chubb, a major insurance company, had followed the provisions of SFAS 60 (1982), as outlined in panel B of the exhibit, but adopted SFAS 115 in 1994.

At December 31, 1993, over $8 billion (79%) of debt securities were classified held-to-maturity. At December 31, 1994, when Chubb adopted SFAS 115, that amount dropped to approximately $3.8 billion (35%) with the available-for-sale portfolio increasing accordingly. As noted by Chubb:

> SFAS 115 establishes more stringent criteria for classifying fixed maturities as held-to-maturity. Therefore, the adoption of SFAS No. 115 resulted in an increase in the portion of the Corporation's fixed maturities classified as available-for-sale and a similar decrease in those classified as held-to-maturity.[8]

As cost approximated market value for Chubb's debt securities at December 31, 1994, the reclassification did not affect Chubb's balance sheet significantly. However, the reclassification did have a significant impact on the December 31, 1995 balance sheet.[9] During 1995, interest rates fell sharply, increasing the market value of Chubb's fixed-income securities. With 65% (at cost) of Chubb's fixed-income securities in its available-for-sale portfolio, the higher market values increased Chubb's reported stockholders' equity. On the other hand, any future declines in market value (when interest rates rise) will also affect reported equity.

Effect on Investment and Financing Decisions

Classification of debt securities as held-to-maturity may also affect a firm's performance in a more subtle way. SFAS 115 states that held-to-maturity securities cannot be sold prior to maturity except under unusual circumstances (see footnote 5). Such sales could force the firm to carry the remaining securities at market rather than cost. Thus, a firm that wants to sell debt securities in anticipation of a rise in interest rates or to increase liquidity must weigh the accounting effects (i.e., increased balance sheet volatility).

Thus, firms must consider the possible future consequences of initial classification of debt securities carefully. With the exception of 1995, there is no "second chance" to reclassify without consequences.

In 1995, the year after SFAS 115 came into effect, interest rates fell sharply, increasing prices of fixed-income securities. Firms with large held-to-maturity portfolios could not realize these gains without taking the (accounting) risk of having the rest of their securities classified as available-for-sale.[10] As part of a special report issued in November 1995,[11] the FASB offered firms an unprecedented second chance. Firms were allowed a six-week (from mid-November to December 31, 1995) "window" to reclassify (and sell those reclassified) securities without "tainting" the rest of the held-to-maturity portfolio. Many firms took advantage of this opportunity, realizing that they had classified too little of their debt portfolio as "available-for-sale," limiting their investment flexibility.[12]

---

[8]*1994 Annual Report,* financial statement Note 2.

[9]See Problem 2, based on Chubb's December 31, 1995 investment portfolio.

[10]Chubb's initial classification decision when adopting SFAS 115 seems to protect it from this constraint.

[11]A Guide to Implementation of Statement 115 on Accounting for Certain Investments in Debt and Equity Securities.

[12]For example, Allied Life Financial, a small insurance company, reclassified $215 million (approximately half) of its held-to-maturity portfolio to available-for-sale on November 30, 1995. This reclassification increased stockholders' equity by $4.4 million at December 31, 1995 (approximately 4.6%).

Analysis of Investment Performance

Panel C of Exhibit 13-3 summarizes Chubb's reported investment income and ROA in total and portfolio-by-portfolio. The reported data suggest that Chubb's overall 1994 investment performance declined from the 1993 level. These results were due to lower returns on the fixed maturity portfolios, partly offset by higher returns on the equity portfolio.

The reported results are, however, misleading, as Chubb changed accounting methods, adopting SFAS 115 in 1994. In addition, portfolio classifications under any accounting standard are meaningless from an analytic standpoint. There is no benefit from recording market values and holding gains and losses only for some investments and not for others. Chubb's balance sheet contains carrying values whose mix of cost and market values changed. In 1992 and 1993, most debt securities were carried at cost; in 1994, most were carried at market. This change limits the comparability of ROA measures between years and portfolios, as the carrying value of the assets is the ROA denominator.

Due to classification effects, reported returns differ from actual portfolio returns. For the available-for-sale portfolio, only realized gains and losses are included in income. As long as the portfolio contains some unrealized gains, management has the ability to determine the amount and timing of (capital) gains recognized in income regardless of the performance of the total portfolio. Management can smooth reported income by realizing some gains each year regardless of market performance. This selective recognition process can be abused by "cherry picking" gains for recognition while allowing losses to remain in the portfolio, unrecognized in income.[13] In Chubb's case, as we show, the improved equity performance reported for 1994 resulted from selective recognition rather than actual investment performance.

To analyze actual investment returns, the analyst must go beyond the reported results. *All securities should be shown at current market value and all gains and losses should be attributed to the period earned rather than the period realized.*[14] The periods in which market values change and those in which they are recognized (by sale) may be completely different. *The analyst should track investment performance on a mark-to-market basis, measuring the actual investment performance for each period.*

Mark-to-Market Accounting

The total return on a firm's portfolio equals the sum of:

- Dividends and interest income
- Realized gains and losses
- Unrealized (holding) gains and losses

Dividends and interest income, as well as realized gains and losses, are always reported. *Thus, calculation of the mark-to-market return requires the unrealized (holding) gains and losses.* When both cost and market values are reported, the calculation of actual portfolio returns is straightforward.

---

[13]The abuse of selective recognition by troubled financial institutions contributed to pressure from some regulators and politicians to use market value accounting for all investments.

[14]Provision should be made, however, for any income tax payable upon sale of the securities.

Calculation of Mark-to-Market Return. If we define the market valuation adjustment (MVA) as the difference between market value and cost at each balance sheet date, then for each time period,

Unrealized Holding Gains and Losses = Change in MVA

This holds true whether or not new securities are added to the portfolio during the year.
Thus, the actual portfolio performance (mark-to-market return) equals the sum of:

- Dividends and interest income
- Realized gains and losses
- Change in the market valuation adjustment

Applying this procedure to Chubb, we use the data in panel A of Exhibit 13-3 to compute the 1994 change in the MVA:

1994 Change in MVA ($ in millions)

| | Fixed Maturity Portfolios | | | |
	Held-to-Maturity	Available-for-Sale	Total	Equity Securities
1994				
Market value	$3,781	$6,954	$10,735	$ 642
Cost	3,768	7,128	10,896	610
MVA	$ 13	$ (174)	$ (161)	$ 32
1993				
Market value	$8,775	$2,149	$10,924	$ 930
Cost	8,058	2,129	10,188	710
MVA	$ 717	$ 20	$ 737	$ 220
Change in MVA				
Fixed maturities			(161) − 737 =	$ (898)
Equity portfolio			32 − 220 =	(188)
Total				$(1,086)

The change in the MVA must now be combined with the reported (realized) returns to calculate the mark-to-market return for 1994:

Calculation of 1994 Mark-to-Market Return

	Fixed Maturities	Equities	Total
Dividend and interest income	$ 741	$ 27	$ 768
Realized gains and losses	(62)	125	63
Reported income	**$ 679**	**$ 152**	**$ 831**
Change in MVA	(898)	(188)	(1,086)
Mark-to-market return	**$(219)**	**$ (36)**	**$ (255)**

The 1994 mark-to-market returns are negative for both the fixed and equity securities portfolios. However, Chubb reported capital gains from its equity portfolio. Although Chubb's equity portfolio MVA decreased by $188 million during 1994, the company realized net gains of $125 million. Panel D of Exhibit 13-3 compares the performance data with those for 1993. Note that the computation of ROA uses market values in the denominator as well.

As only realized gains and losses are reported, 1994 results are overstated (but 1993 results are understated). The failure to recognize gains until realized shifts gains "earned" in 1993 to 1994, the year management decided to sell the gain securities. In 1995 (see Problem 2), reported results again understate investment performance. Chubb appears to be smoothing reported earnings, a common practice among firms with large securities portfolios.

Summary of Analytical Procedures

The following steps should be followed to:

- Segregate operating and investment results.
- Eliminate the effects of selective recognition and inconsistent accounting rules on the measurement of investment results.

1. Identify the existence of marketable securities portfolios from financial statement data and footnote disclosures. Obtain information regarding the risk and income characteristics of each portfolio.

2. Identify the valuation method used in the financial statements. When investments are not valued at market, obtain actual or estimated market values. When adjusting stockholders' equity and equity-based ratios such as debt-to-equity and turnover ratios, substitute market value for cost or other carrying value whenever possible. Provision for capital gains tax on unrealized gains and losses should be made where applicable.

3. Remove realized gains and losses and any valuation adjustments from reported earnings. The result should be an earnings trend that represents the actual operating results, unaffected by selective recognition decisions by management.

4. If dividend and interest income are significant, you may remove them (after-tax) from reported earnings and operating cash flows as well. These adjustments will leave only the results of operating activities and enable the computation of return on equity excluding the impact of investments. This separation generally makes sense for firms whose investment activities are incidental to their operations. However, the investment activities of banks, insurance companies, and other financial intermediaries must be examined on an enterprise basis; investment income must be analyzed relative to the cost of funds.

5. Examine the actual mark-to-market returns on the investment portfolio over an appropriate time period—at least one market cycle. Compare the results with the risk level of the portfolio and with benchmark returns for portfolios of the same type.

6. When using earnings to value a company, normalize investment returns by including in earnings the average return over the cycle rather than returns only for that time period.

7. For companies with large investment portfolios, management should be held accountable, as would any investment manager, for returns on the portfolio.

Financial Reporting for Marketable Securities Outside the United States

IAS 25 allows firms to report current investments at market value or use the lower of cost or market calculation on a security-by-security basis. Noncurrent investments must be reported at cost; nontemporary declines are reported as a component of equity. In exposure draft E32, Comparability of Financial Statements, the IASC proposed prohibition of the portfolio basis in applying LOCOM. The IASC has deferred reconsideration of the valuation of MES pending completion of its Financial Instruments project.

Accounting rules in the Netherlands are similar to those specified in IAS 25 with one exception: Nonmarketable current investments must be carried at cost. France, Japan, Canada, and the United Kingdom use LOCOM (on an individual security basis). Germany allows revaluation after write-downs, and firms must report the write-down in the financial statements if it is required for taxes. However, financial statement treatment is discretionary if write-downs are not required for tax purposes. In the United Kingdom as in the United States, nontemporary declines are treated as realized losses, and the excess of market value over cost may be taken to a revaluation reserve.

EQUITY METHOD OF ACCOUNTING

Conditions for Use

The equity method must be used when the investor can exercise significant influence on the management, operations, and investing and financing decisions of the investee. The investor must report its proportionate share of the investee's net assets and recognize a proportionate share of the income of the investee, regardless of whether it is received as a dividend or is reinvested.

APB 18 (1971), which governs the use of the equity method, requires the investor to have significant influence over the operations of the investee; ownership of 20% is presumed to meet that test. FASB Interpretation 35 (1981) of APB 18 prohibits the use of the equity method, despite 20% (or greater) ownership, if *any* of the following conditions is present:

- Litigation between the investor and investee prevents the investor from exercising influence.
- A "standstill agreement" or similar restriction precludes the investor from voting its shares or influencing management of the investee.
- The investee has a majority holder that controls its operations.
- There are other indicators of a lack of ability to influence the investee such as lack of seats on the board of directors or lack of ability to obtain financial and operating data.

In practice, the equity method has been applied to holdings as low as 10% when "significant influence" has been demonstrated. On the other hand, holdings of well over 20% may be insufficient. The user of financial statements cannot take for granted that the equity method will be used if and only if the voting interest is in the range of 20 to 50%.

Harnischfeger Industries, for example, owned 18.83% of Measurex on October 31, 1990. An agreement limited Harnischfeger to a 20% interest, but gave the company one seat on the board of directors. The equity method was used to account for the investment in Measurex, allowing Harnischfeger to report its proportionate share of Measurex's earnings rather than only dividends received.

Illustration of the Equity Method

The following events are used to illustrate the application of the equity method:

1. On December 31, 19X0, Company P invests $300 in Company S and receives 30% of the shares of Company S in return.
2. During the year ended December 31, 19X1, Company S earns $100 and pays common stock dividends of $20.
3. Company S earns $150 and pays cash dividends of $60 in 19X2.

The Equity Method: At Acquisition and the First Year of Investment. On its balance sheet at December 31, 19X0, Company P reports the purchased asset at its acquisition cost:

Investment in Company S	**$300**

To account for its investment in Company S for the year ended December 31, 19X1, Company P must consider *both* the income earned and the dividends paid by Company S. The equity of Company S (or, equivalently, its net assets) increases by $100 as a result of the income earned during the year. Company P's share of that income (alternatively, its share in the increased equity of Company S) is $30 (30% of $100).

Using the equity method of accounting, Company P will report this $30 in its income statement and increase its "Investment in Company S" account by $30, thereby reflecting its 30% share of the earnings (and increase in the net assets) of Company S:[15]

Investment in Company S	**$30**	
Equity in net income of Company S		**$30**

Company P receives $6 in cash dividends (30% of $20). In contrast to the cost and market methods, these dividends are not included directly as part of its income. Under the equity method, investment income is a function of the earnings of the investee and is independent of dividends received. Company P records dividends received as a reduction in the "Investment in Company S" account.

Cash	**$6**	
Investment in Company S		**$6**

The rationale for this reporting method is that Company S's equity and net assets decline due to the declaration of dividends. The dividend of $20 reduces Company S's equity by $20; Company P's share of that decrease in equity is $6.

---

[15]When the subsidiary has losses, the equity method requires a write-down of the carrying value of the investment. However, the carrying value cannot be written down below zero, unless the investor has economic exposure in addition to its investment (such as a loan guarantee). Subsequent profits cannot be recognized until any unrecognized losses have been made up.

The net effect is that Company P's share of the undistributed (reinvested) earnings of Company S ($100 − $20 = $80) is added to the Investment in Company S account on Company P's balance sheet. That is, the account is increased by $24 ($30 − $6, or 30% of $80). Company P will report the following asset on December 31, 19X1:

Investment in Company S   **$324**

The investment account, therefore, contains the original cost of the investment plus the equity in the undistributed earnings of the investee. When the investment is sold, any realized gain or loss (for financial reporting only, the tax basis is unaffected by the accounting method applied) is based on a comparison of the proceeds with the adjusted cost basis of $324, not the original cost of $300.

The Second Year of Investment. Company P receives cash of $18 (30% of $60) but recognizes earnings of $45 (30% of $150). The excess of income recognized over dividends received ($45 − $18 = $27) increases the investment account to $351, at December 31, 19X2. The account balance reflects the following events:

Original investment in Company S	$300
Equity in reinvested 19X1 income	24
Equity in reinvested 19X2 income	27
Investment in Company S	**$351**

Comparison of the Equity Method and SFAS 115

The differences between SFAS 115[16] and the equity method for the previous example follow:

Year	Income Reported		Cash Received	
	SFAS 115	Equity	SFAS 115	Equity
19X1	$ 6	$30	$ 6	$ 6
19X2	18	45	18	18

Under SFAS 115, Company P's income includes only dividends received. Use of the equity method results in higher earnings for Company P as it reports its proportionate share of the reinvested earnings of Company S. *Whenever the investee has earnings and a dividend payout ratio of less than 100%, use of the equity method will increase the earnings of the investor relative to those reported under SFAS 115.*

Cash flows, however, are unchanged. Although under SFAS 115, income and cash flow are identical (if we assume no write-down of the investment), they differ under the equity method. In the indirect method cash flow statement, there is an adjustment to (subtraction from) net income for the difference between the equity income recognized and the dividends received.

---

[16]As investments in affiliates are not made for "trading" purposes, in the absence of the equity method this security would be classified available-for-sale and (unrealized) market value changes would be ignored in the income statement. Thus, income and cash flow effects under SFAS 115 would be equivalent to the cost method.

When the equity method recognizes income in excess of dividends received, interest coverage and return on investment ratios for Company P improve. Its total assets and stockholders' equity rise due to recognition of its share of the reinvested earnings of Company S. This higher base may, in time, reduce the return-on-investment and return-on-equity ratios if the profitability of Company S declines. The increase in stockholders' equity also increases Company P's book value per share. *Moreover, as only assets and equity are affected, without any recognition of the investee's debt, the investor's debt-to-equity and debt-to-total capital ratios improve.*

The preceding discussion assumes that the investee is profitable. When it reports losses, the equity method will report less favorable results.

Box 13-1 suggests that, as the criterion of "significant influence" is subject to some discretion, firms select the side of the 20% line that obtains the desired accounting treatment. If the investee is not profitable, a firm may avoid the adverse effect (recognizing its share of investee losses) of the equity method by purchasing less than 20%; if the investee is profitable, the firm prefers the equity method, and it purchases just over 20%. For comparative purposes, it may be appropriate to adjust reported earnings to the equity method. This adjustment should be made when companies, although they have "significant influence" over their affiliates, account for them as marketable securities using SFAS 115.

Equity Accounting and Analysis

The differences between accounting for an investment under the equity method and as a marketable security under SFAS 115, illustrated in Exhibit 13-1, are striking. Given a profitable investee and a low dividend payout ratio, the equity in reinvested earnings is a significant factor in the carrying amount under the equity method. In years when the market value of the investee changes significantly, reported investor earnings are quite different depending on the choice of accounting method.

Even when an investee's shares are publicly traded, changes in market price are not recognized by the equity method unless there is a permanent impairment. *For financial analysis, however, the value placed by the securities markets on the investee should be considered a better indicator of value than the carrying amount in the financial statements of the investor.*

Only under the equity method do the earnings of the investee directly affect the reported performance of the parent. The underlying premise is that the parent has or will have access to the earnings, *directly* or *indirectly*. This is a basic principle of accrual accounting, the assumption that the accrual measure is a better indicator of the cash-generating ability of the firm.

The equity method was mandated by APB 18 (1971) as an alternative to the cost method. Ricks and Hughes (1985) offer evidence consistent with the assumption that the equity method provides data used for valuation purposes by the market. They found positive market reaction when financial statements using the equity method were first issued. The positive reaction was positively correlated to both the size of the equity earnings as well as the degree to which analysts underestimated earnings in their forecasts. Ricks and Hughes concluded the market found the information useful, as "the equity method provided information concerning affiliate earnings not previously available from other sources."[17]

[17]William E. Ricks and John S. Hughes, "Market Reactions to a Non-Discretionary Accounting Change: The Case of Long-Term Investments," *The Accounting Review,* Jan. 1985, p. 50.

BOX 13-1
Equity Accounting and Its Impact on Ownership Position

Comiskey and Mulford (1986) tested whether "the inclusion in APB 18 of the 20 percent ownership criterion for application of the equity method (hereafter the 20 percent standard) influences the ownership position taken by investing firms."* Figure 13-1, from their study, shows the distribution of ownership positions taken by investing firms in 1982. The solid line indicates the actual percentage positions taken, and the dashed line depicts the predicted "fitted" distribution.†

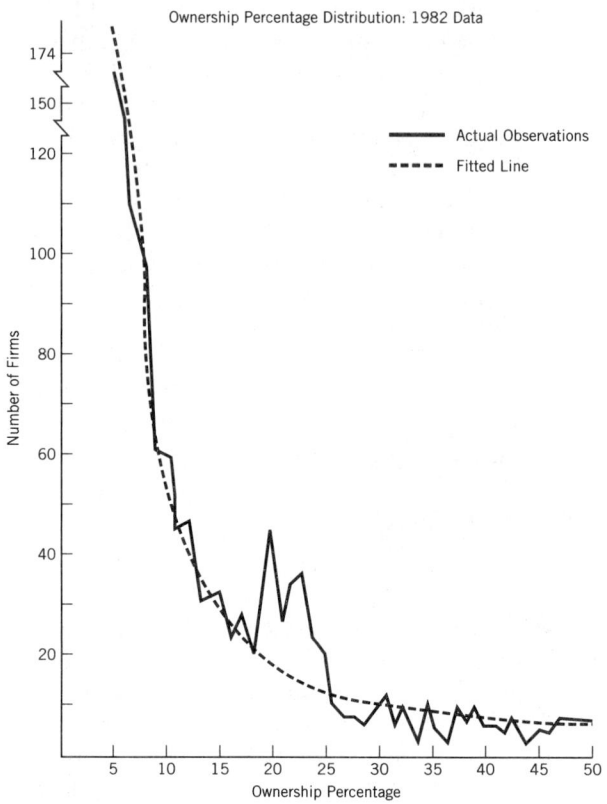

FIGURE 13-1 Ownership Percentage Distribution, 1982 Data.

Source: Eugene Comiskey and Charles W. Mulford, "Investment Decisions and the Equity Accounting Standard," *The Accounting Review,* July 1986, pp. 519–525 (Fig. 1, p. 521).

As indicated in Figure 13-1, the actual concentration of firms in the 16 to 24% range is significantly greater than expected. Comiskey and Mulford argue that the 20% standard mandated by APB 18 may be responsible for the abnormal concentration. Different firms may have different motivations with respect to whether they want to report on the cost or equity basis and stake out positions accordingly.

In further support of this contention, they found that affiliates in the 19 to 19.99% ownership range had reported (on average) a net loss 30.4% of the time in the previous four years. Firms in the 20 to 20.99% range reported losses only 16.1% of the time. As the equity method is increasingly preferable as the subsidiary's income (or more precisely, the undistributed income) increases, these results make sense. Owners of affiliates that are less likely to report losses are more likely to choose an ownership interest permitting use of the equity method. Alternatively, firms facing losses and holding over 20% may decide to sell some of their holdings to bring them below the 20% level.‡

---

*Eugene Comiskey and Charles W. Mulford, "Investment Decisions and the Equity Accounting Standard," *The Accounting Review,* July 1986, p. 519.

†The "fitted" line was determined on the basis of extrapolation of the patterns existing below 16% and above 24%.

‡As discussed later, similar possibilities exist for firms that want to avoid consolidation (i.e., they acquire only 49% of the subsidiary).

In some cases, however, the parent does not have access to permanently reinvested (i.e., undistributed) earnings (or cash flows). It is questionable whether the reinvested earnings should be considered income; analysts should adjust equity earnings by including as income of the parent only actual dividends received from the investee.

Box 13-2 discusses the impact of equity method earnings on deferred taxes; management's assumptions regarding realization of the (undistributed) earnings affect the rate used to calculate deferred taxes. This information can be used to assess whether the parent will have access to the undistributed earnings.

This line of reasoning can be extended further. If the parent does not have access to the earnings of the subsidiary, then the subsidiary should be treated as any other investment in marketable securities. The carrying value and earnings from the subsidiary should be evaluated on a mark-to-market basis.

The appropriateness of mark-to-market analyses of equity investments depends, therefore, on the relationship between the two firms. When investee operations are related to the parent's core business (supplier, distributor, or customer), the investee is arguably an extension of the parent. The equity method is applicable but it may not be adequate because the assets, liabilities, and components of income of the investee are included in summary form only. We return to this issue after first examining consolidation accounting.

BOX 13-2
The Equity Method and Deferred Taxes

The equity method of accounting is used for financial reporting only. Because it cannot be used on corporate tax returns, it creates temporary differences between financial income and taxable income.* In the United States, dividends received by corporations from qualifying domestic corporations are taxed at a low effective tax rate due to the dividends received exclusion available to eligible corporate investors.† Thus, the income tax payable on the dividend component of equity method income can be computed quite precisely. However, estimating the deferred tax expense related to undistributed income (income recognized under the equity method less that portion received as dividends) is difficult because any tax paid depends on future events.

Two different assumptions can be made about reinvested income:

1. It will be received in the form of future dividends in excess of future earnings; the deferred component of tax expense is computed using the effective tax rate on dividends (currently 7% if ownership exceeds 20%).

2. It will be realized via sale of the investment, requiring the use of the corporate capital gains rate (currently 35%) to compute deferred taxes.

If the proportion of reinvested (undistributed) income is significant, then the choice of tax rate applied to reinvested income can materially affect reported income. Unfortunately, explicit disclosure of the choice is almost never made. In some cases, analysis of the income tax footnote (see Chapter 9) will provide the information needed to evaluate the impact of the choice made on reported income.‡

For example, Corning's income tax footnote for 1990 disclosed deferred taxes of $8.7 million on $107.5 million of equity in earnings of associated companies. This disclosure suggests that Corning assumed that reinvested earnings would be received as future dividends ($8.7 million/$107.5 million = 8.1%).

A second issue arises upon sale of the investment. As the equity method is not applied for income tax purposes, the tax basis (cost) of the investment remains unchanged. In the financial statements, however, cost is augmented by reinvested income recognized under the equity method (net of dividends received and deferred tax expense). When the investment is sold, the capital gain for income tax purposes will, in all likelihood, be far greater than the capital gain for financial accounting purposes. In some cases, there is an accounting loss despite the income tax gain.

If the corporate investor has accrued deferred taxes based on the dividend assumption and later sells the investment, the deferred tax provision is inadequate. Thus, even if there is a pretax capital gain (sales price exceeds the sum of original cost and the recorded reinvested earnings), there may be an after-tax loss.§

Thus, if it appears that a major investment accounted for under the equity method may be sold, the tax issue must be considered. The analyst should try to estimate the tax basis (cost for income tax purposes) of the investment; footnotes sometimes disclose the original cost. Look for information regarding the company's tax rate and the existence of any capital loss carryforwards that might shelter the gain from taxation. Most important, be aware that the accounting gain and taxable gain might be quite different.

---

*See Chapter 9 for a detailed discussion of temporary differences and deferred taxes.

†The exclusion is 70% if the investee is less than 20% owned, 80% if ownership exceeds 20%. If ownership exceeds 80%, the investee must be consolidated and dividends to the parent are tax-free. These rules have changed from time to time in recent years.

Thus, at the current tax rate of 35%, the effective tax rate is 10.5% (35% × 30%) on less than 20% owned investees and 7% (35% × 20%) when ownership exceeds 20%.

‡SFAS 109 continued the APB 23 indefinite reversal criteria and does not require deferred tax liabilities for the undistributed earnings of a domestic subsidiary or corporate joint venture that arose in fiscal years beginning prior to December 15, 1992. Tax effects must be recognized when these temporary differences are expected to reverse in the foreseeable future.

However, SFAS 109 requires that deferred taxes be provided on such undistributed earnings effective in 1993.

§If the investee is a foreign corporation, the issues and analysis are slightly different. The preferential tax treatment for dividends does not apply to foreign investees. On the other hand, credits for foreign income taxes paid may be available to offset the U.S. tax liability when reinvested income is received as dividends. More significantly, no deferred tax provision is required for reinvested foreign earnings because of the "permanent reinvestment" option of SFAS 109. Thus, for foreign investees, no deferred tax provision may be made.

CONSOLIDATION

When we see the financial statements of Exxon, Honda, Royal Dutch, or any other huge enterprise, we are viewing a consolidated set of statements that includes a large number of individual corporate entities. Each account in a set of consolidated financial statements consists of the sum (less any intercompany eliminations) of the corresponding amounts for each included entity.[18] The inventories shown, for example, are the inventories of each corporate entity, added together, and adjusted for any intercompany transactions.

The "parent-only" statement reports its investment in each subsidiary on the equity basis, in which the assets and liabilities of the subsidiary are netted in a single investment account. When the firms are consolidated, it is implicitly assumed that the

---

[18]See Chapter 15 for an analysis of requirements when some of those entities keep their records in a currency other than that of the parent.

assets and liabilities of the subsidiary are controlled by the parent company. As we shall see, there are times when that assumption must be questioned.

Conditions for Use

Under SFAS 94 (1986), all entities in which the parent controls (directly or indirectly) more than 50% of the voting shares of the subsidiary must be consolidated. There are two exceptions to this rule:

- Temporary control.
- Subsidiaries that are not considered controlled, despite majority ownership, due to governmental action, a nonconvertible currency, or civil disorder. The legal status of the subsidiary, such as bankruptcy or reorganization, may also preclude consolidation.

Exceptions are made because under these circumstances, the parent company does not have unrestricted use of the subsidiary's assets or cannot be considered to exercise control. An example of the second type of exception is presented in Exhibit 13-4.

Because of concern that the mechanistic 50% rule enabled firms to avoid consolidation despite effective control, the FASB reconsidered its criteria for consolidation. Box 13-3 summarizes the FASB exposure draft, Consolidated Financial Statements: Policy and Procedures (1995), which defines control by whether the parent has *effective control of the assets* of the subsidiary. Box 13-3 also explains the consequences of the proposed new standard.

Illustration of Consolidation

In Exhibit 13-5, Company P, the parent, purchases an 80% interest in Company S, the subsidiary. To simplify matters, we assume that the amount paid ($2,000) equals

---

EXHIBIT 13-4

Exception to Consolidation Rule: The Acquisition of Avdel plc by Textron

---

An exception to the requirement to consolidate subsidiaries occurred with the acquisition by Textron of Avdel plc, a British manufacturer, in 1989. The acquisition was challenged by the Federal Trade Commission, and Textron was enjoined by a court order from exercising control over Avdel. As a result, Textron's *1990 Annual Report* included the following footnote:

> While Textron's results of operations for 1990 and 1989 do not include the results of Avdel, (a) they do include interest expense of $21 million and $22 million, respectively, on the borrowings related to the purchase of Avdel and (b) they include in 1990 $7 million of cash dividends received from Avdel. Avdel's sales and earnings before taxes (unaudited) were $163 million and $22 million, respectively. Avdel's sales were $149 million in 1989 and its earnings before income taxes were $23 million. Such results do not reflect any purchase adjustments which would be required as a result of Textron's acquisition of Avdel, principally amortization of goodwill.

As Textron reported earnings before income taxes of approximately $410 million and $459 million for 1989 and 1990, respectively, the inclusion of Avdel would have increased such earnings by more than 5% in 1989 and by more than 3% in 1990 ($22 million less the $7 million received as a dividend), ignoring any goodwill amortization.

Source: Textron, *1990 Annual Report.*

BOX 13-3
FASB Exposure Draft: Consolidated Financial Statements: Policy and Procedures

The exposure draft (ED) would change the criterion for consolidation from majority ownership to control:

> Control of an entity is an exclusionary power over its assets—power to use or direct the use of the individual assets of another entity in essentially the same ways as the controlling entity can use its own assets. Control enables a parent to use or direct the use of the assets of a subsidiary by:
>
> a. Establishing the controlled entity's policies as well as its capital and operating budgets.
> b. Selecting, determining the compensation of, and terminating personnel responsible for implementing its policies and decisions.*

Conditions for Assessing the Existence of Control

The ED states that control is a factual determination and goes beyond legal control. It discusses factors that lead to the presumption of control:

1. Ownership of the dominant, even when not a majority, voting interest (such as 40%) when no other stockholder (or group) has a significant interest.
2. The ability to dominate the selection of the board of directors.
3. The ability to achieve majority ownership, through rights or convertible securities.
4. For an entity that it has established but has no owners (e.g., a trust), provisions in its charter, bylaws, or trust instrument effectively convey control and cannot be changed without approval of the creator.
5. The unilateral ability to dissolve an entity and assume control of its assets.
6. An entity is the sole general partner in a limited partnership.

The ED also points out that control need not be absolute. There may be restrictions due to regulatory authorities or debt covenants, just as in the case of wholly owned subsidiaries.

Effects on Financial Reporting

The proposed standard would change current financial reporting in a number of ways, including:

- Minority interest is called "noncontrolling interest," which would be included in stockholders' equity on the balance sheet and shown as an allocation of net income on the face of the income statement.
- When less then 100% is purchased, goodwill would be inferred for and allocated to the noncontrolling interest.
- Once an affiliate is consolidated, changes in ownership that do not result in a loss of control would be equity transactions, with no effect on reported income.
- Transactions or events resulting in a loss of control or the sale of subsidiaries would require a reversal of the paid-in capital recorded for transactions in shares of subsidiaries. These amounts are components of the gain or loss on sale or disposal.
- Accounting policies of consolidated affiliates must be conformed to those of the parent, except when differences within a consolidated group are permitted (e.g., inventory).

The new standard was expected to be issued in 1997.

---

*Para. 10 (continuation of part a omitted).

EXHIBIT 13-5
Comparison of Equity Method and Consolidation

Balance Sheet at Acquisition Date

	Preacquisition		After Acquisition of 80% of Company S for $2,000 Company P	
	Company P	Company S	Equity Method	Consolidated
Current assets	$12,000	$4,000	$10,000	$14,000
Investment in Company S	—	—	2,000	—
Other assets	8,000	2,000	8,000	10,000
	$20,000	$6,000	$20,000	$24,000
Current liabilities	$10,000	$3,500	$10,000	$13,500
Minority interest	—	—	—	500
Common stock	7,000	1,500	7,000	7,000
Retained earnings	3,000	1,000	3,000	3,000
	$20,000	$6,000	$20,000	$24,000

Results of First Year After Acquisition

Additional information:
    Dividends paid by S equal $250.
    There are no changes in noncash working capital.
    There are no noncash expenses.
    Company P loaned Company S $350.

		Company P	
	Company S	Equity Method	Consolidated
Revenue	$5,000	$15,000	$20,000
Expense	4,000	10,000	14,000
Operating income	$1,000	$ 5,000	$ 6,000
Equity in income of Company S	—	800	—
Minority interest	—	—	(200)
Net income	$1,000	$ 5,800	$ 5,800
Noncash adjustment		(600)*	200†
Cash from operations	$1,000	$ 5,200	$ 6,000
Cash from affiliates	350	(350)	—
Dividends paid/received	(250)		(50)‡
Change in cash	$1,100	$ 4,850	$ 5,950

    *Reinvested earnings of Company S ($800 earned − $200 dividends received).
    †Minority interest.
    ‡Paid to minority investors.

EXHIBIT 13-5 (continued)

Balance Sheet, End of First Year

		Company P	
	Company S	Equity Method	Consolidated
Current assets	$5,100	$14,850	$19,950
Investment in Company S	—	2,600	—
Receivable from Company S	—	350	
Other assets	2,000	8,000	10,000
	$7,100	$25,800	$29,950
Current liabilities	$3,500	$10,000	$13,500
Payable to Company P	350	—	
Minority interest	—	—	650
Common stock	1,500	7,000	7,000
Retained earnings	1,750	8,800	8,800
	$7,100	$25,800	$29,950

the proportionate share of the book value of the subsidiary (80% of $2,500) purchased. When this is not the case, the subsidiary accounts are restated at their fair market values, and goodwill may be recorded.[19] The exhibit shows both the equity method and full consolidation, allowing for a comparison of the two methods.

COMPARISON OF CONSOLIDATION WITH THE EQUITY METHOD

The first part of Exhibit 13-5 shows the balance sheet under both the equity method and consolidation immediately following the acquisition. The second part shows the income statement, cash flows, and balance sheets after one year.

The equity method incorporates the parent's share of the net income and net assets of the investee in parent company results, reporting them as equity in the earnings of the subsidiary and investment in the subsidiary, respectively. Under consolidation, all the assets, liabilities, revenues, expenses, and cash flows of the subsidiary are included in the corresponding accounts of the parent. When ownership is less than 100%, a "minority interest" (discussed shortly) results.

Note that only the assets and liabilities are changed by consolidation; *the common equity of the consolidated firm remains equal to the equity of the parent.* Similarly, while consolidation results in inclusion of the revenues and expenses of Company S in the income statement of Company P, *net income is unchanged.*

Under the equity method, only the investment account and the net income are affected by investee results. In consolidated statements, virtually every account and the accompanying footnotes include the subsidiary's operating, investing, and financing activities.

[19] A discussion of goodwill is contained in Chapter 14.

Reported cash flows also differ. Under the equity method, parent company cash flow includes only capital flows between parent and investee (dividends, additional investments, and redemptions). When the investee is consolidated, parent company cash flow includes all cash flows of the investee *except* those between parent and investee. Consolidated operating cash flow is $800 higher, equal to the cash flow of Company S less the dividends received by Company P. Thus, consolidation includes all the subsidiary's cash flows, not just payments to the parent. In some cases, such inclusion may result in misleading measures of the resources available to the parent.

The addition of a subsidiary to (or subtraction from) the consolidated group also changes financial statement ratios. Less obviously, financial statement footnote data now include subsidiary data. Although the parent owns only 80% of the subsidiary, 100% of the subsidiary's accounts are included, reflecting the control perspective in consolidated financial reporting.[20]

As the parent owns less than 100% of the subsidiary, however, it does not derive all the benefit from the subsidiary's assets and earnings (and it is not at risk for all subsidiary liabilities). Consolidated financial statements reflect this fact through accounts known as *minority interest.*[21] On the consolidated balance sheet, the share of the subsidiary's equity that does not accrue to the parent is shown as a liability (strictly speaking, it is a credit balance rather than a liability), normally just above stockholders' equity. In Exhibit 13-5, minority interest is $500 (20% of $2,500) at acquisition. After one year, it is $650 (20% of $3,250). On the income statement, minority interest of $200 (20% of $1,000) is shown as a deduction.[22] We consider minority interest further later in this chapter.

Depending on the financial characteristics of the subsidiary, consolidation may result in financial statements that look either better or worse than those resulting from use of the equity method. Parent ownership levels just below 50% may signal a desire to avoid consolidation;[23] ownership of 50% or more may indicate a preference for consolidation.

Consolidation Versus the Equity Method: Analytic Considerations

Consolidation combines different operating segments, obscuring their individual characteristics. The equity method, on the other hand, can result in oversummarization as significant operating and financial characteristics are reported "off-balance-sheet."

Footnotes and other data may permit restatement of financial statements to a form better suited to the desired analysis. At times, the analyst may want to restate from the equity method to pro rata or full consolidation. At other times, deconsolidation is desirable. In the balance of this chapter, we discuss and provide several examples of "do-it-yourself" restatement. The nature of the restatement often depends on the

---

[20]In some cases, however, proportionate consolidation may be more appropriate; that method is discussed later in this chapter.

[21]The FASB exposure draft uses the term *noncontrolling interest.*

[22]Generally, minority interest is shown as a separate line item in both balance sheet and income statement; some firms include it in other accounts. The FASB exposure draft would require that it be shown as part of equity in the balance sheet and as an allocation of net income in the income statement.

[23]After the issuance of SFAS 94, which required the consolidation of finance subsidiaries (discussed below), some companies reduced ownership of their finance subsidiaries to 49%, and did not consolidate them. In these cases, the analyst should apply the proportionate consolidation method, discussed shortly.

degree to which the subsidiary's operations are integrated with those of a parent. Two contrasting types of subsidiaries are representative:

1. Nonhomogeneous subsidiaries
2. Joint ventures

Nonhomogeneous Subsidiaries

One drawback of consolidation is that nonhomogeneous (dissimilar) subsidiaries may be combined, masking the characteristics of individual segments of the firm. In these cases, fully disaggregated information is preferable (or necessary) for analysis. This is especially true when the subsidiary is in an unrelated line of business whose financial and operating characteristics differ from those of the remaining lines, for example, an oil company owned by a chemical or steel company or an insurance company owned by a manufacturer or retailer. In addition, the existence of subsidiary debt or other restrictions (e.g., regulatory) on the ability of the enterprise to draw on the assets of the subsidiary may further strengthen the case for separate analysis.

Prior to the adoption of SFAS 94, which became effective in 1988, credit, insurance, leasing, and other nonhomogeneous subsidiaries were excluded from the consolidated financial statements. This exclusion was the subject of much debate. Proponents of exclusion argued that the operating activities and capital structure of financial subsidiaries differ significantly from those of their manufacturing or retailing parents. Even the form of financial statements is different: Financial companies, for example, have unclassified balance sheets with no distinction between current and noncurrent assets or liabilities. Bond covenants and the degree of control over and claims on assets and cash flows may also differ. Consolidation of such dissimilar entities, it was argued, would confuse financial statement users.

On the other hand, proponents of full consolidation argued that it is illogical to segregate some subsidiaries from the consolidated group, especially when the operations of the subsidiary are integral to the business of the parent. For example, when a finance subsidiary provides credit to the dealers and customers of the parent, its assets are, in effect, the parent's accounts receivable. Financing those receivables through a separate subsidiary may facilitate the parent's borrowing activities, but it does not justify exclusion of the subsidiary from the consolidated financial statements.

The most serious limitation of consolidation is the loss of detailed operating results for the firm's different lines of business. Aggregation often disguises disparate trends and profitability among business segments.

USX, for example, comprises three distinct operating groups: U.S. Steel, its original business; Marathon Oil, an oil producer and refiner; and Delhi, a natural gas producer and distributor. USX has issued three different classes of shares, corresponding to each of the groups, and the company presents financial statements for each in addition to consolidated statements.

Exhibit 13-6 demonstrates, using selected data, how individual operating characteristics of the individual groups are camouflaged by consolidation. Given the relatively small size of the Delhi Group, we focus our discussion on U.S. Steel and Marathon Oil.

The company's (USX) 1993 gross and operating margins were 25 and 0.3%, respectively. Over the 1991 to 1993 period, consolidated sales declined. These overall results, however, mask considerable differences among individual groups. Marathon's gross margin percentage of 31% was more that two and one-half times the Steel group's 12%. Marathon's operating income of $169 million was almost offset by the Steel group's operating loss of $149 million.

EXHIBIT 13-6. USX
Disaggregated Income Statement Data

1993 Sales ($ in millions) and Profitability

| | Consolidated | Individual Components | | |
	USX	Marathon	U.S. Steel	Delhi
Sales	$18,064	$11,962	$5,612	$535
Cost of goods	13,552	8,209	4,962	427
Gross profit	$ 4,512	$ 3,753	$ 650	$108
Gross margin %	25%	31%	12%	20%
Operating income	$ 56	$ 169	$ (149)	$ 36
Operating margin %	0.3%	1.4%	(2.7%)	6.7%

1991 to 1993 Sales Data ($ in billions)

| | Consolidated | Individual Components | | |
	USX	Marathon	U.S. Steel	Delhi
1991	$18.8	**$14.0**	**$4.9**	**$0.4**
1992	17.8	**12.8**	**4.9**	**0.5**
1993	18.1	**12.0**	**5.6**	**0.5**

Source: USX, *1993 Annual Report.*

In addition, the two groups show different sales trends. Marathon, the more profitable division, reported declining sales; Steel group sales rose. As Marathon is the larger and more profitable of the two groups, the difference in trend is important to a forecast of USX's future performance.

The unusual capital structure (different classes of publicly held common stock) of USX provides investors with detailed information about each division. Other firms operating in more than one business must provide segment data, with considerably less detail. The analysis of segment data is discussed in a later section of this chapter.

Joint Ventures

Joint ventures are frequently found in the business world and are often extensions of the firm's core businesses. They offer advantages of economies of scale and allow companies to share technological, operating, and financial risk. They may also facilitate access to developing markets in Eastern Europe and emerging economies. The legal forms of these ventures vary due to tax, legal, and operational requirements. As a result, accounting sometimes follows form rather than substance, and the financial statements may need adjustment to reflect the economic nature of the joint venture and its impact on the venturers more appropriately.

Some joint ventures are primarily contractual arrangements whereby the venturers agree to cooperate toward a common goal but no new entity is created. Each venturer maintains its own assets and liabilities and recognizes revenues and expenses separately. This type of joint venture creates neither accounting nor analysis difficulties as each venturer already reflects the results of the venture in its financial statements. However, disclosure of the impact of the venture is highly variable across firms given the absence of specific reporting requirements.

Other joint ventures result in common ownership of assets, without the formation of a separate legal entity. Each venturer recognizes its proportionate share of common assets, liabilities, revenues, and expenses. Here again, because each venturer already reflects its share of the operations in its financial statements, neither accounting nor analysis is required to go further. Pipelines (oil and gas) and electric utility plants are common applications of this form of joint venture.

Madison Gas and Electric, for example, has an interest in two electric generating plants, which accounted for 54% of capacity at December 31, 1993. The combined investment of $68.5 million (net of depreciation) was included in Madison's balance sheet although its ownership interest was 22% in one case, and 18% in the other.

Jointly Controlled Entities. In many cases, however, the joint venture is a separate entity, either a corporation or partnership. The entity is created by capital contributions (cash and/or operating assets) from two or more venturers and is governed by a contract. The contract will generally specify how operating, investing, and financing decisions are to be made by the venturers.

Because the joint venture is a separate legal entity, it prepares its own financial statements; these may be available if it has issued publicly traded debt. However, if the venture is financed with bank debt, the statements are not public documents. The venturers, in most cases, account for their interests in such jointly controlled entities using the equity method of accounting, reporting their proportionate share of both net income and net investment in the venture.

Use of the equity method means that the gross assets and liabilities, as well as revenues and expenses, are excluded from the financial statements of the venturers. Footnotes of the venturers will also exclude data relating to the joint venture in such areas as leases, retirement plans, and contingent obligations (including off-balance-sheet financing).[24]

However, the operations of the joint venture may be as much a part of the integrated operations of the parent companies as those of other, wholly owned subsidiaries. Mead, a major paper and paperboard manufacturer, included most of the earnings of its joint ventures (primarily suppliers of raw materials and intermediate products for Mead's manufacturing process) as adjustments to cost of goods sold, in recognition of the integrated nature of these operations. In such cases, the "one-line consolidation" resulting from use of the equity method understates the importance of the operations of the joint venture to the parent company and analysts must evaluate the appropriateness of the equity method.

In addition, the venture's often significant debt is excluded because the equity method includes only the net assets of the investee in the investor's balance sheet; this debt may have been an important incentive to use the equity method rather than consolidate. In such cases, proportionate consolidation depicts the higher risk level as we shall see shortly.

Thus, the equity method can distort firm performance in several ways:

1. *Profitability measures.* Although net income includes investee income, the assets that generate them are excluded. Thus, *the investor's ROA is overstated.* (Note that ROE is not affected.)

   As investee revenues and expenses are excluded, *investor return on sales measures are overstated.*

---

[24]Any debt guarantees by coventurers must be disclosed separately in the footnotes.

Similarly, *interest coverage ratios are overstated* as the numerator includes investee income, while the denominator excludes investee interest expense.

2. *Solvency measures.* Investee assets and liabilities are excluded from the balance sheet. This has important implications for credit analysis as:

- *Liabilities are hidden in investees.*
- *The nature of the investee's assets is unknown; are they tangible or intangible?*

3. *Information Loss.* The investor's footnotes exclude information relating to the investee in such areas as leases, derivatives, debt covenants, and employee benefit plans.[25]

Proportionate Consolidation

Because the equity method inadequately conveys the risk and return characteristics of investments in unconsolidated affiliates, alternative accounting methods have been developed for such ventures. These alternatives can provide better information to financial statement users whether they are used by the reporting entity or produced by the financial analyst. Two alternatives to the equity method are:

- Proportionate consolidation (sometimes called pro rata consolidation)
- The expanded equity method

These alternatives gained support from IAS 31, adopted in 1990, which states that proportionate consolidation is the preferred method of accounting for jointly controlled entities:

> Proportionate consolidation better reflects the substance and economic reality of a venturer's interest in a jointly controlled entity, that is control over the venturer's share of the future economic benefits.[26]

Under the expanded equity method, the proportionate shares of assets, liabilities, revenues, and expenses are separated from those of the consolidated group. IAS 31, which became effective in 1992, considers the expanded equity method to be a reporting variant of proportionate consolidation and allows companies to use either method. Although use of the equity method is an allowed alternative under IASC 31, the strong endorsement of proportionate consolidation is likely to lead to greater use of the method. As such, we illustrate this method in the next section.

Comparison of Proportionate Consolidation and the Equity Method

Exhibit 13-7 illustrates proportionate consolidation and compares it with the equity method. Although both net income and equity of Petroleum Corp. are the same under these two methods, virtually all other financial statement amounts are different.

Under proportionate consolidation, the parent company includes its share of *each* asset and liability account of the affiliate in the corresponding account of the parent. For example (if we assume 40% ownership of the joint venture), the parent includes 40% of the cash, inventories, receivables, and debt of the joint venture in the parent's

---

[25]See Case 11-1, regarding the Caltex joint venture between Chevron and Texaco, for an example.
[26]IAS 31, Financial Reporting of Interests in Joint Ventures (1990), para. 24.

EXHIBIT 13-7
Illustration of Proportionate Consolidation

Assume that Petroleum Corp. owns 40% of a joint venture (Supply Corp.). The investment in Supply Corp., exactly equal to 40% of Supply Corp.'s net worth, is $16 on December 31, 19X0. The condensed 19X1 income statement and year-end 19X1 balance sheet follow:

Income Statements, Year Ended December 31, 19X1

	Petroleum	Supply
Revenues	$1,000	$ 200
Equity in earnings of Supply Corp.	4	—
Cost of goods sold	(800)	(140)
Selling, general, and administrative expenses	(80)	(26)
Interest expense	(20)	(17)
Pretax earnings	$ 104	$ 17
Income tax expense	(40)	(7)
Net income	$ 64	$ 10

As Petroleum owns 40% of Supply, its equity in the 1991 earnings of Supply equals $4 (40% of $10).

Balance Sheets, December 31, 19X1

Petroleum

Assets		Liabilities	
Cash	$100	Accounts payable	$200
Inventory	200		
Accounts receivable	300		
Property	280	Long-term debt	200
Investment	20	Equity	500
Totals	$900		$900

Supply

Assets		Liabilities	
Cash	$ 20	Accounts payable	$ 80
Inventory	50		
Accounts receivable	50		
Property	180	Long-term debt	170
		Equity	50
Totals	$300		$300

If we apply the proportionate consolidation method to Petroleum's accounting for its investment in Supply, and compare the resulting financial statements with those prepared under the equity method:

Petroleum Corp. Income Statements, Year Ended December 31, 19X1

	Proportionate Consolidation	Equity Method
Revenues	$1,080	$1,000
Equity in earnings of Supply Corp.		4
Cost of goods sold	(856)	(800)
Selling, general, and administrative expenses	(90)	(80)
Interest expense	(27)	(20)
Pretax earnings	$ 107	$ 104
Income tax expense	(43)	(40)
Net income	$ 64	$ 64

Petroleum Corp. Balance Sheets, December 31, 19X1

Proportionate Consolidation

Cash	$ 108	Accounts payable	$ 232
Inventory	220		
Accounts receivable	320		
Property	352	Long-term debt	268
		Equity	500
Totals	$1,000		$1,000

Equity Method

Cash	$100	Accounts payable	$200
Inventory	200		
Accounts receivable	300		
Property	280	Long-term debt	200
Investment	20	Equity	500
Totals	$900		$900

EXHIBIT 13-7 (continued)

Under the proportionate consolidation method, 40% of the assets and liabilities of Supply are added to the corresponding assets and liabilities of Petroleum. For example, consolidated cash equals $100 + (0.40 × $20).

The investment in Supply is replaced by Petroleum's proportionate share of each asset and liability account of the affiliate. In the income statement, the equity in earnings of Supply has been replaced by a proportionate share of each revenue and expense line of Supply. These changes are identical to those made for a full consolidation except that only 40% of the accounts of the affiliate have been included.

This example assumes, thus far, that there are no intercompany transactions. If the venture is either a supplier to or a customer of the investor company, there are intercompany payables/receivables and intercompany sales. To complete the proportionate consolidation, we must eliminate these items from the consolidated statements. To make these eliminations, assume that:

- Petroleum purchases 30% of Supply's output.
- Supply has accounts receivable from Petroleum of $10 at December 31, 19X1.

As intercompany sales are $60 (.03 × $200), we must eliminate that amount from the consolidated revenues. Consolidated revenues are, therefore, $1,000 + (0.4 × $200) − [0.4 × (0.3 × $200)] = $1,056. The third item is the subtraction of intercompany sales.

Similarly, consolidated cost of goods sold are computed as $800 + (0.4 × $140) − [0.4 × (0.3 × $200)] = $832. The third item, which represents (the proportionate share of) sales from Supply to Petroleum, must also have been included in Petroleum's cost of goods sold. Whenever there are intercompany sales, we must eliminate them from the sales of the seller and the COGS of the buyer.

The second elimination, of intercompany payables, is simpler. We simply reduce the accounts receivable of Supply by 0.4 × $10 and, at the same time, reduce the accounts payable of Petroleum by the same amount. Consolidated accounts receivable are $300 + [0.4 × ($50 − $10)] = $316; accounts payable are $200 + (0.4 × $80) − (0.4 × $10) = $228.

The following compares Petroleum's income statement and balance sheet under the proportionate consolidation method with those statements prepared using the equity method:

Petroleum Corp. Income Statements, Year Ended December 31, 19X1
After Adjustment for Intercompany Transactions

	Proportionate Consolidation	Equity Method
Revenues	$1,056	$1,000
Equity in earnings of Supply Corp.		4
Cost of goods sold	(832)	(800)
Selling, general, and administrative expenses	(90)	(80)
Interest expense	(27)	(20)
Pretax earnings	$ 107	$ 104
Income tax expense	(43)	(40)
Net income	$ 64	$ 64

Petroleum Corp. Balance Sheets, December 31, 19X1 After Adjustment for Intercompany Transactions

Proportionate Consolidation				Equity Method			
Cash	$108	Accounts payable	$228	Cash	$100	Accounts payable	$200
Inventory	220			Inventory	200		
Accounts receivable	316			Accounts receivable	300		
Property	352	Long-term debt	268	Property	280	Long-term debt	200
		Equity	500	Investment	20	Equity	500
Totals	$996		$996	Totals	$900		$900

cash, inventories, receivables, and debt. Only stockholders' equity is unaffected as the investment in the affiliate account is eliminated against the parent's share of the affiliate's equity. To some extent, this procedure is similar to the adjustments made for debt of an unconsolidated subsidiary in the off-balance-sheet analysis in Chapter 11. Here, however, adjustments are made for *all* financial statement accounts.

Similarly, the parent includes 40% of *each* affiliate revenue and expense category in its income statement. There is no impact on parent company net income, as the parent's share of affiliate income is eliminated in consolidation.

As a result of the differences between the two methods, most financial ratios are changed, as shown in the following examples derived from Exhibit 13-7:

Petroleum Corp. Ratio Comparison, 19X1

	Proportionate Consolidation (After Eliminations)	Equity Method
Current ratio	2.82	3.00
Long-term debt to equity	0.54	0.40
Interest coverage*	4.96	6.20
Return on total capital†	0.174	0.177

*EBIT (earnings before interest and taxes)/interest expense.
†EBIT/(long-term debt + equity).

However, note that return on equity is the same ($64/$500 = 12.8%) under both methods, as net income and equity are unchanged.

Use of Proportionate Consolidation in Practice

Neither proportionate consolidation nor the expanded equity method is widely used; in the United States, it is unclear whether these methods are permitted under GAAP. This, of course, should not deter the analyst from making analytic adjustments.

Within the construction industry, however, where joint ventures are the dominant form of doing business, proportionate consolidation is frequently used. Morrison Knudsen, for example, used proportionate consolidation in its income statement for its construction joint ventures. As a result, revenues of $157 million (nearly 10% of total corporate revenues) and costs of $136 million were included in its 1990 income statement rather than the net operating income of $21 million. On its balance sheet, however, Morrison Knudsen reported its net equity in construction joint ventures of $62 million, using the equity method rather than its share of gross assets and liabilities.

Impact of Proportionate Consolidation. Brascan is a large Canadian conglomerate. One of its basic business principles is to own approximately half the shares of its major affiliates. In 1990, Brascan owned less than 50% of its principal operating companies and accounted for them using the equity method. Exhibit 13-8 compares its consolidated financial statements with supplementary statements prepared using the proportionate consolidation method. Note that all Brascan financial data are presented in Canadian dollars.

Most Brascan operations were accounted for using the equity method, and we refer to these as the equity method statements. The company stated in its *1990 Annual*

EXHIBIT 13-8
Brascan Comparison: Equity Method Versus Proportionate Consolidation
($ C in millions)

A. Balance Sheet, December 31, 1990

	Equity Method	Proportionate Consolidation
Assets		
Cash and short-term investments	$ 456	$ 7,072
Loans and accounts receivable	384	16,760
Inventories	—	1,043
Corporate investments	4,637	1,804
Property and equipment	211	5,924
Other assets	30	930
Totals	**$5,718**	**$33,533**
Liabilities		
Bank indebtedness	$ 18	
Savings deposits		$18,564
Accounts payable	47	1,686
Dividends and interest payable	53	
Term debt	1,384	5,507
Deferred credits	81	848
Totals	**$1,583**	**$26,605**
Equity and minority interest		
Minority interests	1,724	4,517
Shareholders' equity	2,411	2,411
Totals	**$5,718**	**$33,533**

B. Statement of Income, Year Ended December 31, 1990

	As Reported, Equity Method
Income before unallocated expenses	
Natural resources	$ 89.9
Consumer and industrial products	87.0
Financial services	31.3
Other operations	37.9
Investment and other	122.6
Subtotal	**$368.7**
Unallocated expenses	
Interest	$119.5
Corporate expenses	5.1
Depreciation and depletion	46.7
Income and resource taxes	1.7
Minority interests	115.4
Subtotal	**$288.4**
Net income for year	**$ 80.3**

EXHIBIT 13-8 (*continued*)

	Proportionate Consolidation
Gross revenues	**$10,275**
Cost of products sold	5,020
Operating income	**$ 5,255**
Selling and other expenses	1,656
Interest expense	2,490
Depreciation and depletion	513
Income and other taxes	296
Minority interests	220
Subtotal	**$ 5,175**
Net income for year	**80**

C. Statement of Changes in Financial Position,
Year Ended December 31, 1990

	Equity Method	Proportionate Consolidation
Provided from operations	**$ 225.2**	**650**
Borrowings	329.9	766
Minority interest	(375.7)	(372)
Increase in savings deposits	—	385
Other	(11.5)	(4)
Provided from financing	**(57.3)**	**775**
Property and equipment	(9.3)	(1,235)
Other	207.5	(260)
Used for investing	**198.2**	**(1,495)**
Dividends paid	**(284.7)**	**(560)**
Net cash flow	**81.4**	**(630)**

Source: Brascan, *1990 Annual Report.*

Report that proportionate consolidation financial statements

provide a greater awareness of the composition of Brascan's underlying assets, earnings base and overall financial strength.[27]

Brascan provided supplementary (unaudited) financial statements prepared using the proportionate consolidation method of accounting for its less than 50% owned affiliates, principally Noranda (minerals, energy, and forest products), John Labatt (brewing and foods), and Trilon (financial services).

We start by comparing the balance sheets, columns 1 and 2 of Exhibit 13-8A. The equity method balance sheet is relatively uninformative as investments constitute

[27]Brascan, *1990 Annual Report.*

81% of total assets. This balance sheet is similar to parent-company-only statements sometimes presented as supplementary data by companies whose primary statements are fully consolidated.

Brascan's equity method balance sheet, however, does provide some insight into the company's financial structure:

1. The large minority interest indicates that those subsidiaries that are consolidated are not wholly owned.

2. Brascan has a substantial debt burden, but also has significant cash and short-term investments.

These circumstances suggest that Brascan's ability to service debt and pay dividends to shareholders depends on its ability to receive dividends from its affiliates or sell investments. As it generally owns less than half the shares of its investees, dividends declared flow largely to outside shareholders. We return to this issue later.

The proportionate consolidation balance sheet is, in some respects, more informative. We see the size of Brascan's financial affiliates, whose large asset categories (cash and securities, and loans and other receivables) and liability for savings deposits dominate the balance sheet. We also get a different view of Brascan's financial structure, with debt and minority interest relatively larger:

Brascan Capital Structure, December 31, 1990 ($C in millions)

	Equity Method		Proportionate Consolidation	
	Amount	% Total	Amount	% Total
Debt	$1,402	25%	$ 5,507	44%
Minority interest	1,724	31	4,517	36
Common equity	2,411	44	2,411	20
Total capital	$5,537	100%	$12,435	100%

This analysis indicates that the leverage of the group is greater than indicated by the equity method statements. Brascan shareholders have four dollars of outside capital for each dollar of stockholders' equity. Although this leverage can result in above-average returns, it also increases risk. Most if not all of that capital ranks prior to Brascan shareholders in claims against both income and assets. Cash must "trickle up" the chain of holding companies before it can be paid out to Brascan shareholders.

Exhibit 13-8B provides the income statements. Here again, the equity method statement has limited utility. Income is shown on a one-line basis, after all expenses except for those of the parent. The proportional income statement, with gross revenues exceeding $C 10 billion, indicates the size of the group. Remember that revenues shown here include only Brascan's proportionate share of group revenues. Gross revenues (disclosed elsewhere in the annual report) exceed $C 21 billion. The proportionate income statement also provides data regarding the composition of expenses. It also indicates the leverage inherent in Brascan's corporate structure:

Brascan Net Income, Year Ended December 31, 1990 ($C in millions)

	Equity Method	Proportionate Consolidation
Earnings before interest, income taxes, and minority interests	$ 317	$ 3,086
Interest expense	(120)	(2,490)
Income tax expense	(2)	(296)
Minority interest	(115)	(220)
Net income	$ 80	$ 80

This analysis indicates that only 2.5% ($C 80 million/$C 3,086 million) of the more than $C 3 billion of earnings before interest, income taxes, and minority interest generated by the group in 1990 accrued to the benefit of Brascan stockholders. Again, this indicates the high degree of leverage inherent in Brascan's financial structure.

Exhibit 13-8C contains the statements of changes in financial position.[28] Once more, note the differences. The equity method statement shows operating cash flow of $C 225.2 million in 1990. New borrowings of $C 329.9 million were more than offset by funds used to reduce minority interests ($C 375.7 million), resulting in a financing outflow of $C 57.3 million. A net investing inflow of $C 198.2 million (largely due to collection of receivables) was more than offset by dividends paid. The net result was an increase in cash of $C 81.4 million.

The proportionate consolidation statement shows an entirely different picture. Operating cash flow is much higher ($C 650 million) than the amount reported under the equity method. Financing provided $C 775 million (increase in debt and savings deposits less the reduction in minority interest). $C 1,495 million was needed for new investment (mainly property) and $C 560 million was paid in dividends. The net result was a cash *decrease* of $C 630 million.

Brascan's presentation of supplementary financial statements using the proportionate consolidation method does, in fact, provide useful data for financial analysis. By providing a broader set of data regarding the company's activities, it helps us to understand the risks and opportunities better. However, it is worth noting that there would be some loss of information if the proportionate consolidation statements were provided in place of the equity method statements. The latter tell us more about the source of Brascan's earnings by line of business. Having both sets allows us to view the company from two different perspectives and results in a richer set of financial data.

Significance of Consolidation: Summary

The preceding sections discussed types of intercorporate investments, different methods of accounting for them, and the analysis of the resulting (significantly different) reported financial data. We now summarize the process and the most significant insights for the financial analyst.

---

[28]Note that these are not cash flow statements; the differences will not concern us here.

First, when examining a set of financial statements, it is essential to determine the accounting methods used for investments in affiliates. This is especially true of non-U.S. companies, as consolidation practices vary widely.

The second step should be to consider whether adjustments are needed to make the financial data more useful. When evaluating several different companies, the most overriding concern is likely to be comparability of basic data. You cannot compare, for example, General Motors, Toyota, Volkswagen, and Hyundai without comparable financial data.

An important aspect of this second step is to ask what form of presentation accords most closely with the objectives of the analysis. For example, current and prospective lenders to financial subsidiaries need separate financial statements for those entities; consolidated statements that include the manufacturing operations of the parent company are less useful.

As we have seen, accounting conventions do not always reflect economic reality. The analyst should determine, for example, which unconsolidated affiliates are integral to the enterprise and should, therefore, be consolidated. Analysts should also be aware of the potential use of "off-balance-sheet" unconsolidated affiliates to obtain financing.

The third step should be to make any required adjustments to the reported financial statements. For U.S. companies, the needed data are often available in 10-K reports or supplemental data (such as "fact books") that companies prepare for financial analysts. Even condensed statements are useful; it is better to be approximately right than precisely wrong!

Adjustments should not be made mechanically. They should be appropriate in the context of the company's operations and the objectives of the analysis. Finally, and most important, adjusted financial statements and ratios should be examined carefully for insights regarding the company's past results, current operations, and future performance. Analysts should concentrate on the differences between adjusted and unadjusted data.

ANALYSIS OF MINORITY INTEREST

Minority interest is the amount of the consolidated net assets and income that does not belong to the parent. The FASB exposure draft on consolidation (see Box 13-3), in keeping with its emphasis on effective control, refers to this as *noncontrolling interest*. We continue to use the term minority interest in our discussion as it is more widely understood.

The balance in the minority interest account shown on the balance sheet and the minority interest in net income are necessarily related. If the subsidiary pays no cash dividends, then the change in the balance sheet account equals the minority interest in net income. If a dividend is paid, then the balance sheet change equals the minority interest in net income less the dividends paid to minority owners; that is, the amount of undistributed earnings for the period. Capital contributions or withdrawals also affect the minority interest shown on the parent company balance sheet.

For example, in 1990, the Aydin Corporation set up a 51% owned subsidiary, Aydin-Aymet, in connection with a major contract with the government of Turkey. This subsidiary generated the following entries in Aydin's 1990 financial statements:

Aydin Corp.: Analysis of Minority Interest

Income statement: Minority interest	$(108,000)
Liability: Minority interest	511,000
Adjustment to operating cash flow*	108,000
Financing cash flow (minority investment in consolidated subsidiary)	403,000

*Under the indirect method, noncash deductions from income are added back to net income to calculate operating cash flow.

From these entries, we can deduce the following transactions:

1. The minority partner invested $403,000 in the subsidiary.
2. The subsidiary earned $220,000 in 1990 ($108,000/0.49), of which 49% (or $108,000) accrued to the minority investor.
3. The subsidiary paid no dividends. Thus, the minority interest at the end of the year was:

Original investment	$403,000
Minority share of 1990 net income	108,000
Total	$511,000

Note that the accounting for minority interest is the mirror image of the equity method. Assuming that the Turkish owner of the 49% interest in Aydin-Aymet used the equity method, it would show its investment as $511,000 and its 1990 earnings from the venture as $108,000.

The Aydin *1990 Annual Report* also contains the following footnote:

Short-term investments . . . include $20.3 million held by the Company's 51% owned Turkish subsidiary.[29]

This footnote reminds us that the assets of a less than wholly owned subsidiary are not as freely available to the parent as those of a 100% owned subsidiary because of the minority investor.

Minority interest can be quite significant. For Aydin, it was less than 1% of stockholders' equity. Alcoa, in contrast, has large majority-owned subsidiaries, and the numbers are far more significant. At December 31, 1995, Alcoa's minority interest was $1.61 billion or more than 36% of equity of $4.44 billion. Minority interest in 1995 earnings was $234 million and reduced net income by 23%. Finally, dividends to the minority shareholders of the majority-owned subsidiaries were $122 million, approaching the $162 million paid to Alcoa's own stockholders.

In some respects, minority interest can be considered equity for purposes of analysis. Minority shareholders have only a residual claim on the assets of the subsidiary.[30] From the point of view of both creditors and stockholders of the parent, however,

---

[29]Aydin Corp., *1990 Annual Report.*

[30]The minority interest is also a residual claim on the assets of the consolidated entity. It is therefore appropriately reported as a component of equity in the consolidated financial statements.

minority interest has the characteristics of a preferred shareholder. Generally, the creditors and shareholders of the parent cannot benefit from the assets of the subsidiary without respecting the claims of its creditors and minority holders. Thus, minority interest occupies a special position and cannot be mechanically aggregated with either liabilities or equity.

CONSOLIDATION PRACTICES OUTSIDE THE UNITED STATES

Although consolidation of majority-owned subsidiaries has been the general rule in the United States for several decades, that has not been the case for other nations. In Japan and parts of Western Europe, parent company reporting has been the norm until quite recently. "Parent-only" financial statements are still considered to be the primary set of statements in Japan because financial reporting there is based on tax reporting.

In Germany, consolidated financial statements normally include only domestic subsidiaries; investments in foreign subsidiaries and affiliates are carried at acquisition cost. In the United Kingdom and Canada, firms may exclude nonhomogeneous subsidiaries from consolidated financial statements. However, current trends indicate that excluded affiliates are limited to those operating in the banking and insurance industries.

Group, or consolidated, financial statements are the norm in France. Generally, consolidation is used when the investor directly or indirectly owns more than 40% of the voting common stock. The equity method is used when control is temporary or restricted by management contract.

The Netherlands, Italy, and France allow firms to exclude nonhomogeneous subsidiaries from consolidated financial statements. Germany and France permit the use of proportionate consolidation.

IAS 27 requires that all controlled subsidiaries be consolidated.[31] As this standard became effective in 1990, all financial statements prepared in accordance with IASC standards should now be comparable in this respect. In time, if we assume increasing conformity with IASC standards, full consolidation should become the norm worldwide.

ANALYSIS OF SEGMENT DATA

The analysis of companies with more than one line of business has inherent difficulties as compared with the analysis of companies engaged in a single business. The aggregation of financial data for businesses with differing financial structures, risk attributes, and indicators of performance obscures the characteristics of each segment. The rise of the conglomerate corporation in the 1960s aggravated the problem as multidivisional corporations proliferated.

With strong encouragement from the financial analyst community, the Financial Accounting Standards Board placed segment reporting on its agenda soon after it was established in 1973. The result was SFAS 14, Financial Reporting for Segments of a

---

[31]The standard allows only rare exceptions to this rule.

Business Enterprise (1974). The stated goal of the standard was to

> assist financial statement users in analyzing and understanding the enterprise's financial statements by permitting better assessment of the enterprise's past performance and future prospects.[32]

The key to segment disclosure is the definition of the segments of the enterprise. The FASB decided that a precise definition could not be written into an accounting standard so SFAS 14 provides for management judgment. Profit centers established for internal management and control purposes are the logical starting point for determining reportable segments. The FASB also suggested that segmentation should consider the similarity of:

- Products
- Production processes
- Markets or marketing methods

Reportable segments are defined as components of the enterprise that account for at least 10% of *any one* of the following:

1. Total revenues (before elimination of intersegment sales).
2. Combined operating profit (of profitable segments), or its operating loss must exceed 10% of the combined operating loss of segments with losses.
3. Combined identifiable assets of all segments.

For each reportable segment, disclosure requirements include:

- Sales to unaffiliated customers and intersegment sales
- Operating profit or some other measure of profitability
- Any unusual income component or any impact of an accounting change
- Identifiable assets
- Depreciation, depletion, and amortization expense
- Capital expenditures

SFAS 14 also requires that companies operating in more than one country disclose data on foreign operations, when significant. For geographic segment reporting, the significance test is slightly different. A reportable geographic segment must exceed 10% of either:

- Sales to unaffiliated customers as compared to consolidated revenues, or
- Identifiable assets as compared to consolidated total assets

Geographic areas may be grouped into segments using management judgment. As in the case of lines of business, precise definition was deemed to be impossible. For each reportable geographic segment, the company must report:

---

[32]SFAS 14, Financial Reporting for Segments of a Business Enterprise (1974), para. 5.

- Sales, with intersegment sales shown separately.
- Operating profit or some other measure of profitability.
- Identifiable assets.
- Export sales from domestic operations, if greater than 10% of consolidated sales.

Firms must also report sales to any customer accounting for more than 10% of sales. Disclosure is also required if 10% of sales comes from domestic government agencies as a group or foreign governments as a group. Note that the name of the major customer need not be disclosed, only the amount of sales.

Illustration of Industry Segments: DuPont

DuPont breaks its operations into five industry segments:

1. Chemicals
2. Fibers
3. Polymers
4. Petroleum
5. Diversified businesses (agricultural products, printing and publishing, electronic materials, films, and medical products)

However, there are really only four *identifiable* segments as diversified businesses is an amalgam of many smaller segments, each of which is not large enough to be reported separately. DuPont's industry segment information is contained in Note 30 of Appendix A.

In compliance with SFAS 14, duPont discloses sales to unaffiliated customers, intersegment sales, operating income, identifiable assets, depreciation, and capital expenditures for each segment for each year. Additionally, duPont discloses income tax expense and the equity in earnings of affiliates accounted for under the equity method for each division.

The low level of intersegment transfers suggests that duPont's industry segments are not significantly integrated. The chemical division has the highest proportion of intersegment sales, approximately 5% of total segment sales. The low level of integration suggests that duPont's acquisitions[33] were not undertaken to achieve synergies through vertical integration. For some companies, the ability to provide inputs for one segment from the output of others has operational advantages that go beyond operating profit in any particular year. However, despite the low level of intersegment transfers, duPont's petroleum business may provide a natural business hedge for segments that use petroleum inputs. Although rising oil prices might reduce the profits of duPont's petrochemical operations, the higher profitability of its petroleum operations would offset that decline.

Analyzing the 1994 segment data, we note first that petroleum is the largest segment in terms of sales and assets, accounting for 44% of consolidated sales and 39% of identifiable assets. However, its contribution to consolidated profits is considerably lower, 22%. The fibers and polymers segments, whose sales and assets are considerably

---

[33]In 1981, duPont acquired Conoco, the base of its petroleum segment.

lower, each show comparable pretax (and larger after-tax) operating income. These relative profitabilities are reflected in the data below:

DuPont Segment Profitability, 1994

Ratio	Chemicals	Fibers	Polymers	Petroleum	Diversified
Operating margin	14%	16%	17%	7%	10%
Return on assets	18	18	21	10	7

The first ratio measures profitability relative to sales.[34] The second, return on average assets (operating income divided by average identifiable assets), is the only available return-on-investment measure by segment. Although petroleum had the lowest return on sales and ROA of any of the four identifiable segments for 1994, profitability had been higher in previous years:

DuPont Segment Profitability, 1992 and 1993

Ratio	Chemicals (%)	Fibers (%)	Polymers (%)	Petroleum (%)	Diversified (%)
OI/Sales, 1993	7	4	4	8	(9)
OI/Sales, 1992	6	9	8	7	(1)
ROA, 1993	8	4	5	10	(9)

Note that the petroleum segment return on sales and ROA were relatively constant at 7 to 8% and 10%, respectively. The other segments outperformed the petroleum segment only in 1994; over the 1992 to 1994 period, profitability measures for the other segments fluctuated widely.

These differences should be viewed in conjunction with the growth in sales and assets of the segments:

Segment Growth Rates, 1992 to 1994

Change in	Chemicals (%)	Fibers (%)	Polymers (%)	Petroleum (%)	Diversified (%)
Sales	4	11	8	5	(8)
Identifiable assets	(10)	5	(5)	(3)	(17)
Capital expenditures	(19)	(37)	(37)	(12)	(49)

Fibers and polymer segment sales grew most rapidly. Interestingly, for all segments, sales grew, while capital expenditures fell. Except for the fibers segment, capital

---

[34]Sales can be defined either as sales to unaffiliated customers (excluding intersegment sales) or as total sales (including intersegment sales). The latter is a better indicator of profitability, especially for segments with large intersegment sales. Presumably, the intersegment sales are profitable; excluding them would overstate segment profitability. In duPont's case, given the low level of intersegment sales, the difference is not material.

expenditures were below depreciation levels, contributing to declines in identifiable assets.

These data indicate that duPont coupled its sales growth with more efficient operations (restructuring[35] and downsizing). The higher 1994 profitability for all segments may indicate the benefits from these efforts. Lower asset levels decrease fixed costs (depreciation) that, when coupled with sales growth, markedly improve profitability.[36] Profitability fluctuated more for the smaller segments; they showed the largest improvement in 1994.

Illustration of Geographic Segments: DuPont

SFAS 14 also requires disclosures regarding geographic areas. Such disclosures often augment insights obtained from industry segment data. As in the case of industry segments, trends that are submerged in consolidated results may become evident from segment breakouts.

DuPont divides its operations into three segments: United States, Europe, and Other Regions (OR), with U.S. operations accounting for just over half of corporate sales. However, U.S. sales remained nearly constant over the 1992 to 1994 period, at just over $20 billion. Non-U.S. sales increased by 7% (Europe 5% and OR 10%) over the same time span. Similarly, identifiable assets decreased in the United States but increased slightly in the non-U.S. segments.

When we look at profitability, we find that European profits steadily increased over the 1992 to 1994 period, whereas profits (in absolute terms and relative to sales) in the United States and OR were volatile. We also note that identifiable assets *increased* in Europe but *decreased* in the United States.

The geographic segment data suggest an additional dimension to our earlier conclusions about the profitability of duPont's industry segments. In Europe, higher sales may have contributed more to higher profitability; in the United States, improved efficiency may have been a more important factor. Lacking geographic data for each industry segment, these questions can be explored only through discussions with management.

Geographic segment data may also highlight the effects of changes in exchange rates and the additional risks that a company faces due to these exposures. Exchange rate changes contributed to the 1993 sales decline for duPont's Europe segment, for example. Chapter 15 contains a detailed discussion of how exchange rates affect reported income statement and balance sheet accounts.

Management Discussion and Analysis

An additional source of information about segments may be found in the required management discussion and analysis (MD&A). In duPont's MD&A, we find the following relevant excerpts:

- 1994 income was . . . up 65%. This increase principally reflects improvements in the chemicals and specialties (i.e., fibers, polymers, and diversified) segments from higher sales volume, lower fixed costs. . . .

---

[35] See Note 6 to duPont's financial statements, "Restructuring Charges and Write-Down of Intangible Assets."

[36] See our discussion of the effects of operating (and financing) leverage in Chapter 4.

- It is estimated that 1994 operating results included about $450 million in pretax savings related to restructuring activities that have been completed.
- Europe was particularly strong, with sales volume up 14% reflecting the economic recovery in that region.
- Sales in 1993 were $37.1 billion, 2 percent below 1992 . . . Lower sales were principally due to lower prices largely the result of adverse exchange effects from a stronger dollar. . . .

The MD&A, often based on segment data, provides further explanation and confirmation of the analysis of those data. The operating results for each segment help the analyst to break down corporate performance into more easily understandable components.

Uses and Limitations of Segment Data

One limitation of segment data is the lack of information on liabilities. Funded debt is, however, not the main issue, unless debt is allocated to segments. As operating income is computed before interest expense, return on total capital by segment should be comparable. The more significant issue is noninterest-bearing liabilities such as payables and accruals and off-balance-sheet obligations. These liabilities reduce the net investment; segment return on assets understates the actual return on capital.

A second limitation is the computation of segment profit, which may be affected by intersegment pricing and any allocation of corporate overhead.

A third problem is the lack of segment cash flow data. Change in assets alone is a poor measure of changes in resources allocated to different segments.

These limitations do not mean that segment data are useless, far from it. They do mean that segment data must be used with some care rather than in a simplistic manner.

Segment data are best used for the examination of trends. We can assume that the computation of segment profitability is consistent from year to year, as is the ratio of liabilities to assets. Therefore, although disclosed levels of profitability may have limited comparability and utility,[37] the trend of profitability is useful and may be more reliable. This is especially true when segment data are presented on a quarterly basis.

Segment trends can, and should, be compared to trends in the sales and operating income of companies in similar businesses and similar segments of multidivisional companies. Again, levels are less reliable indicators than changes over time. It is also important to adjust for any differences in accounting methods (especially for inventories) and for any unusual items included in reported earnings. Many companies report the allocation of unusual items to individual segments. For example, see the footnotes to duPont's segment disclosures in Notes 29 and 30.

Perhaps most important, segment data enable the analyst to obtain a better understanding of a company's operations. Segment disclosures can be used to ask questions that will better illuminate the determinants of sales growth and profitability. This understanding can then be applied to expected future business conditions, resulting in better forecasts of sales and earnings.

Thus, segment data are not an end in themselves but a means to better understanding of a firm's sources of profitability and growth.

---

[37]Empirical results discussed later in the chapter suggest that segment data are most useful for forecasting sales. The aggregated sales forecast can then be used to forecast consolidated earnings.

Proposed Changes in Segment Reporting

In practice, the segment reporting mandated by SFAS 14 worked reasonably well. Management judgment, auditor involvement, and oversight from the SEC produced disclosures that generally achieved the desired objective.

However, the "line of business" orientation of SFAS 14 meant that some firms reported data based on segmentation different from the firm's organizational structure. In addition, analysts lobbied for additional segment disclosures. In early 1996, as part of a joint project with the Canadian Accounting Standards Committee, the FASB issued an exposure draft proposing substantial changes in segment reporting. At the same time, the IASC issued an exposure draft on segment reporting. Box 13-4 discusses these proposals.

BOX 13-4
Proposed Changes in Segment Reporting

In December 1995, the IASC Issued Exposure Draft E51, Reporting Financial Information by Segment. Shortly thereafter, the FASB issued a joint exposure draft (the FASB/AcSB ED) with the Accounting Standards Board (AcSB) of the Canadian Institute of Chartered Accountants: Reporting Disaggregated Information about a Business Enterprise.

The FASB/AcSB ED changes segment reporting from the "risks and rewards" focus of SFAS 14 to the *management approach*

> based on the way that management disaggregates the enterprise for making operating decisions.*

This approach responds to both analyst requests for segmentation "the way that the business is managed" and the expectation that

> financial statement preparers can provide the information in a cost-effective and timely manner.†

The IASC proposal (E51) also adopts the management approach but requires that, when that approach fails to provide useful data about the firm's different business segments, alternate segmentation must be provided.

Both exposure drafts are intended to expand the amount of segment data provided. The FASB/AcSB ED would require disclosure of:

1. Revenues from external sales
2. Intersegment sales
3. Segment profit or loss
4. Interest income and expense‡
5. Research and development expense
6. Depreciation, depletion, and amortization expense
7. Other noncash items
8. Unusual and extraordinary items
9. Equity in income of investees
10. Income tax expense

E51 (IASC) requires income statement data by segment similar to the FASB/AcSB ED except for research and development expense.

Both exposure drafts require the following balance sheet data for each segment:

- Total assets
- Total liabilities
- Investment in equity method investees
- Capital expenditures

For both income statement and balance sheet data, reconciliations between total segment data and enterprise data are required. These reconciliations are intended to help analysts discern the impact of income, expense, assets, and liabilities not included in reported segments.

There are several important differences between the two proposals. First, the FASB/AcSB ED permits firms to report segment data using internal financial reporting systems, even when accounting methods used to prepare such data differ from GAAP. For example, if the firm applies the LIFO method of inventory accounting only at the parent level, but uses FIFO at the division level, segment data could be FIFO-based. E51 requires that segment data use the same accounting methods used to report consolidated financial statements.

A second difference is that the FASB/AcSB ED appears to require disclosure of some segment data only if such data are used by management. The IASC proposal contains no such provision.

Both exposure drafts provide limited segment data for secondary segments. When the primary segmentation is by line of business, secondary segmentation would be based on geography. For each secondary segment, the following must be disclosed:

- Revenues
- Assets§
- Capital expenditures

For U.S. companies, segment profitability by geographic area (required by SFAS 14) would no longer be reported.

The FASB/AcSB ED has two requirements absent from E51:

1. Interim reporting of segment revenues and segment profit or loss, as well as a reconciliation of segment results to consolidated pretax income. This requirement has been a longstanding analyst goal.

2. Continuation of the SFAS 14 requirement to disclose the existence of customers accounting for more than 10% of enterprise revenue.

---

*Para. 6 of the exposure draft.
†Ibid.
‡Items 4 through 10 would be reported only when included in the measurement of segment profit or loss.
§The FASB/AcSB exposure draft requires disclosure of fixed assets only.

Using Segment Data to Estimate Consolidated Earnings and Risk

Segment data can be used to assess both the expected return (profitability) and risk characteristics of a multidivisional firm. After elimination of intercompany transactions, the expected earnings of the total firm is the sum of the expected earnings of the individual segments. Similarly, the overall risk of the entity is a weighted average of the risk of the individual segments.

A number of studies have compared the forecasting accuracy of models that predict consolidated earnings directly with those that predict individual segment earnings first and then combine those results to forecast firm earnings. The earliest of these studies, Kinney (1971), found that segment-based forecasts were more accurate than direct forecasts.

Although intuitively one would expect segment data to improve forecast accuracy, in practice the results depend on the interrelationships among the various segments and on the forecasting models used. Hopwood et al. (1982) note that no gains in forecasting ability result from the use of segment data if either:

1. The time-series models of the component segments are identical, or

2. None of the component series leads or lags the consolidated series.

If the various industries that make up the segments are influenced by similar factors (e.g., they tend to move together during the business cycle), then a forecast based on consolidated data should be just as good as a forecast based on segment data. The more dissimilar the series or the greater the lag effects among segments, the greater the benefits of forecasting with segment data. Thus, the degree of improvement in forecasting ability should depend on the nature of the firm's segments.

However, even under the best of conditions (disparate segments), knowledge of the parameters of the forecasting model is needed. As segment-based models require the estimation of more parameters (a set for each segment) than do consolidated-based models, measurement error may affect the results. Measurement error in estimating the parameters dilutes the benefits of segment data.

Chapter 19 discusses the time-series models used to forecast accounting earnings. Many (extrapolative models) are based on the previous time-series history of the variables being predicted. Thus, forecast earnings are a function of past earnings. As will be seen, there has been very little success in distinguishing firm-specific models for this class of models. That is, a firm-specific model does not forecast any better than a single model applied to all firms. Measurement error has been suggested as one reason for this finding. Thus, given the first condition specified by Hopwood et al., for extrapolative models, it is unlikely that forecasts would be improved by segment data.[38]

Improvement would be more likely for models that exploit the differences between segments. For example, Collins (1976) combined firm-specific and industrywide data to forecast sales and earnings as follows:

1. The estimated percentage increase in shipments (sales) for the following year was obtained from the U.S. Industrial Outlook for industrial sectors corresponding to the individual segments of the consolidated firm.

---

[38]This is consistent with Silhan (1982), who simulated "mergers" of existing companies and tested (using extrapolative models) whether the individual series or the aggregated series better forecast the aggregated series. His results indicated no difference between the two approaches.

2. The percentage increase obtained in step 1 was multiplied by current year sales for each segment; these forecasts were then aggregated to obtain a segment-based consolidated sales forecast (SBCSF).

3. The sales forecast obtained in step 2 was multiplied by the current year profit margin to produce the segment-based consolidated earnings forecast (SBCEF).

These segment-based forecasts were then compared to seven consolidated-based earnings and sales forecasts (CBCEF and CBCSF) generated purely on the basis of consolidated sales and earnings. These latter forecasts were generated from six extrapolative models and a consolidated-based model that mirrored the procedure used for the segment-based data. The expected increase in GNP was used to forecast increases in sales and earnings. The segment-based earnings forecasts had the lowest prediction errors. The results, however, suggested that improvement was due mainly to better sales forecasts and there was little marginal benefit in segment data beyond that of sales.

Baldwin (1984) provided other evidence that segment data can be used to improve forecasts by comparing analyst forecast accuracy before and after the disclosure of segment-based data was first required in 1971. Three groups were compared:

1. Multisegment firms that had previously not provided segment data

2. Multisegment firms that had previously (voluntarily) provided segment data

3. Single-segment firms that continued to report only on a consolidated basis

Forecast accuracy improved for all three groups. However, the most significant improvement was for those firms that had not provided segment data previously. The results indicate that analysts were able to use the segment data to improve their forecasting ability. Similarly, Swaminathan (1991) noted a reduction in the dispersion of analysts' forecasts.

Segment information can also be used to assess a firm's risk. A firm's overall market beta is the weighted average of the beta of the individual segments. These, in turn, are a function of the industries in which they operate. Knowledge of the importance of each segment should provide information as to the relative risk class or beta of the overall firm.[39]

Collins and Simonds (1979) found that when segment data were first provided in 1971, there was a significant downward shift in the betas of firms reporting segment data for the first time.[40] Similarly, Greenstein and Sami (1994) found that bid-ask spreads decreased significantly for those firms reporting segment data for the first time and that the magnitude of the decrease was positively related to the number of segments reported.

These results should be viewed in the context of Swaminathan's finding of a reduction in the dispersion of analysts' forecasts, and Cragg and Malkiel (1982), who showed that firms' overall risk levels are highly correlated with the dispersion of analysts' forecasts.

Balakrishnan et al. (1990) examined whether or not geographic segment disclosures

---

[39]In a related study of insurance companies, Foster (1975) found that the market discriminated between them on the basis of the performance of their three primary subearnings series: underwriting results, investment results, and capital gains results.

[40]Horwitz and Kolodny (1977) did not find any beta shifts. However, their methodology was criticized by Collins and Simonds (1979).

could be used to enhance predictions of sales and income. Specifically, they forecast sales and income by geographic region and compared the aggregated regional forecasts with a forecast based on consolidated sales and income data alone. The regional forecasts considered macroeconomic factors characteristic of each region, such as exchange rates, regional GNP growth, and region-specific inflation rates.

They found that using geographic segment data improved forecasts, but that the improvement, not surprisingly, depended on the ability to forecast the macroeconomic factors. Income forecasts were best when perfect foreknowledge of the macroeconomic factors was assumed; when this assumption was relaxed, they found reduced improvement.

Surprisingly, they found that sales forecasts were better when expectations (rather than perfect foreknowledge) were used for macroeconomic factors. They surmised that

> sales policies (e.g., prices) may be based on predicted exchange rates, and these cannot be adjusted quickly for unexpected exchange rate changes. Thus, the sales forecasts using exchange rate predictions do quite well.[41]

Empirical evidence on the usefulness of segment data for forecasting purposes is mixed. In practice, analyst forecasts use segment data. Particularly in the case of firms operating in different industries, sales and earnings forecasts are based on a segment-by-segment analysis. Segment data provide information regarding the source of revenue and earnings growth and indications of the future direction of the firm.

Segment Reporting Outside the United States

France, Germany, and the Netherlands require segment data by sector and market. Firms in the United Kingdom provide sales and pretax profit by location (geographic segment) and by industry. Better disclosure has been available in the United Kingdom primarily due to listing requirements of the International Stock Exchange in London. A recent Accounting Standards Board (UK) exposure draft proposed disclosures of sales, pretax profits, and capital employed.

As discussed in Box 13-4, the IASC has proposed major changes in segment reporting requirements. Current IASC standards are similar to SFAS 14 in the United States, but rules defining segments are vague and inconsistently applied.

SUMMARY

Intercorporate investments can be accounted for in different ways, depending on ownership structure. As accounting standards often set arbitrary boundaries between accounting methods, transactions may be structured to achieve the desired accounting objective. In some cases, accounting choices are available within a given structure (e.g., the classification of marketable securities).

The analyst must examine accounting and structural choices to understand how they impact reported financial statements. In some cases, good analysis requires that the firm's financial statements be recast using a different accounting method.

---

[41]R. Balakrishnan, T. Harris, and P. Sen, "The Predictive Ability of Geographic Segment Disclosures," *Journal of Accounting Research*, Autumn 1990, p. 316.

CASE 13-1

Coca-Cola

CONSOLIDATION VERSUS EQUITY METHOD

Coca-Cola (Coke) is the largest worldwide soft drink firm, with a 47% market share. However, Coke does not bottle and distribute its beverages; that activity is carried out by affiliates in which Coke has a large equity interest.

Coca-Cola Enterprises (Enterprises) is the world's largest marketer and distributor of Coke products. The relationship between the two firms is complex:

1. Enterprises produces virtually all its products under license from Coke and buys soft drink syrup, concentrates, and sweeteners directly from or through Coke.
2. Coke provides national advertising as well as local marketing support for Enterprises' products.
3. Approximately 90% of Enterprises' sales volume is generated through the sale of products of The Coca-Cola Company; raw materials purchased from Coke account for over 50% of Enterprises' cost of goods sold. To a great extent, Coke controls Enterprises' products and input costs.
4. The chairman and three members of Enterprises' board of directors are current or former officers of Coke.

In the "Management Financial Review" section of its 1995 10-K report, Enterprises states that

> The Coca-Cola Company is an integral partner in our success.

It would not be an understatement to suggest that Enterprises (and Coke's other affiliated bottling companies) are an integral part of Coke's success, providing an outlet for its products. However, by keeping its ownership below 50%, Coke has been able to use the equity method to report its interest in Enterprises and the other bottlers.

Exhibit 13C-1 contains the 1995 financial statements of Coke and Coca-Cola Enterprises. The following excerpts from Coke's financial statements are also relevant to an analysis of the bottling affiliates:

- Coca-Cola Enterprises is the largest soft drink bottler in the world. The Company (Coke) owns approximately 44 percent of the outstanding common stock of Coca-Cola Enterprises and, accordingly, accounts for its investment by the equity method of accounting.
- In January 1994, the Company sold common stock representing a 9 percent voting interest in The Coca-Cola Bottling Company of New York, Inc. (CCNY) to Coca-Cola Enterprises, thereby reducing the Company's ownership in CCNY below 50 percent.
- At December 31, 1994, the Company owned approximately 50 percent of Coca-Cola Amatil, an Australia-based bottler of Company products that operates in 12 countries. In 1995, the Company reduced its ownership in Coca-Cola Amatil to approximately 40 percent and, accordingly, the investment is accounted for by the equity method.
- In 1993, the Company acquired a 30 percent equity interest in Coca-Cola FEMSA, which operates bottling facilities in Mexico and Argentina.

Additional 1995 Financial Information ($ in millions)

Intercompany sales	From Coke to Enterprises	$1,828
	From Enterprises to Coke	253
Net marketing payments	From Coke to Enterprises	343

Condensed 1995 Financial Statements (in millions)

Balance Sheets at December 31, 1995

	Coke	Enterprises
Current assets		
Cash and marketable securities	$ 1,315	$ 8
Trade accounts receivable	1,695	510
Amounts due from The Coca-Cola Company	—	6
Finance subsidiary receivables	55	—
Inventories	1,117	225
Prepaid expenses and other assets	1,268	233
	$ 5,450	$ 982
Investments		
Equity method Investments		
Coca-Cola Enterprises	556	—
Coca-Cola Amatil Limited	682	—
Other, principally bottling companies	1,157	—
Cost method investments, principally bottling companies	319	—
Finance subsidiary receivables	351	—
Marketable securities	1,246	—
	$ 4,311	
Property, plant and equipment (net)	4,336	2,158
Intangible assets	944	5,924
Total assets	**$15,041**	**$ 9,064**
Current liabilities		
Accounts payable and accrued liabilities	$ 4,425	$ 796
Notes payable and current debt	2,923	63
	$ 7,348	$ 859
Noncurrent liabilities		
Long-term debt	1,141	4,138
Other noncurrent liabilities	966	600
Deferred taxes	194	2,032
	$ 2,301	$ 6,770
Shareholders' equity		
Preferred stock	—	30
Common stock	428	145
Paid-in-capital	1,291	1,346
Retained earnings	12,882	144
Other	(410)	38
Treasury stock	(8,799)	(268)
	$ 5,392	$ 1,435
Total liabilities and equity	**$15,041**	**$ 9,064**

Note: Intangible assets for Coke consist primarily of goodwill

Intangible assets for Enterprises consist primarily of franchise rights to bottle Coca-Cola products

EXHIBIT 13C-1. (*continued*)

Income Statements, Year Ended December 31, 1995

	Coke	Enterprises
Net operating revenues	$18,018	$ 6,773
Cost of goods sold	(6,940)	(4,267)
Gross profit	**$11,078**	**$ 2,506**
Selling, administrative and general expenses	(6,986)	(2,038)
Operating income	**$ 4,092**	**$ 468**
Interest income	245	
Interest expense, net	(272)	(326)
Equity income	169	—
Other Income	94	3
Income before taxes	**$ 4,328**	**$ 145**
Income taxes	1,342	63
Net income	**$ 2,986**	**$ 82**
Preferred dividends	—	2
Net income Applicable to Common Share Owners	**$ 2,986**	**$ 80**

Cash Flow Statements, Year Ended December 31, 1995

	Coke	Enterprises
Cash flow from operations		
Net Income	$ 2,986	$ 82
Equity Income, net of dividends	(25)	—
Other Adjustments	154	562
	$ 3,115	**$ 644**
Cash flow from investing activities	**$(1,013)**	**$ (620)**
Cash flow from financing activities		
Debt financing	542	—
Issuance and repurchase of stock	(1,710)	(31)
Dividends on preferred and common stock	(1,110)	(7)
	$(2,278)	**$ (38)**
Effect of Exchange Rate Changes	**(43)**	—
Change in Cash	**$ (219)**	**$ (14)**

Source: Adapted from 1995 annual reports of The Coca-Cola Company and Coca-Cola Enterprises

EXHIBIT 13C-2. THE COCA-COLA COMPANY AND SUBSIDIARIES
Supplementary Data

Notes to Consolidated Financial Statements

Other Equity Investments

On December 31, 1995, the Company owned approximately 40 percent of Coca-Cola Amatil Limited (Coca-Cola Amatil), an Australian-based bottler of Company products that operates in 16 countries. Accordingly, the Company accounts for its investment in Coca-Cola Amatil by the equity method.

In July 1995, Coca-Cola Amatil completed a public offering in Australia of approximately 97 million shares of common stock. This transaction resulted in a non-cash pretax gain of approximately $74 million for the Company.

In the fourth quarter of 1993, Coca-Cola Amatil issued approximately 8 million shares of stock to acquire the Company's franchise bottler in Jakarta, Indonesia. This transaction resulted in a pretax gain for the Company of approximately $12 million.

On December 31, 1995, the excess of the Company's investment over its equity in the underlying net assets of Coca-Cola Amatil was approximately $91 million, which is being amortized on a straight-line basis over 40 years.

During 1995, the Company's finance subsidiary invested $160 million in The Coca-Cola Bottling Company of New York, Inc. (CCNY), in return for redeemable preferred stock. As of December 31, 1995, the Company held a 49 percent voting and economic interest in CCNY. Accordingly, the Company accounts for its investment in CCNY by the equity method.

In 1993, the Company acquired a 30 percent equity interest in Coca-Cola FEMSA, S.A. de C.V. (Coca-Cola FEMSA), which operates bottling facilities in Mexico and Argentina, for $195 million. On December 31, 1995, the excess of the Company's investment over its equity in the underlying net assets of Coca-Cola FEMSA was approximately $31 million, which is being amortized over 40 years.

Operating results include the Company's proportionate share of income from equity investments since the respective dates of investment. A summary of financial information for the Company's equity investments, other than Coca-Cola Enterprises, is as follows (in millions):

December 31,	1995	1994
Current assets	$ 2,954	$ 2,747
Noncurrent assets	6,637	5,316
Total assets	$ 9,591	$ 8,063
Current liabilities	$ 2,944	$ 2,382
Noncurrent liabilities	2,849	2,669
Total liabilities	$ 5,793	$ 5,051
Share-owners' equity	$ 3,798	$ 3,012
Company equity investment	$ 1,839	$ 1,808

Year Ended December 31,	1995	1994	1993
Net operating revenues	$ 11,563	$ 9,668	$ 8,168
Cost of goods sold	7,646	6,397	5,385
Gross profit	$ 3,917	$ 3,271	$ 2,783
Operating income	$ 846	$ 783	$ 673
Operating cash flow	$ 1,403	$ 1,076	$ 984
Net income	$ 355	$ 323	$ 258
Company equity income	$ 134	$ 104	$ 97

Equity investments include certain non-bottling investees.

Net income for the Company's equity investments in 1993 reflects an $86 million after-tax charge recorded by Coca-Cola Beverages Ltd., related to the restructuring of its operations in Canada:

Net sales to equity investees other than Coca-Cola Enterprises were $1.4 billion in 1995 and $1.2 billion in 1994 and 1993. The Company also participates in various marketing, promotional and other activities with these investees, the majority of which are located outside the United States.

If valued at the December 31, 1995, quoted closing prices of shares actively traded on stock markets, the calculated value of the Company's equity investments in publicly traded bottlers other than Coca-Cola Enterprises would have exceeded the Company's carrying value by approximately $1.2 billion.

Required:

1. Given the relationship between Coke and Enterprises, discuss the appropriateness of Coke's use of the equity method to account for its investment in Enterprises.

2. Prepare a 1995 balance sheet, income statement, and cash flow statement for Coke, with Enterprises fully consolidated.

3. Compute the following ratios for Coke (as reported), Enterprises, and Coke after full consolidation of Enterprises:

   (a) Current ratio   (h) Return on assets
   (b) Debt-to-equity   (i) Return on tangible assets
   (c) Debt-to-tangible equity   (j) Return on equity
   (d) Debt-to-assets   (k) Return on tangible equity
   (e) Debt-to-tangible assets   (l) Times interest earned
   (f) Gross profit margin   (m) Inventory turnover
   (g) Return on sales   (n) Receivable turnover

4. Discuss the differences in the ratios in part 3 between Coke as reported and after the consolidation of Enterprises.

5. Repeat parts 2 through 4, but using proportionate consolidation for Enterprises.

6. Exhibit 13C-2 contains summarized data regarding Coke's other bottling affiliates (excluding Enterprises) accounted for using the equity method. Discuss the expected effect of:

   (a) Full consolidation   (b) Proportionate consolidation

   on Coke's financial statements.

7. Discuss the expected effect of the FASB exposure draft on consolidation (Box 13-3) on Coke's accounting treatment of its bottling affiliates.

8. As a financial analyst, discuss the advantages and disadvantages of viewing Coke, with its bottling affiliates:

   (a) On the equity method   (c) Proportionately consolidated
   (b) Fully consolidated

Chapter 13

Problems

1. [Marketable securities: accounting versus mark-to-market returns; 1992 CFA adapted] Bart, a U.S. company, owns the following marketable securities on December 31, 19X1:

| Firm | Shares Owned | Ownership Percentage | Carrying Value* | Investee Data (per share except earnings) | | 19X1 Dividend | 19X1 Earnings |
| | | | | Market Value | | | |
				12/31/X0	12/31/X1		
X	100,000	15%	$50.00	$46.00	$49.00	$0.10	$100,000
Y	800,000	40	35.00	30.00	32.00	0.09	900,000
Z	150,000	10	25.00	27.00	30.00	0.00	100,000

*At 1/1/X0.

Note: Assume that none of the securities are held for trading purposes.

A. Compute the following effects of Bart's investment in marketable securities for 19X1 on reported:

(i) Dividend income

(ii) Unrealized gains and losses

(iii) Equity in income of affiliates

B. Describe the U.S. GAAP accounting method applicable to each investment.

C. Compute Bart's 19X1 reported income from its marketable securities.

D. Compute where possible the balance sheet carrying amount of each security at December 31, 19X1.

E. Calculate Bart's total investment return (mark-to-market basis) on each investment for 19X1.

F. Discuss how each of the following accounting methods would change your answers to parts B, C, and D:

(i) Lower of cost or market for marketable securities

(ii) Consolidation when ownership is 40% or higher

2. [Analysis of investment portfolio] Chubb's 1995 financial statements report the following data regarding its investments:

At December 31, 1995 ($ in millions)	Cost	Market
Fixed maturities		
Held-to-maturity	$3,229	$3,439
Available-for-sale	8,891	9,374
Equity securities	493	588

**Investment Income,
Year Ended December 31, 1995
($ in millions)**

Interest income	$813
Dividend income	16
Realized gains	
Fixed maturities	31
Equity securities	100
Total	$960

The following questions should be answered using the data in Exhibit 13-3 as well as that given above.

A. Describe how each of the three portfolio components listed above is measured (cost or market value) on Chubb's balance sheet.

B. Compute the reported 1995 ROA for each portfolio component (as in Exhibit 13-3C) and compare the results to the reported 1994 ROA.

C. Compute the mark-to-market 1995 ROA for each portfolio component (as in Exhibit 13-3D) and compare the results to the mark-to market 1994 ROA and the reported 1995 ROA.

D. During 1995, U.S. stock and bond prices rose sharply. Discuss whether the reported ROA or mark-to-market ROA provides a better means to evaluate the 1995 performance of Chubb's portfolio. Describe the additional data required to properly evaluate that performance relative to appropriate benchmarks.

3. [Analysis of investment portfolio and effect on financial statements] Exhibit 13P-1 contains data regarding the marketable securities portfolios of Safeco, a large U.S. insurance company. Use these data to answer the following questions.

EXHIBIT 13P-1. SAFECO
Marketable Securities ($ in millions)

Marketable Securities

	December 31		
	1993	1994	1995
Fixed maturities			
Held-to-maturity (at amortized cost)*	$10,721	$ 2,053	$ 2,045
Available-for-sale (at market)†	—	9,509	11,928
Subtotal	$10,721	$11,562	$13,973
Equity securities			
Available-for-sale (at market)‡	910	855	1,119
Total	$11,631	$12,417	$15,092

Note: Preferred shares with fixed redemption dates are included in fixed maturities; all other preferred shares are included in equities.

Gross Investment Income

	December 31	
	1994	1995
Fixed maturities		
Interest income	$908	$ 981
Realized gains (losses)	(9)	29
Subtotal	$899	$1,010
Equity securities		
Dividend income	$ 44	$ 45
Realized gains (losses)	48	36
Subtotal	$ 92	$ 81
Total investment income	$991	$1,091

*Market values: $11,966, $1,948, and $2,388.
†Cost: $0, $9,608, and $10,856.
‡Cost: $513, $565, and $598.
Source: Safeco, *1994–1995 Annual Reports.*

A. Compute the reported ROA for each portfolio component (as in Exhibit 13-3C) for 1994 and 1995. What do these data suggest about investment performance for 1995 compared with 1994?

B. Compute the mark-to-market ROA for each portfolio component (as in Exhibit 13-3D) for 1994 and 1995. What do these data suggest about investment performance for 1995 compared with 1994?

C. U.S. stock and bond prices rose sharply in 1995. Discuss which measure of investment performance (reported ROA or mark-to-market ROA) provides a better measure of the performance of Safeco's portfolios.

D. Discuss how you would evaluate the performance of Safeco's portfolio relative to the markets in which it is invested.

E. In 1995, Safeco reclassified a portion of its held-to-maturity portfolio to the held-for-sale category, in accordance with the FASB implementation guide. These securities had a carrying amount of $331 million and market value of $358 million.

   (i) Describe the effect of the reclassification on reported income and stockholders' equity.

   (ii) Describe the effect of an identical future reclassification on reported income and stockholders' equity.

   (iii) Discuss the likely motivation of Safeco management for this reclassification.

F. Safeco reported pretax income (including securities gains) of $137 million in 1994 and $141 million in 1995.

   (i) Compute the effect on pretax income for both years if Safeco reported its actual return on assets (mark-to-market basis) rather than the returns actually reported.

   (ii) Discuss why managements generally oppose mark-to-market accounting for marketable securities.

   (iii) Discuss how the recognition of only realized gains and losses permits managements to manage reported income.

G. Safeco management suggested at a 1996 meeting with financial analysts that its corporate return on equity should be evaluated with all investments measured at historical cost. Discuss whether you agree with that statement.

4. [Comparison of SFAS 115 and equity method] Company P acquires 100 shares of Company S on January 1, 1996 at $40 per share. Relevant data of S for 1997 are:

Earnings per share	$ 3.00
Dividend per share	1.00
Market price at 12-31-96	37.00

P sells all its shares of S on January 2, 1997 at $39 per share.

A. Compute the carrying amount on December 31, 1996, assuming that P accounts for its investment in S as each of the following:

   (i) Trading security

   (ii) Available-for-sale investment

   (iii) Equity investment

B. Compute the investment income reported by P for 1996, assuming that P accounts for its investment in S as each of the following:

(i) Trading security

(ii) Available-for-sale investment

(iii) Equity investment

C. Compute the total income reported by P on its investment in S over the entire holding period. Discuss the effect of the choice of accounting method on this amount.

5. [Comparison of cost and equity methods; 1988 CFA adapted] Burry acquired 19% of Bowman for $10 million on January 1, 19X0. Bowman's securities are not publicly traded. On January 1, 19X1, Burry purchased an additional 1% share in Bowman for $500,000.

For the years ended December 31, 19X0, and December 31, 19X1, Bowman reported earnings and paid dividends as follows:

	Net Income (Loss)	Dividends Paid
1990	$ (600,000)	$ 800,000
1991	2,000,000	1,000,000

A. Under a strict reading of U.S. GAAP, which method should Burry use to account for its investment in Bowman in 19X0? 19X1?

B. Based on the accounting choices made in part A, how would Burry's financial statements be affected by Bowman's operating results for 19X0 and 19X1?

C. Repeat part B, assuming that Burry applied SFAS 115 in both 19X0 and 19X1.

D. Repeat part B, assuming that Burry used the equity method in both 19X0 and 19X1.

E. Which of the three answers (parts B, C, or D) provides the most useful information in Burry's financial statements regarding its investment in Bowman?

6. [Marketable securities: comparison of cost, equity method, and consolidation; 1989 CFA adapted] The following data are derived from the annual report of the San Francisco Company, a manufacturer of cardboard boxes:

	19X6	19X7	19X8
Sales	$25,000	$30,000	$35,000
Net income	2,000	2,200	2,500
Dividends paid	1,000	1,200	1,500
Book value per share (year-end)	$11.00	$12.00	$13.00

San Francisco had 1,000 common shares outstanding during the entire period. There is no public market for San Francisco shares.

Potter Company, a manufacturer of glassware, made the following acquisitions of San Francisco common shares:

January 1, 19X6   10 shares at $10 per share
January 1, 19X7   290 shares at $11 per share, increasing ownership to 300 shares
January 1, 19X8   700 shares at $15 per share, resulting in 100% ownership of
                   San Francisco

When answering the following questions, ignore income tax effects and the effect of lost income on funds used to make these investments:

A. Calculate the effect of these investments on Potter's reported sales, net income, and cash flow for each of the years 19X6 and 19X7.

B. Calculate the carrying amount of Potter's investment in San Francisco as of December 31, 19X6, and December 31, 19X7.

C. Briefly discuss how Potter would account for its investment in San Francisco during 19X8. State the additional information needed to calculate the effect on Potter's 19X8 financial statements.

Problems 7 to 9 are extensions of the Helmerich & Payne (HP) example in the chapter. Exhibit 13-P2 contains information about HP's marketable securities investments taken from its 1993 through 1995 financial statements. Note that HP carried those investments as noncurrent assets at the lower of cost or market, as required by SFAS 12 prior to the adoption of SFAS 115.

7. [Marketable securities: assessing investment performance]

A. Disaggregate HP's reported income for 1993 and 1994 into the following components:

  (i) Income from operations

  (ii) Income from short-term investments and marketable securities

  (iii) Income from affiliates carried on equity basis

B. Calculate the reported ROA for each component of income calculated in part A (for each year) as well as HP's overall ROA.

C. Discuss the usefulness of the results of parts A and B in explaining HP's operating results for the two years.

D. Calculate each of the following for HP's short-term investments and marketable securities carried at LOCOM, for 1993 and 1994:

  (i) Dividends and interest earned

  (ii) Realized gains and losses

  (iii) Unrealized gains and losses

E. Calculate the mark-to-market return and ROA for HP's short-term investments and marketable securities carried at LOCOM, for 1993 and 1994.

EXHIBIT 13P-2. HELMERICH & PAYNE
Financial Data

Condensed Balance Sheet

December 31	1992	1993	1994	1995
Short-term investments*	$ 13,128	$ 9,109	$ 8,997	$ 8,989
Other current assets	105,553	141,390	113,942	106,005
Current assets	$118,681	$150,499	$122,939	$114,994
Investment in marketable securities	87,780	84,945	87,414	148,596
Property, plant, and equipment	379,043	375,491	414,474	446,575
Total assets	$585,504	$610,935	$624,827	$710,165
Current liabilities	35,881	46,414	46,701	69,611
Noncurrent liabilities	56,337	55,594	53,792	78,119
Stockholders' equity	493,286	508,927	524,334	562,435
Total liabilities and equity	$585,504	$610,935	$624,827	$710,165

* Cost = market value

Condensed Income Statement

Years Ended December 31	1993	1994	1995
Sales	$306,047	$322,698	$314,930
Income from investments	9,050	6,303	10,846
	$315,097	$329,001	$325,776
Operating costs	270,941	298,317	311,660
Interest cost	925	385	407
	$271,866	$298,702	$312,067
Income before taxes and equity income of affiliate	43,231	30,299	13,709
Income tax expense	18,279	10,232	5,044
	$ 24,952	$ 20,067	$ 8,665
Equity in income of affiliate	(402)	904	1,086
	$ 24,550	$ 20,971	$ 9,751

F. HP did not receive any dividends from Atwood Oceanics. Calculate the mark-to-market return and ROA for HP's investment in Atwood for 1993 and 1994.

G. Compare HP's overall mark-to-market returns on its investments (capital appreciation plus dividends and interest) and ROA with those reported for 1993 and 1994.

H. Discuss whether the equity method or mark-to-market return provides a better measure of the performance of Atwood shares over the 1992 to 1994 period.

I. Compute the pretax effect on HP's stockholders' equity of the adoption of SFAS 115 at September 30, 1994.

8. [Equity method, tax rate assumption] HP reports its equity in Atwood's income net of income tax. HP did not receive any dividends from 23.8% owned Atwood.

EXHIBIT 13P-2. (*continued*)

Marketable Securities Held by Helmerich & Payne ($ in thousands)

September 30	1992			1993			1994			1995		
	Shares	Carrying Cost	Market Value	Shares	Carrying Cost	Market Value	Shares	Carrying Cost	Market Value	Shares	Carrying Cost	Market Value
	Equity Basis			*Equity Basis*			*Equity Basis*			*Equity Basis*		
Atwood Oceanics	1,600,000	$19,720	$ 15,200	1,600,000	$19,285	$ 17,200	1,600,000	$20,743	$ 22,800	1,600,000	$22,495	$ 32,100
	LOCOM			*LOCOM*			*LOCOM*			*Available-for-Sale*		
Schlumberger	740,000	23,511	50,043	740,000	23,511	49,303	740,000	23,511	40,238	740,000	23,511	48,378
Sun Company	907,164	10,637	22,112	907,164	10,637	25,854	907,164	10,637	26,081	795,506	8,934	21,184
Phillips Petroleum	300,000	7,470	8,250	300,000	7,470	10,125	300,000	7,470	10,275	240,000	5,976	7,800
Liberty Bancorp	700,000	10,178	18,725	500,000	7,270	17,000	500,000	7,270	16,750	395,000	5,743	14,516
Oryx Energy	756,124	7,271	18,525	700,000	6,683	17,150	675,000	6,433	9,366	625,000	6,032	8,125
Oneok	230,000	2,812	3,996	225,000	2,751	5,006	225,000	2,751	3,796	225,000	2,751	5,231
Other		6,181	6,412		7,338	10,737		8,599	15,706		11,857	20,868
		$68,060	$128,063		$65,660	$135,175		$66,671	$122,212		$64,804	$126,102
Total		$87,780	$143,263		$84,945	$152,375		$87,414	$145,012		$87,299	$158,202
Realized capital gains (pretax)		**$ 1,920**			**$ 2,914**			**$ 124**			**$ 5,697**	

Source: Helmerich & Payne, *1993–1994 Annual Reports.*

A. Calculate Atwood's pretax loss for 1993 and 1994. (*Hint:* Consider the change in HP's carrying amount.)

B. Determine HP's 1993 assumption as to how it would eventually receive income earned by Atwood. (*Hint:* Compute the effective tax rate used for equity income.)

C. Determine HP's 1994 assumption as to how it would eventually receive income earned by Atwood. Discuss a possible reason for the apparent change from the 1993 assumption.

D. Suggest why HP reported its net-of-tax equity in Atwood's income (loss) separately, below after-tax income from other operations.

9. [SFAS 115 and mark-to-market accounting] Helmerich & Payne adopted SFAS 115 on October 1, 1994. Income statement and marketable securities data for the year ended September 30, 1995 are contained in Exhibit 13P-2.

A. HP's reported investment in marketable securities at September 30, 1995 was $148,596,000. Show how that amount was calculated.

B. Net unrealized holding gains included in stockholders' equity at September 30, 1995 were $48,436,000 (net of deferred income tax). Calculate:

(i) The unrealized gains when SFAS 115 was adopted at October 1, 1994

(ii) The change in unrealized gains for the year ended September 30, 1995

Use a 38% tax rate for these calculations.

C. Calculate HP's reported return and ROA on its (combined) short-term investments and available-for-sale portfolio for the year ended September 30, 1995. Discuss how these amounts were affected by the adoption of SFAS 115.

D. Calculate HP's mark-to-market return and ROA on its (combined) short-term investments and available-for-sale portfolio for the year ended September 30, 1995. Discuss how these amounts were affected by the adoption of SFAS 115.

Problems 10 and 11 are based on Moore Motors and Exhibit 13P-3.

Exhibit 13-P3 presents the consolidated financial statements of Moore Motors Company (Moore). Its 100% owned finance subsidiary, MM Finance (MMF), provides financing for the dealers and customers of Moore. MMF's separate balance sheet and income statement are also included.

10. [Finance subsidiaries] Moore's consolidated statements aggregate Moore's manufacturing and its financing operations. The consolidated statements are more useful for some purposes, but it has drawbacks for other types of analysis, and it may be more useful to treat the subsidiary on an equity basis.

A. Prepare a balance sheet for Moore Motors at December 31, 19X8 to 19X9 using the equity method of accounting for MMF.

B. Prepare an income statement for Moore Motors for 19X9 using the equity method of accounting.

EXHIBIT 13P-3. MOORE MOTORS

Balance Sheets, at December 31, 19X8 to 19X9 ($ in thousands)

	Moore Motors Consolidated Balance Sheet		MM Finance	
	19X8	19X9	19X8	19X9
Cash and equivalents	$ 10,181	$ 10,213	$ 3,272	$ 3,143
Accounts receivable				
Trade	4,541	5,447		
Parent			14,840	14,460
Finance receivables	87,477	92,355	74,231	79,120
Inventories	10,020	10,065		
Fixed assets (net)	36,936	39,125	6,698	6,839
Miscellaneous assets	14,908	16,092		
Total assets	$164,063	$173,297	$99,041	$103,562
Accounts payable				
Trade	$ 7,897	$ 7,708		
Parent			$ 3,515	$ 2,898
Bank debt	88,130	93,425	81,875	86,868
Accrued liabilities	27,434	29,861	6,380	6,014
Accrued income tax	4,930	5,671		
Total liabilities	$128,391	$136,665	$91,770	$ 95,780
Common stock	6,702	5,401	500	500
Retained earnings	28,970	31,231	6,771	7,282
Total equity	$ 35,672	$ 36,632	$ 7,271	$ 7,782
Total liabilities and equity	$164,063	$173,297	$99,041	$103,562

Income Statements, for Year Ended December 31, 19X9 ($ in thousands)

	Moore Motors Consolidated	MM Finance
Sales	$110,448	—
Finance revenues	14,504	$14,504
Interest income	1,980	—
Total revenues	$126,932	$14,504
Cost of goods sold	94,683	—
Selling and administrative expense	9,926	3,540
Interest	8,757	7,908
Depreciation and amortization	7,168	1,504
Total expenses	$120,534	$12,952
Pretax income	6,398	1,552
Income tax expense	(2,174)	(441)
Net income	$ 4,224	$ 1,111

EXHIBIT 13P-3. (continued)

Statement of Cash Flows, for Year Ended December 31, 19X9 ($ in thousands)

	Moore Motors Consolidated
Net income	$ 4,224
Depreciation and amortization	7,168
Change in accounts receivable	(906)
Change in inventory	(45)
Change in accrued liabilities	2,427
Change in accrued income tax	741
Change in accounts payable	(189)
Other	(414)
Operating cash flow	$ 13,006
Investment in fixed assets	(9,938)
Sale of fixed assets	228
Investment in finance receivables	(100,689)
Liquidation of finance receivables	95,394
Investing cash flow	$ (15,005)
Increase in bank debt	15,267
Decrease in bank debt	(9,972)
Repurchase of shares	(1,474)
New shares issued	173
Dividends paid	(1,963)
Financing cash flow	$ 2,031
Net change in cash and equivalents	$ 32

C. Compute each of the following ratios for Moore on a fully consolidated basis, and for Moore (with MMF on an equity basis):

    (i) Gross profit margin

    (ii) Return on assets

    (iii) Return on equity

    (iv) Receivables turnover

    (v) Times interest earned

    (vi) Debt-to-equity

D. For each of the six ratios in part C, discuss which of the two reporting methods results in ratios that are most useful for analytic purposes. Justify your choices.

11. [Finance subsidiaries, cash flow analysis] MMF's finance (credit) receivables arise from long-term financing provided by MMF to Moore's customers. MMF "pays" Moore, and the customer repays the loan plus interest to MMF.

A. Discuss Moore's classification of the cash received from such transactions in its cash flow statement. Discuss an adjustment to Moore's cash flow statement that would make that statement a more useful indicator of Moore's ability to generate cash from operations.

B. In Chapter 3, we argue that interest payments should be included in financing cash flows rather than operating cash flows. Evaluate this argument as applied to Moore's (consolidated) interest payments.

C. Moore's consolidated cash flow statement combines cash flows from Moore's manufacturing and MMF's financing activities. Using the data in Exhibit 13P-3 and your answers to parts A and B, prepare 19X9 statements of cash flows (using the direct method) for:

(i) MMF

(ii) Moore's manufacturing operations

D. Using the cash flow statements prepared in part C, compute the cash flow from MMF to Moore's manufacturing operations (from all sources) during 19X9.

E. Discuss how the segmentation of Moore's financial statements aids your understanding of the company's financial condition.

12. [Control requirement for consolidation] On April 12, 1996, Ford Motor announced an increase in its ownership of Mazda Motor, a Japanese company, from 25 to 33.4%. The infusion of $481 million of additional equity was required by Mazda's weak financial condition. The announcement also stated that:

- Henry Wallace, a Ford executive, would be President of Mazda.
- Additional Ford personnel would be added to Mazda management.
- Mazda's board contains seven Ford-nominated directors, four of whom hold executive positions in Mazda.

The Economist (April 20, 1996, p. 57) stated that these changes give Ford "de facto control" over Mazda. Ford accounts for its investment in Mazda using the equity method of accounting.

A. Discuss the effect of the increase of ownership on Ford's accounting for the Mazda investment under current U.S. GAAP.

B. Discuss whether the new definition of control in the FASB exposure draft (Box 13-3) would change the answer to part A. Your answer should include a discussion of any additional information required.

C. Regardless of GAAP requirements, discuss whether the analysis of Ford would be improved by:

(i) Applying proportionate consolidation to the investment in Mazda

(ii) Fully consolidating Mazda

13. [Proportionate consolidation] Mobil uses the equity method to account for its investments in affiliates owned 50% or less. Exhibit 13P-4 contains condensed financial statements for Mobil and summarized financial information for its unconsolidated equity affiliates.

A. Prepare a *pro forma* 1995 balance sheet and income statement for Mobil with its affiliates:

(i) Fully consolidated

(ii) Proportionately consolidated

EXHIBIT 13P-4. MOBIL CORPORATION
Condensed Financial Statements ($ in millions)

Consolidated Balance Sheet

At December 31	1995
Assets	
Current assets	$12,056
Investments and long-term receivables	4,184
Other assets	25,898
Total assets	$42,138
Liabilities and Shareholders' Equity	
Current liabiiities	$13,054
Long-term debt	4,629
Other long-term liabilities	6,504
Total liabilities	$24,187
Shareholders' equity	17,951
Total liabilities and equity	$42,138

Consolidated Statement of Income

Year ended December 31	1995
Revenues	
Sales and services[1]	$73,413
Income from equity investments, and other	1,957
Total revenues	$75,370
Costs and expenses	
Operating costs and expenses	51,960
Taxes other than income taxes[1]	19,019
Income taxes	2,015
Total costs and expenses	$72,994
Net income	$ 2,376

[1]Includes excise and state gasoline taxes of $8,646
Source: Adapted from Mobil 1995 Annual Report

B. Compute the following ratios for Mobil (as reported) and, using the *pro forma* statements prepared in parts A(i) and A(ii):

    (i) Current ratio

    (ii) Long-term debt-to-equity

    (iii) Pretax income to sales

    (iv) Effective tax rate

    (v) Pretax return on assets

C. Summarize the impact on Mobil of the *pro forma* adjustments, using the results of part B.

EXHIBIT 13P-4. (*continued*)

12. Summary Financial Information of Unconsolidated Equity Affiliates

Summary financial information for affiliated companies (owned 50% or less) accounted for on the equity method is shown in the table below. Mobil's investment in these companies is included in Investments and Long-term Receivables. The equity affiliates are primarily engaged in producing, refining and marketing in Germany, the Middle East, Japan and elsewhere in the Asia-Pacific region, and petrochemical and lube manufacturing in the Middle East. Also included are interests in several pipeline ventures.

Undistributed earnings of the equity affiliates included in Earnings Retained in the Business were $735 million at December 31, 1995. Dividends received from these companies were $276 million in 1993, $203 million in 1994 and $346 million in 1995.

Accounts and Notes Receivable in the Consolidated Balance Sheet include $171 million and $227 million at December 31, 1994 and 1995, respectively, of amounts due from equity affiliates. Accounts Payable include $459 million and $531 million at December 31, 1994 and 1995, respectively, of amounts due to equity affiliates.

Equity method affiliates (In millions)	1993		1994		1995	
	Total	Mobil Share	Total	Mobil Share	**Total**	**Mobil Share**
Current assets	$ 9,565	$ 2,954	$ 8,559	$ 2,639	**$ 8,345**	**$ 2,678**
Noncurrent assets	9,449	3,121	11,366	3,637	**12,220**	**3,735**
Current liabilities	(7,437)	(2,373)	(7,865)	(2,493)	**(8,027)**	**(2,643)**
Long-term debt	(2,179)	(791)	(2,271)	(822)	**(2,520)**	**(758)**
Other liabilities	(1,909)	(518)	(2,101)	(576)	**(2,122)**	**(595)**
Net assets	$ 7,489	$ 2,393	$ 7,688	$ 2,385	**$ 7,896**	**$ 2,417**
Gross revenues	$ 25,766	$ 8,125	$ 27,600	$ 8,696	**$ 31,324**	**$ 9,835**
Income before taxes	$ 1,370	$ (105)	$ 1,175	$ 349	**$ 1,360**	**$ 466**
Net income	857	11	578	187[1]	**1,088**	**397**
Capital expenditures	$ 824	$ 238	$ 1,711	$ 421	**$ 1,650**	**$ 337**

[1] Includes $56 million charge related to the LCM change in accounting principle (see Note 4 on page 38).

Source: Mobil, *1995 Annual Report.*

14. [Minority interest] The following data were obtained from the *1991 Annual Report* of Nucor Corporation, which has a 51% owned consolidated subsidiary:

Minority interest at December 31, 1990	$105,441,000
Minority interest at December 31, 1991	124,048,000
Distribution to minority interest (1991 financing cash flow)	(7,507,000)

A. Nucor's operating cash flow reported minority interest for 1991. From the data given, compute that amount and explain its significance.

B. Using the data provided and the result of part A, compute the net profit and return on average equity of the subsidiary for 1991.

EXHIBIT 13P-5. LUMEX
Segment Data

NOTE H — BUSINESS SEGMENT INFORMATION

The Company conducts manufacturing operations principally in two industries, the medical equipment industry through its Lumex division ("Lumex") and the exercise equipment industry through its Cybex division ("Cybex"). In addition, the Company's wholly-owned captive finance subsidiary, Cybex Financial Corp. ("CFC"), provides capital equipment financing to customers of both Lumex and Cybex.

Operating results and other financial data are presented for each business segment of the Company for the three years ended December 31, 1994, 1993 and 1992:

| | Year ended December 31, | | |
(in thousands)	1994	1993	1992
Net sales:			
Lumex	$ 60,764	$ 54,187	$ 50,038
Cybex	70,420	54,781	53,850
Consolidated	131,184	108,968	103,888
Operating profit (loss):			
Lumex	4,012	3,881	3,445
Cybex	2,218	(692)	3,690
CFC	543	215	9
Corporate & other	(2,194)	(1,446)	(1,119)
Non recurring charges	–	(3,160)	–
Consolidated	4,579	(1,202)	6,025
Identifiable assets:			
Lumex	28,659	24,756	24,297
Cybex	37,087	32,117	31,452
CFC	12,128	13,223	2,868
Corporate & other	16,294	15,670	10,420
Consolidated	94,168	85,766	69,037
Capital expenditures:			
Lumex	1,532	1,481	603
Cybex	2,047	1,736	1,550
Corporate & other	35	46	10
Consolidated	3,614	3,263	2,163
Depreciation & amortization:			
Lumex	1,568	1,283	1,142
Cybex	1,671	1,523	1,382
Corporate & other	(15)	22	19
Consolidated	3,224	2,828	2,543

Intersegment sales are immaterial. CFC provides financing for certain capital equipment sales as further described in Note G. CFC treats these lease transactions as direct finance leases whereby the equipment sales and cost of sales are reflected on the books of the respective manufacturing segment while CFC retains all financing revenue.

Operating profit (loss) by segment represents, for Lumex and Cybex, net sales less operating expenses including certain administrative costs allocated on a reasonable basis consistently applied. The operating profit of CFC reflects financing revenue.

Source: Lumex, *1994 Annual Report.*

C. Discuss the conditions under which the proportionate consolidation method would be more appropriate for this subsidiary.

D. Discuss the advantages and disadvantages of the proportionate consolidation method in this case from the point of view of:

(i) Nucor's management

(ii) A financial analyst

15. [Analysis of segment data] Exhibit 13P-5 contains industry segment data reported by Lumex in its *1994 Annual Report*. Use these data to answer the following questions.

A. Compute the following ratios for each segment for the years 1992 to 1994:

(i) Operating profit margin

(ii) Return on assets

(iii) Asset turnover

(iv) Capital expenditures-to-depreciation

B. For each ratio calculated in A, discuss what information the level and trend of that ratio convey about the business segment.

C. Discuss the limitations of segment data, both in terms of trends within the company over time and comparisons with similar segments of other companies.

D. Discuss what additional information you would require to improve your analysis of segment operations.

E. In 1996, Lumex sold its Lumex segment for cash and restated its financial statements to show the Lumex segment as a discontinued operation. Discuss whether the segment data shown in Exhibit 13P-5 permitted financial statement users to anticipate the effect of that divestiture on the company.

16. [Analysis of geographic segment data] Exhibit 13P-6 contains geographic segment data from the *1995 Annual Report* of Coca-Cola. Use the exhibit data to answer the following questions.

A. Compute the following ratios for each segment for the years 1993 to 1995:

(i) Operating profit margin

(ii) Return on assets

(iii) Asset turnover

(iv) Capital expenditures-to-depreciation

B. For each ratio calculated in A, discuss what information the level and trend of that ratio convey about the business segment.

C. Discuss the limitations of segment data, both in terms of trends within the company over time and comparisons with similar segments of other companies.

D. Discuss what additional information you would require to improve your analysis of segment operations.

EXHIBIT 13P-6. THE COCA-COLA COMPANY AND SUBSIDIARIES
Geographic Segment Data

19. Operations in Geographic Areas

Effective February 1, 1996, the Company's operating management structure will consist of five geographic groups and Coca-Cola Foods, and the International and North America Business Sectors will cease to exist. Information about the Company's operations by geographic area is as follows (in millions):

	United States	Africa	Greater Europe	Latin America	Middle & Far East & Canada	Corporate	Consolidated
1995							
Net operating revenues	$ 5,261	$ 595	$ 6,025	$ 1,920	$ 4,162	$ 55	$ 18,018
Operating income	840[2]	206	1,300[2]	797	1,437	(488)	4,092
Identifiable operating assets	3,384	348	4,301	1,294	1,539	1,461[1]	12,327
Equity income						169	169
Investments (principally bottling companies)						2,714	2,714
Capital expenditures	285	19	383	88	85	77	937
Depreciation and amortization	146	8	180	31	23	66	454
1994							
Net operating revenues	$ 5,092	$ 522	$ 5,047	$ 1,928	$ 3,551	$ 41	$ 16,181
Operating income	869	182	1,173	713	1,208	(429)	3,716
Identifiable operating assets	2,991	357	3,958	1,164	1,437	1,456[1]	11,363
Equity income						134	134
Investments (principally bottling companies)						2,510	2,510
Capital expenditures	252	27	330	129	51	89	878
Depreciation and amortization	128	6	160	36	21	60	411
1993							
Net operating revenues	$ 4,586	$ 255	$ 4,456	$ 1,683	$ 2,957	$ 26	$ 13,963
Operating income	782[3]	152	1,029[3]	582	1,005	(442)[3]	3,108
Identifiable operating assets	2,682	153	3,287	1,220	1,184	1,280[1]	9,806
Equity income						91[3]	91
Investments (principally bottling companies)						2,215	2,215
Capital expenditures	165	6	366	141	45	77	800
Depreciation and amortization	127	3	120	33	18	59	360

Intercompany transfers between geographic areas are not material.

Certain prior year amounts related to net operating revenues and operating income have been reclassified to conform to the current year presentation.

Identifiable liabilities of operations outside the United States amounted to approximately $2.7 billion on December 31, 1995, $2.5 billion on December 31, 1994, and $1.9 billion on December 31, 1993.

[1]*Corporate identifiable operating assets are composed principally of marketable securities, finance subsidiary receivables and fixed assets.*

[2]*Operating income for the United States and Greater Europe was reduced by $61 million and $25 million, respectively, for provisions to increase efficiencies.*

[3]*Operating income for the United States, Greater Europe and Corporate was reduced by $13 million, $33 million and $17 million, respectively, for provisions to increase efficiencies. Equity income was reduced by $42 million related to restructuring charges recorded by Coca-Cola Beverages Ltd.*

Compound Growth Rates Ending 1995	United States	Africa	Greater Europe	Latin America	Middle & Far East & Canada	Consolidated
Net operating revenues						
5 years	6%	24%	14%	19%	15%	12%
10 years	5%	9%	20%	16%	15%	12%
Operating income						
5 years	14%	16%	12%	22%	17%	16%
10 years	10%	9%	20%	24%	20%	18%

Source: The Coca-Cola Company, *1995 Annual Report.*

14

ANALYSIS OF BUSINESS COMBINATIONS

CHAPTER OUTLINE

CHAPTER OBJECTIVES

INTRODUCTION

ACCOUNTING FOR ACQUISITIONS
Conditions Necessary for Use of the Pooling of Interests Method

ILLUSTRATION OF THE PURCHASE AND POOLING METHODS
The Purchase Method
The Pooling of Interests Method

EFFECTS OF ACCOUNTING METHODS
Comparison of Balance Sheets
Comparison of Income Statements
Cash Flow Statement Effects
  Deducing Assets and Liabilities Acquired
  Distortion of Cash from Operations
Impact on Ratios

COMPLICATING FACTORS IN PURCHASE METHOD ACQUISITIONS
Contingent Payments
In-Process Research and Development

INCOME TAX EFFECTS OF BUSINESS COMBINATIONS

INTERNATIONAL DIFFERENCES IN ACCOUNTING FOR BUSINESS COMBINATIONS
Differences in Treatment of Goodwill

ILLUSTRATION OF INTERNATIONAL DIFFERENCES: THE ACQUISITION ACTIVITIES OF SMITHKLINE BEECHAM
Differences in Accounting Methods
The Merged Balance Sheet
  Comparison of Stockholders' Equity
Balance Sheet Restatement
Income Statement Effects
Income Statement Restatement
Financial Ratio Effects
Summary

ANALYSIS OF GOODWILL
Goodwill Amortization

CHOOSING THE ACQUISITION METHOD
Income Maximization as Motivation for the Pooling/Purchase Choice
Market Reaction and the Pooling/Purchase Choice
Interpreting the Research Results

Other Factors Influencing Mergers, Bid Premia,
and the Pooling/Purchase Choice
  Characteristics of the Transaction
  Characteristics of the Acquirer
  Characteristics of the Target
Summary

PUSH-DOWN ACCOUNTING

Push-Down in Practice: The GM–Hughes
Transaction
Impact on the Balance Sheet
Impact on the Income Statement
Effect on Cash Flows
Effect on Financial Ratios
Push-Down Summed Up

SPINOFFS

Analysis of Spinoffs
Reasons for Investment in Spinoffs
Example: Emerson Electric's Spinoff of ESCO
Electronics

SUMMARY

**CASE 14-1: ANALYSIS OF A PURCHASE
METHOD ACQUISITION: GEORGIA PACIFIC'S
PURCHASE OF GREAT NORTHERN NEKOOSA**

**CASE 14-2: ANALYSIS OF A POOLING METHOD
ACQUISITION: THE CONAGRA–GOLDEN
VALLEY MERGER**

CHAPTER OBJECTIVES

Chapter 14 examines the accounting and analysis issues related to business combinations, spinoffs, and other forms of corporate reorganization. In this chapter, we:

1. Explain the mechanics of the pooling of interests and purchase methods of accounting for business combinations.

2. Consider the conditions that determine which method is used.

3. Compare the effects of the two methods on post-acquisition balance sheet, income, and cash flow statements.

4. Describe the effects of the two methods on financial ratios.

5. Consider the analytical significance of acquisition goodwill.

6. Discuss international differences in acquisition accounting and the treatment of goodwill.

7. Review factors that affect management motivations when choosing an acquisition accounting method.

8. Explain how push-down accounting affects financial statements and ratios.

9. Describe the special factors in the analysis of corporate spinoffs.

INTRODUCTION

Corporate reorganizations have become an increasingly important aspect of the international financial landscape in recent years. Acquisitions and divestitures of portions of operating segments or entire lines of business are used to modify existing levels of horizontal and vertical integration, diversify, increase market share, improve operating efficiency, and increase the market value of the firm.

Financial restructuring, on the other hand, alters the capital structure of a firm, increasing its debt burden. Capital structure may also be changed through reorganizations in bankruptcy, quasireorganizations, recapitalizations, and initial public offerings or secondary issues of stock in subsidiaries.

In the case of mergers or acquisitions, the use of a new accounting basis or continuation of the historical carrying amounts affects the preparation of subsequent financial statements for the combined operations of the two entities. The most significant issue for financial analysts is the comparability of reported results before and after acquisitions, given different reporting methods. Since sales, income, and return measures of the combined entity following the combination differ from those of the acquirer alone, the question is whether and how to restate reported results to facilitate comparisons of pre- and postmerger operations.

When a subsidiary acquired using the purchase method provides separate financial statements, another issue arises. Should the new basis be "pushed down" into those separate statements? This issue is important because these transactions often generate substantial goodwill and the implications for equity and liability valuation can be quite complex.

Many economic and financial reporting considerations affect the accounting method chosen to report acquisitions; it is important to understand management incentives for these choices. Much has been written in recent years regarding the comparative merits of the different methods of accounting for business combinations, their differential ability to obscure the "true" operating results, and their impact on international competition because of international tax and reporting differences. Although this chapter shows how each of these methods may have these effects, its objectives are to enable the financial analyst to interpret postacquisition financial statements prepared using either method and to provide some insights into management decisions.

The chapter begins with an explanation and simplified illustration of the purchase and pooling methods of accounting for mergers and acquisitions, followed by a comparison of their impact on financial statements and ratios. The SmithKline Beecham merger shows how differences in acquisition accounting methods hamper the comparison of firms in different countries. Next, we provide a discussion of the issue of acquisition goodwill followed by a review of empirical research into market reaction and management incentives to engage in acquisition activities.

The following sections examine push-down accounting and the significant accounting and analysis issues raised by spinoffs.

The chapter contains two cases that extend the analysis to two actual business combinations. The first case, based on the purchase method acquisition of Great Northern Nekoosa by Georgia Pacific, requires restatement to the pooling method, with very different financial statement effects. The second case reverses direction, asking for the restatement of the ConAgra–Golden Valley merger, which was reported using the pooling method, as a purchase. These restatements facilitate a comparison of financial statements and ratios resulting from the use of these two methods.

ACCOUNTING FOR ACQUISITIONS

Financial reporting rules for acquisitions in the United States depend on whether the transaction results in a change in control. Transactions in which one entity acquires the ownership interest of the stockholders of another entity trigger changes in control, requiring a new accounting basis for the acquired assets and liabilities. The *purchase method* of accounting treats such acquisitions as a purchase of the assets and assumption of the liabilities of the acquired or target firm, by the buyer.

The purchase method requires the allocation of the purchase price to all identifiable tangible and intangible assets and liabilities, regardless of whether they were recognized in the financial statements of the acquired company. *As a result, the assets and liabilities of the acquired company are received into the financial statements of the acquirer at their fair market values at the acquisition date.* The resulting postmerger balance sheets are not comparable to the preacquisition balance sheet of the acquirer.

The income and cash flow statements include the operating results of the acquired company effective with the date of acquisition. Operating results prior to the merger are not restated, although pro forma *data on a combined basis may be disclosed.* Like the balance sheet, pre- and postmerger income and cash flow statements are not comparable.

Some business combinations are assumed to merge the ownership interests of two firms rather than transfer control from the stockholders of one entity to those of the surviving firm. When such transactions meet certain restrictive conditions, they are reported using the *pooling of interests method* (merger accounting). The nature of the pooling of interests method is clearly defined in para. 12 of APB 16 (1970):

> The pooling of interests method accounts for a business combination as the uniting of the ownership interests of two or more companies by exchange of equity securities. No acquisition is recognized because the combination is accomplished without disbursing resources of the constituents. Ownership interests continue and the former bases of accounting are retained.

Pooling differs from the purchase method in the following respects:

1. The two parties are treated identically; there is no acquirer or acquired firm.
2. The financial statements are consolidated without adjustment; fair market values are not recognized for either company.
3. Operating results for the combined firm are restated for periods prior to the merger date.

Conditions Necessary for Use of the Pooling of Interests Method

APB 16 sets the conditions under which the pooling method can be used to account for an acquisition. The major requirements follow:

1. Each of the combining companies is independent; pooling is precluded when either has been a subsidiary or division of another company within two years prior to the merger. Significant intercompany stockholdings also preclude pooling.
2. Only voting common shares can be issued; the use of multiple classes of common or other securities (e.g., nonvoting preferred) violates the risk sharing that underlies the pooling concept.
3. Stock reacquisitions (other than normal purchases, such as for use in employee benefit plans) are prohibited, as are special distributions or other changes in

capital structure prior to the merger. These provisions are also intended to preserve the "uniting of equity interests." In the SmithKline Beecham example, discussed later in the chapter, special distributions to stockholders prior to the merger precluded pooling in the United States.

4. Absence of planned transactions that have the effect of benefiting some shareholders. For example, the combined company could not agree to tender for shares to guarantee some stockholders a fixed price for their shares.

5. The combined company must not intend to dispose of a significant portion of the existing businesses of the combining companies, other than duplicate facilities or excess capacity.

The pooling of interests method of accounting can be used only if *all* these conditions are met. The purchase method is required if any one of the conditions is violated. Thus, strictly speaking, the methods are not alternatives for any given transaction.

In practice, however, transaction terms are usually designed to achieve specific reporting objectives. Companies planning an acquisition prepare *pro forma* financial statements to estimate the impact of a proposed transaction and evaluate different terms and their different accounting consequences.[1] Even in the case of unfriendly acquisitions, for example, American Telephone's acquisition of NCR in 1991, pooling treatment can be obtained by restructuring the terms after the surrender.

ILLUSTRATION OF THE PURCHASE AND POOLING METHODS

The application of the purchase and pooling methods of accounting is illustrated by the Acquire Corporation's acquisition of the Target Company for $490 million on June 30, 1996. Scenario A assumes that Acquire raises the funds by selling new common stock. This assumption isolates the accounting effects of the two methods so that their impact on the financial statements and ratios of the combined firm can be seen. In practice, purchase transactions are rarely financed by equity alone. Scenario B assumes that the acquisition of Acquire by Target is financed by a mix of cash, debt, and equity.

Exhibit 14-1 presents the preacquisition balance sheets of both companies and the fair market values of Target's assets and liabilities on the acquisition date. Prior to the acquisition, Target has common equity of $250 million ($500 million assets less $250 million liabilities). The adjustments of Target's assets and liabilities to fair market value are typical of those found in real companies.

The Purchase Method

Application of the purchase method requires that all assets and liabilities of the target entity be revalued to fair market value. In addition, previously unrecognized contingencies and off-balance-sheet items must also be recognized. Examples include lawsuits and environmental contingencies as well as employee benefit plans.

---

[1]See, for example, Michael S. Devine, "Using Pro Forma Allocations to Evaluate Business Purchases," *Financial Executive*, June 1981, pp 15–18.

EXHIBIT 14-1. ACQUIRE AND TARGET
Comparative Balance Sheets at June 30, 1996 ($ in millions)

| | Historical Cost | | | | Fair Value | |
	Acquire		Target		Target	
Cash	$100		$ 75		$ 75	
Inventories	200		100		150	
Receivables	200		75		75	
Current assets		$ 500		$250		$300
Property		500		250		350
Goodwill*		0		0		70
Total assets		$1,000		$500		$720
Payables	150		50		50	
Accrued liabilities	100		50		50	
Current liabilities		$ 250		$100		$100
Long-term debt		250		150		130
Common stock	400		225			
Retained earnings	100		25			
Common equity		500		250		490†
Total equities		$1,000		$500		$720

*See text discussion of the purchase method for allocation rules.

†Acquire has agreed to pay $490 million for Target's net assets; the $490 million presented for common equity reflects that purchase price.

Inventories carried at the lower of cost or market value are frequently reported at amounts below fair value, especially when the last-in, first-out (LIFO) inventory method is employed. Property is another common area of adjustment; in an inflationary world, fair value usually exceeds historical cost. The use of accelerated depreciation methods by the acquired firm may also result in understated asset values.

The adjustment to long-term debt depends on the current level of interest rates, as compared with the interest rate imbedded in the company's long-term debt. In the case of Target, we assume that the interest rate on the company's long-term debt is below current rates. The fair market value of this debt is the present value, at the current interest rate, of the cash flows (both principal and interest) required by the company's debt or $130 million in this case, which is below the face amount ($150 million) of the debt. When the current interest rate is below the historic rate, then the present value exceeds the face amount.[2]

[2]Note that SFAS 107, Disclosures About Fair Value of Financial Instruments, requires footnote disclosures of the fair value of debt and other financial assets and liabilities.

Having determined the fair values of assets and liabilities, we compare the net amount with the purchase price:

Assets at fair market value	$650 million
Liabilities at fair market value	(230)
Net assets at fair market value	$420 million

The purchase price of $490 million is $70 million higher than the fair value of net assets. Once all tangible assets and liabilities are restated at fair market value, any excess, residual purchase price must be allocated to intangible assets. Identifiable intangibles include:

- Patents
- Customer lists
- Licenses
- Brand names

Any excess purchase price that cannot be attributed to identifiable intangibles must be accounted for as a general intangible, usually called goodwill.[3] In Target's case, we cannot attribute any of the purchase price to identifiable intangibles and the $70 million excess purchase price must be treated as goodwill.

Alternatively, the fair value of the net assets acquired may exceed the purchase price of the entire company.[4] In this case, the purchase method requires that the fair value of property be reduced to the extent necessary to equate the net fair value of assets to the purchase price. In such cases, the new carrying amount of property may be less than its fair market value.

Exhibit 14-2A (column 5) shows the postmerger consolidated balance sheet under the purchase method. Note that Target's common equity has not been carried forward; it has been eliminated as a result of the merger. The combined common equity equals the sum of Acquire's preacquisition and newly issued equity, the latter stated at market value.

The combined balance sheet carries forward the assets and liabilities of Acquire without any change; adjustments are made only to the assets and liabilities of Target. If Target had purchased Acquire, the results would be quite different. Acquire's assets and liabilities would be restated, and Target's would remain unchanged.

The application of the purchase method of accounting to the balance sheet can be summarized as follows:

1. The purchase price is allocated to the assets and liabilities of the acquired firm; all assets and liabilities are restated to their fair market value.

---

[3]Goodwill is the excess purchase price over the fair market value of all identifiable assets net of all identifiable liabilities. It is one of the most controversial subjects in the accounting literature, as discussed in a later section of this chapter. Both the FASB and U.K. Accounting Standards Board have undertaken projects on accounting for goodwill.

[4]This may be due to unrecognized obligations or a low rate of return on assets.

EXHIBIT 14-2A
Comparison of Purchase and Pooling Methods: Scenario A (All Stock)

Consolidated Balance Sheets at June 30, 1996 ($ in millions)

	(1)		(2)	(3)	(4)		(5)
	Historical Cost			Pooling	Purchase Method		
	Acquire		Target	Consolidated	Adjustments		Consolidated
Cash	$ 100		$ 75	$ 175	$ 0		$ 175
Inventories	200		100	300	50		350
Receivables	200		75	275	0		275
Current assets	$ 500		$250	$ 750	$ 50		$ 800
Property	500		250	750	100		850
Goodwill*	0		0	0	70		70
Total assets	$1,000		$500	$1,500	$220		$1,720
Payables	150		50	200	0		200
Accrued liabilities	100		50	150	0		150
Current liabilities	$ 250		$100	$ 350	0		$ 350
Long-term debt	250		150	400	(20)		380
Common stock	400	225		625	265	890	
Retained earning	100	25		125	(25)	100	
Common equities	500		250	750	240†		990
Total equity	$1,000		$500	$1,500	$220		$1,720
Current ratio	2.00X		2.50X	2.14X			2.29X
Debt-to-equity ratio	50.00%		60.00%	53.33%			38.38%

*See text discussion of the purchase method for allocation rules.
†The net adjustment of $240 million reflects the purchase and retirement of all Target's equity ($225 million common stock + $25 million retained earnings) and the issuance of Acquire common stock with a market value of $490 million: $490 million − $250 million = $240 million.

2. The restated net fair value is compared with the purchase price; any excess purchase price over net fair value is attributed to identifiable intangible assets when possible, otherwise to goodwill.

3. If the restated net fair value exceeds the purchase price, then the write-up of property is reduced until equality is achieved.

4. The common equity of the acquired firm is eliminated.

The Pooling of Interests Method

The pooling method is illustrated using the same purchase method transaction. However, to meet the pooling method's requirement for an exchange of common stock, we restructure the transaction. We now assume that Acquire exchanges its shares directly for those of Target. The postmerger balance sheet is also shown in Exhibit 14-2A (column 3) and is simply the summation of Target and Acquire's balance sheets.

Notice that the pooling method is similar to consolidation of a previously unconsolidated subsidiary, as discussed in Chapter 13. All assets and liabilities of the two firms are combined (and intercompany accounts eliminated), without any adjustment for fair values. When the pooling method is used, fair market values are irrelevant to recording the combination. *The actual market price and premium paid for the acquired firm are suppressed from both the balance sheet and income statement.*

Unlike the purchase method, the pooling method is symmetrical. The accounting result is identical whether Target is being acquired or is the firm making the acquisition. Note that the common equity of the two firms is simply combined. Neither company's share price has any bearing on the accounting result.[5]

EFFECTS OF ACCOUNTING METHODS

Comparison of Balance Sheets

Scenario A: Acquisition Funded by Sales of Common Stock. Exhibit 14-2A shows that the two methods produce very different postmerger balance sheets. Yet the economic reality resulting from the transaction is identical (if we ignore, for the moment, income tax effects), regardless of the accounting method used.

The differences between the balance sheets under the purchase method (column 5) and the pooling method (column 3) result from recognition of the market value of the transaction and the fair values of Target's assets and liabilities. As a result, a number of financial ratios are changed; we show two examples within the exhibit.

The current ratio is higher under the purchase method because of the adjustment of the acquired firm's current assets to their higher fair market value. The debt-to-equity ratio is lower under the purchase method because the newly issued equity of Acquire is reported at market value rather than at the preacquisition equity of Target.

These ratio effects are dependent on the use of equity as the acquisition medium. We now evaluate the differences between the purchase and pooling method using a more realistic purchase transaction involving the use of a mixture of cash, debt, and equity.

Scenario B: Acquisition Funded by Cash, Debt, and Equity. Exhibit 14-2B depicts the balance sheets under the two methods when the purchase is funded with the following mixture of cash, debt, and equity:

---

[5]Share prices have no effect on the accounting result once the terms of the deal have been set. They do, however, affect the basic terms of the transaction and the exchange ratio and may affect, as will be discussed, the choice of accounting method.

EXHIBIT 14-2B
Comparison of Purchase and Pooling Methods: Scenario B (Cash + Debt + Stock)

Consolidated Balance Sheets at June 30, 1996 ($ in millions)

	(1)	(2)	(3)	(4)	(5)
	Historical Cost		Pooling Consolidated	Purchase Method	
	Acquire	Target		Adjustments	Consolidated
Cash	$ 100	$ 75	$ 175	$(100)	$ 75
Inventories	200	100	300	50	350
Receivables	200	75	275	—	275
Current assets	$ 500	$250	$ 750	$ (50)	$ 700
Property	500	250	750	100	850
Goodwill*	0	0	0	70	70
Total assets	$1,000	$500	$1,500	$ 120	$1,620
Payables	150	50	200	0	200
Accrued liabilities	100	50	150	0	150
Current liabilities	$ 250	$100	$ 350	0	$ 350
Long-term debt†	250	150	400	170	570
Common stock‡	400	225	625	(25)	600
Retained earning	100	25	125	(25)	100
Common equity	500	250	750	(50)	700
Total equities	$1,000	$500	$1,500	$ 120	$1,620
Current ratio	2.00X	2.50X	2.14X		2.00X
Debt-to-equity ratio	50.00%	60.00%	53.33%		81.43%

*See text discussion of the purchase method for allocation rules.
†The net adjustment of $170 million reflects the issuance of $190 million of debt less the write-down of Target's debt by $20 million to its fair value.
‡The net adjustment of $(50) million is the issuance of $200 million of Acquire common stock less the elimination of Target's equity ($225 million of common stock and $25 million of retained earnings).

Cash	$100 million
Debt (issued at the current interest rate[6])	190
Equity	200
Total purchase price	$490 million

As in Exhibit 14-2A, the balance sheet differences reflect the recognition of the market value of the transaction and the fair values of Target's assets and liabilities. The use of cash depresses the current ratio, but that decline is partially offset by the recognition of the fair value of Target's current assets. The net impact is a function

[6]Note that the actual cost of borrowing depends on market and firm-specific factors including, but not limited to, postacquisition leverage, market perceptions of the acquisition, and the debt maturity.

of the proportion of cash and other current assets used relative to the adjustment for fair value of the target's current assets.

The use of debt generates a substantial increase in leverage as depicted by the higher reported debt-to-equity ratio. The lower equity and total assets also affect return measures after the acquisition.

The pooling method balance sheet, *which* (consistent with APB16) *still assumes an all-stock transaction,* is unchanged from Exhibit 14-2A.

Comparison of Income Statements

The acquisition method also affects the income statement. The funding mix is another factor; we will discuss the impact of both purchase method scenarios. Exhibit 14-3

EXHIBIT 14-3. ACQUIRE AND TARGET
Income Statements, 1995 to 1997 ($ in millions)

| | Years Ended December 31 | | | |
	1995	1996	1996*	1997
Target				
Sales	$ 600	$ 660	$ 340	$ 726
Cost of goods sold	(300)	(330)	(170)	(363)
Gross margin	$ 300	$ 330	$ 170	$ 363
Selling expense	(115)	(125)	(65)	(135)
Depreciation expense	(25)	(28)	(14)	(32)
Interest expense	(10)	(10)	(5)	(10)
Pretax income	$ 150	$ 167	$ 86	$ 186
Income tax expense	(50)	(56)	(29)	(62)
Net income	$ 100	$ 111	$ 57	$ 124
Gross margin as a % of sales	50.00%	50.00%	50.00%	50.00%
Interest coverage ratio	16.00	17.70	18.20	19.60
Acquire				
Sales	$1,000	$1,000	$ 500	$1,000
Cost of goods sold	(600)	(600)	(300)	(600)
Gross margin	$ 400	$ 400	$ 200	$ 400
Selling expense	(130)	(130)	(65)	(130)
Depreciation expense	(50)	(50)	(25)	(50)
Interest expense	(20)	(20)	(10)	(20)
Pretax income	$ 200	$ 200	$ 100	$ 200
Income tax expense	(68)	(68)	(34)	(68)
Net income	$ 132	$ 132	$ 66	$ 132
Gross margin as a % of sales	40.00%	40.00%	40.00%	40.00%
Interest coverage ratio	11.00	11.00	11.00	11.00

*Six months ended December 31.

EXHIBIT 14-4
Purchase Method Consolidated Income Statements: Scenario B, 1996 and 1997
($ in millions)

I. Year Ended December 31, 1996

	Acquire	Target	Adjustments	Consolidated
Sales	$1,000	$ 340	$—	$1,340
Cost of goods sold	(600)	(170)	(30)	(800)
Gross margin	$ 400	$ 170	$(30)	$ 540
Selling expense*	(130)	(65)	(1)	(196)
Depreciation expense	(50)	(14)	(5)	(69)
Interest expense	(20)	(5)	(10)	(35)
Pretax income	$ 200	$ 86	$(46)	$ 240
Income tax expense	(68)	(29)	15	(82)
Net income	$ 132	$ 57	$(31)	$ 158
Gross margin (% of sales)	40.00%	50.00%	NA	40.30%
Interest coverage ratio	11.00	18.20	NA	7.86

II. Year Ended December 31, 1997

	Acquire	Target	Adjustments	Consolidated
Sales	$1,000	$ 726	$—	$1,726
Cost of goods sold	(600)	(363)	(20)	(983)
Gross margin	$ 400	$ 363	$(20)	$ 743
Selling expense*	(130)	(135)	(2)	(267)
Depreciation expense	(50)	(32)	(10)	(92)
Interest expense	(20)	(10)	(22)	(52)
Pretax income	$ 200	$ 186	$(54)	$ 332
Income tax expense	(68)	(62)	17	(113)
Net income	$ 132	$ 124	$(37)	$ 219
Gross margin (% of sales)	40.00%	50.00%	NA	43.05%
Interest coverage ratio	11.00	19.60	NA	7.38

*Includes goodwill amortization.

contains condensed income statements for Target and Acquire for 1995, 1996, and 1997 as well as for the second half of 1996. Exhibit 14-4 contains combined income statements for Scenario B. We have assumed that Acquire is in a steady state, reporting a constant gross margin (40%) and interest coverage ratio (11X). Target reports annual sales growth of 10%, constant gross margin of 50%, and interest coverage that increases from 16X in 1995 to 19.6X in 1997.

Under the purchase method, Acquire's income statement includes Target's operations only after the effective date of the merger. Thus, the 1996 combined income statement (see panel I of Exhibit 14-4) includes the operations of Acquire for the entire year, but the operations of Target only for the six months following the merger on June 30, 1996. The restatement of Target's assets and liabilities to their fair market values affects certain categories of expense as well. These include:

- Cost of goods sold (COGS), which may increase as inventory that has been written up in value is sold.
- Higher depreciation expense, due to recognition of the higher fair values of Target's property.
- Amortization of goodwill recognized in the allocation of the purchase price.
- Higher interest expense due to amortization, over the remaining life of the debt, of the debt discount created by revaluing long-term debt. As Exhibit 14-4 shows, when debt is used to fund the acquisition, the additional cost of borrowing is another adjustment.[7]

When inventory is accounted for by using either first-in, first-out (FIFO) or average cost, written-up inventory values flow into the cost of goods sold fairly quickly, depressing gross margins. Although reported income is reduced, some of the acquisition cost is recovered quickly as the higher costs reduce taxable income in a taxable purchase transaction. When last-in, first-out (LIFO) inventory accounting is used, the higher costs remain in inventory indefinitely unless a LIFO invasion (reduction of inventory quantities) takes place.

For the acquisition of Target, we assume use of the average cost method, and that $30 million of the inventory write-up flows through COGS prior to the end of 1996. The remainder ($20 million) flows through COGS in 1997.

Additional depreciation expense is a consequence of the higher depreciable base of property assets. The same depreciation methods and lives applied to that higher cost increase depreciation expense and lower reported income, but also generate income tax savings in taxable purchases.

If we assume use of the straight-line method, it appears that Target's fixed assets have an average life of 10 years (property/depreciation expense). Applying this factor to the property write-up of $100 million increases depreciation expense by $10 million per year, or $5 million (one-half) for the six months ended December 31, 1996.[8]

Amortization of goodwill is deductible for tax purposes in the United States only in some cases. Unless goodwill is tax-deductible, companies prefer to allocate the cost of an acquisition to depreciable property, even though this results in faster amortization in the financial statements. Under APB 17 (1970), goodwill may be amortized over any period from 10 to 40 years.

For Target, we assume a write-off over 35 years; this is within the normal range in the United States. This assumption results in a goodwill amortization expense of $2 million for 1997 and $1 million (one-half) for the last six months of 1996.

---

[7]The derivation of income statements for 1996 and 1997 under Scenario A is not shown in the interest of brevity. The only difference is that, under Scenario A, there is no additional interest expense as the acquisition is financed entirely by issuing shares.

[8]Note that this assumes all Target's property is written up by the same percentage. If the write-up is disproportionately high in a class of property with an average life significantly different from the company average, this assumption does not hold.

The treatment of debt discount follows the method used when a bond is issued at a discount (see Chapter 10). The effective interest rate is higher as it reflects the stated (coupon) interest rate as well as amortization of the discount. This principle, when applied to discounted debt, increases interest expense. Otherwise, the reported debt liability would be insufficient at maturity, resulting in a loss. We assume an increase in interest expense of $1 million for the second half of 1996 and $3 million for 1997. The purchase method debt of $190 million under Scenario B generates additional interest expense of $9 million during the second half of 1996 and a further $19 million in 1997.

The purchase method income statement for the year ended December 31, 1996 includes Acquire's operations for the full year, Target's operations for the six months following the merger, and the effects of the purchase method adjustments (net of applicable tax savings). Panel II of Exhibit 14-4 shows the income statement for 1997 for the combined firm, also under Scenario B.

We see the full impact of purchase accounting from Acquire's income statements for the three years ended December 31, 1997, shown in Exhibit 14-5 for both scenarios. 1995 sales and expenses are those of Acquire only; 1996 and 1997 data include Target for the period following the merger on June 30, 1996 (for Scenario B, their derivation is shown in Exhibit 14-4).

First, note the distortion of the sales trend. From 1995 to 1997, Acquire reports a sales increase of 72.6%, none of which is due to its own internal growth. Most of the growth is due to the inclusion of Target's sales starting with the second half of 1996; part is due to the sales growth of Target following its acquisition.

The second problem is the distortion of profitability ratios. Acquire alone (see Exhibit 14-3) has a constant gross margin (sales less COGS) of 40% of sales; Target has a constant gross margin of 50% of sales. The combined gross margin percentage (Exhibit 14-5) shows a rising trend, reflecting Target's growing importance.

The reported interest coverage ratio, however, declines for Scenario B. The additional debt reduces the coverage ratio to 7.38X in 1997 from the 11X reported for 1995. The decline is a function of the proportion of debt used to finance the purchase, the assumption of Target's debt, and the relative cost of debt. For Scenario A (panel A of Exhibit 14-5), the assumption that the acquisition is financed by selling equity results in higher interest coverage and net income due to lower interest expense.

Without the underlying data (from Exhibits 14-3 and 14-4), it is impossible to determine whether the rising profitability of Acquire is due to improvement in its own operations, the higher profitability of Target, efficiencies from the merger, or the impact of purchase method adjustments. In some cases, we can keep track of an acquired company through the use of segment data (see Chapter 13). However, as the frequency of acquisition rises, the ability to discern the impact of any single acquisition diminishes. When there are many small acquisitions or acquisitions within existing segments, their effect cannot be isolated.

For comparison purposes, we now examine the income statements for the years 1995 through 1997 that result from accounting for the merger as a pooling of interests. These income statements, presented in Exhibit 14-6, are obtained by simply adding together (without any adjustment) the income statements of Acquire and Target for the respective years.

Exhibits 14-5 and 14-6 show considerable differences. When the pooling method is used, the operating results of Target are included for all three years, including the

EXHIBIT 14-5. ACQUIRE CORP.
Purchase Method Consolidated Income Statements, 1995 to 1997,
Years Ended December 31 ($ in millions)

Scenario A: All Equity

	1995	1996	1997
Sales	$1,000	$1,340	$1,726
Cost of goods sold	(600)	(800)	(983)
Gross margin	$ 400	$ 540	$ 743
Selling expense*	(130)	(196)	(267)
Depreciation expense	(50)	(69)	(92)
Interest expense	(20)	(26)	(33)
Pretax income	$ 200	$ 249	$ 351
Income tax expense	(68)	(85)	(119)
Net income	$ 132	$ 164	$ 232
Gross margin (% of sales)	40.00%	40.30%	43.05%
Interest coverage ratio	11.00	10.58	11.64

Scenario B: Cash, Debt, and Equity

	1995	1996	1997
Sales	$1,000	$1,340	$1,726
Cost of goods sold	(600)	(800)	(983)
Gross margin	$ 400	$ 540	$ 743
Selling expense*	(130)	(196)	(267)
Depreciation expense	(50)	(69)	(92)
Interest expense	(20)	(35)	(52)
Pretax income	$ 200	$ 240	$ 332
Income tax expense	(68)	(82)	(113)
Net income	$ 132	$ 158	$ 219
Gross margin (% of sales)	40.00%	40.30%	43.05%
Interest coverage ratio	11.00	7.86	7.38

*Includes goodwill amortization.

periods prior to the merger. The restatement of prior period results is one of the salient features of the pooling of interests method of accounting, and it facilitates comparability.

Because the operating results of all three years include both Acquire and Target, the purchase method's "illusion of growth" is absent. Sales growth over the period 1995 to 1997 is 7.9%, reflecting only the internal sales growth of Target. All categories of expense are comparable as well. The gross margin percentage shows small year-to-year increases, reflecting the growing importance of Target's higher margin operations. The interest coverage ratio reflects the addition of Acquire's higher cost debt.

EXHIBIT 14-6. ACQUIRE CORP.
Pooling Method Income Statements, 1995 to 1997,
Years Ended December 31 ($ in millions)

	1995	1996	1997
Sales	$1,600	$1,660	$1,726
Cost of goods sold	(900)	(930)	(963)
Gross margin	$ 700	$ 730	$ 763
Selling expense	(245)	(255)	(265)
Depreciation expense	(75)	(78)	(82)
Interest expense	(30)	(30)	(30)
Pretax income	$ 350	$ 367	$ 386
Income tax expense	(118)	(124)	(130)
Net income	$ 232	$ 243	$ 256
Gross margin (% of sales)	43.75%	43.98%	44.21%
Interest coverage ratio	12.67	13.23	13.87

However, the pooling of interests method can also mislead. The first problem is that it creates a fictitious history. Results for 1995 have been restated as if the two companies were combined in that year. In reality, they were separate enterprises, with different managements. The pooling method permits the management of Acquire to take credit for the operating results of Target for the period prior to its acquisition.

The pooling method allows companies whose shares sell at high price/earnings ratios to improve earnings per share via acquisition. When a company uses its highly valued shares (i.e., high price/earnings multiple) to acquire a company whose shares sell at a low multiple of earnings under the pooling method, then earnings per share increase. This technique is sometimes known as "bootstrapping," as the acquired company can raise earnings per share through financial engineering rather than operating improvement. This effect is illustrated in Case 14-2, using the ConAgra acquisition of Golden Valley. In theory, this technique should fail as the market assigns a lower price/earnings ratio to the postmerger firm to reflect the inclusion of "lower-quality" earnings.[9] In practice, the technique can be effective for many years.

In the extreme case, an acquisition can be made after the close of the fiscal year to meet sales and earnings objectives. Because of the restatement feature of the pooling method, a company can include in its reported results the operations of firms acquired after the end of the year but before release of the annual report.[10]

Another serious problem with the pooling method of accounting *is the suppression of the true cost of the acquisition.* Since the pooling method carries forward historical

---

[9]The efficient markets hypothesis suggests that the market price of the acquirer should adjust instantaneously.

[10]National Student Marketing, a "high-flyer" in the late 1960s and early 1970s until its collapse, was reported to have made acquisitions *after the end of each fiscal year* to bring reported earnings up to the forecasted level.

costs, *no recognition is given to the true value of the assets acquired or any securities used to pay for the acquired company* (see Exhibit 14-2A, column 3).

There are several consequences of this failure to recognize the fair values acquired and paid for. One is that the acquiring company may sell acquired assets whose carrying cost is well below fair or market value. As a result, reported income includes fictitious gains. Although the acquirer presumably paid the full value of the assets acquired, the price paid was not recognized by the pooling method. Similarly, depreciation and amortization reflect the historical cost of assets acquired rather than their market value. As a result, income is overstated.[11]

Cash Flow Statement Effects

When the pooling method is used, the merger itself (an exchange of shares) is not reported in the cash flow statement as no cash flows have taken place. The postacquisition cash flow statement is the sum of the individual cash flow statements. As in the case of the income statement, previously issued cash flow statements are restated on a combined basis.

Under purchase method accounting, however, cash flows associated with the acquisition are reported on the cash flow statement, but in abbreviated form. The net assets acquired are reported as cash used for investment and the applicable financing sources as cash from financing. To illustrate this recognition in a simplified setting, assume that Acquire prepares a cash flow statement for the acquisition date of June 30, 1996, reflecting only the acquisition (during that short time period, no operations take place). The balance sheet changes and cash flow statement for Scenario B are presented in Exhibit 14-7.

The purchase method balance sheet (panel I) reflects the acquisition of the assets and liabilities (at their fair values) of Target. However, the cash flow statement (panel II) shows only cash outflows for investing of $415 million, equal to the purchase price of $490 million less $75 million of preacquisition cash on Target's balance sheet. None of the individual assets and liabilities acquired (shown in italics in panel I) are reported in the cash flow statement. Financing cash flow includes Acquire's issuance of $190 million of debt and $200 million of equity, for a total of $390 million generated from lenders and owners. The decrease in cash of $25 million is the net amount of cash used by Acquire to complete the acquisition. If we assume that the transaction was financed entirely with equity (Scenario A), the cash flow statement would report cash for investment of $415 million and cash from equity financing equal to $490 million with a net increase in cash of $75 million.

SFAS 95 (see Chapter 3) specifically requires that reported cash flows exclude the effect of acquisitions (other than actual cash flows). The failure to report the

---

[11]Abraham J. Briloff has written extensively over the years on the problems associated with the use of the pooling method. For example, see Briloff, "Distortions Arising from Pooling-of-Interests Accounting," *Financial Analysts Journal*, March–April 1968, pp 71–80. Despite the venerable age of this article, it remains a superb illustration of the suppression of the fair value of the acquisition in the pooling method, permitting the reporting of "gains" on acquired assets.

EXHIBIT 14-7
Impact of the Acquisition of Target on Statement of Cash Flows of Acquire,
Scenario B: Cash + Debt + Stock

I. Acquire Corp. Pre- and Postacquisition Balance Sheets

$ in millions	Preacquisition*	Postacquisition†	Change
Cash	$ 100	$ 75	($ 25)
Inventories	*200*	*350*	*150*
Receivables	*200*	*275*	*75*
Current assets	$ 500	$ 700	$200
Property	*500*	*850*	*350*
Goodwill	*0*	*70*	*70*
Total assets	$1,000	$1,620	$620
Payables	*150*	*200*	*50*
Accrued liabilities	*100*	*150*	*50*
Current liabilities	250	350	100
Long-term debt	*250*	*570*	*320*
Common stock	400	600	200
Retained earnings	100	100	0
Common equity	500	700	200
Total equities	$1,000	$1,620	$620

II. Effect of Acquisition on Acquire's Statement of Cash Flows

($ in millions)

Cash from operations		
Net income	$0	
Changes in operating accounts	0	$ 0
Cash for investment		(415) Net assets of Target (net of cash)
Cash from financing		
Debt financing	$190	
Equity financing	200	390
Net change in cash		($ 25)

*Exhibit 14-2B, column 1.
†Exhibit 14-2B, column 5.
Changes not shown explicitly in cash flow statement shown in italics; note that new debt is reported although assumed debt of Target is ignored.

individual asset and liability changes for purchase method acquisitions has two consequences:

1. Consecutive balance sheets and the cash flow statement can be used to deduce the assets and liabilities acquired.

2. Operating cash flow (CFO) can be distorted.

We consider each of these consequences in turn.

Deducing Assets and Liabilities Acquired

Because SFAS 95 requires the exclusion of acquisition balance sheet changes from the cash flow statement, balance sheet changes for any period have three components:

1. Operating changes for the period
2. Effect of acquisitions
3. Effect of foreign currency changes

For companies with no foreign operations, only the first two components exist. In that case, we can deduct the operating change component from the total change and deduce the acquisition effects.

Exhibit 14-7 illustrates this process in a simplified way. Panel I shows the balance sheet of Acquire just before and just after its acquisition of Target. We have assumed that the period is so short that there are no operations. In this case, therefore, the balance sheet changes are due entirely to the acquisition. If we did not have the consolidating balance sheet (Exhibit 14-2B) for Scenario B, we could deduce it.

For example, inventories rose by $150 million. As the operating change was zero, the acquired inventories of Acquire must have been $150 million (at fair value). This same analysis can be applied to receivables, property, goodwill, and payables.

The analysis of debt is more complicated. The total change is $320 million, of which $190 is new debt issued to finance the acquisition. The assumed debt of Target must be $130 million (reflecting the $20 million write-down to fair value).

The debt example illustrates the general procedure used to deduce acquisition assets and liabilities: Subtract the operating change shown in the cash flow statement from the actual balance sheet change for the period. The difference should be the effect of acquisitions or divestitures.

Use of this procedure is illustrated in Case 14-1 (Georgia Pacific) and Problem 8. Its accuracy, however, depends on an absence of foreign currency effects; these are discussed in Chapter 15.

Distortion of Cash from Operations

Although the acquisition increases operating assets and liabilities, that increase is not included in cash from operations (CFO). The cash flow change in operating accounts does not equal the actual balance sheet change. Because the additional inventories and receivables are acquired as part of an acquisition, the cash paid for their acquisition is included in cash for investment.

However, CFO reported in the year of the acquisition (and in subsequent years) may still be distorted. The degree of distortion depends on whether the levels of operating assets and liabilities immediately after the acquisition are maintained over time.

The potential distortion can be illustrated by considering the inventory acquired. Although the cash paid for the acquisition of the inventory does not flow through cash from operations, the cash received when the inventory is sold does. Thus, CFO is inflated as the proceeds of sale are included, whereas the cost of acquiring the inventory is not.

This distortion is minimal if inventory is continually replaced, as the cash outflows for new inventory offset cash inflows from sales. However, if there is a reduction in the acquired firm's net operating assets, CFO may be distorted, and careful analysis is required to understand the impact. An example appears in Case 14-1, the analysis of Georgia Pacific's acquisition of Great Northern Nekoosa.

Impact on Ratios

Financial statement ratios under the two methods differ, reflecting recognition of the purchase price and the fair values of the assets and liabilities of Target by Acquire under the purchase method; the pooling method suppresses both the purchase price and fair values.

Exhibits 14-2A and 14-2B show that the purchase method reports higher asset values and higher common equity (for the all-equity Scenario A) than the pooling of interests method when the purchase price exceeds the stated net worth of the acquired company. As a result, the base for activity and return ratios is higher. In addition, adjustments required by the purchase method usually reduce reported earnings. (Acquire's 1997 earnings are $256 million under the pooling method, but only $232 million under the purchase method for Scenario A.) The result is that profitability ratios are generally lower when the purchase method is used. Interest coverage ratios are reduced in this case by the increase in interest expense and further lowered when the acquisition is financed with debt.

The purchase method makes financial ratios difficult to interpret in other ways. Acquire's assets and liabilities are carried forward at historical cost, whereas Target's are restated to fair market values,[12] generating a mixture of historical costs and market values in the combined accounts. As a result, activity ratios are difficult to compare with those of other companies.

In addition, postacquisition ratios are not comparable with preacquisition ratios, because:

- Target may have had a different turnover ratio than Acquire (both the level and trend may differ), reflecting the nature of its business; the postmerger ratio is a blend of the ratios of the two companies.
- Turnover ratios are reduced solely because of the fair value adjustments required by the purchase method.

Comparison of a company that has made a purchase method acquisition with one that has made a pooling acquisition (or none at all) is also affected by these same problems.

A purchase method acquisition creates a discontinuity throughout the financial statements of the acquiring company. Comparison with preacquisition data for the same company and comparison with other companies are hampered by the inclusion of the acquired entity at the acquisition date (balance sheet effects), and by the subsequent purchase method adjustments (balance sheet and income statement effects).

---

[12]Property, however, is restated to an amount less than fair value when the purchase price is below the fair value of net assets.

Because the pooling method restates preacquisition financial statements, it produces comparable financial statements. However, this comparability is fictitious; the combined companies were not operated as one or by the same management prior to the combination. The restated levels and trends in ratios may not represent expected performance over time under different management.

The reader is cautioned that ratio effects described in this section are company- and transaction-specific. Depending on the purchase price relative to book value, the fair values of assets and liabilities acquired, the means of financing, and the earnings of the target firm, the effect on ratios of use of the purchase method or pooling method will vary in practice. Use of trend data for such companies can easily lead to misleading conclusions. *We can, however, make the general statement that the choice of method does affect the ratios of the combined enterprise, often significantly.*

COMPLICATING FACTORS IN PURCHASE METHOD ACQUISITIONS

The Target–Acquire scenarios are both simplistic. In actual transactions, there are two complicating factors that sometimes appear:

- Contingent payments
- In-process research and development

We discuss each issue briefly.

Contingent Payments

Some acquisition agreements provide that the acquisition price is dependent on future earnings of the acquired entity or other future events. APB 16 states that the additional purchase price is recognized by the acquirer as soon as those conditions are met.

The purchase price increase must be allocated to the assets and liabilities acquired. If some assets (e.g., property) were not fully written up to fair value, then a further write-up would occur. The usual case, however, is that the contingent compensation increases goodwill.

For example, Russ Berrie, a gift and toy marketer, reported that

> in October 1993, the Company acquired substantially all of the assets of Cap Toys, Inc., a toy company based in Ohio, and $13,606,000 of goodwill was recorded. Under the purchase agreement, additional payments may be required based on the attainment of certain operating profit levels of Cap Toys, Inc. During the years ended December 31, 1995 and 1994, $1,047,000 and $2,563,000, respectively, was charged to goodwill related to these additional payments.[13]

As Russ Berrie amortizes acquisition goodwill over 15 years, the additional goodwill increases amortization expense, offsetting some of the increased profitability of the

---

[13]Russ Berrie, *1995 Annual Report,* Note 1.

acquired firm. Such disclosures are also helpful indications of the performance of acquisitions in following years.

In-Process Research and Development

The acquisition price of computer, biotechnology, and other firms with high technological content recognizes that such firms have significant assets in the form of research and development in progress. APB 16 requires that such "in-process research and development" be expensed immediately when the purchase method of accounting is used. For example, when IBM acquired Lotus in 1995, $1,840 million (more than half) of the purchase price was expensed.

There are two important effects of such expensing:

1. Reported income of the acquirer is reduced in the period of the acquisition. As this effect is nonoperating, it should be considered a nonrecurring expense for analysis purposes.

2. The immediate write-off reduces the amount of goodwill that would otherwise be recognized, reducing future goodwill amortization. In effect, there is an immediate write-off of goodwill. This may create an incentive for firms to allocate as much of the purchase price as possible to in-process research and development.[14]

INCOME TAX EFFECTS OF BUSINESS COMBINATIONS

The income tax aspects of accounting for business combinations have always been complex. Changes in U.S. tax laws in recent years have only increased that complexity. A thorough discussion of this subject is well beyond the scope of this book. However, a few general comments may be helpful.

Most pooling of interests acquisitions are nontaxable events under the Internal Revenue Code (the Code) of the United States. Nontaxability has two consequences:

1. Shareholders of the acquired company do not recognize gain or loss as a result of the merger. They transfer the cost basis of their shares in the acquired company to the shares of the acquirer that they receive in exchange.

2. The cost basis of the assets and liabilities of the acquired company is not affected by the merger. There is no income tax recognition of the fair value of assets and liabilities and no change in tax benefits or deductibility as these assets are used or liabilities paid.

A purchase method acquisition, in contrast, is usually a taxable event under the Code. In a taxable exchange, selling shareholders must recognize gain or loss on the sale of their shares, even if they receive securities of the acquiring company. In addition,

---

[14]See the discussion in Elizabeth McDonald, "More Firms Write Off Acquisition Costs," *Wall Street Journal,* Dec. 2, 1996, p. A2.

the tax basis of assets and liabilities of the acquired firm is changed from original cost to fair value, reflecting the price paid for the company.

In most cases, the accounting treatment and the income tax treatment are identical. In these circumstances, the postmerger accounting and tax basis of assets and liabilities are the same. However, the accounting and tax rules do differ in some respects, and there are times when the tax treatment of an acquisition is different from the accounting treatment. In such cases, care must be taken to discern the impact of the difference on future earnings and cash flows. Careful reading of the income tax footnote (see Chapter 9) may reveal different tax and accounting bases for some assets and liabilities. Differential merger treatment is usually the cause of such differences.

When a merger is tax-free, but accounted for as a purchase, the tax basis of the assets is below the accounting basis (if we assume that the purchase price exceeds historical equity). As a result, the additional depreciation and other expenses resulting from purchase method adjustments are not tax-deductible. This increases the firm's effective tax rate.

Another effect is that recognized gains on the sale of assets are higher for tax purposes than for accounting purposes, reducing after-tax cash proceeds and adversely affecting the after-tax gain or loss from the sale.

INTERNATIONAL DIFFERENCES IN ACCOUNTING FOR BUSINESS COMBINATIONS

IAS 22 (revised in 1993) generally requires the use of the purchase method to account for acquisitions. It allows pooling (merger or uniting of interests) accounting only in exceptional circumstances, when it is not possible to identify the acquirer. However, pooling continues to be used in practice as the criteria governing the identification of the acquirer are provided only as background material and implementation guidance. Requirements for the application of the pooling method are similar to those in APB 16, but the rules are not as detailed, permitting a wider range of interpretations.

U.K. standards effectively make pooling or merger accounting optional, as they do not contain the detailed conditions spelled out in APB 16 for pooling. Generally, application of the purchase method in the United Kingdom results in the allocation of a higher proportion of the purchase price to goodwill for two reasons. First, the U.K. standard contains only a broad description of the process of allocating the purchase price to the acquired assets and liabilities; second, goodwill may be charged directly to equity through any type of reserve account or one created specifically for goodwill. Future results are not reduced by goodwill amortization, increasing reported income relative to firms that must amortize goodwill.

Accounting standards in the United Kingdom and many other countries also permit firms to recognize future costs of the merged firm, further augmenting reported income in subsequent years. This process of *provisioning* (accruing future expenses) at the acquisition date increases the fair values of liabilities and reduces residual goodwill (and its write-off or subsequent amortization).

U.S. accounting rules prohibit the acquisition date recognition of costs to close duplicate facilities of acquired companies (see FASB Technical Bulletin No. 85-5). The Emerging Issues Task Force Issue No. 94-3 specifies criteria for the recognition of costs to exit an activity and costs of involuntary termination or relocation of the employees of acquired companies. IAS 22 also limits provisioning. Again, practice varies because the proscription is part of implementation guidance and not the standard itself.[15]

In France, only the purchase method is used, but the price is rarely allocated to tangible assets to avoid tax penalties; the resulting, comparatively higher goodwill amounts can be immediately charged to equity. A 1993 survey showed that 55 out of 98 firms amortized goodwill over periods ranging from 20 to 40 years. Canadian standards are similar to IAS 22.

The purchase method is the norm in Germany and the Netherlands; pooling or merger accounting is allowed but used rarely. However, there are no specific rules governing revaluations through the allocation of the purchase price to individual assets and liabilities. Postacquisition income can therefore be manipulated by selectively allocating the acquisition cost to current, tangible long-term, or intangible assets as desired.

Differences in Treatment of Goodwill

Accounting standards related to goodwill outside of the United States reflect differing views of financial reporting, cultural differences, and legal requirements.[16] In Germany, laws specify a four-year amortization period. However, a range of 0 to 40 years is used in practice. In the Netherlands, goodwill may be amortized, charged to income, or charged directly to reserves (method used by most firms).

In the United Kingdom, the ASB has proposed[17] that acquisition goodwill be amortized:

- Over its useful life, when that life is 20 years or less
- Over its useful life, when that life exceeds 20 years and is expected to remain measurable
- Over 20 years, when its useful life exceeds 20 years, but is difficult to measure

Goodwill whose life is indefinite need not be amortized, but is subject to annual review for possible impairment.

IAS 22 permits amortization of purchased goodwill over a 5-year period or its expected economic life (not to exceed 20 years). Goodwill may not be charged directly to equity, but an immediate write-off to income is required when that goodwill is not expected to provide future economic benefits.

The maximum 40-year amortization period allowed in the United States is at odds with trends in international practice, which ranges from a minimum of 5 years to a ceiling of 20 years under IAS standards. We expect practice to move closer to the IAS model.

The information on acquisitions provided by cash flow statements in the United States is generally lacking in non-U.S. financial statements, although the IASC cash flow standard encourages disclosures to alleviate this problem. Footnote disclosures

---

[15]In 1995, the IASC joined with Australian, Canadian, U.K., and U.S. standard setters to issue a special report, Provisions: Their Recognition, Measurement, and Disclosure in Financial Statements, with the objective of eliminating the prerecognition of future operating losses.

[16]See *Issues in Accounting Education*, Fall 1996 (vol. 11, no. 2) for articles presenting the U.S., U.K., German, and Japanese perspective on goodwill accounting.

[17]Financial Reporting Exposure Draft 12 (1996).

outside the United States rarely provide detailed information regarding acquisitions. This absence of data is compounded by the lack of adequate segment disclosures.

As a result, it may be difficult to analyze acquisitions made by foreign companies. Analysts should try to determine which method is used, the treatment of goodwill, and any restatement of previously issued financial statements (this is forbidden in some countries) as these are the key issues in acquisition accounting. Applying the principles discussed in this chapter should permit the analyst to draw some inferences regarding the impact of acquisitions and, if management can be questioned, indicate the questions that should be asked. As the SmithKline Beecham example shows, the choice of acquisition method can radically affect the reported results of operations and financial condition of the combined entity.

ILLUSTRATION OF INTERNATIONAL DIFFERENCES: THE ACQUISITION ACTIVITIES OF SMITHKLINE BEECHAM

In July 1989, SmithKline Beckman, an American health care company, merged with Beecham Group, a similar U.K. company; the resulting firm is SmithKline Beecham (SKB). The transaction was accounted for as a pooling of interests under U.K. GAAP (merger accounting in U.K. terminology), but would be reported as a purchase acquisition under U.S. GAAP because of differences in the accounting standards of the two countries. SKB reconciles its stockholders' equity and net income between U.K. and U.S. GAAP on Form 20-F[18] to show the effects of the different accounting principles of the two jurisdictions. *This merger provides an unusual opportunity to compare the effects of both accounting methods on the same transaction, without recourse to estimates or assumptions.*

SKB continued to make acquisitions following the 1989 transaction. These later transactions were treated as purchase method acquisitions under U.K. GAAP. Differences between U.S. and U.K. GAAP in the application of the purchase method provide additional reconciling items between stockholders' equity and net income. *These acquisitions allow us to see the effect of different treatments of acquisition goodwill on financial statements.*

Differences in Accounting Methods

We begin with a review of some of the principal differences between U.S. and U.K. accounting standards:

1. The most critical difference is that APB 16 has detailed criteria (previously discussed) governing the use of the pooling of interests method. The Securities and Exchange Commission, in recent years, has been diligent in enforcing these rules. U.K. standards, similar to non-U.S. standards in this respect, are broad, without detailed guidance.

2. Under U.S. GAAP, acquisition goodwill must be capitalized and amortized over no more than 40 years. Under U.K. GAAP, goodwill can be amortized over its expected economic life (generally ranging from 5 to 20 years), charged immediately to stockholders' equity, or reserved for.[19]

---

[18]Annual report filed by non-U.S. companies with the Securities and Exchange Commission (see Chapter 1).

[19]See the discussion of proposed changes in U.K. accounting for goodwill in the previous section of this chapter.

3. Under U.S. GAAP, the purchase price must be allocated to identifiable intangible assets such as customer lists and amortized over their estimated economic lives. U.K. GAAP does not require separate identification of such identifiable intangible assets in the allocation of purchase price; they are components of recognized goodwill.

4. U.K. GAAP permits independent valuation and capitalization of brand names acquired in transactions with unrelated parties, where the brands have significant, long-term values and can be sold separately from the business acquired. Such capitalized amounts are not amortized, but must be reviewed annually for permanent declines in value that are charged to income in the period recognized. U.S. GAAP does not allow capitalization of brand names; they remain part of goodwill, recognized and amortized over a maximum of 40 years.

5. U.S. GAAP requires treatment of acquisition-related reorganization (restructuring) costs as components of the fair value adjustments. Under U.K. GAAP, FRS 7, Fair Values in Acquisition Accounting, prohibits such treatment for future losses or reorganization costs expected to be incurred as a result of the acquisition.

6. Under U.S. GAAP, the portion of the purchase price attributable to purchased intangible assets under development (e.g., research or software) is charged directly to income. Under U.K. GAAP, the purchase price allocable to the costs of separately identifiable intangibles such as patents, licenses, and marketing rights to develop specific products for commercial application can be capitalized and must be amortized over their useful lives, not to exceed 20 years.

7. Revaluation of property is not permitted under U.S. GAAP; it is common practice in the United Kingdom to replace historical cost with revalued amounts, with the difference credited to equity.

The Merged Balance Sheet

Exhibit 14-8 reproduces the merged company's (SKB) U.K. GAAP-based consolidated balance sheets (condensed) from its Form 20-F report.[20] Because the pooling method was used, the December 31, 1988, balance sheet was restated to include SmithKline, the acquired firm. As a result, the year-to-year changes in total assets and liabilities are not significant.

Cash, debt, and stockholders' equity are significantly different, however. Stockholders of both SmithKline and Beecham received special cash dividends in connection with the merger. These special dividends (which preclude use of the pooling method under U.S. GAAP) reduced cash and increased debt. The decline in equity was due to the special dividends and the immediate write-off of acquisition goodwill.

Comparison of Stockholders' Equity

Exhibit 14-9 reconciles SKB's shareholders' equity under U.K. GAAP to that under U.S. accounting methods. Although our discussion focuses initially on the effects of the 1989 merger, the exhibit shows the reconciliation for the 1989 to 1994 period. To simplify the presentation, we have aggregated the effect of all other accounting differences in a single line item in part A.

---

[20]The 20-F financial statements are presented in the more familiar U.S. format and in both pounds sterling and U.S. dollars (most recent year only).

**EXHIBIT 14-8. SMITHKLINE BEECHAM PLC
AND SUBSIDIARIES**
Condensed Balance Sheets

	December 31	
	1988	1989
	£m	£m
Assets		
Cash and cash equivalent	$ 879.9	$ 233.2
Other current assets	1,645.8	1,958.2
Total current assets	$2,525.7	$2,191.4
Property and investments	1,368.4	1,555.2
Total assets	$3,894.1	$3,746.6
Liabilities and equity		
Short-term debt	$ 501.7	$ 984.1
Other current liabilities	1,071.1	1,550.4
Total current liabilities	$1,572.8	$2,534.5
Long-term debt	550.9	999.5
Other noncurrent liabilities	410.4	509.1
Total liabilities	$2,534.1	$4,043.1
Ordinary (common) shares	322.0	331.3
Reserves	208.0	(852.6)
Retained earnings	1,798.6	1,220.3
Goodwill reserve	(968.6)	(995.5)
Total equity	$1,360.0	$ (296.5)
Total liabilities and equity	$3,894.1	$3,746.6

Source: Adapted from SmithKline Beecham, Form 20-F, 1989.

Premerger Differences: 1988. At December 31, 1988, prior to the merger date, equity under U.S. GAAP was approximately 21% higher than under U.K. GAAP (£1,647 million versus £1,360 million). The major difference is Beecham's policy of writing off goodwill immediately following an acquisition. The write-off effect is partly offset by the:

- Equity increase resulting from the revaluation of fixed assets.
- Inclusion (under U.K. GAAP) of SmithKline's retained earnings through 1988, as required by the pooling method. Under U.S. GAAP (purchase method), SmithKline is not included in the consolidated group at December 31, 1988.

Postmerger Differences: 1989. At December 31, 1989, following the merger, the preexisting goodwill and revaluation differences persist. However, they are dwarfed by new ones arising from the differential treatment of the merger under the accounting principles of the two countries.

EXHIBIT 14-9. SMITHKLINE BEECHAM PLC AND SUBSIDIARIES
Stockholders' Equity (U.K. Versus U.S. GAAP) and Tangible Equity (U.S. GAAP)

A. Effect on Stockholders' Equity of Differences Between U.K. and U.S. GAAP (£ in millions)

	Years Ended December 31						
	1988	1989	1990	1991	1992	1993	1994
Stockholders' equity—U.K. GAAP	1,360	(297)	373	743	910	1,254	570
U.S. GAAP adjustments:							
Preacquisition SmithKline equity	(98)	—	—	—	—	—	—
Beecham goodwill	441	461	344	354	519	547	—
Intangible assets	—	—	—	—	—	(50)	(88)
Revaluation reserve	(108)	(156)	(140)	(145)	(145)	(89)	(78)
Purchase accounting adjustments							
Property, plant, and equipment	—	69	52	50	50	46	—
Intangible assets	—	754	551	486	501	409	369
Goodwill	—	2,665	2,598	2,526	2,456	2,389	3,634
Other, net	—	35	27	38	41	38	—
Restructuring costs	—	—	—	—	—	—	305
Other differences, net	52	14	50	61	53	52	57
Stockholders' equity—U.S. GAAP	1,647	3,545	3,855	4,113	4,385	4,596	4,769

B. Computation of Tangible Equity (U.S. GAAP)

Stockholders' equity—U.S. GAAP	1,647	3,545	3,855	4,113	4,385	4,596	4,769
Less: Beecham goodwill	(441)	(461)	(344)	(354)	(519)	(547)	—
Acquisition intangibles	—	(754)	(551)	(486)	(501)	(409)	(369)
Acquisition goodwill	—	(2,665)	(2,598)	(2,526)	(2,456)	(2,389)	(3,634)
Equals: Tangible equity—U.S. GAAP	1,206	(335)	362	747	909	1,251	766
Stockholders' equity—U.K. GAAP	1,360	(297)	373	743	910	1,254	570

Source: Adapted from SmithKline Beecham, Form 20-Fs, 1989–1994.

Under U.K. GAAP (pooling), the assets and liabilities of SmithKline were consolidated without change, and SmithKline's equity was added to the tangible equity of Beecham (SmithKline's preexisting goodwill was written off against equity at the time of the acquisition, conforming the accounts of the acquired company to U.K. GAAP). Stockholders' equity fell from £1,360 million at December 31, 1988, to a negative £297 million at December 31, 1989. The additional earnings resulting from the inclusion of SmithKline were small compared with the special dividends to shareholders, which reduced equity by more than £1,800 million.

The purchase method recognized the value of the acquisition (£3,205 million based on stock prices at the acquisition date of July 27, 1989). (In comparison, the pooling method measured the transaction at SmithKline's tangible equity of £98 million!) SmithKline's assets and liabilities were restated to fair market value. Almost all the purchase price was allocated to intangible assets (partly, we can assume, patents and brand names), with goodwill alone accounting for three-quarters of the total. These allocations (less amortization between the date of the acquisition and year-end) account for the large purchase accounting adjustments in Exhibit 14-9. Equity rises £1.9 billion, from £1,647 million to £3,545 million, in sharp contrast to the decrease in equity of nearly £1.7 billion under U.K. accounting principles.

1994 Differences. In 1994, SKB acquired Diversified Pharmaceutical Services for a cash payment of £2,300 million, of which £1,508 million was capitalized as intangible assets, to be amortized over 40 years. The company also acquired Sterling-Winthrop for £2,925 million in 1994. This transaction resulted in the recognition of £332 million of goodwill (written off to equity); £776 million attributed to brand names will not be amortized. However, U.K. GAAP requires that brand names be reviewed for impairment and any permanent declines recorded in income.

Tangible Equity. Many analysts remove acquisition goodwill and other intangible assets from the balance sheet for analysis, for reasons discussed later in the chapter. The resulting tangible equity under U.S. GAAP is quite close to equity computed under U.K. GAAP, as shown in part B of Exhibit 14-9. Over the 1988 to 1994 period, the treatment of goodwill under the two accounting methods is the main difference. We examine this issue shortly.

Balance Sheet Restatement

The data provided in Exhibit 14-9 are sufficient to restate the balance sheets (Exhibit 14-8) to U.S. GAAP. The restatement for December 31, 1989, is shown in Exhibit 14-10.

The adjustment entries come directly from the GAAP reconciliation and descriptions provided in Exhibit 14-9.[21] (Each adjustment appears twice: once in the equity account and once in the appropriate asset or liability account. The increase in the assets plus the decrease in the liabilities must, necessarily, be equal to the change in the stockholders' equity.)

The restatement doubles the assets of the company. The allocation of the purchase price of SmithKline, combined with the reinstatement of goodwill (written off under U.K. GAAP), results in the addition of £3,769 million to consolidated assets. Because most of the purchase price was allocated to intangible assets (mostly goodwill), few other accounts are materially affected by this restatement.

However, most financial ratios based on the restated balance sheet are significantly different. The debt-to-equity ratio (including short- and long-term debt) is a moderate

---

[21]The following three items relate to accounting differences unrelated to acquisitions:

1. Current assets are decreased by the (net) increase in deferred tax (£66 million − £5 million) because of footnote disclosure that current assets include deferred taxes.

2. Another footnote indicates that dividends payable are included in current liabilities. This adjustment is made because, under U.S. GAAP, dividends are not accounted for until actually declared.

3. The "other" adjustments (− £12 million + £35 million = £23 million) are nowhere described; we arbitrarily reduce other liabilities by this amount.

EXHIBIT 14-10. SMITHKLINE BEECHAM
Balance Sheet Conversion to U.S. GAAP, at December 31, 1989 (£ in millions)

	U.K. GAAP	Adjustments	U.S. GAAP
Cash	£ 233.2		£ 233.2
Other current assets	1,958.2	£ (61.0)	1,897.2
Current assets	£2,191.4	£ (61.0)	£2,130.4
Investments	90.6	69.0	90.6
Property (net)	1,464.6	(156.0)	1,414.6
		37.0	
Intangible assets	—	754.0	754.0
Goodwill	—	461.0	3,126.0
		2,665.0	
Total assets	£3,746.6	£3,769.0	£7,515.6
Short-term debt	984.1		984.1
Other current liabilities	1,550.4	(50.0)	1,500.4
Current liabilities	£2,534.5	£ (50.0)	£2,484.5
Long-term debt	999.5		999.5
Accrued pensions	64.3		64.3
Restructuring	300.1		300.1
Other liabilities	123.2	(23.0)	100.2
Minority interest	21.5		21.5
Total liabilities	£4,043.1	£ (73.0)	£3,970.1
Stockholders' equity	(296.5)	3,842.0	3,545.5
Total equities	£3,746.6	£3,769.0	£7,515.6
Current ratio	0.86		0.86
Debt-to-total assets	0.53		0.26
Debt-to-equity	NMF*		0.56

*Not meaningful.

0.56. If we use U.K. GAAP data, the negative equity makes this ratio meaningless.[22] Debt-to-total assets falls from 0.53 (U.K. GAAP) to 0.26 (U.S. GAAP). The current ratio, however, is unchanged at 0.86 as current assets and liabilities are both reduced only slightly.

Exhibit 14-11 compares the U.S. GAAP balance sheet (December 31, 1989) just derived with the U.S. GAAP balance sheet at December 31, 1988.[23] *These balance sheets reflect the purchase method as it would be applied under U.S. GAAP.* Total assets nearly triple over the course of the year, whereas total liabilities increase to four times their previous level. Stockholders' equity more than doubles. The ratio

[22]The ratio of U.S. GAAP debt-to-tangible equity is similarly meaningless.

[23]This 1988 balance sheet cannot be derived from the 1988 balance sheet shown in Exhibit 14-8 because the latter has been restated to include SmithKline. Under the purchase method, the December 31, 1988, balance sheet is the actual 1988 balance sheet of Beecham. We have taken that balance sheet (from the 20-F filing) and, using the data in Exhibit 14-9, adjusted it to U.S. GAAP (mainly by restoring goodwill).

EXHIBIT 14-11. SMITHKLINE BEECHAM
Comparative Balance Sheets on U.S. GAAP Basis,
at December 31, 1988 to 1989 (£ in millions)

	1988	1989
Cash	£ 735.5	£ 233.2
Other current assets	899.0	1,897.2
Current assets	£1,634.5	£2,130.4
Investments	11.5	90.6
Property (net)	505.5	1,414.6
Intangible assets		754.0
Goodwill	441.4	3,126.0
Total assets	£2,592.9	£7,515.6
Short-term debt	238.2	984.1
Other current liabilities	434.8	1,500.4
Current liabilities	£ 673.0	£2,484.5
Long-term debt	127.3	999.5
Accrued pensions	38.9	64.3
Restructuring	27.1	300.1
Other liabilities	64.4	100.2
Minority interest	15.3	21.5
Total liabilities	£ 946.0	£3,970.1
Shareholders' equity	1,646.9	3,545.5
Total equities	£2,592.9	£7,515.6
Current ratio	2.43	0.86
Debt-to-total assets	0.14	0.26
Debt-to-equity	0.22	0.56

differences reflect the purchase method adjustments. This comparison illustrates how the purchase method creates discontinuity in the pattern of asset and liability growth. Users of (computerized) databases must be especially wary of the effect of purchase method acquisitions.

Income Statement Effects

The alternative methods of accounting for the merger also result in considerable differences in reported income. As in the case of the balance sheet, SKB reconciles net income between accounting standards, as shown in Exhibit 14-12.[24]

Before we discuss the reconciliation, two major differences in the income statement require comment:

1. U.S. GAAP requires exclusion of the sales of discontinued operations. Under U.K. GAAP, such sales are included, with a separate disclosure provided.

2. Extraordinary items reported under U.K. GAAP are not treated as such under the more restrictive U.S. standards.

---

[24]As in Exhibit 14-9, we present data for the entire 1988 to 1994 period.

EXHIBIT 14-12. SMITHKLINE BEECHAM PLC AND SUBSIDIARIES
Income Under U.K. and U.S. GAAP

	1988	1989	1990	1991	1992	1993	1994
A. Effect on Net Income of Differences Between U.K. and U.S. GAAP (millions)							
Net income—U.K. GAAP	367	130	745	619	711	813	72
U.S. GAAP Adjustments							
SmithKline premerger income	(62)	(144)	—	—	—	—	—
Transaction and restructuring costs	—	281	—	—	—	—	—
Goodwill	(36)	(26)	14	(9)	(11)	(13)	—
One-off items taken to goodwill	—	—	—	—	—	—	458
Intangible assets	—	—	—	—	—	(50)	(39)
Restructuring costs	—	—	—	—	—	—	305
Purchase Accounting Adjustments							
Amortization of intangible assets	—	(60)	(85)	(85)	(86)	(101)	(97)
Amortization of goodwill	—	(28)	(67)	(67)	(67)	(67)	(82)
Depreciation and other	—	(42)	(7)	(5)	(5)	(4)	—
Other, net	(12)	(24)	29	21	(157)	(60)	(17)
Net income—U.S. GAAP	257	87	629	474	385	518	600
Represented by							
Pretax income before nonrecurring items	412	349	680	691	582	862	890
Nonrecurring items	—	(115)	124	—	—	—	—
Income tax expense	(181)	(162)	(300)	(255)	(261)	(389)	(344)
Income from continuing operations	231	72	504	436	321	473	546
Income from discontinued operations	26	15	125	38	64	192	54
Cumulative effect of accounting changes						(147)	
Net income—U.S. GAAP	257	87	629	474	385	518	600
Average A and B shares (millions)	665	952	2,652	2,656	2,666	2,675	2,684
Per Share—U.S. GAAP							
Income from continuing operations	34.7p	7.5p	19.0p	16.4p	12.0p	17.7p	20.3p
Net income	38.6p	9.1p	23.7p	17.8p	14.4p	19.4p	22.4p
Per Share—U.K. GAAP							
Income excluding exceptional items			20.1p	23.3p	26.2p	29.1p	32.3p
Net income			27.7p	23.3p	26.2p	30.4p	2.7p
B. Adjustment for Extraordinary Items							
Extraordinary Items							
Restructuring and rationalization costs		(578)					
Other	(102)	232	201	—	36	35	—
After-tax extraordinary items	(102)	(346)	201	—	36	35	—
Continuing operations (U.S. GAAP)	231	72	504	436	321	473	546
Extraordinary charges	102	346	(201)	—	(36)	(35)	—
Continuing operations (adjusted)	333	418	303	436	285	438	546
Per Share (pence)							
Continuing operations (U.S. GAAP)	34.7p	7.5p	19.0p	16.4p	12.0p	17.7p	20.3p
Extraordinary charges	15.4p	36.4p	(7.6)p	—	(1.3)p	(1.3)p	—
Continuing operations (adjusted)	50.1p	43.9p	11.4p	16.4p	10.7p	16.4p	20.3p

The 1988 difference in net income reflects two main factors. First is the impact of differences in accounting methods, with amortization of (existing) goodwill the most important. If Beecham had capitalized goodwill, its amortization would have reduced 1988 net income by 10%. The second main difference is the elimination, under U.S. GAAP, of the 1988 income of SmithKline.[25] U.S. GAAP net income reflects the different accounting methods and excludes the earnings of SmithKline for the portion of 1989 prior to the effective date of the merger.

But the most important differences in 1989 income stem from the differential accounting treatment of the merger itself. Under the purchase method (U.S. GAAP), the write-up of property and intangible assets requires amortization of £130 million (£60 million + £28 million + £42 million) over the last five months of 1989. Full-year amortization would be much higher. That effect can be seen in the 1990 to 1992 reconciliations, where the full-year amortization of goodwill and intangibles is £153 million compared with the £88 million recorded for 1989.

As a result of these differences, U.S. GAAP net income fell by two-thirds in 1989 to £87 million. Income from continuing operations fell by nearly 70% to £72 million. Although net income under U.K. GAAP (Exhibit 14-12) also declines sharply, much of that decline is classified as extraordinary; 1989 income before extraordinary items slightly increases (not shown in Exhibit 14-12). The reported earnings per share reflect this disparity:

Reported Earnings per Share (in pence)

	1988	1989
U.K. GAAP before extraordinary items	36.5	36.5
U.S. GAAP from continuing operations	34.7	7.5

Note that the number of shares used to compute EPS under U.S. and U.K. GAAP differ. Under U.S. GAAP, the additional shares issued to acquire SmithKline are outstanding only following the merger; under U.K. GAAP, they are considered outstanding for the entire period, as the 1988 results have been restated to include SmithKline. For 1989, however, the number of shares outstanding are the same under both GAAPs.

Which earnings per share figure is a more appropriate measure of 1989 operating results? The major difference is the extraordinary items, shown in part B of Exhibit 14-12. The largest is the "group restructuring and rationalization" charge that may have a positive impact on future earnings. Such charges often include severance pay for discharged employees and write-downs of redundant facilities and other assets (reducing future amortization). The size of this charge suggests that both companies had overvalued assets, but in the case of SmithKline, this does not square with the huge premium relative to stated book value paid for the company.

---

[25]Under the pooling method, 1988 is restated to include SmithKline. Under the purchase method, the results of SmithKline prior to the acquisition data are excluded. In 1989, SmithKline is included only following the date of the merger.

From an earnings perspective, the extraordinary items do appear to be mostly nonrecurring, Thus, we can add them back to net income under U.S. GAAP, resulting in adjusted 1989:

	Earnings (£ in millions)	Per Share (in pence)
Continuing operations (U.S. GAAP)	72.0	7.5
Extraordinary charges	346.3	36.4
Continuing operations (adjusted)	418.3	43.9

We can make the same adjustment for 1988:

Continuing operations (U.S. GAAP)	231.0	34.7
Extraordinary charges	102.3	15.4
Continuing operations (adjusted)	333.3	50.1

Note: All data used for these computations are derived from Exhibit 14-12.

Using this net income definition, we observe that SKB's 1989 earnings from continuing operations rose, but earnings per share fell. In other words, the higher earnings from the inclusion of SmithKline were more than offset by additional shares outstanding; the merger was dilutive.

Income Statement Restatement

The U.K. GAAP income statements can be converted to U.S. GAAP with the following adjustments:

- Apply the purchase method of accounting by including the results of SmithKline only following the acquisition date (July 26, 1989) and by including the purchase method adjustments to income.
- Adjust for other differences in accounting methods between U.S. GAAP and U.K. GAAP.

Exhibit 14-12 contains the adjustments to net income, but it does not show the other necessary adjustments (e.g., sales and cost of goods sold). The inclusion of the results of discontinued operations in the U.K. statements is especially difficult to deal with analytically. Thus, many assumptions and adjustments would be required to recast the entire income statement to a U.S. GAAP basis. We can, however, easily restate sales.

Under U.S. GAAP, the 1988 sales of SKB are those of Beecham only (since the acquisition of SmithKline took place in 1989). Further, we must exclude sales of discontinued operations. The 1988 data in Exhibit 14-13 were obtained from the 1988 Beecham income statement (not shown here).

EXHIBIT 14-13. SMITHKLINE BEECHAM
U.S. Versus U.K. GAAP, for Years Ended December 31, 1988 to 1990 (£ in millions)

	1988	1989	1990
A. Sales Comparisons			
U.S. GAAP—Purchase	£1,939	£3,011	£4,501
U.K. GAAP—Pooling (from continuing operations)	3,672	4,276	4,501
B. Return on Total Capital			
Earnings before interest and taxes (from continuing operations, before nonrecurring items)			
U.S. GAAP		451	790
U.K. GAAP		826	970
Average total capital (total debt plus total equity)			
U.S. GAAP		3,771	5,417
U.K. GAAP		2,050	1,963
Return on total capital (EBIT/average total capital)			
U.S. GAAP		12.0%	14.6%
U.K. GAAP		40.3%	49.4%

1989 sales under U.S. GAAP include the full-year sales of Beecham (excluding discontinued operations) plus the sales of SmithKline for the period July 27 to December 31. We use seven-twelfths of SmithKline's actual 1989 sales ($3,591 million) as estimated sales for the first seven months of 1989. We multiply this amount ($2,095 million) by the average exchange rate for the pound sterling versus the dollar for the same seven-month period (0.604) to obtain estimated sales in pounds (£1,265 million). Subtracting this number from the reported consolidated sales for 1989 yields the estimated sales on a purchase basis, which include those of SmithKline only for the period following the merger.

In 1990, however, SmithKline's sales are included for the full year under both methods. 1990 sales from continuing operations shown in Exhibit 14-13 are identical to those reported under U.K. GAAP.

As we can see from part A of Exhibit 14-13, the difference between the pooling and purchase method is not just the variation in reported income already discussed. Because, under the purchase method, the sales of the acquired company (SmithKline) are included only following the merger date, the sales trend is quite different as well. The sales trend reported under U.K. GAAP reflects the combination of the two firms for periods prior to the merger as well. Comparability is preserved. Under the purchase method, the "phase-in" of SmithKline's sales results in the illusion of growth, which we observed in the Acquire–Target example.

Financial Ratio Effects

Not surprisingly, the financial ratios reported by SKB also depend on the accounting method used. Exhibit 14-13, part B, provides one example, the return on total capital under both methods for the year of the merger (1989) and the following year (1990).

The difference in earnings before interest and taxes (EBIT) mainly reflects the absence, under U.K. GAAP, of the amortization of goodwill and the other asset write-ups resulting from the use of the purchase method. The difference in average total capital is due to the absence of the purchase method adjustments and the U.K. practice of immediate write-off of goodwill against equity. The U.K. total capital is (as we have already noted) very close to tangible capital.

The return ratios under each method are quite different. The U.S. ratio is much lower due to lower income and the higher capital base. The 1989 to 1990 trend is, however, quite similar. Neither set of ratios is inherently more correct than the other; each reflects the method and data from which it was computed. Analysis requires an understanding of financial reporting differences and their impact on financial statements; the analysis of a single company, such as SKB, and, even more important, comparisons with other companies in the industry (other drug companies in the case of SKB) should not be mechanical.

Summary

This section illustrates the hazards of making company comparisons without adjusting for the impact of the acquisition accounting method on reported data. When the companies compared are subject to different national accounting systems, the acquisition problem is compounded by differences in presentation and other accounting methods. With attention to the differences and with adequate disclosure, adjustments can be made to achieve some semblance of comparability. The analysis of unadjusted data is unlikely to result in sound investment decisions.

ANALYSIS OF GOODWILL

Goodwill is one of the most controversial subjects in all of accounting and has been so for at least three decades. In most cases, goodwill and other intangible assets arise in purchase method acquisitions; they are the residual portion of the purchase price that cannot be allocated to other, tangible assets. Goodwill is the premium paid for the target's reputation, brand names, or other attributes that enable it to earn an excess return on investment, justifying that premium price. Hence, the name goodwill.

Since goodwill arises as a residual, it cannot be measured directly. It can be independently appraised only by measuring the "excess" return earned by the enterprise; such measurements require many assumptions, making such appraisals controversial.

Proponents of goodwill recognition argue that goodwill is simply the capitalized present value of excess returns some companies are able to earn and no more subjective than the present value of future cash flows connected with tangible assets. Jennings et al. (1996), using an asset-based valuation framework, found that *on average*, the market views goodwill as an asset.

Opponents of the goodwill concept dislike the subjective nature and indirect measurement of this "asset." They argue that it often turns out to be ephemeral;

write-offs of goodwill are common (see Chapter 8). Prices paid for acquisitions often turn out to be based on unrealistic expectations rather than true earnings prospects.

Both arguments, in our view, have merit both when stated in the abstract and when applied to specific companies. We believe that goodwill can, and should, be examined only with respect to a specific enterprise. There are many companies that are able to earn above-normal returns over long periods of time. The common shares of such companies usually sell at prices well above tangible book value, even after tangible assets are revalued to current cost.

In such cases, investors are paying for intangible assets, such as reputation, brand names, patents, management expertise, or other factors. The allocation of the excess purchase price to these factors can only be arbitrary; accounting cannot measure every attribute of an enterprise.

In other cases, companies earn below-normal returns despite the intangible assets on their balance sheet. These assets may be overstated; share prices of such companies are often below stated book value. The fact that an intangible asset originated in an acquisition does not guarantee that it will have continuing value any more than if the intangible asset were self-generated.

To sum up, the existence of economic goodwill is largely independent of the existence of accounting goodwill. The former is a function of economic performance; the latter is a function of accounting standards. Investors and financial analysts are primarily interested in economic goodwill, yet accounting goodwill exists in abundant quantity in the financial statements of many companies.

For purposes of analysis, therefore, the analyst should remove goodwill from reported balance sheets. When a company clearly earns excess returns, this factor will enter into the valuation of the company's shares.

Goodwill Amortization

For companies whose statements are subject to U.S. GAAP and for some others, the recognition of acquisition goodwill necessarily leads to its amortization. Standards are flexible; goodwill can be amortized over a period as long as 40 years under APB 17. As companies are free to choose the period of amortization and in practice make different choices, comparability is poor.

When present, goodwill amortization is a noncash charge; it is merely the amortization of a past expenditure.[26] In the United States, most classes of goodwill are not deductible expenses under the Internal Revenue Code so there is no income tax benefit. In short, the amortization of goodwill is a nonevent, with no real consequences.

Goodwill amortization does, however, affect reported income. When goodwill is written off (such write-offs are often part of restructuring provisions), future reported income increases. For example, consider the following abbreviated income statement of Gardner Denver Machinery:

---

[26]Some believe that goodwill amortization should remain a deduction from net income, similar to depreciation expense (also an allocation of a past expenditure).

Gardner Denver Machinery Income Statement ($ in thousands)

| | Years Ended December 31 | | |
	1994	1995	% Change
Revenues	$175,854	$191,541	8.9%
Costs excluding goodwill amortization	165,220	169,665	2.7%
Income before goodwill and nonrecurring expense	$ 10,634	$ 21,876	105.7%
Goodwill amortization	$ 5,151	$ 2,056	−60.1%
Nonrecurring expense*	99,710	—	
Pretax income	$(94,227)	$ 19,820	
Pretax income before nonrecurring expense	5,483	19,820	261.5%

*Includes goodwill of $72,126.

In 1994, Gardner Denver recorded nonrecurring expense of $99.7 million (pretax), most of which was a write-off of goodwill. That write-off reduced amortization in 1995, contributing to higher reported earnings in that year.

Many analysts would simply add back the nonrecurring charge to reported 1994 results and use the last line (pretax income before nonrecurring expense) to compare results. By that measure, it appears that operating income rose 261% in 1995. However, the 60% decline in goodwill amortization accounted for a significant part of that gain. Using pretax income before goodwill and nonrecurring expense, we find an increase of 105.7%. This measure allows for better estimates of future income as the analyst can separate the effect of the goodwill write-off from operating gains.

For purposes of analysis, therefore, the amortization of goodwill should be added back to net income. By comparing income before amortization to the total cost of the acquisition (including goodwill), the analyst can evaluate the return on the acquisition in the same manner as the return on other investments.

CHOOSING THE ACQUISITION METHOD

The analyses of Acquire–Target and SmithKline Beecham may suggest that the purchase and pooling methods of acquisition accounting are optional alternatives. Strictly speaking, that is not the case; the conditions mandating the use of the purchase or pooling method in the United States are delineated in APB 16. However, it is naive to believe that acquirers ignore the accounting consequences of planned acquisitions.

APB 16 (1970)[27] was intended to eliminate abuses of the pooling method during the acquisition binge of the 1960s and the optional nature of acquisition accounting by defining the conditions under which each method would be applicable. For example,

[27]On August 21, 1996, the FASB added a project to its agenda that will reconsider APB Opinions 16 and 17.

to be eligible for pooling treatment, 12 separate criteria related to the structure of the transaction, its tax effect, and the mode of payment must be satisfied. Thus, the accounting method depends on the characteristics of the transaction.

From the corporate viewpoint, the pooling method is usually preferred under the following conditions:

1. Purchase price greatly exceeds stated equity or book value of target.

2. Target does not have significant depreciable assets that can be written up substantially for tax purposes, creating higher tax deductions.

3. Acquiring company does not wish to increase its leverage or has limited borrowing power.

4. Target has securities or other assets with market values above historic cost. Under pooling, the cost is unchanged; after the acquisition these assets can be sold, increasing reported income.

Under the purchase method, the first two conditions would generate a large amount of goodwill and subsequent amortization reducing reported earnings without a cash (tax reduction) benefit. The SmithKline-Beecham merger is a good example of the adverse impact of purchase accounting on acquisitions meeting the first two conditions.

The third condition needs some elaboration. Purchase method acquisitions can substantially increase the acquiring company's debt load (see Exhibit 14-2B) as compared with the result under a stock transaction. Case 14C-1 illustrates this issue using Georgia Pacific's acquisition of GNN. Apparently, GP felt that the large cash flow of GNN, combined with asset sales, would make the debt load manageable.

In general, acquisitions of service companies and others with low asset intensity (few assets to write up) and targets with high returns on equity (implying purchase prices well above stated equity) lend themselves to pooling.

On the other hand, purchase accounting can be advantageous under different conditions:

1. Target is "asset rich" allowing write-ups, consequent tax reduction, and quick recovery of the investment. Allocation of the purchase price to inventory is a good example.

2. Purchase price is below stated book value facilitating a write down of assets, reducing depreciation and increasing reported earnings.

3. Purchase accounting includes the Target's "off-balance-sheet" obligations (e.g., underfunded postretirement plans) in the allocation of the purchase price, reducing future charges to earnings.

4. Shareholders of the acquirer do not wish to dilute their voting control or equity interest by issuing additional shares. They may prefer to use cash or securities with little or no voting power to effect the acquisition.

Thus, the accounting method is a consequence of the acquisition terms and the specific circumstances of the acquirer, target company, and shareholders. Although not truly optional, it is subject to management control, and the terms of the merger can be fashioned to achieve the desired accounting alternative. Anecdotal evidence suggests that the accounting treatment can significantly affect the negotiated terms[28] and that certain mergers would not have been consummated if pooling could not be used.

Both the choice of accounting method and different market reactions to mergers accounted for as pooling or purchases must, therefore, be understood in the context of the overall motivation for mergers. These issues can be illustrated by examining the income maximization hypothesis often used to explain the accounting choice.

Income Maximization as Motivation for the Pooling/Purchase Choice

Many researchers have explored income maximization and price (P) to book value (BV) ratio as motivations for the pooling/purchase choice. Under this hypothesis, when the price paid exceeds the target's book value ($P > BV$), pooling is preferred as subsequent reported income, return on equity (ROE), and return on assets (ROA) will be higher. On the other hand, when $P < BV$, purchase accounting is preferred.

Robinson and Shane (1990) summarize the results of a number of studies of this hypothesis. They find that when $P > BV$ there is a strong preference for the pooling method (84% overall). For $P < BV$, although the purchase method does not dominate, there is clearly less of a preference for the pooling method. Thus the results are generally consistent with the overall hypothesis, albeit in an asymmetric fashion.

Davis (1990) also documents that the price to book value differential is considerably larger for poolings. This differential is related to the bid premium (the price paid for the target relative to the premerger price of the target) Robinson and Shane found to be larger for poolings.

Thus, consistent with the income maximization hypothesis, the evidence indicates that pooling is the preferred method of accounting for mergers where:

1. $P > BV$ and
2. Relatively higher prices are paid for targets.

Market Reaction and the Pooling/Purchase Choice

For mergers in general, Morck et al. (1990) report that

> average returns to bidding shareholders are at best slightly positive and significantly negative in some studies.[29]

Hong et al. (1978) compared the abnormal returns of acquiring firms using the pooling method with those using the purchase method to evaluate the impact of the choice of accounting method. They also tested whether the market reacts positively to the higher income reported when the pooling method is used.

Little or no market reaction was observed for pooling firms, either in the period

---

[28]The AT&T–NCR merger is an example. Moreover, the FASB Discussion Memorandum, An Analysis of Issues Relating to Accounting for Business Combinations and Purchased Intangibles (August 19, 1976), reports that two-thirds of its respondents concurred with the statement that many of the mergers that used the pooling of interests would not have been consummated had they been required to use the purchase method. Only 14% disagreed with the statement.

[29]Randall Morck, Andrei Shleifer, and Robert W. Vishny, "Do Managerial Objectives Drive Bad Acquisitions?," *Journal of Finance,* March 1990, pp. 31–48. These results contrast with those of target shareholders, who generally fare well as a result of the merger.

leading up to the merger or around the first post-merger earnings announcement. However, for a smaller sample of purchase method firms, they found significant positive reaction in the 12-month period preceding the effective date of the merger.

Davis (1990), using weekly data and an expanded sample of firms, found similar results. Unlike pooling firms, purchase method acquirers show abnormal positive returns over a 26-week period prior to the merger announcement.

Hong et al. and Davis studied two separate time periods (1954 to 1964 and 1971 to 1982, respectively), but both found positive returns to bidder firms using the purchase method. Bradley et al. (1988),[30] noted that although target firms almost always earn abnormal positive returns, acquiring firms realized a significant positive reaction only during the unregulated period 1963–1968 and in fact suffered a significant loss during the sub-period 1981–1984.[31]

Interpreting the Research Results

It is difficult to draw conclusions from this research for two reasons. First, as cash or debt (taxable) transactions cannot be accounted for by use of the pooling method, comparable purchase method transactions are confined to nontaxable acquisitions using shares of the acquirer. In many cases, however, factors that preclude the use of pooling are characteristic of higher bid premia. When cash is used, the bid premium tends to be higher.[32] Moreover, when the transaction is taxable to the target shareholders, a higher bid premium may be required to compensate them for the tax consequences.

Thus, these studies are limited to those transactions where the bid premia are *a priori* smaller. This self-selection bias may explain smaller price to book value differentials associated with purchase accounting and limit the generalizability of these results.

Similarly, the positive market reaction to the purchase acquisitions may be associated with the bargain purchase implied by the low bid premia. On the other hand, relatively higher payments for the pooling transactions may indicate overpayment (or at least no bargain) and hence the muted market reaction. Thus, the market reaction may be related to the level of payment rather than the choice of accounting method.

This explanation assumes that the market reacts to mergers that had been anticipated because of leaks in the weeks leading up to the merger announcement.[33] An alternative explanation offered by Hong et al. was that the firms that instigated purchase transactions were better performing firms and that

> firms who choose the purchase method can "afford" to report the lower earnings caused by the use of this method.[34]

We return to this point later.

---

[30]Bradley et al. (1988) did not differentiate between purchase and pooling transactions.

[31]J. Bradley, A. Desai, and E. H. Kim, "Synergistic Gains from Corporate Acquisitions and Their Division Between the Stockholders of Target and Acquiring Firms," *Journal of Financial Economics,* May 1988, pp. 3–40.

[32]See Robinson and Shane (1990), p. 81.

[33]As most of the reaction was in the 11-week period leading up to the merger announcement this is a plausible explanation.

[34]Hai Hong, Robert S. Kaplan, and Gershon Mandelker, "Pooling vs. Purchase: The Effects of Accounting for Mergers on Stock Prices," *The Accounting Review,* Jan. 1978, pp. 31-47.

The second issue in interpreting research results is related to the question of *cause and effect*. First, we explore reasons why firms are interested in income maximization. One possibility is that managers with compensation plans based on earnings, ROA, or ROE are motivated to choose pooling over purchase to enhance their compensation.

This line of reasoning is consistent with theories of merger activity that argue that managers initiate mergers for their own self-interest and consequently may overpay for the target. They enter into mergers to "buy" growth or to diversify their own risk even if this growth or diversification is not (necessarily) in the best interests of their shareholders.[35]

This underlying motivation may explain (1) the merger, (2) the accounting choice, and (3) the degree of overpayment. If the accounting choice is deemed desirable, then it may be that the accounting choice itself was one of the terms of the negotiation. The acquirer may have paid more for the target to obtain a deal structure permitting it to use the pooling method.

Thus, the choice of accounting method cannot be viewed separately from the acquisition itself. In many ways it is endogenous to the overall terms of the merger. This is true not only for the effects implied by the income maximization theory and the differential market reactions discussed above. Similar patterns can be shown in the context of other merger characteristics. These are discussed in the next section.

Other Factors Influencing Mergers, Bid Premia, and the Pooling/Purchase Choice

Exhibit 14-14 lists a number of factors that can impact the pooling/purchase choice either directly or indirectly (through its influence on the bid premium). In addition, (some of) these factors have been found in other studies to be associated with positive market reaction to mergers. The discussion of these categories should serve to illustrate the complexities involved in analyzing the relationship of accounting choice and economic characteristics of mergers.

The three categories are characteristics of:

1. The transaction
2. The acquiring firm
3. The target firm

Characteristics of the Transaction

(1) Cash Transaction and (2) Tax Status. These were discussed earlier. Under APB 16, pooling is permissible only if the merger is a noncash transaction. Moreover, pooling transactions tend to be nontaxable acquisitions. Generally, higher bid premia are associated with mergers that involve cash payments and are taxable to the target's shareholders. These factors result in higher bid premia for purchase rather than pooling transactions and also preclude the use of pooling.

(3) Percentage Acquired. The larger the percentage of the target acquired, the larger the bid premium. Under APB 16, unless the acquisition exceeds 90% of the shares of the target, it must be accounted for as a purchase. Thus a higher bid premia is implied for a pooling rather than purchase transaction.

---

[35]See Morck et al. (1990) pp. 31–36. Roll (1986) goes so far as to suggest that managers suffer from hubris and are convinced that they can do a better job with the target than its current management.

EXHIBIT 14-14
Merger Characteristics, Bid Premia, and Choice of Accounting Method

	+ Indicates Preference for Pooling	+ Indicates Larger Bid Premia
Characteristics of Transaction		
1. Cash payment	−	+
2. Tax status	−	+
3. Small percentage acquired	−	−
Characteristics of Acquirer		
4. $P > BV$ and management compensation contract	+	
5. $P > BV$ and bond covenant, debt constraint	−	
6. $P > BV$ and bond covenant, dividend constraint	+	
7. "Good" managers Owner versus manager control	−	−
Characteristics of Target		
8. Low leverage High liquidity		+
9. Relative size of target to acquirer	−	−
10. "Poor" managers Low market to book ratio Low Q ratio		−
11. Low price-earnings multiple	+	

Characteristics of Acquirer

The first three aspects of the acquirer are tied to the nature of the price to book value differential.

(4) Compensation Plans. When $P > BV$, compensation plans can induce managers to increase their compensation by choosing the pooling method (Dunne, 1990).

(5) and (6) Effects of Bond Covenants. The firm's debt covenants may affect preference for the purchase or pooling method. When $P > BV$, the purchase method reports higher assets and equity. This improves the current and debt-to-equity ratios. Thus, firms with binding debt covenants in terms of liquidity and leverage ratios prefer the purchase method.[36] Davis, for example, found that purchase method firms had significantly higher leverage ratios than pooling firms.[37]

---

[36]However, Leftwich (1981) argues that firms with high leverage ratios prefer pooling as it reports higher income. His argument, it seems to us, ignores the increased equity reported at the time of the purchase and focuses on the income stream realized over time.

[37]Davis did not discuss whether the firms had bond covenants based on leverage ratios. Thus, we cannot speculate whether the positive market reaction associated with the choice of the purchase method was in any way related to wealth transfers from bondholders to equityholders.

On the other hand, if restrictions on dividends are related to levels of retained earnings, then the pooling method may be preferred. Although it reports lower total equity, the pooling method reports higher retained earnings, as the retained earnings of the acquirer and target are combined. Under purchase accounting, only the acquirer's retained earnings are carried forward. Because debt covenants usually contain liquidity, leverage, and dividend restrictions, both the terms of the merger and accounting method preference depend on the most limiting of these covenants.

(7) Type of Management. Empirical evidence (e.g., Servaes, 1991) indicates that better managers make better acquisitions. One of the signs of better managers is superior market performance of their firms. Thus, the evidence with respect to acquisitions using the purchase method may indicate a combination of:

1. Firms with better managers (making better acquisitions) explaining the abnormal positive reaction prior to the merger;
2. Since better managers make better acquisitions, they do not tend to overpay, explaining lower bid premia;
3. Better managers do not need or use artificial income increasing methods. This argument was advanced earlier by Hong et al. (1978).

Consistent with these propositions, Dunne (1990) found that owner-controlled firms were more prone to choose the purchase method. They are more likely to take actions that are beneficial to the welfare of the firm, as opposed to manager-controlled firms that may attempt to maximize their own welfare at the expense of the firm.

Characteristics of Target

(8) High Liquidity/Low Leverage. Firms with excess cash are often acquisition targets and would likely receive higher bid premia as the acquiring firm wants to capture the liquid assets. Firms with excess liquidity may have been strong performers in the past in industries whose growth potential has declined.

(9) Relative Size of Target. Robinson and Shane note that the larger the size of the target relative to the acquirer, the less likely the acquirer would be willing to give the target's shareholders common shares with full voting rights. The acquirer's shareholders would be fearful of losing control of the firm. Under APB 16, lack of voting rights precludes use of the pooling method. Robinson and Shane cite empirical evidence that bid premia tend to be lower when the target is relatively large. Again, we have a situation when lower bid premia are consistent with the accounting choice of purchase, independent of any income/asset manipulation motivation.

(10) Type of Management. Firms run by poor managers are often viewed as prime takeover targets. The new managers feel they can do a better job of running the firm. The relationship of the firm's price to its book value is often viewed as an indicator of poor management, as the firm is not valued favorably by the market.

Tobin's Q ratio, the ratio of a firm's market value to the replacement value of its assets, is another indicator of poor managerial performance. Low Q ratios (below 1, for example) indicate that a dollar invested internally in the firm will generate a return whose present value is less than $1.

There are alternative explanations (to poor management) for low market price to book value ratios and low Q's. Such firms may be in industries with few growth opportunities as it is too expensive to grow by investing internally. The efficient way to expand is to acquire another company in the same industry. It may be cheaper to buy a firm with existing assets than to replace the assets directly. In any event, target firms with low market to book value and/or low Q ratios can typically be bought with low bid premia.

(11) Low P/E Ratios. A low P/E ratio may be another manifestation of the poor performance noted earlier. However, we discuss it separately as it is often given another dimension relating to the bootstrapping phenomenon noted earlier. It is hypothesized that a firm with a high P/E ratio can increase its own market price by acquiring companies with low P/E ratios. The newly acquired earnings will be valued by the market at the acquirer's higher P/E ratio. For this to work, the market has to be naive. When companies using this technique make many insignificant mergers (with little disclosure), however, it may be hard for analysts to see through the technique.[38]

Summary

The discussion indicates that the relationship between choice of accounting method and the underlying motivation for mergers is quite complex. One should, therefore, not draw immediate conclusions as to managers' motivations and/or potential market reaction. The effects and implications of the accounting method cannot be understood without a thorough examination of the merger's economic characteristics.

PUSH-DOWN ACCOUNTING

Firms that have been acquired in purchase method acquisitions (in effect subsidiaries of new parents) often continue to issue their own financial statements, due to such factors as:

- Statutory or regulatory reporting requirements
- Minority equity interest, including preferred shareholders
- Need to provide information to creditors

The issuance of such financial statements raises an important accounting issue. Should they reflect the operations of the firm, as if it had not been acquired, or should the financial statements be adjusted to reflect the purchase method adjustments shown in its (new) parent company statements? In other words, should the parent company's purchase method adjustments be "pushed down" into the financial statements of the subsidiary?

---

[38]This phenomenon is discussed in "After the Party," *The Economist,* May 18, 1996, p. 65. It argues that Softbank, a Japanese computer software firm, has successfully taken advantage of the fact that price-earnings ratios are higher in Japan than the United States. By making acquisitions (using the purchase method) in the United States, it increases reported earnings and its stock price, allowing it to sell shares to fund further acquisitions.

Push-down accounting has a controversial history. The SEC requires its use when all the equity of a company is sold to the public, thus marking a complete change in ownership.[39] The SEC also requires push-down accounting:

- When separate financial statements of a company are included in its parent's SEC filings, or
- The subsidiary is registering stock or debt offerings.

The discussion that follows focuses on the impact of the use of push-down accounting rather than the theoretical concerns with the new basis of accounting.

Push-Down in Practice: The GM–Hughes Transaction

Effective December 31, 1985, General Motors (GM) acquired the Hughes Aircraft Company (Hughes) in a purchase transaction for $2.7 billion in cash and 50 million shares of GM Class H stock, with a stated value of $2,561 million, making the total cost $5,261 million. The purchase price was allocated as follows:

Allocation of Purchase Price of Hughes

Net assets of Hughes at historical cost	$1,016 million
Patents and technology	500
Future benefit of Hughes incentive plan	125
Intangible assets (goodwill)	3,620
Total	$5,261 million

Because Hughes was a defense contractor and there was substantial uncertainty whether asset values exceeding historical cost would be recoverable under the company's contracts with the U.S. government, there was no revaluation of Hughes' tangible assets; the entire excess of purchase price over stated equity was, therefore, assigned to intangible assets, mostly goodwill.

The GM Class H shares were entitled to dividends based on the earnings of Hughes. As a result, Hughes continued to publish its own separate financial statements, although it was a subsidiary of GM. The Securities and Exchange Commission required that the purchase method adjustments shown be pushed down into the separate financial statements of Hughes.

Impact on the Balance Sheet

If Hughes had not been required to reflect the purchase method adjustments in its financial statements, those statements would have been unchanged except for the merger-related expenses and a requirement to fund the executive incentive plan. The impact of push-down accounting can be seen in the condensed balance sheet at December 31, 1985, shown in Exhibit 14-15. Push-down accounting nearly doubles the assets (because of goodwill) of Hughes and triples its stockholders' equity.

[39]The SEC requires push-down accounting when the change in ownership is greater than 95% (unless public debt, preferred stock, or significant minority interest affects control), permits it for changes between 80 and 95%, and objects to it for changes below 80%. See SEC Staff Accounting Bulletins No. 54 (1983) and No. 73 (1987).

EXHIBIT 14-15. GM HUGHES
Effect of Push-Down Adjustments on Balance Sheet (Condensed),
at December 31, 1985 ($ in millions)

	Historical*	Adjustments†	Fair Value
Current assets	$3,062	—	$3,062
Property	2,578	—	2,578
Intangible assets	—	$4,245	4,245
Total assets	$5,640	$4,245	$9,885
Current liabilities	3,070	—	3,070
Long-term liabilities	449	—	449
Stockholders' equity	2,121	4,245	6,366
Total equities	$5,640	$4,245	$9,885

*The historical data shown include the assets and liabilities of Delco Electronics, a GM subsidiary merged into Hughes as part of the merger transaction.

†Excess of purchase price of Hughes over net assets at historical cost ($5,261 million − $1,016 million).

Source: GM Hughes, 1985 *Annual Report.*

Impact on the Income Statement

The large intangible assets on the balance sheet of Hughes following the merger as a result of push-down accounting also affected the income statement. GM decided to amortize the acquired patents over 15 years, the incentive plan benefit over 5 years, and the remaining intangibles over 40 years. This amortization sharply reduced the reported earnings of Hughes, shown in Exhibit 14-16.

Because the amortization of the purchase method adjustments was constant, its percentage effect would diminish as income grows. But as income declined during the period 1988 to 1991, the percentage reduction rose. The annual amortization in dollars was unchanged, however, until 1991 (when amortization decreased by $25 million as

EXHIBIT 14-16. GM HUGHES
Effect of Push-Down Accounting on Net Income, Years Ended December 31, 1988 to 1994 ($ in millions)

		1988	1989	1990	1991	1992	1993	1994
Net income before push-down		$ 802	$ 781	$ 726	$ 559	$ (922)	$ 922	$1,049
Purchase method adjustments*		(149)	(149)	(149)	(124)	(124)	(124)	(124)
Reported net income		$ 653	$ 632	$ 577	$ 435	$(1,046)	$ 798	$ 925
Percentage reduction		−18.6%	−19.1%	−20.5%	−22.2%	NMF	−13.4%	−11.8%
*Amortization of								
Incentive plan, over 5 years	$125/5 =	$ 25.0	$ 25.0	$ 25.0	$ —	$ —	$ —	$ —
Patents, over 15 years	$500/15 =	33.3	33.3	33.3	33.3	33.3	33.3	33.3
Goodwill, over 40 years	$3,620/40 =	90.5	90.5	90.5	90.5	90.5	90.5	90.5
		$148.8	$148.8	$148.8	$123.8	$123.8	$123.8	$123.8

the incentive plan benefit was fully amortized in 1990). In 2001, it decreases by a further $33 million as the acquired patents arc fully amortized. The goodwill amortization of $90.5 million will continue, however, through the year 2015 unless written off earlier. Over time, therefore, the effect of the purchase method adjustments decreases, more rapidly if net income grows. This effect can be seen in 1993 and 1994 when income grew substantially.

Effect on Cash Flows

As amortization of the purchase method adjustments that are pushed down into the financial statements of Hughes are noncash charges, they have no impact on the company's cash flow. There would be an indirect impact if dividend policy and capital spending decisions were based on reported earnings, but that is unlikely. In the case of Hughes, the purchase method adjustments were explicitly ignored when computing income available for dividends.

Effect on Financial Ratios

The effects of push-down accounting on financial ratios are similar to those of the purchase method from whence it derives. Activity ratios decline. Return ratios are affected by the change in both numerator (income) and denominator (total capital). Exhibit 14-17 shows the impact of push-down accounting for 1988 to 1994, based on data from Hughes annual reports.

Exhibits 14-16 and 14-17 provide the data required to compute the debt-to-total capital ratio and the return on average equity ratios.

Financial Ratios of GM Hughes, 1989, 1990, and 1994

	As Reported			Adjusted		
	1989	1990	1994	1989	1990	1994
Debt-to-total capital	10.4	10.8	5.7	19.6	18.9	9.2
Return on average equity	8.2	7.2	12.1	21.6	18.2	24.2

EXHIBIT 14-17. GM HUGHES
Effect of Push-Down Accounting on Condensed Balance Sheet, December 31, 1988 to 1994 ($ in millions)

	1988	1989	1990	1991	1992	1993	1994
As Reported (Push-Down)							
Total debt	$1,019	$ 918	$ 983	$ 850	$ 978	$ 495	$ 479
Equity	7,550	7,898	8,098	8,218	6,815	7,328	7,976
Total capital	$8,569	$8,816	$9,081	$9,068	$7,793	$7,823	$8,455
Adjusted* (Excluding Intangibles)							
Total debt	$1,019	$ 918	$ 983	$ 850	$ 978	$ 495	$ 479
Equity	3,469	3,768	4,212	4,451	3,194	3,954	4,704
Total capital	$4,488	$4,686	$5,195	$5,301	$4,172	$4,449	$5,183

*Assumes that purchase method adjustments had not been pushed down to the financial statements of GM Hughes.

The debt-to-total capital ratio is always higher when the reported data are adjusted to exclude the push-down effect, because equity is lower. (Of course, if the "as reported" data are used to compute debt to tangible capital, the ratio also rises.) The trend may also change. Tangible equity grew faster than total debt in 1990. As a result, the debt ratio declined. When the as reported data are used, debt grew faster, increasing the debt ratio. The 1994 ratio reflects the reduced debt burden under both measures.

For return on average equity, the trend is the same, but the levels are very different. Removing the goodwill pushed down into Hughes increases earnings, reduces equity, and thus increases the return on equity. ROE is very high when the push-down adjustments are excluded, suggesting that although Hughes is a good company, GM paid too high an acquisition price; the ROE based on what GM paid is mediocre.

Push-Down Summed Up

Although push-down accounting is no more than an application of the purchase method to the separate statements of the acquired firm, it remains a controversial topic. From the analyst's perspective, push-down accounting replaces historical cost with current values, which may be more useful for making investment decisions.

It is important to understand the effects of push-down because it radically changes the financial statements (and ratios) of affected companies. Consistency over time and comparability with other companies are destroyed by push-down; if the impact of push-down adjustments is not understood, financial data may be misinterpreted.

SPINOFFS

A spinoff occurs when a company separates a portion of its business into a newly created subsidiary and distributes shares of that subsidiary to its shareholders pro rata. The accounting for such spinoffs is quite simple and can be characterized as a "reverse pooling." The assets and liabilities of the subsidiary to be spun off are removed from the balance sheet of the parent company at their historical amounts, that is, without adjustment. The spinoff's balance sheet "inherits" the historical cost of the assets and liabilities transferred. The stockholders' equity of the parent company is reduced by the stockholders' equity (net assets) of the spinoff. The only adjustment will be for any capital transactions (debt repayment, equity infusion, or dividend) with the parent that are part of the spinoff transaction.

The income statement of the spinoff is little changed from what it would have been if it had remained part of its former parent. The only differences are the effects of any capital transactions (e.g., reduced interest expense on debt forgiven by the parent) and the additional administrative expenses borne by the subsidiary as a public company. The *pro forma* income statements issued in connection with the spinoff disclose these impacts.

From the parent company perspective, spinoffs offer some advantages. First, a spinoff can be an easy way to dispose of a "problem" subsidiary without recognizing any gain or loss. Sometimes, the spinoff will have a higher market value as a public company than could have been realized via sale, for reasons discussed in the paragraphs that follow. Thus, stockholders are better off receiving the spinoff shares than if the subsidiary had been sold, especially if its sale would have resulted in capital gains tax payable by the parent.

Second, spinoffs often pay special dividends to their parent as part of the spinoff transaction. In addition, the debt of the spinoff is removed from the parent company's balance sheet. The result is lower parent company debt and, possibly, reduced financial leverage.

Third, if the spinoff was losing money (or had very low profitability), the parent company reports either higher net income or, at least, higher profit margins. Fixed income coverage may also improve.

Analysis of Spinoffs

When analyzing a spinoff, it is important to look for the following information, usually found in the financial statement footnotes:

1. Has the spinoff company paid a special dividend to the parent or, alternatively, has the parent forgiven debt or contributed capital? Such transactions alter the financial structure of the spinoff and its profitability going forward.

2. How have postretirement benefits been dealt with? If the parent company retains responsibility for all benefits for retirees, for example, the spinoff company will have a reduced burden. Also evaluate the allocation of pension plan assets and liabilities.

3. Examine income tax sharing agreements, which detail the impact of additional tax assessments or refunds covering periods prior to the spinoff. Also consider that the spinoff company inherits the tax basis as well as the accounting basis of assets and liabilities. If tax depreciation of fixed assets has exceeded depreciation expense, then future tax deductions will be below depreciation expense. Although the deferred tax liability in the balance sheet should provide for the reversal of this and other timing differences, there may still be a cash flow consequence if income taxes paid exceed future income tax expense.

4. Look for other transactions between parent and spinoff that may affect future profitability or cash flow. Possible problem areas include:

   - Contingent liability for debt or other obligations of the parent company.
   - Guarantees of spinoff obligations by the parent, but with the spinoff company paying a fee for the guarantee.
   - Parent company charges for administrative or other services.
   - Higher rental costs due to spinoff company occupancy of parent company office space or operating facilities.
   - Intercompany supply agreements, which can be either positive or negative for the spinoff, depending on their terms. Such agreements often have "sunset" provisions providing for termination or diminishment over time.

5. Read the footnotes of the spinoff carefully, even if you are familiar with the operations of the parent. Some data (e.g., off-balance-sheet financing) may not have been significant for the parent, but are significant to the spinoff company because of its smaller size.

EXHIBIT 14-18. EMERSON ELECTRIC
Effect of Spinoff of Esco, for Years Ended September 30, 1986 to 1990 ($ in millions)

	1986	1987	1988	1989	1990
Sales (as reported)	$5,242	$6,170	$6,652	$7,071	$7,573
Sales of Esco	(511)	(599)	(607)	(599)	(538)
Pro forma sales	$4,731	$5,571	$6,045	$6,472	$7,035
Net income (as reported)	$ 427	$ 467	$ 529	$ 588	$ 613
Net income of Esco	(30)	(24)	(2)	(12)	2
Pro forma net income	$ 397	$ 443	$ 527	$ 576	$ 615

Growth Rate, 1986 to 1990 (%)	As Reported	*Pro Forma*
Sales	9.63%	10.43%
Net income	9.46	11.56

Source: Emerson Electric, *1990 Annual Report.*

Reasons for Investment in Spinoffs

Although some investors immediately sell the shares of spinoffs they receive, others find spinoffs to be attractive investment opportunities. The following factors may make spinoffs profitable investments:

1. Operations that are "lost" in a large corporation may benefit from the focus of a management undistracted by other activities. Spinoff firms frequently provide stock options and other incentives for managers to improve profitability.

2. The smaller size of a spinoff may increase the flexibility of managers no longer bound by the bureaucracy of the former parent.

3. The spinoff may attract investors who wish to invest in its industry, but were deterred by the other operations of the former parent. The spinoff may also attract customers not previously accessible because they are competitors of the parent.

4. Even if the spinoff company has poor current profitability, investors may be attracted by high book value, cash flow, or other attributes.

As a result, a spinoff may increase shareholder wealth as the combined market value of the spinoff and parent company shares exceeds the prespinoff market value of the parent. Although financial theory says that should not happen, in practice it often does.[40] Operations that contributed little or nothing to the parent company's market value (because of low profitability, or lack of visibility) may have substantial market value as a stand-alone company.

[40]For example, see Schipper and Smith (1983).

Example: Emerson Electric's Spinoff of ESCO Electronics

In September 1990, Emerson Electric spun off Esco Electronics, a wholly owned subsidiary, to its stockholders. The effect on Emerson was small; Esco accounted for only 7% of consolidated sales and 15% of stockholders' equity prior to the spinoff. Esco showed a small loss for the year ended September 30, 1990.

Emerson accounted for the spinoff by reducing its stockholders' equity by $523 million. The assets and liabilities of Esco were removed from the balance sheet of Emerson, but that company did not restate its previously issued financial statements for the spinoff.

Because Esco's sales had been stagnant over the period 1986 to 1990, and its profitability had declined, the restatement of Emerson's income statement to exclude the result of Esco increased Emerson's growth rates of both sales and net income, as shown in Exhibit 14-18.

The spinoff clearly enhanced Emerson's reported growth rate. The reduction of stockholders' equity probably had little effect; Emerson's shares already sold at a high multiple of book value because of its high return on equity. Moreover the spinoff, by reducing profitability only slightly (actually increasing net income for 1990) while reducing equity by 15%, increased Emerson's return on equity.

Thus, the spinoff of the poorly performing Esco subsidiary may have enhanced the value (if we assume a constant price/earnings ratio) of Emerson shares. If the higher growth rate ex-Esco increased Emerson's price/earnings multiple, then the positive effect would be greater. In addition, Emerson stockholders received shares of Esco.

From June 30, 1990 (three months prior to the spinoff) to June 30, 1991 (nine months after), the price of Emerson common shares (excluding the value of the spinoff shares) rose by 13.7%, as compared with a 3.7% increase in the Standard & Poor's 500 stock index for the same time period. When the value of the Esco shares is included, the gain in Emerson was 14.5%. Although comparisons of this type are imprecise (there may have been other factors at work), the superior performance of Emerson does suggest that the company may have increased the value of its shares by "giving away" part of its operations.

Although spinoffs have become increasingly common in recent years, most companies still dispose of unwanted operations by selling them. The accounting for such discontinued operations is discussed in Chapter 2.

SUMMARY

This chapter reviews the accounting and financial analysis issues posed by business combinations and other types of corporate reorganizations. The two reporting methods for mergers, purchase and pooling, are not strictly speaking alternatives. However, their financial statement and ratio effects are so significantly different that they are clearly important variables in any acquisition decision.

The differences between these two methods are illustrated using the simplified Target–Acquire example. This illustration is followed by an evaluation of Beecham's acquisition of SmithKline. This transaction was reported as a merger (pooling) in the United Kingdom, but as a purchase transaction in the United States, providing the opportunity to analyze the difference between these methods.

Two cases extend the chapter analysis. Case 14-1 is concerned with restating the purchase of Great Northern Nekoosa by Georgia Pacific from the purchase to the pooling method. Case 14-2 reverses the process, as the acquisition of Golden Valley by ConAgra is restated from the pooling to the purchase method. These cases highlight the impact of the accounting method on financial statements and ratios and suggest why each transaction was structured to achieve the desired accounting objective.

The chapter goes on to review the effect of push-down accounting on the financial statements of firms acquired in transactions requiring use of the purchase method. The GM Hughes case illustrates the transforming effect of these adjustments on reported income, book value, and financial ratios. Spinoffs, which appear to create shareholder value from unwanted subsidiaries, are examined next.

The transactions discussed in this chapter are particularly troublesome for financial analysts as they create a discontinuity. The firm's business and financial statements may be radically changed overnight. The goal of the chapter was to present analytical tools to help financial statement users separate the effects of these transactions from ongoing operating results.

Chapter 15 deals with another source of discontinuity, changes in exchange rates. Our goal in that chapter is to separate changes in operating activities from the effects of changing exchange rates.

CASE 14-1

Analysis of a Purchase Method Acquisition: Georgia Pacific's Purchase of Great Northern Nekoosa

In March 1990, Georgia Pacific (GP), a major forest products firm, purchased Great Northern Nekoosa (GNN), a pulp and paper company, pursuant to a tender offer for shares of that company. The merger was accounted for as a purchase. The sales of GNN were approximately 40% of those of GP.

The historical cost balance sheet of GNN as of December 31, 1989, relevant sections of GNN's 10-Q report for the quarter ended March 31, 1990, and selected disclosures regarding GNN from GP's *1990 Annual Report* were used to develop the data on purchase method adjustments depicted in Exhibit 14C-1.

The first two adjustments shown in Exhibit 14C-1 reflect the recognition of fair market values of inventories, timber, and property. Adjustment (3) eliminates deferred taxes and (4) recognizes the increase in long-term liabilities. Finally, adjustment (5) relates to the elimination of $482 million of goodwill and the recognition of the residual goodwill from this acquisition computed as follows:

Fair value of tangible assets acquired	$ 3,992 million
Fair value of liabilities assumed	(2,294)
Fair value of net assets acquired	$ 1,698
Purchase Price	$ 3,699
Fair value of net assets acquired	(1,698)
Goodwill	$ 2,001 million

EXHIBIT 14C-1
Acquisition of Great Northern Nekoosa, Purchase Method Adjustments, March 8, 1990
($ in millions)

	GNN (Historical)	Adjustments	GNN (Fair Value)
Cash	$ 96	—	$ 96
Accounts receivable	484	—	484
Inventories	271	117 (1)	388
Other current assets	44	—	44
Current assets	$ 895	$ 117	$1,012
Timber and timberlands	338	98 (2)	436
Property	2,460	20 (2)	2,480
Goodwill	482	(482) (5)	—
		2,001 (5)	2,001
Other assets	109	(45)	64
Total assets	$4,284	$1,709	$5,993
Short-term debt	146	—	146
Payables and accruals	400	—	400
Current liabilities	$ 546	—	$ 546
Long-term debt	1,513	3	1,516
Deferred income taxes	460	(421) (3)	39
Other liabilities	31	162 (4)	193
Total liabilities	$2,550	$ (256)	$2,294
Equity (net worth)	$1,734		
Total adjustments		$1,965	
Net assets acquired including goodwill			$3,699

Note: See text for discussion of adjustments (1–5). The GNN data and adjustments are approximations. The data available do not permit precise allocations in some cases. For simplicity, it is assumed that such accounts as accounts receivable and payables and accruals are already stated at fair value, requiring no further adjustment.

1. (a) GNN reported a LIFO reserve of $94 million. Explain why the adjustment to inventories could be greater than that reserve.

   (b) Discuss two reasons that would explain why GP allocated a higher proportion of the purchase price to goodwill than to timber and property.

   (c) Explain why GP eliminated the $482 million of goodwill on GNN's preacquisition balance sheet.

   (d) Explain why GP eliminated the deferred tax credits on GNN's preacquisition balance sheet.

2. Exhibit 14C-2 contains GP's condensed balance sheet as of December 31, 1990.

   (a) Use Exhibits 14C-1 and 14C-2 to recast the 1990 purchase method balance sheet as a pooling of interests, assuming that GP issued common stock to acquire GNN. To replicate the capital structure and cash position under the purchase method, assume that GP repurchased $3,699 million of common stock. (Note that such repurchase would preclude use of the pooling method under U.S. GAAP; the assumption is made here for educational purposes only.)

**EXHIBIT 14C-2. GEORGIA PACIFIC CORPORATION
AND SUBSIDIARIES**
Balance Sheets, as of December 31, 1989 to 1990

December 31	1989	1990
Assets		
Cash	$ 23	$ 58
Accounts receivable	890	409
Inventories	876	1,209
Other current assets	40	90
Total current assets	$1,829	$ 1,766
Timber and timberlands	1,246	1,630
Property	3,691	6,341
Goodwill	91	2,042
Other assets	199	281
Total assets	$7,056	$12,060
Liabilities		
Short-term debt	$ 210	$ 1,444
Payables and accruals	714	1,091
Current liabilities	$ 924	$ 2,535
Long-term debt	2,336	5,218
Deferred income taxes	841	928
Other liabilities	238	404
Total liabilities	$4,339	$ 9,085
Equity	2,717	2,975
Total liabilities and equity	$7,056	$12,060

Source: Adapted from Georgia Pacific, *1990 Annual Report.*

EXHIBIT 14C-3. GEORGIA PACIFIC
Sales and Income Data, 1988 to 1990 ($ in millions)

	1988	1989	1990
A. Sales			
Sales as reported	$9,509	$10,171	$12,665
GNN sales prior to acquisition	3,566	3,853	710
B. Net Income			
Net income (as reported)	$ 467	$ 661	$ 365
GNN income prior to acquisition*	342	321	(57)

*Reported earnings of GNN for 1988, 1989, and 1990 through March 8.

    (b) Compare the current and debt-to-equity ratios under the purchase and pooling methods.

    (c) Compute the tangible equity (equity less goodwill) under the two methods.

3. Exhibit 14C-3 provides sales and income data for the 1988 to 1990 period.

    (a) Georgia Pacific reported sales were $12,665 and $11,524 million in 1990 and 1991 respectively. GP states that sales for 1989 and 1990 would have been $13,944 and $13,350 million respectively, if the acquisition had been completed on January 1, 1989. Compare the sales trend reported by GP and that suggested by the *pro forma* disclosures.

    (b) Explain why GP's reported income would have differed if the pooling method had been used.

4. **(a)** Reconcile the difference between the change in the inventory balance reported on the balance sheet (increase of $333 million) and the change in inventories reflected in the cash flow statement (decrease of $34 million). Assume that no inventories are denominated in foreign currencies.

    (b) Reconcile the difference between the increase in the property accounts reported on the balance sheet and the change expected given the following transactions during 1990:

Capital expenditures	$833 million
Depreciation expense	622

    (c) Reconcile the difference between the decrease in receivables of $481 million shown on the balance sheet and the decrease of $929 million reported in the cash flow statement.

    (d) GP reported an increase of 53% in CFO from $1,358 million in 1989 to $2,073 million in 1990. Evaluate this increase in CFO in the context of part C and GP's footnote disclosures indicating that the firm sold $850 million of GNN's trade accounts receivable during 1990.

CASE 14-2

Analysis of a Pooling Method Acquisition: The ConAgra–Golden Valley Merger

In July 1991, Golden Valley Microwave Foods, a manufacturer of popcorn and other microwave foods, was merged into ConAgra, a diversified food company. The merger was accounted for using the pooling of interests method of accounting. Exhibit 14C-4 contains a *pro forma* combined, condensed balance sheet from the June 10, 1991 proxy statement that was sent to shareholders of Golden Valley.

    ConAgra and Golden Valley had a joint venture (Lamb-Weston, a manufacturer of frozen potato products) that each firm accounted for using the equity method of accounting. As a result of the merger, Lamb-Weston was now 100% owned and had to be consolidated.

1. Recreate the journal entries required to eliminate the investment in Lamb-Weston and consolidate the joint venture.

2. **(a)** On the merger date (July 11, 1991), ConAgra shares closed at a price of $40.875 per share. Use the following assumptions and additional data to recast the postacquisition combined balance sheet as if the purchase method of accounting had been used. Allocate any excess purchase price paid to goodwill.

    • Golden Valley uses the first-in, first-out method of accounting for its inventories. Assume that the fair value of the inventories exceeds cost by 20%.

EXHIBIT 14C-4. CONAGRA, INC. AND SUBSIDIARIES
Pro Forma Combined Condensed Balance Sheet: Unaudited ($ in thousands)

The following unaudited pro forma combined condensed balance sheet for ConAgra, Golden Valley and Lamb-Weston has been prepared based upon the historical consolidated balance sheets for ConAgra, Golden Valley and Lamb-Weston as of February 24, 1991, March 30, 1991, and February 24, 1991, respectively. The pro forma combined condensed balance sheet gives effect to the Merger as if it had occurred as of February 24, 1991 and as if it had been accounted for as a pooling of interests.

	ConAgra, Inc. and Subsidiaries	Golden Valley Microwave Foods, Inc. and Subsidiaries	Pro Forma Adjustments Lamb-Weston, Inc.	Other	Pro Forma Combined
ASSETS					
Current Assets:					
Cash and Cash Equivalents	$ 115,386	$ 275	$ 22,792	$ 8,308 (5)	
				(31,100)(6)	$ 115,661
Receivables, Net	1,396,592	22,927	30,298	—	1,449,817
Inventories	2,387,066	34,869	76,833	—	2,498,768
Other Current Assets	382,844	150	12,970	—	395,964
Total Current Assets	4,281,888	58,221	142,893	(22,792)	4,460,210
Property, Plant and Equipment	1,853,294	65,185	171,602	2,842 (3)	2,092,923
Brands, Trademarks and Goodwill, Net	2,707,742	—	23,319	4,560 (2)	
				4,763 (3)	2,740,384
Investments in Unconsolidated Subsidiaries	166,754	54,843	—	(104,847)(2)	116,750
Other Assets	272,132	2,591	14,496	(22,328)(4)	266,891
	$9,281,810	$180,840	$352,310	$(137,802)	$9,677,158
LIABILITIES AND STOCKHOLDERS' EQUITY					
Current Liabilities:					
Notes Payable	$915,274	$ —	$ —	$ —	$ 915,274
Current Installments of Long-Term Debt	422,867	413	9,428	—	432,708
Accounts Payable, Accrued Expenses and Other Current Liabilities	2,661,160	17,972	46,806	(667)(2)	
				8,308 (5)	2,733,579
Total Current Liabilities	3,999,301	18,385	56,234	7,641	4,081,561
Long-Term Debt	1,947,660	52,649	172,593	(31,100)(6)	2,141,802
Deferred Income Taxes	—	1,843	17,595	2,890 (3)	
				(22,328)(4)	—
Other Noncurrent Liabilities	1,230,842 (7)	—	1,025	5,243 (2)	1,237,110
Preferred Shares Subject to Mandatory Redemption	356,162	—	—	—	356,162
Common Stockholders' Equity					
Common Stock	697,392	175	53,255	(53,255)(2)	
				49,619 (1)	747,186
Additional Paid-in Capital	435,837	27,768	—	(49,619)(1)	413,986
Retained Earnings	623,184	80,020	51,608	(51,608)(2)	
				4,715 (3)	707,919
Foreign Currency Translation Adjustment	4,204	—	—	—	4,204
Less Cost of Treasury Shares	(3,160)	—	—	—	(3,160)
Less Unearned Restricted Stock	(9,612)	—	—	—	(9,612)
Total Common Stockholders' Equity	1,747,845	107,963	104,863	(100,148)	1,860,523
	$9,281,810	$180,840	$352,310	$(137,802)	$9,677,158

EXHIBIT 14C-4 (*continued*)

(1) Reflects the assumed conversion of 17,545,333 shares of Golden Valley Common Stock into 9,958,731 shares of ConAgra Common Stock (assuming an Exchange Ratio of .5676 of a share of ConAgra Common Stock for each share of Golden Valley Common Stock and assuming no fractional shares of ConAgra Common Stock are created upon the conversion of Golden Valley Common Stock).

(2) Reflects elimination of equity of Lamb-Weston upon consolidation—previously carried at equity.

(3) Reflects adjustment to conform Golden Valley accounting practices to those followed by ConAgra, including capitalization of certain acquired intangible assets and depreciation policies.

(4) Reclassification of deferred income taxes.

(5) Reclassification of Lamb-Weston cash overdraft.

(6) Reflects an assumed prepayment of a portion of Lamb-Weston long-term debt from Lamb-Weston excess cash.

(7) Other noncurrent liabilities of ConAgra consist principally of estimated liabilities of Beatrice Company for post-retirement health care, pensions, income taxes and various litigation, environmental and other matters. See ConAgra's Quarterly Report on Form 10-Q for the quarter ended February 24, 1991.

This table should be read in conjunction with the other pro forma financial information contained in this Proxy Statement/Prospectus and the consolidated financial statements of the companies and the notes thereto incorporated herein by reference.

Source: Golden Valley Microwave Foods, Inc. Proxy Statement, June 10, 1991.

- Schedule V in Golden Valley's 1990 10-K report shows that most of the company's property (mostly machinery and equipment rather than real estate) had been acquired within the past three years. Assume the fair value to be 15% higher than historical cost.
- Lamb-Weston was established by a purchase of assets in June 1988. Assume that fair values of the individual assets and liabilities of Lamb-Weston are unchanged.
- Lamb-Weston reports a defined benefit pension plan underfunded by $2.67 million (projected benefit obligation less assets and accruals) on July 31, 1990 (most recent data available).
- Lamb-Weston reports a $17.6 million deferred income tax liability.

  (b) Describe what other information would be needed to prepare an accurate purchase method balance sheet.

3. Exhibit 14C-5, taken from the proxy statement, shows the combined income statement for the year ended February 24, 1991. Use the same assumptions and data provided in Question 2, and the following additional assumptions, to prepare a *pro forma* income statement under the purchase method.

- Schedules V and VI of Golden Valley's 10-K show an average life of approximately 10 years for its property.
- Assume a life of 30 years for any recognized goodwill.

4. (a) Use Exhibits 14C-4 and 14C-5 and the *pro forma* balance sheets and income statements prepared in Questions 2 and 3 to compute the following financial ratios for *both* accounting methods:

EXHIBIT 14C-5. CONAGRA, INC. AND SUBSIDIARIES
Pro Forma Combining Condensed Statement of Income: Unaudited 12 Months Ended February 24, 1991
(\$ in thousands Except per Share Amounts)

	ConAgra	Golden Valley	Lamb-Weston	Pro Forma Adjustments	Pro Forma Combined
Net sales	\$ 20,571,236	\$ 178,863	\$ 499,311	\$ —	\$ 21,249,410
Cost of goods sold	(17,814,315)	(147,384)	(377,217)	4,290 (3)	(18,334,626)
Other expenses	(2,037,569)	(17,803)	(54,584)	(2,822) (2)	(2,112,778)
Interest expense	(352,400)	(2,767)	(19,322)	—	(374,489)
Equity income	22,736	12,631	—	(26,090) (2)	9,277
Pretax income	\$ 389,688	\$ 23,540	\$ 48,188	\$(24,622)	\$ 436,794
Income tax expense	(163,580)	(3,989)	(19,276)	(1,630) (3)	(188,475)
Net income	\$ 226,108	\$ 19,551	\$ 28,912	\$(26,252)	\$ 248,319
Preferred dividends	(24,018)	—	—	—	(24,018)
Net for common	\$ 202,090	\$ 19,551	\$ 28,912	\$(26,252)	\$ 224,301
Average shares	137,512	18,031		10,236 (1)	147,747
Earnings per share	\$ 1.47	\$ 1.08			\$ 1.52

(1) Reflects the assumed conversion of Golden Valley Common Stock into ConAgra Common Stock (assuming an Exchange Ratio of .5676 of a share of ConAgra Common Stock for each share of Golden Valley Common Stock and assuming no fractional shares of ConAgra Common Stock are created upon the conversion of Golden Valley Common Stock).
(2) Elimination of equity of Lamb-Weston upon consolidation—previously carried at equity.
(3) Adjustment to conform Golden Valley accounting practices to those followed by ConAgra, including capitalization of certain acquired intangible assets and depreciation policies.
   Source: Adapted from Golden Valley Microwave Foods, Inc. Proxy Statement, June 10, 1991.

- Debt to total capital
- Return on ending common equity
- Return on ending total capital
- Net profit margin

(b) Discuss the differences in the ratios computed in part A that result from different accounting methods for the same transaction.

5. (a) Determine the effect of the acquisition of Golden Valley on ConAgra's earnings per share under both accounting methods.

(b) Discuss the implications of the results in part A.

Chapter 14

Problems

1. [Pooling versus purchase] The Ace Co. and Tar Co. merged on January I of year 2, forming the Acetar Co. Ace issued stock worth \$1,500 to effect the merger. The merger was accounted for as a pooling of interests.

Balance sheets for the individual companies at the end of year 1 and for the combined entity at the end of year 2 are presented below. Estimates of the fair value of inventory and fixed assets of the two companies at the end of Year 1 are also provided.

| | Ace (Year 1) | | Tar (Year 1) | | |
	Historical Cost	Fair Value	Historical Cost	Fair Value	Acetar (Year 2)
Cash	$ 100		$ 50		$ 200
Inventory	1,000	1,200	300	330	1,400
Fixed assets (net)	3,000	3,500	1,000	1,050	4,100
Total assets	$4,100		$1,350		$5,700
Current liabilities	1,000		250		1,300
Equity	3,100		1,100		4,400
Liabilities and equity	$4,100		$1,350		$5,700

Acetar generated the following cash flow statement for year 2:

Acetar Cash Flow Statement: Year 2

Net income	$200
Depreciation expense	400
Change in inventory	(100)
Change in accounts payable	50
Cash from operations	**$550**
Cash for investing	
Capital expenditures	**(500)**
Change in cash	**$ 50**

Additional information:

- Acetar uses the FIFO inventory method.
- Acetar depreciates its assets using the straight-line method with an average life of ten years.
- Year 2 dividends paid = 0.

A. Prepare Acetar's pooling method balance sheet at the merger date.
For parts B through E, assume that the merger was accounted for as a purchase with Ace acquiring Tar.

B. Prepare the balance sheet of the merged company at the merger date.

C. Calculate reported net income for year 2. Explain all differences from the $200 reported net income under the pooling method.

D. Prepare the balance sheet of the merged company at the end of year 2.

E. Prepare the statement of cash flows for year 2.

2. [Pooling versus purchase] On January 1, 1996, the Hawk Company acquired the Dove Company. The acquisition was treated as a purchase. The historical cost balance sheets of Hawk and Dove at the acquisition date follow, along with the consolidated balance sheet at December 31, 1996, consolidated cash flow statement for 1996, and relevant information about the company's accounting policies.

Balance Sheet Data

	Hawk	Dove		Consolidated
	Historical 1/1/96	Historical 1/1/96	Fair Value 1/1/96	12/31/96
Cash	$1,000			$ 1,800
Accounts receivable	300	$ 200	?	550
Inventory	1,200	300	?	1,600
Fixed assets (net)	5,000	500	?	6,400
Goodwill			?	390
Total assets	$7,500	$1,000	?	$10,740
Accounts payable	1,000	500	?	1,700
Long-term debt	2,000	700	?	2,750
Equity	4,500	(200)	?	6,290
Liabilities and equity	$7,500	$1,000	?	$10,740

1996 Consolidated Statement of Cash Flows

Net income	$1,240
Depreciation and amortization	600
Increase in accounts payable	200
Increase in accounts receivable	(50)
Cash from operations	$1,990
Cash for investments: January 1 purchase of plant, property, and equipment	(1,290)
Cash from financing: debt issued	100
Change in cash	$ 800

Significant Noncash Financing and Investment Activities. The company acquired the Dove Company on January 1 by issuing shares whose market value was $550.
    Additional information:

- The Hawk Company uses the LIFO inventory method.
- Goodwill is amortized over 40 years on a straight-line basis.
- 1996 combined depreciation expense equals $580.
- Dove's long-term debt is due in five years.

A. Calculate the fair value of Dove's assets and liabilities at the acquisition date.

B. Determine the goodwill recorded at the acquisition date.

C. Assuming that the acquisition of Dove had been treated as a pooling of interest, calculate Hawk's net income for 1996. *Explain all assumptions and adjustments made.*

D. Prepare the 1996 cash flow statement under the pooling assumption.

3. [Purchase versus pooling; 1994 CFA adapted] Aspen Pharmaceuticals (Aspen) is a major worldwide producer of prescription drugs with an outstanding record of sales and earnings growth. Aspen has just announced plans to acquire 100% of the common stock of Pharmacy Services, Inc. (PSI). PSI is much smaller than Aspen, but is a leading factor in mail-order delivery of pharmaceuticals and also provides related cost-containment services.

EXHIBIT 14P-1. ASPEN PHARMACEUTICALS
Condensed Financial Statements

Balance Sheet, December 31, 1996 ($ in millions)

Assets

Current assets	$ 4,500
Property, plant, and equipment	5,000
Total assets	$ 9,500

Liabilities and Stockholders' Equity

Current liabilities	$ 3,500
Long-term debt	1,000
Deferred taxes	1,000
Stockholders' equity*	4,000
Total liabilities and equity	$ 9,500

Income Statement, Years Ended December 31
($ in millions except per share data)

	1996 Actual	1997 Estimated
Sales	$10,000	$10,500
Cost of goods sold	(2,000)	(2,500)
Marketing and administration	(2,700)	(2,700)
Depreciation	(200)	(200)
Interest	(100)	(100)
Research	(1,000)	(1,000)
Pretax income	$ 4,000	$ 4,000
Income tax expense	(1,200)	(1,200)
Net income	2,800	2,800
Earnings per share*	$2.80	$2.80
Dividends per share	$1.10	$1.14

*One billion shares outstanding.

EXHIBIT 14P-2. PHARMACY SERVICES, INC.
Condensed Financial Statements

Balance Sheet, December 31, 1996 ($ in millions)

Assets

Current assets	$1,000
Property, plant, and equipment	200
Total assets	$1,200

Liabilities and Stockholders' Equity

Current liabilities	$ 300
Long-term debt	300
Stockholders' equity*	600
Total liabilities and equity	$1,200

Income Statement, Years Ended December 31
($ in millions except per share data)

	1996 Actual	1997 Estimated
Sales	$ 2,500	$ 3,360
Cost of goods sold	(2,130)	(2,880)
Marketing and administration	(80)	(110)
Depreciation	(20)	(20)
Interest	(20)	(20)
Pretax income	$ 250	$ 330
Income tax expense	(100)	(130)
Net income	$ 150	$ 200
Earnings per share*	$1.50	$2.00
Dividends per share	None	None

*100 million shares outstanding.

Aspen's stock is currently selling at $30 per share and that of PSI at $25 per share. Both companies are U.S.-based. Exhibit 14P-1 contains financial data on Aspen and Exhibit 14P-2 provides data for PSI.

Aspen is considering two alternative approaches to making the acquisition of PSI. Assume the following:

- All assets and liabilities of PSI have fair market values equal to their carrying cost on the balance sheet except property, plant, and equipment that have a fair market value of $1.2 billion.
- PSI depreciates its property, plant, and equipment over 10 years using the straight-line method.
- The marginal tax rate is 40%.
- Any acquisition goodwill would be amortized over 20 years.

A. Assuming that Aspen uses a share-for-share exchange to acquire PSI and accounts for the transaction as a pooling of interests:

  (i) Prepare a *pro forma* December 31, 1996 balance sheet for Aspen reflecting the acquisition and calculate the resulting book value per share.

  (ii) Prepare a *pro forma* estimated 1997 income statement for Aspen reflecting the acquisition and calculate the resulting earnings per share.

B. Assume that Aspen pays $30 per share for all the outstanding shares of PSI and accounts for the transaction as a purchase. The $3 billion purchase price would be financed by debt with a 10% interest rate.

  (i) Prepare a *pro forma* December 31, 1996 balance sheet for Aspen reflecting the acquisition and calculate the resulting book value per share.

  (ii) Prepare a *pro forma* estimated 1997 income statement for Aspen reflecting the acquisition and calculate the resulting earnings per share.

C. (i) Compare the debt-to-total capital and debt-to-tangible equity ratios under the two alternatives.

  (ii) Compare the reported interest coverage under the two alternatives.

  (iii) Briefly discuss three reasons Aspen would prefer to use a share-for-share exchange and pooling of interests accounting method to acquire PSI.

  (iv) Briefly discuss three criticisms of pooling of interests accounting many financial analysts make.

4. [Purchase method of accounting for acquisitions; 1995 CFA adapted] Wholesale prices of auto parts have been rising over the past five years. One company operating in this industry, B Corp., has made several acquisitions with newly issued stock over the past five years, using the purchase method of accounting. In each case, the purchase price has greatly exceeded the fair value of the net assets of the acquired company. Another company in this industry, WAH, has made no acquisitions. Both firms use the first-in, first-out (FIFO) method to account for inventories.

A. Briefly explain why B Corp.'s acquisition history makes it difficult to analyze trends of its financial data and ratios.

B. Briefly explain why B Corp.'s acquisition history makes it difficult to compare its ratios with those of WAH.

C. For each of the following measures, state the effect (higher, lower, or no effect) that using the purchase method has on the financial measures of B Corp. compared with the effect of using the pooling method. Briefly explain why each effect occurs.

  (i) Gross profit margin percentage

  (ii) Long-term debt-to-equity ratio

  (iii) Pretax earnings

5. [Effects of purchase acquisition; 1989 CFA adapted] After the market closed on October 17, 1988, Philip Morris announced a $90-per-share cash offer for all outstanding Kraft shares. At the time of the announcement, your supervisor handed you Exhibit 14P-3 and asked you to complete the "merged company *pro forma*" column. Assume that Philip Morris raises the funds required for the takeover by issuing 11% notes and the excess purchase price over the equity of Kraft is allocated entirely to goodwill, amortized over a period of 40 years.

EXHIBIT 14P-3. PHILIP MORRIS AND KRAFT
Selected Financial Data ($ in millions except per share data)

| | Current | | Merged Company |
	Philip Morris	Kraft	(*Pro Forma*)
Common shares outstanding	234	120	
Long-term debt	$ 4,700	$ 800	
Stockholders' equity	7,394	1,920	
Earnings before interest and tax	4,340	796	
Interest expense	(475)	(81)	
Pretax income	$ 3,865	$ 715	
Income tax expense	(1,623)	(279)	
Net income	$ 2,242	$ 436	
Cash flow from operations	$ 2,974	$ 607	
Capital expenditures	(850)	(260)	
Dividends paid	(892)	(251)	
Earnings per share	$9.58	$3.63	
Debt-to-equity	0.64	0.42	
Times interest earned	9.14	9.82	

Source: Adapted from Annual Reports of Phillip Morris and Kraft.

Discuss the effect of the purchase on Philip Morris' financial quality. Your answer should include a discussion of ratios from each of the following categories:

   (i) Profitability

   (ii) Solvency

   (iii) Activity

   (iv) Liquidity

6. [Push-down accounting, extension of Problem 5] Assume that Kraft continued to issue separate financial statements following the merger with Philip Morris. Using the data in Problem 5 and Exhibit 14P-3 and assuming that Kraft applies push-down accounting to its financial statements, answer the following questions from the point of view of a Kraft bondholder.

   A. Compute the following ratios immediately prior to and immediately following the merger (state any assumptions made):

   (i) Debt-to-equity

   (ii) Return on total capital

   (iii) Interest coverage ratio

   (iv) Net profit margin

   B. Discuss the comparability of Kraft financial data before and after the merger.

   C. Discuss the comparability of Kraft financial data (postmerger) with that of companies that have not been acquired.

EXHIBIT 14P-4. ALLWASTE, INC., AND SUBSIDIARIES
Selected Financial Data

During fiscal 1989, the company acquired nine companies in transactions accounted for as poolings of interest. Aggregate consideration consisted of 8,615,960 shares of common stock. As an integral part of each acquisition, all former shareholders signed noncompete agreements, and key management entered into agreements with the company to continue managing these businesses.

Net revenues, net income, and stockholders' equity of the company are shown below, both at August 31, 1988 and (after restatement) at August 31, 1989. Operations of the pooled companies are included for their fiscal year ending closest to that of the company's.

Financial Data, for Years Ended August 31, 1987 to 1989 ($ in thousands except per share data)

Report Date	1987			1988			1989		
	Net Revenues	Net Income	Earnings per Share	Net Revenues	Net Income	Earnings per Share	Net Revenues	Net Income	Earnings per Share
8-31-88	$45,894	$2,667	$0.16	$ 67,804	$5,329	$0.27	—	—	—
8-31-89	$86,771	$5,205	$0.22	$125,258	$9,877	$0.35	$165,689	$11,797	$0.40

	Stockholders' Equity	Shares Outstanding	Stockholders' Equity	Shares Outstanding	Stockholders' Equity	Shares Outstanding
8-31-88	$14,562	17,242	$33,814	20,154	—	—
8-31-89	$17,820	25,858	$38,077	28,770	$52,359	29,594

Source: Allwaste, Inc., *1988–1989 Annual Reports.*

D. Discuss any insights regarding Kraft that you might draw from the push-down adjustments themselves.

E. Discuss the pros and cons of Kraft's use of push-down accounting following the merger.

7. [Analysis of series of pooling of interest acquisitions; adapted from an article by Abraham Briloff, *Barron's,* October 8, 1990, p. 14 (courtesy of Professor Ashiq Ali)] Exhibit 14P-4 contains excerpts from the 1988 and 1989 annual reports of Allwaste, Inc., a firm that has grown rapidly through acquisitions. Generally, it uses the pooling of interests method for these acquisitions. During fiscal 1989, Allwaste issued 8.6 million shares with an estimated market value of $70 million to acquire nine companies.

A. Discuss how the pooling method acquisitions changed the level and trend of the following for the 1987 to 1989 period:

(i) Revenues

(ii) Net income

(iii) Return on equity

B. Recast Allwaste's 1989 acquisitions using the purchase method, assuming that:

· Allwaste sold common stock and used the proceeds to acquire these firms.

· The excess of the purchase price over book value of the acquired firms was goodwill, amortized over a 40-year life.

· The acquisitions were made on the first day of the fiscal year.

C. Using the recast data from part B, repeat part A. Comment on your results.

D. Discuss the impact on your answer to part C of each of the following changes in assumptions:

   (i) Goodwill amortization over a 10-year life

   (ii) Acquisitions made halfway through the fiscal year

E. (i) Using the exhibit data (pooling method), compute the impact of the acquisitions on earnings per share for 1987 and 1988.

   (ii) Repeat part (i) using the results of part C (purchase method).

   (iii) Discuss how the choice of accounting method affected the impact of the acquisitions on Allwaste's earnings per share.

F. (i) Describe the impact of the acquisitions (pooling method) on Allwaste's statement of cash flows in the acquisition years.

   (ii) Using the results of part B, estimate the reported cash from financing in the acquisition years under the purchase method and compare them to the amounts reported under the pooling method.

   (iii) Discuss any other differences in reported cash flows between the pooling and purchase methods in the acquisition years.

   (iv) Discuss how reported cash flows in the years following the acquisitions vary with the accounting method used.

8. [Derivation of acquisition data from cash flow statement] On June 24, 1992, Roadway Services, a large U.S. motor carrier, acquired Cole Enterprises, a regional carrier. Exhibit 14P-5 contains the financial statement footnote describing the transaction. Elsewhere, Roadway states that 1991 revenues of Cole were approximately $19 million. Roadway's 1991 revenues were $3,177 million.

Exhibit 14P-5 also contains Roadway's statement of cash flows (1992) and balance sheets (1991 to 1992).

A. Using the data in Exhibit 14P-5, derive the balance sheet of Cole at the date of its acquisition. (*Hint:* You must compare each balance sheet change with the corresponding cash flow; some aggregation is required. Remember that noncash transactions are excluded from the cash flow statement.)

B. Using the data in Exhibit 14P-5 and the results of part A, compute the following ratios for Cole (postacquisition) and Roadway (at December 31, 1991):

   (i) Fixed asset turnover

   (ii) Accounts receivable turnover

   (iii) Equity-to-assets

C. Discuss the possible reasons for the ratio differences in part B. Describe the possible implications of the ratio differences for future cash flows.

D. Roadway has insignificant non-U.S. operations. Discuss how this impacts the accuracy of your answer to part A.

E. Discuss how you would measure the future return on Roadway's acquisition of Cole.

9. [Goodwill amortization] Hanson Industries is a U.K.-based conglomerate with operations in the United Kingdom and United States. In July 1989, it acquired Consoli-

Note B — Acquisitions

On June 24, 1992, the company acquired Cole Enterprises, Inc., the parent company of Coles Express, Inc., a New England regional motor common carrier based in Bangor, Maine, for $4,617,000 in cash and 235,892 shares of the company's common stock valued at $15,127,000. The acquisition was accounted for as a purchase and the cost in excess of net assets acquired was $3,441,000. Earnings of Coles since its acquisition are included in the accompanying statement of consolidated income, and are not material in relation to consolidated operations.

A. Statement of Consolidated Cash Flows

	Year Ended December 31 1992
CASH FLOWS FROM OPERATING ACTIVITIES	
Net Income	$ 147,407
Adjustments to reconcile net income to net cash provided by operating activities:	
Depreciation and amortization	172,695
(Gain) loss on sale of carrier operating property	23
Issuance of treasury shares for stock plans	18,507
Changes in assets and liabilities, net of effects from the purchase of Cole Enterprises, Inc.:	
(Increase) in accounts receivable	(39,999)
(Increase) decrease in prepaid expenses and supplies	7,925
Increase in accounts payable and accrued items	34,269
Increase (decrease) in current income taxes payable	3,022
Increase (decrease) in other liabilities	(4,984)
Total adjustments	191,458
NET CASH PROVIDED BY OPERATING ACTIVITIES	338,865
CASH FLOWS FROM INVESTING ACTIVITIES	
Purchases of carrier operating property	(211,073)
Sales of carrier operating property	10,062
Purchases of marketable securities	(197,263)
Sales of marketable securities	124,787
Purchase of Cole Enterprises, Inc., net of cash acquired	(866)
NET CASH USED IN INVESTING ACTIVITIES	(274,353)
CASH FLOWS FROM FINANCING ACTIVITIES	
Dividends paid	(48,984)
Purchases of common stock for treasury	—
Proceeds from exercise of stock options	186
NET CASH USED IN FINANCING ACTIVITIES	(48,798)
NET INCREASE (DECREASE) IN CASH	15,714
CASH AT BEGINNING OF YEAR	25,322
CASH AT END OF YEAR	$ 41,036

EXHIBIT 14P-5 (*continued*)

B. *Consolidated Balance Sheet (dollars in thousands)*

ASSETS

Current assets	December 31 1992	December 31 1991
Cash	$ 41,036	$ 25,322
Marketable securities	274,898	201,917
Accounts receivable, net	304,645	261,252
Prepaid expenses and supplies	55,954	61,650
	$ 676,533	$ 550,141
Property, plant and equipment		
Original cost	2,044,451	1,850,411
(allowances for depreciation)	(1,148,791)	(998,217)
	$ 895,660	$ 852,194
Goodwill	87,330	86,297
Total assets	$ 1,659,523	$1,488,632

LIABILITIES AND SHAREHOLDERS' EQUITY

Current liabilities	1992	1991
Accounts payable	$ 225,361	$ 186,496
Salaries and wages	149,501	154,514
Income taxes payable	25,792	22,712
Freight and casualty claims payable within one year	81,395	78,747
Dividend payable	12,803	11,664
	$ 494,852	$ 454,133
Noncurrent liabilities		
Deferred taxes	41,096	49,507
Future equipment repairs	21,321	18,572
Casualty claims payable after one year	80,894	76,164
	$ 143,311	$ 144,243
Shareholders' equity		
Common stock	39,898	39,898
Additional capital	50,392	31,271
Retained earnings	966,061	868,777
Treasury stock	(34,991)	(49,690)
	$ 1,021,360	$ 890,256
Total liabilities and equity	$ 1,659,523	$1,488,632

Source: Roadway Services, Inc., *1992 Annual Report.*

EXHIBIT 14P-6. HANSON INDUSTRIES
Data Derived from "Reconciliation to U.S. Accounting Principles," for Years Ended
September 30, 1988 to 1991 (£ in millions)

	1988	1989	1990	1991
U.K. GAAP income				
Continuing operations	£ 676	£ 813	£ 971	£1,035
Extraordinary income	445	288	29	71
Total	£1,121	£1,101	£1,000	£1,106
Estimated adjustments				
Goodwill on disposals	(180)	(92)	(171)	(46)
Goodwill amortization	(50)	(56)	(97)	(95)
Other adjustments*	(11)	(26)	218	(9)
U.S. GAAP, net income	£ 880	£ 927	£ 950	£ 956
Continuing operations	523	759	955	972
Extraordinary income	357	168	(5)	(16)
Total	£ 880	£ 927	£ 950	£ 956
Profit on sales of business units	445	288	168	115
(included above)				
U.K. GAAP				
Stockholders' equity	£2,192	£1,046	£2,834	£3,325
Estimated adjustments				
Goodwill	1,811	3,724	3,550	3,438
Other*	(42)	55	248	330
U.S. GAAP				
Stockholders' equity	£3,961	£4,825	£6,632	£7,093

*Other adjustments include foreign currency translation, pensions, revaluation of land, buildings and timberlands, and taxes.
Source: Hanson Industries, *1989–1991 Annual Reports.*

dated Gold Fields, PLC, for £3.3 billion, of which £2.1 billion was allocated to goodwill. Hanson charged this goodwill to reserves, in keeping with its normal practice and U.K. GAAP. Exhibit 14P-6 contains data derived from the "Reconciliation to U.S. Accounting Principles" provided by the firm in its 1989 and 1991 annual reports.

A. Recompute reported income and return on equity for 1988 to 1991, assuming use of a 10-year life for all goodwill.

B. Compare and discuss the differences in the levels and trends of reported income and return on equity for 1988 to 1991 under the three methods: U.K. GAAP, U.S. GAAP (from the exhibit), and your answer to part A.

C. The U.K. Financial Reporting Standard (FRS) 3 now requires (effective 1992) that all remaining goodwill relating to a unit sold or disposed of be written off at the time of sale or discontinuation. Recalculate profits on the sale of businesses in 1988 through 1991 on this basis.

D. Discuss the impact of your results in part C on reported earnings and return on equity for 1988 to 1991.

10. [Analysis of spinoffs] Exhibit 14P-7A contains reported segment data from the *1991 Annual Report* of Adolph Coors Company. In December 1992, Coors spun off ACX Technologies, consisting of virtually all the nonbeer operations of Coors, including aluminum and packaging operations that supply the beer operations. Exhibit 14P-7B contains selected data from the *1991 Annual Report* of Coors and an information statement on the spinoff of ACX.

A. Using the data in Exhibit 14P-7A, prepare an estimated *pro forma* income statement for Coors (excluding ACX) for the period 1989 through 1991. Discuss the additional information required to prepare a more accurate *pro forma* income statement for the period.

B. Compute the following reported and *pro forma* (excluding ACX) statistics for Coors for the 1989 to 1991 period:

   (i) Debt-to-equity

   (ii) Times interest earned

   (iii) Return on sales

EXHIBIT 14P-7. ADOLPH COORS AND ACX TECHNOLOGIES
Selected Financial Data, for Years Ended December 31, 1989 to 1991 ($ in thousands)

A. Segment Data, Adolph Coors Company

Segment Information

The Company's operations include four reportable segments: beer business, ceramics business, aluminum business and packaging business. The beer segment is composed of those operations principally involved in the manufacture, sale and distribution of malt beverage products. The ceramics segment is made up of those operations which manufacture ceramic products. The aluminum segment is involved in the manufacture of aluminum rigid container sheet products and reclamation and recycling of used beverage containers and other secondary metals. The packaging segment produces high-performance folding cartons and flexible packaging.

Developmental businesses include those subsidiaries that produce corn syrup, vitamin products and other food ingredients; manufacture and assemble standard electronic modules (SEM) and multilayer interconnect boards (MIB); develop innovative technologies based on expertise in engineering and technology; and develop oil and gas proper-

ties. In 1991, the nature of operations changed for the subsidiary that manufactures and assembles SEMs and MIBs. This subsidiary was reclassified to developmental businesses from the ceramics business segment. All segment data for prior years have been restated to reflect this change. The operating loss for developmental businesses in 1991 included asset write-downs in the oil and gas operations (Note 7).

The operating results for the beer business in 1990 included a special charge for remediation costs associated with the Lowry Landfill Superfund site (Note 7).

The operating loss for developmental businesses in 1989 includes asset write-downs in oil and gas, coal and snack foods operations (Note 7).

Intersegment activity is composed of sales, accounts receivable and profit on the transfer of inventory between segments. Operating income (loss) for reportable segments is exclusive of certain corporate expenses.

Corporate assets primarily include cash, short-term interest bearing investments, and certain fixed assets.

	Net sales	Operating income (loss)	Assets	Depreciation, depletion and amortization	Additions to properties
1991		*(In thousands)*			
Beer business	$1,530,347	$ 59,126	$1,285,311	$100,992	$235,044
Ceramics business	180,146	1,983	167,330	10,969	25,589
Aluminum business	95,996	6,346	252,691	8,061	67,552
Packaging business	188,141	17,185	109,831	9,291	11,217
Developmental businesses	111,309	(44,158)	111,970	13,684	10,266
Intersegment activity	(188,517)	(819)	(28,546)	—	—
Corporate	—	(17,979)	87,722	892	4,861
	$1,917,422	$ 21,684	$1,986,309	$143,889	$354,529

EXHIBIT 14P-7 (*continued*)

1990

Beer business - continuing	$1,477,271	$100,662	$1,114,962	$ 90,757	$175,199
- Special charge	—	(30,000)	—	—	—
Ceramics business	179,796	2,214	147,848	9,858	14,356
Aluminum business	113,445	16,322	194,152	7,620	83,236
Packaging business	155,809	9,804	102,800	9,141	4,187
Developmental businesses	105,547	(9,684)	142,749	12,181	20,550
Intersegment activity	(193,302)	1,531	(31,666)	—	—
Corporate	—	(16,465)	90,819	819	4,493
	$1,838,566	$ 74,384	$1,761,664	$130,376	$302,021

1989

Beer business	$1,366,108	$ 71,081	$ 967,486	$ 85,249	$ 81,499
Ceramics business	166,215	14,802	150,908	8,051	32,957
Aluminum business	94,173	9,110	93,572	6,822	15,826
Packaging business	136,848	772	110,961	8,281	3,108
Developmental businesses	104,069	(48,290)	130,570	12,761	14,407
Intersegment activity	(176,710)	(2,300)	(18,574)	—	—
Corporate	—	(11,429)	95,860	1,275	1,819
	$1,690,703	$ 33,746	$1,530,783	$122,439	$149,616

B. Selected Financial Data

	1989	1990	1991
Adolph Coors Company			
Net sales	$1,690,703	$1,838,566	$1,917,422
Operating income	33,746	74,384	21,684
Interest expense	(1,699)	(371)	(589)
Other income (expense), net	(6,415)	(9,813)	2,122
Income tax expense (benefit)	12,500	25,300	(700)
Net income	13,132	38,900	23,917
Total assets	1,530,783	1,761,664	1,986,309
Working capital	193,590	201,043	110,443
Long-term debt	—	110,000	220,000
Stockholders' equity	1,060,900	1,091,547	1,099,420
Number of shares	$ 36,900	$ 37,484	$ 37,482
ACX Technologies, Inc.			
Net sales	$ 466,818	$ 521,229	$ 543,503
Operating income	14,881	15,948	8,897
Interest expense	(2,997)	(4,681)	(8,653)
Other income (expense), net	(3,951)	(4,708)	3,301
Income tax expense	2,900	3,000	2,200
Net income	5,033	3,559	1,345
Total assets	422,757	576,435	640,951
Working capital	78,850	124,356	100,999
Debt to parent (Coors)	19,676	131,737	185,782
Stockholders' equity	$ 286,827	$ 294,657	$ 294,709

Source: Coors, *1991 Annual Report;* ACX Technologies information statement, Dec. 9, 1992.

    (iv) Return on equity

    (v) Book value per share

    (vi) Asset turnover

    (vii) Working capital

    (viii) Growth rate of sales, operating income, and net income, for 1989 to 1991

    C. Discuss the limitations of your *pro forma* results (parts A and B) as indicators of the future results of Coors.

    D. Assume that ACX consists entirely of the nonbeer segments of Coors, as shown in Exhibit 14P-7B.

    (i) Under that assumption, describe how the Coors segment data could have been used to estimate the *pro forma* balance sheet and income statement data for ACX.

    (ii) Describe the missing data required to complete the estimate.

    (iii) Discuss the usefulness of the historic segment data as predictors of the future operating results of ACX.

    E. ACX shares more than doubled in price after trading commenced in December 1992. The total share value (Coors after the spinoff plus ACX) rose by 25% from November 30, 1992, to January 29, 1993.

    (i) Using data in Exhibit 14P-7 and your answers to earlier parts, discuss why investors may have been attracted to ACX.

    (ii) Discuss the implications of the behavior of stock prices described here for the efficient market hypothesis.

    F. Using your answers to parts A through E, discuss why Coors may have chosen to spin off ACX rather than sell it to another company or through an initial public offering.

11. (Goodwill—immediate write down) Sandoz, a Swiss conglomerate, charges goodwill to reserves in the year of the acquisition. Exhibit 14P-8 contains selected financial data from the *1994 Annual Report.*

    A. Discuss the impact of Sandoz' acquisitions and the treatment of goodwill on the reported changes in sales and operating income.

    B. Discuss whether the reported return (as measured by operating income) on equity accurately reflects the profitability and return on investment of Sandoz.

    C. Assume that Sandoz capitalized goodwill and amortized it over a 10-year life.

    (i) Recompute the 1994 return on equity.

    (ii) Discuss whether this adjusted return on equity is a better measure of profitability and return on investment.

12. (Goodwill—Alternative Accounting Methods) Alcatel Alsthom, a French telecommunications company, amortizes acquisition goodwill over a maximum life of 20 years. In exceptional cases and for acquisitions for equity securities, goodwill is charged to equity. Acquired trademarks are not amortized.

EXHIBIT 14P-8. SANDOZ
Selected Financial Data for the Years Ended Dec. 31, 1993
and 1994 (CHF millions)

	1994	1993
Consolidated Income Statement		
Sales	15,870	15,100
Operating Income	2,451	2,189
Net Income	1,734	1,706
Consolidated Balance Sheet		
Equity	6,887	10,557
Goodwill writeoff to reserves	4,827	115
Cost and Effect of the August 1994 Acquisition of Gerber Products Company, USA		
Cost*	4,718	
Goodwill	4,582	
Effect On Consolidated:		
Sales	552	
Operating Income	98	

*Net of cash and short-term deposits acquired.

Note: Other 1994 acquisitions contributed CHF 534 million to consolidated sales, resulting in CHF 4,827 million of goodwill and cost of CHF 4,991 million.

Source: Sandoz, *1994 Annual Report.*

The company recognizes restructuring costs relating to severance payments, early retirement of employees, and asset write-offs at the acquisition date. In 1991 and 1992, acquired companies made provisions (5.2 and 3.8 billion French francs, respectively) for postacquisition restructuring. At the same time, Alcatel charged a significant amount of goodwill to equity. Exhibit 14P-9 contains selected data from Alcatel's *1994 Annual Report.*

A. Compare the accounting treatment of goodwill and restructuring costs under French GAAP to that under U.S. GAAP. Discuss the impact of the differences on postacquisition:

   (i) Total assets

   (ii) Total equity

   (iii) Cash flow from operations (CFO)

   (iv) Net income

B. Recompute net income, earnings per share (EPS), and CFO for 1992, 1993, and 1994:

   (i) Applying U.S. GAAP to the restructuring reserve

   (ii) Capitalizing acquired goodwill and assuming a 20-year life

EXHIBIT 14P-9. ALCATEL ALSTHOM
Acquisition Effects, Years Ended December 31, 1990 to 1994 (French francs in millions except per share data)

	1990	1991	1992	1993	1994
Restructuring Reserve					
Opening balance	5,929	6.452	10,656	10,912	7,776
Expenditures during the year	(1,712)	(3,698)	(6,183)	(4,869)	(4,068)
New plans and adjustments to estimates*	2,154	2,727	3,160	2,488	2,898
Effect of acquisitions and disposals	(2)	5,194	3,778	324	506
Currency translation adjustment	83	(19)	(499)	(1,079)	165
Closing balance	6,452	10,656	10,912	7,776	7,277
Increase during the year		4,204	256	(3,136)	(499)
Goodwill					
Ending balance (gross)			39,391	42,428	50,966
Less: accumulated amortization			(4,559)	(6,615)	(9,006)
Ending balance (net)			34,832	35,813	41,960
Amortization of goodwill			(1,625)	(2,053)	(2,557)
Goodwill charged to equity			(2,974)	(6,305)	(1,024)
Other intangible assets					
Specific software			2,528	2,744	3,556
Trademarks			1,405	1,405	1,405
Other			802	941	1,002
Less: Cumulative amortization			(2,043)	(2,050)	(2,786)
Net other intangible assets			2,692	3,040	3,177
Financial Data					
Net income	5,035	6,180	7,053	7,062	3,620
Fully diluted EPS	47.00	51.00	53.17	49.77	26.05
Growth in FDEPS	18.60%	8.51%	4.25%	−6.39%	−47.66%
Cash from operations (CFO)			15,360	16,613	12,481
Stockholders' equity	34,403	42,291	49,895	57,844	59,784
Total assets	194,548	231,090	244,336	260,071	273,942

*Charge reported in the income statement.
   Source: Alcatel Alsthom, *1994 Annual Report.*

      C. Compare the levels and trends of the following under U.S. and French GAAP:
        (i) Net income
       (ii) EPS
      (iii) CFO
      (iv) Return on equity

15

ANALYSIS OF MULTINATIONAL OPERATIONS

CHAPTER OUTLINE

CHAPTER OBJECTIVES

INTRODUCTION

EFFECTS OF EXCHANGE RATE CHANGES

BASIC ACCOUNTING ISSUES

FOREIGN CURRENCY TRANSLATION UNDER SFAS 52
Role of the Functional Currency
The Temporal Method or Remeasurement
The All-Current Method or Translation
Treatment of Exchange Rate Gains and Losses
Remeasurement Versus Translation

ILLUSTRATION OF TRANSLATION AND REMEASUREMENT
Translation: The All-Current Method
Cumulative Translation Adjustment
   Using the CTA to Estimate Exchange Rate Changes
Remeasurement: The Temporal Method

COMPARISON OF TRANSLATION AND REMEASUREMENT
Income Statement Effects
   Effect on Gross Profit Margin
   Effect on Net Income

Balance Sheet Effects
Impact on Financial Ratios
   Comparison of Ratios Under Translation and Remeasurement
   Comparison of Translated and Local Currency Ratios
Impact on Reported Cash Flows

ANALYSIS OF FOREIGN CURRENCY DISCLOSURES
Exchange Rate Changes: Exposure and Effects
   Balance Sheet
   Income Statement
   Cash Flow Statement

HYPERINFLATIONARY ECONOMIES
Alternative Accounting Methods for Hyperinflationary Subsidiaries
Effects of Debt Denominated in Hyperinflationary Currencies

CHANGES IN FUNCTIONAL CURRENCY
Example: Alcoa of Australia

ANALYTIC DIFFICULTIES RELATED TO FOREIGN OPERATIONS
Relationship Among Interest Rates, Inflation, and Exchange Rates
   Nonmonetary Assets
   Monetary Assets

Consistency in Reporting
Economic Interpretation of Results
  Example: Whirlpool
Impact of SFAS 8 and SFAS 52 on Management and Investor Behavior

FINANCIAL REPORTING OUTSIDE OF THE UNITED STATES
Foreign Currency Translation
Foreign Currency Transactions
International Accounting Standards

SUMMARY

CASE 15-1: AFLAC
Analysis of Exchange Rate Effects: Single Currency

CASE 15-2: IBM
Analysis of Exchange Rate Effects: Multiple Currencies

CHAPTER OBJECTIVES

Changes in exchange rates have pervasive effects on the financial statements of multinational enterprises. In this chapter, we examine those effects, with particular attention to the following issues:

1. The difference between the two reporting methods used to account for exchange rate changes with respect to the:

   - Exchange rates used to translate financial statement data
   - Measurement of firm exposure to exchange rate changes
   - Disposition of translation gains and losses

2. The impact of both accounting methods on the income statement, especially the trend of reported revenue and income

3. The differential impact of the two methods on the balance sheet including the role of the currency translation adjustment under the all-current rate method

4. The effects of exchange rate changes on reported cash flow

5. How financial statement ratios are affected by the choice of accounting method, with emphasis on the differences between ratios based on translated data and those based on local currency data

6. How hyperinflation affects financial statement data and the two different methods used to account for subsidiaries in hyperinflationary economies

7. The importance of the choice of functional currency and the effects of changes in that choice

8. How financial statement disclosures can be used to analyze the firm's exposure to exchange rate changes and the effect of such changes on reported financial statements

9. How reported data can give false signals about the economic effect of exchange rate changes on the firm

10. The differences between U.S. GAAP, IASC GAAP, and foreign accounting methods dealing with recognition of the effect of rate changes

Cases 15-1 (AFLAC) and 15-2 (IBM) apply the chapter material to the analysis of firms with exposure to one currency and many currencies, respectively.

INTRODUCTION

The globalization of the economic world is almost a cliché. International trade has expanded significantly in recent years, aided by such factors as the entry of the Eastern European bloc into world markets, the growth of the Pacific Rim countries, and the expansion of the European Economic Community.

Trade has led to investment, as multinational companies (MNCs) add manufacturing capacity in foreign countries. Trade frictions and political considerations join economic factors such as access to low-cost labor or raw materials as incentives for international expansion. Expanding international capital markets facilitate this growth by allowing MNCs to borrow and lend in foreign currencies and markets and to hedge foreign operations with an array of complex instruments, including options, forward contracts (futures), and currency swaps.

MNCs conduct operations in countries where local financial reporting regulations may be quite different from those governing parent company financial statements. Foreign operations are carried out under varied economic conditions and in currencies whose relative prices (exchange rates) fluctuate widely, with significant effects on both actual and reported operating performance, financial position, and cash flows. Hedging operations often involve innovative instruments for which the financial reporting requirements are still under development, making it difficult for investors to evaluate the risk/return trade-offs.

MNCs prepare financial statements that consolidate their domestic and foreign operations that are based on different sets of accounting principles (with varying methods and estimates), and different measurement units (currencies) with fluctuating exchange rates. The foreign currency-denominated financial statements of foreign subsidiaries must be translated into their parent's reporting currency to permit consolidation.

This chapter considers the impact of the translation of operations denominated in foreign currencies on the consolidated financial statements of MNCs. We discuss U.S. standards, IASC requirements, and the standards of selected countries for foreign currency transactions and translation.

EFFECTS OF EXCHANGE RATE CHANGES

Exchange rate changes result in two effects on a firm's actual and reported performance:

1. "Flow" effects
2. Holding gain/loss effects

These effects can be illustrated by the following example.

■ Example

Assume that a foreign subsidiary generates revenues in its local currency (LC) of LC 10,000 in year 1 and LC 11,000 in year 2. On the subsidiary's income statement, this will appear as:

Year	1	2	Total
Revenues (LC)	10,000	11,000	21,000

The subsidiary reports a revenue growth rate of 10%. If the exchange rate between the LC and dollar is constant, at, say, LC 1 = $1, then when the U.S. parent consolidates the foreign subsidiary, the same 10% growth will be shown with revenues of $10,000 in year 1 and $11,000 in year 2.

Flow Effect. If the exchange rate, however, fluctuates, the parent will show a corresponding variation in its (consolidated) results. Thus, if we assume exchange rates of:

Year 1   LC 1 = $1.00
Year 2   LC 1 = $1.30

the subsidiary's results will be reflected in the parent's statements as:

Year	1	2	Total
Revenues ($)	10,000	14,300	24,300

The parent statement now reports revenue growth of 43% although the subsidiary's revenues only grew by 10%. The "additional" 33% is the *flow effect* on the income statement, the result of changes in the exchange rate. *The analyst should unbundle the effects of the exchange rate changes from the results of the subsidiary's operations.* In this example, the $4,300 revenue growth is the sum of the:

• $1,000 increase in local currency revenue
• $3,300 (LC 11,000 × 30% change in exchange rate) exchange rate effect

Holding Gain/Loss Effect. The effect on revenue, however, is not the only consequence of the change in exchange rates. If we assume that the subsidiary retains all cash receipts, then the cash balance in LC (on the subsidiary's statements) and in dollars (on the parent's statements) at the end of each year is:

Year	0	1	2
Subsidiary			
Cash (LC)	0	LC 10,000	LC 21,000
Exchange rate		LC 1 = $1	LC 1 = $1.30
Parent—Consolidated			
Cash ($)		$10,000	$27,300

For the subsidiary, the increase in cash in year 2 is equal to the revenue/income of LC 11,000 earned that year and the cash balance at the end of the second year equals the cumulative two-year revenue/income of LC 21,000.

This relationship does not hold, however, for the dollar cash balances. At the end of year 2, in dollar terms, the cash balance equals $27,300. Cumulative revenues/income, however, only equal $24,300. The difference of $3,000 is the *holding gain.* As the dollar weakened relative to the LC, the LC 10,000 *earned in year 1* and *held* to the end of year 2 appreciated in value. Specifically:

Dollar Value at Year-End

	1	2	Holding Gain
LC 10,000 earned in year 1	$10,000	$13,000	$3,000

The two effects of exchange rate changes can be summarized as follows:

Amount in dollars if we assume exchange rate stayed constant		$21,000
Exchange Rate Effects		
Flow effect on *year 2* income	3,300	
Holding gain on amount earned in *year 1*	3,000	6,300
Amount including exchange rate effect		$27,300

Accounting standards and public discussion largely focus on the treatment of holding gains and losses. *For analytic purposes, however, although the holding gain/loss effect is relevant, the income statement "flow" effect has the most direct effect on reported income.*

BASIC ACCOUNTING ISSUES

Given fluctuating exchange rates, the accounting for operations conducted in foreign currencies creates issues not present in single-currency statements. Accounting for foreign operations raises three basic issues.

The first issue is the choice of exchange rate used to translate foreign currency transactions and financial statements into the parent company currency, the *reporting currency*. For convenience, we use the U.S. dollar as the parent currency in the examples that follow. However, the principles apply equally whether the reporting currency is U.S. dollars, Swiss francs, or Japanese yen.

All transactions denominated in currencies other than the parent currency must be translated into the parent or reporting currency as part of the process of preparing consolidated financial statements. There are two *obvious* choices of exchange rate:

1. The *historical rate,* the exchange rate at the time the transaction (sale of output, purchase of inventory, borrowing, etc.) took place
2. The *current rate,* the exchange rate at the balance sheet date or for the income statement period

Further, the rate chosen may be used for all transactions not denominated in the reporting currency, or different rates may be used for different types of transactions. We discuss the implications of these choices shortly.

The other two issues are the definition of exposure to exchange rate changes (i.e., which assets or liabilities should be adjusted for exchange rate changes) and the treatment of translation gains and losses. Both are a consequence of fluctuating exchange rates. When exchange rates change, financial data recorded in the parent currency (after translation) change, even when the local currency data have not. The translated financial statements of the subsidiary commingle the effects of exchange rate changes with the results of operating, investment, and financing activities on the consolidated financial statements. Further, these exchange rate effects, *translation gains and losses*, must be accounted for. They can be recognized immediately as a component of net income in the period of change, deferred (and possibly amortized), or accounted for as adjustments to stockholders' equity.

Ideally, the translation gain or loss should capture the impact of changing exchange rates on the parent's economic exposure related to its foreign operations. In practice, however, the reported translation gain or loss depends on two characteristics of the reporting method:

1. The transactions selected for translation
2. The exchanges rate(s) chosen for translation

In other words, the reported translation gain or loss reflects the impact of changing exchange rates on the parent's "accounting" rather than its "economic" exposure.

The interaction of the choice of exchange rate, the definition of exposure, and the disposition of the resulting translation adjustments can significantly affect the reported earnings and financial condition of MNCs.

FOREIGN CURRENCY TRANSLATION UNDER SFAS 52

SFAS 52 (1981), Foreign Currency Translation, prescribes reporting requirements for the translation of the financial statements of foreign operations. The primary objectives of SFAS 52 are set out in para. 4:

a. Provide information that is generally compatible with the expected economic effects of a rate change on an enterprise's cash flows and equity.
b. Reflect in consolidated statements the financial results and relationships of the individual consolidated entities as measured in their functional currencies in conformity with U.S. GAAP.[1]

We discuss whether the standard achieves both objectives later in the chapter.

SFAS 52 provides two translation methods:

1. The *temporal* method or the *remeasurement* process, and
2. The *all-current* method or the *translation* process

and delineates the conditions when each method is appropriate. Generally, the choice of method follows from the choice of *functional currency* for each subsidiary. The functional currency reflects the primary currency with which the foreign subsidiary

---

[1]Statement of Financial Accounting Standards 52, Foreign Currency Translation, Financial Accounting Standards Board, December 1981.

operates. The choice depends on the operating characteristics of that subsidiary and (in some cases) the economy in which it operates.

Role of the Functional Currency

Management must determine the functional currency (primary currency) of each foreign subsidiary based on an evaluation of the unit's operating environment. The functional currency may be the foreign subsidiary's local currency, the parent's reporting currency, or a third currency. Factors to be considered in the choice of functional currency include sales markets, input sources, and financing sources.[2] Ultimately, however, the choice of functional currency is based on management judgment and may not be completely objective.[3]

SFAS 52 defines three categories of foreign operations:

1. Relatively self-contained, independent entities operating primarily in local markets. Operating, financing, and investing activities are primarily local, although there may be reliance on the parent's patents and managerial or technological expertise and there may be some exports. *The functional currency for such an "autonomous" affiliate is generally the local currency. The all-current method is used.*

2. Foreign subsidiaries may be significantly integrated operations serving as sales outlets for the parent's products and services with substantially all the operating, financing, and investing decisions based on the reporting (parent) currency. *In such cases, the functional currency should be the parent (reporting) currency and the temporal method is used.*

3. Finally, SFAS 52 *mandates the use of the parent (reporting) currency as the functional currency for foreign operations in highly inflationary economies* (an economy with cumulative inflation of 100% or more over three years).

Management's choice of functional currency determines which accounting method is used.

The Temporal Method or Remeasurement

The temporal method or remeasurement is used when the functional currency of the foreign subsidiary is the reporting (parent) currency. In this situation, the operations of the subsidiary are deemed to be an integral part of those of the parent and the

---

[2] Appendix A of SFAS 52 lists the following indicators to be used when choosing the functional currency: cash flows, output markets and prices, inputs, financing, and intercompany transactions. The general principle is that functional currency should be the primary currency for most of these indicators.

The functional currency designated for a foreign operation must be used consistently unless changing economic circumstances require change to a different functional currency. No restatement of prior financial statements is required, since a change in functional currency reflects new economic circumstances and, as such, does not qualify as a change in accounting principle. However, the change should be disclosed in the financial statement footnotes. See the later discussion of Alcoa of Australia.

[3] At times, management may be able to justify the choice of either one of two functional currencies. In such cases, the functional currency that produces the better reported operating result is likely to be chosen. For example, in the early 1980s, companies with operations in Mexico could justify either the Mexican peso or the U.S. dollar as the functional currency for those operations. Employees of major drug companies told one of the authors that "we looked at the numbers both ways and chose the better result."

accounting method is designed to reflect that relationship. To understand this method, first consider a situation where a (U.S.) firm (without a subsidiary) carries out transactions denominated in a foreign currency:

Acquisition of Inventory or Fixed Assets. If a U.S. firm purchases inventory or fixed assets and pays for the transaction in a foreign currency, it carries the asset on its balance sheet in U.S. dollars, converting the foreign currency amount paid at the exchange rate *in effect at the time of the transaction.* Under the historical cost principle, that carrying cost remains unchanged (no matter what happens to the exchange rate subsequently) and is the amount used to compute COGS or depreciation expense.

Acquisition of Monetary Assets or Liabilities. If a U.S. firm incurs debt denominated in a foreign currency, the debt is reported on the balance sheet in dollars using the exchange rate *in effect at the time of the balance sheet date.* Any gains or losses since the previous balance sheet date as a result of changes in the exchange rate are reported in the income statement. Similarly, the carrying value of any monetary assets denominated in a foreign currency will be measured at the current exchange rate.

The temporal method extends this approach to a foreign subsidiary deemed to be an integral part of the parent's operations and deals with the three basic accounting issues as follows:

1. Nonmonetary assets (mainly inventories and fixed assets) are translated using the historical rate,[4] whereas almost all other (monetary) assets and liabilities are translated using the current rate.

2. The standard defines the accounting exposure as the net monetary asset or liability position since nonmonetary assets (inventories and fixed assets) are translated at historical rates and therefore are not affected by changing exchange rates.[5]

3. The resulting translation gains and losses are included in net income as they are considered to be part of the parent's income. Thus, the effects of volatile exchange rates are transmitted directly to reported earnings quarterly.[6]

---

[4]This results in these assets being carried at the same (historical) cost as they would have been had they been purchased directly by the parent company.

[5]As noted in the next section, this is true only for unrealized gains and losses on nonmonetary assets. Realized gains and losses on nonmonetary assets are recognized and commingled with operating income.

[6]These concepts can be illustrated with a simple example. Assume that a U.S. parent acquires a foreign subsidiary for $500 on December 31, 1990, when the exchange rate between the local currency (LC) and the U.S. dollar is LC 1 = $1. The subsidiary has cash = LC 400 and inventory = LC 100. The inventory is sold, during 1991, when the exchange rate is LC 1 = $1.50, for LC 200 ($300). At year-end 1991, the exchange rate is LC 1 = $2. The subsidiary now has cash of LC 600 ($1,200) and the parent reports total profit of $700 ($1,200 − $500) during the year, which includes both operating and translation gains.

Under the temporal method, only the cash has any accounting exposure to exchange rate changes. The actual translation gain on the cash is $500. (The original LC 400 increased in dollar terms from $400 to $800 for a gain of $400. The LC 200 received from the sale of inventory increased from $300 to $400 for an additional translation gain of $100.) The remaining $200 profit is from operations. (Revenues from the sale are $300 and COGS equals $100, the original cost of the inventory, since under the temporal method inventories are not adjusted for exchange rate changes.)

Prior to SFAS 52, the prevailing accounting standard was SFAS 8 (1975), Accounting for the Translation of Foreign Currency Transactions and Foreign Currency Financial Statements. Under this standard, the temporal method was the only method permitted. Because of the resulting earnings volatility, SFAS 8 was one of the most unpopular standards issued by the FASB. Because the accounting exposure and economic exposure to a currency are frequently quite different, companies wishing to hedge were forced to choose between hedging their accounting exposure and hedging their "real" exposure. As a result,[7] within a few years, the FASB reexamined the accounting for foreign operations and issued SFAS 52.[8]

The All-Current Method or Translation

SFAS 52 requires use of the all-current rate method to translate foreign currency financial data into the parent currency when the functional currency is the local currency. In this case, the subsidiary in its entirety (its operations and assets) is deemed "independent" of the parent's operations and viewed as an "investment" of the parent. As such:

- The exchange rate as of the balance sheet date is employed for *all* assets and liabilities.
- Since all assets and liabilities are translated at the current rate, the accounting exposure becomes the parent's net investment in the foreign operations.
- Gains and losses arising from the translation process are reported separately as a component of stockholders' equity and excluded from reported net income.[9]

As we shall see shortly, the differences between the two methods have significant implications for the financial statements of MNCs. Before proceeding, however, it is important to note where the two methods differ (and where they do not) in the recognition of the effects of changes in exchange rates.

Treatment of Exchange Rate Gains and Losses

Exchange rate holding gains and losses result from the net asset or liability position (the exposure) of the foreign subsidiary. However, as shown in our example, even if the foreign subsidiary liquidated its asset and liability positions each day, leaving no foreign currency assets or liabilities, the parent's reported performance would still be affected by changes in exchange rates as a result of the flow effect. This effect would prevail, regardless of accounting method.

---

[7]These criticisms also led Canadian regulators to suspend the issuance of their equivalent of SFAS 8.

[8]Appendix B to SFAS 52 contains additional information on changes in the temporal method from SFAS 8.

[9]Under the all-current method, the example in footnote 6 would be reported as follows.

Both cash and inventory are exposed to exchange rate changes. The total translation gain is $550. (Translation gain on cash is $500 as calculated in footnote 6. The translation gain on inventory is $50 as its dollar value increases from $100 to $150 between the date of purchase and the date of sale.) Operating profit is $150. Revenues from the sale are $300, and COGS equals $150, the cost of the inventory in dollars at the time of sale (under the all-current method, all assets and liabilities are adjusted for exchange rate changes). Only the operating profit of $150 is included in reported income; the $550 translation gain is added to the cumulative translation adjustment in the stockholders' equity section.

EXHIBIT 15-1
**Summary of Differences Between Temporal and All-Current Methods in Treatment of
Exchange Rate Holding Gains and Losses**

Asset/ Liability	Nature of Gain/Loss	Treatment	
		Temporal Method	All-Current Method
Monetary	Realized and unrealized	Income statement, explicit disclosure of translation gain/loss	Equity, cumulative translation adjustment
Nonmonetary	Realized	Income statement, implicit within operating income	Equity, cumulative translation adjustment
	Unrealized	Ignored	Equity, cumulative translation adjustment
Summary		All gains and losses except unrealized nonmonetary in income statement	All gains and losses in cumulative translation adjustment

The crux of the difference between the temporal and all-current method lies in the treatment of the effect of exchange rate changes on assets held—the holding gains/ losses. Exhibit 15-1 summarizes these differences.

Under the all-current method, all exchange rate holding gains and losses, whether realized or not, are recognized. However, they are not reported in the income statement but flow into the cumulative translation adjustment account in stockholders' equity.

Under the temporal method, only some exchange rate holding gains and losses are recognized. Gains and losses on monetary assets, both realized and unrealized, are given separate disclosure. Unrealized gains and losses on nonmonetary assets are ignored. Realized gains and losses on nonmonetary assets are recognized, but "buried" within reported operating profits.[10] This important distinction is often overlooked, and it is incorrectly assumed that only gains and losses derived from monetary assets are explicitly recognized in the income statement under the temporal method.[11]

Note that the gains and losses on monetary items and the realized gains and losses on nonmonetary items are identical under both methods. *Thus, in terms of which holding gains/losses are recognized, the one difference between the two methods is the treatment of unrealized gains and losses on nonmonetary assets and liabilities.* As these include inventories and fixed assets, the difference may be highly significant; we return to this subject later.

Remeasurement Versus Translation

Much of the confusion that surrounds the accounting for foreign operations under SFAS 52 concerns the two terms, *remeasurement* and *translation*. Remeasurement

---

[10]Returning to our previous example of footnotes 6 and 9, under the temporal method, we see that the amount of operating profit is $200. Under the all-current method, operating profit is $150. The difference of $50 is the realized exchange rate gain on the inventory held from the beginning of the year to the time of sale. Under the temporal method, this $50 is part of operating income; under the current rate method, it is calculated separately, removed from operating income, and added to the cumulative translation adjustment.

[11]The situation is analogous to LIFO and FIFO. FIFO includes holding gains due to inflation as part of operating income, whereas LIFO removes them.

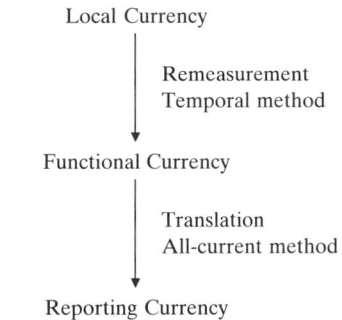

FIGURE 15-1 Accounting for foreign operations.

refers to the process of converting local currency transactions into the functional currency either by a firm with transactions in a foreign currency or with a foreign subsidiary. Translation refers to conversion of the functional currency data of a subsidiary into the reporting currency.

As Figure 15-1 implies, accounting for foreign operations can be a two-step process. The first step is the remeasurement of the subsidiary's financial data into its functional currency. For example, a subsidiary located in Germany, whose functional currency is the deutsche mark (DM), may have transactions denominated in other currencies. If it sells its output in other European countries, it will have cash and accounts receivable in the currency of each market. If it purchases inputs outside Germany, it will have accounts payable in other currencies.

At year-end, a balance sheet in the functional currency (deutsche marks) must be prepared, and each non-deutsche mark (e.g., French francs) asset and liability must be converted into the functional currency. This is the process of remeasurement under SFAS 52, and it is carried out using the temporal method with all translation gains and losses recognized in reported income. The second step is the translation of all functional currency statements into the parent (reporting) currency. Translation gains and losses arising at the translation stage do not appear in the income statement but flow directly to stockholders' equity. However, translation gains or losses that result from remeasurement remain in the income statement even after the translation stage.

Figure 15-1 is an overall representation of the process. In most cases, only one step is needed. If the foreign subsidiary conducted business only in deutsche marks and the local currency is the functional currency, the remeasurement step is not required. Only translation is required. (See Figure 15-2).

Alternatively, if the functional currency for a subsidiary is the parent currency (e.g., a subsidiary operating in a highly inflationary economy), then it is only necessary

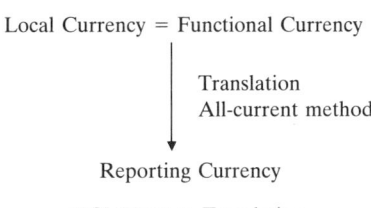

FIGURE 15-2 Translation.

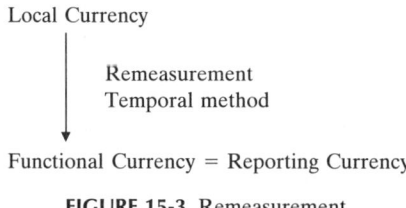

FIGURE 15-3 Remeasurement.

to remeasure its accounts into the parent (reporting) currency and no further translation is required. (See Figure 15-3).

There is an important consequence of this two-step process of remeasurement and translation. The accounting for a particular transaction may depend on geography—its location within the consolidated group. For example, if the German subsidiary (whose functional currency is the deutsche mark) has DM-denominated debt, changes in the exchange rate between the deutsche mark and the dollar do not impact reported earnings. The gains or losses arising from translation of the DM debt into dollars flow directly into stockholders' equity.

If the DM-denominated debt is incurred by the parent company [or by another subsidiary whose functional currency is the dollar (or another currency)] then fluctuations in the exchange rate between the dollar and the deutsche mark will affect reported earnings. Gains and losses arising from remeasurement of the DM debt into the functional currency are included in net income.

Thus, consolidated financial statements may incorporate various types of foreign operations with different functional currencies remeasured and/or translated into the reporting currency. The processes and effects of remeasurement and translation on consolidated financial statements are described next.

ILLUSTRATION OF TRANSLATION AND REMEASUREMENT

Exhibit 15-2 provides balance sheets and exchange rates for the three years ended December 31, 1992, for Foreign Subsidiary, Inc. (FSI), a hypothetical foreign subsidiary of a U.S. multinational. It is assumed that FSI was acquired on December 31, 1990. Exhibit 15-3 contains the subsidiary's income statements for 1991 and 1992. These statements are used to illustrate remeasurement and translation. The different effects of these methods are presented in Exhibits 15-4 through 15-7 under the heading of all-current for translation and temporal for remeasurement.

Translation: The All-Current Method

If management designates the local currency (LC) as the functional currency of Foreign Subsidiary, Inc. (FSI), then the all-current rate method is used to translate the LC-based financial statements into U.S. dollars (the reporting currency). All assets and liabilities are translated using the exchange rate in effect at the balance sheet date. This process is illustrated in Exhibit 15-4 in the columns headed all-current. All assets and liabilities are translated at LC 0.95 = $1.00 (LC 0.85 = $1.00) at December 31, 1991 (1992). For example:

- Accounts receivable at December 31, 1991, equal LC 410 (Exhibit 15-2). With the exchange rate of LC 0.95 = $1.00 on that date, the U.S. dollar equivalent

EXHIBIT 15-2. FOREIGN SUBSIDIARY, INC.
Comparative Balance Sheets, at December 31, 1990 to 1992 (LC in millions)

	1990		1991		1992	
Cash	LC 34		LC 170		LC 333	
Accounts receivable	300		410		475	
Inventory	175		220		310	
Current assets		509		800		1,118
Fixed assets	860		1,260		1,690	
Accumulated depreciation	(150)		(360)		(610)	
Fixed assets—net		710		900		1,080
Total assets		LC 1,219		LC 1,700		LC 2,198
Operating payables	LC 255		LC 290		LC 240	
Current debt	110		130		180	
Long-term debt	140		440		790	
Total liabilities		505		860		1,210
Common stock		230		230		230
Retained earnings		484		610		758
Total equities		LC 1,219		LC 1,700		LC 2,198

Exchange Rates

Fixed assets and stock-holders' equity	LC 1.06 = $U.S. 1.00			
Inventory	LC 1.06 = $U.S. 1.00			
Year-end	LC 1.06 = $U.S. 1.00	LC 0.95 = $U.S. 1.00	LC 0.85 = $U.S. 1.00	
Average	N/A	LC 1.02 = $U.S. 1.00	LC 0.90 = $U.S. 1.00	

N/A = not applicable.

is LC 410/0.95 = $431. This result is shown as accounts receivable in dollars on December 31, 1991 in the all-current column in Exhibit 15-4.

· Inventory at December 31, 1992, equals LC 310 (Exhibit 15-2). If we use the exchange rate of LC 0.85 = $1.00 on that date, the U.S. dollar equivalent is LC 310/0.85 = $364. This result is shown as inventory in dollars in the all-current column in Exhibit 15-4.

EXHIBIT 15-3. FOREIGN SUBSIDIARY, INC.
Income Statements, for Years Ended December 31, 1991 to 1992 (LC in millions)

	1991	1992	% Change
Revenues	LC 1,290	LC 1,430	10.9%
Less: Cost of goods sold	(540)	(611)	
Gross margin	750	819	
Other expenses	(414)	(421)	
Depreciation expense	(210)	(250)	
Net income	LC 126	LC 148	17.5%

EXHIBIT 15-4. FOREIGN SUBSIDIARY, INC.
Translated Balance Sheets, at December 31, 1990 to 1992 ($U.S. in millions)

	1990		1991		1992	
	Temporal	All-Current	Temporal	All-Current	Temporal	All-Current
Cash	$U.S. 32	$U.S. 32	$U.S. 179	$U.S. 179	$U.S. 392	$U.S. 392
Accounts receivable	283	283	431	431	559	559
Inventory	165	165	216	232	344	364
Current assets	480	480	826	842	1,295	1,315
Fixed assets	811	811	1,203	1,327	1,680	1,988
Accumulated depreciation	(141)	(141)	(341)	(379)	(590)	(717)
Fixed assets—net	670	670	862	948	1,090	1,271
Total assets	$U.S. 1,150	$U.S. 1,150	$U.S. 1,688	$U.S. 1,790	$U.S. 2,385	$U.S. 2,586
Operating liabilities	$U.S. 241	$U.S. 241	$U.S. 305	$U.S. 305	$U.S. 282	$U.S. 282
Current debt	103	103	137	137	212	212
Long-term debt	132	132	463	463	929	929
Total liabilities	476	476	905	905	1,423	1,423
Common stock	217	217	217	217	217	217
Retained earnings	457	457	566	581	745	745
Cumulative transaction adjustment	—	—	—	87	—	201
Total equities	$U.S. 1,150	$U.S. 1,150	$U.S. 1,688	$U.S. 1,790	$U.S. 2,385	$U.S. 2,586

Components of the income statement (Exhibit 15-3) should, in theory, be translated at the exchange rates in effect at the dates of the underlying transactions. However, the weighted-average exchange rate for the period is more practical and has been used instead in our example, as it is in practice. All revenues and expenses are translated at the average rate for each year, as listed in Exhibit 15-2. For example:

- Revenue for 1991 is LC 1,290 (Exhibit 15-3). If we use the average exchange rate of LC 1.02 = $1.00 for 1991 (Exhibit 15-2), the U.S. dollar revenue for that year is LC 1,290/1.02 = $1,265. That result is shown in Exhibit 15-5.
- Other expenses for 1992 equal LC 421 (Exhibit 15-3). If we use the average exchange rate of LC 0.90 = $1.00 (Exhibit 15-2), the U.S. dollar equivalent is LC 421/0.90 = $468, shown in Exhibit 15-5.

Note that for these two items, the temporal and all-current results are identical. For the columns headed all-current in Exhibit 15-5, all the U.S. dollar equivalents can be easily computed by dividing the LC amounts by the appropriate exchange rate. Note that some of the numbers in the temporal columns are different; we will see why shortly.

The translation process generates gains or losses since assets and liabilities are translated at different exchange rates at the beginning and end of the period. In addition, income statement components are translated at average rates, but their contribution to equity (change in retained earnings) is translated at the year-end rate.

EXHIBIT 15-4. (*continued*)

Computation of Translation Adjustment Under Temporal Method

	1990	1991	1992
Net monetary liability (year end)	LC 171	LC 280	LC 402
Increase during year	—	109	122

1991:	Loss on December 31, 1990, liability		1992:	Loss on December 31, 1991, liability	
	LC 171 [(1/1.06) − (1/0.95)] =	19		LC 280 [(1/0.95) − (1/0.85)] =	35
	Loss on 1991 increase in liability			Loss on 1991 increase in liability	
	LC 109 [(1/1.02) − (1/0.95)] =	8		LC 122 [(1/0.90) − (1/0.85)] =	8
	Total translation loss	27		Total translation loss	43

Note: The translation loss appears in the income statement. See Exhibit 15-5.

Computation of Translation Adjustment Under All-Current Method

Net assets	December 31, 1991	LC 840	December 31, 1992	LC 988
	December 31, 1990	714	December 31, 1991	840
Increase for the year		LC 126		LC 148

1991:	Gain on December 31, 1990, net assets		1992:	Gain on December 31, 1991, net assets	
	LC 714 [(1/1.06) − (1/0.95)] =	78		LC 840 [(1/0.95) − (1/0.85)] =	104
	Gain on 1991 increase in net assets			Gain on 1992 increase in net assets	
	LC 126 [(1/1.02) − (1/0.95)] =	9		LC 148 [(1/0.90) − (1/0.85)] =	10
	Total translation gain	87		Total translation gain	114

In 1991, the subsidiary begins operations with net assets (stockholders' equity) of LC 714 and ends the year with net assets of LC 840. The beginning balance of net assets translates to $U.S. 674, as the exchange rate is LC 1.06 = $U.S. 1.00 on December 31, 1990. These assets are held for the year, at the end of which they translate to $U.S. 752 (LC 0.95 = $U.S. 1.00), for a gain of $U.S. 78.

However, net assets have increased during the year by LC 126, the net income for the year (if we assume no dividend payout). We assume this income is generated evenly throughout the year, at the average exchange rate of LC 1.02 = $U.S. 1.00, or $U.S. 124. At the end of the year, the net income translates to $U.S. 133 (LC 126/0.95), an increase of $U.S. 9. Thus, the change in the local currency/dollar exchange rate has increased the net assets expressed in dollars by a total of $U.S. 87 ($U.S. 78 + $U.S. 9); this amount is reported as the translation gain in the equity section of the translated balance sheet.

The 1992 translation gain of $U.S. 114 is computed using the procedures just described. This translation gain is added to the 1991 gain of $U.S. 87, and the aggregate translation gain of $U.S. 201 ($U.S. 87 + $U.S. 114) is reported as the cumulative translation adjustment (CTA) in the equity section of the 1992 balance sheet.

Cumulative Translation Adjustment

The cumulative translation adjustment (CTA) is a separate component of stockholders' equity for the all-current method used to accumulate translation gains and losses, excluded from net income. Thus, volatility due to fluctuating exchange rates does not affect reported income, but is permanently accumulated in the CTA. When the foreign operation is sold, liquidated, or considered impaired, the translation adjustment is recognized as a component of the resulting gain or loss.

EXHIBIT 15-5. FOREIGN SUBSIDIARY, INC.
Translated Income Statements, for Years Ended December 31, 1991 to 1992 ($U.S. in millions)

	1991		1992	
	Temporal	All-Current	Temporal	All-Current
Revenues	$U.S. 1,265	$U.S. 1,265	$U.S. 1,589	$U.S. 1,589
COGS	(523)	(529)	(650)	(679)
	742	736	939	910
Depreciation expense	(200)	(206)	(249)	(278)
	542	530	690	632
Other expenses	(406)	(406)	(468)	(468)
Net income before translation	136	124	222	164
Translation loss	(27)	—	(43)	—
Net income	$U.S. 109	$U.S. 124	$U.S. 179	$U.S. 164

Rate of Increase, 1991 to 1992

Sales	= 25.6%
Net Income	
Temporal method	= 64.0
All-current method	= 32.3

In theory, accumulated gains and losses should balance out over time. If the CTA account consistently reports significant translation losses, this may signal a failure to manage currency exposure. As accumulated losses must be recognized in income if the foreign operations are sold or liquidated, a negative CTA also represents a potential loss.

Computation of the translation gain or loss under the all-current method is shown in Exhibit 15-4. Note that under the all-current rate method, the accounting exposure is defined as the net asset position (the financial statement-based measure of the parent's reported net investment in the subsidiary). However, this accounting definition of exposure may not reflect the economic exposure. We discuss the effects of this lack of congruence later in this chapter.

The more immediate question is what analysts should do with the CTA. The prevailing practice is simply to accept it, to use the financial statement data without any adjustment. Few analysts argue that the change in the CTA should be added to net income.

We concur with the latter practice, for two reasons. First, it is not clear that the change in the CTA represents economic gain or loss. Neither theory nor evidence suggests that adding the change to reported earnings produces a better measure of corporate performance.

Second, analysis that considers the CTA alone is incomplete. The CTA is nothing more than an accounting "plug," accumulating the effect of exchange rate changes on assets and liabilities denominated in foreign currencies. It is the effect of rate changes on those assets and liabilities (and on reported sales and net income) that distorts financial statements. Our emphasis, therefore, is on understanding how that distortion occurs and how adjustments can be made to offset it.

Notwithstanding the above, the next section shows how changes in the CTA can provide useful information as to the exchange rate effects facing a firm.

Using the CTA to Estimate Exchange Rate Changes

In 1991, the LC appreciated by 11.6% relative to the dollar.[12] Similarly, in 1992, the LC appreciated by 11.8%. Unless the firm has only one foreign subsidiary, the information as to the (average) change in the "basket" of LCs used by the firm's foreign subsidiaries is usually not known.

The change in the CTA, however, can be used to estimate the (average) change in the exchange rate of the local currencies used by the firm's subsidiaries.

$$\text{Change in Exchange Rate} = \frac{\text{Change in CTA}}{\text{Net Assets of Foreign Subsidiary}}$$

Applying this formula to the example of Exhibit 15-4 yields[13]

	1990	1991	1992
Change in CTA		$87 − 0 = $87	$201 − 87 = $114
Net assets	$1,150 − 476 = $674	$1,790 − 905 = $885	$2,586 − 1,423 = $1,163
Average net assets		$780	$1,024
Change in exchange rate			
Estimated		$87/$780 = 11.2%	$114/$1,024 = 11.1%
Actual		11.6%	11.8%

This procedure provides a good approximation of the average change in the exchange rate. We make use of it later in the chapter and in our cases. However, as Case 15-1 illustrates, the procedure may not be appropriate if:

1. The direction of the change in the exchange rate shifts dramatically during the year.
2. The firm radically shifts the composition of the subsidiary's net assets prior to the shift in the direction of the exchange rate changes.

Remeasurement: The Temporal Method

The principles of remeasurement apply under *each* of the following conditions:

1. The reporting currency (the U.S. dollar in our examples) is the functional currency of Foreign Subsidiary, Inc.
2. The unit operates in a hyperinflationary economy.
3. The foreign operation's records are kept in a currency other than its functional currency.

---

[12] At the end of 1990, LC 1 was equivalent to $0.943. At the end of 1991, LC 1 = $1.053, an 11.6% increase.

[13] We use average net assets. If net assets have not changed dramatically, then using opening net assets provides a reasonable estimate.

SFAS 52 mandates remeasurement into the reporting currency (also the functional currency in the first two cases) or the designated functional currency (in the third case) using the temporal method.

Unlike the current rate method, the temporal method applies the current rate only to monetary assets and liabilities, such as accounts receivable, marketable securities carried at market, current liabilities, and long-term debt. Exhibit 15-4 depicts this translation process for the FSI balance sheet, if we assume that the U.S. dollar is the functional currency and remeasurement is therefore required.

Note that the process for monetary assets and liabilities is the same as under the all-current method. However, nonmonetary accounts are translated at the rates in effect when the transaction occurred. As a result, inventories and fixed assets have been translated at their historical rates. The derivation of U.S. dollar inventories and fixed assets is shown in Exhibit 15-6.

EXHIBIT 15-6. FOREIGN SUBSIDIARY, INC.
Analysis of Inventory and Fixed Assets: Temporal Method ($ millions)

	LC	Rate	$U.S.		LC	Rate	$U.S.
			Analysis of Inventory				
December 31, 1990	175	1.06	165	COGS (FIFO):	175	1.06 =	165
1991 purchases	585	1.02	574		365	1.02 =	358
1991 COGS (at right)	(540)		(523)	Total	540		523
December 31, 1991	220	1.02	216				
1992 purchases	701	0.90	779	COGS (FIFO):	220	1.02 =	216
1992 COGS (at right)	(611)		(650)		391	0.90 =	434
December 31, 1992	310		345	Total	611		650
			Analysis of Fixed Assets				
December 31, 1990	860	1.06	811				
1991 investment	400	1.02	392				
December 31, 1991	1,260		1,203				
1992 investment	430	0.90	477				
December 31, 1992	1,690		1,680				
			Analysis of Accumulated Depreciation				
December 31, 1990	150	1.06	141				
1991 expense	210	1.047*	200				
December 31, 1991	360		341				
1992 expense	250	1.005†	249				
December 31, 1992	610		590				

*December 31, 1991, blended rate for fixed assets.
†December 31, 1992, blended rate.

Note: The exchange rate used to translate depreciation expense is a blend of the historical rates at the time fixed assets were acquired. Under the temporal method, depreciation expense is determined in U.S. dollars; the blended rate is derived by dividing U.S. dollar depreciation expense by LC depreciation expense.

Similarly, cost of goods sold and depreciation expense are translated at historical rates (also shown in Exhibit 15-6), whereas all other revenues and expenses are translated at the weighted-average exchange rate for the period.

The translation adjustment resulting from remeasurement is based on the net monetary assets or liabilities (the accounting exposure under the temporal method) rather than the net assets of the foreign operation. The reported translation adjustment, therefore, ignores the impact of changing exchange rates on inventories and fixed assets even though they may be effective hedges for major components of the net monetary position, that is, accounts payable and long-term liabilities.[14]

Under the temporal method, remeasured income statements also include the translation gain or loss on net monetary assets and liabilities, thereby adding significant volatility to reported income. Moreover, where the translation gain or loss does not reflect the economic exposure, the accounting-induced volatility reduces the utility of financial statements.

These calculations for FSI are shown in Exhibit 15-4. *As the local currency has appreciated against the dollar during the period, the net monetary liability has increased in U.S. dollar terms, resulting in a translation loss.* Like the SFAS 52 calculation, the adjustment occurs in two parts. There is a loss from the increase in the beginning balance of the net monetary liability (due to the appreciating local currency). There is an additional loss from the impact of the rising local currency on the *increase* in the net monetary liability during the year. The first portion of the loss is based on the change in the local currency/dollar exchange rate during the year. The second part results from the difference between the *average rate* during the year (the rate at which the incremental liability is assumed to have been incurred) and the *year-end rate*.

The resulting translation losses are included in net income under remeasurement rather than as part of equity under translation. *Note that under the current rate method, there is a translation gain, whereas under the temporal method, there is a translation loss. The choice of the functional currency defines the accounting exposure, thereby determining the amount of the reported translation gain or loss and its accounting treatment (income versus equity). The choice of functional currency matters!*

COMPARISON OF TRANSLATION AND REMEASUREMENT

Income Statement Effects

As shown in Exhibit 15-5, the current rate method translates all revenues, expenses, gains, and losses at the weighted-average rate. The temporal method also uses the weighted average for all the elements of the income statement *except* cost of goods sold and depreciation expense. Thus, these two expense lines differ, reflecting the choice of functional currency.

Effect on Gross Profit Margin

The temporal method, when combined with the use of first-in, first-out (FIFO) inventory accounting (the method generally used outside of the United States), can distort

---

[14]As inventories are sold for cash, it can be argued that a change in the exchange rate changes the expected amount of cash to be received when inventories are sold. In that sense, inventories can be considered monetary assets, hedging accounts payable, which will be repaid from the sale proceeds of the inventories. A similar argument can be made for fixed assets, which are used to produce inventories.

EXHIBIT 15-7. FOREIGN SUBSIDIARY, INC.
Financial Ratios,* 1991 to 1992

	Year	LC Units	All-Current	Temporal
Gross margin percentage	1991	58.1%	58.1%	58.7%
	1992	57.3%	57.3%	59.1%
Net income as % of sales	1991	9.8%	9.8%	10.8%
(Before translation loss)	1992	10.3%	10.3%	14.0%
Net income as % of sales	1991	9.8%	9.8%	8.6%
	1992	10.3%	10.3%	11.3%
Debt as % of equity	1991	67.9%	67.9%	76.6%
	1992	98.2%	98.2%	118.6%
Inventory turnover	1991	2.73X	2.66X	2.75X
	1992	2.31X	2.27X	2.43X
Receivable turnover	1991	3.63X	3.54X	3.54X
	1992	3.23X	3.21X	3.21X
Fixed asset turnover	1991	1.60X	1.56X	1.65X
	1992	1.44X	1.43X	1.63X
Total asset turnover	1991	0.88X	0.86X	0.89X
	1992	0.73X	0.72X	0.78X
Return on average equity	1991	16.2%	15.9%	18.7%
(Before translation loss)	1992	16.2%	16.0%	25.4%
Return on average equity	1991	16.2%	15.9%	15.0%
	1992	16.2%	16.0%	20.5%
Return on average assets	1991	8.8%	8.4%	9.5%
(Before translation loss)	1992	7.6%	7.5%	10.5%
Return on average assets	1991	8.8%	8.4%	7.7%
	1992	7.6%	7.5%	8.8%

*See Chapter 4 for definitions of ratios.

reported earnings. Use of the historical rate for inventories delays recognition of the effects of rate changes, just as FIFO delays the recognition of price level changes.[15] In the case of FSI, with an appreciating local currency, historical-cost-basis cost of goods sold is lower than the cost of goods sold translated at the average rate. If the local currency declined, cost of goods sold would be higher under the temporal method.

In either case, use of the temporal method distorts gross profit margins. We can see the distortion by comparing the gross profit margin under each method (shown in Exhibit 15-7) with the actual gross profit margin in local currency units.

The gross margin after remeasurement for 1992 is higher than the actual gross margin in local currency (59.1% compared to 57.3%). Equally important, it appears

---

[15]Problem 10 explores the relationship between the translation method and inventory method further.

BOX 15-1
Parent Versus Local Currency Relationships

The temporal method is often criticized for distorting local currency relationships. This box illustrates that, in situations the temporal method was designed for, it is the (remeasured) parent currency relationship that is relevant rather than the local currency relationship.

Assumptions:

- Company charges 50% markup over cost or 33% gross profit margin.
- When inventory is produced, the exchange rate is $1 = LC 1.
- When inventory is sold, the exchange rate is $1.20 = LC 1.
- Cost of inventory is $1.

If pricing decisions are made in dollars, when inventory is sold, its price will be $1.50. The local currency price will be LC 1.25 ($1.50/1.20). The local currency income statement is:

Sales	LC 1.25
COGS	LC 1.00
Gross profit	LC 0.25
Gross margin	20%

The local currency gross margin of 20% does not reflect the underlying economic relationship.* Under the temporal method, the income statement is remeasured as

Sales	$1.50
COGS	$1.00
Gross profit	$0.50
Gross margin	33%

The gross margin reported in dollars (in the parent's income statement) differs from the local currency relationship. It does, however, better reflect the economics of the transaction!

---

*Essentially, the local currency relationship distorts the parent relationship rather than the other way around. Further examples of this nature are discussed in the section entitled, "Analytic Difficulties Related to Foreign Operations."

---

that the gross margin percentage in 1992 increased slightly from that in 1991, 59.1% versus 58.7%; in local currency units, the gross margin percentage declined to 57.3% in 1992 from 58.1% in 1991. The gross margin percentage after translation, however, preserves the trends and relationships of the functional currency of the subsidiary. This preservation of local currency trends and relationships is often viewed as an important advantage of the all-current rate method.

It should however be noted that preservation of the local currency ratio may not be appropriate. Box 15-1 illustrates one situation the temporal method was designed for; with the U.S. dollar as the functional currency, the remeasured dollar ratio rather than the local currency ratio reports the underlying economics with less distortion.

Effect on Net Income

Depreciation expense is also significantly altered when the temporal method is used. Again, an appreciating local currency results in depreciation expense that is lower as compared with that resulting from the current rate method (see Exhibit 15-5). Net income before the effect of translation is again inflated by this effect.

Once again, the all-current rate method faithfully reproduces the net profit margin (as shown in Exhibit 15-7) from the original local currency statements, whereas the temporal method results in higher profit margins and a larger increase in the net profit margin in 1992.

The inclusion of translation (holding) gains and losses in net income under the temporal method results in further distortion. Translation losses in both 1991 and 1992 reduce the positive impact of the temporal method. The fact that the operating effects and translation effects are opposite, it must be noted, is a function of the asset and liability composition of FSI and the direction of change in exchange rates. Specifically, FSI had a net monetary *liability* combined with an increase in the value of the local currency relative to the dollar.

If the local currency had declined, both cost of goods sold and depreciation expense would be higher under the temporal method. The resulting lower reported income would be offset by the inclusion of translation gains on the monetary liability in income. Although the situation described here is not unusual, some companies have operating effects and translation effects in the same direction.

Although the remeasurement net profit margin for 1991 (Exhibit 15-7) falls below the original local currency results, the exaggerated profit margin improvement in 1992 remains. Translation still does the better job of reflecting the local currency operating results in U.S. dollars.

These income effects relate to the *holding gains/losses* resulting from exchange rate changes. Additionally, the use of weighted-average rates to translate the income statement creates the *flow effect* (discussed at the beginning of the chapter) on reported sales and net income. A strengthening (declining) local currency creates the illusion of higher (lower) sales and earnings of foreign operations.

FSI's sales increased by 10.9% in 1992 in local currency units (Exhibit 15-3) but by 25.6% in U.S. dollars (Exhibit 15-5). Net income increased by 17.5% in local currency units but by 32.3% in dollars (all-current).[16] The 13% appreciation of the local currency against the dollar inflates both the sales and earnings comparisons. For companies with significant foreign operations, the effect of changing exchange rates can make it difficult to discern true operating trends.

Balance Sheet Effects

The choice of functional currency also affects the balance sheet of the foreign operation and, after consolidation, that of the parent company. Exhibit 15-4 shows the FSI balance sheets for 1990, 1991, and 1992 under both methods.

Since the subsidiary was acquired on December 31, 1990, the balance sheets as of December 31, 1990, are identical under both methods. For 1991 and 1992, many of the asset and liability accounts are still identical as both methods translate monetary

---

[16]Note that under remeasurement, the increase in net income (even after translation losses) was 64%: twice the growth rate under translation and close to four times the rate reported in local currency terms! This is partly due to the computation of cost of goods sold and depreciation expense at historical exchange rates.

assets and liabilities at the current (balance sheet date) exchange rate. There are, however, some significant differences.

When the reporting currency (here, the U.S. dollar) is the functional currency, the temporal method requires that inventories, fixed assets, and other nonmonetary accounts be translated at historic rates. Exhibit 15-6 provides detailed calculations for both the inventory and fixed asset accounts.

Because the local currency has appreciated against the dollar, the historical costs of both inventories and fixed assets are below their stated amounts under the current rate method. As a result, total assets are lower under the temporal method. The asset turnover ratio increases, as discussed in the next section.

Turning to the right side of the balance sheet, we see that stockholders' equity is also lower under the temporal method. Under the current rate method, equity includes the cumulative translation adjustment gains for 1991 and 1992. Retained earnings at December 31, 1991 are lower under the temporal method as earnings have been reduced by translation losses resulting from the impact of the appreciation of the local currency on the net monetary liability. However, retained earnings are, by coincidence, the same under both methods at December 31, 1992.

Impact on Financial Ratios

We have already seen how the choice of functional currency affects income statement ratios. Because the balance sheet and income statement are both affected, many financial ratios vary with the choice of the functional currency. Exhibit 15-7 includes a number of examples.

Reviewing this exhibit leads to two conclusions: First, the ratios are quite different under translation and remeasurement, and second, the ratios under translation are often different from those in the local currency. Although the first conclusion should not surprise us, the second is disturbing given the objectives of SFAS 52. Let us examine each conclusion in detail.

Comparison of Ratios Under Translation and Remeasurement

As can be seen by comparing the translation ratios with the remeasurement ratios, they give quite different indications of the performance of FSI. Note that:

- The distortion of ratios and financial statement relationships arises from the foreign subsidiary component of consolidated financial statements.
- When a firm uses more than one foreign currency, it is very difficult to predict the financial statement and ratio effects, especially when the currencies move in different directions relative to the parent or reporting currency. Basket indices may or may not reflect the firm's exposure (the IBM case discusses this problem).

We have already discussed the differences in the gross margin and net margin ratios. The debt/equity ratio (current and long-term debt) is significantly higher under remeasurement. Although the debt is the same, the lower level of equity results in a higher debt ratio.

The asset turnover ratios are also different, with one exception. The receivable turnover ratio is identical under both translation and remeasurement because both methods translate receivables and sales at the same rates (year-end rate and average rate, respectively).

For inventory turnover, however, that is not true. Under remeasurement, both cost of goods sold and average inventories are lower, reflecting the lagged effect of the higher value of the local currency against the dollar. The result is a higher turnover ratio for both years. This result, however, reflects the assumed turnover rate and exchange rate changes in this example. It does not hold in all cases.

The fixed asset turnover ratio is significantly higher under remeasurement, reflecting the lower historic cost of fixed assets under the temporal method (given the appreciating local currency). This is a universal result; a rising local currency always increases fixed asset turnover for remeasurement as compared with translation. A depreciating local currency would result in higher fixed assets under remeasurement and a lower turnover ratio.

Total asset turnover is also higher under remeasurement, reflecting the lower historic costs of inventory and fixed assets. As in the case of all turnover ratios except inventory, the numerator (sales) is the same under both methods. Thus, the difference in the turnover ratio is driven by the denominator. Given a rising local currency, assets are higher under translation, resulting in lower turnover ratios.

Return ratios are also different under the two methods, as both the numerator and denominator are different. Under translation, return on equity is virtually unchanged; under remeasurement, return on equity shows a sharp increase in 1992. Both the levels and trend are therefore affected by the choice of functional currency.

This is also true of the return-on-assets ratio. This ratio (before translation losses) is higher under remeasurement than under translation for both years. The trend is also different: Return on assets (ROA) rises in 1992 under translation but declines under remeasurement.

Comparison of Translated and Local Currency Ratios

Turning to our second (perhaps surprising) conclusion that ratios under translation are often different from those in the local currency, compare the U.S. dollar ratios with the local currency ratios in Exhibit 15-7. In most cases, the translation ratios differ from the local currency ratios. The exceptions are the pure income statement (e.g., gross margin) and pure balance sheet (e.g., debt-to-equity) ratios. As all income statement components are translated at the average rate and all balance sheet components are translated at the ending rate, it is mathematically true that the LC ratios and U.S. dollar ratios are identical.

When ratios combine income statement and balance sheet components, however, the equality is disturbed. That is because the numerator and denominator do not rise or fall by the same percentage. Thus, turnover and return ratios are changed by translation. The differences between the ratios under translation and the local currency ratios are not large, and the 1991 to 1992 trends are similar, but the ratios are different.

One more effect of changing exchange rates on ratios deserves comment. When foreign operations have different trends and ratio characteristics than domestic operations, then exchange rate changes can distort consolidated ratios by changing the weight of foreign data. For example, if the local currency appreciates, foreign data will constitute a larger percentage of the consolidated group, and consolidated ratios will be affected. We can see this from the following example.

Assume that a foreign subsidiary has the following debt and equity levels:

	Foreign Subsidiary	
	1991	1992
Debt	LC 570	LC 570
Equity	840	840
Ratio	0.679	0.679

Also assume that the parent company has domestic (U.S.) operations with the following debt and equity levels:

	U.S. Parent	
	1991	1992
Debt	$ 200	$ 200
Equity	1,000	1,000
Ratio	0.20	0.20

There has been no real change in debt, equity, or the debt-to-equity ratio. However, assume the exchange rate has changed from LC 0.95 = $1.00, at the end of 1991, to LC 0.85 = $1.00, at the end of 1992. The appreciation of the local currency increases the foreign subsidiary's U.S. dollar debt and equity. After consolidation (and translation), the total debt and equity are

	Consolidated	
	1991	1992
Debt	$ 800	$ 871
Equity	1,884	1,988
Ratio	0.425	0.438

In consolidation, the debt-to-equity ratio increases only because of the change in exchange rates. *Whenever a financial ratio differs between the foreign subsidiary and the remainder of the consolidated group, a change in exchange rate will affect the consolidated ratio even if there has been no change in the underlying ratios.*

We therefore conclude our discussion of ratios with the following observations:

1. For pure income statement and pure balance sheet ratios, translation using the all-current rate method maintains the local currency relationships.

2. For ratios using both income statement and balance sheet components, the all-current method ratios do not exactly maintain the local currency relationships, but usually do not differ greatly.

3. Ratios computed under the temporal method, in most cases, differ markedly from both the local currency ratios and those computed from translated data.

4. Changes in exchange rates can affect consolidated ratios, even when there is no real change, by increasing or decreasing the "weighting" of the foreign subsidiary.

Impact on Reported Cash Flows

Subsequent to SFAS 52, the FASB issued SFAS 95, Statement of Cash Flows (1987), which affects the reporting of cash flows for foreign operations. SFAS 95 provides that cash flows in the parent (reporting) currency must replicate the cash flows in the local currency. To accomplish this objective, cash flows in the reporting currency must exclude the effects of exchange rate changes. This requirement means that the cash flow statement should be unaffected by whether the temporal or all-current rate method is used.

To understand the consequences of this requirement, compare the statement of cash flows with the balance sheet and income statement. Exhibit 15-8 contains FSI cash flow statements for 1991 and 1992, both in local currency units and U.S. dollars. First, look at the local currency statements.

The local currency cash flow statements were prepared from the balance sheet (Exhibit 15-2) and income statement (Exhibit 15-3) of FSI. The cash flows in Exhibit 15-8 consist of a mixture of income statement data and changes in balance sheet accounts. For example, the 1992 change in receivables is the difference between the balance of accounts receivable at December 31, 1991 and the balance at December 31, 1991 (LC 475 − LC 410 = LC 65).

Investing cash flow equals capital spending, or the change in fixed assets (before depreciation). Financing cash flow equals the increase in current and long-term debt. The net cash flow is necessarily equal to the change in cash for the year.

When local currency cash flows are translated into U.S. dollars, these relationships break down because of the impact of exchange rate changes. For example, the U.S. dollar cash flow statement for 1992 shows an increase of $72 in accounts receivable, whereas the year-to-year increase in accounts receivable on the U.S. dollar balance sheet (Exhibit 15-4) is $128 under either method of translation. How can we reconcile this difference?

Although the $56 difference between $72 and $128 can easily be reconciled,[17] it is important to understand why these two numbers are different. The year-to-year increase in accounts receivable in U.S. dollars is the result of two changes. First is the change in accounts receivable in LC units. Second is the impact of changing exchange rates on the balance.

Given the change in the value of the local currency against the dollar, this difference exists for every balance sheet account. In each case, the reported U.S. dollar cash flow must exclude the impact of exchange rate changes; the cash flow in dollars is simply the cash flow in the local currency, translated at the average rate for the year (LC 0.90 = $1.00 for 1992). For accounts receivable, the change is

$$\frac{LC\,65}{0.90} = \$72$$

As a result of SFAS 95, the U.S. dollar cash flow statement replicates the local currency statement, consistent with the objectives of SFAS 52. Prior to that standard, cash flow statements were distorted by the inclusion of exchange rate effects. Cash flow

---

[17]Effect of exchange rate change on December 31, 1991 balance = LC 410 (1/0.95 − 1/0.85) = $51. Effect on 1992 increase = LC 65 (1/0.90 − 1/0.85) = $4. Total effect is $51 + $4 = $55. Difference from $56 is rounding error. This computation is analogous to the translation adjustments computed in Exhibit 15-4.

EXHIBIT 15-8. FOREIGN SUBSIDIARY, INC.
Cash Flow Statements, 1991 to 1992 (in millions)

	LC		$U.S.	
	1991	1992	1991	1992
Revenues	LC 1,290	LC 1,430	$U.S. 1,265	$U.S. 1,589
Change in receivables	(110)	(65)	(108)	(72)
Collections	LC 1,180	LC 1,365	$U.S. 1,157	$U.S. 1,517
Cost of goods sold	(540)	(611)	(529)	(679)
Change in inventories	(45)	(90)	(44)	(100)
Change in payables	35	(50)	34	(56)
Inputs	LC (550)	LC (751)	$U.S. (539)	$U.S. (835)
Expenses	(414)	(421)	(406)	(468)
Operating cash flow	LC 216	LC 193	$U.S. 212	$U.S. 214
Investing cash flow	(400)	(430)	(392)	(478)
Financing cash flow	320	400	313	445
Effect of translation on cash*	—	—	14	32
Net cash flow	LC 136	LC 163	$U.S. 147	$U.S. 213

*1991:	Opening cash balance	LC 34/1.06 = $U.S.	32
	1991 increase in cash	136/1.02 =	133
	Total	170	165
	Actual cash balance	170/0.95 =	179
	Effect of translation	—	14
*1992:	Opening cash balance	LC 170/0.95 = $U.S.	179
	1992 increase in cash	163/0.90 =	181
	Total	333	360
	Actual cash balance	333/0.85 =	392
	Effect of translation	—	32

1992: Alternative Computation

Beginning cash balance	LC 170	
Effect of change in exchange rate*	$\dfrac{170}{0.95} - \dfrac{170}{0.85} =$	$U.S. 21
Cash flow from operations (CFO)	LC 193	
Effect of change in exchange rate†	$\dfrac{193}{0.90} - \dfrac{193}{0.85} =$	13
Cash flow from investing activities	LC (430)	
Effect of change in exchange rate†	$\dfrac{(430)}{0.90} - \dfrac{(430)}{0.85} =$	(28)
Cash flow from financing activities	LC 400	
Effect of change in exchange rate†	$\dfrac{400}{0.90} - \dfrac{400}{0.85} =$	26
Total effect of exchange rate changes on cash		$U.S. 32

*The revaluation of the LC cash balance to reflect the change in exchange rate during the year.

†The difference between the amount shown on the cash flow statement (translated at the average rate for the year) and the U.S. dollar equivalent of that cash flow at the year-end rate.

statements not prepared in accordance with standards containing rules similar to SFAS 95 (non-U.S. GAAP) retain the distortion resulting from exchange rate changes.[18]

According to the provisions of SFAS 95, the consolidated cash flows of MNCs should represent the reporting currency equivalent of local currency cash flows of foreign operations that are therefore unaffected by the choice of functional currency.[19]

The U.S. dollar cash flows all exclude the impact of exchange rate changes. The net cash flow, however, will not equal the year-to-year change in cash unless the effect of rate changes on cash is recognized. This effect is computed in Exhibit 15-8.[20]

The effect of exchange rate changes on cash ($32 for 1992) may also be broken down into its components, the effects on the opening cash balance and on cash flows for operating, investing, and financing activities. This breakdown is also shown in Exhibit 15-8.

Although we have stated that SFAS 95 mandates the removal of the effects of exchange rate changes on cash flows, that statement is not entirely true. Reported cash flows exclude only the impact of changing exchange rates on assets and liabilities (holding effect).

However, as local currency cash flows are translated at the average exchange rate for the year, changes in currency rates do affect reporting currency cash flows. This flow effect is similar to the impact on reported sales and earnings previously discussed. When a foreign currency rises in value, the parent currency equivalent of cash flows in that currency will also rise; when a currency falls, the translated cash flows decline. So although the provisions of SFAS 95 do provide us with a cash flow statement that replicates the local currency cash flow statement, the parent company cash flow statement is still affected by changes in currency rates.

ANALYSIS OF FOREIGN CURRENCY DISCLOSURES

We now turn to the analysis of disclosures typically found in the financial statements of multinational firms. Our goal is to use the disclosures and our understanding of the accounting for foreign operations to discern the effect of exchange rate changes on reported financial statements. The ultimate objective is to understand the firm's economic exposure to exchange rates, the effects of rate changes on this exposure, and whether or not the effects reported in financial statements reflect the economic effects appropriately.

---

[18]IAS 7 (1992) on cash flow is largely consistent with SFAS 95. Use of that standard outside the United States would make cash flow statements similar to those prepared in the United States under SFAS 95.

[19]Discussions with some preparers and a review of reported cash flow statements convince us that this is not true in all cases. We believe that, in some cases, consolidated cash flow statements are prepared from translated functional currency cash flow statements rather than local currency statements. We conclude that, in these cases, the choice of functional currency does affect reported cash flows!

[20]A simplified way to view the issue is to assume that all LC cash flows are received in the middle of the year; that is the implicit assumption of the cash flow statement. However, between the middle of the year and year-end, there is an exchange gain on the cash received as the LC rises. In addition, the opening balance of LC currency increases in dollar terms. These gains total $32. We can use the method shown in Exhibit 15-4 to confirm this answer.

The effect on December 31, 1991 cash is LC 170 $(1/0.95 - 1/0.85) = \$21$. The effect on the 1992 increase in cash is LC 163 $(1/0.90 - 1/0.85) = \$11$. The total effect for 1992 is $\$21 + \$11 = \$32$.

Exchange Rate Changes: Exposure and Effects

The starting point for any analysis is the determination of exposure to currencies other than the parent (reporting) currency. The next step is to estimate the effects of exchange rate changes. These effects are the consequence of two factors, exposure and rate changes. What is most important, however, is not the precise measurement of the distortions resulting from exchange rate changes, but the recognition that they exist. Once you recognize the issues, you can usually estimate the financial statement effects. Given the imprecision of financial statements to begin with, even a general understanding of the effects of changing exchange rates should improve investment decisions.

Information about exposure can be obtained from:

- Financial statement references to exchange rate effects
- Footnote disclosures about translation gains and losses
- Geographic segment disclosures
- Management discussion and analysis
- Listings of subsidiaries or divisions
- Descriptive material about business operations

From such references, the analyst should seek to determine the following:

1. In which currencies is business conducted?
2. How much exposure does the company have to each currency?
3. What accounting method does the firm use for its foreign operations?
4. What functional currencies does the firm use?
5. How does the firm hedge its exposure to exchange rate effects?

Hedging is deferred to Chapter 16; we focus our discussion on the first four items. As exchange rate changes affect all three financial statements, we must examine the accounting exposure to rate changes for each in turn.

Balance Sheet

A company's balance sheet exposure depends on:[21]

1. The choice of functional currency
2. Composition of foreign subsidiaries' balance sheets

Choice of Functional Currency. **When the parent currency is the functional currency, then exposure equals net monetary assets (the temporal method). When the local currency is the functional currency, exposure equals net assets by currency (the all-current rate method).**

Some large U.S. multinationals use the U.S. dollar as functional currency for all foreign operations. Examples include duPont, Caterpillar, Merck, and Texaco. In other

---

[21]The effect of these factors can be mitigated by hedging activities.

cases, the functional currency choice is made for each foreign operation. For example, the following disclosure appears in the Major Accounting Policies footnote of Mobil's *1995 Annual Report:*

> The functional currency for most foreign operations is the local currency. . . . The U.S. dollar is used as the functional currency for operations in highly inflationary foreign economies and for exploration and producing operations in Indonesia, Nigeria, and Australia.

The choice of functional currency is a management decision. Despite the criteria laid down by SFAS 52, there is disparity even among companies with similar operations. Among U.S.-based oil multinationals, Chevron and Texaco use the U.S. dollar as their functional currency worldwide; Exxon and Mobil use local currencies.

Royal Dutch/Shell and British Petroleum use local currencies as functional currencies. Elf, the French oil multinational, states:

> Each foreign entity's financial statements are prepared in the currency in which that entity primarily conducts its business (the functional currency). For most of the Group's foreign subsidiaries the local currency is the functional currency, with the exception of certain exploration-production subsidiaries, where the U.S. dollar is the most representative currency.[22]

This disclosure illustrates that the functional currency can be a currency other than the local or parent currencies.

Financial statement disclosures regarding exposure are typically poor, as neither SFAS 52 nor IAS 21 have meaningful disclosure requirements. DuPont is a notable exception, as Note 27 reports the company's principal exposures. (As duPont uses the dollar as functional currency, all exposures are measured by the net monetary assets or liabilities.) As will be discussed in Chapter 16, duPont has hedged all these exposures on an after-tax basis. Although there is no disclosure of exchange gains and losses included in income, they are probably not material.

When the firm does not explicitly state its choice of functional currency, then the absence of a cumulative translation adjustment on the balance sheet indicates that the firm is using the temporal method and the functional currency for all its foreign subsidiaries is the parent currency. If a CTA appears on the balance sheet, then the analyst knows that for at least some of the subsidiaries the firm is using the all-current method and the local currency is the functional currency.

Balance Sheet Composition. Balance sheet exposure is also affected by the asset/liability structure of foreign operations. Subsidiaries with few liabilities are heavily exposed to exchange rate effects. Exposure can be reduced by borrowing in the local currency or through hedging activities.

Once exposures are known or estimated, the exchange effects can be computed, following the Foreign Subsidiary example earlier in the chapter. The effect has two parts, similar to those shown in Exhibit 15-4:

1. The opening balance (in local currency) multiplied by the rate change over the entire time period.

---

[22]Note 1 to 1995 financial statements of Elf Aquitaine.

2. The change in balance (in local currency) multiplied by the rate change from the date of the change to the end of period. Absent better information, assume that the local currency change occurred evenly and use the average rate for the period.

Translation adjustments for operations with nonparent functional currencies are accounted for in the cumulative translation adjustment section of equity; adjustments for operations with the parent currency as functional currency are included in reported income.

Example: Pepsico Mexico. Part A of Exhibit 15-9 contains data regarding Pepsico's Mexican operations from its *1995 Annual Report;* year-end and average peso-dollar exchange rates are given in part B. Exhibit 15-9 shows that identifiable assets declined from $995 to $637 in 1995. To ascertain how much of this change resulted from exchange rate changes rather than an actual asset decline in pesos, we use the year-end rates to translate identifiable assets into pesos:

	1994	1995	% Change
Assets ($ in millions)	995	637	−36.0
× Year-end exchange rate	5.075	7.695	
Assets (pesos in millions)	5,050	4,902	−2.9

The sharp decline in assets of PepsiCo's Mexican subsidiary was due almost entirely to the peso's decline. Although the (undisclosed) net investment in Mexico is undoubtedly smaller, Pepsico states that the peso devaluation was the primary factor in the 1995 negative CTA of $337 million. We can compute the translation loss on the identifiable assets:

$$\text{Opening balance} \quad 5,050 \times \left[\frac{1}{7,695} - \frac{1}{5.075} \right] = \$(338)$$

$$\text{Change } (4,902 - 5,050) \quad (148) \times \left[\frac{1}{7.695} - \frac{1}{6.418} \right] = \underline{\quad 4 \quad}$$

$$\text{Translation loss on identifiable assets[23]} \qquad \$(334)$$

In this case, the currency and exposure are known. However, because most firms do not disclose exposures by currency, analysts must use the available data about foreign operations, supplemented by discussions with management, to estimate major exposures and their effects. When foreign operations are limited to one currency, the analysis shown in Case 15-1 (AFLAC) can be employed. For some multinationals, an index approach can be used (see Case 15-2 on IBM). In other cases, the change in the CTA for the firm can be used to estimate the year-end to year-end change in foreign currency rates weighted by the operations of the firm itself. This firm-specific index can then be used to discern the effect of exchange rate changes on assets and liabilities.

---

[23]The closeness of this amount to the actual change in the CTA suggests that Pepsico's peso liabilities were small and the CTA change for all other functional currencies balanced out.

EXHIBIT 15-9. PEPSICO MEXICO
Effects of Devaluation

A. Selected Financial Data

Mexico is an important foreign market for Pepsico and the 1995 decline in the value of the peso had a significant negative impact on operating profit. To explain that impact, PepsiCo's *1995 Annual Report* included the following data:

	1994	1995	% Change
$U.S. millions			
Net sales	$2,023	$1,228	−39.3%
Operating profit	261	80	−69.3
Identifiable assets	995	637	−36.0

PepsiCo's Management's Analysis states that:

- Operations were adversely impacted by the effects of the approximately 50% devaluation of the Mexican peso.
- Consumer demand shrank dramatically.
- [Management actions] resulted in only a modest decline in local currency segment operating profit for Mexico.

B. Peso-Dollar Exchange Rate

	1994	1995	% Change
Year-end rate, December 31	$1 = 5.075	7.695	−51.6%
Average rate during year*	$1 = 3.397	6.418	−88.9

*Average of month-end rates.
Source: PepsiCo, *1995 Annual Report.*

Income Statement

As in the case of the balance sheet, income statement exposure depends on the choice of functional currency. Generally, revenues and most expense categories are translated at the average rate for the period regardless of the choice of functional currency. When the local currency is the functional currency, then all revenue and expense categories are translated at the average rate. When the parent currency is the functional currency, then inventories and fixed assets and consequently COGS and depreciation expense are translated at historical rates (see Exhibits 15-5 and 15-6). In addition, translation gains and losses are included in reported income, as the temporal method is used.

Exchange rate changes affect reported income because the average rate used to translate the income statement is different each period. Analysis of the effect of exchange rate changes on the income statement requires an "average for the period" index. In some cases, a trade-weighted index will serve the purpose. For companies whose operations are concentrated in one or a few countries, it may be possible to construct a firm-specific index. Despite the difficulty of the approximations required, some effort must be made to gauge the income statement exposure to rate changes.

The most pervasive income statement effect of exchange rate changes is the flow effect of rate changes on revenue and expense. This effect must be disaggregated from the effect of operations:

1. *The exchange rate effect is estimated by multiplying the income statement component (in local currency) by the change in the average exchange rate.*

2. *The operational effect is estimated by multiplying the change in the income statement component (in local currency) by the previous period's average exchange rate.*

The exchange rate effect is always present, although it is frequently omitted from management comments about operating results. DuPont's Management Discussion and Analysis, for example, has only some general comments about the effect of exchange rate changes on segment revenues.

When making international comparisons, it is important to remember that exchange rate effects on the income statement depend on the point of view. To cite one example, the *1994 Annual Report* of Merck, which reports in U.S. dollars, states that

the effect of a weakening U.S. dollar against foreign currencies increased 1994 sales growth by one percentage point. . . .

On the other hand, Roche, reporting in Swiss francs, reported that 1994 sales rose 3% despite a 10% increase in local currency sales, implying a negative 7% currency effect.

When comparing the sales growth of firms with different reporting currencies, therefore, the analyst must consider differences in the impact of exchange rates. Differences in both the reporting currency and geographic business mix affect sales comparisons.

Cases 15-1 and 15-2 contain extensive analyses of the effect of exchange rate changes on the revenue and income trends of AFLAC and IBM, respectively. We illustrate the procedure using Pepsico Mexico. The analysis will allow us to check the accuracy of management's statements quoted in Exhibit 15-9. Multiplying the Pepsico Mexico data by the *average rate* produces income statement data in millions of pesos:

Pesos (in millions)	1994	1995	
Net sales	6,872	7,881	14.7%
Operating profit	887	513	−42.1%
Operating margin	12.9%	6.5%	

PepsiCo's statements (Exhibit 15-9) do not match the data:

· Consumer demand did not shrink. Peso sales actually rose 14.7%. The only way to reconcile these statements is to assume that peso prices rose sharply.

· The decline in local currency segment operating profit was not moderate. Peso operating profit fell 42%.

These observations can be confirmed when we disaggregate the decline in sales ($795) and operating income ($181) into the exchange rate flow effect and operational effect as follows:

Sales	Operating Income

Exchange Rate Flow Effect

$$7,881 \times \left[\frac{1}{6.418} - \frac{1}{3.397}\right] = \$(1,092) \qquad 513 \times \left[\frac{1}{6.418} - \frac{1}{3.397}\right] = \$\ (71)$$

Operational Effect

$$(7,881 - 6,872) \times \left[\frac{1}{3.397}\right] = \underline{\quad 297 \quad} \qquad (513 - 887) \times \left[\frac{1}{3.397}\right] = \underline{(110)}$$

$$(795) \qquad\qquad\qquad\qquad\qquad (181)$$

For sales we have a positive operational effect, whereas for operating income it is negative.

Cash Flow Statement

As all cash flows must be translated at the average rate for the period, the choice of functional currency does not matter. Period-to-period changes in average rates directly affect reported cash flows. However, seasonal cash flow patterns or other timing differences can result in cash flow effects that differ from income statement effects, even when the local currency is the functional currency.

For recurring transactions, the exchange rate effects on reported cash flows are quite simple. Cash flows are translated at the average rate for the period, regardless of the choice of functional currency. Almost all operating cash flows and many investing and financing cash flows occur relatively evenly over the year. However, such transactions as payments for acquisitions, and major debt issuance or retirements are occasional and their timing is important. See Case 15-1 (AFLAC) where the timing of major investment and debt changes significantly changed currency exposure.

The index used to measure rate change effects on cash flows should be the same one used to measure the income statement effects. It is important to keep a clear distinction between period-end rates used for balance sheet analysis and period-average rates that affect income and cash flow data.

The devaluation's effect on PepsiCo's cash flows from its Mexican operations can only be guessed at, given the lack of disclosure. Given the decline in the average peso-dollar rate during 1995, we can assume that the Mexican subsidiary contributed little to corporate cash flow in 1995, although Management's Discussion and Analysis is silent on this point.

HYPERINFLATIONARY ECONOMIES

Countries experiencing very high rates of inflation present problems for both accountants and financial analysts. Because the currencies of high-inflation countries normally depreciate at a rapid rate (reflecting the diminishing purchasing power of the currency), translation of the financial statements of companies operating in such countries into "strong" currencies creates special difficulties.

If the current exchange rate is used to translate the assets and liabilities of subsidiaries located in high-inflation countries, their translated amounts quickly become insignificant. Such accounting would misrepresent the financial condition of the subsidiary, suggesting that its assets are disappearing.

In most cases, however, the real value of nonmonetary assets is not destroyed by the high rate of inflation. Inventories and fixed assets generally rise in value (in local currency) enough to offset the rate of inflation. This is to be expected as, otherwise, such assets could be transported to other countries where their value would be higher. This effect is usually explicitly recognized in the accounting system of such countries by indexing the carrying value of nonmonetary assets by the rate of inflation. (See the discussion of constant dollar accounting in Appendix 8-A.)

Alternative Accounting Methods for Hyperinflationary Subsidiaries

There are two solutions to the accounting problem:

1. The reporting (parent) currency can be the functional currency for all operations in highly inflationary economies. Nonmonetary assets and liabilities of the subsidiary, under this method, are effectively accounted for in the parent currency.

2. The indexed value of nonmonetary assets and liabilities can be translated at the current exchange rate. This method has the effect of approximately maintaining the carrying amount of subsidiary assets and liabilities in the reporting currency.

SFAS 52 takes the first approach. It defines hyperinflationary as cumulative three-year inflation exceeding 100%.

With the parent (reporting) currency as the functional currency, use of the temporal method maintains the historical cost of nonmonetary assets and liabilities (most significantly, inventory and fixed assets) in the parent currency. Neither exchange rates nor price changes affect that carrying value. Cost of goods sold and depreciation expense are also measured in the parent currency. The temporal method includes gains and losses resulting from the remeasurement process in reported earnings. Companies operating in high-inflation countries generally try to balance their exposure (net monetary position) to the local currency by borrowing locally if necessary. Because they are frequently unable to do so, or the interest cost is too high, companies with large operations in hyperinflationary economies frequently report translation losses.

IAS 21 takes the second approach to accounting for subsidiaries in hyperinflationary economies. The IASC standard does not, however, explicitly state when a country is considered hyperinflationary.

The two methods are broadly similar as they eliminate the problem of disappearing assets and liabilities. However, the two approaches are different and produce different measures of equity and income. As the IASC method does produce different results and the U.S. Securities and Exchange Commission does not require reconciliation to U.S. GAAP for these differences, analysts must determine whether the effect on comparability is material on a case-by-case basis.

Effects of Debt Denominated in Hyperinflationary Currencies

Borrowing in a high-inflation currency creates another analysis problem. Such currencies normally have extremely high nominal interest rates, as the lender must be compensated for the loss of purchasing power (due to high inflation). The high interest rate is acceptable because the borrower invests in comparatively inflation-proof assets and reduces its net monetary asset exposure. The high interest expense, in reality, is mostly offset by the purchasing power gain from the diminishing real value of the debt.

For example, consider Note 4 to duPont's financial statements, which explains that

> interest expense is reduced by exchange gains associated with local currency borrowing in hyperinflationary economies. These amounts effectively offset the related inflationary interest expense arising from currency devaluations.

This adjustment effectively replaces nominal interest expense with real interest expense, much closer to the interest measure in countries with lower inflation rates (and therefore low inflation premia in nominal rates). It also, incidentally, reduces interest expense, increasing the interest coverage ratio. When companies have not made this adjustment, the analyst should do so to obtain more useful income statement data.

Example: Alcoa Aluminio. Aluminio is Alcoa's 59% owned Brazilian affiliate. As Brazil's inflation rate is very high, the hyperinflationary economy rule applies, and the U.S. dollar is the functional currency. Application of the temporal method results in translation losses in most years if the firm has net monetary assets.

In 1995, however, there was a small translation gain. How was this possible given the continual decline in the Brazilian currency during this period? Presumably, the gain was due to a net monetary liability; the declining exchange rate would then result in a gain.

Approximately three-quarters of Aluminio's assets consist of fixed assets and inventories, which are translated at the historic rate. Since only the net monetary assets or liabilities are exposed to changes in the exchange rate under the temporal method, companies operating in hyperinflationary economies seek to minimize their monetary asset position.

CHANGES IN FUNCTIONAL CURRENCY

The choice of functional currencies for a firm's foreign operations has a pervasive effect on the accounting for exchange rate effects. Companies do, on occasion, alter their choice for one or more foreign affiliates. A change in functional currency is considered a change in accounting estimate and may not be clearly disclosed. Even when the change is disclosed, the financial statement effects of that change are generally not disclosed, except when considered highly material.

Changes in functional currency are generally the result of one of the following:

1. Change in subsidiary operations, resulting in determination that the functional currency is no longer the same. (The factors that determine the choice of functional currency are discussed earlier in this chapter.)

2. Change in inflation rates that either classify the subsidiary currency as hyperinflationary, or remove it from that category. In recent years, the major example has been Mexico, which moved into the hyperinflationary category in the early 1980s and moved out of it (according to some observers) in the early 1990s.

Example: Alcoa of Australia

Aluminum Company of America (Alcoa), the world's largest aluminum company, has a majority owned affiliate in Australia, Alcoa of Australia (AA). AA is consolidated as required by SFAS 94 (see Chapter 13), although it is not wholly owned. Through the end of 1990, the U.S. dollar was the functional currency for AA. As a result, the temporal method was used to remeasure the financial statements of Alcoa of Australia into U.S. dollars, generating significant translation gains and losses and adding to the volatility of reported earnings.

Effective January 1, 1991, however, Alcoa adopted the Australian dollar as the functional currency for its Australian operations (AA). The press release announcing the change stated the following:

> Based on significant changes in the economic facts and circumstances related to Alcoa of Australia's financial operations, among them substantially eliminating its exposure to currencies other than the Australian dollar, the change in the functional currency is required under the guidelines in Financial Accounting Standard No. 52 regarding Foreign Currency Translation.
>
> Alcoa expects the change will reduce the effect that wide exchange rate fluctuations have on Alcoa of Australia's earnings. Gains or losses from translating Alcoa of Australia's financial statements to U.S. dollars now will be reflected in a separate stockholders' equity account on the balance sheet rather than in the income statement.
>
> Alcoa indicated that Alcoa of Australia's earnings in 1990 would have totaled $624.7 million with the change, compared to the reported $614.0 million.
>
> The change also had the effect of reducing Alcoa's consolidated shareholders' equity by $133 million, effective January 1, 1991.[24]

The immediate effect of the change was the reduction in equity of $U.S. 133 million alluded to. More detail is provided in the company's 10-Q Report:

> As of January 1, 1991 Alcoa adopted the Australian dollar as the functional currency for translating financial statements of Alcoa of Australia. The change reduced Alcoa's consolidated shareholders' equity at January 1 by $133 million and minority interests by $128 million. These amounts were offset principally by a reduction in properties, plants, and equipment.[25]

What does all this mean? The Australian dollar had generally declined against the U.S. dollar in recent years. With the U.S. dollar as the functional currency, this decline had no impact on the nonmonetary assets of AA, which were remeasured into U.S. dollars at the historical rate, as required by the temporal method. With the adoption of the Australian dollar as the functional currency for these operations, the nonmonetary assets were now translated at the (lower) current exchange rate, reducing their U.S. dollar equivalent. As fixed assets account for more than half of the assets of AA, these assets accounted for most of the decline in reported equity.

The total impact of the change in functional currency was to reduce the U.S. dollar equivalent of AA's net assets by $U.S. 261 million. The minority interest (49% of AA was owned by outside shareholders) was reduced by $128 million (49% of $261 million), with the remainder accounted for as an adjustment to Alcoa's equity as of January 1, 1991.

The change in functional currency had several financial statement effects on Alcoa. First, by reducing assets and equity, the return-on-assets and return-on-equity ratios were enhanced. Second, the quarterly volatility resulting from changes in the exchange rate between the U.S. and Australian dollars was largely removed from Alcoa's income statement. Further declines in the value of the Australian dollar would impact stockholders' equity but not reported income.

---

[24]Alcoa press release, April 3, 1991.

[25]Alcoa 10-Q, quarter ended March 31, 1991.

In addition, the accounting exposure to rate changes is different. With the U.S. dollar as the functional currency, the exposure (temporal method) was net monetary assets. With the Australian dollar as functional currency, the exposure is defined as net assets. We can see the difference by looking at the balance sheet of AA:

ALCOA OF AUSTRALIA LIMITED (AA)
Summarized Balance Sheets, at December 31, 1989 to 1990
($U.S. millions)

	1989	1990
Cash and equivalents	$ 297	$ 394
Other current assets	525	671
Fixed assets	1,585	1,559
Other assets	165	173
Total assets	$2,572	$2,797
Current liabilities	588	696
Long-term debt	228	179
Other liabilities	351	367
Total liabilities	$1,167	$1,242
Net assets	$1,405	$1,555

Source: Alcoa, *1990 Annual Report* (amounts rounded).

Assuming that all monetary assets and liabilities are denominated in Australian dollars and that inventories account for half of other current assets, we can compute the accounting exposure under each method for both years:

	1989	1990
Temporal method		
Cash and equivalents	$ 297	$ 384
Other current assets	262	235
Other assets (monetary)	165	173
Total liabilities	(1,167)	(1,242)
Accounting exposure (net monetary assets)	$ (143)	$ (450)
Current rate method exposure (net assets)	$ 1,405	$ 1,555

With the U.S. dollar as the functional currency, use of the temporal method created a negative exposure to the Australian dollar; depreciation of the Australian dollar would result in a translation gain (included in reported income). With the Australian dollar as the functional currency, there is a positive exposure measured by the net assets: depreciation of the Australian dollar would result in a translation loss (included in the currency translation adjustment).

We can, therefore, see that the choice of functional currency affects both the amount of the exposure and the disposition of the translation gain or loss. By changing the functional currency of AA to the U.S. dollar, Alcoa may have increased its accounting exposure, but it removed the translation effects from reported earnings.

Prior to 1991, translation gains and losses were included in reported earnings. In 1988 and 1987, for example, AA (using the temporal method) reported foreign currency losses of $U.S. 105.6 million and $U.S. 89.9 million, respectively, due to strength in the Australian dollar. Had the Australian dollar been the functional currency, there would have been translation gains based on the net asset position.

However, there is one additional factor affecting the analysis: Our assumption that all monetary items are in Australian dollars is not correct. In the 1980s, AA's long-term debt was primarily denominated in U.S. dollars. As AA exported much of its output and pricing was in U.S. dollars, the company hedged its revenue exposure by borrowing in the same currency. This decision complicated its accounting.

Had the Australian dollar been the functional currency in the past, AA would have recognized translation gains or losses on its $U.S.-denominated debt. If, for example, the U.S. dollar rose against the Australian dollar (as it did during most of the 1980s), the company's debt would have risen in Australian dollars. This increase would have been a translation loss (under the temporal method). Upon translation of AA's results into U.S. dollars, the translation loss would have remained a component of income. Thus, the parent company (Alcoa) would have gains or losses on liabilities denominated in the parent company's currency (U.S. dollars). This anomalous result occurs whenever the parent company uses the local currency as the functional currency for a subsidiary with assets or liabilities in the parent currency.

Over the period 1985 to 1990, AA sharply reduced its U.S. dollar-denominated debt, reducing Alcoa's exposure to translation gains or losses from this source. Changing the functional currency to the Australian dollar therefore no longer exposed the company to these phantom translation adjustments. (Because the source of financing is one factor in the choice of functional currency, the decline in the importance of U.S. dollar debt helped to justify the change.)

As a result of the change in functional currency, AA's reported income is no longer affected by significant translation adjustments. Over the three-year period 1993 to 1995, total translation and exchange adjustments included in reported income were $U.S. 5.8 million. Effects included in stockholders' equity may remain significant, however.

ANALYTIC DIFFICULTIES RELATED TO FOREIGN OPERATIONS

The provisions of SFAS 52 lower the volatility of reported earnings and produce financial statements and ratios similar to those under the local currency. However, they also generate two types of problems:

1. The lack of consistency or symmetry in the accounting for equivalent transactions
2. The economic interpretation of the financial statements generated by SFAS 52

These problems can be illustrated using the highly stylized environment of perfect markets. The following exposition summarizes work by Beaver and Wolfson (1982, 1984). The analysis is used to demonstrate the relationships among inflation, interest rates, and exchange rates that form the basis for much of the discussion that follows.

Relationships Among Interest Rates, Inflation, and Exchange Rates

Consider two countries, A and B, where the ratio of exchange rates between their currencies is $1:1$ ($1\ LC_A = 1\ LC_B$). Let $i_A = 1\%$ and $i_B = 6.8\%$ equal the inflation rates of countries A and B, respectively. If we assume a real interest rate of r (equal in both countries) of 3%, inflation will result in a higher nominal interest rate R. In equation form, the relationship among inflation and real and nominal interest rates is

$$R = [(1 + i)(1 + r)] - 1$$

The (nominal) interest rates in countries A and B, respectively, are

$$R_A = [(1 + 0.01)(1 + 0.03)] - 1 = 4\%$$
$$R_B = [(1 + 0.068)(1.03)] - 1 = 10\%$$

Given these conditions, *ceteris paribus,* the exchange rate at the end of the year should be $1\ LC_A = 1.058\ LC_B$. This can be demonstrated by examining the effects on either nonmonetary or monetary assets.

Nonmonetary Assets

A nonmonetary asset with a cost of $P(0)$ at the beginning of a year will cost

$$P(1) = P(0)(1 + i)$$

at the end of the year. An asset that cost 1 LC (in each country's currency) at the beginning of the year (when the exchange rate is $1\ LC_A = 1\ LC_B$) now costs $1.01\ LC_A$ in Country A and $1.068\ LC_B$ in Country B. Since in real terms the assets are identical, they should carry an equivalent real price. That is, $1.01\ LC_A = 1.068\ LC_B$ or, equivalently, $1\ LC_A = 1.058\ LC_B$, the year-end exchange rate.

Monetary Assets

Under perfect markets, investors are indifferent as to where they invest. At the year-end exchange rate of $1\ LC_A = 1.058\ LC_B$, as the following table indicates, investors would be indifferent about investing in country A or B.[26]

Comparison of Return on $100 Investment

	Country A	Country B
Interest rate	4%	10%
Return on LC 100 after 1 Year		
In local currencies	$104\ LC_A$	$110\ LC_B$
Converted to Common Currency at Exchange Rate $1\ LC_A = 1.058\ LC_B$		
To currency A	$104\ LC_A$	$110/1.058 = 104\ LC_A$
To currency B	$104 \times 1.058 = 110\ LC_B$	$110\ LC_B$

[26]Otherwise, arbitrage opportunities would exist with money flowing into one currency from the other until the equilibrium of $1\ LC_A : 1.058\ LC_B$ was reached.

This illustration can now be used to discuss the two analytic problems presented at the beginning of this section.

Consistency in Reporting

When the local currency is the functional currency, local currency-denominated assets and liabilities are translated at the current exchange rate at each balance sheet date. For monetary assets and liabilities, the result is reasonable: The parent company balance sheet includes the assets and liabilities in the parent currency at amounts similar to their fair value. For nonmonetary assets and liabilities, that is not the case.

If a nonmonetary asset is purchased at the beginning of year 1 by a subsidiary located in Country B, it will be carried at the end of the year on the subsidiary's books at either:

- The historical cost of 1 LC_B, or
- The current cost (if permitted) of 1.068 LC_B

Similarly, if the parent (located in Country A) had purchased the asset, it would carry it at either:

- The historical cost of 1 LC_A, or
- The current cost (if permitted) of 1.01 LC_A

However, SFAS 52 requires the assets of the foreign subsidiary to be reported on the parent's books at the historical cost divided by the current exchange rate or $(1\ LC_B/1.058 = 0.95\ LC_A)$, which is neither the historical cost (in LC_A) nor the current cost. The accounting result conflicts with the expectation, just discussed, that the real price should be the same in both countries.

This point can be reinforced through another example. Assume that a company builds two identical factories, at identical initial cost, one in the United States and one in Country G, where it has a subsidiary. Assume also that the currency of Country G appreciates relative to the dollar, rising by 50% over the next five years. If the currency of Country G is the functional currency for that subsidiary, the "cost" of the factory in that country will be 50% higher than the cost of the U.S. plant.

Presumably, the rise in Country G's currency is due to a lower rate of inflation. But the inflation rate does not change the asset's historical cost. The higher carrying amount for the factory in Country G (and higher depreciation expense as well) is not logical. It is equally absurd for a factory in a country whose currency depreciates against the dollar to decline steadily in carrying amount. Yet this is the consequence of the application of the all-current rate method. Financial ratios are also affected, giving improper signals regarding the performance of operations in different countries.

Selling and Sorter (1983) make this argument as follows:

The balance sheet (and income) numbers provided under Statement No. 52 may be difficult to interpret. Under Statement No. 8, a historical cost . . . would be multiplied by the exchange rate prevailing at the time of the transaction to yield a dollar-denominated amount that is easy to interpret: it is simply a description of the actual cash flow that occurred in order to acquire an asset, translated at the dollar equivalent of that time period. The same local-currency-denominated historical cost multiplied by the current exchange rate (per Statement No. 52) yields a number that defies description: It is not a meaningful description of past cash flows, nor is it a description of future flows.

Statement No. 52 further confounds interpretation . . . by requiring that these meaningless balances be consolidated with the accounts of the parent company. The result is an aggregation of parent company figures representing a history of the cash flows with a number that is neither fish nor fowl.[27]

In extreme cases, when a factory is located in a hyperinflationary economy, the parent currency must be used as the functional currency, and the problem is solved. Both factories are accounted for at historical cost in the parent currency and retain identical carrying amounts and depreciation expense.

This problem results from the use of historical cost for nonmonetary assets. If current cost were used and assets and liabilities were translated at current exchange rates, then balance sheet carrying amounts would have more meaning. Until current cost accounting is adopted, analysts must simply be aware that the carrying amounts of nonmonetary assets in nondollar functional currencies (and the original or reporting currency) are not representative of fair value and are distorted by changes in price levels and exchange rates.

These issues are compounded by generally inadequate disclosure in the financial statements of companies with significant foreign operations. Some firms provide extensive data on exchange rates but provide no data on their exposures to changes in those rates.

The second and more serious problem created by SFAS 52: The accounting data may provide false signals regarding the economic impact of currency changes on foreign operations.

Economic Interpretation of Results

We noted earlier that one of the stated objectives of SFAS 52 was to provide information "compatible with the expected economic effects of a rate change." The standard does not meet that objective in many cases.

Using our previous example of a 100 LC investment in monetary assets, assume that the parent firm in Country A has a subsidiary in Country B whose functional currency is LC_B. Then, if we use the temporal method, the investment would be reported as follows:

	Subsidiary	Parent
Interest income	LC_B 10	$10/1.058 = LC_A$ 9.5
Translation loss		$100 \times [(1/1.058) - 1] = \underline{(5.5)}$
Net gain		LC_A 4.0

This accounting reflects the economics of the transaction as the parent has earned (and reported) LC_A 4 during the year. Under SFAS 52, however, the translation loss is not reported in the income statement. Income reflects only the interest income of 9.5 LCA. Since the (monetary) asset is restated to 95 LCA, the 10% nominal return relationship is maintained. However, the accounting result no longer accords with the economic reality.

---

[27]Thomas Selling and George Sorter, "FASB Statement No. 52 and Its Implications for Financial Statement Analysis," *Financial Analysts Journal,* May/June 1983, pp. 66–67.

Although this example is constructed in the realm of perfect markets, Beaver and Wolfson (1984) report on the association of high interest rates with weak currencies. An examination of spot and forward exchange rates, as well as prime rates, indicates that markets anticipate currency weakening and compensate for it by requiring higher *nominal* interest rates.

> First, note that the German mark, Swiss franc and Japanese yen are all expected to strengthen against the dollar throughout the year; the French franc and Italian lire are expected to weaken; and the Canadian dollar and British pound are expected to remain approximately stable. Second, note that the currencies that are expected to strengthen all have prime rates below the United States rate of 11 per cent (6.0, 5.5 and 5.75 per cent); the currencies expected to weaken both have prime rates above the U.S. rate (12.25 and 18.75 per cent); and the stable currencies have approximately the same prime rates (11 and 10 per cent).[28]

Other plausible scenarios also lead to accounting that distorts economic reality. First, consider a foreign subsidiary operating within the local environment, with no exports and no import competition. Such an operation is well served by SFAS 52. The parent company data largely replicate (in the reporting currency) the performance of the subsidiary in its local currency. The net investment in the subsidiary, the measure of exposure under SFAS 52, rises or falls depending on the exchange rate. When the local currency rises, the net investment increases in the reporting currency. The net investment is a fair proxy for the value of the investment to the parent.

However, consider a Canadian manufacturing subsidiary that exports all output to the United States. All revenues are in U.S. dollars, whereas costs are incurred entirely in Canadian dollars.

If the Canadian dollar rises against the U.S. dollar, the subsidiary's profit margins will be squeezed. Its Canadian dollar revenues decline (if we assume that U.S. dollar prices remain the same), while costs remain unchanged. To the extent that the subsidiary tries to maintain revenues in Canadian dollars, by raising U.S. dollar prices, it may lose volume. Either way, sales and earnings are likely to fall.

Yet with the Canadian dollar as the functional currency, the accounting consequences are identical to those of the previous example. The U.S. parent translates Canadian dollar assets and liabilities at the higher exchange rate, and the U.S. dollar equity increases (despite lower earnings). However, the economic impact of the rising Canadian dollar is to reduce the subsidiary's revenues, net income, and cash flows (in either currency) and therefore its value to the parent company.

Consider a third case, a British manufacturing subsidiary whose output is sold entirely within Great Britain and whose costs are incurred entirely in pounds sterling. If the value of the pound sterling rises, imports will enter, taking market share from the British subsidiary. The result is likely to be lower sales, lower earnings (price cutting may be necessary to keep market share), and lower cash flows. Once again, with sterling as the functional currency, the U.S. dollar net assets will increase. Yet the value of the British subsidiary has almost certainly declined, despite the higher currency exchange rate.

A partial answer to these contradictions is that accounting net worth is not meant to represent the value of a business. The role of accounting is to provide data that

[28]William Beaver and Mark Wolfson, "Foreign Currency Translation Gains and Losses: What Effect Do They Have and What Do They Mean?", *Financial Analysts Journal,* March/April 1984, p. 29.

help users to make better investment decisions. Analysis of that data, and conclusions regarding the value of investments, are not part of that role. Analysts must not fall into the trap of believing that preparers and auditors have done their job for them. Although the examples given are superficial, they should suggest the need for a thorough analysis of the economic impact of exchange rate changes.

Example: Whirlpool

On June 5, 1996, Whirlpool, a multinational appliance manufacturer, reported that second quarter earnings would be disappointing. Whirlpool's press release stated that

> . . . the strengthening in the lira's position relative to the German mark and other major currencies had been more persistent and profound than economic projections called for. Since December, the Italian currency's position against the Deutsche mark has increased by about 9 percent; the lira is also up significantly versus other European currencies. . . .

Whirlpool Europe has about 50% of its manufacturing base in Italy. About 80% of the volume from the company's Italian plants is exported to other markets; the profit margin on that volume is reduced when the lira strengthens. Yet, with the lira as the functional currency for these operations,[29] appreciation of the lira results in a higher carrying value of Whirlpool's Italian subsidiary.

Impact of SFAS 8 and SFAS 52 on Management and Investor Behavior

SFAS 8 was one of the most unpopular standards ever issued by the FASB. Much corporate criticism was due to the volatility introduced into net income. Ziebart and Kim (1987) note that a number of studies reported that, as a result of SFAS 8, MNCs increased their hedging activities in the currency markets to hedge their "paper" (accounting) gains and losses rather than their underlying economic exposure. Such hedging activities are costly and can actually add to the firm's economic exposure. One can speculate about the motivations underlying this "irrational" hedging in terms of the various theories concerning investor and management behavior discussed throughout this book:

1. Management believed (rightly or wrongly) that its investors or creditors were fooled by volatile reported income.
2. The added volatility adversely affected the firm's contractual arrangements such as management compensation and debt covenants. At the very least, the volatility adversely affected the monitoring role played by financial statements.
3. The volatility lowered the predictability of the firm's income and future cash flows as the reported exchange gains and losses masked the underlying economic events. This added to the firm's uncertainty and risk.

Empirical studies did not address these motivational issues.[30] Rather they examined market reaction, hypothesizing that SFAS 8 was viewed adversely by the market and

---

[29]Whirlpool's financial statements are silent on its choice of functional currencies, but it appears that the company uses local currencies as functional currencies for its European operations.

[30]Some of these studies were commissioned by the FASB in response to the criticism of SFAS 8.

the introduction of SFAS 52, with its dampening of earnings volatility, would result in positive market reaction.

Early studies (e.g., Dukes, 1978) could not document a negative market reaction to the introduction of SFAS 8. Ziebart and Kim[31] extensively analyzed the major events surrounding the inception of SFAS 8 in 1974 and its eventual replacement by SFAS 52 in 1980. They hypothesized that, in addition to issuance of exposure drafts and standards, other events that led to SFAS 52 also had positive market effects.

For the introduction of SFAS 8, its implementation, and the FASB's initial refusal to reconsider it, the authors expected negative market reaction for MNC firms. For events leading to the introduction of SFAS 52, they expected positive reaction.

The results found the expected market reaction to the actual pronouncements. For two of the three events associated with SFAS 8, there is significant negative market reaction. The lack of any significant reaction to the initial SFAS 8 exposure draft may indicate, the authors argue, that the market did not fully understand the implications of SFAS 8 until later.[32]

The market reaction to the SFAS 52 exposure draft was significantly positive (as expected). For other, prior events, the results are inconclusive. The authors explain these results by arguing that, although in retrospect we know that these events led to SFAS 52, the outcome was not clear at the time. These events may have been viewed as delaying tactics by the FASB that would result in maintenance of the status quo. Ziebart and Kim's results were generally consistent with negative effects associated with SFAS 8 and positive effects with SFAS 52.

Bartov and Bodnar (1994) demonstrated that the market found it difficult to understand the effects of changes in foreign currencies. They examined a sample of MNCs for which weakness (strength) in the dollar should translate into higher (lower) income.[33] Market prices would be expected to react in the quarter when the (known) changes in exchange rates occur. They found no significant reaction until the following quarter, when financial results for the previous quarter were reported. This lagged reaction suggests that mispricing does occur and a trading strategy designed to take advantage of this phenomenon generated significant abnormal returns.

Financial analysts also did not seem to appreciate fully the effect of the exchange rate changes. Examining whether analysts incorporated these effects in their forecasts, the authors note that analysts could have improved

> the accuracy of their estimates by using information contained in the past movements of the U.S. dollar. These results also give further credence to the view that investors fail to correctly characterize the contemporaneous relation between dollar fluctuations and firm value when they form future expectations of the value of the firm.[34]

---

[31]Their methodology differed from previous studies in their calculation of abnormal returns. In addition, and perhaps more important, they used a shorter test period. Although previous studies used time periods ranging from five months to two years, Ziebart and Kim used (for all event dates) a two-month test period. Use of a shorter test period increases the possibility of finding abnormal returns since, if they exist, they are not "swamped" by other events.

[32]Prior to SFAS 8, companies used a variety of accounting methods, and disclosure was minimal. Thus, it is possible that the market could not discern the impact of SFAS 8 on companies with foreign operations prior to its adoption.

[33]This higher income effect, as noted earlier, is not necessarily a function of the accounting method used.

[34]Eli Bartov and Gordon M. Bodnar, "Firm Valuation, Earnings Expectations and the Exchange-Rate Exposure Effect," *Journal of Finance,* December 1994, p. 1782.

Interestingly, the study found that the lagged reaction, although it still remained, was somewhat mitigated after the issuance of SFAS 52. In a subsequent paper, Bartov and Bodnar (1995) found that the results depend on the firm's choice of functional currency. For firms using the temporal method, the lagged reaction remained; for firms using the all-current method, the lagged reaction disappeared. They hypothesize that these results reflect lower income statement volatility (inherent in the all-current method), perhaps enabling investors to assess more accurately the impact of exchange rate changes on firm income.

FINANCIAL REPORTING OUTSIDE THE UNITED STATES

Foreign Currency Translation

Translation practices outside the United States may be quite different from the requirements of SFAS 52. Major areas of variation are:

1. In some countries (the United Kingdom, France, and the Netherlands), the balance sheet rate ("closing rate") is used to translate the income statement as well. During periods of significant change in exchange rates, use of the closing rate rather than the average rate will exaggerate the effects of rate changes on reported sales and earnings.

2. The "functional currency" concept is not explicitly used outside of the United States. However, many countries differentiate between foreign operations that are "autonomous" and those that are "integral" (branches). The all-current rate method is used for autonomous operations (local currency is functional currency under U.S. GAAP), whereas the temporal method is used for branches (parent currency is functional currency under U.S. GAAP). However, few countries have standards defining autonomous, leaving much to management judgment.

3. Translation gains and losses may be deferred regardless of the translation method. Deferrals are usually contained in reserves and are not separately disclosed. In some countries (Germany, for instance), gains are deferred, but losses are immediately charged against earnings. Lack of disclosure may make it difficult to discern the impact of translation gains and losses from published financial statements alone.

4. Definitions of "hyperinflationary" economies are vague, even where the concept is specifically used (Canada and the United Kingdom). The designation is consequently more discretionary.

As a result of these differences from U.S. practice, the financial statements of foreign firms frequently reflect changes in exchange rates differently. Although disclosures are generally poor in this area, careful reading of footnotes may provide clues to the financial statement impacts of these changes. When management can be questioned, additional information can be obtained, especially if the analyst understands the issues well enough to ask the right questions.

Foreign Currency Transactions

U.S. GAAP requires remeasurement at the current rate for assets and liabilities denominated in (nonfunctional) foreign currencies, with gains or losses reported as components of current income. The increasing issuance of debt denominated in foreign currency affects many multinationals.

In Canada, unrealized gains and losses on long-term foreign currency assets and liabilities are deferred and amortized over their lives. One example is note H to Suncor's 1994 financial statements:

> Long-term monetary liabilities are translated to Canadian dollars at rates of exchange in effect at the end of the period. Unrealized exchange gains and losses arising on translation are deferred and amortized over the remaining terms of the liabilities.

In Germany and France, unrealized gains may also be deferred until realized, but unrealized losses are recognized immediately.

In Japan, these transactions are translated at historical rates. In Sweden, foreign currency transactions are translated at year-end rates. Unrealized gains and losses are offset, and any remaining unrealized losses are recognized currently. However, unrealized losses are defined net of foreign exchange contracts that are expected to be covered by foreign currency flows generated by operations. Most companies have followed IAS 21 since 1993 and recognize the difference between unrealized gains and losses currently.

These differences result in vastly different reported income for similar transactions in different countries, and analysts should use reported income numbers with care in their decision models. Another difference arises when a portion of unrealized gains or losses is designated as extraordinary: The definition of extraordinary items is highly variable across countries, and the use of reported income before extraordinary items can be misleading. The latter problem is particularly acute when price/earnings (P/E) ratios are compared using computerized databases.

International Accounting Standards

IAS 21 (1993) is similar to SFAS 52. Although the IASC does not use the term *functional currency*, it does classify subsidiaries into operations that are *integral* and those that are *foreign entities*. The clear implication of this distinction is that parent companies should use the temporal method to account for integral operations and the all-current method for foreign entities. For the latter, exchange gains and losses flow directly into stockholders' equity, bypassing the income statement as in SFAS 52.

For foreign currency transactions and integral operations, the temporal method is required, with gains and losses on monetary items included in income (except for those arising from hedges and some long-term intercompany items). Recognizing that revaluations (e.g., fixed assets) are permitted in some countries, the standard requires that any revalued assets and liabilities be translated at the exchange rate at the date of revaluation.

IAS 21, like SFAS 52, requires use of the average exchange rate to translate all income and cash flow statement accounts of "foreign entities." The same analytical techniques used to assess the effect of exchange rate changes on U.S. companies can be applied to foreign firms using IASC GAAP.

IAS 21 has several important differences from SFAS 52:

1. Its treatment of foreign subsidiaries in hyperinflationary economies. That difference was discussed earlier in this chapter.

2. When goodwill and other fair value adjustments under the purchase method of accounting are carried only on the parent company balance sheet,[35] they may be translated either at the current exchange rate or the rate at the acquisition date.

3. Exchange losses resulting from acquisition of an asset invoiced in a foreign currency can either be charged to income (as required by SFAS 52) or added to the carrying value of the asset in exceptional circumstances, that is, the currency cannot be hedged.

SUMMARY

Changing exchange rates introduce an additional layer of complication to the analysis of financial statements. The most significant insights in this chapter follow:

1. The choice of functional currency is an important determinant of the accounting for foreign operations.

2. Translation and remeasurement are fundamentally different accounting processes—both the definition of exposure and the disposition of exchange adjustments differ.

3. Exchange rate changes distort all financial data for nonparent currency operations.

4. The goal is to separate the effects of currency changes from actual operating changes; analysis can often approximate the currency effects.

5. Accounting effects of currency changes are frequently different from the economic effects; analysis of the business is required to discern the impact of exchange rate changes on the value of a business.

CASE 15-1. AFLAC

Analysis of Exchange Rate Effects: Single Currency

INTRODUCTION

AFLAC (American Family Life) is a major specialty insurance company. Although the company is American, its Japanese subsidiary, AFLAC Japan, accounted for 85% of 1995 revenues and 90% of assets. Because AFLAC presents its financial statements in U.S. dollars, changes in the yen-dollar exchange rate have important effects on reported income, net worth, cash flow, and financial ratios.

With only a single foreign currency, the complexity that often characterizes the analysis of exchange effects is eliminated. The yen is one of the world's major currencies, and exchange rate data are widely available. As a result, the impact of exchange rate changes is easier to calculate and understand.

---

[35]In the United States, such adjustments must also be made on the subsidiary balance sheet. See discussion of pushdown accounting in Chapter 14.

CASE OBJECTIVES

The objectives of this case are to use AFLAC to:

1. Show the effects of exchange rate changes on levels and trends of revenue, income, cash flow, and financial position.
2. Calculate translation gains and losses.
3. Show how currency exposure can be managed.

EXCHANGE RATE EFFECTS ON INCOME STATEMENT

As AFLAC Japan dominates corporate results, we start with an examination of that subsidiary. Exhibit 15C-1 shows the revenues and pretax income of AFLAC Japan over the 1986 to 1995 period, in both Japanese yen and U.S. dollars. The average annual yen-dollar exchange rates are also provided. The Japanese yen rose from 168 to the dollar (1986 average) to 94 to the dollar (1995 average) over this time span, rising in seven of the nine years. The strengthening yen magnified the growth rate of AFLAC Japan, as yen results were translated into U.S. dollars at ever higher rates. Revenues rose from 154 billion yen (1986) to 575 billion yen in 1995, an

EXHIBIT 15C-1. AFLAC JAPAN
Exchange Rate Effects on Revenues and Pretax Operating Income (Japanese yen and U.S. $ in billions)

	Revenues			Pretax Operating Income		
	Yen	Rate	Dollars	Yen	Rate	Dollars
1986	153.9	168.56	0.913	19.2	168.56	0.114
1987	194.1	144.67	1.342	21.0	144.67	0.145
1988	218.7	128.19	1.706	23.5	128.19	0.183
1989	242.1	138.00	1.754	27.8	138.00	0.201
1990	286.7	144.83	1.980	31.8	144.83	0.220
1991	339.8	134.52	2.526	35.6	134.52	0.265
1992	399.6	126.67	3.155	40.3	126.67	0.318
1993	456.3	111.21	4.103	44.4	111.21	0.399
1994	524.3	102.26	5.127	48.2	102.26	0.471
1995	575.5	94.10	6.116	52.8	94.10	0.561

	Percent Change (%)			Percent Change (%)		
	Yen	Rate	Dollars	Yen	Rate	Dollars
1987	26.1	−14.2	46.9	9.4	−14.2	27.4
1988	12.7	−11.4	27.2	11.9	−11.4	26.3
1989	10.7	7.7	2.8	18.3	7.7	9.9
1990	18.4	4.9	12.8	14.4	4.9	9.0
1991	18.5	−7.1	27.6	11.9	−7.1	20.5
1992	17.6	−5.8	24.9	13.2	−5.8	20.2
1993	14.2	−12.2	30.1	10.2	−12.2	25.5
1994	14.9	−8.0	25.0	8.6	−8.0	18.1
1995	9.8	−8.0	19.3	9.5	−8.0	19.0
Average	15.9	−6.0	24.1	11.9	−6.0	19.5

Source: AFLAC, 1995 Annual Report.

increase of 274%; the nine-year increase in U.S. dollars was 570%. Due to an average 6% increase in the value of the yen, average revenue growth of less than 16% (in yen) was reported as more than 24% in dollars.

The effect of the yen's rise on reported pretax earnings was equally dramatic. Over the 1986 to 1995 period, AFLAC Japan's pretax earnings increased 175% in yen but 392% after translation to U.S. dollars. It should be noted that the effect of the exchange rate on revenue and pretax income is not affected by the choice of functional currency in this case; all the subsidiaries' revenues and expenses are monetary.[1]

However, the exchange rate effect was not beneficial every year. As shown in Exhibit 15C-1, the U.S. dollar revenue growth rate was only 2.8% in 1989, as 10.7% revenue growth (in yen) was mostly offset by a 7.7% decline in the yen relative to the dollar. A further yen decline in 1990 again resulted in a lower growth rate in dollars than in yen. Pretax income gains in 1989 to 1990 were also depressed (when reported in dollars) by the falling yen.

AFLAC Japan's growth rate has declined (in yen) in recent years. Strong gains by the yen, however, made the revenue growth rate accelerate (in dollars) in the 1990s.

EXCHANGE RATE EFFECTS ON CASH FLOW

As AFLAC Japan's cash flows are translated into dollars at the average exchange rate, the strengthening yen also increased reported cash flow, as can be seen from the following data:

Cash Flow from Operations ($ in billions)

	1993	1994	1995
Consolidated	$1.8	$2.4	$2.9
AFLAC Japan	1.7	2.1	2.7
% Increase	N/A	24%	28%
Exchange rate effect	N/A	9%	9%

Exchange rates accounted for approximately one-third of the increase in AFLAC Japan's cash from operations over the 1993 to 1995 period; AFLAC Japan accounted for more than 90% of consolidated cash from operations.

EXCHANGE RATE EFFECTS ON BALANCE SHEET

Because AFLAC Japan has no inventories and almost no fixed assets, its assets and liabilities are virtually all translated at current exchange rates.[2] Thus, changes in the yen-dollar exchange rate directly affect the consolidated balance sheet as AFLAC Japan accounts for 90% of corporate assets.

The effect on total assets can be seen in Exhibit 15C-2. Appreciation of the yen against the dollar increased the growth rate of total assets. Although assets grew 476% in yen over the 1986 to 1995 period, the growth rate in dollars was 799%. The yen appreciated in six of the nine years. Note that the exchange rate effects each year differ from the income statement effects shown in Exhibit 15C-1. The reason is that balance sheet accounts are translated at the *closing rate* for the year, whereas income statement (and cash flow) accounts are translated at the *average rate*. For example, although the yen's average rate *appreciated* 8% during 1995, its closing rate at December 31, 1995 *declined* 3.1% from the rate one year earlier.

Although liabilities also increased as the yen rose, significant net assets in yen had a positive effect on stockholders' equity in dollars. As the Japanese yen is the functional currency for AFLAC Japan, translation gains and losses are accumulated in the cumulative translation adjustment (CTA) mandated by SFAS 52. At December 31, 1995, the CTA was $213 million, or 10% of AFLAC consolidated equity.

---

[1] As an insurance company, AFLAC has immaterial depreciation and no cost of goods sold.

[2] This is true regardless of whether the functional currency is the yen or dollar.

EXHIBIT 15C-2. AFLAC JAPAN
Exchange Rate Effects on Total Assets (Japanese yen and
U.S. $ in billions)

	Total Assets		
	Yen	Rate	Dollars
1986	408.1	160.60	2.541
1987	511.5	123.05	4.157
1988	631.0	126.00	5.008
1989	760.5	143.55	5.298
1990	909.3	134.60	6.756
1991	1,093.4	125.25	8.730
1992	1,285.8	124.70	10.311
1993	1,523.0	112.00	13.598
1994	1,822.9	99.85	18.256
1995	2,351.0	102.95	22.836

	Percent Change (%)		
	Yen	Rate	Dollars
1987	25.3	−23.4	63.6
1988	23.4	2.4	20.5
1989	20.5	13.9	5.8
1990	19.6	−6.2	27.5
1991	20.2	−6.9	29.2
1992	17.6	−0.4	18.1
1993	18.4	−10.2	31.9
1994	19.7	−10.8	34.3
1995	29.0	3.1	25.1
Average	21.5	−4.3	28.4

With the yen as the functional currency, the CTA is a function of changes in the yen-dollar exchange rate and the net assets (in yen) of AFLAC Japan. Given the substantial size (and net worth) of AFLAC Japan, we would expect the CTA to increase when the yen rises and decline when it falls. Changes in the CTA over the 1993 to 1995 period were

	12/31/93	12/31/94	12/31/95
Opening CTA	$ 68,978	$123,294	$174,091
Increase during year	54,316	50,797	39,228
Closing CTA	$123,294	$174,091	$213,319

Given the *depreciation* in the yen during 1995, it is surprising that the CTA *increased* in that year. That increase can be explained, however, using information provided in AFLAC's annual report and an understanding of how exchange rate changes impact the CTA.

AFLAC's yen exposure decreased sharply, from 60 billion yen at December 31, 1994, to 29 billion yen one year later. The reduced exposure resulted from two management decisions:

• AFLAC incurred yen debt, designated as a hedge of its investment in AFLAC Japan.
• AFLAC Japan increased its U.S. dollar investments by more than $300 million.

But AFLAC's yen exposure remained positive, suggesting that the CTA should still have declined in 1995. The timing of these decisions, however, is crucial to an analysis of their impact.

These transactions apparently took place in the summer of 1995 (the borrowing took place in August), when the yen rose to approximately 85 per dollar, before declining to the year-end level of 103 per dollar. The change in CTA during the year, therefore, has two components:

1. An increase due to the yen's rise from 100 to 85 (per dollar) from January through August
2. A decline (but with sharply reduced exposure) over the balance of the year

The following calculations approximate the 1995 CTA change:

Dollar exposure at December 31, 1994	$601.9 million
Exchange rate	99.85 yen/dollar
Yen exposure at December 31, 1994[3]	Y 60.1 billion

If we assume the yen borrowing and increase in dollar investments took place August 15, 1995, at an exchange rate of 85 yen per dollar, the CTA change from January 1 to August 15, 1995 would be

$$Y\,60.1 \left(\frac{1}{99.85} - \frac{1}{85} \right) = \$105 \text{ million } \textit{Increase}$$

If the yen exposure was reduced to Y 29 billion on August 15, 1995, the CTA change over the balance of 1995 (August 15 to December 31) would be

$$Y\,29.3 \left(\frac{1}{85} - \frac{1}{102.95} \right) = \$60 \text{ million } \textit{Decrease}$$

The *net increase* in the CTA for 1995 would be $105 − $60 = $45 million. This increase exceeds the actual increase in the CTA during 1995; some of the investment changes were probably made at exchange rates closer to 90 yen per dollar, reducing their positive impact on the CTA.

Anticipating the reversal of the yen-dollar exchange rate, AFLAC was able to reduce its exposure to the yen sharply and mitigate the effect of the yen's decline on the CTA and consolidated stockholders' equity. AFLAC describes the critical transactions in its annual reports. However, the surprising change in the CTA would have alerted a perceptive analyst that a significant alteration in AFLAC's yen exposure must have taken place. This is another example of how financial analysis can focus attention on management actions, even when those actions have not been reported.

QUESTIONS FOR FURTHER DISCUSSION

1. The yen continued to decline, reaching nearly 110 per dollar by June, 1996. Predict the effect of this decline on AFLAC's:
   (a) Revenue growth for the second quarter (ending June 30) of 1996 as compared with the second quarter of 1995
   (b) Growth in pretax income for the second quarter (ending June 30) of 1996 as compared with the second quarter of 1995
   (c) CTA change for the six months ended June 30, 1996
   (d) Asset growth for the six months ended June 30, 1996
2. AFLAC carries all investments as available-for-sale under SFAS 115 (see Chapter 13). AFLAC Japan's fixed income investments (including those purchased in 1995) are, there-

---

[3]$601.9 times 99.85.

fore, reported at their market value in U.S. dollars. The current yield (interest) on these $U.S. investments is far higher than that on yen investments of comparable quality.

Discuss the effect of the 1995 shift from yen investments to dollar investments on 1996 growth in investment income (and pretax income) of *both*:

- AFLAC Japan (in yen)
- The consolidated enterprise (in U.S. dollars)

3. AFLAC accounts for the U.S. dollar investments of its Japanese subsidiary by reporting them at market value and ignoring any exchange effects. Yet one might argue that, under SFAS 52, the U.S. dollar investments of AFLAC Japan should be *remeasured* into yen, the functional currency for AFLAC Japan, and then *translated* into dollars.

Discuss how this accounting approach would alter the reported effects of yen-dollar changes on reported income.

CASE 15-2. IBM

Analysis of Exchange Rate Effects: Multiple Currencies

INTRODUCTION

IBM is one of the world's largest multinational corporations, and changes in currency rates have pervasive effects on the firm's financial statements. As IBM provided supplementary data regarding its foreign operations for many years, we can use the company to illustrate the analysis of multinational corporations.

CASE OBJECTIVES

The objectives of this case are to use IBM to:

1. Show the effects of exchange rate changes in levels and trends of revenue, income, cash flow, and financial position.
2. Show the effect of exchange rate changes on financial ratios.
3. Calculate the effect of exchange rate changes on assets and liabilities.
4. Calculate translation gains and losses resulting from exchange rate changes.

IBM DISCLOSURES RELATED TO FOREIGN OPERATIONS

Exhibit 15C-3 contains IBM's balance sheet at December 31, 1989, and 1990. Within the stockholders' equity section, we see "translation adjustments" of $1,698 and $3,266 billion (4.4 and 7.6% of net assets), respectively. These entries tell us that the company has significant non-U.S. operations and it uses foreign functional currencies. If the company used the U.S. dollar as the functional currency for all foreign operations, all gains and losses would have been included in income.

Exhibit 15C-4 contains IBM's consolidated statement of cash flows for the three years ended December 31, 1990. The only reference to translation in the cash flow statement is the "effect of exchange rate changes on cash and cash equivalents" near the bottom.

Exhibit 15C-5, which provides the primary raw material for our analysis, is supplementary data on IBM's non-U.S. operations. Although much of this disclosure is not required (and, unfortunately, rarely provided), it enables us to obtain an understanding of the effect of changing exchange rates on the company's financial condition and operating performance.

The first part of Exhibit 15C-5 contains summarized balance sheets and income statements for IBM's non-U.S. operations. These data suggest steady growth in foreign revenue, net earnings, and net assets over the period 1988 to 1990. Comparison of these data with IBM's consolidated

EXHIBIT 15C-3. IBM
Balance Sheet

At December 31:	1990	1989
(Dollars in millions)		
Assets		
Current Assets:		
Cash	$ 1,189	$ 741
Cash equivalents	2,664	2,959
Marketable securities, at cost, which approximates market	698	1,261
Notes and accounts receivable—trade, net of allowances	20,988	18,866
Other accounts receivable	1,656	1,298
Inventories	10,108	9,463
Prepaid expenses and other current assets	1,617	1,287
	38,920	35,875
Plant, Rental Machines and Other Property	53,659	48,410
Less: Accumulated depreciation	26,418	23,467
	27,241	24,943
Investments and Other Assets:		
Software, less accumulated amortization (1990, $5,873; 1989, $4,824)	4,099	3,293
Investments and sundry assets	17,308	13,623
	21,407	16,916
	$87,568	$77,734
Liabilities and Stockholders' Equity		
Current Liabilities:		
Taxes	$ 3,159	$ 2,699
Short-term debt	7,602	5,892
Accounts payable	3,367	3,167
Compensation and benefits	3,014	2,797
Deferred income	2,506	1,365
Other accrued expenses and liabilities	5,628	5,780
	25,276	21,700
Long-Term Debt	11,943	10,825
Other Liabilities	3,656	3,420
Deferred Income Taxes	3,861	3,280
Stockholders' Equity:		
Capital stock, par value $1.25 per share	6,357	6,341
Shares authorized: 750,000,000		
Issued: 1990—571,618,795; 1989—574,775,560		
Retained earnings	33,234	30,477
Translation adjustments	3,266	1,698
	42,857	38,516
Less: Treasury stock, at cost (Shares: 1990—227,604; 1989—75,723)	25	7
	42,832	38,509
	$87,568	$77,734

Source: IBM Corporation, *1990 Annual Report.*

EXHIBIT 15C-4. IBM
Statement of Cash Flows

For the year ended December 31:	1990	1989	1988
(Dollars in millions)			
Cash Flow from Operating Activities:			
Net earnings	$ 6,020	$ 3,758	$ 5,806
Adjustments to reconcile net earnings to cash provided from operating activities:			
Depreciation	4,217	4,240	3,871
Amortization of software	1,086	1,185	893
Loss (gain) on disposition of investment assets	32	(74)	(133)
(Increase) in accounts receivable	(2,077)	(2,647)	(2,322)
Decrease (increase) in inventory	17	(29)	(1,232)
(Increase) in other assets	(3,136)	(1,674)	(1,587)
Increase in accounts payable	293	870	265
Increase in other liabilities	1,020	1,743	519
Net cash provided from operating activities	7,472	7,372	6,080
Cash Flow from Investing Activities:			
Payments for plant, rental machines and other property	(6,509)	(6,414)	(5,390)
Proceeds from disposition of plant, rental machines and other property	804	544	409
Investment in software	(1,892)	(1,679)	(1,318)
Purchases of marketable securities and other investments	(1,234)	(1,391)	(2,555)
Proceeds from marketable securities and other investments	1,687	1,860	4,734
Net cash used in investing activities	(7,144)	(7,080)	(4,120)
Cash Flow from Financing Activities:			
Proceeds from new debt	4,676	6,471	4,540
Payments to settle debt	(3,683)	(2,768)	(3,007)
Short-term borrowings less than 90 days—net	1,966	228	1,028
Payments to employee stock plans—net	(76)	(29)	(11)
Payments to purchase and retire capital stock	(415)	(1,759)	(992)
Cash dividends paid	(2,774)	(2,752)	(2,609)
Net cash used in financing activities	(306)	(609)	(1,051)
Effect of Exchange Rate Changes on Cash and Cash Equivalents	131	(158)	(201)
Net Change in Cash and Cash Equivalents	153	(475)	708
Cash and Cash Equivalents at January 1	3,700	4,175	3,467
Cash and Cash Equivalents at December 31	$ 3,853	$ 3,700	$ 4,175
Supplemental Data:			
Cash paid during the year for:			
Income taxes	$ 3,315	$ 3,071	$ 3,405
Interest	$ 2,165	$ 1,605	$ 1,440

Source: IBM Corporation, *1990 Annual Report.*

EXHIBIT 15C-5. IBM
Data on Non-U.S. Operations

Non-U.S. Operations	1990	1989	1988
(Dollars in millions)			
At end of year:			
Net assets employed:			
Current assets	$24,337	$20,361	$20,005
Current liabilities	15,917	12,124	11,481
Working capital	8,420	8,237	8,524
Plant, rental machines and other property, net	11,628	9,879	9,354
Investments and other assets	9,077	6,822	5,251
	29,125	24,938	23,129
Long-term debt	5,060	3,358	2,340
Other liabilities	2,699	2,607	2,505
Deferred income taxes	2,381	1,814	1,580
	10,140	7,779	6,425
Net assets employed	$18,985	$17,159	$16,704
Number of employees	168,283	167,291	163,904
For the year:			
Revenue	$41,886	$36,965	$34,361
Earnings before income taxes	$ 7,844	$ 7,496	$ 7,088
Provision for income taxes	3,270	3,388	3,009
Net earnings	$ 4,574	$ 4,108	$ 4,079†
Investment in plant, rental machines and other property	$ 3,020	$ 2,514	$ 2,389

† 1988 net earnings before cumulative effect of accounting change for income taxes.

Non-U.S. subsidiaries which operate in a local currency environment account for approximately 90% of the company's non-U.S. revenue. The remaining 10% of the company's non-U.S. revenue is from subsidiaries and branches which operate in U.S. dollars or whose economic environment is highly inflationary.

As the value of the dollar weakens, net assets recorded in local currencies translate into more U.S. dollars than they would have at the previous year's rates. Conversely, as the dollar becomes stronger, net assets recorded in local currencies translate into fewer U.S. dollars than they would have at the previous year's rates. The translation adjustments, resulting from the translation of net assets, amounted to $3,266 million at December 31, 1990, $1,698 million at December 31, 1989, and $1,917 million at December 31, 1988. The changes in translation adjustments since the end of 1988 are a reflection of the strengthening of the dollar in 1989 and the weakening of the dollar in 1990.

Source: IBM Corporation, *1990 Annual Report.*

balance sheet and income statement indicates that foreign operations accounted for 60% of revenue for 1990. We return to the analysis of these data shortly.

ESTIMATION OF COMPOSITE EXCHANGE RATES

Before starting our analysis, we need data on the exchange rates that affect IBM's financial statements. For a company operating in a single currency (such as Foreign Subsidiary, in the chapter, or AFLAC in Case 15-1), we can obtain year-end and average exchange rates covering the period being analyzed. For a multinational such as IBM, we need data on many currencies and a breakdown of IBM's operations by functional currency. The latter is unavailable (to an external user), and the analysis of many currencies is very time-consuming.[1] We need a shortcut.

Fortunately, there are indices of the value of the U.S. dollar against a basket of foreign currencies, normally computed on a trade-weighted basis. Using such a series for IBM requires us to make the assumption that IBM's business has the same currency mix (distribution over various currencies) as U.S. trade flows. Although that assumption might be untenable for a smaller company with more limited foreign operations, it appears reasonable for a giant multinational such as IBM. Exhibit 15C-6 shows average and year-end exchange rates for the period covered by our analysis.

BALANCE SHEET EFFECTS

Exhibit 15C-5 states that IBM had non-U.S. net assets of approximately $19 billion. What functional currencies did the company use to account for its foreign operations? The exhibit reports that

> non-U.S. subsidiaries which operate in a local currency environment account for approximately 90% of the company's non-U.S. revenue. The remaining 10% . . . is from subsidiaries and branches which operate in U.S. dollars or whose economic environment is highly inflationary.

In other words, the local currency is the functional currency for 90% of IBM's foreign operations. The U.S. dollar is the functional currency for the remainder, including subsidiaries operating in hyperinflationary economies.

Assuming that the 90% figure applies equally to the balance sheet, we conclude that IBM had net assets in nondollar functional currencies of $17.086 billion (90% of total nondollar net assets of $18.985 billion) at December 31, 1990. The corresponding figures for year-end 1989 and 1988 were $15.443 billion (0.90 × $17.159 billion) and $15.034 billion (0.90 × $16.704 billion), respectively. These amounts represent IBM's exposure to changes in exchange rates under SFAS 52.

Translation gains and losses resulting from exchange rate fluctuation have been accumulated as a component of stockholders' equity, in accordance with SFAS 52. The text of Exhibit 15C-5 gives us the cumulative translation adjustments at each year-end:

December 31	Cumulative Translation Adjustments
1988	$1.917 billion
1989	1.698
1990	3.266

[1]In some cases, annual reports for foreign subsidiaries of multinational companies are available, either because of local filing requirements or subsidiary financing. These reports can shed light on significant foreign operations. However, these reports are generally prepared in local currencies according to local accounting standards, not in U.S. dollars under U.S. GAAP. In some cases, reports are available only in the local language, further hampering use. Nonetheless, when a company has one or a few highly significant foreign subsidiaries, the subsidiary annual report may provide insights not available from the parent's consolidated financial statements.

EXHIBIT 15C-6
Dollar's Trade-Weighted Exchange
Index, 1988 to 1990 (1973 = 100)

December 31	Index
1988	92.8
1989	93.7
1990	83.7

Average Rates for Year, 1980 to 1990

Year	Index
1980	87.4
1981	103.4
1982	116.6
1983	125.3
1984	138.2
1985	143.0
1986	112.2
1987	96.9
1988	92.7
1989	98.6
1990	89.1

Sources: Economic Report of the President, February 1991 (annual data) and Federal Reserve Bank of St. Louis (December 31 data).

These calculations enable us to compute the actual increase in IBM's foreign net assets in functional currencies. By taking the reported change and subtracting the effects of translation (change in accumulated adjustment), we get the real change ($ in millions):

Year	Reported	− Translation	= Real
1989	$ 455	$ (219)	$674
1990	1,826	1,568	258

From the reported change, it appears that IBM's foreign net assets increased more rapidly in 1990 than 1989. The reality is that the large 1990 increase was mostly due to the appreciation of foreign currencies against the dollar; before translation (in real terms), the 1989 increase was larger.

The year-to-year change in the cumulative translation adjustment account is the effect of translation for each year. Compare those changes with IBM's exposure:

$$1989: \frac{\$1.698 \text{ billion} - \$1.917 \text{ billion}}{\$15.034 \text{ billion}} = -1.46\%$$

$$1990: \frac{\$3.266 \text{ billion} - \$1.698 \text{ billion}}{\$15.443 \text{ billion}} = +10.15\%$$

These calculations reveal that the IBM-weighted functional currency composite declined by 1.46% against the dollar in 1989 and rose by 10.15% against the dollar in 1990.[2]

Turning to our trade-weighted index in Exhibit 15C-6, we see that the percentage changes are

1989: −1.0%
1990: +11.9%

These changes approximate the IBM-weighted changes, reassuring us that our index is a good proxy. But when possible, we use the IBM-weighted index that we have now derived.

First, consider the company's inventories. Exhibit 15C-5 does not break out non-U.S. inventory, so we must assume that inventories are a constant percentage of current assets.[3] At December 31, 1989, consolidated inventories were 26.4% of consolidated current assets (Exhibit 15C-3). We assume that non-U.S. inventories also were 26.4% of non-U.S. current assets of $20.361 billion or $5.375 billion, of which $4.838 billion (90%) were in nondollar functional currencies.

Applying the IBM-weighted exchange rate change of 10.15% results in an estimated increase in non-U.S. inventories of $491 million due to changing exchange rates. This accounts for most of the $645 million ($10.108 billion − $9.463 billion) increase in IBM's consolidated inventories during 1990 (data from Exhibit 15C-3). These calculations suggest that most of the 1990 inventory increase was due to the impact of changing exchange rates rather than to operating changes.

We can confirm this result from the company's cash flow statement. In Exhibit 15C-4, we find that IBM's inventory change, excluding the effect of translation, was a decrease of $17 million, suggesting that the true effect of exchange rate changes was $662 million [$645 million actual change less (−$17 million) real change].[4]

Although our estimated effect of $491 million is not equal to the true effect of $662 million for 1990, they are not unreasonably far apart. Clearly, our assumptions did not precisely hold. But even if we did not have the true figure, our estimate would still have told us that IBM's inventory increase in 1990 was mostly due to currency effects rather than operating causes. It is this conclusion that makes the analysis worthwhile. This technique, although superfluous when the cash flow statement excludes the impact of exchange rate changes, is useful when cash flow statements (such as those for non-U.S. firms) are not adjusted to exclude that impact.

We can perform this same analysis for IBM's fixed assets. Exhibit 15C-5 shows that non-U.S. fixed assets were $9.879 billion; we estimate that $8.891 billion (90% of $9.879 billion) was in nondollar functional currencies. The estimated effect of currency changes is $902 million (10.15% of $8.891 billion).

The actual impact of currency changes on fixed assets was disclosed in IBM's 10-K report in Schedules V and VI. These reconciliations of fixed assets (gross) and accumulated depreciation reveal that translation increased fixed assets by $963 million ($2,143 million for gross fixed assets less $1,180 million for accumulated depreciation).

Again, our estimate is approximately correct, despite the assumptions required. Consolidated net fixed assets rose by $2.298 billion in 1990 (Exhibit 15C-3), or 9.2%. Nearly half the gain resulted from exchange rate changes rather than new investment. Even if the 10-K data had not been available (Schedules V and VI are no longer required), we would have the same knowledge.

---

[2]Perceptive readers will note that we have omitted the effect of changing exchange rates on the *increase* in IBM's net assets in functional currencies. Given the small change in those assets (in functional currency terms) over the period 1988 to 1990, we have opted for simplification.

[3]IBM uses the FIFO inventory method worldwide. For companies with significant LIFO inventories, this calculation should be made on a FIFO basis by adding back the LIFO reserve (see Chapter 6).

[4]This computation, and similar computations in this case, are possible only because IBM made no purchase method acquisition during 1990. Chapter 14 discusses the impact of purchase method acquisitions on the statement of cash flows.

INCOME STATEMENT EFFECTS

Turning to the income data (Exhibit 15C-5), we note that IBM had revenues of $41.886 billion in currencies other than the dollar, an increase of 13.3% from the 1989 level of $36.965 billion. On the surface, it appears that the 1990 gain in foreign sales was much larger than the 1989 increase (up 7.6% from the 1988 level of $34.361 billion). However, analysis reveals that exchange rate effects distort the data.

In 1990, non-U.S. sales of $37.697 billion (90% of $41.886) were in operations with nondollar functional currencies (FC) (with the remainder in operations with nondollar local currencies but the dollar as functional currency). These revenues (and all expenses) were translated into dollars at the average rate for 1990. Using the data in Exhibits 15C-5 and 15C-6, we can compute the effect of rate changes for each year:

	($ in millions)		
	1988	1989	1990
Non-U.S. revenues ($, Exhibit 15C-5)	$34,361	$36,965	$41,886
Non-$ FC revenues ($, 90%)	30,925	33,268	37,697
% Increase	—	+7.6%	+13.3%
Dollar index (Exhibit 15C-6)	92.7	98.6	89.1
FC revenues	FC 28,667	FC 32,802	FC 33,588
% Increase	—	+14.4%	+2.4%

The last entry, FC revenues, is an artificial index, derived by multiplying estimated non-$ FC revenues by the dollar index.[5] The result is a measure of revenue from which the impact of changes in the value of the dollar has been removed. As a result, we can estimate the "real" change in foreign revenues.

We find that the decline in the value of the dollar accounted for most of the gain in foreign revenues in 1990; the increase is only 2.4% when that factor is removed. Conversely (since the dollar rose in value in 1989), the real (FC) gain is 14.4% as compared with a gain of 7.6% in dollars. The rise in the dollar in 1989 resulted in a smaller percentage sales gain in dollars than local currencies. (These calculations assume that local currency prices were unaffected by exchange rate changes.)

This exercise, therefore, approximates the impact of changing exchange rates on IBM's nondollar revenues. A similar calculation approximates the effect on net income. IBM's annual report to shareholders provides virtually no disclosure of this impact.

Exhibit 15C-7 contains the result of this analysis for the 11-year period 1980 to 1990.[6] Comparison of the reported data with the adjusted data reveals differences that are quite significant.

---

[5]We must use the index because we do not have average "IBM weights," only year-end to year-end data. As we have shown that the index tracked the IBM weights well, we can use it to examine the trend of revenues and pretax income.

[6]The analysis in Exhibit 15C-7 uses total non-U.S. sales rather than the proportion for which IBM uses nondollar functional currencies. This proportion has declined over the 1980 to 1990 period, but the disclosure on this point is vague. For simplicity and because we believe the analysis would not be significantly affected, we omit that step in our analysis.

In principle, it is preferable to use only sales in nondollar functional currencies, as in the 1988 to 1990 computations above. Although other foreign sales are also affected by exchange rate changes, there is an important difference. Foreign sales for which the dollar is the functional currency are likely to be in hyperinflationary countries or where local selling prices are the local currency equivalent of dollar prices. In these cases, changes in exchange rates may affect volume but do not affect dollar prices; they do not create income statement distortion as discussed in this section. In addition, the index derived from changes in the cumulative translation adjustment is not applicable to these situations.

In practice, however, the proportion of sales for which the dollar is the functional currency is rarely available and, therefore, the analyst must use total foreign sales for analytic purposes.

EXHIBIT 15C-7
Analysis of IBM's Foreign Operations, 1980 to 1990

Year	Revenues	% Change	Pretax Income	% Change
	Reported Data ($U.S. in millions)			
1980	$U.S. 13,787		$U.S. 2,772	
1981	13,982	+1.4%	2,664	−3.9%
1982	15,336	+9.7	3,226	+21.1
1983	17,053	+11.2	3,841	+19.1
1984	18,566	+8.9	4,640	+20.8
1985	21,545	+16.0	5,546	+19.5
1986	25,888	+20.2	5,871	+5.9
1987	29,280	+13.1	5,683	−3.2
1988	34,361	+17.4	7,088	+24.7
1989	36,965	+7.6	7,496	+5.8
1990	41,886	+13.3	7,844	+4.6
	Adjusted Data (FC units in millions)			
1980	FC 12,050		FC 2,423	
1981	14,457	+20.0%	2,755	+13.7%
1982	17,882	+23.7	3,762	+36.6
1983	21,367	+19.5	4,813	+27.9
1984	25,658	+20.1	6,412	+33.2
1985	30,809	+20.1	7,931	+23.7
1986	29,046	−5.7	6,587	−16.9
1987	28,372	−2.3	5,507	−16.4
1988	31,853	+12.3	6,571	+19.3
1989	36,447	+14.4	7,391	+12.5
1990	37,320	+2.4	6,989	−5.4

The year-to-year percentage changes in both revenues and pretax income are, in most years, quite different after adjustment for changes in the value of the dollar. We have already discussed the impact on the period 1988 to 1990. For a broader perspective, we have summarized the data for the entire period:

Percentage changes in IBM Foreign Results, 1980 to 1990

Period	Revenues		Pretax Income	
	Reported	Adjusted	Reported	Adjusted
1980–85	+56.3%	+155.7%	+100.1%	+227.3%
1985–90	+94.4	+21.1	+41.4	−11.9
1980–90	+203.8	+209.7	+183.0	+188.4

Source: Data in Exhibit 15C-7.

Over the entire ten years, the reported and adjusted trends are quite similar. As the dollar showed a very small increase in value over the period, we conclude that local currency revenue growth was only slightly greater than revenue growth reported in dollars.

But for the two subperiods, the adjusted data tell a completely different story from the reported data. During the period 1980 to 1985, the value of the dollar rose sharply; the data in

Exhibit 15C-6 show that the average value of the dollar in 1985 was 63.6% higher in 1985 than 1980 (143.0/87.4 = 1.636). Thus, revenues and earnings in foreign currencies were continuously devalued when translated into dollars. The growth in revenues during this period was 155.7% in local currencies, but only 56.3% after translation into dollars. Pretax income was similarly devalued; the local currency growth was 227.3%, whereas the dollar growth was only 100.1%.

The individual year-to-year changes also reflect the impact of the strengthening dollar. In 1981, for example, reported pretax income declined by 3.9%; after adjustment, there was a gain of 13.7%. In every year during the period 1980 to 1985, the performance of IBM's foreign operations was better in local currencies than U.S. dollars.

During the second half of the decade, 1985 to 1990, the impact of exchange rates reversed. The value of the dollar declined in most years, and by 1990 it had returned to a level very close to 1980. The declining value of the dollar inflated foreign currency revenues and income when translated into dollars.

Over the 1985 to 1990 period, IBM's foreign revenues (in dollars) increased by 94.4%, higher growth than in the 1980 to 1985 period. The adjusted data suggest that the reverse was true; IBM's local currency revenues grew by only 21.1% over the second half of the decade, a marked slowing from the 155.7% growth during the first half.

Although the decline of the dollar was not consistent, some of the individual year data echo this conclusion. In both 1986 and 1987, foreign revenues (in dollars) rose sharply, suggesting favorable performance trends. The adjusted data show that, for both years, foreign currency revenues declined.

The pretax income data also appear significantly different after adjustment for changes in the value of the dollar. Over the period 1985 to 1990, foreign pretax earnings rose by 41.4% in dollars, but declined by 11.9% in local currencies. The years 1986 and 1990 are the clearest examples of this effect in individual years: In both cases, pretax income rose in dollars but declined in local currencies.

It is important to caution, however, that this analysis makes a crucial assumption—that IBM's foreign operations were unaffected by exchange rate changes. For some firms, selling prices (and, therefore, revenues and earnings) are affected by variations in exchange rates, which impact the cost of imported components, and the prices of competitive products. We cannot assume that local currency results are always independent of exchange rates.

Nonetheless, it is apparent that the rising value of the dollar during the 1980 to 1985 period disguised the excellent performance of IBM's foreign operations. It is equally clear that the dollar decline during the second half of the decade masked the deterioration of the operating performance of the company's foreign subsidiaries.

These conclusions show that analysis of a multinational enterprise is seriously deficient unless the impact of changing exchange rates is taken into account. Despite the approximations and assumptions required, the analyst gains important insights into operating trends and can use these to question management more perceptively about its real operating performance.

RATIO EFFECTS

The impact of foreign currency changes on IBM's financial ratios is hard to determine, because of inadequate data. Since IBM uses functional currencies other than the U.S. dollar for 90% of its non-U.S. operations, we can conclude that income statement ratios in dollars largely replicate the local currency data. This would also be true of ratios using only balance sheet data, such as the current or debt-to-equity ratios.

The increased importance of foreign operations in 1990, resulting from the weakness of the dollar, gave foreign operations more weight in the consolidated total in 1990 than 1989. Without details of the income statement and balance sheet for foreign operations, we cannot easily tell which ratios are improved (or worsened) by this effect.[7]

---

[7]By using cash flow data and the technique previously employed to estimate the effect of exchange rate changes on various balance sheet and income accounts, we can approximate ratios for IBM's foreign operations.

CONCLUDING COMMENTS

As stated at the outset, the analysis of IBM was made possible by the voluntary disclosures (the first part of Exhibit 15C-5) regarding its non-U.S. operations. Few companies provide similar data; IBM stopped providing extensive disclosures after its *1991 Annual Report.* Why, then, have we devoted a case to this analysis?

Our major objective is to illustrate how changing currency rates distort financial statements in the context of a real company. The analysis issues exist for all companies with significant foreign operations. Our goal is to enable analysts and other readers of this text to apply portions of this analysis of IBM to other companies.

REQUIRED:

Note: Make the simplifying assumption that IBM uses local currencies as the functional currency for all foreign subsidiaries.

1. Using Exhibit 15C-5, the balance sheet and income statement for IBM's non-U.S. operations after translation to U.S. dollars:
   (a) Convert the 1989 and 1990 balance sheets to FC units.
   (b) Convert the 1990 income statement to FC units.
   (c) Using only FC net income, try to reconcile the change in FC equity (net assets) during 1990. Provide one possible reason for the discrepancy.
2. Exhibit 15C-5 states that IBM invested $3,020 million in plant, rental machine, and other properties during 1990. Calculate the amount in FC units. Using this result, estimate depreciation expense (in FC units) for IBM's non-U.S. operations.
3. [Cash flow analysis of IBM foreign operations]
   (a) Assume that cash is 5% of the current assets shown in Exhibit 15C-5. Prepare a 1990 cash flow statement in FC units for IBM's non-U.S. operations.
   (b) Convert the FC unit cash flow statement prepared in part (a) to a U.S. dollar cash flow statement.
   (c) (i) Compute the percentage of IBM's 1990 consolidated cash from operations that came from its non-U.S. operations.
      (ii) Compute the percentage of IBM's 1990 consolidated borrowings made by its non-U.S. operations.
      (iii) Compute the percentage of IBM's 1990 investment in fixed assets that took place in its non-U.S. operations.
      (iv) Discuss how your answers to parts (i) through (iii) contribute to your understanding of the importance of IBM's non-U.S. operations to the company.
      (v) Discuss the limitations of your answers to parts (i) through (iii).
   (d) Using the cash flow data calculated in part (c) estimate the effect of exchange rate changes on cash and cash equivalents. Compare your result to the amount shown in IBM's statement of cash flows (Exhibit 15C-4).

Chapter 15

Problems

1. [Effects of functional currency choice; 1991 CFA adapted] Bethel Company uses the U.S. dollar as its functional currency worldwide. Star Company uses the local currency for each country in which it operates as its functional currencies. Explain how the choice of functional currency affects each of the following:

(i) Reported sales

(ii) Cash flow from operations

(iii) Computation of translation gains and losses

(iv) Reporting of translation gains and loss

2. [Disaggregating operating and exchange rate effects] Consolidated income statements for the E&O Corporation follow ($ in millions):

	19X0	19X1	19X2
Revenues	$100.0	$110.0	$120.0
Operating expenses	70.0	72.0	74.0
Income taxes	9.0	11.4	13.8
Net income	$ 21.0	$ 26.6	$ 32.2

These statements include the operations of E&O's foreign subsidiary, Erzi Limited, which operates in a country whose currency is the LC. Erzi has no inventory and no fixed assets. Excluding the effects of Erzi, E&O's income statement was constant in years 19X0 to 19X2 at:

Revenues	$50.0 million
Operating expenses	45.0
Income tax	2.0
Net income	$ 3.0 million

Average and year-end exchange rates for the years 19X0 through 19X2 follow:

	19X0	19X1	19X2
Average	LC 1 = $1.00	LC 1 = $1.50	LC 1 = $0.75
Year-end	LC 1 = $1.50	LC 1 = $2.00	LC 1 = $0.50

As E&O's (unconsolidated) revenues and income were constant over the three-year period, all variations must result from the operations of Erzi.

A. Calculate how much of the observed growth in consolidated revenues and income over the 19X0 to 19X2 period resulted from Erzi's operations and how much was due to exchange rates changes.

B. Discuss how the choice of functional currency affected the U.S. dollar income statement.

3. [Effects of functional currency choice; 1990 CFA adapted] On December 31, 1988, U.S. Dental Supplies (USDS) created a wholly owned foreign subsidiary, Funimuni,

EXHIBIT 15P-1. FUNIMUNI, INC.
1989 Financial Statements

	Ponts (millions)	Exchange Rate (ponts/U.S.$)	U.S.$ (millions)
Balance Sheet, at December 31, 1989			
Cash	82	4.0	20.5
Accounts receivable	700	4.0	175.0
Inventory	455	3.5	130.0
Fixed assets (net)	360	3.0	120.0
Total assets	1,597		445.5
Accounts payable	532	4.0	133.0
Capital stock	600	3.0	200.0
Retained earnings	465		112.5
Total liabilities and shareholders' equity	1,597		445.5

	Ponts (millions)	Exchange Rate (ponts/U.S.$)	U.S.$ (millions)
Income Statement, for Year Ended December 31, 1989			
Sales	3500	3.5	1000.0
Cost of sales	(2345)	3.5	(670.0)
Depreciation expense	(60)	3.0	(20.0)
Selling expense	(630)	3.5	(180.0)
Translation gain (loss)	—		(17.5)
Net income	465		112.5

Inc. (FI), located in the country of Lumbaria. The balance sheet of FI as of December 31, 1988, stated in local currency (the pont), follows:

Funimuni, Inc.
Balance Sheet, at December 31, 1988
(ponts in millions)

Cash	180
Fixed assets	420
Total assets	600
Capital stock	600

FI initially adopted the U.S. dollar as its functional currency and translated its 1989 balance sheet and income statement in accordance with SFAS 52 (shown in Exhibit 15P-1). USDS subsequently instructed FI to change its functional currency to the pont.

Assume the following exchange rates:

January 1, 1989	3.0 ponts/U.S. dollar
1989 average	3.5
December 31, 1989	4.0

A. Prepare a balance sheet as of December 31, 1989, and a 1989 income statement for FI, both in U.S. dollars, using the pont as the functional currency for FI.

B. Describe the impact of the change in FI's functional currency to the pont on FI's U.S. dollar:

(i) Balance sheet as of December 31, 1990

(ii) 1990 income statement

(iii) Financial ratios for 1990

4. [Effect of remeasurement and translation on financial ratios; 1995 CFA adapted] Company C has a 100% owned foreign subsidiary, whose local currency is the LC and whose functional currency is the FC. Company C reports its results in Swiss francs. The LC is appreciating versus the FC, and the FC is appreciating versus the Swiss franc. The subsidiary uses the first-in-first-out method of inventory accounting.

A. Compare *each* of the following ratios for the foreign subsidiary in its *functional currency after remeasurement (temporal method)* to the same ratio in the *local currency before remeasurement:*

(i) Gross profit margin percentage

(ii) Operating profit margin

(iii) Net profit margin

B. Briefly explain any differences between the LC and FC ratios in part A.

C. Compare *each* of the following ratios for the foreign subsidiary in Swiss francs *after translation (all-current method)* to the same ratio in the *functional currency before translation:*

(i) Gross profit margin percentage

(ii) Long-term debt-to-equity

5. [Analysis of foreign operations] Exhibit 15P-2 contains extracts from the *1991 Annual Report* of Commercial Intertech regarding its foreign operations. The effect of exchange rate changes on cash for 1991 was $(2,075,000); inventories at October 31, 1990 and 1991 were $59,762,000 and $51,777,000, respectively.

The foreign currency translation footnote discusses a subsidiary in Switzerland.

A. What was the functional currency used to account for that subsidiary? Explain.

B. What economic events caused the $3,213,000 gain to appear in the company's financial statements?

C. Discuss whether the $3,213,000 gain:

(i) Should be considered operating income.

(ii) Should be considered 1991 income.

D. Using the change in the cumulative translation adjustment, compute the composite effect of exchange rate changes on the company's foreign assets in nondollar functional currencies. (*Hint:* Don't forget about the Swiss subsidiary.)

EXHIBIT 15P-2. COMMERCIAL INTERTECH
Selected Footnotes

Foreign Currency Translation

The cumulative effects of foreign currency translation gains and losses are reflected in the translation adjustment account of the balance sheet. Translation adjustments decreased shareholders' equity by $6,405,000 and $3,607,000 in 1991 and 1989, respectively, and increased equity in 1990 by $13,246,000. The translation adjustment account was further reduced by $3,213,000 in the current year due to the liquidation of an inactive subsidiary located in Switzerland. The liquidation, which was completed during the first quarter, increased income from continuing operations by $3,213,000 ($.31 per share after related taxes) as a result of recognizing deferred translation gains in income. The gain is recorded as nonoperating income in the income statement.

Foreign currency transaction gains and losses, as well as U.S. dollar translation gains and losses in Brazil, are reflected in income. For the three-year period reported herein, foreign currency losses have decreased income from continuing operations before income taxes as follows:

	(in thousands)
1991	$1,790
1990	95
1989	2,154

Net assets of foreign subsidiaries at October 31, 1991 and 1990 were $94,709,000 and $100,146,000, respectively, of which net current assets were $47,320,000 and $56,795,000, also respectively.

E. Using the result of part D, estimate Commercial Intertech's cash balances in nondollar functional currencies.

F. Using the result of part D, estimate the effect of exchange rate changes on the company's inventories during fiscal 1991. Compare your result with the estimate derived from cash flow data and explain any discrepancy.

G. Do you agree with the statement that Commercial Intertech reduced its investment in its foreign subsidiaries? Why or why not?

H. The company's foreign sales declined from $233.5 million (fiscal 1991) to $229.1 million (fiscal 1992).

   (i) Considering only exchange rate changes, does this result surprise you? Why or why not?

   (ii) What additional information would be required to determine the effect of exchange rate changes on the trend of sales?

   (iii) Briefly discuss the other factors that affect the sales trend.

6. [Analysis of foreign operations] The following information was extracted from the financial statements of General Motors (GM) (all data in $ millions):

	1991	1992	1993
Total Non-U.S. sales	$36,000	$38,000	$35,000
Total Non-U.S. net income	2,600	2,200	2,200
Non-U.S. net assets	12,000	12,000	13,000
Cumulative translation adjustment	467.4	(155.9)	(494.4)
Effect of exchange rate changes on cash	(56.4)	58.1	76.2

Note: As GM reports a cumulative translation adjustment, we know that it uses the all-current method for at least some foreign subsidiaries. When answering parts A and B, assume that the all-current method is used for all GM's foreign subsidiaries.

A. Assuming an exchange rate of $1 = 1 LC in 1991, estimate GM's exchange rate (for the composite LC) for 1992 and 1993.

B. Use the result of part A to estimate the effect of exchange rate changes on GM's non-U.S. sales and net income for 1992 and 1993.

C. Disaggregate the total change (on an absolute or percentage basis) in GM's non-U.S. sales and net income for 1992 and 1993 relative to 1991 between operating and exchange rate effects.

D. Discuss two reasons why the results of part C should be used with caution.

E. (i) Using the result of part A, calculate the expected effect of exchange rate changes on cash for 1992 and 1993.

(ii) Explain any discrepancy between your calculations in part (i) and the reported effect of exchange rate changes on cash.

7. [Currency effect on revenues] Stora, a Swedish forest products firm, reports sales by market and currency rates for those markets, both shown in Exhibit 15P-3.

A. Using the data in Exhibit 15P-4, compute external sales by market in local currencies. Ignore markets for which no currency data are provided. *Suggestion:* Assume that "U.S. and Canada" sales occur entirely in the United States.

B. Using the result of part A, compute the percentage change in local currency sales for each market.

C. Compare the percentage changes in local currencies (part B) with those in Swedish krona (Exhibit 15P-4) and discuss the differences.

D. Discuss the pitfalls of using the "local currency" data to draw conclusions about relative growth rates. Consider that much of Stora's output consists of commodity products that are easily transported from one market to another.

8. [Interaction of inflation, inventory valuation, and foreign exchange effects; 1989 CFA adapted] The Emerald Company has a wholly owned subsidiary in Hibernia,

EXHIBIT 15P-3. STORA
External Sales by Market (krona in millions)

Sales	1993	1994	Change	% Change
Germany	9,895	10,424	529	5.3
Sweden	7,577	8,017	440	5.8
Great Britain	4,694	5,564	870	18.5
France	4,045	4,469	424	10.5
Denmark	2,225	2,502	277	12.4
Netherlands	1,943	2,422	479	24.7
Italy	1,709	2,100	391	22.9
Belgium	1,256	1,759	503	40.0
Norway	1,286	1,614	328	25.5
Other Europe	3,164	4,021	857	27.1
Total Europe	37,794	42,892	5,098	13.5
U.S./Canada	2,359	2,378	19	0.8
Other markets	2,602	3,182	580	22.3
Total	42,755	48,452	5,697	13.3

Currency Rates

Country	Currency	Average Rate, Jan.–Dec.		Year-End Closing Rate, December 31	
		1994	1993	1994	1993
Austria	100 ATS	**67.84**	67.12	**68.45**	68.59
Australia	1 AUD	**5.61**	5.30	**5.79**	5.62
Belgium	100 BEF	**23.16**	22.62	**23.45**	23.22
Canada	1 CAD	**5.66**	6.04	**5.31**	6.24
Chile	100 CLP	**1.81***	1.91*	**1.83***	1.93*
Denmark	100 DKK	**121.70**	120.61	**122.60**	123.65
Finland	100 FIM	**148.57**	137.12	**157.25**	144.45
France	100 FRF	**139.57**	138.05	**139.50**	142.15
Germany	100 DEM	**477.17**	472.11	**481.65**	482.20
Great Britain	1 GBP	**11.83**	11.71	**11.65**	12.35
Hong Kong	1 HKD	**1.00**	1.01	**0.97**	1.08
Ireland	1 IEP	**11.56**	11.52	**11.53**	11.79
Italy	1,000 ITL	**4.80**	4.95	**4.59**	4.88
Netherlands	100 NLG	**425.54**	420.38	**430.05**	430.85
Norway	100 NOK	**109.70**	109.98	**110.30**	111.25
Portugal	100 PTE	**4.66**	4.86	**4.69**	4.74
Spain	100 ESP	**5.79**	6.13	**5.66**	5.86
Switzerland	100 CHF	**565.60**	529.67	**568.75**	568.00
Thailand	100 THB	**30.69**	28.63	**29.00**	33.00
United States	1 $U.S.	**7.73**	7.80	**7.46**	8.33

*Reported in accordance with the monetary/nomonetary method.
Source: Stora, *1994 Annual Report.*

whose currency is the hib. Emerald reports its financial results in U.S. dollars. The exchange rate between the dollar and the hib follows:

December 31, 1987	$1 = 4 hib
December 31, 1988	$1 = 6 hib
1988 average	$1 = 5 hib

On December 31, 1987, the subsidiary acquired 100 units of inventory at a cost of 60 hib per unit. During 1988, 100 additional units were purchased at a cost of 75 hib per unit. On December 31, 1988, 100 units were sold at a price of 150 hib per unit.

A. Assume that the hib is the subsidiary's functional currency. Calculate the cost of goods sold and closing inventory in U.S. dollars using both the first-in, first-out (FIFO) and the last-in, first-out (LIFO) inventory methods.

B. Assume that the U.S. dollar is the subsidiary functional currency. Calculate the cost of goods sold and closing inventory in U.S. dollars using both the FIFO and LIFO methods.

C. Briefly discuss how *both* the choice of inventory method and the choice of functional currency impact reported income *and* inventory valuation during periods of rising prices.

9. [Effect of alternative accounting method] Suncor, a Canadian oil producer, reports the following accounting policy in its *1994 Annual Report:*

Foreign Currency Translation
Long-term monetary liabilities are translated to Canadian dollars at rates of exchange in effect at the end of the period. Unrealized exchange gains and losses arising on translation are deferred and amortized over the remaining terms of the liabilities.

Assume that Suncor's long-term monetary liabilities are denominated in a currency that has risen against the Canadian dollar.

A. Compare the following amounts reported under this policy with the amounts mandated by SFAS 52:

(i) Long-term monetary liabilities shown on Suncor's balance sheet

(ii) Net income

(iii) Stockholders' equity

B. Answer part A, assuming that the liabilities are those of a Suncor subsidiary whose functional currency is the currency in which those liabilities are denominated.

C. Answer part A, assuming that the liabilities are those of a Suncor subsidiary whose functional currency is the Canadian dollar.

10. [Interaction of accounting for intercorporate investments and effect of exchange rate changes.] The Ace Company uses the *equity method* to account for its foreign subsidiary (FC). (Note that the same accounting principles that apply to a consolidated foreign subsidiary apply to a foreign subsidiary on the equity method.) The subsidiary's functional currency is determined to be the local foreign currency.

Ace purchased shares of FC, a company whose shares are traded on a stock exchange, for $1,000 at the end of year 0. At that time, the exchange rate was $1 = LC 1. Based on the subsidiary's past performance, Ace expected its equity in FC's income to be $100 per year.

Ace reported the following amounts with respect to its investment in FC:

	Year 1	Year 2
Income Statement		
Equity in income of affiliate	$140	$225
Cash Flow Statement		
Dividends from subsidiary	28	150

The company did not make any additional purchases (or sales) of shares in FC in years 1 and 2.

The applicable exchange rates were:

Year 1	$1.40 = LC 1
Year 2	$1.50 = LC 1

To simplify the problem, assume that the average and year-end rates were identical.

A. Ace's equity in the net income of FC exceeded original expectations. Calculate how much of that excess was due to operations and how much to exchange rate effects.

B. The market value of Ace's investment in FC at year-end was:

Year 1	LC 1,200
Year 2	LC 1,300

(i) Calculate Ace's mark-to-market return (capital gains plus dividends) *in LC* on its investment in FC for years 1 and 2. Calculate the mark-to-market rate of return earned in those years.

(ii) Calculate Ace's mark-to-market return (capital gains plus dividends) *in U.S. dollars* on its investment in FC for years 1 and 2. Calculate the mark-to-market rate of return earned in those years.

C. Ace's balance sheet reported the following investment in FC:

	Year 1	Year 2
Investment in affiliate	$1,512	$1,695

(i) Show how these amounts were calculated.

(ii) Calculate the balance in the cumulative translation adjustment account at the end of years 1 and 2.

(iii) In the problem, you were given the exchange rates for each year. Explain how you could have derived the exchange rates from the other data provided (investment in affiliate, equity in income of affiliate, dividends from affiliate).

Note that (i), (ii), and (iii) are really the same question, asked three different ways.

11. [Interaction of acquisition methods and foreign currency effects] The AMREK Company acquired its foreign subsidiary, the FX Company, on January 1, 19X1. AMREK issued shares whose market value was $2,000. The acquisition was accounted for as a purchase. No goodwill was recorded and the only asset to be restated to fair value was net fixed assets.

The balance sheets of AMREK (in U.S. dollars) and FX (in LCs) just prior to the merger follow:

	AMREK	FX
Cash	$ 2,000	LC 500
Accounts receivable	3,000	2,000
Inventory	1,500	500
Net fixed assets	5,500	1,000
Total assets	$12,000	LC 4,000
Long-term debt	7,000	500
Stockholders' equity	5,000	3,500
Total liabilities and equity	$12,000	LC 4,000

At the time of the merger, $1 = LC 2.

Note: To simplify the problem, assume that any exchange rate changes occurred immediately following the merger and rates remained unchanged thereafter.

A. Prepare AMREK's balance sheet after the merger.

B. Explain how the acquisition will be reported on AMREK's cash flow statement in 19X1.

C. Briefly discuss how future income statements would differ if the acquisition were treated as a pooling.

The AMREK balance sheet on December 31, 19X1 (including the assets and liabilities of FX) follows:

Cash	$ 1,000
Accounts receivable	4,500
Inventory	1,500
Net fixed assets	6,700
Total assets	$13,700
Long-term debt	$ 7,300
Stockholders' equity*	6,400
Total liabilities and equity	$13,700

*Includes cumulative translation adjustment of $200.

D. Estimate the LC versus U.S. dollar exchange rate as of December 31, 19X1.

E. Calculate the following amounts shown on AMREK's 19X1 cash flow statement:

(i) Change in accounts receivable

(ii) Change in inventory

12. [Pooling versus purchase of foreign subsidiary] The ASU Company acquired the COL Company, its first foreign subsidiary, on January 1, 1995. To effect the acquisition of COL, ASU issued shares whose market value was $3,500.

COL's net assets (before restatement to fair value) at the time of the merger were 3,000 LC and the exchange rate at that time was LC 1 = $1.

The December 31, 1995 financial statements of ASU contained the following:

From the balance sheet	
Cumulative translation adjustment	$300
From the income statement	
Sales revenue	$600,000
From the statement of cash flows	
Exchange rate effect on cash	$20
From the geographic segment information	
Sales revenue of foreign subsidiary	$33,000

Note: To simplify the problem, assume that any exchange rate changes occurred immediately following the merger and rates remained unchanged thereafter.

A. Calculate the shareholder's equity of the merged company (at the time of the acquisition) if the merger was accounted for as a pooling rather than a purchase.

B. Assuming that the acquisition was accounted for as a pooling:

(i) Compute the amount of COL's cash when it was acquired.

(ii) Explain how the acquisition affected the statement of cash flows at the acquisition date and for 1995.

C. Assuming that the acquisition was accounted for as a purchase:

(i) Compute the amount of COL's cash when it was acquired.

(ii) Explain how the acquisition affected the statement of cash flows at the acquisition date and for 1995.

D. Your economic forecasters predicted that:

(i) Exchange rates would be LC 1 = $1.65 for 1996 and LC 1 = $1.32 for 1997.

(ii) Sales in the U.S. market will remain stable for 1996 and 1997.

(iii) Sales volume in the foreign market will decrease by one-third in 1996 and rebound 25% (from 1996 levels) in 1997.

Using these assumptions, estimate the reported sales of ASU in 1996 and 1997, assuming that the acquisition was accounted for as a:

- Pooling
- Purchase

16

DERIVATIVES AND HEDGING ACTIVITIES

CHAPTER OUTLINE

CHAPTER OBJECTIVES

INTRODUCTION

DEFINING RISK
Foreign Currency Risk
Interest Rate Risk
Commodity Risk
Risk of Changes in Market Value

HEDGING TECHNIQUES
Forward Contracts
Options
Economic Hedges
   Interest Rate Matching
   Foreign Currency Matching

ACCOUNTING FOR HEDGING ACTIVITIES
Recognition Issues
Measurement Issues

Forecasted Transactions
   Example: American Home Products
Hedging Portfolios
Rolling Hedges
Imperfect Hedges
Current Accounting Standards for Hedging
Activities

ANALYSIS OF HEDGING DISCLOSURES
Analysis of du Pont Risk Management
Disclosures

**NON-U.S. FINANCIAL REPORTING OF
HEDGING ACTIVITIES**

SUMMARY

**CASE 16-1: ENRON CORP.: ANALYSIS OF RISK
MANAGEMENT ACTIVITIES**

CHAPTER OBJECTIVES

This chapter is concerned with transactions that firms use to manage the effect of price changes on assets, liabilities, reported income, and future cash flows. Our goal is to:

1. Define the primary risks that firms may hedge, including foreign currency risk, interest rate risk, and commodity price risk.

2. Examine the hedging techniques used to manage these risks, including forward contracts, options, and economic hedges.

3. Discuss the recognition and measurement issues connected with hedge accounting, including hedges of forecasted transactions, portfolio hedging, rolling hedges, and imperfect hedges.

4. Analyze financial statement disclosures for insight into risks faced by the firm, its risk management activities, and the impact of these activities on reported financial statements.

5. Discuss the hedging activities of non-U.S. enterprises, including differences in methods used to account for these activities.

INTRODUCTION

Businesses, faced with myriad risks, seek to protect themselves from the consequences of adversity. The purchase of property (damage) and casualty (liability) insurance is the most common risk management technique, one that is used by virtually all firms.

Some risks relate to the effect of price changes on the value of assets and liabilities and the amounts of contractual and forecasted future cash flows. The management of these risks is often referred to as hedging; in this chapter, we use the terms hedging and risk management identically.

Hedging is designed to protect the firm against adverse movements in prices, interest rates, and foreign currency exchange rates. Hedging transactions include, but are not limited to, futures contracts, options, forward commitments, interest rate swaps, currency swaps, and combined interest rate and currency swaps. Firms may hedge existing assets and liabilities, firm commitments, and forecasted transactions.

The growth in hedging activities has paralleled the increased volatility of prices, interest rates, and foreign currency exchange rates. As financial markets have developed and instruments suitable for hedging have become more available, firms have increasingly used hedging techniques to control their exposure to these risks.

Hedges are employed to control or reduce price, interest rate, or currency exchange rate risks associated with:

1. Physical or tangible assets such as inventories of commodities
2. Assets with interest rate and/or currency exposure
3. Liabilities with interest rate and/or currency exposure
4. Firm commitments to purchase or sell raw materials or financial instruments, borrow funds, or repay debt
5. Forecasted transactions such as acquisitions and repatriation of funds, in addition to items included in 4.

The primary financial reporting issue is the timing of the recognition of gains and losses on the hedge transaction as compared with gains and losses on the assets or liabilities, firm commitments, or anticipated transactions being hedged. Current U.S. standards are incomplete and inconsistent; in 1996, the FASB issued an exposure draft (see Box 16-2) to establish comprehensive standards. Other standards setters are also engaged in projects to set recognition, measurement, and disclosure standards for hedge activities (see later sections of this chapter).

This chapter addresses the financial statement effects of hedging transactions. Our goal is the assessment of the:

- Risks inherent in the business
- Hedging strategies used
- Outcome of these hedging activities

DEFINING RISK

For purposes of this chapter, we define risk as potential variability of financial outcomes, or uncertainty. Future financial outcomes of firm activities are uncertain because they depend on unknown future prices. In some cases, this price risk is uncontrollable as it depends on factors such as technological change. For example, the continuous decline in the cost of semiconductor chips has rapidly driven down computer prices.

Some price risks, however, relate to standardized commodities, interest rates, and foreign currency exchange rates. These risks can be managed by using *derivatives*[1] and other hedging techniques. We say managed rather than reduced because risk management often involves replacing one risk with a different one rather than reducing risk in an absolute sense.

In the sections that follow, we examine each of the following risk categories:

- Foreign currency risk
- Interest rate risk
- Commodity risk
- Risk of changes in market value

Thereafter, we turn to the hedging techniques used to manage these risks.

Foreign Currency Risk

Firms that operate across national borders are exposed to the risk of changes in currency exchange rates. DuPont, for example, reported that 47% of 1994 sales (and 45% of assets) were outside the United States.[2]

In Chapter 15, we examined the effects of exchange rate changes on reported sales, income, cash flows, assets, liabilities, and net worth. These effects also distort financial ratios based on these data. The accounting risks faced by multinationals can be summarized as follows:

1. Reported earnings denominated in foreign currencies vary after translation, depending on the *average* exchange rate for the period.
2. Reported cash flows denominated in foreign currencies vary after translation, depending on the *average* exchange rate for the period.

[1]Derivatives and other terms used in this chapter are italicized when first used and defined in the glossary in Box 16-1.

[2]See Geographic Information in Note 29. Although some portion may be denominated in U.S. dollars, Note 27 reports significant currency exposures in seven nondollar currencies.

BOX 16-1
Glossary

Combined interest rate and currency swap (CIRCUS)	Interest rate and currency swap may be combined to convert both the nature (fixed or floating rate) and the currency of a series of payments. For example, an obligation to make variable rate payments in Japanese yen may be swapped for the obligation to make fixed interest payments in U.S. dollars.
Collar	A derivative that limits the effects of (foreign currency or interest rate) fluctuations beyond a predetermined range.
Counterparty or credit risk	Potential for loss due to the failure of the other party to discharge its obligations under a contract, for example, uncertainty that firm will collect unrealized gain on a derivative from other party to the transaction.
Currency swap	Contract that requires one firm to make payments in one currency in exchange for the obligation to make payments in another currency. Counterparties exchange the underlying notional (principal) amounts. (See interest rate swaps.)
Derivatives	Financial instruments deriving their value from changes in the value of an index, interest or exchange rates, or another financial instrument (the underlying).
Duration	Weighted-average maturity of cash flows associated with bond. The market value of bonds with high duration is more sensitive to fluctuations in interest rates. For bonds with similar maturity and yield-to-maturity, a zero coupon bond (duration is equal to maturity) has a higher duration than a coupon-paying bond.
Enterprise risk approach	Under SFAS 80, items to be hedged must contribute to the overall interest rate, market, or currency risk of the enterprise. In applying this criterion, the enterprise must determine whether other assets, liabilities, firm commitments, and forecasted transactions offset or reduce the risk. (See transaction risk approach.)
Firm commitment	Generally, a legally enforceable contract under which performance is probable because of significant penalties for nonperformance.
Forecasted transaction	One that is expected to occur, but is not subject to a firm commitment or contract.
Forward contract	Contractual agreement between a buyer and a seller to deliver an asset in exchange for cash or another financial instrument at a specified future date. Price is fixed at the contract date for the life of the contract. Forwards may be customized to fit the needs of the counterparties (see *counterparty risk*).
Futures contract	Standardized *forward contract* normally traded on an organized exchange. The contract is marked to market daily, and margin is required. There is little or no default (counterparty) risk since the exchange guarantees the contracts.
Hedge	Financial instrument or transaction used to manage risk exposure.
Interest rate swap	Contractual agreement to exchange fixed for floating rate interest payments to effectively convert fixed to floating rate debt. Alternatively, to exchange floating for fixed rate interest payments to effectively convert floating to fixed rate debt.

	In effect, an interest rate swap is a series of forward contracts based on interest rates (net payments must be made at specified intervals). Counterparties do not exchange or deliver the notional (principal) amount of the underlying debt instrument. The counterparties exchange only the interest payments resulting in a payment (net cash flow reflecting the difference between the fixed and floating rate interest on the notional amount) by one counterparty to the other.
Option	An agreement that gives one party the unilateral right to buy (call option) or sell (put option) a specified quantity at a specified price (the exercise price) until a specified maturity date.
Premium	Amount paid by one party to the other in return for an option.
Risk exposure	Vulnerability to adverse consequences; uncertainty, potential for loss, or degree of variability of outcomes.
Spot contract	Contractual agreement between a buyer and a seller to deliver an asset in exchange for cash or another financial instrument. However, delivery may occur at a later (settlement) date. For example, U.S. equity securities purchased in spot contracts are settled three days after the trade date.
Swap	Contract that exchanges one series of payments for another. See interest rate swaps, foreign currency swaps, and combined interest rate and currency swaps.
Swaption	An option that gives one party the right (upon exercise) to require the other party to enter into a swap contract.
Transaction risk approach	Under SFAS 52, firms may hedge an exposure to risk on an individual item or transaction basis without regard to whether other assets, liabilities, firm commitments, and forecasted transactions reduce or offset that exposure.

3. Reported assets and liabilities denominated in foreign currencies vary after translation, depending on the *closing* exchange rate for the period.

4. Expected foreign currency cash flows (e.g., a dividend expected from a foreign subsidiary) depend on the *actual* exchange rate when the cash flow takes place.

In Chapter 15, we also discussed the economic effects of exchange rate changes, which may be different from their accounting effects. Only in the second and last of these four cases is the economic risk necessarily equal to the accounting risk.

Firms with foreign currency risk must, therefore, first decide whether to hedge the accounting risk or the economic risk of foreign operations. Some critics of SFAS 8 stated that it encouraged firms to hedge accounting risk (the effect of exchange rate changes on reported income). As discussed in Chapter 15, SFAS 52 redefined accounting risk rather than eliminated it.

Interest Rate Risk

When businesses borrow funds, the interest rate may be either fixed or variable, as discussed in Chapter 10. When the interest rate is variable, future interest expense and interest paid are uncertain as they depend on the future level of the reference rate (often LIBOR or the bank's prime rate).[3] From the lender (investor) point of view, variable rate loans or investments make future interest income and interest received uncertain. When the interest rate is fixed, however, future interest expense (income) and interest paid (received) are known.

Commodity Risk

In Chapter 7, we discussed duPont's petroleum operations, which accounted for 43% of 1994 sales (39% of assets).[4] The revenues, expenses, and cash flows of this business depend on the price of oil, a commodity whose price is the same for all producers and consumers.[5] DuPont cannot control that price and the related uncertainty of future financial results.

Other commodities have similar effects on firms that either produce or use them, including:

- Other energy sources such as natural gas and coal
- Industrial metals such as iron, steel, aluminum, and copper
- Precious metals such as gold, silver, and platinum
- Agricultural commodities such as cotton, wool, coffee, and sugar

Risk of Changes in Market Value

Fluctuations in foreign currency exchange rates, interest rates, and commodity prices can also affect the market value of assets and liabilities. For example, when the coupon rate is fixed, the market value of a bond varies inversely with interest rate changes.

One consequence of the interrelationship of income/cash flow risk and market value risk is that managing one risk necessarily changes the other. The fixed rate bond has certain future interest payments (ignoring currency, credit, and prepayment risk), but uncertain future market value. Transactions that eliminate the market value risk (such as interest rate swaps) increase the income/cash flow risk. That is why we discuss risk management rather than risk reduction.

A second issue is that the accounting risk is often different from the market risk. When the fixed rate bond is carried at cost, changes in its market value have no impact on the reported balance sheet. But the economic (market) risk remains.

HEDGING TECHNIQUES

Having discussed the risks that firms face, we turn to the techniques available to hedge them. These techniques fall into two general categories: derivatives and natural hedges. We start with a discussion of derivatives.

---

[3]In some cases, the spread may also vary. For example, it may depend on specified financial ratios or the debtor's credit rating.

[4]See Industry Segment Data in Note 30.

[5]We ignore, in this discussion, the fact that there are different grades of oil whose price varies (as does the spread among them). These differences do not change the fundamental issues.

Forward Contracts

One way to eliminate the price risk of future transactions is to fix the transaction price in advance. Forward contracts accomplish that goal by fixing the:

· Amount and nature of the transaction
· Maturity date
· Price

For example, Exhibit 16-1 contains the hedging footnote from Homestake Mining's 1995 financial statements.

The last paragraph in the footnote tells us that Homestake used forward contracts to fix the sales price of future production of its Nickel Plate gold mine. What was the effect of the hedge on 1995 revenues? Nickel Plate mine output was 88,800 ounces in 1995. Homestake's average 1995 per ounce sales price (reported elsewhere) was $386. If we assume that Nickel Plate production would have been sold at that same average price, the benefit of the hedge was ($398 − $386) or $12 per ounce. This equates to just over $1 million ($12 × 88,800 ounces) of additional revenue and pretax profit.

Note also that part of the hedge turned out to be unnecessary as 1995 production fell short of expected levels. Homestake realized an additional gain of $0.8 million by closing out (buying back) this excess at a price less than the contracted sales price.

Forward contracts can be used to fix input costs as well. For example, a bread manufacturer (baker) whose inputs include wheat might enter into a forward contract to buy wheat at a fixed price. If the price of wheat rises, the baker will use the contracted wheat instead of buying more expensive wheat in the open market. Alternatively, the profit on the forward contract offsets the higher cost of wheat.

Forward contracts can also be used to hedge commitments. Exhibit 16-2 contains an example from the *1995 Annual Report* of Ameritech.

Ameritech purchased Belgian francs to hedge the U.S. dollar cost of its Belgian franc investment. This was a partial hedge, as only 35% of the francs needed were purchased.

The Belgian franc (Bfr) depreciated nearly 7% during the first half of 1996, rising from approximately 29.50 Bfr/$U.S. on December 31, 1995 to approximately 31.50 Bfr/$U.S. on June 30, 1996. In this case, Ameritech's forward franc purchase proved to be unnecessary. Its effect was to increase the U.S. dollar cost of its investment in Belgacom. The cost of the insurance was $19.3 million, computed as follows:

$$35\% \times \text{Bfr } 25.6 \text{ billion}/29.50 = \quad \$303.7 \text{ million}$$
$$35\% \times \text{Bfr } 25.6 \text{ billion}/31.50 = \quad \underline{284.4}$$
$$\$ \ 19.3 \text{ million}$$

where 35% of Bfr 25.6 billion is the amount of the hedge.

Forward contracts are private contracts between the buyer and seller and are often customized to meet the needs of the buyer. Both the buyer and seller assume *counterparty risk*, the risk that the other party to the contract will default. This risk is significant only to the party that has a gain on the contract; the party with a loss is unconcerned about the ability of the counterparty to perform.

Counterparty risk requires firms to use credit policies to minimize credit risk. Therefore, parties to forward contracts must evaluate the credit risk of the other party;

EXHIBIT 16-1. HOMESTAKE MINING
Hedging Activities

Note 21: Foreign Currency and Other Commitments
Under the Company's foreign currency protection program, the
Company has entered into a series of foreign currency option
contracts which established trading ranges within which the
United States dollar may be exchanged for foreign currencies
by setting minimum and maximum exchange rates. The
Company does not require or place collateral for these contracts. However, the Company minimizes its credit risk by
dealing with only major international banks and financial
institutions. The contracts are marked to market at each balance sheet date. Net unrealized gains on contracts outstanding
at December 31, 1995 and 1994 totaled $0.3 million and $0.7
million, respectively. Other income for the years ended
December 31, 1995, 1994 and 1993 included income (loss) of
$(0.2) million, $4.6 million and $(1.4) million, respectively,
related to the foreign currency protection program.

At December 31, 1995 the Company had outstanding forward currency contracts as follows:

Currency	Amount Covered (U.S. Dollars)	Exchange Rates to U.S. Dollars		Expiration Dates
		Minimum	Maximum	
Canadian	$111,400	0.67	0.77	1996 - 1997
Australian	33,300	0.68	0.76	1996
	$144,700			

In addition to amounts related to the foreign currency
option contracts, the Company realized foreign currency transaction losses of $0.6 million in 1995, $6.6 million in 1994, and
$1.5 million in 1993, which were included in other income.

During 1994, the Company entered into forward sales for
183,200 ounces of gold it expected to produce at the Nickel
Plate mine during 1995 and 1996. The purpose of the forward
sales program was to allow for recovery of the Company's
remaining investment in the mine and provide for estimated
reclamation costs. Gold sales for the year ended December 31,
1995 included 88,800 ounces sold under this program at an
average price of $398 per ounce. In October 1995, the
Company closed out forward sales covering 24,400 ounces at
an average price of $435 per ounce for delivery in 1996, realiz-
ing a gain of $0.8 million. At December 31, 1995 forward
sales for 70,000 ounces at an average price of $421 per ounce
remain outstanding.

Source: Homestake Mining, *1995 Annual Report.*

EXHIBIT 16-2. AMERITECH
Hedge of Commitment

INVESTMENT COMMITMENTS The company is committed to invest 25.6 billion Belgian francs (about $875 million) in a consortium that will purchase 49.9% of Belgacom S.A., the principal telecommunications company in Belgium. Closing of this transaction is anticipated to be completed by June 30, 1996. The company intends to fund its commitment with cash and debt and is purchasing forward contracts to acquire Belgian francs in order to manage its foreign currency risk. At December 31, 1995, about 35% of the commitment had been purchased with forward contracts.

Ameritech participates in the *Americast* joint venture, as previously discussed. The investment will be funded by the partners with $500 million over a five-year period. Video services will ultimately include movies-on-demand, interactive home shopping, educational programs, games and more. The company has not invested significant funds in *Americast* as of December 31, 1995.

Source: Ameritech, *1995 Annual Report.*

---

collateral is often required. Firms may also use standardized agreements that enable them to offset positive and negative exposures with a specific counterparty.

Futures contracts are standardized forward contracts normally traded on organized commodity exchanges. Since the exchange clearinghouse is between the two parties, it bears the counterparty risk. For this reason, exchange-listed futures contracts are marked to market daily, requiring additional collateral (margin) from the party with a loss on the contract.

Swaps are combination forward contracts. In an interest rate swap, for example, one party promises to pay the other a fixed interest rate on a specified (nominal) amount in return for a variable rate on the same base.[6] This agreement encompasses two contracts: one covering the fixed rate payment, the other the variable rate payment. Swaps are frequently used for foreign currencies as well as interest rates. Interest rate and currency swaps can also be used in tandem.

Exhibit 16-3 contains the hedge transactions footnote from the 1994 financial statements of SPAR Handels-Aktiengesellschaft, a German wholesaler and retailer. SPAR entered into interest rate swaps that fixed the interest rate on some of its debt. Note the 1994 reduction in the swap position; the company repaid some of its debt in that year, making part of the swap speculative rather than a hedge. The footnote reports a realized gain on the closed out swap and an unrealized gain on the remaining swap. No information is provided, however, about the effect of the swap on interest expense. That effect depends on whether the fixed interest rate paid was greater or less than the floating rate received.

Options

An option gives one party the right to buy (call) or sell (put) a specified amount at a fixed price until a fixed maturity date. In contrast to a forward contract that requires

---

[6]See Chapter 10 for a discussion and illustration of interest rate swaps.

EXHIBIT 16-3. SPAR
Interest Rate Swap Disclosure

42. Hedge Transactions

In order to hedge our interest expenses from short-term fluctuating financial requirements, we entered into a swap agreement for the period 17th November 1993 to 17th November 1998 for an underlying financial amount of DEM 300.0 m based on an interest rate of 5.3 % p.a. and an interest income based on the amount of the revolving three-month London Interbank Offered Rate (LIBOR).

In the past financial year 1994, a fractional amount of DEM 100.0 m, which was no longer needed due to the decline in our financial requirements, was terminated. This resulted in a gain of DEM 3.8 m.

Had the remaining amount of DEM 200.0 m been terminated as of 31st December 1994, a gain of about DEM 12.0 m would have been realized.

A further swap agreement was entered into for an underlying financial amount of DEM 35.0 m based on fixed interest income of 8.0 % p.a. and a variable interest rate based on the six-month LIBOR plus a premium of 1.46 bp for the period from 30th August 1994 until 30th December 1997.

The swap agreement was terminated in full as of 11th April 1995. This resulted in a gain of DEM 0.5 m. Apart from the above-stated interest hedges, we are not engaged in any other activities with derivatives.

Source: SPAR, *1994 Annual Report.*

performance (even when the transaction is unfavorable), an option provides its holder with flexibility. If the option is favorable (there is a gain) at maturity, it can be exercised. If the call option (strike) price is above the market price at the maturity date, the option is allowed to lapse without exercise.

The option buyer pays a *premium* to the seller to induce it to accept the price risk. If the option is not exercised, the premium is lost; flexibility does have a cost.

Exchange-traded options, like futures, have no counterparty risk. However, when option agreements are private, the buyer must consider counterparty risk. The seller, which receives its premium at inception of the transaction, has no such risk.

Returning to Exhibit 16-1, we see that Homestake used options on the Canadian dollar and the Australian dollar (both versus the U.S. dollar) to manage its foreign currency risk. Homestake's mines in Canada and Australia produce gold, a commodity priced in U.S. dollars. But production costs are largely incurred in local currencies. Thus, Homestake's (local currency) profit margins depend on both the U.S. dollar selling price and the U.S. dollar equivalent of local currency costs.

We previously discussed Homestake's forward gold sales. The simple way to hedge its currency risk would be to either:

- Sell U.S. dollars forward for Canadian and Australian dollars, thus fixing the local currency price of gold, or
- Buy an option to sell U.S. dollars for Canadian and Australian dollars, intending to exercise the (put) option if the U.S. dollar fell relative to the other currencies.

Instead, Homestake entered into options (a *collar*) that fix exchange rates within the ranges shown in the table. The maximum exchange rate (minimum U.S. dollar rate) has the effect of putting a floor on the local currency proceeds from gold sales. The minimum exchange rate (maximum U.S. dollar rate) is the apparent result of giving the counterparty an option. Although Homestake's disclosures do not say this, it appears that the premium from selling this option reduced the cost of buying the protection Homestake wanted. In other words, Homestake is willing to sacrifice the upside (higher U.S. dollar) in order to protect against the downside (lower U.S. dollar).

Economic Hedges

An alternative risk management device is the economic or natural hedge. Such hedges exist when the effects of a price change on a firm offset each other. For example, if a firm can immediately pass through input price changes to its customers, such changes increase or decrease revenue and expense equally, leaving income unchanged.[7] For example, many gas and electric utilities in the United States are permitted to pass through changes in fuel prices to customers automatically.

Such pure economic hedges are rare. More commonly, output prices may reflect changes in input prices, but with both a time lag and variable effect. For example, changes in the price of crude oil impact the retail price of gasoline, but the spread between the two can vary significantly, making the profits of oil refiners quite volatile.

When the all-current rate method is used for foreign subsidiaries, foreign currency assets and liabilities are pure accounting hedges; the exposure to changes in currency rates is the net investment in the subsidiary. As discussed in Chapter 15, however, the economic exposure may be significantly different.

Interest Rate Matching

Financial intermediaries (banks, insurance companies, finance companies) devote considerable attention to their vulnerability to interest rate changes. Such intermediaries usually seek to maintain a fixed spread between their return on assets and their cost of funds (interest). Management must be concerned with both:

- Fixed versus variable interest rates on both assets and liabilities
- *Duration* of assets and liabilities

In an ideal situation, a given change in interest rates would have the same effect on revenue (interest income) and interest expense, leaving income unchanged. But revenue is unpredictable and its sensitivity to interest rates may depend on customer decisions (e.g., preference for fixed rate versus variable rate mortgages). Similarly, the cost of funds may depend on whether bank depositors prefer fixed rate certificates of deposit or variable rate money market accounts.

Duration is an important indicator of the sensitivity of the market value of assets and liabilities to interest rate changes. It reflects stated maturity as well as the coupon and call (prepayment) characteristics.

Financial intermediaries seek to match the interest rate sensitivity of their assets and liabilities through product pricing and financing decisions. Mismatches can be rectified by using derivative instruments (forwards and options).

Exhibit 16-4 contains the *interest rate sensitivity* section from the financial review in the *1995 Annual Report* of J. P. Morgan, a major international bank. The interest

---

[7]However gross margin percentage and similar ratios are affected even though the amount of gross margin remains unchanged.

EXHIBIT 16-4. J. P. MORGAN
Interest Rate Sensitivity Disclosures

Interest rate sensitivity

J.P. Morgan is exposed to interest rate risk related to the use of interest-rate-sensitive assets, liabilities, and derivatives. While the matching of assets and liabilities of similar interest rate sensitivity would reduce the risk associated with interest rate changes, this approach would not allow the firm to benefit from anticipated changes in interest rates. Net interest revenue may be generated from our asset and liability management activities by creating maturity and repricing imbalances between assets, liabilities, and derivatives. The resulting interest-rate-sensitivity gap is the net effect of assets, liabilities, and derivatives maturing or repricing in a given period. Interest-rate-sensitivity gaps are adjusted by changing repricing profiles through the use of derivatives as well as by changing funding strategies and repositioning assets.

A liability sensitive position results when more liabilities than assets reprice or mature within a given period. Under this scenario, as interest rates decline, increased net interest revenue will be generated. Conversely, an asset sensitive position results when more assets than liabilities reprice within a given period; in this instance, net interest revenue would benefit from an increasing interest rate environment. In addition to generating revenue from maturity and repricing imbalances, net interest revenue may also be generated by matching assets, liabilities, and derivatives of similar maturity and repricing profiles at a positive margin.

The following table provides J.P. Morgan's interest-rate-sensitivity gaps at December 31, 1995 and 1994, including the asset and liability interest-rate-sensitivity gaps and the effect of derivatives on the gaps. The resulting interest-rate-sensitivity gap is presented by U.S. dollar and non-U.S. dollar currency components and reflects J.P. Morgan's market outlook at these points in time. Significant variances in interest rate sensitivity may exist at other dates not presented in the table. Amounts in parentheses reflect liability sensitive positions.

By repricing or maturity dates

In millions	Within six months	After six months but within one year	After one year but within five	After five years
December 31, 1995				
Asset and liability interest-rate-sensitivity gap	$ (3 530)	$(2 403)	$12 240	$ 3 037
Derivatives affecting interest rate sensitivity .	8 384	(4 113)	(7 262)	2 991
Interest-rate-sensitivity gap [a]	4 854	(6 516)	4 978	6 028
(a) Components of interest-rate-sensitivity gap:				
U.S. dollar	*2 017*	*(6 220)*	*5 180*	*3 580*
Non-U.S. dollar *	*2 837*	*(296)*	*(202)*	*2 448*
Total	*4 854*	*(6 516)*	*4 978*	*6 028*
December 31, 1994				
Asset and liability interest-rate-sensitivity gap	(8 885)	(811)	2 361	13 422
Derivatives affecting interest rate sensitivity .	14 324	3 154	280	(17 757)
Interest-rate-sensitivity gap [b]	5 439	2 343	2 641	(4 335)
(b) Components of interest-rate-sensitivity gap:				
U.S. dollar	*17 359*	*2 772*	*(4 752)*	*(4 259)*
Non-U.S. dollar *	*(11 920)*	*(429)*	*7 393*	*(76)*
Total	*5 439*	*2 343*	*2 641*	*(4 335)*

* *Primarily yen, deutsche mark, French franc, Belgian franc, and sterling positions.*

Source: J. P. Morgan, *1995 Annual Report.*

rate sensitivity gap measures the net effect of assets, liabilities, and derivatives that will be repriced within a given period. Three points are especially noteworthy:

- Morgan's interest rate sensitivity gap, roughly the bank's exposure to future interest rate changes, varies considerably over time and by currency (although nondollar components are not provided or discussed).
- Derivatives are used to radically change the underlying exposures, in both direction and amount. For example, the December 31, 1995 "within six months" negative gap of $3.53 billion is changed into a positive gap of more than $4.8 billion.
- The disclosure states quite clearly that these exposures reflect management expectations about future interest rate changes. Changing the negative gap to a positive gap reflects management expectations that interest rates will rise. These comments reinforce our view that hedging is often concerned with risk management (changing exposure) rather than pure risk reduction.

Foreign Currency Matching

Multinational enterprises have assets and liabilities in many currencies. They can minimize the effect of exchange rate changes on foreign subsidiary equity by minimizing their exposure to specific currencies, especially those expected to decline. One way of accomplishing this is to borrow in the weak currency, reducing the net asset exposure (subject to translation) or the net monetary exposure (subject to remeasurement).[8]

Revenues and expenses can be similarly matched, although it is difficult to do so for subsidiaries with many cross-border transactions. When unusual cross-border cash flows are anticipated, derivatives can be used to fix the exchange rate.

ACCOUNTING FOR HEDGING ACTIVITIES

SFAS 52, Foreign Currency Translation, contains accounting guidance for foreign exchange forward contracts, currency futures, and currency swaps. Accounting for all other futures is delineated in SFAS 80, Accounting for Futures Contracts. Additionally, SFAS 105, SFAS 107, and SFAS 119 specify required footnote disclosures. However, Stewart (1989) points out that:

- There are no reporting standards for interest rate forwards, nearly all categories of options, and interest rate swaps.
- Existing standards are inconsistent.

The lack of adequate accounting standards and the growing use of derivative instruments led the FASB to place hedging on its agenda, issuing an initial research report in September 1991. In June 1996, it issued an exposure draft on accounting for derivative and similar financial instruments and for hedging activities, summarized in Box 16-2. A final standard was scheduled to be issued in the second quarter of 1997.

---

[8]See Chapter 15 for an explanation of these concepts.

BOX 16-2
FASB Exposure Draft on Derivatives and Hedge Accounting

In June 1996, the FASB issued an exposure draft, Accounting for Derivatives and Similar Financial Instruments and for Hedging Activities. The proposed standard was intended, for the first time, to establish comprehensive reporting standards for risk management activities. The major provisions of the exposure draft (ED) are:

1. All derivatives* must be recognized as assets (or liabilities) with measurement at fair (market) value.

2. Derivatives may be designated (at inception) as a *fair value hedge*. They may hedge a single item (asset, liability, or a firm commitment) or a portfolio of similar items, whose fair value is measurable and is expected to correlate closely with changes in the fair value of the hedging derivatives. Changes in the fair value of such hedges would be recognized in net income, but not exceeding recognized changes in the fair value of the hedged items.

   The most common application of fair value hedge accounting would be to investments in or liabilities for fixed rate debt obligations. This accounting could *not* be used for held-to-maturity debt portfolios, leases, insurance liabilities, or equity method investments.

3. Derivatives may be designated (at inception) as a *cash flow hedge*, when intended to hedge a probable *forecasted transaction*. The cash flows of the hedging derivatives must be expected to offset the same risk element of the cash flows of the hedged transaction. (A transaction may have several risk elements; the derivative may hedge only one of those risks.) Market value changes of such derivatives must be recognized in comprehensive income† until the projected date of the forecasted transaction. At that time, such cumulated gains or losses must be reported in net income.

4. Derivatives designated (at inception) as hedges of net investments in foreign operations are eligible for hedge accounting, even though such "portfolios" do not meet the ED's portfolio test. Market value changes of such derivatives must be reported as part of the cumulative translation adjustment component of stockholders' equity.‡

5. Changes in the fair value of derivatives that are not part of a hedging strategy must be recorded in net income.

6. The ED requires substantial disclosures about derivatives and risk management activities, including:

   • Description of risk management activities and classes of derivatives used for such activities

   • Gains and losses (from both hedges and hedged items) included in net income

   • For gains and losses not recognized in income, disclosure of amounts and where (in the balance sheet) those amounts are reported

As we went to press, a final standard was expected in the second quarter of 1997, with an effective date of calendar 1998. Due to the complexity of this subject and substantial opposition to ED provisions from corporate preparers, the final standard may differ significantly from the ED.§ Given the strong interest in this subject from the SEC, its input may also change or delay a final standard.

---

*Consistent with prior FASB standards, derivatives that must be settled by delivery of the underlying commodity are excluded.

†See Chapter 1 for a discussion of this concept, the subject of another FASB exposure draft.

‡When the foreign investment is sold, the cumulative translation adjustment balance is included in reported income. See Chapter 15 for further discussion of this component.

§Two of the seven members of the FASB changed subsequent to the issuance of the ED, adding another element of uncertainty to the process of completing work on the standard.

Given the likelihood that new accounting standards will be in place shortly, we focus first on the accounting issues in general followed by a brief discussion of existing standards. We believe that the analysis of hedging activities will remain complex regardless of what standard the FASB adopts.

Recognition Issues

The primary accounting issue in hedging activities is the timing of recognition of the gains or losses on the hedge and those on the underlying assets or liabilities, firm commitments, or anticipated transactions being hedged. SFAS 80 defines two criteria that must be met for an instrument to qualify as a hedge:

1. The hedged item exposes the firm to interest rate or price risk.

2. The hedging instrument reduces that exposure and is designated as a hedge.

When the instrument qualifies as a hedge, gains and losses on the instrument are recognized concurrently with the hedged item:

- Gains and losses (both realized and unrealized) are recognized in current income when the gains and losses on the hedged items are also reported in income in the period of occurrence; that is, when the hedged items are carried at market value.
- For forecasted transactions and hedged items reported at historical cost or lower of cost or market, gains and losses on hedges are deferred and recognized when changes in value in the hedged item are recognized.
- In some cases, gains or losses on the hedged item are reported in a valuation allowance in the stockholders' equity section, for example, net investment in foreign subsidiaries and long-term investments in securities. Gains or losses on hedges of such items must also be reported the same way.

Hedging instruments that do not meet hedge criteria are "marked to market" on each financial statement date. Gains and losses are reported in net income.

Measurement Issues

The fundamental measurement issue is whether all derivatives should be reported at market value at each balance sheet date. The FASB exposure draft would require such measurement, as discussed in Box 16-2.

Forecasted Transactions

Hedging firm commitments is relatively uncontroversial; there is reasonable certainty that the transaction being hedged will occur. However, the hedging of forecasted (anticipated) transactions raises the question of what happens if the hedged transaction does not take place. Hedges of forecasted transactions are also more subjective, and management may improperly characterize speculative activities as such hedges.

Example: American Home Products

Exhibit 16-5 contains footnote disclosure from the *1995 Annual Report* of American Home Products regarding its hedge of anticipated financing of its acquisition of Ameri-

EXHIBIT 16-5. AMERICAN HOME PRODUCTS
Hedge of Forecasted Transaction

In October 1994, the Company entered into $4.75 billion notional amount of simple, unleveraged interest rate swap agreements as a means of (1) locking in the underlying U.S. treasury security rates to be paid in connection with long-term debt planned to be issued during 1995 and (2) converting a portion of the commercial paper issued in connection with the acquisition of ACY from a floating rate obligation to a fixed rate obligation.

The swap agreements are contracts under which the Company pays a fixed rate of interest and receives a floating rate of interest over the term of the swap agreements without the exchange of the underlying notional amounts. During 1995, the weighted average interest rates paid and received on these agreements were 7.8% and 6.0%, respectively. The swap agreements have maturities ranging from 1996 to 2005.

In February 1995, the Company terminated $2.0 billion of interest rate swap agreements in connection with the $2.0 billion issuance of five- and 10-year notes, as discussed above. The effect of terminating these swap agreements was deferred and is being amortized to interest expense over the five- and 10-year terms of the related notes. At December 31, 1995, the fair value of the remaining $2.75 billion of interest rate swap agreements was a payable of $216,906,000.

Source: American Home Products, *1995 Annual Report.*

can Cyanamid (ACY). That acquisition (for $9.6 billion) was completed on November 21, 1994. The $4.75 billion swap agreement was entered into the previous month. When the acquisition was completed, it was financed with (variable rate) commercial paper. The swap had the effect of fixing the interest rate on $4.75 billion of that commercial paper.

In February 1995, American Home issued $2.0 billion of (fixed rate) five- and ten-year debt, and terminated an equal amount of the swap, which was no longer appropriate. The remaining swap agreements ($2.75 billion) remained in effect.

What were the financial statement effects of the swap transactions?

During 1995, the swap (excluding the portion terminated) increased interest expense by the difference between the 7.8% paid and 6.0% received. We can estimate the net increase as:

$$(0.078 - 0.060) \times \$2.75 \text{ billion} = \$49.5 \text{ million}$$

From October 31, 1994 to February 28, 1995, interest rates on five- and ten-year U.S. treasury notes declined by 44 basis points (one-hundredths of 1%) and 61 basis points, respectively. As American Home was locked into a swap requiring it to pay higher fixed rates, the swap resulted in a liability.[9] The (undisclosed) loss on the $2 billion of swap terminated in February 1995 was deferred and amortized over the life of the two bond issues.

What were the economic effects of the swap transactions?

The swap had no effect on the debt issuance in February 1995. As interest rates declined throughout 1995, the swap "insurance" that American Home bought in October 1994 turned out to be unnecessary.

However, the *total* cost of that insurance remains unrecognized. The cost of partially terminating the swap in February 1995 is being amortized over the life of the fixed rate debt; similarly, the loss on the remainder of the swap will appear as higher interest expense over the life of the swap.

Hedging Portfolios

Hedges of portfolios of assets or liabilities also raise difficult accounting problems. For example, consider a mortgage portfolio. The interest rate risk of each mortgage depends on such factors as coupon, maturity, and prepayment provisions. The interest rate risk of the portfolio is a composite of the risk of each mortgage. It may be possible to hedge that composite risk with reasonable precision. Yet, the following problems arise:

1. How should any gains or losses from the hedge be allocated to individual mortgages?
2. What is the effect on the hedge (and unrealized gains and losses) if some mortgages are sold?

Because of these concerns, the FASB exposure draft would not permit portfolio hedges, with the exception of hedges of foreign currency exposures, to be accounted for as hedges; they must be marked to market.

Rolling Hedges

Assume that a company must pay 100 million French francs one year from now and wishes to fix the dollar amount now. It can purchase 100 million francs for delivery one year from now. Under hedge accounting, the gain or loss on the hedge would be deferred until the transaction is completed.

However, it may be easier (due to liquidity constraints) or cheaper to purchase the francs for delivery in three months, intending to roll over the hedge for successive three-month periods. Since the maturity of the hedge is different from that of the commitment, hedge accounting may not apply, and hedge gains and losses would be reported in income. Yet, in the end, the two hedging strategies accomplish the same goal.

On the other hand, there is some uncertainty about the firm's ability to roll over the hedge, as well as the cost of doing so. The FASB exposure draft, therefore, would not permit hedge accounting for rollover hedges.

---

[9]Exhibit 16-5 reports a liability of $217 million at December 31, 1995 on the remaining $2.75 billion swap; on that date, five- and ten-year rates were more than two percentage points below their level at October 31, 1994.

Imperfect Hedges

Some hedges work perfectly. For example, the one-year French franc forward purchase described in the previous section totally eliminates the risk of fluctuation in the dollar/ franc exchange rate. Any change in that rate will be perfectly offset by gains or losses on the forward contract.

In other cases, however, the hedge is not perfect. Consider a firm that wishes to hedge a currency that either has no futures market or an illiquid one. It can hedge using forwards in another currency (perhaps that of a neighboring country) that has historically moved in tandem.[10]

Similar situations arise for:

- Raw materials and refined products, such as crude oil and gasoline, whose prices tend to move together but not perfectly
- Government bonds and other long-term debt obligations
- Interest rates of countries in the same economic block

Such imperfect hedges do sometimes work. When they fail, they can fail spectacularly.

Current Accounting Standards for Hedging Activities

Exhibit 16-6, from Stewart (1989), compares hedge accounting criteria in SFAS 52 and SFAS 80 with those used in accounting practice for interest rate swaps and the AICPA recommendations for accounting for options. Some of the differences and inconsistencies warrant brief comment.

First, both standards allow hedge accounting when risk is reduced, except that SFAS 80 uses an *enterprise approach*, whereas SFAS 52 is based on a *transaction approach*. Gains and losses on economically similar transactions may, therefore, receive different accounting treatment.

Under SFAS 80, futures contracts may be treated as hedges of anticipated transactions, but SFAS 52 does not allow such hedges. Movements in different foreign currencies may be highly correlated, and firms may use them as hedges, but SFAS 52 does not allow imperfect hedging. Again, similar transactions may produce different results.

When the FASB put hedge accounting on its agenda, it started with disclosure-only standards to permit financial statement users to obtain additional information about risk management activities.

SFAS 105 (1990) requires disclosures about financial instruments with off-balance-sheet risk of accounting loss and those with concentrations of credit risk. For all financial instruments with off-balance-sheet credit or market value risk, SFAS 105 requires disclosure of the contractual or notional principal amount, nature and terms of the instruments, and a discussion of their credit and market risk, accounting loss in the event of complete default by the counterparty, collateral policy, and a description of collateral held by the firm. The disclosures in this chapter reflect those requirements.

SFAS 105 also requires firms to disclose concentrations of credit risk from individual or groups of counterparties. Exhibit 16-7 contains Monsanto's disclosure of concen-

---

[10]For example, the Austrian schilling tends to move with the German deutche mark. As financial markets in Germany are much more liquid than those in Austria, firms may use mark financial instruments to hedge schilling exposures. Under SFAS 52, such transactions are not considered hedges.

EXHIBIT 16-6
Comparison of Hedge Accounting Requirements

	FASB 52*	FASB 80†	AICPA Issues Paper on Options‡	Interest Rate Swaps in Practice§
Hedge Accounting Criteria				
Designation as a hedge	Yes	Yes	Yes	Frequently but not always
Risk reduction basis	Transaction	Enterprise	Transaction	Sometimes
Degree of correlation	Not explicit	High	High	Matching
Ongoing assessment	Not explicit	Yes	Yes	Usually
Hedge of anticipated transaction (not firm commitment)	No	Yes	Yes	Yes
Cross hedges	Usually not	Yes	Yes	Yes
Hedge of an asset carried at cost	NA	Yes	No	Yes
Application of Accounting				
Split accounting for inherent elements (premium or discount)	Yes	Usually not	Yes	Frequently not necessary
Amortization of premium on hedge of net investment in a foreign entity	Income or equity	NA	Income	NA
Cap on deferred losses to fair value	No	No	Yes	No
Accounting if hedge criteria not met	Formula value	Market	Market	Market or lower of cost or market

NA = Not applicable. *Statement 52 covers foreign exchange forwards, futures, and swaps, but not options explicitly. †Statement 80 covers all (and only) exchange-traded futures except foreign currency futures, which are covered by Statement 52. ‡The recommendations included in the AICPA issues paper cover all options (whether or not exchange-traded). These recommendations do *not* constitute authoritative generally accepted accounting principles. The chart covers only purchased options. §There is no authoritative GAAP for interest rate swaps, although the emerging issues task force has dealt with several swap issues. Existing practice for interest rate swaps is not uniform. Summarized here is the author's perception of practice. The federal banking regulators are working on a release that would provide guidance for regulatory accounting.
Source: John E. Stewart, "The Challenges of Hedge Accounting," *Journal of Accountancy,* November 1989, Exhibit 2, p. 54.

trations in its trade accounts receivable. Although these data reflect vulnerability that could be inferred from the company's segment disclosures, there is some additional information. Note, for example, the large increase in receivables from pharmaceutical distributors and the decrease from customers in the former Soviet Union. These changes may reflect changing sales patterns.

SFAS 107 (1991) requires the disclosure of market values for all financial instruments (on and off balance sheet). It exempts insurance contracts, leases, equity investments, and trade receivables and payables. Firms must disclose assumptions and methods used to develop estimates of fair values. Additional narrative disclosures are required if it is not practicable to estimate fair values. In keeping with the exploratory

EXHIBIT 16-7. MONSANTO
Credit Risk Disclosures

Commitments and Contingencies

The more significant concentrations in Monsanto's trade receivables at year-end were:

	1995	1994
U.S. agricultural product distributors	$257	$295
European agricultural product distributors	117	103
Pharmaceutical distributors worldwide	357	287
Customers in the former Soviet Union	21	40

Management does not anticipate incurring losses on its trade receivables in excess of established allowances.

Source: Monsanto, *1995 Annual Report.*

nature of these standards, the board did not specify or limit estimation methods but instead asked for qualitative information.

Exhibit 16-8, from Monsanto's *1995 Annual Report*, shows the fair values of financial instruments, as required by SFAS 107. As interest rates declined in 1995, the fair value of Monsanto's mostly fixed rate long-term debt rose relative to the carrying amount.[11] In addition, Monsanto swapped variable rate for fixed rate debt. The decline in interest rates increased Monsanto's interest expense and increased the fair value of the interest rate swap liability.

On the other side of the balance sheet, the market value of investments exceeded the carrying amount by $55 million, an increase of $64 million from the (negative) difference in 1994. Monsanto's investments footnote (not shown here) reports a mix of debt and equity investments; the 1995 swing came primarily from debt holdings that rose in value as interest rates fell.

SFAS 119 (1994) took another step forward. It requires:

1. For derivatives held for trading, disclosure of the:
   - Average fair value
   - End-of-period fair value
   - Net gains or losses disaggregated by class, business activity, or risk.

[11]The effect of interest rate changes on long-term debt is discussed in Chapter 10.

EXHIBIT 16-8. MONSANTO
Fair Value Disclosures

Fair Values Of Financial Instruments

The estimated fair values of Monsanto's financial instruments were:

	1995		1994	
	Recorded Amount	Fair Value	Recorded Amount	Fair Value
Assets:				
Investments in securities and other assets	**$378**	**$433**	$409	$400
Foreign currency option contracts			7	5
Liabilities:				
Currency swaps	**1**	**4**	2	9
Interest-rate swaps	**5**	**19**	1	17
Long-term debt	**1,667**	**1,781**	1,405	1,408

The recorded amounts of cash, trade receivables, discounted receivables, third-party guarantees, foreign currency forward contracts, accounts payable, and short-term debt approximate their fair values.

Fair values are estimated by the use of quoted market prices, estimates obtained from brokers, and other appropriate valuation techniques based on information available as of Dec. 31, 1995. The fair-value estimates do not necessarily reflect the values Monsanto could realize in the current market.

Source: Monsanto, *1995 Annual Report.*

2. For derivatives held for nontrading purposes, a description of:
   - The firm's objectives, strategies, and classes of derivatives used
   - The recognition and measurement policies used for accounting purposes
   - Where recognized amounts are reported in the balance sheet
   - Hedges of forecasted transactions, including hedging methods, the maturity of such transactions, hedging gains or losses deferred, and the events that would trigger recognition of such deferrals
3. For derivatives excluded from the scope of SFAS 105:
   - Their face, contract, or notional amounts
   - Their nature and terms, including credit and market risk, cash requirements, and accounting method.

SFAS 119 also encourages (but does not require) quantitative information about the risk of its derivative financial instruments. Possible disclosures would include:

- Detailed data regarding positions and transactions
- Hypothetical effect of changes in market prices
- Gap analysis of interest rate repricing or maturity dates[12]
- Duration data
- Value at risk

There is considerable controversy regarding the relative usefulness of these data. The SEC requires firms to provide either specific contract data, sensitivity analysis, or value-at-risk disclosures, effective for fiscal years ending after June 30, 1997 (one year later for firms with market capitalizations below $2.5 billion).

ANALYSIS OF HEDGING DISCLOSURES

At this point, the reader may well be overwhelmed by the profusion of risks, hedging techniques, and accounting variations discussed thus far. In this section, we try to bring some order into this jungle by examining corporate disclosures. Our goal is to use these disclosures to understand:

- Risks faced by the firm
- Activities, including the use of derivatives, undertaken to manage those risks
- The financial statement effects of risk management activities
- Differences between accounting and economic hedging

We start with the 1994 financial statements of duPont in Appendix A of the text.

Analysis of duPont Risk Management Disclosures

Multinational enterprises such as duPont are subject to a number of financial risks that can be managed through hedging. We start with the effects of foreign currency exchange rates on revenues, expenses, cash flows, assets, and liabilities.

Note 1, Summary of Significant Accounting Policies, states (under foreign currency translation) that:

- The U.S. dollar is duPont's functional currency worldwide. This tells us that duPont's accounting exposure to exchange rate changes is measured by the net monetary assets or liabilities of each nondollar currency.
- The company uses forward contracts to hedge some firm commitments. Gains and losses on such hedges are deferred and included in the measurement of the related foreign currency transactions.

---

[12]Banks routinely provide this data.

Note 27, Derivatives and Other Hedging Instruments, provides tabular data on duPont's foreign currency hedging activities. That table shows, for each major currency at December 31, 1994, the:

- Net (asset or liability) exposure before hedging
- Open contracts to buy or sell foreign currency, both pretax and aftertax
- Net exposure, equal to the prehedging exposure less the aftertax contracts

DuPont's largest exposure is to the British pound, a net monetary liability of $1,428 million. The after-tax contract to buy pounds (in exchange for U.S. dollars) virtually eliminates this exposure. DuPont's exposure to other currencies is similarly hedged.

This hedging activity effectively sterilizes duPont's balance sheet exposure to changes in the exchange rate between the dollar and the principal currencies in which duPont holds assets or incurs liabilities. Given that the effect of rate changes is a component of reported income under the temporal method, duPont has eliminated a source of volatility from its reported results. Of course, duPont also gives up the possibility of gains if currencies in which it has net monetary assets gain, or those in which it has net monetary liabilities decline against the dollar. The decision to hedge may also require some capital (margin requirements) and management effort.

DuPont's 1995 financial statements (not shown) report a similar fully hedged position. However, effective January 1, 1996, duPont adopted local currencies as functional currencies. This change required a substantial adjustment to the hedge. Now duPont must hedge its net asset exposure in each currency rather than the net monetary exposure.[13]

As discussed in Chapter 15, both the temporal and all-current rate methods generate accounting exposures that may differ from the economic exposure. DuPont provides no discussion of this issue.

It is also important to note that duPont has hedged only the balance sheet exposures of its foreign operations. The hedging disclosures, by indicating significant currencies, help analysts focus on the currencies that matter. As duPont records revenues, expenses, and cash flows in these nondollar currencies, fluctuations in exchange rate continue to affect reported income and cash flows. These effects were discussed in Chapter 15.

Returning to Note 1, we see that duPont enters into interest rate swap agreements.[14] Notes 17 and 19 contain details of these contracts. Note 17 (short-term debt) reports that duPont swapped:

1. $50 million of (variable rate) commercial paper for a fixed rate of 8.3%.
2. 125 billion Italian lira (12.375% fixed rate) obligation for $100 million with a 7.45% rate.

The first swap eliminates the risk that interest rates could rise, increasing interest expense. Although the interest rate received is not disclosed, examination of the yield

---

[13]See the discussion of the all-current rate method in Chapter 15.

[14]Interest rate swaps are discussed in detail in Chapter 10.

curve suggests that interest expense was higher as a result of the swap as variable rates remained low.

The second swap replaced lira-denominated debt with dollar-denominated debt. As Note 27 shows that duPont has net lira monetary assets, it is surprising that it would swap a lira obligation for a dollar obligation, increasing the net lira assets to be hedged.

Note 19 (long-term debt) shows swaps of:

1. $775 of various maturity fixed rate debt to floating rate obligations. This swap would appear to be partly offset by the first short-term debt swap.
2. 150 million Swiss franc 6.25% (fixed) notes for $103 million of 6.9% notes.
3. 160 million Australian dollar 16.5% debt for a Canadian dollar 12.43% obligation.

In addition, duPont wrote a swaption agreement that permits the counterparty to put duPont into an interest rate swap that would convert $300 million of notes into floating rate obligations. DuPont received a premium for entering into this transaction. The put would presumably be exercised if short-term rates rose sharply. The swaption agreement and the first long-term debt swap suggest that duPont expects low interest rates for an extended time period and is willing to run the risk of higher rates in order to lower its current borrowing costs. In effect, $1.075 billion of fixed rate debt is at risk. These transactions suggest that the difference between hedging and speculation is often unclear.

NON-U.S. FINANCIAL REPORTING OF HEDGING ACTIVITIES

The International Accounting Standards Committee (IASC) and the Canadian standards body, the Canadian Institute of Chartered Accountants (CICA), have undertaken a joint project on financial instruments. Both the IASC and CICA issued two exposure drafts with similar proposals for the measurement of financial instruments and accounting for hedges. Australian standard setters also issued an exposure draft on these issues and the U.K. Accounting Standards Board (ASB) published a discussion paper in July 1996. Our discussion focuses on the IASC standard and proposals.[15] A revised exposure draft is expected late in 1997 with a final standard in 1998.

Recognition and Measurement. The IASC's definition of financial instruments is broader than that used by the FASB: It includes instruments that may be settled by delivery of the underlying commodity.

E48 called for the use of hedge accounting for all hedges, including anticipated transactions that are "highly probable" to occur. The FASB ED has similar provisions.

---

[15]IAS 32, Financial Instruments: Disclosure and Presentation, and the latest exposure draft E48, Financial Instruments, issued in January 1994.

E48 would allow entities to choose from two alternative measurement methods for financial instruments. The first, or "benchmark treatment," would allow financial assets and liabilities intended to be held for the long term or to maturity to be carried at historical costs. All other financial assets and liabilities would be measured at fair value. Hedges would be accounted for on the same basis as the hedged item. The proposed hedging criteria are similar to those in the FASB ED. The Canadian ED limits measurement to this approach.

Under the "allowed alternative," all financial assets and liabilities would be reported at fair value. The IASC intends to reissue this exposure draft; a final standard is expected in 1998.

Disclosure Requirements. IAS 32 disclosure requirements apply to all financial instruments (FI). Note that SFAS 105 applies to all FI with off-balance-sheet risk. Fair value disclosures are required for all FI under SFAS 107, and SFAS 119 is limited to derivatives.

With respect to interest rate risk, IAS 32 requires disclosure of effective interest rates and the earlier of contractual repricing or maturity dates for each class of FI. U.S. standards do not call for these disclosures. However, limited information may be available in the discussions of the market risk for each category of derivative FI. Both standards encourage disclosure of interest rate sensitivity.

For each class of FI, IAS 32 requires disclosure of both the maximum credit risk (ignoring collateral) and concentrations of credit risk. Under U.S. standards, firms must disclose credit risk of FI with off-balance-sheet risk and concentrations of credit risk for all FI along with a discussion of collateral policy. Fair value disclosures are comparable across standards. However, the IASC allows more judgment and the disclosure of ranges.

SFAS 119 and IAS 32 prescribe similar disclosure rules for hedges of anticipated transactions. However, unlike IAS 32, which applies to all FI designated as hedges of such transactions, SFAS 119 is limited to derivative FI. Also, IAS 32 calls for quantitative disclosure of all gains and losses, whereas SFAS 119 is limited to explicitly deferred gains and losses.

SUMMARY

In this chapter, we examined the use of derivatives and other hedging activities to manage the firm's foreign currency, interest rate, and commodity risks. As in other areas of financial analysis, the accounting for such transactions may not mirror their economic effect. Our emphasis has been on understanding both the accounting and economic effects of risk management activities and using disclosures to obtain a better understanding of the risks faced by the firm and its efforts to manage those risks. Case 16-1 focuses on the activities of Enron, a firm that has widespread hedging activities, to examine these issues further.

Chapter 16 was the last to examine specific subject areas. Having completed our survey of major topics in financial statement analysis, we turn to a synthesis of these topics in Chapter 17, which includes comprehensive adjustments to financial statements.

CASE **16-1**

Enron Corp.: Analysis of Risk Management Activities

Exhibit 16C-1 contains selected financial statement footnotes of Enron Corp. The firm operates in four business segments:

1. *Transportation and operation.* Interstate transmission of natural gas
2. *Domestic gas and power services.* Purchase, marketing, and financing of natural gas, natural gas liquids, crude oil, and power
3. *International gas and power services.* Development and acquisition of power plants
4. *Exploration and production.* Natural gas and crude oil exploration and production

Enron, and its subsidiary ECT, engage in price risk management activities for both trading and nontrading purposes. The range of trading activities is quite unusual; in effect, Enron serves as an exchange providing various risk management tools to other firms in the energy markets.

TRADING ACTIVITIES

The trading activities usually involve forward contracts, options, and swap agreements for natural gas, crude oil, and electricity and may include interest rate swaps and foreign currency contracts. These financial instruments are marked to market, net of future servicing costs. Unrealized gains and losses are reported as "assets and liabilities from price risk management activities" in the balance sheet and as a component of "other revenues" in the income statement.

Exhibit 16C-2 shows that the net assets (including unrealized gains) from trading activities amounted to $478,123 at December 31, 1995. For the year, net assets from price risk management activities increased by $98,037, which is reported as a component of "other revenues" in the income statement (not disclosed separately) and as a deduction in the reconciliation of net income to net cash provided by operations in the cash flow statement.

Market risk disclosures are primarily qualitative in nature. Note 2 describes the internal control and risk measurement procedures used by the firm. Enron measures and controls risk using value-at-risk (VAR) techniques,[1] which provide an estimate of the expected future losses over a given holding period based on a simulation of the impact of price changes.

VAR measures are highly variable depending on the time horizon, underlying data, correlations assumed, and quantitative models used.[2] VAR[3] can be measured as

$$\text{Daily Earnings at Risk (DEAR)} = \text{Dollar Value of Position} \times \text{Price Volatility}$$

Clearly, the risk measure depends on assumptions used to compute price volatility. The DEAR measure can be converted to different time horizons as a one-week or ten-day holding period. This conversion requires the correlation between price changes over time. One simple approach assumes that price changes are unrelated; the DEAR measure can then be converted to a VAR measure as follows:

$$\text{VAR} = \text{DEAR} \times \sqrt{N}$$

where N is the selected horizon.

---

[1] VAR methods are used by bank regulators to determine the amount of capital banks must have relative to market risk. For a discussion of different VAR methods, see Chapter 9 of Anthony Saunders, *Financial Institutions Management: A Modern Perspective*, 2nd ed. (Chicago, IL: Richard D. Irwin, 1996).

[2] In "VAR: Seductive but Dangerous," *Financial Analysts Journal,* September–October, 1995, pp. 12–24, Tanya Styblo Beder demonstrates that VAR measures are extremely variable and highly dependent on assumptions used.

[3] This section is based on the Saunders text cited in footnote 1 and J. P. Morgan, *Introduction to Risk Metrics* (New York: 1994).

NOTES TO THE CONSOLIDATED FINANCIAL STATEMENTS

1 SUMMARY OF SIGNIFICANT ACCOUNTING POLICIES

G. Accounting for Price Risk Management

Enron engages in price risk management activities for both trading and non-trading purposes. Activities for trading purposes, generally consisting of services provided to the energy sector through Enron Capital & Trade Resources (ECT), are accounted for using the mark-to-market method. Under each method, changes in the market value of outstanding financial instruments are recognized as gain or loss in the period of change. The market prices used to value these transactions reflect management's best estimate considering various factors including closing exchange and over-the-counter quotations, time value and volatility factors underlying the commitments. The values are adjusted to reflect the potential impact of liquidating Enron's position in an orderly manner over a reasonable period of time under present market conditions.

Activities for non-trading purposes consist of transactions entered into by Enron's other business units to hedge the impact of market fluctuations on assets, liabilities, production or other contractual commitments. Changes in the market value of these transactions are deferred until the gain or loss on the hedged item is recognized. See Note 2 for further discussion of Enron's price risk management activities.

2 PRICE RISK MANAGEMENT AND FINANCIAL INSTRUMENTS

Trading Activities

Enron, through ECT, offers price risk management services to the energy sector. These services primarily relate to commodities associated with the energy sector (natural gas, crude oil, natural gas liquids and electricity), but in some instances also include financial products (interest rate swaps and foreign currency contracts). ECT provides these services through a variety of financial instruments including forward contracts involving physical delivery of an energy commodity, swap agreements, which require payments to (or receipt of payments from) counterparties based on the differential between a fixed and variable price for the commodity, options and other contractual arrangements.

ECT accounts for these activities using the mark-to-market method of accounting. Under mark-to-market accounting, forwards, swaps, options and other financial instruments with third parties are reflected at market value, net of future servicing costs, with resulting unrealized gains and losses recorded as "Assets and Liabilities From Price Risk Management Activities" in the Consolidated Balance Sheet. Terms regarding cash settlements of these contracts vary with respect to the actual timing of cash receipts and payments. The amounts shown in the Consolidated Balance Sheet related to price risk management activities also include assets or liabilities which arise as a result of the actual timing of settlements related to these contracts. Current period changes in the assets and liabilities from price risk management activities (resulting primarily from newly originated transactions, restructurings and the impact of price movements) are recognized as net gains or losses in "Other Revenues."

Notional Amounts and Terms. The notional amounts and terms of these financial instruments at December 31, 1995 are set forth below (volumes in trillions of British thermal units eqivalent (TBtue), dollars in millions):

Product	Fixed Price Payor	Fixed Price Receiver	Maximum Terms in Years
Energy Commodities			
Gas	3,741	4,933	19
Crude and liquids	606	743	10
Electricity	33	165	5
Financial Products			
Interest rate[a]	$14,364	$1,465	19
Foreign currency	1,040	1,045	19

(a) The interest rate fixed price receiver represents the net notional dollar value of the interest rate sensitive component of the combined commodity portfolio. The interest rate fixed price payor represents the notional contract amount of a portfolio of various financial instruments used to hedge the net present value of the commodity portfolio. The effectiveness of a hedge on the net present value of the combined commodity portfolio is not a function of notational hedge value but, rather, of cash flows resulting from the notional hedge value. Accordingly, the notional dollar values will not be equal. However, the portfolio is substantially balanced from a cash flow perspective and is not sensitive to movements in interest rates.

ECT also has sales and purchase commitments associated with contracts based on market prices totaling 4,432 TBtue, with terms extending up to 20 years.

Notional amounts reflect the volume of transactions but do not represent the amounts exchanged by the parties to the financial instruments. Accordingly, notional amounts do not accurately measure ECT's exposure to market or credit risks. The maximum terms in years detailed above are not indicative of likely future cash flows as these positions may be offset in the markets at any time in response to the company's risk management needs.

The volumetric weighted average maturity of ECT's entire portfolio of price risk management activities as of December 31, 1995 was approximately 2.3 years.

Fair Value. The fair value of the financial instruments as of December 31, 1995 and the average fair value of those instruments held during the year are set forth below (amounts in millions):

	Fair Value as of 12/31/95		Average Fair Value for the Year Ended 12/31/95[a]	
Product	Assets	Liabilities	Assets	Liabilities
Energy Commodities				
Gas	$1,217	$744	$1,190	$477
Crude and liquids	249	363	293	495
Crude and liquids	97	62	29	14
Financial Products				
Interest rate	357	92	225	60
Foreign currency	64	38	58	35

(a) *Computed using the ending balance at each month end.*

The net change in the value of ECT's portfolio of price risk management activities for the year ended December 31, 1995, primarily attributable to financial instruments fixing energy commodity pricing, was $98 million and is included in "Other Revenues". All of ECT's operations relate to providing price risk management services. Accordingly, earnings for this operating segment appropriately reflect the net gain arising from trading activities for the year ended December 31, 1995.

Market Risk. To provide solutions to energy problems worldwide, ECT serves a diverse customer group that includes independent power producers, industrials, gas and electric utilities, oil and gas producers, financial institutions and other energy marketers. This broad customer mix generates a need for a variety of financial structures, products and terms. This diversity requires ECT to manage, on a portfolio basis, the resulting market risks inherent in these transactions subject to pa-

rameters established by Enron's Board of Directors. Market risks are monitored by a risk control group operating separately from the units that create or actively manage these risk exposures to ensure compliance with Enron's stated risk management policies at both the corporate and subsidiary levels. Risk measurement is also supplemented with stress testing and scenario analysis. ECT's fixed price contract portfolio is typically balanced to within approximately 1% of the gross position at the end of each day.

ECT measures the risk in its portfolio on a daily basis in accordance with value-at-risk methodologies, which simulate forward price curves in the energy markets to estimate the size and probability of future potential losses. The quantification of market risk using value-at-risk provides a consistent measure of risk across diverse energy markets and products. The use of this methodology requires a number of key assumptions including the selection of a confidence level for losses, the holding period chosen for the value-at-risk calculation and the treatment of risks outside the value-at-risk methodologies, including liquidity risk and event risk.

ECT expresses value-at-risk as a percentage of Enron's earnings based on a 95% confidence level using one day holding periods. On a one day basis as of December 31, 1995, ECT's value-at-risk for its price risk management activities was less than 2% (unaudited) of Enron's total income before interest, minority interest and income taxes. Since this is not an absolute measure of risk under all conditions for all products, ECT performs alternative scenario analyses to estimate the economic impact of a sudden market movement on the value of the trading portfolio (stress testing). The results of the stress testing, along with the professional judgments of experienced business and risk managers, are used to supplement the value-at-risk methodology and capture additional market-related risks, including liquidity, event, concentration and correlation reliance risk.

Based upon the ongoing policies and controls discussed above, Enron does not anticipate a materially adverse effect on financial position or results of operations as a result of market fluctuations.

Credit Risk. Credit risk relates to the risk of loss that Enron would incur as a result of nonperformance by counterparties pursuant to the terms of their contractual obligations. The counterparties associated with ECT's assets from price risk management activities as of December 31, 1995 and 1994 are summarized as follows (amounts in millions):

	December 31, 1995 Assets from Price Risk Management Activities		
	Investment Grade[a]	Below Investment Grade	Total
Independent Power Producers	$ 573	$105	$ 678
Gas and Electric Utilities	234	45	279
Oil and Gas Producers	318	109	427
Industrials	35	43	78
Financial Institutions	38	5	43
Energy Marketers	132	103	235
Other	202	42	244
Total	$1,532	$452	1,984
Credit and Other Reserves			(207)
Assets from Price Risk Management Activities[b]			$1,777

	December 31, 1994 Assets from Price Risk Management Activities		
	Investment Grade[a]	Below Investment Grade	Total
Independent Power Producers	$ 447	$ 44	$ 491
Gas and Electric Utilities	287	37	324
Oil and Gas Producers	310	26	336
Industrials	24	21	45
Financial Institutions	176	—	176
Energy Marketers	20	25	45
Other	158	33	191
Total	$1,422	$186	1,608
Credit and Other Reserves			(130)
Assets from Price Risk Management Activities[b]			$1,478

(a) "Investment Grade" is primarily determined using publicly available credit ratings along with consideration of collateral, which encompass standby letters of credit, parent company guarantees and property interests, including oil and gas reserves. Included in "Investment Grade" are counterparties with a minimum Standard & Poor's or Moody's rating of BBB- or Baa3, respectively.

(b) Three customers' exposures at December 31, 1995 and 1994 each comprise greater than 5% of Assets From Price Risk Management Activities.

This concentration of counterparties may impact ECT's overall exposure to credit risk, either positively or negatively, in that the counterparties may be similarly affected by changes in economic, regulatory or other conditions.

ECT maintains credit policies with regard to its counterparties that management believes significantly minimize overall credit risk. These policies include an evaluation of potential counterparties' financial condition (including credit rating), collateral requirements under certain circumstances and the use of standardized agreements which allow for the netting of positive and negative exposures associated with a single counterparty.

ECT maintains a credit reserve which is based on management's evaluation of the credit risk of the overall portfolio. This reserve is objectively determined using an implied risk profile based on the difference between risk-free rates of return and each counterparty's cost of borrowing. This implied risk is then used to evaluate the exposure (based on current market value) to each counterparty adjusted for collateral provisions and overall concentration of exposure. Based on ECT's policies, its exposures and the credit reserve, Enron does not anticipate a materially adverse effect on financial position or results of operations as a result of counterparty nonperformance.

Non-Trading Activities. Enron's other businesses also enter into forwards, swaps and other contracts to hedge the impact of market fluctuations on assets, liabilities, production or other contractual commitments. Changes in the market value of these transactions are deferred until the gain or loss is recognized on the hedged item.

Interest Rate Swaps. At December 31, 1995, Enron had entered into interest rate swap agreements with a notional principal amount of $4,005 million to manage interest rate exposure. Swap agreements relating to notional amounts of $1,315 million, $700 million and $1,990 million are scheduled to terminate in 1996, 1997 and thereafter, respectively.

Energy Commodity Price Swaps. At December 31, 1995, Enron was a party to energy commodity price swaps covering approximately 233 TBtu, 169 TBtu and 427 TBtu of natural gas for the years 1996, 1997 and the period 1998 through 2004, respectively, and 4 million, 4 million and 6 million barrels of crude oil for the years 1996, 1997 and the period 1998 through 2000, respectively. During the first quarter of 1996, Enron removed substantially all of its natural gas commodity price swaps for 1996 by entering into offsetting positions.

Foreign Currency Contracts. At December 31, 1995, foreign currency contracts with a notional principal amount of $11.9 million were outstanding. Such contracts will substantially expire in 1996.

EXHIBIT 16C-1. (*continued*)

Credit Risk. While notional amounts are used to express the volume of various derivative financial instruments, the amounts potentially subject to credit risk, in the event of nonperformance by the third parties, are substantially smaller. Counterparties to the forwards, futures and other contracts discussed above are investment grade financial institutions. Accordingly, Enron does not anticipate any material impact to its financial position or results of operations as a result of nonperformance by the third parties on financial instruments related to non-trading activities.

Financial Instruments

The carrying amounts and estimated fair values of Enron's financial instruments, excluding trading activities which are marked to market, at December 31, 1995 and 1994 were as follows:

(In Millions)	1995		1994	
	Carrying Amount	Estimated Fair Value	Carrying Amount	Estimated Fair Value
Long-term debt (Note 5)	$3,065	$3,360	$2,805	$2,752
Company-obligated preferred stock of subsidiaries (Note 9)	377	386	377	348
Interest rate swaps	—	(18)	—	5
Energy commodity price swaps	—	90	—	80
Foreign currency contracts	—	—	—	(1)

Source: Enron 1995 Annual Report

Enron used the following methods and assumptions in estimating fair values: (a) Long-term debt - the carrying amount of variable-rate debt approximates fair value, the fair value of marketable debt is based on quoted market prices, and the fair value of other debt is based on the discounted present value of cash flows using Enron's current borrowing rates; (b) Company-obligated preferred stock of subsidiaries - the fair value is based on quoted market prices; and (c) Interest rate swaps, Energy commodity price swaps and Foreign currency contracts - estimated fair values have been determined by using available market data and valuation methodologies. Judgment is necessarily required in interpreting market data and the use of different market assumptions or estimation methodologies may affect the estimated fair value amounts (see "Non-Trading Activities" above).

The fair market value of cash and cash equivalents, accounts receivable and accounts payable are not materially different from their carrying amounts.

Guarantees of liabilities of unconsolidated entities and residual value guarantees have no book value associated with them and the fair values of these items are not readily determinable (see Note 15).

Note that the multiple ($\sqrt{N}$) applied to DEAR results in VAR measures that are nonlinear as $\sqrt{10}$ is not twice as large as $\sqrt{5}$. In summary, VAR measures are not comparable across companies or over time unless the assumptions used have been disclosed.

Enron reports that on December 31, 1995, its VAR (using a one-day holding period and at a 95% confidence level) for price risk management activities was less than 2% of its total income before interest, minority interest and income taxes. Thus, the maximum loss according to Enron's VAR calculations is less than 2% or $23.3 million of the $1,165 million of 1995 income before interest, minority interest, and income taxes.

Note 2 also states that Enron is aware of the limitations of VAR measures and it performs

EXHIBIT 16C-2. ENRON CORP. AND SUBSIDIARIES
Price Risk Management Activities

($ in thousands)	December 31		
	1993	1994	1995
Assets from price risk management activities			
Short-term	$ 279,715	$ 449,588	$ 579,749
Long-term	887,342	1,027,945	1,197,029
	$1,167,057	$1,477,533	$1,776,778
Less			
Liabilities from price risk management activities			
Short-term	$ 609,403	$ 522,070	$ 708,353
Long-term	330,209	575,377	590,302
	$ 939,612	$1,097,447	$1,298,655
Equals			
Net assets from price risk management activities	$ 227,445	$ 380,086	$ 478,123
Change in net assets from price risk management activities	$ 115,415*	$ 152,641	$ 98,037

*Derivation not shown; amount obtained from 1994 cash flow statement.
   Source: Enron Corp., *1994–1995 Annual Reports.*

additional sensitivity analysis to assess the impact of other market-related, nonprice risks[4] such as concentration, liquidity, credit, event, and correlation risks.

NONTRADING ACTIVITIES

In addition to providing risk management services to other companies, Enron also uses various FI to manage risk exposures arising in its own operations. Changes in the market value of these contracts and arrangements are deferred until the gain or loss is recognized on the hedged item. The instruments and hedging techniques used are quite similar to those discussed in the chapter for duPont.

REQUIRED

1. The net assets of ECT include unrealized gains and losses on derivatives. These amounts are affected by new contracts entered into during the year, restructuring of existing contracts, and the effects of price changes. These components are, however, not disclosed separately.

   A. Discuss why these components would assist the analysis of ECT's trading activities.

   B. Describe the effect on the level and trend of ECT earnings of immediate recognition of unrealized gains and losses on new contracts.

[4]Liquidity risk reflects the potential losses when counterparties demand settlement of their claims forcing the firm to liquidate assets at unfavorable prices. Event risk is a consequence of unexpected changes in any market due to political or financial events, for example, wars or currency devaluation.

C. Enron's income tax disclosures (not shown here) report deferred tax liabilities related to risk management activities of:

December 31, 1995	$427 million
December 31, 1994	256 million

Explain why these deferred tax liabilities exist and the factors that affect their change over time.

D. Discuss the implications of the growing deferred tax liability for Enron's earnings quality.

2. Enron's note 2 reports the Notional Amounts and Terms of its financial instruments at December 31, 1995. The disclosure shows that, with respect to gas, Enron is a net fixed price receiver.

Explain what this means with respect to Enron's exposure to changes in future gas prices.

3. On July 22, 1996, Enron announced plans to merge with Portland General (PGE), an electricity retailer serving the Portland, Oregon area. Enron's press release stated that the merger would offer Enron additional growth opportunities, as the electricity market deregulates, because of PGE's expertise in

• managing the generation and delivery of electricity;

• serving the end users of electricity.

A. Explain how the acquisition of PGE might assist the expansion of ECT's business as an independent electricity marketer.

B. Discuss the expected effects of this expansion on Enron's use of derivatives.

C. Discuss the expected effect of this expansion on Enron's deferred income tax liabilities.

4. Note 2 contains data regarding the credit risk of ECT's trading activities.

A. Discuss the change in the mix (non-investment grade versus investment grade) of ECT's portfolio during 1995.

B. Explain why it would be useful to know:

(i) The amount of credit reserves separately.

(ii) The amounts of any collateral held.

C. Discuss the expected effect of the change in mix on ECT's 1995 profitability.

5. After Enron and PGE announced their plans to merge, Standard and Poor's placed Enron on credit watch, with positive implications. Enron's senior unsecured debt was rated BBB+ and PGEs debt rated A−.

Discuss the expected effect of an upgrade of Enron's debt rating on the level and profitability of ECT's trading activities.

6. Enron's nontrading activities also use derivatives. Note 2 reports the fair value of Enron's financial instruments, excluding trading activities, at December 31, 1995 and 1994.

A. Describe the relationship between the carrying amount and fair value of Enron's long-term debt at each year-end.

B. State whether the change in that relationship reflects the decline in interest rates during 1995. (Note: Enron's long-term debt is virtually all fixed rate.)

C. Explain how Enron's description of its interest rate swap agreements could have been more informative.

D. Discuss what the change in fair value of interest rate swaps suggests about their nature.

7. On December 13, 1996, Enron Oil and Gas (59% owned by Enron) announced a $10 million hedging loss. Bloomberg quoted one analyst who stated:

> The loss occurred because Enron arranged to sell [gas] futures contracts . . . at $2.50 per thousand cubic feet, believing the price would rise no higher. When gas prices continued to increase, the company bought back the contracts rather than sell the gas at the lower price. The result was a $10 million loss on the gas hedge.

Bloomberg quoted another analyst:

> That expense . . . would not have been there had they not had to close out their hedge.

Assuming that the contracts hedged current production, discuss any possible offsets to the hedging loss. (Note: consider the possible timing of the offset.)

Chapter 16

Problems

Questions 1–4 are based on Exhibit 16P-1, which contains Note 9, Financial Instruments, from the *1995 Annual Report* of Becton Dickinson (BD), a multinational manufacturer of medical supplies and devices.

1. [Analysis of fair value disclosures]

A. BD has debt denominated in both U.S. dollars and other currencies. Explain how the difference between the fair value of long-term debt is affected by variations in:

(i) Interest rates

(ii) Exchange rates

B. Given that interest rates fell in 1995, what inference can you draw from BD's fair value disclosures about the maturity and interest rate characteristics (variable or fixed) of its long-term debt?

C. Given that interest rates fell in 1995, what inference can you draw from BD's fair value disclosures about the interest rate characteristics (variable or fixed) of its investments in marketable securities?

2. [Foreign currency hedging] Exhibit 16P-1 contains extensive data regarding BD's foreign currency hedging activities.

A. From the disclosures provided, explain what appears to be BD's primary reason for these activities.

B. BD reported net assets of $881 million for foreign operations with non-U.S. dollar functional currencies. Those currencies generally rose against the dollar during fiscal 1995. BD's cumulative translation adjustment (CTA) balance declined from $8.6 million at September 30, 1994 to $6.8 million at September 30, 1995. Explain whether this change is surprising and give your reasons.

C. BD states that

> the company does not generally hedge these [operations with non-dollar functional currencies] translation exposures since such amounts are recorded as cumulative translation adjustments.

Evaluate this statement using the foreign currency hedging disclosures in Note 9.

D. For fiscal 1993, BD reported a negative CTA of $109 million, followed by a positive CTA of $38 million for fiscal 1994. What inference might be drawn from these data?

EXHIBIT 16P-1. BECTON DICKINSON
Financial Instruments Footnote

Note 9 - Financial Instruments

Fair Value Of Financial Instruments

The carrying values of cash equivalents, short-term investments, other long-term investments and short-term debt approximate fair values. Fair values were estimated based on market prices, where available, or dealer quotes. The fair value of certain long-term debt is based on redemption value. Investments in marketable securities were primarily composed of Puerto Rico government bonds.

The estimated fair values of the Company's financial instruments at September 30, 1995 and 1994 were as follows:

	1995		1994	
	Carrying Value	Fair Value	Carrying Value	Fair Value
Assets:				
Investments in marketable securities (non-current) (A)	$ 44,400	$ 43,509	$ 71,527	$ 70,093
Forward exchange contracts (B)	3,969	3,084	(630)	(473)
Purchased currency option (B)	360	311	112	112
Interest rate cap	—	13	—	—
Liabilities:				
Long-term debt	$557,595	$604,537	$669,157	$689,181
Interest rate swaps	55	1,155	68	(524)
Interest rate collars	—	—	32	49

(A) Included in Other assets.
(B) Included in Prepaid expenses, deferred taxes and other.

Off-Balance-Sheet Risk

The Company has certain receivables, payables and short-term borrowings denominated in currencies other than the functional currency of the Company and its subsidiaries. During the year, the Company hedged substantially all of these exposures by entering into forward exchange contracts and purchased currency options for the future purchase and sale of foreign currencies. Gains or losses related to these hedges are recognized in income as part of, and concurrent with, the hedged transaction. In addition, the Company hedged a portion of its investment in a foreign subsidiary by entering into forward exchange contracts with a net notional amount of $21,037 at September 30, 1995 to sell French francs and buy U.S. dollars forward. The Company does not use derivative financial instruments for trading or speculative purposes.

At September 30, the stated or notional amounts of the Company's outstanding forward exchange contracts and purchased currency options were as follows:

	1995	1994
Forward exchange contracts	$738,541	$665,945
Purchased currency options:		
German mark put, U.S. dollar call	$ 5,000	$ 9,416
Brazilian real put, U.S. dollar call	7,000	—
Italian lira put, German mark call	11,021	—

At September 30, 1995, $425,367 of the forward exchange contracts mature within 90 days and $313,174 at various other dates in fiscal 1996. The purchased currency options at September 30, 1995 expire within 120 days.

Significant forward exchange contracts and the purchased currency options which represent hedges of currency transaction exposures at September 30, 1995 were as follows:

	U.S. Dollar Equivalents		
	September 30, 1995		
	Notional Amount	Currency Transaction Exposure – Asset (Liability)	Average Contracts During Fiscal 1995
Commitments to sell foreign currencies:			
French francs	$ 78,809	$ 80,214	$ 81,256
Italian lira	58,386	59,073	56,253
Belgian francs	22,653	22,653	44,996
Spanish pesetas	46,952	46,952	45,245
British pounds	17,035	17,035	21,579
Japanese yen	43,704	43,733	14,427
German marks	20,073	20,375	9,223
Commitments to purchase foreign currencies:			
Irish pounds	$219,361	$(221,428)	$195,862
Singapore dollars	72,881	(72,881)	56,911
Japanese yen	18,669	(18,669)	8,443
Belgian francs	10,811	(11,986)	19,555
German marks	34,914	(34,914)	19,554
Canadian dollars	14,859	(15,535)	5,418

The Company's foreign exchange hedging activities do not generally create exchange rate risk since gains and losses on these contracts generally offset losses and gains on the related non-functional currency denominated receivables, payables and short-term borrowings.

The Company enters into interest rate swap and interest rate cap agreements in order to reduce the impact of fluctuating interest rates on its foreign currency short-term floating rate debt outside the U.S. At September 30, 1995 and 1994, the Company had foreign interest rate swap agreements, with maturities at various dates through 1998. Under these agreements the Company agrees with other parties to pay, at specified intervals, fixed rate payments in exchange for variable rate payments, calculated on an agreed-upon notional amount.

	Notional Amount U.S. Dollar Equivalent	Fixed Rate	Average Variable Rate
Interest Rate Swaps:			
September 30, 1995			
French francs	$ 20,312	5.00%	6.39%
Japanese yen	8,521	2.48	1.11
Japanese yen	5,013	2.61	1.83
Japanese yen	10,025	2.61	1.84
Japanese yen	4,010	1.87	1.23
Japanese yen	9,023	1.74	1.05
Japanese yen	8,521	2.44	1.19
September 30, 1994			
French francs	$ 18,886	8.16%	6.41%
French francs	18,886	5.00	6.80
British pounds	15,795	5.85	5.40
Japanese yen	5,041	2.61	2.23
Japanese yen	10,082	2.61	2.25

At September 30, 1995, the Company had a foreign interest rate cap agreement with a notional amount of $9,023 which limits the potential interest rate fluctuations on a portion of the Company's Japanese yen denominated short-term debt. It effectively entitles the Company to receive from a bank the amount, if any, by which the Company's interest payments on $9,023 of its floating rate short-term debt exceed 2%. The cap expires in May 1997.

At September 30, 1994, the Company had a foreign interest rate collar agreement with a notional amount of $15,800 which limited the potential interest rate fluctuations on a portion of the Company's British pound denominated short-term debt to a range of 6.5%-8.0%. The premium paid on the collar agreement was amortized to interest expense over the term of the agreement. The collar agreement expired in October 1994.

Concentration Of Credit Risk

Substantially all of the Company's trade receivables are due from entities in the health care industry. Due to the large number of these entities and diversity of the Company's customer base, concentrations of credit risk with respect to trade receivables are limited. The Company does not normally require collateral. The Company is exposed to credit loss in the event of non-performance by financial institutions with which it conducts business. However, the Company minimizes exposure to such risk by dealing only with major international banks and financial institutions.

Source: Becton Dickinson, *1995 Annual Report.*

E. BD had three purchased currency options outstanding at September 30, 1995. Suggest one motivation for each option.

3. [Interest rate swaps and caps]

A. Suggest the motivation for BD's interest rate swaps in place at September 30, 1995.

B. Explain the effect of these swaps on current interest expense.

C. The fair value of these swaps is higher (liability) than their carrying amount. State whether this fact is consistent with your answer to part B and explain why or why not.

D. Explain the relationship between the interest rate cap (Japanese yen) and the Japanese yen interest rate swaps.

4. [Effect of interest rate collar on interest expense] At September 30, 1994, BD had an interest rate collar agreement on British debt.

A. Explain the effect of this agreement on interest expense, assuming that interest rates:
  (i) Remain between 6.5% and 8.0% over the entire period.
  (ii) Equal 6.0% over the entire period.
  (iii) Equal 9.0% over the entire period.

B. Explain the effect of the collar on interest expense, assuming that the collar has a two-year term and interest rates
  (i) Remain between 6.5% and 8.0% during the first year and equal 6.0% during the second year.
  (ii) Remain between 6.5% and 8.0% during the first year and equal 9.0% during the second year.

C. Given your answers to parts A and B, suggest BD's motivation to enter into the collar agreement.

5. [Effect of functional currency on hedging] At December 31, 1995, duPont had fully hedged its foreign currency exposures, similar to the status shown in Note 27 to the *1994 Annual Report* (Appendix A). DuPont, however, changed the functional currency for its European petroleum operations from the U.S. dollar to local currencies effective January 1, 1996. In its *1995 Annual Report*, the company states that

> in connection with the change to local currency . . . the company entered into contracts to sell forward . . . foreign currency in December, 1995.

A. Explain why the change in functional currencies would result in changes in duPont's foreign currency hedges.

B. Explain why the change in functional currencies would be expected to increase the forward currency sales required to hedge its currency exposure.

EXHIBIT 16P-2. SUNCOR
Swap Contract Disclosures

($ millions except for average price)	Contract Amounts		Revenue hedged $ Canadian	Hedge period
	Quantity	Average Price* $ Canadian		
AS AT DECEMBER 31, 1994				
Crude oil swaps*	35 000 bbl/day	26	326	1995
	3 000 bbl/day	27	29	1996
	2 000 bbl/day	28	21	1997
U.S. dollar swaps	U.S.$60	1.37	80	1995
	U.S.$240	1.38	329	1996
	U.S.$155	1.40	216	1997

Source: Suncor, *1994 Annual Report.*

6. [Hedges of firm commitments] Alcoa, the world's largest aluminum producer, reports in its annual report that:

- Alcoa enters into long-term contracts with a number of its fabricated products customers.
- As a hedge against the economic risk of higher prices for metal needs associated with these long-term contracts, Alcoa entered into long positions, principally using futures and option contracts.
- Alcoa intends to close out the hedging contracts at the time it purchases the metal from third parties. The deferred gains on the closed hedging contracts of $466 million at December 31, 1995 are expected to offset the increase in the price of the purchased metal.
- The expiration dates of the call options and delivery dates of the forward contracts do not always coincide exactly with the dates by which Alcoa is required to purchase metal to meet its contract commitments. Accordingly, some of the futures and option positions will be rolled forward.

A. Discuss Alcoa's motivation for buying futures and options on aluminum.

B. Discuss whether the deferred gains of $466 million should be considered additional stockholders' equity.

C. Some of these deferred gains have been realized as the positions have been closed out. Discuss whether, if Alcoa had recognized these gains, they should be considered operating income or nonrecurring items.

D. The FASB exposure draft (Box 16-2) would forbid rolling hedges. How would this requirement affect Alcoa's reported earnings:

 (i) During the hedge period

 (ii) When contractual commitments are met

E. Discuss the effects of Alcoa's hedging activities on cash from operations:

   (i) During the hedge period

   (ii) When contractual commitments are met

7. [Hedges of forecasted transactions] Suncor is a Canadian oil and gas producer. Note 17 to its *1994 Annual Report* states that

> periodically, the company also is a party to certain off-balance-sheet derivative financial instruments, such as crude oil, natural gas, and foreign currency swap agreements. The company enters into these agreements for hedging purposes only, in order to protect its Canadian dollar earnings and cash flow. . . .

Exhibit 16P-2 shows outstanding swaps at December 31, 1994.

A. Identify and explain the *two* risks to reported earnings and cash flows that Suncor wishes to protect.

B. 1994 revenues were Canadian $1,635 million including local taxes of Canadian $634 million. Compute how much of its earnings exposure Suncor has hedged (assuming no change volumes) for 1995, 1996, and 1997 for each of the two risks identified in part A.

C. Evaluate the effect of Suncor's hedging activities on reported earnings and cash flows for 1995 and 1996, assuming that:

   (i) Oil prices rose to Canadian $30 per barrel.

   (ii) Oil prices fell to Canadian $20 per barrel.

   (iii) The Canadian dollar exchange rate rose to $1.25.

   (iv) The Canadian dollar exchange rate fell to $1.45.

17

ANALYSIS OF FINANCIAL STATEMENTS: A SYNTHESIS

CHAPTER OUTLINE

CHAPTER OBJECTIVES

INTRODUCTION

ANALYSIS OF AND ADJUSTMENTS TO THE BALANCE SHEET
Analysis of Book Value
Adjustments to Assets
Adjustments to Liabilities
Balance Sheet Adjustments for duPont
    Adjustments to Current Assets
    Adjustments to Long-Term Assets
    Adjustments to Current Liabilities
    Adjustments to Long-Term Liabilities
Adjustments to Stockholders' Equity
Adjusted Book Value per Common Share
Analysis of Capital Structure
Balance Sheet Adjustments for Non-U.S. Companies

ADJUSTMENTS TO REPORTED INCOME
Normalization of Reported Income
    Normalized Net Income
Analytic Treatment of Nonrecurring Items
    Earnings Normalization for Interfirm Comparisons
Income Normalization for Non-U.S. Firms

Normalization Over the Economic Cycle
Acquisition Effects
Exchange Rate Effects
Effect of Accounting Changes
Quality of Earnings
Comprehensive Income

ANALYSIS OF CASH FLOW
Analysis of Cash Flow Components
Free Cash Flow
International Cash Flow Comparisons

ADJUSTED FINANCIAL RATIOS
International Ratio Comparisons

SUMMARY

CASE 17-1. COMPARISON OF DOW AND ICI WITH DUPONT

CASE 17-2. ALCOA: ANALYSIS OF CURRENT COST BALANCE SHEET AND NORMALIZED INCOME

CASE 17-3. A. M. CASTLE: ANALYSIS OF A CYCLICAL COMPANY

CASE 17-4. DEERE: CASH FLOW ANALYSIS

CHAPTER OBJECTIVES

This chapter addresses debt and equity analysis and provides a bridge between financial statement and security analysis. It shows how to:

1. Adjust the balance sheet for current values and off-balance-sheet activities.
2. Compute adjusted book value per common share.
3. Adjust the capital structure to reflect current values and off-balance-sheet activities.

4. Normalize reported income.
5. Estimate the earning power of the firm.
6. Assess the quality of earnings.
7. Adjust cash from operations for analysis purposes.
8. Compute free cash flow.
9. Adjust financial ratios for noncomparability.

INTRODUCTION

This chapter is both a review and synthesis of the concepts and techniques discussed in prior chapters. It shows how reported financial data can be adjusted to create more useful input for valuation models; those models are discussed in Chapter 19. The financial analysis in this chapter is illustrated using duPont, whose financial statements are given in Appendix A.

The objectives of equity and credit analysis are similar, with differences only in emphasis. Creditors are primarily concerned with evaluating the firm's ability to service and repay its debt, both when extending credit and while credit is outstanding. Credit analysis is an important factor in setting the interest rate and debt covenants.

Short-term creditors, such as banks, were historically most concerned with liquidity, as they expected to be repaid in a short time period. Insurance companies, pension plans, and other investors in long-term bonds focused on long-term profitability and asset protection, given their longer time horizon. As more bank credit consists of revolving credits and term loans, the required analysis encompasses both short- and long-term credit risk.

Equity investors bear the residual risk of the firm. Their investment return depends on the long-term profitability and growth of the firm, and equity analysts may be tempted to ignore credit risk. However, equity investors should also be concerned with the firm's credit risk since financial distress may result in the loss of some or all of their investment. Firms with excellent long-term prospects may not survive if they cannot manage their credit needs.

However, the ultimate objective of equity analysis is valuation. Such valuation techniques as price/book value, price/earnings, price/cash flow, and discounted cash flow all use financial statement data. Research cited in earlier chapters shows that adjusted financial data often have greater value relevance and predictive value than reported data. Our view is that all financial statement data used to make investment and credit decisions should be adjusted to reflect accounting differences, current values, and the use of off-balance-sheet financing techniques. These adjustments should be made regardless of whether the objective is credit or equity analysis. We start with the balance sheet.

ANALYSIS OF AND ADJUSTMENTS TO THE BALANCE SHEET

The balance sheet shows the recorded assets, liabilities, and equity of the firm. As illustrated throughout the text, the reported balance sheet suffers from two defects:

1. Some assets and liabilities are not recorded.
2. The amounts at which assets and liabilities are measured may differ significantly from their economic value.

For these reasons, the usefulness of the reported balance sheet for investment decisions is limited. Its utility can be enhanced by the following adjustments to address those deficiencies:

1. Off-balance-sheet assets and liabilities are added to the balance sheet.
2. All assets and liabilities are measured at current values.

The first part of this chapter is concerned with the adjustments required to prepare a current value balance sheet. One of the objectives of that exercise is a better estimate of book value per share.

Analysis of Book Value

Book value is the reported stockholders' equity of the company, less the liquidating value of any preferred shares. Although book value per common share is often displayed in corporate and investment reports, it is frequently misunderstood. *Except by coincidence, book value equals neither the market value of the firm nor the fair value of its net assets.* It is primarily the accumulation of accounting entries and adjustments over the lifetime of the company and contains the following elements:

1. Original capital used to start the firm, plus proceeds from any additional shares issued, less the cost of shares repurchased.
2. Retained earnings accumulated over the firm's life.
3. Accounting adjustments. Certain accounting standards result in entries directly to equity, without flowing through the income statement. Examples include the minimum liability provision for pension plans, changes in the market value of long-term marketable securities, and foreign exchange rate effects.

Firms do not distinguish between original capital and subsequent share issuance. The *treasury stock* account accumulates the cost of shares repurchased, although firms may, from time to time, retire treasury shares, eliminating this account. Such technical retirement has no analytic significance.

The direct-to-equity accounting adjustments reflect accounting standards that delay recognition of the income statement impact of economic events. As preparation of a current value balance sheet requires recognition of all such events, the accounting adjustments are replaced by direct adjustments to assets and liabilities. These adjustments replace arbitrary accounting adjustments, some based on management discretion, with recognition of all known economic effects.

Because of the accounting choices available and the selective recognition inherent in GAAP, book value after adjustment may be more useful for decision making. The balance sheet adjustments required to compute adjusted book value are discussed in the following sections.

Adjustments to Assets

The reported book values of assets should be adjusted to current market value to approximate their value as collateral for creditors and resources available to equityholders. The current market value also facilitates an assessment of the earning power and cash-generating potential of the assets. The assets must also be adjusted for the impact of accounting choices, for example, adjustment of last-in, first-out (LIFO) inventories to first-in, first-out (FIFO).

GAAP-required accruals and deferrals may impact reported asset amounts and must be evaluated for their relevance to value. Examples include the reserve for bad debts, asset impairment, the valuation reserve for deferred tax assets, and the impact of exchange rate changes.

In principle, market values should be used for all assets and liabilities that have a determinable market. Financial reporting standards increasingly require the recognition or disclosure of market value for such financial assets as marketable securities, bank loans, mortgages, and private placement debt.

Some nonfinancial assets, including real estate, timberland, and mineral properties, should also be marked to market. These assets have alternative uses and their market values can be estimated with sufficient reliability. However, the estimated current value of an operating facility (such as a steel mill) is far more subjective as its value is derived primarily from its ability to produce (steel). Even if precision of measurement is not a problem, it is not clear which measure of current value should be used (see Appendix 8-A for a discussion of this issue).

For other assets, notably such intangible assets as brand names, customer relationships, and technology, reliable valuation may be difficult if not virtually impossible. Valuing the intangible by valuing the firm and working backward (subtracting all tangible assets and liabilities) serve no useful purpose when performed by financial statement preparers or auditors. If the purpose is firm valuation, the process becomes circular. Applying models such as those discussed in Lev and Sougiannis (1996) (see Chapter 7) to *individual* firms may be feasible, albeit fraught with statistical difficulties.

Thus, somewhere a line must be drawn between those assets (and liabilities) that are revalued and those that are not. This line is easier to draw in practice than in theory. The right decision depends on the purpose of the analysis and a judgment of the reliability of the current value data.

Adjustments to Liabilities

Market value adjustments and recognition of the effect of accounting choices are equally applicable to liabilities for the same reasons given earlier for assets. The recognition of off-balance-sheet activities, including all off-balance-sheet debt, consolidation of unconsolidated affiliates deemed to be integral to the firm's operations, and replacement of the balance sheet accrual for pensions and other postemployment benefits with the actual status of the plan are especially important.

These adjustments recognize obligations that do not meet the accounting definition of debt or whose recognition is not required under current GAAP. Note that some of these adjustments affect both assets and liabilities; for example, the capitalization of operating leases increases both assets (property) and liabilities.

Finally, some reported liabilities must be eliminated or reclassified. Some liability balances are not debt, as they will not require cash repayment, but will be satisfied by the delivery of goods or services. They are indicators of a firm's future sales or profitability rather than cash outflow. Examples of liabilities that should be excluded from debt follow.

Advances from Customers. Income from the sale of syndication rights for films to be shown on television or cable, for example, is recognized over the term of the contract, with the unearned amount shown as a liability. The cost of creating the film has already been incurred. The deferred amount is unearned income, not debt.

Investment Tax Credits. Credits recognized under the deferral method are another example; they are purely unrecognized income, not debt.

Deferred Income Taxes. This liability estimates future taxes payable if the tax basis of income measurement "catches up" to the accounting basis. The deferred tax liability balance may continuously grow, especially if arising from depreciation, and the net timing difference will not reverse in the near future. When the deferred tax liability (or asset) is significant, the analyst should examine its source and the likelihood of its reversal. Components that are likely to reverse should be included, but restated to present value.[1]

Balance Sheet Adjustments for duPont

Box 17-1 lists the most common balance sheet adjustments. Such adjustments generate measures of book value and debt that are more useful for analytical purposes. The adjusted measures, and ratios derived from them, should be better indicators of shareholder wealth and risk than measures based on unadjusted data. We now illustrate these adjustment techniques by applying them to duPont.

Exhibit 17-1 shows duPont's reported balance sheet at December 31, 1994, and applies a number of adjustments to derive a current cost balance sheet. All adjustments are based on data disclosed in duPont's financial statements and discussed in the appropriate chapter of this text.

Adjustments to Current Assets

Each asset account should be evaluated for possible adjustments ranging from recognition of market value to the effects of accrual accounting and management choices.

Cash, Cash Equivalents, and Marketable Securities. Cash and cash equivalents require no adjustment as they represent current cash balances (with foreign currency

---

[1]Some analysts treat deferred taxes as equity. But deferred taxes result from the use of different accounting methods and estimates for financial reporting than for tax purposes. The deferred tax liability partially offsets the different amounts of income recognized for financial reporting and tax purposes. If income recognized in the financial statements is overstated (e.g., by using depreciation lives that are too long), retained earnings are overstated. Adding the deferred tax liability to equity would increase the overstatement. For that reason, the components of the deferred tax asset or liability must be analyzed, rather than blindly added to debt or equity.

EXHIBIT 17-1. E. I. DUPONT DENEMOURS
Current Cost Balance Sheet, December 31, 1994

Assets

	Reported	Adjusted	Adjustment
Cash and cash equivalents	$ 856	$ 856	$ —
Marketable securities	253	253	—
Accounts and notes receivable, net	5,213	5,213	—
Inventories*	3,969	4,788	819
Prepaid expenses	259	259	—
Deferred income taxes†	558	—	(558)
Current assets of affiliates‡		1,627	1,627
Total current assets	**$ 11,108**	**$12,996**	**$ 1,888**
Gross property, plant, and equipment	48,838		
Less: accumulated depreciation	(27,718)		
Net property, plant, and equipment§**	**$ 21,120**	**$23,757**	**$ 2,637**
Investment in affiliates‡	1,662	4,153	2,491
Prepaid pension cost††	1,502	1,920	418
Long-term investments, net	508	508	—
Deferred taxes†	82	—	(82)
Miscellaneous	685	685	—
Total other assets	**$ 4,439**	**$ 7,266**	**$ 2,827**
Intangible assets‡‡	**225**	**—**	**(225)**
Total Assets	**$ 36,892**	**$44,019**	**$ 7,127**

*Addition of LIFO reserve on 12/31/94 (Note 12).
†Elimination of deferred tax assets and liabilities.
‡Recognition of duPont's proportionate share of affiliate assets and liabilities instead of net equity (Note 14).
§Capitalization of operating leases.
**Adjustment of oil and gas properties to discounted present value.
††Excess of pension plan assets over projected benefit obligation (Note 26).
‡‡Elimination of intangible assets.
§§Recognition of fair values (Notes 17 and 19).
***Restatement to market value at December 31, 1994.
†††Net adjustment of assets, liabilities, and preferred stock.
****Replace accrual with plan status.

amounts translated at current exchange rates). Marketable securities are carried at market value (Note 10) and require no further adjustment.

Accounts and Notes Receivable. This total includes both trade (customer) receivables and those from other transactions (such as from asset sales). Both credit risk and interest rate risk must be considered.

The underlying credit risk (the probability that trade receivables will not be collected on time, or at all) is related to duPont's customer base. The allowance for uncollectable accounts (shown in parentheses in duPont's Note 11) is the company's estimate of that risk. The low level of that reserve (2% of gross receivables) suggests

EXHIBIT 17-1 (*continued*)

Liabilities and Stockholders' Equity

	Reported	Adjusted	Adjustment
Accounts payable	$ 2,734	$ 2,413	$ (321)
Payables to banks		321	321
Short-term debt§§	1,292	1,300	8
Short-term debt of affiliates‡		324	324
Taxes payable†	409	346	(63)
Other current liabilities	3,130	2,797	(333)
Postretirement benefits other than pensions****	—	333	333
Current liabilities of affiliates‡		1,032	1,032
Total current liabilities	**$ 7,565**	**$ 8,866**	**$ 1,301**
Bonds, notes, and debentures§§	6,376	6,600	224
Capitalization of operating leases§	—	980	980
Long-term debt of affiliates‡	—	1,295	1,295
Total long-term debt	**$ 6,376**	**$ 8,875**	**$ 2,499**
Accrued postretirement benefits cost****	6,058	3,735	(2,323)
Other liabilities	2,380	2,380	—
Other long-term liabilities of affiliates‡		1,467	1,467
Deferred income tax liabilities†	1,494	—	(1,494)
Total other liabilities	**$ 9,932**	**$ 7,582**	**$(2,350)**
Total Liabilities	**$ 23,873**	**$25,323**	**$ 1,450**
Stockholders' Equity			
Preferred stock***	237	135	(102)
Common stock	5,179	5,179	
Retained earnings	7,406	7,406	—
Minority interest	197	197	—
Adjustments to assets and liabilities†††	—	5,779	5,779
Total stockholders' equity	**$ 13,019**	**$18,696**	**$ 5,677**
Total Liabilities and Equity	**$ 36,892**	**$44,019**	**$ 7,127**
Book value per common share	**$ 18.48**	**$ 26.97**	**$ 8.49**

low credit risk, presumably because duPont sells to other major businesses. Companies that sell to consumers or small businesses generally provide higher loss reserves. *When customers suffer from financial distress, an additional loss provision may be required.*

When a firm has sold receivables with partial or full recourse, the allowance for bad debts must include the expected recourse obligation. As a result, the allowance will be higher (as a percent of gross receivables) than if no receivables had been sold.[2]

---

[2]As discussed in Chapter 11, although book value will not be affected, the accounts receivable and current liability balances should be adjusted to reflect the financing nature of the transaction.

BOX 17-1
Checklist of Balance Sheet Adjustments

Account Area of Analysis or Adjustment Required*	Asset	Liability	Equity
Marketable securities			
Mark to market (13)	x		x
Accounts receivable			
Revenue recognition methods (2)	x		x
Analysis of bad debts (2)	x		x
Interest rate effects (10)	x		x
Sale of receivables (11)	x	x	x
Inventories			
Capitalization policy (6)	x		x
Addback of LIFO reserve (6)	x		x
Foreign currency effects (15)	x		x
Property, plant, and equipment			
Capitalization policy (7)	x		x
Capitalization of interest (7)	x		x
Foreign currency effects (15)	x		x
Effects of inflation (8)	x		x
Computer software (7)	x		x
Natural resource assets (7)	x		x
Depreciation methods and lives (8)	x		x
Impairment (8)	x		x
Long term investments			
Proportionate consolidation (13)	x	x	
Mark to market (13)	x		x
Intangible assets			
Treatment of goodwill (14)	x		x
Brand names (7)	x		x
Research and development (7)	x		x
Deferred charges			
Expense recognition policy (2)	x		x
Advances from customers			
Deferred revenue (10)		x	x
Long term debt			
Capitalization of leases (11)	x	x	x
Guarantees (11)	x	x	x
Take-or-pay contracts (11)	x	x	
Convertible debt (10)		x	x
Redeemable preferred stock (10)		x	x
Employee benefits			
Pension plans (12)	x	x	x
Health and life insurance (12)	x	x	x
Stock option plans (12)			x
Deferred income taxes			
Probability of reversal (9)	x	x	x
Valuation allowance (9)	x		x
Tax loss carryforwards (9)	x		x
Discount to present value (9)	x	x	x

*In many cases the adjustment may be either pretax or aftertax.
Note: The chapter where the issue is discussed is shown in parentheses after each item.

Interest rate risk refers to the possibility that the interest rate on receivables is below the appropriate (risk-related) market rate, resulting in fair value below cost. As Note 11 states that "receivables are carried at amounts which approximate fair value," and no information on interest rates charged on receivables is available no adjustment can be made in this case.

Inventories. DuPont's Summary of Significant Accounting Policies (Note 1) states that

> substantially all inventories are valued at cost as determined by the last-in, first-out (LIFO) method

indicating that an adjustment to current cost is required. Note 12 discloses that the LIFO reserve is $819 million. In our current cost balance sheet, we simply add the LIFO reserve to historic (LIFO) cost.

Should the adjustment be made on a pre- or posttax basis? For tax purposes, the LIFO cost is still relevant; if all LIFO inventories were liquidated, the company would be forced to pay income tax on the realization of the current value of its inventories. Although duPont had a small LIFO invasion in 1993 (Note 12), we cannot assume that its inventories will be completely liquidated without violating the going concern assumption. Thus, complete tax recognition of the LIFO reserve is an unrealistic assumption, and we do not make any adjustment for taxes.[3]

Deferred Income Taxes. We eliminate this current asset account, as explained in the discussion of duPont income tax liability account below.

Current Assets of Affiliates. For reasons discussed shortly, we add duPont's share of the current assets of its affiliates: $1,627 million.

Adjustments to Long-Term Assets

The adjustments to duPont's long-term assets are more complex. We start with duPont's fixed assets.

Property, Plant, and Equipment. There are two issues to consider: off-balance-sheet financing and valuation. Because duPont has significant operating leases (Note 20), some facilities and equipment are not shown on duPont's balance sheet. The present value of these leases (calculated in Problem 15 of Chapter 11) of $980 million has been added to property to reflect their omission.

The valuation issue is more difficult. As discussed in Chapters 7 and 8, the carrying value of property, plant, and equipment (PPE) is determined by accounting choices related to capitalization, depreciation method, and accounting estimates (lives and salvage values). Thus, comparability among companies is poor, reflecting different accounting choices. On the other hand, the current cost of PPE may have little relation to historical cost, regardless of accounting choices.

Oil and gas properties are an excellent example. DuPont uses the successful efforts method, more conservative than the full cost method. As a result, the carrying amount of its oil and gas properties is low. But the current cost of these properties is indepen-

---

[3] Any adjustment would equal the present value of estimated tax payments, as discussed in Chapter 9.

dent of the accounting method. Thus, we replace the carrying amount of duPont's oil and gas properties with their discounted present value, increasing those assets by $1,657 billion.[4]

The current value of duPont's other PPE is unknown. As duPont used an accelerated depreciation method, the carrying value is low relative to that value under the straight-line method. But the real value of PPE is the output it can produce. As duPont breaks out its PPE (Note 13) by segment rather than type, we do not know the proportion of those assets that consists of land, buildings, trucks, or other assets with alternative uses. Lacking any basis for an adjustment, none is made.[5]

The total adjustment to PPE, therefore, is:

Capitalization of operating leases	$ 980 million
Adjustment for oil and gas properties	1,657
Total	$2,637 million

Investment in Affiliates. DuPont uses the equity method to account for its investments in unconsolidated affiliates. Note 14 shows summarized data for these companies. These data are typically vague, in that they aggregate data for several affiliates. We assume that duPont owns exactly 50% of the affiliates.[6]

Our analytic objective is to replace the equity method accruals with proportionate consolidation (see Chapter 14). Taking one-half of each balance sheet component in Note 14 results in the following adjustments to duPont's balance sheet (all $ in millions):

Current assets	$1,627	
Noncurrent assets	4,073	
Total assets		$5,700
Short-term borrowings	$ 324	
Other current liabilities	1,032	
Total current liabilities	$1,356	
Long-term borrowings	1,295	
Other long-term liabilities	1,467	
Total liabilities		4,118
Net equity		$1,582
Advances*		80
DuPont investment (Note 14 total)		$1,662

*Deduced [noncurrent assets]

[4]The derivation of these data is given in Appendix 7-B.

[5]Appendix 8-A contains further discussion of the difficulty of estimating the current cost of PPE.

[6]Our assumption is based on duPont's statement (in Note 14) that the most significant of these affiliates are CONSOL Energy and the DuPont Merck Pharmaceutical Company of which they have a 50% share. Further, the note indicates that duPont's share of the net income of affiliates of $732 million was $361 million or 49.3%. (See, however, footnote 7.)

These adjustments, although approximations,[7] indicate the significance of these affiliates to duPont.

Other Assets. Note 15 breaks out this balance sheet category; we deal with each component separately.

Prepaid pension cost is the result of the smoothing devices of SFAS 87. Using data from duPont's Note 26,[8] we replace the accrual with the actual plan status:

Excess of assets over projected benefit obligation	$1,920
Prepaid pension cost on balance sheet	1,502
Unrecognized net assets	418

A similar adjustment for duPont's medical, dental, and life insurance benefits is shown as a liability adjustment below.

The adjustment for intangible assets is quite simple, total elimination. As goodwill has no value separate from the business, we eliminate it from our current cost balance sheet.

Note 15 states that most "other securities and investments" are reported at market value, whereas the remainder (carried at cost) have no determinable market. If available fair values differed from cost, we would replace cost with fair value.

We eliminate the long-term deferred income tax asset, as we consider all deferred taxes together shortly. Miscellaneous assets have not been adjusted, as we lack information with which to do so. When such assets are material, the analyst should always try to obtain further information regarding their nature and current value, and make any required adjustment using the principles articulated in this chapter.

Some firms show deferred charges that reflect unrecognized expenses, such as the deferral of financing fees, start-up expenses, or major maintenance expenditures. When cash outlays have occurred but have yet to be recognized as expenses, they should not be considered assets for purposes of analysis and should be removed from the adjusted balance sheet.

The net effect of these adjustments has been to increase duPont's assets by $7.127 billion (more than 19%) from $36,892 billion to $44,019 billion. We now turn to adjustments applicable to the firm's liabilities.

Adjustments to Current Liabilities

Current liabilities are generally stated at the amount expected to be paid, making adjustment unnecessary. Given the short time period to liquidation, any interest rate adjustment is usually immaterial (as shown below). The major change, therefore, is the additional current liabilities resulting from the proportionate consolidation of

---

[7]The footnote to Note 14 states that duPont's *pro rata* share of affiliate borrowings is $1,220 million, which is lower than the sum of short- and long-term borrowings calculated above. We are unable to resolve this discrepancy from duPont's disclosures.

[8]When making this adjustment, the company's discount and compensation growth rate assumptions should be compared with similar companies. In some cases, analytical adjustment of the projected benefit obligation may be required. In addition, consideration should be given to the historical pattern of plan amendment, especially for flat benefit plans, to ensure that the PBO does not understate the company's obligation (see Case 12-1 on General Motors for an example).

duPont's equity method affiliates. Income taxes payable have not been removed as the amount shown is the estimated cash outflow over the next year and is not dependent on accounting choices. The postretirement benefit component of other current liabilities has been segregated to facilitate the adjustment for these liabilities (under other long-term liabilities).

Short-Term Borrowings. The liability is increased by $8 million, to reflect the excess fair value of short-term debt as disclosed in Note 17. Although the adjustment is not material for duPont, we show it for instructional purposes. There are two other adjustments:

1. Accounts payable include $321 of payables to banks (Note 16). We consider these payables as financial debt (rather than an operating liability) and show it separately for analysis purposes.
2. DuPont's estimated share of the short-term debt of its affiliates has been added.

Adjustments to Long-Term Liabilities

As these liabilities are longer in duration and some reflect accounting choices rather than economic events, significant adjustments are required.

Long-Term Borrowings and Capital Lease Obligations. DuPont's Note 19 contains details of the company's long-term debt, including the fair value disclosure mandated by SFAS 107. The carrying amount of $6,376 million is replaced by the fair value of $6,600 million in the fair value balance sheet.[9]

The second adjustment is the recognition of the debt associated with the capitalization of duPont's operating leases. As Note 20 reveals, these leases are long-lived and indistinguishable from those leases that have been capitalized.

The third adjustment is the recognition of duPont's proportionate share of the debt of its equity method affiliates, as computed earlier in this chapter.

There is no adjustment for duPont's "indirect guarantees" disclosed in Note 28. Although the footnote wording is vague, these appear to be "take-or-pay" obligations. Given their small amount and the probable overlap with the recognition of duPont's share of affiliate assets and liabilities, no adjustment is made.

Other Liabilities. Note 21 shows that the largest component is a $6,058 million accrual for postretirement medical, dental, and life insurance benefits, accounted for under SFAS 106.

In the current value balance sheet, we replace the accrued cost with the actual plan obligation, shown in Note 25:

Accrued postretirement benefit cost	$ 6,391
Accumulated postretirement benefit obligation	(4,068)
Excess accrual	$ 2,323

[9]When fair value is not disclosed (such as for non-U.S. firms), it should be estimated using the method shown in Chapter 10 and in Case 10-1.

Because duPont has amended its plans, but the effect of that amendment on the benefit obligation has not been recognized, duPont's accrual is overstated. Thus, we reduce the long-term accrual by $2,323 million from $6,058 million to $3,735 million. When the current portion (see current liabilities above) is included, the total balance sheet accrual of $4,068 ($3,735 + $333) million now equals the accumulated obligation.

The second component of other liabilities in Note 21 is reserves for employee-related costs. With no further explanation provided, no adjustment can be made. Similarly, "miscellaneous" (the third category) is left unchanged.

Finally, we include $1,467 million to recognize the other long-term liabilities of duPont's affiliates.

Deferred Income Taxes. DuPont adopted SFAS 109 in 1992. Note 7 reports deferred tax assets of $4,235 million (net of a $357 million valuation allowance) and deferred tax liabilities of $5,152 million, for a net deferred tax liability of $917 million. That net liability is reported on duPont's balance sheet in four pieces:

Deferred income taxes (current asset)	$ 558 million
Deferred taxes (long-term asset)	82
Income taxes (current liabilities)[10]	(63)
Deferred taxes (long-term liabilities)	(1,494)
Net Liability	$ (917) million

As discussed in Chapter 9, depreciation is the major factor in duPont's net deferred tax liability. As depreciation timing differences are unlikely to reverse, we assume zero deferred taxes on the current value balance sheet. Thus, all tax assets and liabilities are eliminated, increasing equity by $917 million.

However, Note 7 also states that

. . .unremitted earnings of non-U.S. subsidiaries totaling $4,333 [million] were deemed to be permanently reinvested. No deferred tax liability has been recognized with regard to the remittance of such earnings. It is not practicable to estimate the income tax liability that might be incurred if such earnings were remitted to the United States.

If analysis of a firm assumes that such "permanently reinvested" earnings would have to be repatriated,[11] then long-term liabilities should be increased by an estimate of the required income tax payments.

Minority Interest. DuPont's balance sheet shows $197 million of minority interest. For analysis purposes, we include this amount in stockholders' equity as it represents the equity interest in duPont's consolidated subsidiaries that belongs to shareholders

---

[10]We assume that the balance sheet caption "income taxes" includes nonincome taxes. Note 7 states that current deferred income tax liabilities equal $63 million. Using this amount results in a total liability ($917 million) which matches that shown in Note 7.

[11]For example, liquidation or a leveraged buyout that would require repatriation of all earnings to service parent company debt.

other than duPont.[12] In a current value balance sheet, the minority interest should be increased by a proportionate share of the asset and liability adjustments that pertain to these subsidiaries. Given the small amount of minority interest and the complete lack of data, we have made no adjustment for duPont.

Commitments and Contingent Liabilities. Every large firm has contracts and other commitments that are not recognized in the financial statements. We have already capitalized operating leases, a common example of such unrecognized "executory contracts." DuPont's Note 28 reports direct and indirect debt guarantees that were discussed under long-term borrowings.

Note 28 also refers to lawsuits and environmental contingencies that are much more difficult to quantify. In the United States, much litigation is routine, and its outcome is rarely material to the firm. However, the analyst should look for footnote references to litigation that may be material, for example, related to:

- Firm patents that are challenged by competitors
- Patents of others that the firm may have violated
- Alleged illegal conduct, such as bribery
- Violations of contracts

Companies rarely disclose the details of such litigation, but court filings are often publicly available.

Environmental obligations are also hard to assess, even from inside the firm. Changing laws and technology hamper estimates of the cost of environmental remediation. Uncertainty as to insurance coverage complicates this issue further. As always, some firms are conservative in accruing such costs; others record these obligations only when they are virtually certain. Disclosures have improved in recent years, but analysts should seek additional information regarding the nature of such obligations and the range of possible cost. DuPont's Note 28 states that it has accrued $616 million at December 31 for environmental remediation.

Adjustments to Stockholders' Equity

The stockholders' equity section of duPont consists of the following components:

1. Preferred stock
2. Common stock
3. Additional paid-in capital
4. Reinvested earnings

The fourth component, often called retained earnings, reflects the reinvestment of more than $7 billion of earnings over duPont's lifetime.

Preferred stock should be restated to either liquidation or market value if it is recorded at some other amount. DuPont's Consolidated Statement of Stockholders' Equity shows two issues of preferred stock carried at $100 per share (their par value).

---

[12]The FASB has proposed this treatment in its exposure draft on consolidation (see Box 13-3).

However, both issues are callable at higher prices (shown in parentheses). In some circumstances,[13] analysis would assume call and the preferreds would be restated to:

$4.50 series:	1,672,594 @ $120 =	$200.7 million	
$3.50 series:	700,000 @ $102 =	71.4	
Total		$272.1 million	

An alternative calculation would use the market values of the two issues at December 31, 1994:

$4.50 series:	1,672,594 @ $60.50 =	$101.2 million	
$3.50 series:	700,000 @ $48.50 =	34.0	
Total		$135.2 million	

As there is no indication that these preferred issues will be called, we use market value in Exhibit 17-1.

The distinction between common stock and additional paid-in capital is legalistic and has no bearing on financial analysis.

The following components of equity are often present in the stockholders' equity section (but are absent in duPont's case):

1. Cumulative translation adjustment (Chapter 15)
2. Unrealized securities gains and losses (Chapter 13)
3. Minimum pension liability

These and any other "smoothing" accounts must be removed from the current cost balance sheet.

The final adjustment is the total of all adjustments to assets and liabilities. In order for the current value balance sheet to balance, this total must be added to stockholder's equity. The adjustment equals:

Net adjustment to assets	$ 7,127 million
Net adjustment to liabilities	(1,450)
Net adjustment to stockholders' equity	$ 5,677

Adjusted Book Value per Common Share

After all balance sheet components have been restated to current cost and any preferred stock deducted, the resulting amount is divided by the number of common shares outstanding at the balance sheet date. The result is adjusted book value per common share, a far better measure of the resources of the firm.

---

[13]For example, in a takeover when existing preferred stock must be retired because of voting rights or restrictive covenants.

For duPont, the adjusted book value per share is computed as:

Adjusted stockholders' equity	$18,696 million
Minority interest	(197)
Preferred stock	(135)
Adjusted common equity	$18,364 million
Number of common shares[14]	681 million

$$\text{Adjusted common equity per share} = \frac{\$18,364}{681} = \quad \$26.97$$

DuPont's reported book value per share equals $18.48, calculated as:

Total stockholders' equity	$13,019 million
Minority interest	(197)
Preferred stock	(237)
Common equity	$12,585 million
Number of common shares	681 million

$$\text{Common equity per share} = \frac{\$12,585}{681} = \quad \$18.48$$

DuPont's adjusted book value per share is 46% higher than the historical cost amount. Although adjusted book value per share is more useful than historical book value per share, it is not an end in itself. This better estimate of the net assets available to the firm is important for current and potential creditors interested in the firm's solvency (see the next section) and for purposes of valuation (see Chapter 19).[15] Additionally, it measures the resources of the firm on which an adequate return must be earned. The next section turns to the analysis of duPont's capital structure to further our understanding of its obligations, liquidity, short- and long-term borrowing needs, and risk.

Analysis of Capital Structure

Exhibit 17-2 compares duPont's reported capitalization at December 31, 1994 with the adjusted amounts. The reported debt-to-equity ratio does not include the impact of off-balance-sheet financing techniques and is a product of management's reporting choices. It can be misleading if used for comparative analysis. The adjustments dis-

---

[14]Remember to use the number of shares outstanding at the period end, net of any treasury shares. The average number of shares outstanding during the period should be used only for earnings per share and cash flow per share calculations.

[15]We note that the extensive discussion in recent years of whether stock prices are "too high" compares market prices with *reported* book values per share. The analysis of duPont illustrates how wide the disparity between reported and adjusted amounts can be.

EXHIBIT 17-2. E. I. DUPONT DENEMOURS
Adjusted Long-Term Debt and Solvency Analysis

Capitalization Table ($ in millions)	12/31/93	12/31/94
Short-term debt	$ 2,796	$ 1,292
Long-term debt	6,531	6,376
Total reported debt	**$ 9,327**	**$ 7,668**
Adjustments		
Payable to banks (Note 16)	264	321
50% of affiliate debt	1,348	1,619
Capitalization of operating leases	1,001	980
Restatement of debt to market value	1,073	232
Adjusted total debt	*$13,013*	*$10,820*
Preferred stock	237	237
Minority interest	187	197
Common equity	10,993	12,585
Total stockholders' equity	**$11,417**	**$13,019**
Adjustments to Equity		
Preferred stock	(68)	(102)
Common equity	134	5,779
Adjusted stockholders' equity	*$11,483*	*$18,696*
Total reported capital	**$20,744**	**$20,687**
Adjusted total capital	*24,496*	*29,516*
Ratios		
Debt-to-equity	0.82	0.59
Debt-to-total capital	0.45	0.37
Adjusted Ratios		
Debt-to-equity	1.13	0.58
Debt-to-total capital	0.53	0.37

Note: See Exhibit 17-1 and text for 1994 adjustments.

cussed in the preceding sections produce a more complete capital structure and ratios that facilitate comparisons with other firms.

Total adjusted stockholders' equity of $18.7 billion is approximately 44% higher than the reported amount of $13 billion. However, duPont's debt obligations are also higher after adjustments, mainly for off-balance-sheet obligations. As a result, the debt-to-equity and debt-to-total capital ratios are virtually unchanged by these adjustments.

However, the 1993 ratios are significantly lower after adjustment. Adjusted total debt is nearly $3.7 billion higher, whereas equity is unchanged.

Balance Sheet Adjustments for Non-U.S. Companies

Adjustments to the balance sheet of an enterprise that does not adhere to U.S. GAAP follow a pattern similar to that of U.S. firms. Special consideration is required, however, for the following issues:

1. Some foreign companies are permitted by local GAAP to revalue fixed assets. The advantage of such revaluation is the restatement of such assets to their current value, providing information generally not available for U.S firms. The disadvantage is the loss of comparability, as foreign assets, equity, and capital are increased relative to those of firms using historical cost for fixed assets. Either such revaluations must be reversed, or (our preference) estimates made of the current value of fixed assets for firms that do not revalue.

2. In some foreign jurisdictions, acquisition goodwill is written off at the acquisition date rather than amortized over time. When intangibles are eliminated, this accounting difference disappears. Similarly, the removal of capitalized research or development costs places all firms on the same basis.

3. Disclosures are generally less informative for non-U.S. firms, especially with respect to operating leases and other off-balance-sheet financing activities. The analyst may have to use any available data to make approximate adjustments; in some cases, management may provide additional disclosures on request.

4. Differences in accounting methods reduce the comparability of balance sheets before adjustment. When possible, adjustment for those differences should be made, using reconciliations to U.S. or IASC standards that are sometimes provided.

ADJUSTMENTS TO REPORTED INCOME

As in the case of book value, reported net income should also be examined for possible adjustments. The objective is to obtain a measure of operating results that better represents the earning power of the firm. The concept of earning power represents the (permanent) net income of the firm, ignoring temporary, nonrecurring, or unusual factors. In theory, the earning power of the firm is stable, but grows at a long-term growth rate. As discussed in Chapter 19, earning power (expected earnings) rather than reported income should be the input in valuation models.

Accounting standards setters have struggled to define such terms as "nonrecurring" and "extraordinary," with a notable lack of success. There is no reason for users of financial statements to be drawn into this semantic morass. Analysts must, however, identify the factors that affect reported operating performance. The objective is to estimate the earning power of the firm by removing nonrecurring factors.

Normalization of Reported Income

In practice, determining the earning power of the firm is difficult, requiring judgment to remove the "noise" that is always present. Part of the difficulty is that one analyst's definition of noise may differ from another's. Normalization is the term applied to the process of estimating normal operating earnings for each period.

For noncyclical companies, the normalization of earnings consists mainly of removing nonrecurring items from reported income. Such items may include:

- Accounting changes
- Realized capital gains or losses
- Gains or losses on the repurchase of debt
- Catastrophes such as natural disasters or accidents
- Strikes
- Impairment or "restructuring" charges
- Litigation or government actions
- Discontinued operations

The impact of some of these items may be segregated as a line item in the income statement. Alternatively, in some cases, it may be disclosed in footnotes or in the Management Discussion and Analysis. Sometimes, the effect is given on a pretax basis only; other times, the after-tax impact on EPS is disclosed.

The analyst should search the financial statements for such items and then remove the effect of those deemed to be nonrecurring from net income. Capital gains or losses, for example, should be segregated from operating earnings. Recurring losses from discontinued operations, impairments, or restructurings suggest that the company's depreciation or other accounting methods may overstate reported income. Because restructurings consist of past and future expenditures, they reflect on either past income or future income. Such write-offs should be segregated from operating earnings but not ignored. Rather, they should be "allocated" to past or future income (as the case may be) to more accurately reflect the trend and level of income.

Exhibit 17-3 normalizes duPont's reported earnings for the five years ended December 31, 1994, using data from financial statement footnotes and the MD&A. Some adjustments are related to the balance sheet adjustments already discussed; others apply only to reported income.

Accounting Changes. The effect of mandated and voluntary accounting changes is another frequent source of nonrecurring items. Most such effects are reported outside of income from continuing operations, making it easy to isolate them. However, the effect of changes in accounting estimates (such as changes in depreciation lives and pension assumptions) is rarely segregated. When material, all such effects should be removed from normalized income.

DuPont adopted both SFAS 106 (postretirement benefits other than pensions) and SFAS 109 (income tax) in 1992 (see Chapters 12 and 9, respectively). The cumulative effect of both adoptions reduced reported income sharply; these effects have been removed from normalized income in Exhibit 17-2.

Early Extinguishment of Debt. When interest rates change, firms may find it advantageous to refinance a portion of their debt. As discussed in Chapter 10, the accounting gains or losses from refinancing may be quite different from the economic effects; for that reason, these gains and losses should be considered nonrecurring, whether or not they are reported as extraordinary items.

EXHIBIT 17-3
Normalization of duPont's Reported Net Income 1990 to 1994 ($ in millions)

	1990	1991	1992	1993	1994	5-Year Total
Reported Net Income	$2,310	$1,403	$(3,927)	$555	$2,727	$3,068
Items Reported After Tax						
Early debt retirement	—	—	69	11	—	80
SFAS 106 adoption	—	—	3,788	—	—	3,788
SFAS 109 adoption	—	—	1,045	—	—	1,045
Tax adjustments	—	(114)	—	(274)	(105)	(493)
LIFO liquidation	—	—	—	(50)	—	(50)
Items Reported Pretax						
Restructuring provisions	94	828	475	1,835	(142)	3,090
Fungicide recall		343	212	200	175	930
Loss (gain) on asset sale	(196)	(833)	(40)	(198)	(92)	(1,359)
Capitalized interest	(207)	(216)	(217)	(231)	(144)	(1,015)
Subtotal	$ (309)	$ 122	$ 430	$1,606	$ (203)	$ 1,646
Tax offset	105	(41)	$ (146)	(546)	69	(560)
Net effect	$ (204)	$ 81	$ 284	$1,060	$ (134)	$1,086
Normalized net income before nonrecurring items	**$2,106**	**$1,370**	**$1,259**	**$1,302**	**$2,488**	**$8,524**
Percentage difference	**−8.8%**	**−2.4%**	**NMF**	**134.6%**	**−8.8%**	**177.8%**
Adjustment (see text)	**(228)**	**(228)**	**(228)**	**(228)**	**(228)**	**(1,140)**
Earnings power	**$1,878**	**$1,142**	**$1,031**	**$1,074**	**$2,260**	**$7,384**
Percentage difference	**−18.7%**	**−18.6%**	**NMF**	**93.5%**	**−17.1%**	**140.7%**

Income Tax Adjustments. In 1991, duPont reported a $114 million tax reduction that related to prior years. In 1993 and 1994, the company had nonoperating tax benefits of $274 and $105 million, respectively.[16] It is important to segregate such amounts because they do not relate to current year operations and distort the relationship between pretax and after-tax income. The use of tax carryforwards and significant changes in the valuation allowance, although not an issue for duPont, are frequent causes of distortions in the reported tax rate.[17]

LIFO Liquidations. DuPont's 1993 net income was increased by $50 million by a LIFO invasion (reduction of LIFO inventory quantities, Chapter 6). As we cannot assume that inventories can be reduced continuously and there has been no other liquidation in recent years, the LIFO reserve reduction should be considered nonrecurring.

[16]See Exhibit 9-6 and related text for the derivation and discussion of these amounts.

[17]See Chapter 9 for a detailed analysis of duPont's income tax rate and a discussion of both tax loss carryforwards and the valuation allowance.

LIFO invasions distort reported gross margins. For this reason, they must be identified so that the analyst can disentangle their impact on the level and trend of gross margins and operating earnings.

Restructuring Provisions. Such provisions have become increasingly common in the United States; non-U.S. firms may report them as well. Restructuring provisions represent either costs of prior periods (e.g., underdepreciation of assets) or of later periods (severance and postemployment benefits, lease costs). These accruals are estimates; note that in 1994, duPont reduced the 1993 accrual. DuPont took restructuring provisions in every year except 1994.

Litigation or Government Actions. In 1991, duPont accrued $343 million for the recall of the fungicide Benlate. Additional accruals were made in 1992 through 1994, for a total accrual of $930 million.

Realized Capital Gains and Losses. Firms frequently report gains and losses on asset sales; duPont reports gains in every year. It is unclear whether these gains result from the sale of fixed assets, investments in affiliates, or marketable securities.

Capital gains and losses are highly variable nonoperating income sources. As discussed in Chapter 13, the timing of capital gains recognition on marketable securities is often discretionary. For this reason, it is preferable to replace recognized gains with actual investment performance. Gains and losses on sales of fixed assets and intercorporate investments also reflect management decisions rather than changes in economic value in that period.

Capitalized Interest. As discussed in Chapter 7, duPont capitalizes interest on fixed assets under construction. Normalized earnings should be adjusted by deducting the capitalized amount.

Normalized Net Income

Subtracting all nonrecurring items from reported net income results in normalized earnings. Note the importance of distinguishing items reported pretax from those whose impact is reported after tax. When the after-tax effect is not reported, the analyst should estimate that effect by applying the marginal tax rate to pretax amounts.[18]

The pattern of normalized earnings is still erratic (duPont's business is, after all, cyclical), but there are significant differences in both level and trend:

- DuPont reported a loss in 1992; normalized income is positive each year.
- Normalized income exceeds reported income in three of the five years.
- The five-year total of normalized income was $8.5 billion, 178% higher than total reported income for the same time span.

Analytic Treatment of Nonrecurring Items

Our analysis thus far has removed nonrecurring items from normalized income in order to obtain the trend of operating earnings. However, if we ignore nonrecurring items, we permit companies to sweep their mistakes under the rug. The purpose of

---

[18]DuPont reported some of these items after tax, but the authors were unable to reconcile the disclosures. For that reason, we used pretax amounts and applied the U.S. marginal tax rate of 34%.

analysis is to understand, not to forgive. Nonrecurring items, in some cases, do change the wealth of the firm's stockholders.

The five-year total of duPont's nonrecurring items is $5.5 billion or about $1.1 billion per year. How should this amount be handled? One approach would allocate $1.1 billion to each year. The reasoning is that, although a given event may be nonrecurring, on average, some such event does occur and must be accounted for.

The better method is to examine major nonrecurring charges on an individual basis. Consider whether each item provides any information regarding:

1. Future cash flows
2. Future reported income
3. Valuation
4. Management behavior

Nonrecurring items with none of these should be ignored. One example is the $1,045 million negative impact from the adoption of SFAS 109 (income taxes). Adoption of the new standard had no cash impact (present or future) and no usefulness for either valuation or forecasting.

The adoption of SFAS 106 (postretirement benefits), however, cannot be ignored. Previously, these benefits were "off-balance-sheet." The accounting change recognized future cash outflows, and in evaluating future trends in income, this discontinuity must be noted.

Restructuring provisions require special scrutiny. Such provisions often contain both noncash write-offs and provisions for future expenditures. The former indicate that prior-year income was overstated; the latter increase future-year income (that will no longer include these costs) and forecast future cash flows. Repeated write-downs suggest that depreciation is inadequate and the firm's quality of earnings is low.

DuPont reported "nonrecurring" charges related to the recall of its fungicide Benlate in each year, 1991 to 1994. It appears that management was slow to recognize the problem and its financial consequences. This pattern is common as firms prefer to expense only the minimum amount required, rather than the full amount at once.

Capital gains are reported every year. It is not surprising that a firm the size of duPont sells some assets each year. Such sales should generally result in gains because of the historical cost bias: Declines in value (impairment) must be recognized when evident, whereas gains can be reported only when the property is sold. DuPont's use of accelerated depreciation methods for most fixed assets should result in gains when those assets are sold.[19] Recurring losses from the sale of operating assets would suggest that depreciation rates are too low.

Capitalized interest is not a nonrecurring item, but an example of how the income statement can be adjusted to a preferred accounting method. Similar adjustments can be made for capitalized software or intangibles, as discussed in Chapter 7.

Nonrecurring items often have implications for securities valuation. Some have a "one-time effect" as they are not expected to recur. Others are recurring in nature; as they effect the estimate of earning power, they can impact both:

• The base to which a price-earnings multiple is applied
• The expected earnings growth rate that determines the multiple itself

---

[19] As discussed in Chapter 8, duPont used accelerated methods for all but oil- and gas-related property. However, it switched to the straight-line method for assets acquired in 1995.

For duPont, the following nonrecurring items should be included in normalized income:

1. Restructuring provisions as adjustments to the firm's portfolio of businesses should be considered a normal operating activity.
2. Gains on asset sales that are clearly recurring in nature and offset some of the losses included in restructuring charges.

Over the five-year period, these two items equal a net expense of $1,731 million pretax, or $1,142 million after tax (if we assume a 34% tax rate). Averaged over five years, there is a $228 million per year reduction. The result is an estimate of earnings power appropriate for valuation purposes.

Earnings Normalization for Interfirm Comparisons

Our discussion thus far has been concerned with normalizing reported earnings in order to discern the operating trend. This process is essential when comparing two or more alternative investments. However, in this case, an additional step is required. Because firms may use alternative accounting methods for similar transactions, normalization must include adjustments for such differences as:

1. Inventory methods
2. Depreciation methods and assumptions
3. Benefit plan assumptions

When the firms in the comparison use different accounting systems (e.g., U.S. versus U.K. GAAP), these adjustments can be highly significant. Case 17-1 illustrates such analysis by comparing duPont with Dow Chemical and ICI, the latter being a U.K. company.

Income Normalization for Non-U.S. Firms

The normalization process applied to non-U.S. firms is complicated by differences in accounting methods. When the goal is comparison of firms from different reporting jurisdictions, an effort must be made to apply the same accounting principles to all firms. In international comparisons, major issues include:

1. Inventory methods, as LIFO is rare outside of the United States.
2. Depreciation; accelerated methods are more common outside of the United States, especially in tax conformity countries.
3. Goodwill amortization is absent when firms charge off acquisition goodwill immediately.
4. Extraordinary and other nonrecurring items; classification rules vary in different jurisdictions.

When data are available (e.g., from reconciliations to U.S. or IASC GAAP), adjustments to reported income should be made to improve comparability.

Normalization over the Economic Cycle

For cyclical firms, there is another complicating factor. The analyst must consider current operating earnings relative to the business cycle. This is true whether earnings are sensitive to the general economy or industry-specific cycles (property and casualty insurance is but one example). Given the varying length of business cycles, the analysis of cyclical firms should encompass a substantial time period—at least one full business cycle. Once these data are assembled, then earning power can be estimated using one of several methods.

One simplistic method is to average operating earnings over the entire cycle and use that average for valuation purposes. A slightly more sophisticated method uses average profitability ratios (such as gross margin or operating margin) or return ratios (return on equity) applied to current period sales or equity to estimate earning power based on the current level of operation.

A better approach is to create an earnings model of the firm based on the economic factors that drive the firm's profitability. For example, industrial production might be an independent variable for a manufacturer of cardboard boxes. Firm sales could then be forecast using regression analysis. That sales forecast, combined with an analysis of the firm's cost structure (see the discussion of fixed and variable costs in Chapter 4), could be used to forecast the firm's earnings.

For conglomerates or other multidivisional firms, analysis needs to be done separately for each segment. Segment data should be used to estimate the future sales and earnings of each line of business. Firm forecasts are arrived at by adding together the segment forecasts and adjusting for corporate overhead (such as debt). We return to these issues, discussed in Chapter 14, in Chapter 19.

Acquisition Effects

Acquisitions affect reported earnings as the results of the acquired firm are included. Both the earnings of the acquired firm and the accounting method used must be examined.

Under the pooling of interests method, the operating results of the two firms are combined retroactively and prospectively. Thus, previously reported earnings are restated. Depending on the profitability of the acquired firm, the growth rate of reported earnings will change in most cases. For example, a firm with a high growth rate (whose shares sell at a high price/earnings ratio) can merge with a low-growth firm (whose shares sell at a low price/earnings ratio). The result will be higher earnings but a lower growth rate.

When the purchase method is used to account for an acquisition, the results of the acquired firm are included only following the merger. Depending on the price paid, the means of payment (cash or stock), the earnings of the acquired firm, and the accounting adjustments required by the purchase method, the acquisition may either increase or dilute reported earnings per share. The trend of reported sales and earnings is always distorted.

Because the sales of the acquired firm are included only following the merger, reported sales and expenses of the acquiring firm appear to rise. Although *pro forma* statements (which are required disclosures) provide some basis of comparison, they are too limited to permit separation of internal growth from the effect of acquisitions. When there are many small acquisitions, it becomes impossible to segregate the impact of each one. Sometimes, segment data can help the analyst track significant acquisitions that are maintained as separate segments.

The earnings trend is also impacted, but not in any predictable fashion. The earnings of the acquired firm are included postmerger. However, these earnings are offset by the impact of purchase method adjustments and financing costs. If the acquisition is partly financed with common stock (directly, or indirectly by selling shares shortly thereafter), then the additional shares dilute reported EPS.

Exchange Rate Effects

When firms operate in foreign countries, changing exchange rates also affect reported earnings. Translation gains and losses may be included in reported income. More subtle, but no less real, is the impact of translating the operating results of foreign subsidiaries into the parent (reporting) currency. When foreign currencies appreciate, the sales and earnings of operations in those currencies translate into more dollars (or other reporting currency), increasing consolidated sales and earnings. This phenomenon is illustrated in Cases 15-1 (AFLAC) and 15-2 (IBM).

Effect of Accounting Changes

Last, but far from least, changes in accounting methods or estimates can significantly influence the trend of reported earnings. Frequently found examples of voluntary changes include:

- Inventory method
- Depreciation method or lives
- Assumptions used for benefit plans
- Accounting method for affiliates

Mandated accounting changes also have had significant effects on reported earnings in recent years. Examples include:

- Impairment
- Income taxes
- Postemployment benefits

DuPont's Accounting Changes. Effective January 1, 1995, duPont adopted the straight-line depreciation method for its nonpetroleum property, plant, and equipment. It had previously used the sum-of-the-years' digits and other accelerated methods for such property. As discussed in Chapter 8, this change increases reported earnings in 1995 and succeeding years.[20]

DuPont has frequently changed the discount rate used to account for pension plan benefits. As the effect of changes in the discount rate is indirect, the effect has not been systematic, although reported income for individual years has been affected. Changes in the assumed rate of return on pension assets have a more direct effect, but duPont has not altered that assumption in recent years.[21]

---

[20]DuPont's *1995 Annual Report* states:

> The effect of this change on net income will be dependent on the level of future capital spending; it did not have a material effect in 1995.

We note that total depreciation, depletion, and amortization was $2,722 million in 1995, 8.5% below the 1994 amount. The decline added approximately $.29 per share to earnings, but disclosures are inadequate to estimate how much of the decline was due to the accounting change.

[21]See Chapter 12 for a discussion of the income statement effects of assumption changes.

As already discussed, duPont adopted SFAS 106 (postretirement benefits) and SFAS 109 (income tax) in 1993; both transition amounts were negative. DuPont's impairment provisions were made prior to the effective date of SFAS 125. It is important to remember that the adoption of new accounting standards affects future income as well as net income in the transition year. For example:

1. Adoption of SFAS 106 resulted in the accrual of estimated benefits earned through the adoption date. Postretirement benefit expense is no longer equal to benefits paid. For mature companies with growing benefit payments, the new standard increases future income by reducing future expense. Plan changes also affect reported postretirement benefit expense. These effects for duPont are illustrated in Chapter 12.

2. As discussed in Chapter 9, SFAS 109 changed the measurement of income tax expense. Changes in tax rates, for example, directly impact reported income.

3. Impairment and other restructuring provisions increase future income because they:

   • Accrue future outflows for such items as employee severance and leases.

   • Reduce the carrying amount of assets, reducing future depreciation expense.

4. DuPont's 1995 depreciation decline reflects prior-year restructuring provisions as well as the accounting change.

Quality of Earnings

The term quality of earnings usually refers to the degree of conservatism in a firm's reported earnings. Indicators of high earnings quality include:

1. Conservative revenue recognition methods
2. Use of LIFO inventory accounting (if we assume rising prices)
3. Bad-debt reserves that are high relative to receivables and past credit losses
4. Use of accelerated depreciation methods and short lives
5. Rapid write-off of acquisition goodwill and other intangibles
6. Minimal capitalization of interest and overhead
7. Minimal capitalization of computer software costs
8. Expensing of start-up costs of new operations
9. Use of the completed contract method of accounting
10. Conservative assumptions used for employee benefit plans
11. Adequate provisions for lawsuits and other loss contingencies
12. Minimal use of off-balance-sheet financing techniques
13. Absence of nonrecurring gains
14. Absence of noncash earnings
15. Clear and adequate disclosures

These issues were discussed in earlier chapters. Indicators listed tend to result in the underreporting of income through a combination of delayed recognition of revenues and accelerated recognition of expenses and losses.

Why is the quality of earnings important?

One reason is that companies with high earnings quality are considered less risky because these firms have "banked" earnings using conservative accounting policies.[22] Such firms frequently are risk averse in other ways, in their financial structures and business plans, for example. High-quality earnings should be accorded a higher price/earnings multiple (all other things being equal) than low-quality earnings. The higher multiple reflects the lower risk as well as the understatement of reported income.

Alternatively, firms with different degrees of earnings quality can be compared by making adjustments to reported earnings so that the earnings of all firms are based on the same accounting principles and estimates. Techniques for making such adjustments appear throughout the book.

It should be noted that the term earnings quality is sometimes used to denote the predictability of earnings. Firms with predictable earnings growth (such as drug and consumer product firms) are sometimes said to have "high-quality" earnings. This usage is, of course, quite different; in some cases, predictability is the result of income manipulation, creating low-quality earnings by our definition. Analysts should be careful to determine which meaning of the term "quality of earnings" is intended when it is used.

In our examination of duPont's quality of earnings, we consider the following issues:

1. DuPont used the more conservative LIFO method for 88% of 1994 inventories (Note 12). The LIFO liquidation in 1993, however, reduced the quality of earnings in that year.

2. The allowance for bad debts (Note 11) equals approximately 2% of trade receivables. The 1994 decline in that allowance despite an increase in gross receivables may reflect a stronger economy (reducing the likelihood of customer default). Changes in that allowance are a frequent "income management" tool, however, and should also be monitored.

3. With the 1995 change, duPont now uses straight-line depreciation for all fixed assets. Depreciation for tax purposes has been considerably higher than for reporting purposes. (This can be seen from the large deferred tax liability related to depreciation revealed in Note 7.) The change to straight-line depreciation moves duPont's policy to the "average" category as firms using accelerated methods (that reduce reported income) are considered to have high earnings quality.

4. Acquisitions have been minimal, with little impact on reported growth.

5. Note 4 reports significant capitalized interest, requiring adjustment when computing normalized earnings.

6. Pension plan assumptions are average. Both pension and postretirement benefit plans are overfunded and that overfunding is not fully recognized on the balance sheet. The current cost balance sheet in Exhibit 17-1 shows significant adjustments for these plans.

---

[22]It has been suggested that firms with conservative accounting methods can increase reported income by changing to less conservative methods. Only when the firm has exhausted this source must it turn to accounting chicanery.

7. DuPont uses off-balance-sheet financing techniques. Exhibit 17-1 adjusts for:
   - Operating leases with an estimated present value of $980 million.
   - Affiliated companies accounted for using the equity method; duPont's proportionate share of the assets and liabilities of the affiliates approximates $4 billion.

8. There is no evidence of revenue recognition problems.

9. The disclosures regarding derivatives and risk management (see Note 27 and Chapter 16) are enlightening; few other companies provide foreign currency exposure data.

10. Segment disclosures (see Notes 29 and 30, and Chapter 13) are appropriate and provide slightly more detail than required by SFAS 14.

11. DuPont's disclosures are generally informative. Their shortcomings are typical of large companies:
    - Overly broad aggregation; duPont reports nearly $3 billion of liabilities that are characterized as "miscellaneous."
    - Insufficient precision; our discussion of normalization indicates that it is difficult to match pretax data in the financial statements with after-tax data in the management discussion and analysis.

Our conclusion is that duPont has, on balance, earnings quality that is above average for large American public companies. The 1995 change in depreciation method is, however, a step down.

Comprehensive Income

In Chapter 2, we discussed the concept of comprehensive income and the FASB exposure draft that would require its inclusion in financial statements. In this section, we consider the application of that concept to duPont.

As defined by current GAAP, comprehensive income for duPont would be little different from reported net income. DuPont does not report any of the following elements of comprehensive income:

- Cumulative translation adjustment
- Unrealized gain or loss on marketable securities
- Minimum pension liability

As discussed in Chapter 16, duPont does use derivative instruments for hedging purposes, generating gains and losses that would be included in comprehensive income under the FASB's proposed standard.

We see comprehensive income, however, in broader terms, encompassing all changes in current cost net worth other than transactions with shareholders. Under this definition, duPont has a number of qualifying elements, as seen in Exhibit 17-1:

1. LIFO reserve on inventory
2. Adjustment of oil and gas properties to discounted present value
3. Funded status of employee benefit plans
4. Adjustment of debt and preferred shares to fair value

By examining the changes in these items during 1994, we can compute a more meaningful measure of comprehensive income:

	1993	1994	Change
LIFO reserve	$ 766	$ 819	$ 53
Adjustment of oil and gas properties	(765)	1,657	2,422
Funded status of employee pension plans	1,055	1,920	865
Funded status of OPEB plans	(6,169)	(4,068)	2,101
Adjustment of debt	(1,073)	(232)	841
Adjustment of preferred shares	68	82	14
Totals	$(6,118)	$ 178	$6,296

In total, these valuation items increased duPont's current cost equity by nearly $6.3 billion in 1994. We use these computations to prepare a statement of current cost comprehensive income for 1994 ($ in millions):

Net income	$2,727
Less: preferred dividends	(10)
Valuation changes	6,296
1994 current cost comprehensive income	$9,013
Comprehensive income per common share	$13.25
Net income per share	$4.00

DuPont's income, as measured using the comprehensive income concept, was nearly three times reported net income for 1994. Although this income measure is far more volatile than reported net income, it captures economic changes that are excluded from income under current GAAP.

ANALYSIS OF CASH FLOW

The adjusted balance sheet reports the current or market value of the resources that are available for firm operations and generate cash flows. We now turn to an analysis of cash flows to evaluate duPont's ability to service debt and generate cash flows for investment or return of capital to the equityholders.

The analysis is based on Chapter 3, where we discuss the use of cash flow analysis to develop insights into a firm's financial position and performance. In other chapters, we show the cash flow implications of different reporting methods. We focus on both the level and trends in cash flow components. Our primary objectives are to:

1. Determine the firm's ability to generate cash flows to meet operating needs.
2. Evaluate the role of different sources of financing for current operations and growth.

Another goal of our analysis is to illustrate the extent to which cash flow classifications are affected by reporting choices. Examples include:

- Capitalization of fixed assets, such as the cost of finding natural resources or developing new products (Chapter 7)
- Exclusion of "off-balance-sheet" obligations from the firm's financial statements (Chapter 11)
- Accounting methods applied to investments in affiliates (Chapter 13)
- Accounting methods used for acquisitions (Chapter 14)

Adjustment for these effects is seldom easy. The first (and most important) step is to recognize that distortion is present. In many cases, the analyst may judge that the degree of distortion is too small to warrant adjustment. In other cases (e.g., accounting for affiliates), analytical techniques (proportionate consolidation) permit approximate adjustment.

As discussed in Chapter 3, the classification of cash flows among operating, investing, and financing activities is the starting point for cash flow analysis. Exhibit 17-4 shows these amounts, obtained from duPont's cash flow statement.

The net change in cash is essentially meaningless; a firm can sell assets or incur liabilities to improve its cash position at the end of an accounting period (often called "window dressing"). What is important is the trend in the components of cash flow and the relationship among them.

Analysis of Cash Flow Components

Cash flow from operations (CFO) reports the cash flows generated by the firm's operating activities. Although duPont's CFO is positive every year and increased over the 1990 to 1994 time period, it declined in three of the five years. There is little correlation with reported net income (before extraordinary items and the effect of accounting changes), which declined each year from 1990 to 1993 and then rose sharply in 1994 (when CFO declined).

Exhibit 17-4 recasts the cash flow statement to a format that provides better insight into cash from operations by:

1. Reclassifying interest paid from CFO to cash from financing (CFF)
2. Segregating capital expenditures from other investment cash flows
3. Estimating cash flows related to nonrecurring items
4. Reporting free cash flow

We discuss each of these issues in turn.

Reclassification of Interest Paid. In Chapter 3, we state that interest paid should be included in CFF rather than CFO because:

1. The cash effects of return on investment should be aggregated with those of return of investment.
2. Excluding interest paid from CFO makes that amount comparable among firms with different degrees of financial leverage.

EXHIBIT 17-4. E. I. DUPONT DENEMOURS
Statement of Cash Flows, 1990 to 1994 ($ in millions)

	1990	1991	1992	1993	1994	Total
As Reported						
Cash and equivalents, January 1	$ 692	$ 611	$ 468	$ 1,640	$ 1,109	
Cash and equivalents, December 31	611	468	1,640	1,109	856	
Change in cash and equivalents	$ (81)	$ (143)	$ 1,172	$ (531)	$ (253)	$ 164
Cash from operations (CFO)	$ 5,146	$ 5,461	$ 4,388	$ 5,380	$ 5,664	$ 26,039
Cash from investment (CFI)	(5,106)	(3,945)	(4,553)	(3,078)	(3,133)	(19,815)
Cash from financing (CFF)	(200)	(1,638)	1,479	(2,744)	(2,878)	(5,981)
Effect of exchange rate changes	79	(21)	(142)	(89)	94	(79)
Change in cash and equivalents	$ (81)	$ (143)	$ 1,172	$ (531)	$ (253)	$ 164
Free cash flow*	$ 40	$ 1,516	$ (165)	$ 2,302	$ 2,531	$ 6,224
Dividends paid	(1,106)	(1,137)	(1,182)	(1,201)	(1,247)	(5,873)
Free cash flow after dividends	$(1,066)	$ 379	$(1,347)	$ 1,101	$ 1,284	$ 351
Adjustments						
Interest paid†	$ 875	$ 909	$ 754	$ 808	$ 741	$ 4,087
Less: income tax offset‡	(306)	(318)	(264)	(283)	(259)	(1,430)
After-tax interest paid	$ 569	$ 591	$ 490	$ 525	$ 482	$ 2,657
Capital expenditures§	$ 5,383	$ 5,065	$ 4,448	$ 3,621	$ 3,050	$ 21,567
After Adjustment						
CFO**	$ 5,715	$ 6,052	$ 4,878	$ 5,905	$ 6,146	$ 28,696
CFI	(5,106)	(3,945)	(4,553)	(3,078)	(3,133)	$(19,815)
CFF††	(769)	(2,229)	989	(3,269)	(3,360)	$ (8,638)
Effect of exchange rate changes	79	(21)	(142)	(89)	94	$ (79)
Change in cash and equivalents	$ (81)	$ (143)	$ 1,172	$ (531)	$ (253)	$ 164
Free cash flow‡‡	$ 332	$ 987	$ 430	$ 2,284	$ 3,096	$ 7,129
Dividends paid	(1,106)	(1,137)	(1,182)	(1,201)	(1,247)	(5,873)
Free cash flow after dividends	$ (774)	$ (150)	$ (752)	$ 1,083	$ 1,849	$ 1,256

*Cash from operations less cash from investment.
†Interest paid plus amount capitalized.
‡35% of interest paid.
§From statement of cash flows.
**Reported CFO plus after-tax interest.
††Reported CFF minus after-tax interest.
‡‡Adjusted CFO less capital expenditures.

The first adjustment in Exhibit 17-4 estimates after-tax interest paid by applying duPont's marginal income tax rate (assumed to be the U.S. statutory rate) to interest paid. Although duPont's disclosure (Note 4) is unclear, we believe that the reported amount of interest paid is *net* of interest capitalized, which we have added back.

This adjustment increases aggregate CFO (5-year total) by more than $2.6 billion. As interest paid is relatively stable, its exclusion does not materially change the trend of CFO; for firms with growing financing costs, the trend would be affected.

Interest received should, under similar reasoning, be reclassified from CFO to CFI. We have not done so because the amount is small ($111 million interest income in 1994).[23]

Segregation of Capital Expenditures. Investing cash flow contains three major components that deserve separate analysis:

1. Marketable securities are investments that do not meet the "cash equivalent" test of SFAS 95. For many firms, such investments also serve as a form of liquidity; changes reflect investment decisions rather than capital requirements.

2. DuPont's acquisition activity has been modest. Segregating expenditures for acquisitions and investments in affiliates, which are presumably optional, is useful when assessing capital requirements. Similarly, proceeds from asset sales (significant for duPont) reflect decisions to eliminate some operating activities in order to devote resources to others.

3. Purchases of property and equipment represent duPont's capital expenditures and are a principal factor in the estimation of free cash flow. Capital expenditures declined steadily, from $5.4 billion in 1990 to $3.0 billion in 1994. DuPont's 1994 MD&A states that

> lower capital expenditures in recent years result from a more focused and rigorous approach to capital spending, combined with the implementation of engineering and design practices that have significantly improved capital productivity.

The real question is whether this decline represents a lack of investment opportunities that meet the firm's required return, or the ability to achieve the same increase in productive capacity with lower capital investment.

An answer to this question requires information about the allocation of capital spending between replacement and growth; duPont provides no data on this issue. The MD&A does state that 1995 capital expenditures are expected to increase to $3.6 billion.[24]

Estimating Nonrecurring Cash Flows. CFO can be distorted by unusual items. Examples include:

1. Changes in normal seasonal patterns. For example, a royalty payment normally received in late December might be received early in January. As a result,

---

[23]There is no information regarding interest received on a cash basis. Lacking other evidence, we would assume that cash received equals the income statement amount.

[24]In fact, 1995 capital expenditures were $3.24 billion, below the management forecast. Analysts should always discuss such discrepancies with management to ascertain the factors that caused them and the implications for future sales and earnings.

current-year CFO would be understated, whereas following-year CFO is over-stated.

2. Sales of receivables. As shown in Chapter 11, changes in the amount of receivables sold (or securitized) distort the pattern of CFO.

3. Nonrecurring cash flows, such as those related to lawsuits.

Nonrecurring income statement items often have no impact on CFO, because either they have no cash flow effect at all (most accounting changes and asset write-downs) or their cash effect is not included in CFO (gains and losses on asset sales).

Reviewing duPont's nonrecurring items in Exhibit 17-3, we see that most had no effect on CFO. The exceptions are:

- Restructuring provisions
- Fungicide recall

Restructuring provisions contain both cash and noncash components. Prior to 1994, duPont's disclosures of cash flow effects were poor. Note 6 in 1994 reports that the 1993 restructuring charge of $1,621 million included $665 of employee separation costs. It appears that the remainder was noncash asset write-downs. $420 million was expended during 1993 and 1994, with $200 million remaining to be paid ($45 million of the provision was reversed during 1994).

These data suggest that CFO was reduced by a total of $420 million during 1993 and 1994 combined. Should we treat these payments as "nonrecurring" cash outflows? Our view is that employee separations are neither unusual nor infrequent and no adjustment is required.

The fungicide recall, on the other hand, should be considered nonrecurring. Du-Pont, however, does not disclose either cash payments or the liability balance at each year-end. It is possible that no cash outflows have been made. If payment data were available, reported CFO should be adjusted by adding back the actual cash outflows.

As duPont provides no other data regarding cash flows that would be considered nonrecurring, there is no adjustment to reported CFO other than for interest paid.

Free Cash Flow

Although widely used in the investment world, free cash flow (FCF) has no uniform definition. With the conventional definition of free cash flow (reported CFO less cash from investment used), duPont's free cash flow totaled $6.2 billion over the 1990 to 1994 period and was positive each year except 1992. The trend is clearly upward. Over the entire period, FCF exceeded dividends paid by only $351 million, but that excess was more than $1 billion in both 1993 and 1994.

As discussed in Chapter 3, we believe that the most useful definition for financial analysis is CFO before interest less capital expenditures. That definition is used in Exhibit 17-4. Adjusted (to that definition) FCF aggregated $7.1 billion over the 1990 to 1994 period, 14.5% higher than conventional FCF. That increase mainly reflects the reclassification of interest paid to cash from financing. The reclassification effect was partly offset, however, by subtracting capital expenditures rather than CFI; as previously discussed, CFI includes proceeds from fixed asset sales and changes in long-term investments.

Adjusted FCF exceeded dividends paid by $1.25 billion over the 1990 to 1994 period. The individual year data show that FCF was insufficient to cover dividends in

1990 to 1992, but grew sharply in 1993 and 1994. This excess cash flow permitted duPont to reduce debt by $1.6 billion and $2.0 billion in 1993 and 1994, respectively (using cash flow statement data). As stockholders' equity rose by more than $1 billion over the same two-year period, duPont's reported debt-to-equity ratio declined sharply.[25]

The import of these changes becomes apparent when we look at duPont's 1995 cash flow statement, which is abstracted below:

Reported CFO	$6,761 million
Add: After-tax interest paid	558
Equals: Adjusted CFO	$ 7,319
Less capital expenditures	(3,240)
Equals: Adjusted FCF	$ 4,079
Less: Dividends paid	(1,196)
Equals: Adjusted FCF after dividends	$ 2,883

This excess, added to the corresponding amounts from 1993 and 1994, represents more than $5.8 billion of discretionary cash flow. In 1993 and 1994, duPont used this surplus cash to reduce debt. In 1995, however, the company paid $8.35 billion cash to re-purchase shares held by Seagram. Shares issued during 1995 generated cash of $1.8 billion, reducing the net cash requirement to $6.54 billion. Total (reported) debt rose $4.17 billion during 1995.

The 1995 stock repurchase illustrates the value of FCF analysis. Excess FCF gives a firm the flexibility to take financial actions that it perceives to be beneficial: It can reduce debt, repurchase shares, or make acquisitions. In the case of duPont, its generation of excess FCF over the 1993 to 1995 period allowed it to purchase the shares held by Seagram.[26]

International Cash Flow Comparisons

Because of accounting differences that limit the comparability of income statements, many analysts focus on cash flows. However, the international comparison of cash flows is also fraught with danger, as noncomparability results from:

1. Consolidation differences that may exclude some operating affiliates.
2. Different definitions of cash from operations. Although the IASC and U.S. definitions are the same, those of other GAAPs differ. In the United Kingdom, for example, interest paid and received is excluded from CFO. Some firms still report funds from operations, which differs considerably from CFO. Reclassification adjustments or use of the transactional analysis method (see Chapter 3) can produce more comparable cash flow statements.
3. Some accounting principle differences do affect reported CFO. Methods that result in more capitalization (interest and research costs are two examples)

---

[25] As shown in Exhibit 17-2, adjusted debt declined by $2.2 billion in 1994, helped by rising interest rates that reduced the market value of debt; duPont's debt-to-equity ratio fell to 0.58 at December 31, 1994 from 1.13 one year earlier.

[26] Whether the share purchase was the best use of this excess liquidity is an important question, but one that is beyond the scope of this text.

increase reported CFO. Lease accounting, which differs from GAAP to GAAP, also changes CFO.

Because of these factors, valid cross-border cash flow comparisons depend on adjustments that restore comparability.

FCF calculations may also be affected by these problems. When FCF is defined as CFO (properly adjusted) less *all* capitalized operating assets, it should be reasonably comparable.

ADJUSTED FINANCIAL RATIOS

The current cost balance sheet shown in Exhibit 17-1 should be used to compute financial ratios that incorporate these better measures of resources (assets) and obligations (liabilities). Exhibit 17-5 shows such computations for some key ratios, using definitions from Chapter 4.

Activity (turnover) ratios are reduced because of the valuation adjustments and the inclusion of off-balance-sheet assets, both of which increase reported assets. Reported sales increase by duPont's share of affiliate sales, offsetting much of the balance sheet effect. Given the firm-to-firm differences in both valuation effects and the use of off-balance-sheet activities, activity ratios using adjusted data provide a better measure of the efficiency with which assets are used. DuPont's total asset turnover declines from 1.06 to 1.04 after adjustment. The inventory turnover ratio decline is greater, reflecting duPont's large LIFO reserve.[27]

Adjusted liquidity ratios may also change, but in less predictable fashion. As both current assets and current liabilities are affected by valuation and off-balance-sheet adjustments, we cannot predict the net result. DuPont's 1994 current ratio is unchanged by these adjustments.

Solvency ratios were recomputed in Exhibit 17-2. For 1994, balance sheet adjustments leave the debt-to-equity ratio unchanged as the highly positive valuation adjustments offset the inclusion of off-balance-sheet liabilities. 1993 solvency ratios, however, are significantly lower after adjustment.

There are two important implications of the differential effects of balance sheet adjustments in 1993 and 1994. First, current cost based data are more volatile than reported data, as the latter ignore many valuation changes. This does not mean that analysts should avoid using adjusted data; such data tell us about real economic effects. It does mean that single-year valuation effects should be used with caution; such effects are best evaluated over longer time periods.

The second implication is that year-to-year comparisons can look very different when adjusted data are used. DuPont's debt-to-total capital ratio declined 18% in 1994 (from 0.45 to 0.37) using reported data. The adjusted ratio fell by 30% (from 0.53 to 0.37). Both valuation changes and changes in off-balance-sheet activities can affect comparisons.

Profitability ratios are also very different after adjustment. Exhibit 17-5 shows pretax return-on-assets, pretax return-on-total-capital, and after-tax return on equity. These ratios decline after adjustment because the denominators are higher, reflecting

---

[27]We have made no adjustment for duPont's affiliates due to lack of data regarding affiliate COGS and inventory methods. When such data are available, the inventory turnover ratio should be adjusted.

EXHIBIT 17-5. E. I. DUPONT DENEMOURS
Adjusted Financial Ratios, Year Ended December 31, 1994 (all data in $ millions)

	Reported	Adjusted
Activity		
Inventory turnover	5.64	4.69
Number of days	65	78
Total asset turnover	1.06	1.04
Liquidity		
Current ratio	1.47	1.47
Solvency		
Debt-to-equity	0.59	0.58
Debt-to-total-capital	0.37	0.37
Profitability		
Return on assets	13.36%	11.74%
Return-on-total-capital	24.07	18.30
Return-on-equity	36.44	29.03

Note: Adjusted ratios based on adjusted data not shown. See text discussion.

both valuation adjustments and the inclusion of off-balance-sheet debt. The numerators are unchanged.[28]

International Ratio Comparisons

As ratios are constructed from reported financial data, ratio comparability depends on comparable underlying data. It should be evident from discussions throughout the chapter that ratios constructed from unadjusted financial data are unlikely to be useful measures of activity, liquidity, solvency, and profitability. Only when balance sheet, income statement, and cash flow data are adjusted for differences in accounting and reporting methods will the resultant ratios be comparable.

SUMMARY

Throughout the text, we emphasize the need to adjust reported financial data for the effects of accounting choice. In this chapter, we have brought all these adjustments together to produce a set of adjusted financial statements and ratios. In Case 17-1, we extend this analysis to a comparison of duPont with Dow and ICI.

The rationale for this adjustment process is the production of data that are useful for investment and credit decisions, the subject matter of the next two chapters.

[28]The numerators of the pretax return ratios, which use EBIT, should be increased by duPont's share of the excess of affiliate EBIT over duPont's equity in net income. These data are not provided in Note 14.

CASE **17-1**

Comparison of Dow and ICI with DuPont

Chapter 17 uses the 1994 financial statements of duPont (Appendix A) to illustrate the adjustments and analysis techniques discussed. The 1994 financial statements of U.S.-based Dow Chemical (Dow), and U.K.-based Imperial Chemical Industries (ICI), are contained in Appendices B and C, respectively. These financial statements and Exhibits 17-1 through 17-5 should be used to answer the following questions.

1. Prepare current cost balance sheets for Dow and ICI as of December 31, 1994, following the format of Exhibit 17-1. List the adjustments made and justify each.

2. Prepare capitalization tables for Dow and ICI, following the format of Exhibit 17-2, as of December 31, 1994, using both reported and adjusted data.

3. (a) Calculate the following ratios as of December 31, 1994, based on both reported and current cost data:
   - Book value per share
   - Debt-to-equity
   - Debt-to-total capital

   (b) Discuss the effect of the current cost adjustments on the:
      (i) December 31, 1994 book value per share of Dow and ICI.
      (ii) Relative price-to-book value ratios of duPont, Dow, and ICI at December 31, 1994. The share prices on that date were $56.125, $67.25, and £7.49, respectively.
      (iii) Relative debt-to-equity ratios of Dow and ICI at December 31, 1994.

   (c) Discuss how the current cost balance sheets alter the reported financial leverage of Dow and ICI relative to duPont.

   (d) Describe the accounting policy differences that significantly affect the comparison of reported book value per share and leverage for duPont, Dow, and ICI. Which of these differences remain in the current cost balance sheets?

4. (a) Prepare a table of normalized net income for Dow and ICI for the two years ended December 31, 1994, following the format of Exhibit 17-3.

   (b) Compute the price-earnings ratios for duPont, Dow, and ICI at December 31, 1994, using:
      (i) Reported net income
      (ii) Net income before nonrecurring items
      (iii) Earnings power

   (c) Discuss the limitations of the normalization process as applied to these three companies.

   (d) Discuss the effect of the Zeneca demerger (spinoff) on the:
      (i) Trend of ICI's sales and net income
      (ii) Earnings power of the firm

5. (a) Compute 1993 and 1994 free cash flow for Dow and ICI, using the format of Exhibit 17-4.

   (b) Discuss the insights obtained from an analysis of the cash flow statements of these two firms.

6. **(a)** Compute *each* of the following ratios for Dow and ICI, using *both* reported and adjusted 1994 data, following the format of Exhibit 17-5:

   (i) Inventory turnover

   (ii) Total asset turnover

   (iii) Current ratio

   (iv) Return on assets

   (v) Return on total capital

   (vi) Return on equity

   (b) For each ratio computed in part (a):

   (i) Compare reported versus adjusted ratios for each firm.

   (ii) Compare the corresponding ratios between firms, both reported and adjusted.

   (iii) Discuss the benefits of using adjusted data, given your answers to (i) and (ii).

7. [Optional] ICI presents a Statement of Value Added as part of its financial statements. Discuss the usefulness of that statement and any insights it provides regarding that firm's profitability and changes in profitability in 1994 versus 1993.

CASE 17-2. ALCOA

Analysis of Current Cost Balance Sheet and Normalized Income

Alcoa is the world's leading producer of aluminum, operating in 28 countries. Exhibits 17C-1 through 17C-3 are extracted from Alcoa's *1995 Annual Report*. The objectives of this case are to:

- Adjust Alcoa's reported balance sheet to currrent cost.
- Normalize reported income.

Use these financial statement data to answer the following questions.

1. Prepare a current cost balance sheet for Alcoa at December 31, 1995 using Exhibits 17C-1 and 17C-2. Justify each adjustment.

2. **(a)** Compute the following ratios for Alcoa using *both* reported and current cost data:

   (i) Book value per share

   (ii) Debt-to-equity

   (b) Compute the price-to-book-value ratio for Alcoa on December 31, 1995 using both stated and current cost book value per share. *Note:* The price of Alcoa shares on that date was $52 7/8.

3. **(a)** Prepare a normalized income statement for Alcoa for the five years ended December 31, 1995, following the format of Exhibit 17-3. Justify each adjustment.

   (b) Compute Alcoa's price-earnings ratio at December 31, 1995 based on:

   (i) 1995 net income per share

   (ii) Normalized 1995 net income per share

   (iii) Average net income per share for the five-year period

   (c) Discuss the advantages and disadvantages of using each price-earnings ratio computed in part (b) to value Alcoa shares.

   (d) Compute Alcoa's return on total capital and return on equity for 1995 using the current cost balance sheet prepared in question 2 and *each* income measure from

EXHIBIT 17C-1. ALCOA
Condensed Balance Sheet at December 31, 1995 ($ in millions)

Assets		Liabilities	
Cash and equivalents	$ 1,055.6	Short-term debt	$ 693.2
Short-term investments	6.8	Income and other taxes	304.7
Customer receivables	1,546.3	Other current liabilities	1,654.3
Inventories	1,418.4	Total current liabilities	$ 2,652.2
Deferred income tax	244.8		
Other current liabilities	469.8	Long-term debt	1,215.5
Total current liabilities	$ 4,741.7	Postretirement benefits	1,827.3
		Deferred hedging gains	466.3
Property (net)	$ 6,929.7	Other liabilities	1,119.4
Intangibles	600.0	Deferred income tax	308.6
Deferred income tax	493.6	**Total Liabilities**	$ 7,589.3
Other assets	878.4		
Total Assets	$13,643.4	Minority interest	1,609.4
		Preferred stock	55.8
		Common stock	816.0
		Translation adjustment	(79.0)
		Retained earnings	3,800.1
		Minimum pension liability	(9.3)
		Treasury stock	(138.9)
		Total Equity	$ 6,054.1
		Total Liabilities and Equity	$13,643.4

Source: Adapted from Alcoa, *1995 Annual Report.*

part (b). *Note:* Since 1994 footnote data are not provided, compute returns on ending balances.

(e) Discuss which return measure computed in part (d) is most useful for comparing Alcoa's performance with that of other firms.

4. Exhibit 17C-3 reports the following data for each year:
   • Alcoa's average realized price per pound for aluminum ingot
   • Average U.S. market price per pound for aluminum ingot

   Discuss the significance of these data for the analysis of Alcoa. Your answer should consider *both* Alcoa's sensitivity to changes in market prices and the effects of price changes on reported income.

EXHIBIT 17C-2. ALCOA
Footnote Data

In December 1994, Alcoa recorded a gain of $400.2 ($300.2 after tax) from the acquisition by Western Mining Corporation Holdings Limited (WMC), located in Melbourne, Australia, of a 40% interest in Alcoa's worldwide bauxite, alumina and inorganic chemicals businesses.

Approximately 50% of total inventories at December 31, 1995 were valued on a LIFO basis. If valued on an average cost basis, total inventories would have been $802.1 and $691.9 higher at the end of 1995 and 1994, respectively.

F. Properties, Plants and Equipment, at Cost

December 31	1995	1994
Land and land rights, including mines	$ 231.3	$ 238.0
Structures	3,941.7	3,860.0
Machinery and equipment	10,452.1	10,003.7
	14,625.1	14,101.7
Less, accumulated depreciation and depletion	8,285.1	7,812.9
	6,340.0	6,288.8
Construction work in progress	589.7	400.6
	$ 6,929.7	$ 6,689.4

G. Other Assets

December 31	1995	1994
Investments, principally equity investments	$ 397.3	$ 355.9
Intangibles, net of accumulated amortization of $253.3 in 1995 and $208.5 in 1994	600.0	396.6
Noncurrent receivables	94.5	67.6
Deferred income taxes	493.6	364.6
Deferred charges and other	386.6	325.9
	$1,972.0	$1,510.6

J. Lease Expense

Certain equipment, warehousing and office space, and oceangoing vessels are under operating lease agreements. Total expense for all leases was $71.9 in 1995, $71.6 in 1994 and $73.7 in 1993. Under long-term operating leases, minimum annual rentals are $46.7 in 1996, $40.5 in 1997, $27.7 in 1998, $22.4 in 1999, $24.9 in 2000, and a total of $39.6 for 2001 and thereafter.

Q. Financial Instruments

The carrying values and fair values of Alcoa's financial instruments at December 31 follow.

	1995		1994	
	Carrying value	Fair value	Carrying value	Fair value
Cash and cash equivalents	$1,055.6	$1,055.6	$ 619.2	$ 619.2
Short-term investments .	6.8	6.8	5.5	5.5
Noncurrent receivables . .	94.5	94.5	67.6	67.6
Short-term debt	693.2	693.2	415.9	415.9
Long-term debt	1,215.5	1,263.3	1,029.8	1,002.3

R. Income Taxes

The components of net deferred tax assets and liabilities follow.

	1995		1994	
December 31	Deferred tax assets	Deferred tax liabilities	Deferred tax assets	Deferred tax liabilities
Depreciation	–	$ 950.6	–	$ 938.8
Employee benefits	$ 838.8	–	$ 822.0	–
Loss provisions	212.0	–	243.9	–
Deferred income	244.0	56.4	112.4	48.4
Tax loss carryforwards . .	113.7	–	212.9	–
Tax credit carryforwards	38.7	–	86.4	–
Other	86.7	20.8	56.0	18.2
	1,533.9	1,027.8	1,533.6	1,005.4
Valuation allowance	(112.1)	–	(170.0)	–
	$1,421.8	$1,027.8	$1,363.6	$1,005.4

EXHIBIT 17C-2 (continued)

T. Postretirement Benefits

The status of the pension plans follows.

December 31	Assets exceed accumulated benefit obligation		Accumulated benefit obligation exceeds assets	
	1995	1994	1995	1994
Plan assets, primarily stocks and bonds at market	$1,959.4	$3,337.7	$1,937.0	$ 231.4
Present value of obligation:				
Vested	1,604.3	2,721.2	1,957.4	335.2
Nonvested	131.7	237.3	155.9	4.9
Accumulated benefit obligation	1,736.0	2,958.5	2,113.3	340.1
Effect of assumed salary increases	72.1	236.1	248.3	32.9
Projected benefit obligation	$1,808.1	$3,194.6	$2,361.6	$ 373.0
Plan assets greater (less than) projected benefit obligation	$ 151.3	$ 143.1	$ (424.6)	$(141.6)
Unrecognized:				
Transition (assets) obligations	(32.7)	21.8	45.3	(8.9)
Prior service costs	19.9	45.9	28.2	32.2
Actuarial (gains) losses, net	(184.9)	(415.9)	36.1	34.0
Minimum liability adjustment	–	–	(38.8)	(23.2)
Accrued pension cost	$ (46.4)	$ (205.1)	$ (353.8)	$(107.5)

Assumptions used to determine plan liabilities and expenses follow.

December 31	1995	1994	1993
Settlement discount rate	7.0%	8.25%	6.75%
Long-term rate for compensation increases	5.0	5.5	5.5
Long-term rate of return on plan assets	9.0	9.0	9.0

The status of the postretirement benefit plans was:

December 31	1995	1994
Retirees	$1,034.0	$1,040.3
Fully eligible active plan participants	136.7	112.5
Other active participants	330.5	307.8
Accumulated postretirement benefit obligation (APBO)	1,501.2	1,460.6
Plan assets, primarily stocks and bonds at market	64.4	53.3
APBO in excess of plan assets	1,436.8	1,407.3
Unrecognized net:		
Reduction in prior service costs	374.3	420.1
Actuarial gains	109.6	103.3
Accrued postretirement benefit liability	$1,920.7	$1,930.7

For measuring the liability and expense, a 9.5% annual rate of increase in the per capita claims cost was assumed for 1996, declining gradually to 5.5% by the year 2003 and thereafter. Other assumptions used to measure the liability and expense follow.

December 31	1995	1994	1993
Settlement discount rate	7.0%	8.25%	6.75%
Long-term rate for compensation increases	5.0	5.5	5.5
Long-term rate of return on plan assets	9.0	9.0	9.0

For 1995 a 1% increase in the trend rate for health care costs would have increased the APBO by 8% and service and interest costs by 9%.

Source: Alcoa, *1995 Annual Report.*

EXHIBIT 17C-3. ALCOA
Summary of Financial and Other Data ($ in millions, except share amounts)

	For the year ended December 31	1995
Operating Results	Sales and operating revenues	$12,499.7
	Other income (loss)	155.2
	Cost of goods sold and operating expenses	9,360.1
	Selling, general administrative and other expenses	707.6
	Research and development expenses	141.3
	Depreciation and depletion	712.9
	Interest expense	119.8
	Taxes on income	445.9
	Other taxes	126.8
	Special items—(income) expense	16.2
	Income from operations	1,024.3
	Minority interests	(233.8)
	Extraordinary gains (losses) and accounting changes*	–
	Net income (loss)	790.5
	Alcoa's average realized price per pound for aluminum ingot	.81
	Average U.S. market price per pound for aluminum ingot (*Metals Week*)	.86
Dividends Declared	Preferred stock	2.1
	Common stock	160.4
Financial Position	Working capital	2,089.5
	Properties, plants and equipment	6,929.7
	Other assets (liabilities), net	(1,749.6)
	Total assets	13,643.4
	Long-term debt (noncurrent)	1,215.5
	Minority interests	1,609.4
	Shareholders' equity	4,444.7
Common Share Data (dollars per share)†	Net income (loss)	4.43
	Dividends declared	.90
	Book value (based on year-end outstanding shares)	24.89
	Price range: High	60¼
	Low	36⅞
	Shareholders (number)	83,600
	Average shares outstanding (thousands)	178,018
Operating Data (thousands of metric tons)	Alumina shipments	6,407
	Aluminum product shipments:	
	Primary	673
	Fabricated and finished products	1,909
	Total	2,582
	Primary aluminum capacity:	
	Consolidated	1,905
	Total, including affiliates and others' share of joint ventures	2,428
	Primary aluminum production:	
	Consolidated	1,506
	Total, including affiliates and others' share of joint ventures	2,037
Other Statistics	Capital expenditures	$887
	Number of employees	72,000
	Return on average shareholders' equity (%)	18.5
	Return on average invested capital (%)	15.9

*Reflects the cumulative effects of the accounting changes for postretirement benefits and income taxes in 1992
†All common share amounts were restated to reflect the two-for-one stock split in February 1995.

EXHIBIT 17C-3. (*continued*)

1994	1993	1992	1991	1990
$ 9,904.3	$ 9,055.9	$ 9,491.5	$ 9,884.1	$10,710.2
487.2	93.0	96.9	97.1	160.3
7,845.7	7,187.0	7,339.1	7,444.8	7,606.2
632.7	603.6	586.8	579.8	592.3
125.8	130.4	212.2	251.9	220.3
671.3	692.6	682.4	697.9	689.9
106.7	87.8	105.4	153.2	184.7
219.2	(10.3)	132.3	192.8	404.0
107.1	105.6	112.3	111.2	105.3
79.7	150.8	251.6	330.9	414.4
603.3	201.4	166.3	218.7	653.4
(160.2)	(196.6)	(143.9)	(156.0)	(358.2)
(67.9)	–	(1,161.6)	–	–
375.2	4.8	(1,139.2)	62.7	295.2
.64	.56	.59	.67	.75
.71	.53	.58	.59	.74
2.1	2.1	2.1	2.1	2.2
142.3	140.2	136.8	151.2	264.9
1,599.7	1,609.6	1,083.0	1,546.0	1,706.3
6,689.4	6,506.8	6,415.8	6,586.1	6,747.0
(1,572.3)	(1,710.9)	(1,733.6)	(701.9)	(413.7)
12,353.2	11,596.9	11,023.1	11,178.4	11,413.2
1,029.8	1,432.5	855.3	1,130.8	1,295.3
1,687.8	1,389.2	1,305.6	1,362.0	1,581.0
3,999.2	3,583.8	3,604.3	4,937.4	5,163.3
2.10	.02	(6.70)	.36	1.70
.80	.80	.80	.89	1.53
22.07	19.96	20.70	28.69	30.10
45⅛	39¼	40⅜	36½	38⅝
32⅛	29½	30½	26⅞	24⅞
55,200	55,300	55,200	55,800	56,300
177,882	175,346	170,948	169,968	172,408
6,660	5,962	5,468	4,898	5,024
ʼ655	841	1,023	1,179	1,179
1,896	1,739	1,774	1,657	1,545
2,551	2,580	2,797	2,836	2,724
1,905	1,905	1,905	1,903	1,903
2,428	2,428	2,428	2,498	2,498
1,531	1,770	1,903	1,919	1,870
2,067	2,315	2,446	2,511	2,395
$612	$757	$789	$850	$851
60,200	63,400	63,600	65,600	63,700
9.9	.1	(26.7)	1.2	5.7
9.3	4.3	(14.0)	4.2	9.7

Source: Alcoa, *1995 Annual Report.*

CASE 17-3. A. M. CASTLE

Analysis of a Cyclical Company

Castle is a distributor of specialty metals including steel, aluminum, titanium, copper, and brass. The objectives of this case are to:

- Adjust Castle's balance sheet to current cost.
- Normalize reported income for both nonrecurring items and cyclicality.
- Extend the analysis of cash flow shown in Box 3-2 (pp. 113–114) through 1995.

The data required for this case are contained in Exhibits 17C-4 through 17C-6.

1. Using Exhibits 17C-4 and 17C-5, prepare current cost balance sheets for Castle for both December 31, 1994 and 1995, following the format of Exhibit 17-1. List the adjustments made and justify each. When 1994 data are not provided, use the 1995 adjustment.
2. Prepare capitalization tables for Castle, following the format of Exhibit 17-2, at December 31, 1994 and 1995, using both reported and adjusted data.
3. (a) Calculate the following ratios at December 31, 1994 and 1995, based on both reported and current cost data:
   - Book value per share
   - Debt-to-equity
   - Debt-to-total capital

EXHIBIT 17C-4. A. M. CASTLE
Condensed Balance Sheets
Years Ended December 31 (data in thousands)

	1994	1995		1994	1995
Assets			**Liabilities**		
Inventories[1]	$ 98,215	$ 97,766	Current debt	$ 3,831	$ 2,756
Other current assets	59,868	64,075	Current income tax	2,321	958
Total current assets	$158,083	$161,841	Other current assets	75,986	73,745
			Total current assets	$ 82,138	$ 77,459
Property (net)	41,190	44,463			
Other assets	13,854	16,245	Long-term debt	38,531	28,015
Total Assets	$213,127	$222,549	Deferred income tax	7,772	10,893
			Postretirement benefits	2,525	2,819
[1] LIFO Reserve	$ 51,700	$ 66,300	**Total Liabilities**	$130,966	$119,186
			Stockholders' equity	82,161	103,363
			Total Liabilities and Equity	$213,127	$222,549
			Shares outstanding	11,080	11,156

Source: Adapted from A. M. Castle, *1995 Annual Report.*

EXHIBIT 17C-5. A. M. CASTLE
Footnote Data

Goodwill – Cost in excess of net assets of acquired companies is amortized on a straight-line basis over a 40 year period. The unamortized balance at December 31, 1995 of $690,000 is reflected on the consolidated balance sheet under prepaid expense and other assets.

(3) Income taxes

Deferred income taxes reflect the net tax effects of temporary differences between the carrying amounts of assets and liabilities for financial reporting purposes and the amounts used for income tax purposes. Significant components of the Company's Federal and state deferred tax liabilities and assets as of December 31, 1995, 1994 and 1993 are as follows (in thousands):

	1995	1994	1993
Deferred tax liabilities:			
Depreciation	$ 5,666	$ 5,119	$ 5,211
Inventory, net	2,799	3,991	1,675
Pension	5,030	2,617	2,644
Other, net	(59)	(101)	400
Net deferred liabilities	13,436	11,626	9,930
Deferred tax assets:			
Postretirement benefits	1,271	1,155	1,132
Net deferred tax liabilities	$12,165	$10,471	$ 8,798

(5) Lease agreements

(a) Description of leasing arrangements – The Company has capital and operating leases covering certain warehouse facilities, equipment, automobiles and trucks, with lapse of time as the basis for all rental payments plus a mileage factor included in the truck rentals.

(b) Capital leases – Obligations under capitalization of leases are not significant.

(c) Operating leases – Future minimum rental payments under operating leases that have initial or remaining noncancelable lease terms in excess of one year as of December 31, 1995, are as follows (in thousands):

Year ending December 31,	
1996	$ 5,888
1997	5,437
1998	4,239
1999	3,483
2000	2,568
Later years	3,727
Total minimum payments required	$25,342

(d) Rental expense – Total rental payments charged to expense were $7.8 million in 1995, $7.4 million in 1994 and $7.0 million in 1993.

(e) Sale and leaseback of assets - During 1995, 1994 and 1993 the Company sold and leased back equipment under operating leases with terms ranging from five to seven years. The assets sold at approximately net book value for proceeds of $4,059,000, $2,618,000 and $2,063,000 respectively. The 1995 and 1994 leases allow for a purchase option at the end of the lease term of $1,349,000 for the 1995 leases and $1,101,000 for the 1994 lease. The 1993 lease allows for a purchase option at the end of six years of $662,000. Annual rentals are $615,000 for the 1995 leases, $482,000 for the 1994 leases, and $342,000 for the 1993 lease transaction.

(6) Retirement, profit-sharing and incentive plans

Substantially all employees who meet certain requirements of age, length of service and hours worked per year are covered by Company-sponsored retirement plans. These retirement plans are defined benefit, noncontributory plans. Benefits paid to retirees are based upon age at retirement, years of credited service and average earnings.

The status of the plans at December 31, 1995, 1994 and 1993, was as follows:

	1995	1994	1993
Actuarial present value of vested benefit obligation	$45,519	$36,617	$38,125
Plus – Nonvested benefit obligation	3,180	2,945	3,703
Vested and nonvested accumulated benefit obligation	48,699	39,562	41,828
Plus – Projected salary increases benefit obligation	9,407	4,816	5,380
Projected benefit obligation	58,106	44,378	47,208
Plan assets at fair market value	57,222	46,508	48,514
Plan assets in excess of (less than) projected benefit obligation	(884)	2,130	1,306
Items not yet recognized in earnings: Unrecognized net transitional assets	(976)	(1,952)	(3,084)
Unrecognized net loss	10,649	4,791	6,336
Unrecognized prior-service cost	1,148	1,353	1,561
Pension prepaid recognized on the consolidated balance sheets at December 31	$ 9,937	$ 6,322	$ 6,119

The assumptions used to measure the projected benefit obligations, future salary increases, and to compute the expected long-term return on assets for the Company's defined benefit pension plans are as follows:

	1995	1994	1993
Discount rate	7.25%	8.75%	7.75%
Projected annual salary increases	4.75	4.75	4.75
Expected long-term rate of return on plan assets	9.50	9.50	9.50

EXHIBIT 17C-5 (*continued*)

The following is a reconciliation between the plan's funded status and the accrued postretirement benefit obligation as reflected on the balance sheet as of December 31, 1995, 1994 and 1993 (in thousands):

	1995	1994	1993
Accumulated postretirement benefit obligation:			
Retirees	**$2,003**	$1,354	$1,491
Fully eligible active plan participants	**147**	149	214
Other active plan participants	**3,088**	1,524	1,560
	5,238	3,027	3,265
Unrecognized prior service cost	**(480)**	238	264
Unrecognized net loss	**(1,523)**	(324)	(647)
Accrued postretirement benefit obligation	**$3,235**	$2,941	$2,882

Future benefit costs were estimated assuming medical costs would increase at a 11.75% annual rate for the first year, with annual increases decreasing by 0.5% per year for two years, and 1% per year thereafter until an ultimate trend rate of 5¾% is reached. A 1% increase in the health care cost trend rate assumptions would have increased the accumulated postretirement benefit obligation at December 31, 1995 by $342,000 with no significant effect on the 1995 postretirement benefit expense. The weighted average discount rate used in determining the accumulated postretirement benefit obligation was 7.25% in 1995, 8.75% in 1994 and 7.75% in 1993.

Source: A. M. Castle, *1995 Annual Report.*

(b) Discuss the effect of the current cost adjustments on Castle's:
  (i) December 31, 1995 book value per share
  (ii) Growth of book value per share in 1995
  (iii) Price-to-book value ratios at December 31, 1994 and 1995
  (iv) Debt-to-equity ratios at December 31, 1994 and 1995
  The share price on those dates was $13.875 and $28.125, respectively.
4. (a) Prepare a table of normalized net income for Castle for the five years ended December 31, 1995, following the format of Exhibit 17-3. Adjustments should be made for *both nonrecurring items and cyclicality*.
  (b) Compute Castle's price-earnings ratios at December 31, 1994 and 1995, using:
    (i) Reported net income
    (ii) Net income before nonrecurring items
    (iii) Earnings power
  (c) Discuss the limitations of the normalization process as applied to Castle.

EXHIBIT 17C-6. A. M. CASTLE
Income Statement Data, 1991 to 1995 ($ in thousands)

	1991	1992	1993	1994	1995
Net sales	$ 436,441	$ 423,913	$ 474,108	$ 536,568	$ 627,826
Cost of material sold	(331,093)	(313,683)	(351,823)	(391,386)	(454,428)
Gross profit	$ 105,348	$ 110,230	$ 122,285	$ 145,182	$ 173,398
Operating expenses	(92,848)	(94,944)	(102,089)	(112,070)	(121,652)
Depreciation	(5,273)	(4,865)	(4,784)	(4,603)	(4,459)
Operating income	$ 7,227	$ 10,421	$ 15,412	$ 28,509	$ 47,287
Interest expense	(6,848)	(4,333)	(3,801)	(3,215)	(2,953)
Pretax income	$ 379	$ 6,088	$ 11,611	$ 25,294	$ 44,334
Income tax expense	(178)	(2,696)	(4,712)	(9,884)	(17,508)
Net income before cumulative effect	$ 201	$ 3,392	$ 6,899	$ 15,410	$ 26,826
Shares outstanding	10,914	10,914	10,917	11,080	11,156
Earnings per share	$ 0.02	$ 0.31	$ 0.63	$ 1.39	$ 2.40
Tons sold (000)	234	249	308	338	343

Source: A. M. Castle, *1991–1995 Annual Reports.*

EXHIBIT 17C-7. A. M. CASTLE
Cash Flow Statements, 1991 to 1995 ($ in thousands)

	1991	1992	1993	1994	1995
Net income	$ 201	$ 3,614	$ 6,899	$ 15,410	$ 26,826
Noncash adjustments	4,257	5,368	4,157	1,563	5,554
Operating changes	20,095	5,633	(9,720)	11,145	(7,671)
Cash from operations	$ 24,553	$ 14,615	$ 1,336	$ 28,118	$ 24,709
Capital expenditures	(3,305)	(1,794)	(4,621)	(7,926)	(11,782)
Proceeds from sales	6,012	1,162	2,083	3,213	4,140
Cash from investing	$ 2,707	$ (632)	$(2,538)	$ (4,713)	$ (7,642)
Net change in debt	(23,329)	(10,817)	4,873	(21,097)	(11,591)
Dividends paid	(3,927)	(2,910)	(2,911)	(3,641)	(6,006)
Stock issue and other	25	106	75	781	221
Cash from financing	$(27,231)	$(13,621)	$ 2,037	$(23,957)	$(17,376)
Net change in cash	$ 29	$ 362	$ 835	$ (552)	$ (309)
Cash at beginning	302	331	693	1,528	976
Cash at end	$ 331	$ 693	$ 1,528	$ 976	$ 667

Source: Adapted from A. M. Castle, *1991–1995 Annual Reports.*

5. (a) Using the data in Exhibit 17C-7, analyze Castle's cash flow for the five years through 1995. Compare these data with those for the five years ended 1991 shown in Box 3-2. Discuss the implications of your analysis for Castle. Be sure to consider Castle's cyclicality in your analysis.

   (b) In 1996, Castle started to diversify into the distribution of plastics. Explain whether the results of part (a) facilitate this diversification.

6. (a) Compute *each* of the following ratios for Castle, using *both* reported and adjusted 1995 data, following the format of Exhibit 17-5:

   (i) Inventory turnover

   (ii) Fixed asset turnover

   (iii) Total asset turnover

   (iv) Current ratio

   (v) Return on assets

   (vi) Return on total capital

   (vii) Return on equity

   (b) For each ratio computed in part (a), explain the difference between the reported and adjusted ratio.

   (c) Discuss the benefits of using adjusted ratios for analysis, given your answers to part b.

CASE 17-4. DEERE & COMPANY

Cash Flow Analysis

Deere & Company is a major manufacturer of agricultural and industrial machinery. The company has a significant finance subsidiary that provides credit to Deere's dealers and customers. Exhibit 17C-8 is the cash flow statement from Deere's *1994 Annual Report*

1. Free cash flow (FCF) can be defined as cash from operations (CFO) less cash used for investment (CFI)

   (a) Using that definition, compute Deere's FCF for each of the three years ended October 31, 1994.

Note: For this and all other questions, three-year totals should be computed as part of the analysis.

   (b) Discuss the level and trend of FCF as an indicator of Deere's financial health.

2. Deere reports changes in credit receivables and operating leases held by its finance subsidiary as part of CFI. Chapter 3 of the text suggests that such assets should be treated as accounts receivable for purposes of analysis and reclassified to CFO. In addition, Deere has securitized some of its receivables, distorting both CFI and cash from financing (CFF) as discussed in Chapter 11. The outstanding balance of such securitized receivables was reported as follows:

1991	$ 242 million
1992	688
1993	1,384
1994	1,195

EXHIBIT 17C-8. DEERE & COMPANY
Statement of Consolidated Cash Flows

	CONSOLIDATED (Deere & Company and Consolidated Subsidiaries)		
	Year Ended October 31		
(In millions of dollars)	1994	1993	1992
Cash Flows from Operating Activities			
Net income (loss)..	$ 603.6	$ (920.9)	$ 37.4
Adjustments to reconcile net income (loss) to net cash provided by operating activities:			
Changes in accounting, cumulative net adjustment................................		1,105.3	
Provision for doubtful receivables	36.1	32.6	55.3
Provision for depreciation	256.7	257.2	250.4
Provision for restructuring costs..		78.5	
Undistributed earnings of unconsolidated subsidiaries and affiliates...............	(12.6)	(7.7)	(7.2)
Provision (credit) for deferred income taxes	26.2	(30.4)	(15.9)
Changes in assets and liabilities:			
Receivables..	(147.8)	82.4	13.9
Inventories..	(164.5)	35.4	(3.0)
Accounts payable and accrued expenses..................................	(60.4)	93.5	(57.3)
Insurance and health care claims and reserves	98.8	27.5	80.8
Other...	82.7	80.7	3.9
Net cash provided by operating activities...........................	718.8	834.1	358.3
Cash Flows from Investing Activities			
Collections of credit receivables..	3,012.5	2,995.5	3,008.9
Proceeds from sales of credit receivables................................	561.9	1,148.3	696.7
Proceeds from sales of marketable securities.............................	222.9	320.9	278.2
Proceeds from sales of equipment on operating leases	49.2	46.5	43.9
Cost of credit receivables acquired......................................	(4,308.8)	(3,635.1)	(3,460.6)
Purchases of marketable securities......................................	(344.8)	(346.5)	(372.2)
Purchases of property and equipment....................................	(228.1)	(206.5)	(285.7)
Cost of operating leases acquired	(102.5)	(106.3)	(63.2)
Acquisition of a business	(119.8)		
Other...	52.2	(1.8)	20.3
Net cash provided by (used for) investing activities	(1,205.3)	215.0	(133.7)
Cash Flows from Financing Activities			
Increase (decrease) in short-term borrowings.............................	934.2	(1,487.1)	(533.9)
Change in intercompany receivables/payables.............................			
Proceeds from issuance of long-term borrowings..........................	188.5	687.1	772.0
Principal payments on long-term borrowings..............................	(590.7)	(546.3)	(359.8)
Proceeds from issuance of common stock.................................	36.9	586.0	2.4
Dividends paid	(171.8)	(152.9)	(152.5)
Other...	(6.2)	(12.9)	(13.8)
Net cash provided by (used for) financing activities.................	390.9	(926.1)	(285.6)
Effect of Exchange Rate Changes on Cash	2.8	(1.6)	(.7)
Net Increase (Decrease) in Cash and Cash Equivalents	(92.8)	121.4	(61.7)
Cash and Cash Equivalents at Beginning of Year	338.2	216.8	278.5
Cash and Cash Equivalents at End of Year	$ 245.4	$ 338.2	$ 216.8

Source: Deere & Company, *1994 Annual Report.*

(a) Adjust the three cash flow components (CFO, CFI, and CFF) as follows:

  (i) Reduce CFO by the sum of the increases in credit receivables, operating leases, and securitized receivables.

  (ii) Increase CFI by the sum of the increases in credit receivables and operating leases.

  (iii) Increase CFF by the increase in securitized receivables.

Note: Be sure that the sum of the three components is unchanged by these adjustments.

(b) Explain why the adjustments improve:

  (i) CFO as a measure of Deere's ability to generate cash from operations

  (ii) CFI as a measure of Deere's investments during the period

(c) Using the revised components from part (a), compute Deere's adjusted FCF (still defined as CFO less CFI) for the three years ended October 31, 1994.

(d) Discuss the level and trend of the adjusted FCF as indicators of Deere's financial health.

3. A more refined cash flow analysis would use the following format:

Adjusted CFO	Net increase in debt
Less: Capital expenditures	Plus: Common stock issued
Equals: Free cash flow	Less: Increase in marketable securities
Less: Dividends paid	Plus: All other cash flows*
Less: Businesses acquired	Plus or minus: Change in cash
Equals: Cash requirements =	Equals: Cash provided

*Miscellaneous investing and financing cash flows plus the effect of exchange rates on cash, where the two totals must be equal.

(a) Use the format provided to analyze Deere's cash flows for the three years ended October 31, 1994.

(b) Explain why this format is useful when analyzing cash flows.

(c) Discuss the insights about Deere's financial health provided by this format.

18

ACCOUNTING- AND FINANCE-BASED MEASURES OF RISK

CHAPTER OUTLINE

CHAPTER OBJECTIVES

INTRODUCTION
Earnings Variability and Its Components
  Operating and Financial Risk
  Measures of Financial and Operating Leverage
  Accounting Beta

THE PREDICTION OF BANKRUPTCY
Usefulness of Bankruptcy Prediction
Research Results
  Univariate Models
  Multivariate Models
Bankruptcy Prediction and Cash Flows
Bankruptcy and Financial Distress: Concluding Comments

THE PREDICTION OF DEBT RISK
The Prediction of Bond Ratings
  Bond Rating Classifications
  The Bond Ratings Process
  Impact of Ratings
Usefulness of Bond Ratings Predictions
  Choice of Explanatory Variables

Model Results
The Z"-Score and Bond Ratings
The Significance of Ratings: Another Look
  Measurement of Financial Variables

EQUITY RISK: MEASUREMENT AND PREDICTION
Risk and Return: Theoretical Models
  The CAPM and Beta (β)
  APT and Multifactor Models
Importance and Usefulness of β
Review of Theoretical and Empirical Findings
  Theoretical Framework
  Empirical Studies
The Attack on the CAPM and β
  Alternative Measures of Equity Risk or Market Inefficiency?
  The Defense of β and the CAPM
  Implications for Accounting Risk Measures

SUMMARY

CASE 18-1: ANALYSIS OF THE DEBT RATINGS AND DEFAULT RISK OF DuPONT, DOW CHEMICAL, AND IMPERIAL CHEMICAL INDUSTRIES

CHAPTER OBJECTIVES

This chapter is concerned with the evaluation of risk and it focuses on different measures of risk suggested by theory and used in practice. Our purpose is to:

1. Define measures of *earnings variability* and examine their use in the prediction and evaluation of risk.

2. Evaluate and review research on the prediction of bankruptcy. We also discuss the role of cash flows in the prediction of bankruptcy.

3. Describe the role of the debt rating process and the resulting debt classifications in the evaluation of default risk.

4. Examine the value of predictions of bond ratings and review empirical research.

5. Discuss equity risk in the context of the capital asset pricing model and the arbitrage pricing theory.

6. Review theoretical and empirical research related to the measurement and prediction of equity risk.

7. Discuss the controversy over the efficacy of CAPM and beta.

INTRODUCTION

An important objective of the analysis of financial statements in general and that of ratios in particular is an assessment of the risk inherent in a firm's operations. Although liquidity, solvency, and profitability analysis implicitly address the probability that a firm's cash will fall below some level, commonly used ratios do not directly measure this uncertainty. A large body of research has examined the utility of accounting-based measures in risk evaluation and prediction. The research can be classified into three broad categories of risk:

1. Risk of financial failure or bankruptcy
2. Default risk as measured by a firm's bond ratings
3. Equity risk

The risk levels indicated by these categories lie along a continuum relative to the probability of the firm attaining a specific level of profit or return commensurate with risk.

The risk of bankruptcy reflects the uncertainty about the ability of the firm to continue operations if its financial condition were to fall below some minimum level.

Bondholders face uncertain returns. The level of uncertainty is not (directly) related to the firm's expected return; rather, it is related to a minimum level of return, that is, the return that is sufficient to avoid default on principal and interest payments.

The equity investor takes on more risk than an investor in the debt securities of that same firm and expects a commensurably higher return. The equity investor's risk relates to the uncertainty of achieving the firm's expected return.

Research in these areas typically involves two phases. The first calibrates the association between the risk measure and a set of financial ratios. The second step uses this association to predict risk. A result of this research is often an equation of the form

$$Y = w_0 + w_1 X_1 + w_2 X_2 + \cdots + w_n X_n$$

which measures the relationship between the dependent variable Y (e.g., bankruptcy, bond rating, or beta) and the independent, explanatory variable X_i's (financial ratios or, more generally speaking, accounting-based measures of risk).

Such research is discussed throughout the chapter, which is divided into three sections corresponding to each of the risk categories. Each section contains a brief discussion of the relevant financial risk measure(s) as well as the accounting-based measures of risk used to forecast those financial risk measures. Exhibits 18-1, 18-2, and 18-3 summarize the explanatory independent variables (financial risk measures) used in key studies in each of the three areas. Some of these measures and their classifications are familiar. The other, new indicators are primarily explicit measures

EXHIBIT 18-1
Independent Variables Used in Bankruptcy Prediction Models

	Ohlson (1980)	Altman et al. (1977)	Deakin (1972)	Altman (1968)
Activity			Four asset categories divided by sales: (1) Current assets (2) Quick assets (3) Working capital (4) Cash	Sales to total assets
Liquidity	Current ratio	Current ratio	Current ratio Quick ratio Cash ratio Four asset categories divided by total assets: (1) Current assets (2) Quick assets (3) Working capital (4) Cash	
	Working capital to total assets			Working capital to total assets
Leverage and solvency	Liabilities to assets	Equity (market) to capital	Debt to assets	Equity (market) to debt (book)
	Funds from operations to total liabilities Dummy variable indicating if net worth is negative	Times interest earned	Funds from operations to debt	
Profitability	Return on assets Dummy variable indicating if net income was negative in last two years	Return on assets Retained earnings to total assets	Return on assets	Return on assets Retained earnings to total assets
Earnings variability	Percentage change in net income	Standard error of return on assets		
Size	Total assets	Total assets		

EXHIBIT 18-2
Independent Variables Used in Bond Ratings Prediction Models

	Belkaoui (1983)	Belkaoui (1980)	Kaplan and Urwitz (1979)	Pinches and Mingo (1973)	Pogue and Soldovsky (1969)	Horrigan (1966)	West (1966)
Activity and liquidity	Current ratio	Current ratio				Working capital to sales; Sales to equity	
Leverage and solvency	Long-term debt to capital; Short-term debt to capital; Fixed charge coverage; Cash flow to investment in fixed assets and inventory plus dividends	Long-term debt to capital; Short-term debt to capital; Fixed charge coverage	Long-term debt to assets; Long-term debt to equity; Times interest earned; Cash flow to debt	Total debt to assets; Times interest earned	Debt to capital; Times interest earned	Equity to debt	Debt to equity (market values)
Profitability			Return on assets	Return on assets	Return on assets	Operating profit	
Earnings variability			Accounting beta; Coefficient of variation—net income	Years of consecutive dividends	Coefficient of variation—ROA		Coefficient of variation—net income
Size	Total assets; Total debt	Total assets; Total debt	Total assets; Issue size	Issue size	Total assets	Total assets	Bonds outstanding
Subordination	0–1 dummy	0–1 dummy	0–1 dummy	0–1 dummy		0–1 dummy	
Market-based	Price to net book value	Price to net book value	Market beta				
Other	Coefficient of variation—total assets				Industry dummy variable		Period of solvency

EXHIBIT 18-3
Independent Variables Used in Beta Prediction Models

		Predictive and Explanatory			Explanatory			
		Hochman (1983)	Rosenberg and McKibben (1973)	Beaver et al. (1970)	Mandelker and Rhee (1984)	Bildersee (1975)	Lev (1974)	Ball and Brown (1968)
Earnings variability	Operating risk†	Accounting beta (operating income)	*		OLE	Accounting beta	Variable cost % (v)	Accounting beta
	Financial risk†	Debt to capital			FLE	Debt to equity Preferred equity to common equity		
	Total risk†			Standard deviation earnings/ price		Standard deviation earnings/price		
Growth		Dividend yield		Asset growth				
Dividends				Dividend payout				
Liquidity						Current ratio		

*See Exhibit 18-12.
†Earnings variability can be measured as the sum of operating risk and financial risk.

of the firm's *earnings variability*. These measures and theoretical justification for their use in the prediction and evaluation of risk are presented below.

Earnings Variability and Its Components

The variance of a firm's earnings is a direct measure of the uncertainty (risk) of its earnings stream. It is surmised that a smooth earnings stream is deemed to be desirable by firms, their creditors, and the financial markets. To the extent that accounting earnings mirror a firm's economic well-being, the variance in that measure would be expected to measure a firm's risk.[1]

[1]Box 18-1 presents a theoretical justification for and a suggested ratio incorporating the variance of a firm's cash flow from operations. This ratio is expressed in terms of CFO and is equal to

$$\frac{\text{Cash Balance} + \text{E(CFO)}}{\text{Standard Deviation of CFO}}$$

where E(CFO) equals expected CFO. The higher the ratio, the less likelihood there is of the firm's cash balance falling below a certain level. The intuitive result emanating from the ratio is that levels of CFO cannot be analyzed alone. Consideration must be given to the variance of the cash flows.

BOX 18-1
A Probabilistic Measure of Liquidity

Emery and Cogger (1982) discussed liquidity in the following theoretical framework. If we let L equal the liquid reserves (e.g., cash)* at the beginning of the period and C equal operating cash flow during the period, insolvency or lack of liquidity is defined as occurring when additional financing is required, that is, when

$$L + C < 0$$

The analytic question becomes one of determining the probability that the foregoing will occur. If we assume that C is normally distributed, the probability† can be found by looking at the normal distribution table for the standardized value

$$-\frac{L + u_C}{s_C}$$

where u_c and s_c are the mean and standard deviation of the operating cash flows. Since this measure is related to the probability of insolvency, Emery and Cogger suggest this as a useful and relevant liquidity ratio. It combines the stock of cash with the flows and the variance of those flows.

---

*The analysis need not be confined to defining L as cash, but it can be extended to include other liquid reserves (such as working capital and accounts receivable) with appropriate definition of terms.
†This measure will be an upwardly biased measure as it ignores the probability of falling below zero before the period ends. However, as Emery and Cogger point out, in short intervals the bias will be small.

Variance is often measured in terms of:

1. The actual level of earnings

2. Year-to-year change in earnings, or

3. Year-to-year percentage change in earnings

Several factors contribute to the variability of a firm's earnings. These components are presented schematically in Figure 18-1.

Earnings variance is primarily related to the underlying uncertainty of demand for the firm's output, the *variance of its sales*. The extent to which the variability of sales impacts earning variability is a function of the firm's *operating and financial leverage*. In addition, earnings variability is affected by uncertainty regarding the prices of outputs and inputs.

If we use identical arguments made with respect to market returns, sales and earnings can be said to depend on general economic conditions as well as firm-specific policies. Thus, earnings variability has a systematic as well as an unsystematic component. The systematic component of earnings (as well as the systematic component of sales) is referred to as the *accounting beta*[2] ($B_{earnings}$ and B_{sales}), which can be defined as the relationship between the firm's operating results and general economic factors.

[2]In order to differentiate between accounting betas and market betas, throughout this chapter we will denote the former as "B" and the latter with the Greek symbol β.

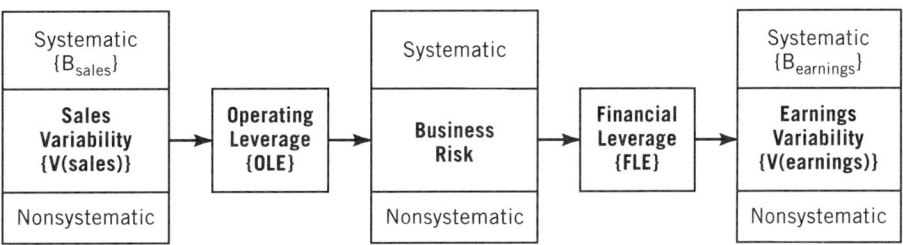

FIGURE 18-1 Relationship of components of earnings variability.

Many of the models use components of variability, that is, operating and financial risk, instead of (or in addition to) overall earnings variability. These components are discussed in greater detail below.

Operating and Financial Risk

Operating (OLE) and financial (FLE) leverage measure the extent to which a firm's income varies as a result of variations in sales. *Operating leverage* is the percentage of fixed operating costs, and *financial leverage* the percentage of fixed financing costs in a firm's overall cost structure. The higher the percentage of fixed costs, the greater the variation in income as a result of variation in sales.[3]

It is important to distinguish between the concepts of operating *leverage* and operating *risk*. The existence of operating leverage does not, by itself, imply risk or uncertainty. If a firm's sales are predictable, then leverage does not create uncertainty. If, on the other hand, a firm's sales are uncertain, high leverage increases operating risk and the variance of income. Operating risk is, therefore, a function of operating leverage and sales variance:

$$\text{Operating Risk} = f\{\text{OLE, Variance (Sales)}\}$$

Operating risk is also referred to as *business risk* as it represents the underlying risk of the firm's operations in the absence of financing. When financial leverage is also considered, the total risk of the firm can be expressed[4] as

$$\text{Variance (Income)} = \text{Total Risk} = f\{\text{FLE, Operating Risk}\}$$
$$= f\{\text{FLE, OLE, Variance (Sales)}\}$$

Two firms, having differing levels of leverage, differ in terms of risk only if the underlying uncertainty (variance) of their sales is equivalent. Leverage and risk are directly associated only for two firms having the same level of uncertainty with respect to sales. The firm with the higher leverage will be the riskier of the two.

---

[3]These concepts were explained in greater detail in Chapter 4.

[4]There is a clear parallel between this expression and the formulation (given in Chapter 4) for the *total leverage effect* (TLE):

$$\% \text{ Change in Income} = \text{TLE} = \text{FLE} \times \text{OLE} \times \% \text{ Change in Sales}$$

Measures of Financial and Operating Leverage

As fixed and variable costs are generally not disclosed, the measurement of leverage often requires the use of surrogate measures. This is less of a problem for financial leverage, where direct measures such as the ratio of interest expense to total expense or earnings before interest and taxes (EBIT) to earnings before taxes (EBT) are available from the financial statements. Nevertheless, some researchers use debt/equity, debt/assets, or debt/capital as surrogate measures of financial leverage, where the higher ratio implies greater financial leverage. The rationale behind the use of these surrogates seems to be reasonable, since higher debt would be expected to result in higher fixed interest charges.[5]

Measuring operating leverage is somewhat more difficult. Appendix 4-A shows how to estimate a firm's fixed and variable costs using regression analysis. A common measure used to estimate operating leverage is the coefficient v derived from the regression equation

$$TC_t = F + vS_t$$

where TC_t and S_t are the firm's total costs and sales, respectively, in period t, and F and v are regression estimates of the firm's fixed and variable costs (the latter as a percentage of sales), respectively. The lower the coefficient v, the greater the operating leverage, as fixed costs are relatively higher.

Another surrogate for operating leverage is the ratio of fixed assets (property) to total assets. Fixed costs (e.g., depreciation) are associated with capital-intensive industries; therefore, high capital intensity increases operating leverage.

An important question is whether the two measures of risk, financial and operating leverage, are independent of each other. Watts and Zimmerman (1986) take the position that the two should be highly (positively) correlated. They posit that capital-intensive industries (and firms) have higher operating leverage. To finance fixed assets (which determine capital intensity), moreover, more debt is required, increasing financial leverage.

> We expect firms' capital structures and operating leverage to be associated (Myers, 1977). Firms with more fixed assets are able to obtain lower-cost, longer term financing and hence will be more highly levered.[6]

Others argue (see Mandelker and Rhee, 1984) that, in general, the amount of total risk a firm should undertake is fixed, commensurate with its expected return. Therefore, if it increases operating risk, it should compensate by reducing financial leverage.[7]

> By changing from a labor-intensive manufacturing process to a capital-intensive one, a significant change would occur in the cost structure of a firm. A rise in fixed costs and a simultaneous decline in variable cost per unit increase the degree of operating leverage

---

[5]It is, however, somewhat mystifying why some researchers resorted to the surrogate measures and did not use the direct measures of financial leverage.

[6]Ross Watts and Jerold L. Zimmerman, *Positive Accounting Theory* (Englewood Cliffs, N.J.: Prentice-Hall, 1986), p. 120.

[7]As noted in Chapter 4, in the late 1980s a number of firms with high operating leverage assumed significantly greater debt. When the economy took a downturn, the combination of financial and operating leverage was too much for many of these firms. They were forced into default or major restructuring to survive.

and thereby increase the relative riskiness of common stocks. However, the firm's decision on the operating leverage can be offset by its decision on its financial leverage. To save portfolio revision costs to the stockholders, the two types of leverage can be chosen so that changes in the level of beta are minimized.[8]

This would imply that the two risk measures are negatively correlated. Using regression estimates of both financial and operating leverage, Mandelker and Rhee report a significant negative correlation (approximately -0.3) between operating and financial leverage, indicating that firms tend to balance the two sources of risk. More interesting, perhaps, is their finding that the trade-off between the two risk sources is not uniform across all firms. Rather, riskier firms [as measured by their systematic beta (β) risk measure] "engage in trade-offs more actively than firms with low betas."[9]

Accounting Beta

Earlier it was noted that the variability in a firm's earnings has two components: one due to (systematic) industry and economywide factors and the other to (nonsystematic) firm-specific factors. The systematic factor reflects the degree to which the earnings of the firm vary with the earnings of other firms in the economy. Its empirical measure is the "accounting beta," $B_{earnings}$, the regression coefficient derived from the following equation[10]:

$$E_t = a + B_{earnings}\, ME_t$$

where E_t is the firm's earnings for period t and ME_t an index of "the market's" earnings for period t. When earnings are defined as operating income, then the corresponding $B_{earnings}$ measures the systematic component of operating or business risk.

Different indices can be used to measure market earnings. One may be the average earnings of the Standard & Poor's 500; others include earnings of another broad stock market index, corporate earnings calculated by the Labor Department, or an index created by the researcher (e.g., the average earnings of a random sample of firms). Since the purpose of the index is to measure general economic conditions, measures of GNP may also be used. The overall objective is to derive a $B_{earnings}$ that best measures the degree to which a firm's earnings (co)vary with general economic conditions. The higher the $B_{earnings}$, the greater the level of systematic risk.

$B_{earnings}$ is, of course, affected by the variability of sales or, more precisely, the systematic portion of sales variability, B_{sales}. Thus, just as we have expressed a firm's earnings variability as a function of FLE, OLE, and variance (sales), we can also express its systematic component as a function of FLE, OLE, and the systematic portion of variance (sales):

$$B_{earnings} = f\{FLE, OLE, B_{sales}\}$$

We will return to these measures and their use in the prediction of risk during the discussions of bankruptcy, debt, and equity risk.

[8]Gershon M. Mandelker and S. Ghon Rhee, "The Impact of the Degrees of Operating and Financial Leverage on Systematic Risk of Common Stock," *Journal of Financial and Quantitative Analysis*, March 1984, pp. 45–57.

[9]Ibid., p. 55.

[10]For statistical purposes, this model is often expressed in terms of changes in earnings, $(E_t - E_{t-1})$ and changes in the earnings index $(ME_t - ME_{t-1})$.

THE PREDICTION OF BANKRUPTCY

Usefulness of Bankruptcy Prediction

The ability to predict which firms will face insolvency in the near term is important to both potential creditors and investors. When a firm files for bankruptcy, creditors often lose a portion of principal and interest payments due; common stock investors may suffer substantial dilution or loss of their equity interest. In addition, bankruptcy imposes significant legal costs and risks on its investors and creditors as well as the firm, even if it survives.

For these reasons, there has been considerable research into the use of ratios and cash flow data to predict bankruptcy. Before reviewing this research, however, we must discuss the appropriate measurement criterion to use in assessing the efficacy of bankruptcy prediction models.

The total percentage of correct predictions provided by a predictive model is not a sufficient criterion. The evaluation of any predictive model is not complete unless the relative costs and benefits of correct versus incorrect predictions are considered. As Exhibit 18-4 indicates, there are two types of misclassification errors:

1. A *type I error* refers to the misclassification of a firm by predicting nonbankruptcy when in reality the firm becomes bankrupt.

2. A *type II error* reflects the misclassification of a solvent firm as bankrupt.

The cost of the two types of error is very different. This is especially relevant for a bankruptcy prediction model, where the costs of incorrectly classifying a firm as solvent when in reality it will go bankrupt (type I) are much larger than if the firm is incorrectly classified as insolvent (type II) [Altman et al., (1977) estimate type I errors to be 35 times as costly as type II errors].

In the first case, the creditor can lose 100% of its investment. In the second case, the loss is limited to the spread between the rate the (incorrectly) rejected firm would have paid and the actual return. This ranges from zero if an equivalent debtor is found, to (worst case) the spread between the forgone rate and the risk-free rate.

To put these arguments in perspective, consider a strategy of forecasting nonbankruptcy for every firm. Since on average, for established firms, the rate of bankruptcy

EXHIBIT 18-4
Types of Misclassification Errors in Bankruptcy Prediction

Predicted Outcome	Actual Outcome	
	Bankrupt	Nonbankrupt
Bankrupt	Correct	Error: Type II Cost: Small 0–10%
Nonbankrupt	Error: Type I Cost: Large Up to 100%	Correct

is only 5%, this strategy would have a 95% success rate. However, it misclassifies every bankrupt firm, and it is precisely this type of costly error one would like to avoid. At the other extreme, predicting bankruptcy for every firm avoids the potential losses associated with lending to a bankrupt firm, but is tantamount to ceasing business as a creditor.

Thus, given the relative magnitudes of the cost of the two error types, one should be willing to make the following trade-off: Lower the accuracy of correctly predicting solvent firms for higher accuracy in the prediction of bankrupt firms.[11] [Figure 18-3 (p. 1040), from Ohlson (1980), illustrates this trade-off.] In evaluating (and designing) a bankruptcy prediction model, therefore, both the percentage correctly classified as bankrupt and the percentage correctly classified as nonbankrupt should be viewed separately.

Research Results

Univariate Models

The early studies of bankruptcy prediction date back to the late 1960s. Beaver (1966) compared patterns of 29 ratios in the five years preceding bankruptcy for a sample of failed firms with a control group of firms that did not fail. The purpose was to see which ratios could forecast bankruptcy and how many years in advance such forecasts could be made.[12]

"Cash flow"/total liabilities proved to be the best predictor overall.[13] Its performance is summarized in Exhibit 18-5.

Overall, in the first year prior to bankruptcy, this model had a 13% misclassification rate. The distribution of errors between type I and type II errors, however, was not uniform. There was a greater frequency of type I errors relative to type II errors as it was more difficult to classify bankrupt firms correctly. This difficulty increased dramatically with the prediction horizon. Given the greater costs associated with type I errors, these results underscore the importance of evaluating each type of error separately.

Beaver's approach was "univariate" in that each ratio was evaluated in terms of how it alone could predict bankruptcy without consideration of the other ratios. Most work in this area, however, is "multivariate," wherein predictive models use a combination of ratios to forecast bankruptcy.

---

[11]It is interesting to note that bankruptcy models have also been used in other contexts, where it can be argued that the relative costs of the different type of errors are radically different. Antitrust laws forbid mergers of certain companies unless one of the companies is deemed to be "failing." Blum (1974) reports a case where a bankruptcy prediction model was used. By the philosophy underlying the antitrust laws, it might be argued that allowing the merger when the firm is not bankrupt (predicting bankruptcy when the firm is solvent, type II error) is more costly to society than stopping the merger even if the firm is failing (but the model incorrectly classified it as nonfailing, type I error).

[12]The procedure involved ranking the ratios of the bankrupt and nonbankrupt firms and finding the optimal cutoff point that discriminated between the two groups. This cutoff point was then tested against a hold-out sample of companies.

[13]We place "cash flow" in quotation marks as, consistent with the definition used at that time, the measure actually uses funds flows (i.e., net income +/− noncash expenses/revenues).

EXHIBIT 18-5
"Cash Flow"/Total Liabilities as Bankruptcy Predictor

Years Prior to Bankruptcy	Error Rate (%)		Overall Correct Classification (%)
	Type I	Type II	
1	22	5	87
2	34	8	79
3	37	8	77
4	47	3	76
5	42	4	78

Source: William Beaver, "Financial Ratios as Predictors of Failure," *Journal of Accounting Research*, Supplement 1966, Table 6, p. 90 (adapted). Reprinted with permission.

Multivariate Models

Exhibit 18-1 presents the variables used in four multivariate studies. Note that liquidity and solvency ratios are most frequently used followed by profitability and activity ratios. A broader summary of 14 studies by Gentry et al. (1984) finds similar ratios relevant for bankruptcy prediction.

Altman's Z-score. The best known of the bankruptcy prediction studies that have withstood the test of time is Altman's (1968) Z-score model. The Z-score is the value resulting from the following discriminant analysis equation:

$$Z = 1.2 \times \frac{\text{Working Capital}}{\text{Total Assets}}$$
$$+ 1.4 \times \frac{\text{Retained Earnings}}{\text{Total Assets}}$$
$$+ 3.3 \times \frac{\text{EBIT}}{\text{Total Assets}}$$
$$+ 0.6 \times \frac{\text{Market Value of Equity}}{\text{Book Value of Debt}}$$
$$+ 1.0 \times \frac{\text{Sales}}{\text{Total Assets}}$$

A Z-score below (above) the critical value of 2.675 signals bankruptcy (solvency). Analysis of the misclassifications resulting from use of this critical value resulted in a more intuitively appealing dichotomy:

> It is concluded that all firms having a Z score of greater than 2.99 clearly fall into the "non-bankrupt" sector, while those firms having a Z below 1.81 are all bankrupt. The area between 1.81 and 2.99 will be defined as the "zone of ignorance" or "gray area" because of the susceptibility to error classification."[14]

[14]Edward I. Altman, "Financial Ratios, Discriminant Analysis and the Prediction of Corporate Bankruptcy," *Journal of Finance*, September 1968, pp. 589–609. Also see Edward I. Altman, *Corporate Financial Distress and Bankruptcy* (New York: John Wiley & Sons, 1993).

The original Z-model was designed for manufacturing firms. Also, the model was only directly applicable to publicly traded companies because one of its inputs was the market value of equity. To remedy these shortcomings, two variations of the Z-model (the Z'- and Z''-models) were developed by Altman. The first, the Z'-model, was developed for nonpublic companies and used the book value of equity in place of the market value of equity. The second, the Z''-model (which omitted the sales turnover ratio), was designed to be applicable to nonmanufacturing (public or private) companies as well.[15] These models and the relevant "cut-off" scores are described in Box 18-2.

The ZETA™ Model. A more refined bankruptcy prediction model, the ZETA™ model, was developed by Altman et al. (1977). However, the parameters and design of the model remain proprietary. The explanatory variables used (see Exhibit 18-1) were, however, disclosed. Although no theoretical bankruptcy model was envisioned in designing this model, Scott (1981) showed that the variables used by Altman's ZETA™ model are consistent with parameters relevant for a theoretical bankruptcy model. Details of this relationship are presented in Box 18-3.

Figure 18-2 illustrates the pattern of ZETA™ scores for bankrupt and nonbankrupt firms for the five years prior to bankruptcy along with the bankrupt, nonbankrupt, and overlap zones.

The classification errors for the two Altman models are as follows:

Years Prior to Bankruptcy	Original Z-Model Classification Errors (%)		ZETA™ Model Classification Errors (%)	
	Bankrupt (Type I)	Nonbankrupt (Type II)	Bankrupt (Type I)	Nonbankrupt (Type II)
1	6	3	4	10
2	18	6	15	7
3	52	NA	25	9
4	71	NA	32	10
5	64	NA	30	18

NA = Not available.

Source: Edward I. Altman, Robert G. Haldeman, and P. Narayanan, "ZETA™ Analysis: A New Model to Identify Bankruptcy Risk of Corporations," *Journal of Banking and Finance*, June 1977, Table 5, p. 41 (adapted).

The predictive accuracy of both models is about equal in the year immediately preceding bankruptcy. Similar to Beaver, classifying bankrupt firms proved to be more difficult than classifying nonbankrupt ones.[16] In addition, the longer the time period

---

[15]As discussed in the next section, this model also has applicability to the bond ratings decision.

[16]More recently, Dambolena and Shulman (1988) found that, *for their sample*, the Z-model was more accurate in classifying *failed* firms. They attempted to improve on the Z-model by adding a variable, the net liquid balance (NLB), defined as

NLB = Cash + marketable securities − (short-term debt + current portion of long-term debt)

to the Z-model. By doing so, they were able to increase one- (two-) year-ahead accuracy of the prediction of *nonfailed* firms from 72 to 86% (76 to 80%).

BOX 18-2
Z′ and Z″: Variations of Altman's Z-score*

The Z′ Model: Application to Private Firms

The Z-model may not be applicable to private firms as it includes as one of its variables the market value of equity. After replacing the market value of equity with book value and reestimating the parameters, the following model was derived:

$$Z' = 0.717 \times \frac{\text{Working Capital}}{\text{Total Assets}}$$

$$+ \ 0.847 \times \frac{\text{Retained Earnings}}{\text{Total Assets}}$$

$$+ \ 3.107 \times \frac{\text{EBIT}}{\text{Total Assets}}$$

$$+ \ 0.420 \times \frac{\text{Book Value of Equity}}{\text{Book Value of Debt}}$$

$$+ \ 0.998 \times \frac{\text{Sales}}{\text{Total Assets}}$$

The appropriate cut-off points for bankruptcy/nonbankruptcy and the gray area are:

Z′ score	Indication
<1.23	Bankruptcy
1.23–2.90	Gray area
>2.90	Nonbankruptcy

The Z″ Model: Application to the Service Sector

The original Z-score had as one of its variables the asset turnover ratio. As this variable is industry sensitive, the Z″-model, which omitted this variable, was developed. This model is applicable to (public and private) firms in the manufacturing, merchandising, and service (*excluding financial*) sector. The model is based on the following equation:

$$Z'' = 6.56 \times \frac{\text{Working Capital}}{\text{Total Assets}}$$

$$+ \ 3.26 \times \frac{\text{Retained Earnings}}{\text{Total Assets}}$$

$$+ \ 6.72 \times \frac{\text{EBIT}}{\text{Total Assets}}$$

$$+ \ 1.05 \times \frac{\text{Book Value of Equity}}{\text{Book Value of Debt}}$$

The appropriate cut-off points for bankruptcy/nonbankruptcy and the gray area are:

Z″-score	Indication
<1.10	Bankruptcy
1.10–2.60	Gray area
>2.60	Nonbankruptcy

---

*The discussion in this box is based on Chapter 8 of Edward I. Altman, *Corporate Financial Distress and Bankruptcy*, New York: John Wiley & Sons, 1993.

BOX 18-3
ZETA™ and a Theoretical Bankruptcy Model

Scott (1981) compares a theoretical model of bankruptcy with the variables used in Altman et al.'s ZETA™ prediction model. In Scott's model, debt (interest) payments (R) can be made from current earnings before interest and taxes (EBIT) or from the firm's equity. This equity is defined as the present value of the firm's future dividends and is symbolized by S. Thus, bankruptcy* occurs when

$$R > \text{EBIT} + S$$

or, alternatively, bankruptcy is defined as

$$\text{EBIT} \leq R - S$$

If we let u_{EBIT} represent the expected (average) EBIT and s_{EBIT} the standard deviation of EBIT, the equation can be standardized, and (as in the Emery and Cogger model of Box 18-2) the probability of bankruptcy will be related to

$$\frac{\text{EBIT} - u_{\text{EBIT}}}{s_{\text{EBIT}}} \leq \frac{R - S - u_{\text{EBIT}}}{s_{\text{EBIT}}}$$

Dividing the numerator and denominator of the right-hand side of this equation by total assets (TA) and rearranging terms yield

$$\frac{\text{EBIT} - u_{\text{EBIT}}}{s_{\text{EBIT}}} \leq \frac{\left[\left(\dfrac{1}{u_{\text{EBIT}}/R} - 1\right)\dfrac{u_{\text{EBIT}}}{TA} - \left(\dfrac{S}{TA}\right)\right]}{s_{\text{EBIT}}/TA}$$

Scott points out that although the functional form differs, all the ratios in the right-hand side are represented (exactly or in surrogate form) in ZETA™.

ZETA™ Variable	Bankruptcy Model Variable
Times interest earned	u_{EBIT}/R
ROA	u_{EBIT}/TA
Standard deviation of EBIT over TA	s_{EBIT}/TA
Common equity to total capital	S/TA

---

*To ease the already cumbersome notation, we have dropped the tax term. With a corporate tax rate equal to t, the model becomes

$$R \geq \text{EBIT} + \frac{S}{(1 - t)}$$

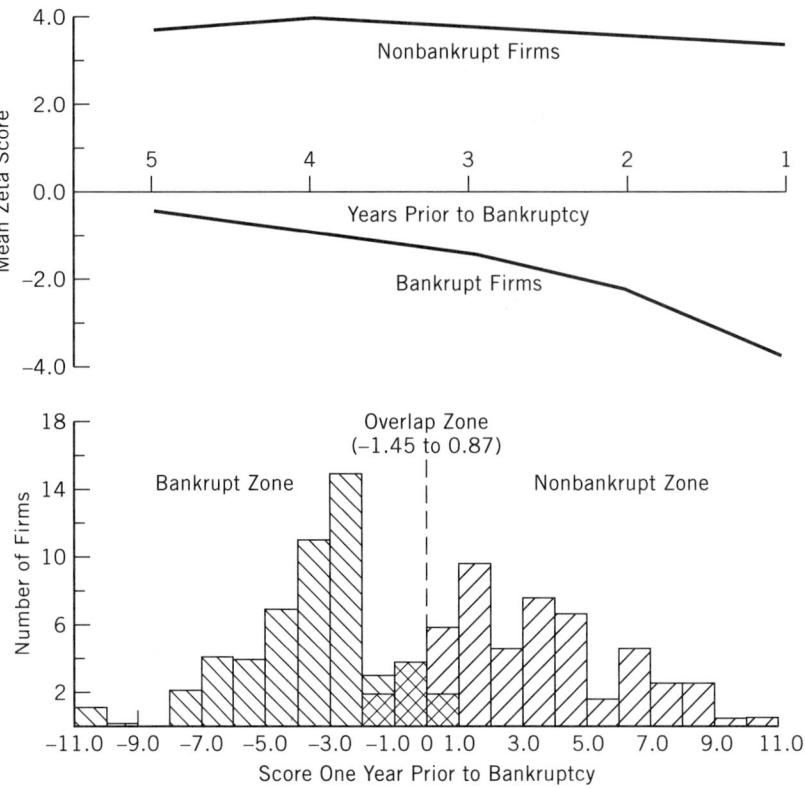

FIGURE 18-2 Zeta scores in years preceding bankruptcy. *Source:* Edward I. Altman, Robert G. Haldeman, and P. Narayann, "ZETA™ Analysis: A New Model to Identify Bankruptcy Risk of Corporations," *Journal of Banking and Finance,* June 1977, Figures 1 and 2, p. 49.

preceding bankruptcy, the less accurate the results. Notwithstanding the foregoing, the ZETA™ model is a major improvement over the original Z-model as it is far more accurate in years 2 through 5 preceding bankruptcy. The original model produced type I errors over 50%, whereas the accuracy of the ZETA™ model is closer to 70%.

An interesting aspect of the ZETA™ model is its use of adjusted rather than reported accounting data. Two of the adjustments are:

Off-balance-sheet debt. All noncancelable operating and capital leases are added to firm assets and liabilities. In addition, finance and other nonconsolidated subsidiaries are consolidated with the parent company.[17]

Intangible assets. Capitalized items such as research and development, interest costs, goodwill, and other intangibles are expensed.

These adjustments, although not comprehensive, are certainly a step in the right direction. Dambolena and Khoury (1980), however, downplay the importance of these adjustments.[18] They argue that Altman's results do not demonstrate that his adjust-

---

[17] Altman's work preceded SFAS 94 (1987), which required consolidation of all subsidiaries.

[18] Also see Elam (1975), who found that lease capitalization did not enhance a model's predictive ability.

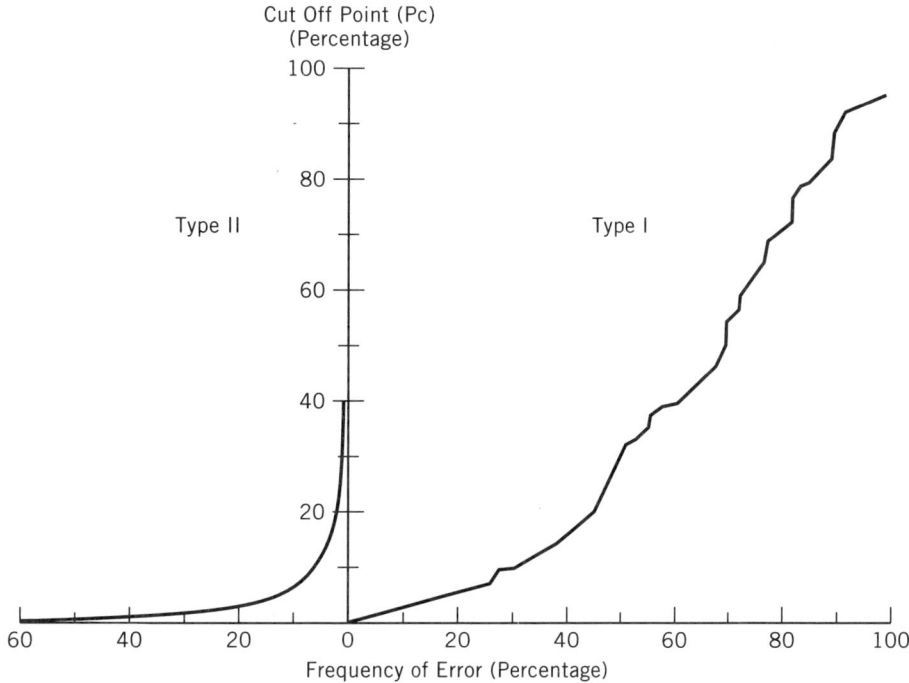

FIGURE 18-3 Trade-offs in classification errors in bankruptcy prediction. *Source:* James A. Ohlson, "Financial Ratios and the Probabilistic Prediction of Bankruptcy," *Journal of Accounting Research,* Spring 1980, Figure 5, p. 127. Reprinted with permission.

ments caused improvement. What would constitute a proof is running a Zeta model without lease capitalization and observing whether the predictive power of the model decreases significantly.[19]

The Probability of Bankruptcy. Ohlson (1980) approached the problem from a different perspective. He used probit analysis, which does not specify a cut-off point delineating a firm as bankrupt or nonbankrupt. Rather, it assigns to each firm a *probability of bankruptcy.* The user of the model can then choose a comfort level in terms of how high a probability he or she is willing to tolerate. The higher (lower) the probability cut-off, the greater the chance of misclassifying a (non)bankrupt company. These trade-offs[20] are illustrated in Figure 18-3. At a cut-off probability of approximately 1%, no type I error occurs, but the type II errors equal 47%. At that low level, essentially all firms are classified as being bankrupt. Raising the cut-off probability increases the chances of making a type I error (misclassifying a bankrupt company) but lowers the type II error. At 3.8% the overall classification errors are minimized with 12% type I errors and 17% type II errors.

---

[19]Ismael G. Dambolena and Sarkis J. Khoury, "Ratio Stability and Corporate Failure," *Journal of Finance*, September 1980, pp. 1017–1026.

[20]Ohlson reverses the nomenclature, calling type I errors type II and vice versa.

Bankruptcy Prediction and Cash Flows

Cash flow variables (or surrogates such as funds flows) are intuitively important factors in bankruptcy analysis. Although the evidence bears this out, both the selection of cash flow measures and interpretation of the results must be made carefully.

Beaver's original study found cash (defined as funds) flows/total debt to be the best *univariate* predictor. Subsequent studies examined whether the use of cash flow variables by themselves or together with a ratio-based model would improve the accuracy of bankruptcy prediction.

Gentry et al. (1985a) found that funds from operations and working capital changes (tested separately) did not aid bankruptcy prediction. Dividend flows were the most significant variable; capital expenditures and debt financing were among the variables that were not significant. However, as dividends are usually a function of cash available from operations after reinvestment (i.e., free cash flow), one measure may subsume the other. In a subsequent study, Gentry et al. (1985b) found that a model that combined (several[21]) cash flow variables with financial ratios performed better than one based on cash flows or financial ratios alone.

Casey and Bartczak (1984, 1985) put the whole bankruptcy classification issue in sharp focus. They concluded that cash flow variables either by themselves or added to a model such as the Z-model did not improve the prediction of bankruptcy. The conclusion, however, was based on *overall* results. A careful examination of their results indicates that an approximation of CFO (which was not reported during the period studied) *clearly aids in the prediction of bankrupt companies*. In the five years prior to bankruptcy, CFO correctly classified bankrupt firms from 83 to 92% of the time (depending on the time period). In contrast, accrual accounting measures correctly classified bankrupt companies only 30 to 83% of the time. On the other hand, CFO did not do as well as accrual measures in predicting nonbankrupt firms as it classified too many of them as bankrupt (47% incorrectly classified one year prior).[22] Given the relative costs of these errors, however, it is the former type of error that must be avoided. The CFO measure, contrary to Casey and Barczak's conclusions, does seem to be useful for bankruptcy prediction.

This ability of cash flow variables to improve the prediction of bankrupt companies (while at the same time not improving the ability to classify nonbankrupt companies) is borne out by other studies. Aziz and Lawson (1989) found that adding cash flow variables to Altman's Z-model and ZETA™ model did not improve the accuracy of the overall (failed and nonfailed) classifications. *However, the combined models did a better job of predicting failures one and two years before bankruptcy.* Thus, when the combined models erred, they did so in a conservative fashion and overpredicted the number of failed firms. Again, as noted earlier, this type of error is less costly.

Bankruptcy and Financial Distress: Concluding Comments

One of the issues raised by Casey and Bartczak was that the misclassification of nonbankrupt companies results from ignoring companies' ability to stay alive. In

---

[21]The use of several cash flow variables may explain their results as opposed to those of Gombola et al. (1987) who did not find an improvement in the ability to predict bankruptcy when they added (*only*) CFO to a set of financial ratios.

[22]CFO classified as bankrupt many financially distressed firms, for example, Chrysler and Massey Ferguson.

spite of lengthy periods of negative CFO, companies can continue to operate by renegotiating credit terms with creditors or selling assets to raise cash.

We do not dispute this point, but rather question the focus of these models on the event of bankruptcy alone. Bankruptcy is a legal, not an economic phenomenon. It is fraught with political and other nonmarket considerations. A better focus would be on whether or not the company is "healthy" or "sick," or on whether or not financial statement information and ratios allow users to forecast future investment performance. From that perspective, CFO is a good indicator of financial distress, raising the question of whether the firm's creditors will be repaid. Staying alive by selling assets or renegotiating ("restructuring") debt is not a sign of success.[23] Creditors and stockholders may suffer large losses even though bankruptcy does not occur.

The evaluation of bankruptcy prediction models requires consideration of two related issues. First, there are different degrees of and criteria for "failure." Indeed, many of the studies define the event of bankruptcy differently. Second, the variables used in the empirical models are not built on an underlying theoretical framework but, rather, rely on the researcher's intuition. Thus, they may be sample- or time-specific. However, some of the models have withstood the test of time and, as Box 18-3 shows, although the ZETA™ model was not designed in the context of a theoretical model, it includes variables used in such a model.

THE PREDICTION OF DEBT RISK

This section addresses the evaluation of debt risk using predictions of bond ratings. The research discussed here was primarily based on publicly traded debt. The results, however, are useful in the analysis of privately held debt.

The Prediction of Bond Ratings

Bond ratings are issued by bond rating agencies, the most prominent of which are Moody's and Standard & Poor's. The ratings attest to the creditworthiness of the firm: The probability that adverse conditions will result in financial difficulties is taken into consideration in assessing the likelihood of the firm defaulting on its interest or principal payments. Bond indentures and the degree of protection afforded in the event of bankruptcy are among other important considerations in the ratings process.

Bond Rating Classifications

The ratings[24] used by Standard & Poor's along with a brief description of each are presented in Exhibit 18-6. A summary of these ratings along with their Moody's

---

[23]In that sense, Ohlson's probabilistic model is useful as the predictive variable is not the ultimate event of bankruptcy, but rather a probability of going bankrupt. A higher probability can be used to assess how poorly the company is doing. Burgstahler et al. (1989), in fact, used Ohlson's model to assess how changes in the probability of bankruptcy affected firms' equity value.

[24]The ratings are further modified by + and − designations, permitting a finer gradation in the rating categories.

EXHIBIT 18-6
Standard & Poor's Corporate and Municipal Rating Definitions

STANDARD & POOR'S Corporate and Municipal Rating Definitions

DEBT

A Standard & Poor's corporate or municipal debt rating is a current assessment of the creditworthiness of an obligor with respect to a specific obligation. This assessment may take into consideration obligors such as guarantors, insurers, or lessees.

The debt rating is not a recommendation to purchase, sell or hold a security, inasmuch as it does not comment as to market price or suitability for a particular investor.

The ratings are based on current information furnished by the issuer or obtained by Standard & Poor's from other sources it considers reliable. Standard & Poor's does not perform any audit in connection with any rating and may, on occasion, rely on unaudited financial information. The ratings may be changed, suspended or withdrawn as a result of changes in, or unavailability of, such information, or based on other circumstances.

The ratings are based, in varying degrees, on the following considerations:

I.   Likelihood of default-capacity and willingness of the obligor as to the timely payment of interest and repayment of principal in accordance with the terms of the obligation;

II. Nature of and provisions of the obligation;

III. Protection afforded by, and relative position of, the obligation in the event of bankruptcy, reorganization or other arrangement under the laws of bankruptcy and other laws affecting creditor's rights.

AAA   Debt rated 'AAA' has the highest rating assigned by Standard & Poor's. Capacity to pay interest and repay principal is extremely strong.

AA   Debt rated 'AA' has a very strong capacity to pay interest and repay principal and differs from the higher rated issues only in small degree.

A   Debt rated 'A' has a strong capacity to pay interest and repay principal although it is somewhat more susceptible to the adverse effects of changes in circumstances and economic conditions than debt in higher rated categories.

BBB   Debt rated 'BBB' is regarded as having an adequate capacity to pay interest and repay principal. Whereas it normally exhibits adequate protection parameters, adverse economic conditions or changing circumstances are more likely to lead to a weakened capacity to pay interest and repay principal for debt in this category than in higher rated categories.

BB, B, CCC, CC, C   Debt rated 'BB', 'B', 'CCC', 'CC' and 'C' is regarded, on balance, as predominantly speculative with respect to capacity to pay interest and repay principal in accordance with the terms of the obligation. 'BB' indicates the lowest degree of speculation and 'C' the highest degree of speculation. While such debt will likely have some quality and protective characteristics, these are outweighed by large uncertainties or major risk exposures to adverse conditions.

BB   Debt rated 'BB' has less near-term vulnerability to default than other speculative issues. However, it faces major ongoing uncertainties or exposure to adverse business, financial, or economic conditions which could lead to inadequate capacity to meet timely interest and principal payments. The 'BB' rating category is also used for debt subordinated to senior debt that is assigned an actual or implied 'BBB –' rating.

B   Debt rated 'B' has a greater vulnerability to default but currently has the capacity to meet interest payments and principal repayments. Adverse business, financial, or economic conditions will likely impair capacity or willingness to pay interest and repay principal. The 'B' rating category is also used for debt subordinated to senior debt that is assigned an actual or implied 'BB' or 'BB –' rating.

CCC   Debt rated 'CCC' has a currently identifiable vulnerability to default, and is dependent upon favorable business, financial, and economic conditions to meet timely payment of interest and repayment of principal. In the event of adverse business, financial, or economic conditions, it is not likely to have the capacity to pay interest and repay principal. The 'CCC' rating category is also used for debt subordinated to senior debt that is assigned an actual or implied 'B' or 'B –' rating.

CC   The rating 'CC' is typically applied to debt subordinated to senior debt that is assigned an actual or implied 'CCC' rating.

C   The rating 'C' is typically applied to debt subordinated to senior debt which is assigned an actual or implied 'CCC –' debt rating. The 'C' rating may be used to cover a situation where a bankruptcy petition has been filed, but debt service payments are continued.

CI   The rating 'CI' is reserved for income bonds on which no interest is being paid.

D   Debt rated 'D' is in payment default. The 'D' rating category is used when interest payments or principal payments are not made on the date due even if the applicable grace period has not expired, unless S&P believes that such payments will be made during such grace period. The 'D' rating also will be used upon the filing of a bankruptcy petition if debt service payments are jeopardized.

Plus (+) or Minus (–): The ratings from 'AA' to 'CCC' may be modified by the addition of a plus or minus sign to show relative standing within the major categories.

r   The 'r' is attached to highlight derivative, hybrid, and certain other obligations that S&P believes may experience high volatility or high variability in expected returns due to non-credit risks. Examples of such obligations are: securities whose principal or interest return is indexed to equities, commodities, or currencies; certain swaps and options; and interest only and principal only mortgage securities.

The absence of an 'r' symbol should not be taken as an indication that an obligation will exhibit no volatility or variability in total return.

NR   indicates that no public rating has been requested, that there is insufficient information on which to base a rating, or that S&P does not rate a particular type of obligation as a matter of policy.

Debt Obligations of issuers outside the United States and its territories are rated on the same basis as domestic corporate and municipal issues. The ratings measure the creditworthiness of the obligor but do not take into account currency exchange and related uncertainties.

Source: Standard & Poor's *Bond Guide*, December 1996. Used by permission of Standard & Poor's Corporation. All rights reserved.

counterparts is presented below:

	Very High-Quality	High-Quality	Speculative	Very Poor
Standard & Poor's	AAA AA	A BBB	BB B	CCC D
Moody's	Aaa Aa	A Baa	Ba B	Caa C

The Bond Ratings Process

Ratings are sought by companies when they issue new debt. The company pays a fee and the agency issues a rating following an examination of the "creditworthiness" of the company. The agency analyzes the company's operations and personnel, its financial statements, and its *pro forma* projections as well as other relevant financial and nonfinancial information.[25]

---

[25]For a more detailed discussion of the rating process, see Chapter 1, Ahmed Belkaoui, *Industrial Bonds and the Rating Process* (Westport, CT: Quorum Books, an imprint of Greenwood Publishing Group, Inc., 1983).

The actual ratings process, however, is shrouded in mystery. How each agency arrives at its rating and the criteria used are not disclosed. The rating agencies go to great lengths to discourage speculation that the rating process is mechanical and based on some mathematical formula. Rather, they stress that ratings are based on the judgment of their analysts who determine their rating after assimilating quantitative as well as available qualitative data.

When the ratings are announced by the agency, the firm, if it is unhappy with the rating, may decide to drop the debt offering and search for alternative financing sources, or alternatively, it may decide to appeal the rating. The appeal may result in a series of negotiations,[26] whereby the terms of the offering are changed. These changes may be with respect to the payment terms or the restrictive covenants attached to the offering.

Impact of Ratings

The ratings process affects a firm's liability position in at least three ways:

1. As Exhibit 18-7 indicates, the higher the rating, the lower the interest rate required. Ratings, therefore, affect real, ongoing costs to the issuing firm.
2. The covenants written into a bond offering are often designed to obtain favorable ratings. As these covenants protect creditors by putting restrictions on the equity shareholders, ratings influence the sharing of risk and reward between equity- and debtholders.
3. Many institutional investors are restricted (legally or by internal policy) as to the type of debt they can hold; that is, the debt must have a minimum rating. Thus, the success or failure of an offering (or whether or not the debt is even issued) is often determined by the rating.

Rating agencies argue that ratings do not cause differential borrowing costs. Rather, they state that ratings and differential borrowing costs reflect the same set of economic conditions indicating the relative risk of the firm. This argument is not without merit. Others, however, contend that, as with any grading device originally designed to measure some attribute, the emphasis tends to shift to the measuring device itself rather than the underlying attribute.[27]

Thus, there is evidence that the ratings themselves can influence bond yields beyond the effect warranted by the firm's economic position. This may be especially true for adjacent ratings such as, for example, AAA versus AA or Baa versus Ba. This argument is bolstered by point 3, which indicates that some investment policies are based on the ratings themselves. To the extent that these factors affect the demand for a debt issue, clearly they influence the yield required for its successful sale.

Notwithstanding the agencies' claims that ratings are not in any sense mechanically or mathematically derived, researchers have constructed mathematical models to pre-

---

[26]The underwriter will play a major role in these negotiations.

[27]Accounting income is, obviously, another example of this phenomenon. A great deal of positive accounting theory is built around this notion. Consistent with the behavior predicted by positive accounting theory as to the existence of incentives to influence accounting numbers (artificially), there is also evidence that firms attempt to cultivate debt ratings agencies to obtain favorable ratings.

EXHIBIT 18-7
Relationship Between Ratings and Bond Yields

STANDARD & POOR'S CORPORATE & GOVERNMENT BOND YIELD INDEX—BY RATINGS

	†PUBLIC UTILITY			INDUSTRIAL						COMPOSITE			U.S. GOVERNMENT			MUNI-CIPALS
	AA	A	BBB	AAA	AA	A	BBB	BB	B	AA	A	BBB	LONG TERM	INTER-MEDIATE	SHORT TERM	
Monthly Averages 1994-1993																
December	8.55	8.70	9.31	8.30	8.62	8.90	9.47	10.34	11.74	8.54	8.81	9.39	7.97	7.76	7.55	6.76
November	8.71	8.84	9.50	8.43	8.60	8.98	9.67	10.07	11.70	8.65	8.90	9.57	8.18	7.49	7.14	6.96
October	8.53	8.66	9.43	8.35	8.54	8.92	9.55	9.84	11.70	8.53	8.79	9.49	8.07	6.90	6.76	6.50
September	8.22	8.39	9.26	8.07	8.35	8.76	9.27	9.89	11.49	8.29	8.57	9.27	7.83	6.69	6.42	6.33
August	8.00	8.28	9.02	7.80	8.07	8.47	8.92	9.84	11.10	8.04	8.36	8.97	7.54	6.55	6.21	6.19
July	8.13	8.33	9.14	7.97	8.19	8.59	9.03	9.89	10.93	8.16	8.46	9.09	7.68	6.69	6.29	6.19
June	7.97	8.21	8.95	7.81	8.05	8.52	8.83	9.76	10.53	8.01	8.37	8.89	7.47	6.48	6.11	6.41
May	8.13	8.27	8.85	7.96	8.10	8.64	8.79	9.76	10.64	8.11	8.45	8.82	7.50	6.62	6.20	6.26
April	8.00	8.28	8.72	7.79	7.92	8.50	8.57	9.54	10.62	7.96	8.39	8.65	7.32	6.29	5.85	6.28
March	7.73	8.06	8.49	7.39	7.59	8.21	8.35	9.12	10.31	7.66	8.15	8.42	6.89	5.78	5.30	5.93
February	7.44	7.96	8.31	6.94	7.33	7.97	8.19	8.91	10.50	7.38	7.97	8.25	6.44	5.23	4.74	5.44
January	7.36	8.12	8.31	6.80	7.26	7.91	8.28	9.01	10.29	7.31	8.01	8.29	6.28	5.02	4.01	5.30
December	7.34	8.69	8.36	6.79	7.28	7.83	8.28	9.06	10.45	7.31	8.26	8.30	6.23	5.08	3.87	5.35
Annual Ranges																
1994 High	8.75	8.87	9.53	8.46	8.64	9.01	9.69	10.41	11.82	8.69	8.94	9.60	8.22	7.83	7.64	7.03
Low	7.26	7.82	8.21	6.66	7.19	7.82	8.06	8.89	10.08	7.23	7.89	8.14	6.15	4.90	3.90	5.27
1993 High	8.34	9.03	8.77	8.12	8.21	8.60	9.03	9.88	11.19	8.23	8.63	8.82	7.35	6.14	4.57	6.22
Low	7.28	7.99	7.65	6.16	7.06	7.48	7.35	8.96	10.37	7.26	7.73	7.50	5.75	4.63	3.63	5.23
1992 High	9.02	9.24	9.32	8.69	8.86	9.38	9.50	11.52	12.53	8.94	9.31	9.39	8.07	7.45	6.03	6.71
Low	8.40	8.63	8.70	7.89	8.08	8.49	8.82	9.84	10.94	8.28	8.56	8.82	7.07	5.53	3.65	5.88
1991 High	9.54	9.75	9.99	9.14	9.55	9.89	11.83	12.58	20.53	9.54	9.80	10.86	8.70	8.13	7.20	7.15
Low	8.77	8.93	8.93	8.05	8.25	8.87	9.13	10.80	12.87	8.51	8.90	9.03	7.36	6.32	5.03	6.50
1990 High	10.17	10.36	10.60	9.76	10.13	10.50	11.48	14.12	19.85	10.15	10.43	10.98	9.32	9.13	8.99	7.56
Low	9.09	9.39	9.68	8.78	9.06	9.55	10.06	11.94	13.80	9.07	9.47	9.87	8.22	7.75	7.22	6.99
1989 High	10.14	10.47	10.56	9.92	10.29	10.70	11.06	12.30	13.95	10.21	10.59	10.81	9.50	9.68	9.97	7.68
Low	8.98	9.28	9.55	8.62	8.91	9.45	9.90	11.20	11.93	8.95	9.36	9.69	7.97	7.71	7.61	6.87

Source: Standard & Poor's *Bond Guide*, January 1995. Used by permission of Standard & Poor's Corporation. All rights reserved.

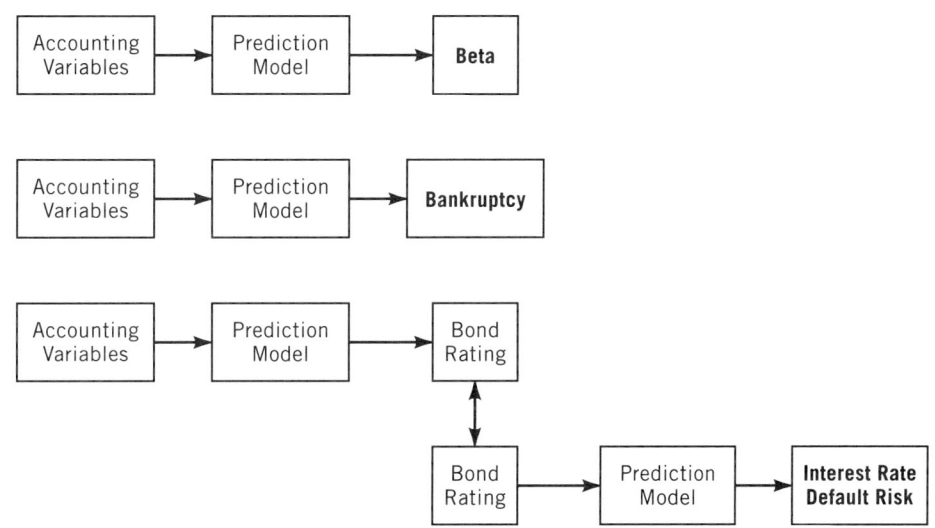

FIGURE 18-4 Comparison of bond rating prediction with bankruptcy and beta prediction (bold indicates variable of interest).

dict bond ratings. Explanatory independent variables, methodology, and the success rates of some of these studies are discussed next.

Usefulness of Bond Ratings Prediction

Figure 18-4 is a schematic representation of the predictive process used to forecast bond ratings in contrast to that used to forecast beta or bankruptcy. The linkages in those models are directly between the accounting variables and the predicted attribute of interest. For bonds, the attributes of interest are the probability of default and the required bond yield. The model does not, however, forecast these attributes. Rather, it forecasts another predictor of these attributes. This raises the following question. If the goal of the mathematical model is simply to duplicate the rating agencies' classification, why bother? Just use the ratings issued by the agency.[28] The responses to this question follow:

1. Some debt offerings (e.g., private placements) are not rated. A mathematical model would, therefore, be a useful surrogate for the ratings process in determining the appropriate yield and indentures. We have previously suggested using predicted ratings to estimate the appropriate market rate at which to discount debt.

2. Ratings are not continuously revised, and there is evidence of a considerable lag between the time conditions change and when ratings agencies respond by

---

[28]The prediction of bond ratings differs from the prediction of beta. The object there is to improve on the predictions of beta readily available. The prediction of bankruptcy is similar; the object is to forecast the event itself, not duplicate someone else's prediction.

revising ratings. Furthermore, there is conflicting evidence[29] as to the extent to which the market anticipates a ratings change. These factors lead to the following interrelated benefits of a bond ratings model:

(a) The model can be used to monitor the debt after the original rating is made. This provides a more accurate prediction of the debt's current risk/return characteristics and whether or not it is over/undervalued.

(b) Given that the market may not fully anticipate a ratings change, the model can be used to forecast a ratings change.

3. Firms sometimes undertake large investment or acquisition programs. These programs usually affect the firm's financial (and operating) structure as a result of the differing characteristics of the acquired firm and/or any new debt required to finance these programs. To the extent that these changes mirror changes in the underlying characteristics of the firm's new and existing debt, the firm's cost of debt capital may change. A ratings model may help the firm (or its investment banker) anticipate these changes in the planning stages of the program.

4. The independent or explanatory variables in a predictive model can shed insight into the important factors that determine the (perceived) riskiness of debt. A firm seeking a favorable rating can take action ahead of time to improve those areas in which it is deficient. This is not to suggest that the firm engage in "window dressing" to spruce up a certain ratio, but rather that it remedy the underlying economic factors that drive the ratio.[30]

5. Finally, as discussed in this section, there exists some evidence that ratings at the lower end of the spectrum, especially for subordinated debt, may be inconsistent and "rigid." This evidence may provide some investment opportunities.

Choice of Explanatory Variables

The relationship between financial performance as measured by accounting ratios and bond rating classification is demonstrated in Exhibit 18-8. The better performers have better ratings and *an initial estimate of a firm's ratings can be derived by mapping the firm's ratios to those found on the table*. It must, however, be noted that the data in this table are based on a large sample. As will be discussed in further detail shortly,[31] these relationships may not necessarily hold for firms on an individual or small-group basis. A firm, for example, may have profitability ratios in the AAA-A categories but leverage ratios that place it in the BBB-B categories.

---

[29]Holthausen and Leftwich (1986) found that an upgrading of a firm's rating is anticipated by the market, whereas downgrades are not fully anticipated. Companies' shares suffer (negative) abnormal returns following downgrades.

[30]This point is reinforced by recalling that ratios in such models are often used as a surrogate for an overall category or factor (see Chapter 4). Thus, the ratio may be masking the actual relationship contributing to the riskiness of the debt.

[31]See the discussion relating to Ang and Patel (1975).

EXHIBIT 18-8
Relationship Between Ratings and Financial Ratios

KEY INDUSTRIAL FINANCIAL RATIOS Three-year (1992–1994) medians	AAA	AA	A	BBB	BB	B
Pretax interest coverage (x)	21.39	10.02	5.67	2.90	2.25	0.74
Pretax interest coverage including rents (x)	6.96	5.31	3.42	2.22	1.62	0.85
EBITDA interest coverage (x)	31.68	14.78	8.25	5.02	3.46	1.56
Funds from operations/total debt (%)	109.80	75.40	49.10	30.30	20.20	9.80
Free operating cash flow/total debt (%)	53.80	27.90	19.60	3.90	0.70	(1.70)
Pretax return on permanent capital (%)	25.10	19.10	16.00	11.80	10.20	6.20
Operating income/sales (%)	21.20	17.10	14.60	12.30	11.90	8.70
Long-term debt/capital (%)	9.70	18.90	28.80	40.70	50.20	62.20
Total debt/capitalization including short-term debt (%)	22.60	28.30	36.70	45.30	55.60	71.40
Total debt/capitalization including short-term debt (including 8 times rents) (%)	36.10	40.10	46.80	56.10	65.50	76.50

Exhibit 18-2 compares models used to predict bond ratings and the variables in these models.[32] Similar to bankruptcy models, formal theoretical models do not exist. Not surprisingly, liquidity, long-term solvency, and leverage ratios feature prominently in these studies. In addition, as bondholders are primarily interested in receiving a (steady) stream of interest and principal payments, variables related to the stability of the firm's earnings stream are included. Similarly, the appearance of "size" variables is explained by the added protection for debtholders, as a result of the greater endurance of larger firms, in the event earnings decline.

Subordination, as seen in the next section, plays a very important role in bond classification. This issue has implications only in the event of financial distress when subordinated bondholders must "wait in line" behind senior claimants. It has no impact on a firm's ongoing interest and principal obligations to the subordinated bondholders.

Model Results

Generally speaking, the models perform quite well; they average anywhere from 60 to 70% accuracy in duplicating the rating arrived at by an agency. Further, when they are in error, it is usually by misclassifying the rating into the immediate adjacent category. When adjacent categories are "allowed," the "success" rate is over 90%.

When we move from the overall rating to specific categories, the results are not as positive. Both Horrigan (1966) and Pinches and Mingo (1973) find the Baa or BBB classification most difficult to predict. This category is important[33] because it is the

---

[32]Generally, the variables used are arrived at by first selecting a set of ratios/variables from the ratio classifications described in Chapter 4. The original set is then scaled down, using techniques such as factor analysis, to a subset of ratios capturing the information contained in the full set. The final set of variables then chosen is the subset that provides the best fit in the model's classification (whether regression, discriminant, or probit) equation. These best-fit results are explanatory in nature as they are based on the same sample companies that were used to develop the models. The model is then tested on a holdout sample to test its predictive ability.

[33]For this reason, firms may work harder to retain the higher rating.

rating that

> has become generally accepted in the investment community as the cutoff between investment and noninvestment grade bonds.[34]

Further, subordination has been found in a number of studies to be the most important variable in the classification model. As the following data from Pinches and Mingo indicate, the importance of subordination and the difficulty in classifying Baa firms are related.

Classification of Pinches and Mingo (Combined) Sample by Subordination Status

	Aa	A	Baa	Ba	B
Subordinated	0	2	20	60	32
Nonsubordinated	18	33	14	1	0
Total	18	35	34	61	32

Source: G. E. Pinches and K. A. Mingo, "A Multivariate Analysis of Industrial Bond Ratings," *Journal of Finance*, March 1973, Table 9, p. 12.

Virtually all Aa and A-rated bonds are nonsubordinated, whereas those rated Ba and B are subordinated. Only at Baa are bonds evenly distributed between subordinated and unsubordinated. Thus, the subordination variable by itself[35] provides the initial pass as to the bond rating. Subordination, however, provides no discriminating power in the Baa category itself. Therefore, the poor classification within the Baa category, where subordination does not play a role, implies that the other variables do not possess strong discriminating power.

The relevance of this point from our perspective is further driven home if we examine the other variables and their relative significance in the classification equations. A size measure (total assets or debt) typically ranks second or third. Depending on the study, the other measure in the top three is either debt/capital (Belkaoui) or a measure of earnings stability (years of consecutive dividends in Pinches and Mingo). Conventional financial ratios thus contribute less than the size or subordination variables:

> The results of this analysis indicate that many traditional financial considerations are fairly insignificant in the bond rating process.[36]

Additionally, for some of the financial variables used in the classification studies the studies found no clear-cut pattern in which higher-rated categories exhibit "better"

---

[34]G. E. Pinches and K. A. Mingo, "A Multivariate Analysis of Industrial Bond Ratings," *Journal of Finance*, March 1973, pp. 1–18.

[35]"If one was only interested in rating bonds as investment quality (Aa, A and Baa) or noninvestment quality (Ba and B) the best single predictor is the subordinated status of the bond. Based on this variable alone, correct ratings (investment versus noninvestment quality) would have resulted 88.6% of the time for the original sample and 83.3% (40/48) of the time for the holdout sample." Pinches and Mingo, p. 12.

[36]G. E. Pinches and K. A. Mingo, p. 13.

ratios. This is a further indication that the relationship between ratings and financial variables is weak.

This weak relationship can be viewed in a number of ways depending on one's perspective. One argument is that financial variables measuring solvency and leverage are not related to the risk of a firm's debt. At face value, this seems contrary to the thrust of this book and the most fundamental tenets of financial analysis. We shall explore this point later. Ratings agencies would argue, as noted earlier, that financial variables are relevant, in a more complex way than can be captured via a linear weighted summation with other selected variables. Others, however, argue that the lack of consistency, as firms with similar financial characteristics obtain different rankings, is a weakness in the ratings process itself and is precisely why the focus on the ratings process needs to be reevaluated.

The Z''-Score and Bond Ratings

In the previous section, we discussed bankruptcy models such as ZETA™ and the Z(' and ")-scores. As higher scores in these models indicate a more solvent firm, a natural extension of these models is to apply them to bond ratings. This was done by Altman for his Z''-model. The relationship between bond ratings in the United States and the Z''-score (augmented by an intercept term of 3.25) is illustrated in Exhibit 18-9. The relationships in the exhibit were determined on an *ex post* basis; that is, calculating the Z''-score for a sample of 750 U.S. firms and finding the average Z''-score within each rating category.

Applications to Emerging Markets. Recently, this model has been used by Salomon Brothers[37] as a *starting point* to determine ratings for corporate bonds issued in "emerging markets" such as Mexico. An initial rating is determined by the Z''-score and then is adjusted up or down after considering factors (e.g., currency risk, inflation, political environment, and industry classification) specific to the firm and country in question.

In a similar vein, Sondhi (1995) used the Form 20-F GAAP reconciliations published by foreign firms to compute ratios used by Standard & Poor's for U.S. firms. The adjusted ratios were used to develop initial estimates of ratings for a sample of emerging market debt securities. The study reported differences among the S&P ratings, ratings based on adjusted local GAAP, and U.S. GAAP-based ratings of emerging market debt.

The Significance of Ratings: Another Look

The explanation for "inconsistencies" in bond ratings is that qualitative factors (raters' judgment) come into play. The rating agencies believe this to be a positive factor. However, from our perspective it is not a very satisfactory answer unless there is an objective evaluation of the efficacy of these qualitative factors. That is, if the purpose of the ratings is to "rank" the probability of timely repayment of interest and principal, then there needs to be evidence that the differentially rated bonds actually do exhibit different risk characteristics.

---

[37]See John M. Hartzell, Matthew B. Peck, and Edward I. Altman, *Emerging Markets Corporate Bonds—A Scoring System*, Salomon Brothers Inc., New York, May 15, 1995 and updates issued July 31, 1995 and December 14, 1995.

EXHIBIT 18-9
Relationship Between U.S. Bond Ratings and (Intercept-Adjusted) Z″-Score

The relationship between bond ratings and the Z″-score adjusted for an intercept of 3.25 is presented in the table below. The purpose of the adjustment was to set zero as the "base" score below which a default is signaled. The relevant Z″-score is

$$Z'' = 6.56 \frac{\text{Working Capital}}{\text{Total Assets}} + 3.26 \frac{\text{Retained Earnings}}{\text{Total Assets}} + 6.72 \frac{\text{EBIT}}{\text{Total Assets}}$$

$$+ 1.05 \frac{\text{Book Value of Equity}}{\text{Total Liabilities}} + 3.25$$

U.S. Bond Rating	Average Z″ Score (with intercept)
AAA	8.15
AA+	7.60
AA	7.30
AA−	7.00
A+	6.85
A	6.65
A−	6.40
BBB+	6.25
BBB	5.85
BBB−	5.65
BB+	5.25
BB	4.95
BB−	4.75
B+	4.50
B	4.15
B−	3.75
CCC+	3.20
CCC	2.50
CCC−	1.75
D(efault)	0

Source: Emerging Market Corporate Bonds—A Scoring System, J. M. Hartzell, Matthew Peck, and E. I. Altman, Salomon Brothers, May 15, 1995, p. 9.

The subordination issue mentioned earlier is a case in point. If ratings measure the probability of repayment, then

> *conventional wisdom suggests that the financial strength of the firm is a better measure of risk than subordination.* However, prior ratings prediction models. . . have identified subordination as an important predictor variable. Such results apparently reflect the actions of bond raters; when a firm has subordinated and unsubordinated bonds, the subordinated issue is invariably rated one grade lower than the nonsubordinated issue. *Apparently, raters automatically downgrade a subordinate bond by one rating.*[38]

[38]L. G. Martin and G. V. Henderson, "On Bond Ratings and Pension Obligations: A Note," *Journal of Financial and Quantitative Analysis*, December 1983, pp. 463–470. Emphasis added.

Is this downgrading justified? That is, do the financial characteristics of the firm suggest that its two issues be rated differently?[39] If not, then the ratings process is at fault, and if the yield on the subordinated bond is higher as a result of the lower rating, an astute investor can take advantage of the higher return without adding any risk to the portfolio.

Our implicit conclusion is that the focus of the research is misguided. The focus should not be on the relationship of financial variables to bond ratings, but rather on their relationship with the actual probabilities of repayment and/or realized yields.[40] Ang and Patel (1975) examined this issue and compared Moody's ratings and ratings predicted by four[41] statistical bond rating models with actual measures of bond default and loss rate on investment yield (defined as the difference between realized and promised yield). They found insignificant differences between the performance of Moody's and the bond ratings models on an overall basis. In fact, in two of the five years examined, a statistical model outperformed Moody's. Ang and Patel concluded that Moody's ratings were inconsistent and should not be relied on in making long-term bond investments. Investors

> should diversify across all rating groups or even concentrate on lower rated bonds if the analyst is confident that the probability of the firm being solvent in the next few years is high.[42]

Ang and Patel demonstrated that Moody's ratings did not outperform models designed to duplicate those same ratings in the prediction of default risk and yield. We suggest, however, that a more relevant comparison of Moody's ratings would be to a model specifically designed to examine the relationship between default risk and yield and a set of explanatory variables. Such a model would, of course, be an original ratings model. Unfortunately, most studies focus on the less interesting case of models that duplicate existing ratings rather than attempting to design a better ratings model.

Measurement of Financial Variables

Earlier, we noted that clear-cut distinctions in financial variables do not exist across bond rating categories. One possible explanation lies in how these ratios are measured. For the most part, no systematic[43] adjustments for differences in accounting policies, off-balance-sheet obligations, unusual items, etc. (as suggested throughout this book and summarized in Chapter 17) are made to the ratios used in these statistical models.

---

[39]Remember, subordination is an issue only in the case of financial distress.

[40]This was an early focus of this line of research. Fisher (1959) examined the factors accounting for differences in corporate bonds' risk premia (i.e., excess yield over the risk-free rate). The explanatory variables used by Fisher were the same four used in West's study (Exhibit 18-2). In fact, West's purpose was to examine whether Fisher's explanatory variables of bond yields could also be used to explain differences in bond ratings.

[41]The Horrigan, West, Pogue and Soldovsky, and Pinches and Mingo models.

[42]James S. Ang and Kiritkumar A. Patel, "Bond Ratings Methods: Comparison and Validation," *Journal of Finance*, May 1975, pp. 631–640.

[43]We stress "systematic" as there have been some isolated adjustments. Belkaoui, for example, capitalized off-balance-sheet leases and included the resultant debt in his ratios. He did not report the effects of this procedure as this was not the thrust of his study.

Bond rating agencies may be presumed to consider all the information available that could and should be used to adjust these ratios. Hence, the ratios used may be misspecified and in that sense may have little or no discriminating value.

EQUITY RISK: MEASUREMENT AND PREDICTION

The last index of risk we examine is the measure of the firm's equity risk. Implicitly, this risk is related to a firm's valuation and expected return.

Exhibit 18-7 indicated the greater the risk of default as measured by the lower rating, the greater the effective yield (return) paid by the bond. This, of course, is in line with a cardinal principle of investment theory; the greater the expected risk, the greater the expected return. The question becomes how to define, measure, and quantify risk.

These issues are important. Theories of the relationship between equity risk and return have come under fire as the definitions of risk embodied by the CAPM and β have not held up empirically. On the other hand, the suggested empirical notions of risk that "outperform" β come with tenuous theoretical underpinnings. In this section of the chapter, we:

1. Review the relationship between accounting variables and β, and then
2. Turn to a discussion of the controversy as to alternative measures of risk that outperform β and, some argue, may supplant β.

Risk and Return: Theoretical Models

In general, the uncertain investment return constitutes the risk borne by equityholders. This risk reflects uncertainty with respect to demand, output prices, input costs, etc. These factors themselves are impacted by global and national economic and political conditions, industrywide and competitive pressures, and conditions endemic to the firm itself. Thus, risk can be classified by its two sources:

1. *Unsystematic risk.* Factors that are specific to the firm.
2. *Systematic risk.* Factors that are common across a wide spectrum of firms.

Portfolio theory suggests that diversification enables investors to eliminate unsystematic risk. Moreover, it argues that, in an efficient market, investors are compensated only for risk that cannot be eliminated by diversification. *Thus, the risk measure that remains relevant is that of systematic risk.*

The CAPM and Beta (β)

As discussed in Chapter 5, both the capital asset pricing model (CAPM), which expresses expected returns as

$$E(R_i) = R_f + \beta_e E(R_m - R_f)$$

or (its empirical counterpart) the market model, which expresses expected returns as

$$E(R_t) = a + \beta_e E(R_m)$$

use beta (β_e), the (standardized) covariance (comovement) between the returns of a given firm and overall market returns, as a measure of systematic risk.

These models predict that a firm's expected return should be positively related to β_e (i.e., the higher the risk, as measured by β_e, the higher the return) and β_e *is sufficient* to describe the cross-sectional variation of expected returns.

APT and Multifactor Models

The theoretical development of the CAPM relies on a number of restrictive assumptions. For example, the CAPM assumes that there exists a market portfolio consisting of *all* risky assets. This portfolio is, by definition, unobservable. Additionally, tests of the model that use different proxies (e.g., the S&P 500 index or the NYSE index) for the market portfolio may give different results depending on the proxy used.

The Arbitrage Pricing Theory (APT), an asset pricing model developed by Stephen Ross in the 1970s, does not require the CAPM assumptions. Its theoretical development is beyond the scope of this book.[44] The intuition behind it, however, is relatively straightforward (and in a sense similar to that of the CAPM). The APT depicts the return of a security as a function of N (macro) factors F and a (micro) firm-specific factor e:

$$R_i = E(R_i) + b_{i1}F_1 + b_{i2}F_2 + \ldots b_{iN}F_N + e_i$$

where

R_i and $E(R_i)$ = the actual and expected (see below) return of the ith asset for a given period.

F_j = a common factor that affects all securities. Examples of such factors are interest rates, inflation, the business cycle, and general economic conditions.

b_{ij} = the sensitivity of the ith security's return to movements of the jth factor.

e_i = the firm-specific portion of the return not explained by the N factors.

In a portfolio of sufficient size, the firm-specific component can be diversified away. The expected return is therefore the risk-free rate plus the sum of the "risk premium" associated with each of the factors times the sensitivity b_{ij} of the ith security to the jth factor.

$$E(R_i) = \text{Risk-free Rate} + b_{i1}f_1 + b_{i2}f_2 + \ldots b_{iN}f_N$$

where f_j is the risk premium associated with the F_j factor.

---

[44]The interested reader is referred to Chapter 10 of Z. Bodie, A. Kane, and A. Marcus, *Investments*, 3rd ed. (Homewood, IL: Irwin, 1996).

In a single-index environment, the CAPM model

$$E(R_t) = R_f + \beta_e E(R_m - R_f)$$

is consistent with the APT relationship with the sensitivity b_1 equal to the β and the risk premium $f_1 = (R_m - R_f)$ *if we assume that the market index is the appropriate single factor.*

The identification of relevant factors is the greatest difficulty in application of the APT. They are not *a priori* specified in the development of the model; they are defined as generic "factors" that influence security returns. Empirical research is, therefore, more difficult. Chen et al. (1986) examined the APT with prespecified factors. Their paper and others have used the following factors to study the APT:

- Level of industrial activity
- Rate of inflation
- Spread between short- and long-term interest rates
- Spread between yields of low- and high-risk corporate bonds

Another problem in specifying relevant factors is that the factors affecting returns need not persist and their role may change over time. Because of these difficulties in testing the APT, it has not proved to be a viable substitute for the CAPM and researchers have focused on tests of the CAPM and β_e. To this end, the studies listed in Exhibit 18-3 were designed to determine accounting-based measures that could be used to explain and/or predict a firm's β_e. However, as we shall see, the recent controversy surrounding the CAPM has important implications for multifactor models such as the APT.

Importance and Usefulness of Beta (β)

Knowledge of beta is important to analysts, investors, and management for a number of reasons:

1. To construct investment portfolios with the desired risk and return characteristics, you must know the beta of individual securities.
2. Discounted cash flow valuation models require an estimate of the firm's expected rate of return. With the CAPM formula, beta can be used to estimate that return (see Chapter 19).
3. Similarly, management, in making capital budgeting decisions, needs to know the firm's cost of capital or hurdle rate. The CAPM formula with beta provides an estimate of the firm's cost of equity capital.

In all three situations, the *ex ante*, or the next period's beta, is required. As this value is not directly observable, it must be estimated. One possibility is to use the past history of firm and market returns. This estimate, the historical beta, is generally the ordinary least-square regression (OLS) estimate of beta derived from actual returns in previous periods.[45]

---

[45] Alternatively, an adjusted beta is derived from a Bayesian adjustment to the OLS beta estimate.

Historical betas, however, are not perfect predictors of future betas, as the regression estimates are subject to measurement error, and the firm's production, investment, and financing decisions change over time. Beta also may not be stable from period to period. Estimating betas on a portfolio basis rather than individually is one remedy for these problems. Additionally, since investors are interested in the systematic risk of portfolios, the prediction of portfolio beta rather than individual beta is of primary importance.[46]

Beaver and Manegold (1975) tested the association between betas in adjacent time periods. They found that betas of one period had a high *ex post* correlation (45%) with betas of the next period. Thus, historical betas could be used to predict the next period's beta. However, that level of correlation means that only about 20% of the (cross-sectional) variation[47] in the second period's betas is explained by the first period's historical beta. On a portfolio basis, the results improve dramatically. For a 5-security portfolio, the correlation is 82% (65% variation explained). At 10 securities, the correlation increases to 91% (82% variation explained).

Note that these correlations and percentage variation explained are derived *ex post*; that is, the "predictive equations" are developed with knowledge of the predicted period's values. In a sense, the equation is developed by asking the following question: "Given the second period beta, what is the best predictive model I can construct using the first period's beta?" The statistics that result define the degree of association between the two periods and not the degree of predictive power between one observation and the next. Predictive ability, on the other hand, is measured with models that do not use data from the predicted period. They address the following question: "Given only the first period's beta, what is the best predictive model I can construct?"

The next section compares the performance of predictive models based on historical betas with those based on accounting-based risk measures. These latter models use accounting measures individually or in conjunction with historical betas in an attempt to improve the forecasting ability of models just using historical betas. Exhibit 18-3 presents an overview of the variables used in the studies. Note the emphasis on the components of earnings variability discussed at the onset of this chapter.

Many of the studies find a more meaningful association between earnings and market returns when earnings are also expressed as a return measure. In the discussion that follows, therefore, the term "earnings" encompasses not only its traditional meaning of net income or EPS, but may also include a return measure such as ROA, ROE, and/or the earnings/price ratio.[48]

Review of Theoretical and Empirical Findings

The literature in this area is both theoretical and empirical. The theoretical papers attempt to link finance-based measures of risk with accounting measures of risk. Not all measures can be justified on a theoretical basis, and the literature indicates those areas where a theoretical relationship should not exist. Empirical studies test these relationships. We first discuss the theoretical underpinnings of the various risk measures and then provide a review of empirical work.

---

[46]The problem of measurement error and the benefits of forecasting on a portfolio basis exist not only for forecasts based on historical betas, but also when accounting variables are used to forecast beta.

[47]The percentage variation explained equals the correlation squared.

[48]When necessary, the exact definition used will be disclosed.

EXHIBIT 18-10
Market and Accounting Betas: Notation and Definitions

Market-Based Betas

β_e = represents the "classical" beta used in finance to measure the systematic risk of an equity security. This is the beta we are attempting to forecast.

β_a = represents the beta of the equity of a firm that has no debt, the unlevered beta. This beta is a function solely of the underlying systematic risk of the firm's assets, that is, its operating risk. It is a theoretical, unobservable construct as few firms have no debt. It is used to demonstrate the contribution of a firm's operating risk to its overall beta.

β_d = represents the beta of a firm's debt. If debt is riskless, β_d equals zero.

Accounting-Based Betas

$B_{earnings}$ = the accounting beta previously defined

B_{sales} = represents the systematic component of the variability of a firm's sales

Theoretical Framework

In this section, beta is used in a number of contexts. The notation and a brief definition of each beta discussed are provided in Exhibit 18-10. Based on our discussion thus far, it should be expected that earnings uncertainty[49] is associated with the stock beta. Thus, operating leverage, financing leverage, the variance of sales or earnings, and the accounting beta should be related to the stock beta. A number of theoretical papers, including those of Hamada (1972) and Bowman (1979), explicitly developed these relationships.

Relationship Among the Stock Beta, Operating Risk, and Accounting Beta. β_a, the unlevered beta, is related to operating risk. Clearly, for an unlevered firm, $B_{earnings}$ is also solely related to operating risk. Bowman (1979) has shown that for an unlevered firm, the relationship between the stock beta and the accounting beta is[50]

$$\beta_a = \beta_e = B_{earnings} \times \frac{1}{\text{Relative Market Value of Firm}}$$

Relationship Among Stock Beta, Financial Leverage, Operating Leverage, and Accounting Beta. Introducing (riskless) debt results in the following relationship:

$$\beta_e = \beta_a + \left[\frac{D}{E}\right]\beta_a$$

[49]This, of course, is true as long as it is not solely due to unsystematic (firm-specific) factors.

[50]The relative market value of firm converts earnings into a return measure. It is the ratio of the firm's market value to the total market value of all firms in the economy.

Thus, adding financial leverage (as measured by the debt-to-equity ratio) to the capital structure of a firm increases its systematic risk.

When debt is risky, the relationship can be expressed as

$$\beta_e = \beta_a + \left\{ \left[\frac{D}{E} \right] \times (\beta_a - \beta_d) \right\}$$

An obvious parallel to this equation is the equation used in Chapter 4 for the disaggregation of ROE into ROA and the cost of debt:

$$\text{ROE} = \text{ROA} + \left[\frac{D}{E} \times (\text{ROA} - \text{Cost of Debt}) \right]$$

This similarity is not coincidental but, rather, is a direct outcome of the risk/return trade-off inherent in all investment opportunities. As higher risks require higher returns, the relationships that determine risk should be similar to those that determine returns.

The foregoing equations imply that equity risk (β_e) is a function of the risk of the underlying assets combined with the risk inherent in financing, that is, the operating and financial leverage. A more direct description of this relationship is given by Mandelker and Rhee (1984), who derive the following expression for systematic risk:

$$\beta_e = \text{FLE} \times \text{OLE} \times \left[\frac{B_{\text{sales}}}{\text{Price/Earnings}} \right]$$

where B_{sales} measures the covariance of the *percentage change in sales* with the market return R_m. Again, note the similarity between the foregoing and the expression for total leverage effect derived in Chapter 4:

$$\text{TLE} = (\% \text{ Change in Income}) = \text{FLE} \times \text{OLE} \times (\% \text{ Change in Sales})$$

The expressions are parallel except for the price/earnings ratio factor that is needed to convert sales to market returns. In the latter expression, we deal with the returns themselves, whereas in the former we are concerned with the uncertainty of these returns. Hence, "% change in sales" is replaced in the former by its (systematic) risk term.

Relationship Between the Stock Beta and Other Risk Measures. Bowman demonstrates that size, growth, and dividend payout have no theoretical relationship to a stock's systematic risk. In addition, earnings variability is related only insofar as its systematic component is related. Thus, although from a theoretical perspective earnings variability is not directly related to β_e, on an empirical level, a relationship is found to the extent that earnings variability captures the systematic risk component of earnings.

Hochman (1983) reviews studies with conflicting views of the theoretical relationship between β_e and various definitions of growth. Furthermore, Hochman argues that dividend yield (dividend/market value) should be low for companies with high growth[51] potential. Thus, if growth is positively associated with β_e, then (empirically) we expect a negative relationship between β_e and dividend yield.

Empirical Studies

Given these theoretical relationships, researchers have attempted to use accounting variables and ratios to explain or predict differences in firm betas. Some studies examine the historical relationship between β_e and accounting measures of risk to see how much of the variation in β_e can be explained *ex post* by the accounting risk measures. The predictive studies, on the other hand, attempt to use the relationships derived to predict future period β_e.

It should be noted that some of the relationships tested were ad hoc in the sense that no strict theoretical underpinning existed to justify the relationship. Their inclusion in the models was based on a combination of researcher intuition and "conventional wisdom."

Explanatory Studies. Ball and Brown (1968) found a high degree of association between the accounting beta and the market beta.[52] Depending on how the accounting beta was measured, its correlation with the market beta ranged from 39 to 46%. Lev (1973) examined the association of operating leverage with both the overall risk (total variance) of a firm's returns as well as the systematic risk component β_e. Using firms in three industries (electric utilities, steel manufacturers, and oil producers), he obtained regression estimates of each firm's variable cost percentage v from the equation

$$TC_t = F + vS_t$$

Lev then regressed the β_e of these companies against these estimates of v. The hypothesized relationship was negative: The lower the variable cost, the higher the total variance of returns and the higher the beta. Empirical results confirmed this negative relationship as the regression coefficient on v was negative (and statistically significant) for all industries and for both risk measures.[53]

Mandelker and Rhee examined the association of beta with the OLE and FLE. They found that (*ex post*) OLE and FLE explain anywhere between 38 and 48% of the variation in beta on a portfolio basis. On an individual basis, only 11% of the variation was explained.

Explanatory and Predictive Studies. The above tests measured association only, not predictive ability. Beaver et al. (1970) tested the association and predictive ability

---

[51]Higher growth means that income is reinvested in the business; dividends are lower. The high growth would be reflected in higher market value and, therefore, a lower dividend yield.

[52]This result was not the main thrust of their study (see Chapter 5 for a detailed discussion of Ball and Brown), and they did not attempt to improve the predictive ability of the market beta by use of the accounting beta.

[53]The percentage variation explained (R^2), however, was meaningful only for the steel manufacturers' risk measures and the overall risk measure for oil producers. The low R^2 may be due to the fact that Lev (1973) examined firms only on an individual rather than portfolio basis.

EXHIBIT 18-11
Predictive Ability of Accounting Risk Measures

	Predicted Association	Findings Confirmed
1. Payout Dividend/income	Negative	Yes
2. Growth Assets (year 5)/assets (year 1)	Positive	Only period 1
3. Leverage (financial) Debt/assets	Positive	Yes
4. Liquidity Current ratio	Negative	Only period 1
5. Size Average assets	Negative	Only period 2
6. Earnings variability Standard deviation of earnings/price ratio	Positive	Yes
7. Accounting beta Beta of firm's ratio of earnings/price with market index of earnings/price	Positive	Yes

Source: William Beaver, Paul Kettler, and Myron Scholes, "The Association Between Market Determined and Accounting Determined Risk Measures," *The Accounting Review*, October 1970, Table 5, p. 669 (adapted).

of seven accounting risk measures[54] and beta on both the individual security level and the portfolio level for two subperiods (1947 to 1956 and 1957 to 1965). The relationship between each accounting risk measure and β_e was first tested individually and then in a multivariate context.

The individual results, presented in Exhibit 18-11, indicate that for four of the seven measures, the correlations were significant on an individual and (five-security) portfolio level over both subperiods in the direction predicted.

The findings for financial leverage, the accounting beta, and earnings variability are consistent with arguments presented earlier in terms of the predicted association with β_e. The theoretical justification stated by Beaver et al. for the findings with respect to the dividend payout ratio is that, since firms are reluctant to cut dividends, those firms that face more uncertainty (i.e., have higher β_e's) pay lower dividends.[55]

These relationships are all univariate as they measure the correlation between β_e and each of the accounting-based measures individually. Beaver et al. then constructed a multivariate model to forecast the next period's β_e. The benchmark forecast to be compared against this forecast was period 1's historic (OLS) β_e:

$$\text{Benchmark Forecast of Period 2 } \beta_e = \text{Period 1 (OLS) } \beta_e$$

[54] The accounting risk measures used in all cases were averaged or calculated over five-year periods.

[55] Watts and Zimmermann (1986) use another justification, based on the leverage ratio, to explain the finding. They argue that since empirically it has been shown that firms with more debt pay lower dividends relative to earnings, then the negative relationship between dividend payout and β is just another manifestation of the positive relationship between β and leverage.

Using only the accounting-based data from the first subperiod in conjunction with the period 1 (OLS) β_e, the following predictive equation resulted[56]:

$$\text{Period 2 } \beta_e = \text{Fitted period 1 } \beta_e$$
$$= 1.016 - (0.584 \times \text{Payout}) + (0.835 \times \text{Growth})$$
$$+ (3.027 \times \text{Earnings Variability})$$

This model thus uses accounting-based data to modify a market-based measure.[57] The period 2 forecast developed with the foregoing model was compared with the benchmark forecast. The accounting-based forecast explained between 63 and 69% (depending on how the portfolios were constructed) of the variation, whereas the benchmark explained only 37 to 42%. The benchmark's forecast error was higher than the accounting-based forecast error 54% (57 to 66%) of the time on an individual (portfolio) basis.

Generally, it is more difficult to forecast variables that are "outliers" relative to the mean of the distribution. For market betas, this means it is easier to forecast stocks of average systematic risk (beta approximately equal to 1) than to forecast high-beta (extremely risky) or low-beta (low-risk) stocks. The accounting-based model did much better than the benchmark model at these extreme values,[58] with smaller forecast errors more than three-fourths of the time.

Professor Barr Rosenberg (by himself or in conjunction with others) undertook comprehensive attempts to forecast "fundamental" β_e's using a variety of accounting as well as nonaccounting variables. Exhibit 18-12 lists the 13 variables used by Rosenberg and McKibben (1973). Using the criterion of which (predicted) beta best forecast future returns, they tested the predictive power of their beta against a number of alternative (return-based) beta forecasts. They found their model to have the best predictive power. The results were statistically significant, although in some cases the additional predictive power was marginal (2% increase in R^2). Rosenberg and Guy (1976) found that the variance of earnings and cash flows, as well as firm size, earnings growth, dividend yield, and the debt-to-asset ratio were useful in predicting betas.

A result of Rosenberg's research was the formation of an investment service company, Barr Rosenberg & Associates (BARRA). The company provides forecasts of betas based on models incorporating accounting-based and other fundamental factors. The actual models used, being proprietary, are not available. This service competes with other investment services that provide beta forecasts based on models incorporating primarily historical stock returns data.

Harrington (1983) tested the forecasting ability of betas provided by such investment services. In all, 12 different predictors of beta were examined. Included in the test were two models based on firm-fundamental characteristics developed by BARRA.

---

[56]The parameters of the model were developed as follows. First, for each firm in the sample, the historic OLS beta for the first period was found using the market model. This OLS beta was then regressed on the firm's accounting variables. The resultant regression equation was then used to determine the next period's market beta. Since only the first period's data were used, the predicted beta is identical to the first period's "fitted" beta, that is, the beta that falls on the regression line.

[57]Note that the multivariate model does not include the same variables that proved to be significant on an individual basis. This happens often in empirical work as interrelationships among independent variables can alter their significance on a univariate level.

[58]The extreme values were defined as the upper and lower deciles (quartiles) on an individual (portfolio) basis.

EXHIBIT 18-12
Variables Used by Rosenberg and McKibben

Accounting-Based Descriptors

1. Standard deviation of a per share earnings growth measure
2. Latest annual proportional change in per share earnings
3. Standard & Poor's quality rating
4. Liquidity (the quick ratio)
5. Absolute magnitude of per share dividend cuts
6. Mean leverage (senior securities/total assets)
7. Growth measure for total net sales
8. Growth measure of per share earnings available for common
9. Gross plant per dollar of total assets

Market-Basd Descriptors

10. Historical beta, a regression of stock return on market return over preceding calendar years in the sample, if we assume alpha equals zero
11. Share turnover as a percentage of shares outstanding
12. Logarithm of unadjusted share price

Market Valuation Descriptors

13. Book value of common equity per share/price

Source: Barr Rosenberg, and Walt McKibben, "The Prediction of Systematic and Specific Risk in Common Stocks," *Journal of Financial and Quantitative Analysis*, March 1973, p. 324.

For the industrial companies, one fundamental BARRA model had the lowest mean-square prediction error over all four time horizons examined. Their other fundamental model finished second over two of the horizons. The results also showed that it is easier to forecast betas calculated over longer horizons. (In all cases, the longer horizons had lower mean-square prediction errors.)

The Attack on the CAPM and β

There is a growing body of (empirical) literature that contradicts the predictions of the CAPM and by extension the usefulness of β. Figure 18-5 (*a* through *d*) based on data from Fama and French (1992) illustrates these issues graphically.

Figure 18-5a plots the average monthly return earned by portfolios formed on the basis of beta. If beta reflects risk, then portfolios with higher (lower) betas should on average earn a higher (lower) return. *The figure, however, indicates very little difference in returns* earned by the various portfolios, with all hovering around 1.2% average monthly returns. On the other hand, Figure 18-5 does show a relationship between returns and portfolios formed on the basis of:[59]

- Size (Figure 18-5b)
- Earnings-to-price (E/P) ratio (Figure 18-5c), or
- Book to market value of equity (B/M) (Figure 18-5d)

[59]The ratios E/P and B/M are inverses of the more familiar P/E and market-to-book ratios because of the computational problems that can occur when small or negative earnings and/or book values appear in the denominator.

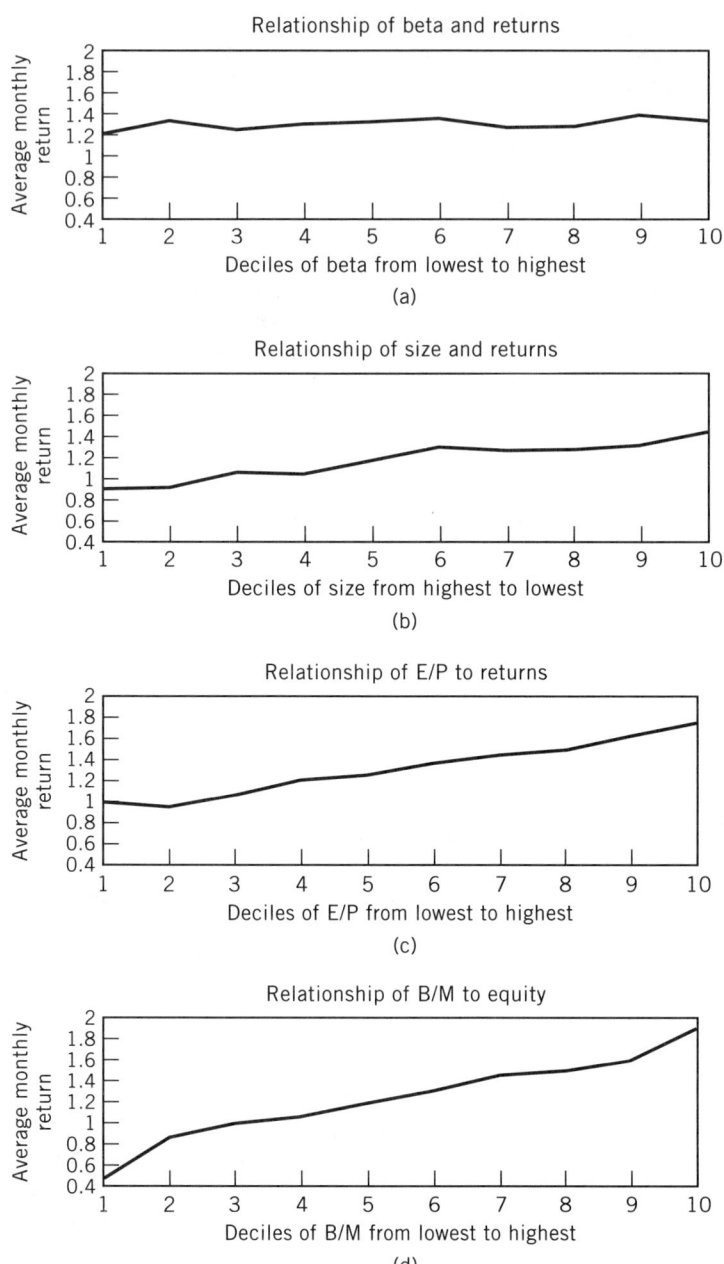

FIGURE 18-5 Relationship of returns and various measures of "risk." *Source:* Adapted from data presented in E. Fama and K. R. French, "The Cross-Section of Expected Stock Returns," *Journal of Finance,* June 1992, pp. 427–65.

These results pose problems for the CAPM (and β) from two perspectives:

1. The CAPM predicts that a firm's returns are determined *solely* by its systematic risk β. These results indicate *that alternative measures of "risk" tend to be (more) closely related to returns.*

2. The results indicate that *returns are not related to β.*

Alternative Measures of Equity Risk or Market Inefficiency?

Fama and French were not the first to examine the relationship between returns and these alternative measures of "risk." The size effect was first documented by Banz (1981). Banz found that market equity, ME (stock price multiplied by outstanding shares), can be used as an additional factor (over β_e) to explain average returns, with smaller firms earning excess returns (over those predicted by β_e) relative to large firms. Similarly, the P/E (the inverse of the E/P ratio) was found by Basu (1983) to explain average returns in tests that also included β_e and size. Rosenberg et al. (1985) documented the relationship of returns and the book to market value of equity ratio. In addition to the measures shown in Figure 18-5, financial leverage has also been shown to be positively related to returns. This in itself is not surprising as β_e is a function of leverage. Thus, we should expect higher leverage to be associated with higher returns. Bhandari (1988), however, determined that leverage had (additional) explanatory power in tests that included β_e (as well as size).[60]

When discussing these alternative measures of "risk," we use quotation marks, because although these variables display empirical properties similar to those of risk (i.e., they are related to expected returns), for the most part, the literature struggles to find convincing explanations for the relationships.

In fact, two views of these findings have emerged. At one extreme, some do not view these measures as "risk." Rather, they view these relationships as evidence of market inefficiency. As discussed in Chapter 5, Lakonishok et al. (1994) argue that the B/M effect is evidence of market *overreaction*. Similarly, the *neglected firm* argument is used to explain the size effect, and the P/E ratio effect is often cited as an example of a market anomaly.

Others argue that whereas the CAPM (and/or the notion of β) may be damaged, market efficiency is not. That is, although they concede that markets may not act in a manner consistent with the CAPM, the relationship between size and B/M and average returns, they argue, is based on risk and return considerations.

Amihud and Mendelson (1986, 1991), for example, argue that the size effect is related to liquidity. As small firms are not traded as often as larger firms, the bid-asked spread on these securities is wider. To compensate for this, a higher expected return (liquidity premium) is required.

Chan and Chen (1991) argue that the B/M effect is due to the fact that firms with high B/M ratios are intrinsically riskier. The market, therefore, discounts their price, accounting for the lower market price (and higher B/M).

Fama and French (1995) also take the position that the B/M and size effects are related to risk and not market inefficiency. As stock prices are discounted future earnings, they note that

> if the size and B/M risk factors in returns (unexpected changes in stock prices) are the result of rational pricing, they must be driven by common factors in shocks to expected earnings that are related to size and B/M.[61]

They proceed to demonstrate that firm profitability (as measured by ROE) is related to differences in size and E/M. However, they concede that

---

[60] Fama and French also examined leverage but argued that its effects were subsumed by the B/M effect.

[61] Eugene F. Fama and Kenneth R. French, "Size and Book-to-Market Factors in Earnings and Returns," *The Journal of Finance*, March 1995, p. 132.

size and B/M remain arbitrary indicator variables, that, for unexplained economic reasons, are related to risk factors in returns.[62]

The Defense of β and the CAPM

The defenders of β and the CAPM respond to Fama and French by taking a closer look at the data and methodology used in their study. They argue that those data suffer from measurement error with respect to:

- How returns were measured
- How β was measured, and/or
- How the market index was measured

Kothari et al. (1995) found that when returns are measured on an annual rather than monthly basis, a positive relationship exists between β and returns. Similarly, Amihud et al. (1992), using a different statistical methodology than Fama and French, also show a significant positive relationship between β and returns.

Kothari et al. also argue that the B/M results may be due to *survivorship bias*. That is, a high B/M ratio indicates a low market price and a potentially distressed firm. If such a firm fails, it (and its low return) will not appear in databases used by researchers such as Fama and French. Thus, only the high B/M firms that recovered and consequently had high returns were included in the sample examined by Fama and French. Omitting the high B/M firms that had low returns (by failing) biased the results in an upward direction.

Other researchers have noted that the CAPM is predicated on the use of a market index that includes *all* risky assets. With an index such as the NYSE or the S&P 500 index, the model used in the empirical tests may be misspecified as it ignores other assets, thus accounting for β's poor showing. Additionally, they argue that historical β's may not be the best estimates of the *ex ante β*.

Jagannathan and Wang (1993), for example, construct a CAPM[63] model that includes, in addition to the standard stock market index, an index to reflect human capital (thus broadening the set of risky assets) and an index to reflect potential changes in β due to shifts in the business cycle. This expanded model shows the expected relationship between β and returns.

Parenthetically, the criticism of the use of historical β's is especially interesting in the context of our earlier discussions. The evidence indicates that accounting variables can be used to estimate β more accurately than historical β's. Thus, the performance of β as a risk measure may be enhanced if one compared "fundamental" β's (rather than historical β's) with average returns.

In response to some of the criticisms levied against their work, Fama and French (1995), in a paper titled "The CAPM: Wanted Dead or Alive," note that even if there were flaws in their tests (which they attempt to disprove) and β is related to returns, at best *that would only save β but not the CAPM*. The fact that measures such as

[62]Ibid., p. 131.

[63]One can debate whether this model should be considered a modified CAPM or a new asset pricing model [see Jagannathan and McGrattan (1995)].

B/M and size are also related to returns contradicts the CAPM, which contends that β (however measured) is the *sole* risk measure.

Implications for Accounting Risk Measures

The need for more research in multifactor models such as the APT is implicit in the arguments that β may not be the sole risk measure and findings that indicate alternative measures of risk may exist. These findings have important implications for accounting based-measures of risk:

1. Research findings indicate a strong explanatory as well as predictive relationship between accounting-based measures of risk and β_e. Although there has been some doubt cast on the relationship of returns to β_e, the use of improperly measured β's may account for the results. This point highlights the potential need (and benefits) of using accounting variables to improve the estimation of β_e.

2. The alternative (empirical) measures that have been suggested as risk proxies, such as the B/M, P/E and leverage ratios, are accounting-based ratios.

3. Given the previous points, it is worth noting that the accounting ratios, used in the empirical studies discussed, were for the most part computed without adjustment for differences in accounting policies, unusual items, and off-balance-sheet information. Such adjustments could potentially improve the models[64] and provide further insight into the nature of the alternative "risk" measures.

SUMMARY

The classification studies have demonstrated strong linkages between accounting-based measures of risk and various forms of risk facing a firm. It is, however, troublesome that the major effort in constructing the models has been devoted to the statistical analysis techniques rather than examination of the inputs going into the models.

Our criticism takes two forms. The first deals with the theoretical underpinnings or motivation for the models. It is one thing when the theory does not really exist, as in the case of bankruptcy prediction. It is another when the theory exists, but is ignored. The prediction of beta and bond ratings are examples of the latter. In the case of beta prediction, many of the models focused only on one or two variables when the theory specifies a larger (available) set of explanatory variables. In the case of bond ratings, the research may be focusing on the wrong variable of interest entirely.

The second criticism deals with the data used in these models. The research focus is on the tools that measure the data rather than the data themselves. It is true that there is no clear-cut evidence that these adjustments would improve the models. That is what should make it such an interesting area for research. Ignoring this issue reminds us of the suggestion by Oskar Morgenstern that working with sophisticated statistics and poor data was equivalent to calculating the circumference of a circle by pacing off the radius with one's feet and multiplying by pi taken to the tenth decimal place.

---

[64]Dhaliwal (discussed in Chapter 12), for example, found that better predictions of β_e could be obtained if the explanatory variable debt/equity was adjusted to reflect off-balance-sheet pension information.

Analysis of the Debt Ratings and Default Risk of DuPont, Dow Chemical, and Imperial Chemical Industries

Dow Chemical and ICI operate in and compete with duPont in certain markets. Appendices B and C contain the financial statements of Dow Chemical and ICI, respectively, for the year ended December 31, 1994.

Case 4-1 called for the preparation of leverage and solvency ratios for these three firms. The objective of this case is to extend the analysis using the adjusted financial data developed in Case 17-1. [Share price data given in 3(b)(ii) of that case.]

Note that the ICI statements are presented in British pounds (£) and prepared according to U.K. GAAP. Case 10-1 required the computation of the market value of the debt of ICI.

1. Compute the Z-score for duPont, Dow Chemical, and ICI at the end of 1994.

2. Use the adjusted financial statements of duPont, Dow Chemical, and ICI developed in Case 17-1 to compute an adjusted Z-score for the three companies.

3. Compare the raw and adjusted Z-scores computed in 1 and 2.

4. Exhibit 18-8 presents the median values of financial ratios according to Standard and Poor's bond rating categories. Using that exhibit and the reported financial statements of the three firms:

   (a) Compute the corresponding ratios for duPont, Dow, and ICI.

   (b) Assign an "appropriate" debt rating to each firm.

5. (a) Use the current cost balance sheet and adjustments made in Case 17-1 to recalculate the ratios in 4(a).

   (b) Determine the bond rating suggested by the adjusted ratios.

   (c) Discuss the limitations of your answer to part b.

6. Use the Z″ score of Exhibit 18-9 to arrive at a bond rating for the three companies. Compare these ratings to those arrived at in 4 and 5.

7. Evaluate the impact of the adjustments discussed in Chapter 17 on your assessment of a firm's default risk. Use the results of 4 to 6 to illustrate your comments.

Chapter **18**

Problems

Problems 1 to 3 relate to the takeover of Kraft by Philip Morris and are based on the data in Exhibit 18P-1.

1. [Ratios and bond ratings; 1989 CFA adapted] Philip Morris Companies is one of the world's largest cigarette manufacturers as well as a major producer and distributor of a broad line of food and beverage products. The company has compiled a steady record of growth in sales, earnings, and cash flow.

In October 1988, Philip Morris announced an unsolicited cash tender offer for all the 124 million outstanding shares of Kraft at $90 per share. Kraft subsequently accepted a $106-per-share all-cash offer from Philip Morris.

Kraft's major products include cheese, edible oils, nonfluid dairy products, and frozen foods. Exhibit 18P-1 provides projected financial data for Philip Morris and Kraft individually and on a consolidated basis.

Exhibit 18P-2 reports the median values, according to bond rating category, for the following three financial ratios:

(i) Pretax interest coverage

(ii) Long-term debt as a percentage of capitalization

(iii) Cash flow as a percentage of total debt (note the definition of cash flow in Exhibit 18P-2)

Using the information provided in Exhibits 18P-1 and 18P-2:

A. Calculate the three ratios listed for Philip Morris for 1989, first, using the figures prior to the Kraft acquisition and, second, using the consolidated figures after the acquisition.

EXHIBIT 18P-1. PHILIP MORRIS COMPANIES, INC.
Projected Financial Data, 1988 to 1989 ($ in millions)

	1988 Estimate Excluding Kraft	1989 Estimate			
		Before Kraft	Kraft Only	Adjustments	Consolidated
A. Selected Income Statement Data					
Total sales	$30,450	$33,080	$11,610		$44,690
Total operating income	$ 4,875	$ 5,550	$ 1,050	$ (210)	$ 6,390
As a % of sales	16.0%	16.8%	9.0%		14.3%
Interest expense	(575)	(500)	(75)	(1,025)	(1,600)
Corporate expense	(200)	(225)	(100)	(40)	(365)
Other expense	(5)	(5)			(5)
Pretax income	$ 4,095	$ 4,820	$ 875	$(1,275)	$ 4,420
As a % of sales	13.4%	14.6%	7.5%		9.9%
Income taxes	(1,740)	(2,000)	(349)	493	(1,856)
Tax rate	42.5%	41.5%	39.9%		42.0%
Net income	$ 2,355	$ 2,820	$ 526	$ (782)	$ 2,564
B. Selected Balance Sheet Data as of Year-End					
Short-term debt	$ 1,125	$ 1,100	$ 683		$ 1,783
Long-term debt	4,757	3,883	895	$11,000	15,778
Stockholders' equity	8,141	9,931	2,150	(2,406)	9,675
C. Other Selected Financial Data					
Depreciation and amortization	$ 720	$ 750	$ 190	$ 295	$ 1,235
Deferred taxes	100	100	10	280	390
Equity in undistributed earnings of unconsolidated subsidiaries	110	125			125

EXHIBIT 18P-2
Median Ratios According to Bond Rating Category

Ratio	AAA	AA	A	BBB	BB	B	CCC
Pretax interest coverage	14.10X	9.67X	5.40X	3.63X	2.25X	1.58X	(0.42X)
Long-term debt as a % of capitalization	11.5%	18.7%	28.3%	34.3%	48.4%	57.2%	73.2%
Cash flow* as a % of total debt	111.8%	86.0%	50.9%	34.2%	22.8%	14.1%	6.2%

*For the purpose of calculating this ratio, Standard & Poor's defines cash flow as "net income plus depreciation, amortization and deferred taxes, less equity in undistributed earnings of unconsolidated subsidiaries."
   Source: Standard & Poor's.

B. Compare these two sets of ratios to the medians for each rating category.

C. Formulate and support an opinion as to the appropriate rating category for Philip Morris (before and after the Kraft acquisition).

2. [Ratios and bankruptcy prediction] Given the variables used in Altman's two bankruptcy models, discuss the impact of the Kraft acquisition on the probability that Philip Morris will become insolvent. (Use the data in Exhibit 18P-1 as part of your answer.)

3. [Effect of acquisition on beta] Describe the expected effect of the Kraft acquisition on Philip Morris' beta. (Your answer should consider the effects on the "unlevered" beta as well as the "levered" beta and should distinguish between operating and financial leverage effects.)

4. [Comprehensive financial analysis; 1989 CFA adapted] The Investment Policy Committee of your firm has decided that the soft drink industry, specifically Coca-Cola Company (KO) and Coca-Cola Enterprises (CCE), qualify as potential purchases for the firm's portfolios. As the firm's beverage industry expert, you must prepare an extensive financial analysis of these two soft drink producers.

KO owns the brands included in its broad product line. It plays almost no direct role in the domestic manufacturing and distribution beyond the output of soft drink extract.

The business of CCE is also dominated by soft drinks. CCE, however, purchases extract from KO and transforms it into completed products sold in a wide variety of retail outlets throughout the United States.

Use the financial statements of KO and CCE provided in Case 13-1 to answer parts A, B, and C.

A. Your comparative analysis of these two soft drink companies requires calculations of various ratios. You have identified four key areas of comparison:

    (i) Short-term liquidity

    (ii) Capital structure and long-term solvency

    (iii) Asset utilization

    (iv) Operating profitability

Compute the ratios required to make these comparisons. Discuss the differences between KO and CCE in these four areas based on the ratios and the financial statements.

B. Using the financial statement data below, identify at least three financial statement adjustments (for each firm) required to enhance their comparability and usefulness for financial analysis.

Data Extracted from Financial Statement Footnotes

Coca-Cola Company (KO)

(1) The market value of the Company's investments in publicly traded equity investees exceeded the Company's carrying value at December 31, 1995, by approximately $2,157 million.

(2) The Company is contingently liable for guarantees of indebtedness owed by some of its licensees and others, totaling approximately $202 million at December 31, 1995.

Coca-Cola Enterprises (CCE)

(1) At December 31, 1995, the fair value of long-term debt was $4,685 million versus carrying value of $4,201 million.

(2) As of December 31, 1995, the company has entered into long-term purchase agreements with suppliers, aggregating approximately $1,310 million in 1996, $1,320 million in 1997, $901 million in 1998, $769 million in 1999, and $779 million in 2000.

C. For each of the adjustments identified in part B, discuss the effects of these adjustments on your answer to part A.

5. [ALCOA; fixed income analysis]

A. Exhibit 18-8 presents median values of financial ratios according to Standard & Poor's bond rating categories. Use this exhibit and the financial statements of ALCOA provided in Case 17-2 to:

(i) Compute the corresponding ratios (where possible) for ALCOA for 1995. (*Note:* ALCOA generated $1,712.5 million in cash flow from operations.)

(ii) Determine the "appropriate" bond rating for ALCOA.

B. (i) Using the current cost balance sheet and normalized income statement developed in Case 17-2, recalculate the ratios in part A.

(ii) What bond rating category is implied by the adjusted ratios?

(iii) Notwithstanding your answer to part (ii), why might these adjustments not make a difference in ALCOA's bond rating?

(iv) Do these adjustments make a difference in assessing ALCOA's default risk?

(v) How do these adjustments affect ALCOA's bankruptcy risk?

6. [Forecasting bond rating changes] Standard & Poor's Corp. states that it places firms on its Creditwatch list when changes in operating profit trends, completed or planned mergers, capital structure changes, or regulatory actions suggest a need for reevaluation of the current credit rating. A listing with negative implications may result in the rating being lowered.

James River is a major manufacturer of paper products. On January 26, 1993, Standard & Poor's Corp. placed James River's debt on Creditwatch with negative implications. It cited weak market conditions and James River's deteriorating operating performance. S&P noted fourth quarter operating losses and each segment's lower

EXHIBIT 18P-3. JAMES RIVER CORP.
Selected Financial Data, for Years Ended December 31, 1991 to
1992 ($ in millions)

	1991	1992
Total debt	$1,891	$2,882
Total equity	2,574	2,112
Sales	4,562	4,728
Operating income	244	(62)
Other income	27	24
Interest expense	(138)	(149)
Income (loss) before taxes	$ 133	$ (187)
Cash from operations*	394	(136)

*Computed using Standard & Poor's definition, not that used through-
out the text.

reported profits. The current debt rating of James River's senior debt was BBB+; its
subordinated debt rating was BBB.

Exhibit 18P-3 provides selected balance sheet and income statement data.

A. Using the data in Exhibits 18P-3 and 18-8, evaluate Standard & Poor's decision
to place James River on its Creditwatch list.

B. What other information would you need to determine whether the firm's debt
should be downgraded? Specify financial statement or footnote information and discuss
how you would use it.

C. Discuss the limitations of comparing James River's ratios with those in Exhibit
18-8.

7. [Bond ratings] Exhibit 18P-4 contains selected data from the financial statements
of Westvaco, a large paper and paperboard producer.

A. Use the data provided to determine the appropriate debt rating for Westvaco.
If different from the actual rating (A), discuss briefly.

B. Exhibit 18P-5 contains a comparison of Westvaco with two other paper companies. Using only the data in Exhibits 18P-5 and 18-8, evaluate the risk that the debt
of the three companies listed will be downgraded.

C. How do the data provided in Exhibits 18P-3 and 18P-4 modify your answer
to part B for James River and Westvaco?

D. 1991 and 1992 were recession years for the paper industry. How should that
affect the evaluation of debt ratings for the three companies?

8. [Debt rating change] On January 4, 1995, Svenska Cellulosa AB (SCA), a large
Swedish paper and forest products company, acquired 60% of the German paper
company, PWA, for SEK 5,888 million. The stake has since been increased to 75%
for an additional cost of SEK 1,447 million, financed by debt. As a result of this

EXHIBIT 18P-4. WESTVACO CORP.
Selected Financial Data, for Years Ended October 31, 1991 to
1992 ($ in millions)

	1991	1992
Total debt	$ 988	$1,079
Total equity	1,699	1,770
Sales	2,301	2,336
Operating income	326	308
Interest expense	(100)	(102)
Income (loss) before taxes	$ 226	$ 206
Cash from operations*	338	356

*Computed using Standard & Poor's definition, not that used throughout the text.

acquisition, SCA became the largest forest products company in Europe and its packaging and hygiene operations were significantly strengthened.

On January 5, 1995, the BBB+ rated SCA was placed on S&P's Creditwatch list. Exhibit 18P-6 provides selected financial statement data for SCA for the 1992 through 1995 period.

A. Use the 1992 to 1994 data to determine the appropriate rating at the end of 1993 and 1994 for SCA. If different from the actual rating, discuss briefly.

B. Do you agree with S&P's decision to place SCA on its Creditwatch list? Discuss major factors you would consider in deciding whether to place SCA on the Creditwatch list.

C. Use the 1995 data in Exhibit 18P-6 to determine an appropriate debt rating for SCA at the end of 1995. Discuss briefly other information that would help you develop this rating.

D. On June 4, 1996, S&P raised the senior debt rating of SCA to A− from BBB+. Discuss major factors that would have influenced this decision.

EXHIBIT 18P-5
Comparison of Paper Company Debt Ratings ($ in millions)

Company (Rating)	1991			Times Interest Earned		
	Capitalization	LT Debt	Debt/Capital (%)	1989	1990	1991
Westvaco (A)	$2,856	$1,205	37.8%	4.24	3.09	2.10
James River (BBB+)	4,556	1,900	43.2	3.15	2.97	1.55
Union Camp (A)	3,750	1,322	48.9	7.41	3.98	1.95

Source: Standard & Poor's *Bond Guide*, March 1993.

EXHIBIT 18P-6. SVENSKA CELLULOSA AKTIBOLAGET
Selected Financial Data, for the Years Ended December 31, 1992 to 1995
(SEK in millions)

	1992	1993	1994	1995
Total debt	15,509	13,674	13,559	22,439
Total equity	18,284	19,963	19,590	22,024
Sales	32,137	33,420	33,676	65,317
Operating income	3,966	4,081	3,578	10,459
Interest expense	(1,580)	(1,154)	(984)	(1,862)
Income before taxes	2,386	2,927	2,594	8,597
Cash from operations	3,407	3,143	2,929	7,574

Source: SCA, *1992–1995 Annual Reports.*

9. [Credit analysis and fixed income investments; 1995 CFA adapted] Margaret O'Flaherty, a portfolio manager for MCF Investments, is considering two fixed-income investment alternatives for her clients' portfolios. Neither bond is callable.

Issuer	Coupon	Maturity	Price
Alpine Chemical	7%	June 30, 2004	100
U.S. Treasury Note	6%	June 30, 2004	100

Currently the spreads between noncallable, 10-year industrial bonds and 10-year U.S. Treasury Notes are as follows:

Treasuries to AAA-rated industrials	25 basis points
Treasuries to AA-rated industrials	50 basis points
Treasuries to A-rated industrials	75 basis points
Treasuries to BBB-rated industrials	100 basis points
Treasuries to BB-rated industrials	125 basis points
Treasuries to B-rated industrials	150 basis points

A. Selected financial ratios for the Alpine Chemical Company are presented below:

Alpine Chemical Company Credit Ratios

Credit Ratios	1989	1990	1991	1992	1993
EBIT/interest expense	3.46X	4.96X	4.79X	4.70X	5.65X
Long-term debt/total capitalization	28%	34%	34%	34%	44%
Funds from operations/total debt	84%	93%	56%	51%	59%
Operating income/sales	13%	13%	14%	12%	13%

Briefly explain the significance of each of the four ratios to the assessment of Alpine Chemical's creditworthiness.

B. Select an appropriate credit rating for Alpine Chemical by relating the level and trend of the four credit ratios to the medians for those ratios shown in Exhibit 18-8.

C. Given your assessment of Alpine Chemical's credit rating, state and justify which of the two bonds (Alpine Chemical or U.S. Treasury) O'Flaherty should recommend for purchase.

19

VALUATION AND FORECASTING

CHAPTER OUTLINE

CHAPTER OBJECTIVES

INTRODUCTION

VALUATION MODELS

OVERVIEW OF MODELS

ASSET-BASED VALUATION MODELS
Market Price and Book Value: Theoretical
Considerations
Book Value: Measurement Issues
Tobin's Q Ratio
Stability and Growth of Book Value
  Earnings Retention
  Effect of New Equity Financing
  Effect of Acquisitions
  Effect of Changing Exchange Rates
  *Effect of Financial Reporting Choices and
  Accounting Changes*
  Restructuring Provisions

**DISCOUNTED CASH FLOW VALUATION
MODELS**
Dividend-Based Models
  Growth Patterns
Earnings-Based Models
  *Relationship Between Earnings-Based and
  Dividend-Based Models*

*The Definition of Earnings and the Valuation
Objective*
No-Growth Model
Growth Model
Estimating Growth
Alternative and Finite Growth Assumptions
*Earnings Valuation and the Price/Earnings
Ratio*
Growth, Risk, and Valuation
*Effects of Permanent and Transitory Earnings
and Measurement Error*
Earnings or Cash Flows?
Free Cash Flow Approach to Valuation
  Adjustments to Reported Cash from Investment
  Dividends, Earnings, or Free Cash Flows?

THE ABNORMAL EARNINGS OR EBO MODEL
EBO Versus DCF Models
  Finite Horizons
  *Relative Importance of Terminal Value
  Calculations*
  Effect of Accounting Policies

The Clean Surplus Relationship
Unbiased Versus Conservative Accounting
Value Drivers

Price/Book Value and Price/Earnings Ratios Revisited
The EBO Model: Concluding Comments

FORECASTING MODELS AND TIME-SERIES PROPERTIES OF EARNINGS

FORECASTING MODELS
Extrapolative Models
  Permanent Versus Transitory Components
Index Models
Forecasting with Disaggregated Data
  Quarterly Forecasting Models
  Segment-Based Forecasts
  Forecasts Using Income or Balance Sheet Components

COMPARISON WITH FINANCIAL ANALYST FORECASTS
Analyst Forecasts: Some Caveats

SUMMARY

CASE 19-1 VALUATION OF DUPONT

APPENDIX 19-A: MULTISTAGE GROWTH MODELS
Valuing a Nondividend-Paying Firm
Shifting Growth Rate Patterns

APPENDIX 19-B: THE EBO AND TERMINAL VALUE ASSUMPTIONS

CHAPTER OBJECTIVES

Chapter 19 concludes the text with an examination of valuation models and forecasting. The chapter:

1. Discusses the use of book value to measure value, and the effects on book value of:
   - Measurement problems
   - Transactions with stockholders
   - Acquisitions
   - Exchange rate changes
   - Financial reporting choices
2. Compares valuation models (DCF models) that are based on discounting estimates of future dividends, earnings, or cash flows.
3. Shows that these models are theoretically equivalent but the choice of model depends on such problems as:
   - Definition of earnings and cash flows

   - Estimating the growth rate
   - The effect of transitory earnings components
   - The inability to reliably forecast far into the future
4. Describes the abnormal earnings or EBO model, which avoids some of the limitations of DCF models and has the following advantages:
   - Short forecast horizon
   - Reliance on book value as a principal input
   - Limited impact of accounting choices
5. Reviews research that compares analyst forecasts to those based on extrapolative or index models that use time-series models. Such research shows that quarterly data, segment data, and financial statement components all improve forecast accuracy under some conditions.

INTRODUCTION

This chapter provides an overview of valuation models. In a perfect world, the models based on assets, dividends, cash flows, and earnings are identical. However, in the real world, this highly stylized environment does not exist and model results can differ. In such settings, the data used in valuation models are estimates of expected future values and their measurement is as important as their predictive ability.

The primary focus of the chapter, therefore, is not the theoretical underpinnings of these models, but rather the relationship of their parameters to information obtainable from the accounting system. In addition, consistent with forecasting requirements of valuation models, the chapter concludes with a discussion of forecasting and the time-series properties of earnings.

VALUATION MODELS

OVERVIEW OF MODELS

The valuation models most commonly used by analysts and investors generally fall into two classes:

1. Asset-based valuation models
2. Discounted cash flow (DCF) models

Additionally, we explore a third class, which has characteristics of the first two:

3. The abnormal earnings or Edwards–Bell–Ohlson (EBO) model.

Asset-based valuation models assign a value to the firm based on the current market value of the individual component assets. Liabilities (also at market value) are deducted to arrive at the (market) value of the firm's equity:

Value = Assets − Liabilities

In DCF models, value at time t is determined as the present value of future cash flows:

$$\textbf{Value}_t = \sum_i \frac{\textbf{CF}_{t+i}}{(1 + r)^i} \tag{1}$$

where CF_{t+i} represents (expected[1]) cash flows i periods from time t and r is the discount factor (the firm's required rate of return). DCF models vary as to the appropriate measure of cash flow CF, defined variously as streams of future dividends, earnings, or free cash flows.

Conceptually, the DCF and asset-based approaches to valuation are related through the actual rate of return r^* earned by a firm on its equity investment. For an

---

[1]Technically, we should use the expectation operator $E(*)$ when discussing future period (as yet unknown) cash flows/earnings to differentiate from current period (known) earnings. This would, however, only add needlessly to the notation. From the context, it should be clear that when we speak of future earnings or cash flows, we are talking about their expected rather than actual values.

infinite (constant) cash flow stream, using the DCF model, we obtain

$$\textbf{Value} = \frac{\textbf{CF}}{r} \qquad (2)$$

But the amount a firm earns, CF, is equal to

$$\textbf{CF} = r\textbf{*}B$$

where B is the book value of the firm. If we assume that the firm earns the required rate of return r, $(r^* = r)$, then CF $= rB$ and

$$\textbf{Value} = \frac{\textbf{CF}}{r} = \frac{rB}{r} = B \qquad (3)$$

This equation suggests that value can be equivalently defined as either a "stock" of assets or the flows those assets generate.

The EBO model, we shall see, determines value as a combination of the stock of assets representing the normal flow that assets generate and the discounted value of abnormal earnings generated by these assets.

The various approaches are equivalent in a highly stylized and perfect world. Such a world has no need for financial analysis as all is known. Analysis is challenging and rewarding, however, in real-world settings, with finite knowledge and horizons and costly information. In the real world, there is uncertainty with respect to both the definition and measurement of the model parameters and their actual outcomes. The equivalence of asset-based, DCF, and EBO models breaks down, and different valuations result. The uncertainties in these models include:

- Difficulties in forecasting over a finite horizon, let alone to infinity
- The random nature of cash flows and earnings and the difficulty in assessing whether reported amounts are *permanent* (will persist in the future) or *transitory* (nonrecurring)
- The measurement of assets, earnings, and cash flows, which can be influenced by the selection of accounting policies and by discretionary management policies

Analysts must be able to circumvent the pitfalls introduced by uncertainty and measurement problems. This chapter will discuss these problems further in the context of the valuation models themselves.

ASSET-BASED VALUATION MODELS

Asset-based models assign a value to the firm by aggregating the current market value of its individual component assets and liabilities. Chapter 17 discussed the steps required to develop an asset-based valuation. As derived in Exhibit 17-1, duPont's adjusted book value on December 31, 1994, was $18.7 billion, or $26.97 per share, approximately 46% higher than the reported book value of $13.0 billion, or $18.48 per share. Both amounts were considerably below the closing market price (at December 31, 1994) of $56.125. How should this discrepancy be interpreted? Should we expect to see the market price equal (the adjusted) book value?

One possibility is that the value of the firm exceeds the sum of its parts. Asset-based valuation calculates that sum; synergistic effects could then result in a premium (economic goodwill) for the going concern. Whether or not this is true depends on the firm's profitability. There may be other reasons for this discrepancy, including but not limited to the nature of the firm's assets, management's choice of financial reporting methods, mandatory and discretionary accounting changes, and other problems in the measurement of book value. We explore these causes to develop our understanding of the insights they provide and the pitfalls in the use of asset-based valuation models.

Market Price and Book Value: Theoretical Considerations

Earlier we showed that when the actual rate of return r^* equals the required rate of return r, then

$$\text{Value} = \frac{\text{CF}}{r} = \frac{rB}{r} = B$$

When r^* is not equal to r, then this equation can be transformed to

$$\text{CF} = r^*B = rB + (r^* - r)\,B$$

and, therefore, if

$$\text{Value} = \frac{\text{CF}}{r}$$

then

$$\begin{aligned}
\text{Value} &= \frac{rB + (r^* - r)\,B}{r} \\
&= \left[1 + \frac{(r^* - r)}{r}\right] B \qquad (4) \\
&= B + \left[\frac{(r^* - r)}{r}\right] B
\end{aligned}$$

Whether or not a firm's stock price is above or below book value depends on the intuitively appealing factor of how high the firm's expected rate of return is. As we shall see, $r^* > r$ is characteristic of a firm with positive growth opportunities, leading to market values greater than book value. Thus, the shares of a firm whose expected r^* is higher (lower) than the required r should sell at a price above (below) book value. The component

$$\left[\frac{(r^* - r)}{r}\right] B$$

is, in effect, a measure of the firm's economic goodwill, the excess of market over book value.[2]

---

[2] As we shall see, this relationship is basic to the EBO model.

Book Value: Measurement Issues

The calculation of duPont's adjusted book value, although detailed, was relatively straightforward for all liabilities and current assets as much of the required information was available. The major difficulty in applying asset-based valuation is the determination of the market (current) value of long-lived assets such as plant, machinery, and equipment. Because this is true for most companies, the relationship between (adjusted) book value and market price is affected by this measurement error.

For some analysts, reported book value is an "index" against which to compare the stock price. Under the assumption that the differential between market price and book value should be similar for firms in the same industry, the analysis turns on whether the relationship for a given firm is "in line" with a comparable population of firms.

When book value is used as an indicator, it is common practice to rely on unadjusted data that are simpler to obtain. These amounts do not measure value directly, but rather are viewed as benchmarks against which market value is compared. The focus is on how close market value is to book value. If it is very close to book value or below book value, then the stock is a "buy," as the downside risk is viewed as negligible.[3]

This comparison is generally conducted under the implicit or explicit assumption that historical cost-based book value reflects the minimum value of the firm. This minimum value assumption is justified by the fact that, since book value is based on historical cost, it does not reflect increases in value caused by inflation. Moreover, when there are adjustments to historical cost, only markdowns (such as impairment) not markups are permitted. (In some cases, such as marketable securities, markups are allowed.) Thus, book value is viewed as a conservative estimate of the firm's value.

Notwithstanding the foregoing, stocks do trade below the firm's book value. On an economy-wide level, Stober (1996) found the average price-to-book ratio to be less than 1 for every year in the 1973 to 1979 period; since that period, it has been greater than 1. Feltham and Ohlson (1995) noted that close to one-third of companies on the COMPUSTAT tape traded below their book values at some time. The relationship between price and book value depends to a great extent on the nature of the firm's assets, its reporting methods, its profitability, and the overall economy.

Firms reporting intangible assets such as goodwill can trade below reported book value. Relating this to the theoretical model earlier, we see that if the economic goodwill component $[(r^* - r)/r]\,B$ is less than the recorded goodwill, then a company can trade below its reported book value.[4] For a company that has no recorded goodwill, if its profitability is poor ($r^* < r$), then it is possible for the firm's shares to trade below even its (historical) book value. Such a firm may have greater value broken up than as a going concern.

Book value is also a function of management's financial reporting choices that affect the allocations of revenues and expenses across time periods and as a result determine reported asset and liability balances. In some cases, these choices result in nonrecognition of economic obligations. These choices affect reported book value over time for a given firm, and at any given point in time, they affect comparisons of book value across firms.

---

[3]The results of Fama and French (1992), discussed in Chapters 5 and 18, imply that one of the variables that best explain differential market returns is the book value/price ratio. They suggest that this ratio may serve as a surrogate risk measure.

[4]This is true even if $r^* > r$.

A final point relates to restructurings and write-offs. It was indicated in Chapter 8 that the decision to write down long-lived tangible assets is somewhat subjective. Management determines the amount and may accelerate or delay the recognition of write-offs and restructurings affecting reported book value and earnings. Thus, if the market anticipates a write-off, the firm's shares could trade below book value.

Tobin's Q Ratio

The relationship between a company's market and book values can be measured by Tobin's q ratio,[5] defined as the market value of the firm divided by its book value on a replacement cost basis.[6] Q values below 1 (price less than replacement book value) imply that the firm earns less than the required rate of return; a (marginal) dollar invested in the firm's assets results in future cash flows whose present value is less than $1. Such firms are poor performers.

However (as discussed in Chapter 14), firms with low q ratios are often seen as prime takeover targets. Firms that want to expand find it cheaper to grow by acquiring an existing firm rather than constructing new production or marketing facilities. Implicit in such takeovers is the assumption that the acquired assets will perform better within the new firm due to diversification, synergistic effects, or better management.

The assumption of poor management can also motivate acquisitions even when the target firm is not in the same line of business. Low q ratios indicate poor firm performance. If this performance is due to poor management, bidders who believe they are better managers can buy the business at an attractive price.

Stability and Growth of Book Value

The growth of equity capital, the base on which shareholder returns are earned, is an important component of firm value. Even a constant return on equity, if applied to a growing capital base, will increase earnings. Thus, the trend of book value per share (BPS) is as important as its level; both are affected by operating, investing, and financing decisions, financial reporting choices, and discretionary or mandatory accounting changes. A brief discussion of factors which affect (and sometimes distort) BPS follows.

Earnings Retention

For most firms, retained earnings provide most of the growth in book value. That growth is affected by the firm's return on equity (ROE) and its dividend policy. If the payout ratio (dividends/net income) equals k, then the increase in book value B is

$$
\begin{aligned}
B_1 - B_0 &= \text{Income} - \text{Dividends} \\
&= (\text{ROE} \times B_0) - (k \times \text{ROE} \times B_0) \qquad (5)\\
&= (1 - k) \times \text{ROE} \times B_0
\end{aligned}
$$

where B_0 is the book value at the beginning of the period and $(1 - k)$ is the *earnings retention rate*. Thus, $(1 - k) \times$ ROE is the growth rate of book value per share due to earnings retention.[7]

---

[5]The ratio was developed by the Nobel prize-winning economist James Tobin.

[6]See Chapter 7 and Appendix 8-A for a discussion of the concepts of current cost and replacement cost.

[7]As we shall see in our discussion of DCF models, this is also one way of estimating earnings growth. We shall also indicate the problems in using these parameters to estimate growth.

Effect of New Equity Financing

Sales of new shares at prices above BPS increase book value per share, whereas sales below BPS result in dilution.[8] Similarly, repurchases of outstanding shares at prices below BPS increase it, whereas repurchases of shares above BPS dilute it.

Effect of Acquisitions

Acquisitions that are made for stock affect book value per share under either the purchase or pooling methods of acquisition accounting (see Chapter 14), although the impact differs.

When the pooling method is used, the newly issued shares are reflected at the book value of the acquired company:

$$\frac{\text{Book Value of Acquired Company}}{\text{Number of Shares Issued}}$$

If the BPS of the newly issued shares exceeds that of the acquirer, then BPS increases. If the BPS of the newly issued shares is lower, the acquirer's BPS is diluted.

Under the purchase method of accounting, the newly issued shares are recorded at market value. Thus, the effect on the acquirer's BPS depends on whether or not the market price of its shares is above or below its own BPS; it is as if the acquirer sold shares for cash and used that cash to purchase the acquired company.

Effect of Changing Exchange Rates

As discussed in Chapter 15, the equity of operations in functional currencies other than the reporting (parent) currency is translated at the exchange rate on the balance sheet date. As a result, when functional currencies appreciate, the firm's BPS rises. Similarly, the remeasurement of foreign operations and translation of foreign currency transactions affect the BPS and need careful evaluation.

Effect of Financial Reporting Choices and Accounting Changes

Much of this text has been devoted to analyses of the effects (including those on book value) of financial reporting choices such as inventory valuation, depreciation, employee benefits, leases, and other capitalization versus expensing decisions. Discretionary changes in these policies can also change the level and trend of growth (or decline) in BPS.

Finally, mandatory accounting changes can have a significant impact on reported book value. In recent years, new accounting standards have had significantly positive (income taxes and marketable securities) and negative (postemployment benefits and impairment) impacts on BPS. As noted in earlier chapters, long transition periods and alternative transition methods affect the level and trend of BPS of a given firm and comparisons across firms.

As a result of duPont's adoption of SFAS 106, Employers' Accounting for Postretirement Benefits Other Than Pensions, in 1992, for example, there was a cumulative negative effect of $4.8 billion ($7.18 per share). DuPont's book value was reduced by 30%!

---

[8]A mathematical formulation of this effect can be found in Cohen et al. (1987), p. 399.

Thus, although the trend of BPS is an important indicator of potential earnings growth, the analyst must discern whether or not BPS growth comes from operations (increases in retained earnings)[9] or the other factors discussed. To the extent that BPS growth evolves from nonoperating factors, that growth may be artificial or nonrecurring. Failure to consider the sources of BPS growth can result in erroneous conclusions regarding future earnings trends.

Restructuring Provisions

In recent years, many companies have reported large restructuring provisions that significantly reduced reported BPS. In the case of duPont, pretax restructuring charges were $828, $475, and $1,835 million in 1991 through 1993, followed by a $142 million reversal in 1994. In total, these charges (if we assume a 35% tax rate) reduced book value per share by approximately $2.90 per share, or 16%.

Although asset-based valuation can be a useful tool, because of the complexities and problems discussed above, analysts have sought to value companies using forecasts of future cash flows rather than the evaluation of the current stock of assets. We now turn to these models.

DISCOUNTED CASH FLOW VALUATION MODELS

The parameters that make up the DCF model

$$\text{Value} = \sum \frac{\text{CF}_{t+i}}{(1 + r)^i}$$

are related to risk (the required rate of return) and the return itself (CF). Chapter 18 dealt with the elements of risk and their impact on the required rate of return. This chapter focuses primarily on measurement of the return or CF measure.

These models (originating in the finance literature) use three alternative CF measures: dividends, accounting earnings, and free cash flows. Just as DCF and asset-based valuation models are equivalent under the assumptions of perfect markets, dividends, earnings, and free cash flow measures can be shown (theoretically) to yield equivalent results. Their implementation, however, is not straightforward.

First, there is inherent difficulty in defining the cash flows used in these models. Which cash flows and to whom do they flow? Conceptually, cash flows are defined differently depending on whether the valuation objective is the firm's equity (denoted as P), or the value of the firm's debt plus equity (V).

Assuming that we can define CF, we are left with another issue. The models need future cash flows as inputs. How is the cash flow stream estimated from present data? More important, are current and past dividends, earnings, or cash flows the best indicators of that stream? These (and other) pragmatic issues determine which model should be used. Before addressing these issues directly, we discuss various models based on these measures. Doing so will highlight some of the difficulties inherent in using them.

---

[9]This source of growth in BPS may also stem from financial reporting choices and the impact of such changes is not necessarily the same as real operating improvements.

Dividend-Based Models

The value of a firm's equity (P) equals the present value of all future dividends paid by the firm to its equity holders:

$$P_0 = \frac{D_1}{(1+r)} + \frac{D_2}{(1+r)^2} + \cdots$$
$$= \sum_{i=1}^{\infty} \frac{D_i}{(1+r)^i} \tag{6}$$

where

P_0 = the value of the firm's equity at the end of period 0
D_i = the dividend paid by the firm in period i
r = the firm's required rate of return based on the firm's risk class

This formulation requires forecasting dividends to infinity (see the discussion below), which is impossible. Thus, different patterns of future dividend payments must be assumed.

Growth Patterns

No-Growth–Constant Dividend Model. In its no-growth form, the dividend discount model assumes a constant dividend rate equal to the current dividend level, and Eq. (6) reduces to

$$P_0 = \frac{D_1}{r} \tag{7}$$

In effect, dividends are capitalized at r to derive the value of the firm.

Constant Growth Model. For a firm with an expected (constant) growth rate g, dividends in the next period are expected to equal $(1 + g)$ times current dividends, $D_1 = D_0(1 + g)$, and the valuation model becomes

$$P_0 = \frac{D_0(1+g)}{r-g} = \frac{D_1}{r-g} \tag{8}$$

Explicit Forecasts with Terminal Value Assumptions. Equation (6) can be rewritten as

$$P_0 = \sum_{i=1}^{T} \frac{D_i}{(1+r)^i} + \frac{P_T}{(1+r)^T} \tag{9}$$

where

$$P_T = \sum_{j=1}^{\infty} \frac{D_{T+j}}{(1+r)^{T+j}}$$

Equation (9) states that firm value in period 0 equals the discounted value of a stream of dividends for T periods plus the (discounted) value of the firm at the end of T periods. Using this form of the model requires *explicit* forecasts of dividends for T

(usually three to five) years, plus a forecast of the terminal price (P_T) at the end of period T. This forecasted price usually incorporates (one of) the previously discussed growth assumptions.

Although the dividend model is easy to use, it presents a conceptual dilemma.[10] Finance theory[11] says that dividend policy does not matter; the pattern of dividends up to the terminal (liquidating) dividend is irrelevant. The model, however, requires forecasting dividends to infinity or making terminal value assumptions. Firms that presently do not pay any dividends are a case in point.[12] Such firms are not valueless. In fact, high-growth firms often pay no dividends, as they reinvest all funds available to them. When firm value is estimated using a dividend discount model, it depends on the dividend level of the firm after its growth stabilizes. *Future dividends depend on the earnings stream the firm will be able to generate.* Thus, the firm's expected future earnings are fundamental to such a valuation. Similarly, for a firm paying dividends, the level of dividends *may be* a discretionary choice of management that is restricted by available earnings.

When dividends are not paid out, value accumulates within the firm in the form of reinvested earnings. Alternatively, firms sometimes pay dividends right up to bankruptcy. Thus, dividends may say more about the allocation of earnings to different claimants than valuation.

Earnings-Based Models

The implementation problems with dividend-based models highlight the crucial role of earnings in valuation. We now proceed to a discussion of earnings-based valuation models by showing the relationship between dividends and earnings models. However, one caveat must be noted: The concept of earnings used in these models and accounting income are the same only under specific simplified assumptions. The notion of earnings in these theoretic models is closer to CFO or free cash flows. For the present, the term "earnings" should be viewed broadly. We shall expand and clarify this issue as we proceed.

Relationship Between Earnings-Based and Dividend-Based Models

An earnings-based model can be derived from the dividend-based model using k, the dividend payout ratio. If $D_i = kE_i$, then, for the *growth case,*

$$P_0 = \frac{kE_0(1 + g)}{r - g} = \frac{kE_1}{r - g} \tag{10}$$

As discussed shortly, a firm with no growth in dividends and earnings is (generally) not making *new* investments. Thus, all earnings are paid out as dividends. The payout ratio k equals 1, and the valuation model becomes

$$P_0 = \frac{E_0}{r}$$

---

[10]Penman labels this paradox the dividend conundrum.

[11]Miller and Modigliani's proposition. We ignore the potentially signaling aspect of dividends. (See footnote 20.)

[12]See Appendix 19-A for a discussion of such firms.

EXHIBIT 19-1
No-Growth Model

Income Statement

	All Years
Operating revenue	$ 350
Operating expense	(150)
	$ 200
Depreciation expense	(50)
Operating income before tax	$ 150
Tax @ 20%	(30)
Net operating income	**$ 120**
Interest expense (net of taxes)	(20)
Net income	**$ 100**

The Definition of Earnings and the Valuation Objective

Earnings-based models can be used to value either:

1. The equity of the firm (P), or
2. The firm as a whole (V), debt plus equity

The definition of earnings used depends on the valuation objective. To measure the value of the firm (V), earnings are defined *prior* to payment of interest, as net operating income. To value equity, earnings are measured *after* payment of interest, net income.[13] *The definition of such other parameters as the rate of return also differs for each case.*

No-Growth Model

For the no-growth case and a simplified income statement (Exhibit 19-1), the appropriate definitions for each case are:

Value	= Earnings	/ Rate of Return
Equity P = Net income		/ Rate of return on equity [e.g., $r = r_f + \beta(r_m - r_f)$]
Firm V = Net operating income		/ Rate of return on debt and equity (weighted-average cost of capital)

(1) Equity Valuation. When the valuation objective is the firm's equity, earnings are defined as net income, the amount available for distribution to equity shareholders. Similarly, the required rate of return is the *equity rate of return.* This rate of return is similar to that used for the dividend-based model and its estimation is discussed in

---

[13]This discussion assumes that there is no preferred stock. When preferred stock exists, a third possibility exists, the valuation of total (common and preferred) equity.

Chapter 18. By estimating the firm's beta,[14] the risk-free rate, and the (excess) market return, the CAPM can be used[15] to estimate r. If we assume r is 10%, the value of equity is

$$P = \frac{E}{r} = \frac{\$100}{0.10} = \$1,000$$

(2) Value of the Firm. Net operating income (before deducting interest), that is, the cash available to all providers of capital, is the appropriate measure of earnings when valuing the firm as a whole. Similarly, the rate of return is a weighted average of the required rates of return of all providers of capital: the weighted-average cost of capital (WACC). The weighting is based on the relative proportions of debt and equity.

In our example, if we assume that the firm has a debt-to-capital ratio of 20% (four-fifths equity and one-fifth debt) and further that the (after-tax) cost of debt is 8%, then the weighted-average cost of capital is

$$\textbf{WACC} = (0.8 \times 0.10) + (0.2 \times 0.08) = 0.096$$

and the value of the firm as a whole is

$$V = \frac{\textbf{Net Operating Income}}{\textbf{WACC}} = \frac{\$120}{0.096} = \$1,250$$

The value of the firm equals the value of its debt plus the value of its equity. The equity value P can be derived from the firm value V by deducting the value of debt. As we have assumed an (after-tax) cost of debt (interest rate) of 8% and the (after-tax) interest expense is $20, then the value of its debt must equal $250 ($20/8%). Thus, the equity value is $1,250 − $250 = $1,000, identical to the value for equity derived directly.[16]

Growth Model

For a growing firm, the relationships between earnings and the amounts flowing to the equity- and debtholders are somewhat more complex. We begin again with the valuation of equity followed by the valuation of the firm.

(1) Equity Valuation and Earnings. The firm's net income is assumed to be used either for (1) payment of dividends or (2) investment in new assets.

With k equal to the payout ratio, then $(1 - k)$ is the fraction of earnings reinvested in new assets. Exhibit 19-2A illustrates the allocation of net income between new investment and dividends given an assumed dividend payout ratio of 80%. If these

---

[14]In Chapter 18, we discuss alternative estimation procedures for beta.

[15]Additional adjustments may also be appropriate to control for such other risk factors as size.

[16]It should be noted that $1,000 equity and $250 debt are consistent with the debt-to-capital ratio of 20% based on the market values of the debt and equity.

EXHIBIT 19-2
Growth Model

A. *Derivation of Amount Available for Equityholders*
for Valuation of Equity

	Year 0
Operating revenue	$ 350
Operating expense	(150)
	$ 200
Depreciation expense	(50)
Operating income before tax	$ 150
Tax @ 20%	(30)
Net operating income	**$ 120**
Interest expense (net of taxes)	(20)
Net income	**$ 100**
New investment (equity)	(20)
Available for equityholders (dividends)	**$ 80**

B. *Derivation of Amount Available for Debt- and*
Equityholders for Valuation of Firm

	Year 0
Operating revenue	$ 350
Operating expense	(150)
	$ 200
Depreciation expense	(50)
Operating income before tax	$ 150
Tax @ 20%	(30)
Net operating income	**$ 120**
New investment	(30)
Available for debt- and equityholders	**$ 90**

Financing Distribution (Cash for Financing)

Dividends	$ 80
Interest expense (net of taxes)	20
New debt	(10)
	$ 90

new assets earn a rate of return $r^* = 20\%$, then the pattern of net income and its distribution between dividends and reinvestment, for $k = 0.80$, is:

Period	Earnings	= Dividend	+ New Investments
0	$E_0 = \$100$	$= 0.8E_0 = \$80$	$+ 0.2E_0 = \$20$
1	$E_1 = \$100 + (r^* \times \$20) = \$104$	$= 0.8E_1 = \$83.2$	$+ 0.2E_1 = \$20.8$
2	$E_2 = \$104 + (r^* \times \$20.8) = \$108.16$	$= 0.8E_2 = \$86.53$	$+ 0.2E_2 = \$21.63$

The firm's earnings, dividends, and investments all grow at a rate of 4%. As the next table indicates, this growth rate is the product of the fraction reinvested $(1 - k)$ times the rate of return the firm can earn on the reinvestment (r^*):

Period	Earnings	= Dividend	+ New Investments
0	E_0	$= kE_0$	$+ (1 - k) E_0$
1	$E_1 = E_0 + r^*(1 - k) E_0$	$= kE_1$	$+ (1 - k) E_1$
	$= E_0[1 + r^*(1 - k)]$	$= kE_0[1 + r^*(1 - k)]$	$+ (1 - k) E_0[1 + r^*(1 - k)]$
2	$E_2 = E_1[1 + r^*(1 - k)]$	$= kE_2$	$+ (1 - k) E_2$
	$= E_0[1 + r(1 - k)]^2$	$= kE_0[1 + r^*(1 - k)]^2$	$+ (1 - k) E_0[1 + r^*(1 - k)]^2$

Note that earnings, dividends, and new investment each grow at the rate $[r^*(1 - k)]$. The firm's growth rate g thus equals

$$g = r^*(1 - k) = 0.2 \times (1 - 0.8) = 0.04$$

This result is intuitively appealing: A firm's growth rate depends on the level of investment and the return on that investment. Thus, a no-growth company is one with no new investment: $k = 1$.

Using the growth formula to find the value of the firm's equity yields

$$P_0 = \frac{kE_0(1 + g)}{r - g} = \frac{kE_1}{r - r^*(1 - k)}$$

$$= \frac{0.8(\$104)}{0.10 - 0.04} = \$1,387$$

(2) Value of the Firm. We continue with our previous example. In the no-growth case, equity value was related to the earnings available to the equity shareholder, net income. To value the firm (total capital), we used the earnings available to the debt holders and shareholders, net operating income.

In the growth model, to value equity, net income is replaced by the amount available to the equity shareholder after new investment of equity (net income − reinvestment of equity). Similarly, to value the firm as a whole, we must determine the earnings available to all providers of capital: the debt- and equityholders. This amount equals net operating income minus *total* new investment. Total new investment is provided by both equity- and debtholders. Given the growth rate of 4% implied by the equity investment of $20, debt[17] must be increased[18] by $10 (4% of $250), making the total new investment equal to $30.

The two approaches are contrasted in Exhibit 19-2. We must carefully distinguish between total new investments and the reinvestment of equity referred to previously. The first is the actual investment in new assets made by the firm ($30, in the example).

[17]The debt-to-capital ratio of 20% developed for the no-growth case can no longer be maintained. That ratio was based on relative market values. Growth opportunities, however, are "captured" by equity shareholders, thereby altering the relative proportions of debt and equity. The new debt-to-capital ratio is 15.8% [$260/($1,387 + $260)], based on equity of $1,387 and debt of $260. This ratio will now be maintained as both the market value of debt and equity grow at a rate of 4%.

[18]The $10 of new debt is consistent with an assumed 4% growth in net income. For interest expense to increase by 4%, debt must increase by 4% from $250 to $260.

Financing for this investment is provided by debt ($10) and equity ($20). For equity valuation, reinvestment refers only to that amount (i.e., $20) provided by equityholders (net income − dividends).

With new debt of $10, total debt is now $260. The market value of equity, we have shown, is $1,387. Therefore, the firm's WACC equals 9.7%.[19]

Exhibit 19-2 provides year 0 data. All year 1 values are 4% higher. The value of the firm using this approach therefore equals

$$\frac{\textbf{(Operating Income − Total New Investment) (1 + g)}}{\textbf{WACC − g}} = \frac{(\$120 − \$30)\,(1.04)}{(0.097 − 0.04)}$$

$$= \frac{93.6}{0.057} = \$1,647$$

The $1,647 value of the firm is the sum of the value of the equity ($1,387) plus the value of the debt ($260).

Estimating Growth

The firm's growth rate can be estimated in one of two ways:

1. Estimating the individual components, k and r^*, that contribute to growth as $g = (1 − k)r^*$
2. Extrapolating the historical growth rate to the future

Defining and Estimating r*: *Return on New (Equity) Investment.* The terms r^* and r both represent rates of return for the equity investor. The former represents the actual return, whereas the latter refers to the required rate of return. *Growth opportunities exist only when expected returns r^* exceed the required rate of return r (i.e., $r^* > r$).* When $r^* = r$, then the growth model reduces to the no-growth case:

$$P = \frac{kE}{[r − r^*(1 − k)]}$$

$$= \frac{kE}{[r − r^* + r^*k]}$$

But $r = r^*$:

$$P = \frac{kE}{(r − r + rk)}$$

$$= \frac{E}{r}$$

[19]With debt of $260 and equity of $1,387, and the (after-tax) cost of debt and equity equal to 8% and 10%, respectively:

$$\text{WACC} = \frac{\$1,387}{\$1,387 + \$260} \times 10\% + \frac{\$260}{\$1,387 + \$260} \times 8\% = 9.7\%$$

This result does not imply that firms cannot make new investments and grow even when $r^* = r$. It does show that it does not make any difference whether or not the firm decides to grow. The value of the firm's equity is not affected whether the firm reinvests its net income or pays dividends. Recall our earlier example for the no-growth model in which we found the value of the equity equal to $100/0.10 = $1,000. That example assumed all income is paid out as dividends. The following table indicates the effect of alternative dividend payout ratios, beginning in period 1, when the remainder is reinvested at the rate $r^* = r = 0.10$:

Payout Ratio k	Reinvested Income $(1 - k) E_1$	Growth Rate $g = (1 - k) r$	Share Value $P_0 = kE_1/(r - g)$
0.75	25	$0.025 = (1 - 0.75) \times 0.1$	$1,000 = 75/(0.1 - 0.025)
0.50	50	$0.050 = (1 - 0.50) \times 0.1$	$1,000 = 50/(0.1 - 0.050)
0.25	75	$0.075 = (1 - 0.25) \times 0.1$	$1,000 = 25/(0.1 - 0.075)

Shareholder's wealth is not affected by the firm's dividend policy.[20]

As r^* measures the actual return earned on (reinvested) equity, it is conceptually equivalent to the familiar ROE measure. Using ROE to measure r^* is reasonable if (along with the other assumptions of our simplified world) the firm's new investment opportunities are similar to past ones.

Estimating k: *The Dividend Payout Ratio.* The current dividend payout ratio is often used to estimate k. This gives us an estimate of the firm's earnings growth rate (often called the sustainable or implicit growth rate) in terms of the same ratios previously used to estimate growth in book value:

$$g = (1 - k) \times r^* = (1 - \text{Dividend Payout}) \times \text{ROE}$$

Using the dividend payout ratio and ROE to estimate future growth rates assumes constant levels for these parameters that can limit the usefulness of this technique. For stable growth companies, k and ROE are relatively constant. For cyclical companies, they are not. Exhibit 19-3 shows growth rate estimates for duPont derived from 1990 to 1994 data.

Given the volatility of these estimates, it is hard to use them with any confidence. Whenever dividends exceed EPS, the projected growth rate is negative. It should also be noted that it is theoretically incorrect to use the dividend payout ratio to estimate k. In the development of these models, no distinction is made among dividends paid

---

[20]We do not intend to review all the literature on dividend policy. Modigliani and Miller, in their famous proposition, note that, given a level of investment (growth opportunities), dividends are irrelevant as they are readily replaced by external financing. We address this issue in the next section by pointing out that dividend payout must be considered net of the raising of additional capital.

The issue of a firm's dividend policy remains controversial in the finance literature. There are those who argue that dividend policy is relevant because investors prefer the security of dividends; others view dividend policy in a "signaling" framework whereby management conveys its intentions and/or forecasts by its level of dividends. These issues are beyond the scope of our discussion. The foregoing argues only that in the context of this model, *ceteris paribus,* dividend policy is irrelevant.

EXHIBIT 19-3. DUPONT
Sustainable Growth Rate Estimates

Year	k	ROE	Growth Rate $(1 - k) \times$ ROE
1990	0.48	0.143	0.074
1991	0.81	0.083	0.016
1992	1.22	0.081	(0.018)
1993	2.22	0.048	(0.059)
1994	0.46	0.227	0.123

Note: Calculations are based on income before extraordinary charges and effects of changes in accounting policy.

out, stock repurchases, and issuance of new equity. That is,

kE = Dividends + Share Repurchases − New Equity Issued

should reflect net cash flows to and from equity shareholders; not just dividends.

Dividend payout measures only one portion of the total flow; it ignores new issues and repurchases and can distort the valuation model. A firm's choice of the form (the mix of dividends and the sale or repurchase of shares) of equity financing should not affect valuation. Thus, the more appropriate definition of k is

$$k = \frac{\textbf{Dividends + Share Repurchases − New Equity Issued}}{\textbf{Earnings}}$$

The potential instability of the individual growth rate components suggests that historical growth trends should not be used blindly to make growth projections. In a similar fashion, dividend policy affects the observed earnings trend.

Dividend Policy and EPS Growth. As stock values are expressed as price per share, many models that estimate earnings trends use earnings per share (EPS). The EPS growth rate can be distorted by a number of factors, not all of them value-related.

Dividend policy has an important impact on earnings growth. A firm with a low payout ratio grows faster than if it paid out most of its earnings, since reinvested earnings generate future earnings. This effect of dividend policy is meaningful. However, by choosing the mode of equity financing, that is, trading off dividends and the sale and repurchase of equity securities, the growth rate in EPS can be distorted. In Chapter 4 we discussed the adjustment of earnings per share for the effect of dividend policy. Exhibit 19-4 applies that methodology to duPont.

The adjustments shown for duPont are not very large for 1994. However, if the analysis is extended over a number of years, the effect is much greater. Dividend policy, by modifying the firm's need for external financing, ultimately affects the number of shares outstanding and, as a result, reported earnings per share. Firms with low dividend payouts should report faster EPS growth than firms with high payout policies.

EXHIBIT 19-4. DUPONT
Effect of Dividend Policy on Earnings per Share Growth

To show the effect of dividend policy on EPS growth, initially assume that duPont pays out earnings as dividends and sells new common shares equal to the increase in retained earnings. For 1994:

Net income	$ 2,727 million
Dividends	(1,237)
Increase in retained earnings	$ 1,490 million

If duPont distributed all its earnings as dividends, it would need to recover $1,490 million by selling new common shares. Using the 1994 mean price of $56 per share, duPont would have sold 26.6 million shares ($1,490/$56), increasing the number of shares outstanding by 4% and reducing EPS by 4%.

This analysis can be used in another way. If duPont paid no dividends in 1994, it would have had an additional $1,237 million of equity. If shares were repurchased (using the same price of $56), duPont would have repurchased 22 million shares ($1,237/$56), reducing the number of shares outstanding by 3% and increasing future EPS.

Alternative and Finite Growth Assumptions

We have demonstrated that the benefits from growth depend on the availability of investment opportunities earning a high rate of return, specifically, $r^* > r$. The valuation formula

$$P_0 = \frac{kE_0(1 + g)}{r - g} = \frac{kE_1}{r - g} \tag{10}$$

can be disaggregated into two components:

$$P_i = \frac{E_{i+1}}{r} + \frac{(1 - k) E_{i+1}}{r} \left[\frac{r^* - r}{r - (1 - k) r^*} \right]$$

The first component is the value of the firm in the absence of growth, the second component is the value of the firm's growth opportunities. Although the models assume infinite growth opportunities, high-return investment opportunities ($r^* > r$) do not exist forever in the real world. Appendix 19-A presents variations of (some of) these models using alternative growth assumptions.

Additionally, as discussed earlier, valuation models may use the following relationship:

$$P_0 = \frac{kE_1}{(1 + r)} + \frac{kE_2}{(1 + r)^2} \cdots \frac{kE_n}{(1 + r)^n} + \frac{P_n}{(1 + r)^n} \tag{11}$$

Explicit short-term horizon forecasts of earnings ($E_1, \ldots, E_n$) for a three-to-five-year period are made and then a terminal value (P_n) at the end of the period is estimated. This terminal value often incorporates the more general growth assumptions discussed. This valuation technique is especially useful under the more realistic assumption of growth opportunities with a finite horizon. We return to this issue later in the chapter.

Earnings Valuation and the Price/Earnings Ratio

The price/earnings (P/E) ratio is often used to compare firm valuations. This ratio is the multiple of earnings used by the market to value the firm. Its relationship to our valuation models is straightforward.

For the no-growth case,

$$P = \frac{E}{r}$$

becomes

$$\frac{P}{E} = \frac{1}{r} \tag{12}$$

The P/E ratio in this case equals the inverse of the firm's capitalization rate. For the growth case,

$$P_i = \frac{kE_i(1 + g)}{r - g}$$

becomes

$$\frac{P_i}{E_i} = \frac{k(1 + g)}{r - g} \tag{13}$$

Price/Earnings cum Dividend. Dividend irrelevancy implies that dividends and price are equivalent, dollar for dollar. Thus, from a pure theoretical perspective, P/E should be expressed as the ratio of *price plus dividends* to earnings. In practice, as dividends are small relative to price, modification does not affect the calculation materially. For discussion, however, we include this modification when necessary to show the development of these models.

Adding k to both sides of Eqs. (11) and (12) yields the *price/earnings cum dividend ratio.* For the no-growth case [Eq. (12)],

$$\frac{P}{E} + k = \frac{1}{r} + k$$

Since in the no-growth case, $k = 1$ and $D = E$:

$$\frac{P + D}{E} = \frac{1 + r}{r} \tag{14}$$

In the growth case [Eq. (13)],

$$\frac{P_i}{E_i} + k = \frac{k(1 + g)}{r - g} + k$$
$$\frac{P_i + D_i}{E_i} = \frac{k(1 + r)}{r - g} \tag{15}$$

Earlier, we showed that, when a firm does not possess extraordinary growth opportunities (i.e., $r^* = r$), although it can still grow by reinvesting dividends, growth does not affect valuation. This can be illustrated with the price/earnings cum dividend ratio. When $r^* = r$, then $g = (1 - k) r$ and Eq. (15) reduces to

$$\frac{P_i + D_i}{E_i} = \frac{1 + r}{r} \tag{16}$$

which is identical to the no-growth relationship. *Thus, in the absence of (extraordinary) growth opportunities, $(1 + r)/r$ is the normal price/earnings relationship.*

Growth, Risk, and Valuation

The preceding discussions imply that the relationship between price and earnings is a function of the firm's growth rate and risk (as captured by r). Beaver and Morse (1978) compared the price/earnings ratios of a sample of firms to see whether growth and/or risk could explain differentials among firms. For 25 portfolios of firms ranked by P/E ratios, they compared the average portfolio P/E ratios over 15 years. Parts A and B of Exhibit 19-5 show P/E ratios and average earnings growth rates for different portfolios. Extreme P/E ratios revert to the mean over the period. Note the trend in the ratio of portfolio 1's P/E to that of portfolio 25.

Initially, at least, some of the differences in P/E ratios are due to the earnings growth rate. Portfolios with high P/E ratios have higher earnings growth in the first

EXHIBIT 19-5
Results of Beaver and Morse: P/E Ratio Patterns

A. Price/Earnings Ratio of Portfolio

Portfolio	Number of Years After Portfolio Formation						
	0	1	2	3	5	10	14
1	50.0	22.7	16.4	13.8	13.2	13.0	8.3
5	20.8	17.5	16.9	15.9	13.7	11.9	8.4
10	14.3	11.9	11.5	10.3	10.1	9.9	8.3
15	11.1	10.8	10.4	10.0	10.0	8.6	7.1
20	8.9	9.1	9.6	9.4	9.3	9.0	7.7
25	5.8	6.9	8.0	7.9	7.9	7.8	8.9
Portfolio 1 / Portfolio 25	8.6	3.3	2.1	1.7	1.7	1.7	0.9

B. Cumulative Earnings Growth (%)

Portfolio	0	1	2	3	5	10	14
1	−4.1	9.53	37.2	28.2	18.9	15.3	11.8
5	10.7	14.9	12.1	13.1	10.9	8.0	18.1
10	9.6	12.9	11.5	12.3	9.2	12.9	29.6
15	10.0	8.8	8.5	8.1	14.3	11.0	33.4
20	10.8	5.2	9.3	12.6	6.0	11.1	18.0
25	26.4	−3.3	7.5	10.8	12.9	16.7	10.1

Source: William Beaver and Dale Morse, "What Determines Price-Earnings Ratios?," *Financial Analysts Journal,* July–August 1978, pp. 65–76. Adapted from Table 3 (p. 68) and Table 5 (p. 70).

few years. However, persistent differences in P/E ratios could not be explained by growth rate differentials (e.g., see year 10).

> Comparing the P/E analysis with the growth analysis, we conclude that some of the initial dissipation of the P/E ratio in the first three years after formation can be explained by differential growth in earnings. Beyond that, however, there clearly exists a P/E differential that cannot be explained by differential earnings growth.[21]

In addition to being unable to explain the long-run differentials using growth rates, Beaver and Morse could not explain variations in P/E ratios by differences in risk. They hypothesized that the long-run differential in P/E ratios was probably due to the effects of different accounting policies.[22]

Zarowin (1990) reexamined Beaver and Morse's findings and came to a different conclusion. Using a database in which earnings had been "normalized" in an effort to remove the effect of accounting differences,[23] Zarowin found[24] that the P/E ratio differences could not be explained (solely) by differing accounting policies. Even with normalized earnings, persistent differences remained among firms' P/E ratios.

To explain these differences, Zarowin used forecasted growth as a growth proxy. This contrasts with Beaver and Morse who used (*ex post*) actual growth. For *ex ante* valuation purposes, forecasted growth is more appropriate. As the model predicted, the differences in P/E ratios were attributable to differences in expected growth. Zarowin argued that Beaver and Morse's nonfindings resulted from using actual growth rather than expected growth rates.

Effects of Permanent and Transitory Earnings and Measurement Error

Beaver and Morse's findings with respect to short-term growth rates provide valuable insight into differential P/E ratios: the filtering of transitory earnings components by the market. In Exhibit 19-5, the high (low) P/E portfolios had low (high) earnings changes in the years that the portfolios were formed. Portfolio 1's earnings change in year 0 was −4%, whereas portfolio 25's exceeded 25%. The following year (year 1), the high- (low-) growth experienced was the opposite of the previous year. These observations indicate that reported earnings when the initial P/E portfolios were formed were abnormally low (high) for the high (low) P/E categories. The following year, earnings returned to their normal level. The market ignored the transitory component of earnings; it multiplied normal earnings by a constant. As a result, firms whose earnings were unusually low (high) appeared to have abnormally high (low) P/E ratios.

On a more general level, academic research has used the earnings response coefficient (ERC) to capture the relationship between prices and earnings. The ERC measures the price change that results from an earnings change. If the relationship between prices and earnings is exactly as the simple models suggest, then the ERC should

---

[21] William H. Beaver and Dale Morse, "What Determines Price-Earnings Ratios?," *Financial Analysts Journal,* July–August 1978, pp. 65–76.

[22] They did not test this hypothesis.

[23] The database used was from Cragg and Malkiel (1982).

[24] In his actual testing procedure, Zarowin used the earnings-to-price (E/P) ratio as the relationship between this ratio and risk and growth is hypothesized to be linear.

equal (or approximate) the P/E ratio. Although Collins and Kothari (1989) show that risk and growth explain some of the cross-sectional differences in ERCs, the ERCs generated are typically much lower than expected.

Explanations for these differences include the points we raised earlier. Collins and Kothari note that "persistence" (the extent to which earnings changes carry into the future) also affects the ERCs. That is, prices will not react as much to changes in earnings caused by transitory components. More specifically (as Box 19-1 indicates), transitory earnings components increase value on a dollar-for-dollar basis,[25] whereas permanent changes increase value by a multiplier (the P/E ratio).

This is consistent with Kormendi and Lipe's (1987) finding that higher persistence increases the ERC. Ryan and Zarowin (1995) demonstrate that measurement error also contributes to low ERCs.[26] The relationship between earnings and price (as Box 19-1 shows) is distorted by both transitory noise and measurement problems resulting from accounting choices. Thus, it is important, when using an earnings-based valuation model, to normalize earnings for nonrecurring items as well as to evaluate the impact of accounting choices, that is, the quality of earnings. Such an analysis and normalization of earnings for duPont are shown in Chapter 17.

Earnings or Cash Flows?

The concept of earnings used in these valuation models is closer to cash flow than GAAP net income. In the theoretical development of these models, earnings are generally defined as cash flow after the replacement of depreciated assets. Net income, as defined by GAAP, is not the appropriate input for these models. Only in a simplified world under stringent assumptions does net (operating) income under GAAP meet the foregoing definition of earnings.

The first assumption required is the equality of funds flow and cash flow. This holds only when working capital levels are kept (relatively) constant over time.[27] Generally, however, this assumption does not hold. Moreover, differences between cash flows and income are not due solely to working capital changes. The second required assumption is that depreciation expense approximates the replacement cost of depreciated assets. This also is generally true only by coincidence. Furthermore, the choice of accounting methods affects the calculation of income. Thus, as soon as we move away from a simplified world, the use of accounting income becomes problematic.

Using reported cash from operations (CFO) rather than income may solve some of the problems inherent in the first assumption. However, as has been shown throughout the book, reported CFO, cash for investments, and cash from financing are also affected by accounting choice. In addition, CFO does not provide for the replacement of depreciated assets. Finally, the classification of capital expenditures between investments made to maintain capacity and those made for growth is not directly available in most cases. Thus, the use of CFO in valuation models is also fraught with difficulties.

---

[25] An example of a transitory component is a holding gain such as an increase in the value of the firm's inventory. If such increases are not expected to be repeated in the future, then the effect on value should be dollar for dollar: A dollar increase in inventory value would result in a dollar increase in firm value.

[26] In the literature, the measurement error is referred to as the valuation-irrelevant component. See Ramakrishnan and Thomas (1991).

[27] Under this assumption, cash from operations and funds (working capital) from operations converge.

BOX 19-1
The Effects of Transitory Components and Measurement Error on Valuation

---

Permanent Versus Transitory Earnings and Valuation

The effects of the permanent/transitory dichotomy on the P/E ratio are described below. The P/E ratio, as we have shown, is consistent with some simplified valuation models. Use of the P/E ratio is meant to be illustrative of the general class of models discussed. The effects are more readily shown on the P/E ratio due to its simplicity.

A firm's permanent earnings are defined as the portion of the earnings stream that is to be carried into the future. For example, if we assume a constant dividend model where a firm pays out all earnings as dividends, the firm's expected earnings (dividends) are $5 per share, and $r = 10\%$, the value of the firm would be $5/0.1 = 50. The P/E ratio would be 10.

At the beginning of period 1, suppose it is known that due to some windfall the firm will actually earn $6.10 but after that the EPS will revert to $5. The value of the firm will be equal to $51 derived as

$$P_0 = \frac{E_1}{1.1} + \frac{P_1}{1.1} = \frac{\$6.10}{1.1} + \frac{\$50}{1.1} = \$51$$

The extra $1.10 earned in period 1 was not capitalized (i.e., the value of the firm did not go to $6.10/0.1 = 61). Only the permanent portion of $5.00 was capitalized. The one-shot or transitory portion of earnings entered into valuation only as a one-period adjustment (adding $\frac{\$1.10}{1.1} = \$1$ to value) without any carryover effects. The observed P/E ratio for this firm will be $51/$6.10 = 8.4$ even though the firm's "true" capitalization rate is 10.

Would this low P/E ratio indicate that the firm is a buy?* It should not. The potential distortion in P/E ratios can be even greater if we consider measurement error inherent in accounting earnings.

Measurement Error and Its Effects on Valuation

Let E_a represent accounting earnings and E_e economic earnings. We will define the difference between them as measurement noise, $M = E_e - E_a$. Further, assume that economic earnings has a permanent and transitory component, that is,

$$E_e = E_{ep} + E_{et}$$

The true relationship between price and earnings will be $P = E_{ep}/r$, with an underlying "unobservable" P/E ratio of $1/r$. The market will fully capitalize only the permanent E_{ep}. Empirically, however, one observes P/E_a, which is equivalent to $P/(E_{ep} + E_{et} + M)$. This observable P/E ratio may be larger or smaller than the "true" P/E_{ep} capitalization rate, depending on the magnitudes and directions of the transitory component (E_{et}) and measurement error (M).

---

*In Chapter 5, we noted that one of the reported anomalies of efficient markets is the abnormal returns that seem to accrue to firms with low P/E ratios.

Free Cash Flow Approach to Valuation

The free cash flow (FCF) approach has been suggested by some as a potential solution to the problems just discussed. Free cash flow, *when the valuation objective is the firm,* is defined as the cash available to debt- and equityholders after investment.

Just as the dividend model is essentially equivalent to the earnings model, the FCF model that follows is equivalent to the earnings-based model of Exhibit 19-2B, where the valuation objective is the value of the firm. To illustrate the free cash flow approach, we return to that example. Free cash flow in that example is equal to $90, derived as follows:

Net operating income	$120
Total new investment	(30)
Free cash flow	$ 90

The problem with this definition in the general case is that, as previously noted, the breakdown between *new* and *replacement* investment is rarely provided. Only the total cash for investment is given in the statement of cash flows. Upon reflection, however, total investment is really the amount we want. There is no need to use depreciation expense, or any other surrogate for that matter, to estimate the cost of replacing depreciated assets. Our objective, in general, is the following calculation of free cash flow:

	Net operating income before replacement of depreciated assets
−	Replacement of depreciated assets
−	New investment
=	Free cash flow

This is equivalent to:

	Adjusted CFO (net operating income plus adjustments)
−	Cash for investment (new + replacement)
=	Free cash flow

Note that adjusted CFO is not the same CFO reported in the statement of cash flows. They differ with respect to the treatment of interest payments: CFO is reduced by interest payments as required by SFAS 95, whereas the adjusted measure is preinterest.

Exhibit 19-6 compares an SFAS 95 Statement of Cash Flows for our hypothetical company (column A) with free cash flow in the form used in this section (column B). The difference between them is the treatment of interest and the related income tax reduction. In column A, cash from operations is reduced by interest paid and income taxes include the related tax effect. In column B, interest paid and the associated tax deduction ($5 = 20% of $25) have been removed, increasing CFO by $20 ($25 − $5). After-tax interest paid is included in cash from financing.

Note that we have assumed no change in cash during the period. If a change had taken place, column B would include the change in cash from operations. By doing so, we explicitly assume that cash is an element of working capital, as is accounts receivable.

Column B calculates free cash flow, which, by definition, equals adjusted cash

EXHIBIT 19-6
Comparison of Statement of Cash Flows and Free Cash Flow

	A	B
	Cash Flow Statement (SFAS 95)	Free Cash Flow For Firm Valuation
Cash from customers	$ 350	$ 350
Cash for operating expenses	(150)	(150)
Cash for interest (pretax)	(25)	NA
Cash for taxes	(25)	(30)
Cash from operations	**$ 150**	**$ 170**
Cash for investment*	**(80)**	**(80)**
Free cash flow		**$ 90**
Interest (net of tax)	NA	(20)
Dividends	(80)	(80)
New debt	10	10
Cash for financing	**(70)**	**(90)**
Net change in cash	$ 0	$ 0

NA = not applicable.
*Cash from investment is equal to the $30 of total new investment plus the $50 of depreciation that in this simplified example is assumed to be equivalent to the replacement cost of depreciated assets.

from financing (CFF). This definition of CFF differs from CFF under SFAS 95 as it includes (after-tax) interest paid.

The free cash flow approach yields an estimated value for the firm. The appropriate discount rate is WACC. To derive the value of equity, subtract the value of debt from the firm value.

The advantage of the FCF approach is that many (but not all) of the issues relating to differences in accounting policies and of income versus cash flows disappear. Whether or not the accounting method defines something as CFO or cash from investment (e.g., capitalization versus expense issues) does not make any difference as the focus is on FCF (the net amount). Similarly, whether or not a cash flow is treated as principal or interest (see Chapter 10) also does not matter as all payments to creditors are excluded from free cash flow.

The remaining problems relate to whether or not to treat an item as operating/investment or financing. Some potential adjustments follow.

Adjustments to Reported Cash from Investment

- All leases should be capitalized and treated as a reduction in free cash flow at the time the lease is entered into even though no cash has yet changed hands.
- Capitalized interest expense should be removed from cash for investment and added to free cash flow.
- Assets acquired in exchange for debt or equity are presently not included in either cash from investment or financing. Such transactions are disclosed as "significant noncash investing and financing activities." The cost of the assets should be deducted from free cash flow.

The free cash flow approach, however, is not without problems. Valuation should not be affected by purely discretionary policies. The model assumes that any cash held within the firm is needed as operating working capital. But firms may decide to hold excess cash for other reasons.[28] Moreover, as shown, free cash flow is equal to financing cash flow. As Penman (1991) states:

> Thus the value increment under this accounting regime would represent (be manipulated by) stock and debt issues or repurchases, and, yes, dividends. This is venturing on the absurd. Free cash flow concerns *the distribution of wealth rather than the generation of wealth.*[29]

Dividends, Earnings, or Free Cash Flows?

All three DCF approaches rely on a measure of cash flows to the suppliers of capital (debt and equity) to the firm. They differ only in the choice of measurement, with the dividend approach measuring these cash flows directly and the others arriving at them in an indirect manner. The free cash flow approach arrives at the cash flow measure (if the firm is all-equity) by subtracting investment from operating cash flows, whereas the earnings approach expresses dividends indirectly as a fraction of earnings.

This begs the question: If the dividend approach can measure cash flows directly, why use a roundabout approach? The answer to this question brings us to the issues of uncertainty and forecasting.

Valuation depends on future CF, not current CF. The firm's future dividends depend on its future earnings. Thus, to forecast future dividends, it is first necessary to forecast future earnings. Similarly, the free cash flow model attempts to avoid the problem of estimating dividends from earnings, given the problems with earnings measurement. Nevertheless, free cash flow forecasts generally require[30] the analyst *to first forecast earnings and then adjust the forecasted earnings to generate free cash flow.* Additionally, in many applications of the free cash flow model, the following formulation is used:

$$V_0 = \sum_{i=1}^{n} \frac{\text{FCF}_i}{(1 + r)^i} + \frac{V_n}{(1 + r)^n} \qquad (17)$$

As with earnings, free cash flows are forecast over a short horizon of n years (usually 5), and then a terminal value V_n is estimated. This terminal value, which can contribute over 60% of the total value, is often earnings-based.

Regardless of which valuation model is used, it relies on the ability to forecast future earnings. Analysts, as well as academics, often use accounting earnings for valuation purposes. The price/earnings ratio is the most widely used valuation measure and is calculated on the basis of accounting earnings. To a great extent, this is because reported earnings are readily available.

---

[28]See, for example, the discussion of financial slack in Box 12-2.

[29]Stephen H. Penman, "Return to Fundamentals," working paper, University of California at Berkeley, November 1991, pp. 29–30 (emphasis added).

[30]See, for example, Tom Copeland, Tim Koller, and Jack Murrin, *Valuation: Measuring and Managing the Value of Companies* (New York: John Wiley & Sons, 1990). They advocate the use of free cash flow for valuation, but arrive at that measure by first forecasting earnings.

Additionally, accounting earnings may yield better forecasts of future earning power or cash flows than historical cash flows. This should not come as a shock. After all, the underlying premise of accrual accounting is just that; recording a credit sale (but one example) provides useful information about future cash flows.

Another factor may make net income a better input for forecasting purposes than cash flows. Period-to-period changes in income and cash flows are random, with some portion transitory and the remainder permanent. For valuation, only permanent earnings are fully capitalized. If cash flow is more subject to random fluctuations due, for example, to the timing of payments, then income may produce better forecasts of permanent earnings than cash flows.

One final point must be reiterated before leaving this section. DCF models are all predicated on the dividend discount model. Finance theory, however, argues that dividends up to the terminal and liquidating dividend are irrelevant to valuation. Thus, applying these models requires growth assumptions to forecast past a finite horizon. As we cannot assume that dividends, earnings, and cash flows will converge (to zero or some steady state-value), the infinite horizon remains a problem. The next section introduces a valuation model that, although derivable from the dividend discount model, has a number of unique characteristics that warrant its own classification.

THE ABNORMAL EARNINGS OR EBO MODEL

The residual or abnormal earnings model, also referred to as the Edwards–Bell–Ohlson (EBO) model, is based on work by Ohlson (1991 and 1995) and Edwards and Bell (1961).[31] This model transforms the dividend discount model into a model based on book values and (abnormal) earnings and defines the value of equity as

$$P_0 = B_0 + \sum_{j=1}^{\infty} \frac{E_j - rB_{j-1}}{(1 + r)^j} \tag{18}$$

As $\text{ROE}_t = E_t/B_{t-1}$ the above is often expressed in its ROE form as

$$P_0 = B_0 + \sum_{j=1}^{\infty} \frac{(\text{ROE}_j - r)\,B_{j-1}}{(1 + r)^j} \tag{19}$$

The model is derived in Box 19-2. The link between book value, earnings, and dividends is based on the accounting identity

$$B_t = B_{t-1} + E_t - d_t$$

known as the *clean surplus relation.* Changes in book value are the result of income and dividends.[32]

---

[31]The origins of the residual income model can be traced to earlier work by Preinreich (1938), Edwards and Bell (1961), and Peasnell (1982). The model is also conceptually similar to the EVA model advocated by G. Bennett Stewart III, *The Quest for Value* (New York: Harper Business, 1991), Chapter 8. Stewart's EVA model is structured to value the firm; the model we discuss focuses on the value of equity. Feltham and Ohlson (1995) expand the EBO model to encompass the value of the firm.

[32]As in our previous discussion, dividends include share issues and repurchases.

BOX 19-2
Derivation of the EBO Model

Our derivation makes use of the following three relationships:

$$B_t = B_{t-1} + E_t - d_t \quad \text{or} \quad d_t = E_t - (B_t - B_{t-1}) \tag{1}$$

$$E_t = \text{ROE}_t B_{t-1} \tag{2}$$

$$\frac{B_t}{(1+r)} = B_t - \frac{rB_t}{(1+r)} \tag{3}$$

Relationships (1) and (2) are definitions: (1) is the clean surplus relationship and (2) defines income as ROE times opening book value. The dividend discount model is

$$P_0 = \sum_{j=1}^{\infty} \frac{d_j}{(1+r)^j}$$

Substituting the clean surplus relationship (1) yields

$$P_0 = \sum_{j=1}^{\infty} \frac{E_j - (B_j - B_{j-1})}{(1+r)^j}$$

For demonstration purposes, we expand the above expression for $j = 1$ and $j = 2$ and find that

$$P_0 = \frac{E_1 - (B_1 - B_0)}{(1+r)} + \frac{E_2 - (B_2 - B_0)}{(1+r)^2} + \sum_{j=3}^{\infty} \frac{E_j - (B_j - B_{j-1})}{(1+r)^j}$$

Using (3) yields

$$P_0 = \left[\frac{E_1}{(1+r)} - \frac{B_1}{(1+r)} + B_0 - \frac{rB_0}{(1+r)} \right] + \left[\frac{E_2}{(1+r)^2} - \frac{B_2}{(1+r)^2} + \frac{B_1}{(1+r)} - \frac{rB_1}{(1+r)^2} \right]$$
$$+ \sum_{j=3}^{\infty} \frac{E_j - (B_j - B_{j-1})}{(1+r)^j}$$

and

$$P_0 = B_0 + \left[\frac{E_1 - rB_0}{(1+r)} \right] + \left[\frac{E_2 - rB_1}{(1+r)^2} \right] - \frac{B_2}{(1+r)^2} + \sum_{j=3}^{\infty} \frac{E_j - (B_j - B_{j-1})}{(1+r)^j}$$

By similarly expanding the summation from $j = 3$ to ∞, we arrive at

$$P_0 = B_0 + \sum_{j=1}^{\infty} \frac{E_j - rB_{j-1}}{(1+r)^j}$$

Now from (2), since earnings in any period $E_t = \text{ROE}_t B_{t-1}$,

$$P_0 = B_0 + \sum_{j=1}^{\infty} \frac{(\text{ROE}_j - r) B_{j-1}}{(1+r)^j}$$

Thus, we have defined the value of the firm in terms of opening book value (B_0), ROE, and abnormal earnings [$(\text{ROE}_j - r) B_{j-1}$].

If we define rB_{t-1} as the required rate of return earned on the firm's (opening) book value in period t, residual or abnormal earnings can be defined as

$$E_t^a = E_t - rB_{t-1}$$

and we can express the valuation formulation as

$$P_0 = B_0 + \sum_{j=1}^{\infty} \frac{E_j^a}{(1+r)^j} \tag{20}$$

The intuition behind the model is perhaps better understood if we consider a firm that only earns the required rate of return r (ROE $= r$) on its book value. Such a firm's shares will sell at a price equal to book value. If it earns more (less) than the required rate of return, the premium (discount) to book value is the present value of those abnormal earnings.[33]

The EBO valuation model can be applied to the example of Exhibits 19-1 and 19-2. Prior to the introduction of "growth," the firm earns a 10% return on its equity investment of $1,000. Using that as our starting point, we set the initial book value (B_{-1}) at the *beginning of period zero* at $1,000. During period zero, the firm's net income is $100 (see Exhibit 19-1). Because it now has growth opportunities, it pays a dividend of $80, leaving book value at the end of period 0; $B_0 = \$1,020$. Recall that net income grows at 4%.

Period i	Book Value Beginning B_{i-1}	Net Income E_i	Abnormal Earnings $E_i^a = E_i - (r \times B_{i-1})$	Dividend kE_i	Book Value End $B_i = B_{i-1} + (1 - k)\,E_i$
0	$1,000	$100	0	$80	$1,020
1	1,020	104	$104 - (0.1)\,(1,020) = 2$	83.2	1,040.8
2	1,040.8	108.16	$108.16 - (0.1)\,(1,040.8) = 4.08$	86.528	1,062.432
3	1,062.432	112.4864	6.2432	. . .	. . .

Therefore, inserting the above into the EBO valuation (20), we obtain

$$P_0 = B_0 + \sum_{i=1}^{\infty} \frac{E_i^a}{(1+r)^i}$$

$$P_0 = 1,020 + \left[\frac{2}{(1.1)^1} + \frac{4.08}{(1.1)^2} + \frac{6.2432}{(1.1)^3} \cdots \right]$$

The series in the right bracket converges to $367, yielding, as before, the value of equity:

$$P_0 = 1,020 + 367 = \$1,387$$

[33]This is, of course, equivalent to our earlier formulation [Eq. (4)] for economic goodwill, albeit in a more rigorous fashion.

EBO Versus DCF Models

As the EBO model is essentially a variation of the DCF model, its result is identical. What then are its advantages? We consider both pragmatic and conceptual answers to this question.

Finite Horizons

In a nondeterministic world, where the future is unknown, valuation depends on forecasts of future dividends, earnings, or cash flows. As discussed earlier, it is not possible to make reliable forecasts to infinity. In practice, therefore, analysts make explicit forecasts for a few (usually five) years and then estimate a terminal value, based on simplifying assumptions, to capture the remaining value. In DCF models, the assumptions made to estimate the terminal value may be crucial, as it may constitute 70% of total value.

Proponents of the EBO model argue that terminal value estimates in that model are less troublesome. If we consider a finite horizon T, the valuation model (19) becomes[34]

$$P_0 = B_0 + \sum_{j=1}^{T} \frac{(\text{ROE}_j - r)\, B_{j-1}}{(1+r)^j} + \frac{(P_T - B_T)}{(1+r)^T} \tag{21}$$

The last expression $(P_T - B_T)$ represents the premium over book value at the end of the finite horizon T. This premium is based on the abnormal earnings earned following period T. *Advocates of the EBO model argue that this premium should disappear as economic factors tend to drive abnormal earnings to zero within a relatively short time.*[35] More formally, as long as T is sufficiently large, $(P_T - B_T) \to 0$.

Recall that Figure 4-6 provides empirical evidence that ROEs converge from extreme positions toward an overall mean within approximately five years. As abnormal earnings are a function of the difference between ROE and the required rate of return r, this convergence in ROE is equivalent to abnormal earnings approaching zero.

Competitive forces are one reason for this convergence, as competitors enter business segments with abnormal profits, eventually reducing those profits to zero. *Even if a company could protect a particular source of abnormal profits indefinitely (through patents or copyrights), it is unlikely that it could find additional sources of abnormal profits indefinitely. Thus, reinvested profits would only earn a normal rate of return.* As reinvested profits increase book value, ROE (a weighted average of normal and abnormal profits) declines and the firm's abnormal earnings converge to a steady-state level.[36] That level can be used to estimate the terminal premium $(P_T - B_T)$.

---

[34]This expression can be derived by expansion of (19) to

$$P_0 = B_0 + \sum_{j=1}^{T} \frac{(\text{ROE}_j - r)\, B_{j-1}}{(1+r)^j} + \sum_{k=T+1}^{\infty} \frac{(\text{ROE}_k - r)\, B_{k-1}}{(1+r)^k}$$

and by using

$$P_T = B_T + (1+r)^T \sum_{k=T+1}^{\infty} \frac{(\text{ROE}_k - r)\, B_{T-1}}{(1+r)^k}$$

[35]Or, at the very least, their discounted values. Our example does not have this property as abnormal growth opportunities are considered to exist to infinity. However, $(\text{ROE} - r)$ does reach steady state at 10% as ROE approaches 20%.

[36]See the following section entitled, "Unbiased Versus Conservative Accounting."

Whatever the firm's current earnings, competitive forces are assumed to reduce the firm's abnormal earnings over time. At some point, the firm will have only zero net present value opportunities and zero abnormal earnings. Because of this convergence property, abnormal earnings play a central role in the valuation function . . .

. . . Although the valuation formula, like the Dividend Discount Model, incorporates the sum of an infinite series, its power derives from the fact that estimating abnormal earnings over a finite horizon can generate reasonable firm valuations.[37]

Simplified Assumptions for ROE, Book Values, and Terminal Value. The convergence of ROE, along with assumptions about the level and growth of ROE, leads to reasonably accurate and simplified valuation calculations. For example, assume $T = 3$ and ROE $= r$ after three periods. Then the valuation model reduces to estimates of ROE for the next three years and book values for the next two:

$$P_0 = B_0 + \frac{(\text{ROE}_1 - r) \, B_0}{(1 + r)} + \frac{(\text{ROE}_2 - r) \, B_1}{(1 + r)^2} + \frac{(\text{ROE}_3 - r) \, B_2}{(1 + r)^3}$$

This model is sometimes expressed in the form of the price/book value ratio, yielding

$$\frac{P_0}{B_0} = 1 + \frac{(\text{ROE}_1 - r)}{(1 + r)} + \frac{(\text{ROE}_2 - r) \, (1 + g_1)}{(1 + r)^2} + \frac{(\text{ROE}_3 - r) \, (1 + g_1) \, (1 + g_2)}{(1 + r)^3}$$

where g_i is the growth in book value in period i. Value equals current book value (B_0) multiplied by the price/book (P/B) ratio. This model requires an estimate of growth in book value. As noted earlier, the growth rate of book value equals $(1 - k)$ ROE; the exercise thus boils down to estimating ROEs and dividend payout ratios.

If we assume that abnormal earnings do not disappear, but reach steady state *after* period 3, then the above can be modified to incorporate the terminal value as

$$\frac{P_0}{B_0} = 1 + \frac{(\text{ROE}_1 - r)}{(1 + r)} + \frac{(\text{ROE}_2 - r) \, (1 + g_1)}{(1 + r)^2} + \frac{(\text{ROE}_3 - r) \, (1 + g_1) \, (1 + g_2)}{(1 + r)^3}$$
$$+ \frac{(\text{ROE}_4 - r) \, (1 + g_1) \, (1 + g_2) \, (1 + g_3)}{r(1 + r)^3}$$

where $(\text{ROE}_4 - r)$ is the terminal steady-state difference between the firm's ROE and its required rate of return r.

This formulation assumes that although the firm has abnormal earnings equal to $(\text{ROE}_4 - r) \, B_3$ after period 3, these abnormal earnings do not grow (although book value grows after period 3); similar reinvestment opportunities do not exist.

If, however, we assume that abnormal earnings do grow as book value grows at a rate equal to g_3, then the P/B ratio can be expressed as

$$\frac{P_0}{B_0} = 1 + \frac{(\text{ROE}_1 - r)}{(1 + r)} + \frac{(\text{ROE}_2 - r) \, (1 + g_1)}{(1 + r)^2} + \frac{(\text{ROE}_3 - r) \, (1 + g_1) \, (1 + g_2)}{(1 + r)^3}$$
$$+ \frac{(\text{ROE}_4 - r) \, (1 + g_1) \, (1 + g_2) \, (1 + g_3)}{(r - g_3) \, (1 + r)^3}$$

[37]Patricia M. Fairfield, "P/E, P/B and the Present Value of Future Dividends," *Financial Analysts Journal,* July–August 1994, p. 24.

Additional formulae for estimates of terminal values under differing growth assumptions and steady-state values are provided in Appendix 19-B.

Relative Importance of Terminal Value Calculations

The relative importance of terminal value calculations is a significant issue. In our previous example, the book value of $1,020 approximates 75% of the $1,387 firm value. *Book value, which often represents a sizable portion of firm value, is given and does not have to be estimated.* Further, when we consider the value derived from forecasts of the first few periods' abnormal earnings, the proportion of the terminal value to total value is small.

In DCF models, as noted, terminal values frequently constitute 60 to 70% of total value. All parameters must be estimated, and those that are most difficult to estimate play a large role in valuation.

The reason for the difference in the relative importance of terminal value relates to the accrual system of accounting. That system essentially quantifies (net) assets in terms of future benefits; that is, will they generate future cash flows? Those future benefits are, therefore, already quantified within the book value of the firm. The EBO model makes use of this quantification; it focuses on the difference between firm value and book value: abnormal earnings.

The DCF model, on the other hand, undoes the accrual process, forecasts future cash flows, and then rebundles them in the present value calculations. Everything must be reestimated. Put differently, DCF models estimate *firm value* itself; the EBO model estimates the *differential between firm value and book value,* a more manageable problem.

To be sure, when the models are applied in a consistent manner, they obtain the same result. The errors in DCF terminal value calculations are expected to appear in the shorter horizons of the EBO model. Pragmatically, however, forecasting is simpler for EBO models.

Effect of Accounting Policies

Both the EBO model and the earnings version of the dividend DCF models use accounting earnings as an input. There is, however, an important distinction between the two. In the DCF model, earnings (together with the payout ratio k) are a surrogate for dividends, and the efficacy of the model depends on the validity of that relationship.

Although the EBO model can be derived (as shown in Box 19-2) from the dividend discount model, it is not dependent on any set of accounting standards. Consistent with its accounting definition, earnings in the EBO model measure the creation of wealth, not as a surrogate for another parameter such as cash flows, dividends, or even economic earnings. As long as the *clean surplus* relationship is maintained, the model is applicable to any set of accounting rules.

At first glance, this may seem illogical. How can value be determined by a number (earnings) that can be manipulated by accounting choices? The answer lies in the *self-correcting* nature of accounting. Value under the EBO model is a function of current book value and (discounted) future abnormal earnings. If a given accounting method recognizes earnings in the current period, *the book value portion of the EBO valuation increases as current book value is higher.* However, in following periods, the higher book value increases the normal (required) earnings (rB). Consequently, *future abnormal earnings are lower (or negative), offsetting the higher book value in the valuation formula.* Thus, *over time,* different accounting choices catch up with each other.[38]

The foregoing does not mean that accounting is irrelevant. On the contrary, it creates an objective measure of "better" accounting policies. Our earlier discussion notes that the strength of the EBO model is its use of finite horizons, as abnormal earnings converge to zero as long as T is *sufficiently* large. The self-correcting process of differing accounting policies is another manifestation of this convergence process. Thus, a better accounting system is one in which this convergence takes place over a shorter horizon T. More important, in terms of adjusting reported financial data:

> . . . the accounting-based valuation methods *provide a motive for adjusting book values and earnings, much as analysts do*; with "better" accounting, value can be summarized with forecasts over shorter horizons.[39]

The Clean Surplus Relationship

The clean surplus relationship requires a definition of income similar to comprehensive income, discussed in Chapters 2 and 17. All changes in book value (other than transactions with stockholders) flow through the income statement without any direct charges to stockholders' equity.

U.S. GAAP is generally consistent with clean surplus accounting. There are exceptions, three of which are discussed in the book:

1. Adjustment for the minimum pension liability (Chapter 12)

2. Recognition of unrealized gains and losses on available-for-sale marketable securities (Chapter 13)

3. Exchange rate gains and losses under the all-current method (Chapter 15).

Thus, applying the EBO to U.S. firms requires adjustments to income for these items.

Unbiased Versus Conservative Accounting

The self-correcting process that drives abnormal earnings to zero and ROE to r is characterized by Ohlson as *unbiased* accounting. Not all accounting methods, however, possess this property.

For example, Chapter 7 compares capitalization versus expense accounting policies. Figure 7-3 shows that for a company that grows and then reaches steady state, ROE for the expensing firm is *higher and remains higher* relative to that of the capitalizing firm. *Conservative* accounting that expenses current expenditures *leads to higher abnormal earnings* (ROE $> r$) *indefinitely.* Thus, firms with high R&D expenditures (that must be expensed) report positive abnormal earnings indefinitely.[40] *The level of these abnormal earnings, however, reach steady state and the analysis discussed earlier and in Appendix 19-B must be adopted.*

---

[38]Problem 14 illustrates this property.

[39]Victor L. Bernard, "Accounting-Based Valuation Methods, Determinants of Market-to-Book Ratios and Implications for Financial Statement Analysis," working paper, University of Michigan, June 1993, p. 8 (emphasis added).

[40]See, for example, Exhibit 7-4, and the analysis of Merck's ROE from Lev and Sougiannis.

Value Drivers

The EBO model also has conceptual advantages. By focusing on earnings rather than dividends, *the model defines value in terms of wealth generation rather than wealth distribution.*

> Value is determined by the *creation* of wealth, measured by aggregate accounting earnings, rather than the *distribution* of wealth, measured as dividends.[41]

This argument can be extended to the valuation of firms that do not pay dividends. The valuation of these firms by EBO models is no different from that of any other firm, as value is determined by the generation of wealth (earnings), not its distribution as dividends.

The value drivers in the EBO model are precisely those attributes that analysts normally consider. Abnormal earnings depend on ROE, a ratio whose disaggregation and analysis are familiar (see Chapter 4). The various DCF models also use many of these drivers to estimate cash flows. However, as the EBO paradigm focuses on the attributes that are important for valuation, the impact of parameter and assumption changes can be seen *directly*. The valuation equation allows us to focus directly on price and its relationship to earnings, book value, ROE, and the growth and persistence of these components.

Price/Book Value and Price/Earnings Ratios Revisited

The EBO model provides a useful framework to revisit the questions addressed earlier: why companies sell at higher or lower price/book value and price/earnings ratios. The model allows us to reevaluate the parameters that are relevant to these ratios.

Price/Book Value Ratios. We begin with expression (19) evaluated at time t:

$$P_t = B_t + \sum_{j=1}^{\infty} \frac{(\text{ROE}_{j+t} - r)\, B_{j+t-1}}{(1+r)^j}$$

Dividing by B_t yields

$$\frac{P_t}{B_t} = 1 + \sum_{j=1}^{\infty} \frac{(\text{ROE}_{j+t} - r)}{(1+r)^j} \frac{B_{j+t-1}}{B_t}$$

This equation implies that the P/B ratio is related to future abnormal earnings (the difference between ROE and r*) and the growth of book value. If future abnormal earnings are zero, then the P/B ratio is "normal" (equal to 1). Note that current profitability is not relevant.*

Price/Earnings Ratios. We begin with expression (20) evaluated at time t:

$$P_t = B_t + \sum_{j=1}^{\infty} \frac{E_{j+t}^a}{(1+r)^j}$$

[41]Bernard, op. cit.

Adding D_t to both sides and dividing by E_t and using the clean surplus relationship, we obtain

$$\frac{P_t + D_t}{E_t} = 1 + \frac{B_{t-1}}{E_t} + \sum_{j=1}^{\infty} \frac{E_{j+t}^a}{(1 + r)^j \, E_t} \tag{22}$$

B_{t-1}/E_t measures current year profitability, (the inverse of) ROE_t. The summation term reflects future (abnormal) earnings relative to current earnings. *Expression (22) states that the P/E ratio is related to both current and future profitability and the extent to which current profitability will persist.*

Since $E_t = E_t^a + rB_{t-1}$, after substituting for B_{t-1}, Eq. (22) reduces to

$$\frac{P_t + D_t}{E_t} = \left[\frac{1 + r}{r}\right] + \frac{1}{E_t}\left[\sum_{j=1}^{\infty} \frac{E_{j+t}^a}{(1 + r)^j} - \frac{E_t^a}{r}\right] \tag{23}$$

The term in the left bracket is the same one derived for "normal" P/E ratios (cum dividend) in the earnings DCF model. The term in the right bracket is the difference between the present value of *future abnormal* earnings and *current abnormal* earnings in perpetuity. That difference determines whether or not P/E ratios are high or low.

We first consider a situation where future abnormal earnings are equivalent to current abnormal earnings for all j; that is, $E_{j+t}^a = E_t^a$. Then

$$\sum_{j=1}^{\infty} \frac{1}{(1 + r)^j} = \frac{1}{r}$$

Equation (23) reduces to

$$\frac{P_t + D_t}{E_t} = \frac{1 + r}{r} \tag{24}$$

the expression for normal P/E ratios. *When future abnormal earnings are equivalent to current abnormal earnings, P/E ratios are normal.*[42]

High (low) P/E ratios are dependent on future abnormal earnings that are higher (lower) than current abnormal earnings. *The P/E ratio is a function of current abnormal earnings, their persistence, and the growth in future abnormal earnings.* Note that it is the *relative*, not absolute, levels of current and future abnormal earnings that matter. Growth affects P/E ratios only if future abnormal earnings exceed current abnormal earnings.

The relationship between P/B and P/E ratios and current and future (abnormal) earnings is illustrated in Figure 19-1.[43] The vertical axis plots future abnormal earnings (FE^a); the horizontal axis plots current abnormal earnings (CE^a).

Figure 19-1*a* shows that P/E ratios are a function of whether or not current levels of profitability persist in the future. The 45° line drawn in the graph represents

---

[42] In equation 16, we showed that P/E ratios are normal when there are no abnormal growth opportunities ($r^* = r$). Our EBO formulation shows that this restriction is too limiting. The important issue is the relative level of current and future abnormal earnings, not whether or not there are abnormal earnings at all.

[43] Figure 19-1 is similar to the analysis of Table 2 in Fairfield (1994) and the matrix of Penman (1996).

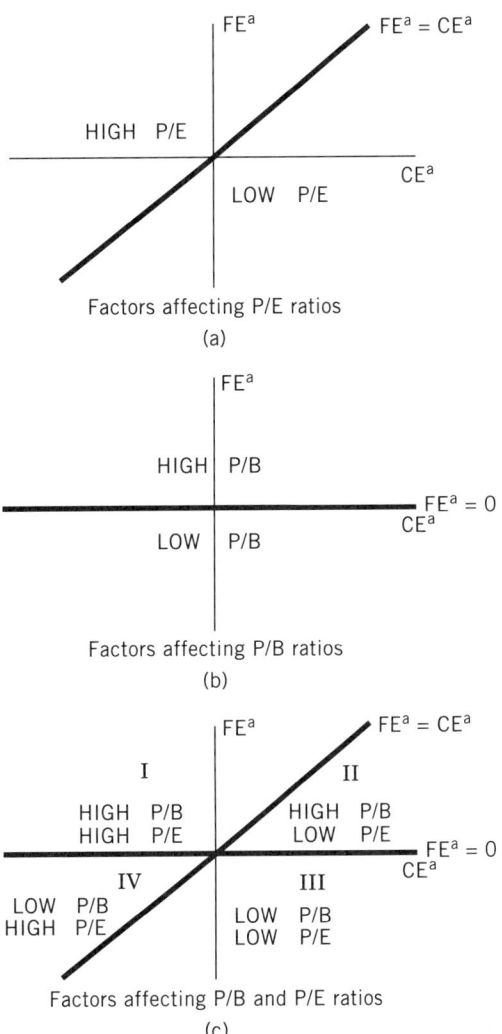

FIGURE 19-1 Factors affecting price/earnings and price/book value ratios.

$CE^a = FE^a$. Along this line, current abnormal earnings are a good indicator of future abnormal earnings (earnings are persistent). The P/E ratio is normal and equal to $(1 + r)/r$.

On either side of this line, current profitability is not a good indicator of future profitability and P/E ratios are high or low. To the right and below the line, current profitability exceeds future profitability. Either current earnings have a transitory positive component or the high abnormal earnings are not sustainable in the future. The result is a low P/E ratio. To the left and above the 45° line, future profitability exceeds current profitability. Current earnings may have a transitory negative component. The P/E ratio is high.

Figure 19-1b shows that the P/B ratio is purely a function of future abnormal earnings. The horizontal axis is equivalent to $FE^a = 0$. When $FE^a = 0$, the P/B ratio is normal (equivalent to 1). When FE^a is positive, P/B ratios are high (exceed 1). When future abnormal earnings are negative, the P/B ratio is below 1.

Figure 19-1c combines Figures 19-1a and 19-1b, showing conditions for all possible combinations of (high or low) P/B and (high or low) P/E ratios. At the origin, the P/B and P/E ratios are normal.

- Region I represents companies with strong growth potential. FE^a is high and future profitability exceeds current levels. These companies have high P/E and P/B ratios.
- Region II contains mature companies in their harvesting years. Current and future E^a is positive; however, future profitability is below current profitability. These companies exhibit high P/B ratios and low P/E ratios.
- Region III represents poor performers. Future profitability is expected to be below normal ($FE^a < 0$) as well as below current levels. These companies exhibit low P/E and P/B ratios.
- Region IV shows distressed companies that are recovering. Future earnings are below normal ($FE^a < 0$); however, they are expected to rise from current levels. Companies that have had major restructurings (or a "big bath") would fall into this category, as current earnings are depressed. Although P/B ratios are low, P/E ratios are high.

The EBO Model: Concluding Comments

The efficacy of the EBO model has been tested in a number of studies. Bernard (1995) shows that a model using book values and forecasts of abnormal earnings for just three years explains variations in market prices far better than a comparable model based on discounted dividends. Penman and Sougiannis (1995) compare (variations of) the EBO model to a free cash flow and dividend discount model. They find the EBO model superior to the dividend model in all cases. Its performance vis-à-vis the free cash flow model depends on the assumption used to estimate terminal value. Only when the free cash flow model uses accrual earnings to calculate terminal value are the models comparable; otherwise, the EBO model dominates.

Frankel and Lee (1996) extend the EBO model to an international framework. They suggest that, since the EBO model is supposedly immune to accounting variations (see the earlier discussion), it can be used to compare firms across countries. To date, research results seem promising, with additional research underway.

FORECASTING MODELS AND TIME SERIES PROPERTIES OF EARNINGS

As the discussion so far indicates, valuation depends to a great degree on the ability to forecast earnings and filter out its transitory and permanent components. A great deal of empirical research has focused on the time-series properties of earnings and the development of appropriate forecasting models. The research has generally been based on income rather than cash flow. Although unfortunate from a theoretical standpoint, from a practical point of view it may be that earnings work as well as or better than (free) cash flow, for reasons discussed earlier. Moreover, available evidence on the time-series properties of cash flows indicates little difference between the properties of income and cash flows. This section reviews some of these results.

FORECASTING MODELS

Generally, there are two classes of forecasting models in the literature: extrapolative models and index models. These are mechanical models in that forecasts use the statistical properties of these models without any further judgment on the part of the forecaster.

Extrapolative Models

Extrapolative models use the previous time series of earnings to forecast the future level of earnings. That is, the forecast of next period's income, defined as $E(Y_t + 1)$, is a function of the past history of earnings:

$$E(Y_{t+1}) = f(Y_t, Y_{t-1}, \ldots, Y_1)$$

Permanent Versus Transitory Components

When using time series of a firm's earnings, it is important to separate the permanent and transitory components. The permanent component is expected to persist into the future. That permanent earnings stream itself can, however, be altered by random events affecting the firm or its environment. If these random occurrences have permanent effects, then they alter the permanent earnings stream.[44] The permanent earnings stream includes all prior permanent random events.

Nonpermanent (transitory) events do not affect the permanent earnings stream. These random shocks disguise the underlying (permanent) stream. Reported income is the sum of the permanent and transitory components. The goal of time-series analysis is to identify the firm's permanent earnings stream.

The following example shows the importance of the difference, for forecasting purposes, between permanent and transitory components. Assume that a company in a no-growth environment had expected earnings of $10 but actual (reported) earnings of $11 for the current period (a positive earnings surprise). What should the estimate of the next period's earnings be? Maintaining the original estimate of $10 assumes that next period the company's earnings will revert from its present level of $11 to the previous expectation of $10. The $1 deviation ($11 − $10) is treated as a one-time, transitory event that will not recur in the future; expectations are not affected by the reported earnings for a given period. Such a process is referred to as mean reverting, as the earnings revert to a constant level.

In general, for a mean-reverting process, the forecast of next period or, for that matter, any period earnings is a constant u. The estimate of u is the mean of all prior period earnings. That is,

$$E(Y_{t+1}) = u$$

where u is estimated as

$$u = \frac{1}{t}(Y_t + Y_{t-1} + \cdots + Y_2 + Y_1)$$

---

[44]For example, an external event may raise oil prices, permanently increasing the earnings of oil producers.

If, on the other hand, the $1 deviation from expected earnings is viewed as permanent, then the next period expectation becomes $11. Such a process is referred to as a *martingale* or *random walk*. For such processes, the only information needed to generate the next period forecast is the prior period result. All earlier information is irrelevant:

$$E(Y_{t+1}) = Y_t$$

In a martingale process, expectations change from period to period based on reported earnings.

The distinction between mean-reverting and martingale processes need not be confined to a no-growth environment. Assume that a company whose income is expected to grow by $2.00 each year had an expected income of $12.00 for this year. The actual earnings of $11.50 were $0.50 below expectation. If this negative earnings surprise is viewed as transitory, then the underlying income of the firm is still assumed to be $12.00. The forecast of next period's income is $12.00 + $2.00 = $14.00:

$$E(Y_{t+1}) = E(Y_t) + d$$

where *d* represents the growth term.

If the $0.50 deviation is viewed as permanent, then the starting point for the next period estimate is the reported $11.50 and the next period forecast is $11.50 + $2.00 = $13.50. This is an example of a *martingale with drift* or a *submartingale,* and can be expressed as

$$E(Y_{t+1}) = Y_t + d$$

The martingale and mean-reverting processes are two extremes on a continuum. In the first case, the forecast of the next period is determined solely by current period results. For the mean-reverting process, current period results are only used to estimate the underlying mean. Choosing between the two extremes of random walk or mean-reverting processes, we see that *the overwhelming empirical evidence indicates that, on average, earnings follow a submartingale process.*

It is, of course, possible that an earnings surprise has both transitory and permanent components. Such a process is described in Box 19-3. Forecasting such a time series places one within the two extremes. The forecast does not depend solely on current period results, but also on all previous reported earnings. At the same time, the weights are not the same for all previous results, as is the case for mean-reverting models. Typically, the forecast should be a weighted average of previous reported earnings. The *exponential smoothing* model is an example; it uses higher weights for more recent data and lower weights for earlier data. A more complex set of forecasting models used in the literature are the *Box-Jenkins models.*[45]

Diagnostic tests, using these models, indicate that, for many firms, the pure (sub) martingale model does not describe the underlying time series. Nevertheless, when forecasting models were designed for these firms individually, they did not, on average, outperform the (sub)martingale process. The best forecast *based solely on the previous time series* was a (sub)martingale forecast.

---

[45]This class of models is beyond the scope of this book. The interested reader is referred to Box and Jenkins (1976).

BOX 19-3
Description of a Time-Series Process Having Transitory and
Permanent Components

The process is described as

$$X_t = X_{t-1} + v_t$$
$$Y_t = X_t + e_t$$

Therefore,

$$Y_t = X_{t-1} + v_t + e_t$$

Let X_t represent the firm's permanent earnings stream. Then the v_t are the periodic random occurrences that become a permanent part of the firm's earnings.* If there are transitory components, symbolized by e_t, the permanent stream X_t would be unobservable. Instead, one would observe Y_t, which is made up of the permanent and transitory components.† If there are no transitory components, the description of the process would stop at the first equation ($X_t = X_{t-1} + v_t$), and we would have a random walk process. If, on the other hand, there are no permanent random components, the underlying permanent earnings stream of the firm is a constant, as $X_t = X_{t-1} = X_{t-2}, \ldots$ and so on. This constant would be the mean, as by definition all random occurrences are represented by the transitory component e_t and the process is mean-reverting.

---

*Note that

$$X_t = X_0 + \Sigma v_i$$

That is, this period's permanent earnings is a summation of all previous permanent random occurrences since period 0.
†Note that

$$Y_t = X_0 + \Sigma v_i + e_t$$

That is, this period's reported earnings is a summation of all previous permanent random occurrences and this period's transitory component.

The only consistent results that belie this point occurred when the previous year deviation was abnormally large.[46] Brooks and Buckmaster (1976) found that such very large deviations are typically transitory and that forecasts based on the exponential smoothing model are better than martingale-based forecasts. These results confirm those of Beaver and Morse discussed earlier.

[46]There are a number of ways to define "abnormally large." Brooks and Buckmaster, for example, define the normalized first difference (nfd) as

nfd $= (Y_t - Y_{t-1})$/Standard Deviation of Earnings

For large absolute values of nfd, they found exponential smoothing parameters ranging from 0.2 to 0.9 (depending on the sign and magnitude of nfd) to be better predictors than a martingale model.

In a similar vein, Freeman et al. (1982) showed that earnings forecasts can be improved by considering the trend in the firm's ROE. ROE, *unlike earnings, is mean-reverting*. ROE measures the rate of return on the firm's book value; if the current ROE is considerably above (below) its recent mean,[47] that indicates current earnings are too high (low) and a reversal can be expected in the next period. This is, of course, consistent with our discussion of EBO models (and Figure 4-6), indicating that ROE reverts to a mean level.

Index Models

The second class of models does not rely on the previous earnings history, but rather uses independent variables or indices to forecast earnings. The earnings forecast is described as $E(Y_{t+1}) = f(Z_{1t}, Z_{2t}, \ldots, Z_{nt})$, where the Z's represent independent variables. The most commonly used model of this sort is described in Chapter 18 in the discussion of the accounting beta. This model, the market model of accounting income, expresses earnings as a function of some overall market index of earnings (ME) such as the S&P 500 earnings index, GNP, corporate earnings, or the average earnings of the sample of firms being examined. Operationally, the model is represented as

$$E(Y_{t+1}) = a + bME_{t+1}$$

where a and b are regression parameters derived from the previous history of earnings and the market index.[48]

Comparisons between this model and the submartingale show that they perform equally well. Fried and Givoly (1982), for example, found that, over an 11-year period (1969 to 1979), the index model had an average percentage forecast error of 20.3%, whereas the (modified[49]) submartingale's percentage forecast error was 19.3%.

Forecasting with Disaggregated Data

The models described here all use time series of annual earnings data to forecast annual earnings. The literature has also examined forecasts of annual income using data disaggregated along three dimensions:

1. By time, using quarterly data
2. By segment, using segment-based data
3. By component, using income statement components

Quarterly Forecasting Models

Forecasting models using quarterly data have been those most commonly examined. Although quarterly models have been used primarily to forecast quarterly earnings, they have also been utilized to forecast annual earnings; such forecasts usually sum the

---

[47]This result assumes stable book values with no major new stock issues, repurchases, or acquisitions.

[48]As noted in Chapter 18, these models are generally expressed in terms of the relationship between the change in earnings and the change in the index.

[49]The model is referred to as modified because it applies the Brooks and Buckmaster criterion when appropriate.

individual quarterly forecasts. These forecasts have been generally found to outperform forecasts based on annual models alone (see Hopwood et al., 1982). Moreover, as expected, the farther along in the year and the more interim periods that have gone by, the greater the accuracy of forecasts using quarterly reports.

Unlike annual earnings data, which seem to follow martingale or submartingale patterns, quarterly earnings are generally better described by more complex models. The seasonality of many businesses makes the task of designing quarterly models more challenging. Box–Jenkins forecasting techniques, mentioned earlier, are designed to detect seasonality components and have been used with some success in quarterly time-series models.

Generally, the extrapolative models for quarterly series find that a quarter's income Q_t (e.g., second quarter of 1996) is related to the immediately preceding quarter Q_{t-1} (first quarter of 1996) and the same quarter of the preceding year Q_{t-4} (second quarter of 1995). Three competing models have been put forward to represent the average firm; individually fitted models were not able to improve on these models in a meaningful way. The models follow. Model 1 is based on Watts (1975) and Griffin (1977):

$$E(Q_t) = Q_{t-4} + (Q_{t-1} - Q_{t-5}) - be_{t-1} - ce_{t-4} + bce_{t-5}$$

Model 2 is based on Foster (1977):

$$E(Q_t) = Q_{t-4} + a(Q_{t-1} - Q_{t-5}) + d$$

Brown and Rozeff (1979) is the basis for Model 3:

$$E(Q_t) = Q_{t-4} + a(Q_{t-1} - Q_{t-5}) - ce_{t-4}$$

where a, b, and c are estimated parameters; d is a drift term (the average seasonal change); and e_t (times the respective parameter) represents the transitory portion of a period's Q_t.

It is interesting to note that an explanation of the post-announcement drift anomaly (see Chapter 5) would seem to lie in the market's (and analyst's) inability to correctly estimate the pattern of serial correlation between quarters. This phenomenon is documented by Bernard and Thomas (1989) as well as Bartov (1992). Ball and Bartov (1996) show that the market is cognizant of the serial correlation between quarters but underestimates its magnitude by up to 50%. Mendenhall (1991) and Abarbanell and Bernard (1992) show that forecasts by (Value Line) analysts do not fully incorporate the quarterly serial correlations.

Segment-Based Forecasts

The merits of forecasting annual earnings using segment-based data are discussed at some length in Chapter 13. For time-series models, the potential improvement is highly dependent on the differences in the underlying time-series behavior of the individual segments. If segments, for example, are similarly affected by the business cycle, that reduces the advantage of using segment data. Moreover (again, for time-series models), the improvement of segment-based forecasts seems not to go beyond the prediction of sales.

Forecasts Using Income or Balance Sheet Components

Studies that use income statement (or balance sheet) components to help forecast income are few and far between. These models come in two forms. The first, similar to segment-based models, generates an earnings forecast from separate forecasts of sales, cost of goods sold, operating expenses, depreciation, and so forth, and then aggregating these components to forecast earnings. The results suggest that this method of forecasting *earnings* is not fruitful for the same reason as for segment-based models.[50] The time series of the individual components are interdependent, which precludes substantial gains in predictive power from disaggregated data. However, Fairfield et al. (1996) show that the use of disaggregated data can improve ROE predictions.

The second model form shows more potential. These explicitly model interrelationships among income and balance sheet components and construct a structural model of the firm. Such *econometric models* were designed by Elliott and Uphoff (1972) and, Wild (1987). Unfortunately, it is difficult to generalize from these models. Although their results improved predictive ability, given the difficulty in constructing such models, studies were usually limited to small samples.[51]

Ou and Penman (1989), in a variation of this approach, use common financial ratios to improve the forecasting ability of a random walk model. Their model forecast the probability that a firm's earnings change would be higher or lower than that forecasted by a random walk (with drift) process. That is, they estimated the probability that a firm's earnings next year (Y_{t+1}) would exceed a random walk (with drift) forecast of earnings:

$$E(Y_{t+1}) = Y_t + d$$

where d represents the drift term calculated as the average change in earnings over the previous four years. More formally, the model generates the following probability (Pr):

$$Pr[Y_{t+1} > (Y_t + d)]$$

A set of 68 financial variables and ratios were first analyzed individually to see which were most associated with earnings changes. The analysis was carried out separately for the two subperiods 1965 to 1972 and 1973 to 1977. The best 18 variables were then incorporated in a multivariate model for each subperiod. The resultant models are presented in Exhibit 19-7. Not all 18 variables are incorporated in the final model(s); the variables incorporated differ from period to period. The model developed over the 1965 to 1972 period was used to forecast the 1973 to 1977 period, and the latter model was used to forecast the 1978 to 1983 period.

The results are presented in Exhibit 19-8. At a cut-off of $Pr = 60\%$, the model correctly predicted the direction of earnings change close to two-thirds of the time. Ou and Penman thus demonstrate that financial ratios can successfully improve predictive power. Their use of ratios, however, is mechanical, in that they do not use any judgment in interpreting their variables. This method is driven in part by the nature of their research process and sample size.

Bernard and Noel (1991) approach forecasting in a less mechanical fashion by using trends in (finished goods and work in process) inventory levels to forecast sales

---

[50]See, for example, Fried (1978).

[51]Wild, for example, is based on one firm.

EXHIBIT 19-7
Variables Used in Ou and Penman

Accounting Descriptor	Included in Model for Subperiod	
	1965–1972	1973–1977
% Δ in current ratio		✔
% Δ in quick ratio		✔
% Δ in inventory turnover	✔	
Inventory/total assets		✔
% Δ in the previous ratio	✔	✔
% Δ in inventory		✔
% Δ in sales		✔
% Δ in depreciation	✔	
Δ in dividend per share	✔	✔
% Δ in depreciation/plant assets	✔	
Return on opening equity		✔
Δ in the previous ratio		✔
% Δ in capital expenditures/total assets	✔	
Previous ratio with a one-year lag	✔	✔
Debt/equity ratio		✔
% Δ in the previous ratio	✔	
% Δ in sales/total assets	✔	
Return on total assets	✔	✔
Return on closing equity	✔	
Gross margin ratio	✔	
% Δ in pretax income/sales		✔
Sales to total cash		✔
% Δ in total assets		✔
Cash flow to debt	✔	
Working capital/total assets		✔
Operating income/total assets	✔	✔
Repayment of long-term debt as % of total long-term debt	✔	✔
Cash dividend/cash flows	✔	

Source: Jane A. Ou and Stephen Penman, "Financial Statement Analysis and the Prediction of Stock Returns," *Journal of Accounting and Economics,* Vol. 11, 1989, pp. 295–329, Table 3 (p. 307).

and earnings.[52] As discussed in Chapter 6, they use these variables to aid prediction. However, they conclude that the nature of the analysis calls for a "contextual" approach. That is, changes in inventory may mean different things to different firms. Knowledge of the firm, the industry, and the overall state of the economy at that time is needed before such models can realize their fullest potential.

Lev and Thiagarajan (1993) allow for such a contextual approach in their forecasting model. That model, discussed in Chapter 5 (along with other forecasting models), however, was designed with a different objective. The original objective of Ou and

[52]Freeman et al., discussed earlier, also qualifies as nonmechanical as it combines the relationship of the firm's book value, ROE, and earnings.

EXHIBIT 19-8
Results of Ou and Penman

Summary of Prediction Performance of Earnings Prediction Models; Earnings Changes are Predicted One Year Ahead on the Basis of $\overline{Pr}$.**

| | Predictions Over 1973–1977 | | Predictions Over 1978–1983 | |
| | $\overline{Pr}$ Cut-off | | $\overline{Pr}$ Cut-off | |
	(0.5, 0.5)	(0.6, 0.4)	(0.5, 0.5)	(0.6, 0.4)
Number of observations	9138	5791	9640	4779
% correct predictions	62%	67%	60%	67%
χ_1^2 from 2×2 table (and *p*-value)	299.94	271.63	387.46	444.54
	(0.000)	(0.000)	(0.000)	(0.000)
% predicted EPS increases correct	62%	67%	59%	66%
% predicted EPS decreases correct	61%	66%	62%	67%

*$\overline{Pr}$ is the estimated probability of an earnings increase indicated by the prediction models.
Source: Jane A. Ou and Stephen Penman, "Financial Statement Analysis and the Prediction of Stock Returns," *Journal of Accounting and Economics,* Vol. 11, 1989, pp. 295–329, Table 4 (p. 308).

Penman was valuation, not "predictive ability." These other models were developed to forecast (abnormal) returns directly.

COMPARISON WITH FINANCIAL ANALYST FORECASTS

Earnings forecasting is a prime activity of financial analysts. Such financial analyst forecasts (FAFs) are important inputs in valuation models and usually use a contextual approach. These forecasts possess two advantages over those generated by time-series models. First, analysts base their forecasts on a broader set of data. Extrapolative models use only historical earnings; index models are limited to the information in the chosen indices.

Analysts are not restricted in the information they can incorporate in their forecasts. Their broader set includes information that time-series models ignore, such as:

- The analysis of financial statements
- Assessment of the competitive environment
- Economic forecasts and company disclosures of current business conditions[53]

In addition, analysts possess a timing advantage in that they update their forecasts based on data available after publication of the annual (or quarterly) report. This information is not available for time-series forecasting until the publication of the next report.

Of course, FAFs are much costlier and time-consuming to generate than simple time-series forecasts. Bhushan (1989) analyzed analyst services as an economic good

---

[53]Few firms explicitly forecast earnings. Many do, however, provide "guidance" regarding future operating results to prevent surprises (especially negative ones) when actual earnings are released.

EXHIBIT 19-9
Factors Influencing Degree of Analyst Coverage

Factors Leading to Increased Analyst Coverage

1. *Firm size.* The larger the firm, the greater the profit that can be earned on any piece of information. This would tend to increase analyst coverage. Additionally, to the extent (brokerage house) analysts are interested in increasing the volume of business for their firms, the larger the firm, the greater the potential for transactions business.

2. *Institutional holdings.* The number of analysts is positively related to both the number of institutions holding shares in a company and the percentage of shares held by institutions.

3. *Greater return variability.* The greater the uncertainty associated with a firm, the greater the need for analysts to provide information that may reduce that uncertainty.

4. *Correlation between firm and market return.* For information relating to macro variables, information acquisition costs are likely to be lower, and the more the firm's returns are correlated with the market. This lower cost would therefore increase analyst coverage.

Factors Leading to Decreased Analyst Coverage

5. *Insider holdings* (manager-controlled). The greater the percentage of shares held by insiders, the less demand there is for analysts as presumably the insiders have direct access to all the information they need.

6. *Degree of diversification.* The greater the number of segments, the more complex and costly it is to follow the company.

Source: Derived from Ravi Bhushan, "Firm Characteristics and Analyst Following," *Journal of Accounting and Economics,* July 1989, pp. 255–274.

by examining the factors that affect the supply and demand for such services. His results are summarized in Exhibit 19-9. These results are only descriptive in the sense that they describe environments calling for more or fewer analyst services. Whether or not the services provided actually prove to be "useful" was not the focus of Bhushan's study.

A number of studies have compared analyst and time-series-based forecasts. These studies generally use publicly available analyst forecasts collected by services such as Zacks Investment Research and the Institutional Brokers Estimate System (IBES). These services collect data from a number of analysts. In addition, investor services such as Value Line, Moody's, and Standard & Poor's publish earnings forecasts.

The results generally indicate that analyst forecasts are superior, but not dramatically. Givoly and Lakonishok (1984) surveyed comparisons of analyst forecasts with mechanical models. Exhibit 19-10A is adapted from this paper.

[the table] summarizes the results of the recent studies. Although the magnitude of the errors varied (because of the different treatment of outliers, the different test periods and the fact that Fried and Givoly employed mean, rather than individual forecasts), the common finding is that analysts predict earnings significantly more accurately than mechanical models.[54]

[54]Dan Givoly and Josef Lakonishok, "The Quality of Analysts' Forecasts of Earnings," *Financial Analysts Journal,* September–October 1984, pp. 40–47.

EXHIBIT 19-10
Comparison of Analysts' Forecasts and Mechanical Models

A. Annual Earnings

Relative Accuracy of Analysts' Forecasts

	Mean Relative Absolute Error		
	Collins and Hopwood*	Brown and Rozeff†	Fried and Givoly‡
Analysts' forecasts	31.7%	28.4%	16.4%
Mechanical models§	34.1	32.2	19.8%

*Value Line forecasts, 50 firms, years 1970 to 1974; errors greater than ±300% are equated to ±300%.

†Value Line forecasts, 50 firms, years 1972 to 1975; errors greater than ±100% are equated to ±100%.

‡Mean forecasts, published in the *Earnings Forecaster,* for 410 firms, years 1969 to 1979; errors greater than ±100% are equated to ±100%.

§Average result for the competing mechanical models. The three studies used four, three, and two naive models, respectively.

Source: Dan Givoly and Josef Lakonishok, "The Quality of Analysts' Forecasts of Earnings," *Financial Analysts Journal,* September–October 1984, pp. 40–47, Table 1 (p. 46).

B. Quarterly Earnings

Mean Percentage Error of Quarterly Forecasts,
Forecasts Carried Out over 24 Quarters, 1975 to 1980*

	Models			
Forecasting Horizon	TS1†	TS2‡	TS3§	FAF
One quarter	27.3%	29.1%	27.9%	20.7%
	(0)	(0)	(0)	(24)
Two quarters	30.7%	32.2%	30.8%	26.3%
	(1)	(0)	(1)	(21)
Three quarters	33.1%	33.6%	33.1%	28.7%
	(0)	(4)	(0)	(18)

*Numbers in parentheses indicate the number of quarters model has lowest mean.

†Quarterly time-series model 1 (Brown and Rozeff, 1979).

‡Quarterly time-series model 2 (Foster, 1977).

§Quarterly time-series model 3 (Watts, 1975, and Griffin, 1977).

Source: Lawrence D. Brown, Robert Hagerman, Paul Griffin, and Mark E. Zmijewski, "Security Analyst Superiority Relative to Univariate Time-Series Models in Forecasting Quarterly Earnings," *Journal of Accounting and Economics,* Vol. 9, 1987, pp. 61–87 (adapted from Table 1, pp. 67 and 68).

Using quarterly data, Brown, Hagerman, Griffin, and Zmijewski (1987) compared the performance of the three quarterly earnings forecasting models listed with those generated by analysts (Value Line) for a sample of over 200 companies. They compared forecasting ability one, two, and three quarters ahead. The results, summarized in Exhibit 19-10B, indicate that analyst forecasts are superior. The authors examined the reasons for the superiority of analyst forecasts of quarterly earnings and conclude that it is:

> due to better utilization of information existing at the forecast initiation date for the TS models, a contemporaneous advantage, and acquisition and use of information after the TS model's forecast initiation date, a timing advantage.[55]

In a subsequent paper, Brown, Griffin, Hagerman, and Zmijewski (1987) noted that analyst expectations seem to be a better surrogate for market expectations than time-series forecasts. Market reaction to earnings announcements is more closely associated with errors in analyst forecasts than with errors emanating from time-series models. The predictive ability of analysts (or at the least the information utilized by them) seems to be recognized by the market in forming its aggregate expectations.[56]

Analyst Forecasts: Some Caveats

Not all the evidence on the issue of analyst superiority is clear-cut. Brown, Griffin, Hagerman, and Zmijewski (1987) show that the outperformance of analyst forecasts as surrogates of market expectation is related to firm size.[57] For smaller firms, it is possible to reduce the measurement error in unexpected earnings proxies by pooling analyst forecasts with those of time-series models. O'Brien (1988) found that, although analyst forecasts are superior to those generated by various quarterly forecasting models:

> Errors from the quarterly autoregressive models, however, appear to be more closely related with excess returns over the forecasting horizon than those of analysts. Because of this anomalous result, it is unclear that analysts provide a better model of the "market expectation" than mechanical models.[58]

Furthermore, some studies indicate that analyst forecasts may follow the market rather than leading it. Thus, if the firm's stock price is moving strongly in one direction, analyst forecasts will be revised in that same direction.[59] Brown, Foster, and Noreen (1985), for example, found that positive (negative) returns *precede* upward (downward) revisions in analyst forecasts by as much as 12 months.

---

[55]Lawrence D. Brown, Robert Hagerman, Paul Griffin, and Mark E. Zmijewski, "Security Analyst Superiority Relative to Univariate Time-Series Models in Forecasting Quarterly Earnings," *Journal of Accounting and Economics,* 1987, pp. 61–87.

[56]Similar findings for annual earnings were reported by Dov Fried and Dan Givoly, "Financial Analysts' Forecasts of Earnings: A Better Surrogate for Market Expectations," *Journal of Accounting and Economics,* October 1982, pp. 85–108. They found that market expectations were more closely associated with analyst forecasts and financial analysts' forecasts of annual earnings were more accurate due to

> the existence of some timing advantage to forecasts that are made well after the end of the fiscal year and which presumably incorporate more recent information. However, the main contributor to the better performance of FAF is their ability to utilize a much broader set of information than that used by the univariate time-series models (p. 102).

[57]These results are consistent with those of Brown, Richardson, and Schwager (1987).

[58]Patricia O'Brien, "Analysts' Forecasts as Earnings Expectations," *Journal of Accounting and Economics,* January 1988, pp. 53–83.

[59]This result, as Zarowin himself noted, could be an alternative explanation for his finding (discussed earlier) that differential P/E ratios are a function of higher expected growth rates. The expected growth rates used in Zarowin's study are based on analyst forecasts. Thus, rather than the higher expected growth rates causing higher P/E ratios, analysts may forecast such rates on the basis of higher P/E ratios.

Brown, Richardson, and Schwager (1987) examined factors accounting for the superiority of analyst forecasts over time-series models. After controlling for the timing effect, they find that analyst superiority is positively related to firm size, which they attribute to the broader information set available for larger firms. On the other hand, they find that the more difficult it was to forecast a given firm in the first place (as measured by the dispersion of the FAF), the smaller the benefit from using analyst forecasts.

These results are especially interesting in light of Bhushan's (1989) findings reported in Exhibit 19-9. Firm size and earnings uncertainty are two factors contributing to increased analyst coverage. For the former, the increased supply of analyst services seems to be justified. For the latter, it is not. This is troublesome as, in precisely the environment (high uncertainty) where there is a need for analyst services, the analyst does not seem to outperform time-series models.

Additionally, accounting changes, as noted in previous chapters, cause problems for analysts as it takes time for analysts to learn the effects of these changes. This is true whether changes are voluntary[60] or mandated.[61]

These results hold for analysts in general based on comparisons between consensus (average or median) forecasts and those generated by time-series models. Such consensus forecasts eliminate the idiosyncrasies of individual forecasters.[62]

With respect to individual forecasters, Stickel (1989, 1990) notes that publicly available forecasts are often "stale." Forecasters may not continually update their forecasts, but rather wait for interim reports or other events (such as company meetings or press releases) to revise forecasts. Using information from interim reports, Stickel demonstrates that it is possible to anticipate forecast revisions of individual analysts.

Stickel does, however, note that those analysts with the best forecasting record were those whose forecasting behavior was the most difficult to predict. These analysts are able to add something to the simple extrapolation of interim results.

SUMMARY

Chapter 19 has two critical objectives.

1. First, together with Chapters 17 and 18, it provides both a summation and integration of the preceding chapters by presenting models that use the variables generated by the analysis in those chapters.
2. Equally important, it introduces the final phase in the use and analysis of financial statements: forecasts of the additional variables required for decision making.

---

[60]See Chapter 6, for example, and the discussion of the difficulty analysts had with the continuing effects of FIFO/LIFO changes.

[61]See Chapter 15, where we discuss analysts' difficulty incorporating exchange rate changes in their forecasts.

[62]Kirt C. Butler and Larry H. P. Lang, "The Forecast Accuracy of Individual Analysts: Evidence of Systematic Optimism and Pessimism," *Journal of Accounting Research,* Spring 1991, pp. 150–156, for example, present evidence that certain analysts tend to be "persistently optimistic or pessimistic relative to consensus forecasts."

These objectives are complementary in that the analyses in the earlier chapters are essential if the variables used in decision models are to reflect the economics of the firm rather than accounting choice. Forecasts based on reported data alone, which ignore the database inherent in financial statements, are mechanical exercises at best.

The first part of this chapter discusses valuation models based on discounted cash flows, earnings, net assets, and abnormal earnings. It is not surprising that these diverse models are conceptually equivalent. Although reported cash flows and earnings can diverge sharply in the short run (and, as we have shown, there may be some permanent differences as well), they tend toward equality over longer time periods. As net assets include the cumulative impact of earnings, changes in net assets reflect earnings (as well as capital transactions).

The discussion of asset-based valuation models includes a reexamination of the impacts of dividend policy, equity transactions, acquisitions, exchange rate changes, and accounting methods on net assets. The discussion of discounted cash flow and earnings models provides a similar reevaluation. These reviews reinforce the view, presented throughout this text, that both economic and accounting factors must be considered when using financial data.

The second part of the chapter is quite unlike the preceding sections of the book in that it describes and evaluates statistical procedures useful in forecasting. However, it relies on the preceding chapters through reminders that financial data used in forecasting models may require adjustment. The discussion of forecasting, as always in this text, is primarily concerned with the rationale for the analytic techniques used rather than the mechanics of forecasting, which is left to technical statistics and econometrics texts.

Chapter 19 closes the cycle that started with the framework for financial statement analysis presented in Chapter 1. Our goal has been to take the reader from the basics of financial reporting through the valuation models that, ultimately, are the basis for investment decisions. The theme of this text has been that the financial analyst, armed with knowledge of the financial reporting system and analytical techniques that exploit the shortcomings of that system, can make better informed investment decisions.

CASE **19-1**

Valuation of DuPont

In this case, we apply the valuation models discussed in the chapter to duPont. We have used duPont to illustrate financial analysis techniques throughout the book. The reader should reference the following:

- DuPont's 1994 financial statements, located in Appendix A
- The financial statement adjustments in Chapter 17, including Exhibits 17-1 through 17-5
- Forecast data provided in Exhibit 19C-1

1. The chapter notes that the market price of duPont's common shares on December 31, 1994, was $56.125, considerably above the asset-based valuation.
   (a) Compare that market price to valuations based on *each* of the three DCF models discussed in the chapter. Your valuations require consideration of the following:
      - The CAPM model is used to estimate the discount rate for equity. DuPont's β is 1.00. At the end of 1994, the risk-free rate was approximately 6.5%. Assume an

EXHIBIT 19C-1. DUPONT
Selected Financial Data—Actual and Forecasted

Beta = 1.00

Annual Rates of Change (per share)

	Past		Forecast
	10 Years (%)	5 Years (%)	Next 5 Years (%)
Sales	2.5	6.0	7.0
Cash Flow	7.0	4.5	11.5
Earnings	6.0	3.0	18.0
Dividends	7.5	9.0	7.0
Book Value	2.5	−0.5	8.0

Per Share Data—Forecasts

	1995	1996	1997–1999
Sales	62.60	67.70	84.10
Cash Flow	9.45	10.60	12.35
Earnings	4.70	5.55	6.65
Dividends	1.88	2.00	2.70
Capital Spending	6.15	6.45	6.65
Book Value	20.70	24.15	30.45
No. of Shares (millions)	685	690	700

Cash Flow is defined by *Value Line* as net income plus depreciation, deferred taxes, and equity in undistributed earnings of affiliates.
Source: Adapted from *Value Line Investment Surveys February 3 and May 5, 1995.*

equity risk premium of 6%. The rate so derived should be applied to the following two models.

(i) *Dividend discount model.* Dividend information is provided in duPont's Five Year Review as well as Exhibit 19C-1.

(ii) *Earnings-based model.* Use reported earnings as well as the normalized stream provided in Exhibit 17-3.

- For the *free cash flow* model, estimate the value of the firm. Subtract the market value of debt to estimate the value of equity. These steps require estimation of WACC and information about the market value of duPont's debt. For the latter, see Chapter 10 and duPont's Notes 17 and 19. DuPont's debt rating was AA (S&P). See Chapters 3 and 17 for information about duPont's free cash flows.

(b) Valuations are sensitive to the parameter estimates. Working backward, estimate the relevant parameters implicit in the $56.125 price of duPont shares.

2. (a) Calculate duPont's reported price/earnings and price/book value ratios at December 31, 1994.

(b) Discuss whether or not these ratios are above or below "normal."

(c) In which sector of Figure 19-1 would you place duPont? What does this imply about duPont's current and future abnormal earnings?

3. (a) Discuss whether or not you should use reported income and book values or the adjusted amounts provided in Chapter 17 to value duPont using the EBO model.

(b) Estimate the value of duPont's equity using the EBO model.

Chapter **19**

Problems

1. [Dividend- versus earnings-based models; 1989 CFA adapted] The Director of Research has asked you to recommend whether the Green Fund should add shares of Emfil stock to its portfolio. Apply the following valuation data to Emfil and determine the attractiveness of its shares, using the:

(i) Dividend discount model

(ii) Earnings discount model

EMFIL COMPANY
Valuation Data, June 30, 19X3

	Amount	Percentage Change from Prior Year
Current price per share	$115	
19X2 earnings per share	10.03	28%
19X2 dividends per share	4.05	29
Current annual dividends per share	4.50	11
19X3 estimated earnings per share	11.40	14
Predicted long-term growth rates		
Dividends per share	15%	
Earnings per share	14	
Discount rate	20	

2. [Permanent versus transitory earnings and growth] The CF company, an all-equity company, has a policy of paying out all earnings as dividends. The company's earnings per share remain constant at $10 per share. CF stock sells at a price/earnings ratio of 12. The company has not issued any shares in recent years.

A. Calculate the firm's cost of (equity) capital.

B. For the most recent year, the firm reports earnings per share of $13. Consider three possible price/earnings ratios (on current year earnings per share):

(i) Below 12

(ii) Equal to 12

(iii) Greater than 12

Discuss what each ratio implies about whether or not the earnings increase is permanent or nonrecurring.

3. [Effect of dividend policy on valuation] The historical earnings per share and dividends per share for the Lo Company (Lo) and Hi Company (Hi) follow:

	19X1	19X2	19X3	19X4	19X5
Lo Company					
Earnings per share	$1.00	$1.04	$1.08	$1.12	$1.17
Dividends per share	0.200	0.208	0.216	0.225	0.234
Hi Company					
Earnings per share	1.00	0.80	0.64	0.51	0.41
Dividends per share	1.00	0.80	0.64	0.51	0.41

A portfolio manager has just handed you these data with a perplexed look, stating:

> Look at these numbers. Both companies are in the same industry. Neither has any debt. The EPS of one are obviously growing; the other's EPS are declining. The funny thing about it is that, although Hi's EPS are declining, its market value is identical to that of Lo, and it is constantly able to sell new shares in the equity market. Lo hasn't obtained external financing in years. I just don't get it!

Preliminary investigation indicates that the capital expenditures of both companies are identical each year. Furthermore, you find that the appropriate discount rate for the industry in question is 10%.

A. Calculate the appropriate price/earnings ratio for Lo, based on the above data.

B. Determine the appropriate price/earnings ratio for Hi. (*Hint:* Consider the P/E ratio of Lo.)

C. Complete the following table. To simplify, assume that 19X1 net income was $1,000 for each company and any new financing by Hi was effected at the end of the year. Further, assume that depreciation expense is sufficient to cover the replacement of assets.

	19X1	19X2	19X3	19X4	19X5
Lo Company					
Earnings per share	$ 1.00	$1.04	$1.08	$1.12	$1.17
Number of shares	1,000	____	____	____	____
Net income	1,000	____	____	____	____
Dividends paid	200	____	____	____	____
New investment	800	____	____	____	____
Firm value at period end	____	____	____	____	____
Price per share	____	____	____	____	____
P/E ratio	____	____	____	____	____

	19X1	19X2	19X3	19X4	19X5
Hi Company					
Earnings per share	$ 1.00	$0.80	$0.64	$0.51	$0.41
Number of shares	1,000	——	——	——	——
Net income	1,000	——	——	——	——
Dividends paid	1,000	——	——	——	——
New investment	800	——	——	——	——
New financing	800	——	——	——	——
Firm value at period end	——	——	——	——	——
P/E ratio	——	——	——	——	——
Price per share before new issue	——	——	——	——	——
P/E ratio	——	——	——	——	——
Shares issued	——	——	——	——	——
Price per share at new issue	——	——	——	——	——

D. Calculate the growth rate of net income, dividends paid, and firm value for both companies. Explain why Hi's earnings per share growth rate is not consistent with these growth rates.

E. The P/E ratio is relatively low for both companies. Explain why. Discuss the companies' returns on new investments.

4. [Extension of previous problem, application of EBO model] The previous problem suggests that when new investments are not profitable, companies are better off paying out all earnings as dividends.

A. Assuming an opening book value of $10,000, show how the EBO model demonstrates this point.

B. Redo part A, assuming an opening book value of:
(i) $9,000
(ii) $11,000

5. [Valuation with free cash flows, alternate financing modes] You are considering investing in a new joint venture. The investment is expected to have a two-year life. In addition to equity financing, the syndicate intends to borrow $10 million at the current market rate of 10%. There is some debate, however, as to whether the debt should be incurred by issuing:
(i) "Conventional" notes with annual interest payments
(ii) Zero-coupon notes

These funds would be borrowed January 1, 19X6, and repaid January 1, 19X8.

Projected income statements and cash flow from operations under both alternatives follow ($ in millions):

	Conventional		Zero-Coupon	
	19X6	19X7	19X6	19X7
Earnings before interest and taxes	$20.00	$20.00	$20.00	$20.00
Interest expense*	(1.00)	(1.00)	(1.00)	(1.10)
Earnings before taxes	$19.00	$19.00	$19.00	$18.90
Income tax expense (30% rate)	(5.70)	(5.70)	(5.70)	(5.67)
Net income	$13.30	$13.30	$13.30	$13.23
Noncash charges*	0	0	1.00	1.10
Cash from operations	$13.30	$13.30	$14.30	$14.33

*Interest expense on the zero-coupon bond, although not paid currently, is tax-deductible.

Some investors support the zero-coupon alternative, given the higher cash from operations in both years.

A. Calculate free cash flow for each year under *both* alternatives.

B. Calculate the cash flows for debtholders and the firm for *each* of the years 19X6 through 19X7 under *both* alternatives.

C. Calculate funds available for dividend payments *each year under both alternatives*. (*Hint:* Consider where the funds required to repay debt will come from.)

D. Discuss whether the zero-coupon note is the better financing alternative from the investor point of view.

6. [Valuation models, calculation of free cash flows] The LZ Company income statement for the current year and the forecast for the coming year follow:

	Current	Forecast
Sales	$100,000	$112,000
Cost of goods sold	(40,000)	(44,800)
Selling expense	(25,000)	(28,000)
Operating income	$ 35,000	$ 39,200
Interest expense	(5,000)	(5,600)
Net income	$ 30,000	$ 33,600

The forecast is based on a projected growth rate of 12% arising from new investment opportunities. To simplify, assume that income taxes are zero and depreciation expense approximates replacement cost. Depreciation for the current year is $8,000 and is included in selling expense.

Assume that the cost of equity capital is 15%, the cost of debt 10%, and the rate of return on the firm's new investment opportunities 20%.

A. Based on the data provided, calculate the firm's implied dividend payout ratio.

B. Calculate the firm's total capital expenditures (for replacement and new investment) for the current year. Calculate how much of the new investment will come from debt and how much from equity.

C. Prepare a statement of cash flows for the current and forecast years.

D. Calculate the company's free cash flow for the current and forecast years.

E. Calculate, as of the end of the current year, the value of:

  (i) The firm

  (ii) Its equity

  (iii) Its debt

7. [Extension of Problem 6, application of EBO model] Estimate the value of the firm's equity using the EBO framework and the data in Problem 6. Assume that the current period's (closing) book value equals:

  (i) $168,000

  (ii) $212,000

8. [Extension of Problem 6, treatment of leases in free cash flow calculations] Use the same basic assumptions as in Problem 6. However, now assume that LZ has decided to lease assets instead of borrowing funds for capital expenditures. Assets exceeding those that the company can acquire using internally generated (equity) funds will be leased. The interest rate on leases is the same as for other debt, 10%.

Current income statements are unchanged from Problem 6. Two forecast statements are shown: One assumes that leases are operating leases; the second assumes that they are capital leases. Both statements assume a five-year lease term. The capital lease forecast assumes straight-line depreciation. (*Note:* No longer assume that straight-line depreciation for leased assets approximates replacement cost.)

		Forecast	
	Current	Operating	Capital
Sales	$100,000	$112,000	$112,000
Cost of goods sold	(40,000)	(44,800)	(44,800)
Selling expense	(25,000)	(29,343)	(28,960)
Operating expense	$ 35,000	$ 37,857	$ 38,240
Interest expense	(5,000)	(5,000)	(5,600)
Net income	$ 30,000	$ 32,857	$ 33,640

A. Calculate the annual lease payments.

B. Reconcile the forecast income statements under *both* the operating and capital lease methods with the forecast income statement in Problem 6.

C. Prepare a statement of cash flows for the current and forecast years, assuming that the leases are reported as *operating* leases. Describe how the "acquisition" of the leased assets is reported in the financial statements.

D. Prepare a statement of cash flows for the current and forecast years, assuming that the leases are reported as *capital* leases. Again, describe how the acquisition of the leased assets is reported in the financial statements.

E. Calculate the company's free cash flows for the current and forecast years, assuming that the leases are reported as:

(i) Operating leases

(ii) Capital leases

F. Redo Problem 6E. Discuss how lease financing affects the value of the firm, its equity, and its debt.

G. Discuss what this problem suggests regarding the treatment of leases in a valuation model.

Problems 9 to 12 are based on the information provided in Exhibit 19P-1, extracted from Value Line's report on FAB Industries.

FAB Industries is a practically all-equity firm, with minuscule debt (1% of total capital). Additionally, for the past two years the company had begun to repurchase its own shares whenever management felt the stock price was too low. In answering these problems, assume a cost of equity of 12%.

9. [Comparison of valuation models, estimating growth and growth assumptions; courtesy of Professor Joshua Livnat]

A. Compare FAB's book value per share with its market price. Discuss the implication of this relationship for the existence of economic goodwill. Describe possible adjustments to book value per share that might reduce the difference between book value per share and market price.

B. **(i)** Estimate FAB's dividend payout ratio and ROE, and use them to estimate the firm's internal growth rate. Compare this estimated growth rate with FAB's historical and projected (by Value Line) growth rates. Discuss the advantages and disadvantages of each of these (three) growth rate estimates.

(ii) Describe how FAB's share repurchase program affects *each* of the three growth rate estimates.

C. **(i)** Using the data in Exhibit 19P-1 and assuming constant growth, estimate the value of FAB shares using (1) a dividend discount model, (2) an earnings-based model, and (3) a free cash flow model.

(ii) Compare these estimates with the market price of FAB shares.

D. Discuss how FAB's large cash position affects the use of discounted valuation models. Describe why such "excess" cash may explain the discrepancy between FAB's stock price and the estimates in part C(i).

E. Redo part C, but this time explicitly forecast the relevant variable (dividend, earnings, free cash flows) through 1991, using a constant growth model thereafter.

F. In the chapter, we note that "growth" does not matter for companies whose expected rate of return r^* equals its required rate of return r. Discuss whether or not FAB fits this description. (*Hint:* Consider the value of FAB, assuming that its dividend payout ratio is 100%.)

10. [Extension of previous problem, EBO valuation] Apply the EBO valuation model to FAB Industries. Discuss whether this model provides better estimates of market value than the models in Problem 9. Discuss what the current P/E and P/B ratios tell you about FAB's current and future profitability. Do the actual and forecasted data bear this out?

EXHIBIT 19P-1. FAB INDUSTRIES, INC.
Selected Financial Data, 1985–1994E
Recent price: $36 per share
Price/earnings ratio: 11.3
Beta: 0.80

A. Annual Rates of Change (per Share)

	Past		Forecast
	10 Years	5 Years	Next 5 Years
Sales	9.5%	7.0%	11.5%
Earnings	11.5	8.0	10.0
Dividends	19.0	15.0	9.5
Cash flow	11.5	10.5	9.5
Book value	16.5	12.5	9.5

B. Earnings per Share Data

	Actual				Value Line Forecast		
	1985	1986	1987	1988	1989	1990	1992–94
Earnings	$ 2.39	$ 2.95	$ 2.94	$ 2.62	$ 3.20	$ 3.50	$ 5.00
Dividends	0.50	0.60	0.60	0.70	0.80	0.90	1.10
"Cash flow"	3.18	3.87	4.13	4.02	4.70	5.10	6.95
Capital spending	1.04	1.71	2.47	0.95	1.15	1.40	2.25
Book value	19.52	21.86	24.70	26.62	28.95	32.30	41.95
No. of shares (millions)	3.63	3.63	3.53	3.43	3.28	3.25	3.10

C. Current Position (in $ millions)

	1987	1988
Cash	$31.9	$32.8
Receivables	25.5	28.5
Inventory (LIFO)	23.7	23.8
Other	2.2	1.2
Current assets	$83.3	$86.3
Accounts payable	9.5	8.4
Other	8.9	8.3
Current liabilities	$18.4	$16.7

Other information:
FAB's P/E ratio is approximately 85% of the P/E of comparable companies.
FAB has no pension liability and insignificant leases.
"Cash flow" is defined by *Value Line* as net income plus depreciation, deferred taxes, and equity in undistributed earnings of affiliates.
Source: Value Line Investment Survey, September 1, 1989.

11. [Extension of previous problems] Answers to the previous problems relied on your own and Value Line forecasts. Differences between the values predicted by the respective models and the actual market price may have been due to market expectations that differ from those of Value Line. The following table presents the actual results of FAB Industries for 1989 through 1992. Discuss whether or not having perfect foreknowledge would have improved the performance of the valuation models.

Per Share*	1989	1990	1991	1992
Earnings	$ 3.26	$ 3.24	$ 5.04	$ 5.30
Dividends	0.80	0.80	1.00	1.00
Cash flow	4.64	4.92	6.60	7.30
Capital spending	1.32	2.18	0.98	2.40
Book value	29.12	31.32	35.40	38.70
Shares outstanding (millions)	3.29	3.12	3.09	3.08

*Number of shares and per share data are restated for stock split after 1989.

12. [Valuation, effects of leverage] In 1989, FAB's pretax cost of debt was approximately 11%; its tax rate was 34%. Assume that FAB borrowed $50 million.

A. Compute the effect of the new debt on the value of FAB's equity.

B. Compute the effect of the new debt on the overall value (debt plus equity) of FAB.

13. [Using ratios as forecasting tools, valuation with changing growth patterns] Exhibit 19P-2 presents comparative income statements (19X1 and 19X2) and comparative balance sheets (19X0 through 19X2) for the EFF Company. At the end of 19X2, the company forecast a dramatic increase in sales for 19X3, 19X4, and 19X5:

Sales Forecast

19X3	$150,000
19X4	180,000
19X5	200,000

After 19X5, the company expects sales to stabilize at the 19X5 level.

A. Prepare the statement of cash flows for 19X2 and an estimate of free cash flow.

B. Using the relationships and ratios implied by the financial statements in Exhibit 19P-2, forecast the income statements and balance sheets for 19X3 through 19X5.

C. Use the forecast balance sheets and income statements to estimate free cash flow for 19X3 through 19X5.

D. Assuming a cost of equity of 15%, estimate the value of the EFF Company at the end of 19X2.

EXHIBIT 19P-2. EFF COMPANY
Selected Financial Data for Years Ended December 31

A. Income Statement

	19X1	19X2
Sales	$100,000	$110,000
Cost of goods sold	(50,000)	(53,000)
Selling and general expense	(20,000)	(22,000)
Operating income	$ 30,000	$ 35,000
Interest expense	(3,000)	(3,000)
Income before tax	$ 27,000	$ 32,000
Tax expense	(10,800)	(12,800)
Net income	$ 16,200	$ 19,200
Earnings per share	$ 16.20	$ 19.20

B. Balance Sheet

	19X0	19X1	19X2
Cash	$ 7,000	$ 9,000	$ 11,000
Accounts receivable	8,000	8,500	9,000
Inventory	6,000	6,000	6,000
Current assets	$ 21,000	$ 23,500	$ 26,000
Fixed assets, gross	83,000	94,000	103,000
Accumulated depreciation	(24,000)	(32,500)	(41,000)
Fixed assets, net	$ 59,000	$ 61,500	$ 62,000
Total assets	$ 80,000	$ 85,000	$ 88,000
Accounts payable	$ 8,000	$ 8,500	$ 9,000
Long-term debt	30,000	30,000	30,000
Stockholders' equity	42,000	46,500	49,000
Total liabilities and stockholders' equity	$ 80,000	$ 85,000	$ 88,000

14. [The EBO model, alternative accounting methods] Selected data for the Expac Company are:

1/1/19X0	Stockholders' equity	$5,000
19X0	Income before restructuring costs	1,000

At the end of 19X0, the company considers a major restructuring. Given the nature of the restructuring, the company has the flexibility to recognize the $300 restructuring cost either:

    (i) As a $300 expense in 19X0, or

  (ii) As expenses of $150 in 19X1, $100 in 19X2, and $50 in 19X3

Under alternative 1, 19X0 net income will be $700, and closing book value B_{19X0} will be $5,700. Under alternative 2, 19X0 net income will be $1,000, and closing book value B_{19X0} will be $6,000.

A. Using the template(s) provided below as a guide, show that the EBO valuation model is immune to the choice of accounting recognition methods. Assume that the valuation is made at the *end* of 19X0 and:

- Income before restructuring costs will grow by $50 in each of the next three years.
- No dividends are paid.
- The discount rate is 10%.
- The recognition method chosen does not affect the actual cash flows associated with the restructuring.

$300 Restructuring Charge Taken in 19X0

	Opening Book Value	Income Before Restructuring	Restructuring Charge	Net Income	0.10 × Opening Book Value	Abnormal Earnings
19X1	$5,700	$1,050	0	$1,050	$570	$480
19X2			0			
19X3			0			

Book value at the end of 19X3 _____

B_{19X0} + present value of abnormal earnings in years 19X1, 19X2, and 19X3 _____

Restructuring Charge Recognized over Next Three Years

	Opening Book Value	Income Before Restructuring	Restructuring Charge	Net Income	0.10 × Opening Book Value	Abnormal Earnings
19X1	$6,000	$1,050	$150	$900	$600	$300
19X2			100			
19X3			50			

Book value at the end of 19X3 _____

B_{19X0} + present value of abnormal earnings in years 19X1, 19X2, and 19X3 _____

B. Now assume that the valuation is made as of the *beginning* of 19X0 and the firm is already aware of its restructuring choices. Opening book value is $5,000 in both cases. However, 19X0 net income differs with the accounting choice.

    (i) Discuss whether abnormal earnings differ for years 19X1, 19X2, and 19X3.

    (ii) Show that the EBO valuation as of the beginning of 19X0 is also immune to the choice of recognition methods.

15. [Valuation; 1989 CFA adapted] Following its October 1988 announcement that it was prepared to purchase all of Kraft's outstanding shares at $90.00 per share, Philip Morris' own shares dropped $4.50 to $95.50 per share. At the time of the announcement, it was assumed that Philip Morris would raise the funds required for the takeover by issuing 11% notes. Prior to the merger, Philip Morris' earnings growth rate approximated 20%; Kraft's earnings growth rate was 8%. Selected financial data follow (in millions, except per share data):

	October 1988	
	Philip Morris	Kraft
Common shares outstanding (millions)	234	120
Price per share (preannouncement)	$ 100	$ 65
Long-term debt	4,700	800
Stockholders' equity	7,394	1,920
Earnings before interest and tax	$ 4,340	$ 796
Interest expense	(475)	(81)
Pretax income	$ 3,865	$ 715
Income tax expense	(1,623)	(279)
Net income	$ 2,242	$ 436
Cash flow from operations	$ 2,974	$ 607
Capital expenditures	850	260
Dividends paid	892	251
Earnings per share	$9.58	$3.63

A. Using an asset-based valuation approach and assuming that market prices prior to the merger were appropriate, predict the price change for Philip Morris shares that should have followed the merger announcement.

B. Suggest why the actual decline in Philip Morris shares following the merger announcement was significantly different from your forecast in part A.

C. The discussion of discounted cash flow (DCF) valuation models in the chapter suggests that the models are identical in theory and the main differences are their ease of application. For *each* of the three DCF models discussed in the chapter:
  (i) Dividend discount model
  (ii) Earnings-based model
  (iii) Free cash flow model

discuss the difficulties in using the model to predict the change in Philip Morris' stock price following the merger announcement. Describe the advantages that one model may have over the others. (*Hint:* Focus on the *change* in the value of Philip Morris rather than the value itself.)

16. [Cash flow and valuation] *The New York Times* "Market Place" column featured an article on March 1, 1993, by Robert Hurtado entitled, "Analysts Urge Investors to Look Beyond Earnings at Cash Flow."

> "Analyzing the cash flow, which is generally defined as net income plus depreciation and amortization costs, of a company enables an investor to see beyond the bottom line and unearth hidden values," said Allison Bisno, director of research for Stephens, Inc., a brokerage firm in Little Rock, Ark. "Cash flows often show a company's future earnings potential, which may be more dramatic than the current net income indicates."
>
> To identify bargain stocks on this basis, an investor needs first to calculate the issue's price-to-cash-flow ratio. . . . Wall Street analysts say that stocks are now trading at about 11 times cash flow and investors should seek companies whose shares are trading below this multiple.
>
> The best opportunities naturally lie in companies that have strong corporate earnings and good cash flow, along with a low stock price.

Comment on the investment approach advocated by the author. Can you find a theoretical basis for a price-to-cash-flow ratio? Describe the advantages and disadvantages of using such a ratio to select investments as compared with the use of the price/earnings ratio.

17. [Earnings and Valuation] The Institute of Investment Management and Research (IIMR) is a British organization of investment and financial analysts. Exhibit 19P-3 contains an article concerning the IIMR's proposal for disclosure of "IIMR headline earnings." (*Note:* FRS3 refers to the U.K. Accounting Standards Board's Standard 3.)

A. Discuss how the IIMR headline earnings envisioned in this article are related to *each* of the following definitions of income: operating income, permanent income, sustainable income, and economic income.

B. The IIMR agrees with FRS3 that "it is not possible to distill the performance of a complex organization into a single measure." Given this statement, what is the purpose of creating IIMR headline earnings? What is the importance of the amounts removed from accounting earnings to arrive at headline earnings?

C. The article notes that comments on the IIMR exposure draft were invited. Prepare a comment letter to be sent to the IIMR. (Be brief and to the point.)

EXHIBIT 19P-3
Measuring Earnings After FRS3

The Institute of Investment Management and Research, formerly the Society of Investment Analysts, has published an exposure draft proposing a standardized treatment of a company's trading earnings for use by analysts, commentators, and other observers. A shortened version of the paper follows:

The first sentence of paragraph 52 of FRS3 states "It is not possible to distill the performance of a complex organization into a single measure." This is manifestly true. The performance of a company is reflected in a complex and interlocking set of figures, which themselves interrelate with the industry and economy.

If FRS3 can begin to unravel the myth that a single number determines share prices, a considerable step forward will have been taken. Nevertheless, there are several reasons why efforts should be made to delineate some clearly acceptable earnings figure (or figures).

First, in evaluating a company the stock market must order published information in some useful way. If this is so, it would be desirable that the information should as far as possible be ordered in that way in the calculations of earnings.

Second, there are a large number of users of accounts who do not have the time or the expertise to make the detailed investigations which are distilled into the final market price.

Whatever other requirement there may be for an earnings figure it is clearly desirable, indeed virtually necessary, to define a figure for the company's earnings for the year which can be used as an unambiguous reference point between users, the press, the statistical services, etc. This raises the possibility that such a figure should also be used in preliminary and interim announcements as a statement of earnings, and how they compare with the previous year.

The figure—to be known as IIMR headline earnings—should for these purposes have certain characteristics.

First, it should be a measure of the company's trading performance in the year, not confused with capital items.

Second, it should as far as possible be robust. That is, the calculation should be one that can be carried through by anyone presented with the building blocks of the calculation.

Third, the figure should be factual, including incomes and costs which actually occurred.

However, headline earnings, because they robustly and factually represent the past, will not necessarily be the best basis for forecasts of future earnings. Such forecasts require a great deal of judgment and this is where individual analysts or research firms can add value on behalf of their clients. The practical usefulness of the headline earnings figure is, however, its justification. No one earnings figure can do everything.

These considerations lead to a standard definition of the headline earnings, calculated for the purposes set out above. It is intended as an additional figure, which can be reconciled to FRS3 figures subject to the points discussed below. The guiding principles follow.

- All the trading profits and losses of the company for the year (including interest) should be included in the earnings number. Items which are abnormal in size or nature are included.
- Profits and losses on the sale of fixed assets or of businesses should be excluded. This does not apply to assets acquired for resale.
- Profit and losses arising in activities discontinued at some point during the year, or in activities acquired at some point during the year, should remain in the earnings figure. The costs of eliminating a discontinued operation, or making an acquisition, and the profits and losses on any disposals, should be excluded.
- Prior period items, and the effect of changes in accounting policies and of past fundamental accounting errors should not affect the current year's calculation of earnings.
- Goodwill should not affect earnings in any way.
- Variations in pension fund contributions (and other post-retirement benefit provisions if any) should be included in earnings, but prominently displayed if of significant size.
- Capital and trading items which arise in currencies other than the reporting currency should be handled in the same way as the equivalent items arising in the domestic currency.
- The calculation of the headline earnings number should include tax adjustments to reflect the fact that certain items are excluded from the headline figure.
- Apart from these adjustments, the calculation of headline earnings should normally reflect the tax charge as shown in the company accounts.
- Companies should be encouraged to ensure that adequate disclosures are made to enable the effect of minority interests to be calculated on any adjustments that may be made to arrive at the headline figure if these are not already required.

The definition of earnings. Exposure Draft published by the Institute of Investment Management and Research, 211–213 High St. Bromley, Kent BR1 1NY. David Damant of Credit Suisse Asset Management chaired the subcommittee which produced the draft. Comments invited by April 30.

Source: Financial Times, March 5, 1993, p. 28.

Appendix 19-A

Multistage Growth Models

The original formulation of the discounted models discussed in the chapter is presented below:

$$P_0 = \sum_{i=1}^{\infty} \frac{kE_i}{(1-r)^i}$$

Theoretically, by predicting each year individually, any assumed growth rate of dividends or earnings payout (even zero dividends) can be accommodated. From a practical point of view, of course, one would not attempt to forecast individual periods over a very long horizon.

One palatable approach is to forecast the near future individually and then impose an assumption as to the appropriate valuation after that period. Recall that the preceding expression is equivalent to

$$P_0 = \frac{kE_1}{(1+r)} + \frac{kE_2}{(1+r)^2} + \cdots + \frac{kE_n}{(1+r)^n} + \frac{P_n}{(1+r)^n}$$

This is the present value of the dividends over the first n years plus the discounted value at the end of year n.

For example, assume that you forecast a firm's net income over the next three years as year 1 = 100, year 2 = 120, and year 3 = 150. The firm's k = 20% and its r = 10%. To use the preceding equation, one must derive a terminal value for the firm at the end of year 3. You may at this point decide to make some general assumptions. One assumption might be that from the third year on the firm will experience growth of 8%. The implicit forecast for year 4's earnings is (1.08 × \$150) = \$162, and the terminal value at the end of year 3 (if we use the constant growth model presented earlier) is equal to

$$P_3 = \frac{0.2 \times \$162}{0.10 - 0.08} = \$1,620$$

The value now will be equal to

$$P_0 = \frac{\$100}{(1.1)} + \frac{\$120}{(1.1)^2} + \frac{\$150}{(1.1)^3} + \frac{\$1,620}{(1.1)^3}$$
$$= \$91 + \$99 + \$113 + \$1,217 = \$1,520$$

VALUING A NONDIVIDEND-PAYING FIRM

A firm paying zero dividends can also be modeled along these lines. A firm that pays zero dividends reinvests everything in the firm. Its growth rate is equal to $[1 - k]r^*$ = r^* since k = 0. Assume that a firm having an r^* of 25% for the next five years does not plan to pay dividends for those five years. If its present earning level is \$10, its earnings in year 5 will equal $\$10(1.25)^5 = \$30.5$. From year 6 and on, assume that its r^* will be 20% and the firm will pay dividends at a rate k = 60%. Its growth rate will therefore equal $(1 - 60\%) \times 20\% = 8\%$. Earnings in year 6 will equal \$30.5(1.08) =

$32.9. The firm's value at the beginning of year 6 will be equal to

$$\frac{0.6 \times \$32.9}{0.1 - 0.08} = \$987$$

The value today will be equal to the $987 discounted (back five years) to the beginning of year 1 or $987/(1.10)^5 = \$613$.

SHIFTING GROWTH RATE PATTERNS

Variations of this approach assume a certain level of growth over some initial phase and different growth rates after the initial phase (Figure 19A-1).

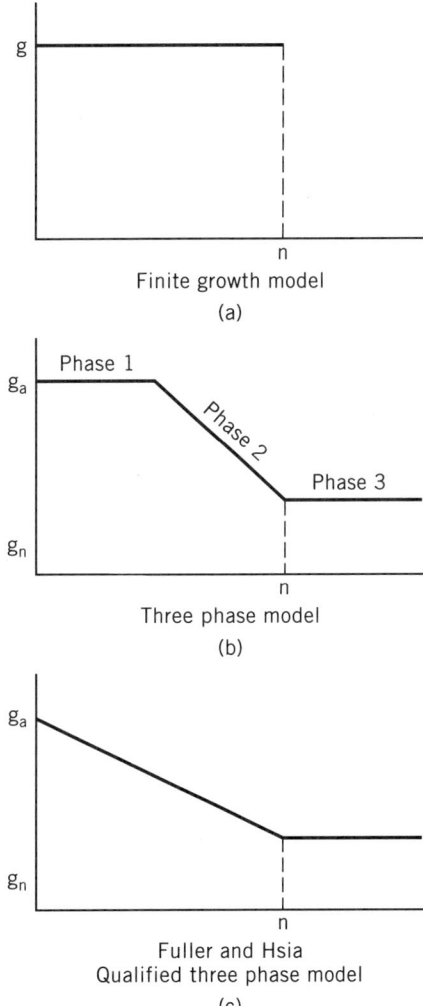

Finite growth model

(a)

Three phase model

(b)

Fuller and Hsia
Qualified three phase model

(c)

FIGURE 19A-1a–c. Simplified three-phase model (Fuller and Hsia, 1984). *Source:* Russel J. Fuller and Chi-Cheng Hsia, "A Simplified Common Stock Valuation Model," *Financial Analysts Journal,* September–October 1984, pp. 49–56 (Figure B, p. 50, and Figure E, p. 53).

The *finite growth model* (Figure 19A-1*a*) assumes that the firm will experience growth of $g = (1 - k)r*$ for *n* years. After that point, the abnormal investment opportunities of $r* > r$ will not exist. The value of equity for such a firm will equal

$$P_0 = \frac{E_1}{r} + \frac{E_1}{r} \left\{ \frac{g - r(1 - k)}{r - g} \left[1 - \left(\frac{1 + g}{1 + r} \right)^n \right] \right\}$$

Other models commonly referred to as *three-phase models* assume (Figure 19A-1*b*) an initial (phase 1) high abnormal growth rate g_a for a number of years that tapers off (in phase 2) to a long-term (phase 3) normal growth pattern of g_n. The calculations for these models are somewhat complex. Fuller and Hsia (1984) simplified these models by assuming a growth pattern as depicted in Figure 19A-1*c*. They start with initial above-normal growth, but assume that it converges gradually to a stable long-term growth pattern. If we stay with the definitions of g_a as the initial growth pattern and g_n as the long-term growth pattern to be reached within *n* years, the value of the equity is equal to

$$P_0 = \frac{kE_0}{r - g_n} \left[(1 + g_n) + \frac{n}{2} (g_a - g_n) \right]$$

Appendix 19-B

The EBO and Terminal Value Assumptions

The terminal value calculations in the chapter assume that ROE remains *constant* after period *T*, at *r* or some other level. Figure 4-6, however, indicates that it is more likely for ROE to *converge asymptotically* to a steady-state level. This appendix presents valuation formulae that can be used when the rate of convergence can be modeled as an autoregressive process, that is,

$$(\text{ROE}_t - \overline{\text{ROE}}) = c(\text{ROE}_{t-1} - \overline{\text{ROE}})$$

or

$$\text{ROE}_t = \overline{\text{ROE}} + c(\text{ROE}_{t-1} - \overline{\text{ROE}}) \qquad \text{where } 0 < c < 1$$

where ROE_t converges to the steady-state level $\overline{\text{ROE}}$. The equation indicates that, in each period, the gap between the actual ROE and the steady-state level narrows as a function of the autoregressive parameter *c*.

Under these assumptions, the valuation formula becomes

$$P_0 = B_0 + \sum_{j=1}^{T} \frac{(\text{ROE}_j - r) B_{j-1}}{(1 + r)^j} + \left\{ \frac{B_{T-1}}{(1 + r)^T} \left[\frac{(\text{ROE}_T - \overline{\text{ROE}}) c}{1 + r - c(1 + g)} + \frac{(\overline{\text{ROE}} - r)}{r - g} \right] \right\}$$

where *g* represents the assumed growth rate in book value. Explicit forecasts of earnings (ROE and book value) are made for *T* periods, followed by the terminal value calculation in the braces.

In the chapter, we note that, even if abnormal earnings were to continue indefinitely ($\overline{\text{ROE}} > r$) because of a special situation such as patent protection, it is unlikely that similar higher returns could be earned on new projects. Thus, the abnormal earnings would not grow as book value increases. Setting $g = 0$ yields

$$P_0 = B_0 + \sum_{j=1}^{T} \frac{(\text{ROE}_j - r)\, B_j}{(1 + r)^j} + \left\{ \frac{B_{T-1}}{(1 + r)^T} \left[\frac{(\text{ROE}_T - \overline{\text{ROE}})\, c}{1 + r - c} + \frac{(\overline{\text{ROE}} - r)}{r} \right] \right\}$$

If competitive pressures force abnormal profits to zero, then at steady state, $\overline{\text{ROE}} = r$ and the valuation formula becomes

$$P_0 = B_0 + \sum_{j=1}^{T} \frac{(\text{ROE}_j - r)\, B_j}{(1 + r)^j} + \left\{ \frac{B_{T-1}}{(1 + r)^T} \left[\frac{(\text{ROE}_T - r)\, c}{1 + r - c} \right] \right\}$$

APPENDIX A

DUPONT FINANCIAL STATEMENTS

Management's Discussion and Analysis

This review and discussion of financial performance should be read in conjunction with the letter to stockholders (pages 1–4), business reviews (pages 16–28) and the consolidated financial statements (pages 39–63).

Analysis of Operations

Sales

Sales in 1994 were $39.3 billion, up 6 percent from 1993. Petroleum segment sales increased 7 percent, while the combined chemicals and specialties segments of Chemicals, Fibers, Polymers and Diversified Businesses were up 6 percent. The chemicals and specialties segments sales increase was 8 percent after adjusting for businesses acquired and divested, reflecting 9 percent higher sales volume, with improvements in every region. Europe was particularly strong, with sales volume up 14 percent, reflecting the economic recovery in that region. Selling prices, while trending upward in 1994, still averaged 1 percent below average 1993 levels. Full-year currency effect on 1994 average prices versus 1993 was negligible.

Sales in 1993 were $37.1 billion, 2 percent below 1992, reflecting 2 percent reductions for the combined chemicals and specialties segments and for the petroleum segment. Lower sales were principally due to lower prices, largely the result of adverse exchange effects from a stronger dollar, partly offset by higher volume.

Earnings

Net income in 1994 was $2,727 million, or $4.00 per share, compared to $555 million, or $.81 per share, in 1993. Results in 1993 included nonrecurring items—principally for restructuring, write-down of intangible assets, product liability charges, asset sales and benefits from tax law changes—which totaled a net charge of $1.65 per share. For similar nonrecurring items in 1994, the total net charge was $.07 per share. Excluding these charges from both years, 1994 net income was $2,775 million, or $4.07 per share, versus $1,677 million, or $2.46 per share, in 1993, up 65 percent. This increase principally reflects improvements in the chemicals and specialties segments from higher sales volume, lower fixed costs and a slightly lower tax rate. The coal business improved, reflecting a full year of normal operations, as compared to prior year results, which had been adversely affected by United

Mine Workers strikes. Petroleum segment earnings were lower, principally reflecting reduced downstream worldwide refined product margins and the adverse impact of refinery downtime, partly offset by better results in upstream operations.

Net income in 1993 was $555 million, or $.81 per share, compared with a loss of $3,927 million, or $(5.85) per share, in 1992. Excluding tax benefits in 1993, nonrecurring and extraordinary items from both years and one-time charges in 1992 for the adoption of new accounting standards, 1993 earnings were $1,677 million, or $2.46 per share, 25 percent higher than the $1,341 million, or $1.98 per share, earned in 1992. The improvement principally resulted from higher petroleum segment earnings from lower costs and increased production outside the United States, partly offset by lower coal results, which were impaired by strikes.

Taxes ($ in millions)

	1994	1993	1992
Income tax expense	**$1,655**	$392	$836
Effective income tax rate (EITR)	**37.8%**	40.9%	46.2%

Over the last three years, the company's EITR exceeded the U.S. statutory rate of 35 percent in 1994 and 1993 and 34 percent in 1992, principally because of the higher tax rates associated with petroleum production operations outside the United States. The 1994 EITR decreased about 3 percentage points from the prior year, reflecting a lower EITR for the chemicals and specialties segments and a lower proportion of higher-taxed petroleum earnings to total company earnings. The decrease in the 1993 EITR versus 1992 reflected a lower effective tax rate in Petroleum operations and a $265 million tax benefit, principally arising from U.K. Petroleum Revenue Tax law revisions, partly offset by an increased proportion of higher-taxed petroleum earnings.

The company paid total taxes of $7.5 billion in 1994, compared to $6.4 billion in 1993 and $6.6 billion in 1992. 1994 total tax payments were higher than 1993, reflecting higher taxes on income and higher gas and oil excise taxes. Tax payments in 1993 were less than 1992, reflecting lower income taxes.

Restructuring

In 1993, restructuring was aimed at improving competitiveness in global markets and focus on the customer. This included plans to eliminate approximately 10,900 positions worldwide and to reduce large internal business sectors in favor of smaller, more responsive, strategic business units. The 1993 pretax charge to earnings for these business restructuring activities was $1.6 billion. At year-end 1994, restructuring reserve balances are about $300 million, approximately two-thirds of which will be paid during 1995. As this program is concluded, these future cash payments are not expected to have a material impact on the company's liquidity. Additional details on these restructuring charges are set forth in Note 6 to the financial statements.

It is estimated that 1994 operating results included about $450 million in pretax savings related to restructuring activities that have been completed. Evaluation of the need for additional restructuring is ongoing and is made in conjunction with corporate strategies to build and maintain globally competitive businesses. However, requisite across-the-board downsizing is believed to be complète, and no additional restructuring costs of the magnitude experienced in recent years are anticipated.

Cash Flows and Financial Condition

During the past three years, cash provided by operations was the primary source of funding for the company's capital investment programs and dividends. Cash flow in excess of these needs was used to reduce borrowings.

CASH PROVIDED BY OPERATIONS

Cash provided by operations totaled $5.7 billion in 1994, about $300 million more than in 1993. In substance, the increase was the result of higher net income partly offset by higher cash payments for restructuring. As shown on the Consolidated Statement of Cash Flows, net income in 1994, adjusted for noncash charges and credits, was up $1.3 billion over that of 1993. Noncash charges in 1993 included asset write-downs and write-offs as part of that year's restructuring program. In 1993, the net change

in operating assets and liabilities resulted in an inflow of more than $900 million, reflecting higher current liabilities, principally due to restructuring charges and reduced inventories and accounts receivable. Cash provided by operations in 1993 totaled $5.4 billion, up $1.0 billion from 1992, reflecting higher net income, excluding restructuring charges, and lower working capital.

CAPITAL EXPENDITURES

Capital expenditures of $3.1 billion in 1994, including investments in affiliates, were 15 percent below the prior year's level. Capital expenditures of $3.7 billion in 1993 were 19 percent lower than in 1992. Lower capital expenditures in recent years result from a more focused and rigorous approach to spending capital, combined with the implementation of engineering and design practices that have significantly improved capital productivity.

In the Petroleum segment, capital expenditures were $1.6 billion, essentially equal to the 1993 level. The most significant Petroleum expenditures in 1994 were for the continued development of the Heidrun field in Norway and the Belida field in Indonesia, the acquisition of an additional interest in the Britannia field in the United Kingdom and for an improvement at the Billings refinery to comply with the U.S. Clean Air Act.

For other segments, capital spending in 1994 continued to concentrate on strengthening and growing strategic businesses outside the United States. This included projects for "Adi-Pure" adipic acid and "Zytel" engineering polymers in Singapore, THF/"Terathane" polyether glycol in Spain and "Tyvek" spunbonded products in Luxembourg. In the United States, significant expenditures were also made for commercialization of CFC alternatives and for modernization of "Dacron" polyester and "Tyvek" spunbonded products facilities. Improvement projects mainly concentrated on enhancing the efficiency and yields of existing refineries and manufacturing facilities.

Capital expenditures are expected to increase to $3.6 billion in 1995, to take advantage of growth opportunities.

PROCEEDS FROM SALES OF ASSETS

Proceeds from sales of assets were $432 million in 1994, versus $1.2 billion in 1993 and $179 million in 1992. In 1994, $212 million came from the sale of petroleum properties, none individually significant, and the balance principally from sales of the "Sclair," Petroleum Additives and "Selar" businesses. Principal proceeds in 1993 were $270 million from connector systems, $280 million from acrylics and $300 million from the sale of the Remington Arms Company.

DIVIDENDS

Dividends per share of common stock in 1994 were $1.82, versus $1.76 in 1993 and $1.74 in 1992. The regular quarterly dividend was increased from $.44 per share to $.47 per share in the third quarter of 1994. The common stock dividend payout in relation to cash provided by operations was 22 percent in 1994 and 1993, as compared to 27 percent in 1992.

BORROWINGS

Borrowings at year-end 1994 were $7.6 billion, as compared to $9.3 billion and $10.9 billion in 1993 and 1992, respectively. Improved cash flow during 1994, principally due to higher cash flow provided by operations and lower capital expenditures, was used to reduce borrowings by $1.7 billion. As a result, the debt ratio* at year-end 1994 was 37 percent, versus 45 percent in 1993.

WORKING CAPITAL INVESTMENT

Working capital investment (excluding cash and cash equivalents, marketable securities, short-term borrowings and capital lease obligations) increased about $700 million in 1994, principally due to accounts receivable and inventory increases related to the exchange effect of a weaker dollar and a decrease in other accrued liabilities resulting from cash payments for "Benlate" DF 50 fungicide settlements and restructuring. These increases in investment were partially offset by higher accounts payable and a decrease in deferred tax asset balances as tax

---

* *Total short- and long-term borrowings and capital lease obligations divided by the sum of these amounts plus stockholders' equity and minority interests in consolidated subsidiaries.*

benefits were realized during the year. In 1993, working capital investment decreased $1.1 billion, reflecting lower inventories and accounts receivable and higher current liabilities, which increased principally due to the 1993 restructuring charge.

The ratio of current assets to current liabilities, including cash and cash equivalents, marketable securties, short-term borrowings and capital lease obligations, at year-end 1994 was 1.5:1, as compared to 1.2:1 in 1993 and 1992.

Financial Instruments

DERIVATIVES AND OTHER HEDGING INSTRUMENTS

The company enters into contractual arrangements (derivatives) in the ordinary course of business to hedge its exposure to foreign currency, interest rate and commodity price risks. The counterparties to these contractual arrangements are major financial institutions. The company is exposed to credit loss in the event of nonperformance by these counterparties. The company manages this exposure to credit loss through credit approvals, limits and monitoring procedures and, to the extent possible, by restricting the period over which unpaid balances are allowed to accumulate. The company does not anticipate nonperformance by counterparties to these contracts, and no material loss would be expected from any such nonperformance. Procedures are in place to regularly monitor and report to management the market and counterparty credit risks associated with these instruments.

FOREIGN CURRENCY

The company routinely uses forward exchange contracts to hedge its net exposures, by currency, related to the foreign currency-denominated monetary assets and liabilities of its operations. The primary business objective of this hedging program is to maintain an approximately balanced position in foreign currencies so that exchange gains and losses resulting from exchange rate changes, net of related tax effects, are minimized.

In addition, from time to time, the company will enter into forward exchange contracts to establish with certainty the U.S. dollar amount of future firm commitments denominated in a foreign currency. Decisions regarding whether or not to hedge a given commitment are made on a case-by-case basis taking into consideration the amount and duration of the exposure, market volatility and economic trends. Forward exchange contracts are also used to manage near-term foreign currency cash requirements and to place foreign currency deposits and marketable securities investments into currencies offering favorable returns.

INTEREST RATES

The company uses a combination of financial instruments, including interest rate swaps, interest and principal currency swaps and structured medium-term financings, as part of its program to manage the fixed and floating interest rate mix of the total debt portfolio and related overall cost of borrowing.

Interest rate swaps involve the exchange of fixed for floating rate interest payments to effectively convert fixed rate debt into floating rate debt based on LIBOR or commercial paper rates. Interest rate swaps also involve the exchange of floating for fixed rate interest payments to effectively convert floating rate debt into fixed rate debt. Interest rate swaps allow the company to maintain a target range of floating rate debt.

Under interest and principal currency swaps, the company receives predetermined foreign currency-denominated payments corresponding, both as to timing and amount, to the fixed or floating interest rate and fixed principal amounts to be paid by the company under concurrently issued foreign currency-denominated bonds. In return, the company pays U.S. dollar interest and a fixed U.S. dollar principal amount to the counterparty, thereby effectively converting the foreign currency-denominated bonds into U.S. dollar-denominated obligations for both interest and principal. Interest and principal currency swaps allow the company to be fully hedged against fluctuations in currency exchange rates and foreign interest rates and to achieve

U.S. dollar fixed or floating interest rate payments below the market interest rate, at the date of issuance, for borrowings of comparable maturity.

Structured medium-term financings consist of a structured medium-term note and a concurrently executed structured medium-term swap that, for any and all calculations of the note's interest and/or principal payments over the term of the note, provides a fully hedged transaction such that the note is effectively converted to a U.S. dollar-denominated fixed or floating interest rate payment. Structured medium-term swaps allow the company to be fully hedged against fluctuations in exchange rates and interest rates and to achieve U.S. dollar fixed or floating interest rate payments below the market interest rate, at the date of issuance, for borrowings of comparable maturity.

COMMODITY HEDGES AND TRADING

The company enters into exchange-traded and over-the-counter commodity futures contracts to hedge its exposure to price fluctuations on anticipated crude oil, refined products and natural gas transactions and certain raw material purchases.

Commodity trading in petroleum futures contracts is a natural extension of cash market trading and is used to physically acquire about 15 percent of North America refining crude supply requirements. The commodity futures market has underlying principles of increased liquidity and longer trading periods than the cash market and is one method of reducing exposure to the price risk inherent in the petroleum business. Typically, trading is conducted to manage price risk around near-term (30–60 days) supply requirements. Occasionally, as market views and conditions allow, longer-term positions will be taken to manage price risk for the company's equity production (crude and natural gas) or net supply requirements. The company's use of futures contracts reduces the effects of price volatility, thereby protecting against adverse short-term price movements, while limiting, somewhat, the benefits of favorable short-term price movements.

From time to time, on a limited basis, the company also purchases and sells petroleum-based futures contracts for trading purposes. After-tax gain/loss from such trading has not been material.

Additional details on these and other financial instruments are set forth in Note 27 to the financial statements.

Environmental Matters

The company operates about 150 manufacturing facilities, five petroleum refineries, 20 natural gas processing plants and numerous product-handling and distribution facilities around the world, all of which are significantly affected by a broad array of laws and regulations relating to the protection of the environment. It is the company's policy to comply fully with or to exceed all legal requirements worldwide. In addition, since some risk to the environment is associated with the company's operations, as it is with other companies engaged in similar businesses, voluntary programs are in place to minimize that risk. These programs are designed to reduce air emissions, curtail the generation of hazardous waste, decrease the volume of wastewater discharges and improve the energy efficiency of operations. The cost of complying with increasingly complex environmental laws and regulations, as well as the company's own internal programs, is significant, and will continue to be so for the foreseeable future, but is not expected to have a material impact on the company's competitive or financial position. The enactment of broader or more stringent environmental laws or regulations in the future, however, could lead to an upward reassessment of the potential environmental costs provided below.

New waste treatment facilities and pollution control and other equipment are routinely installed to satisfy both legal requirements and the company's waste elimination and pollution prevention goals. About $400 million was spent for capital projects related to environmental requirements and company goals in 1994. The company currently estimates expenditures for environmental-related capital projects will total about the same in 1995. The company anticipates significant capital expenditures may be required over the next decade for treatment, storage and disposal facilities for solid and hazardous waste and for compliance with the 1990 Amendments to the Clean Air Act (CAA). For example, environmental capital costs in 1993 and 1994 related to the CAA Amendments included expenditures in the Petroleum segment to meet federal requirements for reformulated gasoline/clean fuels, and additional environmental capital expenditures are anticipated for plant air emission controls, primarily in the Chemicals and Petroleum segments. Although considerable uncertainty will remain with regard to future estimates of capital expenditures until all new CAA regulatory requirements are known, related capital costs over the next two years are currently estimated to total approximately $20 million.

Estimated pretax environmental expenses charged to current operations totaled about $950 million in 1994, as compared to $1 billion in 1993 and $900 million in 1992. These expenses included the remediation accruals discussed below, operating, maintenance and depreciation costs for solid waste, air and water pollution control facilities and costs incurred in conducting environmental research activities. The largest of these expenses resulted from the operation of water pollution control facilities and solid waste management facilities, each of which accounted for about $200 million. About 75 percent of total annual expenses resulted from the operations of the company's Chemicals, Fibers, Polymers and Diversified Businesses segments in the United States, primarily the Chemicals and Polymers segments. Expenses are expected to increase over the next several years as a result of additional operating costs associated with new pollution prevention and control equipment.

REMEDIATION ACCRUALS

The Comprehensive Environmental Response, Compensation and Liability Act (CERCLA, often referred to as Superfund) and the Resource Conservation and Recovery Act (RCRA) both require that the company undertake certain remediation activities at sites where the company conducts or once conducted operations or at sites where company-generated waste was disposed. DuPont accrues for those remediation activities when it is probable that a liability has been incurred and reasonable estimates can be made. Accrued liabilities are exclusive of claims against third parties and are not discounted. During 1994 the company accrued $185 million for environmental remediation activities, compared to $183 million and $160 million in 1993 and 1992, respectively. At December 31, 1994, the company's balance sheet included an accrued liability of $616 million as compared to $522 million and $465 million at year-end 1993 and 1992, respectively. Approximately 75 percent of the company's environmental accrual is attributable to RCRA and similar remediation liabilities and 25 percent to CERCLA liabilities. Expenditures for such previously accrued remediation activities were $91 million in 1994, $126 million in 1993 and $121 million in 1992.

The company's assessment of the potential impact of these two principal remediation statutes is subject to considerable uncertainty due to the complex, ongoing and evolving process of generating estimates of remediation costs. The various stages of remediation include initial broad-based analysis of a site, on-site investigation, feasibility studies to select from among various remediation methods, approval by applicable authorities and, finally, the actual implementation of the remediation plan. Remediation activities occur over a relatively long period of time and vary in cost substantially from site to site depending on the mix of unique site characteristics, the development of new remediation technologies and the evolving regulatory framework. The company's assessment of those costs is a continuous process which takes into account the factors affecting each specific site. DuPont Environmental Remediation Services, a wholly owned subsidiary, provides technical capability to address the company's remediation needs in a cost-effective manner, while protecting human health and the environment.

RCRA, as amended in 1984, provides for extensive regulation of the treatment, storage and disposal of hazardous waste.

The regulations currently provide that companies seeking to periodically renew RCRA permits, or close facilities with permits, must, as a condition of renewal or closure, undertake certain corrective measures to remediate contamination caused by prior operations. The RCRA corrective action program affects the company differently than the CERCLA program in that the cost of RCRA corrective action activities is typically borne solely by the company. The company anticipates that significant ongoing expenditures for RCRA corrective actions may be required over the next two decades. Annual expenditures for the near term are not expected to vary significantly from the range of such expenditures over the past few years. Longer term, expenditures are subject to considerable uncertainty and may fluctuate significantly, perhaps between $50 million and $300 million in any one year. The company's expenditures associated with RCRA and similar remediation activities were approximately $70 million in 1994, $90 million in 1993 and $103 million in 1992.

The company from time to time receives requests for information or notices of potential liability from the Environmental Protection Agency (EPA) and state environmental agencies, alleging that the company is a "potentially responsible party" (PRP) under CERCLA or equivalent state legislation. In addition, the company has on occasion been made a party to cost recovery litigation by those agencies. These requests, notices and lawsuits assert potential liability for remediation costs of various waste treatment or disposal sites that are not company owned but allegedly contain wastes attributable to the company from past operations. As of December 31, 1994, the company was aware of potential liability under CERCLA or state laws at about 310 sites around the United States. The CERCLA or state remediation process is actively under way at one stage or another at about 145 of those sites. In addition, the company has resolved its liability at 48 sites either by completing necessary remedial actions with other PRPs or by participating in "de minimis buyouts" with other PRPs whose waste, like the company's, only represented a small fraction of the total waste present at a site.

Management's Discussion and Analysis

The company's expenditures associated with CERCLA or state remediation activities were approximately $21 million in 1994, $36 million in 1993 and $18 million in 1992. Over the next decade the company may incur significant costs under CERCLA. Considerable uncertainty exists with respect to these costs, and under the most adverse circumstances potential liability may exceed amounts accrued as of December 31, 1994. The company's share of the remediation cost at these sites in many instances cannot be precisely estimated due to the large number of PRPs involved, the scarcity of reliable data pertaining to many of these sites, uncertainty as to how the laws and regulations may be applied to these sites and the multiple choices and costs associated with diverse technologies that may be used in remediation. For most sites, the company's potential liability will be significantly less than the total site remediation costs because the percentage of material attributable to the company versus that attributable to other PRPs is relatively low. There are a few sites where the company is a major participant, but neither the cost to the company of remediation at those sites, nor at all CERCLA sites in the aggregate, is expected to have a material impact on the competitive or financial position of the company. The process of estimating CERCLA remediation costs, the financial viability of other PRPs and the PRPs' respective shares of liability is ongoing. Often these estimates are performed by third parties and, thus far, have not been subject to material uncertainty or dispute. Moreover, other PRPs at sites where the company is a party typically have the financial strength to meet their obligations and, where they do not, or where certain PRPs cannot be located, the company's own share of liability has not materially increased. The company's general experience has been that, in most cases, its share of estimated costs at any given site has trended downward as this process has matured.

Although future remediation expenditures in excess of current reserves could be significant, the effect on future financial results is not subject to reasonable estimation because considerable uncertainty exists as to the cost and timing of expenditures. The company is actively pursuing claims against insurers with respect to RCRA and CERCLA liabilities. Potential recoveries in this litigation have not been offset against the accruals discussed above.

Financial Statements

E. I. du Pont de Nemours and Company and Consolidated Subsidiaries

Consolidated Income Statement

(Dollars in millions, except per share)

	1994	1993	1992
Sales*	**$39,333**	$37,098	$37,799
Other Income (Note 2)	**926**	743	553
Total	**40,259**	37,841	38,352
Cost of Goods Sold and Other Operating Charges (Notes 3 and 12)	**21,977**	21,624	22,046
Selling, General and Administrative Expenses	**2,888**	3,081	3,553
Depreciation, Depletion and Amortization	**2,976**	2,833	2,655
Exploration Expenses, Including Dry Hole Costs and Impairment of Unproved Properties	**357**	361	416
Research and Development Expense	**1,047**	1,132	1,277
Interest and Debt Expense (Note 4)	**559**	594	643
Taxes Other Than on Income* (Note 5)	**6,215**	5,423	5,476
Restructuring (Note 6)	**(142)**	1,621	475
Write-Down of Intangible Assets (Note 6)	**–**	214	–
Total	**35,877**	36,883	36,541
Earnings Before Income Taxes	**4,382**	958	1,811
Provision for Income Taxes (Note 7)	**1,655**	392	836
Income Before Extraordinary Item and Transition Effect of Accounting Changes	**2,727**	566	975
Extraordinary Charge from Early Extinguishment of Debt (Note 8)	**–**	(11)	(69)
Transition Effect of Changes in Accounting Principles (Notes 1, 7 and 25)	**–**	–	(4,833)
Net Income (Loss)	**$ 2,727**	$ 555	$ (3,927)
Earnings Per Share of Common Stock (Note 9)			
Income Before Extraordinary Item and Transition Effect of Accounting Changes	**$ 4.00**	$ .83	$ 1.43
Extraordinary Charge from Early Extinguishment of Debt (Note 8)	**–**	(.02)	(.10)
Transition Effect of Changes in Accounting Principles (Notes 1, 7 and 25)	**–**	–	(7.18)
Net Income (Loss)	**$ 4.00**	$ .81	$ (5.85)

* Includes petroleum excise taxes of $5,291, $4,477 and $4,508 in 1994, 1993 and 1992, respectively.

See pages 43–63 for Notes to Financial Statements.

Financial Statements

E. I. du Pont de Nemours and Company and Consolidated Subsidiaries

Consolidated Balance Sheet

(Dollars in millions, except per share)

December 31	1994	1993
Assets		
Current Assets		
Cash and Cash Equivalents (Note 10)	$ 856	$ 1,109
Marketable Securities (Note 10)	253	85
Accounts and Notes Receivable (Note 11)	5,213	4,894
Inventories (Note 12)	3,969	3,818
Prepaid Expenses	259	231
Deferred Income Taxes (Note 7)	558	762
Total Current Assets	11,108	10,899
Property, Plant and Equipment (Note 13)	48,838	47,926
Less: Accumulated Depreciation, Depletion and Amortization	27,718	26,503
	21,120	21,423
Investment in Affiliates (Note 14)	1,662	1,607
Other Assets (Notes 7 and 15)	3,002	3,124
Total	**$36,892**	$37,053
Liabilities and Stockholders' Equity		
Current Liabilities		
Accounts Payable (Note 16)	$ 2,734	$ 2,444
Short-Term Borrowings and Capital Lease Obligations (Note 17)	1,292	2,796
Income Taxes (Note 7)	409	321
Other Accrued Liabilities (Note 18)	3,130	3,878
Total Current Liabilities	7,565	9,439
Long-Term Borrowings and Capital Lease Obligations (Notes 19 and 20)	6,376	6,531
Other Liabilities (Note 21)	8,438	8,200
Deferred Income Taxes (Note 7)	1,494	1,466
Total Liabilities	23,873	25,636
Minority Interests in Consolidated Subsidiaries	197	187
Stockholders' Equity (see page 41)		
Preferred Stock	237	237
Common Stock, $.60 par value; 900,000,000 shares authorized;		
issued at December 31: 1994—681,004,944; 1993—677,577,437	408	407
Additional Paid-In Capital	4,771	4,660
Reinvested Earnings	7,406	5,926
Total Stockholders' Equity	12,822	11,230
Total	**$36,892**	$37,053

See pages 43–63 for Notes to Financial Statements.

Financial Statements

E. I. du Pont de Nemours and Company and Consolidated Subsidiaries

Consolidated Statement of Stockholders' Equity

(Dollars in millions, except per share)

	1994	1993	1992
Preferred Stock, without par value—cumulative;			
23,000,000 shares authorized; issued at December 31:			
$4.50 Series—1,672,594 shares (callable at $120)	$ 167	$ 167	$ 167
$3.50 Series—700,000 shares (callable at $102)	70	70	70
	237	237	237
Common Stock (Notes 22 and 23), $.60 par value;			
900,000,000 shares authorized; issued at December 31:			
1994—681,004,944; 1993—677,577,437; 1992—675,008,236	408	407	405
Additional Paid-In Capital (Notes 22 and 23)			
Balance at Beginning of Year	4,660	4,551	4,418
Common Stock Issued in Connection with Compensation Plans	111	109	133
Balance at End of Year	4,771	4,660	4,551
Reinvested Earnings			
Balance at Beginning of Year	5,926	6,572	11,681
Net Income (Loss)	2,727	555	(3,927)
	8,653	7,127	7,754
Preferred Dividends	(10)	(10)	(10)
Common Dividends (1994—$1.82; 1993—$1.76; 1992—$1.74)	(1,237)	(1,191)	(1,172)
Total Dividends	(1,247)	(1,201)	(1,182)
Balance at End of Year	7,406	5,926	6,572
Total Stockholders' Equity	**$12,822**	$11,230	$11,765

See pages 43–63 for Notes to Financial Statements.

Financial Statements

E. I. du Pont de Nemours and Company and Consolidated Subsidiaries

Consolidated Statement of Cash Flows

(Dollars in millions)

	1994	1993	1992
Cash and Cash Equivalents at Beginning of Year	**$1,109**	$1,640	$ 468
Cash Provided by Operations			
Net Income (Loss)	**2,727**	555	(3,927)
Adjustments to Reconcile Net Income to Cash Provided by Operations:			
Extraordinary Charge from Early Extinguishment of Debt (Note 8)	**–**	11	69
Transition Effect of Accounting Changes (Notes 1, 7 and 25)	**–**	–	4,833
Depreciation, Depletion and Amortization	**2,976**	2,833	2,655
Dry Hole Costs and Impairment of Unproved Properties	**152**	201	185
Other Noncash Charges and Credits—Net	**(140)**	843	(174)
Decrease in Operating Assets:			
Accounts and Notes Receivable	**30**	103	104
Inventories and Other Operating Assets	**19**	664	219
Increase (Decrease) in Operating Liabilities:			
Accounts Payable and Other Operating Liabilities	**(432)**	686	907
Accrued Interest and Income Taxes (Notes 4 and 7)	**332**	(516)	(483)
Cash Provided by Operations	**5,664**	5,380	4,388
Investment Activities (Note 24)			
Purchases of Property, Plant and Equipment	**(3,050)**	(3,621)	(4,448)
Investments in Affiliates	**(90)**	(70)	(127)
Payments for Businesses Acquired	**(5)**	(409)	–
Proceeds from Sales of Assets	**432**	1,160	179
Investments in Short-Term Financial Instruments—Net	**(379)**	(85)	(70)
Miscellaneous—Net	**(41)**	(53)	(87)
Cash Used for Investment Activities	**(3,133)**	(3,078)	(4,553)
Financing Activities			
Dividends Paid to Stockholders	**(1,247)**	(1,201)	(1,182)
Net Increase (Decrease) in Short-Term Borrowings	**(517)**	(2,024)	2,310
Long-Term and Other Borrowings:			
Receipts	**824**	1,806	2,976
Payments	**(2,032)**	(1,392)	(2,711)
Common Stock Issued in Connection with Compensation Plans	**94**	67	86
Cash Provided by (Used for) Financing Activities	**(2,878)**	(2,744)	1,479
Effect of Exchange Rate Changes on Cash	**94**	(89)	(142)
Cash and Cash Equivalents at End of Year	**$ 856**	$1,109	$1,640
Increase (Decrease) in Cash and Cash Equivalents	**$ (253)**	$ (531)	$1,172

See pages 43–63 for Notes to Financial Statements.

Notes to Financial Statements

(Dollars in millions, except per share)

1. Summary of Significant Accounting Policies

DuPont observes the generally accepted accounting principles described below. These, together with the other notes that follow, are an integral part of the consolidated financial statements.

Accounting Changes

In 1992, DuPont adopted Statement of Financial Accounting Standards (SFAS) No. 106, "Employers' Accounting for Postretirement Benefits Other Than Pensions" and SFAS No. 109, "Accounting for Income Taxes." The company recorded charges to net income of $3,788 ($5.63 per share) and $1,045 ($1.55 per share), respectively, as of January 1, 1992 for the effects of transition to these two new standards. See also Notes 7 and 25.

Basis of Consolidation

The accounts of wholly owned and majority-owned subsidiaries are included in the consolidated financial statements. Investments in affiliates owned 20 percent or more and corporate joint ventures are accounted for under the equity method. Investments in noncorporate joint ventures of petroleum operations are consolidated on a pro rata basis. Other securities and investments, excluding marketable securities, are generally carried at cost.

Inventories

Substantially all inventories are valued at cost as determined by the last-in, first-out (LIFO) method; in the aggregate, such valuations are not in excess of market. Elements of cost in inventories include raw materials, direct labor and manufacturing overhead. Stores and supplies are valued at cost or market, whichever is lower; cost is generally determined by the average cost method.

Property, Plant and Equipment

Property, plant and equipment (PP&E) is carried at cost and, except for petroleum, PP&E is generally classified in depreciable groups and depreciated under the sum-of-the-years' digits method and other substantially similar methods. Depreciation rates range from 4 percent to 12 percent per annum on direct manufacturing facilities and from 2 percent to 10 percent per annum on other facilities; in some instances appropriately higher or lower rates are used. Generally, for PP&E acquired prior to 1991, the gross carrying value of assets surrendered, retired, sold or otherwise disposed of is charged to accumulated depreciation and any salvage or other recovery therefrom is credited to accumulated depreciation. For disposals of PP&E acquired after 1990, the gross carrying value and related accumulated depreciation are removed from the accounts and included in determining gain or loss on such disposals.

Beginning in 1995, nonpetroleum PP&E placed in service will be depreciated using the straight-line method. This change in accounting principle is being made to reflect management's belief that the productivity of such PP&E will not appreciably diminish in the early years of its useful life, and it will not be subject to significant additional maintenance in the later years of its useful life. In these circumstances, straight-line depreciation is preferable in that it provides a better matching of costs with revenues. Additionally, the change to the straight-line method will conform to predominant industry practice. Although the effect of this change on net income will be impacted by the level of future capital spending, the change is not expected to have a material effect on 1995 results.

Petroleum PP&E, other than "Oil and Gas Properties" described below, is depreciated on the straight-line method at various rates calculated to extinguish carrying values over estimated useful lives. When petroleum PP&E is surrendered, retired, sold or otherwise disposed of, the nature of the assets involved determines if a gain or loss is recognized, or the gross carrying value is charged to accumulated depreciation, depletion and amortization and any salvage or other recovery therefrom is credited to accumulated depreciation, depletion and amortization.

Maintenance and repairs are charged to operations; replacements and betterments are capitalized.

Oil and Gas Properties

The company's exploration and production activities are accounted for under the successful-efforts method. Costs of acquiring unproved properties are capitalized, and impairment of those properties, which are individually insignificant, is provided for by amortizing the cost thereof based on past experience and the estimated holding period. Geological, geophysical and delay rental costs are expensed as incurred. Costs of exploratory dry holes are expensed as the wells are determined to be dry. Costs of productive properties, production and support equipment and development costs are capitalized and amortized on a unit-of-production basis.

Notes to Financial Statements

(Dollars in millions, except per share)

Intangible Assets

Identifiable intangible assets such as purchased patents and trademarks are amortized on a straight-line basis over their estimated useful lives. Goodwill is amortized over periods up to 40 years on the straight-line method. The company continually evaluates the reasonableness of its amortization for intangibles. In addition, if it becomes probable that expected future undiscounted cash flows associated with intangible assets are less than their carrying value, the assets are written down to their fair value.

Environmental Liabilities and Expenditures

Accruals for environmental matters are recorded in operating expenses when it is probable that a liability has been incurred and the amount of the liability can be reasonably estimated. Accrued liabilities are exclusive of claims against third parties and are not discounted.

In general, costs related to environmental remediation are charged to expense. Environmental costs are capitalized if the costs increase the value of the property and/or mitigate or prevent contamination from future operations.

Income Taxes

The provision for income taxes has been determined using the asset and liability approach to accounting for income taxes. Under that approach, deferred taxes represent the future tax conse-quences expected to occur when the reported amounts of assets and liabilities are recovered or paid. The provision for income taxes represents income taxes paid or payable for the current year plus the change in deferred taxes during the year. Deferred taxes result from differences between the financial and tax bases of the company's assets and liabilities and are adjusted for changes in tax rates and tax laws when changes are enacted. Valuation allowances are recorded to reduce deferred tax assets when it is more likely than not that a tax benefit will not be realized.

Provision has been made for income taxes on unremitted earnings of subsidiaries and affiliates, except in cases in which earnings of foreign subsidiaries are deemed to be permanently invested. Investment tax credits or grants are accounted for in the period earned (the flow-through method).

Foreign Currency Translation

The company has determined that the U.S. dollar is the "functional currency" of its worldwide operations. Foreign currency asset and liability amounts are translated into U.S. dollars at end-of-period exchange rates, except for inventories, prepaid expenses and property, plant and equipment, which are translated at historical rates. Income and expenses are translated at average exchange rates in effect during the year, except for expenses related to balance sheet amounts that are translated at historical exchange rates. The company routinely uses forward exchange contracts to hedge its net exposures, by currency, related to the foreign currency-denominated monetary assets and liabilities of its operations. Exchange gains and losses, net of their related tax effects, are included in income in the period in which they occur.

In addition, the company from time to time enters into forward exchange contracts and similar agreements to effectively convert firm foreign currency commitments to U.S. dollar-denominated transactions. Gains and losses on these specific commitment hedges are deferred and included in the measurement of the related foreign currency transactions.

In the Consolidated Statement of Cash Flows, the company reports the cash flows resulting from its hedging activities in the same category as the related item that is being hedged.

Interest Rate Swap Agreements

The company enters into interest rate swap agreements as part of its program to manage the fixed and floating interest rate mix of its total debt portfolio and related overall cost of borrowing. The dif-ferential to be paid or received is accrued as interest rates change and is recognized in income over the life of the agreements.

Commodity Hedges and Trading

The company enters into commodity futures contracts to hedge its exposure to price fluctuations on anticipated crude oil, refined products and natural gas transactions and certain raw material purchases. Gains and losses on these hedge contracts are deferred and included in the measurement of the related transaction. From time to time, on a limited basis, the company also purchases and sells petroleum-based futures contracts for trading purposes. Changes in the market values of these trading contracts are reflected in income in the period the change occurs.

Reclassifications

Certain reclassifications of prior years' data have been made to conform to 1994 classifications.

Notes to Financial Statements

(Dollars in millions, except per share)

2. Other Income

	1994	1993	1992
Royalty income	$ 95	$111	$118
Interest income, net of miscellaneous interest expense	111	160	178
Equity in earnings of affiliates (see Note 14)	361	121	216
Sales of assets	92	198	40
Miscellaneous income and expenses—net	267	153	1
	$926	$743	$553

3. Fungicide Recall and Claims Provision

During 1991, the company initiated a stop-sale and recall of "Benlate" DF 50 fungicide. The company accrued $175, $200 and $212 in 1994, 1993 and 1992, respectively, for estimated costs in excess of insurance coverage. The related liability included in the Consolidated Balance Sheet is not reduced by the amounts of any expected insurance recoveries. Adverse changes in estimates for such costs could result in additional future charges.

4. Interest and Debt Expense

		1994	1993	1992
Interest and debt cost incurred		$703	$825	$860
Less:	Interest and debt cost capitalized	143	194	194
	Foreign currency adjustments*	1	37	23
		$559	$594	$643

* *Represents exchange gains associated with local currency borrowings in hyperinflationary economies. These amounts effectively offset the related inflationary interest expense arising from currency devaluations.*

Interest paid (net of amounts capitalized) was $598 in 1994, $614 in 1993 and $611 in 1992.

5. Taxes Other Than on Income

	1994	1993	1992
Petroleum excise taxes (also included in Sales):			
U.S.	$1,049	$ 803	$ 709
Non-U.S.	4,242	3,674	3,799
Payroll taxes	424	443	459
Property taxes	202	201	201
Import duties	159	151	146
Production and other taxes	139	151	162
	$6,215	$5,423	$5,476

6. Restructuring Charges and Write-Down of Intangible Assets

Restructuring charges are directly related to management decisions to reduce worldwide employment levels and realign worldwide production and support facilities in order to improve productivity and competitiveness. Charges principally reflect employee separation costs, costs of shutting down certain facilities and contract cancellation costs.

In the third quarter of 1993, the company recorded a restructuring charge of $1,621. The principal component of this charge related to employee separation costs of $665. This charge was for the involuntary and voluntary termination of approximately 10,900 employees, and was based on plans that identified the number of employees to be terminated, their functions and their businesses. Substantially all of this charge was for estimated termination payments and enhanced benefit costs for terminated employees. As of December 31, 1994, almost 9,000 employees have been terminated under this program and about $420 has been settled and charged against the related $665 liability. In addition, during the fourth quarter 1994, the restructuring reserve balance was reduced by $45 principally to reflect lower estimates for employee separation costs and a reduction of about 500 in the number of employees to be terminated. As a result, about $200 remains as a liability in the company's Consolidated Balance Sheet at December 31, 1994. This $200 balance includes certain termination payments for former employees that extend beyond December 31, 1994 under the terms of various separation

Notes to Financial Statements

(Dollars in millions, except per share)

agreements, in addition to the liability for employees yet to be terminated. All restructuring plans have been announced, and most of the remaining 1,400 employee terminations will be in Europe. The majority of these employees will be terminated during 1995, and the program will be completed in 1997 concurrent with the last plant closing.

The remaining portion of the restructuring charge, $956, is related to asset write-downs and facility shutdowns, principally:

a) The decision to discontinue the manufacture of silver halide films in New Jersey and to consolidate manufacturing at existing facilities in Germany and North Carolina. A charge of $330 was recorded to fully reserve discontinued facilities and to cover other costs directly associated with manufacturing and product line rationalizations of the printing and publishing business;

b) Write-downs of operating assets to be sold, specifically, certain North American petroleum-producing properties. The petroleum properties were written down by $233 to their estimated net realizable value, generally based on their respective estimated selling prices;

c) The write-down of a polymers plant in Texas by $102 to its estimated net realizable value. This charge covered the net book value of the facilities and estimated dismantlement costs less estimated salvage proceeds since it was uncertain at that time whether an appropriate buyer could be identified. This plant was subsequently sold as discussed below;

d) Charges of $108 related to restructuring by an equity affiliate, write-off of chlorofluorocarbon (CFC) manufacturing facilities in South America, and contract cancellations; and

e) A write-off of $70 associated with rationalization of certain fibers facilities in the United States, Europe and South America.

This portion of the restructuring, after 1994 adjustments described below, is expected to be essentially completed in 1995. The related reserve balances at year-end 1994 were about $100.

In the fourth quarter 1992, the company recorded charges of $475 for termination incentives and payments, as well as certain other charges, related to business restructuring. During 1994, an additional $25 charge was recorded to reflect higher-than-projected employee termination costs. This restructuring is complete.

Adjustments of 1993 Restructuring Charges

1994 earnings included a $167 benefit associated with several adjustments of restructuring provisions established in September 1993. Revisions related to asset write-downs and facility shutdowns totaled $122 and reflected higher-than-anticipated proceeds from the disposal of a portion of a plant previously written down, continuation of CFC operations in South America, at the request of local government, to allow for an orderly transition to alternative products, and further refinement of certain of the other items reflected in the 1993 restructuring charge. In addition, an adjustment of $45 was made to reflect lower estimates for employee separation costs.

Write-Down of Intangible Assets

A charge of $214 was recorded in the third quarter 1993 for the write-down of intangible assets (technology and goodwill) associated with a series of acquisitions made by the printing and publishing business in 1989. Such action was taken when it became probable that undiscounted future cash flows would not be adequate to support carrying values. (See Note 1, "Intangible Assets.")

Notes to Financial Statements

(Dollars in millions, except per share)

7. Provision for Income Taxes

Effective January 1, 1992, the company adopted SFAS No. 109, "Accounting for Income Taxes." On adoption, the company recorded an increase in deferred tax liabilities at January 1, 1992 and a charge to income of $1,045, principally to provide deferred taxes for purchase business combinations consummated prior to 1992 for which it was not practicable to adjust all remaining assets and liabilities to pretax amounts. Total income taxes paid worldwide were $1,344 in 1994, $896 in 1993 and $1,213 in 1992.

	1994	1993	1992
Current tax expense:			
U.S. federal	$ 337	$ 321	$ 34
U.S. state and local	47	21	5
Non-U.S.	1,023	758	857
Total	1,407	1,100	896
Deferred tax expense:			
U.S. federal	497	(486)	(319)
U.S. state and local	(55)	(53)	(35)
Non-U.S.	(136)	(198)	133
Total	306	(737)	(221)
Other[1]	(58)	29	161
Provision for Income Taxes (Excluding Extraordinary Item and Transition Effect of Accounting Change)	1,655	392	836
Extraordinary Item	–	(7)	(39)
Transition Effect of Change in Accounting for Postretirement Benefits Other Than Pensions	–	–	(2,130)
Stockholders' Equity[2]	(26)	(20)	(11)
Total Provision	$1,629	$ 365	$(1,344)

1 *Represents exchange (gains)/losses associated with the company's hedged non-U.S. tax liabilities. These amounts offset the tax effect arising from related hedging activities. The 1992 amount also includes $97 representing exchange gains on unhedged non-U.S. deferred tax liabilities established in conjunction with the adoption of SFAS No. 109. Excluding this item, exchange gains and losses, net of their related tax effects, were not material in the periods presented.*

2 *Represents tax benefit of certain stock compensation amounts that are deductible for income tax purposes but do not affect net income.*

Deferred income taxes result from temporary differences between the financial and tax bases of the company's assets and liabilities. The tax effects of temporary differences and tax loss/tax credit carryforwards included in the deferred income tax provision (excluding extraordinary item and transition effect of accounting change) are as follows:

	1994	1993	1992
Depreciation	$144	$(105)	$ 232
Accrued employee benefits	(19)	(69)	(69)
Other accrued expenses	185	(346)	(67)
Intangible drilling costs	(48)	(68)	10
Inventory	(87)	109	(53)
Unrealized exchange gains/(losses)	103	(22)	(125)
Investment in subsidiaries and affiliates	(7)	(4)	–
Other temporary differences	33	30	(55)
Tax loss/tax credit carryforwards	90	4	(103)
Valuation allowance change—net	17	8	9
Tax rate changes	–	(274)	–
Tax status changes	(105)	–	–
	$306	$(737)	$(221)

The significant components of deferred tax assets and liabilities at December 31, 1994 and 1993 are as follows:

	1994		1993	
Deferred Tax	Asset	Liability	Asset	Liability
Depreciation	$ –	$2,940	$ –	$2,808
Accrued employee benefits	2,873	630	2,875	651
Other accrued expenses	782	4	963	–
Intangible drilling costs	–	289	–	337
Inventory	174	310	107	330
Unrealized exchange gains	–	19	85	–
Tax loss/tax credit carryforwards	395	–	590	–
Investment in subsidiaries and affiliates	37	125	34	130
Other	331	835	352	878
Total	4,592	$5,152	5,006	$5,134
Less: Valuation allowance	(357)		(445)	
Net	$4,235		$4,561	

Notes to Financial Statements

(Dollars in millions, except per share)

Current deferred tax liabilities (included in the Consolidated Balance Sheet caption "Income Taxes") were $63 and $67 at December 31, 1994 and 1993, respectively. In addition, deferred tax assets of $82 and $198 were included in Other Assets at December 31, 1994 and 1993, respectively (see Note 15).

An analysis of the company's effective income tax rate (excluding extraordinary item and transition effect of accounting changes) follows:

	1994	1993	1992
Statutory U.S. federal income tax rate	35.0%	35.0%	34.0%
Higher effective tax rate on non-U.S. operations (principally Petroleum)	9.9	51.9	20.5
Lower effective tax rate on operations within U.S. possessions	(1.1)	(5.6)	(2.4)
Alternative fuels credit	(2.1)	(6.9)	(2.0)
Tax rate changes	–	(28.6)[1]	–
Tax status changes	(2.4)[2]	–	–
Other—net	(1.5)	(4.9)	(3.9)
Effective income tax rate	37.8%	40.9%	46.2%

1 *Reflects a net tax benefit of $265, arising principally from U.K. Petroleum Revenue Tax law revisions.*
2 *Reflects a tax valuation allowance benefit of $105 related to a change in tax status resulting from a transfer of properties among certain North Sea affiliates.*

Earnings before income taxes shown below are based on the location of the corporate unit to which such earnings are attributable. However, since such earnings are often subject to taxation in more than one country, the income tax provision shown above as U.S. or non-U.S. does not correspond to the earnings set forth below.

	1994	1993	1992
U.S. (including exports)	$2,651	$ (167)	$ 136
Other regions	1,731	1,125	1,675
	$4,382	$ 958	$1,811

At December 31, 1994, unremitted earnings of non-U.S. subsidiaries totaling $4,333 were deemed to be permanently invested. No deferred tax liability has been recognized with regard to the remittance of such earnings. It is not practicable to estimate the income tax liability that might be incurred if such earnings were remitted to the United States.

Under the tax laws of various jurisdictions in which the company operates, deductions or credits that cannot be fully utilized for tax purposes during the current year may be carried forward, subject to statutory limitations, to reduce taxable income or taxes payable in a future year. At December 31, 1994, the tax effect of such carryforwards approximated $395. Of this amount, $176 has no expiration date, $20 expires in 1995, $139 expires after 1995 but before 2001 and $60 expires between 2001 and 2010.

8. Extraordinary Charge from Early Extinguishment of Debt

In 1993, there was a charge of $11, net of a tax benefit of $7, for the redemption of $285 of outstanding debentures. In 1992, outstanding debt of $603 was redeemed with a resulting charge of $69, net of a tax benefit of $39. Charges principally represent call premium and unamortized discount, respectively.

9. Earnings Per Share of Common Stock

Earnings per share are calculated on the basis of the following average number of common shares outstanding: 1994—679,999,916; 1993—676,622,115; and 1992—673,454,935.

10. Cash and Cash Equivalents and Marketable Securities

Cash equivalents represent investments with maturities of three months or less from time of purchase. They are carried at cost plus accrued interest, which approximates fair value because of the short maturity of these instruments. Cash and cash equivalents are used in part to support a portion of the company's commercial paper program.

Marketable securities represent investments in fixed and variable rate financial instruments classified as available-for-sale securities and reported at fair value.

11. Accounts and Notes Receivable

December 31	1994	1993
Trade—net of allowances of $86 in 1994 and $97 in 1993	$4,244	$4,020
Miscellaneous	969	874
	$5,213	$4,894

Accounts and notes receivable are carried at amounts which approximate fair value.

See Note 30 for a description of business segment markets and associated concentrations of credit risk.

Notes to Financial Statements

(Dollars in millions, except per share)

12. Inventories

December 31	1994	1993
Chemicals	$ 237	$ 250
Fibers	677	571
Polymers	617	550
Petroleum	1,365	1,367
Diversified Businesses	1,073	1,080
	$3,969	$3,818

The excess of replacement or current cost over stated value of inventories for which cost has been determined under the LIFO method approximated $819 and $766 at December 31, 1994 and 1993, respectively. In the aggregate, the market value of the company's vertically integrated petroleum and petroleum-based chemical products exceeds cost. Inventories valued at LIFO comprised 88 percent and 87 percent of consolidated inventories before LIFO adjustment at December 31, 1994 and 1993, respectively.

The liquidation of LIFO inventory quantities carried in the aggregate at lower costs prevailing in prior years increased 1993 net income by about $50 ($.07 per share).

13. Property, Plant and Equipment

December 31	1994	1993
Chemicals	$ 5,086	$ 4,984
Fibers	10,574	10,280
Polymers	7,827	7,742
Petroleum	17,999	17,698
Diversified Businesses	5,377	5,265
Corporate	1,975	1,957
	$48,838	$47,926

Property, plant and equipment includes gross assets acquired under capital leases of $148 and $72 at December 31, 1994 and 1993, respectively; related amounts included in accumulated depreciation, depletion and amortization were $88 and $57 at December 31, 1994 and 1993, respectively.

14. Summarized Financial Information for Affiliated Companies

Summarized combined financial information for affiliated companies for which DuPont uses the equity method of accounting (see Note 1, "Basis of Consolidation") is shown below on a 100 percent basis. The most significant of these affiliates are CONSOL Energy Inc. and The DuPont Merck Pharmaceutical Company; DuPont has a 50 percent equity ownership in each of these companies. Dividends received from equity affiliates were $326 in 1994, $243 in 1993 and $124 in 1992.

	Year Ended December 31		
Results of operations	1994	1993	1992
Sales*	$9,161	$8,030	$8,173
Earnings before income taxes	947	446	771
Net Income	732	252	568
DuPont's equity in earnings of affiliates (see Note 2)	361	121	216

* Includes sales to DuPont of $828 in 1994, $752 in 1993 and $803 in 1992.

	December 31	
Financial position	1994	1993
Current assets	$ 3,254	$2,703
Noncurrent assets	8,147	6,813
Total assets	$11,401	$9,516
Short-term borrowings*	$ 648	$ 475
Other current liabilities	2,065	1,820
Long-term borrowings*	2,590	2,220
Other long-term liabilities	2,934	2,847
Total liabilities	$ 8,237	$7,362
DuPont's investment in affiliates (includes advances)	$ 1,662	$1,607

* DuPont's pro rata interest in total borrowings was $1,220 in 1994 and $985 in 1993, of which $599 in 1994 and $388 in 1993 was guaranteed by the company. These amounts are included in the guarantees disclosed in Note 28.

Notes to Financial Statements

(Dollars in millions, except per share)

15. Other Assets

December 31	1994	1993
Prepaid pension cost (see Note 26)	$1,502	$1,384
Intangible assets	225	278
Other securities and investments	508	474
Deferred income taxes (see Note 7)	82	198
Miscellaneous	685	790
	$3,002	$3,124

Other securities and investments includes $351 and $391 at December 31, 1994 and 1993, respectively, representing marketable securities classified as available for sale and reported at fair value. The remainder represents numerous small investments in securities for which there are no quoted market prices and for which it is not practicable to determine fair value. Such securities are reported at cost.

16. Accounts Payable

December 31	1994	1993
Trade	$1,847	$1,675
Payables to banks	321	264
Compensation awards	222	94
Other	344	411
	$2,734	$2,444

Payables to banks represents checks issued on certain disbursement accounts but not presented to the banks for payment. The reported amounts approximate fair value because of the short maturity of these obligations.

17. Short-Term Borrowings and Capital Lease Obligations

December 31	1994	1993
Commercial paper[1]	$ 450	$ 325
Bank borrowings:		
U.S. dollars	–	25
Other currencies[2]	264	395
Master notes	–	495
Medium-term notes payable within one year	519	853
Long-term borrowings payable within one year[3]	–	636
Industrial development bonds payable on demand	51	50
Capital lease obligations	8	17
	$1,292	$2,796

1 *An interest rate swap effectively converted $50 of these floating rate borrowings to a fixed rate obligation at December 31, 1994 and 1993, as part of the program to manage the fixed and floating interest rate mix of total borrowings. The interest rate was 8.3 percent and the remaining maturity was 1.2 years at December 31, 1994.*

2 *1993 includes 1,173 million Norwegian krone borrowing ($158 at the December 31, 1993 exchange rate) with an average interest rate of 5.9 percent.*

3 *1993 includes notes denominated as 125 billion Italian lire with a 12.375 percent Italian lira fixed interest rate. Concurrent with the issuance of these notes, the company entered into interest and principal currency swaps that effectively established a $100 fixed principal amount with a 7.45 percent U.S. dollar fixed interest rate.*

The estimated fair value of the company's short-term borrowings, including interest rate financial instruments, based on quoted market prices for the same or similar issues or on current rates offered to the company for debt of the same remaining maturities, was $1,300 and $2,900 at December 31, 1994 and 1993, respectively.

Unused short-term bank credit lines were approximately $1,360 and $2,100 at December 31, 1994 and 1993, respectively. These lines support short-term industrial development bonds, a portion of the company's commercial paper program and other borrowings.

Notes to Financial Statements

(Dollars in millions, except per share)

18. Other Accrued Liabilities

December 31	1994	1993
Payroll and other employee benefits	$ 725	$ 694
Taxes other than on income	422	380
Postretirement benefits other than pensions (see Note 25)	333	343
Restructuring charges	219	810
Miscellaneous	1,431	1,651
	$3,130	$3,878

19. Long-Term Borrowings and Capital Lease Obligations

December 31	1994	1993
U.S. dollar:		
Industrial development bonds due 2001–2024	$ 295	$ 234
Medium-term notes due 1995–2005[1]	592	837
8.50% notes due 1996	251	252
8.45% notes due 1996	300	300
8.65% notes due 1997	300	300
8.50% notes due 1998	302	302
7.50% notes due 1999	303	304
9.15% notes due 2000[2]	306	307
6.00% debentures due 2001 ($660 face value, 13.95% yield to maturity)	430	411
6.75% notes due 2002[3]	299	299
8.00% notes due 2002	253	254
8.50% notes due 2003[2]	300	300
8.13% notes due 2004	331	349
8.25% notes due 2006	282	299
8.25% debentures due 2022	372	399
7.95% debentures due 2023[3]	299	299
7.50% debentures due 2033[3]	247	247
6.25% Swiss franc notes due 2000[4]	103	103
Other loans (various currencies) due 1995–2005[5]	725	701
Capital lease obligations	86	34
	$6,376	$6,531

1 *Average interest rates at December 31, 1994 and 1993 were 7.5 percent and 6.8 percent, respectively.*

2 *The company entered into an interest rate swaption agreement for each of these notes as part of the program to manage the fixed and floating interest rate mix of total borrowings. Each agreement gives the swaption counterparty the one-time option to put the company into an interest rate swap with a notional amount of $300, whereby the company would, over the remaining term of the notes, receive fixed rate payments essentially equivalent to the fixed interest rate of the underlying notes, and pay the counterparty a floating rate of interest essentially equivalent to the rate the company pays on its commercial paper. If exercised, the swaptions would effectively convert the notes to a floating rate obligation over the remaining maturity of the notes. The premium received from the counterparties for these swaptions is being amortized to income, using the effective interest method, over the remaining maturity of the notes. The fair value and carrying value of these swaptions at December 31, 1994 and 1993 were not material.*

3 *Interest rate swaps effectively converted $775 of these notes and debentures to a floating rate obligation as part of the program to manage the fixed and floating interest rate mix of total borrowings. The remaining average maturity of these swaps was 2.2 years at December 31, 1994.*

4 *Represents notes denominated as 150 million Swiss francs with a 6.25 percent Swiss franc fixed interest rate. Concurrent with the issuance of these notes, the company entered into an interest and principal currency swap that effectively established a $103 fixed principal amount with a 6.9 percent U.S. dollar fixed interest rate.*

5 *Includes notes denominated as 160 million Australian dollars with a 16.5 percent Australian dollar fixed interest rate issued by the company's majority-owned Canadian subsidiary, which were effectively converted to a Canadian dollar borrowing with an implicit 12.43 percent Canadian dollar fixed interest rate. Also includes a loan of 190 million pounds sterling ($296 and $292 at the respective 1994 and 1993 year-end exchange rates) with a floating money market-based interest rate.*

Notes to Financial Statements

(Dollars in millions, except per share)

Average interest rates on industrial development bonds and on other loans (various currencies) were 6.1 percent and 7.3 percent at December 31, 1994, and 6.0 percent and 7.4 percent at December 31, 1993.

Maturities of long-term borrowings, together with sinking fund requirements in each of the four years after December 31, 1995, are as follows:

1996—$908	1998—$407
1997—$798	1999—$443

The estimated fair value of the company's long-term borrowings, including interest rate financial instruments, based on quoted market prices for the same or similar issues or on current rates offered to the company for debt of the same remaining maturities was $6,600 and $7,500 at December 31, 1994 and 1993, respectively.

20. Leases

The company uses various leased facilities and equipment in its operations. The company's future minimum lease payments under operating and capital leases, together with the present value of the net minimum capital lease payments at December 31, 1994, are as follows:

	Capital Leases	Operating Leases*
Minimum lease payments for years ending December 31:		
1995	$ 20	$ 290
1996	16	224
1997	11	182
1998	11	156
1999	11	124
Remainder	104	673
	173	$1,649
Less: Estimated executory costs	7	
Net minimum lease payments	166	
Less: Imputed interest	72	
Present value of net minimum lease payments	94	
Due in 1995	8	
Due after 1995	$ 86	

* *Minimum lease payments have not been reduced by minimum sublease rentals due in the future under noncancelable subleases related to operating leases in the amount of $102.*

Rental expense under operating leases was $355 in 1994, $429 in 1993 and $453 in 1992.

21. Other Liabilities

December 31	1994	1993
Accrued postretirement benefits cost (see Note 25)	$6,058	$5,998
Reserves for employee-related costs	937	989
Miscellaneous	1,443	1,213
	$8,438	$8,200

22. Stockholders' Equity

Shares of new common stock issued in connection with employee compensation and benefit plans were 3,427,507 in 1994, 2,569,201 in 1993 and 3,766,099 in 1992.

Notes to Financial Statements

(Dollars in millions, except per share)

23. Compensation Plans

In 1990, the Board of Directors approved the adoption of a world-wide Corporate Sharing Program. Under the program, in February 1991, essentially all employees each received a one-time grant of options to acquire 100 shares of DuPont common stock at the fair market value ($38.25 per share) at date of grant. Common shares subject to option under this Plan are as follows:

	1994	1993	1992
Outstanding at January 1	8,916,709	10,525,892	12,693,600
Options:			
Exercised	2,199,142	1,534,403	1,960,028
Terminated	43,215	74,780	207,680
Outstanding at December 31	6,674,352	8,916,709	10,525,892

In January 1995, the Board of Directors approved the worldwide 1995 Corporate Sharing Program and awarded to essentially all employees a one-time grant of options to acquire 100 shares of DuPont common stock at the fair market value ($57 per share) on the date of grant.

Awards for 1994 under the DuPont Stock Performance Plan (granted to key employees in 1995) consisted of 3,133,091 options to acquire DuPont common stock at fair market value of $55.50 per share. Payment of the purchase price must be made in cash or in DuPont common stock (at fair market value on the date of exercise). Common shares subject to option under this Plan are as follows:

	1994	1993	1992
Outstanding at January 1	14,553,921	13,594,606	13,822,375
Options granted	2,324,720	2,160,360	2,425,130
Average price	$52.50	$46.01	$49.21
Options exercised	1,954,064	1,092,473	2,456,592
Average price	$32.46	$27.77	$26.78
Options expired or terminated	229,677	108,572	196,307
At December 31:			
Participants	1,318	1,226	1,188
Options outstanding	14,694,900	14,553,921	13,594,606
Average price	$40.83	$37.62	$35.47
Options exercisable	12,384,780	12,418,711	11,202,016
Shares available for option	27,527,631	26,215,426	25,092,886

At December 31, 1994, there were 559,463 stock appreciation rights (SARs) outstanding, at an average option price of $32.51 per share. SARs may be exercised only in tandem with the exercise of an accompanying stock option. As each SAR is exercised, one additional stock option is cancelled. Expiration dates for outstanding options and SARs ranged from February 17, 1995 to September 20, 2004.

Awards under the Variable Compensation Plan may be granted in stock and/or cash to employees who have contributed most in a general way to the company's success, consideration being given to ability to succeed to more important managerial respon-sibility. Such awards were $208 for 1994, $87 for 1993 and $87 for 1992. Amounts credited to the Variable Compensation Fund are dependent on company earnings, and are subject to maximum limits as defined by the Plan. The amounts credited to the fund were $220 in 1994, $89 in 1993 and $85 in 1992. In accordance with the terms of the Variable Compensation Plan and similar plans of subsidiaries, 1,326,922 shares of common stock were awaiting delivery from awards for 1994 and prior years.

24. Investment Activities

Payments for businesses acquired in 1993 include $380 as part of the third quarter acquisition of Imperial Chemical Industries P.L.C.'s worldwide nylon business. In addition to the cash pay-ment, a deferred payment of $93 was reflected in Other Liabilities. Of the total purchase price, $259 and $170 were reflected in property, plant and equipment and inventories, respectively.

In 1994, there were no individually material items included in Proceeds from Sales of Assets. Proceeds from sales in 1993 principally include $270 from the sale of the connector systems business, $280 from the sale of the acrylics business and $300 from the sale of the Remington Arms Company. Assets sold in connection with these sales amounted to $656, of which $336 was property, plant and equipment with the remainder divided about equally between inventories and other current assets.

Notes to Financial Statements

(Dollars in millions, except per share)

25. Other Postretirement Benefits

The parent company and certain subsidiaries provide medical, dental and life insurance benefits to pensioners and survivors. The associated plans are unfunded, and approved claims are paid from company funds. Under the terms of the benefit plans, the company reserves the right to change, modify or discontinue the plans.

In 1992, the company adopted SFAS No. 106, "Employers' Accounting for Postretirement Benefits Other Than Pensions." Medical, dental and life insurance costs for these plans and related disclosures are determined under the provisions of SFAS No. 106. Cash expenditures are not affected by this accounting change. At January 1, 1992, the accumulated postretirement benefit obligation was $5,990, and related accrued liabilities were $68, resulting in a transition charge of $5,922. Other postretirement benefits cost includes the following components:

	Health Care	Life Insurance	Total
1994			
Service cost—benefits allocated to current period	$ 56	$ 17	$ 73
Interest cost on accumulated postretirement benefit obligation	288	77	365
Amortization of net gains and prior service credit	(78)	8	(70)
Other postretirement benefits cost	$266	$102	$368
1993			
Service cost—benefits allocated to current period	$ 55	$ 12	$ 67
Interest cost on accumulated postretirement benefit obligation	305	69	374
Amortization of net gains and prior service credit	(94)	–	(94)
Other postretirement benefits cost	$266	$ 81	$347
1992			
Service cost—benefits allocated to current period	$ 82	$ 11	$ 93
Interest cost on accumulated postretirement benefit obligation	431	67	498
Other postretirement benefits cost	$513	$ 78	$591

The lower health care costs in 1994 and 1993 versus 1992 were due to changes in the company's health care benefits programs in the United States, which were announced on December 31, 1992. These changes provide for increased cost control through prevention and managed care, and for increased cost sharing by employees and pensioners. The impact of these changes resulted in an unrecognized prior service credit of $1,219 at the beginning of 1993; the accumulated postretirement benefit obligation was reduced by a similar amount.

The following provides a reconciliation of the accumulated postretirement benefit obligation to the liabilities reflected in the balance sheet at December 31, 1994 and 1993.

	Health Care	Life Insurance	Total
1994			
Accumulated postretirement benefit obligation for:			
Current pensioners and survivors	$(2,366)	$ (570)	$(2,936)
Fully eligible employees	(139)	–	(139)
Other employees	(674)	(319)	(993)
	(3,179)	(889)	(4,068)
Unrecognized net loss/(gain)	(1,267)	3	(1,264)
Unrecognized prior service credit	(1,059)	–	(1,059)
Accrued postretirement benefits cost	$(5,505)	$ (886)	$(6,391)
Amount included in Other Accrued Liabilities (see Note 18)			$ 333
Amount included in Other Liabilities (see Note 21)			$ 6,058
1993			
Accumulated postretirement benefit obligation for:			
Current pensioners and survivors	$(2,993)	$ (692)	$(3,685)
Fully eligible employees	(146)	–	(146)
Other employees	(934)	(404)	(1,338)
	(4,073)	(1,096)	(5,169)
Unrecognized net loss/(gain)	(285)	252	(33)
Unrecognized prior service credit	(1,139)	–	(1,139)
Accrued postretirement benefits cost	$(5,497)	$ (844)	$(6,341)
Amount included in Other Accrued Liabilities (see Note 18)			$ 343
Amount included in Other Liabilities (see Note 21)			$ 5,998

Notes to Financial Statements

(Dollars in millions, except per share)

The health care accumulated postretirement benefit obligation was determined at December 31, 1994 using a health care cost escalation rate of 8 percent decreasing to 5 percent over 8 years and at December 31, 1993 using a health care escalation rate of 10 percent decreasing to 5 percent over 10 years. The assumed long-term rate of compensation increase used for life insurance was 5 percent. The discount rate was 9 percent at December 31, 1994 and 7.25 percent at December 31, 1993. A one-percentage-point increase in the health care cost escalation rate would have increased the accumulated postretirement benefit obligation by $251 at December 31, 1994, and the 1994 other postretirement benefit cost would have increased by $44.

26. Pensions

The company has noncontributory defined benefit plans covering substantially all U.S. employees. The benefits for these plans are based primarily on years of service and employees' pay near retirement. The company's funding policy is consistent with the funding requirements of federal law and regulations.

Pension coverage for employees of the company's non-U.S. consolidated subsidiaries is provided, to the extent deemed appropriate, through separate plans. Obligations under such plans are systematically provided for by depositing funds with trustees, under insurance policies or by book reserves.

Net pension cost/(credit) for defined benefit plans includes the following components:

	1994		1993		1992	
Service cost—benefits earned during the period		$ 380		$ 301		$ 283
Interest cost on projected benefit obligation		1,079		1,038		980
Return on assets:						
Actual (gain)/loss	$ 214		$(1,880)		$(1,055)	
Deferred gain/(loss)	(1,540)	(1,326)	617	(1,263)	(164)	(1,219)
Amortization of net gains and prior service cost		(91)		(123)		(127)
Net pension cost/(credit)		$ 42		$ (47)		$ (83)

The change in the annual pension cost/(credit) was primarily due to the discount rate used to determine the present value of future benefits and the return on pension trust assets.

The funded status of these plans was as follows:

December 31	1994		1993	
Actuarial present value of:				
Vested benefit obligation	$(10,342)		$(11,681)	
Accumulated benefit obligation	$(10,744)		$(12,177)	
Projected benefit obligation		$(12,303)		$(14,195)
Plan assets at fair value		14,223		15,250
Excess of assets over projected benefit obligation		1,920		1,055
Unrecognized net (gains)[1]		(877)		(35)
Unrecognized prior service cost		459		364
Prepaid pension cost[2]		$ 1,502		$ 1,384

1 Includes the unamortized balance of $(1,339) and $(1,513) at December 31, 1994 and 1993, respectively, of unrecognized net gain at January 1, 1985, the initial application date of Statement of Financial Accounting Standards No. 87, "Employers' Accounting for Pensions."

2 Excludes the pension liability for unfunded plans of $820 and $744 and the related projected benefit obligation of $1,213 and $1,228 at December 31, 1994 and 1993, respectively.

Notes to Financial Statements

(Dollars in millions, except per share)

For U.S. plans, the projected benefit obligation was determined using a discount rate of 9 percent at December 31, 1994 and 7.25 percent at December 31, 1993, and an assumed long-term rate of compensation increase of 5 percent. The assumed long-term rate of return on plan assets is 9 percent. Plan assets consist principally of common stocks and U.S. government obligations. For non-U.S. plans, no one of which was material, similar economic assumptions were used.

The Omnibus Budget Reconciliation Act of 1990 permits employers to transfer some of the excess funds from an overfunded pension trust to pay the company portion of certain postretirement health care benefits. The company transferred $260 during 1993 to a special retiree health care account to be used toward the payment of these benefits. This transfer had no impact on earnings (see Note 25).

27. Derivatives and Other Hedging Instruments

The company enters into contractual arrangements (derivatives) in the ordinary course of business to hedge its exposure to foreign currency, interest rate and commodity price risks. The counterparties to these contractual arrangements are major financial institutions. The company is exposed to credit loss in the event of nonperformance by these counterparties. The company manages this exposure to credit loss through credit approvals, limits and monitoring procedures and, to the extent possible, by restricting the period over which unpaid balances are allowed to accumulate. The company does not anticipate nonperformance by counterparties to these contracts, and no material loss would be expected from any such nonperformance. Procedures are in place to regularly monitor and report to management the market and counterparty credit risks associated with these instruments. The company's accounting policies with respect to these financial instrument transactions are set forth in Note 1.

Foreign Currency

The company routinely uses forward exchange contracts to hedge its net exposures, by currency, related to the foreign currency-denominated monetary assets and liabilities of its operations. The primary business objective of this hedging program is to maintain an approximately balanced position in foreign currencies so that exchange gains and losses resulting from exchange rate changes, net of related tax effects, are minimized.

Principal foreign currency exposures and related hedge positions at December 31, 1994 were as follows:

Currency	Net Monetary Asset/(Liability) Exposure	Open Contracts To Buy/(Sell) Foreign Currency		Net After-Tax Exposure
		Pretax	After-Tax	
British Pound	$(1,428)	$2,306	$1,427	$ (1)
German Mark	$ (593)	$ 955	$ 595	$ 2
Norwegian Krone	$ (564)	$ 914	$ 567	$ 3
French Franc	$ 451	$ (620)	$ (453)	$ (2)
Italian Lira	$ 205	$ (333)	$ (206)	$ (1)
Dutch Guilder	$ 273	$ (355)	$ (271)	$ 2
Japanese Yen	$ (205)	$ 285	$ 204	$ (1)

Notes to Financial Statements

(Dollars in millions, except per share)

In addition, the company from time to time will enter into forward exchange contracts to establish with certainty the U.S. dollar amount of future firm commitments denominated in a foreign currency. Decisions regarding whether or not to hedge a given commitment are made on a case-by-case basis, taking into consideration the amount and duration of the exposure, market volatility and economic trends. At December 31, 1994, no such commitments were hedged. Forward exchange contracts are also used to manage near-term foreign currency cash require-ments and to place foreign currency deposits and marketable securities investments into currencies offering favorable returns. Net cash inflow/(outflow) from settlement of forward exchange contracts was $139, $(84) and $146 for the years 1994, 1993 and 1992, respectively.

Interest Rates

The company uses a combination of financial instruments, includ-ing interest rate swaps, interest and principal currency swaps and structured medium-term financings, as part of its program to manage the fixed and floating interest rate mix of the total debt portfolio and related overall cost of borrowing.

Interest rate swaps involve the exchange of fixed for floating rate interest payments that are fully integrated with underlying fixed rate bonds or notes to effectively convert fixed rate debt into floating rate debt based on LIBOR or commercial paper rates. Interest rate swaps also involve the exchange of floating for fixed rate interest payments that are fully integrated with commercial paper or other floating rate borrowings to effectively convert floating rate debt into fixed rate debt. Both types of interest rate swaps are denominated in U.S. dollars. Interest rate swaps allow the company to maintain a target range of floating rate debt. Notional amounts do not represent the amounts exchanged by the counterparties, and thus are not a measure of market or credit exposure to the company. The amounts exchanged by the counterparties are calculated on the basis of the notional amounts and the fixed and floating interest rates.

The following interest rate swaps were outstanding at December 31, 1994:

Type of Swap	Notional Amount	Weighted Average Rate Paid	Weighted Average Rate Received
Pay Fixed, Receive Floating	$ 50	8.3%	4.5%
Pay Floating, Receive Fixed	$775	5.4%	5.8%

These interest rate swaps mature in 1 to 3 years, with a weighted average maturity of 2.1 years.

Under interest and principal currency swaps, the company receives predetermined foreign currency-denominated payments corresponding, both as to timing and amount, to the fixed or floating interest rate and fixed principal amount to be paid by the company under concurrently issued foreign currency-denominated bonds. In return, the company pays a U.S. dollar-denominated fixed or floating interest rate and a U.S. dollar-denominated fixed principal amount to the counterparty, thereby effectively converting the foreign currency-denominated bonds into U.S. dollar-denominated obligations for both interest and principal. Interest and principal currency swaps allow the company to be fully hedged against fluctuations in currency exchange rates and foreign interest rates and to achieve U.S. dollar fixed or floating interest rate payments below the market interest rate, at the date of issuance, for borrowings of comparable maturity.

One interest and principal currency swap was outstanding at December 31, 1994 that effectively converted a 150 million Swiss franc borrowing with a 6.25 percent Swiss franc fixed interest rate and a maturity of 2000 to a U.S. dollar fixed principal amount of $103 with a 6.9 percent U.S. dollar fixed interest rate.

Structured medium-term financings consist of:

a) A structured medium-term note with interest and/or principal pay-ments (denominated in either U.S. dollars or foreign currencies) determined using a specified calculation incorporating changes in currency exchange rates or other financial indices; and

Notes to Financial Statements

(Dollars in millions, except per share)

b) A concurrently executed structured medium-term swap that, for any and all calculations of the note's interest and/or principal payments over the term of the note, provides a fully hedged transaction such that the note is effectively converted to a U.S. dollar-denominated fixed or floating interest rate with a U.S. dollar-denominated fixed principal amount. Structured medium-term swaps allow the company to be fully hedged against fluctuations in exchange rates and interest rates and to achieve U.S. dollar fixed or floating interest rate payments below the market interest rate, at the date of issuance, for borrowings of comparable maturity.

The face amount of these structured medium-term financings outstanding at December 31, 1994 was $522, with a weighted average interest rate of 6.1 percent, and a weighted average maturity of 1.9 years.

In addition, the company's majority-owned Canadian subsidiary had a structured medium-term financing outstanding at December 31, 1994 that effectively converted a 160 million Australian dollar borrowing, with a 16.5 percent Australian dollar fixed interest rate and a maturity of 1996, to a Canadian dollar borrowing with an implicit 12.43 percent Canadian dollar fixed interest rate.

It is the company's policy that foreign currency bonds and structured medium-term notes will not be issued unless a hedge of the market risks inherent in such borrowings is executed simultaneously with a management-approved, highly credit-worthy counterparty to provide a fully hedged transaction.

Interest rate financial instruments did not have a material effect on the company's overall cost of borrowing at December 31, 1994 and 1993.

See also Notes 17 and 19 for additional descriptions of interest rate financial instruments.

Summary of Outstanding Derivative Financial Instruments

Set forth below is a summary of the notional amounts, estimated fair values and carrying amounts of outstanding financial instruments at December 31, 1994 and 1993.

Notional amounts represent the face amount of the contractual arrangements and are not a measure of market or credit exposure. Estimated fair values represent a reasonable approximation of amounts the company would have received from/(paid to) a counterparty at December 31 to unwind the positions prior to maturity. Estimated fair value of forward exchange contracts is based on market prices for contracts of comparable time to maturity. Estimated fair value of swaps represents the present value of remaining net cash flows to maturity under swap agreements, discounted using market-implied future interest rates existing at December 31, 1994 and 1993, respectively. At December 31, 1994, the company had no plans to unwind these positions prior to maturity. Carrying amounts represent the receivable/(payable) recorded in the Consolidated Balance Sheet. See also Notes 10, 11, 15, 16, 17 and 19 for fair values and carrying amounts of other financial instruments.

Notional Amount, Estimated Fair Value and Carrying Amount of Outstanding Derivative Financial Instruments

Type of Instrument	Notional Amount	Estimated Fair Value	Carrying Amount
Forward Exchange Contracts			
December 31, 1994	$7,978	$ 62	$ 73
1993	9,181	7	10
Interest Rate Swaps			
December 31, 1994	$ 825	$(47)	$ (1)
1993	775	(3)	2
Interest and Principal Currency Swaps			
December 31, 1994	$ 103	$ 21	$ 11
1993	204	(24)	(31)
Structured Medium-Term Swaps			
December 31, 1994	$ 646	$ 23	$ 36
1993	1,172	30	38

Estimated fair values shown above only represent the value of the hedge or swap component of these transactions, and thus are not indicative of the fair value of the company's overall hedged position. The estimated fair value of the company's total debt portfolio, based on quoted market prices for the same or similar issues or on current rates offered to the company for debt of the same remaining maturities, was $7,900 and $10,400 at December 31, 1994 and 1993, respectively. The improvement in fair value of $2,500 in 1994 was primarily due to lower borrowing levels and the change in the interest rate environment. As fully hedged transactions, the estimated fair values of the integrated debt and interest rate financial instruments do not affect income and are not recorded in the financial statements, but rather only represent the amount to unwind the debt and financial instruments at a specific point in time prior to maturity.

Notes to Financial Statements

(Dollars in millions, except per share)

Commodity Hedges and Trading

The company enters into exchange-traded and over-the-counter commodity futures contracts to hedge its exposure to price fluctuations on anticipated crude oil, refined products and natural gas transactions and certain raw material purchases.

Commodity trading in petroleum futures contracts is a natural extension of cash market trading and is used to physically acquire about 15 percent of North America refining crude supply requirements. The commodity futures market has underlying principles of increased liquidity and longer trading periods than the cash market and is one method of reducing exposure to the price risk inherent in the petroleum business. Typically, trading is conducted to manage price risk around near-term (30–60 days) supply requirements. Occasionally, as market views and conditions allow, longer-term positions will be taken to manage price risk for the company's equity production (crude and natural gas) or net supply requirements. These positions may not exceed anticipated equity production or net supply requirements for the hedge period. The company's use of futures contracts reduces the effects of price volatility, thereby protecting against adverse short-term price movements, while limiting, somewhat, the benefits of favorable short-term price movements. Open hedge positions and deferred gains/losses for petroleum futures contracts were immaterial at December 31, 1994 and 1993.

From time to time, on a limited basis, the company also purchases and sells petroleum-based futures contracts for trading purposes. After-tax gain/loss from such trading has not been material.

28. Commitments and Contingent Liabilities

The company has various purchase commitments for materials, supplies and items of permanent investment incident to the ordinary conduct of business. In the aggregate, such commitments are not at prices in excess of current market.

The company is subject to various lawsuits and claims with respect to such matters as product liabilities, governmental regulations and other actions arising out of the normal course of business. While the effect on future financial results is not subject to reasonable estimation because considerable uncertainty exists, in the opinion of company counsel, the ultimate liabilities resulting from such lawsuits and claims will not materially affect the consolidated financial position of the company.

The company is also subject to contingencies pursuant to environmental laws and regulations that in the future may require the company to take action to correct the effects on the environment of prior disposal practices or releases of chemical or petroleum substances by the company or other parties. The company has accrued for certain environmental remediation activities consistent with the policy set forth in Note 1. At December 31, 1994, such accrual amounted to $616 and, in management's opinion, was appropriate based on existing facts and circumstances. Under the most adverse circumstances, however, this potential liability could be significantly higher. In the event that future remediation expenditures are in excess of amounts accrued, management does not anticipate that they will have a material adverse effect on the consolidated financial position of the company.

The company has indirectly guaranteed various debt obligations under agreements with certain affiliated and other companies to provide specified minimum revenues from shipments or purchases of products. At December 31, 1994, these indirect guarantees totaled $13. In addition, at December 31, 1994, the company had directly guaranteed $832 of the obligations of certain affiliated companies and others. No material loss is anticipated by reason of such agreements and guarantees.

Notes to Financial Statements

(Dollars in millions, except per share)

29. Geographic Information

	United States	Europe	Other Regions	Consolidated
1994				
Sales to Unaffiliated Customers[1]	$20,769	$14,216	$ 4,348	$39,333
Transfers Between Geographic Areas[2]	2,044	673	507	–
Total	$22,813	$14,889	$ 4,855	$39,333
After-Tax Operating Income	$ 1,993	$ 874	$ 240	$ 3,107
Identifiable Assets at December 31	$16,933	$10,232	$ 3,857	$31,022
1993				
Sales to Unaffiliated Customers[1]	$20,342	$12,639	$ 4,117	$37,098
Transfers Between Geographic Areas[2]	2,260	395	522	–
Total	$22,602	$13,034	$ 4,639	$37,098
After-Tax Operating Income	$ 133	$ 721	$ 63	$ 917
Identifiable Assets at December 31	$17,117	$ 9,995	$ 3,812	$30,924
1992				
Sales to Unaffiliated Customers[1]	$20,331	$13,571	$ 3,897	$37,799
Transfers Between Geographic Areas[2]	2,477	298	469	–
Total	$22,808	$13,869	$ 4,366	$37,799
After-Tax Operating Income	$ 528	$ 624	$ 89	$ 1,241
Identifiable Assets at December 31	$19,197	$ 9,667	$ 3,827	$32,691

1 *Sales outside the United States of products manufactured in and exported from the United States totaled $3,625 in 1994, $3,500 in 1993 and $3,509 in 1992.*
2 *Products are transferred between geographic areas on a basis intended to reflect as nearly as practicable the "market value" of the products.*

Consolidated Geographic Data

(Dollars in millions)

	Capital Expenditures		Total Assets December 31		Average Employment	
	1994	1993	**1994**	1993	**1994**	1993
United States	**$1,520**	$1,842	**$19,857**	$20,610	**73,507**	81,587
Europe	**1,317**	1,277	**11,957**	11,315	**22,624**	22,427
Other Regions	**404**	606	**5,078**	5,128	**14,376**	15,395
Total	**$3,241**	$3,725	**$36,892**	$37,053	**110,507**	119,409

Capital expenditures, total assets and average employment are assigned to geographic areas, generally based on physical location.

Notes to Financial Statements

(Dollars in millions, except per share)

30. Industry Segment Information

The company has five principal business segments that manufacture and sell a wide range of products to many different markets, including the energy, transportation, textile, construction, automotive, electronics, printing, health care, packaging and agricultural markets. The company's sales are not materially dependent on a single customer or small group of customers. The Fibers and Polymers segments, however, have several large customers in their respective industries that are important to these segments' operating results.

	Chemicals	Fibers	Polymers	Petroleum	Diversified Businesses	Consolidated
1994						
Sales to Unaffiliated Customers[1]	$ 3,760	$ 6,767	$ 6,318	$16,815[2]	$ 5,673	$39,333
Transfers Between Segments	208	44	181	388	36	–
Total	$ 3,968	$ 6,811	$ 6,499	$17,203	$ 5,709	$39,333
Operating Profit	$ 536	$ 1,083	$ 1,084	$ 1,141	$ 595	$ 4,439
Provision for Income Taxes	(208)	(412)	(423)	(486)	(191)	(1,720)
Equity in Earnings of Affiliates	58	30	56	25	219	388
After-Tax Operating Income[3]	$ 386	$ 701	$ 717	$ 680	$ 623	$ 3,107[4]
Identifiable Assets at December 31	$ 2,880	$ 6,020	$ 5,160	$11,961	$ 5,001	$31,022[5]
Depreciation, Depletion and Amortization	$ 412	$ 512	$ 403	$ 1,191	$ 434	$ 3,106[6]
Capital Expenditures	$ 298	$ 541	$ 310	$ 1,576	$ 283	$ 3,151[7]

	Chemicals	Fibers	Polymers	Petroleum	Diversified Businesses	Consolidated
1993						
Sales to Unaffiliated Customers[1]	$ 3,546	$ 6,188	$ 5,869	$15,771[2]	$ 5,724	$37,098
Transfers Between Segments	475	14	23	428	1	–
Total	$ 4,021	$ 6,202	$ 5,892	$16,199	$ 5,725	$37,098
Operating Profit	$ 237	$ 258	$ 255	$ 1,195	$ (495)	$ 1,450
Provision for Income Taxes	(99)	(144)	(108)	(428)	162	(617)
Equity in Earnings of Affiliates	28	55	30	45	(74)	84
After-Tax Operating Income[8, 9, 10]	$ 166	$ 169	$ 177	$ 812[11]	$ (407)[12]	$ 917[4]
Identifiable Assets at December 31	$ 2,960	$ 5,771	$ 5,226	$11,938	$ 5,029	$30,924[5]
Depreciation, Depletion and Amortization	$ 303	$ 658	$ 527	$ 1,379	$ 460	$ 3,451[6]
Capital Expenditures	$ 294	$ 751	$ 428	$ 1,659	$ 329	$ 3,655[7]

Notes to Financial Statements

(Dollars in millions, except per share)

	Chemicals	Fibers	Polymers	Petroleum	Diversified Businesses	Consolidated
1992						
Sales to Unaffiliated Customers[1]	$ 3,617	$ 6,074	$ 5,856	$16,065 [2]	$ 6,187	$37,799
Transfers Between Segments	187	6	51	414	5	–
Total	$ 3,804	$ 6,080	$ 5,907	$16,479	$ 6,192	$37,799
Operating Profit	$ 324	$ 591	$ 471	$ 1,008	$ (182)	$ 2,212
Provision for Income Taxes	(128)	(246)	(185)	(707)	101	(1,165)
Equity in Earnings of Affiliates	30	64	32	36	32	194
After-Tax Operating Income[13]	$ 226	$ 409	$ 318	$ 337	$ (49)[14]	$ 1,241[4]
Identifiable Assets at December 31	$ 3,201	$ 5,738	$ 5,412	$12,307	$ 6,033	$32,691[5]
Depreciation, Depletion and Amortization	$ 317	$ 592	$ 409	$ 1,006	$ 410	$ 2,839[6]
Capital Expenditures	$ 366	$ 856	$ 642	$ 1,781	$ 558	$ 4,397[7]

1 Sales of refined petroleum products of $12,853 in 1994, $12,403 in 1993 and $12,681 in 1992 exceeded 10 percent of consolidated sales.

2 Excludes crude oil and refined product exchanges and trading transactions totaling $2,254 in 1994, $3,808 in 1993 and $3,881 in 1992.

3 Includes the following (charges)/benefits[a]:

Chemicals[b]	$ (5)
Fibers	25
Polymers	11
Petroleum[c]	(26)
Diversified Businesses[d]	(53)
	$ (48)

a Reflects a net benefit of $112 from adjustments in estimates associated with the third quarter 1993 restructuring charge of which $88 relates to adjustments for other than employee separation costs. The $112 is reflected in Chemicals $22; Fibers $25; Polymers $11; and Diversified Businesses $54.

b Includes a charge of $27 associated with the discontinuation of certain products, asset sales and write-downs.

c Includes a charge of $58 for employee separation costs, a loss of $95 from the write-down of certain North Sea oil properties to be sold and a benefit of $127 principally related to a favorable change in tax status resulting from a transfer of properties among certain North Sea affiliates.

d Includes charges of $110 associated with the "Benlate" DF 50 fungicide recall and $27 for the write-down of assets and discontinuation of certain products, and a benefit of $30 from an adjustment of prior-year tax provisions.

4 The following reconciles After-Tax Operating Income to Net Income:

	1994	1993	1992
After-Tax Operating Income	**$3,107**	$ 917	$1,241
Interest and Other Corporate Expenses Net of Tax[a]	**(380)**	(351)	(266)
Net Income[b]	**$2,727**	$ 566	$ 975

a Includes interest and debt expense and other corporate expenses such as exchange gains and losses (including the company's share of equity affiliates' exchange gains and losses), minority interests in earnings of consolidated subsidiaries and amortization of capitalized interest. The year 1992 includes an exchange gain of $97 related to unhedged non-U.S. deferred tax liabilities, which were established on the adoption of SFAS No. 109.

b Before extraordinary item and transition effect of accounting changes. See the Consolidated Income Statement on page 39.

Notes to Financial Statements

(Dollars in millions, except per share)

5 *The following reconciles Identifiable Assets to Total Assets:*

	1994	1993	1992
Identifiable Assets at December 31	**$31,022**	$30,924	$32,691
Investment in Affiliates	**1,662**	1,607	1,746
Corporate Assets	**4,208**	4,522	4,433
Total Assets at December 31	**$36,892**	$37,053	$38,870

6 *Includes depreciation on research and development facilities, impairment of unproved properties and depreciation reflected in 1993 and 1992 restructuring charges.*

7 *Excludes investments in affiliates.*

8 *Includes the following third-quarter charges for asset write-downs, employee separation costs, facility shutdowns and other restructuring costs (see Note 6):*

Chemicals[a]	$ 112
Fibers[b]	266
Polymers[c]	148
Petroleum[d]	172
Diversified Businesses[e]	413
	$1,111

a *Includes $59 for asset write-downs and facility shutdowns for the fluorochemicals and specialty chemicals businesses.*

b *Includes $46 for facility shutdowns and asset write-downs, primarily for the nylon business.*

c *Includes $64 for shutdown of a portion of a polymers plant in LaPorte, Texas.* ·

d *Includes $147 for asset write-downs, primarily for certain North American petroleum-producing properties sold in the fourth quarter.*

e *Includes $264 for asset write-downs, principally facilities for the printing and publishing business.*

9 *Includes a net benefit of $265 resulting from tax law changes. The Petroleum segment reflects $230, primarily due to a reduction in deferred U.K. petroleum revenue taxes, and $35 is reflected in the remaining segments (Chemicals $6; Fibers $10; Polymers $10; and Diversified Businesses $9).*

10 *Includes a net charge of $92 related to certain product liability claims and litigation costs ($144, of which $126 is associated with the "Benlate" DF 50 fungicide recall) and a loss on the sale of a polyethylene business ($17), partly offset by a gain from the sale of the Remington Arms Company ($69). The foregoing amounts are reflected in the Chemicals ($10), Polymers ($25) and Diversified Businesses ($57) segments.*

11 *Includes a $21 loss from sale of petroleum-producing properties and a $32 gain from exchange of several proved and unproved North Sea petroleum properties for an interest in a Norwegian offshore pipeline and cash; since these are not "similar productive assets" as defined under Accounting Principles Board Opinion No. 29, a gain was recognized on the exchange.*

12 *Includes a charge of $184 for the write-down of intangible assets (technology and goodwill) associated with the printing and publishing business.*

13 *Includes the following fourth-quarter charges for termination incentives and payments, as well as other charges, related to business restructurings (see Note 6):*

Chemicals[a]	$ 51
Fibers[b]	69
Polymers	22
Petroleum[c]	96
Diversified Businesses[d]	91
	$329

a *Includes $38 charge for project and facility shutdowns.*

b *Includes $38 charge principally for shutdown of fire-damaged facilities.*

c *Includes $17 charge for shutdown of refinery facilities.*

d *Includes $42 charge principally for withdrawal from certain printing and publishing business lines.*

14 *Includes charge of $134 associated with "Benlate" DF 50 fungicide recall.*

See segment discussions on pages 16–28 for a description of each industry segment. Products are transferred between segments on a basis intended to reflect as nearly as practicable the "market value" of the products.

Supplemental Petroleum Data

(Dollars in millions)

Oil and Gas Producing Activities

The disclosures on pages 64–70 are presented in accordance with the provisions of Statement of Financial Accounting Standards No. 69. Accordingly, volumes of reserves and production exclude royalty interests of others, and royalty payments are reflected as reductions in revenues.

In January 1989, the U.S. Treasury Department was authorized by the President to modify the sanctions levied against Libya in 1986. In June 1989, Conoco was granted a license by the Treasury Department to resume its activities in Libya, and commenced negotiations with the Libyan government's national oil company. Although negotiations are continuing, Conoco has not resumed its participation in Libyan operations. Accordingly, disclosures for 1994 continue to exclude petroleum reserve data applicable to the company's petroleum assets in Libya.

Results of Operations for Oil and Gas Producing Activities

	Total Worldwide			United States			Europe			Other Regions[1]		
	1994	1993	1992	**1994**	1993	1992	**1994**	1993	1992	**1994**	1993	1992
Consolidated Companies												
Revenues:												
Sales to unaffiliated customers	**$ 2,196**	$ 2,177	$ 1,990	**$ 552**	$ 538	$ 535	**$ 1,015**	$ 1,000	$ 874	**$ 629**	$ 639	$ 581
Transfers to other company operations	**733**	930	1,003	**401**	558	583	**332**	372	407	–	–	13
Exploration, including dry hole costs	**(323)**	(329)	(347)	**(130)**	(107)	(82)	**(110)**	(109)	(165)	**(83)**	(113)	(100)
Production	**(786)**	(868)	(1,039)	**(327)**	(424)	(492)	**(377)**	(363)	(473)	**(82)**	(81)	(74)
Depreciation, depletion, amortization and valuation provisions	**(957)**	(1,140)	(786)	**(334)**	(591)[2]	(433)	**(533)**[3]	(468)	(296)	**(90)**	(81)	(57)
Other[4]	**67**	(20)	(55)	**38**	(17)	(8)	**25**	9	(28)	**4**	(12)	(19)
Income taxes	**(463)**	(281)	(626)	**7**	84	2	**(122)**[5]	(16)[6]	(219)	**(348)**	(349)	(409)
Total consolidated companies	**467**	469	140	**207**	41	105	**230**	425	100	**30**	3	(65)
Equity Affiliates												
Results of operations of equity affiliates	**(16)**	(13)	(13)	**1**	(1)	(1)	**(17)**	(12)	(12)	–	–	–
Total	**$ 451**	$ 456	$ 127	**$ 208**	$ 40	$ 104	**$ 213**	$ 413	$ 88	**$ 30**	$ 3	$ (65)

1 *Comprises exploration costs in all areas outside the United States and Europe and production operations primarily in Canada, Dubai and Indonesia.*

2 *Includes a charge of $219 ($137 after taxes) for impairment of certain U.S. petroleum-producing properties to be sold.*

3 *Includes a charge of $115 ($95 after taxes) for impairment of certain North Sea oil properties to be sold.*

4 *Includes gain/(loss) on disposal of fixed assets and other miscellaneous revenues and expenses.*

5 *Includes a tax benefit of $127 principally related to a favorable change in tax status resulting from a transfer of properties among certain North Sea affiliates.*

6 *Includes a benefit of $241 resulting from tax law changes in the United Kingdom.*

Supplemental Petroleum Data

(Dollars in millions)

Costs Incurred in Oil and Gas Property Acquisition, Exploration and Development Activities[1]

	Total Worldwide			United States			Europe			Other Regions[2]		
	1994	1993	1992	**1994**	1993	1992	**1994**	1993	1992	**1994**	1993	1992
Consolidated Companies												
Property acquisitions:												
Proved[3]	**$ 139**	$ 111	$ 16	**$ 14**	$ 93	$ 16	**$115**	$ 5	$ –	**$ 10**	$ 13	$ –
Unproved	**36**	11	23	**18**	8	7	**5**	–	–	**13**	3	16
Exploration	**403**	352	432	**151**	83	99	**136**	158	221	**116**	111	112
Development	**713**	864	806	**174**	195	206	**466**	567	498	**73**	102	102
Total consolidated companies	**1,291**	1,338	1,277	**357**	379	328	**722**	730	719	**212**	229	230
Equity Affiliates												
Property acquisitions:												
Proved	–	43	–	–	43	–	–	–	–	–	–	–
Development	**75**	70	38	**12**	16	19	**63**	54	19	–	–	–
Total equity affiliates	**75**	113	38	**12**	59	19	**63**	54	19	–	–	–
Total	**$1,366**	$1,451	$1,315	**$ 369**	$438	$347	**$785**	$784	$738	**$212**	$229	$230

1 These data comprise all costs incurred in the activities shown, whether capitalized or charged to expense at the time they were incurred.

2 Includes Canada, Dubai and Indonesia.

3 Does not include properties acquired through property exchanges.

Capitalized Costs Relating to Oil and Gas Producing Activities

	Total Worldwide			United States			Europe			Other Regions*		
	1994	1993	1992	**1994**	1993	1992	**1994**	1993	1992	**1994**	1993	1992
Consolidated Companies												
Gross costs:												
Proved properties	**$11,057**	$11,663	$11,356	**$ 4,806**	$4,934	$5,587	**$4,950**	$5,582	$4,732	**$1,301**	$1,147	$1,037
Unproved properties	**790**	701	1,152	**291**	321	471	**323**	218	461	**176**	162	220
Accumulated depreciation, depletion, amortization and valuation allowances:												
Proved properties	**6,173**	6,467	6,171	**3,073**	3,023	3,244	**2,122**	2,604	2,169	**978**	840	758
Unproved properties	**185**	261	347	**110**	162	235	**6**	13	13	**69**	86	99
Total net costs of consolidated companies	**5,489**	5,636	5,990	**1,914**	2,070	2,579	**3,145**	3,183	3,011	**430**	383	400
Equity Affiliates												
Net costs of equity affiliates:												
Proved properties	**253**	177	66	**93**	92	36	**160**	85	30	–	–	–
Total	**$ 5,742**	$ 5,813	$ 6,056	**$ 2,007**	$2,162	$2,615	**$3,305**	$3,268	$3,041	**$ 430**	$ 383	$ 400

* Includes Canada, Dubai and Indonesia.

Supplemental Petroleum Data

(In millions of barrels)

Estimated Proved Reserves of Oil[1]

	Total Worldwide			United States			Europe			Other Regions[2]		
	1994	1993	1992	**1994**	1993	1992	**1994**	1993	1992	**1994**	1993	1992
Proved Developed and Undeveloped Reserves of Consolidated Companies												
Beginning of year	**964**	1,034	1,112	**344**	421	470	**390**	391	392	**230**	222	250
Revisions and other changes	**51**	14	26	**14**	(6)	(13)	**26**	13	37	**11**	7	2
Extensions and discoveries	**50**	83	23	**8**	19	9	**21**	41	10	**21**	23	4
Improved recovery	**10**	7	3	**9**	5	3	**–**	–	–	**1**	2	–
Purchase of reserves[3]	**43**	25	5	**14**	7	5	**29**	2	–	**–**	16	–
Sale of reserves[4]	**(33)**	(64)	(12)	**(20)**	(62)	(12)	**(13)**	(2)	–	**–**	–	–
Production	**(132)**	(135)	(123)	**(33)**	(40)	(41)	**(59)**	(55)	(48)	**(40)**	(40)	(34)
End of year	**953**	964	1,034	**336**	344	421	**394**	390	391	**223**	230	222
Proved Developed and Undeveloped Reserves of Equity Affiliates												
Beginning of year	**19**	19	–	**–**	–	–	**19**	19	–	**–**	–	–
Revisions and other changes	**6**	–	–	**–**	–	–	**6**	–	–	**–**	–	–
Extensions and discoveries	**11**	–	19	**–**	–	–	**11**	–	19	**–**	–	–
Production	**(1)**	–	–	**–**	–	–	**(1)**	–	–	**–**	–	–
End of year	**35**	19	19	**–**	–	–	**35**	19	19	**–**	–	–
Total	**988**	983	1,053	**336**	344	421	**429**	409	410	**223**	230	222
Proved Developed Reserves of Consolidated Companies												
Beginning of year	**708**	750	778	**332**	397	441	**160**	153	118	**216**	200	219
End of year	**706**	708	750	**324**	332	397	**171**	160	153	**211**	216	200

1 Oil reserves comprise crude oil and condensate and natural gas liquids (NGL) expected to be removed for the company's account from its natural gas deliveries.

2 Includes Canada, Dubai and Indonesia.
3 Includes reserves acquired through property exchanges.
4 Includes reserves disposed of through property exchanges.

Supplemental Petroleum Data

(In billion cubic feet)

Estimated Proved Reserves of Gas

	Total Worldwide			United States			Europe			Other Regions[1]		
	1994	1993	1992	**1994**	1993	1992	**1994**	1993	1992	**1994**	1993	1992
Proved Developed and Undeveloped Reserves of Consolidated Companies												
Beginning of year	**3,680**	3,445	3,619	**1,802**	1,928	2,149	**1,752**	1,417	1,321	**126**	100	149
Revisions and other changes	**317**	72	(36)	**121**	(22)	(55)	**187**	54	56	**9**	40	(37)
Extensions and discoveries	**514**	712	307	**139**	196	127	**356**	507	172	**19**	9	8
Improved recovery	**–**	1	–	**–**	1	–	**–**	–	–	**–**	–	–
Purchase of reserves[2]	**375**	53	37	**42**	53	37	**321**	–	–	**12**	–	–
Sale of reserves[3]	**(71)**	(122)	(51)	**(37)**	(49)	(51)	**(34)**	(68)	–	**–**	(5)	–
Production	**(485)**	(481)	(431)	**(318)**	(305)	(279)	**(151)**	(158)	(132)	**(16)**	(18)	(20)
End of year	**4,330**	3,680	3,445	**1,749**	1,802	1,928	**2,431**	1,752	1,417	**150**	126	100
Proved Developed and Undeveloped Reserves of Equity Affiliates												
Beginning of year	**586**	368	128	**586**	368	128	–	–	–	–	–	–
Revisions and other changes	**255**	72	167	**255**	72	167	–	–	–	–	–	–
Extensions and discoveries	**–**	–	75	**–**	–	75	–	–	–	–	–	–
Purchase of reserves	**2**	151	–	**2**	151	–	–	–	–	–	–	–
Production	**(13)**	(5)	(2)	**(13)**	(5)	(2)	–	–	–	–	–	–
End of year	**830**	586	368	**830**	586	368	–	–	–	–	–	–
Total	**5,160**	4,266	3,813	**2,579**	2,388	2,296	**2,431**	1,752	1,417	**150**	126	100
Proved Developed Reserves of Consolidated Companies												
Beginning of year	**2,570**	2,539	2,750	**1,717**	1,837	2,013	**738**	618	602	**115**	84	135
End of year	**2,496**	2,570	2,539	**1,687**	1,717	1,837	**683**	738	618	**126**	115	84

1 Includes Canada, Dubai and Indonesia.
2 Includes reserves acquired through property exchanges.
3 Includes reserves disposed of through property exchanges.

Supplemental Petroleum Data

Standardized Measure of Discounted Future Net Cash Flows Relating to Proved Oil and Gas Reserves

The information on the following page has been prepared in accordance with Statement of Financial Accounting Standards No. 69, which requires the standardized measure of discounted future net cash flows to be based on year-end sales prices, costs and statutory income tax rates and a 10 percent annual discount rate. Specifically, the per-barrel oil sales prices used to calculate the December 31, 1994 data averaged $14.38 for the United States, $15.81 for Europe and $16.08 for Other Regions, and the gas prices per thousand cubic feet averaged approximately $1.59 for the United States, $2.87 for Europe and $1.34 for Other Regions. Because prices used in the calculation are as of December 31, the standardized measure could vary significantly from year to year based on market conditions at that specific date.

The projections should not be viewed as realistic estimates of future cash flows nor should the "standardized measure"

be interpreted as representing current value to the company. Material revisions to estimates of proved reserves may occur in the future, development and production of the reserves may not occur in the periods assumed, actual prices realized are expected to vary significantly from those used and actual costs may also vary. The company's investment and operating decisions are not based on the information presented on the following page, but on a wide range of reserve estimates that includes probable as well as proved reserves, and on different price and cost assumptions from those reflected in this information.

Beyond the above considerations, the "standardized measure" is also not directly comparable with asset balances appearing elsewhere in the financial statements because any such comparison would require reconciling adjustments, including reduction of the asset balances for related deferred income taxes.

Supplemental Petroleum Data

(Dollars in millions)

Standardized Measure of Discounted Future Net Cash Flows Relating to Proved Oil and Gas Reserves

	Total Worldwide			United States			Europe			Other Regions*		
	1994	1993	1992	1994	1993	1992	1994	1993	1992	1994	1993	1992
Consolidated Companies												
Future cash flows:												
Revenues	$23,836	$19,558	$24,439	$ 7,201	$ 7,199	$10,027	$12,945	$ 9,380	$10,785	$ 3,690	$ 2,979	$ 3,627
Production costs	(8,967)	(9,117)	(10,011)	(3,411)	(4,361)	(5,228)	(4,719)	(4,005)	(4,119)	(837)	(751)	(664)
Development costs	(1,693)	(1,802)	(1,719)	(184)	(515)	(534)	(1,439)	(1,143)	(1,001)	(70)	(144)	(184)
Income tax expense	(6,084)	(3,607)	(6,022)	(873)	(414)	(1,060)	(2,893)	(1,514)	(2,585)	(2,318)	(1,679)	(2,377)
Future net cash flows	7,092	5,032	6,687	2,733	1,909	3,205	3,894	2,718	3,080	465	405	402
Discounted to present value at a 10% annual rate	(2,817)	(1,818)	(2,379)	(1,154)	(655)	(1,239)	(1,522)	(1,021)	(1,000)	(141)	(142)	(140)
Total consolidated companies	4,275	3,214	4,308	1,579	1,254	1,966	2,372	1,697	2,080	324	263	262
Equity Affiliates												
Standardized measure of discounted future net cash flows of equity affiliates	211	99	70	102	96	55	109	3	15	–	–	–
Total	$ 4,486	$ 3,313	$ 4,378	$ 1,681	$ 1,350	$ 2,021	$ 2,481	$ 1,700	$ 2,095	$ 324	$ 263	$ 262

*   *Includes Canada, Dubai and Indonesia.*

Supplemental Petroleum Data

(Dollars in millions)

Summary of Changes in Standardized Measure of Discounted Future Net Cash Flows Relating to Proved Oil and Gas Reserves for Fully Consolidated Companies

	1994	1993	1992
Balance at January 1	$3,214	$4,308	$3,558
Sales and transfers of oil and gas produced, net of production costs	(2,143)	(2,239)	(2,053)
Development costs incurred during the period	713	864	833
Net changes in prices and in development and production costs	1,275	(3,017)	765
Extensions, discoveries and improved recovery, less related costs	775	915	453
Revisions of previous quantity estimates	796	130	178
Purchases (sales) of reserves in place—net	333	(120)	(42)
Accretion of discount	529	791	689
Net change in income taxes	(1,174)	1,493	(369)
Other	(43)	89	296
Balance at December 31	$4,275	$3,214	$4,308

Five-Year Financial Review[1]

(Dollars in millions, except per share)

	1994	1993	1992	1991	1990
Summary of Operations					
Sales	**$39,333**	$37,098	$37,799	$38,695	$40,047
Earnings Before Income Taxes	**$ 4,382**	$ 958	$ 1,811	$ 2,818	$ 4,154
Provision for Income Taxes	**$ 1,655**	$ 392	$ 836	$ 1,415	$ 1,844
Net Income[2]	**$ 2,727**	$ 566	$ 975	$ 1,403	$ 2,310
As Percent of Average Stockholders' Equity[2]	**22.6%**	4.8%	8.1%	8.3%	14.3%
Earnings Per Share of Common Stock[2,3]	**$ 4.00**	$ .83	$ 1.43	$ 2.08	$ 3.40
Financial Position at Year End					
Working Capital	**$ 3,543**	$ 1,460	$ 2,002	$ 3,381	$ 2,210
Total Assets	**$36,892**	$37,053	$38,870	$36,559	$38,128
Borrowings and Capital Lease Obligations:					
Short Term	**$ 1,292**	$ 2,796	$ 3,799	$ 1,841	$ 3,928
Long Term	**$ 6,376**	$ 6,531	$ 7,193	$ 6,456	$ 5,663
Stockholders' Equity	**$12,822**	$11,230	$11,765	$16,739	$16,418
Total Debt as Percent of Total Capitalization	**37%**	45%	48%	33%	37%
General					
For the Year:					
Capital Expenditures	**$ 3,241**	$ 3,725	$ 4,524	$ 5,246	$ 5,513
Depreciation, Depletion and Amortization	**$ 2,976**	$ 2,833	$ 2,655	$ 2,640	$ 2,625
Research and Development Expense	**$ 1,047**	$ 1,132	$ 1,277	$ 1,298	$ 1,428
As Percent of Combined Segment Sales for:					
Chemicals, Fibers, Polymers and Diversified Businesses	**4.5%**	5.1%	5.6%	5.8%	6.2%
Petroleum	**0.3%**	0.3%	0.4%	0.4%	0.3%
Average Number of Shares Outstanding (millions)	**680**	677	673	671	676
Dividends Per Common Share	**$ 1.82**	$ 1.76	$ 1.74	$ 1.68	$ 1.62
Dividends as Percent of Earnings on Common Stock[2]	**46%**	212%	122%	81%	48%
Common Stock Prices:					
High	**$ 62⅜**	$ 53⅞	$ 54⅞	$ 50	$ 42⅜
Low	**$ 48¼**	$ 44½	$ 43½	$ 32¾	$ 31⅜
Year-End Close	**$ 56⅛**	$ 48¼	$ 47⅛	$ 46⅝	$ 36¾
At Year End:					
Employees (thousands)	**107**	114	125	133	144
Common Stockholders of Record (thousands)	**172**	181	188	195	199
Book Value Per Common Share	**$ 18.48**	$ 16.22	$ 17.08	$ 24.58	$ 24.16

1 See Management's Discussion and Analysis on pages 30–36, Consolidated Income Statement on page 39, Notes to Financial Statements on pages 43–63 and Quarterly Financial Data on page 71 for information relating to significant items affecting the results of operations and financial position.

2 Before effect on income of extraordinary item (1993 and 1992) and transition effect of accounting changes (1992). See the Consolidated Income Statement on page 39.

3 Based on the average number of common shares outstanding.

APPENDIX B

DOW CHEMICAL COMPANY

CONSOLIDATED BALANCE SHEETS

In millions		December 31 1994	December 31 1993
	Assets		
Current Assets	Cash and cash equivalents	$ **569**	$ 407
	Marketable securities and interest-bearing deposits	**565**	430
	Accounts and notes receivable:		
	Trade (less allowance for doubtful receivables– 1994, $104; 1993, $93)	**3,359**	2,587
	Other	**1,099**	1,245
	Inventories:		
	Finished and work in process	**2,079**	1,984
	Materials and supplies	**633**	542
	Deferred income taxes receivable–current	**389**	457
	Total current assets	**8,693**	7,652
Investments	Capital stock at cost plus equity in accumulated earnings of 20%-50% owned companies	**931**	1,019
	Other investments	**1,529**	1,726
	Noncurrent receivables	**330**	369
	Total investments	**2,790**	3,114
Plant Properties	Plant properties	**23,210**	21,608
	Less accumulated depreciation	**14,484**	13,028
	Net plant properties	**8,726**	8,580
Other Assets	Goodwill (net of accumulated amortization– 1994, $676; 1993, $563)	**4,365**	4,434
	Deferred income taxes receivable–noncurrent	**1,132**	933
	Deferred charges and other assets	**839**	792
	Total other assets	**6,336**	6,159
Total Assets		**$26,545**	$25,505

See Notes to Financial Statements.

In millions, except for share amounts		December 31	
		1994	*1993*
	Liabilities and Stockholders' Equity		
Current Liabilities	Notes payable	$ 741	$ 877
	Long-term debt due within one year	534	165
	Accounts payable:		
	Trade	1,928	1,479
	Other	634	765
	Income taxes payable	664	245
	Deferred income taxes payable–current	56	199
	Dividends payable	202	200
	Accrued and other current liabilities	1,859	1,721
	Total current liabilities	6,618	5,651
Long-Term Debt		5,303	5,902
Deferred Taxes and	Deferred income taxes payable–noncurrent	644	372
Other Liabilities	Pension and other postretirement benefits–noncurrent	1,987	1,918
	Other noncurrent obligations	1,253	1,173
	Total deferred taxes and other liabilities	3,884	3,463
Minority Interest in Subsidiary Companies		2,506	2,439
Temporary Equity	Preferred stock (authorized 250,000,000 shares of $1.00 par value each; issued Series A–1994: 1,549,014; 1993: 1,566,677) at redemption value	133	135
	Less guaranteed ESOP obligation	111	119
	Total temporary equity	22	16
Stockholders' Equity	Common stock (authorized 500,000,000 shares of $2.50 par value each; issued 1994: 327,125,854; 1993: 327,125,854)	818	818
	Additional paid-in capital	326	366
	Retained earnings	8,857	8,645
	Unrealized gains (losses) on investments	(21)	105
	Cumulative translation adjustments	(330)	(304)
	Treasury stock, at cost (shares 1994: 50,002,967; 1993: 52,640,015)	(1,438)	(1,596)
	Net stockholders' equity	8,212	8,034
Total Liabilities and Stockholders' Equity		$26,545	$25,505

See Notes to Financial Statements.

CONSOLIDATED STATEMENTS OF INCOME

In millions, except for share amounts		**1994**	1993	1992
Net Sales		**$20,015**	$18,060	$18,971
Operating Costs	Cost of sales	**13,219**	12,195	12,704
and Expenses	Insurance and finance company operations, pretax income	**(40)**	(98)	(15)
	Research and development expenses	**1,261**	1,256	1,289
	Promotion and advertising expenses	**658**	678	795
	Selling and administrative expenses	**2,403**	2,230	2,328
	Amortization of intangibles	**169**	179	147
	Special charge (Note B)	**–**	180	433
	Total operating costs and expenses	**17,670**	16,620	17,681
Operating Income		**2,345**	1,440	1,290
Other Income (Expense)	Equity in earnings (losses) of 20%-50% owned companies (Note Q)	**63**	(111)	71
	Interest income	**131**	167	109
	Capitalized interest	**66**	66	78
	Interest expense and amortization of debt discount	**(603)**	(666)	(773)
	Net gain (loss) on foreign currency transactions	**7**	(10)	11
	Net gain (loss) on investments (Note C)	**(60)**	592	–
	Sundry income–net	**103**	47	86
	Total other income (expense)	**(293)**	85	(418)
Income before Provision for Taxes on Income and Minority Interests		**2,052**	1,525	872
Provision for Taxes on Income		**779**	606	274
Minority Interests' Share in Income (Note K)		**335**	275	322
Income before Cumulative Effect of Accounting Change		**938**	644	276
Cumulative Effect of Accounting Change, Net of Taxes on Income (Note B)		**–**	–	(765)
Net Income (Loss)		**938**	644	(489)
Preferred Stock Dividends		**7**	7	7
Net Income (Loss) Available for Common Stockholders		**$ 931**	$ 637	$ (496)
Average Common Shares Outstanding		**276.1**	273.6	271.6
Earnings (Loss)	Before cumulative effect of accounting change	**$ 3.37**	$ 2.33	$ 0.99
per Common Share:	Cumulative effect of accounting change (Note B)	**–**	–	(2.82)
	Net earnings (loss) per common share	**$ 3.37**	$ 2.33	$ (1.83)
Common Stock Dividends Declared per Share		**$ 2.60**	$ 2.60	$ 2.60

See Notes to Financial Statements.

CONSOLIDATED STATEMENTS OF STOCKHOLDERS' EQUITY

In millions		1994	1993	1992
Common Stock	Balance at beginning and end of year	$ **818**	$ 818	$ 818
Additional Paid-in Capital	Balance at beginning of year	**366**	350	346
	Tax benefit of contingent value rights	**–**	34	45
	Issuance of treasury stock at less than cost	**(40)**	(18)	(41)
	Balance at end of year	**326**	366	350
Retained Earnings	Balance at beginning of year	**8,645**	8,720	9,920
	Net income (loss)	**938**	644	(489)
	Unfunded pension obligations	**–**	–	3
	Preferred stock dividends declared	**(7)**	(7)	(7)
	Common stock dividends declared	**(719)**	(712)	(707)
	Balance at end of year	**8,857**	8,645	8,720
Unrealized Gains (Losses) on Investments	Balance at beginning of year	**105**	(2)	(2)
	Unrealized gains (losses)	**(126)**	107	–
	Balance at end of year	**(21)**	105	(2)
Cumulative Translation Adjustments	Balance at beginning of year	**(304)**	(107)	194
	Translation adjustments	**(26)**	(197)	(301)
	Balance at end of year	**(330)**	(304)	(107)
Treasury Stock	Balance at beginning of year	**(1,596)**	(1,715)	(1,835)
	Purchases	**(38)**	(17)	(10)
	Issuance to employees and employee plans	**196**	136	130
	Balance at end of year	**(1,438)**	(1,596)	(1,715)
Net Stockholders' Equity		$ **8,212**	$ 8,034	$ 8,064

See Notes to Financial Statements.

CONSOLIDATED STATEMENTS OF CASH FLOWS

In millions		1994	1993	1992
Operating Activities	Income before cumulative effect of accounting change	$ **938**	$ 644	$ 276
	Adjustments to reconcile net income to net cash provided by operating activities:			
	Depreciation and amortization	**1,525**	1,552	1,487
	Provision (credit) for deferred income tax	**34**	24	(295)
	Undistributed (earnings) losses of 20%-50% owned companies	**(48)**	147	(27)
	Minority interests' share in income	**335**	275	322
	Net (gain) loss on investments (Note C)	**60**	(592)	–
	Net gain on sales of plant properties	**(73)**	(58)	(22)
	Net (gain) loss on foreign currency transactions	**(7)**	10	(11)
	Special charge (Note B)	**–**	180	433
	Other	**6**	13	10
	Changes in assets and liabilities that provided (used) cash:			
	Accounts receivable	**(513)**	(8)	(17)
	Inventories	**(171)**	207	195
	Accounts payable	**238**	139	(275)
	Other assets and liabilities [1]	**311**	(440)	(45)
	Cash provided by operating activities	**2,635**	2,093	2,031
Investing Activities	Purchases of plant properties	**(1,183)**	(1,414)	(1,608)
	Investments in unconsolidated affiliates	**(43)**	(103)	(90)
	Purchases of consolidated companies (net of cash acquired) (Note C)	**(88)**	(307)	(397)
	Proceeds from sales of plant properties	**111**	100	62
	Proceeds from outside investors in limited partnerships (Note K)	**–**	380	855
	Purchases of investments	**(1,171)**	(237)	(127)
	Proceeds from sales of investments (Note C)	**1,179**	959	–
	Cash used in investing activities	**(1,195)**	(622)	(1,305)
Financing Activities	Changes in short-term notes payable	**(62)**	121	(248)
	Proceeds from issuance of long-term debt	**108**	969	1,231
	Payments on long-term debt	**(391)**	(1,675)	(791)
	Purchases of treasury stock	**(38)**	(17)	(10)
	Proceeds from sales of common stock	**110**	82	82
	Distributions to minority interests	**(281)**	(198)	(143)
	Dividends paid to stockholders	**(723)**	(719)	(710)
	Cash used in financing activities	**(1,277)**	(1,437)	(589)
Effect of Exchange Rate Changes on Cash		**(1)**	(2)	2
Summary	Increase in cash and cash equivalents	**162**	32	139
	Cash and cash equivalents at beginning of year	**407**	375	236
	Cash and cash equivalents at end of year	$ **569**	$ 407	$ 375

See Notes to Financial Statements.

[1] *Excludes cumulative effect of accounting change.*

NOTES TO FINANCIAL STATEMENTS

In millions, except for share amounts

Table of Contents

A   Summary of Significant Accounting Policies 30
B   Special Charge and Accounting Change 31
C   Acquisitions and Divestitures 32
D   Taxes on Income 33
E   Inventories 34
F   Related Company Transactions 34
G   Plant Properties 34
H   Leased Properties 34
I   Notes Payable, Long-Term Debt and
        Available Credit Facilities 35

J   Financial Instruments 36
K   Limited Partnerships 37
L   Stockholders' Equity 37
M   Stock Option Plans 38
N   Redeemable Preferred Stock 38
O   Pension Plans 38
P   Other Postretirement Benefits 39
Q   Commitments and Contingent Liabilities 40
R   Supplementary Information 42
S   Industry Segments and Geographic Areas 42

A   Summary of Significant Accounting Policies

Principles of Consolidation The accompanying consolidated financial statements of The Dow Chemical Company and its subsidiaries (the Company) include the assets, liabilities, revenues and expenses of all majority-owned subsidiaries. Intercompany transactions and balances are eliminated in consolidation. Investments in companies 20%-50% owned (related companies) are accounted for on the equity basis.

Reclassifications Certain reclassifications of prior years' amounts have been made to conform to the presentation adopted for 1994.

Foreign Currency Translation The local currency has primarily been used as the functional currency throughout the world. Translation gains and losses of those operations that use local currency as the functional currency, and the effects of exchange rate changes on transactions designated as hedges of net foreign investments, are included as a separate component of stockholders' equity. Where the U.S. dollar is used as the functional currency, foreign currency gains and losses are reflected in income currently.

Cash and Cash Equivalents Cash and cash equivalents include time deposits and readily marketable securities with original maturities of three months or less.

Inventories Inventories are stated at the lower of cost or market. The method of determining cost is used consistently from year to year at each subsidiary and varies among the last-in, first-out (LIFO) method; the first-in, first-out (FIFO) method; and the average cost method.

Plant Properties, Investments and Other Assets Land, buildings and equipment, including property under capital lease agreements, are carried at cost less accumulated depreciation. Depreciation is based on the estimated service lives of depreciable assets and is generally provided using the declining balance method. Fully depreciated assets are retained in property and depreciation accounts until they are removed from service. In the case of disposals, assets and related depreciation are removed from the accounts and the net amount, less proceeds from disposal, is charged or credited to income.

The excess of the cost of investments in subsidiaries over the carrying value of assets acquired is shown as goodwill, which is amortized on a straight-line basis over its estimated useful life with a maximum of 40 years.

The Company evaluates long-lived assets for impairment based on the recoverability of the asset's carrying amount. When it is probable that undiscounted future cash flows will not be sufficient to recover the asset's carrying amount, the asset is written down to its fair value.

Gain Recognition on Sale of Subsidiaries' Stock Company policy is to record gains from the sale or other issuance of previously unissued stock by its subsidiaries.

Financial Instruments Interest differentials on swaps and forward rate agreements designated as hedges of exposures to interest rate risk are recorded as adjustments to interest expense over the contract period. Premiums for early termination of derivatives designated as hedges are amortized as adjustments to interest expense over the original contract period. Interest derivatives not designated as hedges are marked-to-market at the end of each accounting period.

The Company calculates the fair value of financial instruments using quoted market prices whenever available. When quoted market prices are not available, the Company uses standard pricing models for various types of financial instruments (such as forwards, options, swaps, etc.) which take into account the present value of estimated future cash flows.

Investments in debt and equity securities are classified as either Trading, Available-for-Sale or Held-to-Maturity. Investments classified as Trading are reported at fair value with unrealized gains and losses included in income. Investments classified as Available-for-Sale are reported at fair value with unrealized gains and losses recorded in a separate component of stockholders' equity. Investments classified as Held-to-Maturity are recorded at amortized cost.

The cost of investments sold is determined by specific identification.

In millions, except for share amounts

A   Summary of Significant Accounting Policies *(continued)*

Environment Accruals for environmental matters are recorded when it is probable that a liability has been incurred and the amount of the liability can be reasonably estimated, based on current law and existing technologies. These accruals are adjusted periodically as assessment and remediation efforts progress or as additional technical or legal information becomes available. Accruals for environmental liabilities are generally included in the balance sheet as "Other noncurrent obligations" at undiscounted amounts and exclude claims for recoveries from insurance or other third parties. Accruals for insurance or other third party recoveries for environmental liabilities are recorded when it is probable that a claim will be realized. Accruals for recoveries are included in the balance sheet as "Noncurrent receivables."

Environmental costs are capitalized if the costs extend the life of the property, increase its capacity, and/or mitigate or prevent contamination from future operations. Costs related to environmental contamination treatment and cleanup are charged to expense.

Taxes on Income The Company accounts for taxes on income using the asset and liability method wherein deferred tax assets and liabilities are recognized for the future tax consequences of temporary differences between the carrying amounts and tax bases of assets and liabilities using enacted rates.

Provision is made for taxes on undistributed earnings of foreign subsidiaries and related companies to the extent that such earnings are not deemed to be permanently invested.

Certain countries provide tax incentives which are granted to encourage new investment. Generally, such grants are credited to income as earned.

Earnings per Common Share The calculation of earnings per share is based on the weighted average number of common shares outstanding during the applicable period.

B   Special Charge and Accounting Change
The second quarter of 1993 included a special pretax charge of $180 by Marion Merrell Dow Inc. (MMDI). The special charge reflected the impact of a number of steps intended to reduce costs and position MMDI for the future, including work force reduction and U.S. business reorganization. The special charge has had total cash expenditures of $107 ($65 in 1994, $42 in 1993), all of which have been funded from operations. Asset write-downs have been $4. At December 31, 1994, the special charge liability was $69. Work force reduction efforts are expected to result in estimated payroll and benefit cost savings in 1995 of $127. The actions intended by the restructuring are expected to be substantially complete by December 1995. The Company owns 71 percent of MMDI.

During the fourth quarter of 1992, opportunities were identified to streamline the Company and a special pretax charge of $433 was taken. This charge reflected asset write-offs and write-downs, plant shutdowns, divestitures and the consolidation of a variety of business activities globally. Included were costs related to work force reductions associated with these activities. The actions

contemplated by the special charge were substantially complete at December 31, 1993, with no significant adjustments required to the estimates.

Effective January 1, 1994, the Company adopted Statement of Financial Accounting Standards (SFAS) No. 112 (Employers' Accounting for Postemployment Benefits). The impact on net income for the year was not material.

Effective January 1, 1992, the Company adopted SFAS No. 106 (Employers' Accounting for Postretirement Benefits Other Than Pensions) and SFAS No. 109 (Accounting for Income Taxes). SFAS No. 106 requires employers to recognize the cost of certain health care and life insurance benefits provided to retirees and their dependents as a liability during the employees' active years of service. In making the transition to adopt this required accounting standard, a charge of $994 or $3.66 per share was made against 1992 net income. SFAS No. 109 requires an asset and liability approach for financial accounting and reporting for income taxes. The favorable cumulative effect of its implementation was $229 or 84 cents per share in 1992. The net impact of adopting SFAS Nos. 106 and 109 was a cumulative charge of $765 against 1992 net income.

NOTES TO FINANCIAL STATEMENTS

In millions, except for share amounts

C   Acquisitions and Divestitures

In 1994, the Company recognized a pretax gain of $90 on its common shares in Magma Power Company (Magma), primarily as a result of the merger agreement between Magma and California Energy Company, Inc.

In the fourth quarter of 1994, the Company recorded a pretax charge of $132 related to the pending sale of the Personal Care business of DowBrands.

During the third quarter of 1994, Dow Deutschland Inc., a subsidiary of the Company, signed a letter of intent to study and evaluate the restructuring potential of several state-owned chemical assets in eastern Germany with the intention of acquiring a majority position.

During January and February of 1994, Marion Merrell Dow Inc. (MMDI) increased its ownership of Kodama Ltd. (Kodama), a Japanese pharmaceutical corporation, to 91 percent. By December 31, 1994, MMDI had further increased its ownership of Kodama to 99.8 percent. The net cash cost for 1994 was $101.

In November 1993, Dow Chemical Canada Inc. (DCCI) sold shares of Crestar Energy Inc. (Crestar). The net proceeds to the Company were $172 and generated a pretax gain of $101. As a result of the sale, DCCI's common share holding in Crestar was reduced from 50 percent to 17.5 percent.

In October 1993, MMDI acquired The Rugby Group, Inc., the U.S.'s largest generic drug company, from the privately held Rugby-Darby Group Companies, Inc. for $285.

In June 1993, the Company sold 3.6 million shares of common stock in Magma for which it received gross proceeds of $116. The sale generated a pretax gain of $62 in 1993. In October 1993, the Company sold its option to purchase 2 million shares of Magma common stock to Magma and received consideration of 857,143 shares of Magma's common stock.

In January 1993, the Company sold its 50 percent ownership in the Dowell Schlumberger group of companies to Schlumberger Limited. The selling price was $675 in cash and a warrant to purchase 7.5 million shares of Schlumberger stock with an exercise price of $59.95 per share. The warrant is fully vested and nontransferable, and expires in the year 2000. The sale generated a pretax gain of $450.

The Company acquired an additional 2.1 million shares of MMDI common stock during 1993 and 1.4 million shares during 1992 at costs of $36 and $43, respectively. The increased interests were accounted for as purchases with increases to goodwill of $21 and $29, respectively.

In millions, except for share amounts

D Taxes on Income

Operating loss carryforwards at December 31, 1994 amounted to $870 of which $108 is subject to expiration in 1995, $176 in 1996, $87 in 1997, $39 in 1998 and $5 in 1999. The remaining balances expire in years beyond 1999 or have an indefinite carryforward period.

Tax credit carryforwards at December 31, 1994 amounted to $100 of which $3 is subject to expiration in 1995, $3 in 1996, $4 in 1997, $1 in 1998 and $2 in 1999. The remaining balances expire in years beyond 1999 or have an indefinite carryforward period.

Undistributed earnings of subsidiaries and related companies which are deemed to be permanently invested amounted to $2,053, $1,782 and $1,989 at December 31, 1994, 1993 and 1992, respectively. It is not practicable to calculate the unrecognized deferred tax liability on those earnings.

The movement in the valuation allowance during 1994 was a net reduction of $37 due primarily to business improvement and an extension in the loss carryforward period in Spain.

Domestic and Foreign Components of Income before
Taxes on Income and Minority Interests

	1994	1993	1992
Domestic	$1,161	$1,099	$632
Foreign	891	426	240
Total	$2,052	$1,525	$872

Reconciliation to U.S. Statutory Rate

	1994	1993	1992
Taxes at U.S. statutory rate	$718	$534	$296
Amortization of nondeductible intangibles	83	45	43
Taxes on foreign operations at rates different from U.S. statutory rate (including FSC)	(4)	29	37
Other–net	(18)	(2)	(102)
Total tax provision	$779	$606	$274
Effective tax rate	38.0%	39.7%	31.4%

Provision (Credit) for Taxes on Income

	1994			1993			1992		
	Current	Deferred	Total	Current	Deferred	Total	Current	Deferred	Total
Federal	$457	$13	$470	$404	$ (8)	$396	$381	$(158)	$223
State and local	23	2	25	63	–	63	39	–	39
Foreign	265	19	284	115	32	147	149	(137)	12
Total	$745	$34	$779	$582	$24	$606	$569	$(295)	$274

Deferred Tax Balances at December 31

	1994		1993	
	Deferred Tax Assets	Deferred Tax Liabilities	Deferred Tax Assets	Deferred Tax Liabilities
Property	$ 83	$ (799)	$ 94	$ (732)
Inventory	104	(102)	103	(95)
Accounts receivable	58	(55)	47	(29)
Pension and other compensation accruals	107	(49)	127	(47)
Tax loss and credit carryforwards	330	–	355	–
Long-term debt	131	(19)	66	(16)
Alternative minimum tax	80	–	102	–
Accrual for postretirement benefit obligations	624	(9)	625	–
Investments	30	(93)	76	(96)
Amortization of intangibles	28	(1)	15	(37)
Other accruals and reserves	379	(9)	305	(10)
Other–net	201	(175)	141	(115)
Subtotal	$2,155	$(1,311)	$2,056	$(1,177)
Less: Valuation allowance	23	–	60	–
Total	$2,132	$(1,311)	$1,996	$(1,177)

NOTES TO FINANCIAL STATEMENTS

In millions, except for share amounts

E Inventories

A reduction of certain inventories resulted in the liquidation of some quantities of LIFO inventory, which increased pretax income by $16 in 1994 and decreased pretax income by $18 in 1993 and $6 in 1992.

The amount of reserve required to reduce inventories from the first-in, first-out basis to the last-in, first-out basis at December 31, 1994 and 1993, was $119 and $106, respectively. The inventories that were valued on a LIFO basis represented 35 and 41 percent of the total inventories at December 31, 1994 and 1993, respectively.

F Related Company Transactions

The Company's investments in related companies accounted for by the equity method at December 31, 1994 and 1993 were $931 and $1,019, respectively, which approximated the Company's equity in the net assets of these companies.

Dividends received from related companies were $15 in 1994, $36 in 1993 and $45 in 1992. All other transactions with related companies, and balances due to or from related companies, were not material in amount.

G Plant Properties

Plant Properties at December 31

	1994	1993
Land	$ 414	$ 359
Land and waterway improvements	660	607
Buildings	2,337	2,177
Transportation and construction equipment	211	199
Machinery and equipment	15,332	14,191
Utility and supply lines	1,315	1,244
Office furniture and equipment	836	757
Wells and mineral reserves	355	240
Other	184	229
Construction in progress	1,566	1,605
Total	$23,210	$21,608

Depreciation expense was $1,321 in 1994, $1,343 in 1993 and $1,342 in 1992. Maintenance and repair costs were $974 in 1994, $1,004 in 1993 and $1,152 in 1992.

H Leased Properties

The Company routinely leases premises for use as sales and administrative offices, warehouses and tanks for product storage, motor vehicles, railcars, computers, office machines and equipment under operating leases. In addition, the Company leases a vinyl chloride plant and a Canadian subsidiary leases an ethylene plant. The Company has the option to purchase these plants and certain other leased equipment and buildings at the termination of the leases.

Rental expenses under operating leases were $459, $482 and $554 for 1994, 1993 and 1992, respectively. The minimum future lease commitments for all operating leases are included at right.

Minimum Operating Lease Commitments

1995	$ 297
1996	272
1997	250
1998	402
1999	360
2000 and thereafter	1,358
Total minimum lease commitments	$2,939

In millions, except for share amounts

▌ Notes Payable, Long-Term Debt and Available Credit Facilities

Notes payable at December 31, 1994 and 1993 consisted of obligations due banks with a variety of interest rates and maturities. The notes payable outstanding at December 31, 1994 and 1993 were $741 and $877, respectively, on which the year-end weighted average interest rates were 4.80 percent and 4.20 percent, respectively, excluding the effects of short-term borrowings in highly inflationary countries. Included in notes payable at December 31, 1994 and 1993 was commercial paper of $191 and $225, respectively.

The average interest rate on long-term debt was 6.64 percent in 1994 compared to 7.43 percent in 1993. Annual installments on long-term debt for the next five years are as follows: 1995, $534; 1996, $387; 1997, $649; 1998, $330; 1999, $230. During 1994, $526 of long-term debt was retired. Included in this amount was $135 of 5.75% subordinated exchangeable notes due in 2001 that were exchanged for shares of Magma Power Company.

The Company had unused and available credit facilities at December 31, 1994, with various U.S. and foreign banks totaling $2,043, which required the payment of commitment fees. Additional unused credit facilities totaling $2,276 at December 31, 1994 were available for use by foreign subsidiaries. These facilities are available in support of commercial paper borrowings and working capital requirements.

Promissory Notes and Debentures at December 31

	1994	1993
4.63%, final maturity 1995	$ 150	$ 150
8.25%, final maturity 1996	150	150
5.75%, final maturity 1997	200	200
5.75%, final maturity 2001	15	150
7.38%, final maturity 2002	150	150
9.35%, final maturity 2002	200	200
7.13%, final maturity 2003	150	150
8.63%, final maturity 2006	200	200
8.55%, final maturity 2009	150	150
9.00%, final maturity 2010	150	150
9.20%, final maturity 2010	200	200
6.85%, final maturity 2013	150	150
7.13%, final maturity 2015	24	150
9.00%, final maturity 2021	300	300
8.85%, final maturity 2021	200	200
8.70%, final maturity 2022	138	150
7.38%, final maturity 2023	150	150
Subtotal	$2,677	$2,950

Guaranteed ESOP Obligations at December 31

	1994	1993
9.42%, final maturity 2004, Dow ESOP	$ 111	$ 119
9.11%, final maturity 2005, MMDI ESOP	90	95
Subtotal	$ 201	$ 214

Foreign Bonds at December 31

	1994	1993
6.75%, final maturity 1995, German mark	$ 194	$ 173
5.63%, final maturity 1996, German mark	194	173
10.87%, final maturity 1997, British pound sterling	374	354
4.00%, final maturity 1998, Japanese yen	201	179
4.75%, final maturity 1999, Swiss franc	152	135
4.63%, final maturity 2000, Swiss franc	114	101
6.38%, final maturity 2001, Japanese yen	251	224
Subtotal	$1,480	$1,339

Other Facilities – Various Rates and Maturities at December 31

	1994	1993
Foreign currency loans	$ 255	$ 339
U.S. dollar loans	4	50
Medium-term notes, final maturity 2022	585	607
Pollution control/industrial revenue bonds, final maturity 2024	707	684
Unexpended construction funds	(20)	(50)
Capital lease obligations	32	40
Subtotal	$1,563	$1,670

Long-Term Debt at December 31

	1994	1993
Promissory notes and debentures	$2,677	$2,950
Guaranteed ESOP obligations	201	214
Foreign bonds	1,480	1,339
Other facilities	1,563	1,670
Less unamortized debt discount	(84)	(106)
Less long-term debt due within one year	(534)	(165)
Long-term debt	$5,303	$5,902

NOTES TO FINANCIAL STATEMENTS

In millions, except for share amounts

J   Financial Instruments

Fair Value of Financial Instruments at December 31

	1994				1993			
	Cost	Gain	Loss	Fair Value	Cost	Gain	Loss	Fair Value
Nonderivatives:								
Interest-bearing deposits	$ 92	–	–	$ 92	$ 105	–	–	$ 105
Marketable equity and debt securities:								
Trading	414	$20	–	434	433	$ 7	–	440
Available-for-Sale								
Debt securities	824	3	$(22)	805	732	38	$ (3)	767
Equity securities	454	64	(45)	473	489	205	(22)	672
Held-to-Maturity	408	1	(1)	408	177	3	(3)	177
Other	337	–	(7)	330	357	–	(4)	353
Total investments	$ 2,529	$88	$(75)	$ 2,542	$ 2,293	$253	$ (32)	$ 2,514
Long-term debt	$(5,303)	$33	–	$(5,270)	$(5,902)	–	$(391)	$(6,293)
Derivatives relating to:								
Foreign currency	–	$52	$(70)	$ (18)	–	$ 9	–	$ 9
Interest	–	37	(45)	(8)	–	176	$(130)	46
Cross-currency swaps	–	15	(93)	(78)	–	–	–	–

The cost approximates the fair value for all other financial instruments.

Investments   Total investments at December 31, 1994 and 1993 included cash equivalents of $455 and $362, marketable securities and interest-bearing deposits of $565 and $430, and other investments of $1,529 and $1,726, respectively.

The proceeds from sales of Available-for-Sale securities were $981 for 1994. These sales resulted in gross realized gains of $55 and losses of $26.

Maturities for most debt securities ranged from one to ten years for the Available-for-Sale classification and one to five years for the Held-to-Maturity classification at December 31, 1994.

Foreign Currency Risk Management   The Company's global operations require active participation in the foreign exchange markets. The Company enters into foreign exchange forward contracts and options to hedge various currency exposures or create desired exposures. Exposures primarily relate to (a) assets and liabilities denominated in foreign currency in Europe, Asia and Canada; (b) bonds denominated in foreign currency; and (c) economic exposure derived from the risk that currency fluctuations could affect the dollar value of future cash flows at the operating margin level. The primary business objective of the activity is to optimize the U.S. dollar value of the Company's assets, liabilities and future cash flows with respect to exchange rate fluctuations. Hedging is done on a net exposure basis. Namely, assets and liabilities denominated in the same currency are netted and only the balance is hedged.

At December 31, 1994 and 1993, the Company had forward contracts outstanding with various expiration dates (primarily in January of the next year) to buy, sell or exchange foreign currencies with a U.S. dollar equivalent of $6,573 and $3,664, respectively. The unrealized gains or losses on these contracts, based on the foreign exchange rates at December 31, 1994 and 1993, were a loss of $18 and a gain of $9, respectively, and were included in income in "Net gain (loss) on foreign currency transactions."

Interest Rate Risk Management   The Company enters into various interest rate contracts with the objective of lowering funding costs, diversifying sources of funding or altering interest rate exposure. In these contracts, the Company agrees with other parties to exchange, at specified intervals, the difference between fixed and floating interest amounts calculated on an agreed upon notional principal amount.

The notional principal on all types of interest derivative contracts at December 31, 1994 and 1993 totaled $4,264 and $9,302, with a weighted average remaining life of 3.3 and 3.8 years, respectively. The $37 in gains and $45 in losses in 1994 related to interest derivatives were not recognized in income as they represented hedges of debt-related exposures. The $15 in gains and $93 in losses in 1994 related to cross-currency swaps were primarily recognized in income in "Net gain (loss) on foreign currency transactions" and offset the gains and losses from the assets and liabilities being hedged. In 1993, there were $176 in gains and $130 in losses related to cross-currency swaps and interest derivatives. Of these amounts, $142 in gains and $103 in losses had not been recognized in income as they represented hedges of debt-related exposures.

Interest Derivatives at December 31, 1994

	Notional Amount	Maturities	Weighted Average Rate	
			Receive	Pay
Cross-currency swaps	$1,427	1995–1999	–	–
Receive Fixed Hedge	1,630	1995–2005	6.1%	5.5%
Receive Floating Hedge	1,024	1996–2005	5.5%	6.8%
Other	183	1995–1998	–	–

The Company's risk management program for both foreign currency and interest rate risk is based on fundamental, mathematical and technical models that take into account the implicit cost of hedging. Risks created by derivative instruments and the mark-to-market valuations of positions are strictly monitored at all times.

In millions, except for share amounts

J   Financial Instruments *(continued)*

The Company uses portfolio sensitivities and stress tests to monitor risk. Because the counterparties to these contracts are major international financial institutions, credit risk arising from these contracts is not significant and the Company does not anticipate any such losses. The net cash requirements arising from risk management activities are not expected to be material. The Company's overall financial strategies and impacts from using derivatives in

its risk management program are reviewed periodically with the Finance Committee of the Company's Board of Directors and revised as market conditions dictate.

The Company's global orientation in diverse businesses with a large number of diverse customers and suppliers minimizes concentrations of credit risk. No concentration of credit risk existed at December 31, 1994.

K   Limited Partnerships

In April 1993, three wholly owned subsidiaries of the Company contributed assets with an aggregate fair value of $977 to Chemtech Royalty Associates L.P. (Chemtech), a newly formed Delaware limited partnership. In August and October 1993, outside investors acquired limited partner interests in Chemtech totaling 20 percent in exchange for $200.

In April 1993, two wholly owned subsidiaries of Marion Merrell Dow Inc. (MMDI) contributed assets with an aggregate fair value of approximately $1 billion to Carderm Capital L.P. (Carderm), a newly formed Delaware limited partnership. Outside investors made contributions of $180 in October 1993 in exchange for limited partner interests in Carderm totaling 15 percent.

In December 1991, three wholly owned subsidiaries of the Company contributed assets with an aggregate market value of $2 billion to DowBrands L.P., a newly formed Delaware limited partnership. Outside investors made cash contributions of $45 in December 1991 and $855 in June 1992 in exchange for an aggregate 31 percent limited partner interest in DowBrands L.P.

The three partnerships (Chemtech, Carderm and DowBrands L.P.) are separate and distinct legal entities from the Company and its affiliates and have separate assets, liabilities, businesses and operations. Each partnership has as a general partner a wholly owned subsidiary of either the Company or MMDI which directs the business activities of the partnership and has

fiduciary responsibilities to the partnership and its other partners.

The outside investors in each partnership will receive a cumulative annual priority return on their investments in the partnership and participate in residual earnings. The annual priority return is $14, $11 and $67 for Chemtech, Carderm and DowBrands L.P., respectively.

The partnerships will not terminate unless a termination or liquidation event occurs. One such event, which is within the control of outside investors, occurs in the year 2000 for Chemtech and Carderm and 1996 for DowBrands L.P. In addition, the partnership agreements provide for various windup provisions wherein subsidiaries of the Company or MMDI may purchase at any time the limited partnership interests of the outside investors. Upon windup, liquidation or termination, the partners' capital accounts will be redeemed at current fair values.

For financial reporting purposes, the assets (other than intercompany loans, which are eliminated), liabilities, results of operations and cash flows of the partnerships and subsidiaries are included in the Company's consolidated financial statements and outside investors' limited partnership interests are reflected as minority interests.

Supplemental contractual disclosures required by the partnership agreements are contained within Note R of the December 31, 1993 Form 10-K of The Dow Chemical Company.

L   Stockholders' Equity

The authorized capital stock consists of 250 million preferred shares with a par value of $1.00 per share, and 500 million shares of common stock with a par value of $2.50 per share. The only preferred shares issued are the convertible preferred shares discussed in Note N. The number of common shares issued has remained at 327,125,854 for the last three years.

There are no significant restrictions limiting the Company's ability to pay dividends.

Undistributed earnings of 20%-50% owned companies included in retained earnings were $269 and $290 at December 31, 1994 and 1993, respectively.

In computing earnings per common share, no adjustment was made for common shares issuable under award, option and stock purchase plans, or conversion of preferred shares issued, because there would be no material dilutive effect.

The Board of Directors has authorized, subject to certain business and market conditions, the purchase of up to 18,000,000

shares of the Company's common stock. At December 31, 1994, the number of shares purchased under this authorization was approximately 3,700,000.

The number of treasury shares purchased was 591,000 in 1994, 300,000 in 1993 and 169,000 in 1992. The number of treasury shares issued to employees was 2,836,000 in 1994, 1,946,000 in 1993 and 2,051,000 in 1992. The number of treasury shares contributed to the pension plan for funding future retiree health care benefits through a 401(h) account was 391,000 in 1994 and 251,000 in 1993.

Reserved Treasury Stock at December 31

In thousands of shares	**1994**	*1993*	*1992*
Stock option plans	**16,517**	15,807	14,171
Employees' stock purchase plan	**894**	1,040	1,120
Total shares reserved	**17,411**	16,847	15,291

NOTES TO FINANCIAL STATEMENTS

In millions, except for share amounts

M Stock Option Plans

The Company has various stock option plans. Options under all plans are granted at the market price of the shares on the date of the grants.

Option Plans

In thousands of shares	1994	1993	1992
Outstanding at January 1	14,059	11,657	9,986
Granted	2,634	3,431	2,688
Exercised	(1,862)	(567)	(801)
Expired	(96)	(462)	(216)
Outstanding at December 31	14,735	14,059	11,657
Price Range	$23.54–$74.63	$18.46–$60.88	$18.46–$60.88
Exercisable at December 31	12,189	10,776	8,869
Available for future grant	559	407	1,177

Stock options were exercised at prices ranging from $18.46 to $65.06 in 1994, $18.46 to $59.75 in 1993 and $18.46 to $60.88 in 1992.

The Company made offerings of common stock to its employees, excluding directors, in 1994, 1993 and 1992 at $54.50, $45.00 and $48.00 per share, respectively, payable generally through payroll deductions. Unfilled subscriptions, cancelable at the option of the employee, were 894,000, 1,040,000 and 1,120,000 shares at December 31, 1994, 1993 and 1992, respectively. Partial payments received on these subscriptions aggregating $32, $28 and $33 at December 31, 1994, 1993 and 1992, respectively, were included in current liabilities.

N Redeemable Preferred Stock

The Company has an employee stock ownership plan (the ESOP), which is an integral part of the Salaried Employees Savings Plan.

The ESOP borrowed funds at a 9.42 percent interest rate with a final maturity in 2004, and used the proceeds to purchase convertible preferred stock from the Company. The preferred stock is convertible into approximately 1.5 million shares of the Company's common stock at $86.125 per common share. The dividend yield on the preferred stock is 7.75 percent of the $86.125 redemption value.

In the event the Company consummates certain merger or consolidation transactions involving the Company's common stock, the preferred stock must be redeemed by the Company for cash at a redemption price equal to 105 percent of the $86.125 per share redemption value, plus accrued and unpaid dividends.

The convertible preferred stock issued to the ESOP is reported as temporary equity in the Company's balance sheet. Since the Company has guaranteed the ESOP's borrowings, the principal amount of the ESOP loan has been reported as long-term debt and a reduction of temporary equity in the Company's balance sheet.

O Pension Plans

The Company has defined benefit pension plans which cover employees in the U.S. and a number of foreign countries. The Company's funding policy is to contribute annually, at a rate that is intended to approximate a level percentage of compensation for the covered employees, to those plans where pension laws and economics either require or encourage funding.

The U.S. funded plan is the largest plan. Its benefits are based on length of service and the employee's three-highest consecutive years of compensation. The weighted average discount rate and rate of increase in future compensation levels used in determining the actuarial present value of the projected benefit obligations were 7.75 and 5.5 percent, respectively, for 1994 and 7.25 and 5.5 percent, respectively, for 1993. The assumed long-term rate of return on assets was 9 percent for 1994 and 1993.

All other pension plans used assumptions in determining the actuarial present value of the projected benefit obligations that are consistent with (but not identical to) those of the U.S. plan.

Defined contribution plans cover employees in some subsidiaries in the U.S. and in other countries, including Australia, France, Spain, and the United Kingdom. In addition, employees in the U.S. are eligible to participate in defined contribution plans (Employee Savings Plans) by contributing a portion of their compensation. The Company matches compensation deferrals, depending on Company profit levels. Contributions charged to income for defined contribution plans were $71 in 1994, $76 in 1993 and $83 in 1992.

The net periodic pension cost for all significant defined benefit plans was as follows:

Net Periodic Pension Cost

	1994	1993	1992
Service cost – benefits earned during the period	$ 170	$ 152	$ 122
Interest cost on projected benefit obligation	347	333	306
Actual (return) on assets	(93)	(494)	(341)
Amortization and deferred amounts	(266)	153	47
Employee contributions to the plans	(8)	(8)	(9)
Net periodic pension cost	$ 150	$ 136	$ 125

In millions, except for share amounts

O Pension Plans *(continued)*

The funded status of significant defined benefit plans for the Company was as follows:

Defined Benefit Plans at December 31	Fully Funded		Partially Funded	
	1994	*1993*	**1994**	*1993*
Actuarial present value of benefit obligation:				
Vested	**$(3,287)**	$(3,173)	**$(467)**	$(361)
Nonvested	**(292)**	(324)	**(40)**	(50)
Accumulated benefit obligation	**(3,579)**	(3,497)	**(507)**	(411)
Effect of projected compensation increases	**(826)**	(838)	**(125)**	(164)
Projected benefit obligation for services rendered to date	**(4,405)**	(4,335)	**(632)**	(575)
Plan assets at market value, primarily publicly traded stocks and bonds	**4,439**	4,534	**221**	208
Plan assets in excess of (less than) projected benefit obligation	**34**	199	**(411)**	(367)
Unrecognized transition obligation	**28**	29	**45**	35
Unrecognized net (gains) losses	**57**	(84)	**(1)**	51
Unrecognized prior service cost	**9**	(4)	**39**	48
Additional minimum liability	**–**	–	**(49)**	(8)
Accrued pension asset (liability)	**$ 128**	$ 140	**$(377)**	$(241)

P Other Postretirement Benefits

The Company provides certain health care and life insurance benefits to retired employees. The Company funds most of the cost of these health care and life insurance benefits as incurred.

The U.S. plan covering the parent company is the largest plan. The plan provides health care benefits, including hospital, physicians' services, drug and major medical expense coverage, and life insurance benefits. The plan provides benefits supplemental to Medicare after retirees are eligible for these benefits, except for employees hired after December 31, 1992. The cost of these benefits is shared by the Company and the retiree, with the Company portion increasing as the retiree has increased years of credited service. The Company has the ability to change these benefits at any time.

Effective October 1993, the Company amended its health care benefits plan in the U.S. to cap the cost absorbed by the Company at approximately twice the 1993 cost per person for employees who retire after December 31, 1993. Effective April 1994, the Company extended this amendment to cover all other retired employees. The effect of the October 1993 amendment was to reduce the net periodic postretirement cost by $21 for 1993 and the accumulated postretirement benefit obligation by $327 at December 31, 1993. The effect of the April 1994 amendment was to reduce the net periodic postretirement cost by $71 for 1994 and the accumulated postretirement benefit obligation by $101 at December 31, 1994.

For 1994, a discount rate of 7.75 percent and weighted average medical cost trend rates starting at 9.47 percent and declining to 5.53 percent in 2004 were assumed. For 1993, the discount rate assumption was 7.25 percent and the medical cost trend rate assumption was 10.65 percent declining to 5.03 percent in 2004. The assumed long-term rate of return on assets was 9 percent for 1994 and 1993. Increasing the assumed medical cost trend rate by 1 percentage point in each year would increase the accumulated postretirement benefit obligation at December 31, 1994 by $33 and the net periodic postretirement benefit cost for the year by $3.

All other postretirement health care and other benefit plans used assumptions in determining the actuarial present value of accumulated postretirement benefit obligations that are consistent with (but not identical to) those of the U.S. parent company plan.

The net periodic benefit cost of all significant plans was as follows:

Net Periodic Postretirement Cost

	1994	*1993*	*1992*
Service costs – benefits earned during the period	**$ 26**	$ 35	$ 38
Interest cost on accumulated postretirement benefit obligation	**89**	122	127
Amortization and deferred amounts	**(43)**	(9)	–
Net periodic postretirement cost	**$ 72**	$148	$165

The postretirement benefit obligations of all significant plans were as follows:

Partially Funded Postretirement Plans at December 31

	1994	*1993*
Accumulated postretirement benefit obligation:		
Retirees	**$ (676)**	$ (792)
Fully eligible active plan participants	**(290)**	(279)
Other active plan participants	**(210)**	(234)
Total accumulated postretirement benefit obligation	**(1,176)**	(1,305)
Plan assets at market value, primarily publicly traded stocks and bonds	**52**	20
Unfunded accumulated postretirement benefit obligation	**(1,124)**	(1,285)
Unrecognized gain from experience favorable to assumptions	**(166)**	(81)
Negative prior service costs	**(373)**	(319)
Accrued postretirement benefit liability	**$(1,663)**	$(1,685)

NOTES TO FINANCIAL STATEMENTS

In millions, except for share amounts

Q Commitments and Contingent Liabilities

In January 1994, Dow Corning Corporation (Dow Corning), in which Dow is a 50 percent shareholder, announced a pretax charge of $640 ($415 after tax) for the fourth quarter of 1993. In January 1995, Dow Corning announced a pretax charge of $241 ($152 after tax) for the fourth quarter of 1994. These charges included Dow Corning's best estimate of its potential liability for breast implant litigation based on the settlement approved by Judge Sam C. Pointer, Jr. of the U.S. District Court for the Northern District of Alabama (the Court); litigation and claims outside of this breast implant settlement; and provisions for legal, administrative and research costs related to breast implants. The charges for 1993 and 1994 included pretax amounts of $1,240 and $441, respectively, less expected insurance recoveries of $600 and $200, respectively. The 1993 amounts reported by Dow Corning were determined on a present value basis. On an undiscounted basis, the estimated liability above for 1993 was $2,300 less expected insurance recoveries of $1,200.

As a result of the Dow Corning actions, the Company recorded its 50 percent share of the charges, net of tax benefits available to Dow. The impact on the Company's net income was a charge of $192 for 1993 and a charge of $70 for 1994.

In March 1994, Dow Corning signed a Breast Implant Litigation Settlement Agreement (the Settlement Agreement) which was preliminarily approved by the Court in April 1994. The Settlement Agreement received final approval by the Court on September 1, 1994. The Company is not a signatory to the Settlement Agreement and is not required to contribute to the settlement. In certain circumstances, if any defendant who is a signatory to the Settlement Agreement considers the number of plaintiffs who have opted out and maintained lawsuits against such defendant to be excessive, such defendant may withdraw from participation in the Settlement Agreement.

Various preliminary estimates of the aggregate number of plaintiffs who have indicated an intent to opt out of the settlement (the Opt Out Plaintiffs) have been made public. Dow Corning has reported that, since July 1, 1994, many former Opt Out Plaintiffs have rejoined the settlement. The Court is continuing to collect information relating to the number of Opt Out Plaintiffs. Dow Corning has stated that, as information is received from the Court, Dow Corning will continue to evaluate the nature and scope of the current or potential future claims of these Opt Out Plaintiffs. Opt Out Plaintiffs may continue to rejoin the settlement until the March 1, 1995 date established by the Court.

The date by which Dow Corning was required to decide whether to remain as a participant in or to exercise the first of its options to withdraw from the Settlement Agreement was extended to September 9, 1994. On September 8, 1994, Dow Corning's Board of Directors approved Dow Corning's continued participation in the Settlement Agreement. Initial claims were required to be filed with the Court by September 16, 1994. After these claims and the supporting medical records have been evaluated by the Court for validity, eligibility, accuracy, and consistency, the Court will determine whether contributions to the settlement are sufficient to pay validated claims. The date by which this process will be completed is uncertain. If contributions are not sufficient, claimants with validated claims may have the ability to become Opt Out Plaintiffs during another specified period. In that event, if any defendant who is a signatory to the Settlement Agreement considers the number of new Opt Out Plaintiffs to be excessive, such defendant may decide to exercise a second option to withdraw from participation in the Settlement Agreement. There can be no assurance that Dow Corning will not withdraw from participation in the Settlement Agreement.

Dow Corning has reported that, as additional facts and circumstances develop, the estimate of its potential liability may be revised, or provisions may be necessary to reflect any additional costs of resolving breast implant litigation and claims not covered by the settlement. Any future charge by Dow Corning resulting from a revision or provision, if required, could have a material adverse impact on the Company's net income for the period in which it is recorded by Dow Corning, but would not have a material adverse impact on the Company's consolidated cash flows or financial position. The Company's maximum exposure for breast implant product liability claims against Dow Corning is limited to its investment in Dow Corning which, at December 31, 1994, was $337.

The Company is separately named as a defendant in many of the breast implant claims and lawsuits. It is the opinion of the Company's management that the possibility is remote that the litigation of these claims will have a material adverse impact on the Company's consolidated financial statements.

Numerous lawsuits have been brought against the Company and other chemical companies alleging that the manufacture, distribution or use of pesticides containing dibromochloropropane (DBCP) has caused, among other things, property damage, including contamination of groundwater. To date, there have been no verdicts or judgments against the Company in connection with these allegations. It is the opinion of the Company's management that the possibility is remote that the resolution of such lawsuits will have a material adverse impact on the Company's consolidated financial statements.

In millions, except for share amounts

Q   Commitments and Contingent Liabilities *(continued)*

The Company has accrued $234 at December 31, 1994, for probable environmental remediation and restoration liabilities, including $29 for the remediation of Superfund sites. This is management's best estimate of these liabilities, although possible costs for environmental remediation and restoration could range up to 50 percent higher. It is the opinion of the Company's management that the possibility is remote that costs in excess of those accrued or disclosed will have a material adverse impact on the Company's consolidated financial statements.

In addition to the breast implant, DBCP and environmental remediation matters, the Company and its subsidiaries are parties to a number of other claims and lawsuits arising out of the normal course of business with respect to commercial matters, including product liabilities, governmental regulation and other actions. Certain of these actions purport to be class actions and seek damages in very large amounts. All such claims are being contested.

Except for the possible effect on the Company's net income for charges which may be taken by Dow Corning for breast implant litigation, it is the opinion of the Company's management that the possibility is remote that the aggregate of all claims and lawsuits will have a material adverse impact on the Company's consolidated financial statements.

On behalf of Destec Energy, Inc. (Destec), a 76 percent owned subsidiary, the Company has guaranteed the lease payments of a Destec subsidiary which leases the Lyondell cogeneration facility near Houston, Texas. Minimum lease payments total $145 for the noncancelable portion of the lease which runs through March 31, 1995. The guarantee is cancelable upon proper notice on any anniversary date of the guarantee.

Destec entered into an agreement with the U.S. Department of Energy, PSI Energy Inc. (PSI), and a third party owner to design, construct, and operate a 262 megawatt syngas facility which will repower an existing PSI turbine. Destec will provide coal gasification services under a 25-year contract. Associated with the above agreement, Destec assumed a construction performance obligation of $161 with project completion scheduled for third quarter 1995, at which time Destec will lease the plant. The lease commitments are included in Note H.

Destec contracted to design, engineer, build and operate a cogeneration facility in central Florida for a partnership in which Destec owns approximately 50 percent. Commercial operations commenced in January 1995 as planned. Destec has guaranteed $33 to fund its equity contribution.

Destec contracted to design, engineer and build a 424 megawatt cogeneration facility in Freeport, Texas and is a 50 percent partner in Oyster Creek Limited which owns the facility. The Company has agreed to purchase steam and power from the facility and estimates that its minimum annual obligation to outside parties is $20, increasing 3 percent annually through 2014.

Eli Lilly and Company (Lilly) is a 40 percent partner with the Company in DowElanco, a global agricultural products joint venture. Lilly holds a put option requiring the Company to purchase Lilly's interest in DowElanco at fair market value. Lilly notified the Company in September 1994 that it did not plan to exercise the put option at that time. No subsequent notification has been received.

A Canadian subsidiary has entered into two 20-year agreements to purchase 89 percent of the output of an ethylene plant (Plant No. 1) and 40 percent of the output of a second ethylene plant (Plant No. 2). The purchase price of the output is determined on a cost-of-service basis which, in addition to covering all operating expenses and debt service costs, provides the owner of the plants with a specified return on capital. Total purchases under the agreements were $252, $237 and $236 in 1994, 1993 and 1992, respectively. The contracts related to Plants No. 1 and No. 2 expire in 1998 and 2004, respectively.

DCS Capital Corporation (the Corporation) is 100 percent owned by DCS Capital Partnership. The Corporation was organized to assist DCS Capital Partnership in raising funds to finance construction of an ethylene plant. DCS Capital Partnership is owned by Shell Canada, Union Carbide and Dow through its 100 percent owned subsidiary, Dofinco, Inc. As part of the ownership agreement, Dofinco indirectly guarantees approximately 52 percent of the debt of the Corporation. Dofinco's indirect guarantee amounted to $68 at December 31, 1994.

At December 31, 1994, the Company had various outstanding commitments for take or pay and throughput agreements, including the Canadian subsidiary's take or pay ethylene contract, for terms extending from one to 20 years. In general, such commitments were at prices not in excess of current market prices. The table below shows the fixed and determinable portion of the take or pay and throughput obligations:

Fixed and Determinable Portion of Obligations

1995	$200
1996	168
1997	155
1998	142
1999	73
2000 through expiration of contracts	197
Total	$935

In addition to the take or pay and throughput obligations, the Company had other outstanding commitments at December 31, 1994, including ship charters, purchase commitments for materials and property, and other purchases used in the normal course of business. Total purchase obligations under the agreements were $244. In general, such commitments were at prices not in excess of current market prices.

NOTES TO FINANCIAL STATEMENTS

In millions, except for share amounts

R   Supplementary Information

Accrued and Other Current Liabilities at December 31

	1994	1993
Accrued vacations	$ 200	$ 196
Employees' retirement plans	163	135
Interest payable	124	126
Accrued payroll	316	154
Accrued miscellaneous taxes	146	142
Insurance companies' reserves	168	155
Sundry	742	813
Total	$1,859	$1,721

Sundry Income — Net

	1994	1993	1992
Royalty income	$ 25	$ 26	$ 21
Gain (loss) on securities	(34)	(55)	24
Gain on sale of assets	73	57	22
Dividend income	36	93	14
Other–net	3	(74)	5
Total	$103	$ 47	$ 86

Other Supplementary Information

	1994	1993	1992
Cash payments for interest	$576	$611	$690
Cash payments for taxes on income	257	454	439
Provision for doubtful receivables	11	18	9

S   Industry Segments and Geographic Areas

The Company conducts its worldwide operations through separate geographic area organizations which represent major markets or combinations of related markets.

Aggregation of products is generally made on the basis of process technology, end-use markets and channels of distribution.

Chemicals and Performance Products contains a wide range of products that are used primarily as raw materials in the manufacture of customer products, or which aid in the processing of customer products and services.

Plastic Products consists of a broad range of thermoplastics, thermosets and plastic fabricated products used in a wide variety of applications in markets which include packaging, automotive, electronics, and construction among many others.

Hydrocarbons and Energy encompasses procurement of fuels and petroleum-based raw materials as well as the production of olefins, aromatics, styrene and cogenerated power and steam for use in the Company's manufacturing operations. Income from the construction of power plants by Destec Energy, Inc. is also recorded in this segment.

Consumer Specialties includes agricultural chemicals, pharmaceuticals, and food care, home care, and personal care products.

The Unallocated segment encompasses the Company's businesses that are not reported elsewhere, including the consolidated insurance and finance companies, and Ventures businesses such as Dow Environmental and advanced electronics materials. This segment also includes activities and overhead cost variances not allocated to other segments.

Transfers between areas and industry segments are generally valued at cost except for movements between Consumer Specialties and the other industry segments. These movements are generally valued at market-based prices.

APPENDIX C

ICI FINANCIAL STATEMENTS

accounting policies

The accounts are prepared under the historical cost convention and in accordance with the Companies Act 1985 and applicable accounting standards. The following paragraphs describe the main policies. The accounting policies of some overseas subsidiaries do not conform with UK Accounting Standards and, where appropriate, adjustments are made on consolidation in order to present the Group accounts on a consistent basis.

Depreciation

The Group's policy is to write-off the book value of each tangible fixed asset to its residual value evenly over its estimated remaining life. Reviews are made periodically of the estimated remaining lives of individual productive assets, taking account of commercial and technological obsolescence as well as normal wear and tear. Under this policy it becomes impracticable to calculate average asset lives exactly; however, the total lives approximate to 22 years for buildings and 17 years for plant and equipment. Depreciation of assets qualifying for grants is calculated on their full cost.

Foreign currencies

Profit and loss accounts in foreign currencies are translated into sterling at average rates for the relevant accounting periods. Assets and liabilities are translated at exchange rates ruling at the date of the Group balance sheet. Exchange differences on short-term currency borrowings and deposits are included with net interest payable. Exchange differences on all other transactions, except relevant foreign currency loans, are taken to trading profit. In the Group accounts, exchange differences arising on consolidation of the net investments in overseas subsidiary undertakings and associated undertakings are taken to reserves, as are differences arising on equity investments denominated in foreign currencies in the Company accounts. Differences on relevant foreign currency loans are taken to reserves and offset against the differences on net investments.

Goodwill

On the acquisition of a business, fair values are attributed to the net assets acquired. Goodwill arises where the fair value of the consideration given for a business exceeds such net assets. UK Accounting Standards require that purchased goodwill be eliminated from the balance sheet either upon acquisition against reserves or by amortisation over a period. Elimination against reserves has been selected as appropriate to the goodwill purchases made during recent years. On the subsequent disposal or termination of a previously acquired business, the profit or loss on disposal or termination is calculated after charging the amount of any related goodwill previously taken to reserves.

Leases

Assets held under finance leases are capitalised and included in tangible fixed assets at fair value. Each asset is depreciated over the shorter of the lease term or its useful life. The obligations related to finance leases, net of finance charges in respect of future periods, are included as appropriate under creditors due within, or creditors due after, one year. The interest element of the rental obligation is allocated to accounting periods during the lease term to reflect a constant rate of interest on the remaining balance of the obligation for each accounting period. Rentals under operating leases are charged to profit and loss account as incurred.

Pension costs

The pension costs relating to UK retirement plans are assessed in accordance with the advice of independent qualified actuaries. The amounts so determined include the regular cost of providing the benefits under the plans which should be a level percentage of current and expected future earnings of the employees covered under the plans. Variations from the regular pension cost are spread on a systematic basis over the estimated average remaining service lives of current employees in the plans.

With minor exceptions, non-UK subsidiaries recognise the expected cost of providing pensions on a systematic basis over the average remaining service lives of employees in accordance with the advice of independent qualified actuaries.

Associated undertakings

The Group's share of the profits less losses of significant associated undertakings is normally included in the Group profit and loss account on the equity accounting basis. The holding value of significant associated undertakings in the Group balance sheet is calculated by reference to the Group's equity in the net tangible assets of such undertakings, as shown by the most recent accounts available, adjusted where appropriate. Proportional consolidation is adopted where this more accurately reflects the Group's interest in an associated undertaking.

Research and development

Research and development expenditure is charged to profit in the year in which it is incurred.

Stock valuation

Finished goods are stated at the lower of cost and net realisable value, raw materials and other stocks at the lower of cost and replacement price; the first in, first out or an average method of valuation is used. In determining cost for stock valuation purposes, depreciation is included but selling expenses and certain overhead expenses are excluded.

Taxation

The charge for taxation is based on the profit for the year and takes into account taxation deferred because of timing differences between the treatment of certain items, including post-retirement benefits, for taxation and for accounting purposes. However, no provision is made for taxation deferred by reliefs unless there is reasonable evidence that such deferred taxation will be payable in the future.

Environmental liabilities

The Group is exposed to environmental liabilities relating to its past operations, principally in respect of soil and ground-water remediation costs. Provisions for these costs are made when expenditure on remedial work is probable and the cost can be estimated within a reasonable range of possible outcomes.

group profit and loss account

for the year ended 31 December 1994

	Notes	1994 Continuing operations Before exceptional items £m	1994 Continuing operations Exceptional items £m	1994 Discontinued operations £m	1994 Total £m	1993† Continuing operations Before exceptional items £m	1993† Continuing operations Exceptional items £m	1993† Discontinued operations £m	1993† Total £m
Turnover	4	**9,189**	**–**	**–**	**9,189**	8,430	–	2,202	10,632
Operating costs	3,5	**(8,691)**	**(67)**	**–**	**(8,758)**	(8,228)	–	(1,941)	(10,169)
Other operating income	5	**90**	**–**	**–**	**90**	123	–	33	156
Trading profit (loss)	3,4,5	**588**	**(67)**	**–**	**521**	325	–	294	619
Share of losses less profits of associated undertakings	3,7	**14**	**(70)**	**–**	**(56)**	45	–	2	47
Losses less profits on sale or closure of operations	3	**–**	**(39)**	**–**	**(39)**	–	(94)	(59)	(153)
Profits on disposal of fixed assets	3	**–**	**70**	**–**	**70**	–	–	–	–
Profit (loss) on ordinary activities before interest	4	**602**	**(106)**	**–**	**496**	370	(94)	237	513
Net interest payable	8	**(88)**	**–**	**–**	**(88)**	(90)	–	(63)	(153)
Profit (loss) on ordinary activities before taxation		**514**	**(106)**	**–**	**408**	280	(94)	174	360
Tax on profit (loss) on ordinary activities	9	**(182)**	**18**	**–**	**(164)**	(101)	(18)	(70)	(189)
Profit (loss) on ordinary activities after taxation		**332**	**(88)**	**–**	**244**	179	(112)	104	171
Attributable to minorities		**(62)**	**6**	**–**	**(56)**	(38)	(4)	–	(42)
Net profit (loss) for the financial year		**270**	**(82)**	**–**	**188**	141	(116)	104	129
Dividends	10								
Cash					**(199)**				(199)
Demerger									(363)
					(199)				(562)
Loss retained for year	23				**(11)**				(433)
Earnings (loss) per £1 Ordinary Share	11	**37.3p**	**(11.3)p**	**–**	**26.0p**	19.6p	(16.1)p	14.4p	17.9p

statement of group total recognised gains and losses

for the year ended 31 December 1994

	Notes	1994 £m	1993† £m
Net profit for the financial year		**188**	129
Currency translation differences on foreign currency net investments and related loans		**(96)**	(23)
Share of other reserve movements of associated undertakings and other items		**(7)**	–
Total recognised gains and losses relating to the year		**85**	106
Prior year adjustment	2	**(95)**	
Total gains and losses recognised since last annual report		**(10)**	

† Restated (note 2)

balance sheets

at 31 December 1994

	Notes	Group 1994 £m	Group 1993† £m	Company 1994 £m	Company 1993† £m
ASSETS EMPLOYED					
Fixed assets					
Tangible assets	12	**3,861**	4,024	**424**	311
Investments					
Subsidiary undertakings	13			**6,883**	6,179
Participating and other interests	14	**171**	458	**56**	268
		4,032	4,482	**7,363**	6,758
Current assets					
Stocks	15	**1,233**	1,199	**88**	70
Debtors	16	**1,980**	1,887	**1,197**	1,033
Investments and short-term deposits	17	**1,524**	1,467	**232**	629
Cash	17	**235**	194	**37**	31
		4,972	4,747	**1,554**	1,763
Total assets		**9,004**	9,229	**8,917**	8,521
Creditors due within one year					
Short-term borrowings	18	**(142)**	(145)	**(50)**	(1)
Current instalments of loans	20	**(181)**	(220)	**(63)**	(62)
Other creditors	19	**(2,285)**	(2,087)	**(4,840)**	(3,774)
		(2,608)	(2,452)	**(4,953)**	(3,837)
Net current assets (liabilities)		**2,364**	2,295	**(3,399)**	(2,074)
Total assets less current liabilities		**6,396**	6,777	**3,964**	4,684
FINANCED BY					
Creditors due after more than one year					
Loans	20	**1,522**	1,717	**200**	263
Other creditors	19	**95**	123	**1,141**	1,190
		1,617	1,840	**1,341**	1,453
Provisions for liabilities and charges	21	**675**	680	**40**	51
Deferred income: Grants not yet credited to profit		**30**	39	**1**	1
Minority interests – equity		**338**	330		
Shareholders' funds – equity					
Called-up share capital	22	**724**	722	**724**	722
Reserves					
Share premium account		**569**	561	**569**	561
Revaluation reserve		**37**	46	**–**	–
Associated undertakings' reserves		**60**	66		
Profit and loss account		**2,346**	2,493	**1,289**	1,896
Total reserves	23	**3,012**	3,166	**1,858**	2,457
Total capital and reserves attributable to parent company (page 14)		**3,736**	3,888	**2,582**	3,179
		6,396	6,777	**3,964**	4,684

† *Restated (note 2)*

The accounts on pages 11 to 37 were approved by the Board of Directors on 6 March 1995 and were signed on its behalf by:

statement of group cash flow

for the year ended 31 December 1994

	Notes	1994 £m	1993 £m
Cash inflow from operating activities			
Net cash inflow from trading operations	24	1,032	1,305
Outflow related to exceptional items	25	(144)	(279)
Net cash inflow from operating activities		888	1,026
Returns on investments and servicing of finance			
Interest and dividends received	26	105	159
Interest paid		(182)	(254)
Dividends paid by parent company		(199)	(318)
Dividends paid by subsidiary undertakings to minority interests		(32)	(20)
Net cash outflow from returns on investments and servicing of finance		(308)	(433)
Tax paid		(98)	(144)
Investing activities			
Cash expenditure on tangible fixed assets	12	(373)	(485)
Acquisitions and new fixed asset investments	27	(37)	(286)
Disposals	28	310	443
Repayment of debt by Zeneca		568	1,364
Purchase of short-term investments and deposits		(175)	(436)
Cash and cash equivalents of Zeneca at date of demerger			(153)
Net cash inflow from investing activities		293	447
Net cash inflow before financing		775	896
Financing			
Issues of ICI Ordinary Shares		10	67
Net decrease in loans		(199)	(379)
Net decrease in lease finance		(30)	(15)
Net increase (decrease) in short-term borrowings		6	(3)
Issue of shares to minorities by subsidiary undertakings		–	6
Net cash outflow from financing	29	(213)	(324)
Increase in cash and cash equivalents	30	562	572

reconciliation of movements in shareholders' funds

for the year ended 31 December 1994

	1994 £m	1993† £m
Net profit for the financial year	188	129
Dividends		
Cash	(199)	(199)
Demerger		(363)
Loss retained for year	(11)	(433)
Issues of ICI Ordinary Shares	10	67
Goodwill movement	(48)	80
Other recognised losses related to the year	(103)	(23)
Net reduction in shareholders' funds	(152)	(309)
Shareholders' funds at beginning of year	3,888	4,197
(1994 originally was £3,983m (1993 £4,286m) before deduction of prior year adjustment of £95m (£89m))		
Shareholders' funds at end of year	3,736	3,888

† Restated (note 2)

notes relating to the accounts

1 Composition of the Group

The Group accounts consolidate the accounts of Imperial Chemical Industries PLC (the Company) and its subsidiary undertakings, of which there were 363 at 31 December 1994. Owing to local conditions and to avoid undue delay in the presentation of the Group accounts, 62 subsidiaries made up their accounts to dates earlier than 31 December, but not earlier than 30 September; one subsidiary makes up its accounts to 31 March but interim accounts to 31 December are drawn up for consolidation purposes.

2 Basis of presentation of financial information

At an Extraordinary General Meeting on 28 May 1993 the shareholders of ICI approved a resolution to demerge its bioscience operations ("Zeneca"). The demerger was effective 1 June 1993 and Zeneca has operated as a separate, publicly listed company since that date.

The results of Zeneca to the date of demerger and of the European nylon fibres business were reported as discontinued operations in the 1993 Group Profit and Loss Account together with the loss on disposal of the fibres business. The 1993 Group Cash Flow Statement includes the cash flows of Zeneca to the date of demerger.

The results reflect the initial adoption of the accounting requirements of pronouncement UITF6 "Accounting for Post-retirement Benefits other than Pensions". The cumulative cost of the benefits relating to previous years

has been recognised in the accounts as a prior year adjustment and comparative figures for 1993 have been restated. The effect on continuing operations of implementing this new accounting policy was to reduce trading profit for the year by £12m (1993 £10m), to reduce the tax charge by £4m (1993 £4m) and to reduce the value of Group reserves at 1 January 1994 by £95m (1993 £89m) (Company £3m, 1993 £3m).

The Accounting Standards Board published Financial Reporting Standard No.4 – "Capital Instruments" in December 1993, No.5 – "Reporting the Substance of Transactions" in April 1994, No.6 – "Acquisitions and Mergers" in September 1994 and No.7 – "Fair Values in Acquisition Accounting" in September 1994 all of which have been applied to the 1994 Accounts.

3 Exceptional items before tax

	1994 Continuing operations £m	1994 Discontinued operations £m	Total £m	1993 Continuing operations £m	1993 Discontinued operations £m	Total £m
Charged in arriving at trading profit (loss)						
Provisions for restructuring in the Explosives business, principally severance costs of £44m and asset write-downs and demolition of £13m	(67)	–	(67)	–	–	–
Charged after trading profit (loss)						
Share of losses of associated undertakings*	(70)	–	(70)	–	–	–
Losses less profits on sale or closure of operations and related provisions						
Losses/provisions*	(78)	–	(78)	(148)	(72)	(220)
Profits	39	–	39	54	13	67
	(39)	–	(39)	(94)	(59)	(153)
Profits on disposal of fixed assets*	70	–	70	–	–	–
Exceptional items within profit (loss) on ordinary activities before taxation	(106)	–	(106)	(94)	(59)	(153)

* Exceptional items include the following relating to the flotation and partial disposal of EVC International NV:
  (i) £70m being a write-down of assets by EVC as part of the flotation (included in share of losses less profits of associated undertakings),
  (ii) £55m being losses on sale of residual operations to EVC (included in losses on sale or closure of operations) and
  (iii) £13m being profit on disposal of shares in EVC (included in profits on disposal of fixed assets).

notes relating to the accounts

4 Segment information

CLASSES OF BUSINESS

	Turnover		Trading profit before exceptional items		Profit before interest and taxation after exceptional items	
	1994 £m	1993 £m	**1994 £m**	1993 £m	**1994 £m**	1993 £m
Continuing operations						
Paints	**1,712**	1,691	**122**	101	**117**	127
Materials	**1,748**	1,494	**76**	14	**83**	(81)
Explosives	**786**	643	**45**	51	**(35)**	51
Industrial Chemicals	**3,881**	3,691	**265**	103	**253**	102
Regional Businesses	**1,477**	1,416	**80**	45	**134**	21
Inter-class eliminations	**(415)**	(373)	**–**	11	**–**	11
Share of losses less profits of associated undertakings					**(56)**	45
	9,189	8,562				
Sales to discontinued operations	**–**	(132)				
	9,189	8,430	**588**	325	**496**	276
Discontinued operations	**–**	2,256	**–**	294	**–**	237
Sales to continuing operations	**–**	(54)				
	–	2,202	**–**	294	**–**	237
	9,189	10,632	**588**	619	**496**	513

The Group's policy is to transfer products internally at external market prices. Inter-class turnover affected several businesses the largest being sales from Industrial Chemicals to Materials of £178m (1993 £163m).

	Total assets less current liabilities		Capital expenditure (note 12)		Depreciation (note 12)	
	1994 £m	1993 £m	**1994 £m**	1993 £m	**1994 £m**	1993 £m
Continuing operations						
Paints	**578**	533	**61**	65	**36**	38
Materials	**1,162**	1,221	**53**	58	**108**	109
Explosives	**333**	302	**50**	46	**43**	24
Industrial Chemicals	**1,995**	2,160	**146**	122	**158**	159
Regional Businesses	**756**	790	**75**	57	**68**	87
Net operating assets	**4,824**	5,006				
Net non-operating assets	**1,572**	1,771				
	6,396	6,777	**385**	348	**413**	417
Discontinued operations	**–**	–	**–**	117	**–**	88
	6,396	6,777	**385**	465	**413**	505

Net non-operating assets include assets in course of construction, investments in participating and other interests, current asset investments, short-term deposits and cash less short-term borrowings and current instalments of loans, and debtors and creditors relating to taxes and dividends.

notes relating to the accounts

4 Segment information (continued)

GEOGRAPHIC AREAS

The information opposite is re-analysed in the table below by geographic area. The figures for each geographic area show the turnover and profit made by, and the net operating assets owned by, companies located in that area; export sales and related profits are included in the areas from which those sales were made.

	Turnover		Trading profit before exceptional items		Profit before interest and taxation after exceptional items	
	1994 £m	1993 £m	1994 £m	1993 £m	1994 £m	1993 £m
Continuing operations						
United Kingdom						
Sales in the UK	1,978	1,927				
Sales overseas	1,644	1,566				
	3,622	3,493	130	38	98	46
Continental Europe	1,392	1,486	56	21	66	32
The Americas	2,567	2,409	169	118	141	(11)
Asia Pacific	2,182	1,871	178	107	202	108
Other countries	414	374	53	40	43	55
	10,177	9,633	586	324	550	230
Sales to discontinued operations	–	(132)				
Inter-area eliminations	(988)	(1,071)	2	1	2	1
Share of losses less profits of associated undertakings					(56)	45
	9,189	8,430	588	325	496	276
Discontinued operations	–	2,256	–	294	–	237
Sales to continuing operations	–	(54)				
	–	2,202	–	294	–	237
	9,189	10,632	588	619	496	513

Inter-area turnover shown above includes sales of £359m (1993 £682m) from the United Kingdom to overseas subsidiaries.

	Net operating assets		Turnover by customer location	
	1994 £m	1993 £m	1994 £m	1993 £m
Continuing operations				
United Kingdom	1,514	1,531	2,001	1,876
Continental Europe	531	575	1,834	1,678
The Americas	1,211	1,362	2,515	2,383
Asia Pacific	1,411	1,424	2,256	1,957
Other countries	157	114	583	536
	4,824	5,006	9,189	8,430
Discontinued operations	–	–	–	2,202
	4,824	5,006	9,189	10,632

EMPLOYEES	1994		1993	
	Continuing operations	Total	Continuing operations	Total
Average number of people employed by the Group in				
United Kingdom	21,200	21,200	24,400	31,600
Continental Europe	6,300	6,300	7,200	11,500
The Americas	15,000	15,000	16,400	20,700
Asia Pacific	13,200	13,200	13,300	14,000
Other countries	11,800	11,800	9,100	9,300
Total employees	67,500	67,500	70,400	87,100

The number of people employed by the Group at the end of 1994 was 64,800 (1993 67,000).

notes relating to the accounts

5 Trading profit (loss)

| | 1994 | | | | 1993 | | |
| | Continuing operations | | Discontinued operations | Total | Continuing operations | | Discontinued operations | Total |
	Before exceptional items £m	Exceptional items £m	£m	£m	Before exceptional items £m	Exceptional items £m	£m	£m
Turnover	9,189	–	–	9,189	8,430	–	2,202	10,632
Operating costs								
Cost of sales	(6,502)	(27)	–	(6,529)	(6,095)	–	(1,124)	(7,219)
Distribution costs	(608)	(5)	–	(613)	(594)	–	(90)	(684)
Research and development	(184)	–	–	(184)	(177)	–	(189)	(366)
Administrative and other expenses	(1,397)	(35)	–	(1,432)	(1,362)	–	(538)	(1,900)
	(8,691)	(67)	–	(8,758)	(8,228)	–	(1,941)	(10,169)
Other operating income								
Government grants	8	–	–	8	10	–	1	11
Royalties	25	–	–	25	25	–	18	43
Other income	57	–	–	57	88	–	14	102
	90	–	–	90	123	–	33	156
Trading profit (loss)	588	(67)	–	521	325	–	294	619
Total charge for depreciation included above	404	7	–	411	398	–	88	486
Gross profit, as defined by the Companies Act 1985	2,687	(27)	–	2,660	2,335	–	1,078	3,413

Forward contracts hedging foreign currency working capital are revalued at year end and gains and losses are included in trading profit. Forward contracts and currency options hedging other anticipated cash flows are not revalued but, on realisation, gains and losses net of option premia are included in trading profit in the period that the hedged cash flow occurs. Net gains/losses deferred at year end were not material. Option premia are included in debtors until realised.

6 Note of historical cost profits and losses
There were no material differences between reported profits and losses and historical cost profits and losses on ordinary activities before tax in either 1994 or 1993.

7 Share of losses less profits of associated undertakings

| | 1994 | | | 1993 | | |
	Continuing operations £m	Discontinued operations £m	Total £m	Continuing operations £m	Discontinued operations £m	Total £m
Share of losses less profits						
Share of undistributed losses less profits	(59)	–	(59)	11	2	13
Dividend income						
Listed companies	2	–	2	8	–	8
Unlisted companies	5	–	5	22	–	22
	7	–	7	30	–	30
Share of losses less profits before taxation	(52)	–	(52)	41	2	43
Amounts written off investments (including provisions raised £8m (1993 £1m) and released £4m (1993 £5m))	(4)	–	(4)	4	–	4
	(56)	–	(56)	45	2	47
Of which accounted for as exceptional	(70)	–	(70)	–	–	–

The reduction in ICI's interest in AECI Ltd, effective from the beginning of the year, and in EVC International NV, in November, has resulted in these investments ceasing to be equity accounted from those dates.

notes relating to the accounts

8 Net interest payable

	Continuing operations £m	1994 Discontinued operations £m	Total £m	Continuing operations £m	1993 Discontinued operations £m	Total £m
Interest payable and similar charges						
Bank loans, overdrafts and other loans wholly						
repayable within five years	100	–	100	151	1	152
Other loans not wholly repayable within five years	86	–	86	101	–	101
Interest between continuing and discontinued operations				–	62	62
	186	–	186	252	63	315
Interest receivable and similar income						
Listed investments	(10)	–	(10)	(4)	–	(4)
Unlisted investments and short-term deposits	(88)	–	(88)	(96)	–	(96)
Interest between continuing and discontinued operations				(62)	–	(62)
	(98)	–	(98)	(162)	–	(162)
Net interest payable	88	–	88	90	63	153

Interest on cross-currency and interest rate swaps is accrued and included with the interest flows of the underlying borrowing. Forward rate agreements are not revalued but, on realisation, gains or losses are spread over the period of the hedged borrowing or deposit. Net gains/losses deferred at year end were not material.

Interest allocated to discontinued operations in 1993 consisted of the interest applicable to Zeneca based on the debt assumed by Zeneca prior to demerger. No interest was allocated in that year in respect of the discontinued fibres business.

9 Tax on profit (loss) on ordinary activities

	1994 Continuing operations Before exceptional items £m	1994 Continuing operations Exceptional items £m	1994 Discontinued operations £m	Total £m	1993 Continuing operations Before exceptional items £m	1993 Continuing operations Exceptional items £m	1993 Discontinued operations £m	Total £m
ICI and subsidiary undertakings								
United Kingdom taxation								
Corporation tax	72	(1)	–	71	2	4	60	66
Double taxation relief	(11)	–	–	(11)	(2)	–	–	(2)
Deferred taxation	5	(13)	–	(8)	7	2	(13)	(4)
	66	(14)	–	52	7	6	47	60
Overseas taxation								
Overseas taxes	110	5	–	115	87	8	34	129
Deferred taxation	2	(9)	–	(7)	(6)	4	(11)	(13)
	112	(4)	–	108	81	12	23	116
	178	(18)	–	160	88	18	70	176
Associated undertakings	4	–	–	4	13	–	–	13
Tax on profit (loss) on ordinary activities	182	(18)	–	164	101	18	70	189

UK and overseas taxation has been provided on the profits (losses) earned for the periods covered by the Group accounts. UK corporation tax has been provided at the rate of 33 per cent (1993 33 per cent).

The exceptional tax credit in 1994 is in respect of the Explosives restructuring costs and the transfer of operations to EVC partially offset by tax on disposals of other operations in the US and Australia. Taxation attributable to discontinued operations in 1993 comprised the taxation on the operating results of the discontinued businesses to the date of demerger/disposal together with tax relief on the losses on sale of the fibres business. The exceptional tax charge in 1993 reflected taxation on profits on disposals; losses on disposals, principally goodwill, did not attract significant tax relief.

notes relating to the accounts

9 Tax on profit (loss) on ordinary activities (continued)

Deferred taxation

The amounts of deferred taxation accounted for at the balance sheet date and the potential amounts of deferred taxation are disclosed below.

	Group		Company	
	1994 **£m**	1993 £m	**1994** **£m**	1993 £m
Accounted for at balance sheet date (note 21)				
Timing differences on UK capital allowances and depreciation	**182**	178	**69**	36
Miscellaneous timing differences	**(92)**	(90)	**(38)**	(17)
	90	88	**31**	19
Not accounted for at balance sheet date				
Timing differences on UK capital allowances and depreciation	**–**	–	**–**	–
Miscellaneous timing differences	**22**	(18)	**–**	(11)
	22	(18)	**–**	(11)
Full potential deferred taxation	**112**	70	**31**	8

10 Dividends

	1994 **pence per** **£1 Share**	1993 pence per £1 Share	**1994** **£m**	1993 £m
Interim, paid 3 October 1994	**10.5p**	10.5p	**76**	76
Second interim, to be confirmed as final, payable 26 April 1995	**17.0p**	17.0p	**123**	123
	27.5p	27.5p	**199**	199
Demerger dividend – This comprised the net assets of Zeneca at date of demerger.				363
			199	562

11 Earnings (loss) per £1 Ordinary Share

	1994 **£m**	1993 £m
Net profit for the financial year before exceptional items – continuing operations	**270**	141
Exceptional items after tax and minorities – continuing operations	**(82)**	(116)
Net profit on discontinued operations		104
Net profit for the financial year	**188**	129
	million	million
Average Ordinary Shares in issue during year, weighted on a time basis	**723**	719
	pence	pence
Earnings per £1 Ordinary Share before exceptional items – continuing operations	**37.3**	19.6
Earnings per £1 Ordinary Share – total operations	**26.0**	17.9

The effect on earnings per £1 Ordinary Share of the issue of shares under option (note 22) would not be material.

Earnings per £1 Ordinary Share before exceptional items for continuing operations has also been calculated to exclude the impact of exceptional items and, in respect of 1993, of discontinued operations as these can have a distorting effect on earnings and therefore warrant separate consideration.

notes relating to the accounts

12 Tangible fixed assets

	Land and buildings	Plant and equipment	Payments on account and assets in course of construction	Total
	£m	£m	£m	£m
GROUP				
Cost or as revalued				
At beginning of year	1,285	6,609	267	8,161
Exchange adjustments	(1)	(14)	3	(12)
New subsidiary undertakings	23	23	4	50
Capital expenditure			385	385
Transfers of assets into use	33	292	(325)	
Disposals and other movements	(93)	(511)	(1)	(605)
At end of year	1,247	6,399	333	7,979
Depreciation				
At beginning of year	458	3,679		4,137
Exchange adjustments	2	4		6
Disposals and other movements	(45)	(393)		(438)
Charge for year	40	373		413
At end of year	455	3,663		4,118
Net book value at end 1994	792	2,736	333	3,861
Net book value at end 1993	827	2,930	267	4,024

The Group depreciation charge of £413m, shown above, comprises £411m charged in arriving at trading profit and £2m charged within losses on sale or closure of operations.

Capital expenditure in the year of £385m includes capitalised finance leases of £7m; creditors for capital work done but not paid for increased by £5m; the resulting cash expenditure on tangible fixed assets was £373m.

The net book value of the tangible fixed assets of the Group includes capitalised finance leases of £24m (1993 £39m) comprising cost of £104m (£114m) less depreciation of £80m (£75m). In respect of capitalised leases the depreciation charge for the year was £5m (1993 £4m) and finance charges were £4m (£7m).

Included in land and buildings is £228m in respect of the cost of land which is not subject to depreciation.

	Land and buildings	Plant and equipment	Payments on account and assets in course of construction	Total
COMPANY				
Cost				
At beginning of year	165	508	11	684
Capital expenditure			23	23
Transfers of assets into use	3	16	(19)	
Transfers from (to) subsidiary undertakings	2	191	(4)	189
Disposals and other movements	(3)	(23)	–	(26)
At end of year	167	692	11	870
Depreciation				
At beginning of year	44	329		373
Transfers from subsidiary undertakings		43		43
Disposals and other movements	6	(30)		(24)
Charge for year	5	49		54
At end of year	55	391		446
Net book value at end 1994	112	301	11	424
Net book value at end 1993	121	179	11	311

notes relating to the accounts

12 Tangible fixed assets (continued)

	Group		Company	
	1994 **£m**	1993 £m	**1994** **£m**	1993 £m
The net book value of land and buildings comprised				
Freeholds	**729**	750	**111**	120
Long leases (over 50 years unexpired)	**64**	71	**1**	1
Short leases	**9**	6	**–**	–
	792	827	**112**	121

	Group			
	Land and buildings		Plant and equipment	
Revalued assets included in tangible fixed assets	**1994** **£m**	1993 £m	**1994** **£m**	1993 £m
At revalued amount	**104**	102	**127**	129
Depreciation	**41**	37	**112**	112
Net book value	**63**	65	**15**	17
At historical cost	**57**	57	**129**	130
Depreciation	**31**	31	**120**	119
Net book value	**26**	26	**9**	11

13 Investments in subsidiary undertakings

	Shares £m	Loans £m	Total £m
Cost			
At beginning of year	4,606	1,721	**6,327**
Exchange adjustments	(10)	(67)	**(77)**
Transfers to subsidiary undertakings	(2,853)	(511)	**(3,364)**
Transfers from subsidiary undertakings	207	29	**236**
New investments/new loans	3,624	582	**4,206**
Disposals/loans repaid/transfers	(12)	(278)	**(290)**
At end of year	5,562	1,476	**7,038**
Provisions			
At beginning of year	(147)	(1)	**(148)**
Exchange adjustments	3	–	**3**
Additions	(21)	–	**(21)**
Disposals	11	–	**11**
At end of year	(154)	(1)	**(155)**
Balance sheet value at end 1994	5,408	1,475	**6,883**
Balance sheet value at end 1993	4,459	1,720	6,179

Cost includes scrip issues capitalised £6m (1993 £6m).

Shares in subsidiary undertakings which are listed investments	**1994** **£m**	1993 £m
Balance sheet value	**5**	5
Market value	**63**	81

None of the listed investments were listed on The London Stock Exchange.

The Company's investment in its subsidiary undertakings consists of either equity or long term loans, or both. Normal trading balances are included in either debtors or creditors. Information on principal subsidiary undertakings is given on page 37.

notes relating to the accounts

14 Investments in participating and other interests

	Associated undertakings		Other investments	Total
	Shares £m	Loans £m	Shares £m	£m
GROUP				
Cost				
At beginning of year	398	7	–	405
Exchange adjustments	(18)	–	–	(18)
Additions	22	6	7	35
Reclassification	(137)	–	137	
Disposals and repayments	(213)	(5)	–	(218)
Other movements	(8)	(5)	–	(13)
At end of year	44	3	144	191
Share of post-acquisition reserves less losses				
At beginning of year	66			66
Exchange adjustments	(11)			(11)
Retained losses less profits	(63)			(63)
Reclassification	74			74
Disposals	3			3
Other movements	(9)			(9)
At end of year	60			60
Provisions				
At beginning of year	(13)	–	–	(13)
Exchange	(1)	–	–	(1)
Net additions in year	(4)	–	–	(4)
Reclassification	–	–	(74)	(74)
Disposals	7	–	(2)	5
Other movements	7	–	–	7
At end of year	(4)	–	(76)	(80)
Balance sheet value at end 1994	100	3	68	171
Balance sheet value at end 1993	451	7	–	458
The above investments included				
1994				
Listed investments – balance sheet value	–		57	57
– market value	–		72	72
1993				
Listed investments – balance sheet value	145	–	–	145
– market value	234	–	–	234

None of the listed investments were listed on The London Stock Exchange.

Information on principal associated undertakings is given on page 36.

notes relating to the accounts

14 Investments in participating and other interests (continued)

	Associated undertakings		Other investments	Total
	Shares	Loans	Shares	
	£m	£m	£m	£m
COMPANY				
Cost				
At beginning of year	271	6	–	277
Exchange adjustments	15	–	–	15
Additions	14	–	–	14
Transfers from subsidiary undertakings	40	–	–	40
Reclassification	(151)	–	151	
Disposals	(184)	(6)	–	(190)
At end of year	5	–	151	156
Provisions				
At beginning of year	(3)	(6)	–	(9)
Additions	–	–	(99)	(99)
Disposals	2	6	–	8
At end of year	(1)	–	(99)	(100)
Balance sheet value at end 1994	4	–	52	56
Balance sheet value at end 1993	268	–	–	268
The above investments included				
1994				
Listed investments - balance sheet value	–	–	52	52
- market value	–	–	66	66
1993				
Listed investments - balance sheet value	–	–	–	–

None of the listed investments were listed on The London Stock Exchange.

15 Stocks

	Group		Company	
	1994	1993	1994	1993
	£m	£m	£m	£m
Raw materials and consumables	418	396	23	18
Stocks in process	75	84	8	4
Finished goods and goods for resale	740	719	57	48
	1,233	1,199	88	70

16 Debtors

	Group		Company	
Amounts due within one year				
Trade debtors	1,360	1,214	42	1
Amounts owed by subsidiary undertakings			993	912
Amounts owed by associated undertakings	9	18	–	–
Other debtors	260	341	26	25
Prepayments and accrued income*	112	104	31	24
	1,741	1,677	1,092	962
Amounts due after more than one year				
Advance corporation tax recoverable	–	–	56	29
Prepayments and other debtors*	239	210	49	42
	239	210	105	71
	1,980	1,887	1,197	1,033

* Includes prepaid pension costs (note 33).

notes relating to the accounts

17 Current asset investments and short-term deposits

	Group		Company	
	1994 **£m**	1993 £m	**1994** **£m**	1993 £m
Securities listed on The London Stock Exchange	75	–	58	–
Other listed investments	187	–	59	–
Total listed investments	262	–	117	–
Unlisted investments and short-term deposits	1,262	892	115	54
	1,524	892	232	54
Amounts owed by Zeneca	–	575	–	575
	1,524	1,467	232	629
Included in cash and cash equivalents (note 30)	941	464		
Market value of listed investments	262	–	117	–

Included in unlisted investments and short-term deposits and cash are amounts totalling £61m (1993 £nil) held by the Group's insurance subsidiaries, of which some £49m (1993 £nil) is not readily available for the general purposes of the Group.

18 Short-term borrowings

	Group		Company	
Bank borrowings				
Secured by fixed charge	3	3	–	–
Secured by floating charge	4	3	–	–
Unsecured	82	56	50	1
	89	62	50	1
Other borrowings (unsecured)	53	83	–	–
	142	145	50	1
Included in cash and cash equivalents (note 30)	136	144		

19 Other creditors

	Group		Company	
Amounts due within one year				
Trade creditors	993	888	128	130
Amounts owed to subsidiary undertakings			4,386	3,341
Amounts owed to associated undertakings	8	6	5	5
Corporate taxation	233	164	97	78
Value added and payroll taxes and social security	76	81	6	8
Other creditors*	539	531	57	62
Accruals	313	294	38	27
Dividends to Ordinary Shareholders	123	123	123	123
	2,285	2,087	4,840	3,774
Amounts due after more than one year				
Amounts owed to subsidiary undertakings			1,136	1,186
Other creditors*	95	123	5	4
	95	123	1,141	1,190

* Includes obligations under finance leases (note 31) and accrued pension costs (note 33).

notes relating to the accounts

20 Loans

	Repayment dates	Group 1994 £m	Group 1993 £m	Company 1994 £m	Company 1993 £m
Secured loans					
US dollars	1995/1998	55	71		
Australian dollars		–	18		
Other currencies	1995/2004	113	135		
Total secured		168	224		
Secured by fixed charge — bank loans		163	205		
— other		–	14		
Secured by floating charge — bank loans		5	5		
Unsecured loans					
Sterling					
9¾% to 11¼% Bonds	1995/2005	263	325	263	325
Others	1995/2002	98	74		
		361	399	263	325
US dollars					
8% eurodollar Bonds	1996	64	68		
8⅞% Debentures	2006	160	169		
7.83% to 8.9% medium-term Notes	1995/2002	61	68		
8¾% Notes	2001	160	169		
7⅝% Notes	1997	144	152		
9½% Notes	2000	192	203		
7½% Notes	2002	128	135		
Others	1995/2005	15	18		
		924	982		
Australian dollars (13.5%)	1995	37	62		
Swiss francs (4½% to 6¾%)	1997/1999	195	220		
Other currencies	1995/2005	18	50		
Total unsecured		1,535	1,713	263	325
Total loans		1,703	1,937	263	325

The Group has entered into currency swap, interest rate swap and forward rate agreements to manage the interest rate and currency exposures arising on borrowings and cash not immediately required by the business. At 31 December 1994, the Group had agreements outstanding with commercial banks which had principal amounts of £1,450m (1993 £1,763m) equivalent at the exchange rate on that date. Principal amounts under cross-currency agreements are revalued to balance sheet rates and any exchange gains or losses arising are included in the total sterling value of Group loans. The amount attributed to cross-currency swaps included in the above total is £9m (1993 (£5m)).

notes relating to the accounts

20 Loans (continued)

	Group		Company	
Loan maturities	**1994 £m**	1993 £m	**1994 £m**	1993 £m
Bank loans				
Loans or instalments thereof are repayable				
After 5 years from balance sheet date				
Lump sums	**8**	–		
Instalments	**53**	82		
	61	82		
From 2 to 5 years	**138**	129		
From 1 to 2 years	**45**	43		
Total due after more than one year	**244**	254		
Total due within one year	**46**	42		
	290	296	**–**	–
Other loans				
Loans or instalments thereof are repayable				
After 5 years from balance sheet date				
Lump sums	**851**	1,018	**200**	200
Instalments	**–**	6	**–**	–
	851	1,024	**200**	200
From 2 to 5 years	**361**	304	**–**	–
From 1 to 2 years	**66**	135	**–**	63
Total due after more than one year	**1,278**	1,463	**200**	263
Total due within one year	**135**	178	**63**	62
	1,413	1,641	**263**	325
Total loans				
Due after more than one year	**1,522**	1,717	**200**	263
Due within one year	**181**	220	**63**	62
Total loans	**1,703**	1,937	**263**	325
Aggregate amount of loans repayable by instalments any of which fall due after 5 years	**180**	200	**–**	–

21 Provisions for liabilities and charges

	At beginning of year £m	Profit and loss account £m	Net amounts paid or becoming current £m	Exchange and other movements £m	At end of year £m
GROUP					
Deferred taxation (note 9)†	88	(15)	–	17	**90**
Advance corporation tax recoverable	(29)	–	–	(40)	**(69)**
Employee benefits * †	292	51	(27)	5	**321**
Reorganisation, environmental and other provisions	329	99	(78)	(17)	**333**
	680	135	(105)	(35)	**675**
COMPANY					
Deferred taxation (note 9)†	19	12	–	–	**31**
Advance corporation tax recoverable	–	–	–	(19)	**(19)**
Other provisions†	32	17	(22)	1	**28**
	51	29	(22)	(18)	**40**

* Includes provisions for unfunded pension costs (note 33).
† Restated at 1 January 1994 to include prior year adjustment in respect of post-retirement healthcare obligations (notes 2 and 34).
No provision has been released or applied for any purpose other than that for which it was established.

22 Called-up share capital of parent company

	Authorised	Allotted, called-up and fully paid	
	£m	**1994 £m**	1993 £m
Ordinary Shares (£1 each)	**724**	**724**	722
Unclassified shares (£1 each)	**126**		
	850	**724**	722

The number of Ordinary Shares issued during the year, wholly in respect of the exercise of options totalled 1.8m.

At 31 December 1994 there were options outstanding in respect of 8.3m Ordinary Shares of £1 under the Company's share option schemes for staff (1993 6.0m) normally exercisable in the period 1995 to 2004 (1994 to 2003) at subscription prices of £4.32 to £13.81 (£3.04 to £13.81). The weighted average subscription price of options outstanding at 31 December 1994 was £6.43.

Options granted to directors are shown in note 39.

During 1994 movements in the number of shares under option comprised new options issued £4.5m, options exercised £1.8m, and options lapsed or waived £0.4m. At the end of 1994 there were 15.3m shares available for the granting of options (1993 19.3m).

notes relating to the accounts

23 Reserves

	Share premium account £m	Revaluation £m	Associated under- takings £m	Profit and loss account £m	**1994 Total £m**	1993 Total £m
GROUP						
Reserves attributable to parent company						
At beginning of year as previously stated						3,572
Prior year adjustment (note 2)						(89)
At beginning of year as restated	561	46	66	2,493	**3,166**	3,483
Profit (loss) retained for year			(63)	52	**(11)**	(433)
Amounts taken direct to reserves						
Share premiums	8				**8**	59
Goodwill				(48)	**(48)**	80
Exchange adjustments		(6)	(11)	(79)	**(96)**	(23)
Share of other reserve movements						
of associated undertakings and other items			(9)	2	**(7)**	–
	8	(6)	(20)	(125)	**(143)**	116
Other movements between reserves		(3)	77	(74)		
At end of year	569	37	60	2,346	**3,012**	3,166

In the Group accounts, £33m of net exchange gains (1993 losses £26m) on foreign currency loans have been offset in reserves against exchange losses (1993 gains) on the net investment in overseas subsidiaries and associated undertakings.

The movement in goodwill includes £54m of goodwill written off on the acquisition of new subsidiaries and £6m relating to goodwill transferred to the profit and loss account on the disposal of subsidiaries.

The cumulative amount of goodwill resulting from acquisitions during 1994 and prior years, net of goodwill attributable to subsidiary undertakings or businesses demerged or disposed of prior to 31 December 1994, amounted to £657m (1993 £609m).

There are no significant statutory or contractual restrictions on the distribution of current profits of subsidiary or associated undertakings; undistributed profits of prior years are, in the main, permanently employed in the businesses of these companies. The undistributed profits of Group companies overseas may be liable to overseas taxes and/or UK taxation (after allowing for double taxation relief) if they were to be distributed as dividends. No provision has been made in respect of potential taxation liabilities on realisation of assets at restated or revalued amounts or on realisation of associated undertakings at equity accounted value.

For the purpose of calculating the basis of the borrowing limits in accordance with the Articles of Association, the total of the sums standing to the credit of capital and revenue reserves of the Company and its subsidiary undertakings, to be added to the nominal amount of the share capital of the Company, was £3,636m at 31 December 1994.

	Share premium account £m	Profit and loss account £m	**1994 Total £m**	1993 Total £m
COMPANY				
Reserves				
At beginning of year as previously stated				3,070
Prior year adjustment (note 2)				(3)
At beginning of year as restated	561	1,896	**2,457**	3,067
Loss retained for year		(579)	**(579)**	(646)
Amounts taken direct to reserves				
Share premiums	8		**8**	59
Exchange adjustments		(28)	**(28)**	(23)
	8	(28)	**(20)**	36
At end of year	569	1,289	**1,858**	2,457

By virtue of S230 of the Companies Act 1985, the Company is exempt from presenting a profit and loss account.

notes relating to the accounts

24 Net cash inflow from trading operations

	1994 £m	1993 £m
Trading profit	521	619
Exceptional charges within trading profit	67	–
Trading profit before exceptional items	588	619
Depreciation	404	486
Stocks (increase) decrease	(65)	130
Debtors increase	(161).	(87)
Creditors increase	210	189
Other non-cash movements, including exchange	56	(32)
	1,032	1,305

Net cash inflow from trading operations in 1993 included £251m relating to discontinued Zeneca operations.

25 Outflow related to exceptional items

This includes expenditure charged to exceptional provisions relating to business rationalisation and restructuring and for sale or closure of operations, including severance and other employee costs, plant demolition and site clearance. The major part of the 1994 expenditure relates to provisions raised in 1992.

Exceptional items outflow in 1993 included £51m relating to discontinued Zeneca operations.

26 Interest and dividends received

	1994 £m	1993 £m
Dividends received from equity accounted associated undertakings	6	31
Other dividends received	2	4
Interest received	97	124
	105	159

27 Acquisitions and new fixed asset investments

	1994 £m	1993 £m
Acquisitions and new fixed asset investments		
Acquisitions of subsidiary undertakings involving		
Fixed assets	50	299
Current assets	56	60
Total liabilities	(36)	(107)
Minority interests	(15)	–
Net assets of subsidiary undertakings acquired	55	252
Goodwill	54	31
Fair value of consideration for subsidiary undertakings	109	283
Investment in equity accounted undertakings	9	11
Other investments	7	1
	125	295
Consideration for acquisitions and new fixed asset investments		
Cash and cash equivalents acquired	1	7
Non-cash consideration	78	–
Deferred consideration	9	2
Net cash investment	37	286
	125	295

Fixed and current assets are adjusted to fair value based on external valuations and internal reviews.

The principal acquisition in the year was a 51% interest in AECI Explosives Limited.

notes relating to the accounts

28 Disposals

	1994 £m	1993 £m
Disposals in the year resulted in the following net asset movements		
Tangible fixed assets	166	263
Investments in participating interests	205	4
Other net current assets	54	205
Creditors due after more than one year	(6)	(2)
Provisions for liabilities and charges	(29)	89
Minority interests	(31)	7
	359	566
Goodwill	(6)	111
Profit and loss account		
Ordinary activities	(9)	–
Exceptional items	44	(140)
	388	537
Satisfied by		
Cash consideration	310	443
Non-cash consideration	78	–
Deferred consideration	–	94
	388	537

The cash consideration for disposals comprises £77m (1993 £408m) in respect of disposals of operations, £120m (£4m) in respect of equity accounted participating interests, £80m (nil) in respect of other investments and £33m (£31m) in respect of tangible fixed assets. £272m (1993 £439m) of the cash consideration was accounted for as exceptional.

Apart from the disposal proceeds, the contribution of the businesses and subsidiary undertakings divested in 1994 to the cash flows for the year was not material.

29 Changes in financing during the year

	Share capital £m	Share premium account £m	Loans £m	Finance leases £m	Short-term borrowings* £m	Total £m
At beginning of 1993	714	502	2,266	94	4	3,580
Exchange adjustments			21	(1)	–	20
New finance	8	59	31	6	–	104
Finance repaid			(410)	(15)	(3)	(428)
Introduced by acquisitions			72†	–	–	72
Zeneca demerger			(62)	(9)	–	(71)
Other movements			19	–	–	19
At beginning of 1994	722	561	1,937	75	1	3,296
Exchange adjustments			(33)	2	–	(31)
New finance	2	8	93	7	6	116
Finance repaid			(292)	(30)	–	(322)
Other movements			(2)	(1)	(1)	(4)
At end of 1994	724	569	1,703	53	6	3,055

* Amount of short-term borrowings repayable more than 3 months from date of advance.

† The increase in loans due to acquisitions includes £69m in respect of the Group's investment in Louisiana Pigment Company, L.P..

No new finance was raised from the issue of shares to minorities in 1994 (1993 £6m).

notes relating to the accounts

30 Cash and cash equivalents

	1994 £m	1993 £m
Balance of cash and cash equivalents		
Cash	235	194
Investments and short-term deposits which were within 3 months of		
maturity when acquired (note 17)	941	464
Short-term borrowings repayable within 3 months from date of advance (note 18)	(136)	(144)
	1,040	514
Change in the balance of cash and cash equivalents		
At beginning of year	514	(56)
Exchange adjustments	(36)	(2)
Increase for year	562	572
At end of year	1,040	514

31 Leases

	1994			1993		
	Continuing operations	Discontinued operations	Total	Continuing operations	Discontinued operations	Total
Total rentals under operating leases, charged as an expense in the profit and loss account	£m	£m	£m	£m	£m	£m
Hire of plant and machinery	67	–	67	69	2	71
Other	41	–	41	43	12	55
	108	–	108	112	14	126

	Group		Company	
Commitments under operating leases to pay rentals during the year following the year of these accounts, analysed according to the period in which each lease expires	1994 £m	1993 £m	1994 £m	1993 £m
Land and buildings				
Expiring within 1 year	7	4	–	–
Expiring in years 2 to 5	14	18	1	1
Expiring thereafter	13	30	1	1
	34	52	2	2
Other assets				
Expiring within 1 year	9	10	1	5
Expiring in years 2 to 5	27	35	1	1
Expiring thereafter	17	7	1	2
	53	52	3	8
Obligations under finance leases comprise				
Rentals due within 1 year	46	31	1	–
Rentals due in years 2 to 5	10	39	2	–
Rentals due thereafter	–	31	1	–
Less interest element	(3)	(26)	(1)	–
	53	75	3	–

Obligations under finance leases are included in other creditors (note 19).

The Group had no commitments under finance leases at the balance sheet date which were due to commence thereafter.

notes relating to the accounts

32 Employee costs

	1994			1993		
	Continuing operations	Discontinued operations	Total	Continuing operations	Discontinued operations	Total
	£m	£m	£m	£m	£m	£m
Salaries	1,340	–	1,340	1,421	405	1,826
Social security costs	132	–	132	138	52	190
Pension costs	154	–	154	137	38	175
Other employment costs	76	–	76	45	23	68
	1,702	–	1,702	1,741	518	2,259
Less amounts allocated to capital and to provisions set up in previous years	(26)	–	(26)	(59)	(21)	(80)
Severance costs charged in arriving at profit before tax	115	–	115	60	17	77
Employee costs charged in arriving at profit before tax	1,791	–	1,791	1,742	514	2,256

The average number of people employed by the Group in 1994 was 67,500 (1993 87,100) all of whom were engaged in continuing operations (1993 70,400).

33 Pension costs

Group

The Company and most of its subsidiaries operate retirement plans which cover the majority of employees (including directors) in the Group. These plans are generally of the defined benefit type under which benefits are based on employees' years of service and average final remuneration and are funded through separate trustee-administered funds. Formal independent actuarial valuations of the Group's main plans are undertaken regularly, normally at least triennially and adopting the projected unit method.

The actuarial assumptions used to calculate the projected benefit obligation of the Group's pension plans vary according to the economic conditions of the country in which they are situated. The weighted average discount rate used in determining the actuarial present values of the benefit obligations was 8.7%. The weighted average expected long-term rate of return on investments was 8.8%. The weighted average rate of increase of future earnings was 5.9%.

The actuarial value of the fund assets of these plans at the date of the latest actuarial valuations was sufficient to cover 92% of the benefits that had accrued to members after allowing for expected future increases in earnings; their market value was £5,747m.

The total pension cost for the Group for 1994 was £154m (1993 continuing operations – £137m). Accrued pension

costs amounted to £29m (1993 £29m) and are included in other creditors (note 19); provisions for the benefit obligation of a small number of unfunded plans amounted to £130m (£119m) and are included in provisions for employee benefits (note 21). Prepaid pension costs amounting to £69m (£48m) are included in debtors (note 16).

ICI Pension Fund

The ICI Pension Fund accounts for approximately 80% of the Group's plans in asset valuation and projected benefit terms.

An actuarial valuation of the ICI Pension Fund was carried out as at 31 March 1994. From that date the Company will make payments into the Fund to reflect the extra liabilities arising from early retirement as retirements occur. In addition, the Company has agreed to make accelerated contributions to the Fund over the next six years commencing with £75m in 1995. The solvency ratio on a current funding level basis which assumes a cessation of operations is 96% and the deficit of £189m in market value terms will be eliminated over a three year period. The deficit in the Fund has been taken into account in arriving at the employers' pension cost charged in the accounts from 1 April 1994 by being amortised as a percentage of pensionable emoluments over the expected working lifetime of existing members.

34 Healthcare costs

The Group provides in North America, and to a lesser extent in some other countries, certain unfunded healthcare and life assurance benefits for retired employees. At 31 December 1994 approximately 28,000 current and retired employees were eligible to benefit from these schemes.

As stated in note 2, the results reflect the initial adoption of the accounting requirements of pronouncement UITF 6 "Accounting for Post-retirement Benefits other than Pensions" and the liabilities in respect of these benefits are now fully

accrued. The total post-retirement healthcare cost for the Group for 1994 was £16m and the provision at the year end was £153m.

In respect of the Group's major US plans the costs and provisions were determined on an actuarial basis using a discount rate of 7.25%. Healthcare cost rate increases range from 9.0% to 11.0% for 1994 and are assumed to gradually decrease to 5.0%.

notes relating to the accounts

35 Commitments and contingent liabilities

	Group		Company	
	1994 **£m**	1993 £m	**1994** **£m**	1993 £m
Commitments for capital expenditure not provided for in these accounts (including acquisitions)				
Contracts placed for future expenditure	**274**	80	**4**	2
Expenditure authorised but not yet contracted	**275**	243	**14**	23
	549	323	**18**	25

Contingent liabilities existed at 31 December 1994 in connection with guarantees and uncalled capital relating to subsidiary and other undertakings and guarantees relating to pension funds, including the solvency of pension funds. The maximum contingent liability in respect of guarantees of borrowings and uncalled capital at 31 December 1994 was £25m (1993 £18m) for the Group; the maximum contingent liability for the Company, mainly on guarantees of borrowings by subsidiaries, was £1,247m (1993 £1,337m).

The Group is also subject to contingencies pursuant to environmental laws and regulations that in the future may require it to take action to correct the effects on the environment of prior disposal or release of chemical substances by the Group or other parties. The ultimate requirement for such actions, and their cost, is inherently difficult to estimate, however provisions have been established at 31 December 1994 in accordance with the accounting policy noted on page 11. It is believed that, taking account of these provisions, the cost of addressing currently identified environmental obligations is unlikely to impair materially the Group's financial position.

The Glidden Company is a defendant, along with numerous other paint and former lead pigment manufacturers, in a number of suits in the US, several of which purport to be class actions, seeking damages for alleged personal injury caused by lead-based paint or for the costs of removing lead-based paint. Glidden stopped manufacturing lead pigments in the 1950s and lead-based consumer paints in the 1960s. The suits involve substantial claims for damages and an adverse ruling against Glidden could lead to additional claims. Several US State legislatures and the US Congress are considering proposed bills that could adversely affect Glidden's position in pending or possible future cases, including proposals that could add additional grounds for legal liability or that would permit suits otherwise time-barred. Glidden believes that it has strong defences and intends to continue to deny all liability and to defend all actions vigorously.

In December 1992, ICI Explosives USA Inc. received a subpoena from a grand jury sitting in Fort Worth, Texas, with respect to what appears to be an industry-wide antitrust investigation of the US explosives business. The company is co-operating with the investigation, the results of which are unlikely to be known for some time. However, violation of US antitrust laws, if established, can result in the payment of substantial penalties and damages.

The Group is also involved in various other legal proceedings, principally in the UK and US, arising out of the normal course of business. The Group does not believe that the outcome of these proceedings will have a material effect on the Group's financial position.

The Company has given certain indemnities in the course of disposing of companies and businesses and also in connection with the demerger of Zeneca. These and other guarantees and contingencies arising in the ordinary course of business, for which no security has been given, are not expected to result in any material financial loss.

Significant take-or-pay contracts entered into by subsidiaries are as follows:

(i) the purchase of electric power which commenced April 1993 for 15 years. The present value of the remaining commitment is estimated at £679m.

(ii) the supply of ethane which will commence May 1996 for 10 years. The present value of this commitment is £105m.

36 Statutory and other information

Included in debtors is an interest-free loan of £45,000 (1993 £45,000) to one (one) officer of the Company. This loan was provided in accordance with the Company's policy of providing housing assistance to staff who have been transferred.

Remuneration of auditors charged in the Group accounts for 1994 was £3.5m (1993 £3.4m); fees paid to the auditors of the parent Company for services other than statutory audit supplied to the Company and its UK subsidiaries during 1994 totalled £0.9m (1993 £2.3m).

In November 1994, as part of the Group's restructuring in Malaysia, ICI disposed of its 50.1% interest in Chemical Company of Malaysia Berhad (CCM), to companies owned by three directors of CCM, Mr Chen Yeng Khan, Mr Oh Kim Sun and Mr Lim Say Chong. The consideration comprised cash of £25m together with 25% of the share capital of ICI Paints (Malaysia) Sdn. Bhd. (value approximately £20m) owned by CCM.

sources and disposal of value added

for the year ended 31 December 1994

| | 1994 | | | | 1993† | |
	Continuing operations £m	Discontinued operations £m	Total £m	Continuing operations £m	Discontinued operations £m	Total £m
SOURCES OF INCOME						
Sales turnover	9,189	–	9,189	8,430	2,202	10,632
Royalties and other trading income	82	–	82	113	32	145
Less materials and services	(6,556)	–	(6,556)	(6,111)	(1,351)	(7,462)
Value added by manufacturing and trading activities	2,715	–	2,715	2,432	883	3,315
Share of profit less losses of associated undertakings	14	–	14	45	2	47
Value added related to exceptional items taken below trading profit	(37)	–	(37)	(52)	(47)	(99)
Total value added	2,692	–	2,692	2,425	838	3,263
DISPOSAL OF TOTAL VALUE ADDED						
Employees						
Employee costs charged in arriving at profit before tax	1,791	–	1,791	1,742	514	2,256
Governments						
Corporate taxes	164	–	164	119	70	189
Less grants	(8)	–	(8)	(10)	(1)	(11)
	156	–	156	109	69	178
Providers of capital						
Interest cost of net borrowings	88	–	88	90	63	153
Dividends to shareholders						
Cash	199	–	199	199	–	199
Demerger				363	–	363
Minority shareholders in subsidiary undertakings	56	–	56	42	–	42
	343	–	343	694	63	757
Re-investment in the business						
Depreciation	413	–	413	417	88	505
(Loss) profit retained	(11)	–	(11)	(537)	104	(433)
	402	–	402	(120)	192	72
Total disposal	2,692	–	2,692	2,425	838	3,263

† Restated (Note 2 to the Annual Accounts)

This table is based on the audited accounts; it shows the total value added to the cost of materials and services purchased from outside the Group and indicates the ways in which this increase in value has been disposed.

TABLE 1
Amount of 1

$$a = (1+i)^n$$

(n) PERIODS	2%	2.5%	3%	4%	5%	6%	8%	9%	10%	12%	15%	(n) PERIODS
1	1.02000	1.02500	1.03000	1.04000	1.05000	1.06000	1.08000	1.09000	1.10000	1.12000	1.15000	1
2	1.04040	1.05063	1.06090	1.08160	1.10250	1.12360	1.16640	1.18810	1.21000	1.25440	1.32250	2
3	1.06121	1.07689	1.09273	1.12486	1.15763	1.19102	1.25971	1.29503	1.33100	1.40493	1.52088	3
4	1.08243	1.10381	1.12551	1.16986	1.21551	1.26248	1.36049	1.41158	1.46410	1.57352	1.74901	4
5	1.10408	1.13141	1.15927	1.21665	1.27628	1.33823	1.46933	1.53862	1.61051	1.76234	2.01136	5
6	1.12616	1.15969	1.19405	1.26532	1.34010	1.41852	1.58687	1.67710	1.77156	1.97382	2.31306	6
7	1.14869	1.18869	1.22987	1.31593	1.40710	1.50363	1.71382	1.82804	1.94872	2.21068	2.66002	7
8	1.17166	1.21840	1.26677	1.36857	1.47746	1.59385	1.85093	1.99256	2.14359	2.47596	3.05902	8
9	1.19509	1.24886	1.30477	1.42331	1.55133	1.68948	1.99900	2.17189	2.35795	2.77308	3.51788	9
10	1.21899	1.28008	1.34392	1.48024	1.62889	1.79085	2.15892	2.36736	2.59374	3.10585	4.04556	10
11	1.24337	1.31209	1.38423	1.53945	1.71034	1.89830	2.33164	2.58043	2.85312	3.47855	4.65239	11
12	1.26824	1.34489	1.42576	1.60103	1.79586	2.01220	2.51817	2.81266	3.13843	3.89598	5.35025	12
13	1.29361	1.37851	1.46853	1.66507	1.88565	2.13293	2.71962	3.06580	3.45227	4.36349	6.15279	13
14	1.31948	1.41297	1.51259	1.73168	1.97993	2.26090	2.93719	3.34173	3.79750	4.88711	7.07571	14
15	1.34587	1.44830	1.55797	1.80094	2.07893	2.39656	3.17217	3.64248	4.17725	5.47357	8.13706	15
16	1.37279	1.48451	1.60471	1.87298	2.18287	2.54035	3.42594	3.97031	4.59497	6.13039	9.35762	16
17	1.40024	1.52162	1.65285	1.94790	2.29202	2.69277	3.70002	4.32763	5.05447	6.86604	10.76126	17
18	1.42825	1.55966	1.70243	2.02582	2.40662	2.85434	3.99602	4.71712	5.55992	7.68997	12.37545	18
19	1.45681	1.59865	1.75351	2.10685	2.52695	3.02560	4.31570	5.14166	6.11591	8.61276	14.23177	19
20	1.48595	1.63862	1.80611	2.19112	2.65330	3.20714	4.66096	5.60441	6.72750	9.64629	16.36654	20
21	1.51567	1.67958	1.86029	2.27877	2.78596	3.39956	5.03383	6.10881	7.40025	10.80385	18.82152	21
22	1.54598	1.72157	1.91610	2.36992	2.92526	3.60354	5.43654	6.65860	8.14027	12.10031	21.64475	22
23	1.57690	1.76461	1.97359	2.46472	3.07152	3.81975	5.87146	7.25787	8.95430	13.55235	24.89146	23
24	1.60844	1.80873	2.03279	2.56330	3.22510	4.04893	6.34118	7.91108	9.84973	15.17863	28.62518	24
25	1.64061	1.85394	2.09378	2.66584	3.38635	4.29187	6.84848	8.62308	10.83471	17.00006	32.91895	25
26	1.67342	1.90029	2.15659	2.77247	3.55567	4.54938	7.39635	9.39916	11.91818	19.04007	37.85680	26
27	1.70689	1.94780	2.22129	2.88337	3.73346	4.82235	7.98806	10.24508	13.10999	21.32488	43.53531	27
28	1.74102	1.99650	2.28793	2.99870	3.92013	5.11169	8.62711	11.16714	14.42099	23.88387	50.06561	28
29	1.77584	2.04641	2.35657	3.11865	4.11614	5.41839	9.31727	12.17218	15.86309	26.74993	57.57545	29
30	1.81136	2.09757	2.42726	3.24340	4.32194	5.74349	10.06266	13.26768	17.44940	29.95992	66.21177	30
31	1.84759	2.15001	2.50008	3.37313	4.53804	6.08810	10.86767	14.46177	19.19434	33.55511	76.14354	31
32	1.88454	2.20376	2.57508	3.50806	4.76494	6.45339	11.73708	15.76333	21.11378	37.58173	87.56507	32
33	1.92223	2.25885	2.65234	3.64838	5.00319	6.84059	12.67605	17.18203	23.22515	42.09153	100.69983	33
34	1.96068	2.31532	2.73191	3.79432	5.25335	7.25100	13.69014	18.72841	25.54767	47.14252	115.80480	34
35	1.99989	2.37321	2.81386	3.94609	5.51602	7.68609	14.78534	20.41397	28.10244	52.79962	133.17552	35
36	2.03989	2.43254	2.89828	4.10393	5.79182	8.14725	15.96817	22.25123	30.91268	59.13557	153.15185	36
37	2.08069	2.49335	2.98523	4.26809	6.08141	8.63609	17.24563	24.25384	34.00395	66.23184	176.12463	37
38	2.12230	2.55568	3.07478	4.43881	6.38548	9.15425	18.62528	26.43668	37.40434	74.17966	202.54332	38
39	2.16474	2.61957	3.16703	4.61637	6.70475	9.70351	20.11530	28.81598	41.14478	83.08122	232.92482	39
40	2.20804	2.68506	3.26204	4.80102	7.03999	10.28572	21.72452	31.40942	45.25926	93.05097	267.86355	40

TABLE 2
Present Value of 1

$$p^n = \frac{1}{(1+i)^n} = (1+i)^{-n}$$

(n) PERIODS	2%	2.5%	3%	4%	5%	6%	8%	9%	10%	12%	15%	(n) PERIODS
1	.98039	.97561	.97087	.96154	.95238	.94340	.92593	.91743	.90909	.89286	.86957	1
2	.96117	.95181	.94260	.92456	.90703	.89000	.85734	.84168	.82645	.79719	.75614	2
3	.94232	.92860	.91514	.88900	.86384	.83962	.79383	.77218	.75131	.71178	.65752	3
4	.92385	.90595	.88849	.85480	.82270	.79209	.73503	.70843	.68301	.63552	.57175	4
5	.90573	.88385	.86261	.82193	.78353	.74726	.68058	.64993	.62092	.56743	.49718	5
6	.88797	.86230	.83748	.79031	.74622	.70496	.63017	.59627	.56447	.50663	.43233	6
7	.87056	.84127	.81309	.75992	.71068	.66506	.58349	.54703	.51316	.45235	.37594	7
8	.85349	.82075	.78941	.73069	.67684	.62741	.54027	.50187	.46651	.40388	.32690	8
9	.83676	.80073	.76642	.70259	.64461	.59190	.50025	.46043	.42410	.36061	.28426	9
10	.82035	.78120	.74409	.67556	.61391	.55839	.46319	.42241	.38554	.32197	.24718	10
11	.80426	.76214	.72242	.64958	.58468	.52679	.42888	.38753	.35049	.28748	.21494	11
12	.78849	.74356	.70138	.62460	.55684	.49697	.39711	.35553	.31863	.25668	.18691	12
13	.77303	.72542	.68095	.60057	.53032	.46884	.36770	.32618	.28966	.22917	.16253	13
14	.75788	.70773	.66112	.57748	.50507	.44230	.34046	.29925	.26333	.20462	.14133	14
15	.74301	.69047	.64186	.55526	.48102	.41727	.31524	.27454	.23939	.18270	.12289	15
16	.72845	.67362	.62317	.53391	.45811	.39365	.29189	.25187	.21763	.16312	.10686	16
17	.71416	.65720	.60502	.51337	.43630	.37136	.27027	.23107	.19784	.14564	.09293	17
18	.70016	.64117	.58739	.49363	.41552	.35034	.25025	.21199	.17986	.13004	.08081	18
19	.68643	.62553	.57029	.47464	.39573	.33051	.23171	.19449	.16351	.11611	.07027	19
20	.67297	.61027	.55368	.45639	.37689	.31180	.21455	.17843	.14864	.10367	.06110	20
21	.65978	.59539	.53755	.43883	.35894	.29416	.19866	.16370	.13513	.09256	.05313	21
22	.64684	.58086	.52189	.42196	.34185	.27751	.18394	.15018	.12285	.08264	.04620	22
23	.63416	.56670	.50669	.40573	.32557	.26180	.17032	.13778	.11168	.07379	.04017	23
24	.62172	.55288	.49193	.39012	.31007	.24698	.15770	.12640	.10153	.06588	.03493	24
25	.60953	.53939	.47761	.37512	.29530	.23300	.14602	.11597	.09230	.05882	.03038	25
26	.59758	.52623	.46369	.36069	.28124	.21981	.13520	.10639	.08391	.05252	.02642	26
27	.58586	.51340	.45019	.34682	.26785	.20737	.12519	.09761	.07628	.04689	.02297	27
28	.57437	.50088	.43708	.33348	.25509	.19563	.11591	.08955	.06934	.04187	.01997	28
29	.56311	.48866	.42435	.32065	.24295	.18456	.10733	.08215	.06304	.03738	.01737	29
30	.55207	.47674	.41199	.30832	.23138	.17411	.09938	.07537	.05731	.03338	.01510	30
31	.54125	.46511	.39999	.29646	.22036	.16425	.09202	.06915	.05210	.02980	.01313	31
32	.53063	.45377	.38834	.28506	.20987	.15496	.08520	.06344	.04736	.02661	.01142	32
33	.52023	.44270	.37703	.27409	.19987	.14619	.07889	.05820	.04306	.02376	.00993	33
34	.51003	.43191	.36604	.26355	.19035	.13791	.07305	.05339	.03914	.02121	.00864	34
35	.50003	.42137	.35538	.25342	.18129	.13011	.06763	.04899	.03558	.01894	.00751	35
36	.49022	.41109	.34503	.24367	.17266	.12274	.06262	.04494	.03235	.01691	.00653	36
37	.48061	.40107	.33498	.23430	.16444	.11579	.05799	.04123	.02941	.01510	.00568	37
38	.47119	.39128	.32523	.22529	.15661	.10924	.05369	.03783	.02673	.01348	.00494	38
39	.46195	.38174	.31575	.21662	.14915	.10306	.04971	.03470	.02430	.01204	.00429	39
40	.45289	.37243	.30656	.20829	.14205	.09722	.04603	.03184	.02209	.01075	.00373	40

TABLE 3
Amount of an Ordinary Annuity of 1

$$A_{\overline{n}|i} = \frac{(1+i)^n - 1}{i}$$

(n) PERIODS	2%	2.5%	3%	4%	5%	6%	8%	9%	10%	12%	15%
1	1.00000	1.00000	1.00000	1.00000	1.00000	1.00000	1.00000	1.00000	1.00000	1.00000	1.00000
2	2.02000	2.02500	2.03000	2.04000	2.05000	2.06000	2.08000	2.09000	2.10000	2.12000	2.15000
3	3.06040	3.07563	3.09090	3.12160	3.15250	3.18360	3.24640	3.27810	3.31000	3.37440	3.47250
4	4.12161	4.15252	4.18363	4.24646	4.31013	4.37462	4.50611	4.57313	4.64100	4.77933	4.99338
5	5.20404	5.25633	5.30914	5.41632	5.52563	5.63709	5.86660	5.98471	6.10510	6.35285	6.74238
6	6.30812	6.38774	6.46841	6.63298	6.80191	6.97532	7.33593	7.52333	7.71561	8.11519	8.75374
7	7.43428	7.54743	7.66246	7.89829	8.14201	8.39384	8.92280	9.20043	9.48717	10.08901	11.06680
8	8.58297	8.73612	8.89234	9.21423	9.54911	9.89747	10.63663	11.02847	11.43589	12.29969	13.72682
9	9.75463	9.95452	10.15911	10.58280	11.02656	11.49132	12.48756	13.02104	13.57948	14.77566	16.78584
10	10.94972	11.20338	11.46388	12.00611	12.57789	13.18079	14.48656	15.19293	15.93742	17.54874	20.30372
11	12.16872	12.48347	12.80780	13.48635	14.20679	14.97164	16.64549	17.56029	18.53117	20.65458	24.34928
12	13.41209	13.79555	14.19203	15.02581	15.91713	16.86994	18.97713	20.14072	21.38428	24.13313	29.00167
13	14.68033	15.14044	15.61779	16.62684	17.71298	18.88214	21.49530	22.95338	24.52271	28.02911	34.35192
14	15.97394	16.51895	17.08632	18.29191	19.59863	21.01507	24.21492	26.01919	27.97498	32.39260	40.50471
15	17.29342	17.93193	18.59891	20.02359	21.57856	23.27597	27.15211	29.36092	31.77248	37.27971	47.58041
16	18.63929	19.38022	20.15688	21.82453	23.65749	25.67253	30.32428	33.00340	35.94973	42.75328	55.71747
17	20.01207	20.86473	21.76159	23.69751	25.84037	28.21288	33.75023	36.97370	40.54470	48.88367	65.07509
18	21.41231	22.38635	23.41444	25.64541	28.13238	30.90565	37.45024	41.30134	45.59917	55.74971	75.83636
19	22.84056	23.94601	25.11687	27.67123	30.53900	33.75999	41.44626	46.01846	51.15909	63.43968	88.21181
20	24.29737	25.54466	26.87037	29.77808	33.06595	36.78559	45.76196	51.16012	57.27500	72.05244	102.44358
21	25.78332	27.18327	28.67649	31.96920	35.71925	39.99273	50.42292	56.76453	64.00250	81.69874	118.81012
22	27.29898	28.86286	30.53678	34.24797	38.50521	43.39229	55.45676	62.87334	71.40275	92.50258	137.63164
23	28.84496	30.58443	32.45288	36.61789	41.43048	46.99583	60.89330	69.53194	79.54302	104.60289	159.27638
24	30.42186	32.34904	34.42647	39.08260	44.50200	50.81558	66.76476	76.78981	88.49733	118.15524	184.16784
25	32.03030	34.15776	36.45926	41.64591	47.72710	54.86451	73.10594	84.70090	98.34706	133.33387	212.79302
26	33.67091	36.01171	38.55304	44.31174	51.11345	59.15638	79.95442	93.32398	109.18177	150.33393	245.71197
27	35.34432	37.91200	40.70963	47.08421	54.66913	63.70577	87.35077	102.72313	121.09994	169.37401	283.56877
28	37.05121	39.85980	42.93092	49.96758	58.40258	68.52811	95.33883	112.96822	134.20994	190.69889	327.10408
29	38.79223	41.85630	45.21885	52.96629	62.32271	73.63980	103.96594	124.13536	148.63093	214.58275	377.16969
30	40.56808	43.90270	47.57542	56.08494	66.43885	79.05819	113.28321	136.30754	164.49402	241.33268	434.74515
31	42.37944	46.00028	50.00268	59.32834	70.76079	84.80168	123.34587	149.57522	181.94342	271.29261	500.95692
32	44.22703	48.15028	52.50276	62.70147	75.29883	90.88978	134.21354	164.03699	201.13777	304.84772	577.10046
33	46.11157	50.35403	55.07784	66.20953	80.06377	97.34316	145.95062	179.80032	222.25154	342.42945	664.66552
34	48.03380	52.61289	57.73018	69.85791	85.06696	104.18375	158.62667	196.98234	245.47670	384.52098	765.36535
35	49.99448	54.92821	60.46208	73.65222	90.32031	111.43478	172.31680	215.71075	271.02437	431.66350	881.17016
36	51.99437	57.30141	63.27594	77.59831	95.83632	119.12087	187.10215	236.12472	299.12681	484.46312	1014.34568
37	54.03425	59.73395	66.17422	81.70225	101.62814	127.26812	203.07032	258.37595	330.03949	543.59869	1167.49753
38	56.11494	62.22730	69.15945	85.97034	107.70955	135.90421	220.31595	282.62978	364.04343	609.83053	1343.62216
39	58.23724	64.78298	72.23423	90.40915	114.09502	145.05846	238.94122	309.06646	401.44778	684.01020	1546.16549
40	60.40198	67.40255	75.40126	95.02552	120.79977	154.76197	259.05652	337.88245	442.59256	767.09142	1779.09031

TABLE 4
Present Value of an Ordinary Annuity of 1

$$P_{n,i} = \frac{1 - \dfrac{1}{(1+i)^n}}{i} = \frac{1 - p^n}{i}$$

(n) PERIODS	15%	12%	10%	9%	8%	6%	5%	4%	3%	2.5%	2%	(n) PERIODS
1	0.86957	0.89286	0.90909	0.91743	0.92593	0.94340	0.95238	0.96154	0.97087	0.97561	0.98039	1
2	1.62571	1.69005	1.73554	1.75911	1.78326	1.83339	1.85941	1.88609	1.91347	1.92742	1.94156	2
3	2.28323	2.40183	2.48685	2.53129	2.57710	2.67301	2.72325	2.77509	2.82861	2.85602	2.88388	3
4	2.85498	3.03735	3.16987	3.23972	3.31213	3.46511	3.54595	3.62990	3.71710	3.76197	3.80773	4
5	3.35216	3.60478	3.79079	3.88965	3.99271	4.21236	4.32948	4.45182	4.57971	4.64583	4.71346	5
6	3.78448	4.11141	4.35526	4.48592	4.62288	4.91732	5.07569	5.24214	5.41719	5.50813	5.60143	6
7	4.16042	4.56376	4.86842	5.03295	5.20637	5.58238	5.78637	6.00205	6.23028	6.34939	6.47199	7
8	4.48732	4.96764	5.33493	5.53482	5.74664	6.20979	6.46321	6.73274	7.01969	7.17014	7.32548	8
9	4.77158	5.32825	5.75902	5.99525	6.24689	6.80169	7.10782	7.43533	7.78611	7.97087	8.16224	9
10	5.01877	5.65022	6.14457	6.41766	6.71008	7.36009	7.72173	8.11090	8.53020	8.75206	8.98259	10
11	5.23371	5.93770	6.49506	6.80519	7.13896	7.88687	8.30641	8.76048	9.25262	9.51421	9.78685	11
12	5.42062	6.19437	6.81369	7.16073	7.53608	8.38384	8.86325	9.38507	9.95400	10.25776	10.57534	12
13	5.58315	6.42355	7.10336	7.48690	7.90378	8.85268	9.39357	9.98565	10.63496	10.98318	11.34837	13
14	5.72448	6.62817	7.36669	7.78615	8.24424	9.29498	9.89864	10.56312	11.29607	11.69091	12.10625	14
15	5.84737	6.81086	7.60608	8.06069	8.55948	9.71225	10.37966	11.11839	11.93794	12.38138	12.84926	15
16	5.95423	6.97399	7.82371	8.31256	8.85137	10.10590	10.83777	11.65230	12.56110	13.05500	13.57771	16
17	6.04716	7.11963	8.02155	8.54363	9.12164	10.47726	11.27407	12.16567	13.16612	13.71220	14.29187	17
18	6.12797	7.24967	8.20141	8.75563	9.37189	10.82760	11.68959	12.65930	13.75351	14.35336	14.99203	18
19	6.19823	7.36578	8.36492	8.95011	9.60360	11.15812	12.08532	13.13394	14.32380	14.97889	15.67846	19
20	6.25933	7.46944	8.51356	9.12855	9.81815	11.46992	12.46221	13.59033	14.87747	15.58916	16.35143	20
21	6.31246	7.56200	8.64869	9.29224	10.01680	11.76408	12.82115	14.02916	15.41502	16.18455	17.01121	21
22	6.35866	7.64465	8.77154	9.44243	10.20074	12.04158	13.16300	14.45112	15.93692	16.76541	17.65805	22
23	6.39884	7.71843	8.88322	9.58021	10.37106	12.30338	13.48857	14.85684	16.44361	17.33211	18.29220	23
24	6.43377	7.78432	8.98474	9.70661	10.52876	12.55036	13.79864	15.24696	16.93554	17.88499	18.91393	24
25	6.46415	7.84314	9.07704	9.82258	10.67478	12.78336	14.09394	15.62208	17.41315	18.42438	19.52346	25
26	6.49056	7.89566	9.16095	9.92897	10.80998	13.00317	14.37519	15.98277	17.87684	18.95061	20.12104	26
27	6.51353	7.94255	9.23722	10.02658	10.93516	13.21053	14.64303	16.32959	18.32703	19.46401	20.70690	27
28	6.53351	7.98442	9.30657	10.11613	11.05108	13.40616	14.89813	16.66306	18.76411	19.96489	21.28127	28
29	6.55088	8.02181	9.36961	10.19828	11.15841	13.59072	15.14107	16.98371	19.18845	20.45355	21.84438	29
30	6.56598	8.05518	9.42691	10.27365	11.25778	13.76483	15.37245	17.29203	19.60044	20.93029	22.39646	30
31	6.57911	8.08499	9.47901	10.34280	11.34980	13.92909	15.59281	17.58849	20.00043	21.39541	22.93770	31
32	6.59053	8.11159	9.52638	10.40624	11.43500	14.08404	15.80268	17.87355	20.38877	21.84918	23.46833	32
33	6.60046	8.13535	9.56943	10.46444	11.51389	14.23023	16.00255	18.14765	20.76579	22.29188	23.98856	33
34	6.60910	8.15656	9.60857	10.51784	11.58693	14.36814	16.19290	18.41120	21.13184	22.72379	24.49859	34
35	6.61661	8.17550	9.64416	10.56682	11.65457	14.49825	16.37419	18.66461	21.48722	23.14516	24.99862	35
36	6.62314	8.19241	9.67651	10.61176	11.71719	14.62099	16.54685	18.90828	21.83225	23.55625	25.48884	36
37	6.62881	8.20751	9.70592	10.65299	11.77518	14.73678	16.71129	19.14258	22.16724	23.95732	25.96945	37
38	6.63375	8.22099	9.73265	10.69082	11.82887	14.84602	16.86789	19.36786	22.49246	24.34860	26.44064	38
39	6.63805	8.23303	9.75696	10.72552	11.87858	14.94907	17.01704	19.58448	22.80822	24.73034	26.90259	39
40	6.64178	8.24378	9.77905	10.75736	11.92461	15.04630	17.15909	19.79277	23.11477	25.10278	27.35548	40

BIBLIOGRAPHY

A

Abarbanell, J., and V. L. Bernard, "Tests of Analysts' Overreaction/Underreaction to Earnings Information as an Explanation for Anomalous Stock Price Behavior," *Journal of Finance* (July 1992), pp. 1181–1208.

Abdel-khalik, A. Rashad, *Economic Effects on Leases of FASB Statement No. 13, Accounting for Leases.* Stamford, CT: Financial Accounting Standards Board, 1981.

Abdel-khalik, A. Rashad, "The Effect of LIFO-Switching and Firm Ownership on Executives Pay," *Journal of Accounting Research* (Autumn 1985), pp. 427–447.

Abdel-khalik, A. Rashad, and James C. McKeown, "Disclosures of Estimates of Holding Gains and the Assessment of Systematic Risk," *Journal of Accounting Research* (Supplement 1978), pp. 46–92.

Abdel-khalik, A. Rashad, Philip R. Regier, and Sara Ann Reiter, "Some Thoughts on Empirical Research in Positive Accounting," in Thomas Frecka (ed.), *The State of Accounting Research as We Enter the 1990's,* pp. 153–189. Urbana-Champaign: University of Illinois, 1989.

Altman, Edward I., "Financial Ratios, Discriminant Analysis and the Prediction of Corporate Bankruptcy," *Journal of Finance* (September 1968), pp. 589–609.

Altman, Edward I., *Corporate Bankruptcy in America.* Lexington, MA: Heath Lexington Books, 1971.

Altman, Edward I., *Corporate Financial Distress and Bankruptcy,* 2nd ed. New York: John Wiley & Sons, 1993.

Altman, Edward I., Robert G. Haldeman, and P. Narayanan, "Zeta™ Analysis: A New Model to Identify Bankruptcy Risk of Corporations," *Journal of Banking and Finance* (June 1977), pp. 29–54.

American Bar Foundation, *Commentaries on Indentures.* Chicago: American Bar Foundation, 1971.

Amihud, Y., and H. Mendelson, "Asset Pricing and the Bid-Ask Spread," *Journal of Financial Economics* (December 1986), pp. 223–249.

Amihud, Y., and H. Mendelson, "Liquidity, Asset Prices and Financial Policy," *Financial Analysts Journal* (November/December 1991), pp. 56–66.

Amihud, Y., B. J. Christensen, and H. Mendelson, "Further Evidence on the Risk-Return Relationship," working paper, New York University, November 1992.

Amir, Eli, "The Effect of Accounting Aggregation on the Value-Relevance of Financial Disclosures: The Case of SFAS No. 106," *The Accounting Review* (October 1996), pp. 573–590.

Amir, Eli, and Baruch Lev, "Value-relevance of Nonfinancial Information: The Wireless Communications Industry," *Journal of Accounting and Economics* (August/December 1996), pp. 3–30.

Amir, Eli, and Joshua Livnat, "Multiperiod Analysis of Adoption Motives: The Case of SFAS No. 106," *The Accounting Review* (October 1996), pp. 513–538.

Ang, James S., and Kiritkumar A. Patel, "Bond Rating Methods: Comparison and Validation," *Journal of Finance* (May 1975), pp. 631–640.

Archibald, T. Ross, "Stock Market Reaction to the Depreciation Switchback," *The Accounting Review* (January 1972), pp. 22–30.

Aziz, A., and G. H. Lawson, "Cash Flow Reporting and Financial Distress Models: Testing of Hypothesis," *Financial Management,* No. 1 (Spring 1989).

B

Balakrishnan R., T. Harris, and P. Sen, "The Predictive Ability of Geographic Segment Disclosures," *Journal of Accounting Research* (Autumn 1990), pp. 305–325.

Baldwin, Bruce A., "Segment Earnings Disclosure and the Ability of Security Analysts to Forecast Earnings per Share," *The Accounting Review* (July 1984), pp. 376–389.

Ball, Ray, "Changes in Accounting Techniques and Stock Prices," *Journal of Accounting Research* (Supplement 1972), pp. 1–38.

Ball, Ray, "Anomalies in Relationships Between Securities' Yields and Yield-Surrogates," *Journal of Financial Economics* (June/September 1978), pp. 103–126.

Ball, Ray, "The Earnings-Price Anomaly," *Journal of Accounting and Economics* (June/September 1992), pp. 319–346.

Ball, R., and E. Bartov, "How Naive Is the Stock Market's Use of Earnings Information?," *Journal of Accounting and Economics* (June 1996), pp. 319–338.

Ball, Ray, and Philip Brown, "An Empirical Evaluation of Accounting Income Numbers," *Journal of Accounting Research* (Autumn 1968), pp. 159–178.

Banz, Rolf W., "The Relationship Between Return and Market Value of Common Stocks," *Journal of Financial Economics,* Vol. 9, 1981, pp. 3–18.

Barlev, Benzion, Dov Fried, and Joshua Livnat, "Economic and Financial Reporting Effects of Inventory Tax Allowances," *Contemporary Accounting Review* (Spring 1986), pp. 288–310.

Barth M. E., and M. F. McNichols, "Estimation and Valuation of Environmental Liabilities," *Journal of Accounting Research* (Supplement 1994), pp. 177–209.

Barth, Mary, William H. Beaver, and Wayne Landsman, "The Market Valuation Implications of Net Periodic Pension Cost Components," *Journal of Accounting and Economics* (March 1992), pp. 27–62.

Bartley, Jon W., and Al Y. S. Chen, "Material Changes in Financial Reporting Attributable to the Tax Reform Act of 1986," *Accounting Horizons* (March 1992), pp. 62–74.

Bartov, Eli, "Patterns in Unexpected Earnings as an Explanation for Post-Announcement Drift," *The Accounting Review* (July 1992), pp. 610–622.

Bartov, Eli, "The Timing of Asset Sales and Earnings Manipulation," *The Accounting Review* (October 1993), pp. 840–855.

Bartov, Eli, and G. M. Bodnar, "Firm Valuation, Earnings Expectations and the Exchange-Rate Exposure Effect," *Journal of Finance* (December 1994), pp. 1755–1785.

Bartov, Eli, and G. M. Bodnar, "Foreign Currency Translation Reporting and the Exchange-Rate Exposure Effect," *Journal of International Financial Management and Accounting* (Summer 1995), pp. 93–114.

Basu, Sanjoy, "The Relationship Between Earnings Yield, Market Value, and Return for NYSE Common Stocks: Further Evidence," *Journal of Finance* (June 1988), pp. 129–156.

Bathke, Allen W., Jr., and Kenneth S. Lorek, "The Relationship Between Time-Series Models and the Security Market's Expectations of Quarterly Earnings," *The Accounting Review* (April 1984), pp. 163–176.

Beatty, A., S. Chamberlain, and J. Magliolo, "Managing the Financial Reports of Commercial Banks: The Influence of Capital, Earnings and Taxes," *The Journal of Accounting Research* (Autumn 1996), pp. 231–261.

Beaver, William H., Financial Ratios as Predictors of Failure," *Journal of Accounting Research* (Supplement 1966), pp. 71–111.

Beaver, William H., "What Should Be the FASB's Objec-

tives?" *Journal of Accountancy* (August 1973), pp. 49–56.

Beaver, William H., *Financial Reporting: An Accounting Revolution.* Englewood Cliffs, NJ: Prentice Hall, 1989.

Beaver, William H., Andrew A. Christie, and Paul A. Griffin, "The Information Content of SEC Accounting Release No. 190," *Journal of Accounting and Economics* (August 1980), pp. 127–157.

Beaver, William H., R. Clarke, and W. F. Wright, "The Association Between Unsystematic Security Returns and the Magnitude of Earnings Forecast Errors," *Journal of Accounting Research* (Autumn 1979), pp. 316–340.

Beaver, William H., and Roland E. Dukes, "Interperiod Tax Allocation, Earnings Expectations, and the Behavior of Security Prices," *The Accounting Review* (April 1972), pp. 320–332.

Beaver, William H., and Roland E. Dukes, "Interperiod Tax Allocation and δ-Depreciation Methods: Some Empirical Results," *The Accounting Review* (July 1973), pp. 549–559.

Beaver, Willliam H., Paul Griffin, and Wayne R. Landsman, "The Incremental Information Content of Replacement Cost Earnings" *Journal of Accounting and Economics* (July 1982), pp. 15–39.

Beaver, William H., Paul Kettler, and Myron Scholes, "The Association Between Market-Determined and Accounting Determined Risk Measures," *The Accounting Review* (October 1970), pp. 654–682.

Beaver, William H., and Wayne R. Landsman, *Incremental Information Content of Statement 33 Disclosures* (Stamford CT: Financial Accounting Standards Board, 1983).

Beaver, William H., and James Manegold, "The Association Between Market Determined and Accounting-Determined Measures of Systematic Risk: Some Further Evidence," *Journal of Financial and Quantitative Analysis* (June 1975), pp. 231–284.

Beaver, William H., and Dale Morse, "What Determines Price-Earnings Ratios?" *Financial Analysts Journal* (July/August 1978), pp. 65–76.

Beaver, William H., and Mark Wolfson, "Foreign Currency Translation and Changing Prices in Perfect and Complete Markets," *Journal of Accounting Research* (Autumn 1982), pp. 528–550.

Beaver, William H., and Mark Wolfson, "Foreign Currency Translation Gains and Losses: What Effect Do They Have and What Do They Mean?" *Financial Analysts Journal* (March/April 1984), pp. 28–36.

Beder, T. S., "VAR: Seductive but Dangerous," *Financial Analysts Journal* (September/October 1995), pp. 12–14.

Belkaoui, Ahmed, "Industrial Bonds Ratings: A New Look," *Financial Management* (Autumn 1980), pp. 44–51.

Belkaoui, Ahmed, *Industrial Bonds and the Rating Process.* Westport, CT: Quorum Books, an imprint of Greenwood Publishing Group, 1983.

Beneish, M., and E. Press, "Costs of Technical Violation of Accounting-Based Debt Covenants," *The Accounting Review* (April 1993), pp. 233–257.

Beneish, M., and E. Press, "The Resolution of Technical Default," *The Accounting Review* (April 1995), pp. 337–353.

Bernard, Victor L., "The Feltham-Ohlson Framework: Implications for Empiricists," *Contemporary Accounting Research* (Spring 1995), pp. 733–747.

Bernard, Victor L., "Capital Market Research During the 1980's: A Critical Review," in Thomas Frecka (ed.), *The State of Accounting Research as We Enter the 1990's,* pp. 72–120. Urbana-Champaign: University of Illinois, 1989.

Bernard, Victor L., "Accounting-Based Valuation Methods, Determinants of Market-to-Book Ratios, and Implications for Financial Statement Analysis," working paper, University of Michigan 1993.

Bernard, Victor L., and James Noel, "Do Inventory Disclosures Predict Sales and Earnings," *Journal of Accounting Auditing and Finance* (March 1991), pp. 145–182.

Bernard, Victor L., and Thomas Stober, "The Nature and Amount of Information in Cash Flows and Accruals," *The Accounting Review* (October 1989), pp. 624–652.

Bernard, V. L., and J. K. Thomas, "Evidence That Stock Prices Do Not Fully Reflect the Implications of Current Earnings for Future Earnings," *Journal of Accounting and Economics* (December 1990), pp. 305–340.

Bernstein, Leopold, *Financial Statement Analysis,* 5th ed. Homewood, IL: Richard D. Irwin 1993.

Bhandari, Laxmi Chand, "Debt/Equity Ratio and Expected Common Stock Returns: Empirical Evidence," *Journal of Finance* (June 1988), pp. 507–528.

Bhushan, Ravi, "Firm Characteristics and Analyst Following," *Journal of Accounting and Economics* (July 1989), pp. 255–274.

Bicksler, James, and Andrew Chen, "An Economic Analysis of Interest Rate Swaps," *The Journal of Finance* (July 1986), pp. 645–656.

Biddle, Gary C., "Accounting Methods and Management Decisions: The Case of Inventory Costing and Inventory Policy," *Journal of Accounting Research* (Supplement 1980), pp. 235–280.

Biddle, Gary C., and Frederick W. Lindahl, "Stock Price Reactions to LIFO Adoptions: The Association Between Excess Returns and LIFO Tax Savings," *Journal of Accounting Research* (Autumn 1982, Part II), pp. 551–588.

Biddle, Gary C., and William E. Ricks, "Analyst Forecast Errors and Stock Price Behavior Near the Earnings Announcement Dates of LIFO Adopters," *Journal of Accounting Research* (Autumn 1988), pp. 169–194.

Bildersee, John S., "The Association Between a Market-Determined Measure of Risk and Alternative Measures of Risk," *The Accounting Review* (January 1975), pp. 81–98.

Bishop, Marguerite L., "Managing Bank Regulation Through Accruals," Stern School of Business, working paper, New York University (1996).

Blankley, Alan I., and Edward P. Swanson, "A Longitudinal Study of SFAS 87 Pension Rate Assumptions, *Accounting Horizons* (December 1995), pp. 1–21.

Blum, Marc, "Failing Company Discriminant Analysis," *Journal of Accounting Research* (Spring 1974), pp. 1–25.

Bodie, Zvi, Alex Kane, and Alan J. Marcus, *Investments,* 3rd ed. Homewood, IL: Richard D. Irwin 1996.

Bowen, Robert M., "Valuation of Earnings Components in the Electric Utility Industry," *The Accounting Review* (January 1981), pp. 1–22.

Bowen, Robert M., David Burgstahler, and Lane A. Daley, "The Incremental Information Content of Accrual Versus Cash Flows," *The Accounting Review* (October 1987), pp. 723–747.

Bowman, Robert G., "The Theoretical Relationship Between Systematic Risk and Financial (Accounting) Variables," *Journal of Finance* (June 1979), pp. 617–630.

Bowman, Robert G., "The Importance of a Market-Value Measurement of Debt in Assessing Leverage," *Journal of Accounting Research* (Spring 1980), pp. 242–254.

Box, G. E. P., and G. M. Jenkins, *Time-Series Analysis: Forecasting and Control,* San Francisco: Holden Day, 1976.

Bradley, J., A. Desai, and E. H. Kim, "Synergistic Gains from Corporate Acquisitions and Their Division Between the Stockholders of Target and Acquiring Firms," *Journal of Financial Economics* (May 1988), pp. 3–40.

Briloff, Abraham J., "Distortions Arising from Pooling-of-Interests Accounting," *Financial Analysts Journal* (March–April 1968), pp. 71–80.

Brooks, Leroy, and Dale Buckmaster, "Further Evidence of the Time Series Properties of Accounting Income," *Journal of Finance* (December 1976), pp. 1359–1373.

Brown, Lawrence D., Paul A. Griffin, Robert L. Hagerman, and Mark E. Zmijewski, "An Evaluation of Alternative Proxies for the Market's Assessment of Unexpected Earnings" *Journal of Accounting and Economics* (July 1987), pp. 159–193.

Brown, Lawrence D., Robert L. Hagerman, Paul A. Griffin, and Mark E. Zmijewski, "Security Analyst Superiority Relative to Univariate Time-Series Models in Forecasting Quarterly Earnings," *Journal of Accounting and Economics* (April 1987), pp. 61–87.

Brown, Lawrence D., Gordon D. Richardson, and Steven J. Schwager, "An Information Interpretation of Financial Analyst Superiority in Forecasting Earnings," *Journal of Accounting Research* (Spring 1987), pp. 49–67.

Brown, Lawrence D., and Michael S. Rozeff, "Univariate Time-Series Models of Quarterly Accounting Earnings per Share: A Proposed Model" *Journal of Accounting Research* (Spring 1979), pp. 179–189.

Brown, Philip, George Foster, and Eric Noreen, *Security Analyst Multi-Year Earnings Forecasts and the Capital Market.* Sarasota, FL: American Accounting Association, 1985.

Brown, Robert M., "Short-Range Market Reaction to Changes to LIFO Accounting Using Preliminary Announcement Dates," *Journal of Accounting Research* (Spring 1980), pp. 38–63.

Bublitz, Bruce, and Michael Ettredge, "The Information in Discretionary Outlays: Advertising, Research and Development," *The Accounting Review* (January 1989), pp. 108–124.

Bulow, Jeremy, "What Are Corporate Pension Liabilities?" *Quarterly Journal of Economics* (August 1982), pp. 435–442.

Burgstahler, David, James Jiambalvo and Eric Noreen, "Changes in the Probability of Bankruptcy and Equity Value," *Journal of Accounting and Economics* (July 1989), pp. 207–224.

Butler, Kirt C., and Larry H. P. Lang, "The Forecast Accuracy of Individual Analysts: Evidence of Systematic Optimism and Pessimism," *Journal of Accounting Research* (Spring 1991), pp. 150–156.

C

Callen, J. L., J. Livnat, and S. Ryan, "Capital Expenditures: Value Relevance and Fourth Quarter Effects," *The Journal of Financial Statement Analysis* (Spring 1996), pp. 13–24.

Canning, John B., *The Economics of Accountancy.* New York: The Ronald Press, 1929.

Carcello, J. V., D. R. Hermanson, and F. F. Huss, "Temporal Changes in Bankruptcy-Related Reporting," *Auditing: A Journal of Practice and Theory* (Fall 1995), pp. 133–143.

Casey, Cornelius J., and Norman J. Bartczak, "Cash Flow, It's Not the Bottom Line," *Harvard Business Review* (July/August 1984), pp. 60–66.

Casey, Cornelius J., and Norman J. Bartczak, "Using Operating Cash Flow Data to Predict Financial Distress: Some Extensions," *Journal of Accounting Research* (Spring 1985), pp. 384–401.

Chambers, R. J., *Accounting, Evaluation and Economic Behavior.* Englewood Cliffs, NJ: Prentice Hall, 1966.

Chan, K. C., and N. Chen, "Structural and Return Characteristics of Small and Large Firms," *Journal of Finance* (September 1991), pp. 1467–1484.

Chen, Kung H., and Thomas A. Shimerda, "An Empirical Analysis of Useful Financial Ratios," *Financial Management* (Spring 1981), pp. 51–60.

Chen, K., and J. Wei, "Creditors' Decisions to Waive Violations of Accounting-Based Debt Covenants," *The Accounting Review* (April 1993), pp. 218–232.

Christie, Andrew, "Aggregation of Test Statistics: An Evaluation of the Evidence on Contracting and Size Hypothesis," *Journal of Accounting and Economics* (January 1990), pp. 127–157.

Clinch, Greg J., and Joseph Magliolo, "Market Perceptions of Reserve Disclosures Under SFAS No. 69," *The Accounting Review* (October 1992), pp. 843–861.

Cohen, Jerome B., Edward D. Zinbarg, and Arthur Zeikel, *Investment Analysis and Portfolio Management,* 5th ed. Homewood, IL: Richard D. Irwin, 1987.

Collins, Daniel W., "Predicting Earnings with Subentity Data: Some Further Evidence," *Journal of Accounting Research* (Spring 1976), pp. 163–177.

Collins, Daniel W., and Warren T. Dent, "The Proposed Elimination of Full Cost Accounting in the Extractive Petroleum Industry: An Empirical Assessment of the Market Consequences," *Journal of Accounting and Economics* (March 1979), pp. 3–44.

Collins, Daniel W., and S. P. Kothari, "An Analysis of Intertemporal and Cross-sectional Determinants of Earnings Response Coefficients," *Journal of Accounting and Economics* (July 1989), pp. 143–181.

Collins, Daniel W., Michael Rozeff, and Dan Dhaliwal, "The Economic Determinants of the Market Reaction to Proposed Mandatory Accounting Changes in the Oil and Gas Industry: A Cross-sectional Analysis," *Journal of Accounting and Economics* (March 1981), pp. 37–71.

Collins, Daniel W., Michael Rozeff, and William K. Salatka, "The SEC's Rejection of SFAS 19: Tests of Market Price Reversal," *The Accounting Review* (January 1982), pp. 1–17.

Collins, Daniel W., and Richard R. Simmonds, "SEC Line-of-Business Disclosure and Market Risk Adjustments," *Journal of Accounting Research* (Autumn 1979), pp. 352–383.

Collins, J., D. Shakelford, and J. Whalen, "Bank Differences in the Coordination of Regulatory Capital, Earnings and Taxes," *The Journal of Accounting Research* (Autumn 1996), pp. 263–291.

Comiskey, Eugene, and Charles W. Mulford, "Investment Decisions and the Equity Accounting Standard," *The Accounting Review* (July 1986), pp. 519–525.

Copeland, R. M., and M. L. Moore, "The Financial Bath: Is It Common?" *MSU Business Topics* (Autumn 1972), pp. 63–69.

Copeland, T., T. Koller, and J. Murrin, *Valuation: Measuring and Managing the Value of Companies,* 2nd ed. New York: John Wiley and Sons, 1996.

Cragg, J. G., and B. G. Malkiel, *Expectations and the Structure of Share Prices.* Chicago: University of Chicago Press, 1982.

Cushing, Barry E., and Marc J. LeClere, "Evidence on the Determinants of Inventory Accounting Policy Choice," *The Accounting Review* (April 1992), pp. 355–366.

D

Daley, Lane A. "The Valuation of Reported Pension Measures for Firms Sponsoring Defined Benefit Plans," *The Accounting Review* (April 1984), pp. 177–198.

Dambolena, Ismael G., and Sarkis J. Khoury, "Ratio Stability and Corporate Failure," *Journal of Finance* (September 1980), pp. 1017–1026.

Davis, H. Z., and Y. C. Peles, "Measuring Equilibrating Forces of Financial Ratios," *The Accounting Review* (October 1993), pp. 725–747.

Davis, Harry Z., Nathan Kahn, and Etzmun Rosen, "LIFO Inventory Liquidations: An Empirical Study," *Journal of Accounting Research* (Autumn 1984), pp. 480–496.

Davis, Michael L., "Differential Market Reaction to Pooling and Purchase Methods," *The Accounting Review* (July 1990), pp. 696–709.

Deakin, Edward B. III, "A Discriminant Analysis of Predictors of Business Failure," *Journal of Accounting Research* (Spring 1972), pp. 167–179.

Deakin, Edward B. III, "An Analysis of Differences Between Non-Major Oil Firms Using Successful Efforts and Full Cost Methods," *The Accounting Review* (October 1979), pp. 722–734.

Deakin, Edward B. III, "Rational Economic Behavior and Lobbying on Accounting Issues: Evidence from the Oil and Gas Industry," *The Accounting Review* (January 1989), pp. 137–151.

DeBondt, W., and R. Thaler, "Does the Stock Market Overreact," *Journal of Finance* (March 1985), pp. 793–805.

Dechow, Patricia M., "Accounting Earnings and Cash Flows as Measures of Firm Performance: The Role of Accounting Accruals," *Journal of Accounting and Economics* (July 1994), pp. 3–42.

DeFond, M., and J. Jiambalvo, "Debt Covenant Violation and Manipulation of Accruals," *Journal of Accounting and Economics* (January 1994), pp. 145–176.

Devine, Michael, "Using Pro Forma Allocations to Evaluate Business Purchases," *Financial Executive* (June 1981), pp. 15–18.

Dhaliwal, Dan S., "Measurement of Financial Leverage in the Presence of Unfunded Pension Liabilities," *The Accounting Review* (October 1986), pp. 651–661.

Dhaliwal, Dan, Gerald Saloman, and E. Dan Smith, "The Effect of Owner Versus Management Control on the Choice of Accounting Methods," *Journal of Accounting and Economics* (July 1982), pp. 89–96.

Dieter, R., and J. A. Heyman, "Implications of SEC Staff Accounting Bulletin 88 for Foreign Registrants," *Journal of Accountancy* (August 1991), pp. 121–125.

Dopuch, Nicholas, and Morton Pincus, "Evidence on the Choice of Inventory Accounting Methods: LIFO Versus FIFO," *Journal of Accounting Research* (Spring 1988), pp. 28–59.

Dreman, David, "Value Will Out," *Forbes* (June 17, 1996), pp. 146.

Duke, Joanne C., and Herbert G. Hunt III, "An Empirical Examination of Debt Covenant Restrictions and Accounting-Related Debt Proxies," *Journal of Accounting and Economics* (January 1990), pp. 45–63.

Dukes, Roland E., *An Empirical Investigation of the Effects of Statement of Financial Accounting Standards No. 8 on Security Return Behavior.* Stamford, CT: Financial Accounting Standards Board, 1978.

Dukes, Roland E., Thomas R. Dyckman, and John A. Elliott, "Accounting for Research and Development Costs: The Impact on Research and Development Expenditures," *Journal of Accounting Research* (Supplement 1980), pp. 1–26.

Dumbolena, I. G., and J. M. Shulman, "A Primary Rule for Detecting Bankruptcy: Watch the Cash," *Financial Analysts Journal* (September/October 1988), pp. 74–78.

Dunne Kathleen M., "An Empirical Analysis of Management's Choice of Accounting Treatment for Business Combinations," *Journal of Accounting and Public Policy* (July 1990), pp. 111–133.

Dyckman, Thomas R., and Abbie J. Smith, "Financial Accounting and Reporting by Oil and Gas Producing Companies: A Study of Information Effects," *Journal of Accounting and Economics* (March 1979), pp. 45–75.

E

Easman, W., A. Falkenstein, and R. Weil, "The Correlation Between Sustainable Income and Stock Returns," *Financial Analysts Journal* (September/October 1979), pp. 44–47.

Easton, Peter D., Trevor Harris, and James Ohlson, "Aggregate Accounting Earnings Can Explain Most of Security Returns: The Case of Long Run Intervals," *Journal of Accounting and Economics* (June/September 1992), pp. 119–142.

Eccher, Elizabeth A., "The Value Relevance of Capitalized Software Development Costs," working paper, Sloan School of Management, April 1996.

Edwards, E. O., and P. W. Bell, *The Theory and Measurement of Business Income.* University of California Press, 1961.

Eggleton, Ian R., Stephen H. Penman, and John R. Twombly, "Accounting Changes and Stock Prices: An Examination of Selected Uncontrolled Variables," *Journal of Accounting Research* (Spring 1976), pp. 66–88.

Elam, Rick, "The Effect of Lease Data on the Predictive Ability of Financial Ratios," *The Accounting Review* (January 1975), pp. 25–53.

Elliott, J. W., and H. L. Uphoff, "Predicting the Near Term Profit and Loss Statement with an Econometric Model: A Feasibility Study," *Journal of Accounting Research* (Autumn 1972), pp. 259–274.

Elliott, John A., and Donna R. Philbrick, "Accounting Changes and Earnings Predictability," *The Accounting Review* (January 1990), pp. 157–174.

Elliott, John A., Gordon Richardson, Thomas R. Dyckman, and Roland E. Dukes, "The Impact of SFAS No. 2 on Firm Expenditures on Research and Development: Replications and Extensions," *Journal of Accounting Research* (Spring 1984), pp. 85–102.

Elliott, John A., and Wayne Shaw, "Write-offs as Accounting Procedures to Manage Perceptions," *Journal of Accounting Research* (Supplement 1988), pp. 91–119.

El-Gazzar, Samir M., Steven Lilien, and Victor Pastena, "Accounting for Leases by Lessees," *Journal of Accounting and Economics* (October 1986), pp. 217–237.

Emery, Gary W., and Kenneth O. Cogger, "The Measurement of Liquidity," *Journal of Accounting Research* (Autumn 1982), pp. 290–303.

F

Fairfield, Patricia, "P/E, P/B and the Present Value of Future Dividends," *Financial Analysts Journal* (July/August 1994), pp. 23–31.

Fairfield, Patricia, R. Sweeney, and T. L. Yohn, "Accounting Classification and the Predictive Content of Earnings," *The Accounting Review* (July 1996), pp. 337–356.

Falkenstein, Angela, and Roman L. Weil, "Replacement Cost Accounting: What Will Income Statements Based on the SEC Disclosures Show? Part I," *Financial Analysts Journal* (January/February 1977a), pp. 46–57.

Falkenstein, Angela, and Roman L. Weil, "Replacement Cost Accounting: What Will Income Statements Based on the SEC Disclosures Show? Part II," *Financial Analysts Journal* (March/April 1977b), pp. 48–57.

Fama, Eugene, "Efficient Capital Markets: A Review of Theory and Empirical Work," *Journal of Finance* (May 1970), pp. 383–417.

Fama, Eugene, and Kenneth R. French, "The Cross-section of Expected Stock Returns," *Journal of Finance* (June 1992), pp. 427–466.

Fama, Eugene, and Kenneth French, "Common Risk Factors in the Returns on Stocks and Bonds," *Journal of Financial Economics* (February 1993), pp. 3–56.

Fama, Eugene, and Kenneth French, "Size and Book-to-Market Factors in Earnings and Returns," *Journal of Finance* (March 1995), pp. 131–155.

Fama, Eugene, and Kenneth French, "The CAPM Is Wanted, Dead or Alive," working paper, Graduate School of Business, University of Chicago, April 1995.

Feldstein, Martin, and Randall Morck, "Pension Funding Decisions, Interest Rate Assumptions and Share Prices," in Zvi Bodie and John B. Shoven (eds.), *Financial Aspects of the United States Pension System.* Chicago: University of Chicago Press, 1983.

Feltham, Gerald, and James A. Ohlson, "Valuation and Clean Surplus Accounting for Operating and Financial Activities," *Contemporary Accounting Research* (Spring 1995), pp. 689–731.

Financial Executives Institute, Committee on Corporate Reporting, "Survey on Unusual Charges" (1986 and 1991).

Foster, George, "Accounting Earnings and Stock Prices of Insurance Companies," *The Accounting Review* (October 1975), pp. 686–698.

Foster, George, "Quarterly Accounting Data: Time Series Properties and Predictive-Ability Results," *The Accounting Review* (January 1977), pp. 1–21.

Foster, George, "Briloff and the Capital Market," *Journal of Accounting Research* (Spring 1979), pp. 262–274.

Francis, Jere R., and Sara Ann Reiter, "Determinants of Corporate Pension Funding Strategy," *Journal of Accounting and Economics* (April 1987), pp. 35–59.

Frankel, Richard, and Charles M. C. Lee, "Accounting Diversity and International Valuation," working paper, University of Michigan, 1996.

Frecka, Thomas J., and Cheng F. Lee, "Generalized Financial Ratio Adjustment Processes and Their Implications," *Journal of Accounting Research* (Spring 1983), pp. 308–316.

Freeman, Robert N., James A. Ohlson, and Stephen H. Penman, "Book Rate-of-Return and Prediction of Earnings Changes: An Empirical Investigation," *Journal of Accounting Research* (Autumn 1982), pp. 639–653.

Fried, Dov, "Aggregation Versus Disaggregation and the Predictive Ability Criterion," unpublished dissertation, New York University, 1978.

Fried, Dov, and Dan Givoly, "Financial Analysts' Forecasts of Earnings: A Better Surrogate for Market Expectations," *Journal of Accounting and Economics* (October 1982), pp. 85–108.

Fried, Dov, Haim Mozes, Donna Rapaccioli, and Allen Schiff, "Earnings Manipulation and the Sale of a Business Segment," *The Journal of Financial Statement Analysis* (Spring 1996), pp. 25–33.

Fried, Dov, Michael Schiff, and Ashwinpaul C. Sondhi, *Impairments and Writeoffs of Long-Lived Assets.* Montvale, NJ: National Association of Accountants, 1989.

Fried, Dov, Michael Schiff, and Ashwinpaul C. Sondhi, "Big Bath or Intermittent Showers? Another Look at Write-offs," working paper, New York University, 1990.

Fuller, Russell J., and Chi-Cheng Hsia, "A Simplified Common Stock Valuation Model," *Financial Analysts Journal* (September/October 1984), pp. 49–56.

G

Gahlon, James M., and James A. Gentry, "On the Relationship Between Systematic Risk and the Degrees of Operating and Financial Leverage," *Financial Management* (Summer 1982), pp. 15–23.

Gaver, J. J., K. M. Gaver, and J. R. Austin, "Additional Evidence on the Association Between Income Management and Earnings-based Bonus Plans," *Journal of Accounting and Economics* (February 1995) , pp. 3–28.

Gentry, James A., Paul Newbold, and David T. Whitford, "Bankruptcy, Working Capital, and Funds Flows," *Managerial Finance.* Vol. 10, No. 3/4, 1984.

Gentry, James A., Paul Newbold, and David T. Whitford, "Classifying Bankrupt Firms with Funds Flow Components," *Journal of Accounting Research* (Spring 1985), pp. 146–160.

Gentry, James A., Paul Newbold, and David T. Whitford, "Predicting Bankruptcy: If Cash Flow's Not the Bottom Line, What Is?," *Financial Analysts Journal* (September/October 1985), pp. 47–58.

Ghicas, Dimitrios C., "Determinants of Actuarial Cost Method Changes for Pension Accounting and Funding," *The Accounting Review* (April 1990), pp. 384–405.

Gibson, Charles H., "Financial Ratios in Annual Reports," *The CPA Journal* (September 1982), pp. 18–29.

Gibson, Charles H., "How Chartered Financial Analysts View Financial Ratios," *Financial Analysts Journal* (May/June 1987), pp. 74–76.

Givoly, Dan, and Carla Hayn, "The Valuation of the Deferred Tax Liability: Evidence from the Stock Market," *The Accounting Review* (April 1992), pp. 394–410.

Givoly, Dan, and Josef Lakonishok, "The Information Content of Financial Analysts' Forecasts of Earnings: Some Evidence of Semi-Strong Inefficiency," *Journal of Accounting and Economics* (December 1979), pp. 165–185.

Givoly, Dan, and Josef Lakonishok, "The Quality of Analysts' Forecasts of Earnings," *Financial Analysts Journal* (September/October 1984), pp. 40–47.

Gombola, M. F., M. E, Haskins, J. E. Katz, and D. D. Williams, "Cash Flow in Bankruptcy Prediction," *Financial Management* (Winter 1987).

Gombola, Michael J., and J. Edward Ketz, "Financial Ratio Patterns in Retail and Manufacturing Organizations," *Financial Management* (Summer 1983), pp. 45–56.

Gonedes, Nicholas J., "Risk, Information and the Effects of Special Accounting Items on Capital Market Equilibrium," *Journal of Accounting Research* (Autumn 1975), pp. 220–256.

Gonedes, Nicholas J., "Corporate Signalling, External Accounting and Capital Market Equilibrium: Evidence on Dividends, Income and Extraordinary Items," *Journal of Accounting Research* (Spring 1978), pp. 26–79.

Gonedes, Nicholas J., and Nicholas Dopuch, "Capital Market Equilibrium, Information Production and Selecting Accounting Techniques: Theoretical Framework and Review of Empirical Work," *Journal of Accounting Research* (Supplement 1974), pp. 48–129.

Gopalakrishnan, V., and T. F. Sugrue, "An Empirical Investigation of Stock Market Valuation of Corporate Projected Pension Liabilities," *Journal of Business Finance & Accounting* (September 1993), pp. 711–724.

Granof, Michael H., and Daniel G. Short, "Why Do Companies Reject LIFO?," *Journal of Accounting Auditing and Finance* (Summer 1984), pp. 323–333.

Greenstein, M. M., and H. Sami, "The Impact of the SEC's Segment Disclosure Requirement on Bid-Ask Spreads," *The Accounting Review* (January 1994), pp. 179–199.

Griffin, Paul A., "The Time-Series Behavior of Quarterly Earnings: Preliminary Evidence," *Journal of Accounting Research* (Spring 1977), pp. 71–83.

H

Hackel, Kenneth S., and Joshua Livnat, "International Investments Based on Free Cash Flow: A Practical Approach," *The Journal of Financial Statement Analysis* (Fall 1995), pp. 5–14.

Hackel, Kenneth S., and Joshua Livnat, *Cash Flow and Security Analysis,* 2nd ed. Homewood, IL: Business One-Irwin, 1995.

Hamada, Robert S., "The Effect of the Firm's Capital Structure on the Systematic Risk of Common Stocks," *Journal of Finance* (May 1972), pp. 435–452.

Hand, John R. M., "Did Firms Undertake Debt-Equity Swaps for Accounting Paper Profits or True Financial Gains?" *The Accounting Review* (October 1989), pp. 587–623.

Hand, John R. M., "A Test of the Extended Functional Fixation Hypothesis," *The Accounting Review* (October 1990), pp. 739–763.

Harrington, Diana R., "Whose Beta Is Best?" *Financial Analysts Journal* (July/August 1983), pp. 67–77.

Harris, Trevor S., and James A. Ohlson, "Accounting Disclosures and the Market's Valuation of Oil and Gas Properties," *The Accounting Review* (October 1987), pp. 651–670.

Harris, Trevor S., and James A. Ohlson, "Accounting Disclosures and the Market's Valuation of Oil and Gas Properties: Evaluation of Market Efficiency and Functional Fixation," *The Accounting Review* (October 1990), pp. 764–780.

Haugen, Robert A., *The New Finance: The Case Against Efficient Markets.* Englewood Cliffs, NJ: Prentice Hall, 1995.

Hauworth, William P. II, and Lailani Moody, "An Accountant's Option Primer: Puts and Calls Demystified," *Journal of Accountancy* (January 1987), pp. 87–97.

Healy, Paul M., "The Effect of Bonus Schemes on Accounting Decisions," *Journal of Accounting and Economics* (April 1985), pp. 85–107.

Healy, Paul M., Sok-Hyon Kang, and Krishna Palepu, "The Effect of Accounting Procedure Changes on CEO's Cash Salary and Bonus Compensation," *Journal of Accounting and Economics* (April 1987), pp. 7–34.

Heian, James B., and James B. Thies, "Consolidation of Finance Subsidiaries: $230 Billion in Off-Balance-Sheet Financing Comes Home to Roost," *Accounting Horizons* (March 1989), pp. 1–9.

Hicks, J. R., *Value and Capital,* 2nd ed. Oxford: Chaundon Press, 1946.

Hirschey, Mark, and Jerry J. Weygandt, "Amortization Policy for Advertising and Research and Development," *Journal of Accounting Research* (Spring 1985), pp. 326–335.

Hochman, Shalom, "The Beta Coefficient: An Instrumental Variables Approach," in Haim Levy (ed.), *Research in Finance,* Vol. 4. Greenwich, CT: JAI Press, 1983.

Holthausen, Robert W., "Evidence on the Effect of Bond Covenants and Management Compensation Contracts on the Choice of Accounting Techniques: The Case of The Depreciation Switch-Back," *Journal of Accounting and Economics* (March 1981), pp. 73–109.

Holthausen, Robert W., and Richard E. Leftwich, "The Effect of Bond Ratings on Common Stock Prices," *Journal of Financial Economics* (September 1986), pp. 57–90.

Holthausen, Robert W., and D. F. Larcker, "The Predic-tion of Stock Return Using Financial Statement Information" *Journal of Accounting and Economics* (June/September 1992), pp. 373–411.

Holthausen, R., D. F. Larcker, and R. G. Sloan, "Annual Bonus Schemes and the Manipulation of Earnings," *Journal of Accounting and Economics* (February 1995), pp. 29–74.

Hong, Hai, Robert S. Kaplan, and Gershon Mandelker, "Pooling vs. Purchase: The Effects of Accounting for Mergers on Stock Prices," *The Accounting Review* (January 1978), pp. 31–47.

Hopwood, William, James C. McKeown, and Paul Newbold, "The Additional Information Content of Quarterly Earnings Reports," *Journal of Accounting Research* (Autumn 1982), pp. 343–349.

Hopwood, William, Paul Newbold, and Peter A. Silhan, "The Potential for Gains in Predictive Ability Through Disaggregation: Segmented Annual Earnings," *Journal of Accounting Research* (Autumn 1982), pp. 724–732.

Horrigan, James O., "Some Empirical Bases of Financial Ratio Analysis," *The Accounting Review* (July 1965), pp. 558–568.

Horrigan, James O., "The Determination of Long-Term Credit Standing with Financial Ratios," *Journal of Accounting Research* (Supplement 1966), pp. 44–62.

Horwitz, Bertrand, and Richard Kolodny, "Line of Business Reporting and Security Prices: An Analysis of an SEC Disclosure Rule," *Bell Journal of Economics* (Spring 1977), pp. 234–249.

Horwitz, Bertrand N., and Richard Kolodny, "The Economic Effects of Involuntary Uniformity in the Financial Reporting of R&D Expenditures," *Journal of Accounting Research* (Supplement 1980), pp. 38–74.

Hull, John , *Introduction to Futures and Options Markets.* Englewood Cliffs, NJ: Prentice Hall, 1995.

Hunt, Herbert G., III, "Potential Determinants of Corporate Inventory Accounting Decisions," *Journal of Accounting Research* (Autumn 1985), pp. 448–467.

I

Imhoff, Eugene A., Jr., and Jacob K. Thomas, "Economic Consequences of Accounting Changes: The Lease Disclosure Rule Change," *Journal of Accounting and Economics* (December 1988), pp. 277–310.

Ingberman, Monroe and George H. Sorter, "The Role of Financial Statements in an Efficient Market," *Journal of Accounting, Auditing, and Finance* (Fall 1978), pp. 58–62.

J

Jagannathan, Ravi, and Z. Wang, "The CAPM Is Alive and Well," *Staff Report 165, Federal Reserve Bank of Minneapolis,* 1993.

Jagannathan, Ravi, and McGrattan, "The CAPM Debate," *Federal Reserve Bank of Minneapolis, Quarterly Report,* Vol. 19(4), 1995, pp. 2–17.

Jennings, Ross, David P. Mest, and Robert B. Thompson II, "Investor Reaction to Disclosures of 1974–75 LIFO Adoption Decisions," *The Accounting Review* (April 1992), pp. 337–354.

Jennings, R., J. Robinson, R. B. Thompson II, and L. Duvall, "The Relation Between Accounting Goodwill Numbers and Equity Values," *Journal of Business, Finance and Accounting* (June 1996), pp. 513–534.

Jensen, M. C. and W. H. Meckling, "Theory of the Firm: Managerial Behavior, Agency Costs, and Ownership Structure," *Journal of Financial Economics* (October 1976), pp. 305–360.

Johnson, W. Bruce, "The Cross Sectional Stability of Financial Ratio Patterns," *Journal of Financial and Quantitative Analysis* (December 1979), pp. 1035–1048.

Johnson, W. Bruce, and Dan S. Dhaliwal, "LIFO Abandonment," *Journal of Accounting Research* (Autumn 1988), pp. 236–272.

Jones, Jennifer J., "Earnings Management During Import Relief Investigations," *Journal of Accounting Research* (Autumn 1991), pp. 193–228.

Joy, O. M., and C. P. Jones, "Earnings Reports and Market Efficiencies: An Analysis of the Contrary Evidence," *The Journal of Financial Research* (Spring 1979), pp. 51–63.

K

Kaplan, Robert S., and Richard Roll, "Investor Evaluation of Accounting Information: Some Empirical Evidence," *Journal of Business* (April 1972), pp. 225–257.

Kaplan, Robert S., and Gabriel Urwitz, "Statistical Models of Bond Ratings: A Methodological Inquiry," *Journal of Business* (April 1979), pp. 231–261.

Kerstein, Joseph, and Sungsoo Kim, "The Incremental Information Content of Capital Expenditures," *The Accounting Review* (July 1995), pp. 513–526.

Kim, Moshe, and Giora Moore, "Economic vs. Accounting Depreciation," *Journal of Accounting and Economics* (April 1988), pp. 111–125.

Kimmel, Paul, and Terry D. Warfield, "Variation in Attributes of Redeemable Preferred Stock: Implications for Accounting Standards," *Accounting Horizons* (June 1993), pp. 30–40.

Kimmel, Paul, and Terry D. Warfield, "The Usefulness of Hybrid Security Classifications—Evidence from Redeemable Preferred Stock," *The Accounting Review* (January 1995), pp. 151–167.

Kinney, M., and R. H. Trezevat, "Taxes and the Timing of Corporate Capital Expenditures," *The Journal of the American Taxation Association* (1993), pp. 40–62.

Kinney, William R., Jr., "Predicting Earnings: Entity Versus Subentity Data," *Journal of Accounting Research* (Spring 1971), pp. 127–136.

Kormendi, Roger, and Robert Lipe, "Earnings Innovations, Earnings Persistence, and Stock Returns," *Journal of Business* (July 1987), pp. 323–345.

Kothari, S. P., Jay Shanken, and Richard G. Sloan, "Another Look at the Cross-section of Expected Stock Returns," *Journal of Finance* (March 1995), pp. 185–224.

L

Lakonishok, Josef, Andrei Shleifer, and Robert W. Vishny, "Contrarian Investment, Extrapolation and Risk," *Journal of Finance* (December 1994), pp. 1541–1578.

Landsman, Wayne, "An Empirical Investigation of Pension and Property Rights," *The Accounting Review* (October 1986), pp. 662–691.

Largay, James A., III, and Clyde P. Stickney, "Cash Flows, Ratio Analysis and the W. T. Grant Bankruptcy," *Financial Analysts Journal* (July/August 1980), pp. 51–54.

Lasman, Daniel A., and Roman L. Weil, "Adjusting the Debt-Equity Ratio," *Financial Analysts Journal* (September/October 1978), pp. 49–58.

Lau, Amy Hing-Ling, "A Five-State Financial Distress Prediction Model," *Journal of Accounting Research* (Spring 1987), pp. 127–138.

Leftwich, Richard W., "Evidence of the Impact of Mandatory Changes in Accounting Principles on Corporate Loan Agreements," *Journal of Accounting and Economics* (March 1981), pp. 3–36.

Leftwich, Richard W., "Accounting Information in Private Markets: Evidence from Private Lending Agreements," *The Accounting Review* (January 1983), pp. 23–42.

Lev, Baruch, "Industry Averages as Targets for Financial Ratios," *Journal of Accounting Research* (Autumn 1969), pp. 290–299.

Lev, Baruch, "On the Association Between Operating Leverage and Risk," *Journal of Financial and Quantitative Analysis* (September 1974), pp. 627–640.

Lev, Baruch, "The Impact of Accounting Regulation on the Stock Market: The Case of Oil and Gas Companies," *The Accounting Review* (July 1979), pp. 485–503.

Lev, Baruch, "On the Usefulness of Earnings and Earnings Research: Lessons and Directions from Two Decades of Empirical Research," *Journal of Accounting Research* (Supplement 1989), pp. 153–192.

Lev, Baruch, and Theodore Sougiannis, "The Capitalization, Amortization and Value-Relevance of R&D," *Journal of Accounting and Economics* (February 1996), pp. 107–138.

Lev, Baruch, and S. Ramu Thiagarajan, "Fundamental Information Analysis," *Journal of Accounting Research* (Autumn 1993), pp. 190–215.

Lilien, Steven, and Victor Pastena, "Determinants of Intra-Method Choice in the Oil and Gas Industry," *Journal of Accounting and Economics* (December 1982), pp. 145–170.

Lindhal, F. W., and W. E. Ricks, "Market Reactions to Announcements of Writeoffs," working paper, The Fuqua School of Business, Duke University, January 1990.

Lipe, Robert C., "The Information Contained in the Components of Earnings," *Journal of Accounting Research* (Supplement 1986), pp. 37–64.

Livnat, Joshua, and Ashwinpaul C. Sondhi, "Finance Subsidiaries: Their Formation and Consolidation," *Journal of Business Finance & Accounting* (Spring 1986), pp. 137–147.

Livnat, Joshua, and Paul Zarowin, "The Incremental Informational Content of Cash-Flow Components," *Journal of Accounting and Economics* (May 1990), pp. 25–46.

Lys, Thomas, "Mandated Accounting Changes and Debt Covenants: The Case of Oil and Gas Accounting," *Journal of Accounting and Economics* (April 1984), pp. 39–65.

M

Malmquist, David H. "Efficient Contracting and the Choice of Accounting Method in the Oil and Gas Industry," *Journal of Accounting and Economics* (January 1990), pp. 173–205.

Mandelker, Gershon M., and S. Ghon Rhee, "The Impact of the Degrees of Operating and Financial Leverage on Systematic Risk of Common Stock," *Journal of Financial and Quantitative Analysis* (March 1984), pp. 45–57.

Martin, L. G., and G. V. Henderson, "On Bond Ratings and Pension Obligations: A Note," *Journal of Financial and Quantitative Analysis* (December 1983), pp. 463–470.

McConnell, J. J., and C. J. Muscarella, "Corporate Capital Expenditure Decisions and the Market Value of the Firm," *Journal of Financial Economics* (1985), pp. 399–422.

Mellman, Martin, and Leopold Bernstein, "Lease Capitalization Under APB Opinion No. 5," *The New York Certified Public Accountant* (February 1966), pp. 115–122.

Mendenhall, R., "Evidence on the Possible Underweighting of Earnings Related Information," *Journal of Accounting Research* (Spring 1991), pp. 170–179.

Mittelstaedt, H. F., W. D. Nichols, and P. R. Regier. "SFAS No. 106 and Benefit Reduction in Employer-Sponsored Retiree Health Care Plans." *The Accounting Review* (October 1995), pp. 535–556.

Mohrman, Mary Beth, "The Use of Fixed GAAP Provisions in Debt Contracts," *Accounting Horizons* (September 1996), pp. 78–91.

Morck, Randall, Andrei Shleifer, and Robert W. Vishny, "Do Managerial Objectives Drive Bad Acquisitions?" *Journal of Finance* (March 1990), pp. 31–48.

Moses, Douglas, "Income Smoothing and Incentives: Empirical Tests Using Accounting Changes," *The Accounting Review* (April 1987), pp. 358–377.

Most, Kenneth S., "Depreciation Expense and the Effect of Inflation," *Journal of Accounting Research* (Autumn 1984), pp. 782–788.

Mulford, Charles W., "The Importance of a Market Value Measurement of Debt in Leverage Ratios: Replications and Extensions," *Journal of Accounting Research* (Autumn 1985), pp. 897–906.

Murdoch, Brock, "The Information Content of FAS 33 Returns on Equity," *The Accounting Review* (April 1986), pp. 273–287.

Myers, Stewart C., and Nicholas S. Majluf, "Corporate Financing and Investment Decisions When Firms Have Information That Investors Do Not Have," *Journal of Financial Economics* (June 1984), pp. 187–221.

N

Nakayama, Mie, Steven Lilien, and Martin Benis, "Due Process and FAS No. 13," *Management Accounting* (April 1981), pp. 49–53.

Nurnberg, Hugo, "Inconsistencies and Ambiguities in Cash Flow Statements Under FASB Statement No. 95," *Accounting Horizons* (June 1993), pp. 60–75.

O

O'Brien, Patricia, "Analysts Forecasts as Earnings Expectations," *Journal of Accounting and Economics* (January 1988), pp. 53–83.

Ohlson, James A., "Financial Ratios and the Probabilistic Prediction of Bankruptcy," *Journal of Accounting Research* (Spring 1980), pp. 109–131.

Ohlson, James A., "Accounting Earnings, Book Value and Dividends: The Theory of the Clean Surplus Equation (Part I)," working paper, Columbia University, 1989.

Ohlson, James A., "Earnings, Book Values and Dividends in Equity Valuation," *Contemporary Accounting Research* (Spring 1995), pp. 661–687.

Ou, Jane A., and Stephen Penman, "Financial Statement Analysis and the Evaluation of Market-to-Book Ratios," working paper, University of California at Berkeley, 1995.

Ou, Jane A., "The Information Content of Nonearnings Accounting Numbers as Earnings Predictors," *Journal of Accounting Research* (Spring 1990), pp. 144–162.

Ou, Jane A., and Stephen H. Penman, "Financial Statement Analysis and the Prediction of Stock Returns," *Journal of Accounting and Economics* (November 1989), pp. 295–329.

P

Pariser, David B., and Pierre L. Titard, "Impairment of Oil and Gas Properties," *Journal of Accountancy* (December 1991), pp. 52–62.

Patell, James M., and Mark A. Wolfson, "Good News, Bad News, and the Intraday Timing of Corporate Disclosure," *The Accounting Review* (July 1982), pp. 509–527.

Patell, James M., and Mark A. Wolfson, "The Intraday Speed of Adjustment of Stock Prices to Earnings and Dividend Announcements," *Journal of Financial Economics* (June 1984), pp. 223–252.

Peasnell, K., "Some Formal Connections Between Economic Values and Yields and Accounting Numbers," *Journal of Business, Finance and Accounting* (October 1982), pp. 361–381.

Peles, Y. C., and M. Schneller, "The Duration of the Adjustment Process of Financial Ratios," *The Review of Economics and Statistics* (November 1989), pp. 527–532.

Penman, Stephen, "An Evaluation of Accounting Rate-of-Return," *Journal of Accounting, Auditing and Finance* (Spring 1991), pp. 233–255.

Penman, Stephen H., "Return to Fundamentals," *Journal of Accounting, Auditing and Finance* (Fall 1992), pp. 465–483.

Penman, Stephen, "The Articulation of Price-Earnings Ratios and Market-to-Book Ratios and the Evaluation of Growth," *Journal of Accounting Research* (Autumn 1996), pp. 235–259.

Penman, Stephen, and Theodore Sougiannis, "A Comparison of Dividend, Cash Flow, and Earnings Approaches to Equity Valuation," working paper, University of California at Berkeley, 1995.

Pinches, George E., and Kent A. Mingo, "A Multivariate Analysis of Industrial Bond Ratings," *Journal of Finance* (March 1973), pp. 1–18.

Pinches, George E., and Kent A. Mingo, "The Role of Subordination and Industrial Bond Ratings," *Journal of Finance* (March 1975), pp. 201–206.

Pinches, George E., Kent A. Mingo, and J. Kent Caruthers, "The Stability of Financial Ratio Patterns in Industrial Organizations," *Journal of Finance* (May 1973), pp. 384–396.

Pinches, George E., A. A. Eubank, Kent A. Mingo, and

J. Kent Caruthers, "The Hierarchical Classification of Financial Ratios," *Journal of Business Research* (October 1975), pp. 295–310.

Pogue, T., and R. Soldovsky, "What's in a Bond Rating," *Journal of Financial and Quantitative Analysis* (June 1969), pp. 201–228.

Preinreich, G. A. D., "Annual Survey of Economic Theory: The Theory of Depreciation," *Econometrica* (July 1938), pp. 219–241.

Press, Eric G., and Joseph B. Weintrop, "Accounting-Based Constraints in Public and Private Debt Agreements," *Journal of Accounting and Economics* (January 1990), pp. 65–95.

R

Rama, D.V., K. Raghunandan, and M. A. Geiger, "Economic Conditions, Audit Reports and Bankruptcies," working paper, University of Massachusetts-Dartmouth, October 1995.

Ramakrishnan, Ram T. S., and Jacob K. Thomas, "Valuation of Permanent, Transitory, and Price-Irrelevant Components of Reported Earnings," working paper, Columbia University, 1991.

Rapaccioli, Donna, and Allen Schiff, "Reporting Segment Sales Under APB Opinion No. 30," *Accounting Horizons* (December 1991), pp. 53–59.

Rayburn, Judy, "The Association of Operating Cash Flow and Accruals with Security Returns," *Journal of Accounting Research* (Supplement 1986), pp. 112–133.

Reilly, Frank K., "Using Cash Flows and Financial Ratios to Predict Bankruptcies," *Analyzing Investment Opportunities in Distressed and Bankrupt Companies.* Charlottesville, VA: The Institute of Chartered Financial Analysts, 1991.

Reeve, James H., and Keith G. Stanga, "The LIFO Pooling Decision: Some Empirical Results from Accounting Practice," *Accounting Horizons* (March 1987), pp. 25–34.

Rendelman, R. J., Jr., C. P. Jones, and H. A. Latane, "Empirical Anomalies Based on Unexpected Earnings and the Importance of Risk Adjustments," *Journal of Financial Economics* (November 1982), pp. 269–287.

Richards, Verlyn D., and Eugene J. Laughlin, "A Cash Conversion Cycle Approach to Liquidity Analysis," *Financial Management* (Spring 1980), pp. 32–38.

Ricks, William E., "The Market's Response to the 1974 LIFO Adoption," *Journal of Accounting Research* (Autumn 1982, Part I), pp. 367–387.

Ricks, William E., and John S. Hughes, "Market Reactions to a Non-Discretionary Accounting Change: The Case of Long-Term Investments," *The Accounting Review* (January 1985), pp. 33–52.

Robert Morris Associates, *Annual Statement Studies.* Philadelphia: RMA, 1994.

Robinson, John R., and Philip B. Shane, "Acquisition Accounting Method and Bid Premia for Target Firms," *The Accounting Review* (January 1990), pp. 25–48.

Roll, Richard, "The Hubris Hypothesis of Corporate Takeovers," *Journal of Business* (April 1986), pp. 197–216.

Ronen, Joshua, and Simcha Sadan, *Smoothing Income Numbers: Objectives, Means, and Implications.* Reading, MA: Addison-Wesley, 1981.

Rosenberg, Barr, and James Guy, "Beta and Investment Fundamentals," *Financial Analysts Journal,* Vol. 32(3) 1976, pp. 60–72.

Rosenberg, Barr, and Walt McKibben, "The Prediction of Systematic and Specific Risk in Common Stocks," *Journal of Financial and Quantitative Analysis* (March 1973), pp. 317–333.

Rosenberg, Barr, Keith Reid, and Ronald Lansten, "Persuasive Evidence of Market Inefficiency," *Journal of Portfolio Management,* Vol. 11, 1984, pp. 9–17.

Roussey, R. S., E. L. Ten Eyck, and M. Blanco-Best, "Three New SASs: Closing the Communications Gap," *Journal of Accountancy* (December 1988), pp. 44–52.

Rue, Joseph C., David E. Tosh, and William B. Francis, "Accounting for Interest Rate Swaps," *Management Accounting* (January 1988), pp. 43–49.

Ryan, Stephen, "Structural Models of the Accounting Process and Earnings," unpublished dissertation, Stanford University, 1988.

Ryan, Stephen G., and Paul Zarowin, "On the Ability of the Classical Errors in Variables Approach to Explain Earnings Response Coefficients and R^2s in Alternative Valuation Models," *Journal of Accounting, Auditing and Finance* (Fall 1995), pp. 767–786.

S

Saunders, Anthony, *Financial Institutions Management: A Modern Perspective,* 2nd ed. (Chicago, IL: Richard D. Irwin) 1997.

Savich, Richard S., and Laurence A. Thompson, "Resource Allocation Within the Product Life Cycle," *MSU Business Topics* (Autumn 1978), pp. 35–44.

Schiff, Allen I., "The Other Side of LIFO," *Journal of Accountancy* (May 1983), pp. 120–121.

Schiff, Michael, "A Closer Look at Variable Costing," *Management Accounting* (August 1987), pp. 36–39.

Schipper, Katherine, and Abbie J. Smith, "Effects of Recontracting on Shareholder Wealth: The Case of Voluntary Spin-offs," *Journal of Financial Economics* (December 1983), pp. 437–467.

Scott, James, "The Probability of Bankruptcy: A Comparison of Empirical Predictions and Theoretical Models," *Journal of Banking and Finance* (September 1981), pp. 317–344.

Selling, Thomas I., and George H. Sorter, "FASB Statement No. 52 and Its Implications for Financial Statement Analysis," *Financial Analysts Journal* (May/June 1983), pp. 64–69.

Selling, Thomas I., and Clyde P. Stickney, "The Effects of Business Environment and Strategy on a Firm's Rate of Return on Assets," *Financial Analysts Journal* (January/February 1989), pp. 43–52.

Selling, Thomas, I., and Clyde P. Stickney, "Disaggregating the Rate of Return on Common Shareholders' Equity: A New Approach," *Accounting Horizons* (December 1990), pp. 9–17.

Selto, Frank H., and Maclyn L. Clouse, "An Investigation of Managers' Adaptations to SFAS No. 2: Accounting for Research and Development Costs," *Journal of Accounting Research* (Autumn 1985), pp. 700–717.

Servaes, Henri, "Tobin's Q and the Gains from Takeovers," *Journal of Finance* (March 1991), pp. 409–419.

Shevlin, Terry, "The Valuation of R&D Firms with R&D Limited Partnerships" *The Accounting Review* (January 1991), pp. 1–21.

Silhan, Peter A. "Simulated Mergers of Existent Autonomous Firms: A New Approach to Segmentation Research," *Journal of Accounting Research* (Spring 1982), pp. 255–262.

Skinner, R. C., "Fixed Asset Lives and Replacement Cost Accounting," *Journal of Accounting Research* (Spring 1982), pp. 210–226.

Sloan, Richard G., "Do Stock Prices Fully Reflect Information in Accruals and Cash Flows About Future Earnings," *The Accounting Review* (July 1996), pp. 289–315.

Smith, Clifford, Jr., and L. Macdonald Wakeman, "Determinants of Corporate Leasing Policy," *Journal of Finance* (July 1985), pp. 895–908.

Smith, Clifford, Jr., and Jerold B. Warner, "On Financial Contracting: An Analysis of Bond Covenants," *Journal of Financial Economics* (June 1979), pp. 117–161.

Solomons, David, "The FASB's Conceptual Framework: An Evaluation," *Journal of Accountancy* (June 1986), pp. 114–124.

Sondhi, Ashwinpaul C., "Analyzing the Credit Risk of Emerging Market Debt," *Credit Analysis of Nontraditional Debt Securities,* AIMR 1995.

Sondhi, Ashwinpaul C., George H. Sorter, and Gerald I. White, "Transactional Analysis," *Financial Analysts Journal* (September/October 1987), pp. 57–64.

Sondhi, Ashwinpaul C., George H. Sorter, and Gerald I. White, "Cash Flow Redefined: FAS 95 and Security Analysis," *Financial Analysts Journal* (November/December 1988), pp. 19–20.

Sorter, George H., and George Benston, "Appraising the Defensive Position of a Firm: The Interval Measure," *The Accounting Review* (October 1960), pp. 633–640.

Sterling, Robert R, *Theory of the Measurement of Enterprise Income.* Lawrence, KS: University Press of Kansas, 1970.

Stewart, G. Bennet, III, *The Quest for Value.* New York: Harper Business, 1991.

Stewart, John E., "The Challenges of Hedge Accounting," *Journal of Accountancy* (November 1989), pp. 48–62.

Stickel, Scott E., "The Timing of and Incentives for Annual Earnings Forecasts Near Interim Earnings Announcements," *Journal of Accounting and Economics* (July 1989), pp. 275–292.

Stickel, Scott E., "Predicting Individual Analysts Earnings Forecasts," *Journal of Accounting Research* (Autumn 1990), pp. 409–417.

Stickney, Clyde P., "Analyzing Effective Corporate Tax Rates," *Financial Analysts Journal* (July/August 1979), pp. 45–54.

Stober, Thomas L., "The Incremental Information Content of Financial Statement Disclosures: The Case of LIFO Liquidations," *Journal of Accounting Research* (Supplement 1986), pp. 138–160.

Stober, Thomas L., "Do Prices Behave as if Accounting Is Conservative? Cross-sectional Evidence from the Feltham-Ohlson Valuation Model," working paper, University of Notre Dame, October 1996.

Strong, John S., and John R. Meyer, "Asset Writedowns: Managerial Incentives and Security Returns," *Journal of Finance* (July 1987), pp. 643–663.

Sunder, Shyam, "Relationship Between Accounting Changes and Stock Prices: Problems of Measurement and Some Empirical Evidence," *Journal of Accounting Research* (Supplement 1973), pp. 1–45.

Sunder, Shyam, "Properties of Accounting Numbers Under Full Costing and Successful-Efforts Costing in the Petroleum Industry," *The Accounting Review* (January 1976), pp. 1–18.

Swaminathan, Siva, "The Impact of SEC Mandated Segment Data on Price Variability and Divergence of Beliefs," *The Accounting Review* (January 1991), pp. 23–41.

T

Thomas, Jacob K., "Why Do Firms Terminate Their Overfunded Pension Plans?," *Journal of Accounting and Economics* (November 1989), pp. 361–398.

Todd, Kenneth R., Jr., "How One Financial Officer Uses Inflation-Adjusted Accounting Data," *Financial Executive* (October 1982), pp. 13–19.

Train, John, *Money Masters.* New York: Harper & Row 1987.

Tse, Senyo, "LIFO Liquidations," *Journal of Accounting Research* (Spring 1990), pp. 229–238.

V

Vigeland, Robert L., "The Market Reaction to Statement of Financial Accounting Standards No. 2," *The Accounting Review* (April 1981), pp. 309–325.

W

Wang, Shiing-Wu, "The Relation Between Firm Size and Effective Tax Rates: A Test of Firms' Political Success," *The Accounting Review* (January 1991), pp. 158–169.

Watts, Ross, "The Time-Series Behavior of Quarterly Earnings," working paper, University of Newcastle, England, 1975.

Watts, Ross, and Richard W. Leftwich, "The Time Series of Annual Accounting Earnings," *Journal of Accounting Research* (Fall 1977), pp. 253–271.

Watts, Ross, and Jerold L. Zimmerman, *Positive Accounting Theory.* Englewood Cliffs, NJ: Prentice Hall. 1986.

Watts, Ross, and Jerold L. Zimmerman, "Positive Accounting Theory: A Ten Year Perspective," *The Accounting Review* (January 1990), pp. 131–156.

West, Richard R., "An Alternative Approach to Predicting Corporate Bond Ratings," *Journal of Accounting Research* (Spring 1970), pp. 118–127.

Wild, John, "The Prediction Performance of a Structural Model of Accounting Numbers," *Journal of Accounting Research* (Spring 1987), pp. 139–160.

Williamson, R. W., "Evidence on the Selective Reporting of Financial Ratios," *The Accounting Review* (April 1984), pp. 296–299.

Wilson, Peter G., "The Relative Information Content of Accruals and Cash Flows: Combined Evidence at the Earnings Announcement and Annual Report Release Date," *Journal of Accounting Research* (Supplement 1986), pp. 165–200.

Z

Zarowin, Paul, "What Determines Earnings-Price Ratios: Revisited," *Journal of Accounting Auditing and Finance* (Summer 1990), pp. 439–454.

Zarowin, Paul, "Does the Stock Market Overreact to Corporate Earnings Information?" *Journal of Finance* (December 1989), pp. 1385–1399.

Zarowin, Paul, "Size, Seasonality and Stock Market Overreaction" *Journal of Financial and Quantitative Analysis* (March 1990), pp. 113–124.

Ziebart, David A., and David H. Kim, "An Examination of the Market Reactions Associated with SFAS No. 8 and SFAS No. 52," *The Accounting Review* (April 1987), pp. 343–357.

Zimmerman, Jerold L., "Taxes and Firm Size," *Journal of Accounting and Economics* (August 1983), pp. 119–149.

Zmijewski, Mark E., and Robert L. Hagerman, "An Income Strategy Approach to the Positive Theory of Accounting Standard Setting/Choice," *Journal of Accounting and Economics* (August 1981), pp. 129–149.

INDEX

A

Abarbanell, J., 1077
Abdel-khalik, A., 316, 319, 536
Abnormal earnings (EBO) model,
  valuation models, 1062–1072,
  1102–1103. *See also* Valuation
  models
Accelerated depreciation:
  methods, 380–381, 382–383
  taxes and, 388
Accounting beta, risk measurement,
  earnings variability, 991
Accounting methods:
  abnormal earnings (EBO) model,
    1067–1068
  accrual accounting concept, 61, 63
    nonrecurring items, 69
  asset-based valuation models,
    1042–1043
  business combinations analysis. *See
    also* Business combinations analysis
  international reporting, 767–768
  U.S., 751–763
  cash flow analysis, 108–109, 116
  efficient market theory, mechanistic
    hypothesis versus, 224–225
  income tax analysis, deferred taxes,
    439–440
  inventory analysis, 258
  long-lived asset analysis (financial
    reporting), 368–376
  market-based research, earnings and
    stock return relationship, 228–229
  positive accounting research, 237–238
  ratio analysis, 143–144
  reported income adjustments,
    955–956
Accounts payable turnover ratio,
  calculation of, 152
Accrual accounting concept, 35–85
  balance sheet, 69–74
    assets and liabilities measurement,
      72–73
    format and classification, 69–72
    uses of, 73–74
  defined, 7
  definitions and relationships, 36–40
  income, 40–58
    generally, 40–43

income statement, 43–48
  recognition issues, 48–58
  Morrison Knudsen Corporation
    example, 80
  nonrecurring items, 58–69
    analysis of, 63–69
    types of, 58–63
  overview, 36
  statement of stockholders' equity,
    74–76
  Thousand Trails, Inc. example, 74–78
Acquisitions:
  asset-based valuation models, 1042
  business combinations analysis,
    745–747. *See also* Business
    combinations analysis
  cash flow statement, 101
  income tax analysis, 449
  pension plan analysis, 623
  reported income adjustments,
    954–955
Activity analysis, ratio analysis, 151–
  155
Actuarial gains/losses, defined benefit
  pension plans, benefit obligations,
  600
Advances, liabilities, balance sheet
  analysis and adjustments, 935
Advertising costs, capitalization versus
  expensing, 334
Affiliates, investment in, off-balance-
  sheet debt, 555–556
Agency theory, positive accounting
  research, 238–239
Alcan, off-balance-sheet debt, 548, 549
Alcoa, financial statement analysis,
  968–973
Alcoa Aluminio, multinational
  operations analysis, 854
Alcoa of Australia, multinational
  operations analysis, 854–857
All-current method. *See* Translation
  (all-current method)
Altman, E. I., 992, 994n14, 995, 996,
  998, 1009n37, 1010
Altman's Z-score, bankruptcy
  prediction, 994–998
A.M. Castle, financial statement
  analysis, 974–979

Amerada Hess:
  capitalization versus expensing,
    329–330
  inventory analysis, 271–273, 277
American Airlines:
  leases, 541–543, 547
  liability financing analysis, long-term
    debt, 486
  off-balance-sheet debt, 551–554
American Family Life (AFLAC),
  multinational operations analysis,
  866–871
American Home Products, derivatives
  and hedging activities, 907–909
American Institute of Certified Public
  Accountants (AICPA):
  reporting systems, 8–9
  risks and uncertainties, 22
Ameritech, hedging techniques, 899, 901
Amihud, Y., 1023, 1024
Amir, E., 249, 338n24, 615, 635
Amortization:
  depreciation, 385–386
  goodwill, business combinations
    analysis, 779–780
Ang, J. S., 1006n31, 1011
Annuity or sinking fund depreciation,
  methods, 379–380
Appreciation, financial statement
  analysis, 3
Arbitrage Pricing Theory (APT), equity
  risk, 1013–1014
Archibald, T. R., 223, 394
Ashland Oil, off-balance-sheet debt,
  557–561
Asset-based valuation models,
  1038–1043. *See also* Valuation
  models
Asset revaluation, capitalization versus
  expensing, 334–335
Assets. *See also* Long-lived asset
  analysis
  balance sheet, 16–17
    analysis and adjustment, 934
    measurement, accrual accounting
      concept, 72–73
  conceptual definitions of, 36–40
  current, balance sheet analysis and
    adjustments, DuPont, 935–939

Assets, *cont.*
  long-term, balance sheet analysis and
    adjustments, DuPont, 939–941
AT&T, 64–65, 85
Auditor, role of, financial statement
  analysis, 24–28
Automobile industry, pension plan
  analysis, 608–610
Average number of days of receivables
  outstanding, calculation of, 151–152
Aydin Coporation, intercorporate
  investment analysis, 709–710
Aziz, A., 1000

B

Balakrishnan, R., 720, 721n41
Balance sheet:
  accrual accounting concept, 69–74
    assets and liabilities measurement,
      72–73
    format and classification, 69–72
    uses of, 73–74
  analysis and adjustments, 933–948
    assets adjustment, 934
    book value analysis, 933–934
    book value per common share
      adjustment, 945–946
    capital structure analysis, 946–947
    DuPont example, 935–944
    international reporting systems, 948
    liabilities adjustment, 934–935
    stockholders' equity adjustment,
      944–945
  business combinations analysis
    international reporting, 768–773
    U.S., 751–753, 788–789
  described, 16–17
  forecasting models, 1078–1080
  inventory analysis, 261
  leases, 538
  liability financing analysis, 475–506.
    See also Liability financing analysis
  multinational operations analysis
    foreign currency disclosure,
      847–850
    methods compared, 840–841
  pension plan analysis, 612
  ratio analysis, 144–147
Baldwin, B. A., 720
Ball, R., 225–226, 227, 228, 229, 230,
  231, 244, 245–248, 316, 1018, 1077
Bankruptcy prediction. *See also* Risk
  measurement
  models, variables in, 985
  risk measurement, 992–1001
Banz, Rolf, 1023
Barlev, B., 279
Bartczak, N. J., 1000
Barth, M. E., 22n22, 615
Bartov, E., 67, 350, 405, 863n34, 864,
  1077
Basu, Sanjoy, 1023
Bathe, A., 228

Beatty, A. S., 249
Beaver, W. H., 40n7, 221n7, 222n9, 227,
  229, 390, 390n10, 445, 857, 861, 993,
  994, 995, 1015, 1018, 1019, 1055,
  1056, 1075
Belkaoui, A., 1002n25
Bell, P. W., 218, 249, 1062n31
Benchmarks:
  industry norms as, ratio analysis,
    196–198
  ratio analysis, 142
Benefits. *See* Pension plans;
  Postemployment benefits;
  Preretirement benefits; Stock
  compensation plans
Beneish, M., 510
Benston, G., 160
Bernard, V. L., 43, 231, 233, 244, 249,
  251, 295, 1068n39, 1072, 1077, 1078
Beta (β):
  critique of, 1021–1024
  defense of, 1024–1025
  equity risk, 1012–1013
  importance and utility of, 1014–1015
Bhandari, Laxmi, 1023
Bhushan, R., 1080, 1081, 1084
Bicksler, J., 488
Biddle, G. C., 279, 280, 317, 318, 319
Bid premia, business combinations
  analysis, 784–787
"Big bath" accounting, accrual
  accounting concept, nonrecurring
  items, 68
Biotech Partners, L.P., long-lived asset
  analysis (financial reporting), 366
Birmingham Steel, inventory analysis,
  297–298
Bishop, M. L., 249
Blankley, Alan, 610
Block, Frank, 9
Blum, M., 993n11
BMC Industries, inventory analysis,
  295–296
Bodie, Z., 237n46, 1013n44
Bodnar, G. M., 863n34, 864
Boeing, liability financing analysis,
  497–498, 500
Bond covenants, liability financing
  analysis, 506–512. *See also* Liability
  financing analysis
Bond ratings, debt risk prediction,
  1001–1012. *See also* Risk
  measurement
Bond ratings prediction models,
  variables in, 986
Bonus plan hypothesis, positive
  accounting research, 239–240
Book/market value estimation, liability
  financing analysis, 497–501
Book-to-market ratio, market-based
  research, 234
Book value:
  abnormal earnings (EBO) model,
    1069–1072
  asset-based valuation models, 1039

  measurements, 1040–1041
  stability and growth, 1041–1043
  balance sheet analysis and
    adjustments, 933–934
Book value per share:
  balance sheet analysis and
    adjustments, 945–946
  ratio analysis, 179–180
Bowen, R. M., 43
Bowman, R. G., 501, 1016
Box, G. E. P., 1074n45
Bradley, J., 783n30
Brands, capitalization versus expensing,
  334
Brascan, intercorporate investment
  analysis, 704–708
Briloff, A. J., 234, 759n11
Briloff effect, market-based research,
  234–235, 236
British Petroleum:
  inventory analysis, 293–294
  pension plan analysis, 627–628
Brooks, L., 1075
Brown, L. D., 229, 1077, 1082, 1083,
  1083n57, 1084
Brown, P., 225–226, 227, 228, 229, 230,
  231, 244, 245–248, 1018, 1083
Brown, R. M., 316
Brown & Sharpe, depreciation methods,
  384
Bublitz, B., 346
Buckmaster, D., 1075
Bulow, J., 594n1
Burgstahler, D., 43, 1001n23
Business combinations analysis, 743–817
  accounting method effects, 751–763
    balance sheet comparison, 751–753
    cash flow statement effects,
      759–762
    income statement comparison,
      753–759
    ratios impact, 762–763
  acquisition method selection, 780–787
    generally, 780–782
    pooling-purchase choice, 782–787
  acquisitions accounting, 745–747
  complicating factors, 763–764
  examples
    ConAgra-Golden Valley merger,
      798–801
    Georgia Pacific-Great Northern
      Nekoosa, 795–798
  goodwill, 778–780
  income tax effects, 764–766
  international reporting systems,
    766–778
    generally, 765–766
    goodwill, 766–767
    SmithKline Beecham example,
      767–778
  overview, 744–745
  pooling of interests method, 750–751
  purchase method, 747–750
  push-down accounting, 787–791
  spinoffs, 791–794

analysis of, 792–793
example, 794
generally, 791–792
rationale for, 793
Butler, K. C., 1084n62

C
Cadbury Schweppes, income tax
analysis, 456–457
Callable bonds, debt retirement prior to
maturity, 504–505
Callen, J. L., 350
Caltex, off-balance-sheet debt, 562–570
Canada, multijurisdictional disclosure
system, 15. *See also* International
reporting systems
Canadian Accounting Standards Board,
9
Canning, J. B., 219
Capital asset pricing model (CAPM):
critique of, 1021–1024
defense of, 1024–1025
equity risk, 1012–1013
modern portfolio theory, 221–222
Capital expenditure:
capitalization versus expensing, 347,
350
ratio analysis, 163–165
Capitalization table, ratio analysis,
162–163
Capitalization versus expensing (asset
analysis), 323–376. *See also* Long-
lived asset analysis (financial
reporting)
analytic adjustments, 342–350
consequences, 345
fixed asset data, 345, 347, 350
rationale for, 342–345
valuation, 345, 346–347
asset revaluation, 334–335
conceptual issues, 323–328
general issues, 328–334
intangible assets, 331–334
interest costs, 328–331
industry issues, 336–342
computer software development,
338–340
oil and gas exploration, 340–342,
367–376
utilities (regulated), 336–338
Capital lease, lease classification,
534–537. *See also* Leases
Capital markets, financial statement
analysis, 5–6
Capital structure:
balance sheet analysis and
adjustments, 946–947
ratio analysis, earnings per share, 173,
176
Casey, C. J., 1000
Cash cycle, length of, liquidity analysis,
156–158
Cash flow. *See also* Discounted cash
flow valuation models

accrual accounting concept,
nonrecurring items, 65
accrual income versus, 42–43
bankruptcy prediction and, 1000
capitalization versus expensing, 327
conceptual definitions of, 36–40
discounted cash flow valuation
models, 1057
inventory analysis, 265
leases, 540, 551–554
liability financing analysis, long-term
debt, 482–485
pension plan analysis, 611–616
profitability analysis, 168
Cash flow analysis, 104–117
classification issues, 112, 115–117
financial statement analysis, 959–965
components analysis, 960–963
free cash flow, 963–964
generally, 959–960
international comparisons, 964–965
free cash flows and valuation,
104–105
income and, 105–110
overview, 104
trends, 110–112, 113–114
Cash flow per share, calculation of, 179
Cash flow statement, 87–137
business combinations analysis,
759–762, 790
described, 19
direct and indirect method, 88–91
direct method, 93–96
DuPont example, 98–100, 102–104
exchange rate changes, 102
indirect method, 97
international perspective, 117–118
multinational operations analysis
foreign currency disclosure, 852
methods compared, 844–846
overview, 88
reported versus operating changes, 97,
101–102
transactional analysis method, 91–93
Cash flow-to-debt ratio, ratio analysis,
163–165
Chambers, R. J., 218
Champion Enterprises, inventory
analysis, 285–289
Chan, K. C., 1023
Chen, A., 488
Chen, K., 193, 510, 1014
Chen, N., 1023
Christie, A., 243
Chubb Corporation, marketable
securities analysis, 680–682, 685
Classical theory, empirical research,
218–219
Clean surplus relationship, abnormal
earnings (EBO) model, 1068
Clinch, G. J., 347, 371
Closure liabilities, environmental costs,
long-lived asset analysis
(accounting), 406–408
Clouse, M. L., 348

Coca-Cola, intercorporate investment
analysis, 722–726
Cogger, K. O., 988
Collins, D. W., 230, 249, 349, 719, 720,
1057
Comiskey, E., 690
Commodity bonds:
liability financing analysis, debt with
equity features, 493–494
off-balance-sheet debt, 556–557
Commodity risk, derivatives and
hedging activities, 898
Common-size statements, ratio analysis,
144–150
Company fact books, financial statement
analysis, 24
Comparability, FASB framework, 11–12
Competitive factors, ratio analysis,
integrated analysis, 190
Completed contract method, accrual
accounting concept, recognition
issues, 50–55
Comprehensive income:
income statement, 18
reported income adjustments,
958–959
Computer services, financial statement
analysis, 24
Computer software development:
amortization, 385–386
capitalization versus expensing,
338–340
ConAgra, business combinations
analysis, 798–801
Consistency, FASB framework, 11
Consolidation:
equity method compared, 696–709,
722–726
intercorporate investment analysis,
692–696. *See also* Intercorporate
investment analysis
Constant dollar method, long-lived asset
analysis (accounting), 415–417, 423
Contingencies, financial statements,
21–22
Contingent payments, business
combinations analysis, 763–764
Continuing operations, accrual
accounting concept, nonrecurring
items, 65
Contracts, financial statement analysis, 3
Contribution margin ratio, calculation
of, 171
Convertible bonds and warrants,
liability financing analysis, debt
with equity features, 490–493
Convertible securities, adjustments for,
earnings per share computation,
177
Cope, Anthony, 9
Copeland, T., 1061n30
Copyrights, capitalization versus
expensing, 333–334
Cost method, securities investment
analysis, 674

Cost recovery method, accrual accounting concept, recognition issues, 55

Costs of goods sold (COGS): adjustment of, inventory analysis, 268–270
adjustment of FIFO and, for current costs, 270–273
inventory analysis, 258, 259–260, 266. *See also* Inventory analysis

Cragg, J. G., 720, 1056n23

Cumulative translation adjustment, described, 833–835

Current assets, balance sheet analysis and adjustments, DuPont, 935–939

Current cost adjustment, FIFO COGS, inventory analysis, 270–273

Current cost method, long-lived asset analysis (accounting), 418–420, 421–423

Current liabilities:
balance sheet analysis and adjustments, DuPont, 941–942
liability financing analysis, 475–476

Curtailments, pension plan analysis, 623–624

Cushing, B. E., 291, 292

Customer advances, liabilities, balance sheet analysis and adjustments, 935

D

Daley, L. A., 43, 615, 616

Dambolena, I. G., 998, 999n19

Davis, H. Z., 196, 197n45, 281

Davis, M. L., 782, 783

DBP Corporation, pension plan analysis, 656–657

Deakin, E. B., III, 369, 370

Debondt, W., 235

Debt, liability financing analysis, 473–530. *See also* Liability financing analysis

Debt analysis, long-term, ratio analysis, 160–165

Debt covenant, ratio analysis, 161–162

Debt covenant hypothesis, positive accounting research, 240

Debt ratios, ratio analysis, 162–163

Debt retirement, prior to maturity, liability financing analysis, 503–506

Debt risk prediction, risk measurement, 1001–1012. *See also* Risk measurement

Debt-to-equity ratio, inventory analysis, LIFO versus FIFO, 279–280

Dechow, P. M., 42

Declining-balance method, accelerated depreciation, 381

Deere & Company, financial statement analysis, 979–981

Defeasance, debt retirement prior to maturity, liability financing analysis, 505–506

Defensive intervals, defined, 160

Deferred tax assets, 430–432
deferred taxes, 444–445
financial statement preparation and disclosure requirements, 438–439
liability method (SFAS 109), 437–438

Deferred tax liabilities:
balance sheet analysis and adjustments, 935
income tax analysis, 430–432

Defined pension plans, 596. *See also* Pension plans

DeFond, M., 511

Delta Airlines:
depreciation methods, 392–393
off-balance-sheet debt, 551–554

Depletion, depreciation, 385

Depreciation, 378–393. *See also* Long-lived asset analysis (accounting)
amortization, 385–386
defined, 378–379
depletion, 385

Depreciation methods, 379–385
accelerated depreciation, 380–381, 382–383, 388
annuity or sinking fund depreciation, 379–380
changes in, 391–393, 394
disclosures, 386–387
financial statements, 387–388
group (composite) methods, 385
inflation and, 388–391
straight-line depreciation, 380, 381
units-of-production and service hours methods, 381, 383–384

Derivatives and hedging activities, 893–930
accounting practices, 905–914
forecasting, 907–909
generally, 905–907
imperfect hedges, 910
measurement issues, 907
portfolios, 909
recognition issues, 907
rolling hedges, 909
standards, 910–914
disclosures, 914–916
examples, Enron Corporation, 918–925
hedging techniques, 898–905
economic hedges, 903–905
forward contracts, 899–901
options, 901–903
international reporting systems, 916–917
overview, 893–895
risk definition, 895, 897–898

Desai, A., 783n31

Devine, M. S., 747n1

Dhaliwal, D. S., 266n9, 394, 614, 1025n64

Dieter, R., 15n15

Digital Equipment, capitalization versus expensing, 351

Direct method, cash flow statement, 88–91, 93–96

Disaggregated data, forecasting models, 1076–1080

Disclosure:
deferred tax assets, income tax analysis, 438–439
depreciation methods, 386–387
foreign currency disclosure analysis, 846–852. *See also* Multinational operations analysis
hedging activities, 914–916
income tax analysis
comprehensive, 459–463
DuPont example, 449–455
leases, 540–547
pension plans, 605–607, 644–657
positive accounting research, 238
postemployment benefits, 632–633, 639
of ratios, ratio analysis, 195–196
stock compensation plans, 643–644

Discontinued operations, accrual accounting concept, 60–61

Discounted cash flow valuation models, 1043–1062
abnormal earnings (EBO) model compared, 1065–1072
dividend-based models, 1044–1045
earnings-based models, 1045–1058
alternative and finite assumptions, 1053–1054
cash flow, 1057
dividend-based models and, 1045–1046
earnings definitions, 1046
earnings valuation and price/earnings ratio, 1054–1055
errors, 1056–1057, 1058
growth, risk, and valuation, 1055–1056
growth estimation, 1050–1053
growth model, 1047–1050
no-growth model, 1046–1047
free cash flow approach, 1059–1062
adjustments, 1060–1061
dividends and earnings, 1061–1062
generally, 1059–1060
multistage growth models, 1100–1102
overview, 1043

Discovery Zone, cash flow analysis, 109–110

Distressed firms, liability financing analysis, 502–503

Distributable earnings, defined, 39

Divestitures:
cash flow statement, 101
pension plan analysis, 623

Dividend-based models:
discounted cash flow valuation models, 1044–1045
earnings-based models and, 1045–1046

Dividend payout ratio, ratio analysis, 180–181

Dividends, cash flow analysis, 116–117

Dodd, David, 219

Dopuch, N., 227n21, 273, 274, 319, 320
Dow Chemical:
   debt risk prediction (bond ratings),
      1026
   financial statements, 1147–1165
   ICI and, compared with DuPont,
      financial statement analysis,
      967–968
   income tax analysis, 459–463
   liability financing analysis, 515–517
   ratio analysis, 145–147
Dreman, D., 236n44
Duke, J. C., 507
Dukes, R. E., 227, 348, 390, 445
DuPont:
   balance sheet, 70–71, 76
   balance sheet analysis and
      adjustments, 935–944
   cash flow analysis, 110–112
      financial statement analysis,
      960–963
   cash flow statement, 98–100, 102–104
   debt risk prediction (bond ratings),
      1026
   depreciation methods, 385
   Dow and ICI compared with,
      financial statement analysis,
      967–968
   financial statements, 1105–1145
   growth estimation, earnings-based
      models, 1053
   hedging activities, 914–916
   income statement, 46–47, 59, 60, 63,
      64, 65
   income tax analysis, 440, 445, 446,
      447, 448, 449–455
   intercorporate investment analysis,
      713–715
   liability financing analysis, 504,
      515–517
   long-lived asset analysis (financial
      reporting), 371–376
   pension plan accounting, 605–607
   pension plan analysis, 616–622
   postemployment benefits analysis,
      634–635, 637–639
   ratio analysis, 145–150, 155, 161, 164,
      169, 183, 186
   reported income adjustments, 950
   valuation models, 1085–1087

E
Earnings, stock return relationship,
   market-based research, 227–230
Earnings-based models, discounted cash
   flow valuation models, 1045–1058.
   See also Discounted cash flow
   valuation models
Earnings before interest, taxes,
   depreciation, and amortization
   (EBITDA):
   calculation of, 179
   firm performance analysis, 183

Earnings manipulation, accrual
   accounting concept, nonrecurring
   items, 66–69
Earnings per share, ratio analysis,
   172–179
Earnings response coefficient, good
   news/bad news classification, 230
Earnings retention, asset-based
   valuation models, 1041
Earnings valuation, discounted cash flow
   valuation models, earnings-based
   models, 1054–1055
Earnings variability, risk measurement,
   987–991. *See also* Risk
   measurement
Easman, W., 390n10
EBITDA. *See* Earnings before interest,
   taxes, depreciation, and
   amortization (EBITDA)
Economic characteristics, ratio analysis,
   integrated analysis, 186–191
Economic cycle, reported income
   adjustments, 954
Economic order quantity (EOQ),
   inventory turnover ratio, 278
Edwards, E. O., 218, 249, 1062n31
Edwards-Bell-Ohlson (EBO) model. *See*
   Valuation models
Efficient market theory:
   described, 220–221
   mechanistic hypothesis versus,
      223–225
Eggleton, I. R., 316
Elam, R., 998n18
El-Gazzar, S., 536
Elliott, J. A., 68, 69, 348, 404
Elliott, J. W., 1078
Emerson Electric, business
   combinations analysis, 792–793, 794
Emery, G. W., 988
Empirical research, 215–256
   bankruptcy prediction, 993–999
   classical approach, 218–219
   equity risk, 1018–1021
   financial statement analysis and,
      250–251
   impaired assets, 403–406
   inventory analysis, LIFO versus
      FIFO, 289–292
   market-based research, 219–237. *See
      also* Market-based research
   overview, 216–218
   positive accounting research, 237–244.
      See also Positive accounting
      research
   trends in, 244–250
Employee Retirement Income Security
   Act of 1974 (ERISA), 594
Employer contributions, defined benefit
   pension plans, plan assets, 601
Environmental costs, long-lived asset
   analysis (accounting), 406–408
EQK Realty Investors, liability
   financing analysis, long-term debt,
   482–485

Equity, income tax analysis, deferred
   taxes, 442–444
Equity adjustments, income tax analysis,
   deferred taxes, 442
Equity financing, asset-based valuation
   models, 1042
Equity method of accounting:
   consolidation compared, 696–709,
      722–726
   intercorporate investment analysis,
      686–692. *See also* Intercorporate
      investment analysis
Equity risk, risk measurement,
   1012–1025. *See also* Risk
   measurement
Ettredge, M., 346
Europe. *See also* International reporting
   systems
   capitalization versus expensing,
      330–331
   income tax analysis, 455–456
   reporting systems, 13–14
European Economic Community
   (EEC), reporting systems, 14
Exchangeable bonds, liability financing
   analysis, debt with equity features,
   492
Exchange rates. *See also* Multinational
   operations analysis
   asset-based valuation models, 1041
   cash flow statement, 102
   cumulative translation adjustment,
      835
   multinational operations analysis
      analytic difficulties, 858–859
      generally, 821–823
   reported income adjustments, 955
Expenses:
   accrual accounting concept,
      recognition issues, 48–58
   income statement, 17–18
Extraordinary items, accrual accounting
   concept, 59–60
Extrapolative forecasting models,
   1073–1076

F
Fabozzi, F. J., 491n27
Fact books, financial statement analysis,
   24
Fairfield, P. M., 1066n37
Fairfield, P. R., 48, 1078
Falkenstein, A., 270, 391n11
Fama, E., 220, 222, 234, 1021, 1022,
   1023, 1024, 1040n3
Feldstein, M., 614
Feltham, G., 179, 180, 249, 1040,
   1062n31
Finance subsidiaries, off-balance-sheet
   debt, 554–555
Financial Accounting Standards Board
   (FASB):
   financial statement analysis, 4, 7
   long-lived assets, 323
   reporting systems, 8–12

Financial analyst forecasts, forecasting models compared, 1080–1084
Financial leverage:
  earnings variability, 990–991
  ratio analysis, 168–172
Financial leverage ratios, capitalization versus expensing, 328
Financial risk, earnings variability, 989
Financial statement(s), 15–23
  balance sheet, 16–17
  cash flow statement, 19
  contingencies, 21–22
  deferred tax assets, income tax analysis, 438–439
  depreciation methods, 387–388
  footnotes, 20
  impaired assets, 402–403
  income statement, 17–18
  inventory analysis, 287–288
  liability financing analysis, long-term debt, 480–482
  long-lived asset analysis, 323–328
  long-lived asset analysis (accounting), inflation, 420–423
  stockholders' equity statement, 19–20
  supplementary schedules, 22–23
Financial statement analysis, 1–32, 931–981
  accrual accounting concept, 35–85. See also Accrual accounting concept
  auditor role, 24–28
  balance sheet analysis and adjustments, 933–948
    assets adjustment, 934
    book value analysis, 933–934
    book value per common share adjustment, 945–946
    capital structure analysis, 946–947
    DuPont example, 935–944
    international reporting systems, 948
    liabilities adjustment, 934–935
    stockholders' equity adjustment, 944–945
  cash flow analysis, 959–965
    components analysis, 960–963
    free cash flow, 963–964
    generally, 959–960
    international comparisons, 964–965
  data sources, 24
  empirical research, 250–251. See also Empirical research
  examples
    Alcoa, 968–973
    A.M. Castle, 974–979
    Deere & Company, 979–981
    Dow and ICI compared with DuPont, 967–968
  financial ratio adjustment, 965–966
  investment decisions, 4–6
  management discussion and analysis, 21, 23–24
  need for, 2–3
  overview, 2, 932
  reported income adjustments, 948–959

accounting changes, 955–956
  acquisition effects, 954–955
  comprehensive income, 958–959
  economic cycle, 954
  exchange rate effects, 955
  international reporting systems, 953
  nonrecurring items analysis, 951–953
  normalization, 948–951
  quality of earnings, 956–958
reporting systems, 6–14
  generally, 6–7
  international, 12–14
  SEC requirements for foreign registrants, 14–15
  U.S., 7–12
statement types, 15–23. See also Financial statement(s)
Financing cash flow, cash flow statement, 88, 92, 96
Firm growth rate, income tax analysis, deferred taxes, 440–442
Firm performance analysis, ratio analysis, 183–186
First-in, first-out (FIFO):
  adjustment of COGS and, for current costs, 270–273
  adjustment to, from LIFO, 267–270
  efficient market theory, 224–225
  international reporting systems, 294
  inventory analysis, 258, 259, 260. See also Inventory analysis
  LIFO versus
    British Petroleum example, 293–294
    empirical and historical perspective, 289–292, 315–320
    financial ratios, 273–280
    inventory analysis, 264–266
    positive accounting research, 242
Fisher, Lawrence, 1011n40
Fixed asset data, capitalization versus expensing, 345, 347, 350
Fixed asset turnover ratio, defined, 153
Fixed-rate debt, variable-rate versus, liability financing analysis, long-term debt, 485–489
Footnotes, financial statements, 20
Forecasting, inventory analysis, 295–296
Forecasting models, 1072–1084
  disaggregated data, 1076–1080
    income statement or balance sheet components, 1078–1080
    quarterly forecasting models, 1076–1077
    segment-based forecasts, 1077
  extrapolative models, 1073–1076
  financial analyst forecasts compared, 1080–1084
  index models, 1076
  overview, 1072
Foreign currencies:
  liability financing analysis, long-term debt, 489–490
  matching, hedging techniques, 905
  risk, derivatives and hedging activities, 895, 896

Foreign currency translation (SFAS 52), multinational operations analysis, 824–830, 864.
Foreign subsidiaries, cash flow statement, 101–102
Forest products industry, fixed asset analysis, 409–410
  depreciation, 396–397
Forward contracts, hedging techniques, 899–901
Foster, G., 228, 236n45, 720n39, 1083
Foster Wheeler, stock compensation plans, 641–643
Franchises and licenses, capitalization versus expensing, 334
Francis, J. R., 595, 596
Frankel, Richard, 1072
Frecka, T. J., 196
Free cash flow:
  discounted cash flow valuation models, 1059–1062
  financial statement analysis, 963–964
  valuation and, cash flow analysis, 104–105
Freeman, R. N., 1076, 1079n52
Freeport-McMoRan, liability financing analysis, 493
French, K. R., 222, 234, 1021, 1022, 1023, 1024, 1040n3
Fried, D., 67, 68, 281, 403, 406n28, 1076, 1078n50, 1081
Functional currency changes, multinational operations analysis, 854–857

G
Gains, income statement, 17–18
Gardner Denver Machinery, business combinations analysis, 779–780
Gaver, J. J., 67, 240
Generally accepted accounting principles (GAAP):
  auditor role, 26
  earnings per share computation, 174–175
  Europe, 14, 15
  financial statement analysis, 3
  inventory analysis, 261, 284
  SEC foreign registrant reporting requirements, 14–15
General Motors:
  business combinations analysis, 788–791
  pension plan analysis, 644–656
Gentry, J. A., 994, 1000
Georgia Pacific:
  business combinations analysis, 795–798
  off-balance-sheet debt, 555–556
Germany, generally accepted accounting principles (GAAP), 14
Ghicas, D. C., 626
Gibson, C. H., 150n8, 195

Givoly, D., 229, 444, 445, 1076, 1081, 1082
Glatfelter, P. H. (PHG):
  impaired asset reporting, 399–401, 402
  liability financing analysis, long-term debt, 486
Globalization. *See* International reporting systems; Multinational operations analysis
Going concern assumption:
  cash flow analysis, 108
  reporting systems, 7
Golden Valley Microwave Foods Company, business combinations analysis, 798–801
Gombola, M. J., 168, 188, 189, 194
Gonedes, N. J., 67n35, 227n21, 228
Good news/bad news classification:
  abnormal returns, 230
  accrual accounting concept, nonrecurring items, 66
  future trends, 245–247
  market-based research, 225–226
  measurement of, 229
Goodwill:
  business combinations analysis
    international reporting systems, 766–767
    U.S., 749, 778–780
  capitalization versus expensing, 334
Gopalakrishnan, V., 615
Graham, B., 219, 220
Granof, M. H., 291n26
Great Northern Nekoosa, business combinations analysis, 795–798
Greenstein, M. M., 720
Griffin, P. A., 1077, 1082, 1083
Gross profit margin, inventory analysis, LIFO versus FIFO, 274–275
Group (composite) methods, depreciation, 385
Growth model, discounted cash flow valuation models, 1047–1050
Guy, James, 1020

H

Hackel, K. S., 118n27
Hagerman, R., 1082, 1083
Hagerman, R. L., 242, 243
Haldeman, R. G., 995, 998
Hamada, R. S., 1016
Hand, J. R. M., 504n54
Harnischfeger Industries, intercorporate investment analysis, 686–687
Harrington, D. R., 1020
Harris, T. S., 346, 347, 721n41
Hartzell, J. M., 1009n37, 1010
Haugen, R. A., 235n42
Hayn, C., 444, 445
Health care benefits, postemployment, estimation of, 631–632
Healy, P. M., 240, 391, 394
Hedging. *See* Derivatives and hedging activities

Heian, J. B., 554
Heico Corporation, 61, 62
Helmerich & Payne, marketable securities analysis, 678–679
Henderson, G. V., 1010n38
Hercules, liability financing analysis, 491
Heyman, J. A., 15n15
Hicks, J. R., 418n3
Hissler, H. L., 185n37
Historical cost:
  accrual accounting concept, 42
  reporting systems, 7
Hochman, S., 1017
Hoechst, pension plan analysis, 628, 629–630
Holthausen, R. W., 67, 240, 247, 248n69, 394, 1006n29
Homestake Mining, hedging techniques, 899–900
Hong, H., 782, 783
Hopwood, W., 719, 1077
Horrigan, J. O., 192, 1007
Horwitz, B., 348, 349, 720n40
Hughes, J. S., 689
Hughes Aircraft Company, business combinations analysis, 788–791
Hunt, H. G., III, 319, 507
Hyperinflation, multinational operations analysis, 852–854

I

IBM:
  amortization, 386
  capitalization versus expensing, 338–340
  multinational operations analysis, 871–881
ICI. *See* Imperial Chemical Industries (ICI)
Imhoff, E. A., Jr., 536
Impaired assets, long-lived asset analysis (accounting), 398–406. *See also* Long-lived asset analysis (accounting)
Impaired debt, liability financing analysis, 502–503
Imperfect hedges, derivatives and hedging activities, 910
Imperial Chemical Industries (ICI):
  debt risk prediction (bond ratings), 1026
  Dow and, compared with DuPont, financial statement analysis, 967–968
  financial statements, 1167–1191
  income tax analysis, 459–463
  liability financing analysis, 515–517
  ratio analysis, 145–147
Income. *See also* Reported income adjustments
  accrual accounting concept of, 40–58. *See also* Accrual accounting concept
  capitalization versus expensing, 327

cash flow analysis and, 105–110, 119–121
  conceptual definitions of, 36–40
Income smoothing, accrual accounting concept, nonrecurring items, 66–68
Income statement:
  accrual accounting concept, 43–48
    net income components, 44–48
    nonrecurring items, 64–65
  business combinations analysis
    international reporting, 773–777
    U.S., 753–759, 789–790
  described, 17–18
  forecasting models, 1078–1080
  inventory analysis, 261–264
  leases, 538–539
  multinational operations analysis
    foreign currency disclosure, 850–852
    methods compared, 837–840
  ratio analysis, 144–147
Income tax:
  business combinations analysis, 764–766
  deferred, liabilities, balance sheet analysis and adjustments, 935
Income tax analysis, 425–472
  acquisitions, 449
  basic issues, 426–432
    deferred tax assets and liabilities, 430–432
    generally, 426–430
  deferral method, 471–472
  deferred taxes, 439–447
    deferred tax asset analysis, 444–445
    effective tax rates, 445–447
    level and trend influences, 439–442
    liability and equity, 442–444
  disclosures analysis
    comprehensive, 459–463
    DuPont example, 449–455
  indefinite reversals, 447–448
  international standards, 455–459
  liability method (SFAS 109), 433–439
    deferred tax assets and valuation allowance, 437–438
    effective date and transition method, 439
    generally, 433
    operating losses, 437
    tax rate and tax law changes, 434–437
  overview, 426–427
  temporary versus permanent differences, 447
Indefinite reversals, income tax analysis, 447–448
Index forecasting models, 1076
Indirect method, cash flow statement, 88–91, 97
Industry characteristics, ratio analysis, integrated analysis, 186–191
Industry norms, as benchmarks, ratio analysis, 196–198
Inflation:
  depreciation and, 388–391

long-lived asset analysis (accounting), 414–423
multinational operations analysis, analytic difficulties, 858–859
Information content studies, market-based research, 226–227
Infrequent items, accrual accounting concept, 58–59
Installment method, accrual accounting concept, recognition issues, 55
Intangible assets, capitalization versus expensing, 331–334
Intel, cash flow analysis, 106, 107, 109
Intercorporate investment analysis, 671–742
    consolidation, 692–696
        conditions for use, 693, 694
        example, 693, 695–696
        generally, 692–693
        international reporting systems, 711
    equity method of accounting, 686–692
        analysis and, 689–692
        conditions for use, 686–687
        example, 687–688
        SFAS 115 compared, 688–689
    marketable securities analysis, 678–686
        classification under SFAS 115, 679–682
        international reporting systems, 686
        procedures summarized, 685
        separation of operating from investment results, 678–679
    methods compared, 696–709
        analytic considerations, 697–701
        Coca-Cola example, 722–726
        generally, 696–697
        proportionate consolidation, 701–708
        summarized, 708–709
    minority interest analysis, 709–711
    overview, 672–673
    securities investment, 673–678
        cost method, 674
        generally, 673–674
        lower of cost or market method, 675
        market method, 674–675
        U.S. requirements, 675–678
    segment data analysis, 711–721
        consolidated earnings and risk estimation by, 719–721
        DuPont example, 713–715
        generally, 711–713
        international reporting systems, 721
        management discussion and analysis (MD&A), 715–716
        reporting changes proposed, 717–719
        uses and limitations, 716
Interest costs:
    capitalization versus expensing, 328–331
    defined benefit pension plans, benefit obligations, 599–600

Interest coverage ratio, ratio analysis, 163
Interest income, cash flow analysis, 116–117
Interest paid, cash flow analysis, 117
Interest rates:
    accrual accounting concept, 37–38
    liability financing analysis, 496–501
    matching, hedging techniques, 903–905
    multinational operations analysis, analytic difficulties, 858–859
    risk, derivatives and hedging activities, 896–898
Interest rate swaps, liability financing analysis, long-term debt, 485–489
Interfirm comparisons, nonrecurring items, reported income adjustments, 953
Interindustry factors, ratio analysis, integrated analysis, 188–191
International Accounting Standards Committee (IASC):
    financial statement analysis, 4, 9
    income tax analysis, 455–456
    inventory analysis, 294
    multinational operations analysis, 865–866
    reporting systems, 12–13
International Organization of Securities Commissions (IOSCO), reporting systems, 12
International reporting systems:
    balance sheet analysis and adjustments, 948
    business combinations analysis, 766–778. See also Business combinations analysis
    cash flow statement, 117–118
    derivatives and hedging activities, 916–917
    earnings per share computation, 175
    financial statement analysis, 12–14
        cash flow analysis, 964–965
    income tax analysis, 455–459
    intercorporate investment analysis, 711, 721
    inventory analysis, 294
    leases, 561–562
    liability financing analysis, 513–515
    marketable securities analysis, 686
    multinational operations analysis, 864–866
    pension plans, 624, 627–628, 629–630
    postemployment benefits, 639
    reported income adjustments, 953
    SEC foreign registrant reporting requirements, 14–15
    securities investment analysis, 675
Inventory analysis, 257–320
    alternative methods compared, 261–264
        balance sheet, 261
        income statement, 261–264
    costs of goods sold, 259–260

FIFO COGS adjustment, for current costs, 270–273
financial ratios, LIFO versus FIFO, 273–280
forecasting, 295–296
international perspective, 294
LIFO
    adjustment from, to FIFO, 267–270
    interim reporting under, 313–315
LIFO adoption and changes to and from, 283–289
LIFO measurement issues, 311–313
LIFO reserve declines, 280–283
LIFO versus FIFO
    British Petroleum example, 293–294
    described, 264–266
    empirical and historical perspective, 289–292, 315–320
Nucor example, 297–298
overview, 258
ratio analysis, 142
Inventory turnover ratio:
    defined, 151
    LIFO versus FIFO, 276–279
Investing cash flow, cash flow statement, 88, 92, 95–96
Investment (long-term) activity ratio, ratio analysis, 153–155
Investment decisions, financial statement analysis, 4–6
Investment-linked bonds, off-balance-sheet debt, 557
Investment tax credits, liabilities, balance sheet analysis and adjustments, 935

J

Jagannathan, R., 1024, 1024n63
January effect, market-based research, 233–235
Jenkins, G. M., 1074n45
Jennings, R., 320, 778
Jensen, M. C., 239n50
Jiambalvo, J., 511
Johnson, W. B., 193, 266n9
Joint ventures:
    intercorporate investment analysis, 699–701
    off-balance-sheet debt, 555–556
Jones, C. P., 228
Jones, J. J., 67
Joy, O. M., 228
J.P. Morgan, hedging techniques, 903–905
Justin Corporation, 51–53
Just-in-time policy, inventory turnover ratio, 278–279

K

Kane, A., 237n46, 1013n44
Kang, S.-H., 394

Kaplan, R. S., 223, 224, 394, 783n34
Kerstein, J., 347
Kettler, P., 1019
Ketz, J. E., 168, 188, 189, 194
Khoury, S. J., 998, 999n19
Kim, D. H., 862, 863
Kim, E. H., 783n31
Kim, M., 389
Kim, S., 347
Kimmel, P., 496
Kinney, M., 350
Kinney, W. R., Jr., 719
Kline, C. A., Jr., 185n37
Kmart:
  cash flow analysis, 106, 107, 108
  ratio analysis, 157, 158
Koller, T., 1061n30
Kolodny, R., 348, 349, 720n40
Kormendi, R., 230, 1057
Kothari, S. P., 222n10, 230, 1024, 1057

L

LAC Minerals, off-balance-sheet debt, 555
Lakonishok, J., 222n10, 229, 235, 1023, 1081, 1082
Landsman, W. R., 390n10, 614, 616
Lang, L. H. P., 1084n62
Larcker, D. F., 247, 248n69
Largay, J. A., III, 118n26
Lasman, D. A., 279n16
Last-in, first-out (LIFO):
  adjustment from, to FIFO, 267–270
  adoption of, and changes to and from, 283–289
  efficient market theory, 224–225
  FIFO versus
    British Petroleum example, 293–294
    empirical and historical perspective, 289–292, 315–320
    financial ratios, 273–280
    inventory analysis, 264–266
  inventory analysis, 258, 259, 260. *See also* Inventory analysis
  interim reporting under, 313–315
  measurement issues, 311–313
  positive accounting research, 242
  reported income adjustments, 950–951
  reserve declines, inventory analysis, 280–283
Lawson, G. H., 1000
Leaseback transactions, financial reporting for sales with, 588–589
Leases, 531–547. *See also* Off-balance-sheet debt
  classifications, 534–537
    capital lease, 534–537
    operating lease, 535–536, 537
  disclosures analysis, 540–547
  financial reporting by lessee, 537–540, 581–589

incentives for, 533–534
international reporting systems, 561–562
overview, 532–533
LeClere, M. J., 291, 292
Lee, C. F., 196
Lee, Charles, 1072
Leftwich, R. W., 509, 1006n29
Length of cash cycle, liquidity analysis, 156–158
Lev, B., 196, 228, 231, 232, 233, 248, 249, 249n70, 332n15, 338n24, 342, 344, 346, 347, 1018, 1068n40, 1079
Leverage:
  operating and financial, earnings variability, 990–991
  ratio analysis, 168–172
Leverage ratios, capitalization versus expensing, 328
Liabilities:
  balance sheet, 16–17
  balance sheet analysis and adjustments, 934–935
  current, balance sheet analysis and adjustments, DuPont, 941–942
  income tax analysis, deferred taxes, 442–444
  long-term, balance sheet analysis and adjustments, DuPont, 942–944
  measurement of, balance sheet, accrual accounting concept, 72–73
Liability financing analysis, 473–530
  bond covenants, 506–512
    accounting-based constraints calculation, 508–512
    nature of, 506–508
  comparative analysis of cases, 515–517
  current liabilities, 475–476
  debt retirement prior to maturity, 503–506
  debt with equity features, 490–496
    commodity bonds, 493–494
    convertible bonds and warrants, 490–493
    perpetual debt, 494–495
    preferred stock, 495–496
  distressed firms, 502–503
  interest rate change effects, 496–501
    market/book value estimation, 497–501
  international reporting systems, 513–515
  long-term debt, 476–490
    financial statement effects, 480–482
    fixed- versus variable-rate debt and interest rate swaps, 485–489
    foreign currencies, 489–490
    generally, 476–480
    project debt, 490
    variable-rate debt, 485
    zero-coupon debt, 482–485
  overview, 474–475
Liability method (SFAS 109), income tax analysis, 433–439. *See also*

Income tax analysis
Lilien, S., 370, 536
Lindahl, F. W., 317, 318, 404, 405
Lipe, R. C., 228, 230, 1057
Liquidity:
  cash flow analysis, 109–110
  inventory analysis, LIFO versus FIFO, 275–276
  probabilistic measure of, 988
Liquidity analysis, ratio analysis, 155–160
Livnat, J., 43, 118n27, 228, 554, 635
Long-lived asset analysis (accounting), 377–423. *See also* Depreciation
  depreciation concept, 378–393
  environmental costs, 406–408
  fixed asset disclosure analysis, 393, 395–397
  forest products industry, 409–410
  impaired assets, 398–406
    empirical findings, 403–406
    financial reporting, 398–402
    financial statement impact, 402–403
    SFAS 121, 403
  overview, 378
  price change analysis, 414–423
Long-lived asset analysis (financial reporting), 321–376. *See also* Capitalization versus expensing (asset analysis)
  acquisition decision, 322–323
  capitalization versus expensing analytic adjustments, 342–350
    asset revaluation, 334–335
    conceptual issues, 323–328
    general issues, 328–334
    industry issues, 336–342
  oil and gas disclosures, 367–376
  overview, 322
  research and development affiliates, 365–367
Long-term (investment) activity ratio, ratio analysis, 153–155
Long-term assets, balance sheet analysis and adjustments, DuPont, 939–941
Long-term debt, liability financing analysis, 476–490. *See also* Liability financing analysis
Long-term debt analysis, ratio analysis, 160–165
Long-term liabilities, balance sheet analysis and adjustments, DuPont, 942--944
Lorek, K. S., 228
Loss contingencies, financial statements, 21
Losses, income statement, 17–18
Lower of cost or market method (LOCOM), securities investment analysis, 675
Lys, T., 349

M

Magliolo, J., 347, 371

Majluf, N. S., 595
Malkiel, B. G., 720, 1056n23
Malmquist, D. H., 369
Management discussion and analysis (MD&A):
  financial statement analysis, 21, 23–24
  intercorporate investment analysis, 715–716
Management strategy:
  accrual accounting concept, nonrecurring items, 66–69
  inventory analysis, 263–264
  multinational operations analysis, 862–864
  ratio analysis, integrated analysis, 187
Mandelker, G. M., 783n34, 990, 991, 1017, 1018
Manegold, J., 1015
Marcus, A. J., 237n46, 1013n44
Maremont, M., 57
Marketable securities analysis, 678–686. *See also* Intercorporate investment analysis
Market anomalies, market-based research, 233–237
Market-based research, 219–237
  anomalies, 233–237
  current status, 230–233
  earnings and stock return relationship, 227–230
  efficient market theory, 220–221
    mechanistic hypothesis versus, 223–225
  generally, 219–220
  "good news"/"bad news" groupings, 225–226
  information content studies, 226–227
  modern portfolio theory, 221–223
Market/book value estimation, liability financing analysis, 497–501
Market method, securities investment analysis, 674–675
Market value:
  asset-based valuation models, generally, 1039
  risk, derivatives and hedging activities, 898
Mark-to-market accounting, marketable securities analysis, 683–685
Martin, L. G., 1010n38
Martin Marietta Corporation, pension plan analysis, 624
Matching principle, 7
  income, 41–43
  recognition issues, 48–49
McConnell, J. J., 347
McDonald, E., 764n14
McDonnel Douglas, pension plan analysis, 624
McGrattan, 1024n63
McKeown, J. C., 316
McKibben, W., 1020, 1021
McNichols, M. F., 22n22
Mechanistic hypothesis, efficient market theory versus, 223–225

Meckling, W. H., 239n50
Mendelson, H., 1023
Mendenhall, M., 1077
Merck, capitalization versus expensing, 342–344
Mergers. *See* Acquisitions
Metropolitan Life, off-balance-sheet debt, 555–556
Meyer, J. R., 404
Miller, Merton, 1045n11
Mingo, K. A., 1007, 1008
Minority interest analysis, intercorporate investment analysis, 709–711. *See also* Intercorporate investment analysis
Mittelstaedt, H. F., 635
Mobil Corporation:
  environmental costs, long-lived asset analysis (accounting), 407–408
  inventory analysis, 312–313
Modern portfolio theory. *See* Portfolio theory
Modigliani, Franco, 1045n11
Mohrman, Mary Beth, 508
Monday effect, market-based research, 234
Monsanto, derivatives and hedging activities, 912–913
Moody's, bond ratings, 1001, 1002, 1011
Moore, G., 389
Morck, R., 614, 782, 784n35
Morgenstern, O., 1025
Morrison Knudseh Corporation, accrual accounting concept example, 80
Morse, D., 1055, 1056, 1075
Most, K. S., 395n15
Mulford, C. W., 501, 690
Multijurisdictional disclosure system, SEC foreign registrant reporting requirements, 15
Multinational operations analysis, 819–866
  accounting issues, 823–824
  analytic difficulties, 857–866
    economic interpretations, 860–862
    interest rates, inflation, and exchange rate interrelationships, 858–859
    reporting consistency, 859–860
    SFAS 8 and SFAS 52 impacts, 862–864
  examples
    American Family Life (AFLAC) example, 866–871
    IBM, 871–881
  exchange rate changes, 821–823
  foreign currency disclosure analysis, 846–852
    generally, 846
  foreign currency translation (SFAS 52), 824–830
    exchange rate gains and losses, 827–828
    functional currency role, 825
    generally, 824–825

methods compared, 828–830
    remeasurement, 825–827
    translation, 827
  functional currency changes, 854–857
  hyperinflation economies, 852–854
  illustrations, 830–837
    cumulative translation adjustment, 833–835
    remeasurement, 835–837
    translation, 830–833
  international reporting systems, 864–866
  methods compared, 837–846
    balance sheet effects, 840–841
    cash flows, 844–846
    financial ratios, 841–843
    income statement effects, 837–840
  overview, 820–821
Multistage growth models, discounted cash flow valuation models, 1100–1102
Murdoch, B., 390n10
Murrin, J., 1061n30
Muscarella, C. J., 347
Myers, S. C., 595

N
Nakayama, M., 536
Narayanan, P., 995, 998
Negative numbers, ratio analysis, 143
Neutrality, FASB framework, 11
Newcor Company, 55, 56
Noel, J., 295, 1078
No-growth model, discounted cash flow valuation models, 1046–1047
Noncash transactions, cash flow analysis, 117
Nonhomogeneous subsidiaries, intercorporate investment analysis, 698–699
Nonrecurring items:
  accrual accounting concept analysis of, 63–69
  income statement, 45–48
  types of, 58–63
  income tax analysis, deferred taxes, 442
  reported income adjustments, 951–953
Nonsmoothed pension cost, 602
NorAm Energy, liability financing analysis, 511, 512
Noreen, E., 1083
Normalization, reported income adjustments, 948–951. *See also* Reported income adjustments
Nucor Corporation, inventory analysis, 297–298, 314–315
Number of days payables are outstanding, calculation of, 152

O
O'Brien, P., 229, 1083n58

Off-balance-sheet debt, 547–561. *See also* Leases
  commodity-linked bonds, 556–557
  examples
    Ashland Oil, 557–561
    Texaco and Caltex, 562–570
  finance subsidiaries, 554–555
  investment-linked bonds, 557
  joint ventures and investment in affiliates, 555–556
  overview, 532–533, 547
  receivables, sale of, 548–554
  take-or-pay and throughput arrangements, 548
Ohlson, J. A., 179, 180, 249, 346, 347, 993, 999, 1001n23, 1040, 1062n31
Oil and gas exploration, capitalization versus expensing (asset analysis), 340–342, 345, 367–376
Operating activities, cash flow statement, 88, 92, 93, 95, 115–116
Operating (short-term) activity ratio, ratio analysis, 151–153
Operating cycle, length of cash cycle, liquidity analysis, 156–158
Operating income, leases, 539
Operating lease, lease classification, 535–536, 537. *See also* Leases
Operating leverage:
  earnings variability, 990–991
  estimation of, ratio analysis, 211–213
  ratio analysis, 168–172
Operating losses, income tax analysis, liability method (SFAS 109), 437
Operating risk, earnings variability, 989
Options:
  adjustments for, earnings per share computation, 177
  hedging techniques, 901–903
Ou, J. A., 218n2, 245, 246, 247, 249, 1078, 1079, 1080
Overfunded pension plans, termination of, 625–626
Overreactive markets, market-based research, 235–237

P

Palepu, K., 394
Panhandle Eastern, off-balance-sheet debt, 556
Pariser, D. B., 368n3
Pastena, V., 370, 536
Patel, K. A., 1006n31, 1011
Patell, J. M., 230n26
Patents, capitalization versus expensing, 333–334
Peasnell, K., 1062n31
Peck, M. B., 1009n37, 1010
Peles, Y. C., 196, 197n45
Penman, S. H., 191, 218n2, 245, 245n62, 247, 249, 1045n10, 1061, 1072, 1078, 1079, 1080
Pension plans, 591–628. *See also* Postemployment benefits;
    Preretirement benefits; Stock compensation plans
  accounting for, 603–607
    costs, 603–605
    disclosure of status, 605–607
  costs and liability analysis, 608–622
    assumptions, 608–611
    DuPont example, 616–622
    plan status, costs, and cash flows, 611–616
  DBP Corporation example, 656–657
  defined, 594
  defined benefit plans, 596–602
    benefit obligations, factors affecting, 599–601
    benefit obligations estimation, 597–599
    funded status, 602
    plan assets, factors affecting, 601
  defined contribution plans, 596
  discontinuities, 623–624, 625–626
  General Motors example, 644–656
  incentives for, 595–596
  international reporting systems, 624, 627–628, 629–630
  overfunded plans, termination of, 625–626
  overview, 592–594
  varieties among, 594
Pepsico, liability financing analysis, long-term debt, 490
Pepsico Mexico, foreign currency disclosure, 849–850
Percentage-of-completion method, accrual accounting concept, recognition issues, 50–55
Permanent differences, income tax analysis, 447
Permanent earnings, defined, 39
Perpetual debt, liability financing analysis, debt with equity features, 494–495
Petroleum, oil and gas exploration, capitalization versus expensing (asset analysis), 340–342
Philbrick, D. R., 68, 69
Philips Electronics N. V., liability financing analysis, 514
Pinches, G. E., 193, 1007, 1008
Pincus, M., 273, 274, 319, 320
Political factors:
  information content studies, 227
  political cost hypothesis, 240–241
  positive accounting research, 238
Pooling of interests method:
  described, 750–751
  example, 798–801
  necessary conditions, 746–747
  selection rationale for, 782–787
Portfolios, hedging activities, 909
Portfolio theory:
  described, 221–223
  equity risk, 1012. *See also* Risk measurement

Positive accounting research, 237–244
  agency theory, 238–239
  bonus plan hypothesis, 239–240
  debt covenant hypothesis, 240
  disclosure and regulatory requirements, 238
  generally, 237–238
  political cost hypothesis, 240–241
  summarized, 241–244
Postannouncement drift, market-based research, 234
Postemployment benefits, 628, 631–639. *See also* Pension plans;
    Preretirement benefits; Stock compensation plans
  assumptions, 633–635
  benefit costs computation, 632
  disclosure of status, 632–633
  generally, 628, 631
  health care benefits, 631–632, 637–639
  international reporting systems, 639
  SFAS 106 disclosures, 639
  transition methods, 635–637
Preferred stock, liability financing analysis, debt with equity features, 495–496
Preinreich, G. A. D., 1062n31
Preretirement benefits, 640. *See also* Pension plans; Postemployment benefits; Stock compensation plans
Present value tables, 1192–1195
Press, E. G., 508, 510
Press releases, financial statement analysis, 24
Price change analysis, long-lived asset analysis (accounting), 414–423
Price-earnings ratio:
  abnormal earnings (EBO) model, 1069–1072
  discounted cash flow valuation models, 1054–1055
  market-based research, 234
Price fluctuations, inventory analysis, 259, 275, 281–283
Price-to-book value ratio, defined, 180
Price-to-earnings ratio, defined, 180
Prior period adjustments, accrual accounting concept, 63
Prior service cost, defined benefit pension plans, benefit obligations, 600–601
Product life cycle, ratio analysis, integrated analysis, 187–189
Profitability:
  capitalization versus expensing, 327
  inventory analysis, LIFO versus FIFO, 274–285
  ratio analysis, 165–168
Project debt, liability financing analysis, long-term debt, 490
Proportionality assumption, ratio analysis, 142
Proportionate consolidation, intercorporate investment analysis, 701–708

Purchase method:
business combinations analysis,
747–750
selection rationale for, 782–787
Push-down accounting, business
combinations analysis, 787–791

Q

Quaker Oats, inventory analysis,
284–285
Quality of earnings, reported income
adjustments, 956–958
Quarterly forecasting models,
1076–1077

R

Ramakrishnan, R. T. S., 1057n26
Ratio analysis, 139–213
book value per share, 179–180
business combinations analysis
international reporting, 777–778
U.S., 762–763, 790–792
cash flow per share, 179
categories, 150–172
activity analysis, 151–155
liquidity analysis, 155–160
long-term debt and solvency
analysis, 160–165
operating and financial leverage,
168–172
profitability analysis, 165–168
common-size statements, 144–150
dividend payout ratio, 180–181
earnings per share, 172–179
EBITDA, 179
financial statement analysis, 965–966
integrated analysis, 182–198
economic characteristics and
strategies, 186–191
firm performance analysis, 183–186
generally, 182–183
patterns of disclosure, definition,
and use, 194–198
ratio selection and classification,
192–194
leases, 538, 539–540
limits of, 141–144
multinational operations analysis,
methods compared, 841–843
operating leverage estimation,
211–213
overview, 140–141
purpose and use of, 141
Rayburn, Judy, 43
Receivables, sale of, off-balance-sheet
debt, 548–554
Receivables turnover ratio, defined, 151
Recognition issues:
accrual accounting concept, 48–58
derivatives and hedging activities, 907
Recurring items, accrual accounting
concept, income statement, 45–48
Reeve, J. H., 311

Regulated utilities, capitalization versus
expensing, 336–338
Regulatory requirements, positive
accounting research, 238
Reiter, S. A., 595, 596
Relevance, FASB framework, 11
Reliability, FASB framework, 11
Remeasurement (temporal method). *See
also* Multinational operations
analysis
illustrated, 835–837
multinational operations analysis,
foreign currency translation (SFAS
52), 825–827
translation compared, 828–830
Rendelman, R. J., Jr., 229
Reported income adjustments, 948–959
accounting changes, 955–956
acquisition effects, 954–955
comprehensive income, 958–959
exchange rate effects, 955
international reporting systems, 953
nonrecurring items analysis, 951–953
normalization, 948–951
quality of earnings, 956–958
Reporting systems, financial statement
analysis, 6–14. *See also* Financial
statement analysis
Representational faithfulness, FASB
framework, 11
Research and development:
affiliates, long-lived asset analysis
(financial reporting), 365–367
business combinations analysis, 764
capitalization versus expensing,
332–333, 342–350
Restructured debt, liability financing
analysis, 502–503
Restructuring, asset-based valuation
models, 1043
Return on assets:
defined benefit pension plans, plan
assets, 601
firm performance analysis, 183–186
ratio analysis, 166–167, 189–190
Return on equity:
firm performance analysis, 183–186
ratio analysis, 167–168, 191
trends in, 191
Return on investment, ratio analysis,
166–168
Return on sales, ratio analysis, 165–166
Return on total capital, ratio analysis,
167
Revenues, income statement, 17–18
Rhee, S. G., 990, 991, 1017, 1018
Richardson, G. D., 1083n57, 1084
Ricks, W. E., 316, 317, 318, 404, 405,
689
Risk:
accrual accounting concept, 37
contingencies, financial statements, 22
derivatives and hedging activities, 895,
897–898. *See also* Derivatives and
hedging activities
earnings-based models, 1055–1056

Risk measurement, 983–1033
bankruptcy prediction, 992–1001
cash flows and, 1000
models, variables in, 985
research results, 993–999
uncertainties in, 1000–1001
usefulness of, 992–993
beta prediction models, variables in,
987
bond ratings prediction models,
variables in, 986
debt risk prediction (bond ratings),
1001–1012
bond classifications, 1001–1002
examples, 1026
impact of ratings, 1003–1005
process of ratings, 1002–1003
uncertainties in, 1009–1012
utility of, 1005–1009
earnings variability, 987–991
accounting beta, 991
generally, 987–989
operating and financial leverage,
990–991
operating and financial risk, 989
equity risk, 1012–1025
Arbitrage Pricing Theory (APT)
and multifactor models,
1013–1014
Beta (β) importance and utility,
1014–1015
CAPM and Beta (β), 1012–1013
CAPM and Beta (β) critiqued,
1021–1024
CAPM and Beta (β) defended,
1024–1025
empirical findings, 1018–1021
theoretical findings, 1015–1018
overview, 984–987
Robinson, J. R., 782, 783n32
Roche, liability financing analysis, 506
Roll, R., 223, 224, 394, 784n35
Rolling hedges, derivatives and hedging
activities, 909
Ronen, J., 66, 67, 228
Rosenberg, B., 1020, 1021
Ross, S., 1013
Rozeff, M. S., 1077
Ryan, S., 218n2, 1057

S

Sadan, S., 66, 67, 228
Sales basis, of revenue recognition,
departures from, 50
Salvage value, depreciation methods,
387
Sami, H., 720
SAS Group, liability financing analysis,
494
Savich, R. S., 187
Schiff, A., 281
Schiff, M., 406n28
Schipper, K., 793n40
Schneller, M., 196
Scholes, M., 1019

Schwager, S. J., 1083n57, 1084
Scott, J., 995, 997
Securities, convertible, adjustments for, earnings per share computation, 177
Securities and Exchange Commission (U.S.):
   foreign registrant reporting requirements of, 14–15
   reporting systems, 7–8
Segment-based forecasting models, 1077
Segment data analysis, intercorporate investment analysis, 711–721. *See also* Intercorporate investment analysis
Selling, T. I., 187n38, 189, 190, 859, 860n27
Selto, F. H., 348
Sen, P., 721n41
Service cost, defined benefit pension plans, benefit obligations, 599
Service hours method, depreciation, 381, 383–384
Settlements, pension plan analysis, 624
SFAS 8, multinational operations analysis, 862–864
SFAS 52:
   foreign currency translation, multinational operations analysis, 824–830. *See also* Multinational operations analysis
   multinational operations analysis, 862–864
SFAS 87, pension plan accounting, 603–605
SFAS 106, postemployment benefits, 639
SFAS 109 (liability method), income tax analysis, 433–439. *See also* Income tax analysis
SFAS 115:
   equity method of accounting compared, 688–689
   marketable securities analysis, 679–682
SFAS 121, impaired assets, 403
SFAS 123 disclosures, stock compensation plans, 643–644
Shane, P. B., 782, 783n32
Shaw, W., 68, 404
Shevlin, T., 346, 365
Shimerda, T. A., 193
Shleifer, A., 782n29
Short, D. G., 291n26
Short-term (operating) activity ratio, ratio analysis, 151–153
Short-term debt, defined, 162
Silhan, P. A., 719n38
Simonds, R. R., 720
Sinking fund depreciation. *See* Annuity or sinking fund depreciation
Size effect, market-based research, 234
Skinner, R. C., 389
Sloan, R. G., 42
Smith, A. J., 793n40

Smith, C., Jr., 506, 507, 536
SmithKline Beecham, business combinations analysis, 767–778
Solvency, inventory analysis, LIFO versus FIFO, 279–280
Solvency analysis, ratio analysis, 160–165
Sondhi, A. C., 91n3, 406n28, 554, 1009
Sorter, G. H., 91n3, 160, 859, 860n27
Sougiannis, T., 332n15, 342, 344, 346, 347, 1072
SPAR Handels-Aktiengesellschaft, hedging techniques, 901–902
Spinoffs, business combinations analysis, 791–794. *See also* Business combinations analysis
Standard & Poor's Corporation, bond ratings, 1001, 1002, 1004, 1007
Stanga, K. G., 311
Statement of cash flows, described, 19
Statement of Financial Accounting Standards (SFAS), FASB and, 9, 10. *See also* SFAS
Statement of stockholders' equity. *See* Stockholders' equity statement
Sterling, R. R., 218
Stewart, G. B., III, 1062n31
Stewart, J. E., 910, 911
Stickel, S. E., 1084
Stickney, C. P., 118n26, 187n38, 189, 190
Stober, T. L., 43, 280, 1040
Stock compensation plans, 640–644. *See also* Pension plans; Postemployment benefits; Preretirement benefits
   Foster Wheeler example, 641–643
   generally, 640–641
   SFAS 123 disclosures, 643–644
Stockholders' equity:
   balance sheet, 16–17
   balance sheet analysis and adjustments, 944–945
   business combinations analysis, 768–771
Stockholders' equity statement:
   accrual accounting concept, 74–76
   described, 19–20
Stock returns, earnings relationship, market-based research, 227–230
Straight-line depreciation, methods, 380, 381
Strong, J. S., 404
Subsidiaries, nonhomogeneous, intercorporate investment analysis, 698–699
Sugrue, T. F., 615
Sum-of-years'-digits method, accelerated depreciation, 381
Sun Company, inventory analysis, 267–269, 272, 276–277, 281
Suncor Company, 63
Supplementary schedules, financial statements, 22–23
Sustainable income, defined, 39
Swaminathan, S., 720

Swanson, Edward P., 610
Swaps, hedging techniques, 901

T
Take-or-pay contracts, off-balance-sheet debt, 548, 549
Temporal method. *See* Remeasurement
Temporary differences, income tax analysis, 447
Terminal value calculations, abnormal earnings (EBO) model, 1067, 1102–1103
Texaco, off-balance-sheet debt, 562–570
Textron Corporation, intercorporate investment analysis, 693
Thaler, R., 235
Thiagarajan, S. R., 248, 249n70, 347, 1068n40, 1079
Thies, J. B., 554
Thomas, J. K., 536, 625, 626, 1057n26, 1077
Thompson, L. A., 187
Thousand Trails, Inc.:
   accrual accounting example, 74–78
   cash flow analysis, 119–121
Throughput agreement, off-balance-sheet debt, 548
Timeliness, FASB framework, 11
Time-series process, extrapolative forecasting models, 1075
Times Mirror Corporation (TMC), liability financing analysis, 492
Timing issue, ratio analysis, 142
Titard, P. L., 368n3
Tobin's q ratio, asset-based valuation models, 1041
Todd, K. R., Jr., 418n3
Trademarks, capitalization versus expensing, 334
Trade publications, financial statement analysis, 24
Train, J., 220n6
Transactional analysis method, cash flow statement, 91–93
Translation (all-current method). *See also* Multinational operations analysis
   illustrated, 830–835
   multinational operations analysis, foreign currency translation (SFAS 52), 827
   temporal method compared, 828–830
Treasury stock method, earnings per share computation, 177
Trezevant, R. H., 350
Type I and II errors, bankruptcy prediction, 992, 993

U
Uncertainty:
   accrual accounting concept, 37–38
   financial statements
      auditor role, 26–28
      contingencies, 22

Union Camp, cash flow analysis, 106, 107
United Kingdom, generally accepted accounting principles (GAAP), 14. *See also* International reporting systems
Units-of-production method, depreciation, 381, 383–384
Unusual items, accrual accounting concept, 58–59
Uphoff, H. L., 1078
Useful life, depreciation methods, 387, 395
User classes, financial statement analysis, 4–5
Utilities (regulated), capitalization versus expensing, 336–338

V

Valuation:
    capitalization versus expensing, 345, 346–347
    free cash flows and, cash flow analysis, 104–105
Valuation allowance, income tax analysis, liability method (SFAS 109), 437–438
Valuation models, 1035–1072
    abnormal earnings (EBO) model, 1062–1072
        DCF models compared, 1065–1072
        overview, 1062–1064
        terminal value assumptions, 1102–1103
    asset-based, 1038–1043
        book value measurements, 1040–1041

book value stability and growth, 1041–1043
    market price and book value, 1039
    Tobin's q ratio, 1041
    discounted cash flow, 1043–1062. *See also* Discounted cash flow valuation models
    DuPont example, 1085–1087
    overview, 1037–1038
Value drivers, abnormal earnings (EBO) model, 1069
Value Line, market-based research, 235, 236
Variable-rate debt:
    fixed-rate versus, liability financing analysis, long-term debt, 485–489
    liability financing analysis, long-term debt, 485
Verifiability, FASB framework, 11
Vigeland, R. L., 349
Vishny, P. W., 782n29

W

Wakeman, L. M., 536
Wang, S.-W., 446n20
Wang, Z., 1024
Warfield, T. D., 496
Warner, J. B., 506, 507
Warrants:
    adjustments for, earnings per share computation, 177
    convertible bonds and, liability financing analysis, debt with equity features, 490–493
Watts, R., 237, 238n49, 239n52, 243n59, 244, 990, 1019n55, 1077
Wei, J., 510
Weil, R. L., 270, 279n16, 391n11

Weintrop, J. B., 508
Westvaco, fixed asset analysis, depreciation, 397
Weygandt, J. J., 346
Whirlpool Europe, multinational operations analysis, 862
White, G. I., 91n3
Wild, J., 1078
Williamson, R. W., 195
Wilson, G. Peter, 43
Window dressing, ratio analysis, 142–143
Winslow, R., 631
Wolfson, M. A., 230n26, 857, 861
Working capital, inventory analysis, 265
    LIFO versus FIFO, 275–276
Working capital ratios, defined, 158–160
WSF Company, cash flow statement, 89, 90, 91, 94–95
Wyman-Gordon, inventory analysis, 282–283

Z

Zarowin, P., 43, 228, 235n42, 1056, 1057, 1083n59
Zero-coupon debt, liability financing analysis, long-term debt, 482–485
ZETA model:
    bankruptcy prediction, 995–999, 1001
    bond ratings, 1009
Ziebart, D. A., 862, 863
Zimmerman, J. L., 237, 238n49, 239n52, 243n59, 244, 446n20, 990, 1019n55
Zmijewski, M. E., 242, 243, 1082, 1083
Z-score:
    bankruptcy prediction, 994–998, 1000, 1001
    bond ratings, 1009, 1010